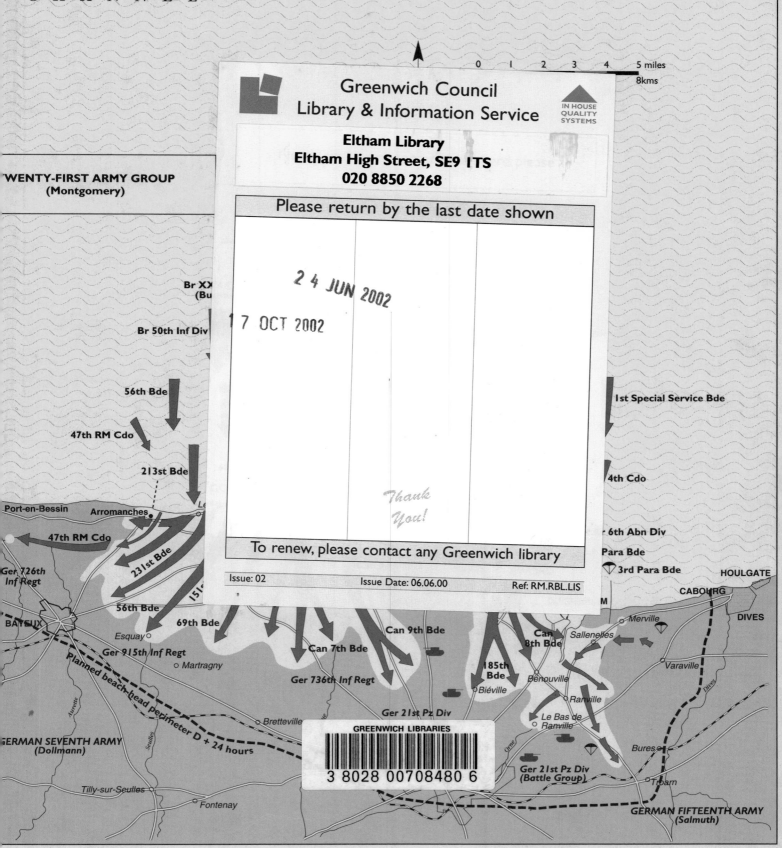

TWENTY-FIRST ARMY GROUP
(Montgomery)

Br XX
(Bu

Br 50th Inf Div

56th Bde

47th RM Cdo

213st Bde

Port-en-Bessin

Arromanches

Le

47th RM Cdo

231st Bde

Ger 726th
Inf Regt

151

56th Bde

BAYEUX

Esquay

Ger 915th Inf Regt

Martragny

Planned beach-head perimeter D + 24 hours

Aure

Seulles

GERMAN SEVENTH ARMY
(Dollmann)

Bretteville

Tilly-sur-Seulles

Fontenay

69th Bde

Can 7th Bde

Ger 736th Inf Regt

Ger 21st Pz Div

Can 9th Bde

1st Special Service Bde

4th Cdo

6th Abn Div

Para Bde

3rd Para Bde

HOULGATE

CABOURG

DIVES

Merville

Can
8th Bde

Sallenelles

185th
Bde

Bénouville

Biéville

Ranville

Le Bas de
Ranville

Orne

Ger 21st Pz Div
(Battle Group)

Varaville

Dives

Bures

Troarn

GERMAN FIFTEENTH ARMY
(Salmuth)

The D-Day
Encyclopedia

Editorial Board

The D-Day Encyclopedia

Edited by

DAVID G. CHANDLER
The Royal Military Academy, Sandhurst

JAMES LAWTON COLLINS, JR.
U.S. Army, Retired

Helicon

Copyright © 1994 by
Simon & Schuster

First published in the
United States of America by
Simon & Schuster
Academic Reference Division
New York, 1994

First published in the
United Kingdom by
Helicon Publishing Ltd.
42 Hythe Bridge Street
Oxford OX1 2EP

ISBN 0–09–178265–1

A catalogue record
for this book is
available from
the British Library

Printed in the United States of America

Editorial and Production Staff

Publisher
Charles E. Smith

Editorial Director
Paul Bernabeo

Project Editor
Dorothy Bauhoff Kachouh

Manuscript Editors
Clifford Browder   John W. Hopper   Cecile Rhinehart Watters

Proofreaders
Clifford Browder   John W. Hopper

Editorial Assistant
Steven J. Tirone

Compositor
Robert Engle Design/
J. Robert Englebright

Illustration Editor
Patricia Brecht

Cartographer
Swanston Publishing Ltd.
Derby, England

Indexer
AEIOU Inc.
Pleasantville, New York

Case Design
Mike McIver

Production Supervisor
Winston Sukhnanand

Contents

Editor's Foreword

David G. Chandler

As I sat at my word processor on 2 April 1993 wondering what I could possibly write by way of an introduction to *The D-Day Encyclopedia,* published to help commemorate the fiftieth anniversary of the single most complex and significant amphibious operation in all history, my eye strayed to the obituary page of the previous day's *Daily Telegraph*—and my problem was at least partially solved. For there was recorded the death, at age eighty-two, of Col. Edward Maxwell Morrison, MC and Bar (or second award), reputedly the first man ashore on Juno Beach on that fateful morning of 6 June 1944, who before midday had earned a recommendation for Britain's third-highest military award for officers, the Military Cross.

Maj. "Max" Morrison was commanding A Company of the 8th (Irish) Battalion of the King's Regiment. At 2 a.m. the "Liverpool Irish" embarked in assault craft from the *Llangibby Castle,* in which they had been heaving in the gale-torn English Channel since 4 June—the seasick culmination of nine months of intensive invasion training. So deep were the troughs of the waves, he later recalled, that they never saw another assault craft on the long, crazily-tossing shoreward journey. He eventually jumped off the boat when it grounded—and found himself in nine feet of water. He managed to struggle ashore near some mined triangular iron beach obstacles and pointed logs of the German beach defenses. As the landings at Utah and Omaha beaches had commenced an hour earlier, there was scant hope of catching the Germans unawares on Juno, and six of his men were at once scythed down by machine-gun fire. There were no DD (Duplex Drive) tanks in sight—many had been swamped between ship and shore—so they could not rely on close fire support to silence the enemy's concrete pillboxes as they struggled up the beach to regroup in the sand dunes beyond. So they fixed bayonets and, firing from the hip, launched a desperate frontal attack to capture the position—and succeeded, killing many Germans and taking more prisoners of war than the Liverpool Irish themselves numbered. Undaunted, Morrison and his men next assaulted a concrete fire-control tower overlooking the beach. Again they were successful, and still more prisoners were put into the bag. Pressing on to clear the beach exit, which was dominated by several defended buildings, they ran into a mine field and suffered more casualties. After enduring the savage hand-to-hand fighting that ensued among and inside the neighboring houses, they cleared and captured their third objective of the morning, taking yet more Germans captive.

Maj. "Max" Morrison had certainly earned the award of his Military Cross, but typically gave the full credit to his seasick men who had—like himself—just received their first baptism of fire. A few days later he would be seriously wounded at Tilly-sur-Seulles and evacuated home to spend six months in hospital. Returning near the year's end as a company commander in the East Lancashire Regiment, he earned his Bar to the MC for "cool leadership and imperturbable behaviour under fire," as the citation reads, during possibly the worst fighting conditions encountered in the whole northwest European campaign—in the grim Reichwald Forest battle. His active war ended on 9 May 1945 after passing the Rhine and reaching the Weser River as Germany surrendered.

Although he came of military stock (his ancestors included the commanding officer of the Liverpool Irish during the Boer War of 1899–1902, and further back still he could claim kinship with the famous Irish rebel of the 1790s, Wolfe Tone), he was by prewar profession a rugby-football-playing advertising executive whose grandfather had built Liverpool's Anglican cathedral. Always a modest man, he had no illusions about fighting. "There is no glamour in war," he would often say. "I took risks to save lives."

This, then, was the story of a single British citizen-soldier in many ways typical of millions of ordinary people called up to wear uniform who eventually fought in the Anglo-American armies in Normandy (and beyond) during that long, hot summer. The incidents that earned him his first decoration were repeated a hundredfold by soldiers of many nations in the drop zones, five beaches, and narrow inland beachheads on that dramatic June day. Only a relative handful received formal recognition of their achievements although Sgt. Stanley Hollis of the Green Howards and Andrew Charles Mynarski of the Royal Canadian Air Force were awarded the Victoria Cross and several Americans received the Medal of Honor. To this day half a century later, many tales have never been told. Collectively they undoubtedly left their mark on history by ensuring the overall success of the initial assault on Adolph

Hitler's Fortress Europe. The story of "Max" Morrison's valor must stand here for one and all of them—soldiers, sailors, airmen, and marines of many Allied nationalities.

My memories of D-day are by any comparative standard totally prosaic and insignificant. As a ten-year-old schoolboy attending preparatory boarding school in the North Riding of Yorkshire between York and Malton, I was on 6 June 1944 confined to the sick room with many of my peers suffering from chicken pox. I remember the wild excitement that swept through the school when the first news broke. The matron had thoughtfully loaned our sick bay her portable battery radio. I can remember the news announcer interrupting a program of "Music-While-You-Work" on the BBC Home Service, portentously asking his audience to stand by for a special announcement, which was then read as follows: "Under Command of General Eisenhower, Allied naval forces, supported by strong air forces, began landing Allied armies this morning. That is the end of this special announcement." All day we crowded around that radio in our dressing gowns, our itching spots forgotten, avid for the least crumb of further information. Later in the evening we heard the recording of General Eisenhower's calm and reassuringly measured tones breaking the news over the air to the population of occupied Europe. "Peoples of Western Europe, early this morning forces of the United Nations under my command began to land in northern France."

One other slightly older contemporary was Her Royal Highness Princess Elizabeth. On 6 June 1944, I have been informed, she spent part of the day having some fillings at the dentist. Her Majesty the Queen has most kindly authorized me to quote the following entry from her personal diary:

> Heard early this morning that invasion of France began. Went up to London, people seemed quite calm. Papa spoke on wireless; we have landed at Caen, fighting there, airborne troops elsewhere.

Her Majesty has added the comment that her experiences on 6 June 1944 were perhaps one better than being in bed with chicken pox! I'm not so sure—I personally would have far preferred to be on the D-day beaches than in the dentist's chair—but with the resilience of youth all our sickroom patients were full of beans that day, itchy spots or no. There is thus no doubt that 6 June 1944 was an important date for both "the Princess in her castle" and "the sick boys in their beds"—freely to adapt part of the well-known hymn "All things bright and beautiful," which we Terrington boys used to sing with as much gusto as our breaking voices would allow at morning assembly or Sunday morning service in Terrington church from time to time.

For young Britons, both boys and girls, who were not in cities subject to bombing or living in countries under enemy occupation—which of course included the British Channel Islands—these were exciting times. Food was rationed and often short—but then few of my age group could remember anything else—and many evenings and nights were spent in air-raid shelters after the wailing sirens had sounded the alert. Many of us had fathers, uncles, elder brothers, or mothers, aunts, sisters, and cousins away "at the war" or performing war work in the factories or "digging for victory" in the Land Army—but the realities of war were barely comprehended except by those who suffered bereavement or, being bombed out, had lost both house and home. We all found the dramatic times we lived in extremely stimulating, to say the least. We liked to think we were "doing our bit" by collecting enamel pans and scrap iron, or saving the silver-foil from our meager sweet rations (two ounces a week) in support of the latest "Build a Spitfire" campaign.

There were other memorable moments, to be sure, in the months leading up to D-day. On one occasion in midmorning, our classes were disrupted by all the din and orchestrated confusion caused by a large-scale army exercise with much firing of blank ammunition and smoke by British infantry and armored cars as they fought along the length of the single street of Terrington village and through the grounds of the school. The headmaster was not best pleased, but you can be assured that we boys loved every minute of it. A common sight by this time were work parties of unguarded Italian prisoners of war, wearing dusty denims with yellow cloth circles stitched on their backs. They were hired out to local farmers to labor on the land—and they showed not the least inclination to try to escape or cause mischief.

This was just as well, for along both grass verges of the road to Castle Howard and through its extensive open parkland there sprouted large numbers of semicircular corrugated iron shelters, perhaps twenty-five yards apart, packed with piles of unfuzed shells and boxes of SAA (Small Arms Ammunition). Some had bricked-up ends with doors painted with yellow symbols denoting that poison-gas shells were stored within (mercifully never used by either side, unlike in World War I), but most were quite open to the elements—and to the prying eyes and fingers of inquisitive schoolboys. Again the dumps were completely unguarded—which, on reflection, must have demonstrated the confidence of the authorities about the unlikelihood of any enemy aerial or saboteur activities by that time in the war. They were more fortunate, perhaps, that even the intense curiosity of British schoolboys was held in check within reasonable bounds.

In any case, we were by this time adopting the role of self-appointed sleuths, eyeing every innocent stranger we met on walks with secret suspicion that he might well be a German secret agent or a disguised Fifth Column saboteur, and we often shadowed him on his way. We once even thought we found a spy station below the floor boards of the school assembly room (we had always suspected the loyalties of our unpopular Latin teacher). One dark night some of us pried up some boards and with beating hearts explored the old foundations by torchlight—but only found several dozen yellowing Ping-Pong balls that generations of boys had lost through nooks and crannies in the floor above. No matter, this was no small booty, but we made the elementary mistake of flooding the school black market with our contraband, which made the headmaster suspicious. Inevitably some individual "sneaked" (the American military honor code had no place in English prep schools of the mid-1940s), and the ringleaders were soon being rather careful when sitting down for some days afterward. But, all in all, these were fascinating times for the young. As William Wordsworth wrote about the outbreak of the French Revolution, "Bliss was it in that dawn to be alive, / But to be young was very heaven!" This was all taking place a full 300 miles from the south coast ports where the invasion preparations were centered, and indicates the extent of the logistical preparations being undertaken to support the coming invasion of France. Indeed, throughout 1944 England had become one immense military encampment with interspersed airfields.

Once or twice the reality of the horrors of war came a trifle closer. I remember a group of us returning by train to school one start of term seeing a group of badly burned airmen at York station in transit to a new hospital. That gave us pause for thought. And one holiday in late 1944 I remember at my seaside home of Withernsea seeing what must have been a V-1 self-propelled bomb (which we called "Doodlebugs") pass straight up the road past our vicarage on its spluttering flight, rocket engine flaming behind, toward Hull (but we later heard it had fallen short of its intended destination, thank goodness, and exploded harmlessly in open fields).

By this time enemy air raids were rare, and I had long become accustomed to spending many night hours in our family bomb shelter under the reinforced stairs, waiting for the ever-welcome single note of the All Clear so that we could safely return to bed. I was also used to seeing rows of bomb-damaged or burnt-out buildings on our occasional shopping visits to Hull (which was badly blitzed in 1941). But even I, blasé to the sights of war as I thought myself to be at the mature age of nine, was impressed when I was taken by my father one early morning in 1942 to see our St. Matthews Church surrounded by fire engines and ARP [Air-Raid Precaution] wardens staring at the roof, where clearly for all to see was the tail fin of a large incendiary oil-bomb (which had fortunately failed to explode) sticking up through the tiles. There were also the occasional treasured visits to smoking wrecks of shot-down enemy bombers to be inspected from a safe distance. These were always under armed guard, I remember—and sometimes small pieces of metal debris smelling strangely sweet were smuggled to me by a friend of my father's in the Home Guard who helped carry out these tedious duties.

Twice our vicarage had whole windows blown in by freaks of bomb explosion blasts from distant exploding land mines (large bombs that came down by parachute, often with delayed fuzes attached), one of which destroyed the church at nearby Hilston. The Yorkshire farmer (and churchwarden)—who lived next door to the churchyard and heard not a sound by another quirk of blast, acoustics, and a smiling fate—next morning drew back the blackout curtains reputedly to make the classic remark to his wife, "Ee, lass! T'church be gorn!" It was indeed.

Once there was a large unexploded bomb at Rimswell corner about two miles from my home that took several days' hard work to defuze. I vividly remember the red mud-guarded three-ton lorries of the bomb disposal squad driving past our house, the Royal Engineers of the new shift riding in the back clinging onto the superstructure and blithely whistling without apparently a care in the world as they returned to face all-too-real mortal danger at the bomb crater. But this is perhaps to reminisce too far . . . and as all historians know only too well who have interviewed veteran servicemen, the passage of time can play strange tricks with the memory. But in the case of the young—vibrantly alive—such events may have been indelibly impressed on our receptive minds. Or so I believe.

It is incredible for me to realize that all of this was happening *fifty* years ago: it often seems like yesterday. Ten years ago there were large commemorations and celebrations for the fortieth anniversary—it being widely stated that by the fiftieth there would be too few veterans left for D-day to be marked properly. I was even summoned from Sandhurst to appear on early-morning BBC TV, interviewed sitting on the sea wall at Arromanches by Frank Bough and Selina Scott to provide a military historian's analysis of what had happened there on 6 June. For me the most memorable event of a packed day was being kissed on the cheek by Dame Vera Lynn, the "Forces' Sweetheart" of World War II. The famous singer is still very much with us ten years later as are an estimated 100,000 veterans of D-day itself (so much for the gloomy prognostications of 1984)—and I look forward with some anticipation to what 6 June 1994 may hold in store for me. Only time will tell, but the approaching anniversary has already involved my participation in preparing this remarkable volume.

I have found it a great honor to be involved, with my coeditor and friend Brig. Gen. J. Lawton ("Jimmy") Collins, Jr., in helping Charles E. Smith, president of the Academic Reference Division of Simon and Schuster—whose original idea this whole project was—together with his dedicated team headed by Paul Bernabeo, not to forget the indispensable and unflappable secretary, Glady Villegas Delgado—to create this impressive *D-Day Encyclopedia*. It has not been a task without its difficulties, to be sure, but with some 150 contributors drawn from a dozen nations—both military personnel and scholars—it would indeed have been strange if this had not been the case. There are still several strong disagreements, national and personal, for example, over the relative contributions of Winston Churchill and Franklin D. Roosevelt to the D-day planning processes, and even more over the way the indubitably controversial General Bernard L. Montgomery chose to carry them into execution as commander of 21st Army Group.

I also wish to thank our editorial board, most especially my good friends Gen. Sir Anthony Farrar-Hockley and Dr. Stephen Badsey, for all the help and advice they have so unselfishly and unflinchingly provided, not forgetting the numerous contributors who responded so effectively to my invitations on behalf of the publisher to participate in our ambitious venture. Heading the list are the Second Viscount Montgomery (like myself, a schoolboy on the great day) and Oberbürgermeister Manfred Rommel (a young recruit in the Luftwaffe on 6 June 1944), who not only agreed to lend their names to the editorial board but also made fascinating contributions based upon their special knowledge of their fathers' respective parts in this great historical drama.

Of course we can hardly claim to have produced the truly definitive work on D-day, although we have all tried our utmost to do so. As Colin F. Baxter wisely remarks in his *Selected Bibliography* devoted to *The Normandy Campaign, 1944* (1992): "Clio [the Muse of History] rarely sleeps in the same bed for long; all historical writing is a progress report, and the reputations of political and military leaders are especially prone to revisionist assessment." Thus opinions can widely differ within the space of a very few years.

It was agreed from almost the start—on the suggestion of General Collins—that we should close our study on D plus 12 (or 18 June). On that day the Allied beachhead was officially declared secure—although the very next day saw the return of the great westerly gale that was to wreck the American Mulberry harbor off Omaha and severely damage the British equivalent off Arromanches and thereby jeopardize, or at least immensely complicate, the success of the huge logistical buildup of men and matériel that was vital to the achievement of success in the impending "Battle of the Breakout" from Normandy into northwest and north-central France and ultimately to the Seine and Paris. In fact, the American gift for improvization saved the day, and as late as September vehicles and stores were still coming over the original beaches.

There will, alas, be some mistakes and errors of commission as well as of omission within the pages that follow, but hopefully these may be put right in future printings of the *Encyclopedia*. We hope we have not offended the susceptibilities of participants or their immediate descendants—but history must surely be in part subjective. Purely objective retailing of facts (even when those can be established beyond any reasonable doubt—no easy matter either) can make for some pretty dull reading. Clearly a careful balance has to be preserved. On reflection, perhaps the great Duke of Wellington made a good point or two when he wrote from Paris to John Wilson Croker on 8 August 1815 (in an attempt to dissuade him from attempting a history of the Battle of Waterloo) in the following terms:

> The object which you propose to yourself is very difficult of attainment, and if really attained, is not a little invidious. The history of a battle is not unlike the history of a ball. Some individuals may recollect all the little events of which the great result is the battle won or lost; but no individual can recollect the order in which, or the exact moment at which, they occurred, which makes all the difference as to their value or importance. Then the faults of the misbehaviour of some gave occasion for the distinction of others, and perhaps were the cause of material losses; and you cannot write a true history of a battle without including the faults and misbehaviour of part at least of those engaged. Believe me that every man you see in a military uniform is not a hero; and that, although in the account given of general action, such as that of Waterloo, many instances of individual heroism must be passed over unrelated, it is better for the general interest to leave these parts of the story untold, than to tell the whole truth.

Of course the duke did not have the advantages (nor the arguable disadvantages either) of having war correspondents, film crews, and tape recorders on the battlefield at the time of the action, nor the facilities for debriefing participants afterward, that are taken for granted today. But make no mistake, D-day and its immediate aftermath form as significant a battle for its time as Waterloo proved to be in the early nineteenth century. At least we may hope not to have condoned deliberate untruths, nor to have committed any injustices of the kind the conscientious Wellington was so anxious to avoid. But there need be no doubt that Maj. (later Col.) "Max" Morrison, a description of whose exploits on D-day served to open this introduction, may be taken as an overall representative standard-bearer for all the heroism displayed by so many soldiers on both sides of the front line during the fluctuating fortunes of that action-packed, windswept day in June 1944 and over the just under two weeks that followed.

In the works of the Apocrypha, "Let us now praise famous men, and our fathers that begat us" (Ecclesiasticus 46:1). For there will in all probability never be such a massive amphibious operation ever again in the history of humankind and its wars.

Editor's Foreword

James Lawton Collins, Jr.

On 6 June 1944 the dawn was dim, wet, and windy at Westergate Woodhouse, a few miles from the English Channel. There the 957th Field Artillery Battalion from North Dakota, armed with 155-mm howitzers, awaited orders to embark for France. I was then a lieutenant colonel commanding this battalion.

The electrifying news that the invasion had been launched crackled over the radio. The officers and men, who had spent the previous weeks in a fever of preparation, rushed to check everything again. They knew that our big guns would soon receive the call to head for the port and the combat that lay ahead. Although all equipment had been renovated, cleaned, and finely tuned only a few days before, the waiting period was consumed by inspections in minute detail to be sure everything was ready. The much-despised dry runs, where everything was packed and loaded aboard the vehicles, then unloaded and unpacked, now paid off. The combat loading of equipment and the packing of personal gear went smoothly and expeditiously and everyone awaited the order to move out. Confined to the vicinity of our quarters, with everything packed and loaded, the battalion chafed at the delay, which was ended three days later when orders were received to move to the staging area.

Plans had been made and rehearsed to split the unit into two echelons. The cross-Channel transportation was to be a Landing Ship, Tank (LST) that could not accommodate the whole unit, so all personnel and equipment not essential to the battalion were stripped out and assigned to the rear echelon to follow as shipping became available.

The advance group left their billets at 0500 on a clear but chilly morning on 11 June and headed for the marshaling area near Southampton. There last-minute items were passed out, such as vomit bags and seasickness pills, in preparation for a rough crossing. Maps of Normandy were issued and four dollars worth of French invasion currency—different from the paper money used in occupied France—was given to each man. Many exchanged their British money for francs, and games of chance were soon in full swing as the men became familiar with the new medium of exchange.

A last-minute change of orders shortly before dawn of the 12th had everyone digging through well-packed barracks bags to unearth the wool olive drab uniforms and long johns that had been impregnated with chemicals to reduce casualties in event of gas attack. These were to be worn for the landings, although it turned out they were not necessary. The unit moved out in the morning and fount *LST 365* beached on the hard sand opposite Cowes on the Isle of Wight. By about 6:00 p.m. the ship was full, but the ammunition train of about six vehicles and a dozen men was not yet loaded! They had to be left behind until a ship with room for them could be found. Fortunately they rejoined us a couple of days later.

LST 365 backed slowly into the choppy English Channel and a blackout journey to France had begun. A peaceful night ensued as the ghostly silhouettes of other ships in the convoy appeared and disappeared against the waves and no enemy challenged the steady progress of the fleet. Although the ship rocked, rolled, and plunged, few men were seasick as the pills did their work and exerted a calming and soporific effect on all.

In the early morning hours the convoy arrived off Juno Beach, where the Canadian 3d Division had landed on D-day. *LST 365* was manned by a British crew, and the skipper tried to convince me to land on Juno so he could return to England for another load. I insisted that we be taken to our destination—Utah Beach—and he finally agreed and we got under way to the east.

Cruising just offshore we passed the British beaches, Gold and Sword, and then Omaha, where the U.S. 1st and 29th divisions had clawed their way ashore on D-day. All the beaches were cluttered with landing craft unloading or stranded. Many ships were half-sunk with whitecaps washing over them, casualties of the underwater mines and beach obstacles as well as the German artillery fire that sporadically landed in the water. Apparently it was then blind fire as I saw no hits scored.

Finally in the early afternoon we arrived and anchored a quarter mile off Utah Beach. The ship's captain did not want to beach the LST because it was high tide. He could not see the underwater obstacles and he would have had to wait for the next high tide to pull off. After a delay of a couple of hours, two Rhino ferries appeared and expeditiously loaded the men and matériel for the short journey to the beach and landed us in only a couple of feet of water. By 2100 the unit was on the way to the dewater-proofing area, where the trucks were cleaned of grease, and the long extensions to the tail pipes and air intakes that allowed the vehicles to come ashore through shallow water were removed. This process took a couple of hours, and it was after dark when the unit reached its first firing position near Sainte-Mère-Église. We were prepared to fire our big guns, but we were not called upon during the remainder of the night.

At dawn the guns were registered on a target in front of the U.S. 9th Infantry Division, which we were supporting. First light also divulged a grisly scene just next to the battalion headquarters: the bodies of two parachutists of the 82d Airborne Division were hanging from a tree, suspended by their parachutes. The had been dropped short of their destination. They were brought down and turned over to the Graves Registration unit for proper burial. Several fire missions were executed that morning in support of the 9th Division, which was starting to move to the west to cut off the Cotentin Peninsula. Resistance was heavy and progress was slow, but gradually the opposition to the front was overcome and the 155-mm howitzers of the 957th pounded the enemy with 100-pound high-explosive shells.

Small pockets of the enemy were found that had been bypassed by the infantry; they were taken prisoner by the 957th. In the first few days thirty-two German prisoners were captured after only token opposition.

Enemy counterbattery fire was sporadic, and we suffered no casualties until the Germans finally found the range as we were attacking the defenses of Cherbourg. There one man was killed and four were wounded, and one 155-mm howitzer was destroyed.

The horrors of war had been brought home to the men in the first few days of combat. Not only were the dead paratroopers a stark reminder that we were in a life-or-death struggle, but on the third night ashore it became apparent that we could kill our own. In the early hours after midnight, one of the men guarding our perimeter heard a sound in the bushes near his position. In the faint light he could see a figure moving slowly toward him. He challenged the individual and told him to stop. He kept coming and again the sentinel ordered him to halt, but to no avail. No response was made, but the figure came closer. After a third challenge, the sentinel fired, dropping the figure in the bushes. At the sound of the shots, the alert squad rushed to the area and there discovered a dead soldier from the 82d Airborne Division, reeking of alcohol. Apparently he had found a cache of the local firewater—

apple brandy called Calvados—and after becoming drunk had blundered into our lines. While we were very sorry to have killed one of our own, it impressed our men with the danger of drinking while in combat.

Another scene in the early days of combat impressed our farm-boy soldiers from North Dakota with an example of the waste of war. A German horse-drawn field artillery unit had been caught on the road by an Allied air squadron and heavily strafed. Not only were many Germans killed and wounded, but most of the horses were also dead and the rest were wounded. This made a powerful impression on the country boys, who had grown up with livestock, almost more than the sight of the dead Germans.

Another event that shocked the men was an attack by American fighter planes on a reconnaissance party selecting a new position for our guns. Fortunately they made but one pass over our clearly marked vehicles and, except for a few bullet holes and one flat tire on a jeep, no damage was done. But after this, we took cover at the sound of any aircraft. Even so, during the war the 957th had more casualties from "friendly" planes than from enemy artillery and German air attacks combined.

By 18 June the 9th Division had reached the sea and cut off the German forces in the northern Cotentin Peninsula and around Cherbourg. This event convinced the Allies that the beachhead was secure and that the Germans could not push them back into the sea. It remained to dispose of the trapped Germans, a task the U.S. VII Corps, of which the 957th Field Artillery Battalion was a part, undertook with gusto.

My esteemed colleague and friend, David Chandler, has expressed much more eloquently than could I, our appreciation and thanks to all those who have contributed so mightily to this endeavor. It would be anticlimactic for me to repeat David's thoughts, which I embrace, and so I shall not attempt to do so.

However, until the Gulf War, World War II was the most recent successful war of any size fought by American servicemen and women, and as such holds a hallowed memory for Americans. It was largely fought by nonprofessionals called to the colors, who had become professional military personnel by the time they finished the job. The plainsmen of North Dakota, as I can attest, had no peers as combat artillerymen. All the American states and territories contributed extraordinary men and women to defeat our antagonists.

We are confident that the spirit, the camaraderie, and the efficiency so evident in Normandy will rise if we must ever go to war again.

David Montgomery, Viscount of Alamein

At the end of 1943 my father, General Sir Bernard Montgomery, or Monty as he was then universally known, was appointed as Allied Ground Forces Commander for the invasion of northwest Europe. This was the most important appointment and challenge of his military career—to be responsible for the largest military operation in the history of warfare. It was the start of the last phase of the war which, following the liberation of France and the Benelux countries, ended eleven months later at Lüneburg Heath.

As with his appointment as commander of the Eighth Army, Monty was not Churchill's first choice, but fortunately the wise views of Alan Brooke, Chief of the Imperial General Staff and the single most important British military figure in World War II, together with P. J. Grigg, then secretary of state for war, prevailed. Thus over New Year 1943–1944 Monty flew via Marrakech, Morocco, where he conferred with Churchill, to take command. Monty had already heard about the plan for the invasion, and his first task was to convince Eisenhower that it was inadequate in breadth, depth, and strength. To this end he had conferred with the Supreme Allied Commander designate in Algiers at the end of December before leaving the Eighth Army. The revised Montgomery plan was finally accepted and became the blueprint for the task that followed. Monty had already proved himself master of the set-piece battle, but the preparations for D-day required a massive effort at planning, coordination, leadership, and dedication to duty.

The first five months of 1944 were a period of tremendous activity, as Montgomery addressed every officer and man who would take part in the battle. Many of the troops were not battle-hardened, but Monty believed that good training and high morale were key ingredients to success. As a result he also visited munition and armament factories, where the workers were mostly women, to encourage them and to demonstrate that their menfolk were in good hands and that they could have confidence in the outcome. The result of all this ceaseless activity was that by early June a massive Allied fighting force comprising American, British, Canadian, Commonwealth, and other participants was ready to penetrate the fortress of Europe.

The whole operation was nearly jeopardized by the weather, with the navy and air force doubting whether it could be achieved. Monty said that the troops could not be delayed, and that there were too many risks to security and morale. Finally Eisenhower, on whom the ultimate responsibility lay, took the momentous decision to go. That same day—5 June, the eve of D-day—Montgomery issued a historic message to his troops, which included a verse from Montrose, the soldier-poet of the seventeenth century:

> He either fears his fate much,
> or his deserts are small,
> who dare not put it to the touch,
> to win or lose it all.

The rest is history, covered elsewhere in this volume, and worthy of close study. I was a fifteen-year-old schoolboy during the first half of 1944, living in the very restricted area of southern England, close to Portsmouth, so it was difficult not to be caught up in the momentous events that were taking place. Reflecting on the subsequent fifty years of peace in Europe, we must always be grateful for the courage and sacrifice of those who gave their lives, and for the leadership that made victory possible.

Reminiscences of the Invasion

Manfred Rommel

My father, Field Marshal Erwin Rommel, arrived at our house in Herrlingen bei Ulm toward evening on 4 June 1944. He intended to see Hitler at Obersalzberg in order to discuss defense strategy for the anticipated Allied landing. There were basic differences of opinion on the German side regarding this strategy. Field Marshal Gerd von Rundstedt, Gen. Heinz Guderian, and the commander of *Panzer Group West,* Gen. Leo Geyr von Schweppenburg, were of the opinion that the German side should concentrate its panzer divisions in central France in order to confront the Allies in a large mobile battle in which the greater combat experience of the German troops would be proven.

My father, who had come to know the effectiveness of the Allies' superior air power in North Africa, had no faith in a battle of movement because he was convinced that Allied air superiority would make regular movements of German motorized troops and panzer units impossible. Events later confirmed his opinion. My father saw only one chance for a successful defense: fortification of the coasts and harbors and the concentration of German panzer units immediately behind the most threatened coastal sections. Hitler, full of mistrust, probably leaned more toward my father's view, but could not decide and agreed first with one and then with the other position. Moreover, he proceeded according to the principle of divide and rule. The military command in France (including Belgium and Holland) was divided among Field Marshal von Rundstedt as Commander in Chief West (Oberbefehlshaber West), my father as supreme commander of army units in northern France, and Gen. Johannes von Blaskowitz as supreme commander of army units in southern France, and General Geyr as supreme commander of panzer units (in regard to tactics, however, panzer command was divided between my father and General Blaskowitz); additionally, there were separate commanders for the navy and air force, and finally, Hitler himself had reserved authority to deploy some units. Thus, considerable disorganization prevailed; each participant, convinced that he was right and the others were not, wanted to see order established on his terms through Hitler as Supreme Commander of the Wehrmacht and Army. The Germans, by the beginning of May at the latest, feared that Normandy, especially the Cotentin Peninsula with its harbor of Cherbourg, could become the focal point of Allied invasion operation. My father thus attempted to achieve substantial reinforcements of German troops deployed near the coast. This largely failed, owing to the strategic disagreements noted.

At the proposed meeting with Hitler at Obersalzberg, my father once again wanted to reach agreement concerning the reinforcement of German troops in Normandy by two panzer divisions, one antiaircraft corps, and a smoke screen brigade. On 5 June 1944 my father learned through a telephone call from Herrlingen to the Führer's headquarters that the conference with Hitler could take place on 8 June at Obersalzberg. My mother's fiftieth birthday was 6 June 1944. This was an occasion for my father to stop in Herrlingen, particularly since they did not know whether they would be able to celebrate any further birthdays together. The German Navy had notified my father that weather conditions, especially the rough sea, did not permit an Allied landing. German long-range reconnaissance could uncover no evidence of the anticipated invasion. Nonetheless, it took place.

I myself was fifteen years old at the time. Since January 1944 I had been a Luftwaffe auxiliary (*Luftwaffenhelfer*) with a 3.7-cm antiaircraft battery in Ulm. When my mother heard that my father was coming for her birthday, she succeeded in getting me two days of leave. Thus I was home and a witness to how my father learned of the Normandy landing.

On 6 June 1944, at 7:30 in the morning, his chief of staff, Maj. Gen. Hans Speidel, telephoned him in Herrlingen and informed him that Allied paratroops had landed in Normandy. It was, however, not yet clear whether this was the invasion and whether the trip to see Hitler would have to be canceled. At ten o'clock my father again called the staff of his army group. Clearly the invasion had begun and the initial battles had gone favorably. My father then canceled his appointment with Hitler and returned immediately to France. Beforehand, he had expressed his skepticism as to German chances of success, particularly because of insufficient troop strength in Normandy. On 7 June he worked out the first tactical moves at his headquarters. On 8 June he went to the front at Caen, where his pessimism was clearly confirmed.

Allied air superiority was overwhelming. My father had to seek cover from bombing and strafing attacks twenty times. The German troops could not move by daylight, or could do so only by accepting high casualties.

By the end of 1942 my father had already known that Germany could not win the war. Hitler, however, would not discuss its termination. This became increasingly clear. In the summer of 1943 he told my father, "Bear in mind, nobody will make peace with me." Hitler was unwilling to step down and thus give Germany a way out. On the contrary, he wanted war to the bitter end.

My father considered it possible that, if Germany did repulse the Allied landing, the Western Allies would offer conditional peace to Germany without Hitler, conditions of increasing consequence the more that information leaked through about mass murder, especially of Jews, in the extermination camps. By the first days of June 1944 my father saw that the Germans had lost the Battle of Normandy. He then worked toward a capitulation of German forces in the West. On 17 July 1944 he was gravely wounded in Normandy in an attack by a low-flying plane. Thus he could not carry through his plans to capitulate at the moment when the Allies breached the German positions in the West and thus end the war. On Hitler's orders, on 14 October 1944 he was murdered as a conspirator. That, too, I experienced.

Introduction

Charles E. Smith

Operation OVERLORD, the largest amphibious landing in human history, followed a historical path across the English Channel. It was from these Norman shores that William the Conqueror, Duke of Normandy, had set forth to conquer the British Isles 878 years earlier. It was here, at Caen, that William and his wife, Matilda, built Église Saint-Étienne in 1066 and it is in this church that he was buried.

Caen, on the Orne River, about nine miles from the coast, was a relatively large town of strategic importance, the site of some of the bitterest fighting during the Normandy invasion. The first bombs fell on Caen on 6 June and it was not liberated until a month later. In the process, seventy-five percent of the city was destroyed, though William's church was spared.

Bayeux, fifteen miles to the west, is the home of the famous tapestry made in England for Bishop Odo, William's half-brother, although some claim that it was made for Queen Matilda. Bayeux, one of the first cities liberated by the Allies, escaped damage. The eponymous tapestry depicts the Norman invasion of England, echoing the invasion nearly a millennium later. As David Chandler notes in his article "British Monuments and Memorials," the British Memorial to the Missing at Bayeux bears a Latin quotation, which translated reads: "We, once conquered by William, have now liberated the land of the conqueror."

On the night of 5–6 June, the Allies returned to Normandy and began the assault on Hitler's Fortress Europe. Within weeks more than two million men were engaged in what will probably be the last battle of its kind. Reconnaissance satellites have removed the degree of surprise the Allies were able to muster in 1944; today nuclear weapons would probably be used to avert a crushing defeat.

Although we have chosen to call this work *The D-Day Encyclopedia,* it actually covers the period to 18 June, the date on which the beachhead was secured. The big storm, or Great Gale, as it is often called, that destroyed the American Mulberry hit on 19 June. The entry titled "Prelude" discusses the beginning of the war with Germany; the period from 18 June to the German surrender is discussed in "Aftermath."

We have chosen as our logo the insignia of Supreme Headquarters, Allied Expeditionary Force. The sword of liberation is shown upon a field of heraldic sable (black), representing the darkness of Nazi oppression. The flames rising from the hilt and leaping up the blade represent avenging justice. Above the sword a rainbow, emblematic of hope, contains all the colors of which the national flags of the Allies are composed. The heraldic chief of azure (blue) above the rainbow symbolizes the restoration of peace and tranquillity to the peoples of Europe.

Although the work appears in alphabetical sequence, the 437 articles were planned systematically. That systematic organization is reflected in the Synoptic Outline of Contents on page 601 of the encyclopedia. At the core of the work are the forty-two articles on the Allied and German army divisions and brigades and the complementary articles on their commanders. Also included are entries on the higher organizational units (army group, army, and corps) to which they belonged. The plan gives similar attention to navy and air force units. Biographies are provided of individuals of one-star rank or higher who commanded a division or its equivalent, and we have included articles on the Allied flagships of commodores or higher.

In general we have followed particular elements of style recommended in the style guide of the Center of Military History, Department of the Army, for example, concerning the use of roman and arabic numerals in names of particular military units and the use of italics for particular German units. We use an English form in naming German units whenever possible; see the Guide to German Military Units for a listing of German names for units and the English forms we have employed. The Guide to Numbered Entries may be helpful in locating numbered units, both Allied and German. In addition, we employ the convention of printing code names for operations and military exercises in small capital letters.

Although only fifty years have passed since this momentous event, it is remarkable how much information is not available. It is understandable that many German records were destroyed, and also that some individuals just disappeared, perhaps to eastern Europe. We were surprised, though, to learn that the first names of junior British officers were not readily available; unless they were peers of the realm, first names were not given in dispatches.

The encyclopedia includes over 350 photographs. In order to achieve the highest possible quality of reproduction, images were scanned electronically by Chapter One; a Pre-Press Company. Some two-thirds of the photographs were acquired from my old friend Mr. Charles Merullo at Hulton Deutsch Collection Limited, London. Several dozen more were gotten through the good offices of Dr. Thomas Weis and Mrs. Irina Renz at the Bibliothek für Zeitgeschichte, Stuttgart.

I would like to thank Mr. Ed Finney, Jr., at the Photographic Section, Naval Historical Center, and Ms. Dale Connelly, Still Picture Section, National Archives, both of Washington, D.C. Their informed and friendly assistance made a difficult job much easier. Many of our contributors graciously supplied illustrations from their private collections, and they are acknowledged in the appropriate photo caption.

The maps were prepared on computer by Ms. Andrea Fairbrass, Swanston Publishing Limited, London. Swanston Publishing also scanned the unit patches and flashes shown herein.

The endpaper is an adaptation of the map in *The Month-by-Month Atlas of World War II* by Barrie and Frances Pitt. The map in "Resistance" is adapted from *La Résistance Normande face à la Gestapo* by Raymond Ruffin. The map in "Navy: Allied Naval Forces" is adapted from *The Invasion of France and Germany, 1944–1945,* Vol. 11 of *History of United States Naval Operations in World War II.*

I am indebted to Dr. Paul Bernabeo, Editorial Director, Academic Reference Division, Paramount Publishing Education Group, for his unique ability to bring order from out of chaos; to Ms. Dorothy Kachouh for persistent attention to detail; and to Mr. Clifford Browder for careful scrutiny of the text. Mr. Steven Tirone and Ms. Sara Simon have offered invaluable assistance in several stages of the project. Mr. J. Robert Englebright did the page makeup to a demanding schedule and Ms. Cynthia Crippen produced an excellent index in record time. Mr. Winston Sukhnanand's assistance regarding production and manufacturing matters was invaluable. Ms. Glady Villegas Delgado, my assistant and friend of many years, has once again helped me through the joyous agony of producing an encyclopedia.

Above all, thanks are due to Dr. David Chandler and Brig. Gen. James Lawton Collins, Jr., for their knowledge and patience. Like OVERLORD itself, this was a grand Anglo-American collaboration on their part.

Thanks are also due the 141 contributors whose accumulated scholarship made this work possible. Their individual contributions bear their names. The reader will note that this work is unique in still another way in as much as many German scholars have participated in this work, both as members of the Editorial Board and as contributors. Their cooperation and assistance have been invaluable. There are also contributors from Canada, the United States, Great Britain, France, Poland, Italy, and the Netherlands.

The cover design of our encyclopedia purposely imitates the famous Green Books, for example, *United States Army in World War II, The European Theater of Operations.* These volumes, produced by the Center of Military History, Department of the Army, Washington, D.C., are invaluable to anyone studying this period.

Again, following the lead of the Green Books, we dedicate this work to

. . . THOSE WHO SERVED

Editors' and Contributors' Biographies

Editors

DAVID G. CHANDLER was awarded the Litt.D. by Oxford University. Head of the Department of War Studies at the Royal Military Academy, Sandhurst, he is president emeritus of the British Commission for Military History, member of the Commission Internationale d'Histoire Militaire, trustee of the Royal Tower of London Armouries, and council member of the British Society for Army Historical Research. He is author of *World War II on Land, Battles and Battlescenes of World War II, Atlas of Military Strategy, The Campaigns of Napoleon,* and *Dictionary of the Napoleonic Wars.*

Brig. Gen. JAMES LAWTON COLLINS, JR. (U.S. Army, ret.), landed on Utah Beach in command of the 957th Field Artillery Battalion. He served in Korea and with the Military Assistance Command, Vietnam, and later headed both the army language program and the Defense Language Institute. Repeatedly recalled to service after retirement, he was made Army Chief of Military History, and was the U.S. member of the international commission to investigate Kurt Waldheim. President emeritus of the U.S. Commission on Military History, he is currently president of the U.S. Council on America's Military Past and an adviser to the U.S. Committee for the Battle of Normandy Museum, Caen, France. He is author of *The Development and Training of the South Vietnamese Army, 1950–1972,* coauthor of *Allied Participation in Vietnam,* and coeditor of *The History of World War II* and *The Green Berets: U.S. Special Forces.*

Editorial Board

STEPHEN BADSEY received his Ph.D. from Cambridge University. Currently a senior lecturer at the Royal Military Academy, Sandhurst, he is author of *Normandy 1944* and has served as military adviser and researcher for numerous television and video productions.

Gen. Sir ANTHONY FARRAR-HOCKLEY (British Army, ret.) rose from private to general, serving for forty-four years through World War II, the Korean War, and numerous campaigns, retiring as Commander in Chief, Allied Forces Northern Europe, NATO. He is author of ten books of biography and military history.

ROLAND G. FOERSTER received his Ph.D. from Ludwig Maximilians University. A colonel of the Bundeswehr and formerly defense attaché at the German Embassy, Ottawa, he is currently director of historical education at the Militärgeschichtliches Forschungsamt, Freiburg im Breisgau. He is coauthor, with

Heinrich Walle, of *Militär und Technik: Wechselbeziehungen zu Staat, Gesellschaft und Industrie im 19. und 20. Jahrhundert.*

RICHARD H. KOHN received his Ph.D. from the University of Wisconsin. Formerly Chief, Office of Air Force History, Bolling Air Force Base, and Chief Historian, United States Air Force, he is currently professor at the University of North Carolina, Chapel Hill. He is coeditor of *Air Superiority in World War II and Korea; Air Interdiction in World War II, Korea, and Vietnam;* and *Strategic Air Warfare.*

ALLAN R. MILLETT received his Ph.D. from The Ohio State University, where he is currently Raymond E. Mason, Jr. Professor of Military History and director of the university's Program in International Security and Military Affairs. A retired colonel of the U.S. Marine Corps Reserve, he is author of *Semper Fidelis: The History of the United States Marine Corps,* coauthor of *For the Common Defense: A Military History of the United States, 1607–1983,* and coeditor, with Williamson Murray, of *Calculations, Net Assessment, and the Coming of World War II* and *Military Effectiveness,* volumes 1–3.

DAVID BERNARD MONTGOMERY, Second Viscount Montgomery of Alamein, is active in business and charitable pursuits. He is patron of the D-Day and Normandy Fellowship and the 8th Army Veterans Association.

JÜRGEN ROHWER received his Ph.D. from Hamburg University. He served in the Kriegsmarine during World War II on a destroyer, a mine destruction vessel, and a fleet minesweeper. Formerly manager and president of the Arbeitskreis für Wehrforschung, he is currently director of the Bibliothek für Zeitgeschichte, Stuttgart. He is author of *Axis Submarine Successes, 1939–1945;* coauthor, with Gerhard Hümmelchen, of *Chronology of the War at Sea, 1939–1945;* and coeditor of *Decisive Battles of World War II: The German View.*

MANFRED ROMMEL is Oberbürgermeister of the city of Stuttgart. Formerly Ministerialdirektor with the state of Baden-Württemberg, he is also currently chairman of the Baden-Württemberg Städtetages and president of the Deutsche Städtetages.

RONALD H. SPECTOR received his Ph.D. from Yale University. Formerly Director of Naval History and director of the Naval Historical Center, Washington, D.C., he is currently a professor of history and international affairs at George Washington University. He is author of *Eagle against the Sun* and *After Tet.*

Contributors

The Rev. P. R. C. ABRAM was a military chaplain with 3 Para, 16th Airborne Brigade. He lives in Salcombe, Devon, England.

ALAN C. AIMONE is the Chief of Special Collections at the U.S. Military Academy Library, West Point. He is active with the Society for Military History, the Association for the Bibliography of History, and the American Committee on the History of the Second World War.

STEPHEN AMBROSE received his Ph.D. from the University of Wisconsin. Formerly Dwight D. Eisenhower Professor of War and Peace at Kansas State University, currently he is Boyd Professor of History and director of the Eisenhower Center at the University of New Orleans. He is author of *Eisenhower: Soldier, General of the Army, President-Elect* and *Band of Brothers: E Company, 506th Regiment, 101st Airborne from Normandy to Hitler's Eagle's Nest,* and assistant editor of *The Papers of Dwight David Eisenhower.*

DUNCAN ANDERSON, a native Australian, received his Ph.D. from Oxford University. Currently a senior lecturer at the Royal Military Academy, Sandhurst, he is author of *D-Day: The Normandy Campaign June to August 1944.*

Air Chief Marshal Sir MICHAEL ARMITAGE (Royal Air Force, ret.) has served in flying and staff positions and commanded No. 17 Squadron and RAF Luqa, Malta. He later was Deputy Commander RAF Germany, Director of Service Intelligence, and Chief of Defense Intelligence. Formerly a council member of the Royal United Services Institute for Defense Studies, he is coauthor of *Illustrated History of the Royal Air Force.*

Col. EDELFRIED BAGINSKI (Bundeswehr, ret.) joined the Wehrmacht in 1944. He later served in the Bundeswehr for thirty-one years as an armor officer. He later helped manage the restoration of the first German tank, the World War I A7V.

Lt. Col. CHARLES M. BAILY (U.S. Army, ret.) received his Ph.D. from Duke University. Having served for twenty-two years as an armor officer, he is currently a defense analyst at the Science Applications Corporation, specializing in arms control.

DONALD E. BAIN received his Ph.D. from the State University of New York at Buffalo. Formerly a visiting scholar with the Defense Intelligence Agency, he is currently a professor at the National Defense University, Washington, D.C.

JOSEPH M. BALKOSKI has served as a historian with the Maryland National Guard. He is author of *Beyond the Beachhead: The 29th Infantry Division in Normandy* and *A History of Maryland's Military Forces.*

JEFFREY G. BARLOW received his Ph.D. from the University of South Carolina. Currently a historian with the Naval Historical Center, Washington, D.C., he is author of *The "Revolt of the Admirals": The Fight for Naval Aviation, 1945–1950.*

Lt. Col. Sir JOHN BAYNES, 7th Baronet (British Army, ret.), was commissioned into the Cameronians (Scottish Rifles) in 1949. He served in Malaya and in Aden, Yemen, was a Defense Fellow at Edinburgh University, and commanded the 52d Lowland Volunteers. He is author of *Soldiers of Scotland* and *The Forgotten Victor: General Sir Richard O'Connor.*

DANIEL R. BEAVER received his Ph.D. from Northwestern University. Currently a professor at the University of Cincinnati, he has served as Harold Keith Johnson Visiting Professor at the U.S. Army Military History Institute, Carlisle Barracks, Pennsylvania, and as distinguished visiting scholar at the Center of Military History, Washington, D.C.

EDWARD N. BEDESSEM joined the Center of Military History, Washington, D.C., in 1986 as a historian in the Field and International Division. He is currently a member of the Center's Organizational History Branch.

Lt. Col. FLORIAN BERBERICH (Bundeswehr, ret.), a former paratrooper and company commander, has served as a historical staff officer at the Militärgeschictliches Forschungsamt, Freiburg im Breisgau, and as an assistant professor at the Offizierschule des Heeres, Hanover.

JOHN D. BERGEN is the president and chief operating officer of GCI Group, an international public relations firm. A former Signal Corps officer who served in Vietnam, Germany, and Korea, he is author of *A Test for Technology: Military Communications in Southeast Asia.*

MARTIN BLUMENSON served with the U.S. Army during World War II and in Korea. He has held the Ernest J. King Chair at the Naval War College, the Mark W. Clark Chair at the Citadel, and the Harold Keith Johnson Chair at the Army War College, and is author of *Patton: The Man behind the Legend, 1885–1945; The Patton Papers,* in 2 volumes; and *The Duel for France.* He lives in Washington, D.C.

DAVID BROWN is a Fellow of the Royal Historical Society. Formerly a naval aviator, he currently heads the Naval Historical Branch, Ministry of Defence, London. He is author of *Warship Losses of World War Two* and *Seafire: The Spitfire That Went to Sea.*

NEVILLE BROWN, formerly a naval meteorologist and a professor of international security at Birmingham University, is currently a scientific consultant with the Environmental Change Unit at Oxford. He is author of *The Strategic Revolution.*

RAY S. CLINE received his Ph.D. from Harvard University. Joining the OSS in 1943, he served as chief of its Current Intelligence Staff from the spring of 1944 to the end of World War II. He later became Deputy Director for Intelligence for the Central Intelligence Agency and Assistant Secretary of State as director of the Bureau of Intelligence and Research. He is currently chairman of the United States Global Strategy Council and a professor at Georgetown University. He is author of *Secrets, Spies and Scholars: Blueprint of the Essential CIA.*

Maj. JAMES S. CORUM (U.S. Army Reserve) received his Ph.D. from Queen's University, Ontario. Currently a professor at the School of Advanced Airpower Studies, Air University, Maxwell Air Force Base, Alabama, he is author of *The Roots of the Blitzkrieg: Hans von Seekt and German Military Reform between the World Wars.*

Lt. Gen. Sir NAPIER CROOKENDEN (British Army, ret.) was commissioned in the Cheshire Regiment in 1935. Brigade major of the 6th Airlanding Brigade in June 1944, he later commanded the 9th Parachute Battalion, 16th Parachute Brigade Group, Royal Military College of Science, and Western Command U.K. He is author of *Drop Zone Normandy* and *Airborne at War.*

RICHARD G. DAVIS received his Ph.D. from George Washington University. Currently with the Office of Air Force History, Washington, D.C., he is author of *The 31 Initiatives,* a study of army–air force efforts at cooperation and reform, and *Tempering the Blade: The Development of American Tactical Air Power in the North African Campaign.*

Maj. GERARD M. DEVLIN (U.S. Army, ret.) served in Korea and Vietnam as a paratrooper and Ranger. He is author of *Paratrooper, Silent Wings,* and *Back to Corregidor.* He lives in Hilton Head, South Carolina.

Lt. Col. KARL DIEFENBACH (Bundeswehr) serves as a helicopter pilot and is currently deputy chief of historical reference at the Militärgeschictliches Forschungsamt, Potsdam.

R. L. DiNARDO received his Ph.D. from the Graduate School, City University of New York. Currently a professor at St. Peter's College, he is author of *Mechanized Juggernaut or Military Anachronism? Horses and the German Army of World War II.*

W. A. B. DOUGLAS, a retired commander in the Royal Canadian Navy, is the official historian of the Canadian armed forces. Currently writing the official history of Canadian naval operations in World War II, he is author of *The Creation of a National Air Force,* volume 2 of *The Official History of the RCAF,* and coauthor of *Out of the Shadows: Canada in the Second World War.* He is editor of *The RCN in Transition, 1910–1985.*

JAMES F. DUNNIGAN is a designer of historical simulations and the founder of Simulations Publications. A consultant for the Department of Defense, the Central Intelligence Agency, and the U.S. Marine Corps, he is author of *The Complete Wargames Handbook* and *How to Make War.* He lives in New York City.

Lt. Col. JOHN A. ENGLISH received his Ph.D. from Queen's University, Canada. Currently serving with Princess Patricia's Canadian Light Infantry, he is author of *A Perspective on Infantry* and *The Canadian Army and the Normandy Campaign: A Study of Failure in High Command,* and editor of *The Mechanized Battlefield: A Tactical Analysis.*

DONNA EVERETT, a military historian with the Center of Military History, Washington, D.C., since 1986, specializes in organizational and unit history.

STANLEY L. FALK received his Ph.D. from Georgetown University. Formerly Chief Historian, U.S. Air Force, and a founding director of the American Committee on the History of the Second World War, he is a member of the board of historians of the Battle of Normandy Foundation.

Gen. Sir MARTIN FARNDALE (British Army, ret.) was commissioned into the Royal Artillery in 1948. He commanded the 1st Royal Horse Artillery, 7th Armoured Brigade, 2d Armoured Division, 1st British Corps, and Northern Army Group. He is currently Master Gunner, St. James's Park, London, and chairman of the Royal United Services Institute for Defence Studies.

Col. ERNEST F. FISHER (U.S. Army, ret.) received his Ph.D. from the University of Wisconsin. In World War II he served with the 501st Parachute Regiment, 101st Airborne Division, at Bastogne, Belgium, in the Netherlands, and in the Rhineland. He was a historian with U.S. Army Headquarters, Europe, and the Center for Military History, Washington, D.C.

M. R. D. FOOT was intelligence officer to the Special Air Service Brigade and a gunner major on combined operations intelligence staff during World War II. While serving in uniform with the Resistance in Brittany, he was severely wounded and captured, and later organized escapes. Formerly a professor at Oxford and Manchester universities, he is author of *SOE in France, Resistance,* and *Six Faces of Courage.*

Lt. Col. BARRY W. FOWLE (U.S. Army, ret.) received his Ph.D. from the University of Maryland. Having served for twenty-three years with the Signal Corps, he is currently a historian with the U.S. Army Corps of Engineers. He is coauthor of *The 51st Again* and editor of *Builders and Fighters: U.S. Army Engineers in World War II.*

ARTHUR L. FUNK received his Ph.D. from the University of Chicago. Currently a professor emeritus of the University of Florida, he is author of *Hidden Ally: The French Resistance, Special Operations, and the Landings in Southern France, 1944.*

MICHAEL GANNON received his Ph.D. from the University of Florida. Currently Distinguished Service Professor of History at the University of Florida, he is author of *Operation Drumbeat: The Dramatic True Story of Germany's First U-Boat Attacks along the American Coast in World War Two.*

MARTIN GILBERT is a Fellow of Merton College, Oxford. He has published six volumes on the life of Winston Churchill with eight volumes of supporting documents. He is currently editing *Churchill's War Papers, 1939–45,* in 8 volumes..

SUSAN H. GODSON received her Ph.D. from American University. A historian in Williamsburg, Virginia, she is author of *Viking of Assault: Admiral John Lesslie Hall, Jr., and Amphibious Warfare.*

MARTIN K. GORDON received his Ph.D. from George Washington University. Currently a historian with the Office of History, U.S. Army Corps of Engineers, he is also executive editor of the White

Mane Publishing Company and a director of the Council on America's Military Past. He is author of *Imprint on the Nation: Stories Reflecting the National Guard's Impact on a Changing Nation.*

GORDON F. GRAHAM is a retired executive of the National Association of Wool Manufactures and Knitted Textile Association. Enlisting in the U.S. Navy as a yeoman, he served in several of Adm. Carleton F. Bryant's fast troop convoys, leaving the service as a lieutenant.

Maj. DAVID R. GRAY received his Ph.D. from The Ohio State University. He has served in command and staff positions in infantry divisions within the U.S. Army's rapid deployment force. Currently an assistant professor at the U.S. Military Academy, he is writing a book on the Ranger experience during the Korean War.

ERIC GROVE was Deputy Head of Strategic Studies and civilian lecturer at the Royal Naval College, Dartmouth, England. Formerly an exchange professor at the U.S. Naval Academy, he is currently visiting lecturer at the Royal Naval College, Greenwich, and a Research Fellow at both Southampton and Lancaster universities. He is author of *Sea Battles in Close-up: World War II,* volume 2.

EKKEHART GUTH received his Ph.D. from Düsseldorf University. Currently an assistant professor at the Führungsakademie der Bundeswehr, Hamburg, he is author of *Sanitätswesen im Zweiten Weltkrieg* and *La Cambe–Deutscher Soldatenfriedhof in der Normandie.*

AMY HACKETT received her Ph.D. from Columbia University. She was general editor and translator of *The Encyclopedia of the Third Reich.* She lives in Brooklyn, New York.

Maj. DONALD E. HALL (U.S. Army Medical Service Corps) served during the Persian Gulf War as command historian of the 3d Medical Command in Riyadh, Saudi Arabia. He is currently assigned as an analyst at the Armed Forces Medical Intelligence Center, Fort Detrick, Maryland.

ALAN HANKINSON is a freelance journalist and author. He has worked for the Nigerian Broadcasting Corporation and Independent Television News, London.

DONALD J. HARVEY received his Ph.D. from Columbia University. In World War II he served as a field artillery captain in the European theater. Professor and chair emeritus at Hunter College and the Graduate School, City University of New York, he is author of *France since the Revolution* and coauthor of *Modern France: Problems of the Third and Fourth Republics.*

Maj. WINFRIED HEINEMANN (Bundeswehr) is currently with the Militärgeschichtliches Forschungsamt, Freiburg im Breisgau. Formerly a company commander, he is coeditor, with Reinhard Stumpf, of *Militärgeschichte.*

Col. PAUL F. HENRY (U.S. Air Force) is a professor of aerospace studies at the University of Virginia. He has flown combat missions in Vietnam and the Persian Gulf, and has served tours of duty in Europe and the Far East.

Capt. GÜNTER HILLER lives in Munich, Germany.

Sir Harry (F. H.) HINSLEY was with the Government Code and Cypher School at Bletchley Park during World War II. Formerly Master of St. John's College and a professor at Cambridge University, he is author of *British Intelligence in the Second World War,* in 4 volumes.

IAN HOGG enlisted in the Royal Artillery during World War II and later served in Korea. Having retired as master gunner and instructor at the Royal Military College of Science, he is currently editor of *Jane's Infantry Weapons* and *Jane's Security & Counter-Insurgency Equipment Yearbook,* joint editor of *Jane's Ammunition Handbook,* and author of *Infantry Weapons of World War II.*

WILLIAM J. HOURIHAN received his Ph.D. from the University of Massachusetts at Amherst. He is currently the U.S. Army Chaplain Branch historian.

THOMAS HUGHES is currently completing his doctoral dissertation on Maj. Gen. Elwood ("Pete") Quesada at the University of Houston.

GERHARD HÜMMELCHEN served in the Luftwaffe during World War II. He has worked for the historical division of the U.S. Air Force and the Studiengruppe Luftwaffe of the Führungsakademie der Bundeswehr, and was managing director of the Arbeitskreis für Wehrforschung. He is currently a member of the Commission Internationale d'Histoire Militaire and of the Komitee der Bundesrepublik für die Geschichte des Zweiten Weltkrieges.

MARK JACOBSEN received his Ph.D. from the University of California, Irvine. Formerly a historian with the Naval Historical Center, Washington, D.C., he is currently an associate professor at the U.S. Marine Corps Command and Staff College, Quantico, Virginia. He is coauthor of *Contingency War Plans for War in Western Europe, 1920–1940.*

ROBERT J. JAKEMAN received his Ph.D. from Auburn University, Alabama, where he is currently an assistant professor. He holds a U.S. Air Force Reserve commission. Formerly archivist at the Air Force Historical Research Agency, Maxwell Air Force Base, Alabama, he is author of *Divided Skies: Establishing Segregated Flight Training at Tuskegee, Alabama, 1934–1942.*

Lt. Col. JOHANNES KINDLER (Bundeswehr) is currently chief of historical reference at the Militärgeschichtliches Forschungsamt, Potsdam.

Gen. DOUGLAS KINNARD (U.S. Army, ret.) received his Ph.D. from Princeton University. He saw combat in Europe during World War II, and in Korea and Vietnam. Formerly a professor at Princeton University, he is currently professor emeritus at the University of Vermont and on the faculty of the National Defense University, Washington, D.C. He is author of *The Certain Trumpet* and *The War Managers.*

BROOKS E. KLEBER received his Ph.D. from the University of Pennsylvania. During World War II he served as an infantry officer and was taken prisoner in Normandy. He was a historian at the Center of Military History, Washington, D.C., retiring as the army's Chief of Military History. He is coauthor of *Chemicals in Combat.*

ANDREW D. LAMBERT, currently lecturer at King's College, London, also serves as councillor of the Navy Records Society and councillor of the British Commission for Maritime History. He is author of *Steam, Steel and Shellfire.*

JAMES LUCAS served with the British Army in Africa and in Italy during World War II. He has worked for the German section of the Foreign Office and was Deputy Head of the Department of Photographs of the Imperial War Museum. A founder and honorary secretary of the British section of the European Confederation of Former Combatants, he is author of *World War Two through German Eyes* and *Experiences of War: The British Soldier,* and coauthor of The *Battle of Normandy: Falaise Gap.*

RAIMONDO LURAGHI served in World War II and in the Italian Resistance. He is currently director of graduate studies in history of the Americas at the University of Genoa and president of the Italian Society for Military History.

J. BRITT MCCARLEY received his Ph.D. from Temple University. He is currently the U.S. Army Test and Evaluation Command historian at Aberdeen Proving Ground, Maryland.

STEPHEN MCFARLAND received his Ph.D. from the University of Texas. Currently an associate professor at Auburn University and a visiting professor at the U.S. Air Force's Air War College, he is author of *Hitting the Broad Side of a Barn: America's Pursuit of Precision Bombing, 1910–1945,* and coauthor of *To Command the Sky: The Battle for Air Superiority over Germany, 1942–44.*

Lt. Col. DAVID MACISAAC (U.S. Air Force, ret.) received his Ph.D. from Duke University. He has taught at the U.S. Air Force Academy, Naval War College, and Air War College, and is author of *Strategic Bombing in World War II.*

SEAN MCKNIGHT is a senior lecturer in the Department of War Studies at the Royal Military Academy, Sandhurst.

Maj. KENNETH MACKSEY (British Army, ret.) served during World War II as a trooper with the Royal Tank Corps, commanding the 141st Regiment RAC (The Buffs) in 1944. He later served in India, Korea, Germany, and Singapore. Currently a freelance author and publisher, he is author of *Armoured Crusader: The Biography of Maj. Gen. Sir Percy Hobart, Tank versus Tank,* and *A History of the Royal Armoured Corps,* coauthor of *The Penguin Encyclopedia of Modern Warfare,* and deputy editor of *Purnell's History of the Second World War* and *History of the Second World War.*

EDUARD MARK received his Ph.D. from the University of Connecticut. He is currently a historian at the Center for Air Force History, Washington, D.C., and is author of *Aerial Interdiction: Air Power and the Land Battle in Three American Wars.*

PHILIPPE MASSON, doctor of letters, is currently head of the historical section of the Service historique de la Marine, Vincennes, and teaches at the École Supérieure de Guerre Navale. He is author of *La Marine française et la guerre 1939–1945* and *Une guerre totale, 1939–1945,* and coauthor of the three naval volumes of *Histoire militaire de la France.*

Lt. Col. PHILLIP S. MEILINGER received his Ph.D. from the University of Michigan. A command pilot with tours in both Europe and the Pacific, he has served with the U.S. Air Force's Doctrine Division in the Pentagon. He is currently Dean of the School of Advanced Air Power Studies at Maxwell Air Force Base, Alabama.

LT. COL. CHARLES MESSENGER (British Army, ret.) served for twenty years as an officer in the Royal Tank Regiment. Currently a military historian and defense analyst, he is author of the *Art of Blitzkrieg;* "*Bomber*" *Harris and the Strategic Bombing Offensive, 1939–1945; The Commandos, 1940–1946;* biographies of "Sepp" Dietrich and Gerd von Rundstedt; and the *World War II Chronological Atlas.*

GEORG MEYER received his Ph.D. from Göttingen University. A lieutenant colonel with the Luftwaffe reserves, he is currently a historian at the Militärgeschichtliches Forschungsamt, Potsdam. He is editor of *Generalfeldmarschall W. Ritter v. Leeb: Tagebuchaufzeichnungen und Lagebeurteilungen aus zwei Weltkriegen.*

JOEL D. MEYERSON received his Ph.D. from Harvard University. He is currently chief of the Operational History Branch at the Center of Military History, Washington, D.C., and is author of *Images of a Lengthy War: The U.S. Army in Vietnam.*

ALFRED C. MIERZEJEWSKI received his Ph.D. from the University of North Carolina, Chapel Hill. Formerly command historian at the U.S. Army Training and Evaluation Command (TRADOC), he is currently an assistant professor at Athens State College, Alabama. He is author of *The Collapse of the German War Economy, 1944–1945: Allied Air Power and the German National Railways.*

Col. PAUL L. MILES (U.S. Army, ret.) was a Rhodes Scholar at Oxford University. He commanded an engineer company during the Vietnam War and served as a research assistant to the Chief of Staff of the Army, later teaching at the U.S. Military Academy.

SAMUEL W. MITCHAM, JR., received his Ph.D. from the University of Tennessee. A former U.S. Army helicopter pilot and combat engineer company commander, he is currently an associate professor at Northeast Louisiana University. He is author of *Hitler's Field Marshals and Their Battles, Men of the Luftwaffe,* and *Hitler's Legions: The German Army Order of Battle, World War II,* and coauthor, with Gene Mueller, of *Hitler's Commanders.*

STEVEN J. MROZEK is currently the historian for the 82d Airborne Division Association. A paratrooper with the parachute badges of several countries, he is a sergeant in a long-range surveillance company of the Michigan National Guard.

GENE MUELLER received his Ph.D. from the University of Idaho. Currently a professor at Henderson State University, Arkansas, he is author of *The Forgotten Field Marshall: Wilhelm Keitel* and coauthor, with Samuel W. Mitcham, Jr., of *Hitler's Commanders*.

MALCOLM MUIR, JR., received his Ph.D. from The Ohio State University. Formerly a visiting professor at the U.S. Naval Academy, he has held the Secretary of the Navy's Research Chair in Naval History, Naval Historical Center, Washington, D.C. Currently professor and chairman at Austin Peay State University, he is author of *The Iowa-Class Battleships*.

RICHARD R. MULLER received his Ph.D. from The Ohio State University. Currently professor at the U.S. Air Force Air Command and Staff College, Maxwell Air Force Base, Alabama, he is author of *The German Air War in Russia*.

Lt. TIM J. MUNDEN (British Army, ret.) is currently with the Royal Military Academy, Sandhurst.

WILLIAMSON MURRAY received his Ph.D. from Yale University. Currently a professor at The Ohio State University, he is author of *Luftwaffe* and *German Military Effectiveness*, and coeditor, with Alan R. Millett, of *Calculations, Net Assessment, and the Coming of World War II* and *Military Effectiveness*, volumes 1–3.

Lt. Col. CLAYTON R. NEWELL (U.S. Army, ret.) served for more than twenty-seven years. His assignments included the Center of Military History, Washington, D.C., and the faculty of the Army War College, where he held the John J. Pershing Chair. He is author of *The Framework of Operational Warfare*.

Lt. Col. S. MICHAEL NEWELL (Canadian Army, ret.) served as both an infantry and an armor officer and taught at the Staff College. Upon retirement from the army, he was appointed Assistant Secretary-General of the Commonwealth War Graves Commission, Canadian Agency, retiring in 1993 as Secretary-General.

Maj. Gen. FRANK W. NORRIS (U.S. Army, ret.) commanded the 345th Field Artillery Battalion, 90th Infantry Division, from the Normandy invasion to V-E Day. He later served in Korea, held senior staff positions, and was commandant of the Armed Forces Staff College. He is coeditor, with Orwin Talbott and Eames Yates, of *War from the Ground Up: The 90th Division in World War II*.

WILLIAM L. O'NEILL received his Ph.D. from the University of California, Berkeley. Currently a professor of history at Rutgers University, New Jersey, he is author of *A Democracy at War: America's Fight at Home and Abroad in World War II*.

Capt. DEREK OAKLEY (Royal Marines, ret.) served for more than forty-two years, seeing action in Malaya, Port Said in Egypt, Northern Ireland, Brunei, and Borneo, and was editor of the regimental journal *The Globe & Laurel*. Currently editor of the Royal Marines Historical Society, he is author of *The Commandos: World War II to the Present*.

VINCENT ORANGE is a Reader in History at the University of Canterbury in Christchurch, New Zealand. He is author of *Coningham: A Biography of Air Marshal Sir Arthur Coningham*.

TADEUSZ PANECKI is currently with the Wojskowy Instytut Historyczny, Warsaw. He is editor of *2 Korpus Polski w Bitwie o Monte Cassino: Z Perspektywy Polwiecza*.

JAMES PARTON served during World War II as an aide to Gen. Ira C. Eaker and as Chief Historian, Mediterranean Allied Air Forces. Founder of the American Heritage Publishing Co., he has served as president of the Encyclopaedia Britannica Educational Co., assistant librarian of Congress, and trustee of the Air Force Historical Foundation. He is author of *"Air Force Spoken Here": Gen. Ira Eaker and the Command of the Air,* and editor and publisher of *IMPACT, the Army Air Forces' Confidential Picture History of World War II,* in 8 volumes.

J. L. PIMLOTT received his Ph.D. from Leicester University, England. Currently Deputy Head of the Department of War Studies at the Royal Military Academy, Sandhurst, he is author of *Strategic Bombing* and *Battle of the Bulge,* and coeditor of *British Military Operations*.

BARRIE PITT served during World War II in both Europe and the Middle East, and worked for the Atomic Energy Authority after the war. He is author of *The Battle of the Atlantic, Churchill and the Generals,* and *The Crucible of War,* and editor of *Ballantine's Illustrated History of World War 2*.

FORREST C. POGUE was a First Army combat historian in World War II. Former director of the George C. Marshall Research Center, he is author of *George C. Marshall,* in 4 volumes.

ALFRED PRICE received his Ph.D. from Loughborough University, England, and is a Fellow of the Royal Historical Society. An officer of the Royal Air Force whose flying career spanned fifteen years, he is author of *Instruments of Darkness,* on electronic warfare deception operations; *Aircraft versus Submarine;* and *The Last Year of the Luftwaffe*.

Air Como. HENRY PROBERT (Royal Air Force, ret.) served as director of the RAF Education Branch. Formerly head of the Air Historical Branch, Ministry of Defence, he currently chairs the Programmes Committee of the RAF Historical Society. He is author of *High Commanders of the RAF*.

Maj. HAROLD E. RAUGH, JR. (U.S. Army), received his Ph.D. from the University of California, Los Angeles. Formerly an assistant professor of history at the U.S. Military Academy, he is currently brigade executive officer in the 7th Infantry Division (Light) at Fort Ord, California.

JOHN C. REILLY, JR., currently heads the Ships' Histories Branch of the Naval Historical Center, Washington, D.C. He is coauthor of *American Battleships, 1886–1923* and editor of *Operational Experience of Fast Battleships*.

OLAV RISTE is director of the Norwegian Institute for Defense Studies, Oslo, and a professor at the University of Bergen. A member of the Norwegian Academy of Science and Letters, the International Commission for the History of International Relations, and the International Commission for Military History, he is author of *Norge i krigsalliansen 1940–1945*, in 2 volumes.

SIMON N. ROBBINS is pursuing his doctorate at King's College, London. Currently with the Department of Documents, Imperial War Museum, he is coeditor of *Staff Officer: The Diaries of Walter Guinness (First Lord Moyne) 1914–1918*.

WILLIAM RODNEY received his Ph.D. from the University of London. During World War II he served in the Royal Canadian Air Force with Four Group, Bomber Command. Dean Emeritus of Royal Roads Military College, he is vice-president of the Bomber Airfield Society and a member of the Aircrew Association.

Col. WILLIAM E. RYAN, JR., is currently Director of Operations and Finance for the American Battle Monuments Commission.

MICHAEL SALEWSKI is currently a professor at Christian Albrechts University, Kiel, and a commander in the Bundesmarine reserve. He is author of *Die deutsche Seekriegslietung 1935–1945, Von der Wirklichkeit des Krieges,* and *Die bewaffnete Macht im Dritten Reich 1933–1935*.

ROBERT J. SAUER received his Ph.D. from Boston College and is preparing his dissertation on I SS Panzer Corps for publication. He is currently teaching at the University of Massachusetts, Boston, and at Mount Ida College, Newton, Massachusetts.

C. M. SCHULTEN is director of the Rijksinstituut voor Oorlogsdocumentatie, Amsterdam, and president of the International Commission of Military History. He is coeditor of *Oranje op de bres: vorstenhuis en leger in de Nederlandse geschiedenis*.

DONALD M. SCHURMAN received his Ph.D. from the University of London. During World War II he served in the Royal Canadian Air Force as wireless air gunner with No. 429 Squadron, Six Group, Bomber Command. Formerly head of the history department at the Royal Military College of Canada, he is author of *The Education of a Navy*.

G. D. SHEFFIELD is pursuing his doctorate at King's College, London. Currently a senior lecturer at the Royal Military Academy, Sandhurst, he also serves as secretary of the Royal Commission for Military History.

B. MITCHELL SIMPSON III received his Ph.D. from the Fletcher School of Law and Diplomacy, Tufts University. A retired career U.S. Navy officer, he is currently a practicing lawyer in Newport, Rhode Island. He is author of *Admiral Harold R. Stark: Architect of Victory, 1939–1945*.

CHARLES E. SMITH is currently the president of Paramount Publishing Education Group, Academic Reference Division, New York. He lives in Colts Neck, New Jersey.

ROGER SMITHER, formerly Keeper of the Department of Information Retrieval, Imperial War Museum, London, is currently Keeper of its Department of Film, one of the two national film archives in the United Kingdom.

Lt. Col. LEWIS SORLEY (U.S. Army, ret.) received his Ph.D. from The Johns Hopkins University. He served in Vietnam, in NATO forces, and at the Pentagon, and as a civilian official of the Central Intelligence Agency. He is author of *Thunderbolt: Gen. Creighton Abrams and the Army of His Times*.

Air Marshall Sir FREDERICK SOWREY (Royal Air Force, ret.) served during World War II in the European theater as a fighter reconnaissance pilot. He was Middle East Senior Air Staff Officer, Commandant of the National Defense College, Director of RAF Training, and the U.K. CENTO representative. Formerly with the Institute for Strategic Studies, he is currently chairman of the RAF Historical Society.

ALAN STEPHENS is a senior research fellow at the Royal Australian Air Force's Air Power Studies Centre, Canberra. He is author of *Power plus Attitude: Ideas, Strategy & Doctrine in the RAAF, 1921–1991*.

PAUL STILLWELL is a U.S. Naval Reserve officer who served on active duty during the Vietnam War. Formerly editor in chief of *Naval History* magazine, he is currently director of the History Division of the U.S. Naval Institute, Annapolis. He is author of *Assault on Normandy*.

TRUMAN R. STROBRIDGE served in the Merchant Marine and the U.S. Army Air Forces. Formerly the historian of the U.S. Coast Guard, he has worked at the Joint Chiefs of Staff (JCS) and as a historian or archivist with various government agencies, including the unified JCS combatant commands in Alaska, Europe, and the Pacific.

REINHARD STUMPF received his Ph.D. from Heidelberg University. Currently Oberregierungsrat with the Bundesministerium der Verteidigung, Bonn, he is author of *Die Wehrmacht-Elite: Rang- und Herkunftsstrucktur der deutschen Generale und Admirale 1933–1945* and coeditor, with Winfried Heinemann, of *Militärgeschte*.

Lt. Gen. ORWIN TALBOTT (U.S. Army, ret.) survived the sinking of the USS *Susan B. Anthony* off Utah Beach to command Company G, 359th Infantry Regiment, 90th Infantry Division. He later commanded the 1st Infantry Division in Vietnam, was Commandant of the Infantry School at Ft. Benning, Georgia, and the deputy commander of the Training and Doctrine Command (TRADOC). He is coeditor, with Frank W. Norris and Eames Yates, of *War from the Ground Up: The 90th Division in World War II*.

PHILIP M. TAYLOR, Ph.D. and Fellow of the Royal Historical Society, is currently deputy director of the Institute of Communications Studies at the University of Leeds, England. He is author of *Britain and the Cinema in the Second World War* and *Munitions of the Mind: War Propaganda from the Ancient World to the Nuclear Age,* and an associate editor of the *Historical Journal of Film, Radio and Television.*

JOHN TERRAINE is a Fellow of the Royal Historical Society. A member of the Royal United Services Institute and honorary president of the Western Front Association, he is scriptwriter of the BBC production *The Life and Times of Lord Mountbatten,* and author of the book of the same name and *The Right of the Line: The Royal Air Force in the European War, 1939–45.* He lives in West Sussex, England.

CHARLES S. THOMAS received his Ph.D. from Vanderbilt University. Currently an associate professor at Georgia Southern University, he is author of *The German Navy in the Nazi Era.*

STEVEN J. TIRONE is pursuing his doctorate at Columbia University. Currently a freelance editor, he is project editor for the forthcoming *Encyclopedia of the Vietnam War.*

FRANCIS TOASE is a senior lecturer at the Royal Military Academy, Sandhurst. He is coeditor of *Armoured Warfare.*

VINCENT A. TRANSANO received his Ph.D. from the University of California. He is command historian of the Naval Facilities Engineering Command (NAVFAC) and director of the NAVFAC Historical Program Office.

DAVID F. TRASK received his Ph.D. from Harvard University. Formerly director of the Office of the Historian, U.S. Department of State, and Chief Historian, Center of Military History, Washington, D.C., he is author of *Captains and Cabinets: Anglo-American Naval Relations, 1917–1918* and *The War with Spain in 1898.*

Lt. Col. DETLEF VOGEL is currently a historian at the Militärgeschichtliches Forschungsamt, Freiburg im Breisgau. He is author of *Das Eingreifen Deutschlands auf dem Balkan 1941* and *La Retraite du Midi de la France août/septembre 1944.*

Lt. Col. JOHN F. VOTAW (U.S. Army, ret.) received his Ph.D. from Temple University. Having served in the army for twenty-five years and commanded cavalry and tank units through battalion level, he is currently executive director of the Cantigny First Division Foundation, Wheaton, Illinois.

HEINRICH WALLE received his Ph.D from Bonn University. A commander in the Bundesmarine, he is currently chief of audio-visual media and commissioner of military museums with the Militärgeschichtliches Forschungsamt, Potsdam. He is coauthor, with Roland G. Foerster, of *Militär und Technik: Wechselbeziehungen zu Staat, Gesellschaft und Industrie im 19. und 20. Jahrhundert.*

THEODORE A. WILSON received his Ph.D from Indiana University. Formerly a visiting professor at the U.S. Army Command and General Staff College and the Center of Military History, Washington, D.C., he is currently a professor at the University of Kansas. He is author of *The First Summit: Roosevelt and Churchill at Placentia Bay, 1941* and editor of *WW2: Critical Issues* and *Makers of American Diplomacy.*

ALAN P. WILT received his Ph.D. from the University of Michigan. Currently a professor at Iowa State University, he is author of *War from the Top: German and British Military Decision Making during World War II, The French Riviera Campaign of August 1944,* and *The Atlantic Wall: German Defenses in the West, 1941–1944.*

GEOFFREY WOOTTEN formerly worked in marketing for Plessy and IBM. He is currently a lecturer at a business school near Bath, England.

HUMPHREY WYNN served as a pilot in the Royal Air Force during World War II and subsequently in the Royal Air Force Volunteer Reserve. Formerly deputy editor and defense correspondent of the aviation magazine *Flight International,* he later served as a historian and deputy head of the Air Historical Branch, Ministry of Defence, London, where he is currently a part-time consultant for a history of Transport Command.

The late Lt. Col. EAMES YATES (U.S. Army, ret.) landed with the 90th Infantry Division headquarters on Utah Beach and served as aide-de-camp to several of the generals commanding the division. He later served in Korea and commanded the 2d Battalion, 27th Infantry. He was coeditor, with Frank W. Norris and Orwin Talbott, of *War from the Ground Up: The 90th Division in World War II.*

BILL YENNE is a writer specializing in aviation and aerospace topics. Based in San Francisco, he is author of *The History of the U.S. Air Force* and *The Pictoral History of American Aircraft,* and coauthor, with Gen. Curtis E. Lemay, of *Superfortress.*

Maj. Gen. A. E. YOUNGER (British Army, ret.) was commissioned into the Royal Engineers in 1939. He commanded a section during the retreat to Dunkirk in 1940 and commanded the 26th Assault Engineer Squadron on D-day. One of the first British soldiers to cross the Rhine, he later served in Burma, Malaya, Norway, Korea, and Kenya. He has taught at the U.S. Army Command and General Staff College and the Royal College of Defence Studies, and was director general of the Royal United Services Institute for Strategic Studies.

EARL F. ZIEMKE received his Ph.D. from the University of Madison. Currently research professor at the University of Georgia, Athens, he is author of *Moscow to Stalingrad: Decision in the East; Stalingrad to Berlin: The German Defeat in the East;* and *The U.S. Army in the Occupation of Germany, 1944–46.*

PROPER NAMES AND ENGLISH EQUIVALENTS USED IN THE PRECEDING BIOGRAPHIES

Arbeitskreis für Wehrforschung	Council for Defense Research
Bibliothek für Zeitgeschichte	Library for Contemporary History
Bundesministerium der Verteidigung	Federal Ministry of Defense
Bundesmarine	German Navy, Federal Republic of Germany (post–World War II)
Bundeswehr	German Army, Federal Republic of Germany (post–World War II)
École Supérieure de Guerre Navale	Naval War College, France
Führungsakademie der Bundeswehr	Bundeswehr Staff and Command College
Komitee der Bundesrepublic für die Geschichte des Zweiten Weltkrieges	Committee of the Federal Republic of Germany for the History of the Second World War
Kriegsmarine	German Navy (World War II)
Luftwaffe	German Air Force
Militärgeschichtliches Forschungsamt	Military History Research Office
Ministerialdirektor	governmental department head
Oberbürgermeister	lord mayor
Oberregierungsrat	senior civil servant
Offizierschule des Heeres	Army Officers' School (Bundeswehr)
Rijksinstituut voor Oorlogsdocumentatie	Netherlands State Institute for War Documentation
Städtetages	municipal authorities
Studiengruppe Luftwaffe	Air Force Study Group
Wehrmacht	German Army (World War II)

Directory of Contributors

A

PAUL ABRAM
Salcombe, England
Chaplains
    British Chaplains

ALAN C. AIMONE
U.S. Military Academy Library, West Point
Bibliography

STEPHEN AMBROSE
University of New Orleans
American Beaches
    Omaha Beach
Cole, Robert G.

DUNCAN ANDERSON
Royal Military Academy, Sandhurst
Australia
New Zealand

MICHAEL ARMITAGE
Bath, England
Air Defence of Great Britain
Hill, Roderic M.

B

STEPHEN BADSEY
Royal Military Academy, Sandhurst
Crocker, J. T.
Czechoslovakia
Great Britain
Greece
Resources, Allied and German Compared

EDELFRIED BAGINSKI
Erftstadt, Germany
Armor and Tracked Vehicles
    German Armor and Tracked Vehicles

CHARLES M. BAILY
Springfield, Virginia
Armor and Tracked Vehicles
    Allied Armor and Tracked Vehicles

DONALD E. BAIN
National Defense University, Washington, D.C.
101st Airborne Division

JOSEPH M. BALKOSKI
Baltimore, Maryland
Gerhardt, Charles H.
Peregory, Frank D.
29th Infantry Division

JEFFREY G. BARLOW
Naval Historical Center, Washington, D.C.
Navy
    Allied Naval Forces

JOHN BAYNES
Llanfyllin, Wales
Bullen-Smith, D. C.
VIII Corps (British)
15th (Scottish) Infantry Division
51st (Highland) Infantry Division
MacMillan, G. H. A.
O'Connor, Richard N.

DANIEL R. BEAVER
University of Cincinnati
Robertson, Walter M.
2d Infantry Division

EDWARD BEDESSEM
Center of Military History, Washington, D.C.
Brooks, Edward H.
2d Armored Division

FLORIAN BERBERICH
Merdingen, Germany
5th Parachute Division
Schimpf, Richard
II Parachute Corps
3d Parachute Division
Wilke, Gustav

JOHN D. BERGEN
GCI Group, New York
Communication

MARTIN BLUMENSON
Washington, D.C.
Patton, George S., Jr.

DAVID BROWN
Naval Historical Branch, Ministry of Defense, London
Air Spotting Pool
Oliver, G. N.
Parry, William E.
Patterson, W. R.
Task Force L
Vian, Philip

NEVILLE G. BROWN
Oxford University, England
Weather

C

DAVID CHANDLER
Royal Military Academy, Sandhurst
Battlefield Tours
Cemeteries, Monuments, and Memorials
    British Monuments and Memorials
George VI
Hollis, Stanley Elton
Montgomery, Bernard L.
Museums
Thierry d'Argenlieu, Georges

RAY S. CLINE
Georgetown University, Washington, D.C.
Office of Strategic Services (OSS)

J. L. COLLINS, JR.
Middleburg, Virginia
Associations and Organizations
    Normandy Foundation
Collins, J. Lawton
McNair, Lesley J.

JAMES S. CORUM
Air University, Maxwell Air Force Base,
    Alabama
Brereton, Lewis H.
Newman, James
IX Air Defense Command
Ninth Air Force
IX Air Force Service Command
IX Engineer Command
Richardson, William L.
Wood, Myron

NAPIER CROOKENDEN
Kent, England
Gale, Richard N.
6th Airborne Division

D

RICHARD G. DAVIS
Office of Air Force History, Washington, D.C.
Air Service Command
Air Strategy
    Allied Air Strategy
Anderson, Frederick L.
Anderson, Samuel E.
Doolittle, James
Eighth Air Force
VIII Air Force Service Command
Fifteenth Air Force
1st Bombardment Division
Goodrich, Donald
Hodges, James P.
Knerr, Hugh J.
XIX Tactical Air Command
IX Bomber Command
IX Troop Carrier Command
2d Bombardment Division
Spaatz, Carl
3d Bombardment Division
U.S. Strategic Air Forces (USSTAF)
Weyland, Otto
Williams, Paul
Williams, Robert B.

GERARD M. DEVLIN
Hilton Head, South Carolina
Gliders

KARL DIEFENBACH
Militärgeschictliches Forschungsamt, Freiburg
    im Breisgau
Chaplains
    German Chaplains

R. L. DiNARDO
St. Peter's College, New Jersey
Horses

W. A. B. DOUGLAS
National Defence Headquarters, Ottawa,
    Canada
Royal Canadian Navy

JAMES DUNNIGAN
New York City
War-Gaming

E

JOHN A. ENGLISH
Canadian Armed Forces
Canada
I Corps
Keller, R. F. L.
King, W. L. Mackenzie
3d Infantry Division (Canadian)

DONNA EVERETT
Center of Military History, Washington,
    D.C.
Barton, Raymond O.
V Corps
Gerow, L. T.
30th Infantry Division

F

STANLEY L. FALK
Alexandria, Virginia
79th Infantry Division
Wyche, Ira T.

MARTIN FARNDALE
Master Gunner, St. James's Park, London
Artillery
    Allied Artillery and Air Defense
Morgan, Frederick

ANTHONY FARRAR-HOCKLEY
Oxford, England
Airborne Forces
British Beaches
    An Overview
British Beaches
    Gold Beach
British Beaches
    Juno Beach
British Beaches
    Sword Beach
Brooke, Alan
Prisoners
Supreme Headquarters Allied Expedi-
    tionary Force (SHAEF)

ERNEST F. FISHER
Arlington, Virginia
Atlantic Wall
Engineers
    German Engineers
Organization Todt
Signal
    Allied Signal
Signal
    German Signal
Supply Corps

M. R. D. FOOT
London, England
Combined Operations Pilotage Parties
Special Operations

BARRY FOWLE
U.S. Army Corps of Engineers, Fort Belvoir,
    Virginia
Engineers
    American Engineers

ARTHUR L. FUNK
Gainesville, Florida
Casualties
    French Casualties
de Gaulle, Charles
French Resistance

G

MICHAEL GANNON
University of Florida, Gainesville
Antisubmarine Warfare

MARTIN GILBERT
Oxford University
Churchill, Winston

SUSAN H. GODSON
Williamsburg, Virginia
Ancon, USS
Hall, John L.

MARTIN K. GORDON
*Office of History, U.S. Army Corps of
Engineers, Columbia, Maryland*
Hoge, W. M.
Shore Party
Wharton, James E.

GORDON F. GRAHAM
Vero Beach, Florida
Bryant, Carleton F.

DAVID GRAY
United States Military Academy, West Point
Rangers

ERIC J. GROVE
Surrey, England
Air Defense Ships
Amphibious Assault Training
Assault Ships
Escort Ships
Landing Ships
R-Boats
Torpedo Boats

EKKEHART GUTH
*Führungsakademie der Bundeswehr,
Hamburg*
Casualties
    German Casualties
Medical Support
    German Medical Support

H

AMY HACKETT
Brooklyn, New York
Cemeteries, Monuments, and Memorials
    German Cemeteries, Monuments, and
    Memorials

DONALD HALL
*U.S. Army Medical Service Corps,
Fort Detrick, Maryland*
Casualties
    Allied Casualties
Medical Support
    American Medical Support

ALAN HANKINSON
Cumbria, England
Associations and Organizations
    D-Day and Normandy Fellowship
Associations and Organizations
    Normandy Veterans' Associations
de Guingand, Francis W.
Ritchie, N. M.

DONALD HARVEY
Winchester, Massachusetts
France
Pétain, Henri Philippe Omer

WINFRIED HEINEMANN
*Militärgeschichtliches Forschungsamt,
Freiburg im Breisgau*
Bayerlein, Fritz
Beach and Coastal Defenses
Lüttwitz, Heinrich von
Panzer Lehr Division
2d Panzer Division
Speidel, Hans

PAUL HENRY
University of Virginia, Charlottesville
VIII Fighter Command
Kepner, William

GÜNTER HILLER
Bad Homburg, Germany
Kraiss, Dietrich
352d Infantry Division

F. H. HINSLEY
Cambridge, England
Deception
Intelligence
ULTRA

IAN HOGG
Worcester, England
Infantry Weapons and Equipment
    Allied Infantry Weapons and
    Equipment

BILL HOURIHAN
*U.S. Army Chaplain Center and School,
Fort Monmouth, New Jersey*
Chaplains
    American Chaplains

THOMAS HUGHES
University of Houston, Texas
Convoy Cover
IX Fighter Command
IX Tactical Air Command
Quesada, Elwood R.

GERHARD HÜMMELCHEN
Winnenden, Germany
Bechtolsheim, Theodor
Blanc, Adalbert von
Breuning, Erich Alfred
Hennecke, Walter
Hoffman, Heinrich
Peterson, Rudolf
Rösing, Hans Rudolf
Ruge, Friedrich
S-Boats

J

MARK JACOBSEN
*U.S. Marine Corps Command and Staff
College, Quantico, Virginia*
Task Force 125
Task Force 124
Western Task Force

ROBERT J. JAKEMAN
Auburn University, Alabama
Air-Sea Rescue
Air Special Operations

K

JOHANNES KINDLER
*Militärgeschichtliches Forschungsamt,
Freiburg im Breisgau*
Archival Sources
    German Archives

DOUGLAS KINNARD
National Defense University, Washington,
D.C.
Taylor, Maxwell

BROOKS KLEBER
Newport News, Virginia
American Beaches
    Utah Beach
VII Corps

L

ANDREW LAMBERT
King's College, London
Ajax, HMS
Belfast, HMS
Bulolo, HMS
Coastal Command
Dalrymple-Hamilton, F. H. G.
Douglas, W. Sholto
Douglas-Pennant, C. E.
Eastern Task Force
England, H. T.
Hawkins, HMS
Hilary, HMS
Largs, HMS
Leatham, Ralph
Longley-Cook, E. W. L.
Mauritius, HMS
Naval Bases
Naval Supply
Ramsay, Bertram H.
Rivett-Carnac, J. W.
Scylla, HMS
Talbot, Arthur G.
Task Force G
Task Force J
Task Force S

JAMES LUCAS
Kent, England
Barker, E. H.
49th (West Riding) Infantry Division
43d (Wessex) Infantry Division
Lammerding, Heinz
Ostendorff, Werner
2d SS Panzer Division "Das Reich"
17th SS Panzer Grenadier Division
Thomas, G. I.
12th SS Panzer Division "Hitlerjugend"
Witt, Fritz

RAIMONDO LURAGHI
University of Genoa, Italy
Poland

M

J. BRITT MCCARLEY
Aberdeen Proving Ground, Maryland
Twining, Nathan

STEPHEN MCFARLAND
Auburn University, Alabama
Air Combat

DAVID MACISAAC
Montgomery, Alabama
LeMay, Curtis E.

SEAN MCKNIGHT
Royal Military Academy, Sandhurst
Planning
    Allied Planning

KENNETH MACKSEY
Dorset, England
Artillery
    Allied Antitank Weapons
Bocage
Erskine, G. W. E. J.
Hobart, Percy C. S.

EDUARD MARK
Center for Air Force History, Washington,
D.C.
Interdiction Operations

PHILIPPE MASSON
École Supérieure de Guerre Navale, France
French Ships
Jaujard, Robert
Montcalm

PHILIP MEILINGER
Air University, Maxwell Air Force Base,
Alabama
Vandenberg, Hoyt

CHARLES MESSENGER
London, England
Blumentritt, Günther
Dietrich, Josef ("Sepp")
LXXXIV Corps
11th Armoured Division
Fahrmbacher, Wilhelm
4th Special Service Brigade
Hitler, Adolf
Infantry Weapons and Equipment
    German Infantry Weapons and
        Equipment
Jodl, Alfred
Klosterkemper, Bernhard
Meyer, Kurt
91st Air Landing Division
Roberts, G. P. B. ("Pip")
Rundstedt, Gerd von
711th Static Division

GEORG MEYER
Militärgeschichtliches Forschungsamt,
Freiburg im Breisgau
Geyr, Leo
Keitel, Wilhelm
Mahlmann, Paul
Obstfelder, Hans von
Reichert, Josef
Schlieben, Karl Wilhelm von

JOEL D. MEYERSON
Center for Military History, Washington,
D.C.
Quartermaster and Ordnance Corps

ALFRED MIERZEJEWSKI
Athens State College, Alabama
Railroads

PAUL L. MILES
Princeton, New Jersey
Bradley, Omar

ALLAN MILLETT
The Ohio State University
Aftermath

SAMUEL W. MITCHAM, JR.
Northeast Louisiana University
Army Group B
Diestel, Erich
Dollmann, Friedrich
LXXXVI Corps
Falley, Wilhelm
Feuchtinger, Edgar
Fifteenth Army
XLVII Panzer Corps
Funck, Hans von
Hellmich, Heinz
Panzer Group West
Richter, Wilhelm
Salmuth, Hans von
Schmidt, Hans
709th Static Division
716th Division
Seventh Army
77th Infantry Division
Stegmann, Rudolf
353d Infantry Division
346th Infantry Division
21st Panzer Division
243d Division
275th Division

STEVEN J. MROZEK
Eastpointe, Michigan
82d Airborne Division
Gavin, James
Ridgway, Matthew B.

GENE MUELLER
Henderson State University, Arkansas
Propaganda
    German Propaganda

MALCOLM MUIR, JR.
Austin Peay State University, Tennessee
Moon, Don P.
Texas, USS

RICHARD R. MULLER
U.S. Air Force Air Command and Staff College, Maxwell Air Force Base, Alabama
Aircraft
    German Aircraft

TIM MUNDEN
Royal Military Academy, Sandhurst
Cass, E. E. E.
Rennie, T. G.
3d Infantry Division (British)

WILLIAMSON MURRAY
The Ohio State University
Air Force
    German Air Force
Air Strategy
    German Air Strategy

N

CLAYTON R. NEWELL
Hedgesville, West Virginia
Butts, John E.
Corlett, Charles
Eddy, Manton
VIII Corps (U.S.)
Hodges, Courtney H.
Middleton, Troy H.
XIX Corps
9th Infantry Division
Roosevelt, Theodore, Jr.

S. MICHAEL NEWELL
Orleans, Ontario, Canada
Cemeteries, Monuments, and Memorials
    Commonwealth Cemeteries

FRANK NORRIS
Ojai, California
Landrum, Eugene M.
MacKelvie, Jay W.
90th Infantry Division

O

WILLIAM O'NEILL
Rutgers University, New Jersey
Roosevelt, Franklin D.
United States of America

DEREK OAKLEY
Hampshire, England
Commandos
1st Special Service Brigade
Leicester, B. W.
Lovat, Lord
Mills-Roberts, Derek

VINCENT ORANGE
University of Canterbury, Christchurch, New Zealand
Tedder, Arthur

P

TADEUSZ PANECKI
Wojskowy Instytut Historyczny, Warsaw
Polish Ships

JAMES PARTON
Hanover, New Hampshire
Air Superiority
Eaker, Ira
POINTBLANK

J. L. PIMLOTT
Royal Military Academy, Sandhurst
Allied Air Bases

BARRIE PITT
Somerset, England
Dempsey, Miles C.
50th (Northumbrian) Infantry Division
Graham, D. A. H.
Second Army
21st Army Group

FORREST C. POGUE
Arlington, Virginia
Marshall, George
Smith, Walter Bedell

ALFRED PRICE
Uppingham, Leicester, England
Bülowius, Alfred
Electronic Warfare
Holle, Alexander
Junck, Werner
IX Air Corps
Peltz, Dietrich
II Air Corps
II Fighter Corps
Sperrle, Hugo
X Air Corps (Fliegerkorps X)
Third Air Force (Luftflotte 3)

HENRY PROBERT
RAF Historical Society, London
Bomber Command
Broadhurst, Harry
Brown, L. O.
Cole-Hamilton, J. B.
85th Composite Group
84th Composite Group
83d Composite Group
Embry, Basil
Harris, Arthur
2d Composite Group

R

HAROLD RAUGH, JR.
Fort Ord, California
Medals
  Allied Medals

JOHN C. REILLY, JR.
Naval Historical Center, Washington, D.C.
Area Screen Ships
Bombardment Ships
Close Gunfire Support
Deyo, Morton L.
Far Shore Service Ships
Kirk, Alan G.
Minesweeper Ships
  Allied Minesweepers
Mine Warfare

OLAV RISTE
University of Bergen, Norway
Norway

SIMON N. ROBBINS
Imperial War Museum, London
Archival Sources
  Allied Archives

WILLIAM RODNEY
Victoria, British Columbia, Canada
McEwen, Clifford M.
Royal Canadian Air Force
Six Group

JÜRGEN ROHWER
Bibliothek für Zeitgeschichte, Stuttgart,
  Germany
Auxiliary Warships
Destroyers
Dönitz, Karl
Krancke, Theodor
Minesweeper Ships
  German Minesweepers
Navy
  German Navy
U-Boats
Western Defense Force

WILLIAM E. RYAN, JR.
American Battle Monuments Commission,
  Washington, D.C.
Cemeteries, Monuments, and Memorials
  American Cemeteries, Monuments,
    and Memorials

S

MICHAEL SALEWSKI
Christian Albrechts University, Kiel, Germany
Germany

ROBERT SAUER
University of Massachusetts, Boston
I SS Panzer Corps

C. M. SCHULTEN
Rijkinstituut voor Oorlogsdocumentatie,
  Amsterdam
Netherlands

DONALD M. SCHURMAN
Sydenham, Ontario, Canada
Mynarski, Andrew Charles

GARY SHEFFIELD
Royal Military Academy, Sandhurst
Medical Support
  British Medical Support

B. MITCHELL SIMPSON III
Newport, Rhode Island
Stark, Harold R.

CHARLES E. SMITH
Simon & Schuster, New York
American Beaches
  An Overview
De Glopper, Charles N.
Musée de l'Ordre de la Libération

ROGER SMITHER
Imperial War Museum, London
Battlefield Film Footage

LEWIS SORLEY
Potomac, Maryland
First Army
4th Infantry Division
Hobbs, Leland

FREDERICK SOWREY
RAF Historical Society, London
Aerial Reconnaissance
Ground Training
Pathfinders
Portal, Charles

ALAN STEPHENS
RAAF Air Power Studies Center, Canberra
Royal Australian Air Force

PAUL STILLWELL
U.S. Naval Institute, Annapolis
Augusta, USS
Bayfield, USS
Salvage and Firefighting
Tuscaloosa, USS
Wilkes, John

TRUMAN R. STROBRIDGE
Alexandria, Virginia
Coast Guard

REINHARD STUMPF
Bundesministerium der Verteidigung, Bonn
Marcks, Erich
Meindl, Eugen
Rommel, Erwin

T

ORWIN TALBOTT
Annapolis, Maryland
Landrum, Eugene M.
MacKelvie, Jay W.
90th Infantry Division

PHILIP TAYLOR
University of Leeds, England
Propaganda
  Allied Propaganda

JOHN TERRAINE
London, England
Air Force
  Allied Expeditionary Air Force
Close Air Support
Coningham, Arthur
Leigh-Mallory, Trafford
Second Tactical Air Force

CHARLES THOMAS
Georgia Southern University
Medals
  German Medals

STEVEN J. TIRONE
New York City
Edgar, Campbell D.
Maloy, USS
Task Force 126
Tennant, William G.

FRANCIS TOASE
Royal Military Academy, Sandhurst
Bucknall, G. C.
7th Armoured Division
XXX Corps

VINCENT TRANSANO
Naval Facilities Engineering Command, Port Hueneme, California
Seabees

DAVID TRASK
Washington, D.C.
Political-Military Relations

V

DETLEF VOGEL
Militärgeschichtliches Forschungsamt, Freiburg im Breisgau
Planning
   German Planning

JOHN F. VOTAW
Cantigny First Division Foundation, Wheaton, Illinois
Barrett, Carlton W.
DeFranzo, Arthur F.
Ehlers, Walter D.
1st Infantry Division
Huebner, Clarence R.
Monteith, Jimmie W., Jr.
Pinder, John J., Jr.

W

HEINRICH WALLE
Militärgeschichtliches Forschungsamt, Freiburg im Breisgau
Artillery
   German Antiaircraft and Antitank Weapons and Artillery

THEODORE A. WILSON
University of Kansas, Lawrence
Eisenhower, Dwight D.

ALAN F. WILT
Iowa State University, Ames
Prelude

GEOFFREY WOOTTEN
Bath, England
Artificial Harbors
PLUTO

HUMPHREY WYNN
Air Historical Branch, Ministry of Defence, London
Hollinghurst, L. N.
Transport Command

Y

EAMES YATES
Denver, Colorado
Landrum, Eugene M.
MacKelvie, Jay W.
90th Infantry Division

BILL YENNE
American Graphic Systems, Inc., San Francisco, California
Aircraft
   Allied Aircraft

A. E. YOUNGER
Twyford near Winchester, Hampshire, England
Engineers
   British Engineers
79th Armoured Division

Z

EARL F. ZIEMKE
University of Georgia, Athens
Stalin, Josef

Alphabetical List of Entries

Guide to Numbered Entries

The names of military units ordinarily include numbers that are indicated in various conventional ways using roman numerals, arabic numerals, or by writing out the number. To assist the reader in finding articles on particular military units, the following list shows all articles beginning with a number in the order in which these articles can be found in the encyclopedia. These entries are alphabetized *as if the numbers were written out in English*. For example, the article on the 82d Airborne Division is alphabetized as if its first word were *eighty-second*.

Eighth Air Force
VIII [Eighth] Air Force Service Command
VIII [Eighth] Corps (U.S.)
VIII [Eighth] Corps (British)
VIII [Eighth] Fighter Command
85th Composite Group
84th Composite Group
LXXXIV [Eighty-fourth] Corps
82d Airborne Division
LXXXVI [Eighty-sixth] Corps
83d Composite Group
11th Armoured Division

15th (Scottish) Infantry Division
Fifteenth Air Force
Fifteenth Army
V [Fifth] Corps
5th Parachute Division
50th (Northumbrian) Infantry Division
51st (Highland) Infantry Division
First Army
1st Bombardment Division
I [First] Corps
1st Infantry Division
1st Special Service Brigade
I [First] SS Panzer Corps
49th (West Riding) Infantry Division
XLVII [Forty-seventh] Panzer Corps
43d (Wessex) Infantry Division
4th Infantry Division
4th Special Service Brigade

XIX [Nineteenth] Corps
XIX [Nineteenth] Tactical Air Command
90th Infantry Division
91st Air Landing Division
IX [Ninth] Air Corps
IX [Ninth] Air Defense Command
Ninth Air Force
IX [Ninth] Air Force Service Command
IX [Ninth] Bomber Command
IX [Ninth] Engineer Command
IX [Ninth] Fighter Command
9th Infantry Division
IX [Ninth] Tactical Air Command

IX [Ninth] Troop Carrier Command

101st Airborne Division

II [Second] Air Corps
2d Armored Division
Second Army
2d Bombardment Division
2d Composite Group
II [Second] Fighter Corps
2d Infantry Division
2d Panzer Division
II [Second] Parachute Corps
2d SS Panzer Division "Das Reich"
Second Tactical Air Force
711th Static Division
709th Static Division
716th Static Division
17th SS Panzer Grenadier Division
7th Armoured Division
Seventh Army
VII [Seventh] Corps
79th Armoured Division
79th Infantry Division
77th Infantry Division
Six Group
6th Airborne Division

X [Tenth] Air Corps (Fliegerkorps X)
Third Air Force (Luftflotte 3)
3d Bombardment Division
3d Infantry Division (British)
3d Infantry Division (Canadian)
3d Parachute Division
XXX [Thirtieth] Corps
30th Infantry Division
352d Infantry Division
353d Infantry Division
346th Infantry Division
12th SS Panzer Division "Hitlerjugend"
21st Army Group
21st Panzer Division
29th Infantry Division
243d Division
275th Division

Common Abbreviations and Symbols Used in This Work

Adm.	admiral; Admiralty
Brig.	brigadier
Capt.	captain
Col.	colonel
cm	centimeter(s)
Comdr.	commander (naval)
Como.	commodore
diss.	dissertation
ed.	editor (pl., eds.); edition
e.g.	*exempli gratia,* for example
et al.	*et alii,* and others
ft.	feet
Gen.	general
GRT	gross register tons
HMCS	His/Her Majesty's Canadian ship
HMS	His/Her Majesty's ship
i.e.	*id est,* that is
in.	inch(es)
km	kilometer(s)
Lt.	lieutenant
m	meter(s)
M.A.	Master of Arts
Maj.	major
mi.	mile(s)
mm	millimeter(s)
n.d.	no date (of publication)
no.	number (pl., nos.)
n.p.	no place (of publication)
p.	page (pl., pp.)
Ph.D.	*Philosophiae Doctor,* Doctor of Philosophy
pl.	plural
pt.	part (pl., pts.)
Pvt.	private
ret.	retired
rev.	revised
sec.	section (pl., secs.)
Sgt.	sergeant
U.K.	United Kingdom
U.S.	United States
USS	United States ship
U.S.S.R.	Union of Soviet Socialist Republics
vol.	volume (pl., vols.)
yd.	yard(s)
?	uncertain; possibly
°	degrees
¢	minutes

Note: for abbreviations of specialized military terms, please see the glossary.

A

AERIAL RECONNAISSANCE. Information about activity on the ground can be collected from the air either photographically or visually. Although the latter had immediacy and was valuable in a rapidly moving battle situation, it was aircraft fitted with vertical- or oblique-facing cameras that provided the images that were used to plan for D-day. Photographs allowed the assessment of the armament of coastal defenses for more effective attack. The strengths and weaknesses of key installations, such as the Merville battery, were analyzed.

Vertical photographs viewed by stereoscope can provide three-dimensional information, and low-level oblique photographs in the hands of trained photographic interpreters reveal much detail. Coverage of specific locations over a period of time can show the development of defenses and the introduction of new weapons. The limitation of aerial photography was that targets could be obscured by cloud or darkness, although night photography was possible by simultaneously launching an illuminating flare.

Aerial reconnaissance before D-day involved the American, British, and German air forces. The air superiority provided by the Royal Air Force (RAF) defensive system over southern England virtually denied the Luftwaffe the opportunity for reconnaissance of the buildup for the invasion. Without strategic objectives, reconnaissance sorties were not given sufficient priority, and this weakness denied the Germans adequate warning of the invasion.

The Allies, in contrast, had begun collecting the photographic information they needed for the invasion two years before the event. The RAF and the U.S. Army Air Forces systematically photographed the coastal area from Holland to the Spanish frontier, often flying for long periods at low level in the face of intense flak. This provided a continuous photographic record of the terrain of various beaches, the routes inland, beach defenses as they developed, and possible enemy approach routes.

The preinvasion demand for aerial reconnaissance came from many sources—Admiralty, War Office, Air Ministry, Ministry of Economic Warfare, Supreme Headquarters Allied Expeditionary Force, and Command Headquarters—and needed to be sorted to match the effort available. The first-level screening was by the Joint Photographic Reconnaissance Committee, composed of British and American officers. The Technical Control Office at RAF Medmenham, on the Thames River, with its British and American service composition decided on priorities and passed the request to the appropriate reconnaissance unit. It was essential that the site for the invasion be kept secret, so for every sortie flown over Normandy, two were flown over the area around the Pas de Calais as part of a comprehensive deception plan to indicate the latter as the intended invasion point.

Once the invasion was launched, air reconnaissance activity was intense. The Allied reconnaissance units charted the progress of the Allied advance; identified the development of German counterattacks; and assessed the movement of German reinforcements to the area. American F-4s (P-38E Lightning) and F-5s (P-38 G&H) together with Royal Air Force Mosquitos and Spitfires provided most of the photo reconnaissance, with F-6s (P-51 Mustang) and RAF Mustangs augmenting the oblique photo cover with visual observations. Early reconnaissance was to observe and correct the fire of naval guns on the shore defenses. The photographic laboratory of the 10th Photo Reconnaissance Group processed nearly 10,000 prints on the night of 6–7 June. Every bomber or ground attack sortie returned with visual reports or photographs from still cameras or from cinecamera guns to augment the overall picture of Allied progress that was being built up in England, and specific information was transmitted by radio to forces in the bridgeheads. Aircraft from Army Observation Post squadrons were in France on 8 June to

RAF SPITFIRE.   With a camera fitted in the fuselage, used for photographic reconnaissance.   IMPERIAL WAR MUSEUM

NORMANDY COAST.   Defensive flooding near Carentan.   HULTON DEUTSCH

NORMANDY BEACHES.   Low-level photograph showing beach defenses.   IMPERIAL WAR MUSEUM

direct artillery fire and provide photographs by hand-held cameras. An advanced landing ground was in use from 10 June, but with the comparatively slow growth of the bridgehead it was not until the end of June that reconnaissance squadrons operated fully from French soil.

Reconnaissance from D-day onward at this high level was only possible if air superiority was sustained. In spite of the barrier of the English Channel between the main airfields and the armies, the Allied air forces did maintain sufficient control of the air to ensure air supremacy, and thus were able to continue providing valuable photographic and visual reconnaissance information.

BIBLIOGRAPHY

Mead, Peter. *The Eye in the Air*. 1983.
Stanley, R. M. *World War II Photo Intelligence*. 1982.
United Kingdom. Royal Air Force Historical Society. *Photographic Reconnaissance in World War II*. 1991.

FREDERICK SOWREY

AFTERMATH. After the invasion of Normandy on 6 June, the U.S. First Army broke the German defensive position in the area with Operation COBRA. On 25 July, 2,500 bombers, most of them American aircraft from the Eighth and Ninth Air Forces, dropped 4,000 tons of bombs in front of the U.S. VII Corps. Although some of the bombs fell short and caused almost 600 American casualties, the bombardment opened a gap in the German positions just west of Saint-Lô and ruined the one available reserve panzer division. Two days later the commander of *Army Group B* (Field Marshal Hans Günther von Kluge) admitted that the *Seventh Army* could not stop the four American army corps on its front and approved a limited withdrawal. (The initiative of the German army high command had been dulled by the purge that followed the unsuccessful attempt on Hitler's life by army officers on 20 July 1944.) As the *Seventh Army* and *Fifth Panzer Army* began to fall back, Field Marshal Bernard L. Montgomery's 21st Army Group (Canadian First Army and British Second Army) advanced beyond the farmlands west of Caen.

With the 21st Army Group as the pivot, the Allied expeditionary force swung westward after American armored forces cleared Avranches on 31 July. General Dwight D. Eisenhower activated a second army (U.S. Third Army) commanded by Lt. Gen. George S. Patton, Jr., and it moved simultaneously east toward Alençon and Le Mans and west toward the ports of Saint-Malo, Brest, Lorient, and Saint-Nazaire, all of which were surrounded during the first week of August. The move into Brittany, which removed valuable divisions from the thrust eastward, reflected a flawed planning assumption that these ports

THE BIG THREE.   Winston Churchill, Franklin D. Roosevelt, and Josef Stalin at the Yalta Conference, February 1945, where the occupation of Germany and the status of eastern Europe were mapped out.   NATIONAL ARCHIVES

would prove invaluable logistical assets. In the meantime, Gen. Omar Bradley moved up to a new command, the U.S. 12th Army Group, and left the First Army to Lt. Gen. Courtney H. Hodges.

Facing disaster in the west, Adolf Hitler ordered Kluge to concentrate his panzer divisions and strike the Americans at the neck of their breakthrough at Avranches. Slowed by Allied air attacks, the seven German corps that mounted the Argentan-Mortain counteroffensive did not attack until 10 August, by which time the Americans (alerted by intercepted Ultra messages) had redeployed to meet the threat. Patton's three Third Army corps were well to the south and west, while Hodges had three other corps massed east of Avranches. The German offensive faltered in only four days; the Allies then massed on the north and south edges of the Mortain salient and battered the surviving German units until they escaped through the Falaise-Argentan gap on 19 August. Both British and American misjudgments allowed the Germans to escape, but with much of their mechanized force destroyed by artillery and air attacks. The disaster left Kluge with only one fully operational army, the *Fifteenth Army,* in western France. The way to the Seine was clear for the Allies.

The German position west of the Rhine came close to collapse in August and September 1944, but by the end of September the Germans had salvaged their position by regrouping and reinforcing the ground forces defending the Siegfried Line (or West Wall), the fortification belt just west of the Rhine. In the meantime, the German armies fell back before the relentless Allied advances spearheaded by armored forces from all four Allied armies under Eisenhower's command. The southern soft under-belly of the German occupation of France ruptured on 15 August when a force of three American and four French divisions invaded the Riviera from just east of Toulon to Fréjus–Saint-Raphaël (DRAGOON) and, aided by the French Resistance, chased the German *Nineteenth Army* up the Rhone and Durance valleys. On 11 September the advance units of the U.S. Third Army and Seventh Army met near Dijon, giving the Allies a continuous front from the Channel to Switzerland. On 15 September Eisenhower added the U.S. Sixth Army Group (U.S. Seventh Army and French First Army) to his command. Lt. Gen. Jacob L. Devers led this group.

The very success of the Allied campaign of August and September generated a crisis in Eisenhower's army, the result of accumulated problems of logistics and personnel policy. The logistical difficulties stemmed from the lack of developed port facilities along the Atlantic-Channel coastline. The Normandy-Brittany operations had not produced a usable port; the British did no better in their attempts to take Le Havre, Dieppe, Boulogne, Calais, Dunkirk, and Ostend. Montgomery's army group captured the best alternative to the Normandy beaches—Antwerp, Belgium—on 4 September, but the British and Canadians did not clear the Schelde Estuary for two more months in the face of a tenacious defense by the German *Fifteenth Army.*

Arguing that the major Allied effort should come in his sector and drive across the lower Rhine, Montgomery won Eisenhower's approval for a bold airborne-armored offensive across Holland to the Rhine at Arnhem. Operation MARKET-GARDEN (17–26 September 1944) pitted a British armored corps and a three-division airborne corps against a misestimated German defensive force of two infantry and two SS armored divisions. The offensive fell short of Arnhem, where the better part of the British First Airborne Division died or was captured. The operational frustration coincided with a gas shortage in the Allied armies, which brought the U.S. First and Third armies to a halt on the outer edges of the Siegfried Line. The combination of river valleys and ridges in eastern France favored the defenders, who also benefited by their reduced dependence on coded radio traffic and, thus, Allied exploitation of Ultra. In addition, increased German resistance inflicted crippling casualties on Allied infantry divisions, who had to bear the burden of the attack in the hills west of the Rhine.

While the Canadians struggled in the Schelde Estuary and the British stalled in Holland, the American First and Third armies battered themselves into exhaustion (abetted by the cold, wet weather) in their effort to reach the Rhine. From Aachen to Strasbourg the Americans faced a revived German army fighting for its homeland and held to its duty by professional standards, Nazi ideology, and the execution of deserters and malcontents. The U.S. Army paid

WILHELM KEITEL.   Surrendering, 9 May 1945 at Karlshorst, a district of Berlin.

ALFRED JODL.   Leaving Lüneburg Heath in Germany on way to Rheims, France, to surrender the German Army.

NATIONAL ARCHIVES

for its unwillingness to mobilize more than eighty-nine divisions, a third of which were in the Pacific. The limited number of divisions and the scarcity of infantry replacements meant that American offensive effectiveness withered in the shell-torn pines of the Huertgen Forest and ebbed away in the flooded valley of the Roer. The 21st Army Group received virtually no replacements at all, and British-Canadian operational concepts reflected the declining numbers in Montgomery's armies. That the Americans activated one more army—the Ninth—and slipped it into the line between the U.S. First Army and the British did not mean that Eisenhower had solved his manpower shortage, only that he had abandoned any effort to liberate southern France with American troops. Instead he wanted to concentrate his divisions and force the Rhine between Köln and Bonn with the Ninth and First armies, with Montgomery and Patton in supporting roles.

Hitler, whose megalomania had now taken him into the twilight zone of sanity, believed that he could duplicate the feats of Frederick the Great and smite his enemies with a winter campaign that would ruin them. He called one of his military geniuses, Field Marshal Gerd von Rundstedt, out of retirement (where he had been relegated for defeats in Russia) and reappointed him Commander in Chief West. Hitler's instructions to Rundstedt were that he was to organize a massive armored counteroffensive through the Ardennes hill country of Belgium and Luxembourg and splinter the Allied armies along the Meuse. Bad weather would minimize the impact of Allied tactical air support, and surprise would allow the nine re-formed panzer and panzer grenadier divisions to penetrate the U.S. First Army positions between Trier and the Losheim gap. Facing the Germans were two full but inexperienced and four understrength, very tired infantry divisions. About 200,000 Germans would attack 83,000 Americans.

The German Ardennes counteroffensive, known as the Battle of the Bulge, started on 16 December with a degree of surprise and ferocity that staggered U.S. commanders. Early American troop losses were equally staggering and included most of the new 106th Infantry Division. Fleeing (or displacing, depending on the degree of control) artillery battalions and service units made the disaster look worse than it was, for the American infantry and tank task forces facing the Germans put up a sturdy resistance, usually until they ran out of gas, ammunition, and soldiers. From the first the German timetable fell victim to the tenacious American defense, which even forced the Germans to penetrate farther south than planned with the *Fifth Panzer Army,* not the *Sixth Panzer Army* in the north. Fixing attacks by the *Seventh Army* and *Fifteenth Army* did not disconcert the U.S. First Army or prevent a counterattack against the southern edge of the Bulge by divisions sent north from the U.S. Third Army. The 101st Airborne Division and parts of the 28th Infantry Division and other units held the road junction at Bastogne and fixed important German elite troops in a siege. On Christmas Day the senior German commanders conceded that they could not reach the Meuse.

Unconvinced that his grand strategic design had failed, Hitler would not allow Rundstedt to disengage, and the fighting in the Bulge continued on its bloody course until the first week of February 1945. From the Allied perspective Hitler's stubbornness was a godsend, for it offered a splendid opportunity to destroy the remaining elite mobile divisions of the Wehrmacht. When the battle ended, the Americans had lost 81,000 men (including 15,000 prisoners), but the Germans had lost more than 100,000 irreplaceable soldiers and more than 800 tanks. Allied tactical aviation had again proved a significant instrument of destruction, and the Germans lost 1,000 aircraft in the attempt to win air superiority over the battlefield.

Eisenhower, whose initial dismay had turned quickly to opportunism, emerged from the crisis a stronger commander, ready to deal even more firmly with Montgomery. The Allied position had been further strengthened by the successful defense of the Colmar-Strasbourg region by the Sixth Army Group against a secondary German counteroffensive. As the Allies prepared to shift to the offensive, they could muster 3 million American and 1 million Commonwealth troops with endless numbers of tanks, trucks, artillery pieces, and tactical aircraft against a shrinking Wehrmacht.

With the Russians moving through Poland and Hungary, the Allied armies on the Western front shifted to the offensive in early February and in four months met the Russians along the Elbe River. Eisenhower's offensive, in which he deployed eighty-five divisions, developed in two phases: the crossing of the Rhine and the mobile warfare of exploitation that followed. The pattern of approach and crossing of the Rhine varied from army to army. With the Canadians and U.S. Ninth Army securing the western bank, Montgomery mounted a set-piece offensive, complete with a two-division air assault and major amphibious attacks by American and British divisions on 23–24 March 1945. The U.S. First Army captured the railroad bridge at Remagen intact on 7 March and then extemporized an operation to open its cross-river enclave between Bonn and Koblenz. The U.S. Third Army had much farther to go before it reached the Rhine, so Patton did not get his first bridgehead until 23 March. The U.S. Seventh Army crossed the river at Worms three days later. With the equivalent of only twenty-six divisions in action along the Rhine, the Germans could do little more than fight delaying actions. As the weather improved with the approach of spring, Allied fighter-bombers made any German military movement a nightmare.

The war's final stage produced grand advances punctuated by occasional desperate defensive actions as the German army either fell back or surrendered, the latter a more popular option than meeting the vengeful Red Army. Montgomery's army group liberated Holland and drove past the base of the Danish peninsula to the Baltic. The U.S. Ninth and First armies headed eastward toward Berlin, although Eisenhower had no intention of taking the city, which was well beyond the agreed-upon "stop line" of the Elbe provided for in the occupation agreement with the Russians. The major accomplishment of General Bradley's army group was the encirclement of *Army Group B* in the Ruhr valley; the 317,000 Germans who surrendered represented the largest number of prisoners taken before V-E Day. In the meantime, the U.S. Third and Seventh armies advanced even more rapidly with Patton's Third Army pointed at Leipzig and Lt. Gen. Alexander M. Patch's Seventh Army wheeling south into Bavaria and toward the border of Austria. Elements of the Third Army reached Czechoslovakia on 4 May, and ele-

AT RAISING OF AMERICAN FLAG IN BERLIN, 28 JULY 1945. From left to right: Dwight D. Eisenhower, George S. Patton, Jr., and Harry S. Truman. NATIONAL ARCHIVES

ments of the Seventh Army reached Salzburg the same day.

With the Russians destroying Berlin above his bunker, Hitler killed himself on 30 April. Several German military leaders then took the initiative to sign unconditional surrender agreements on 4 and 7 May 1945. Other German armies surrendered to the Russians and to Allied forces and Yugoslav partisans at the head of the Adriatic Sea. The last Germans to yield were the occupying forces on Crete and several Aegean islands, who capitulated on 11 and 12 May. The Thousand-Year Reich had ended in its second decade of horror, and only a handful of unreconstructed Nazis mourned its passing.

BIBLIOGRAPHY

Ambrose, Stephen E. *Eisenhower: Soldier, General of the Army, President-Elect, 1890–1952.* 1983.

Bradley, Omar N., and Clay Blair. *A General's Life.* 1983.

Chief of Staff of the United States Army. *Atlas, Supplement to the Biennial Report to the Secretary of War, July 1, 1943 to June 30, 1945.* 1945.

MacDonald, Charles B. *The Mighty Endeavor: American Armed Forces in the European Theater in World War II.* 1969.

Weigley, Russell F. *Eisenhower's Lieutenants: The Campaigns of France and Germany, 1944–1945.* 1981.
Willmott, H. P. *The Great Crusade.* 1989.

ALLAN R. MILLETT

AIRBORNE FORCES. In 1918, an American plan to parachute part of the 1st Division behind German lines at Metz was broken off when the armistice was signed. Attempts to revive this form of maneuver after the war were stifled by defense economies. In the meantime, the Soviet Union, aided by the secret German *Fliegerzentrale* (Central Flying Office) was modernizing the air arm of the Red Army, and one outcome of this was the adoption of gliders and parachutes for military use. By 1936, a regiment had been dropped by parachute during maneuvers, and the dropping of vehicles was under trial.

Well informed of these advances, Germany began its own trials in airborne warfare as soon as it evaded the constraints of the Versailles treaty. In 1938, the *Luftwaffe 7th Air Division* was formed under Brig. Gen. Kurt Student to collect all parachute and glider units in an operational formation. This force subsequently stormed the Low Countries in 1940.

Their success persuaded both the British and the Amer-

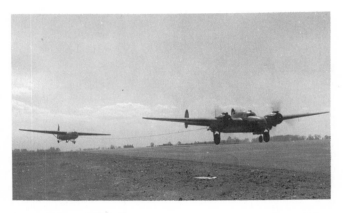

ALBEMARLE ("TUG") AIRCRAFT.   Towing a Horsa glider.
IMPERIAL WAR MUSEUM

ican military authorities to form their own airborne arms. Neither had technical expertise in parachutes and gliders to launch men, weapons, vehicles, and equipment onto the battlefield, but intensive trials began. During 1941–1943, the 1st and 6th Airborne Divisions were developed in Britain, and the 82d and 101st in the United States. The men to fill them were found among volunteers from the respective armies. A Polish parachute brigade increased their number.

America had a considerable advantage in possessing with-

BRITISH HORSA GLIDER.   Carrying airborne reinforcements to Normandy.   IMPERIAL WAR MUSEUM

PARATROOPERS.   Over Normandy, camouflaged in preparation for descent.   IMPERIAL WAR MUSEUM

in the Army Air Corps a suitable transport aircraft, the Douglas C-47 Dakota. The British army had nothing comparable and was obliged to rely upon Royal Air Force (RAF) bomber aircraft converted to drop men and tow gliders. With limited resources to meet huge commitments, Bomber Command was reluctant to provide the numbers required, but Prime Minister Winston Churchill insisted on their cooperation. Ultimately, these difficulties were resolved by the formation of Royal Air Force Transport Command and, from 1943, British purchase of C-47s.

By trial and error, sometimes involving death among the pioneers in both nations, equipment was developed. The American "statichute" was adopted, the parachute being attached to an aircraft strong point by a webbing static line. The weight of the falling parachutist pulled out the canopy and rigging lines and finally broke the tie to the static line. This automatic process permitted the dropping of troops some five hundred feet from the ground, reducing the exposure of the descending parachutist to ground

fire to less than thirty seconds. British and American parachutes were developed separately, the former on the basis that paratroops would not wear reserve parachutes.

Glider construction progressed from types able to carry a section or squad to the American CG-4A Waco carrying fifteen men or 1.7 tons and the British Horsa carrying twenty-nine men or 3.1 tons. The American gliders were built around a tubular metal frame; the British, on plywood modules. The American gliders were stronger, but the British believed that it was better to accept wing and even fuselage fracture to absorb the shock of striking an obstacle on landing.

The parachutist landed with his personal weapon, ammunition, and equipment attached to his body, adding eighty-five pounds to his body weight. British crew-served weapons, radios, and other bulky loads were dropped in cylindrical containers released from bomb racks under the aircraft wings. Similar American loads were discharged as door bundles. Vehicles and guns could

"Coup de Main" gliders.   Used for Pegasus Bridge operation.   Imperial War Museum

be delivered only by glider, and thus the parachute units relied on some allocation of glider aircraft to bring in the essentials of these supporting items. Similarly, the air-landing—gliderborne—formations were obliged to trade troop space for heavy loads. The nature of the operation decided the balance between them. All expected to receive their remaining vehicles, weapons, and equipment when the ground forces reached their positions. Until then, airborne forces also relied on resupply by air, and were obliged to hold their casualties within local perimeters until the main ground forces reached them.

From the outset of planning the invasion of Normandy (OVERLORD), political and military leaders anticipated heavy casualties in the seaborne assault. By 1944, with the experience of a major operation in Sicily behind them and enjoying air supremacy, the Allied airborne forces had provided a means of vaulting over enemy defenses. Lack of armor and mobility limited their role on landing, but air-borne landings would at least dissipate the enemy. More-

over, the quality of the men suggested their ability to seize and hold ground to facilitate the beach landings. Weather apart, the principal limitation was air transport resources. Initial plans had allocated two parachute brigades to OVER-LORD. Gen. Bernard L. Montgomery's expansion of the beach limits included three airborne divisions, a concept opposed by Air Chief Marshal Sir Trafford Leigh-Mallory, Allied air commander in chief, who anticipated heavy losses to the transport aircraft from antiaircraft fire in the delivery phase, Operation NEPTUNE. General Dwight D. Eisenhower supported Montgomery, but the total of Dakotas and converted bombers (Albemarles, Halifaxes, and Stirlings)—1,270 aircraft in all—was insufficient to lift simultaneously the formations chosen: the 6th British, 82d and 101st American Airborne Divisions. A second lift would thus be required on D-day, requiring some reduction in the number of air resupply sorties. Reinforcing the RAF 38th and 46th Groups were IX Troop Carrier Command C-47s. British Horsa and some of the new heavy

Hamilcar gliders lifted a number of the American vehicles and guns. A Combined Troop Carrier Command was instituted to control all air transport operations.

During April, air photos showed that antiglider obstacles were being erected in the glider landing zones. At first it was feared that the enemy had discovered the airborne plan, but it was soon seen that this was a general policy across the countryside. Gliders required adequate open spaces to land but delivered complete subunits. Parachute delivery was by streams; the troops had to rendezvous after landing but did not depend as much on large open spaces. The obstacles obliged the 82d and 101st to reduce the number of gliders in the first lift from 410 and 260 to 50 each. Similarly, the 6th Airborne Division changed from an air landing and a parachute brigade assault to one of two parachute brigades, but retained glider detachments for vital coup de main operations, such as Pegasus Bridge. The tasks of the Pathfinders, specialists in independent companies who operated the Rebecca-Eureka radar homing system to the aircraft, were adjusted accordingly. The air-landing brigade was to follow in the second and third phases to hold the southern perimeter.

The landings were remarkable on at least three counts. Damage to aircraft and gliders was minimal—about 5 percent: 23,000 airborne troops were landed, including the glider forces in the second lift. Despite the considerable scattering on all dropping zones, essential tasks were completed on D-day and thereafter, and ground was held until the sea-landing forces arrived. As the divisions concentrated, they were able to play a crucial role in the defense of the bridgehead immediately after D-day and in the break-out battle that followed. These were the results of what Air Chief Marshal Leigh-Mallory had rated as a "highly speculative operation."

[See also 82d Airborne Division; Gliders; 101st Airborne Division; Pathfinders; 6th Airborne Division.]

BIBLIOGRAPHY

Brereton, Lewis. *The Brereton Diaries*. 1946.
Crookenden, Napier. *Drop Zone Normandy*. 1976.
Otway, Terence. *Airborne Forces*. 1951.

ANTHONY FARRAR-HOCKLEY

AIR COMBAT. The success of the Normandy invasion (OVERLORD) hinged on Allied air forces fending off Luftwaffe attacks in the landing area. The commander of the U.S. Strategic Air Forces (USSTAF), Lt. Gen. Carl Spaatz, believed that air superiority could be won through gradual attrition—destroying German aircraft production on the ground while shooting down German aircraft defending the skies over the Reich. British Air Chief Marshal Trafford Leigh-Mallory, commander of the tactical Allied Expeditionary Air Force (AEAF), wanted to use the strategic air forces to support Professor Solly Zuckerman's Transportation Plan—interdicting lines of communication in and around the invasion area and winning air superiority in a great swirling battle over the beachhead on D-day. At a meeting on 25 March 1944 Supreme Allied Commander General Dwight D. Eisenhower supported the Transportation Plan but allowed Spaatz to continue striking into Germany to weaken the Luftwaffe.

Field Marshal Hugo Sperrle's *Third Air Force* in France bore the responsibility of slowing the invaders until the Luftwaffe High Command could initiate "Impending Danger West," the plan to send day fighter units of the *I Fighter Corps*, defending Germany against the Allied strategic bombing campaign, to dispersed fields in France. Together the two forces, with panzer divisions on the ground, were to counterattack and drive the invaders back into the English Channel.

In the four months before D-day, the American Eighth Air Force, augmented by Royal Air Force (RAF) and American Ninth Air Force units, bled the *I Fighter Corps*, downing 1,300 fighters and pushing the remainder west of Hamburg, more than eight hundred kilometers (five hundred miles) from Normandy. When Allied forces came ashore on D-day, Sperrle's two fighter wings had less than 100 serviceable Me 109 and FW 190 fighters to challenge 5,400 British and American fighters and 6,000 other Allied aircraft. American P-38 Lightnings provided a protective umbrella over the invasion fleet, replaced by RAF aircraft at night. Covering the beaches were P-47 Thunderbolts and Spitfires. Long-range P-51 Mustangs patrolled far inland to intercept German aircraft heading for the invasion area. Additional fighters escorted bombers and transport aircraft. Sperrle's *Third Air Force* launched a meager three hundred sorties to challenge fifteen thousand Allied sorties for air superiority over the invasion area. Only two German fighters appeared over the beaches on 6 June, testimony to the success of Spaatz's campaign to weaken the Luftwaffe before the invasion.

In Germany Luftwaffe leaders failed to respond to the invasion, struck by the same indecision that delayed the deployment of the panzer divisions. On its own, the *I Fighter Corps* ordered some 400 single-engine day fighters to move to previously prepared bases in France over the next two days. Together the two German forces began launching an average of but 350 to 400 fighters per day to challenge Allied domination in the air. Intercepts by ULTRA (the top-secret Allied operation to intercept and decipher German radio transmissions) revealed that P-51 patrols destroyed between 30 and 50 percent of the reinforcements before they reached forward bases already heavily damaged by Allied bombers. After ten days the *I Fighter Corps* returned to Germany in tatters.

Eisenhower's preinvasion promise to his men, "If you see fighting aircraft over you, they will be ours," was borne out. German soldiers asked repeatedly, "Where is the Luftwaffe?" German losses amounted to nearly 600 aircraft of all kinds in the first ten days of OVERLORD. Allied losses were considerably heavier, most of them to ground fire.

[*See also* Third Air Force; U.S. Strategic Air Forces (USSTAF); *and biographies of numerous figures mentioned herein.*]

BIBLIOGRAPHY

McFarland, Stephen L., and Wesley Phillips Newton. *To Command the Sky: The Battle for Air Superiority over Germany, 1942–1944.* 1991.
Wynn, Humphrey, and Susan Young. *Prelude to Overlord.* 1984.

STEPHEN L. MCFARLAND

AIRCRAFT. [*This entry includes two articles:* Allied Aircraft *and* German Aircraft. *See also* Air Force; Air Strategy.]

Allied Aircraft

Air power was essential to the Allied victory in World War II and an integral part of the success of OVERLORD.

The aircraft available in England on 5 June 1944 to support OVERLORD included 5,049 fighters, 3,467 heavy bombers, 1,645 light and medium bombers, 2,316 transports, 2,591 gliders, and 698 aircraft of other types. These were, for the most part, divided into three types: strategic (long-range) bombers, troop carriers, and tactical (battlefield-support) aircraft. The strategic bombers were operated and managed by the RAF Bomber Command and the Eighth Air Force. The tactical aircraft were under an entity known as the Allied Expeditionary Air Force (AEAF), which was formed on 1 November 1943 as an umbrella for tactical air operations for OVERLORD. The components of the AEAF included the U.S. Ninth Air Force and its constituents (especially the IX Air Command), the Second British Tactical Air Force, and the First Tactical Air Force (authorized by Supreme Headquarters Allied Expeditionary Force on 6 April 1945), which was a multinational organization that included the I French Air Corps and the XII Tactical Air Command. Most troop carrier transport squadrons were under the IX Troop Carrier Command, which was part of the U.S. Ninth Air Force but was later transferred to the First Allied Airborne Army, which was created after OVERLORD.

Those aircraft of all types intended for action over the actual invasion area on, and immediately after, 6 June

RAF BOSTON.   A pair of RAF Douglas Boston MkIII attack bombers prepare for take-off in England. The bold black-and-white invasion stripes indicate involvement in OVERLORD.   IMPERIAL WAR MUSEUM

MOSQUITO.   This RAF de Havilland Mosquito, MkXVIII, is marked with invasion stripes.   IMPERIAL WAR MUSEUM

were marked with several bold, alternating black and white "invasion stripes" that were painted around the aft fuselage and the wings, so that these aircraft would be immediately recognizable to Allied antiaircraft gunners on the ground. The invasion stripes were also intended to aid Allied pilots in keeping track of "friendlies" during the intense air-to-air combat environment that was anticipated, but which failed to materialize.

The heavy, or strategic, bombers were the first aircraft to be used in support of OVERLORD. Their typical missions prior to May 1944 had involved striking strategic targets, which included factories, fuel depots, and railroads deep inside Germany and occupied Europe. Several weeks before D-day, however, they were reassigned to the task of "isolating the battlefield." Managed under the code name Operation COVER, isolating the battlefield involved severing the Normandy area and all northern France from sources of supply. This entailed destroying rail yards, highways, bridges, and trestles that the enemy could use to resupply their forces facing the invasion beaches and to bring in reinforcements. An especially large number of missions were flown against the Pas de Calais area as a diversion: the Germans expected the invasion there; COVER was designed to reinforce this belief.

The heavy bombers were under the command of the RAF Bomber Command and the U.S. Eighth Air Force.

The principal bomber types used in this operation included the British Avro Lancaster and Handley Page Halifax, as well as the American Boeing B-17 Flying Fortress and Consolidated B-24 Liberator. They each cruised at over 320 kph (200 mph) and had a range of over 3,200 km (2,000 mi.) with a typical bomb load in the neighborhood of 2,700 kg (6,000 lb.), except for the Halifax, whose range was about a third less than that of the others. For shorter missions less weight in fuel was required, so a greater weight in bombs could be carried. Each of these aircraft types dated from the late 1930s, but the specific subvariants in use in 1944 had been introduced since 1942.

On 2 through 5 June the B-17s and B-24s of the Eighth Air Force averaged 693 sorties daily over northern France and suffered only six losses. On 6 June alone, 1,729 Eighth Air Force heavy bombers delivered 3.3 million kg (7.2 million lb.) of bombs with only three losses. A thousand-plane raid was flown on 7 June, but weather conditions prohibited heavy bomber missions on 8 and 9 June. From 10 through 13 June, when the heavy bombers were redirected back to their strategic targets within Germany, Eighth Air Force bombers averaged 658 daily missions against northern France.

The light and medium bombers also flew some "isolating the battlefield" missions, but they were likewise committed to directly supporting the Allied troops on

RAF MITCHELL.   A North American Aviation Mitchell in RAF markings releases a string of 500-lb. bombs over a target in northern France about six weeks before OVERLORD. The USAAF Mitchell was designated the B-25.

IMPERIAL WAR MUSEUM

the battlefield by attacking nearby enemy forces and supply lines. Like the heavy bombers, they were active throughout northern France prior to 6 June, but they shifted their primary focus to Normandy after there was no need to continue the Pas de Calais deception.

Light bombers included the American Douglas A-20 Havoc (designated "Boston" by the RAF) and the Douglas A-26 Invader and the British de Havilland Mosquito. The latter two aircraft carried typical bomb loads of 900 kg (2,000 lb.) for about 2,400 km (1,500 mi.) at cruising speeds of 400 kph (250 mph). The Havoc (Boston), which was the direct predecessor of the A-26, had about half the range capability. Both aircraft were outstanding. The Mosquito was a relatively light airplane built of plywood to conserve weight and was powered by two Merlin engines. The Mosquito also saw service as a long-range fighter and a high-altitude reconnaissance aircraft. The Invader was a versatile attack aircraft that had entered service less than a year before OVERLORD, and would go on to see combat in both the Korean and Vietnam wars.

Allied medium bombers included the North American Aviation B-25 Mitchell and the Martin B-26 Marauder. Both were twin-engine aircraft that typically carried bomb loads of up to 1800 kg (4,000 lb.) for 2,400 km (1,500 mi.) at cruising speeds above 320 kph (200 mph). Like the A-26, both the B-25 and B-26 were armed with guns as well as bombs. While heavy bombers carried .50-caliber machine guns as defensive armament, the light

and medium bombers used them as offensive weapons for attacking enemy ground targets. For example, one Mitchell variant, the B-25H, carried eight forward-firing machine guns, as well as a 75-mm cannon.

During 3 to 5 June the Ninth Air Force light and medium bombers averaged over 220 missions daily, and on 6 June over 800 missions. From 7 through 18 June (excluding 9 and 16 June, when bad weather canceled all missions), an average of over 400 light and medium bomber missions were flown daily. Ninth Air Force operational control moved its advanced headquarters from Britain to Normandy on 17 June.

The first aircraft to take part in the actual invasion were the troop carrier transports that took off from England on the evening of 5 June carrying the paratroopers or pulling gliders (primarily Waco CG-4s). The vast majority of these transports had been built in the United States by Douglas Aircraft and were a class of large, twin-engined craft based on the successful DC-3 airliner. These were designated as C-47 Skytrain by the U.S. Army Air Forces (USAAF) and known as Dakota by the RAF. A variation on the C-47 was the C-53 Skytrooper, which though basically identical, was specially configured to carry 18 to 20 paratroopers, and had a small airliner-size door rather than a large cargo door like the C-47. The C-47s, C-53s, and Dakotas had a range of over 3,200 km (2,000 mi.) at 320 kph (200 mph) with an average load. They were designed with a load capacity (fuel and cargo) of 3,600 kg (8,000 lb.) but often carried up to twice that amount, especially during OVERLORD when the distances were relatively short and less fuel was necessary. As a group, these aircraft types had an excellent reputation for reliability, and General Eisenhower, among others, rated them as the most important Allied aircraft in the war. The durable Douglas transports flew over 1,400 missions on the night of 5–6 June, and more than 400 resupply flights to the paratroopers on the ground on 7 June.

During OVERLORD the Allied fighter aircraft provided a variety of services ranging from maintaining air superiority over the beaches to attacking German positions behind those beaches. British fighter types included the Supermarine Spitfire and Hawker Hurricane, which had performed so heroically in the Battle of Britain in 1940, as well as the newer Hawker Typhoon, which had entered service in 1943. The Hawker Tempest, which was actually an advanced variation on the Typhoon, saw its first combat action on 8 June 1944, two days after OVERLORD. The American fighters included the Lockheed P-38 Lightning, the Republic P-47 Thunderbolt, and the North American P-51 Mustang. The Allied fighters were each armed with at least six machine guns and were also configured to carry rockets and 227-kg (500-lb.) bombs. The Typhoon

NORTH AMERICAN AVIATION B-25 MITCHELL BOMBER.

COURTESY OF BILL YENNE

C-47 SKYTRAIN.   The Douglas C-47, which served the USAAF as the Skytrain and the RAF as the Dakota, was deemed by Eisenhower the most important aircraft of World War II.

COURTESY OF BILL YENNE

MUSTANG MkIII.   The RAF Mustang MkIII was the British equivalent of the North American Aviation P51C.

IMPERIAL WAR MUSEUM

and Tempest had 20-mm cannons. The P-47, P-51, Typhoon, and Tempest all had top speeds well in excess of 720 kph (450 mph). All the Allied fighters had a service ceiling near or exceeding 12,200 meters (40,000 ft.) and a range exceeding 1,600 km (1,000 mi.). The newest subvariants of the American fighters—the P-47D and P-51D—had appeared in 1943 and could fly twice as far. With extra fuel tanks attached, the P51-D was the first Allied fighter capable of regularly escorting heavy bombers all the way from England to Berlin.

The P-51D accounted for the greatest number of Luftwaffe aircraft defeated in air-to-air combat by the USAAF Forces (4,950), and the P-47 held the record for bomb tonnage dropped by a USAAF fighter type (104 million kg/113,963 tons). Indeed, the P-47 was an amazingly effective fighter-bomber during OVERLORD and other operations in both the European and Mediterranean theaters.

On 7 June (D plus 1), when the Luftwaffe attacked in greater numbers, the Eighth Air Force fighters—mainly P-51Ds—shot down 31 German fighters for a loss of only 4 of their own. From 8 through 18 June (D plus 12)—excluding 9 June, when operations were grounded because of bad weather—the USAAF alone flew more than 1,000 fighter sorties a day over northern France, most of them as fighter-bomber, or ground-attack, missions. Because Luftwaffe opposition ranged from minimal to nonexistent over northern France, the fighters were able to devote more time than expected to attacking ground targets such as bridges, barracks, troops, and vehicles. The Allied fighters had achieved total air superiority over Normandy on 6 June and were never effectively threatened by the Luftwaffe.

BIBLIOGRAPHY

Carter, Kit C., and Robert Mueller. *The Army Air Forces in World War II: Combat Chronology. 1941–1945.* 1973.
Eisenhower, Dwight David. *Crusade in Europe.* 1949.
Green, William. *Famous Bombers of the Second World War.* 1960.
Green, William. *Famous Fighters of the Second World War.* 1960.

P-47 "RAZORBACK."   This Republic P-47D-22 "Razorback" of the U.S. Ninth Air Force made an emergency landing on one of the Normandy invasion beaches in June 1944.   NATIONAL ARCHIVES

Wagner, Ray. *American Combat Planes*. 1960. Reprint, 1982.
Yenne, Bill. *Black '41: The West Point Class of 1941 and the American Triumph in World War II*. 1991.

BILL YENNE

German Aircraft

The Luftwaffe, although heavily committed to the defense of the Reich and the campaign against the Soviet Union, planned to resist the invasion of occupied Europe with all available fighter, fighter-bomber, long-range bombardment, and antishipping units. As was true of the entire Luftwaffe in mid-1944, these formations operated a mixture of obsolescent and technically advanced aircraft types. Their numbers—only 815 total aircraft on 5 June 1944—were inadequate for the task. While Luftwaffe aircraft achieved isolated successes against Allied forces, the lack of sufficiently trained crews, a chaotic command situation, and overwhelming Allied air superiority rendered the German air response irrelevant.

Fighters and Fighter-Bombers. The most capable and numerous type among the 170 German single-seater fighter aircraft in northern France in June 1944 was the Focke-Wulf FW 190A. The FW 190A, a single-engine air superiority fighter, equipped elements of *Jagdgeschwader (Fighter Wings) JG 2* and *JG 26*. A common variant, the FW 190A-8, armed with two 13-mm machine guns and four MG 151 20-mm cannon, possessed a top speed of 653 km/h (408 mph) at 6,000 meters (20,000 ft) altitude.

The 190s were augmented by lesser numbers of Messerschmitt Bf 109G-6 and G-10 fighters, the former armed with one 20-mm cannon and two 13-mm machine guns and capable of a top speed of 620 km/h (386 mph) at 6,792 meters (22,640 ft). Both fighter types could carry a variety of conversion sets, installed at the factory or in the field, that augmented their armament with additional cannon, rockets, or bombs.

Seventy-five FW 190F and G fighter-bombers equipped elements of *Schlachtgeschwader (Ground Attack Wings) SG 4* and *SG 10*. These formidable variants were similar to the fighter versions but were fitted with center-line and/or wing-mounted bomb racks carrying up to 1,800 kg (2 tons) of bombs. Despite the great need for ground attack aircraft in northern France, the Luftwaffe high command was compelled to keep nearly 600 FW 190 fighter-bombers on the Eastern front, in anticipation of the Red Army's summer 1944 offensive.

The Luftwaffe leadership intended to deploy ten Messerschmitt Me 262A jet-propelled fighter-bombers, with a top speed of 869 km/h (540 mph), four 30-mm cannon, and a 500-kg bomb load, but engineering, production, and training delays prevented the appearance of these advanced aircraft until August 1944.

The Luftwaffe hoped to contest the Allied air forces' air superiority over the landing beaches, but against overwhelming Allied air power, the German fighter force could achieve little. On D-day itself Luftwaffe fighters flew only seventy sorties, and although steadily rein-

FOCKE-WULF FW 190.   BIBLIOTHEK FÜR ZEITGESCHICHTE, STUTTGART

forced, could make little contribution to the German cause. FW 190s and Bf 109s generally flew close cover for troop movements, rather than operating offensively against Allied air and ground forces. The fighter-bombers rarely managed to penetrate the Allied fighter screens and frequently jettisoned their bombs before reaching their targets. The Germans estimated their fighter losses as three times greater than those of the Allies.

Bombers. The Luftwaffe's long-range striking arm operated a mixture of types with which it had begun the war in 1939, and newer designs that were finally coming off the production lines. In early 1944, *IX Air Corps* carried out a series of costly reprisal raids against the British Isles. Attrition was such that the force available to repel the invasion had dwindled to about 130 bombers. These included the Heinkel He 177, a heavy bomber powered by two Daimler-Benz 610 coupled engines driving two propellers. Although the aircraft possessed excellent performance characteristics and a large bomb load of 5,900 kg maximum (6.5 tons), it was technically unreliable. Derided by Adolf Hitler as "obviously the worst junk ever manufactured," the plane was prone to engine fires, and losses were heavy. More conventional types

included the Junkers Ju 88 (A and S models) and Ju 188 twin-engine medium bombers. The former had entered service in late 1939. Although one of the most successful multirole aircraft in aviation history, by 1944 the Ju 88 was obsolete and of limited use in the Western theater. The Ju 188 was a greatly improved redesign—renumbered, in the words of the Luftwaffe's chief of air armament, "so the enemy gets the impression it's something new." The Messerschmitt Me 410 twin-engine fighter-bomber and Dornier Do 217 heavy bomber equipped the remainder of the force.

Luftwaffe bombers were likewise unable to influence the outcome of the Normandy invasion. The mission of the *IX Air Corps* was to attack the Allied sea lines of communication as well as the beachhead itself. On D-day it managed only a paltry nine sorties by day and fifteen by night. Losses over the landing beaches during the first days of OVERLORD proved prohibitive, and the remainder of the bomber force subsequently carried out aerial minelaying duties in the Thames Estuary. In addition, Me 410 fighter-bombers engaged in ineffectual night-fighting operations and hit-and-run harassing attacks against the Allied landing zone.

MESSERSCHMITT BF-109G-6.

COURTESY OF BILL YENNE

HEINKEL HE 177.

BIBLIOTHEK FÜR ZEITGESCHICHTE, STUTTGART

JUNKERS JU 88A.

BIBLIOTHEK FÜR ZEITGESCHICHTE, STUTTGART

MESSERSCHMITT ME 410.

COURTESY OF ALFRED PRICE

Focke-Wulf FW 200.

Reconnaissance Aircraft. The long-range reconnaissance units were armed primarily with a version of the Ju 188 bomber, equipped with special night camera equipment and flash bombs. With a 5 June strength of seventy aircraft, they were far too weak to provide thorough photographic coverage of Allied preparations and deployments. The lack of reconnaissance aircraft was in part responsible for OVERLORD's achieving such a high degree of strategic and operational surprise.

Antishipping Aircraft. The Luftwaffe command concentrated its 200 antishipping aircraft in southern France under the command of the *X Air Corps* and the *2d Air Division*. The units, most notably *Kampfgeschwader (Bomber Wings) KG 26, KG 40,* and *KG 100,* were equipped with Do 217 and He 177 bombers armed either conventionally or with the Henschel Hs 293 (500-kg warhead) and Fritz X (1,400-kg warhead) radio-controlled bombs. These early guided missiles had gained some successes against British and Italian warships in the Mediterranean, but Allied fighter cover and electronic jamming greatly hindered their use against the invasion fleet. Ju 88s armed with the LT 350 aerial torpedo scored several hits on Allied shipping, but torpedo shortages restricted their employment. Approximately twenty-five Focke-Wulf FW 200 Condors, converted airliners serving as maritime patrol planes, were still in service with *KG 40* in mid-1944, but they were too vulnerable to risk in combat operations against the Allied fleet.

The Luftwaffe's most unusual (and notably unsuccessful) antishipping weapon was the Mistel (Mistletoe) 1, a composite aircraft consisting of a Ju 88 bomber, its crew compartment replaced by a 7,800-kg (8.5-ton) warhead, controlled by an attached Bf 109 fighter. Altogether, antishipping aircraft accounted for only five Allied vessels, with air-dropped mines sinking an additional twenty-six.

[*See also* Air Combat; Air Superiority.]

BIBLIOGRAPHY

Green, William. *Warplanes of the Third Reich.* 1970. Reprint, 1986.
Irving, David. *The Rise and Fall of the Luftwaffe: The Life of Field Marshal Erhard Milch.* 1973.
United Kingdom. Air Ministry. *The Rise and Fall of the German Air Force: A History of the Luftwaffe in World War II.* 1946. Reprint, 1986.

RICHARD R. MULLER

AIR DEFENCE OF GREAT BRITAIN. After its narrow victory over the Luftwaffe during the Battle of Britain from August through October 1940, the Royal Air Force concentrated on the Combined Bomber Offensive against Germany and on preparations for the Normandy invasion (overlord). One result of these preparations was the allocation of more than half the squadrons of the Fighter Command to the Allied Expeditionary Air Force,

HAWKER TEMPEST. A development of the Typhoon, this aircraft was used by RAF Fighter Command to intercept German V-1 bombs, or "Flying Bombs," over England.

IMPERIAL WAR MUSEUM

with the rest forming part of a new command, the Air Defence of Great Britain (ADGB). Air Marshal Roderic Hill was appointed to command this formation, with its headquarters at Bentley Priory. By 6 June 1944 Hill's force, in terms of aircraft, included twenty-eight squadrons of day fighters, nine of night fighters, two of intruder aircraft, and four air-sea rescue squadrons. Spitfires made up eighteen of these units, two were equipped with Hurricanes, two with flying Typhoons, and nine with Mosquitos. The ADGB Command also included the ground-based air defenses of the country: the air-raid warning system, the chain of radar stations, over 1,700 barrage balloons, and the army's Anti-Aircraft Command, with over 2,800 heavy guns and many more of light caliber.

Hill's command had three tasks. The first was simply air defense against attacks by the Luftwaffe. Although the German air force had suffered a considerable defeat at the hands of the Fighter Command in the summer of 1940, and by 1944 the bulk of the Luftwaffe effort was deployed on the Russian front and in the air defense of Germany itself, the Luftwaffe in the West was by no means a spent force. Even as late as February 1944, there had been five night bombing attacks against London, and as many as 170 German aircraft had been over the capital in a single night. Second, the ADGB was directed to prevent the Luftwaffe from making reconnaissance flights over the

south of England, where massive Allied forces were assembling for the invasion. And third, Hill was given the task of defending the United Kingdom against an expected attack by V-1s (Vergeltungswaffen 1 or Vengeance Weapons 1), also known as the Flying Bombs.

As it turned out, the last threat was the most serious one as well as the most difficult to counter. But the V-1 campaign was late in starting, and it was in any case directed against the London area rather than against the gathering Allied invasion forces. When the anticipated bombardment with these weapons began, Hill responded on 16 June by deploying almost all his defenses in the southeast of England. This removed effective air defense from many key targets on the south coast connected with the support of OVERLORD, leaving them vulnerable to air attack. But by this time the invasion was well under way, and the modest resources available to the Luftwaffe were directed against the invasion area in Normandy rather than against the supporting effort in the south of England. Apart from the V-1 attacks against London, the forces defending Britain against air attack were never seriously challenged.

[See also Hill, Roderic M.]

BIBLIOGRAPHY

Saunders, Hilary St. G.. *The Fight Is Won*. Vol. 3 of *The Royal Air Force, 1939–1945*. 1954.

Terraine, John. *The Right of the Line: The Royal Air Force in the European War, 1939–1945*. 1985.

MICHAEL ARMITAGE

AIR DEFENSE SHIPS. Two specialized types of air defense ship were used in the Normandy landings. Three fighter direction tenders (FDTs) were converted and deployed, *FDT 13* in the main convoy approach area, *FDT 216* in the Western Task Force area, and *FDT 217* with the Eastern Task Force. They were American-built tank landing ships of the LST(2) type operated by the Royal Navy and fitted with special radar and communications equipment to allow embarked RAF parties to act as forward fighter controls. The numbers were those they bore as LSTs (Landing Ships, Tank), whose characteristics they otherwise shared. Fears were expressed over the vulnerability of the FDTs, and the headquarters landing ships were prepared to act as backups. This proved unnecessary during the landings, but *FDT 217* was eventually sunk by an aircraft torpedo on 7 July.

To strengthen the antiaircraft defenses of the invasion anchorage, it was decided to send over nine so-called eagle ships. These were auxiliary antiaircraft vessels, mostly converted from pleasure steamers, to defend coastal convoys and anchorages; some had originally been minesweepers. The name came from the first such conversions, HMS *Royal Eagle* and HMS *Crested Eagle*. Because their antiaircraft weapons were individually aimed, these ships were considered more useful for barrage fire and breaking up attacks than for shooting aircraft down. The nine ships deployed off Normandy were:

Aristocrat: a paddle vessel built in 1935 with diesel-electric propulsion; 544 gross register tons (GRT); 17 knots; single 2-pounder pom-poms fore and aft, a single 20-mm gun forward and two on each beam, two quadruple 0.303-inch Browning machine-gun–armed aircraft turrets aft, and one twin and four single 0.303-inch Lewis guns; station: Mulberry B, Arromanches.

Golden Eagle: a genuine paddle steamer with reciprocating engines built in 1909; 793 GRT; 2,700 horsepower (hp), 18 knots; two 2-pounders and four 20-mm guns; one quadruple 0.303-inch machine-gun turret over each paddle, twin Lewis guns on the bridge roof; two quadruple rocket projectors; station: Port-en-Bessin.

Douwe Aukes: a former Royal Netherlands Navy (RNN) minelayer of 748 tons, launched in 1922; twin-shaft (screw), coal-fired, triple-expansion engines, 1,000 hp, 13 knots; one 75-mm gun aft, a single 2-pounder in each bridge wing, 20-mm guns on "bandstands" fore and aft; station: Port-en-Bessin (returned to RNN after the war).

Thames Queen: a 517-GRT paddle steamer built in 1898; 17 knots; one 12-pounder forward, two single 2-pounders before the funnel, four 20-mm guns, quadruple Browning turrets on each beam, a Lewis gun, a quadruple rocket projector; station: Ouistreham.

Whippingham: an 824-GRT paddle steamer built in 1930; 16 knots; armament generally like the others; station: Courseulles.

Goatfell: a 624-GRT paddle steamer built in 1934; a single 2-pounder fore and aft, six single 20-mm guns, two quadruple Browning turrets amidships; station: Western Task Force.

Scawfell: a 642-GRT paddle steamer built in 1937; 2,000 hp, 17 knots; armament generally like the others; station: Western Task Force; also used as a control vessel for Mulberry.

Sandown: a 684-GRT paddle steamer built in 1934; 14 knots; three 2-pounders, six 20-mm guns; station: Western Task Force; also a control vessel for the bombardons, the outer floating breakwater of the Mulberry harbor.

Ryde: a 603-GRT paddle steamer built in 1937; 14 knots; two 2-pounders, six 20-mm guns, two quadruple Browning turrets, three Lewis guns; station: Western Task Force.

[*See also* Antiaircraft and Artillery, *article on* Allied Antiaircraft and Artillery; Navy, *article on* Allied Naval Forces.]

BIBLIOGRAPHY

Lenton, H. T., and J. J. Colledge. *Warships of World War Two.* 1964.

Macdermott, Brian. *Ships without Names.* 1992.

ERIC J. GROVE

AIR FORCE. [*This entry includes two articles:* Allied Expeditionary Air Force *and* German Air Force.]

Allied Expeditionary Air Force

From the beginning of planning for Operation OVERLORD, the decisive role of air forces had been acknowledged. The very location of the Anglo-American landings in northwest Europe depended upon obtaining fighter cover by achieving air supremacy. Close air support of the ground forces, during both the landing and subsequent buildup, was also seen as essential. Equally important was the disruption of German communications in order to isolate the battlefield ("interdiction"), thus preventing the supply, reinforcement, and maneuver of German forces.

Experience in the Mediterranean theater had taught the lesson that "when critical land operations are in progress,

ARTHUR TEDDER.   NATIONAL ARCHIVES

army cooperation is not simply a specialized activity of part of an air force. It is the function of the entire force, with all its available strength" (John Terraine, *Time for Courage,* pp. 385–386). The OVERLORD planners rediscovered this truth. The multiplicity of tasks awaiting the British and American air forces called for the participation of every United Kingdom–based command of the Royal Air Force (RAF): Bomber, Fighter, Coastal, Transport, and Balloon, in addition to the mixed elements of the U.S. Army's Eighth (Strategic) and Ninth (Tactical) air forces.

The Allied Expeditionary Air Force (AEAF) was a new element whose specific purpose was to support the Allied armies through the northwest Europe campaign. Its commander, Air Chief Marshal Trafford Leigh-Mallory, was selected at the QUADRANT conference in Quebec in August 1943; he was the first Allied force commander to be named. This appointment appeared logical, since Leigh-Mallory was at that time the air officer commanding (AOC) Fighter Command, and the opinion of the Combined Chiefs of Staff was, as noted in the British official history, *The Strategic Air Offensive against Germany,* vol. 3 (1961), that "the most important aspect of the air contribution to OVERLORD would be the attainment of air superiority over the beachheads" (p. 16).

It was above all the necessary inclusion of the strategic bomber forces, the 1,970 aircraft of the U.S. Eighth Air Force and the 1,470 aircraft of RAF Bomber Command, in the OVERLORD air program that exposed the unsatisfactory character of this command arrangement. Neither Gen. Carl ("Tooey") Spaatz, commanding the U.S. Strategic Air Forces in Europe (USSAFE), nor Air Chief Marshal Arthur Harris, AOC Bomber Command, was willing to take orders from Leigh-Mallory. To resolve this serious difficulty, it was agreed that "direction" of all the OVERLORD air components should be vested in the Supreme Allied Commander, General Dwight D. Eisenhower, to be exercised by his deputy, Air Chief Marshal Arthur Tedder, who thus became, as the official air historians Charles Webster and Noble Frankland say, "a real Commander-in-Chief of the air."

In the final constitution for D-day, Tedder's jurisdiction contained:

U.S. Eighth Air Force
RAF Bomber Command
RAF Coastal Command
Air Defence of Great Britain (ADGB, ex-Fighter Command)
AEAF (under Leigh-Mallory)

The AEAF itself consisted of an Advance Force under Air Marshal Arthur Coningham, comprising:

U.S. Ninth Air Force (Maj. Gen. Lewis H. Brereton) containing IX (Light and Medium) Bomber Command, two tactical air commands, one troop carrier command, No. 10 Reconnaissance Group
Second Tactical Air Force, containing No. 2 (Light and Medium) Group of Bomber Command, three composite fighter groups, two special reconnaissance wings
In association with these as occasion demanded, four ADBG day and night fighter groups, and two RAF troop-carrying groups

The total Allied air strength available on 6 June 1944 was:

	Aircraft
Heavy bombers (Strategic Forces)	3,440
Medium and light bombers (Tactical Forces)	930
Fighter-bombers and fighters (day and night)	4,190
Troop carriers and transports	1,360
Coastal Command (including 40 U.S. aircraft attached)	1,070
Reconnaissance	520
Air/sea Rescue	80
	11,590

Of this total, 6,080 aircraft were American, and 5,510

ALLIED AIR STRATEGY.   Left to right: Roderic M. Hill; Maj. Gen. William C. Butler, deputy commander in chief, Allied Expeditionary Air Force (pointing); Trafford Leigh-Mallory (standing); Air Vice Marshal H. Wigglesworth; Brig. Gen. Aubrey C. Strickland; Lewis H. Brereton; Arthur Coningham.
IMPERIAL WAR MUSEUM

were British or from other Allied contingents. In addition to the powered aircraft, the Allies disposed of 3,500 troop transport gliders.

OVERLORD air operations, especially those concerned with the interdiction program and the destruction of the German fighter arm, began long before the Normandy landings. During the intensive phase, 1 April–5 June, the Allied air forces flew approximately 195,200 sorties, during which they dropped over 195,000 tons of bombs. Their losses were 1,953 aircraft (1,251 American, 702 British and Allied), totaling over 12,000 aircrew. On D-day itself the Allied air forces flew a further 14,674 sorties at a cost of 127 aircraft (chiefly caused by antiaircraft fire). During the whole day the Luftwaffe flew only 319 sorties. This was air supremacy indeed, already won when

the assault began and never lost throughout the whole of the ensuing campaign.

[See also Air Superiority; Air Strategy, article on Allied Air Strategy; Coningham, Arthur; Leigh-Mallory, Trafford; Tedder, Arthur; and articles on the units mentioned herein.]

BIBLIOGRAPHY

Ellis, L. F., et al. The Battle of Normandy. Vol. 1 of Victory in the West. 1962.
Saunders, Hilary St. G. The Fight Is Won. Vol. 3 of The Royal Air Force, 1939–1945. 1975. Official history.
Terraine, John. A Time for Courage: The Royal Air Force in the European War, 1939–1945. 1985.
Wynn, Humphrey, and Susan Young. Prelude to Overlord. 1983.

JOHN TERRAINE

German Air Force

In 1944 the Luftwaffe's organization reflected the framework with which it had gone to war in 1939, rather than the realities of the military situation or adaptation to the changing nature of the war. Hermann Göring remained as its commander in chief despite his growing dependency on drugs and arrogant incompetence—realities that were apparent even to Hitler. But the Führer still valued Göring, an old Nazi party colleague, for his loyalty and his unstinting willingness to toe the military lines that Hitler laid down. By 1944 Göring's sycophancy had disastrous consequences for Germany's conduct of the war. But Göring's greatest failure had been his optimistic calculations on the direction that the air war was taking in 1942 and 1943.

Before World War II the Luftwaffe's structure had aimed at providing balanced air fleets to support the Wehrmacht's march of conquest. By 1944 the Wehrmacht was in the midst of its long retreat back to the Reich, while the Luftwaffe confronted a massive aerial assault from Anglo-American air forces in England as well as in

Italy. Despite that terrible threat, already apparent as early as the summer of 1943, Göring persisted in leaving a splintered organization in place to defend the western frontiers of the Reich.

As German forces shifted to the east for the invasion of the Soviet Union in 1941, *Third Air Force (Luftflotte 3)* had remained behind to protect the occupied territories and the western Reich from British air attacks. Field Marshal Hugo Sperrle, similar to his boss Göring in both girth and devotion to the Nazi cause, remained as *Third Air Force*'s chief. By 1941 the threat had grown beyond one organization's capabilities. A new air force, eventually named *Home Air Force*, assumed control of the air defenses in northern Germany, while *Third Air Force* held responsibility for France, Holland, and Belgium.

This did not prove an altogether effective arrangement in dealing with either nighttime or daytime attacks. A number of generals commanding fighter divisions urged Göring to establish an organization akin to Fighter Command in England, but the Reichsmarshal resolutely refused, believing that such an organization would diminish his powers. The assault on the Reich in the summer of 1943 by the Anglo-American air forces, however, did tend to concentrate the Luftwaffe's scarce resources in the Reich. By early 1944 *Third Air Force* had lost most of its force structure to *Home Air Force*. While the bombing offensive against London, starting in January 1944, took place from French bases, *Third Air Force* played virtually no role in its planning.

Third Air Force's last gasp came with plans to concentrate the fighter squadrons on French air bases, from which they could strike the invasion. But that planning took place in an atmosphere of general unreality: those charged with the defense of the Reich believed that they were waging a life-and-death struggle for the survival of Germany's industry and cities, whereas Sperrle's staff were looking at the coming invasion. In fact, by the spring of 1944 the weakened Luftwaffe was capable of fighting neither battle. Wherever it placed its strength, it was going to lose.

[*See also* Sperrle, Hugo.]

BIBLIOGRAPHY

Murray, Williamson. *Luftwaffe*. 1985.
Overy, Richard J. *The Air War, 1939–1945*. 1980.

WILLIAMSON MURRAY

HERMANN GÖRING.   NATIONAL ARCHIVES

AIR-SEA RESCUE. Over one hundred aircraft and a similar number of surface vessels provided air-sea rescue support for the invasion. Primary responsibility fell to the Royal Air Force (RAF), although U.S. controllers and aircraft from a new U.S. rescue unit supported the operation.

HERMANN GÖRING WITH ADOLF HITLER.

Air-sea rescue— coordinated operations by aircraft and surface vessels to rescue aircrews downed in offshore waters—had become a priority for Britain early in the war. The British system consisted of three components: spotter aircraft, surface vessels, and a communication network. By mid-1942 the RAF had developed an effective air-sea rescue organization that saved approximately one-third of the aircrews who bailed out over or made forced landings on water. It included over 100 surface vessels and 95 spotter aircraft. The aircraft were divided between Fighter Command, responsible for search missions within forty miles of the coast, and Coastal Command, which conducted the longer-range "deep search" missions. Initially, U.S. aircrews based in England relied on the British air-sea rescue organization. In June 1943, however, the Americans established a communication network, and thereafter occasionally used their own aircraft as spotters when they could be spared from operational missions.

During the winter and spring of 1943–1944, the RAF reorganized and strengthened its air-sea rescue capability in preparation for OVERLORD. To ensure unity of command in the invasion area, the Air Staff assigned responsibility for all air-sea rescue operations in the English Channel—regard-less of distance from the coast—to Air Defence of Great Britain Command (ADGB, formerly Fighter Command); Coastal Command assumed responsibility for rescue operations in all other areas. The RAF also upgraded the aircraft of its rescue squadrons; although the Hudsons and Walruses remained, the aging Lysanders, Defiants, and Ansons were replaced by Spitfires and Warwicks.

As the invasion approached, ADGB concentrated its spotter aircraft and surface vessels in southern England. In May the 80 aircraft of the ADGB's spotter units—Air/Sea Rescue Squadrons 275–278—were positioned at key locations along the coast of southern England to ensure adequate coverage for the assault area. Units of Coastal Command—Air/Sea Rescue Squadrons 279–282— provided 89 aircraft to cover operations outside the assault area. The RAF squadrons were augmented by the 25 P-47s of a newly formed U.S. spotter unit—Detachment B of the 65th Fighter Wing (later redesignated the 5th Emergency Rescue Squadron). By the end of May, RAF rescue planners had concentrated 136 rescue vessels along the southern coast of England, 90 high-speed launches, 6 seaplane tenders, and 40 Royal Navy rescue motor launches, supplemented by 60 U.S. Coast Guard cutters responsible for

U.S. COAST GUARD RESCUE CRAFT.   Operating off landing beaches.   NATIONAL ARCHIVES

assisting distressed ships in the invasion area.

Allied air-sea rescue operations for D-day and its aftermath were highly successful. Although statistics on the number of forced landings and crashes in the Channel are unavailable, very few Allied airmen perished at sea. By D plus 10, RAF air-sea rescue aircraft and surface vessels had rescued 163 Allied airmen and sixty others, including two Germans. As of 30 June 1944, ADGB's four air-sea rescue squadrons had flown 1,471 sorties in support of OVERLORD and had helped rescue approximately 350 individuals.

[See also Air Defence of Great Britain; Coastal Command.]

BIBLIOGRAPHY

Ransom, Frank E. *Air-Sea Rescue, 1941–1952*. U.S. Air Force Historical Study No. 95. 1954.
United Kingdom. Air Ministry. *Air/Sea Rescue*. Air Publication 3232. 1952.

ROBERT J. JAKEMAN

AIR SERVICE COMMAND. The Air Service Command, U.S. Strategic Air Forces in Europe (ASC, USSAFE, later USSTAF), came into existence 6 January 1944, when Lt. Gen. Carl Spaatz established Headquarters USSTAF at Bushy Park near London. Its organization reflected its dual responsibilities: operational control of the American Eighth and Fifteenth air forces, and administrative control of the American Eighth and Ninth air forces. The Ninth Air Force was under the operational control of the Allied Expeditionary Air Force (AEAF). Headquarters USSTAF had a unique dual deputy organization with a deputy commanding general, operations, who coordinated the operations of the Eighth and Fifteenth air forces, and a deputy commanding general, administration, Brig. Gen. Hugh J. Knerr (promoted to major general in March 1944), who exercised theater-wide authority over U.S. Army Air Force logistics.

General Knerr also served as the commander of ASC, USSTAF, which absorbed VIII Air Force Service Command. The Base Area Depot became its chief component, while the Strategic Air Depot Area became the new VIII Air Force Service Command. Both the VIII and IX air force service commands operated under the technical control of ASC, USSTAF, which by June 1944 provided all base services for both commands. Depots of ASC, USSTAF, performed much of the fourth-level or most complicated maintenance for the Eighth and Ninth air forces. By shortly after D-day, ASC, USSTAF, had also assumed complete responsibility for receipt, assembly, and modification of all aircraft arriving from the United States. General Knerr had not only theater-wide logistical authority but also direction of the theater air logistical components. Much to the confusion of his subordinate commands, Knerr did not draw a hard-and-fast distinction between his two roles, but he did delegate much of the day-to-day work to the Base Area Depot, while emphasizing his advisory and policy-making functions.

Headquarters USSTAF's organization, by placing logistics on the same level as operations, illustrated the importance of administration to the smooth functioning of air warfare. It further prevented both avoidable duplications of effort by the Eighth and Ninth air forces and excessive competition between them in setting supply priorities and obtaining the supplies themselves, thus reducing waste and inefficiency. The new organization was instrumental in allowing the two air forces to absorb the massive preinvasion air buildup. As a secondary purpose, the tying of the Ninth Air Force to the major American air headquarters in Europe by means of firm administrative bonds enabled Spaatz to resist both the desire of the Ninth Air Force to operate more independently, and the wishes of the commander of the AEAF to acquire more complete control over the Ninth. Although one cannot measure tangibly the contribution of the logistical organization of USSTAF to the Allied effort, it undoubtedly helped to ensure the efficiency of U.S. air operations for the Normandy campaign and beyond—an important factor in the defeat of Germany.

[See also VIII Air Force Service Command; Goodrich, Donald; Knerr, Hugh J.]

BIBLIOGRAPHY

Goldberg, Alfred. "Air Logistics in the ETO." In vol. 2 of *The Army Air Forces in World War II*, edited by Wesley Frank Craven and James Lea Cate. 1949.

RICHARD G. DAVIS

AIR SPECIAL OPERATIONS. Allied air special operations in support of D-day fell into three general categories: support of clandestine forces, propaganda and deception missions, and other special operations.

Support of Clandestine Forces. After the fall of France, special duty units of the Royal Air Force (RAF) were formed to support the clandestine efforts of Britain's Special Operations Executive (SOE) to direct and supply the French Resistance. By 1942 these secret units constituted two squadrons—Nos. 138 and 161—based at a camouflaged field at Tempsford and equipped with an assortment of specially modified aircraft that included Lysanders, Stirlings, and Hudsons. The special duty units conducted virtually all their operations under cover of darkness. When feasible, supplies and agents were dropped into France by parachute, but pickups—and some deliveries—required landings in remote areas, usually with Lysanders.

At the end of 1943, in anticipation of the coming invasion, the SOE intensified its efforts to supply the Resistance. Consequently, the RAF special duty squadrons were enlarged, and the U.S. Army Air Forces (USAAF) provided four B-24 units—the 36th, 406th, 788th, and 850th bombardment squadrons—to fly CARPETBAGGER missions, the U.S. code name for airdrop supply missions to the Resistance. During the first half of 1944, RAF and USAAF units flew almost two thousand sorties in support of the French Resistance, more than double the number flown since the beginning of the war. This preinvasion supply campaign paid unexpected dividends: according to the official SOE history, Resistance forces were responsible for almost one thousand railway cuts on the night of 5–6 June, disrupting railroad traffic on a scale that rivaled the effectiveness of conventional air strikes.

After D-day the pace of aerial supply missions accelerated even more: between July and September, Allied aircraft flew approximately four thousand Resistance supply sorties. Once the invasion began, the experienced crews of the special duty squadrons were also called on to insert a wide variety of intelligence agents and special forces behind the lines, including Jedburgh teams (three-man Anglo-French-American units), Special Air Service (SAS) commandos, and U.S. special operations groups.

Propaganda and Deception Missions. Millions of propaganda leaflets were dispensed by the USAAF's special leaflet unit, the 422d Bombardment Squadron, and by other air units during the course of regular combat sorties. Aircraft also played key roles in the deception operations conducted during the initial phases of the invasion, part of the overall deception plan code-named FORTITUDE. On the morning of 6 June, aircraft of RAF's 617 and 218 squadrons dispensed chaff (metallic strips) over the Channel while flying carefully rehearsed patterns as part of TAXABLE and GLIMMER, coordinated air-sea operations that convinced German radar operators that invasion fleets were approaching Cap d'Antifer and Boulogne, well north of the actual route of the seaborne assault. To conceal the real route of the huge stream of transports carrying paratroopers of the U.S. 82d and 101st airborne divisions, RAF Stirlings used chaff (metallic strips) to create a radar illusion of a sky train well to the south of the actual drop zone. Other deceptions regarding the airborne forces were carried out under the code name TITANIC, which involved RAF aircraft dropping small, mechanical "dummy" airborne troops together with small, specially trained SAS units equipped to replicate the sights and sounds of an airborne assault. To the north, a force of thirty Lancasters and B-17s laid a chaff corridor west of Amiens to simulate a bomber stream headed toward Berlin, so as to disrupt and confuse German air defenses over northern France.

Other Special Operations. Shortly after midnight 5–6 June, RAF Halifaxes towed six Horsa gliders, containing an independent company of Britain's 6th Airborne Division, across the Channel to the mouth of the Orne River. Their mission was to seize and hold a key bridge across the Orne River and canal between Bénouville and Ranville. These glider-borne troops became the first Allied company to see action on D-day, as they successfully took and held their bridgehead until relieved by main assault forces almost twenty-four hours later. Thus Pegasus Bridge—as it is now called—was preserved for Allied use in the critical first days of the invasion by a daring aerial coup de main.

Farther inland, the Germans were denied use of another key transportation choke point by Lancasters from 617 Squadron. On the evening of 7 June, aircrews from this renowned "dam buster" unit—having completed their chaff mission the previous day—dropped massive 12,000-pound bombs (the largest of the war) that destroyed an important railway tunnel under the Loire River, cutting the last route open between southern France and Normandy and further disrupting the flow of German forces to the invasion area.

[*See also* Deception; French Resistance; Office of Strategic Services (OSS); Propaganda, *article on* Allied Propaganda; Special Operations.]

PEGASUS BRIDGE.   The bridge across the Orne River, renamed Pegasus Bridge, was captured by a glider-borne patrol commanded by Maj. John Howard. At the top right of the photograph are two Horsa gliders.

IMPERIAL WAR MUSEUM

BIBLIOGRAPHY

Ambrose, Stephen A. *Pegasus Bridge: June 6, 1944.* 1985.
Brickhill, Paul. *The Dam Busters.* 1951.
Brown, Anthony Cave. *Bodyguard of Lies.* 1975.
Foot, M. R. D. *SOE in France: An Account of the Work of the British Special Operations Executive in France, 1940–1944.* 1966.
Saunders, Hilary St. G. *Royal Air Force, 1939–1945.* 3 vols. 1954.
Tickell, Jerrard. *Moon Squadron.* 1956.
Warren, Harris. "Air Support for the Underground." In vol. 3 of *The Army Air Forces in World War II*, edited by Wesley Frank Craven and James Lea Cate. 1951.

ROBERT J. JAKEMAN

AIR SPOTTING POOL. The use of aircraft for spotting and correcting ships' gunfire dates back to 1915, when they were employed with some success in the Gallipoli campaign. During the early years of World War II, the U.S. Navy and Royal Navy (RN) operated seaplanes carried on the catapults of capital ships and cruisers in actions against ships and shore targets. By 1943 most RN spotting flights had been removed, to make way for additional antiaircraft weapons. They were retained in the U.S. Navy, but during the Sicilian invasion in July 1943, the slow floatplanes had suffered severe losses to the efficient German flak. Over the Normandy coastal areas not only would the flak be more intense, but there was also likely to be fighter opposition. It was therefore decided that, for Operation NEPTUNE, fighter-type aircraft would be used for spotting; they were organized as No. 34 Tactical Reconnaissance Wing, Royal Air Force (RAF), Second Tactical Air Force (TAF).

The Supermarine Seafire pilots of No. 3 Naval Fighter Wing (Nos. 808, 885, 886, and 897 naval air squadrons) began specialized training on 25 February 1944, the pilots learning tactical reconnaissance and army cooperation techniques in addition to spotting for large-caliber ships' guns; they were joined by two RAF "Army Co-op" squadrons, Nos. 26 and 63, equipped with Spitfire LVB aircraft similar to the Seafire FIII. A third service was represented in the Air Spotting Pool, which was commanded by Como. E. C. Thornton, RN: seventeen U.S. Navy floatplane pilots were taught to fly borrowed Spitfires and operated as VCS-7, the only U.S. Navy squadron to fly this famous aircraft.

Based at RN air station Lee-on-Solent, near Portsmouth, the 101 Seafires and Spitfires of the pool flew 339 sorties on D-day, the first spotting pair taking off before dawn and the last landing after dusk. Six aircraft were lost to flak, but on the opening day the fighter pilots contributed markedly to the accuracy of the long-range naval gunnery against targets as far as twenty-four kilometers (fifteen miles) inland. Three Seafires were lost to German fighters over the next two days, but the naval pilots evened the score with two "kills" and a "probable."

Low clouds over Normandy and fewer calls for spotting missions led to a considerable reduction in flying intensity from D plus 3. The Western Task Force's bombardment of Cherbourg on 25 June provided an exception, requiring 142 sorties by the pool: one U.S. Navy cruiser underlined the reason for using fighters, launching a floatplane only to see it shot down as soon as it came within range of the defenses. VCS-7 handed in its Spitfires after this operation and on 29 June RAF No. 63 Squadron was withdrawn from the pool. The naval bombardment of the defenses of Caen was spotted by the five remaining squadrons from 27 June until 8 July. Additional tasks had been found for the Seafires, which escorted C-47 Dakota supply-dropping missions and undertook fighter sweeps over central Normandy.

Operation NEPTUNE ended officially on 7 July, but No. 3 Fighter Wing was not released until the 15th, the naval pilots' final task being antisubmarine patrols around the eastern anchorage, where they destroyed at least four Biber midget submarines by 20-mm cannon fire.

The Air Spotting Pool flew a total of 2,408 combat sorties between 6 June and 15 July. Twenty-seven Seafires and Spitfires were lost to enemy action and two to friendly fire; accidents cost four more aircraft, but pilot losses were fewer than a dozen killed or taken prisoner. Tactically, the use of fighters was regarded as successful, and the U.S. Navy went as far as forming escort carrier fighter squadrons for this specific role, the first seeing action in the subsequent invasion of the south of France.

[*See also* Bombardment Ships; Second Tactical Air Force.]

BIBLIOGRAPHY

Saunders, Hilary St. G. *The Fight Is Won.* Vol. 3 of *The Royal Air Force, 1939–1945.* 1975. Official history.
Terraine, John. *A Time for Courage: The Royal Air Force in the European War, 1939–1945.* 1985.
Wilmot, Chester. *The Struggle for Europe.* 1952.

DAVID BROWN

AIR STRATEGY. [*This entry includes two articles:* Allied Air Strategy *and* German Air Strategy.]

Allied Air Strategy

Determination of Allied air strategy before OVERLORD sparked a controversy within the alliance. The strategic bomber commanders, Lt. Gen. Carl Spaatz, who was in charge of the American Eighth Air Force in Britain, and the Fifteenth Air Force in Italy, and Air Chief Marshal (ACM) Arthur Harris, who led the RAF Bomber Command, opposed other air and ground leaders, such as General Dwight D. Eisenhower's deputy supreme commander, ACM Arthur Tedder, and his tactical air commander, ACM Trafford Leigh-Mallory. Spaatz and Harris wished to strike targets in Germany, whereas Tedder and Leigh-Mallory, employing the Transportation Plan advanced by Prof. Solly Zuckerman, a British bombing expert, proposed an attritional attack on German lines of communication in Belgium and France, particularly rail systems.

Since the Transportation Plan would not begin until sixty to ninety days before the invasion, the fortunes of the strategic air forces during early 1944 played a crucial role in their attitudes toward it. Bomber Command suffered disastrous losses and after the 30 March 1944 attack on Nuremberg, ceased operations over Germany. That made it available for transportation raids, undercutting Harris's objections. The Americans had more success. The introduction of long-range P-51 fighters and of larger jettisonable gas tanks extended the range of American P-38 and P-47 fighters and allowed the Eighth Air Force to crush the Luftwaffe in a four-month battle of attrition. American fighters drove the Germans from the skies and descended to low altitudes to damage German airfields and other targets. By 1 March Spaatz concluded that he could strike any target in Germany. Fearing the Germans might conserve fighter aircraft to oppose the invasion instead of defending against American raids, he favored selecting crucial targets that would force a Luftwaffe response. The synthetic oil industry provided the perfect target, being small and vital to the German military effort.

Spaatz's Oil Plan offered two advantages to the invasion: it would eviscerate the German fighters, preventing interference with the invasion, and reduce the mobility of the German land forces, preventing rapid reinforcement of the troops opposing the invasion. The competing Oil and Transportation plans each gained adherents. On 25 March

BOMBED RAILWAY YARDS AND BRIDGE.   Saumur, 1 June 1944.   AIR HISTORICAL BRANCH, RAF, CROWN COPYRIGHT RESERVED

Eisenhower selected the Transportation Plan, because it guaranteed tremendous damage to the rail and road system supporting the German land response to the invasion. Bomber Command began raiding its assigned targets and continued hitting them until after the invasion.

Spaatz delayed sending the Eighth Air Force to France. On 19 April he met with Eisenhower and obtained his consent to mount two raids on synthetic oil plants prior to the invasion. Both generals knew that the European weather patterns would provide instances of clear days over Germany and clouds over France (and vice versa), so that bombing the one need not interfere with bombing the other. On 22 April the Eighth Air Force flew its first Transportation Plan mission. On 12 and 28 May American bombers struck and damaged synthetic oil targets, halving total production. Ultra, the Allied code-breaking organization, intercepted messages revealing the Germans' great alarm. Two weeks after the invasion the Allies commenced a strategic bombing campaign against synthetic oil plants.

Shortly after Eisenhower made his choice, British Prime Minister Winston Churchill intervened. When the prime minister saw RAF estimates of 60,000 French civilian dead caused by transportation bombing, he balked. He insisted the raids produce less than 150 casualties each. Eisenhower objected: the restriction would emasculate the plan and leave the beachhead open to counterattack. Churchill remained adamant, remarking that he had not realized "our use of air power before OVERLORD would assume so cruel and remorseless a form" (Arthur Tedder, *With Prejudice*, 1966, p. 529). Finally, the prime minister appealed to President Franklin D. Roosevelt, who replied that he would not interfere with Eisenhower's judgment. The plan went forward. Fortunately, the rail center and bridge attacks killed less than 5,750 French civilians.

Before the invasion Allied aircraft dropped 71,000 tons of bombs on rail centers, attacked airfields, and destroyed numerous bridges. At the same time they maintained Operation FORTITUDE, a deception scheme whereby two bombs were dropped outside the invasion area for each one dropped in it, in order to mislead the Germans as to the invasion site. The destruction of rail centers and the unrestricted strafing of trains reduced the rolling stock, train crews, and shipping capacity available to the Germans. The Transportation Plan imposed great injury on German mobility and logistics, which undoubtedly hurt their effort on D-day and afterward.

[*See also* Air Superiority; Bomber Command; Eighth Air Force; Fifteenth Air Force; Harris, Arthur; Railroads; Spaatz, Carl.]

BIBLIOGRAPHY

Kingston-McClourghry, E. J. *The Direction of War: A Critique of the Political Direction and High Command in War.* 1956.

Rostow, W. W. *Pre-Invasion Bombing Strategy: General Eisenhower's Decision of March 25, 1944.* 1981.

Zuckerman, Solly. *From Apes to Warlords.* 1978.

RICHARD G. DAVIS

German Air Strategy

By the spring of 1944 the Allies' Combined Bomber Offensive had placed the Luftwaffe in an impossible strategic situation. Allied air attacks had done much damage to the aircraft industry; Allied escort fighters had depleted the Luftwaffe's fighter force; German bomber raids on the British Isles had suffered insupportable losses, while inflicting minimal damage on enemy cities; and finally, in May the Americans had begun striking the synthetic oil sites and by the end of May had already achieved significant results against oil production—an essential resource for the further prosecution of the war.

Only against Bomber Command's nighttime attacks had the Luftwaffe held its own. But even that success had a double edge: Bomber Command switched its emphasis to attacking the transportation system of France, and achieved significant success in isolating the defended coast and fortifications of Fortress Europe from the supplies and logistical support necessary for a successful defense.

Thus even in defense of the Reich, the Luftwaffe was losing the struggle. But the looming strategic threat in 1944 was that of the Allied assault on Fortress Europe, Operation OVERLORD. To counter it, the Germans planned to move their fighter forces from their bases in the Reich westward to bases in France from which they could contest the air over the invasion beaches. Hitler had also calculated that the Me 262, a revolutionary new jet fighter, would be ready in sufficient numbers for use as a fighter-bomber, and that its appearance over Allied ground forces fighting their way ashore would have a shattering impact on enemy morale.

Finally, over the winter of 1943–1944 the Germans began construction of launching sites in France for their equivalent to the modern-day cruise missile, the V-1 (Vergeltungswaffe) or Flying Bomb. From that weapon the Germans hoped for two results. First, they hoped it would terrorize the British population and force a cessation of the combined bomber offensive that was ravaging the cities and industry of Germany. And if that should fail, they hoped the V-1s could disrupt the concentration of troops and supplies that the invading armies would require.

In fact, every aspect of German air strategy conflicted with reality. Through intelligence sources and aerial reconnaissance, the Allies learned of the construction program of launch ramps throughout northern France that early versions of the V-1 required. In response Allied air forces, including strategic bombers, conducted Operation

BOMBED V-1 LAUNCH SITE IN THE PAS DE CALAIS.   AIR HISTORICAL BRANCH, RAF, CROWN COPYRIGHT RESERVED

CROSSBOW, thus delaying the launch date for the V-1 offensive against southern England until after the invasion. Consequently the V-1 had no impact on the concentration and movement of invading forces up to and across the Channel.

Air power enthusiasts have often ascribed the nonappearance of the Me 262 until late 1944 to Hitler's insistence that German industry fit the world's first operational jet as a fighter-bomber. That is not, however, why the Me 262 failed to enter the Luftwaffe's inventory at its scheduled time. In early 1944 the Germans were having serious problems with the production power plant of the Me 262: turbine blades were coming off compressors so early in engine life cycles that it made no sense to put the aircraft into full-time production and equip fighter squadrons with aircraft that—not surprisingly, given the technology—were still going through teething troubles.

The failure of the V-1 and the Me 262 to appear on the scene in the spring of 1944 left the fighter and bomber squadrons as the sole weapons in the Luftwaffe's arsenal.

But German aircraft had been going through a rough time in early 1944. The German bomber force had carried out a series of retaliatory raids beginning in January, but the results had been minimal in terms of the damage inflicted on the British. On the other hand, attacking bombers suffered catastrophic losses. Over a three-month period the Germans lost 329 heavy bombers, having begun their attacks on London with only 550. By May the Germans possessed only 144 bombers on airfields in France—too few to interfere with the invasion.

The movement of daylight fighters to forward operating bases in France was thus the final operational course left. But the fighter force was having its own difficulties in the spring of 1944. In February the U.S. Eighth Air Force had launched a massive assault on the Luftwaffe. "Big Week" aimed to destroy the entire base of German aircraft production by attacking and wrecking the factories and their power plants.

In 1943 the German fighter defenses had mastered such

American attacks, because Allied escort fighters lacked the range to accompany bomber formations beyond the Rhine. But in February 1944 the formations of American bombers had returned with an escort fighter, the P-51, that could accompany bombers all the way to Berlin. Ironically, the Germans managed to increase the production of fighters despite the bombing, but the savage air battles took a horrific toll of the Luftwaffe's qualified pilots. By the end of February, the Germans had lost 18 percent of the fighter pilots available at the beginning of the month killed, wounded, or missing; that number rose to 22 percent in March, 20 percent in April, and 25 percent in May. No combat force in the world could sustain such losses and retain its combat effectiveness; about all the Luftwaffe high command could offer was the statement that "our pilots must attempt to counterbalance the obvious disadvantage [in skill level] by greater enthusiasm and courage."

Moreover, the movement of Luftwaffe fighters from the Reich had little prospect of affecting the invasion. By 6 June the Luftwaffe had already lost control of its base structure in France. Allied air forces had blasted Luftwaffe bases across the breadth of France through incessant air attacks. With Ultra, the program decrypting coded German radio messages, Allied air commanders had gained a thorough knowledge of all major bases in France. They could judge the success of Allied air attacks and monitor the progress that the Germans were making in repairing those airfields. Moreover, Ultra indicated German plans to move fighter squadrons forward from the Reich and the proposed locations for these forces in France. As if that were not enough, none of the fighter pilots arriving from Germany had trained to attack ground forces; the ground attack squadrons were on the Eastern front awaiting the Soviet summer offensive.

In the first two days of the invasion, 200 fighters were moved from the Reich to airfields in France; 100 more followed by 10 June—hardly enough to tip the balance. The movement to forward operating locations in France collapsed in confusion. Its failure suggests how much Allied air attacks had wrecked the Luftwaffe's organization. A German after-action report indicated: "The airfields that had long been earmarked for the emergency day fighter squadrons from the Reich in the event of an invasion . . . were completely inadequate. In almost every case no headquarters buildings had been constructed, and dispersal points had not been organized."

The movement of these inexperienced fighter pilots only served to swell impossibly heavy pilot losses. In the invasion's first two weeks, the Germans lost 594 aircraft. *Third Air Force* had 815 aircraft on 5 June, of which only 600 were battle-ready. Even when reinforced with aircraft from the Reich, its fighters were hardly able to put in an appearance over the invasion beaches. Moreover, by moving so many fighters to Normandy, the Luftwaffe further reduced its potential to defend the synthetic fuel plants in Germany that were under increasing attack by the Eighth Air Force's heavy bombers.

Within the first week of the invasion the Luftwaffe abandoned attempts to use its fighters as fighter-bombers and ordered its squadrons to convert back to air-to-air tactics. The hope was that, as fighters, Bf 109s and FW 190s might take some pressure off frontline troops under increasing attack by Allied tactical and strategic air power. The change did little good, except to allow the Germans to slip small flights of aircraft into Allied territory on strafing runs. An Ultra report from 14 June, based on decrypts of messages from Field Marshal Gerd von Rundstedt's headquarters, underlined the general and complete inadequacy of the Luftwaffe's strategic response to the invasion:

C in C West report morning ninth included: In large-scale operations by thousands of bombers and fighter bombers, Allied air forces stifled German tank attacks and had harassing effect on all movement. High losses in wireless equipment by fighter bomber attacks (I SS Corps had, for example, only four wireless trucks, and Panzer Group West had lost 75 percent of its wireless equipment) were noticeable in making reporting difficult.

[*See also* Air Force, *article on* German Air Force; Third Air Force.]

BIBLIOGRAPHY

Murray, Williamson. *Luftwaffe*. 1985.
Overy, Richard J. *The Air War, 1939–1945.* 1980.
Terraine, John. *The Right of the Line: The Royal Air Force in the European War, 1939–1945.* 1985.
United Kingdom. Air Ministry. *The Rise and Fall of the German Air Force, 1933–1945.* 1983.

WILLIAMSON MURRAY

AIR SUPERIORITY. Allied command of the air over Normandy and, indeed, all of Europe was won well before D-day. But it took two years to achieve in the face of conflicting target concepts, huge logistic problems, and diversions to other theaters.

In April 1942, Gen. George C. Marshall, chief of the U.S. general staff, came to England and spent a day with Brig. Gen. Ira C. Eaker, commander of the embryonic VIII Bomber Command, the spearhead of the Eighth Air Force, destined to become the mightiest air force ever assembled. With no planes and only twenty-two officers, Eaker was sharing headquarters space with his British opposite number, Air Chief Marshal Arthur T. Harris, head of the Royal Air Force Bomber Command.

General Marshall told Eaker that he did not believe the

Allies would ever successfully invade the Continent unless they first defeated the Luftwaffe, and Eaker concurred. But it was not until July that he received his first heavy bombers (forty B-17s) and not until August that he could dispatch a daylight precision attack—by twelve B-17 "Flying Fortresses" escorted by RAF fighters—on a French railroad yard.

Since the RAF had tried daylight precision attacks two years before and been slaughtered, causing them to switch to night bombing of cities, Harris expected the Americans to meet daylight disaster, too. But Eaker's planes returned unscathed, as they did for nine more small attacks in France before the first loss. Meanwhile, Harris was sending as many as a thousand bombers deep into Germany almost every night. The American effort seemed to Harris puny by comparison, and he urged Eaker to switch to night bombing. Eaker refused.

But just as he began getting enough bombers for missions of a hundred or more, the Allies decided to invade North Africa in November. To support that invasion, a new air force, the Twelfth, headed by Maj. Gen. James Doolittle, was created out of units allotted to the Eighth.

With the Eighth seemingly stalled, Harris persuaded Winston Churchill to ask Franklin D. Roosevelt at the Casablanca Conference in January 1943 to order the Eighth into night operations. Eaker, who knew the prime minister well, was summoned to make the rebuttal. In his half-hour talk he stressed round-the-clock bombing. As Churchill wrote in *The Second World War*: "I decided to back Eaker and his theme and I turned around completely and withdrew all my opposition to daylight bombing by the Fortresses." Thus began the Combined Bomber Offensive, code-named POINTBLANK.

Upon his return from Casablanca and now in command of the entire Eighth Air Force, Eaker left Bomber Command largely in the hands of Maj. Gen. Frederick L. Anderson while bomber strength mounted to a peak dispatch of 710 heavies on 30 December 1943. Many missions were bull's-eyes, including two on ball-bearing plants at Schweinfurt, though at heavy cost—sixty bombers down on each, or 20 percent. The overall loss rate for the year, however, was 5.2 percent.

The VIII Fighter Command was Eaker's most critical problem. Each B-17 or B-24 had six to fourteen 50-caliber machine guns, reinforcing each other in tight formation. Air force plans called also for fighter escort, but the two fighters available, the P-47 and P-38, could fly only part way into Germany. Not until early 1944 did the marvelous P-51, capable of round trips all the way into Germany, reach England in quantity.

In 1944, General Dwight D. Eisenhower brought many of his North African commanders to England, including Doolittle, who succeeded Eaker in command of the Eighth and directed pilots of the new P-51 fighter to aban-

don close protective escort of bombers and attack approaching German fighters.

Simultaneously, Eaker was appointed commander in chief of the Allied air forces in the Mediterranean, comprising two U.S. units (the Fifteenth, strategic, and the Twelfth, tactical) and two British air forces (Desert and Balkan). The Fifteenth was commanded by Maj. Gen. Nathan Twining. Coordinating the strategic missions of the Fifteenth and Eighth was assigned to Lt. Gen. Carl Spaatz on Eisenhower's staff.

As D-day neared, Eisenhower's basic air force plan was to cut German communication lines to Normandy. But Spaatz, Eaker, and Doolittle believed the key objective remained the elimination of the Luftwaffe. Leaving the attacks on transportation primarily to medium (B-26 and A-20) and fighter bombers (P-47, P-38, and P-51), the American generals concentrated their heavy bombers, primarily the B-17, in two offensives: (1) the renowned "Big Week" of 20–25 February 1944, when good weather permitted devastating blows by the Eighth from England and the Fifteenth from Italy on fighter factories in southern Germany; and (2) a subsequent blitz of synthetic oil refineries, also in southern Germany. Meanwhile the Fifteenth devastated the city of Ploesti in Romania, Germany's biggest source of natural oil, plus synthetic plants too far for the Eighth to reach. Oil proved to be Hitler's Achilles' heel. Without fuel, planes cannot fly and tanks and trucks cannot move.

In the first twenty-four hours over Normandy, the Allies mounted 14,674 sorties, the Luftwaffe only 319. It was unable to counter the expanding beachhead and the conquest of Germany. The only air weapons left to Hitler were the V-1 and V-2 rockets, which killed many civilians but had no impact on the war's outcome. Churchill wrote in his history of World War II: "For our air superiority . . . full tribute must be paid to the United States Eighth Air Force."

[*See also* Bomber Command; Eighth Air Force; Fifteenth Air Force; Interdiction Operations; POINTBLANK; *and biographies of numerous figures mentioned herein.*]

BIBLIOGRAPHY

Arnold, Henry H. *Global Mission*. 1949.
Craven, Wesley, and James Lea Cate. *The Army Air Forces in World War II*. Vols. 2 and 3. 1949, 1951.
Murray, Williamson. *Strategy for Defeat: The Luftwaffe, 1933–1945*. 1983.
Parton, James. *"Air Force Spoken Here": General Ira Eaker and the Command of the Air*. 1946.

JAMES PARTON

AJAX, HMS. A Leander-class light cruiser with a weight of 7,400 tons, armament of eight 6-inch and eight

HMS *Ajax*.   IMPERIAL WAR MUSEUM

4-inch guns, and speed of 32 knots, *Ajax* was built by Vickers at Barrow and completed in 1935. The flagship of Commodore Harwood at the Battle of the Plate River on 13 December 1939, *Ajax* was badly damaged by *Admiral Graf von Spee*'s 11-inch shells. Thereafter it served in the Mediterranean, including the Battle of Matapan on 26 March 1941, and sustained bomb damage off Crete later that year and in Bône harbor, Tunisia, on 1 January 1943. After a major refit and radar upgrade at New York from March to October 1943, *Ajax* returned to the Mediterranean, but was recalled in May 1944.

As part of Capt. E. W. L. Longley-Cook's Fire Support Force K in Task Force G, *Ajax* supported the assault of the 50th (Northumbrian) Division on Gold Beach. In 1944 its crew of 570 was commanded by Capt. J. J. Weld. On D-day *Ajax* and *Argonaut* engaged and disabled the four-gun 155-mm battery at Longues that threatened both Gold and Omaha beaches. Opening fire at 0530, after Longues fired on *Bulolo*, *Ajax* first neutralized and by 0845 had knocked out the battery with three direct hits on the guns through their embrasures. This was achieved with a total of 114 rounds at a range of 12,000 yards, a remarkable piece of naval gunnery. Return fire from the German batteries in this sector was negligible.

Ajax was transferred to Force S (Sword Beach) on 13 June; Rear Adm. W. R. Patterson and his staff shifted to *Ajax* on the following day. Released from Operation NEPTUNE on 27 June, *Ajax* returned to the Mediterranean as a unit of Task Force 84. It opened the naval bombardment to cover the landings in the south of France during Operation DRAGOON on 15 August. In September it took part in the occupation of Greece, and on 21 December 1944 bombarded Greek Communist positions close to Piraeus. It was broken up in 1949.

[*See also* Longley-Cook, E. W. L.; Task Force G.]

BIBLIOGRAPHY

London. Public Record Office. "Overlord Plans and Preparations." Cabinet Office Papers, CAB 44/242.
Raven, Alan, and John Roberts. *British Cruisers of World War Two*. 1980.

ANDREW LAMBERT

ALANBROOKE. *See* Brooke, Alan.

ALLIED AIR BASES. Until 10 June 1944 (D plus 4), tactical support and air cover to the Allied armies in Normandy was provided exclusively from airfields in England. Although some ground control units had gone ashore on D-day itself—in the British sector, for example, No. 15083 Ground Control Interception Unit, drawn from No. 85 Group Royal Air Force (RAF), had landed near Meuvaines at noon on 6 June—it was to take time for air bases in the lodgment area to be either created or captured. Even then, such bases would be available for fighters or fighter-bombers only; the medium and heavy bombers needed for more sustained fire support would have to remain across the Channel.

The heavy bombers were concentrated principally in the east of England. RAF Bomber Command had groups in Yorkshire, Lincolnshire, and East Anglia, while the Eighth U.S. Army Air Force (USAAF) was stationed slightly farther south, around Bedford, Cambridge, Norwich, and Ipswich. The fighters, fighter-bombers, and medium bombers of the British Second Tactical Air Force and Ninth USAAF occupied bases on the south coast, as close to the invasion area as possible. One of the planning considerations for D-day was the fact that such aircraft had to be within range of the beachhead, with sufficient fuel reserves to carry out close-support missions or interceptions.

But these arrangements could only be temporary, for the provision of air bases in Normandy would clearly shorten reaction times and increase air flexibility. As early as 20 March 1944, Air Chief Marshal Trafford Leigh-Mallory, commander of the Allied Expeditionary Air Forces, had pressed for the early capture of airfield sites. Although General Bernard L. Montgomery had refused to commit himself to priority attacks into the Caen-Falaise area, where the ground was most suitable, arrangements were made for the construction of temporary air bases as soon as the ground troops went ashore. The RAF, for example, formed special construction wings, aided by the army's Royal Engineers, and U.S. construction squads satisfied the same need in their invasion sectors.

Some success was achieved. Bearing in mind the adverse weather conditions and the fact that fighting was going on around them as they worked, the construction teams did remarkably well. As early as 10 June the first British airfield, built by Nos. 3207 and 3209 construction wings of the RAF at Sainte-Croix-sur-Mer, was ready for use. Such facilities were initially available simply for refueling, but as the Allies consolidated their hold on the beachhead, they were transformed into semipermanent bases for entire squadrons of support aircraft. No. 144 Wing of the Royal Canadian Air Force, for example, had three Spitfire squadrons operating in Normandy by D plus 9. Some fighter-bombers were called upon to mount attacks on locations less than 1,000 meters (1,093 yards) from their new bases, which entailed flying out over the Channel to gain altitude before returning to engage the targets. By the end of June thirty-one Allied squadrons were based in Normandy.

BIBLIOGRAPHY

Freeman, Roger A. *Mighty Eighth War Manual*. 1984.
Saunders, Hilary St. G. *The Fight Is Won*. Vol. 3 of *The Royal Air Force, 1939–1945*. 1954.

J. L. PIMLOTT

ALLIED EXPEDITIONARY AIR FORCE. *See* Air Force, *article on* Allied Expeditionary Air Force.

AMERICAN BEACHES. [*The following entry includes three articles:*
An Overview
Omaha Beach
Utah Beach.
For discussion of Gold, Juno, and Sword beaches, see British Beaches.]

U.S. COAST GUARD LANDING BOAT.   NATIONAL ARCHIVES

An Overview

The U.S. First Army (under Lt. Gen. Omar Bradley) landed the U.S. V Corps (under Maj. Gen. Leonard T. Gerow) and the U.S. VII Corps (under Maj. Gen. J. Lawton Collins) on Omaha and Utah beaches respectively. While the British Second Army took and held the area south and east of Caen, the U.S. First Army was to cut off the Cotentin Peninsula and capture Cherbourg by D plus 15, so that the port could be used as a major supply channel. They were also to attack south and capture the Cerisy Forest by D plus 5 or 6 and Saint-Lô and Caumont by D plus 9.

V Corps landed at Omaha Beach. Widely separated from Utah Beach, Omaha was 7,000 yards (6,300 meters) long and was divided into five sectors, from west to east: Charlie, Dog, Easy, Fox, and George. It ran from Pointe de la Percée in the east to Saint-Honorine in the west and it had terrain that was made for defense.

Historian Samuel Eliot Morison said that Omaha "was defended by every device and weapon that a resourceful enemy could think up, and that withering defense called forth the highest qualities of courage and decision on the part of the attacking force." The beaches of the farm villages of Saint-Laurent, Colleville, and Vierville-sur-Mer are now known as Omaha on most maps "as homage to the American soldiers of the 1st Division who fell in the most costly battle of D-Day," according to the Michelin Guide.

Utah Beach was the westernmost point of the Normandy invasion. It included the Uncle and Victor sectors from the dam and lock just north of Carentan to Quinnéville in the west and formed a part of the east Cotentin Peninsula. The dominant terrain feature was the Douve River and its principal tributary, the Merderet.

The landing of VII Corps at Utah Beach was made comparatively easier by the earlier landings of the 82d (under Maj. Gen. Matthew B. Ridgway) and 101st (under Maj. Gen. Maxwell D. Taylor) airborne divisions, which had dropped several miles inland of the beach beginning at about H minus 5. Although they were scattered over a broad area, they did manage to seize crossings and bridges. They also secured important beach exits and the 82d Airborne Division captured Sainte-Mère-Église.

But, as historian Max Hastings has noted, the greatest achievement of the American airborne forces "was to bring confusion and uncertainty to the Germans across the whole breadth of the Cherbourg [Cotentin] peninsula."

SOLDIERS HELPING GI TO SHORE.   American soldiers help a GI whose landing craft was sunk off Utah Beach. Around their waists are inflatable life preservers.
COURTESY OF BARRY W. FOWLE

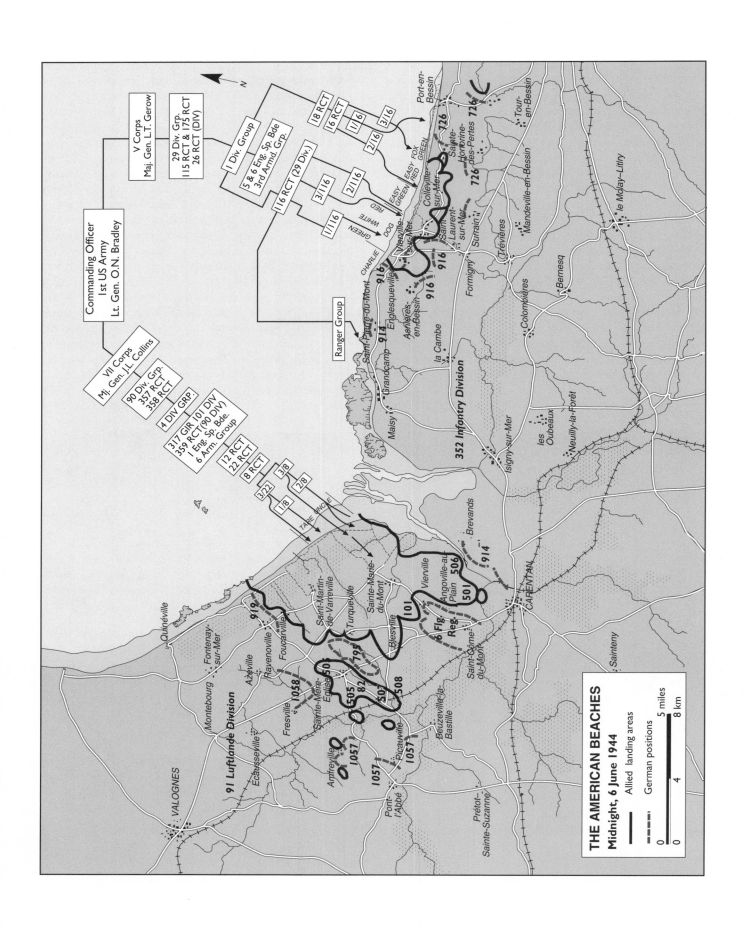

THE AMERICAN BEACHES
Midnight, 6 June 1944

Allied landing areas
German positions

0   4   5 miles
0   8 km

Commanding Officer
1st US Army
Lt. Gen. O.N. Bradley

V Corps
Maj. Gen. L.T. Gerow

29 Div. Grp.
115 RCT & 175 RCT
26 RCT (DIV)

1 Div Group

5 & 6 Eng. Sp. Bde.
3rd Armd. Grp.

116 RCT (29 Div.)

18 RCT
16 RCT
1/16
3/16
2/16
2/116
3/116
1/116

Ranger Group

VII Corps
Mj. Gen. J.L. Collins

90 Div. Grp.
357 RCT
358 RCT

4 DIV GRP.

317 GIR 101 DIV
359 RCT (90 DIV)
1 Eng. Sp. Bde.
6 Arm. Group

12 RCT
22 RCT
8 RCT
3/8
2/8
3/22
1/8

EASY GREEN
EASY FOX GREEN
EASY RED
RED
WHITE
GREEN
DOG
CHARLIE

TARE UNCLE

VALOGNES
Quinéville
Montebourg
Fontenay-sur-Mer
Azeville
Ecausseville
Ravenoville
Amfreville
Pont-l'Abbé
Prétot-Sainte-Suzanne
Picauville
Fresville
Sainte-Mère-Eglise
Foucarville
Saint-Martin-de-Varreville
Turqueville
Beuzeville-la-Bastille
Sainte-Marie-du-Mont
Blosville
Saint-Côme-du-Mont
Vierville
Angoville-au-Plain
Brevands
CARENTAN
Sainteny
le Molay-Litry

91 Luftlande Division
1057
1057
1057
1058
505
82
505
508
507
919
919
6 Flg. Reg.
101
501
506
914

Saint-Pierre-du-Mont
Grandcamp
Maisy
Isigny-sur-Mer
la Cambe
Asnières-en-Bessin
Englesqueville
Vierville
Colleville-sur-Mer
Saint-Laurent-sur-Mer
Surrain
Formigny
Trévières
Colombières
Bernesq
les Oubeaux
Neuilly-la-Forêt
Port-en-Bessin
Sainte-Honorine-des-Pertes
Tour-en-Bessin
Mandeville-en-Bessin
914
916
916
916
916
726
726
726

352 Infantry Division

N

Naval control during the landings was exercised by the Western Task Force under Rear Adm. Alan G. Kirk in USS *Augusta*. Two Assault Forces, O (TF 124) for Omaha Beach and U (TF 125) for Utah Beach, were commanded by Rear Adm. John L. Hall in USS *Ancon* and Rear Adm. Don P. Moon in USS *Bayfield,* respectively.

Assault Force O had all the troops loaded by 3 June and the main convoy cleared Portland Harbor on the afternoon of 5 June. *Ancon,* headquarters ship for Admiral Hall and General Gerow, anchored at 0251 on D-day, 23,000 yards (20,700 meters) off the beach. It included the 1st Division (under Maj. Gen. Clarence R. Huebner) and the 29th Division (under Maj. Gen. Charles H. Gerhardt) and the Rangers. It numbered almost 35,000 men and over 3,000 vehicles. More than 1,000 men were killed by nightfall.

Three companies of the 2d Ranger Battalion attacked German gun emplacements at Pointe du Hoc in an isolated action three miles to the west of the Omaha Beaches, between Vierville-sur-Mer and Grandcamp-les-Bains. Two hundred and twenty-five Rangers scaled a sheer cliff 85 to 100 feet high covered by fire from the American destroyer *Satterlee*. Their mission was to destroy the German battery of six 105-mm howitzers, which could have wreaked havoc on both Omaha and Utah beaches. Accomplishing this, they moved inland to secure the road between Vierville and Grandcamp. In two days, they suffered casualties of almost 60 percent. Two other Ranger units also suffered heavy casualties in the Pointe du Hoc area.

USS *Bayfield,* flagship of Assault Force U, dropped anchor eleven and one half miles off the Cotentin Peninsula four hours before H-hour. The 4th Infantry Division (under Maj. Gen. Raymond O. Barton) had some difficulty with the rough sea, but over 23,000 men were landed on D-day with less than 200 dead.

BIBLIOGRAPHY

Harrison, Gordon A. *Cross-Channel Attack.* U.S. Army in World War II: The European Theater of Operations. 1951.

Hastings, Max. *OVERLORD: D-Day, June 6, 1944.* 1984.

Morison, Samuel E. *The Invasion of France and Germany, 1944-1945.* Vol. 11 of *History of the United States Naval Operations in World War II.* 1957.

U.S. Army, Center of Military History. *Omaha Beachhead: 6 June–13 June 1944.* 1945. Facsimile reprint, 1989.

U.S. Army, Center of Military History. *Utah Beach to Cherbourg: 6–27 June 1944.* 1948. Reprint, 1990.

CHARLES E. SMITH

Omaha Beach

If the Germans were going to stop the Allied invasion of the Continent anywhere, it would be at Omaha Beach. It was an obvious landing site, the only sand beach between the mouth of the Douve River to the west and the village of Arromanches-les-Bains to the east, a distance of almost forty kilometers. On both ends of Omaha the cliffs were more or less perpendicular. The beach itself was slightly crescent-shaped, about ten kilometers (six miles) long overall. At low tide there was a stretch of firm sand of two hundred to three hundred meters in distance. At high tide, the beach was but a few meters wide. In 1944 there was a two- or three-meter-high stretch of shingle (smooth, round rocks, impassable to vehicles; gone today) and then a part-wood, part-stone masonry seawall of from one to four meters in height.

Inland of the seawall was a paved, promenade beach road, then a V-shaped antitank ditch as much as two meters deep, then a flat swampy area, and then a steep bluff that ascended to fifty meters or more. A man could climb the bluff, but not a vehicle. There were four small "draws"—ravines that sloped gently to the tableland above the beach. A paved road led off the coast to Vierville; at Moulins a dirt road led up to Saint-Laurent-sur-Mer; the third draw had only a path leading up to the plateau; the fourth draw had a dirt road leading to Colleville.

No tactician could have devised a better defensive situation: a narrow, enclosed battlefield, with no possibility of outflanking it; many natural obstacles for the attacker to overcome; an ideal place to build fixed fortifications and a trench system on the slope of the bluff and on the high ground looking down on a wide-open killing field for infantry trying to cross the beach. The Allied planners hated the idea of assaulting Omaha, but it had to be done; without Omaha the gap between Utah and the British beaches would be too great.

That was as obvious to Field Marshal Rommel as to General Eisenhower. Rommel prepared an extensive defense, installing mines offshore; beach obstacles (more than at any of the other beaches); fortified positions on the beach, up the slope, and on the top that held 88-mm, 75-mm, and 20-mm cannons; pillboxes for machine guns; and an extensive trench system. Every inch of the beach was covered by presited flanking cross fire.

The German defenders consisted of three battalions of the *352d Infantry Division* under the command of Maj. Gen. Dietrich Kraiss. It was an ordinary infantry division, without transport or mobility, and with a high percentage of conscripted troops from Poland, Russia and elsewhere. The words of one private in the *352d* summed up the experience of most members of the division: "It was the first time I shoot at living men. I don't remember exactly how it was: the only thing I know is that I went to my machine gun and I shoot, I shoot, I shoot."

The Allied plan to assault this all-but-impregnable position relied heavily on a presunrise air bombardment by B-17s, followed by a naval bombardment from Allied warships. Then the assault waves would come in, led by the

TROOPS LANDING FROM *LCI 412*.   NATIONAL ARCHIVES

116th Regiment on the right (part of the 29th Infantry Division, Maj. Gen. Charles H. Gerhardt commanding) and the 16th Regiment on the left (part of the 1st Infantry Division, Maj. Gen. Clarence R. Huebner commanding). The first waves would include some sixteen specialized units, ranging from DD (Duplex Drive) amphibious tanks to demolition teams to engineers to communications sections. Their job was to open the draws and get up to the plateau so that follow-up waves could drive off the beach. Some forty thousand men with thirty-five hundred motorized vehicles were scheduled to land at Omaha on D-day. Briefers told the infantry that the air and naval bombardments would so disrupt and destroy the German defenders that their problems would not begin until they got to the top and started to move inland toward their D-day objectives.

In the event, nothing in the plan worked. The B-17s, fearful of hitting their own men, dropped their bombs three kilometers or more inland. The naval bombardment was too brief to provide significant help. The first waves were all but wiped out by machine-gun fire before the men got across the beach. Company A of the 116th lost 96

percent of its effective strength before it fired even one shot. Other companies fared almost as badly. Pvt. Harry Parley of the 16th recalled, "As our boat touched sand and the ramp went down, I became a visitor to hell."

The assault began at 0630. By 0730 the 16th and 116th were supposed to have the draws open and be at the top of the bluff; in fact, at 0730 the pathetic remnants of the regiments were huddled behind the seawall, leaderless, shell-shocked, generally without weapons.

It got worse. The follow-up waves were cut down. Tanks, trucks, half-tracks, bulldozers, jeeps, and other vehicles piled up on the shrinking beach (the tide rose eight feet between 0630 and 0830), causing a massive traffic jam and providing German artillery with stationary targets. None of the draws had been attacked, much less opened. At 0830 the navy beachmaster suspended the landing of reinforcements; there simply was no place to put them. A German officer at Vierville reported by telephone to Kraiss that the invasion at Omaha had been stopped. He anticipated an attempt to withdraw. That would not have been possible, but Gen. Omar Bradley did contemplate sending the follow-up waves to Utah or the British beaches.

Two things happened to make Omaha a success nevertheless. First, the destroyers came in close, some of them touching sand, to deliver intense and brutally effective point-black fire at the German fortified positions. Second, the individual initiative of the men at the seawall, ranging from general officers (especially Brig. Gen. Norman Cota of the 29th Division) to junior and noncommissioned officers, got the troops organized and started up the bluff. They did so by setting a personal example and by pointing out the obvious, that to stay at the seawall was certain death and retreat was impossible. The 5th Ranger Battalion, landing at 0800, provided much-needed support on the right flank. Cota gave the Rangers their motto when he told them, "Rangers lead the way!"

The men, organized into ad hoc groups that mixed companies and regiments, moved up the bluff—between the draws, not up them. In innumerable firefights, they cleared out the trenches and then attacked the fortified artillery emplacements from the rear. By afternoon, incoming fire was long-range artillery only. The draws were not yet open and functioning (precious few vehicles made it to the plateau on D-day), but the Americans had taken Colleville, Vierville, and Saint-Laurent-sur-Mer. That was far short of the D-day objective—the 29th and 1st Divisions were but a couple of kilometers inland, instead of the ten kilometers called for in the plan. Still, the Americans had prevailed in what was by far the best defended of the D-day beaches. It was one of the great feats of arms in the history of the U.S. Army.

Over the next two days the attackers expanded the beachhead. The 1st Division linked up with the British at Port-en-Bessin and moved across the N-13, the main highway running from Caen through Bayeux to Carentan and on to Cherbourg. The 29th linked up with the 2d Ranger Battalion at Pointe du Hoc and moved into Isigny. From 9 to 11 June the two divisions pushed farther south, fighting from hedgerow to hedgerow—slow going—while reinforcements piled into Omaha. By 13 June the lodgment was secure from the far right to the far left, as the 29th and the 2d Infantry and 2d Armored divisions made contact with the 101st Airborne at Carentan (as was supposed to have happened on 6 June).

The Americans paid a fearful price for Omaha, more than half the casualties coming on D-day and most of those in the first two hours. In the 29th Division, 2,440 men became casualties at Omaha; the 1st Division had 1,744. The divisions took 2,500 German prisoners and virtually eliminated the *352d Division*. Omaha was one of the hardest amphibious assault landings in military history, but it was a success. Without Omaha, the Allies would have had a huge gap between the Americans at Utah and the British at Gold, a gap which the Germans might have been able to

OMAHA BEACH.   Rifles crossed in tribute, afternoon of 6 June 1944.   NATIONAL ARCHIVES

exploit to the point of defeating the invasion as a whole.

[*See also* Task Force 124 *and articles on units mentioned herein.*]

BIBLIOGRAPHY

Balkoski, Joseph. *Beyond the Beachhead: The 29th Infantry Division in Normandy*. 1989.

Black, Robert W. *Rangers in World War II*. 1992.

Harrison, Gordon A. *Cross-Channel Attack*. U.S. Army in World War II: The European Theater of Operations. 1951.

U.S. Army, Center of Military History. *Omaha Beachhead: 6 June–13 June 1944*. 1945. Facsimile reprint, 1989.

STEPHEN E. AMBROSE

Utah Beach

Utah Beach, on the east side of the Cotentin Peninsula of France, was the westernmost of five Allied D-day assault areas in Normandy. This beach was not in the original invasion plans, but in early 1944, the Allies increased the sea-assault forces from three to five divisions, and Utah Beach was added. With this, OVERLORD, the Allied plan for securing lodgment in France, was just about complete.

The Peninsula. The lower half of the Cotentin Peninsula is dominated by two rivers—the Merderet, running roughly north to south, and the Douve, running west to east. They join above the city of Carentan, located at the southeast corner of the peninsula. Swamps, dams, and generally low terrain made the area behind Utah Beach susceptible to flooding. The hedgerows, or bocage, were another significant feature of the terrain. Small irregular fields, separated by mounds of earth surmounted by trees and heavy brush, would complicate military operations in the area. The beach itself was the least intimidating terrain feature. This broad expanse of shoreline was backed not by dominating terrain as in the case of Omaha Beach but by a man-made seawall ranging in height from four to twelve feet. The beach gradient was fairly flat, and the distance between low and high tides was from nineteen to twenty-five feet. In addition to this wall, many more man-made obstacles abounded in the beach area.

German defenses on the Channel west of France were influenced largely by Field Marshal Erwin Rommel, who arrived in the area late in 1943. Rommel knew from his experience in North Africa that massed armored formations, as well as mobile operations, would suffer in the absence of air superiority. This certainly would be the case in any cross-Channel attack. Consequently, he favored using natural terrain close to potential assault areas, augmented by a variety of mines and other man-made obstacles. Troops were to be located near the coast.

Coastal areas from surf to the back of the beaches were dotted with hedgehogs, tetrahedra, and Belgian gates, all formidable obstacles constructed of iron and steel. And then there were a multitude of stakes—some of them mined—in the water, on the beach, and in fields usable as landing areas for gliders.

Plans and Preparations. The cross-Channel attack was an undertaking of unprecedented size and difficulty. Special training preceded the operation including dress rehearsals at Slapton Sands on England's Channel coast. Exercise TIGER (27–28 April 1944) provided joint training for the land and sea forces slated for Utah Beach. It was a memorable exercise. Not only was there a normal amount

of problems of coordination, but one of the assaulting convoys, simulating the landings that were to take place on Utah Beach, was attacked by nine German E-boats; American losses were estimated at over 700 dead.

The VII Corps, commanded by Maj. Gen. J. Lawton Collins, received the Utah Beach mission. Briefly put, the VII Corps had three tasks: make a successful landing on D-day; link up with the V Corps, which would land at Omaha Beach at the southeast corner of the Cotentin; and take the port of Cherbourg on the northern tip of the peninsula as quickly as possible. Cherbourg would be instrumental in providing logistical support.

The 4th Infantry Division, commanded by Maj. Gen. Raymond O. Barton, was to make the D-day assault, supported by one battalion of the 90th Infantry Division. The remainder of the 90th would land on D plus 1. Appropriate supporting troops also would land on D-day, including the familiar artillery and engineer units, as well as a not-so-familiar chemical mortar battalion, which, in the absence of gas warfare, would support the infantry with high explosives and smoke. The 9th and 79th infantry divisions would land later. Preceding all this, the 82d and 101st airborne divisions would land behind the beach area in the early darkness of D-day. Their roles would be pivotal.

Task Force U (for Utah, TF 125), commanded by Rear Adm. Don P. Moon, would transport the assault forces to Utah Beach. The task force elements were to provide protection en route and fire support against the German land defenses. They would also breach the enemy's underwa-

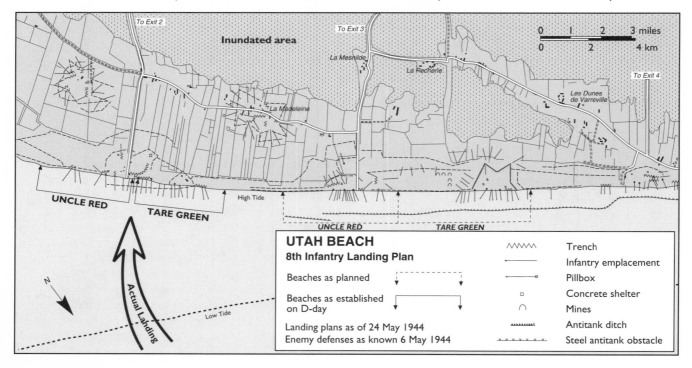

UNCLE RED

TARE GREEN

High Tide

UNCLE RED   TARE GREEN

Actual Landing

Low Tide

UTAH BEACH
8th Infantry Landing Plan

Beaches as planned

Beaches as established
on D-day

Landing plans as of 24 May 1944
Enemy defenses as known 6 May 1944

⋀⋀⋀⋀	Trench
—	Infantry emplacement
—□	Pillbox
□	Concrete shelter
∩	Mines
⋯⋯⋯	Antitank ditch
××××××	Steel antitank obstacle

To Exit 2

To Exit 3

Inundated area

La Meshilde

La Recherie

To Exit 4

Les Dunes
de Varreville

La Madeleine

0   1   2   3 miles
0   2   4 km

VIEW OF UTAH BEACH FROM COLLEVILLE, FRANCE, 9 JUNE 1944.

HULTON DEUTSCH

ter obstacles at the beach. Moon, Collins, and their staffs worked together with harmony and skill.

The Ninth Air Force provided the third element of the assault equation, taking part in the massive preinvasion bombardment of rail centers and military targets and providing tactical support during and after the invasion.

Col. Gen. Friedrich Dollman's German *Seventh Army* controlled the Cotentin Peninsula. Two mediocre infantry divisions, containing some non-German nationals, were the heart of his force. Shortly before the invasion, Allied planners became aware of a third division in the area generally behind Utah Beach, a situation that caused a change in the 82d Airborne Division mission. Despite indications from interception of a message for the French Resistance of a possible invasion, Dollman was not overly concerned about a cross-Channel attack. Rommel was home in Germany.

D-Day. D-day was to have been 5 June 1944, but nasty weather forced postponement. This resulted in perhaps the bravest decision ever made by General Dwight D. Eisenhower, the Supreme Allied Commander. The invasion would begin on the next day—6 June—despite a weather forecast that was far from comforting.

Actually, the invasion began during the final hours of 5 June when some 13,000 men from the 82d and 101st Airborne Divisions set out in 822 transport planes from nine English airfields. Reinforcements were to come in by glider at dawn and dusk of D-day. Although its drop was widely scattered, the 101st, under Maj. Gen. Maxwell D. Taylor, quickly secured the far edge of an inundated area to the west of Utah. At the end of the day, the division had carried out the most important D-day objective, even though only 2,500 of the 6,600 men who had made the initial drop had been assembled.

The 82d Airborne Division, commanded by Maj. Gen. Matthew B. Ridgway, was less successful, although it did capture the town of Sainte-Mère-Église, one of its initial missions. As D-day ended, the division had failed to make contact with either the 101st or the 4th Infantry Division, which had assaulted the beach at 0630 that morning.

Forty minutes before the 4th Infantry Division troops hit the beach, warships shelled the enemy positions and Ninth Air Force planes dropped bombs on German defenses. Assault craft mixed in with the landing craft sprayed the beach with rockets. Duplex Drive (DD) amphibious tanks left their ships and headed toward the shore. Engineer and naval demolition experts cleared mines and obstacles. Enemy opposition was incredibly light. And even though the first two battalions came ashore 2,000 yards south of their objective, the new area was better because of less destruction and fewer shore defenses. Brig. Gen. Theodore Roosevelt, Jr., who came ashore with an infantry company, took charge on the beach and found a causeway that would lead troops off it.

Except for the 82d Airborne Division, all VII Corps elements were in pretty good shape as D-day ended. Casualties for the 4th Infantry Division were amazingly low—197, of whom 60 were missing at sea. The two airborne divisions were hit much harder. The 101st casualties totaled 1,240, of whom 182 were fatalities. The 82d suffered 1,259 casualties, including 156 deaths.

By D plus 1, 32,000 men, 3,200 vehicles, and 2,500 tons of supplies had come over Utah Beach. It must be noted, however, that planners had estimated that these numbers would be 39,722 men, 4,732 vehicles, and 7,000 tons of supplies. Supplies were of particular concern. Until natural ports were taken, Allies on the French coast had to rely on artificial facilities. These included protective lines of sunken ships called Gooseberries, and a process of beaching supply ships and then unloading them at low tide called "drying out." Obviously, natural ports were a matter of great urgency.

Wrap-up. Having secured its beachhead, the VII Corps prepared to fulfill its further missions—the capture of Carentan and, of even greater importance, the capture of the port of Cherbourg on the northern tip of the Cotentin Peninsula. Carentan was taken on 14 June, thus completing the link-up with V Corps. Taking Cherbourg proved to be more difficult.

The 4th, 9th, 79th, and 90th infantry divisions and the 82d Airborne Division all participated in the drive for Cherbourg. By 9 June Gen. Omar Bradley was concerned about the lack of progress in the effort and ordered General Collins to seal off the peninsula. This was done on 14 June, thereby ensuring that German troops could neither reinforce nor escape from the Cherbourg pocket. Its fate thus determined, the stubborn German force at Cherbourg surrendered to the American VII Corps on 27 June. With Cherbourg taken, the first phase—the one that had begun on Utah Beach—of the VII Corps operations on the continent of Europe was over.

[*See also* Task Force 125 *and articles on units mentioned herein.*]

BIBLIOGRAPHY

Collins, J. Lawton. *Lightning Joe: An Autobiography.* 1974.

Harrison, Gordon A. *Cross-Channel Attack.* U.S. Army in World War II: The European Theater of Operations. 1951.

U.S. Army, Center of Military History. *Utah Beach to Cherbourg: 6–27 June 1944.* 1948. Reprint, 1990.

BROOKS E. KLEBER

AMPHIBIOUS ASSAULT TRAINING. An amphibious operation of the size and complexity of NEPTUNE/OVERLORD required an enormous amount of training at all levels. The main center for amphibious training in Britain up to 1943 was the Combined Operations Training Centre, HMS *Quebec*, at Inveraray on Loch Fyne on the west coast of Scotland. Opened for commando training on 15 October 1940 under the command of Vice Adm. Theodore Hallett, it provided facilities for training in embarkation and disembarkation and landing under fire. Exercises were carried out beginning with platoons and ending with a brigade landing using a two-mile-long beach near Strathlachan where two companies could land simultaneously. Some 130 battalions passed through *Quebec* before D-day, including twenty-nine Canadian and six American units.

NIGHT EXERCISES.   Exploding charges and tracer ammunition were fired within a few feet of these British soldiers.

Landing craft training was carried out at a converted holiday camp at Hayling Island, HMS *Northney*, and at HMS *Tormentor* at Warsash on Southampton Water, the former Household Brigade Yacht Club. As D-day came closer, a special cadet training establishment for landing craft officers was set up at Lochailort between Mallaig and Fort William in western Inverness-shire, Scotland. In addition, many different forms of bombardment and landing craft were exercised at Studland Bay near Poole and at Portland and Ringstead Bay near Weymouth. The specialized techniques of controlling supporting bombardments were learned at the Royal Artillery establishment at Larkhill and at the Royal Navy's gunnery school at Whale Island. Divisional assault training also took place at Southwold in East Anglia and at Newhaven and Gosport, both in the south of England.

More areas were required for large-scale landing exercises, so in late 1943 five were chosen where conditions were similar to those in Normandy. Three amphibious training areas were cleared on both sides of the Moray Firth in Scotland. Around Tarbat Ness in eastern Ross, nine hundred inhabitants had to leave their homes by 1 December. At the two sites on the southern shore, Culbin Sands and Burghead Bay, the local impact was less. These facilities were used by the British Force S (Sword Beach), though not without difficulty in the stormy weather of the winter of 1943–1944. In the southwest a training area was set up on the Gower Peninsula in south Wales, but the most important area cleared of its normal population was Slapton Sands in south Devon. Since this involved uprooting some 2,750 people, there was considerable British pressure for the Americans, for whom it was intended, to make the most of the facility.

From August 1943 onward the Americans also opened eight amphibious training centers at Rosneath, Plymouth,

LANDING EXERCISES.   In this realistic exercise, the soldier being carried to shore was a casualty; the man on the right has lost his helmet and rifle and appears dazed.   HULTON DEUTSCH

Falmouth, Dartmouth (in the evacuated Royal Naval College), Salcombe, Appledore/Instow, Milford Haven /Penarth, and Teignmouth. In addition there were two advanced amphibious training subbases, both in Cornwall, at St. Mawes and Fowey. Particularly important for assault training was Appledore, where German fortifications were simulated at an assault training center at Woolacombe. This center's other duties were training landing craft crews and accustoming soldiers to boat work. Much useful experience was gained at Woolacombe before larger exercises began under the command of Adm. John L. Hall, USN, commander of the Eleventh Amphibious Force, and his subordinate commander, Rear Adm. John Wilkes, USN.

Pressed by Churchill to use Slapton as much and as soon as possible, Hall carried out Exercise DUCK 1 on 3 and 4 January 1944, only days after the last inhabitants had been evacuated. The U.S. 29th Infantry Division was landed, covered by live firing. A number of lessons were learned about the numbers of ships required, the loading of troops and vehicles, and the need for specialized gunfire support craft. During DUCK 2, held with a regimental combat team in February, Rhino pontoon ferries were used for the first time. The exercise was more of a success than its predecessor, but there was clearly much room for improvement in traffic control and landing craft handling. In Exercise FOX in March, troops from the U.S. V Corps experimented with the use of DUKW amphibious trucks to carry ammunition ashore and with various ways of waterproofing vehicles. The high-ranking officers, both American and British, observing the exercise were quite impressed. After each event the commanding officers involved attended a "wash-up" session with Hall to analyze the lessons learned.

Less successful was Operation BEAVER at the end of March. A simulated airborne landing was carried out by "dropping" troops of the U.S. 101st Airborne Division by jeep and landing the U.S. 5th Infantry Division under a heavy bombardment to relieve them. The units got badly confused and failed to accomplish their missions. A two-day wash-up was held at the beginning of April to distill the lessons for the next event planned for later in the month, Operation TIGER.

TIGER was a large-scale rehearsal of Force U, the U.S. forces planning to assault Utah Beach; the 4th Infantry Division with two supporting engineer special brigades, together with the two airborne divisions, the 101st and 82d. On "D-day," 26 April, the initial landings were confused. The promised air support never appeared and the beach engineers moved too slowly, causing a vulnerable buildup off the beaches. The fire support plan could not be executed in the confusion and only the DD (Duplex Drive) tanks, used for the first time, gave effective support. The exercise lost its realism but then became all too real overnight, when the follow-up convoy of eight LSTs due off Slapton on "D plus 1" was attacked by German S-boats; LSTs 507 and 531 were sunk and LST 289 damaged. Over 600 soldiers and sailors were reported lost, heavier casualties than Force U (Utah Beach) would suffer on D-day itself. (Some historians estimate that over 700 were lost during this attack.) Despite these losses, 25,000 troops and 2,750 vehicles were landed in TIGER and much was learned about the realities of amphibious assault, notably the crucial importance of timing, of good communications between ships, landing craft, and shore, and good troop control and traffic organization on the beaches. There was no time to give Force U another exercise before D-day, but its performance then showed that

the chastening experience of TIGER had not been wasted.

The final assault rehearsals were designated FABIUS and took place in the first week in May. FABIUS 1 was held at Slapton on 3 through 6 May with Force O (Omaha Beach) and was an improvement on TIGER. Force G (Gold Beach) landed at Hayling Island in FABIUS 2. Force J (Juno Beach) used the long beach running from the Witterings to Selsey Bill on Bracklesham Bay in FABIUS 3, and Force S (Sword Beach) landed to the west of Littlehampton in FABIUS 4. (FABIUS 5 was an embarkation exercise in the Thames Estuary.) One feature of the FABIUS series was the opportunity to improve the organization of air cover as well as to reassure the troops that such cover would protect them.

All this realistic assault training was vital to the success of the Allied forces on 6 June; as Admiral Hall said, "We were ready."

[See also Assault Ships; Landing Ships.]

LST 289.   Entering Dartmouth harbor, England, after being attacked during Exercise TIGER.

BIBLIOGRAPHY

Edwards, Kenneth. *Operation Neptune*. 1946.
Fergusson, Bernard. *The Watery Maze*. 1961.
Godson, Susan G. *Viking of Assault: Admiral John Leslie Hall, Jr., and Amphibious Warfare*. 1982.
Hoyt, Edwin P. *The Invasion before Normandy*. 1987.

ERIC J. GROVE

ANCON, USS.

Ancon (AGC-4) was the flagship of Rear Adm. John L. Hall, Jr., commander, Assault Force O and headquarters ship for Maj. Gen. Leonard T. Gerow, commander, U.S. V Corps; Maj. Gen. Clarence R. Huebner, commander, U.S. 1st Infantry Division; and Brig. Gen. William M. Hoge, commander, U.S. Engineer Special Brigade.

Built in 1938, *Ancon* was a privately owned passenger ship until commandeered by the U.S. military in 1942 and used as a transport. Converted to an amphibious command ship in 1943, *Ancon* carried a crew of 707. The 493-foot vessel mounted two 5-inch, four 40-mm, and fourteen 20-mm guns, plus modern communications equipment. It took part in the invasions of Sicily and Salerno, then became flagship of the Eleventh Amphibious Force.

Captained by Comdr. Mead S. Pearson, *Ancon* departed Portland, England, on 5 June 1944, and at 0251 on D-day anchored in the transport area eleven miles off Omaha Beach. Throughout D-day *Ancon* successfully operated its vast communications systems for army and naval commanders, lent its LCVPs (Landing Craft, Vehicle and Personnel) for special missions, and stood ready to repel enemy air attacks. After the army commanders went ashore, *Ancon* remained off Normandy until D plus 21. This modern amphibious command ship ensured the presence of the assault force commander in the area until the landing force was securely established ashore and the buildup phase was well under way.

After *Ancon* returned to England, it soon sailed for the Pacific, where it took part in the invasion of Okinawa and was present in Tokyo Bay when the Japanese surrendered. It received five battle stars for wartime service.

[*See also* Hall, John L.]

BIBLIOGRAPHY

Commander Assault Force "O" [J. L. Hall, Jr.]. Action Report: Assault on the Vierville-Colleville Sector, Coast of Normandy. Serial 00876 of 27 July 1944. Operational Archives, Naval Historical Center, Washington, D.C.
Commanding Officer, USS *Ancon* [Mead S. Pearson]. Action Reports. Serial 0044 of 21 June 1944 and Serial 048 of 30 June 1944. Operational Archives, Naval Historical Center, Washington, D.C.
Mooney, James L., ed. *Dictionary of American Naval Fighting Ships*. Vol. 1, pt. A, 1991.

SUSAN H. GODSON

ANDERSON, FREDERICK L. (1905–1969),

American, deputy commanding general, operations, U.S.

USS *ANCON*.   At right, standing off Omaha Beach, 7 June 1944.   NATIONAL ARCHIVES

Strategic Air Forces (USSTAF). Having graduated from West Point in 1928, Anderson transferred to the Air Corps in 1929. He specialized in bombardment aviation and attended the Air Corps Tactical School in 1940. In 1940–1941 he organized and established the first Air Corps School for bombardier instruction. Later in 1941 he served as an Army Air Forces (AAF) observer of bombing tactics in Great Britain. Upon his return he rose to the rank of brigadier general while serving in the office of the chief of the Air Corps as the deputy director of bombardment until early 1943, when the commander of the AAF, Lt. Gen. Henry H. Arnold, sent him to Africa and England as his personal representative on bombardment matters. While in England Anderson became head of the Eighth Air Force's 4th Bomb Wing. In July 1943 he took over VIII Bomber Command and in November 1943 was promoted to major general. As head of VIII Bomber Command, Anderson conceived and advocated shuttle bombing missions, such as the first Schweinfurt-Regensburg mission in August 1943 and the shuttle to the Soviet Union in the summer of 1944 (Operation frantic). He worked closely with Lt. Gen. Ira C. Eaker, Eighth Air Force commander, and the RAF chief of staff, Air Chief Marshal Charles A. Portal, in the development of plans for the Combined Bomber Offensive against Germany.

When Lt. Gen. Carl Spaatz established USSAFE (later USSTAF) in early January 1944, he recognized Anderson's expertise and selected him as his deputy commanding general, operations, and charged him with coordinating the activities of the U.S. Eighth and Fifteenth air forces. Anderson retained the post until the end of the war in Europe. In late February 1944 he was instrumental in directing and carrying out Operation ARGUMENT, known as "Big Week," which damaged a significant percentage of Germany's aircraft assembly plants. Anderson was a workaholic who kept a cot in his office, and a hard-driving believer in strategic bombing. His practical and emotional support of Spaatz during USSTAF's attempts to avoid Transportation Plan bombing and to substitute bombing of the German synthetic oil industry further strengthened Spaatz's resolve.

By helping to keep USSTAF focused on strategic bombing, Anderson contributed to maintaining the Eighth Air Force's successful campaign of attrition, which destroyed the German day fighter force in the months before D-day. The German fighter force would only suffer losses in the defense of strategically valuable targets in Germany itself; it would not commit itself to defend French and Belgian transportation targets. If the Germans had retained the capacity for massive aerial intervention, which they lost in defending their homeland from American bombing raids, and used it against the beachhead, then D-day, at the very least, might have been more costly and less successful. [See also U.S. Strategic Air Forces (USSTAF).]

BIBLIOGRAPHY

Copp, Dewitt S. *Forged in Fire: Strategy and Decisions in the Air War over Europe, 1940–1945.* 1982.
Craven, Wesley Frank, and James Lea Cate, eds. *Europe: ARGUMENT to V-E Day, January 1944 to May 1945.* Vol. 3 of *The Army Air Forces in World War II.* 1951.

RICHARD G. DAVIS

ANDERSON, SAMUEL E. (1906–1982), American, brigadier general, commanding general, IX Bomber Command. Samuel E. Anderson graduated from West Point in 1928, and for the next ten years served as an instructor pilot in pursuit units. During 1939–1941 he commanded the 6th Pursuit Group and served as plans and training officer, 18th Composite Wing, in Hawaii. In October 1941 he joined the U.S. Army Air Forces Air Staff and in March 1942 he transferred to the prestigious Operations Division of the War Department General Staff. While on tour at Port Moresby, New Guinea, in the spring of 1943 he won a Silver Star for gallantry.

In July 1943 Anderson arrived in England to command the Eighth Air Force's 3d Bombardment Wing of medium bombers. Within two weeks he earned a Distinguished Flying Cross for leading multiple combat missions. When his division was reassigned to the reestablished Ninth Air Force Bomber Command (Medium) in October 1943, he became commander. In the winter of 1943–1944 General Anderson directed bombers against German airfields to aid the heavy bombers attacking Germany, and against German V-1 launch sites that were under construction. In mid-April the general's forces began violent and effective interdiction attacks against German transportation in France. During the last week of May 1944 the medium bombers carried out an orchestrated assault on large German anti-invasion guns, some in use and others under construction. The Allies carefully planned these attacks so as not to reveal the actual invasion site.

On 6 June, rather than cancel missions because of low clouds, General Anderson asked for and received permission for his planes to fly at 1,060 meters (3,500 feet). At 0500 they attacked outlying targets and at 0605 they attacked Utah Beach with 278 aircraft that dropped 500,000 kilograms (550 tons) of bombs. Forty-three percent of the bombs fell within 90 meters (300 feet) of their targets (Craven and Cate, 1951). For the remainder of the campaign the IX Bomber Command participated in interdiction and attacks in direct support of ground operations, such as Operations CHARNWOOD and GOODWOOD.

On 25 July 380 medium bombers joined in Operation

COBRA, which assisted the American breakout from the Normandy beachhead. Forty-two bombers misidentified their target, however, and dropped bombs on American forces, causing casualties and confusion, but not significantly delaying the ground assault.

Following World War II Anderson continued a long and distinguished career. In 1948–1950 he occupied the post of U.S. Air Forces Air Staff deputy chief of staff, Plans and Operations. In May 1953 he assumed command of the Fifth Air Force, the principal U.S. Air Force combat organization in Korea. Afterward he commanded the U.S. Air Force Air Matériel Command before retiring as a four-star general, in 1963, from the post of air deputy to Supreme Allied Commander, Europe. He died on 12 September 1982 and was buried at the Air Force Academy in Colorado Springs, Colorado.

[See also IX Bomber Command.]

BIBLIOGRAPHY

Craven, Wesley Frank, and James Lea Cate, eds. *Europe: ARGU-MENT to V-E Day, January 1944 to May 1945.* Vol. 3 of *The Army Air Forces in World War II.* 1951.

U.S. Ninth Air Force. *Condensed Analysis of the Ninth Air Force in the European Theater of Operations.* 1984.

RICHARD G. DAVIS

ANTIAIRCRAFT WEAPONS. *See* Artillery.

ANTISUBMARINE WARFARE. Between 22 March and 6 June 1944 Grand Admiral Karl Dönitz, Commander in Chief of the German Navy *(Kriegsmarine),* assigned thirty-six U-boats, nine of them equipped with snorkels (air intake and exhaust pipes protruding above the surface of the water), to anti-invasion duty in the Channel. Based at Brest, Lorient, Saint-Nazaire, and La Pallice on the Bay of Biscay, these U-boats constituted *Group Landwirt,* the most formidable German naval force in the Channel area, the other vessels available being torpedo boats, including E-boats (105-ft. *Schnellboote*), minesweepers, patrol craft, and gun carriers.

Another five snorkel-equipped boats, each with a meteorologist on board, formed a weather picket patrol in mid-Atlantic to provide D-day predictions. Their guesses proved futile, as Dönitz acknowledged on 11 June, when he described the date of the Allied assault as a complete surprise.

Against the U-boat threat, the Allies' Operation NEPTUNE plan for providing cover to the assault forces and their follow-up shipping called for the deployment of four antisubmarine-warfare support groups—mainly destroy-

ers, destroyer escorts, frigates, and corvettes—in the southwestern approaches to the Channel. Six more groups, including three escort carriers, stood guard west of Land's End, at the southwestern tip of England, and mines were laid along the Brittany shore to interdict U-boats seeking the protection of coastal batteries. In addition, reinforced bomber squadrons of 19th Group RAF Coastal Command patrolled the southwestern approaches from the air in such density that surface operation by U-boats, their preferred cruise and attack mode, was not possible. As a result, long periods of travel while submerged used up the battery power of nonsnorkel boats, while crews in snorkel boats were subjected to debilitating levels of carbon monoxide and other noxious vapors.

First to sortie after invasion alert sounded at 0309 on 6 June at the German Navy's Group Command West at Paris, were seventeen boats from Brest, seven of them with snorkels, followed by fourteen boats from Saint-Nazaire, four from La Pallice, and one from Lorient. By the end of D-day, Coastal Command had reported fourteen sightings and made eight depth bomb attacks. Three boats were forced back to base. Not only the *Landwirt* boats but boats returning to Biscay bases from Atlantic missions met particularly intense Allied fire, all of it from the air, during the four-day period of 7 through 10 June. Bombers from 19th Group sank *U 373* and *629* (both hit within a half hour by the same B-24 Liberator), *740, 821, 955,* and *970,* while sending U *256, 413, 415, 963,* and *989* home damaged. On 12 June all nonsnorkel boats were recalled from operations.

In their turn, various of the *Landwirt* boats launched torpedoes at Allied targets: on 7–8 June *U 984* launched four, *621* two, and *953* four against the four Canadian destroyers (*Qu'Appelle, Saskatchewan, Skeena,* and *Restigouche*) of Support Group 12, but all the warheads exploded harmlessly. The U-boats' run of bad luck continued on 9 June when *U 764* launched four without a hit, and on 11 June when *U 269, 275,* and *621* missed with torpedoes aimed at destroyer groups in the western Channel. Likewise on the 11th, *U 821* fell victim to a British air attack. On 14 June *U 984* launched yet another abortive attack, but on the following day *U 621* sank the landing ship *LST 280; U 767* sank the frigate *Mourne* operating with Support Group 5 off Land's End; and *U 764* torpedoed the destroyer escort *Blackwood* northwest of Cape de la Hague. On 18 June the British destroyers *Fame, Constant,* and *Havelock* avenged the *Blackwood*'s loss by sinking *U 767* off the Brittany coast. Also on the 18th *U 621* missed two U.S. battleships with a multiple launch (*Fächerschuss,* or "fan shot"), and a Polish-manned RAF Wellington bomber sank *U 441* off Ushant, an island off the tip of Brittany. During the second half of June, Allied forces sank four more boats, *U 269, 971,*

DEPTH CHARGE DROPPED BY WARSHIP DURING SUBMARINE ATTACK.

988, and 1191, while suffering the loss of one corvette and three Liberty ships (a fourth Liberty ship was beached and salvaged).

Except for the Liberty ships torpedoed on 29 June by a single boat, U 984, the Group Landwirt boats were as unsuccessful in interrupting the dense flow of shipping to and from the invasion beaches as they had been in frustrating the initial assaults on 6 June. Principal credit for their failure must go to the air squadrons of Coastal Command, which not only scored the greatest number of kills, but caused most of the U-boat commanders to keep their heads down and out of the hunt. By 18 September all the Landwirt survivors would be in Norwegian ports.

[See also U-Boats.]

BIBLIOGRAPHY

Hessler, Günther. *German Naval History: The U-Boat War in the Atlantic, 1939–1945.* 3 vols. 1989.

Rohwer, Jürgen, and Gerhard Hümmelchen. *Chronology of the War at Sea, 1939–1945.* Translated by Derek Masters. Vol. 2, 1992.

Roskill, Stephen W. *The Offensive.* Vol. 3, pt. 2, of *The War at Sea, 1939–1945.* 1961.

MICHAEL GANNON

ANTITANK WEAPONS. *See* Artillery.

ARCHIVAL SOURCES. [*This entry includes separate discussions of Allied and German archives.*]

Allied Archives

There are a large number of sources now available in different countries, covering the experiences of the World

War II frontline soldier as well as the deliberations of the high command. These sources increasingly reflect the interest of historians and the general public in the experiences of ordinary people and how they were affected by events. In the United States, operational records and U.S. War Department documents are held at the Modern Military Branch of the National Archives in Washington, D.C. Private papers such as diaries and correspondence, including those kept by the senior defense personnel, are retained at the Manuscript Division of the Library of Congress in Washington, D.C.; the Dwight D. Eisenhower Library in Abilene, Kansas; the Hoover Institute on War, Revolution and Peace at Stanford University in Palo Alto, California; and the U.S. Military Academy Library at West Point, New York. Information on the respective services can be found at the U.S. Army Military Institute in Carlisle Barracks, Pennsylvania; the Naval Historical Center, Naval History Division, and the Operational Archives, Naval History Division, in Washington, D.C.; and the Office of Air Force History in Washington, D.C.

Official British and Commonwealth documents and unit war diaries are deposited at the Public Record Office at Kew, just outside London. Private papers, such as letters and personal diaries of all ranks, are held at Churchill College, Cambridge; the Imperial War Museum, London (which also has sound recordings of oral interviews); and the Liddell Hart Centre for Military Archives at King's College, London. Material relating to the British Navy, Army, and Air Force are held respectively at the National Maritime Museum in Greenwich, London; the National Army Museum in London; and the Royal Air Force Museum at Hendon, London. Records open to the public in Canada include private papers, including those of high-ranking officers, held at the National Archives of Canada in Ottawa and the Royal Military College of Canada at Kingston. Official and military documents are held at the Directorate of History, National Defence Headquarters, in Ottawa. Material relating to Polish armed forces is held in the Archives Department of the Polish Institute and Sikorski Museum and the Polish Library in London. The Public Record Office, Kew, also holds official papers relating to operations of Canadian and Polish forces.

Members of the public wishing to discover the whereabouts of the grave or memorial of a relative or friend should contact the Battle Monuments Commission in Washington, D.C., or the Commonwealth War Graves Commission in Maidenhead, Berkshire, in the United Kingdom, for U.S., and British and Commonwealth forces respectively.

BIBLIOGRAPHY

Foster, Janet, and Julia Sheppard. *British Archives: A Guide to Archive Resources in the United Kingdom*. 1989.

National Historical Publications and Records Commission. *Directory of Archives and Manuscript Repositories in the United States*. 1988.

SIMON N. ROBBINS

German Archives

Germany's central archive system, the National Archive (Reichsarchiv) for government and military documents, had been founded in 1919 in Berlin. That same year it was moved to Potsdam in order to make it independent of the Prussian Secret State Archive (Preussisches Geheimes Staatsarchiv).

In 1937 military records were separated from the National Archive and collected in the Army Archive (Heeresarchiv), also in Pottsdam. In World War II, commanding officers and troop divisions down to the independent unit level were required to maintain war diaries and, along with formations, commands, and reports, deposit them quarterly in the Army Archive. Many documents were lost through wartime contingencies, then through a bombing raid on Potsdam in April 1945 as well as a command to destroy military documents to prevent them from being captured. With few exceptions, only those diaries that had been sent elsewhere for storage were preserved; these came from the divisional level or higher and cover the period to the middle or end of 1943. A partial substitute resource is the Foreign Military division of the U.S. Army Historical Division.

After the war the archives in the Allied occupation zones were reorganized without the Wehrmacht documents. This changed in 1949 with the founding of the Federal Republic of Germany (West Germany) and the German Democratic Republic (East Germany). In Potsdam the East German Central Archive (Deutsches Zentralarchiv in der DDR) was established, while in Bonn the government in March 1950 established the Federal Archive (Bundesarchiv) to collect the documents of the Federal government and agencies as well as maintain the functions of the former national, Prussian and army archives. It thus was given a division for military records.

West Germany's military archive (Bundesarchiv-Militärarchiv—BA-MA) initially suffered from a lack of material; many records were located in archives in East Germany, were in the hands of the victorious Allied nations, or were scattered throughout the Federal Republic and first had to be collected. Archival records returned by the Allies went first to the documentation center of the Military History Research Office in Freiburg (Dokumentationszentrale des Militärgeschichtlichen Forschungsamtes—MGFA); military documents were thus divided between the BA-MA and the MGFA. In 1968 the BA-MA moved from Koblenz to Freiburg, taking over the MGFA document office. Since then, the BA-MA has been the central military archive, making documents available to researchers at one location. The volume of documents has been increased by further returns from various nations. With the reunification of Germany in 1990, the East German military archive in Potsdam was attached to the BA-MA as a branch.

The holdings of the BA-MA are divided into several sections: RW, Wehrmacht command and central Wehrmacht affairs; RH, Reichsheer (pre-Wehrmacht army) and Wehrmacht; RM, German navy from the Imperial period to the Third Reich; RL, Luftwaffe; RS, Waffen-SS. These major sections are subdivided into further categories, for example, RW 4, Wehrmacht High Command, Wehrmacht general staff; RH 26, infantry divisions; RH 26-91, *91st Infantry Division;* RH 27, panzer divisions; RH 27-2, *2d Panzer Division.* In order to locate the records of a particular topic or military event, the researcher must know which troop unit was involved. Archive catalogs then help locate the documents. The catalogs organize the documents by content, chronology, and provenance, for example, Operations Report Ic of the *91st Infantry Division* (with supplements), March to July 1944, is numbered RH 26-91/6.

In accordance with West Germany's Archives Law, the BA-MA is open for use by the general public. All materials must be used on the premises. Not all documents are available in the original; some are on microfiche. A prior request in writing is required so that a workplace can be reserved and a determination made as to the availability of the documents. The BA-MA's photo-reproduction office can make copies on request, including large-format maps, microfilms, and reproductions. Information concerning the BA-MA can be obtained by writing to Bundesarchiv-Militärarchiv, Wiesentalstrasse 10, D-79115 Freiburg.

BIBLIOGRAPHY

Granier, Gerhard. *Das Bundesarchiv-Militärarchiv: Funktion, Geschichte, Bestände.* 1989.

JOHANNES KINDLER
Translated from German by Amy Hackett

AREA SCREEN SHIPS. OVERLORD's planners expected considerable opposition from more than 500 minor German surface ships (destroyers and smaller vessels) based along the Atlantic and Channel coasts and the 49 German submarines designated for invasion defense. The landing forces had their own escort ships, but the principal goal of air and naval forces was to deny German attackers access to the Spout (the name given to the cross-Channel convoy route to the landing beaches).

Channel waters east and west of the invasion area were guarded by an extensive screen of light forces so effective that OVERLORD's naval operations, code-named NEPTUNE, were able to proceed almost without interference.

The "deep defense" of the invasion route was commanded by Adm. Charles J. C. Little, commander in chief, Portsmouth. In the eastern Channel four destroyers and coastal forces (motor torpedo boats and motor launches) screened coastal convoy routes. Two frigates with coastal craft operated east of the Spout.

In the open waters of the western Channel, stronger defense was required against submarines and surface craft out of Cherbourg and other western bases. To protect this area three groups of four destroyers each were stationed south of Lyme Bay, in midchannel between Start Point and the Cotentin Peninsula, and between Falmouth and Ushant; they were reinforced at night by coastal craft. Convoy routes from western British ports were protected by antisubmarine groups south of Falmouth. Two destroyers, two frigates, and coastal forces operated north of the Cotentin Peninsula. Off Land's End three British escort aircraft carriers of Western Approaches Command operated with six antisubmarine escort groups of frigates. The Admiralty kept other North Atlantic convoy escort groups available, in case U-boats succeeded in entering the Channel. Finally, distant cover was provided by the British Home Fleet, which had ready three battleships, three fleet carriers, seven cruisers, and ten destroyers, in case German heavy ships should sortie into the Atlantic.

German surface forces were able to accomplish only one counterattack on D-day. Off Sword Beach three torpedo boats from Le Havre sank the Norwegian destroyer *Svenner,* but missed the British battleships *Warspite* and *Ramillies.* During the nights that followed, German light forces repeatedly attempted to attack invasion shipping but could inflict no more than a few casualties and suffered heavy losses themselves.

U-boats had an even harder time of it. Thirty-five submarines left their bases on 6 June, to be followed by others, but nine were sunk or damaged in the first forty-eight hours. Heavy air patrol proved such an obstacle that all surviving U-boats, except seven with snorkels (ventilation tubes protruding above the surface), were ordered back to port on 12 June. The surface escort groups skirmished with the approaching U-boats, and were rearranged to form a barrier west of the Cotentin Peninsula. U-boats finally succeeded in working their way into the Allied defensive area by 14 June but accomplished little, sinking frigates *Blackwood* and *Mourne* on the 15th and damaging frigate *Goodson* on the 25th. Throughout the operation thirty-six U-boats were lost and fourteen more were damaged

Comprehensive control of the narrow sea kept Allied naval losses to a remarkable minimum, and prevented the

German Navy from being more than a minor nuisance to the invasion and support fleets.

BIBLIOGRAPHY

Lenton, H. T., and J. J. Colledge. *British and Dominion Warships of World War II.* 1968.

Roskill, Stephen W. *The Offensive.* Vol. 3, pt. 2, of *The War at Sea, 1939–1945.* 1961.

JOHN C. REILLY, JR.

ARMOR AND TRACKED VEHICLES. [*This entry includes two discussions of armor and tracked vehicles, the first focusing on Allied and the second on German equipment.*]

Allied Armor and Tracked Vehicles

American. The backbone of the Allies' armored formations, the American M4 medium tank (34 tons), named "Sherman" by the British, was the standard U.S. medium tank and equipped two-thirds of Britain's armored units. The M4 was criticized after the Normandy invasion because its armor and gunpower could not match Germany's Panther and Tiger, but in the days just after the landings its ability to support infantry was far more important than its shortcomings in tank duels. Its virtues were mechanical reliability, versatility, mobility (42 k/h, or 26 mph), good high-explosive (HE) performance from its 75-mm gun, efficient turret power traverse, and numerical superiority. During the fighting following D-day, these virtues were more important than tank-killing firepower, particularly in the bocage hedgerows, which robbed the Germans of their ability to kill tanks at long range.

Neither Allied army had ignored the problem of dealing with heavy German tanks. To penetrate German armor, the British converted part of their Shermans into Fireflies by mounting the 17-pounder gun, and the Americans had sent 76-mm-gunned versions of the M4 to England before D-day. But neither army was anxious to replace all 75-mm guns with these heavier weapons, since both were less efficient for infantry support. Less

BRITISH SHERMAN TANK.   Advancing through a French village. Spare track hanging on the front was intended to increase armor protection.

IMPERIAL WAR MUSEUM

AMERICAN SHERMAN M4 TANK.

HULTON DEUTSCH

BRITISH M3 STUART TANK. On a road west of Caen.

IMPERIAL WAR MUSEUM

BRITISH CROMWELL TANKS.   In an assembly area for an attack east of the Orne River.   IMPERIAL WAR MUSEUM

explosive filler, and excessive muzzle blast that obscured targets for subsequent shots, were sufficient to keep the 76-mm M4s out of the invasion force, while the 17-pounder had no HE round at all. However, combat soon after D-day demonstrated that both armies had underestimated the problem of killing German Panther and Tiger tanks, and this crisis came to the attention of both Eisenhower and Montgomery.

One reason for American lack of concern about the M4s' ability to destroy tanks was the fact that the U.S. Army doctrinally assigned this task to its Tank Destroyer (TD) battalions. About half of these battalions, one of which generally supported each division, had self-propelled guns, while the remainder towed 3-inch guns. Most of the self-propelled guns, called "TDs" by the troops, were open-turreted M10s (33 tons; 48 k/h, or 30 mph) carrying the 3-inch gun (same ballistic performance as the 76-mm). In addition, some TD battalions had the light, fast M18 (20 tons; 80 k/h, or 50 mph), which carried the 76-mm gun in its open turret. Unfortunately, the Normandy campaign revealed that even these more powerful guns could not penetrate the frontal armor of heavy German tanks.

Supplementing the principal U.S. tanks were a wide array of other armored vehicles. The versatile M4 provided the chassis for self-propelled 105-mm artillery and, with a turret-mounted 105, served as an assault gun. Reconnaissance and cavalry units in both Allied armies employed the American M5 (Stuart) light tank (17 tons; 72 k/h, or 40 mph), which was thinly armored and carried only a 37-mm gun. Half-tracks, whose cross-country mobility was never completely satisfactory, served in a variety of roles such as troop carriers in armored divisions, gun tractors, and self-propelled antiaircraft guns. Finally, the U.S. Army used the six-wheeled M8 (8.5 tons; 64 k/h, or 40 mph), which had a turret mounting the 37-mm gun; without its turret the M8 became the M20 utility and command vehicle.

British. British designs reflected the concept of complementary "cruiser or cavalry" tanks for exploiting breakthroughs and "infantry" tanks to support infantry units. Along with Shermans, the fast Cromwell (27.5 tons; 58 k/h, or 36 mph), equipped Britain's armored divisions. The slower, more heavily armored Churchill (39 tons; 24 k/h, or 15 mph) served in separate regiments supporting infantry. Both originally carried the 6-pounder as main

M3 Stuart light tank.   In British service.

Army. The Bren was a mobile fire unit carrying a Bren light machine gun, 3-inch mortar, or flamethrower, while the Loyd towed 6-pounder antitank guns or carried a mortar. Finally, the British Army made greater use of armored cars than did the Americans. In most general use were the Daimler and Humber (both about 7 tons; 72–80 k/h, or 45–50 mph), which mounted 2-pounder (40-mm) and 37-mm guns, respectively.

No discussion of D-day would be complete without mentioning Britain's "Funnies," a collection of innovative adaptations of tanks inspired by the Dieppe disaster, intended to support both the landings and subsequent operations. A collapsible screen for flotation and propellers for propulsion turned the M4 into the amphibious Duplex Drive or DD, which both armies employed. However, heavy seas swamped those used at Omaha Beach, where they probably would have done the most good. A rotating drum with chains to detonate mines turned the Sherman into the Crab or Flail. Churchills provided the basis for the AVRE (Armoured Vehicle Royal Engineers), which substituted a 290-mm bunker-busting spigot mortar, or Petard, for the main gun. AVREs could also carry bridges or fascines, large bundles of brushwood to fill antitank ditches. Towing an armored fuel trailer, the Churchill became the flame-throwing Crocodile.

Summary. Overall, Britain and the United States equipped their soldiers with a variety of effective and versatile armored vehicles well-suited to most of their tactical missions. In hindsight, history has probably made too much of the problem of killing Panthers and Tigers. Large tank battles were the exception in northwest Europe, especially on D-day and in the initial fighting in

armament, but this gun was largely replaced by a British adaptation of the U.S. 75-mm, illustrating British respect for the versatility of the latter weapon. In an adaptation similar to the Americans', the British used the M4 chassis and their 25-pounder howitzer to create self-propelled artillery. To improve antitank capability, the British produced the Challenger version of Cromwell by mounting a large turret with the 17-pounder. In addition, the M10 TD, some armed with the 17-pounder, served in British units. Britain's light tracked carriers, the Bren and Loyd (4 tons; 48 k/h, or 30 mph), had no counterparts in the U.S.

Column of British Cromwells.   Southeast of Caen.

AVRE.   The bunker-busting Petard is evident on this AVRE (Armoured Vehicle Royal Engineers). An M10 tank destroyer is in the background.   IMPERIAL WAR MUSEUM

AMERICAN SHERMAN TANK.   "Cannon Ball" mired on an invasion beach, 12 June 1944. The special air intakes were for semisubmerged operations.   NATIONAL ARCHIVES

Normandy. Suffice it to say that the Allies never suffered an *operational* reverse because of tank quality. However, at the tactical level Allied tank crews paid in blood for the superiority of German tanks.

BIBLIOGRAPHY

Baily, Charles M. *Faint Praise: American Tanks and Tank Destroyers during World War II.* 1983.

Chamberlain, Peter, and Chris Ellis. *British and American Tanks of World War II.* 1969.

Crow, Duncan, ed. *American AFV's of World War II.* Vol. 4 of *Armoured Fighting Vehicles in Profile.* 1972.

Crow, Duncan, ed. *British and Commonwealth AFV's, 1940–46.* Vol. 3 of *Armoured Fighting Vehicles in Profile.* 1972.

Ellis, L. F., et al. *The Battle of Normandy.* Vol. 1 of *Victory in the West.* 1962.

CHARLES M. BAILY

German Armor and Tracked Vehicles

In 1944 the situation of German armor was gloomy. Although the production rate of armored vehicles, in spite of heavy Allied bombing attacks, was the highest since the outbreak of World War II, it was a fraction of that of the United States, Great Britain, and the Soviet Union. Germany could not compensate for heavy loss-

PANTHER.   Originally designated Panzerkampfwagen V. The nickname "Panther" was adopted as its official nomenclature in February 1944. Probably the most successful German tank.

COURTESY OF EDELFRIED BAGINSKI

es on the Russian front and at the same time equip numerous newly formed units with the necessary armored vehicles. Owing to the shortage of rare metals for alloys, the quality of components was often reduced and caused cracks above all in propulsion units and armor plates, which in combat often resulted in the abandonment of the vehicles. Also, the production of HVAP (hypervelocity-armor-piercing) ammunition had long ceased, because there was little tungsten carbide available, and the training of many new units was severely impaired by lack of fuel. Armor warfare had changed more and more to defensive actions without air cover, as the Luftwaffe was exhausted.

The following German tanks and tracked vehicles were engaged in the Normandy fighting. (Insignificant vehicles and captured vehicles used by German troops are not included.)

Panzer IV, Make H. Make H, produced in 1943–1944, was the most advanced version of this tank, which was developed before World War II. Because of upgrading of guns and armor, its combat weight had increased from 18.5 to 26 tons. Every German panzer division contained in its panzer regiment at least one battalion of these tanks. 1944 witnessed the highest output of this vehicle—3,454 tanks.

Thanks to many improvements, Panzer IV had become a reliable battle tank, well suited for mass production. It had a good reputation among tank crews because of its controllability and availability. Fielding the 75-mm gun L/48, it could match any Western tank except the Sherman Firefly armed with the British 17-pounder (76.2-mm) gun. Its fundamental drawbacks were the vertical armor plates and the susceptibility to wear and tear of the small road wheels. With its thin side armor it frequently fell victim to concealed Allied antitank guns.

3,076 derivatives of this tank were developed and pro-

duced for specialized armor in 1944. They included tank destroyer IV, assault gun IV, the self-propelled 150-mm howitzer Hummel, self-propelled antitank guns, and antiaircraft tanks.

Panzer V (Panther). International experts agree that the Panther was one of the best, most likely the best, medium battle tank in World War II. Meeting the Russian T-34 in 1941 was a shock for German armor. The Panther was then developed in great haste and consequently suffered from a lack of testing, material problems, and the hurried start of production with new manufacturing techniques.

With its long-barreled 75-mm gun, Panzer V could defeat the British Churchill III and the Cromwell at a range of 2,000 meters (2,200 yards), and the U.S. General Sherman tank frontally at 1,000 meters (1,100 yards), although the hedges and villages of Normandy often impaired the exploitation of its superior range, and in street fighting the long barrel was even a hindrance. Further advantages were the strong frontal sloping armor, and the effective suspension system allowing a high cross-country speed. Drawbacks were the high silhouette, the weaker flank protection, maintenance of the road wheel suspension system, and difficulties with the quality of alloy steel. After fighting, abandoned Panthers were frequently found with broken final drives and transmission or engine trouble. In 1944 each German panzer division contained one battalion of Panthers. 3,717 tanks of this type were produced in 1944, and a further 453 derivatives.

Panzer VI (Tiger E). In May 1941 the German High Command required a superior heavy tank to be used as a spearhead for armored formations. As a result, after

PANZER IV, MAKE H.   Of the four tank types employed by the Germans at the start of the war, only the Panzer IV remained in service by 1944 as a main battle tank. This picture was taken in Russia in the winter of 1943–1943.

COURTESY OF EDELFRIED BAGINSKI

SCHÜTZENPANZERWAGEN.   Sd Kfz 251 towing a 75-mm antitank gun.
COURTESY OF EDELFRIED BAGINSKI / PANZERMUSEUM MÜNSTER

precipitate development the Tiger came out. Compared with other tanks in service, it was outstandingly well armed and protected and soon gained a legendary repute. The gun was a modified 88-mm antiaircraft gun with a remarkable accuracy and penetration power. Its great drawback, however, was limited mobility. Because of its excessive fuel consumption and short cruising range, longer road marches were avoided and Tiger units were moved by rail whenever possible. In these cases, the combat tracks had to be exchanged for narrower transport tracks because of the tank's width. As the suspension and propulsion system was overloaded, the cross-country speed of 10 to 20 kilometers (6 to 12 miles) per hour was slow. Therefore this powerful tank could be outmaneuvered and attacked from the flanks or rear. Recovery and repair of this heavy tank was difficult. Tigers were organized in independent battalions of forty-five tanks and were attached to divisions for action. From January to August 1944, 623 Tiger E tanks left the assembly lines. From then on, only the Tiger B (Königstiger) was produced.

The Sturmgeschütz 40 Assault Gun. This derivative of Panzers III and IV was originally meant to give close support to attacking infantry by suppressing field fortifications, pillboxes, and such. The limited antitank capability of German infantry against mass tank attacks led to the conversion of the *Sturmgeschütz* into an antitank

weapon. Forgoing the rotating turret made production quicker and cheaper, but these guns were strictly defensive in concept. They were organized in battalions or brigades and were allocated to support of infantry. Sometimes they were included in the antitank battalions of panzer divisions. This assault gun was mounted on the chassis of Panzer III and of Panzer IV. Although Panzer III was slightly lighter than Panzer IV, the technical data of both for mobility and armor were roughly equal. As

SCHÜTZENPANZERWAGEN SPW.   Armored infantry fighting vehicle (AIFV) used by the German panzer grenadiers.
COURTESY OF EDELFRIED BAGINSKI

Main Battle Tanks (MBT)

TECHNICAL DATA	PANZER IV MAKE H	PANZER V PANTHER	PANZER VI TIGER E
GENERAL			
Combat weight	26 tons	44.8 tons	56.9 tons
Length (gun at 12 o'clock) / Height	7.15 m / 2.68 m	8.66 m / 2.99 m	8.45 m / 3.00 m
Width (with skirts)	3.19 m (3.33 m)	3.27 m (3.42 m)	3.70 m
Crew	5	5	5
FIRE POWER			
Main gun caliber / Barrel length	75 mm/48 calibers	75 mm/70 calibers	88 mm/56 calibers
Penetration at range 1,000 meters against rolled homogeneous armor (RHA) at an oblique angle of 30° with AP[1]/HVAP[2] ammunition	87 mm/97 mm	110 mm/136 mm	100 mm/138 mm
Muzzle-velocity AP/HVAP ammunition[3]	790 mps/990 mps	925 mps/1,120 mps	773 mps/990 mps
Ammunition stowage	87 rounds	82 rounds	92 rounds
Machine guns	2	3	2
Ammunition stowage for machine guns	3,150 rounds	5,100 rounds	3,920 rounds
Traversing system	Electric + hand	Hydraulic + hand	Hydraulic + hand
Elevating system	Hand	Hand	Hand
Elevation arc	−10°/+20°	−8°/+18°	−8°/+15°
MOBILITY			
Engine	Maybach HL 120TRM	HL 230 P30	HL 210 P45
Cylinders / Rated horsepower	12/265–300 hp	12/600–700 hp	12/650 hp
Maximum road speed[4]	38 kph	55 kph	45 kph
Ground pressure[5]	0.89	0.88	1.02
Power/weight ratio	11.5 hp/t	15.5 hp/t	12.2 hp/t
Fuel capacity	470 liters	720 liters	540 liters
Road / Terrain range	200 km / 130 km	250 km / 100 km	100 km / 60 km
Trench crossing	2.20 m	2.45 m	2.30 m
Vertical obstacle	0.6 m	0.9 m	0.8 m
Shallow fording	1.20 m	1.90 m	1.20 m
ARMOR PROTECTION[6]			
Turret front / Angle	80 mm / 9°	110 mm / 12°	100 mm / 0°
Turret side / Angle	30 mm / 25°	45 mm / 25°	80 mm / 0°
Turret roof	25–16 mm	30 mm	25 mm
Hull glacis / Angle	80 mm / 9°	80 mm / 5°	100 mm / 0–15°
Hull side / Angle	30 mm / 0°	40 mm / 0–40°	80–60 mm / 0°
Hull cover	15–20 mm	16–30 mm	25 mm
Hull, rear turret / Angle	30, 20 mm/0°	40 mm/30°, 45 mm/25°	80 mm/9°, 80 mm/0°
Skirts	5 mm	5mm	—

[1]Armor-piercing
[2]High-velocity armor-piercing
[3]In meters per second (mps)
[4]In kilometers per hour (kph)
[5]In kilograms per square centimeter
[6]An angle of impact (for instance, 60°) doubles the traveling path of a shot through armor plate. Furthermore, AP projectiles frequently ricocheted without effect when hitting at an angle of impact above 45°.

STURMGESCHÜTZ 40.   Assault gun (Make F with Sturmkanone 75-mm L/43, later L/48). From 1943 on, Make G had a commander's cupola and another gun shield (the so-called *Saukopfblende*).

COURTESY OF EDELFRIED BAGINSKI

TIGER E.   First encountered by the Western Allies in Tunisia in 1943, Tiger E required very skilled driving and maintenance for optimum performance. With the 88-mm tank gun, it had remarkable firepower.

COURTESY OF EDELFRIED BAGINSKI

the 75-mm gun L/48 was identical with Panzer IV's armament, the main differences were the reduced height of 2.16 meters compared to the tanks' heights of 2.50 and 2.68 meters respectively, and the limited traverse of the gun of 11 degrees to each side owing to the lack of a traversable turret. Frontal armor was 50 + 30 mm thick, and that of the flanks 30 mm thick. The crew consisted of four men. The gun's advantage was the low silhouette, above all when it could fight from defilade positions. The driver was always involved in fire conduct, as he had to turn the vehicle for target acquisition or when engaging a target outside the 11-degree traverse. Nevertheless, the *Sturmgeschütz* was quite successful and very often the backbone of infantry antitank defense. 5,751 of them were produced in 1944.

Half Tracks. These were the workhorses of the panzer and panzer grenadier divisions. Varying in weight from one to eighteen tons, they were used to tow guns of all types, and served as self-propelled antiaircraft guns, rocket launchers, flamethrowers, and armored command, reconnaissance, radio, ambulance, observer, recovery, and supply vehicles. The best-known was the Schützenpanzerwagen SPW (armored infantry fighting vehicle, AIFV), intended for combined tank-infantry operations. Technical data as follows:

Combat weight	up to 9 tons
Length/Width/Height	4.56/1.95/1.66 m
Crew	1 infantry or engineer squad
Engine	Maybach HL 42; 100 hp
Maximum speed	52.5 kph
Cruising range, Road/Terrain	300 / 150 km
Fuel capacity	160 liters
Trench crossing / Fording	2.0 / 0.5 m
Armor: frontal/side/rear	14.5 / 8 / 8 mm

The varied armament included all light and heavy weapons of the infantry such as machine guns, mortars, light antiaircraft guns, and anti-infantry and antitank guns. Each German panzer division contained at least one battalion of armored infantry with SPWs, which were very reliable vehicles. The roofless SPWs did not protect the crews from airbursts of the superior Allied artillery and mortars or from air attacks, however. 7,800 of them were produced in 1944.

[*See also* Artillery: *article on* German Antiaircraft and Antitank Weapons and Artillery.]

BIBLIOGRAPHY

Foss, Christopher. *Die Panzer des zweiten Weltkrieges.* 1988.
Hahn, Fritz. *Waffen und Geheimwaffen des deutschen Heeres 1933–1945.* Vols. 1 and 2, 1992.
Lefèvre, Eric. *Panzers in Normandy Then and Now.* 1990.
Meyer, Hubert. *Kriegsgeschichte der 12.SS-Panzerdivision "Hitlerjugend."* Vols. 1 and 2, 1987.
Ritgen, Helmut. *Die Geschichte der Panzer-Lehr-Division im Westen 1944–1945.* 1979.
Spielberger, Walter. *Der Panzerkampfwagen PANTHER und seine Abarten.* 1978.
Spielberger, Walter. *Der Panzerkampfwagen IV und seine Abarten.* 1988.
Spielberger, Walter. *Der Panzerkampfwagen TIGER und seine Abarten.* 1987.

EDELFRIED BAGINSKI

ARMY GROUP B. *Headquarters, Army Group B,* was formed in Munich on 19 July 1943 under the command of Field Marshal Erwin Rommel. It was sent to northern Italy in August, where it assumed control of the *LI Mountain, II SS Panzer,* and *LXXXVII* corps. In September it was charged with the task of disbanding the Italian forces north of Rome, which it did with minimal difficulty. In November, however, Hitler decided to place Field Marshal Albert Kesselring in charge of all German forces in Italy, and Rommel and his staff were ordered to conduct an inspection of the Atlantic Wall. During this assignment Rommel conferred with Field Marshal Gerd von Rundstedt, Commander in Chief West, and the two agreed that *Army Group B* should be subordinated to OB West, Rundstedt's headquarters. Hitler acceded to this request and *Army Group B* assumed control of the *7th* and *15th* armies and *Armed Forces Command Netherlands,* with the task of defending northern France, Belgium, and the Netherlands against the Allied invasion under the general supervision of Rundstedt. *Panzer Group West* was also placed under the command of *Army Group B* on 6 June 1944. (*See tables on following pages.*)

Army Group B was the German headquarters primarily responsible for dealing with the Allied landing and the subsequent campaign in Normandy. Later it fought in the retreat through France and Belgium and directed the German offensive in the Ardennes in December 1944. It was finally destroyed in the battle of the Ruhr pocket in April 1945.

[*See also* Rommel, Erwin; Rundstedt, Gerd von; *and articles on units mentioned herein.*]

BIBLIOGRAPHY

Mehner, Kurt, comp. *Die geheimen Tagesberichte der deutschen Wehrmachtführung im Zweiten Weltkrieg, 1939–1945.* Vol.10, 1985.
Tessin, Georg. *Verbände und Truppen der deutschen Wehrmacht und Waffen-SS im Zweiten Weltkrieg, 1939–1945.* Vol. 14, 1980.

SAMUEL W. MITCHAM, JR.

Army Group B
15 May 1944

Armed Forces Command Netherlands (LXXXVIII Corps)

347th Infantry Division
16th Luftwaffe Field Division
719th Infantry Division

Seventh Army

LXXXIV Corps
  716th Infantry Division
  352d Infantry Division
  709th Infantry Division
  243d Infantry Division
  319th Infantry Division
LXXIV Corps
  77th Infantry Division
  266th Infantry Division
XXV Corps
  343d Infantry Division
  265th Infantry Division
  275th Infantry Division
  353d Infantry Division
Army Reserve
  II Parachute Corps
    2d Parachute Division
    3d Parachute Division
    5th Parachute Division
    91st Air Landing Division
Army Group B Reserve
  LXIV Reserve Corps
  LXV Corps
  2d Panzer Division
  21st Panzer Division
  116th Panzer Division

Fifteenth Army

LXXXIX Corps
  165th Reserve Division
  712th Infantry Division
  48th Infantry Division
LXXXII Corps
  18th Luftwaffe Field Division
  47th Infantry Division
  49th Infantry Division
LXVII Corps
  344th Infantry Division
  348th Infantry Division
LXXXI Corps
  245th Infantry Division
  17th Luftwaffe Field Division
  711th Infantry Division
Army Reserve
  19th Luftwaffe Field Division
  182d Reserve Division
  326th Infantry Division
  346th Infantry Division
  84th Infantry Division
  85th Infantry Division
  331st Infantry Division

SOURCES: *Die geheimen Tagesberichte der deutschen Wehrmachtführung im Zweiten Weltkrieg, 1939–1945*, vol. 10, *1. März 1944–31. August 1944* (Osnabruck: Biblio Verlag, 1985), p. 501; Georg Tessin, *Verbände und Truppen der deutschen Wehrmacht und Waffen-SS im Zweiten Weltkrieg, 1939–1945*, vol. 3, *Die Landstreitkrafte 6–14* (Osnabruck: Biblio Verlag, 1974), p. 51.

ARTIFICIAL HARBORS. One of the hard-taught lessons of the Dieppe raid by Commonwealth forces in 1942 was that no major port was likely to be captured early or intact during an invasion of Continental Europe. With a view to Normandy itself, even if Cherbourg could be seized within two weeks, the clearing of mines and repair of damage could easily take two months. OVER-LORD forces would therefore have to be supplied across open—possibly congested—beaches, in uncertain weather conditions, and at the mercy of the tides. With German forces rushing to converge in force on the beachheads from across northern France, the race to build up resources of men, armor, and matériel ahead of the German response would determine success. Without adequate matériel the invasion would certainly reach an early culmination point, or, worse, be thrown back into the sea.

With no port available, an alternative solution had to be found if OVERLORD was to succeed. The solution came in the form of two British-designed and built prefabricated harbors, called Mulberries, which were to be towed across the channel and assembled in the vicinity of the landing areas. Initially a three-division assault was intended, and to that end the throughput capacity of a Mulberry harbor was set at 7,000 tons per day. Two were ultimately built, one to support the American landings and one to support the British and Commonwealth forces.

Each harbor enclosed over five square kilometers of water (two square miles)—roughly the size of Dover har-

Army Group B
15 May 1944

Armed Forces Command Netherlands (LXXXVIII Corps)

347th Infantry Division
16th Luftwaffe Field Division
719th Infantry Division

Fifteenth Army

LXXXIX Corps
  165th Reserve Division
  712th Infantry Division
  48th Infantry Division
LXXXII Corps
  18th Luftwaffe Field Division
  47th Infantry Division
  49th Infantry Division
LXVII Corps
  344th Infantry Division
  348th Infantry Division
LXXXI Corps
  245th Infantry Division
  17th Luftwaffe Field Division
  711th Infantry Division
  346th Infantry Division
  Elements, 21st Panzer Division
Army Reserve
  LXIV Reserve Corps
  1st SS Panzer Division (in transit)
  182d Reserve Division
  326th Infantry Division
  331st Infantry Division (in transit)
  85th Infantry Division
  84th Infantry Division

Seventh Army

I SS Panzer Corps
  21st Panzer Division (-)
  12th SS Panzer Division

Panzer Lehr Division
716th Infantry Division
LXXXIV Corps
  II Parachute Corps
    Elements, 2d Panzer Division
    3d Parachute Division
    352d Infantry Division (+KG 275)
    6th Parachute Regiment
    KG 265i
    17th SS Panzer Grenadier Division (-)
  KG Hellmich
    243 Infantry Division
    91st Air Landing Division
    77th Infantry Division
    709th Infantry Division
    752d Infantry Division
    319th Infantry Division *
LXXIV Corps
  266th Infantry Division
  353d Infantry Division (in transit)
XXV Corps
  265th Infantry Division
  275th Infantry Division (in transit)
  343d Infantry Division
  2d Parachute Division (in transit)
Seventh Army Reserve
  XLVII Panzer Corps
  5th Parachute Division
  Elements, 17th SS Panzer Grenadier Division (in transit)

(-) Elements of the unit detached or not present
* Stationed on the Channel Islands and not engaged in the Normandy campaign
KG *Kampfgruppe* (battle group; approximately regimental strength)
SOURCE: *Die geheimen Tagesberichte der deutschen Wehrmachtführung im Zweiten Weltkrieg, 1939–1945*, vol. 10, *1. März 1944–31. August 1944* (Osnabruck: Biblio Verlag, 1985), p. 503.

bor. Outer floating breakwaters sheltered an inner fixed breakwater made of huge concrete caissons five stories high and displacing up to 6,000 tons each. These were towed into position and submerged to form the harbor shell. When completed, each Mulberry would contain over six kilometers (four miles) of piers, and almost ten kilometers (six miles) of floating roadway attached to fifteen pier heads to allow landing. Small coaster and landing ships could unload directly into army lorries on the pier heads, while other vessels could transfer their cargoes onto barges within the shelter of the installation.

The five main assault areas, as well as the Mulberries, were protected by lines of blockships scuttled bow-to-stern. These additional breakwaters, known as Gooseberries, provided extra sheltered unloading capacity supporting additional forces added to the invasion.

The first components of the Mulberries were towed across the Channel on D plus 1, the American Mulberry to a point near Saint-Laurent in the center of U.S. V Corps, the British Mulberry near Arromanches.

By D plus 5 Gooseberries had been set up in the assault sectors, where they made an immediate impact on logistical support; without them the Americans had been able to unload less than one-third of their planned tonnage of

CONCRETE MULBERRY CAISSON.   In tow after construction.   NATIONAL ARCHIVES

GOOSEBERRY HARBOR.   Off Omaha Beach.   NATIONAL ARCHIVES

MULBERRY HARBOR.   Used to assist in the unloading of Allied supplies at Colleville, France.   HULTON DEUTSCH

ammunition and supplies along that treacherous coast.

By D plus 12 both Mulberry harbors were in use, the concrete caissons of the main breakwaters had been planted, and the floating piers were half finished. Bad weather had prevented the towing of the comparatively frail floating roadways to complete the harbors, but nonetheless with the advent of the Gooseberries and opening of the Mulberries, American unloading had been able to make up for lost time, and was only 25 percent behind schedule.

Bottlenecks were still experienced, however, and the LSTs (Landing Ships, Tank) were turned around slowly until the Mulberry piers were completed, which then allowed an LST to offload 60 vehicles in 30 minutes or less.

On 17 June a favorable meteorological report presented an opportunity to tow much of the remaining roadway across the Channel. But, within actual sight of the harbors, a furious and unforeseen gale blew up and the roadways were sunk. For three days and nights the storm continued. All Channel convoys remained in port, and in

Normandy ships were broken from their anchorages and dashed onto the shore.

By the third day, the Mulberries started to break up, especially the more hastily erected U.S. Mulberry, which was effectively destroyed; only the Gooseberry blockships prevented a total disaster there as the storm waters poured into the breaches and broke the ferry craft into pieces. The remains of the U.S. Mulberry were used to repair the less established but more painstakingly assembled British Mulberry, which, further along the coast, had withstood the storms.

Nonetheless, in three days the weather had inflicted a serious reverse on Allied shipping—five times as much damage as the enemy had been able to inflict since D-day. Among the 800 craft put out of action were almost half of the available LCTs (Landing Craft, Tank), and the Allied unloading rate fell from 24,000 tons a day to 4,500 tons, almost all of it through the Arromanches Mulberry.

For the Americans, everything had to come directly

onto the beaches, and it says much for the Gooseberry blockships and American improvisation on the beaches that by the middle of July some 35,000 tons a day were coming across the U.S. beach sectors. The British Mulberry had by this time stepped up its throughput to near its 7,000-tons-a-day capacity, and a further 10,500 tons were landed on British sector beaches in the shelter of the Gooseberries.

During the ten months that the Arromanches Mulberry was needed, some two and a half million men, half a million vehicles, and four million tons of supplies passed through.

[See also Tennant, William G.]

BIBLIOGRAPHY

Ellis, L. F., et al. *The Battle of Normandy.* Vol. 1 of *Victory in the West.* 1962.
Packenham-Walsh, R. P. *History of the Corps of Royal Engineers.* Vol. 9, 1958.
Wilmot, Chester. *The Struggle for Europe.* 1971.

GEOFFREY WOOTTEN

ARTILLERY. [*The following entry includes three articles:*
Allied Antitank Weapons
Allied Artillery and Air Defense
German Antiaircraft and Antitank Weapons and Artillery.*]

Allied Antitank Weapons

Antitank defenses are based on natural and man-made obstacles (including mines) secured by infantry armed with light antitank weapons, by field and self-propelled artillery, and by tanks. They are also occasionally supported by bombers and fighter bombers. Because the Allies mostly were on the offensive in Normandy, they had less need for obstacles and mines than did the Germans.

Obstacles. Esplanades, bocage, rivers, and built-up areas provided the best obstacles, which could be improved by the hasty felling of trees and laying of mine fields. The British Mark IV mine contained 4.5 pounds of explosive; the Mark VII, 20 pounds; and the Hawkins No. 75, 1.5 pounds. The American T6E1 contained 11 pounds of explosive; the Light T7 (similar to the Hawkins), 1.5 pounds; and the Mark V only 5.6 pounds. All were pressure-detonated by a tank's tracks at approximately 350 to 450 pounds per square inch. And all were made of metal except for the American Mark V, which was made of ceramic and thus more difficult to detect.

Infantry weapons. British troops were armed with the hand-held projector infantry antitank (PIAT), a spigot mortar that threw a 3-pound hollow-charge warhead to

PIAT. Projector, Infantry, Antitank.   IMPERIAL WAR MUSEUM

a range of about 350 yards, but was more likely to hit a tank at 115 yards. The Americans had the tube-launched 2.36-inch bazooka (named after U.S. comedian Bob Burns's homemade trombone) with a range of about 600 yards, and also a hollow-charge warhead. The PIAT was a slightly better penetrator of armor than the bazooka. Both were liable to fail against thicknesses of approximately 100 millimeters (3.9 inches).

Artillery. Medium and field artillery pieces were usually supplied with armor-piercing projectiles (solid, high-explosive, or hollow-charge). These projectiles, however, with their relatively low velocities, had large zones of dispersion and therefore were less likely to score direct hits than specialized high-velocity antitank guns. Nevertheless, British 4.2-inch, 5.5-inch, and 25-pounder guns and American 155-mm and 105-mm gun/howitzers were frequently fired at tanks, if only to cause external damage and persuade them to shift position.

On D-day the principal American high-velocity antitank guns were the 57-mm (muzzle velocity 2,700 ft/sec with a 6.28-lb shot), 75-mm (muzzle velocity 2,030 ft/sec with a 14-lb shot), and 3-inch (muzzle velocity 2,800 ft/sec with a 12.65-lb shot). The British guns were the 57-mm (muzzle velocity 2,950 ft/sec with a 6-lb shot) and 76.2-mm (muzzle velocity 2,950 ft/sec with a 17-lb shot). None of these would penetrate the Panther tank's glacis plate point-blank, and all failed against Tiger 1 frontally at 200 yards, except for the British 76.2-mm, when using the new armor-piercing discarding sabot (APDS) shot with a muzzle velocity of 3,950 ft/sec. All, however, could penetrate the latest version of Panzerkampfwagen IV tanks and most armored self-propelled guns at ranges up to and beyond 1,000 yards. One should always bear in mind that, in bocage and therefore in most of Normandy, the vast majority of antitank engagements took place at less than 500 yards.

BRITISH 5.5-INCH GUN.   Frequently fired at tanks, although not very effective.

BRITISH FIREFLY.   Proved most effective in antitank warfare in Normandy.

FOUR-INCH ROCKETS.   Being loaded onto RAF Typhoon.

IMPERIAL WAR MUSEUM

Field antitank guns were mounted on wheeled carriages towed by tracked or wheeled vehicles. In that mode the small 57-mm was easiest to man-handle and conceal, while the larger 76.2-mm, more difficult to conceal, often required its prime mover to get it into and out of position—a vital factor when flash and smoke caused by discharge invited immediate enemy countermeasures.

Hence the best carrier was a self-propelled, armored vehicle—a tank or something resembling it. The Americans depended upon large numbers of Sherman tanks with the 75-mm gun, but gradually received modified Shermans with the improved 76-mm gun. In addition, they had T10 tank destroyers with a 3-inch gun, but these had thin armor and an open-topped turret, and were therefore more vulnerable than a tank. The British, on the other hand, mounted 57-mm guns in many of the Churchill tanks, besides 75-mms in their Shermans and Cromwells. But difficulties in mounting the big 76.2-mm (17-pounder) in Cromwell had led to the production of the farcically clumsy Challenger I tank and the much more practical

Sherman Firefly. The latter was an ordinary Sherman with the 75-mm gun replaced by the 76.2-mm, and the front gunner replaced by the larger ammunition. Proven feasible as late as Christmas Day 1943, Fireflies were ready in sufficient numbers by 6 June to be issued to one out of four 75-mm Shermans; they saved the day for the otherwise outgunned British antitank forces in Normandy.

Aircraft. Needless to say, the bombing of German lines of communication and troop concentrations had an indirect logistic and operational effect on antitank warfare. But low-level fighter attacks on tanks, especially by 4-inch rockets fired from the Typhoon, were grossly overrated. Twenty-mm cannon fire could only inflict light damage. The rocket had to score a direct hit to kill; however, being ballistically unstable, it had only a 5-percent chance of a hit. As a result, RAF claims were discovered to be five times in excess of the truth, although, like low-velocity artillery, the Typhoons often induced an unsettled enemy to redeploy.

On balance, therefore, the Allies were inferior to the Germans in antitank capability both in striking power and in gun control, this last because their optical equipment also was inadequate. Morale therefore suffered. In the final analysis it was superior numbers that proved decisive, though at excess cost in lives.

[See also Armor and Tracked Vehicles.]

BIBLIOGRAPHY

Ellis, L. F., et al. *The Battle of Normandy.* Vol. 1 of *Victory in the West.* 1962.

Harrison, Gordon A. *Cross-Channel Attack.* U.S. Army in World War II: The European Theater of Operations. 1951.

KENNETH MACKSEY

Allied Artillery and Air Defense

All military operations are some combination of "fire and movement," and none were more so than the D-day landings on 6 June 1944. Firepower to cover maneuver forces is provided by naval gunfire, aircraft, and artillery. The role of this firepower is to destroy as much of the enemy as possible and to neutralize the remainder to such an extent that they cannot interfere with the assaulting forces. But such firepower has to be carefully coordinated with ground operations. The American, British, and Canadian artillery had three broad tasks: to find, locate, and destroy or neutralize the enemy on the ground and in the air. It was to this end that the artillery of the invading forces was organized. It was structured to cover the three main phases: to provide air defense and bombardment of the coastal defenses during the approach; to provide air defense and artillery attacks during the landings and the establishment of the beachhead; and to provide air defense and artillery attacks for the breakout. A top priority within all these phases was the location and destruction of enemy artillery.

During the Channel crossing to the Normandy beaches, army 40-mm and 20-mm antiaircraft (AA) guns and machine guns were in action on all non-naval ships (naval ships had their own guns) and on the great floating pontoons that were to make up the Mulberry harbor. Both

ANTIAIRCRAFT HALF-TRACKS.   *LST 47* loads cargo of half-tracks with quadruple 50-mm machine guns at Dartmouth, England, on 1 June 1944.

NATIONAL ARCHIVES

BRITISH 40-MM BOFORS ANTIAIRCRAFT GUN.   In action in a gun site captured on the "Hindenburg Bastion." A German 88-mm gun formerly stood in this position.

IMPERIAL WAR MUSEUM

light (40-mm and 0.5-in. machine guns) and heavier caliber guns, 3.7-inch with the British and Canadians and 90-mm with the Americans, landed in the immediate follow-up waves to provide air defense on the beaches in that critical and vulnerable phase.

For the assault landings, field artillery joined the naval and air bombardment as it closed with the beaches. They did this by firing for thirty minutes from the landing ships. Six regiments with either Sexton self-propelled 25-pounders or Priest self-propelled 105-mm guns, a total of 144 guns, were allotted to each army front. A troop of four guns per Landing Craft, Tank (LCT) covered the British and Canadian assault, while a similar number covered the American assault. Artillery forward observing officers (FOOs) landed with the leading waves and controlled the fire onto targets on their beaches. Each group of six craft (one regiment) under naval command was kept on a straight and steady course toward its appointed beach. Firing started at 0655 at 11,000 meters out to sea and continued up to 3,000 meters. Thus the navy kept the guns on target for bearing while the gunners reduced

elevation as the range closed, using a clock device that was set to the speed of the LCT: as the pointer passed each hundred-yard indicator, range was reduced. Each gun fired 65 rounds, making a total of some 9,360 rounds on the British and Canadian sector alone. The regiments that carried out the shoot-in were as follows:

British Sector

3d British Divisional Artillery
7th Field Regiment
33d Field Regiment
76th Field Regiment

3d Canadian Divisional Artillery
12th Canadian Field Regiment
13th Canadian Field Regiment
14th Canadian Field Regiment

50th British Divisional Artillery
86th Field Regiment from corps troops
90th Field Regiment
147th Field Regiment from corps troops

AMERICAN 155-MM SELF-PROPELLED GUN.   The 987th Field Battery in action near Bayeux. The gun is mounted on an M3 chassis and fires a 95-lb. shell.

American Sector

Field artillery support came from the divisional artilleries of the 1st, 4th, 29th, and 90th U.S. infantry divisions.

But the gunners were already ashore. During the night of 5–6 June the British 213th Airlanding Light Battery had landed accurately by glider with their 75-mm pack howitzers, and were soon joined on both sides of the Orne River by their comrades of the British 6th Airborne Division with 6- and 17-pounder antitank and 40-mm antiaircraft guns. Similarly, 75-mm pack artillery was landed with the American 82d and 101st airborne divisions on their objectives south of Carentan.

During the first four days it was planned to land 18 field regiments (432 25-pounder guns), 4 medium regiments (96 5.5-in. guns), 20 heavy guns, and 18 antiaircraft regiments (432 3.7-in. and 40-mm AA guns) on the British and Canadian beaches, and a similar number of guns on the American beaches. This great buildup of firepower was vital to the success of the operation and by and large it went well, once the problems on the American beaches were resolved. As soon as suitable landing sites were cleared, the little Auster aircraft flew the Channel to provide the vital air observation for the guns. The next problem was to locate the enemy guns and silence them. This was done initially from Britain, firing data being passed across the Channel to the batteries ashore and afloat by special high-powered radio. A unified Anglo/American/Canadian system of controlling AA fire was established.

The guns started to land at about 0900. Lt. Col. N. P. H. Tapp, commanding the 7th Field Regiment of the Royal Artillery, later wrote: "As we landed the beach was packed with armoured vehicles, guns and tanks. 76th and 33rd Field Regiments were unable to get off the beach so were firing from the water's edge. The houses screened them so most enemy shells either hit the houses or passed overhead into the sea. As the tide was still coming in, guns and vehicles were edging forwards so increasing the congestion on the beach." Once ashore and forward of the

AMERICAN 105-MM HOWITZER.   Shelling German forces retreating near Carentan, 11 July 1944.   NATIONAL ARCHIVES

beaches, the guns formed into their divisional groups of about 120 guns and then into corps groups of about 360. This enabled the fire of a whole division's guns or even those of a whole corps to engage one target. As a result of these huge concentrations of fire, the German artillery, although active, never really interfered with the landing operations. By this time the antitank regiments were ashore with their 17-pounder self-propelled guns, together with the light antiaircraft regiments with their 40-mm Bofors guns. These moved forward with the tanks to secure ground already won.

On the American front disaster struck the gunners as they attempted to ferry the guns ashore in assault boats. All but one of the guns of the 111th Field Artillery Battalion and six of the 7th Battalion were sunk; five out of six howitzers of the 16th Cannon Company were lost, and three guns of the 58th Battalion that had taken part in the shoot-in hit mines and were destroyed. This shortage of guns

for the breakout from the beaches was a severe blow.

Casualties were high: in the first week the British alone had to send in over 2,000 artillerymen as battle casualty replacements. But by the end of D-day guns were ashore all along the beaches. Antiaircraft guns were having a busy time and F Troop of the 93d Light Anti-Aircraft (LAA) Regiment brought down seventeen enemy aircraft in the first six days. A self-propelled gun of the 147th Army Field Regiment hit a nest of snipers and antitank guns at Le Hamel at point-blank range, and the 90th Field Regiment destroyed four 88-mm German guns on D-day that were holding up the advance. FOOs were moving inland with the leading British tanks and infantry and directing both naval and artillery fire onto enemy positions holding up the advance. Battery commanders were alongside their battalion commanders, artillery commanding officers alongside brigade commanders, and senior artillery commanders alongside divisional and corps commanders. This system ensured maximum coordination of firepower of all types with ground operations and worked with great success.

The American system was slightly different but achieved similar success. Much of the equipment of all assaulting gunners was American anyway, and this simplified coordination. But since the American beaches were steeper and overlooked by higher cliffs than those of their allies, the Americans suffered greater casualties and had more difficulty in getting their guns inland. However, once they broke in, their 105-mm Priest self-propelled guns and their 155-mm medium guns, coordinated with air power, played a large part in the expansion of the bridgehead.

Colonel Tapp describes the scene on D-day:

Everyone was cheering and the sun was shining as 7th Field Regiment passed through Hermanville to come into action just in front of the leading infantry. The whole Regiment was in action by 1200 hours that day. . . . We were held up by a German Battery of 122mm guns near Perrier. Major Rae went off with a company of the King's Shropshire Light Infantry and eventually silenced it. We were then held up by a strong enemy position which we called "Hillman" just south of Colleville. At the close of D-Day we were counter attacked by about a dozen German Mark IV tanks but these were beaten off.

But soon resistance hardened and exploitation became more difficult. The British 3d Infantry Division was held up by strong enemy forces around Lébisey Wood; Colonel Tapp reports; "I moved the Regiment into new positions just north of Beuville, it was only intended that we stay there for 24 hours, in fact we stayed there for 7 weeks!" Thus all along the front the artillery settled down to a period of constant action. The force built up as more and more regiments came ashore, waiting for the breakout that did not come until well into July.

So the artillery of the British 21st Army Group and the U.S. First Army played a vital role in both the landings and the subsequent operations and did so with great courage and effect.

[*See also* Bombardment Ships.]

BIBLIOGRAPHY

Bell, G., and Sons, Ltd. *The Royal Artillery Commemoration Book, 1939–45.* 1950.

Ellis, L. F., et al. *The Battle of Normandy.* Vol. 1 of *Victory in the West.* 1962.

Harrison, Gordon A. *Cross-Channel Attack.* U.S. Army in World War II: The European Theater of Operations. 1951.

North, John. *Northwest Europe, 1944–45.* 1953.

BRITISH 25-POUNDER FIELD GUN BATTERY.   Laying down a smoke screen to cover an infantry advance at Tilly-sur-Seulles a few days after the landings.

IMPERIAL WAR MUSEUM

British Sector

<u>3d British Divisional Artillery</u>
7th Field Regiment
33d Field Regiment
76th Field Regiment

<u>3d Canadian Divisional Artillery</u>
12th Canadian Field Regiment
13th Canadian Field Regiment
14th Canadian Field Regiment

<u>50th British Divisional Artillery</u>
86th Field Regiment from corps troops
90th Field Regiment
147th Field Regiment from corps troops

American Sector

Field artillery support came from the divisional artilleries of the 1st, 4th, 29th, and 90th U.S. infantry divisions.

But the gunners were already ashore. During the night of 5–6 June the British 213th Airlanding Light Battery had landed accurately by glider with their 75-mm pack howitzers, and were soon joined on both sides of the Orne River by their comrades of the British 6th Airborne Division with 6- and 17-pounder antitank and 40-mm antiaircraft guns. Similarly, 75-mm pack artillery was landed with the American 82d and 101st airborne divisions on their objectives south of Carentan.

During the first four days it was planned to land 18 field regiments (432 25-pounder guns), 4 medium regiments (96 5.5-in. guns), 20 heavy guns, and 18 antiaircraft regiments (432 3.7-in. and 40-mm AA guns) on the British and Canadian beaches, and a similar number of guns on the American beaches. This great buildup of firepower was vital to the success of the operation and by and large it went well, once the problems on the American beaches were resolved. As soon as suitable landing sites were cleared, the little Auster aircraft flew the Channel to provide the vital air observation for the guns. The next problem was to locate the enemy guns and silence them. This was done initially from Britain, firing data being passed across the Channel to the batteries ashore and afloat by special high-powered radio. A unified Anglo/American/Canadian system of controlling AA fire was established.

The guns started to land at about 0900. Lt. Col. N. P. H. Tapp, commanding the 7th Field Regiment of the Royal Artillery, later wrote: "As we landed the beach was packed with armoured vehicles, guns and tanks. 76th and 33rd Field Regiments were unable to get off the beach so were firing from the water's edge. The houses screened them so most enemy shells either hit the houses or passed overhead into the sea. As the tide was still coming in, guns and vehicles were edging forwards so increasing the congestion on the beach." Once ashore and forward of the beaches, the guns formed into their divisional groups of about 120 guns and then into corps groups of about 360. This enabled the fire of a whole division's guns or even those of a whole corps to engage one target. As a result of these huge concentrations of fire, the German artillery, although active, never really interfered with the landing operations. By this time the antitank regiments were ashore with their 17-pounder self-propelled guns, together with the light antiaircraft regiments with their 40-mm Bofors guns. These moved forward with the tanks to secure ground already won.

On the American front disaster struck the gunners as they attempted to ferry the guns ashore in assault boats. All but one of the guns of the 111th Field Artillery Battalion and six of the 7th Battalion were sunk; five out of

ANTIAIRCRAFT ARTILLERY. An 8.8-cm (88-mm) Flugabwehrkanone 41 (8.8-cm Flak 41 "Eisenerz").

"NASHORN."   With an 8.8-cm (88-mm) Flak 18 antitank gun.

HULTON DEUTSCH

six howitzers of the 16th Cannon Company were lost, and three guns of the 58th Battalion that had taken part in the shoot-in hit mines and were destroyed. This shortage of guns for the breakout from the beaches was a severe blow.

Casualties were high: in the first week the British alone had to send in over 2,000 artillerymen as battle casualty replacements. But by the end of D-day guns were ashore all along the beaches. Antiaircraft guns were having a busy time and F Troop of the 93d Light Anti-Aircraft (LAA) Regiment brought down seventeen enemy aircraft in the first six days. A self-propelled gun of the 147th Army Field Regiment hit a nest of snipers and antitank guns at Le Hamel at point-blank range, and the 90th Field Regiment destroyed four 88-mm German guns on D-day that were holding up the advance. FOOs were moving inland with the leading British tanks and infantry and directing both naval and artillery fire onto enemy positions holding up the advance. Battery commanders were alongside their battalion commanders, artillery commanding officers alongside brigade commanders, and senior artillery commanders alongside divisional and corps commanders. This system ensured maximum coordination of firepower of all types with ground operations and worked with great success.

The American system was slightly different but achieved similar success. Much of the equipment of all assaulting gunners was American anyway, and this simplified coordination. But since the American beaches were steeper and overlooked by higher cliffs than those of their allies, the Americans suffered greater casualties and had more difficulty in getting their guns inland. However, once they broke in, their 105-mm Priest self-propelled guns and their 155-mm medium guns, coordinated with air power, played a large part in the expansion of the bridgehead.

Colonel Tapp describes the scene on D-day:

Everyone was cheering and the sun was shining as 7th Field Regiment passed through Hermanville to come into action just in front of the leading infantry. The whole Regiment was in action by 1200 hours that day. . . . We were held up by a German Battery of 122mm guns near Perrier. Major Rae went off with a company of the King's Shropshire Light Infantry and eventually silenced it. We were then held up by a strong enemy position which we called "Hillman" just south of Colleville. At the close of D-Day we were counter attacked by about a dozen German Mark IV tanks but these were beaten off.

But soon resistance hardened and exploitation became more difficult. The British 3d Infantry Division was held up by strong enemy forces around Lébisey Wood; Colonel Tapp reports; "I moved the Regiment into new positions just north of Beuville, it was only intended that we stay there for 24 hours, in fact we stayed there for 7 weeks!" Thus all along the front the artillery settled down to a period of constant action. The force built up as more and more regiments came ashore, waiting for the breakout that did not come until well into July.

So the artillery of the British 21st Army Group and the U.S. First Army played a vital role in both the landings and the subsequent operations and did so with great courage and effect.

[*See also* Bombardment Ships.]

BIBLIOGRAPHY

Bell, G., and Sons, Ltd. *The Royal Artillery Commemoration Book, 1939–45.* 1950.
Ellis, L. F., et al. *The Battle of Normandy.* Vol. 1 of *Victory in the West.* 1962.
Harrison, Gordon A. *Cross-Channel Attack.* U.S. Army in World War II: The European Theater of Operations. 1951.
North, John. *Northwest Europe, 1944–45.* 1953.
Pemberton, A. L. *The Development of Artillery Tactics and Equipment.* 1950.
Tapp, Nigel. *"Account of Operations of 7th Field Regiment RA during the Invasion of France, June 1944."* Paper, 1984.

MARTIN FARNDALE

German Antiaircraft and Antitank Weapons and Artillery

German land forces in France in June 1944 had artillery ranging from the horse-drawn battery of light 10.5-cm (105-mm) Model 16 field howitzers, whose construction stemmed from World War I, up to modern self-propelled carriages, such as the Panzer Howitzer Hummel armed with heavy 15-cm (150-mm) Model 18 field howitzers. The models reflected not only the technological developments of the three prior decades, but also a broad variety of calibers and types of artillery. The German weapons were augmented by a diversity of plundered matériel.

In March 1944 in the West (France, Belgium, and the Netherlands), some 3,823 artillery pieces of foreign manufacture were being used by German troops. They

ABANDONED GERMAN 50-MM ANTITANK GUN.   A 5-cm Panzerabwehrkanone 38 (5 cm PAK 38).

IMPERIAL WAR MUSEUM

Nebelwerfer Rocket launcher.

included 61 different models, ranging in caliber from 7.5 to 27.4 cm (75 to 274 mm). More than 1,000 guns of German manufacture were deployed, divided among various models from 7.5 to 28 cm (75 to 280 mm). This tally from March does not include antiaircraft guns or special antitank weapons, self-propelled gun carriages, assault weapons, or infantry guns.

The weapons counted included:

- 7.5-cm (75-mm) modern field guns (7.5-cm Feld-kanone neuer Art; 7.5 cm FK nA): 46 deployed on land; 177 in coastal defense
- 7.5-cm (75-mm) Model 36 mountain guns (7.5-cm Gebirgsgeschütz 36; 7.5 cm Geb.G 36; "Grune-wald"): 6 deployed on land; 53 in coastal defense
- 10.5-cm (105-mm) Model 18 light field howitzers (leichte 10.5-cm Feldhaubitze 18; 10.5 cm le FH 18; "Opladen") and Model 16 (10.5 cm le FH 16): 550 deployed on land; 10 in coastal defense (the older Model 16s)
- 10-cm (100-mm) Model 18 heavy guns (schwere 10-cm Kanone 18; s 10 cm K 18; "Bleiglanz"): 33 deployed on land; 9 in coastal defense
- 15-cm (150-mm) Model 18 heavy field howitzers (schwere 15-cm Feldhaubitze 18; 15 cm s FH 18; "Immergrün"): 190 deployed on land
- 15-cm (150-mm) Model 16 guns (15-cm Kanone 16; 15 cm K 16): 12 in coastal defense
- 17-cm (170-mm) Model 18 guns on howitzer carriages (17-cm Kanone 18 in Mörserlafette; 17 cm K 18 in

Mrs Laf; "Matterhorn"): 15 deployed on land; 46 in coastal defense
- 21-cm (210-mm) Model 18 mortars (21 cm Mörser 18; 21 cm Mrs 18; "Brummbär"): 18 deployed both on land and on railroads; 39 deployed on land; 8 in coastal defense

These numbers may have increased somewhat by the time of the invasion.

German artillery deployed on 6 June 1944 included the following. A 7.5-cm (75-mm) Model 18 light infantry gun (leichtes Infanteriegeschütz; "Forelle"), developed by Rheinmetall (Rheinische Metallwaren-und Maschinen-fabrik) in 1927, was standard equipment with the German infantry until 1945. Its tilting breech action resembled that of a shotgun: on loading, the breechblock remained stationary and the barrel moved away. Its box trail had wooden-spoke wheels for drawing by horses, which were later replaced by steel disk-wheels with rubber tires. The barrel was 885 mm (35.4 in.) in length. The gun weighed 570 kg (1,254 lb.) and fired a 5.5-kg (12-lb.) shell a maximum of 3,495 meters (3,845 yd.).

After May 1944 the infantry possessed the new Krupp 7.5-cm (75-mm) Model 37 infantry gun (Infanteriegeschütz). This weapon had a horizontally sliding breechblock and a split trail with tubular spars. The barrel was 1,798 mm (6 ft.) in length; its range with the same ammunition used by the Model 18 was 5,150 meters (5,665 yd.). With hollow-charge shells it could be used in antitank combat.

The standard German artillery piece was the 10.5-cm (105-mm) Model 18 light field howitzer, which was developed between 1929 and 1932 by Rheinmetall. After 1935 it replaced its precursor, the Model 16, remaining in use

20-MM QUADRUPLE ANTIAIRCRAFT GUN.   A 20-mm quadruple antiaircraft gun mounted on an eight-ton half-track tractor (Zugmaschine, SdKfz 7/1).

GERMAN 8.8-CM (88-MM) GUN.   IMPERIAL WAR MUSEUM

until 1945. It weighed 1,985 kg (4,367 lb.). The barrel, 2,941 mm (9.8 ft.) in length, had a horizontally sliding breechblock. The howitzer had a split trail with hinged spades. It was outfitted first with wooden-spoked wheels, then with pressed metal ones. It used 50 different types of ammunition, including hollow-charge shells for antitank combat. Its maximum range was 10,675 meters (11,743 yd.).

The 10-cm (100-mm) Model 18 heavy gun was developed jointly by Krupp (the carriage) and Rheinmetall (the gun) between 1926 and 1930. It was supplied to the troops in 1934. The barrel, 5,460 mm (18.2 ft.) in length, had a horizontally sliding breechblock. The gun carriage had a split trail. Its maximum range was 19,075 meters (20,983 yd.).

The counterpart to this heavy gun was the 15-cm (150-mm) Model 18 heavy field howitzer, also developed jointly by Krupp and Rheinmetall in the same years. This weapon weighed 5,412 kg (11,906 lb.). The barrel was 4,440 mm (14.8 ft.) in length and had a horizontally sliding breechblock. Its maximum range was 13,325 meters (14,658 yd.). Both weapons saw use into

1945.

The 17-cm (170-mm) Model 18 gun mounted on a howitzer carriage, along with the 21-cm (210-mm) Model 18 mortar, was the backbone of the Wehrmacht's heavy artillery. Given to troops in 1941, the 17-cm gun was the only new artillery piece introduced to troops during the war. This "mortar" (Mörser)—an old-fashioned term for howitzer—was developed by Krupp and produced both by that firm and by Hanomag. Ready to fire, it weighed 17,525 kg (38,555 lb.); limbered, 23,375 kg (51,425 lb.). The barrel was 8,530 mm (28.4 ft.) in length and had a horizontally sliding breechblock. The box carriage had a dual recoil system; after firing, the barrel recoiled in the cradle, and then the top carriage recoiled on the whole mounting. The undercarriage rested on a platform, allowing the gun to be traversed through 360 degrees. Its maximum range was 31,000 meters (34,100 yd.).

The 21-cm (210-mm) mortar, also built by Krupp, was introduced in the field in 1939. Its carriage was similar to that of the 17-cm gun, but the mortar could elevate its barrel up to 70 degrees. It weighed 16,700 kg (36,740 lb.) when fired. The barrel was 6,510 mm (21.7 ft.) in length and had a horizontally sliding breechblock. The weapon had a maximum range of 16,700 meters (18,370 yd.). Because its effectiveness seemed too modest for its cost, production was halted in 1942.

There is no need here to discuss the recoilless light guns, such as the 10.5-cm (105-mm) Model 40 gun ("Olpe"), since this weapon, developed for the parachute troops, was numerically insignificant.

The 21-cm (210-mm) Model 38 gun was a masterpiece of modern arms technology. Developed by Krupp, the weapon weighed 25,435 kg (55,957 lb.) when fired and 34,825 kg (76,615 lb.) limbered. The carriage was an improved version of that used for the 21-cm mortar and 17-cm gun, in that it could be raised and lowered without a hoist. The barrel, 11,635 mm (38.8 ft.) in length, had a horizontally sliding breechblock. Its maximum range was 33,900 meters (37,290 yd.). Despite its effectiveness, this weapon was also too expensive to produce; only ten guns were issued, and two of these were deployed to combat the Allied landings in Normandy.

The Wehrmacht in 1944 had no artillery units as large as a division. The matériel described was organized in artillery regiments, which were part of their respective divisions. These regiments consisted of two or three artillery detachments that were themselves divided into batteries. Because all artillery models described up to 17 cm (170 mm) inclusive could be pulled by horses if necessary, the artillery regiments of nonmotorized infantry divisions continued to have a considerable number of horse-drawn batteries. The artillery regiments of motorized infantry divisions had motorized batteries. The artillery regiments of armored divisions had armored artillery detachments with batteries equipped with self-propelled carriages. As replacements for heavy artillery, after 1943 infantry divisions were given an assault gun battalion, which will not be discussed here.

"Wespe" (Wasp) was a weapons system in which the 10.5-cm (105-mm) Model 18 light field howitzer was installed on the undercarriage of the Panzer II tank. Developed in 1942 by Alkett, "Wespe" carried 32 rounds. The Panzer Howitzer Hummel, also developed by Alkett, consisted of the undercarriage of the Panzer III, on which was mounted the 15-cm (150-mm) heavy field howitzer Model 18/1, a variant of the previously mentioned howitzer. The Hummel carried only 18 rounds.

To prepare for the expected Allied landing, rocket launcher batteries (*Werferbatterien*) were relocated to France in the spring of 1944. These units were equipped with the so-called "smoke projector" (*Nebelwerfer*), which was simply a code name for a launcher of unguided solid-fuel rockets. A "smoke troop" (*Nebeltruppe*) constituted a

heavy attack or defense force within a corps or army. In 1944 they were equipped with the 15-cm (150-mm) Model 41 rocket launcher (Nebelwerfer 41), an assembly of six smoothbore barrels, 1,300 mm (4.3 ft.) in length, mounted on the split trail of the 3.7-cm (37-mm) antitank gun. From this launcher six projectiles, 158.5 mm (6.3 in.) in caliber and each weighing 34.2 kg (75.2 lb.), could be fired 6,900 meters (7,590 yd.) within 10 seconds. The solid-fuel projectiles were stabilized by rotation imparted by diagonally placed gas exhaust nozzles. A 15-cm (150-mm) rocket launcher unit could fire 108 projectiles in 10 seconds. The 21-cm (210-mm) Model 42 rocket launcher had only five barrels, but fired a projectile of 21-cm (210-mm) caliber, weighing 110 kg (242 lb.), a distance of 7,850 meters (8,635 yd.). The trail was the same as for the 15-cm launcher. The Model 41 heavy launcher (Schweres Wurfgerät 41), of simple steel-frame construction, fired a 28-cm (280-mm) high-explosive shell weighing 82 kg (180.4 lb.), of which 50 kg (110 lb.) were explosives, a distance of 1,925 meters (2,118 yd.). Thus in 30 seconds a rocket launcher unit could land 24,000 kg (52,800 lb.) of explosives in a tight pattern. The 32-cm (320-mm) flame projectile (*Wurfkörper Flamm*) could be fired from the same equipment and also from its packing case (though with less accuracy) a distance of 2,200 meters (2,420 yd.). This projectile weighed 79 kg (174 lb.) and contained 40 kg (88 lb.) of incendiary fluid.

The German forces on 6 June 1944 also had a variety of other weapons that were effective against aircraft and tanks. Army and Luftwaffe antiaircraft weapons (*Flugabwehrkanone,* or *Flak*) were used in ground combat and

CAPTURED GERMAN ANTITANK WEAPONS.   A British sergeant holds a Panzerfaust 30 (left) and a Panzerfaust 60 (right). An 8.8-cm (88-mm) Model 54 rocket launcher (*Panzerschreck*) is in the left foreground. In the right foreground are grenades and Teller mines.   IMPERIAL WAR MUSEUM

against tanks as well as planes. There were fewer different models than was the case with artillery pieces, but in sheer numbers they were the most numerous Wehrmacht weapon.

The standard light antiaircraft gun was the 2-cm (20-mm) weapon. The basic model was the Model 30 2-cm antiaircraft gun, a recoil-loader with rocking-lever bolt action, which was developed in Switzerland in the late 1920s and early 1930s by Rheinmetall-Borsig in collaboration with Oerlikon. In 1939 an improved variant, the 2-cm (20-mm) Model 38 antiaircraft gun ("Erika"), was produced. Its barrel length was 1,300 mm (4.3 ft.) and its theoretical rate of firing was 420–480 shots per minute. With a muzzle velocity of 830–900 meters per second (913–990 yd./sec.), a cartridge would reach a maximum distance of 4,800 meters (5,280 yd.) and a maximum ceiling of 3,800 meters (4,180 yd.). The ammunition was loaded in magazines that contained 20 cartridges. The weapon rested on a three-legged platform and had a swivel compass of 360 degrees. The entire weapon, which weighed 406 kg (893 lb.), was transported on a special two-wheeled trailer from which it could also be fired. The gun could also be mounted on trucks, self-propelled gun carriages, chain-driven vehicles, railroad cars, or even buildings.

In 1940 four 2-cm (20-mm) Model 38 antiaircraft guns were mounted together on one carriage to create the 2-cm Flakvierling 38, thereby nearly quadrupling the rate of fire. This carriage consisted of a swivel attached to a triangular base on which was mounted the rotating upper chassis. The weapon, which weighed 1,509 kg (3,320 lb.), was moved on a special two-wheeled trailer, but it could also be positioned on vehicles or buildings. This gun first saw action in late 1943 mounted on the chassis of the Panzer IV to form the self-propelled weapons "Möbelwagen" and "Wirbelwind." The 2-cm guns were outfitted with artillery shields. To attack armored targets, they used armor-piercing explosive shells or hard-core shot.

The 3.7-cm (37-mm) Model 36 and Model 37 antiaircraft gun ("Westerwald") was developed in 1938 by Rheinmetall from the precursor 3.7-cm (37-mm) Model 18 as a recoil-loader with sliding barrel and central bolt action. The barrel was 2,112.2 mm (7 ft.) long; the theoretical rate of fire was 160 shots per minute and the effective rate 80. Depending on the type of cartridge used, the muzzle velocity was 770–820 meters per second (847–902 yd./sec.). The maximum range was 6,600 meters (7,260 yd.), and the maximum ceiling 4,800 meters (5,280 yd.). The ammunition was in 6-round clips. The weapon's carriage stood on a triangular base. Weighing 1,544 kg (3,397 lb.), the gun could be moved on the Model 52 trailer. The Model 37 was differentiat-

ed from its precursors by its aiming sight. The 3.7-cm gun could also be installed on vehicles and buildings. After 1944 it saw action with the self-propelled antiaircraft weapon "Ostwind," on the chassis of the Panzer IV.

The 3.7-cm (37-mm) Model 43 antiaircraft gun ("Schwarzwald"), developed in 1943 by Rheinmetall-Borsig, was a gas-pressure recoil-loader with the same ballistic characteristics as the Models 36 and 37. Its rate of fire, however, was higher: 250 shots per minute theoretically and 150 effectively. In ground combat all 3.7-cm weapons used artillery shields. Firing antitank shells, they could pierce 37-mm (1.5-in.) steel armor at 500 meters (550 yd.).

Probably the most legendary artillery piece in the Wehrmacht was the 8.8-cm (88-mm) antiaircraft gun, Models 18, 36, and 37, which were also deployed to great effect against tanks. The gun was developed in the late 1920s and early 1930s by Krupp engineers in collaboration with the Swedish Bofors firm. It was introduced to the troops in 1933 as Model 18; Models 36 and 37 came in 1939. The carriage consisted of a cruciform platform resting on two two-wheeled trails, the Special Trailer 201. Before firing, the weapon had to be emplaced. The actual pedestal rested on the baseplate, which permitted a swivel compass of 360 degrees. The barrel was 4,930 mm (16.4 ft.) in length. It had a semiautomatic, horizontally sliding breechblock. With a muzzle velocity of 820–840 meters per second (902–924 yd./sec.), depending on the type of cartridge used, the gun's maximum range was 14,860 meters (16,346 yd.) and its maximum ceiling 9,900 meters (10,890 yd.), although the maximum effective ceiling was 8,000 meters (8,800 yd.). The rate of fire was 15 shots per minute. The choice of ammunition depended upon the type of engagement, but at 1,000 meters (1,100 yd.) at an angle of impact of 60 degrees, hard-core shot could pierce armor 103 mm (4 in.) thick. Contributing greatly to the effectiveness of the 8.8-cm gun, which weighed 4,985 kg (10,967 lb.), were such special equipment as fuze setters, devices to facilitate loading at high elevations, and data transmission equipment for ballistic calculations. The 8.8-cm Model 18 gun was also mounted on the chassis of the Panzer IV after early 1944, creating the "Nashorn" (Rhinoceros) antitank gun. In 1943 the troops received a more effective variant in the 8.8-cm (88-mm) Model 41 antiaircraft gun. With a barrel 6,545 mm (21.8 ft.) in length, it had a range of 19,735 meters (21,709 yd.), a maximum ceiling of 15,000 meters (16,500 yd.), and a maximum effective ceiling of 10,675 meters (11,743 yd.).

The most important antitank guns deployed in 1944 were the 5-cm (50-mm) PAK (*Panzerabwehrkanone*) 38, the 7.5-cm (75-mm) PAK 40, and the 8.8-cm (88-mm)

CORRIGENDUM

Due to an error in electronic data transmission, there is a duplication of text from page 78 to page 80.
Please note that the end of page 77 continues at the top of the second column of page 80.
The following material should be inserted between page 84 and page 85.

PAK 40. The 5-cm gun, developed by Rheinmetall, was given to the troops in 1940. It had a barrel 3,187 mm (10.6 ft.) in length with semiautomatic horizontally sliding breechblock. The gun had a split trail with tubular spars. Although production was halted in 1943, the weapon was used until 1945.

The 7.5-cm (75-mm) Model 40 antitank gun ("Hünengrab"), also developed by Rheinmetall, was given to troops in 1942. With 23,303 such guns produced between 1942 and 1945, it was the most numerous weapon of its type. It was also used as a field gun in divisional artillery in large units. The barrel was 3,450 mm (11.5 ft.) in length and had a semiautomatic horizontally sliding breechblock. Like the 5-cm gun, it had a split trail and a double artillery shield. Its maximum armor-piercing capability was 91 mm (3.6 in.) of steel at 500 meters (550 yd.) and 80 mm (3.2 in.) at 1,000 meters (1,100 yd.). With improved ammunition, these numbers could be increased to 108 or 87 mm (4.3 or 3.5 in.) respectively. With hollow-charge projectiles, 90 mm (3.6 in.) of armor could be penetrated at any combat distance to a maximum of 1,800 meters (1,980 yd.). The 8.8-cm (88-mm) PAK 43 ("Neuntöter") was developed by Krupp; it was introduced to the troops in large numbers in 1944. The carriage rested on a cruci-form platform, but was lower than that of the similar 8.8-cm Model 18 antiaircraft gun. The barrel was 6,280 mm (20.9 ft.) in length, with a drop breech mechanism. This gun also fired cartridges. Depending on the type of ammunition used, the gun's maximum penetration capability was 274 mm (11 in.) of armor at 500 meters (550 yd.) and 241 mm (9.6 in.) at 1,000 meters (1,100 yd.). Its maximum range was 17,500 meters (19,250 yd.).

In 1943 new types of antitank weaponry came to the front. With hollow-charge rounds, which were available up to a caliber of 17 cm, the armor piercing no longer depended on the kinetic energy of the projectile's mass, but rather on the peculiar physical characteristics of the explosive detonated. This permitted effective attacks against targets to the outer limits of the weapon's range. Hollow-charge cartridges were also used with the close-range antitank weapons introduced after 1943. In technical terms these were simple, unguided solid-fuel projectiles that carried a hollow-charge round to its target at relatively close range. Analogous to the *Nebelwerfer* rounds, these rockets were fired using primitive and cheaply produced launchers. American bazookas captured in Tunisia provided the basis for the development in 1943 of the similar 8.8-cm (88-mm) Model 54 rocket launcher known as the *Panzerschreck*. The weapon was a thin metal barrel 1,640 mm (5.5 ft.) in length, with a small metal shield as flame protector for the gunner. The weapon fired a rocket projectile of which there were several 3.3-kg (7.3-lb.) varieties. The maximum range was 180 meters (198 yd.), with the hollow charge capable of piercing 160 mm (6.4 in.) of armor with an angle of impact of 60 degrees. The weapon required two gunners and, because of a three-meter-long rear jet of flame, was dangerous. The *Panzerschreck* saw action in Normandy in June 1944.

A little later what were probably the first disposable antitank launchers (*Panzerfäuste,* or "Armored Fists") were introduced in Normandy. In mid-1944 the Model 30 Panzerfaust was put in the field. A hollow-charge shell with solid-fuel propellant was fired from a simple 44-mm (1.8-in.) diameter tube. Weighing 2.9 kg (6.4 lb.), the shell could pierce 200 mm (8 in.) of armor at 30 meters (33 yd.). The Panzerfaust 30 was 1,045 mm (3.5 ft.) in length and weighed 5.1 kg (11.2 lb.).

BIBLIOGRAPHY

Hahn, Fritz. *Waffen und Geheimwaffen des deutschen Heeres, 1935–1945.* 2d ed. Vol. 1, *Infanteriewaffen, Pionierwaffen, Artilleriewaffen, Pulver-, Spreng- und Kampfstoffe.* Vol. 2, *Panzer- und Sonderfahrzeuge, "Wunderwaffen", Verbrauch und Verluste.* 1992.

Hogg, Ian. *Deutsche Artilleriewaffen im Zweiten Weltkrieg.* 1978.

Kosar, Franz. *Infanteriegeschütze und rückstrossfreie Leichtgeschütze, 1915–1978.* 1979.

Kosar, Franz. *Panzerabwehrkanonen, 1916–1977.* 1978.

Müller, Werner. *Die leichte und mittlere Flak 1906–1945, eingesetzt bei den Waffengattungen an allen Fronten.* 1990.

HEINRICH WALLE
Translated from German by Amy Hackett

ASSAULT FORCE O. *See* Task Force 124.

ASSAULT FORCE U. *See* Task Force 125.

ASSAULT SHIPS.

The assault ships used in the Normandy landings were almost all merchantmen of various sizes converted to carry troops and their equipment, which they unloaded over the side into small landing craft carried aboard. These ships were designated LSI (Landing Ships, Infantry) by the British, and APA (Attack Transports) by the Americans. The command and communications role was carried out by units designated LSH (Landing Ship, Headquarters) by the Royal Navy (RN), and AGC (Command Ship) by the U.S. Navy (USN). Only two purposely built LSDs (Landing Ships, Dock) were deployed, and these were used to provide repair support for landing craft. Most assault ships were British, some of them commissioned RN vessels, others merchant vessels manned and operated by the Ministry of War Transport (MOWT). They were supplemented by ten large USN transports, an American headquarters vessel, and two Canadian medium LSIs. The assault ships were as follows:

Landing Ships, Infantry (Large)—LSI (L)

HMS *Glenroy* and *Glenearn*: 9,800 gross register tons (GRT); 18-knot cargo liners built in 1938–1939 and taken over by the RN as fast transports on the outbreak of war; converted to LSI(L)s in 1941. They could carry about 1,100 troops and were each equipped with 24 LCAs (Landing Craft, Assault).

SS *Empire Anvil*, Empire Arquebus, Empire Battleaxe, Empire Broadsword, Empire Crossbow, Empire Cutlass, Empire Gauntlet*, Empire Halberd, Empire Javelin*, Empire Lance, Empire Mace, Empire Rapier,* and *Empire Spearhead*: 6,711–7,080 GRT; built in the United States to U.S. Maritime Commission type C1-S-AY1 in 1943 and supplied under the Lend-Lease Act for operation by MOWT; 14 knots; 900–1,450 troops; 18 LCAs. (Asterisk indicates that those carrying American troops carried two extra landing craft, probably LCMs [Landing Craft, Mechanized].)

SS *Clan Lamont*: 7,250 GRT; built 1939, converted 1945; 14 knots; 800 troops, 17 LCAs.

SS *Monowai*: 10,852 GRT; built 1924, commissioned as an armed merchant cruiser 1940, converted to troopship 1943, and to LSI(L) 1944; 19 LCAs.

MV *Llangibby Castle*: 11,951 GRT; built 1929, diesel-powered; 20 LCAs.

Attack Transports—APA

(Unless otherwise stated, standard load about 1,400 troops, 26 LCVPs [Landing Craft, Vehicle and Personnel], and 2 LCMs.)

USS *Joseph T. Dickman* (APA13): 13,869 tons standard; built 1921, former transatlantic liner *President Roosevelt,* commissioned USN 1941; 17 knots; about 1,750 troops, 33 LCVPs.

USS *Samuel Chase* (APA26): 10,812 tons standard; built 1941, Maritime Commission C3P cargo liner, commissioned USN 1942; 18 knots.

USS *Thomas Jefferson* (APA30): 10,210 tons standard; built 1940, Maritime Commission C3A cargo liner; commissioned USN 1942; 18 knots.

USS *Barnett* (APA5): 9,432 tons standard; British-built in 1928 as liner *Santa Maria,* commissioned USN 1940; 15 knots.

USS *Charles Carroll* (APA28): 8,409 tons standard; built and commissioned 1942, Maritime Commission C3D cargo liner; 16 knots.

USS *Bayfield* (APA33) and *Henrico* (APA45): 7,845 tons standard; Maritime Commission C3S-type ships built and commissioned USN 1942; 18 knots. *Bayfield* used as command ship, Force U (Task Force 125).

Transports—AP (fitted with LCVP for use as Assault Transports)

USS *Dorothea L. Dix* (AP67): 6,736 tons standard; built 1940, commissioned USN 1942; 16 knots.

USS *Thurston* (AP77): 6,131 tons standard; built 1941, commissioned USN 1942; 16.5 knots.

USS *Anne Arundel* (AP76): 7,500 tons standard; built 1940, commissioned USN 1942; 18 knots.

Landing Ships, Infantry (Medium)—LSI (M)

HMS *Queen Emma*: 4,136 GRT; former Dutch passenger ferry, built 1939; diesel-powered, 23 knots; 372 troops; 6 LCAs, 2 LCMs.

HMCS *Prince David* and *Prince Henry*: 6,890 GRT; former armed merchant cruisers, built 1930, commissioned 1940, and converted 1943; 22 knots; 538 troops, 6 LCAs, 2 LCMs.

Landing Ships, Infantry (Small)—LSI (S) (Asterisk indicates that craft was used to carry American troops in the Assault Groups for Omaha [TF 124] and Utah [TF 125].)

HMS *Prince Charles**, *Prince Leopold**, *Princess Astrid*, *Princess Josephine Charlotte*: 2,950 GRT; former Belgian Channel ferries, built 1929–1930 and converted 1941; 24 knots; 250 troops, 8 LCAs.

HMS *Prince Baudouin**: 3,219 GRT; former Belgian Channel ferry, built 1933 and converted 1942; diesel-powered, 23 knots; 196 troops, 8 LCAs.

Landing Ships, Infantry (Hand)—LSI (H) (Channel and Irish Sea ferries with simple hand-operated davits; 400–485 troops and 6 LCAs, except where stated. Asterisk indicates that craft was used to carry American troops in Force O4.)

HMS *St. Helier*: 1,952 GRT; built 1925, converted 1942; 18 knots (coal-burning).

HMS *Brigadier*: 2,294 GRT; built 1928, converted 1942; 21 knots.

HMS *Ulster Monarch*: 3,791 GRT; built 1929, converted 1942; diesel-powered, 18 knots; 580 troops, 5 LCAs.

HMS *Duke of Wellington*: 3,743 GRT; built 1935, converted 1942; 21 knots (coal-burning).

HMS *Royal Ulsterman*: 3,244 GRT; built 1936, converted 1942; diesel-powered, 16 knots. Used as the headquarters ship of Amphibious Group J3.

HMS *Invicta*: 4,178 GRT; built 1939 and taken over

LCVP. Landing Craft, Vehicle and Personnel, from USS *Thomas Jefferson*.

while building; 22 knots (coal-fired).

SS *Amsterdam**: 4,220 GRT; built 1930. SS *Princess Margaret*: 2,552 GRT; built 1931. SS *Lairds Isle*: 1,929 GRT; built 1911. SS *Isle of Thanet*: 2,701 GRT; built 1925. SS *Isle of Guernsey*: 2,143 GRT; built 1925. SS *Canterbury*: 2,910 GRT; built 1929. SS *Duke of Argyll*: 3,814 GRT; built 1928. SS *Mecklenburg*: 2,907 GRT; built 1922. SS *Biarritz*: 2,388 GRT; built 1915. SS *Lady of Man*: 3,104 GRT; built 1930. SS *Ben-My-Chree**: 2,586 GRT; built 1927. SS *Maid of Orleans*: 2,386 GRT; built 1918. SS *Princess Maud**: 2,883 GRT; built 1934. SS *Victoria*: 1,641 GRT; built 1907.

Landing Ships, Dock—LSD

HMS *Northway* and *Oceanway*: 4,270 tons light, 7,930 tons ballasted; launched 1943 at Newport News, Va., and transferred under Lend-Lease; a British concept of a fast (16-knot) floating dry dock; capacity 36 LCMs or 2 to 3 large LCTs. *Northway* was used as a landing craft repair ship off Juno Beach, *Oceanway* off Omaha Beach.

Landing Ships, Emergency Repair—LSE

In addition to converted tank landing ships, the former minelayer HMS *Adventure* (6,740 tons standard, commissioned 1927, converted to LSE 1944) and the former seaplane carrier HMS *Albatross* (4,800 tons standard, commissioned Royal Australian Navy 1929, transferred RN 1938, converted to LSE 1943) were deployed off Normandy.

Landing Ships, Headquarters, Large—LSH (L)

HMS *Bulolo*: 6,257 GRT; built 1938, commissioned as armed merchant cruiser 1940, and converted 1942; 15 knots; Task Force G.

HMS *Hilary*: 7,403 GRT; built 1931, commissioned as ocean boarding vessel 1940, and converted 1943; 14 knots; Task Force J.

HMS *Largs*: 4,504 GRT; built 1938, commissioned as ocean boarding vessel 1940, and converted 1942; 17 knots; Task Force S.

Command Ship—AGC

USS *Ancon* (AGC4): 6,812 tons standard; built 1938, commissioned as transport (AP66) in 1942, and converted 1943; 18 knots; Force O (Task Force 124).

Landing Ships, Headquarters (Small)—LSH(S)

These were converted warships, the 625-ton standard former river gunboat HMS *Locust*, completed in 1940 (with Amphibious Group S), and the following RN escort ships (amphibious groups commanded by the LSHs are in parentheses):

Type III Hunt-class escort destroyers: *Albrighton* (G1) and *Goathland* (S3).

River-class frigates: *Nith* (G1) and *Waveney* (J2).

Captain-class frigates (Lend-Lease GMT DEs): *Dacres* (S2), *Kingsmill* (G2), and *Lawford* (J1).

[*See also* Escort Ships *and articles on ships and task forces mentioned herein.*]

BIBLIOGRAPHY

Conway's All the World's Fighting Ships, 1922–1946. 1980.
Dictionary of American Naval Fighting Ships, vols. 1–8. 1959–1991.
Lenton, H. T., and J. J. Colledge. *Warships of World War Two.* 1964.

ERIC J. GROVE

ASSAULT TRAINING. *See* Amphibious Assault Training.

ASSOCIATIONS AND ORGANIZATIONS.

[*The following entry includes three articles:*
D-day and Normandy Fellowship
Normandy Foundation
Normandy Veterans' Association.]

D-Day and Normandy Fellowship

The D-Day Fellowship was formed in England in 1968 to raise money to complete Portsmouth Cathedral as a memorial to the invasion, since it was from Portsmouth Naval Command that the operation was launched. Although the scheme ran into difficulties and had to be abandoned, the Fellowship survived as the D-Day and Normandy Fellowship, with Field Marshal Montgomery as its patron.

The aims of the Fellowship are described in its leaflet: "(1) To foster understanding between all who were involved, whether in the Services, Civilians or their families and those who may be interested. (2) To meet together from time to time for special events and social functions."

Membership is open to men and women of the Allied forces and merchant navies that were engaged from D-day until the end of the Battle of Normandy, to their relatives, and to anyone else associated with or interested in the events of June–August 1944. Life membership costs a minimum of £10. There are over 2,000 members from all services and several countries, notably, the United Kingdom, the United States, Australia, Canada, Greece, and the Netherlands. There are thirty corporate members such as regiments, regimental associations, and naval establishments.

Members receive a tie and a badge, both of which incorporate the emblem of SHAEF. A service is held in the cathedral each year for members, their relatives, and friends. There is also an annual function commemorating the D-day anniversary.

Their address is 9 South Parade, Southsea, Portsmouth, Hampshire P05 2JB, England.

ALAN HANKINSON

Normandy Foundation

The Battle of Normandy Foundation was formed in 1985 to promote in the United States a greater understanding of the causes, events, and effects of World War II. The foundation is guided by a board of directors and a board of trustees that include business, academic, political, and military leaders, and is advised by a board of military historians and a group of war correspondents. It has approximately 45,000 members. The foundation is solely dependent on private donations for its activities and has received the endorsement of the president and the Congress of the United States.

The foundation supports numerous projects. Its first undertaking was to help build the Battle of Normandy Memorial Museum at Caen, which is located directly above the underground German headquarters. Working with French, British, and other authorities, it helped to plan and build the large modern teaching museum in Normandy known as Le Mémorial, which tells the story of World War II in films, recordings, photographs, and artifacts.

Le Mémorial is closely associated with the University of Caen and is becoming an education and research center for scholars from around the world. Nearby the twelfth-century Abbaye d'Ardennes and its outbuildings are being reconstructed to create the United States Campus in Normandy. This will allow students to live and study at the Abbaye as well as at Le Mémorial and allow the expansion of the Normandy Scholar Program. Sponsored by the foundation, and with students from the University of Texas at Austin, Texas A & M University, and the University of Tennessee, it is expected to grow to some 2,500 students from universities throughout the United States.

Another project of the foundation, in cooperation with the "50th Anniversary Commission of D-day, the Battle of Normandy and Liberation of Europe," as well as with the French government, is to create a traveling exhibit, The Freedom Tour, which will visit cities in the United States to commemorate the achievement of veterans and to give a better understanding of the meaning of war to the American people and to tomorrow's leaders.

The United States Armed Forces Memorial in Normandy, adjacent to Le Mémorial Museum, is expected to be built by the spring of 1994. The foundation was named by the U.S. Congress's 50th Anniversary Commission for D-day to be its planning and executive arm. The Battle of Normandy Foundation's Executive Offices are at 1730 Rhode Island Avenue, N.W., Washington, D.C., 20036.

BIBLIOGRAPHY

Congressional Record. Vol. 132, no. 136, 6 October 1986.
The Fiftieth Anniversary Commission. D-Day: The Battle of Normandy and the Liberation of Europe. 1992. Pamphlet.

JAMES LAWTON COLLINS, JR.

The Normandy Veterans' Association

The association was launched in England in April 1981. Arthur Flodman, who landed in Normandy with the Durham Light Infantry, put a paragraph in the local papers of Cleethorpes and Grimsby, inviting veterans who had served in the campaign to attend a meeting in Grimsby. Twenty-nine people turned up and the association began. In the summer of 1985, with thirty-five branches in the United Kingdom, Flodman decided to form a national organization. At a meeting in London, Gen. John Mogg, who had been Flodman's commanding officer on D-day, was installed as national president. Flodman became general secretary but died only a few weeks later.

The aims of the association are: to encourage the 1944 spirit of comradeship; to promote contacts between old comrades by branch meetings, reunion dinners, and annual conferences; to organize trips; and to give practical help to members, or to the dependents of deceased members, who are in need.

By 1992 the association had eighty-five branches, most in the United Kingdom, but some also in Australia, New Zealand, Nova Scotia, Belgium, and France.

Local branches run their own affairs and organize pilgrimages to Normandy. Each branch sends an annual levy, based on the number of members it has, to the National Council, which meets three times a year and runs the annual general meeting. Their address is 53 Normandy Rd., Cleethorpes, South Humberside DN35 9JE, England.

ALAN HANKINSON

ATLANTIC WALL. Up until the end of 1941 the only German fortifications along the French Atlantic coast had been seven heavy coastal batteries between Boulogne and Calais. These had been constructed for bombardment of England during preparations for Operation SEELÖWE (SEA LION), the planned invasion of England. In addition to these emplacements there were a few naval coastal batteries and fortified U-boat pens. After the cancellation of SEA LION, Hitler directed Organization Todt, then under

ATLANTIC WALL.   Steel bars were inserted into the wall and barbed wire was affixed to them.

HULTON DEUTSCH

CASEMATED GUN.   Near Utah Beach.

NATIONAL ARCHIVES

GERMAN BLOCKHOUSE. IMPERIAL WAR MUSEUM

Dr. Fritz Todt, to continue construction of U-boat pens and fortify the French Atlantic coast, especially at Brest, Lorient, and Saint-Nazaire, absorbing most of the labor and matériel available to the organization for fortifications in the West. In September 1941 Field Marshal Erwin von Witzleben, Commander in Chief West, proposed to the Wehrmacht High Command that the army begin work on permanent defenses along the Atlantic coast. In December 1941 Witzleben ordered his command to begin a reconnaissance of defense sites along the coast as a first step toward construction. This was all that could be done at that time because of the shortage of labor and matériel. Then, early in March 1942, Hitler replaced Witzleben with Field Marshal Gerd von Rundstedt. On 23 March Hitler issued his basic order for a defense of the Atlantic and Channel coasts. Wehrmacht High Command (Oberkommando der Wehrmacht—OKW) now had responsibility for this task, while the Army High Command (Oberkommando des Heeres—OKH) had sole responsibility for operations on the Eastern front. In his directive to the OKW, Hitler ordered that the coastal defenses be so organized and troops so deployed that any Allied invasion be halted on the coast or shortly thereafter.

In the summer of 1942 Hitler estimated that ten to twelve additional divisions would be needed for the main defenses in areas considered most suitable for large-scale Allied landing. Those beaches where only small-scale surprise landings were possible were to be defended only by strong points tied in, if possible, with existing coastal batteries. The rest of the coastline would be covered by army patrols.

As a result of the High Command's admission that the

elastic defense principles applied so successfully by the Russians on their vast territories could not be adopted in the West, Hitler decided to expand his notion of an Atlantic Wall. In September 1942 he ordered a fortification along the French coast similar to the West Wall, or Siegfried Line, along the Franco-German frontier. This new wall would consist of 15,000 concrete strong points manned by 300,000 men. Concrete pens for U-boats were to be built first. Then harbors suitable for Allied landings would be fortified, then the Channel Islands, and finally those beaches on the open coast most likely to be used in a major invasion.

During the coming winter, coastal fortress construction in France was to proceed, said Hitler, with "fanatic energy." His object was to build many small concrete strong points, housing thirty to seventy men each armed with machine guns and antiaircraft weapons. Hitler himself designed many of these strong points. The intervening ground would be covered by a continuous belt of interlocking fire from these structures, which were also designed to withstand air bombardment and naval shelling.

Hitler ordered that these tasks be completed by 1 May 1943. Albert Speer, now head of Organization Todt following Dr. Todt's death, thought that he would be lucky to get 40 percent of the defenses finished by that time. Even though the Wehrmacht High Command believed the Channel coast to be the most likely place for major Allied landings, defenses in this area were not completed before the Allies attacked.

In spite of this, Hitler assigned construction priority to those portions of the Atlantic Wall defending rocket-launching areas. Although the strongest fortified portion of the French coast never became anything like the impregnable fortress that Hitler desired, he nevertheless believed it to be so. As a matter of fact, he never inspected any portion of the Atlantic Wall, nor set foot again on French soil until June 1944, a week after D-day. Hitler declared that the German armies in the West must hold the Atlantic Wall when attacked. This was also Field Marshal Erwin Rommel's view, for he believed that the battle for France would be decided in front of the coastal defense zone. (In November 1943 Rommel, under the nominal command of Field Marshal Gerd von Rundstedt, had been selected by Hitler to speed up completion of the coastal defenses, and to command the initial resistance in case of an Allied landing.)

On the eve of D-day there was a maximum of seventy-three large-caliber guns located in fixed concrete emplacements and capable of firing on an Allied attack. Rommel had ordered that mines and other obstacles be laid so thickly as to prevent any enemy penetrations. As the expected invasion season drew near, Rommel, because of shortages of labor and matériel, was compelled to concentrate on numerous field-type defenses, emphasizing mines, rather than on a few complex fortifications.

In late 1943 Rundstedt, whose tactics differed sharply from those of Rommel, had ordered a so-called *Zweite Stellung,* or second position, to be built a few kilometers from the coast in order to give the earlier coastal defenses some depth. This was in addition to the staking of open fields in the interior to deter glider and parachute landings. But in April 1944 Rommel ordered all work halted on the *Zweite Stellung,* preferring to concentrate on coastal defenses. But of the minimum of 50 million mines needed for a continuous defense along the coast, only 5 million had been emplaced by D-day.

Shortly before the Allied invasion on the east coast of the Cotentin Peninsula, strong points and resistance nests were spaced about 800 meters apart, but between there and the Orne and Vire rivers they were about 1,800 meters apart. Most of these were field fortifications, sometimes with concrete troop shelters and casemated guns. By D-day, however, these were far from complete. For example, in the *352d Division*'s sector overlooking Utah Beach, only 15 percent of the coastal positions had been bombproofed; the rest remained unprotected. Because of Hitler's earlier delay in initiating it, and shortages of labor and matériel, Rommel, despite his best efforts, was unable to complete the Atlantic Wall. This undoubtedly contributed to the success of the Allied landing on D-day.

[*See also* Beach and Coastal Defenses; Organization Todt.]

BIBLIOGRAPHY

Harrison, Gordon A. *Cross-Channel Attack.* U.S. Army in World War II: The European Theater of Operations. 1951.
Irving, David. *The Trail of the Fox: The Search for the True Field Marshal Rommel.* 1977.
MacDonald, Charles B. *The Mighty Endeavor: The American War in Europe.* 1969.
Speer, Albert. *Erinnerungen.* 1969.

ERNEST F. FISHER

AUGUSTA, USS. A heavy cruiser of the Northampton class, *Augusta* was 600 feet long and 66 feet in width, and had a standard displacement of 9,050 tons. It was armed with nine 8-inch guns and eight 5-inch antiaircraft guns. Commissioned in January 1931, *Augusta* had served as a flagship throughout much of its service life, and during the Allied invasion of North Africa in November 1942 had carried the flag of the commander, Western Naval Task Force.

In the Normandy landings *Augusta* was the principal flagship—and thus a floating command post—for Rear Adm. Alan G. Kirk, commander of Task Force 122. Also on board were Lt. Gen. Omar Bradley, commanding general of the U.S. First Army; Maj. Gen. Ralph Royce, deputy commander of the U.S. Ninth Air Force; and a number of news media representatives.

In June 1944 *Augusta* carried a crew of approximately 1,100 men and was commanded by Capt. Edward H. Jones. Its primary mission was to provide accommodations and communications facilities for the embarked commanders and their staffs as the invasion force moved across the English Channel and carried out the assault on Normandy. *Augusta* departed Plymouth, England, on 5 June and steamed to within 3,000 meters of the French

USS *Augusta* in the Channel.

coast. On 6 June it participated in the preinvasion bombardment off Omaha Beach and then remained off the coast until the end of the month to provide shore bombardment and antiaircraft gunfire. The cruiser was not damaged when an enemy bomb exploded 800 yards off the port beam on the morning of 11 June. The ship shot down a German plane on 13 June and drove away several others during the days offshore.

Once the beachhead was secure, *Augusta* transferred Admiral Kirk to another ship on 1 July and proceeded to the Mediterranean. There it became the flagship of the Bombardment Support Group for the invasion of southern France in August 1944. In July 1945 it transported President Harry S. Truman and his advisers from the United States to Europe for the Potsdam Conference.

[*See also* Kirk, Alan G.]

BIBLIOGRAPHY

Brown, John Mason. *Many a Watchful Night.* 1944.
Dictionary of American Naval Fighting Ships. Vol. 1, pt. A, 1991.

PAUL STILLWELL

AUSTRALIA. Shortly before D-day Maj. Gen. Francis de Guingand was reputed to have said to General Bernard L. Montgomery, "I'd feel a lot happier if the Australian 9th Division was going ashore with us." The Australian government had withdrawn the last of its divisions, the 9th, from the Mediterranean theater early in 1943 in order to concentrate its forces against the Japanese, but as late as June 1944 there were still 11,000 Australian aircrew serving with the Royal Air Force (RAF) and in the ten squadrons designated Royal Australian Air Force (RAAF) and 1,100 officers and enlisted men of the Royal Australian Naval Volunteer Reserve (RANVR) serving with the Royal Navy.

Most of the 1,100 men of the RANVR were serving on Royal Navy ships on D-day. Several served aboard the cruisers HMS *Enterprise, Glasgow, Scylla,* and *Ajax;* on *Ajax* a RANVR officer commanded the 6-inch-gun bombardment of Langues in the British sector. In addition, Australians served aboard the destroyers HMS *Ashanti, Eskimo,* and *Mackay,* and RANVR officers commanded several of the flotillas of landing craft and motor torpedo boats.

Virtually all 11,000 Australian RAF aircrew took part in the invasion of Normandy. RAAF personnel serving either in the RAF or in RAAF squadrons were present at every phase of the operation. RAAF pilots commanded six Lancasters of the famous No. 617 Squadron in a deception operation on the night of 5–6 June that involved dropping metallic strips (code-named Window) in carefully calculated amounts to create the illusion that a vast congregation of ships was heading for the Pas de Calais area. Far-

ther west over the Bay of the Seine, RAAF pilots flew five of the Stirlings of No. 199 Squadron in an operation to jam German early warning radar. Just after midnight RAAF officers piloted forty-one transports of the ten squadrons of No. 38 Group for the drop of the British 6th Airborne Division, the RAAF providing about one in seven of the pilots.

In the preinvasion aerial bombardment of coastal fortifications culminating on 5–6 June, Australian squadrons and crews provided 168 of the 1,136 aircraft committed by Bomber Command, nearly 15 percent of the total. In the attacks on coastal batteries on 5–6 June, RAAF Lancasters flew sixty-seven missions, the majority of them against German gun emplacements on the Pointe du Hoc, the fire from which could enfilade Omaha Beach. In the week following the landings, Bomber Command carried out nearly 3,000 sorties against communication centers. RAAF bomber squadrons were heavily committed. No. 460 Squadron flew on five of the seven nights, and despatched sixty-nine missions against rail centers and thirty-eight against other targets; each of the three other RAAF heavy bomber squadrons operated on four nights. Many crews flew consecutive trips, and Flying Officer J. D. Perfrement, who began his operation tour at the beginning of June, flew ten raids in thirteen nights.

On 6 June Australian-piloted Typhoons of Nos. 121 and 247 squadrons carried out ground attack missions south of Caen, while Mosquitos of No. 464 Squadron attacked transport farther east across the Seine. Enemy antiaircraft fire was intense; three Australian Typhoons were shot down, although the pilot of one managed to make it back through German lines to the beachhead despite severe burns and a broken leg. On the same day an Australian-crewed Mosquito was brought down farther east. The navigator, Flight Lt. D. M. Shanks, survived the crash and hid out in German-occupied France until advancing Allied armies reached him toward the end of August. On 16 June he had the rare opportunity of watching one of the first German V-1 rockets take off from a ramp near his hiding place bound for Britain.

BIBLIOGRAPHY

Gill, G. Hermon. *Royal Australian Navy, 1942–1945.* 1968.
Herington, John. *Air Power over Europe, 1944–1945.* 1963.

DUNCAN ANDERSON

AUXILIARY WARSHIPS. The German Navy made much use of auxiliary warships, most of them rebuilt or specially equipped merchant ships or fishing vessels. They came from the German merchant marine, but a great number of vessels captured in the Netherlands, Belgium, and France were also used in this way. The vessels were assigned to the flotillas of the defense divisions of the commander of the Western Defense Force (Befehlshaber der Sicherung West), Rear Adm. Erich Alfred Breuning.

Mine Destruction Vessels (*Sperrbrecher*). There were two general types of *Sperrbrecher*. The first type comprised former freighters of 2,500 to 8,200 gross tons. They had a speed between 9 and 16 knots, an armament of normally two 10.5-cm guns and up to six 37-mm anti-aircraft (AA) guns in twin or single mounts and up to fourteen 20-mm AA guns in quadruple, twin, or single mounts. Some also had four to eight rocket launchers for firing wires against aircraft, and one or two barrage balloons or flamethrowers at the aft mast top. The crew averaged about 8 officers and 226 men. The vessels were numbered *Sperrbrecher 1* to *37*. They were used to escort ships and U-boats to protect them from mines in the Bay of Biscay, but not in the Channel.

The second type of *Sperrbrecher* included medium or small freighters or coasters from 1,000 to 2,500 gross tons. Their speed was 9 to 15 knots, and the armament consisted of a great variety of German and foreign weapons. On average there were one or two 10.5-cm or 8.8-cm guns, and one or two 37-mm and up to eight 20-mm AA guns. The crew included 3 to 5 officers and 60 to 111 men. These ships were used mainly in the river estuaries and off the French coast, but only to a limited extent in the Channel. They were numbered *Sperrbrecher 60* to *189* (with many gaps in the numbering).

All *Sperrbrecher* were equipped with a VES-Anlage, strong electrical equipment to form a heavy magnetic field in front of the ship so as to sweep magnetic ground mines. They also had equipment to explode acoustic mines.

The ships were organized in the *2d* and *6th Sperrbrecher* flotillas at Royan and Concarneau. In June 1944 the *2d Flotilla* had *Sperrbrecher 3, 5, 7, 16, 20, 32, 37, 122, 146, 168,* and *175,* and the *6th Flotilla* had *Sperrbrecher 1, 6, 8, 9, 19, 121, 134, 135, 157, 162,* and *180*. Of the twenty-two ships, one was decommissioned on 1 July in Brest and scuttled as a block ship. Eight were sunk by Allied aircraft off or inside the ports of the Bay of Biscay in August. One was sunk in August by the cruiser HMS *Mauritius* and the destroyers HMS *Ursa* and HMCS *Iroquois,* and another, after damage from air attack, by the Polish destroyer *Piorun*. One was lost to a mine, and ten were scuttled when the ports were evacuated, or remained in the besieged fortresses until the end of the war. These ships did not directly participate in the defense against the invasion.

Auxiliary Minesweepers. These included former French fishing trawlers of 200 to 450 gross tons; former French tugs of 100 to 250 gross tons; and a great number of former French, Belgian, and Dutch fishing luggers of 80 to 150 gross tons; and luggers (*Kriegsfischkutter,* or *KFKs*) of 150 tons built specifically for wartime service.

They were armed with a great variety of weapons, the bigger ones mostly with one 8.8-cm or 10.5-cm gun, and all vessels with 37-mm and 20-mm AA guns. Mostly they towed their minesweeping equipment, but to some extent they also had equipment for detonating acoustic mines. The number of the crew varied; most were commanded by senior noncommissioned officers.

The *2d Defense Division* had the *36th* and *38th* minesweeper (*Minensuch*) flotillas; the *3d Defense Division,* the *40th* and *46th* flotillas; and the *4th Defense Division,* the *42d* and *44th* flotillas. They had about eight to ten trawlers, a few tugs, and about twenty luggers and ten *KFKs*. The flotillas of the *2d Defense Division* were used for minesweeping and escort duties along the French and Belgian coasts from Le Havre to Ostend. *The 38th Flotilla* took great losses in the Allied air raid on Le Havre on 15–16 June. The flotillas of the *3d Defense Division* were used off the north coast of Brittany; in early June it lost two ships to mines off Brest, and more later to Allied air raids against Brest and Saint-Malo. The flotillas of the *4th Defense Division* in the Bay of Biscay suffered a few losses to mines and air attacks, but most of the vessels had to be scuttled when the ports were evacuated, or they were laid up in the besieged fortresses.

Auxiliary Patrol Boats (*Vorpostenboote*). These too consisted of former German or French fishing trawlers of 250 to 450 gross tons; some flotillas also had *KFKs*. Their armament was similar to but sometimes somewhat greater than that of the minesweepers, but without the minesweeping equipment. They too were to some extent commanded by reserve officers and senior noncommissioned officers.

The *2d Defense Division* had the *15th Patrol (Vorposten) Flotilla* at Le Havre and the *18th Flotilla* in Boulogne. The *15th Flotilla* lost *V 1509* on 6 June in an engagement with the invasion forces, and another on 12 June to a mine; nine vessels were destroyed during the Allied air raid on Le Havre on 15–16 June. The *3d Defense Division* had the *2d Patrol Flotilla* at Saint-Malo, which was later engaged in the Channel Islands area, and the *7th Patrol Flotilla* at Brest. The *4th Defense Division*'s *4th* and *6th* flotillas, at Bordeaux and Saint-Nazaire respectively, were used in the Bay of Biscay.

Auxiliary Submarine Chasers (*U-bootjäger*). These were mostly former German or French whalers of 300 to 450 gross tons, but also some newly built *Kriegs-U-Jäger,* a whaler-type vessel of 542 gross tons and 12.8 knots equipped with one 8.8-cm gun, one 37-mm and nine 20-mm AA guns, sonar, and a great load of depth charges. They had 1 officer and 60 men; the ex-civilian whalers had a smaller crew. In France there was only the *14th Flotilla* at Lorient and Saint-Nazaire. *UJ 1401* was in repair in Caen and had to be scuttled on 12 June. Most other boats were in the Bay of Biscay; two were sunk by air attacks in late June and early July, and three more in actions with Allied surface forces in July and August. The other boats were scuttled or remained in besieged French ports.

Gun Carriers (*Artillerie-Fähren*, or *AF*). These were modified *Marine-Fähr-Prähme (MFP)*, seagoing barges similar to the Allied LCTs (Landing Craft, Tank). They displaced 400 tons full load, had a maximum speed of 8.7 to 9 knots, and an armament of two 8.8-cm guns, one single-mounted 37-mm AA gun, and two quadruple-mounted 20-mm AA guns. The crew consisted of 1 or 2 officers and 47 to 51 men. The *2d Gun Carrier Flotilla* was at Boulogne, and the *6th Flotilla* in the Channel Islands. Between 6 June and 31 August 1944 they lost fourteen vessels to air attacks, ten in surface engagements, and two by mines. Three were scuttled in ports to avoid capture.

BIBLIOGRAPHY

Gröner, Erich, *Die deutschen Kriegsschiffe 1815–1945*. Edited by Dieter Jung and Martin Maass. Vol. 3, 1985; vol. 7, 1990. (Vol. 8, in preparation, covers auxiliary minesweepers, patrol boats, and submarine chasers.)

JÜRGEN ROHWER

B

BARKER, E. H. (1894–1983), British, major general, commander of the 49th (West Riding) Infantry Division. Barker entered the Royal Military College in Sandhurst, from which he graduated in 1913 with a commission in the elite King's Royal Rifle Corps (KRRC). In 1914 he fought with his regiment and as a captain held the post of battalion adjutant from February 1916 to August 1917. He was then posted to the Mediterranean theater of operations and served in the Aegean area as a staff officer until January 1918. He was promoted to brigade major, a position he held until 1919, during which time he fought in southern Russia. In the postwar years Barker held staff appointments in the War Office and in Southern Command. From 1931 to 1933, he was brigade major of the 8th Infantry Brigade before taking over command of the 2d Battalion in the KRRC in Palestine. In 1937, he brought his battalion back to the United Kingdom for conversion to a lorried infantry unit as part of the first mobile division in the British army.

In August 1938, holding the temporary rank of brigadier, Barker was given the 10th Infantry Brigade and upon the outbreak of the Second World War took it to France. When, during May and June 1940, the Allies were forced back to the beaches at Dunkirk, Barker's brigade conducted a spirited defense and carried out counterattacks against the encircling German forces. He was one of those junior commanders who escaped through Dunkirk.

In 1943 Barker passed from commanding the 54th Infantry Division to become commanding general of the 49th (West Riding) Division, which he led during the northwestern Europe campaign. Barker had always stressed in briefings to his officers that although the division was not in the assault wave, hard fighting was to be expected. The 49th did not reach Normandy until 13 June, but Barker had already liaised with the commanders of the neighboring divisions and had reconnoitered the ground across which

his 146th Brigade was to attack on 16 June. He planned a brigade attack to be followed by a two-brigade operation. The opening attack on 16 June met no opposition because the units of *12th SS Division* had withdrawn to a shorter line, but the two-brigade advance in the Boislande sector was involved in bitter fighting that continued until 25 June.

In December 1944, he was promoted to lieutenant general and subsequently given command of the British VIII Corps, which he led over the Rhine and across northern Germany as far as the Baltic. Barker took Adm. Karl Doenitz's government into custody and was governor of Schleswig-Holstein for almost a year.

In April 1946, Barker became general officer commanding Palestine and the Transjordan, a post he held until February 1947. He then served as aide de camp to King George VI before taking up the post of general officer commanding Eastern command in 1950. Barker retired from the Army on 18 March 1950 with the rank of general. He died on 23 November 1983.

[*See also* 49th (West Riding) Infantry Division.]

BIBLIOGRAPHY

Ellis, L. F., et al. *The Battle of Normandy.* Vol. 1 of *Victory in the West.* 1962.
Headquarters, 2d Army. *An Account of Operations of 2nd Army in Europe, 1944–45.* 1945.
Hughes, F. K. *A Short History of 49th (West Riding) Infantry Division, 1944–45.* 1958.

JAMES LUCAS

BARRETT, CARLTON W. (1919–1986), American, private; Medal of Honor recipient. Carlton W. Barrett was born in Fulton, New York. At the time of the Normandy invasion, he was assigned to the intelligence and reconnaissance platoon of the headquarters and headquarters company, 18th Infantry Regiment, 1st Infantry Division. On 6 June 1944 Barrett and several members of his platoon made up one of two radio teams that accompanied elements of the 2d Battalion, 16th Infantry Regiment, ashore in the initial waves. He waded ashore in neck-deep water under intense enemy fire, then repeatedly returned to the surf to rescue floundering comrades from certain drowning. He risked his life repeatedly, with fierce determination, by carrying wounded soldiers to an evacuation boat offshore.

During the course of the first day on Omaha Beach, Barrett performed his mission as a guide, carried dispatches under fire, and assisted the wounded and those unable to care for themselves. His personal heroism and cool behavior under withering fire were a source of inspiration to his fellow soldiers. For these actions on D-day he was later awarded the Medal of Honor, one of five presented to men of the 1st Infantry Division for their heroism in the early days of the Normandy invasion.

Carlton Barrett survived the war and married in 1946. He died in 1986 in California.

BIBLIOGRAPHY

U.S. Congress. Senate. Committee on Veterans' Affairs. *Medal of Honor Recipients, 1863–1978.* 96th Cong., 1st sess., 1979. S. Committee Print No. 3.

JOHN F. VOTAW

BARTON, RAYMOND O. (1889–1963), American, major general, commander of the 4th Infantry Division. A 1912 graduate of the U.S. Military Academy, Barton was first assigned as a second lieutenant with the 30th Infantry in Alaska. In August 1919, Barton, then a captain, transferred overseas to France, serving with the 8th Infantry. Following his tour with the 8th, Major Barton returned to the United States and attended the Command and General Staff School at Fort Leavenworth, Kansas, and the Army War College in Washington, D.C. Promoted to lieutenant colonel in 1935, Barton commanded the 8th Infantry from the end of 1938 to July 1940, when he became chief of staff for the 4th Infantry Division. Two years later, in June 1942, he returned to the 4th as its new commander.

Barton, a noted trainer, devoted himself to preparing his men for their coming mission, the assault on Europe. The 4th Infantry Division, under Barton's careful watch, made several amphibious landings at Camp Gordon Johnson, Florida, and up to June 1944, at Slapton Sands on the English coast practicing for their role in the coming invasion of France.

The plan for the Allied invasion of Normandy called for the VII Corps to capture and hold Utah Beach, using the 4th Infantry Division as its main assault force. As planned, the division's lead elements landed early in the morning on D-day, and General Barton went ashore that afternoon. Although resistance on Utah Beach had been light compared to the resistance on Omaha Beach, Barton still worried about moving his men and equipment off Utah and farther inland to link up with the airborne troops. This became increasingly difficult since the flooded terrain behind the beach made the causeways the only escape inland. Barton, at one point during the afternoon, was directing traffic through the only open causeway off the beach. His apprehensions were somewhat alleviated when the Allies were able to open other exits.

Barton led the 4th Division inland, where divisional elements relieved 82d Airborne Division troops isolated at Sainte-Mère-Église. During the following days the division fought to enlarge and strengthen the beachhead against surprisingly stubborn resistance. One apocryphal story of this period tells of Barton visiting a division unit to encourage their progress with the news that the Germans they faced were not capable of first-rate opposition. The unit's intelligence officer remarked to Barton that the Germans should be put on the distribution list for this news, because they did not realize they were second-rate.

After leading his division during some of the most significant actions of the war—through Normandy, the capture of Paris, the Huertgen Forest, and the opening blows of the Battle of the Bulge—Barton, troubled by illness, gave up command of the 4th Infantry Division in late December 1944 and transferred back to the United States. In March 1945 he became the commanding general for infantry training at Fort McClellan. Major General Barton retired from the army in 1946 and became vice president of the Chamber of Commerce of Augusta. He died 27 February 1963 at Fort Gordon, Georgia.

[*See also* 4th Infantry Division.]

BIBLIOGRAPHY

Obituary. *Assembly,* vol. 22, no. 2 (Summer 1963).
Ryan, Cornelius. *The Longest Day: June 6, 1944.* 1959.
Weigley, Russell F. *Eisenhower's Lieutenants.* Vol. 1, 1981.

DONNA C. EVERETT

BATTLEFIELD FILM FOOTAGE. Surviving film provides a fascinating though incomplete record of the D-day battles. It is important to remember that cameramen can only film where they happen to be, and within limits imposed by their equipment, their fitness, and the fortunes of war. In Normandy, cameramen like any other soldiers were killed and wounded, were pinned down in the wrong position, or found their intelligence (information about where stories were breaking), equipment (cameras), or movement of supplies (film) inadequate or unreliable.

Film footage came from two sources: newsreel operators working as accredited war correspondents and service cameramen. The British Army and Royal Air Force both had well-established film units set up specifically to record military operations and the Royal Navy also had two small camera teams covering D-day. Other Allied forces filmed their own involvement in the campaign. Canadian, Czechoslovak, French, Dutch, Norwegian, and Polish units all generated film of its later stages, although none contributed significant amounts of film of D-day itself. All this effort by the other Allies was small compared to that of the United States. Coverage by the Signal Corps, the navy, the air forces, and U.S. newsreels has been calculated to account for two-thirds of the film received by SHAEF.

For the Germans, Normandy before the invasion was an inactive front in a losing war, and their record is consequently much less complete. Available coverage is restricted to the newsreel *Deutsche Wochenschau,* which reported the invasion in an issue (composed largely of stock footage) passed by censors on 14 June.

Both original unedited footage and documentaries (such as the 1945 Oscar winner *The True Glory*) are preserved in film archives around the world, and newsreel libraries preserve contemporary reports. The largest collections of D-day footage are housed at the U.S. National Archives and Records Administration in Washington, D.C., and the Imperial War Museum in London, England. Copies of the *Wochenschau* are available in several archives, but the principal source is the Bundesarchiv-Filmarchiv in Koblenz and Berlin, Germany. Supplemented by interviews with survivors, this material is regularly used in television series like *The World at War.*

BIBLIOGRAPHY

Bull, Donald. "Filming the European Campaign." *Documentary News Letter* 49 (1945): 90–91.

Coultass, Clive. *Images for Battle: British Film and the Second World War, 1939–1945.* 1989.

Manvell, Roger. *Films and the Second World War.* 1974.

ROGER SMITHER

BATTLEFIELD TOURS.

BATTLEFIELD TOURS. Although soldiers and military historians have always visited the "haunted acres" of historical engagements, organized battlefield touring for the general public effectively began—albeit in an intermittent and haphazard way—after World War I, when growing numbers of relatives and friends of the fallen wished to visit war cemeteries.

After 1945 the demand grew still further, and from 1984 on an ever-increasing number of divisional and formation organizations planned tours to Normandy for veterans who wished to revisit the battlefields and attend the inauguration or rededication of a memorial to their comrades of yesteryear. Battlefield tours of D-day sites and the Normandy beachhead for old soldiers and the public alike really got under way on a large scale with the foundation of Major and Mrs. Holt's Battlefield Tours in England in 1976.

At first this company specialized in World War I battle anniversary visits, but soon demands for D-day and 1944-oriented tours began to grow. The company responded to the challenge, including in 1992, for instance, six-day Operation Overlord and five-day Battle for Normandy (Caen/Hill 112) tours in their program. These were among a total of one hundred tours to battlegrounds all over the world, including Hong Kong, Malaysia, and the Falklands, with at least thirty-five of them devoted to World War II subjects. Of these, six were dedicated to introductory D-day tours and two more to the Battle for Normandy. Other companies have sprung up since 1976—for instance Sandhurst Staff Rides, Garner Horrocks Travel, and Grapeshot Tours, to name but three, several of them offering more specialized tours and other periods. But few can rival Holt's in terms of value or frequency.

There are also many firms in the United States offering tours of Normandy. Worth mention is Galaxy Tours of Wayne, Pennsylvania.

Normandy is particularly rich in relics, museums, and memorials of all kinds pertaining to the dramatic events of June 1944, which makes it unlikely indeed that tours, whether in large groups by coach or in smaller parties using cars or bicycles, will be uninteresting. Watershed dates, such as the fortieth or fiftieth anniversary of D-day, always inspire increased numbers of tours and observances.

[*See also* Museums.]

BIBLIOGRAPHY

Holt, Tonie, and Valmai Holt. *The Visitor's Guide to Normandy Landing Beaches.* 1989.

Holt, Tonie, and Valmai Holt. *Holt's Battlefield Guides: Normandy-Overlord.* 2d ed., 1988.

DAVID G. CHANDLER

BAYERLEIN, FRITZ (1899–1970), German, major general, commander of the *Panzer Lehr Division.* Bayerlein, who joined the army shortly before the end of World War I, served throughout the Reichswehr period and was trained to be a general staff officer. During both the 1939 and 1940 campaigns, he was operations officer of the *XIX Army Corps* under Colonel General Heinz Guderian. In September 1941, he was appointed chief of staff of the *Africa Corps* under Generals Ludwig Crüwell and, later, Walther Nehring. In Africa, he was awarded the Knight's

Cross. In December 1942, he was appointed Field Marshal Erwin Rommel's chief of staff in the German-Italian *Panzer Army Africa*. After promotion to brigadier general, he was decorated with the Oak Leaves in July of that year. From August 1943 to early 1944, he commanded the *3d Panzer Division* on the Eastern front. On Guderian's personal intervention, he was put in charge of the newly formed elite *Panzer Lehr Division* in February 1944. On 1 May 1944, he was promoted to major general.

Bayerlein was thus well acquainted with the war experience of the German panzer force in all the major theaters. He had served under Rommel for a long time and had come to know him and his preferences well. Moreover, unlike many other commanders, he had had the experience of operating under conditions of Allied air superiority. Bayerlein was considered a brilliant general staff officer, but before taking over the *3d Panzer Division*, he had never held an independent command in the war. Still, working under Rommel, who was away most of the time and left day-to-day decisions to his chief of staff, must have prepared Bayerlein well enough for what was to come.

Bayerlein's *Panzer Lehr Division* was one of the strongest in the German Army and one of the first to be sent to the front after the Normandy invasion. On 8 June, while still on the road to Normandy, Bayerlein was injured in an air attack that killed his driver and his adjutant. Even so, the next morning Bayerlein personally led his division into the attack against British forces around Ellon (near Caen). After an initial success, Bayerlein took it upon himself to abort the attack because of Allied pressure on his right wing.

The next day, 9 June, he launched another attack, which faltered owing to the intervention of Allied naval artillery. From then on, Bayerlein's division was employed in defensive roles for which it had not been designed. The *Panzer Lehr Division* had to be pulled out of the line on 26 June, by which time the division had lost 78 percent of its combined tank and assault gun total. It had been hit hard by American bombers while advancing toward Saint-Lô. For his role in containing the Allied advance, Bayerlein was mentioned in the *Wehrmachtsbericht* Daily Army Report on 26 June and was decorated with the Swords to the Oak Leaves of the Knight's Cross on 20 July 1944.

Bayerlein, with the *Panzer Lehr Division*, took part in the Ardennes offensive and in February 1945, he was given command of the *LIII Army Corps*. Bayerlein was eventually taken prisoner by the Americans in the battle for the Ruhr pocket. He was widely involved in the early historiography of World War II, working for the U.S. Operational History (German) Section. He never joined the Bundeswehr (the army of the Federal Republic of Germany) and he died in Würzburg in March 1970.

[*See also* Panzer Lehr Division.]

BIBLIOGRAPHY

Keilig, Wolf. *Deutsche Generale des Zweiten Weltkrieges.* 1964.
Ritgen, Helmut. *Die Geschichte der Panzer-Lehr-Division im Westen, 1944–1945.* 1979.

WINFRIED HEINEMANN

BAYFIELD, USS. The name ship of its class, the USS *Bayfield* was 492 feet long, 70 feet in width, and had a standard displacement of 8,100 tons. Launched originally as the cargo ship *Sea Bass*, it was taken over by the navy and put into full commission as an attack transport on 30 November 1943. It was manned by a Coast Guard crew of nearly 600, including the first skipper, Capt. Lyndon Spencer, who was still in command in June 1944. During the Normandy invasion the *Bayfield* served as flagship for Rear Adm. Don P. Moon, who commanded Task Force 125 for the assault on Utah Beach. Maj. Gen. J. Lawton Collins, commanding U.S. VII Corps, was also embarked.

The ship sortied from Plymouth Harbor on 5 June 1944 and steamed as part of a convoy to the transport area off Utah Beach. All hands went to general quarters at 2230, and then the ship anchored about eighteen and a half kilometers (eleven and a half miles) off the beach at 0230 on

USS *BAYFIELD*.   NATIONAL ARCHIVES

D-day. The *Bayfield* sent twelve of her LCVPs (Landing Craft, Vehicle and Personnel) to load troops from the transport *Barnett*. The other LCVPs operated in assembly circles to embark troops from other ships. The troops debarked from the *Bayfield* were sent ashore in land-based LCMs (Landing Craft, Mechanized), which began loading at 0525 and proceeded to the beach. The remainder of troops and vehicles were later loaded aboard an LCT (Landing Craft, Tank) for the trip ashore.

In succeeding days the *Bayfield* remained on the scene, moving progressively closer to the beach. It served as command information ship for Admiral Moon, while also providing logistic support, repair and maintenance of landing craft, and medical care. In addition, it became a treatment and evacuation center for captured prisoners of war. While off the beach, the transport was attacked twice by bombers and suffered slight engine room damage as the result of a near miss. On 25 June the *Bayfield* returned to England. In August and September it was the flagship for the commander of Task Force 87 during the invasion of southern France (Operation DRAGOON).

[*See also* Moon, Don P.]

BIBLIOGRAPHY

Bayfield Action Report. Serial 00218 of 17 June 1944. Operational Archives, Naval Historical Center, Washington, D.C.
Dictionary of American Naval Fighting Ships. Vol. 1, 1959.

PAUL STILLWELL

BEACH AND COASTAL DEFENSES. After the conquest of France, German intentions in the West remained offensive throughout 1940. It was only in the winter of 1940–1941 that the German strategic effort was shifted toward the East. As a consequence, the first fortification works to be undertaken on the French, Belgian, and Dutch coasts were the installation of naval batteries designed to support Operation SEELÖWE (SEA LION), the intended landing in Britain. They usually consisted of naval guns removed from German shore fortifications.

Preparations for Operation BARBAROSSA, the invasion of Russia, led to the transfer of most German units stationed in France, leaving the French coast virtually undefended. To make up for this weakness, in December 1941 Hitler ordered the construction of permanent fortifications. These were originally designed not against a major invasion, but against British raids on individual German installations. Only during the course of 1943 did the task of the Atlantic Wall change from purely tactical to strategic.

These origins help to explain some of the Atlantic Wall's major characteristics. Its most impressive fortifications were clustered in the Pas de Calais, partly because they had been part of the original Operation SEA LION, and partly because that was where German planners expected the invasion. These fortifications included naval guns of up to 40.6 centimeters (16 inches) under heavy concrete shelters up to 7 meters (23 feet) thick. However, these spectacular batteries accounted for only a minor part of the overall effort.

CASEMATED GUN.   Near Utah Beach.   NATIONAL ARCHIVES

MINE-TIPPED POLES SLANTING SEAWARD.   NATIONAL ARCHIVES

Most of the works were based on experiences gathered during the construction of the West Wall, or Siegfried Line, along the Franco-German border. Unlike the French Maginot Line, the West Wall had been built deploying a limited number of types of bunkers, slightly varied according to local conditions. This procedure did not provide perfect tactical solutions, but it permitted rapid construction because supply and personnel could be more easily organized. Even more important, these preplanned buildings could be effected with less qualified manpower—an important consideration in the later stages of the war. Unlike the West Wall, however, which had been a continuous line, the Atlantic Wall was initially clustered around sensitive areas, in particular the major ports that the Allies were supposed to be targeting for their invasion.

Most of the work was done by the Organization Todt assisted by the *Reichsarbeitsdienst* (German compulsory labor service) and German army engineers. At the peak of the effort, up to 260,000 men were employed, only 10 percent of whom were German, the others being forced laborers, prisoners of war, and West European volunteers. In April 1943 alone, more than 769,000 tons of concrete were poured. Altogether, some 13 millions tons were used.

Building of the wall was marked by interservice rivalry, particularly between army and navy. The navy wanted its guns emplaced within sight of the sea so they could fire at moving targets and under direct control, although they would often be ineffective against enemy already on the beach. The army preferred gun sites in the rear, from where they could sweep wide sectors of the beach. Army methods of indirect fire control, however, would then not permit effective shelling of fast-moving naval units.

In the autumn of 1943 Field Marshal Erwin Rommel was put in charge of German defenses in the West. His arrival on the scene marked a decided change in emphasis. Rommel insisted on easy-to-build field fortifications supported by a wide variety of obstacles. It was only then that the wall became a continuous system along the entire coast.

Rommel was particularly interested in mines, which he had used skillfully in North Africa. By October 1943 about two million mines had been laid; by the end of May 1944, the figure had risen to more than six million. Entire sectors of the beach had been mined in depth; others had been designated as dummy minefields. In addition, stakes driven into open fields at intervals of about

OMAHA BEACH.   Afternoon of 6 June 1944.   NATIONAL ARCHIVES

ten meters (about 30 feet) were designed to make these fields unusable for airborne landings.

Rommel also insisted that obstacles be built on the sea floor in front of the beaches. Wooden or concrete stakes driven into the beach and angled outward, sometimes with explosive devices attached, were meant to rip the bottom out of landing craft. Concrete tetrahedrons, steel "hedgehogs," and similar structures were derived from the West Wall, but these too were usually mined. Where sufficient quantities of explosives could not be obtained, Rommel made use of captured French artillery shells.

The wide variety of obstacles, mines, and field fortifications were designed not only to enhance the defensive value of the Atlantic Wall, close gaps between strongpoints, and render entire sectors of beach unusable. It was also hoped that they would force the Allies to spend more time training and preparing, thus giving the Germans additional time for their own preparations.

The Wehrmacht defenses in Normandy were considerably weaker than in most other areas along the coast. Only

a few heavy batteries had been installed. Most notable of these were the six 6-inch guns at Riva-Bella (Sword Beach), the army coastal battery of four 5-inch guns at Graye (Juno Beach), the naval battery of four 5.9-inch guns at Longues (Gold Beach), the five operational 6-inch guns at the top of the Pointe du Hoc (Omaha Beach), and the naval battery of three impressive 8-inch guns at Marcouf (Utah Beach), which held out against repeated American attacks until 11 June and was then evacuated. These were enhanced by field fortifications and extensive mining.

Even among Rommel's subordinates, a number of officers had always had their doubts as to the value of the manifold efforts to fortify the beaches. After all, the experience of the war so far had indicated the uselessness of permanent linear fortifications. German evaluations even in mid-June 1944 were that the Atlantic Wall had not lived up to expectations. Its heavy works had been swiftly destroyed by Allied naval guns and aerial bombardment, and its field fortifications had only been effective when manned by first-rate units. The majority of Allied losses were inflicted by regular German army units.

[*See also* Atlantic Wall; Organization Todt; Planning, *article on* German Planning.]

BIBLIOGRAPHY

Rolf, Rudi. *Der Atlantikwall.* 1983.
Wilt, Allan F. *The Atlantic Wall: Hitler's Defenses in the West, 1941–1944.* 1975.

WINFRIED HEINEMANN

BECHTOLSHEIM, THEODOR (1902–198?), German, commander, *8th Destroyer Flotilla*. Theodor Freiherr (Baron) von Mauchenheim, known by the name Bechtolsheim, was born on 26 August 1902 at Castle Mainsondheim in Franconia. He joined the German Navy in 1922 and in October 1927 was promoted to lieutenant. During the 1930s he held various commands, including two destroyers. He became first naval staff officer with the commander of destroyers in August 1942, and chief of staff in September 1943. He was promoted to captain in October 1943.

After a brief interim appointment as chief of the *5th Destroyer Flotilla*, Bechtolsheim became chief of the *8th Destroyer Flotilla* at Brest. The *8th Destroyer Flotilla* was the strongest German unit in the West on D-day, but it never reached the invasion area. During the night 8–9 June, Bechtolsheim tried to make a sortie against the invasion forces with *Z 32, Z 24, ZH 1,* and *T 24.* (*Z 23* and *Z 37* were not ready for action). Northwest of the Île de Batz he was intercepted by the British 10th Destroyer Flotilla (Capt. B. Jones) with *Tartar, Ashanti, Haida, Huron, Blyscawica, Piorun, Eskimo,* and *Javelin. ZH 1* was sunk by torpedoes from *Ashanti, Z 32* was beached and blown up after a duel with the Canadian *Haida* and *Huron,* and *Tartar* was severely damaged. The surviving destroyer *Z 23* of the 8th Flotilla was sunk in August 1944 after an Allied air attack, and the damaged *Z 24* and *Z 37* never saw service again.

From July 1944 until the end of the war, Bechtolsheim served as the Navy High Command's liaison officer to the SS Reich Security Main Office. Released from internment as a prisoner of war in November 1946, he lived in Stuttgart until his death.

[*See also* Navy, *article on* German Navy.]

BIBLIOGRAPHY

Harnack, Wolfgang. *Zerstörer unter deutscher Flagge 1934 bis 1945.* 1978.
Lohmann, Walter, and Hans H. Hildebrand. *Die deutsche Kriegsmarine 1939–1945.* 1956–1964.

GERHARD HÜMMELCHEN

Z 24 AND *Z 32*.   The destroyers *Z 24* and *Z 32* of the *8th Destroyer Flotilla* on a sortie in the Bay of Biscay in April 1943.

BIBLIOTHEK FÜR ZEITGESCHICHTE, STUTTGART

BELFAST, HMS. An improved Town-class cruiser with a weight of 10,000 tons and a speed of 32 knots, and armed with twelve 6-inch and twelve 4-inch guns, *Belfast* was built by Harland & Wolff, Belfast, and completed in 1939. Its crew of 850 was commanded by Capt. G. F. R. Parham. Badly damaged by a magnetic mine in the Firth of Forth, Scotland, *Belfast* returned to service in late 1942, serving with the Home Fleet covering Arctic convoys, and took part in the destruction of the German battleship *Scharnhorst* on 24 December 1943. On 3 April 1944 it escorted a Home Fleet aircraft carrier strike against the battleship *Tirpitz*. It was refitted at Rosyth, Scotland, prior to D-day.

As part of Task Force J, *Belfast* was to provide fire support for Juno Beach. It was the flagship of Fire Support Force E (Rear Adm. F. H. G. Dalrymple-Hamilton) and the 10th Cruiser Squadron. On D-day *Belfast* engaged the batteries at Ver-sur-Mer and Courseulles-sur-Mer in the sector of the 3d Canadian Division, opening fire at 0527. After 0930 it fired on Montfleury. On 7 through 9 June it fired on infantry concentrations, and on the tenth successfully engaged the battery on Cape Antifer. Between D-day and 14 June *Belfast* fired 1,996 6-inch rounds. On 27 June and 8 through 11 July it provided fire support for the British and Canadian assault on Caen.

After the war *Belfast* supplied United Nations operations in Korea from 1950 to 1952. Since 1971 it has been a museum ship in the Pool of London, one of the last major ships to survive from Operation NEPTUNE.

[*See also* Dalrymple-Hamilton, F. H. G.; Task Force J.]

BIBLIOGRAPHY

London. Public Record Office. Ship Log Books, HMS *Belfast*, ADM 53/118968-9.
Watton, Ross. *HMS Belfast*. 1985.

ANDREW LAMBERT

BIBLIOGRAPHY. Literature in English about D-day is extensive. Stephen T. Powers, "The Battle of Normandy: The Lingering Controversy," *Journal of Military History* 56 (July 1992): 455–471, updates the growing number of publications. For an in-depth analysis of much of the literature pertaining to D-day, see G. E. Patrick Murray, "Eisenhower and Montgomery: Broad Front versus Single Thrust: The Historiography of the Debate over Strategy and Command, August 1944–April 1945," Ph.D. diss., Temple University, 1945 (Ann Arbor, Mich.: University Microfilms, 1991); and Colin F. Baxter, *The Normandy Campaign, 1944: A Selected Bibliography* (New York, 1992).

The best general books about the invasion have had a popular readership. All the Allied official histories are well written and illustrated and provide insights into the invasion. Gordon A. Harrison, *Cross-Channel Attack* (Washington, D.C., 1951, repr., 1984), is the U.S. Army account of D-day. Although new information has come to light on the political and intelligence backgrounds of D-day, this book remains the best survey. Lionel F. Ellis, G. R. G. Allen, A. E. Warhurst, and James Robb, *The Battle of Normandy*, vol. 1 of *Victory in the West* (London, 1962), is not as detailed as U.S. official histories, but is more interpretive and literary in style. Albert Norman, *Operation Overlord, Design and Reality: The Allied Invasion of Western Europe* (Westport, Conn., 1952, repr., 1970), is a well-documented account by Gen. Omar Bradley's staff historian.

Carlo D'Este, *Decision in Normandy: The Unwritten Story of Montgomery and the Allied Campaign* (London and New York, 1991), is well researched. Max Hastings, *Overlord: D-Day and the Battle for Normandy, 1944* (London and New York, 1985), is a superb narrative history. Russell F. Weigley, *Eisenhower's Lieutenants: The Campaigns of France and Germany, 1944–1945* (Bloomington, Ind., 1990), provides an analysis of command at both the strategic and tactical levels. U.S. Army Center of Military History, *Utah Beach to Cherbourg, 6 June –27 June 1944*, American Forces in Action Series (Washington, D.C., 1948, repr., 1990), is a description of the VII Corps landings by Roland G. Ruppenthal. Charles H. Taylor wrote the companion narrative, *Omaha Beachhead: 6 June–13 June 1944* (Washington, D.C., 1945, fascimile repr., 1989), which emphasizes the assault and consolidation by units of the U.S. First Army.

The OVERLORD leadership role of General Dwight D. Eisenhower is evaluated in Stephen E. Ambrose, *Supreme Commander: The War Years of General Dwight D. Eisenhower* (Garden City, N.Y., 1970). Eisenhower's best-seller, *Crusade in Europe* (New York, 1948, repr., 1990), reviews the D-day landing and describes the factors that influenced his coalition command decisions. David Eisenhower, *Eisenhower: At War, 1943–1945* (New York, 1986), is a well-researched and well-written account of Ike's invasion role by his grandson.

Field Marshal Bernard L. Montgomery has been written about extensively in his leadership of British and Allied forces. In *Master of the Battlefield: Monty's War Years, 1942–1944* (New York, 1983), Montgomery's godson, Nigel Hamilton, contributes significantly to the understanding of Montgomery. Alexander McKee, *Last Round against Rommel: The Battle of the Normandy Beachhead* (New York, 1964), and *Caen: Anvil of Victory* (London, 1985), reconstruct the British-Canadian campaign phase of Operation OVERLORD, including the Eisenhower-Montgomery debate on strategy and tactics.

Gen. Omar Bradley played a significant role in the successful D-day invasion. *General's Life: An Autobiography by General of the Army Omar N. Bradley and Clay Blair* (New York, 1989) contains more personal impressions, opinions, and controversy than *A Soldier's Story* (London and New York, 1951), which was based on the diaries of Bradley's staff officer, Chester B. Hansen, and on Bradley's conversations. Blair also interviewed Bradley and used his testimonies and papers.

The largest armada in history is covered in Samuel E. Morison, *Invasion of France and Germany, 1944–1945* (Boston, 1957). It is vol. 11 of the fifteen-volume *History of the United States Naval Operations in World War II* and continues to be the best existing naval account of the invasion. The official British historian, Stephen W. Roskill, *The Offensive* (London, 1961), vol. 3, pt. 2, of *The War at Sea, 1939–1945,* analyzes the role of the Royal Navy in Operation OVERLORD.

Allied air force operations have been narrated in Wesley Frank Craven and James Lea Cate, eds., *Europe: ARGUMENT to V-E Day, January 1944 to May 1945* (Washington, D.C., 1983), vol. 3 of *The Army Air Forces in World War II*. Vincent Orange, *Coningham: A Biography of Air Marshal Sir Arthur Coningham* (London, 1990), discusses the Royal Air Force's role in Operation OVERLORD. W. W. Rostow, *Pre-Invasion Bombing Strategy: General Eisenhower's Decision of March 25, 1944* (Austin, Tex., 1981), outlines the dynamics behind one facet of the air plans.

A number of planning and technical operations studies have been published. The Eisenhower Foundation, ed., *D-Day: The Normandy Invasion in Retrospect* (Lawrence, Kans., 1971), includes essays by former commanders and scholars that evaluate planning, weather, logistics, equipment, gunfire support, and air support. A new edition, *D-Day in Retrospect: The Normandy Invasion after Fifty Years,* has been announced for 1994. Maurice Matloff, *Strategic Planning for Coalition Warfare, 1943–1944* (Washington, D.C., 1959, repr., 1970), is part of the official U.S. Army World War II "green book" series (*U.S. Army in World War II: The European Theater of Operations*), as is Forrest C. Pogue, *The Supreme Command* (Washington, D.C., 1954, repr., 1983). R. G. Ruppenthal, *Logistical Support of the Armies: May 1941–September 1944*, vol. 1 (Washington, D.C., 1953, repr., 1982), reviews the role of logistics in Operation OVERLORD planning and supply activities.

Ultra and other reconnaissance aspects of Operation OVERLORD have been a fascinating topic. F. H. Hinsley, E. E. Thomas, C. A. G. Simkins, and C. F. G. Ranson, *British Intelligence in the Second World War: Its Influence on Strategy and Operations*, vol. 3, pt. 2 (London and New York, 1988), is the official British assessment of intelligence's role in the Normandy campaign. Harold C. Deutsch, ed., *Basic Deception and the Normandy Invasion* (New York, 1989), is a study of eighteen documents concerning directives, equipment, and methods used for the landing.

Unit histories of Allied forces during the Normandy campaign include some of the most widely read books about World War II. Cornelius Ryan's postwar interviews with participants led to *The Longest Day: June 6, 1944* (West Yorkshire, U.K., 1962, New York, 1967), the most popular D-day history. John Keegan, *Six Armies in Normandy: From D-Day to the Liberation of Paris, June 6th–August 25th, 1944* (London and New York, 1983), is a probing discovery of the common infantryman's experience. Murdoch C. McDougall, *Swiftly They Struck: Story of No. 4 Commando* (London, 1954, repr., 1957), covers the unit's action during the invasion. John A. English, *The Canadian Army and the Normandy Campaign: A Study of Failure in High Command* (London and New York, 1991), presents new information and a critical analysis of the Canadian army's performance in the war. The airborne troops have been well represented by such monographs as George E. Koskimaki, *D-Day with the Screaming Eagles*, 2d ed. (Kalamazoo, Mich., 1989), which is a collection of eyewitness narratives by U.S. Army 101st Airborne Division participants. John Golley, *The Big Drop: The Guns of Merville, June 1944* (New York, 1986), interviews soldiers in the British 6th Airborne Division.

[*See also* Archival Sources.]

ALAN C. AIMONE

BLANC, ADALBERT VON

BLANC, ADALBERT VON (1907–1976), German, commander, *2d Defense Division.* Adalbert von Blanc was born on 11 July 1907 in Wilhelmshaven. He joined the German Navy in 1926, became a lieutenant in October 1930, and thereafter served on various ships. At the outbreak of World War II Blanc was first officer on the armed merchant cruiser *Orion,* which operated successfully in the Atlantic and Pacific in 1940 and 1941.

As first naval staff officer of the *2d Defense Division* (December 1941 to September 1943), Blanc learned about the problems of coastal defense in the West. After an interlude as commander of the *2d Minesweeper Flotilla* from September 1943 to March 1944, Blanc was promoted to commander and on 1 April 1944 assumed command of the *2d Defense Division* in Souvrain-Moulin near Boulogne. The division, responsible for the area from the English Channel to the Schelde Estuary, consisted of 163 minesweepers (*Minensuchboote*), fifty-seven patrol boats, and thirty-two gun carriers (*Artillerieträger*), mostly auxiliary vessels. Most of the division's vessels were lost in June and July 1944; 46% were sunk by air attacks, 27% were scuttled by their own crews when their bases were captured, 21% were sunk in action, and 6% were lost to mines and other causes. They never received necessary reinforcements, and the division was dissolved.

At the war's end Blanc commanded the *9th Defense Division* in the Baltic. From January 1948 to April 1951 he commanded the West German minesweeper group at Cuxhaven. Promoted to captain in 1956, from October 1958 to July 1961 he was commander of minesweepers. Until his retirement in 1964 he was flotilla admiral in charge of naval training. He died in Hamburg on 7 November 1976.

[See also Navy, article on German Navy.]

BIBLIOGRAPHY

Lohmann, Walter, and Hans H. Hildebrand. *Die deutsche Kriegsmarine 1939–1945*. 1956–1964.

Rohwer, Jürgen, and Gerhard Hümmelchen. *Chronology of the War at Sea, 1939–1945*. Translated by Derek Masters. 1992.

GERHARD HÜMMELCHEN

BLUMENTRITT, GÜNTHER (1892–1967), German, general, chief of staff to Commander in Chief West.

After service as a young officer during World War I, Blumentritt was selected to remain in the slimmed-down postwar German Army and began to make his mark as a staff officer, known for his ability to work quickly and accurately. In spring 1939, now a colonel, he joined Gen. Gerd von Rundstedt's planning team for the invasion of Poland and served as the latter's chief of operations in both that campaign and that in France in 1940. In the autumn he became chief of staff of Field Marshal Hans Günther von Kluge's *Fourth Army* for the invasion of Russia and then was posted to be the OKH (Army High Command) chief of operations. At the end of 1942 he rejoined Rundstedt in France as his chief of staff and as such was largely responsible for planning the defense of the West. Like his commander, Blumentritt believed that the main Allied landings would be north of the Seine River.

During the battle for Normandy, Rundstedt used him as his mouthpiece to OKW (Wehrmacht High Command), but Blumentritt stayed on as chief of staff after Rundstedt was sacked. In September 1944, when Rundstedt returned as Commander in Chief West, Blumentritt, despite Rundstedt's wish to retain him, was given command of the *XII SS Corps* and, in January 1945, the *Twenty-Fifth Army* in Holland. He finished the war as commander of the *First Parachute Army*.

After 1945 Blumentritt worked for the U.S. Army Historical Division in Europe, contributing monographs on aspects of the war. He also wrote a biography of Rundstedt, for whom he had much respect, likening their relationship to that of father and son.

BIBLIOGRAPHY

Blumentritt, Günther. *Von Rundstedt: The Soldier and the Man*. 1952.

CHARLES MESSENGER

GÜNTHER BLUMENTRITT.
BIBLIOTHEK FÜR ZEITGESCHICHTE, STUTTGART

BOCAGE.

Bocage is a French word for a copse, grove, or as applied to Normandy, a wooded region. In that province it mainly consisted of small fields or apple orchards bounded by thick, usually uncut, and often double, hedges set on high banks. In the invasion area these fields, intersected by rivers, streams, and narrow lanes and dotted with stone-built farms and villages, created formidable obstacles dominated by hills and ridges, except to the north and south of Caen, where the ground was more open.

Bocage provided excellent cover and therefore was ideal for blocking, ambush, and infiltration tactics. It thus offered greater advantages to defensive than to offensive operations, and also inhibited airborne operations, land movement, and the construction of airfields (of which Carpiquet, near Caen, was the only one in the invasion area and therefore a strategic objective).

The existence and nature of bocage had been noticed

during the 1940 French campaign by, among others, Field Marshal Erwin Rommel and Lt. Gen. J. T. Crocker, and therefore came as no surprise. But while it naturally favored the Germans, who in 1944 were on the defensive, its effects were underestimated by the Allies, even though some of their troops had been given training in similar country in England. With observation and ranges of engagement limited to between 400 and 500 yards, tanks were severely hampered, and infantry were compelled to play the predominant role. Troops trying to attack through the thick hedges and orchards suffered heavy casualties from well-protected and concealed opponents at close range. Artillery and mortar fire often was the more deadly when it was air-burst among the trees. Tanks pushing through the hedges and climbing the banks were slowed down and picked off with relative ease by an enemy they never even sighted. The tempo of operations was slowed and casualties multiplied.

To overcome the bocage, the Allies were compelled to practice extremely close cooperation between tanks and escorting infantry and to expend unexpectedly large quantities of ammunition. Every village, farm, copse, and hedgerow became an objective demanding a carefully prepared assault. Engineers' efforts with bulldozers to clear gaps and widen roads were immense. Specialized armor, particularly AVREs (Armoured Vehicle Royal Engineers) to blast holes and Crocodile flamethrowers to burn out the enemy, assumed important roles. Short-range antitank weapons, such as the bazooka and *Panzerfaust,* were notably effective. The invention by an American sergeant of the "Rhinoceros"—a set of shears welded to tanks' bows to cut through the banks—was very effective in the breakout. For the Allies, it was a relief when eventually the claustrophobia of bocage became a bad memory of the past.

KENNETH MACKSEY

BOMBARDMENT SHIPS. An assault landing is one of the most difficult military operations, requiring the heaviest available firepower. Naval guns and aircraft support the landing force until army artillery can land and go into action. Naval guns then supplement field artillery as long as suitable targets remain within range. World War II battleships and cruisers had heavier guns than any mobile land artillery unit, and these proved valuable against fortified positions.

Naval guns destroy or damage defensive works, help isolate the landing beaches by hitting reinforcement routes, and support assault minesweeping. Bombardment continues as the first waves approach the beaches, shifting inland during the final minutes—on D-Day, at H minus 5 minutes—to avoid danger to one's own forces. At this point fire support is taken up by gun- and rocket-armed small ships and craft.

Gunfire support at Normandy was provided by 106 British, American, Canadian, French, Polish, Norwegian, and Dutch warships: 6 battleships, 2 monitors (small, shallow-draft ships with two 380-mm [15-inch] guns), 23 cruisers, 73 destroyers, and 2 gunboats. British and American pilots spotted fire from Spitfires, which were judged to be the only suitable type of aircraft in the face of expected Luftwaffe opposition.

Though the particulars varied considerably, a typical warship's guns were controlled by a fire-control system usually including an optical director, which measured the bearing and elevation of line-of-sight targets; an optical range finder; and a form of gunnery radar, some of which could measure bearing as well as range. An electromechanical computer took in information from director, range finder, and radar, and combined this with such factors as wind direction and velocity and the firing ship's own movements to produce continuous bearing and elevation orders to the guns. Spotters in the ship's elevated

405-MM (16-INCH) GUN.   Taken by the 3d Canadian Division, this gun was put out of action by Allied guns, as evidenced by the split barrel.   HULTON DEUTSCH

USS *NEVADA*.   This battleship in Admiral Deyo's Bombardment Group provided naval gunfire at Utah Beach.

THE ROBERT HUNT LIBRARY, LONDON

tops, ashore with ground troops, and in airplanes observed the fall of shot and called corrections that were then fed into the computer to bring fire onto the target. The ship's own directors and spotters could handle fire to the visible horizon, but shore fire-control parties and air spotting were needed for the precise shooting required for close support, and for accurate shooting beyond the horizon.

An early study of the proposed Normandy landing stated that 20 or more battleships or cruisers would be needed to silence German fortified gun batteries, while another 20 cruisers and 100 destroyers would be required to cover the landing beaches and their defenses. These were not available, and planners doubted if even this number of ships could do the entire job. British experience at Dieppe and American experience at Tarawa showed heavy gunfire to be essential, if assault troops were to break through beach defenses without crippling losses. Planners drew pessimistic lessons about the effectiveness of naval guns against shore defenses, so that more fire-support ships were made available.

Initial estimates had called for a fire-support force for the Eastern Task Force of 3 battleships, 2 heavy and 8 light cruisers, and 36 destroyers; American warships were later added. As finally formed, the Eastern Task Force was primarily supported by British ships, reinforced by a number of other Allied vessels; the Western Task Force received support from American ships, with two French cruisers

and a Dutch gunboat. Each of the five assault beaches had its assigned bombardment force. These were commanded by Rear Adm. M. L. Deyo, USN (Utah Beach); Rear Adm. C. F. Bryant, USN (Omaha); Capt. E. W. L. Longley-Cook, RN (Gold); Rear Adm. F. H. G. Dalrymple-Hamilton, RN (Juno); and Rear Adm. W. R. Patterson, RN (Sword). Numbers of gunfire ships were still thought insufficient, and produced such expedients as LCTs (Landing Craft, Tank) modified so that tanks and self-propelled guns could fire from them as they approached the beaches.

Since tactical surprise was essential, naval gunfire could not begin until D-day itself. Preinvasion bombing had to be spread thin to avoid giving away the landing area, and much of it was aimed at the Pas de Calais; in all, about 3 percent of the overall air effort was directed against Normandy coastal batteries. On the morning of 6 June, individual battleships and cruisers were assigned to each of the identified heavy batteries. Some destroyers and gunboats fired on the beach defenses, while others attacked the flanks of the landing beaches or stood ready to answer calls for fire support.

Field Marshal Erwin Rommel had predicted that the landing would be accompanied by heavy air and naval attack, and doubted if he could defeat the invasion after this pounding. He noted that Allied air and naval attack hampered his defense, or made it impossible. He reported that naval gunnery's "effect is so immense that no operation of any kind is possible in the area commanded by this rapid-fire artillery, either by infantry or tanks." When Rommel and his superior, Field Marshal Gerd von Rundstedt, Commander in Chief West, reported this to Hitler, Hitler responded that destruction of the Allied battleships was of "outstanding importance." This, of course, was not feasible; the Allied navies continued to support the battle for the beachhead until the fighting had moved inland. Rear Adm. Alan G. Kirk, commander of the Western Task Force, reported that "the performance of battleships, cruisers, and destroyers in support of the landing was magnificent," while Adm. Bertram H. Ramsay, the Allied naval commander in chief, wrote that "by common consent, the shooting was uniformly good and it is considered that the initial advances of our armies were helped in no small measure by the naval supporting fire."

[See also Air Spotting Pool; Close Gunfire Support.]

BIBLIOGRAPHY

Conway's All the World's Fighting Ships, 1922–1946, 1980.
Ellis, L. F., et al. The Battle of Normandy. Vol. 1 of Victory in the West. 1962.
Morison, Samuel Eliot. The Invasion of France and Germany, 1944–1945. Vol. 11 of History of United States Naval Operations in World War II. 1957. Reprint, 1988.
Padfield, Peter. Guns at Sea. 1974.
Schofield. B. B. Operation Neptune. 1974.

JOHN C. REILLY, JR.

BOMBER COMMAND. RAF Bomber Command was placed under General Dwight D. Eisenhower's command on 14 April 1944. Until then it had been largely committed to the strategic bombing of Germany, a campaign that started when France and the Low Countries were attacked in May 1940. Directed from their headquarters at High Wycombe (about 16 kilometers or 10 miles northwest of London), the bomber squadrons operated almost entirely by night, experience having shown that they could not do so by day without suffering unacceptable losses. Since precise objectives could not be identified and hit at night, they were compelled to concentrate mainly on area targets. Consequently, up to 1944 Bomber Command had devoted most of its attention to the attack on German cities; its equipment and tactics were thought ill-suited to precision bombing.

When, however, it was decided to adopt the Trans-

RAF AVRO LANCASTER MkIII.   Strategic bombers such as the Lancaster were able to reach deep into German-held Europe to strike bridges and rail heads.
IMPERIAL WAR MUSEUM

RAF DE HAVILLAND MOSQUITO OVER ENGLAND.   The fast and durable Mosquito was one of the best overall combat aircraft ever built in Britain.   IMPERIAL WAR MUSEUM

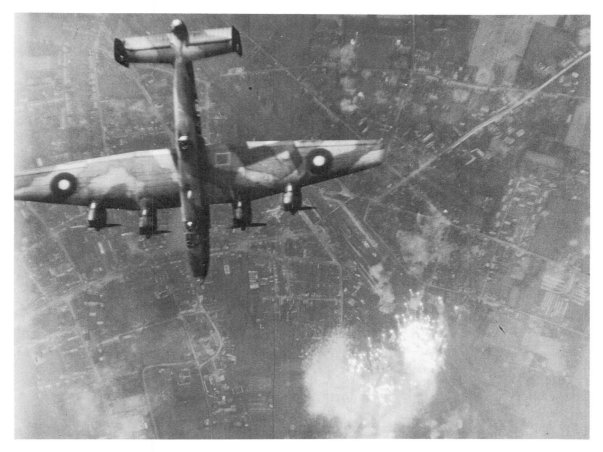

RAF HANDLEY PAGE HALIFAX.   Strategic bomber en route to its target in occupied Europe on 6 June 1944.
                                                                                             IMPERIAL WAR MUSEUM

TANK DEPOT AT MAILLY.   Tank and truck depot in northeastern France, 40 miles southeast of Rheims, before the Bomber Command attack on the night of 4–5 May 1944.   IMPERIAL WAR MUSEUM

portation Plan and attack rail communications in France in preparation for OVERLORD, the use of the strategic air forces, both British and American, was considered essential. Bomber Command was now equipped with some 1,400 heavy bombers, Lancasters and Halifaxes, together with a force of light Mosquito bombers, all based in eastern England on sixty-one airfields stretching from East Anglia through Lincolnshire and Yorkshire to Durham. The commander in chief, Air Chief Marshal Arthur Harris, exercised command through seven subordinate headquarters. Nos. 1, 3, 4, 5, and 6 Groups provided the main striking force, No. 8 Group contained the pathfinder squadrons, and No. 100 Group comprised the specialist radio countermeasures units that sought to confuse the German air defenses. Altogether there were 83 squadrons, 14 of them belonging to the Royal Canadian Air Force and, mostly in 6 Group, 4 belonging to the Royal Australian Air Force, and 4 others with New Zealand, Rhodesian, French, and Polish personnel.

The offensive against the French railways began with a series of experimental attacks on six major marshaling yards starting on the night of 6–7 March 1944; their great success confirmed the practicality of the full plan, and Bomber Command was allocated 37 of the 79 centers that were to be knocked out by the Anglo-American air forces in order to paralyze the railway system before the invasion. The subsequent attacks, delivered mainly in April and May, were "astonishingly accurate," to quote Harris. Coupled with the bombing of coastal defenses and supply depots, the Command's total offensive prior to D-day entailed 24,600 sorties and the dropping of 87,000 tons of bombs—a major contribution to the preliminary air campaign that was critical to the success of the invasion.

The night before D-day saw Bomber Command out in force. The main effort, involving over 1,000 aircraft, was against ten heavy gun batteries in the landing area, but just as important in their own way were the diversionary and support operations, not least the carefully controlled

TANK DEPOT AT MAILLY.   After Bomber Command attacked in strong force, dropping 1,500 tons of high-explosive and incendiary bombs.   IMPERIAL WAR MUSEUM

dropping of bundles of narrow metal foil strips (code-named Window) over the Straits of Dover in a successful attempt to simulate the reaction a large convoy would produce on the German radar. Altogether some 1,200 bombers operated that night, including the radio countermeasures squadrons and a force of Mosquitos that attacked Germany itself.

Bomber Command was out again in force every night over the next twelve days. Its prime task continued to be the attack on railway communications either just behind the front line, as on the night of 6–7 June when 1,065 aircraft took part, or farther to the rear in order to impede the flow of German reinforcements. On the night of 8–9 June the targets included the important tunnel at Saumur, where the new 12,000-pound Tallboy bombs were used to such effect that the Germans were never able to clear the line. In addition, at the request of the army there were attacks on key road junctions, troop concentrations, and ammunition and fuel dumps: on 9–10 June a group of

airfields was bombed, and on the 14th and 15th the E-boat bases at Le Havre and Boulogne were targeted with great success. Over the same period the new strategic offensive against oil refineries in Germany was begun with raids on Gelsenkirchen and Sterkrade. The commencement of the German V-weapon assault on southern England compelled diversion of some of the effort to the V-1 launching sites in the Pas de Calais, but Mosquitos continued to operate over Germany as far east as Berlin. Altogether this twelve-day offensive entailed over 8,500 sorties and cost some 150 aircraft.

Thereafter there was a pause, largely owing to bad weather, but soon the effort was resumed and Bomber Command remained at the Supreme Commander's disposal until September. General Bernard L. Montgomery, thanking them for their readiness to cooperate in the tactical battle, asked Harris to tell his pilots how greatly the Allied soldiers admired and applauded their work, and Eisenhower had no doubts about the value of their contribution.

[*See also* Harris, Arthur; Railroads.]

BIBLIOGRAPHY

Middlebrook, Martin. *Bomber Command War Diaries*. 1985.
Terraine, John. *The Right of the Line*. 1985.
Wynn, Humphrey, and Susan Young. *Prelude to Overlord*. 1983.

HENRY PROBERT

BRADLEY, OMAR (1893–1981), American, lieutenant general, commander of U.S. First Army. Omar Nelson Bradley was born on 12 February 1893 in Clark, Missouri. He was the son of a farmer who supplemented his income by teaching school. Because of the family's limited financial means, the prospect of a college education was remote, but in 1911 Bradley secured an appointment to the U.S. Military Academy at West Point. Upon graduation from West Point in 1915, he was commissioned a second lieutenant in the infantry.

During the 1920s and 1930s Bradley's career followed a pattern typical for officers of his generation. His assignments included service with the National Guard in Hawaii and two tours of duty at West Point. One assignment was of particular significance: while serving as an instructor at the army's Infantry School, he impressed the deputy commandant, Lt. Col. George Marshall. As the army's Chief of Staff during World War II, Marshall would recall Bradley's grasp of tactics.

Advancement had been slow in the peacetime army, but the outbreak of World War II catapulted Bradley into the senior ranks of American military leaders. He was promoted to brigadier general in 1941 and appointed commandant of the Infantry School. He became a major general and division commander in 1942, and in 1943 was promoted to lieutenant general and given command of II Corps in North Africa. As commander of II Corps, Bradley gained valuable experience in the conduct of amphibious operations when the Allies invaded Sicily in July 1943.

In October 1943 Bradley arrived in England to assume command of U.S. First Army, which was earmarked for Operation OVERLORD, the invasion of Normandy. At this time a general plan for the cross-Channel attack had been developed by the office of the Chief of Staff to the Supreme Allied Commander (COSSAC). Nevertheless, Bradley and his subordinate commanders were responsible for developing plans at the operational and tactical levels. Moreover, Bradley was charged with bringing the First Army troops to a high state of combat readiness.

As D-day approached, Bradley's staff refined plans for an assault against the German defenses. Although a subordinate of Field Marshal Bernard L. Montgomery, commander of 21st Army Group, Bradley enjoyed consider-

OMAR BRADLEY.   THE ROBERT HUNT LIBRARY, LONDON

able autonomy in preparing First Army for its mission.

On 6 June 1944 elements of First Army's V Corps and VII Corps landed on beaches that were code-named Utah and Omaha. The landing on Utah Beach proceeded smoothly, but combat on Omaha was intense. After overcoming resistance, Bradley's forces gradually expanded the beachheads, and by mid-June a massive buildup of men and matériel was under way. During this period, Bradley maintained close contact with his corps and division commanders, but generally deferred to their tactical judgment and initiative. On 26 July, First Army broke through the German lines at Saint-Lô and opened the way for an advance to the Seine River.

As commander of First Army, Bradley did not project a charismatic image. He was firm and decisive, but also soft-spoken and inclined toward deliberate decisions. War correspondents observed that Bradley evaluated the multiple factors that determine success on the battlefield with the mind of a mathematician. Because of his unpretentious demeanor and reserved style, Bradley earned the sobriquet of "the GI's general."

In August 1944 Bradley was given command of the newly formed 12th Army Group, which included U.S. First Army and U.S. Third Army. As army group commander, Bradley devised the campaign strategy that enabled American forces to sweep across France to the Siegfried Line. In December Bradley's armies participated in the counteroffensive that foiled the German attack in the Ardennes, and by March 1945 12th Army Group was poised to cross the Rhine. When First Army units seized a bridgehead at Remagen, General Dwight D. Eisenhower, the Supreme Commander, made Bradley responsible for the main attack into the heart of Germany.

Bradley's military career and public service did not end with the defeat of Germany. In August 1945 President Harry S. Truman called upon Bradley to head the Veterans Administration, and in 1948 he succeeded Eisenhower as Chief of Staff of the U.S. Army. The following year Bradley was elevated to the post of chairman, Joint Chiefs of Staff. As chairman of the JCS he was instrumental in developing military strategy to support the policy of containing the U.S.S.R. In September 1950 President Truman promoted Bradley to the five-star rank of general of the army.

When Bradley relinquished his military duties in 1953, he became chairman of the board of the Bulova Corporation. While involved in the business community, he remained active in public affairs also. During the Vietnam War he served as one of the elder statesmen who advised President Lyndon B. Johnson on policy and strategy.

Omar Nelson Bradley died on 8 April 1981. He was buried at Arlington National Cemetery.

[*See also* First Army.]

BIBLIOGRAPHY

Bradley, Omar N. *A Soldier's Story.* 1951.
Harrison, Gordon A. *Cross-Channel Attack.* U.S. Army in World War II: The European Theater of Operations. 1951.
Weigley, Russell F. *Eisenhower's Lieutenants: The Campaigns of France and Germany, 1944–1945.* 1981.

PAUL L. MILES

BRERETON, LEWIS H. (1890–1967), American, lieutenant general, commander of the Ninth Air Force. Brereton graduated from the U.S. Naval Academy in 1911, but soon transferred to the army, where he became one of its first pilots. He served as a squadron commander in France in World War I, where he won the Distinguished Service Cross for shooting down four German planes. By the end of the war, he was operations officer for the American Expeditionary Air Service.

In the interwar period, Brereton was closely associated with Gen. William ("Billy") Mitchell. He taught at the Air Corps Tactical School and commanded various units, including the 2d Bombardment Group. He was promoted to brigadier general in 1939, and major general in 1941. Late in 1941, he was ordered to command the U.S. Air Forces in the Philippines, which were largely destroyed when the Japanese attacked Clark Field on 8 December 1941.

LEWIS H. BRERETON.   NATIONAL ARCHIVES

In 1942, Brereton was sent to command the U.S. Air Forces in the Middle East. A year later, he arrived in England to command the Ninth Air Force, which would provide tactical air support for the U.S. ground armies during D-day, and later across Europe.

Promoted to lieutenant general in April 1944, Brereton was an able organizer and administrator. He had built up the Ninth Air Force from only a few air groups in 1943 to a force of eleven bomber groups, eighteen fighter groups, and fourteen troop carrier groups by D-day. Brereton and the Ninth Air Force were heavily involved in pre-invasion air planning and operations. Brereton showed himself to be a capable air tactician by planning much of the highly successful air campaign that paralyzed the French rail net and consequently crippled the Germans' ability to move troops and supplies after the Normandy landings. He ordered the use of his P-47 fighters as dive bombers, a very effective role, and directed his medium bombers to destroy the French rail bridges. His greatest accomplishment was his direction of the Ninth Air Force interdiction campaign from May to July 1944, which effectively sealed the Normandy area and hampered all Wehrmacht movement.

Brereton nevertheless was hampered by his weaknesses as a commander, which lay in his leadership and his acidic personality. He got along badly with his peers, superiors and subordinates. Gen. Henry H. Arnold, chief of the Army Air Forces, blamed Brereton for the debacle in the Philippines in 1941. Gen. Omar Bradley disliked Brereton intensely and accused him of not training the Ninth Air Force for close air support of ground troops. Bradley also personally blamed Brereton for the hundreds of U.S. casualties inflicted by American bombers during the COBRA operation of July 1944.

Brereton was removed from command of the Ninth Air Force in August 1944 and given command of the First Allied Airborne Army. But his unpopularity was such that, although he had commanded one of America's largest air forces in combat, he was never promoted to full general and retired shortly after the war in 1948. He died in 1967.

[See also Ninth Air Force.]

BIBLIOGRAPHY

Brereton, Lewis H. *The Brereton Diaries*. 1946.
DuPre, Flint. *U.S. Air Force Biographical Dictionary*. 1978.
Keegan, John. *Who Was Who in World War II*. 1978.

JAMES S. CORUM

BREUNING, ERICH ALFRED (1897–1978), German, rear admiral, commander of *Western Defense Force*. Erich Alfred Breuning was born on 16 October 1897 in Rottweil, Württemberg. He joined the Imperial Navy in January 1916. He served on several warships in World War I, and was promoted to lieutenant in March 1918. After the war he transferred to the new German navy, where he held various posts. In 1936 he was made an expert on mines in the Operations Division of the Navy High Command, where he remained until September 1942, meanwhile advancing to captain in 1940.

In September 1942 Breuning became head of the *3d Defense Division,* then in June 1943 commander in chief of the *Western Defense Force* (Befehlshaber der Sicherung West—BSW) with headquarters in Paris. A rear admiral as of 1 June 1944, Breuning was responsible for overall defense of the western coast of France, Belgium, and southern Holland. For this task he commanded a total of 309 minesweepers, 116 patrol boats and submarine chasers, and 42 gun carriers (*Artillerieträger*), of which a third lay in dock with some kind of damage. At the height of the invasion Breuning, in his Paris headquarters, was inadequately informed about the fate of his forces, which suffered heavy losses, especially through air attacks. Surviving vessels remained in the West after the cordoning off of the German-held Atlantic ports. Thus the command for Germany's *Western Defense Force* had to be dissolved on 30 September 1944.

On 28 October 1944 Breuning was named chief of staff on the National Socialist Command Staff in the Wehrmacht High Command, formed after the 20 July 1944 attempt on Hitler's life. He retained this post until 8 May 1945. Captured, on 12 May he was brought to Felixtown-Harwich, England, as an expert on mines, in order to provide information on German minefields from documents and his own knowledge. After release from internment as a POW in May 1948, Breuning lived in St. Peter-Ording. He died on 28 November 1978 in Las Palmas, Grand Canary Island.

[See also Western Defense Force.]

BIBLIOGRAPHY

Hildebrand, Hans H., and Ernest Henriot. *Deutschlands Admirale*. Vol. 1, 1988.
Lohmann, Walter, and Hans H. Hildebrand. *Die deutsche Kriegsmarine 1939–1945*. 1956–1964.
Rohwer, Jürgen, and Gerhard Hümmelchen. *Chronology of the War at Sea, 1939–1945*. Translated by Derek Masters. 1992.

GERHARD HÜMMELCHEN

BRITAIN. *See* Great Britain.

BRITISH BEACHES. [*The following entry includes four articles:*

    An Overview
    Gold Beach
    Juno Beach
    Sword Beach.

For discussion of Omaha and Utah beaches, see American Beaches.]

An Overview

The British Second Army (under Lt. Gen. Miles Dempsey) landed the I and XXX corps on Gold, Juno, and Sword beaches with the dual aim of securing a lodgment in France and placing a powerful force around Caen. Unlike Utah and Omaha beaches, which were widely detached, these three were all of a piece. Running continuously for forty kilometers (twenty-five miles), they were subdivided into sectors: Item, Jig, King, Love, Mike, Nan, Oboe, Peter, Queen, and Roger. Port-en-Bessin lay on the western edge, the projected junction point with the First U.S. Army. Ouistreham at the mouth of the Orne River was the eastern extremity, the junction point with the 6th British Airborne Division. Equally unlike Omaha, a considerable stretch of this coastline was low lying with sandy beaches descending gradually to the sea. The *LXXXIV Corps* within the German *Seventh Army* (Gen. Friedrich Dollmann commanding) was responsible for the defense of the area, its *716th Infantry Division* holding the coast from the Orne River to Le Hamel, and the *352d Infantry Division* from Le Hamel westward to include part of Omaha. Eight infantry battalions from these formations manned the shoreline, over which the British and Canadians would land, and the support belt immediately behind. From these, ten companies, reinforced by one hundred light guns, fifty mortars, and some five hundred machine guns covered the beaches directly. Twenty-seven batteries of artillery, numerous self-propelled and towed antitank guns lay within and behind the coastal belt together with a reserve of five more infantry battalions. All were well supplied with ammunition, concentrated progressively since the appointment of Field Marshal Erwin Rommel in his concurrent appointment as inspector of defenses in the west. Dollmann assured the *LXXXIV Corps* commander, Lt. Gen. Erich Marcks, during April and May that if his sector was pressed, armored forces would immediately counter any penetration.

None among the corps expected to be attacked across the British beaches on the morning of 6 June, notwithstanding reports of airborne landings to the east and west. Some hours passed before Dollmann was able to relate the seaborne to the airborne landings and to order priorities for counterattack, the British landing sites appearing to be more important than those at Omaha since Maj. Gen. Walther Krauss, commanding the *352d Infantry Division,* was confident of holding the coastal defenses there. Though this was a misjudgment, the regrouping and redeployment of the *21st Panzer Division* remained a prime requirement. Urgent requests were also made for additional armored forces; but first the movement forward and then the authority to commit to operations the *12th Panzer* and *Panzer Lehr Divisions* were denied by Adolf Hitler to Commander in Chief West Gerd von Rundstedt, until 1600 on D-day.

In the organization of forces for the seaborne assault, the British and their Canadian partners formed brigade groups, formations of all arms within their divisions on the same basis as the American regimental combat teams.

Naval control during the landings was exercised commonly for all beaches by Eastern Task Force under Rear Adm. Philip Vian in HMS *Scylla.* Three subordinate forces served the beaches: G for Gold, J for Juno, and S for Sword. Light craft shuttling between beach and deep-draft vessels were also controlled by the Royal Navy, and naval teams ashore directed these craft in and out of cleared lanes. Naval teams in cooperation with specialist army engineers also cleared beach obstacles to enlarge access.

On each beach an army area headquarters and two or three working groups—specially trained infantry battalions—were established as soon as the assault forces had cleared the foreshore. Their task was to provide dispersal sites, maintain beach exits, control traffic, and establish

a main beach signal station. Rearward movement—chiefly the wounded, in the early stages—was similarly coordinated with the Royal Navy beach masters. For some days, the beach organizations worked under intermittent enemy shellfire.

The weight and frequency of German artillery fire and, no less, air strikes were constrained initially, however, by the abiding air supremacy of the Allied air forces. Luftwaffe attacks were limited to hit and run. While batteries in casemates were more effectively hit by naval gunfire, those in the open were picked up and attacked principally from the air. As operations developed, German batteries in the bocage, replete with cover, became the targets of British and Canadian artillery. The Second Tactical Air Force was then better employed in attacking troops moving to reinforce the German defense line, which it did by day and night.

BIBLIOGRAPHY

Ellis, L. F., et al. *The Battle of Normandy.* Vol. 1 of *Victory in the West.* 1962.
Wilmot, Chester. *The Struggle for Europe.* 1952.

ANTHONY FARRAR-HOCKLEY

Gold Beach

Gold was the British western beach, sixteen kilometers (ten miles) across. Half of it was useless for landings; from Port-en-Bessin to Arromanches-les-Bains steep bluffs overlooked a rock-strewn shore. But between Arromanches and the seaside village of La Rivière, the sea broke on gently shelving sand and clay.

The XXX British Corps was ordered to break open the Gold defenses and advance to capture Bayeux and the high ground immediately east and west of it on D-day. The commander, Lt. Gen. G. C. Bucknall, decided to employ one division on this task to simplify the chain of command in the opening phase. He chose the 50th (Northumbrian) under Maj. Gen. D. A. H. Graham, which he reinforced with an armored and an infantry brigade.

The western section of Gold, Item sector, was reserved for early development of a Gooseberry—followed by a Mulberry—prefabricated harbor. The 231st Brigade Group of the 50th Division landed on Jig, the central sector, just after 1730 on 6 June, the 15-knot wind and flowing tide carrying the 1st Battalion, Royal Hampshire Regiment (Hampshires), eastward. Sea and wind held back the landing of its supporting armor. The commanding officer, his artillery support officers, and many in his forward headquarters became casualties; shortly afterward, his second-in-command was killed. Their headquarters radios were smashed, and thus the battalion lacked the means to call for fire support from ships or aircraft. Even so, the Hampshires closed

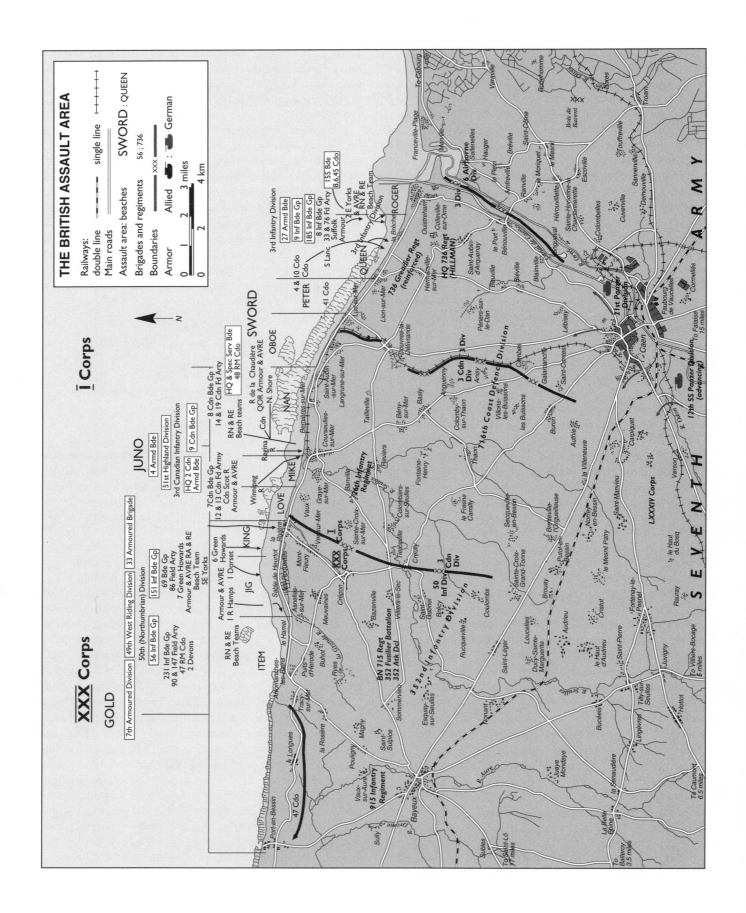

THE BRITISH ASSAULT AREA

Railways:
double line ⟶ single line
Main roads
Assault area: beaches — **SWORD : QUEEN**
Brigades and regiments — 56 : 736
Boundaries — xxx
Armor — Allied — German

0 1 2 3 miles
0 2 4 km

N

XXX Corps

GOLD

| 7th Armoured Division | 49th West Riding Division | 33 Armoured Brigade |

50th (Northumbrian) Division

| 56 Inf Bde Gp | 151 Inf Bde Gp | 69 Bde Gp |

231 Inf Bde Gp
90 & 147 Field Arty
47 RM Cdo

86 Field Arty
7 Green Howards
Armour & AVRE RA & RE
Beach Team
SE Yorks

Armour & AVRE
I R Hamps
I Dorset

6 Green
Howards
I Devons

RN & RE
Beach teams

ITEM

JIG KING

I Corps

JUNO

| 4 Armd Bde |

51st Highland Division

3rd Canadian Infantry Division

| HQ 2 Cdn Armd Bde | 9 Cdn Bde Gp |

7 Cdn Bde Gp
12 & 13 Cdn Fd Army
Cdn Scot R
Armour & AVRE

8 Cdn Bde Gp
14 & 19 Cdn Fd Army
RN & RE
Beach teams

R de la Chaudière
QOR Armour & AVRE
N. Shore
Cdn

HQ & Spec Serv Bde
48 RM Cdo

LOVE MIKE NAN

OBOE

SWORD

3rd Infantry Division

| 27 Armd Bde | 9 Inf Bde Gp |

| 185 Inf Bde Gp |

2 E Yorks
33 & 76 Fd Arty
Suffolk

4 & 10 Cdo

S Lanc

PETER 41 Cdo QUEEN ROGER

155 Bde
8.6.45 Cdo

8 Inf Bde Gp
AVRE & RE
Beach Team

Ī Corps

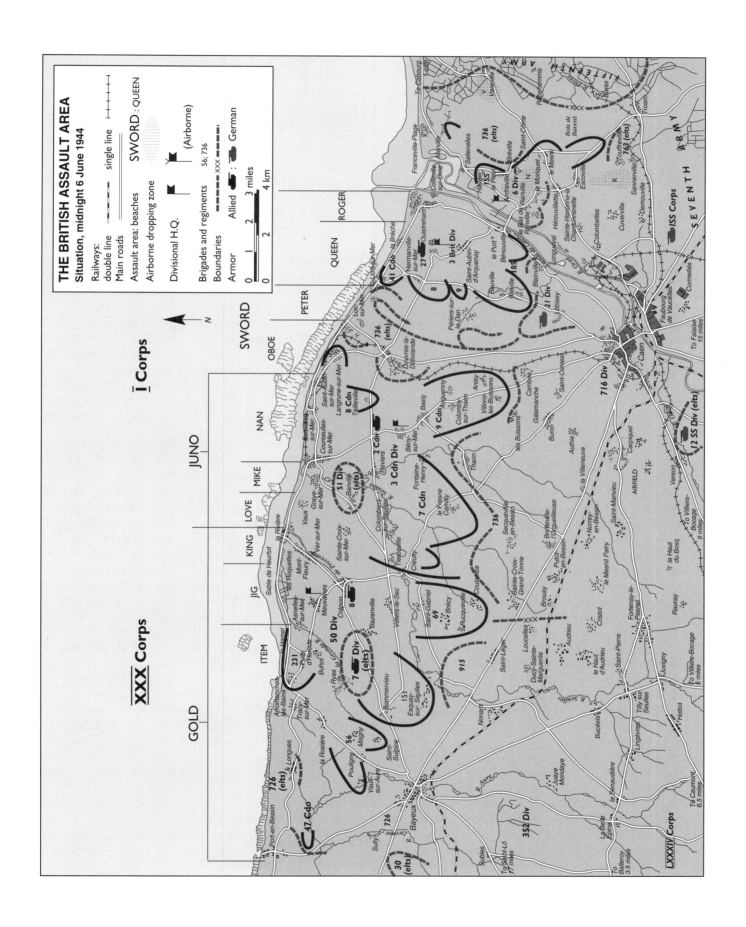

THE BRITISH ASSAULT AREA
Situation, midnight 6 June 1944

Railways:
double line
Main roads   single line

Assault area: beaches
Airborne dropping zone

Divisional H.Q.   (Airborne)

Brigades and regiments   56: 736
Boundaries   xxx

Armor   Allied   : German

SWORD : QUEEN

0   1   2   3 miles
0   2   4 km

N

XXX Corps   GOLD

I Corps

SWORD   OBOE

PETER   QUEEN   ROGER

JUNO   NAN

MIKE   LOVE   KING   JIG   ITEM

with the reinforced concrete defenses of Le Hamel.

Farther to the east in Jig sector, the 1st Battalion, the Dorset Regiment (Dorsets), passed successfully through Les Roquettes and began to push inland. Behind them flail tanks and armored engineer assault vehicles (AVRE) began to open paths through the mine fields. The 2d Battalion, the Devonshire Regiment (Devons), and the 47th Royal Marine Commando (47th Commando) followed between 0800 and 0900, though three of the latter's landing craft foundered on obstacles. Forty-three marines were lost together with numerous radios.

In King sector, easternmost on Gold, the 69th Brigade Group of the 50th Division landed at 0730. The 6th Battalion, Green Howards (6th Green Howards) and AVREs rapidly cleared the post at Hable de Heurtot and advanced on the fortified but heavily shelled complex of Mont Fleury. The 5th Battalion, the East Yorkshire Regiment (5th East Yorks), were halted at La Rivière, where a corner of the shell-torn defenses remained intact. Machine guns raked the beach and an 88-mm gun in a ferroconcrete bunker began to pick off the AVREs. A lone AVRE drew in on the blind side of the barrel aperture, braved exposure at a hundred meters (one hundred and ten yards), and fired directly into the opening. This permitted the 5th East Yorks, sheltering under the seawall, to clear the area. But it took several more hours to sweep the remainder of La Rivière village, building by building. Bypassing this battle, the reserve battalion, the 7th Green Howards, landed at 0820 to follow the 6th Green Howards and to establish with tanks a hold on the Meuvaines ridge.

The arrival of tanks in the latter part of the morning—the Nottinghamshire Yeomanry and the 4th and 7th Dragoon Guards—greatly increased General Graham's opportunities to push inland. More flail tanks of the 22d Westminster Dragoons joined those beating out routes through the second mine field belt. Three self-propelled field artillery regiments followed, providing thereafter a close support and counterbattery capability. Several Royal Marine Centaurs, mounting 95-mm howitzers, were also concentrating, but they had lost three-quarters of their complement on the sea passage.

At noon Gold Beach was in full use as a reception and dispersal site, except in the area of Le Hamel, where the Hampshires assisted by the Devons battled on until 1600 to clear machine-gun nests, many of which, tucked behind concrete curtains, were firing in enfilade. As mine and booby trap clearance developed, unit assembly areas were allocated south of the coast road; a mass of unit directional signboards appeared along the tracks. The 56th Brigade Group landed and, as planned, set off to the southwest to capture Bayeux. The 151st Brigade Group entered the line between the 56th and 69th Brigades to advance toward occupation of the main road between Bayeux and Caen.

German opposition fell away as the 50th Division advanced from Gold during the morning and afternoon but revived for several hours from about 1600. The most serious encounters involved a battle between two German battalions with antitank support—part of *352d Infantry Division*'s reserve—and the 69th Brigade in the area of Villiers le Sec and Bazenville at 1600, which the latter decisively won. But, if anything, the advance from Gold on D-day was hampered by an excess of caution in the evening. The battalions of the 56th Brigade could have taken Bayeux that night without a struggle but were restrained. The commanders of both the 56th and the 151st Brigades were concerned to secure their gains in expectation of counterattack, while the *LXXXIV Corps* commander was unhappily aware that he had no forces in the area to take the offensive.

On the coast, the Hampshires, joined by the remainder of the 231st Brigade, turned westward, clearing the defenses to Arromanches. This secured the anchorage for the first phase of harbor construction, the placement of Gooseberry breakwaters and Whale piers within them by Royal Engineer Port Construction units. No. 47 Commando, which had landed with the 50th Division on Jig, infiltrated successfully to capture Port-en-Bessin on 7 June after many adventures. It welcomed the arrival of the American First Army the next day, when Omaha and Gold were effectively joined.

Almost 25,000 troops had landed on D-day. During the following week, the 50th Division was strengthened by the arrival of the British 7th Armoured Division, ensuring the lodgment despite early and daunting enterprise by the *Panzer Lehr Division* and later the *2d Panzer*, counterattacking from among various infantry, artillery, and antitank groups on the XXX Corps front. Weather and some degree of confusion ashore delayed subsequent landings, yet by D plus 12, the whole of the XXX Corps had passed across Gold Beach, with the 49th (West Riding) Division under Maj. Gen. E. H. Barker taking its place in the line. The British VIII Corps formed up behind them with the 11th Armoured and 15th (Scottish) Divisions. By 18 June, the American 1st Infantry Division and British 7th Armoured held the foremost extension of the bridgehead, 35 kilometers (22 miles) from the beaches they had crossed to begin the liberation of France and Europe.

[*See also* Task Force G *and articles on units mentioned herein.*]

BIBLIOGRAPHY

Clay, Ewart W. *The Path of the 50th: The Story of the 50th (Northumbrian) Division in the Second World War, 1939–1945.* 1950.

Spiedel, Hans. *We Defended Normandy*. 1951.

ANTHONY FARRAR-HOCKLEY

Juno Beach

Together with Sword, the central beach Juno, ten kilometers (six miles) in width, was allotted to Lt. Gen. J. T. Crocker to land his I British Corps. Offshore reefs obscured the greater part of Juno's seaward approaches, screening altogether the westernmost Love sector. The adjacent Mike, however, was readily accessible through a central passage, as was the eastern part of Nan sector.

The 3d Canadian Division (Maj. Gen. R. F. L. Keller commanding), reinforced by an armored brigade, AVREs, and Royal Marine Centaurs, was to land two brigades almost simultaneously on Juno from 0735, the 7th Canadian on Mike and the edge of Nan, the 8th Canadian on Nan. Force J lowered the assault craft without serious mishap from 0617, but the assault engineers were delayed by misdirection through the swept channel of another group, to which they had to defer. The heavy swell and current from the west contributed to other delays as the first wave of landing craft, assault (LCA), weaved through the various obstructive devices to put the infantry ashore—but not without loss.

A Canadian naval officer later reported, "About three quarters of the troops had been disembarked from *LCA 1150* when an explosion . . . blew in the port side. . . . The port side of *LCA 1059* was blown in by one of the mined obstructions after about one third of the troops had been disembarked. . . . two soldiers were killed. Another explosion holed *LCA 1137* and stove in the starboard bow. All troops had been cleared from the craft without casualties. . . . *LCA 1138* was about to leave the beach when a wave lifted it on to an obstruction. The explosion which followed ripped the bottom out of the craft. . . . An obstruction ripped the bottom out of *LCA 1151*. The crews then transferred to an LCT [landing ship, tank] and were eventually brought back to the [parent] ship."

Twenty of 24 LCA were lost in one battalion landing; altogether 90 of 306 LCA were lost or disabled during the morning. Still, they landed the majority of the infantry in the right area, and between 0800 and 0900 the four assault battalions were engaged in opening the Atlantic Wall.

The 7th Canadian Brigade straddled the Seulles River. A company of the Royal Winnipeg Rifles (Winnipeg), assisted by tanks, assailed the buildings of Courseulles-sur-Mer on the western bank while the remainder pressed on to Graye-sur-Mer a kilometer inland. Bombardment from the sea had damaged the beach defenses in this area, though there were still numerous pockets of enemy to be overcome. The greater part of Courseulles, lying on the east bank, was largely intact. Despite supporting fire from the Sherman tanks of the 6th Canadian Armoured Regiment, which had swum ashore, elements of the Regina Rifles were obliged to clear it piecemeal. Assisted later by AVREs and Centaurs, they triumphed finally in midafternoon. Meantime, the Winnipeg and part of the Canadian Scottish had cleared Vaux, Graye, and Sainte-Croix-sur-Mer. A follow-up company of the Regina Rifles, much diminished by losses on landing, had marched around the Courseulles battle to capture Reviers.

The sea was too rough for the tanks of the Canadian 10th Armoured Regiment to swim ashore with the 8th Brigade's leading infantry. Their landing craft drew in to shallow water, attracting shellfire that destroyed six Sherman tanks. The Queen's Own Rifles and the North Shore Regiment storming the seawall at Bernières-sur-Mer and Saint-Aubin-sur-Mer, respectively, found both villages alive with enemy. The ferroconcrete strongpoint commanding the Bernières beach resisted all assaults until it was broken up by renewed naval gunfire, but its flanking positions were combed out by the Queen's Own during this action. The village was cleared by 0930, but when the reserve battalion, the Regiment de la Chaudière, sought to move south to Bény-sur-Mer it was halted by machine guns and antitank guns sited on a spur immediately ahead. It was noon before this ground was cleared. Saint-Aubin was captured by 1030, though snipers operated until nightfall.

Meanwhile, landings continued, though somewhat more slowly owing to the impediments of broken landing craft and vehicles overlying the beach defenses. Random mortar and small-arms fire across the strand delayed the flail tanks and assault engineers clearing and opening routes inland. The third wave of vehicles and men became progressively packed together in and between Bernières and Saint-Aubin as the artillery, 9th Canadian Brigade, remaining armor, and divisional headquarters landed but were unable to deploy. The beach here was particularly narrow at high tide. Warnings of the situation notwithstanding, the Canadians wanted to get ashore.

The assault engineers opened two routes and then another through the shore obstructions. From 1400, the reserve brigade, four regiments of field artillery, and a third armored regiment were all engaged in expansion of the divisional bridgehead. Free of the shore defenses, the Canadian armor and infantry advanced aggressively. The 7th Brigade swept over a battalion of the *726th Infantry Regiment*, closing their western flank with the British 50th Division at Creully. Intermittently under shellfire, they stalked a series of antitank guns to cut the Caen-Arromanches road at Le Fresne–Camilly. The 8th Brigade cleared the fortified villages of Tailleville, Basly, and Colomby-sur-Thaon and were succeeded by the 9th at 1830, when the North Nova Scotia Highlanders and 27th Armoured Regiment pushed on through German mortar and antitank gunfire to capture Villons—les Buissons and Anisy at sunset. Opposed now by the remaining local defenses reinforced by a battle group from the *21st Panzer Division* (under Generalleutnant Edgar Feuchtinger), the brigade was ordered to hold its foremost positions overnight.

A total of 21,400 troops had landed on Juno Beach on 6 June. The delays on the beaches denied the 3d Canadian Division its D-day objective, Carpiquet airfield, but it had secured a considerable bridgehead and joined up with the 50th Northumbrian and Gold Beach. That evening at Bény, however, the divisional commander discovered that the enemy still held a corridor to the coast, dividing him from the British 3d Division to the east. The 48th Commando supported by Centaurs had captured the greater part of Langrune-sur-Mer after a day-long battle, but the German coastal garrison and part of the *736th Grenadier Regiment* still held the coast eastward for four kilometers (two and a half miles).

A battle group of the *21st Panzer Division* was probing in this direction early in the evening of 6 June, although, all communication having been lost with this sector of the *716th Infantry Division*, its commander was unaware of the

corridor. A rifle company and six tanks succeeded in reaching the coast, and this force reported the opening. Shortly afterward, however, a substantial air transport stream under fighter escort—destined for the 6th Airborne Division—appeared falsely to be dropping in the area and the battle group drew back. In any case, orders had arrived for a major counterattack next day to destroy the British bridgehead.

Obergruppenführer Joseph ("Sepp") Dietrich, *I SS Panzer Corps* commander, was ordered to mount this attack. He launched all he could muster of the *12th SS Panzer Division* (it was still concentrating in the area and required fuel) against the Canadians between 0900 and 1000 on the seventh. The latter had advanced the 7th Brigade across the Bayeux-Caen road and the 9th Brigade was approaching Authie when a battle group of the *12th SS Panzer* (Brigadeführer Kurt Meyer) appeared from Authie, driving into the Canadian positions. Surprised, the 9th Brigade was forced back into Buron after considerable losses. There it held, eventually forcing the SS battle group to withdraw. Meyer's other venture that day, a thrust down the corridor between Juno and Sword beaches, was frustrated by the junction of the Canadian and British divisions on either side.

Rommel ordered Dietrich to attack again on 8 June,

CANADIANS DISEMBARKING.   The second wave of the 7th Canadian Brigade lands on the western side of Juno Beach at 0730 on D-day.
HULTON DEUTSCH

effectively with the *12th SS Panzer* and *21st Panzer* divisions, and Meyer chose to strike at the 7th Canadian Brigade holding Putot and Bretteville-l'Orgueilleuse. A battle group drove the Winnipeg Rifles and their supporting tanks from Putot after a long and costly fight; and that evening a second group under Meyer's personal direction attempted to drive the Regina Rifles from Bretteville. It failed. Having lost a third of his tanks, Meyer drew back. The Canadians reoccupied the ground they had conceded.

During the next two weeks, the 3d Canadian Division had a crucial role in the operations around Caen, denying all attempts to throw them back toward Juno Beach and, by the pressure they exerted, drawing enemy reinforcements onto their front.

On the beach itself landings continued, but not at the pace planned. In the week following the landings, the harbor at Courseulles was rapidly opened. Two piers, each seven hundred feet in length, were installed on Juno. As the beach hazards were progressively cleared, landing ships and even small coasters were grounded at high water to discharge on the ebb. But on Juno, as elsewhere, persistent winds, the scale of obstacles, errors, and misunderstandings between shore and ship controls delayed the buildup of men, equipment, and supplies, including concentration of the 51st (Highland) Division. Even before a storm rising on the night of D plus 12 devastated landing operations, these were two days behind schedule.

Extraordinary efforts overcame the principal movement difficulties. Juno Beach was to remain a vital link in the reinforcement and supply chain for many weeks after D-day.

[*See also* Task Force J *and articles on units mentioned herein.*]

BIBLIOGRAPHY

Edwards, Kenneth. *Operation Neptune.* 1946.
Stacey, C. P. *The Canadian Army: 1939–1945.* 1948.

ANTHONY FARRAR-HOCKLEY

Sword Beach

The shoreline between the village of Saint-Aubin-sur-Mer and the mouth of the Orne River was designated Sword and subdivided west to east as Oboe, Peter, Queen, and Roger sectors. Offshore rocks denied direct access to Oboe, Peter, and part of Queen. Shoaling complicated landing on Roger. General Crocker thus decided to land the 3d Infantry Division, the left hand of the two assault formations in his I Corps, on Queen, between the eastern outskirts of Lion-sur-Mer and the Riva-Bella extension of Ouistreham, some three kilometers off the flat sandy shore. The narrow frontage restricted the divisional commander, Maj. Gen. T. G. Rennie, to use of a single brigade for the break-in operation. And—a not unimportant fac-tor—it involved separation of four kilometers (two and a half miles) from the Canadians.

The division was ordered to capture Caen, or at least the high ground overlooking the city, and to secure the Orne canal and river crossings into the 6th Airborne Division area. But the first requirement was to capture a bridgehead.

It fell to the 8th Infantry Brigade Group, specifically to the 1st Battalion, the South Lancashire Regiment (South Lancashire), 2d Battalion, the East Yorkshire Regiment (2 E. Yorks), and the armor of the 13th/18th Royal Hussars (13/18H). Among this group were two squadrons of assault engineers, the Westminster Dragoons' Flail tanks, Royal Marine Centaurs, and the devoted naval and army beach clearance and control teams.

Force S carrying the 3d Division was the only sea transport group to rendezvous to the east of the Solent. After a night in the Channel swell, the leading infantry companies boarded their LCAs at 0530 and were lowered into the turbulent sea. Seasickness became widespread. Heading for the enemy shore, Maj. C. K. King read extracts from Shakespeare's *Henry V* to his company of 2 E. Yorks over the Tannoy system. Close by, the LCTs carrying the Duplex Drive tanks and AVREs steamed on, closing to 5,000 yards before launching, owing to the wave heights.

Maj. Hendrie Bruce of the 9th (Irish) Field Battery, accompanying the infantry, noted:

> Further out to sea came the group carrying the Divisional Artillery and about 0630 hours, when they were about 15,000 yards (13,600 meters) from the shore, they began to change formation in readiness for the "Run In Shoot." . . . In close attendance was a Motor Launch equipped with a radar to calculate the opening range. The radio links were working perfectly and all was now ready for ranging to begin at H-42 [0643 hours]. . . . The bombardment of shore targets by naval gunfire from battleships, monitors, cruisers, and destroyers had already begun and promptly at H-35 [0650 hours] the seventy two 105-mm self-propelled guns of 3 Div Arty opened fire at just over 10,000 yards, (9,000 meters) firing high explosive.

Maj. A. D. Rouse with the South Lancashire recounted:

> The boat crews had been ordered to go in at 4 knots and hit the beach hard. During the last 100 yards (91 meters) of the run in everything seemed to happen at once. Out of the haze of smoke, the underwater obstacles loomed up. We had studied them on air photographs and knew exactly what to expect but somehow we had never realised the vertical height of them, and as we weaved in between iron rails and ramps and pickets with Teller mines on top like gigantic mushrooms we seemed to be groping through a grotesque petrified forest. . . . Mortar fire was coming down on the sands, an 88-mm gun was firing along the line of the beach and there was continuous machine-gun and rifle fire. Immediately ahead of us a DD tank, its rear end enveloped in flames, unable to get off the beach, continued to fire its guns.

The bombardment suppressed but did not destroy the forward companies of the *736th Grenadier Regiment*. As the guns lifted, the commanding officer and two company commanders of the South Lancashire were killed. Maj. A. R. Rouse noted that Lt. R. Bell-Walker, assuming a company command, "lobbed a grenade through a gun port and then gave it a burst of fire. He himself was killed by a burst of fire from strong point COD over on our left. He had, however, opened a way for the rest of his company to get off the beach." In confused fighting, a corporal of the antitank platoon maneuvered his gun at the water's edge to destroy a machine-gun post with a 6-pounder shell.

By 0900, the South Lancashire had overcome the beach defenses and captured their next objective, the village of Hermanville-sur-Mer, a thousand meters inland. Close behind, the 41st Commando suffered considerably during the landing before they moved westward to attack Lion-sur-Mer, while the 10th (Inter-Allied) Commando struck in the opposite direction for Ouistreham. For a time, they were engaged with the East Yorks in clearing the remainder of La Brèche, a battle that continued until 1000. Meanwhile, the foreshore, narrowed by the flowing wind-driven tide, was packed with those following, including the 1st Battalion, the Suffolk Regiment (Suffolk), the reserve battalion of the 8th Brigade.

While the East Yorks cleared the southern outskirts of Ouistreham and captured a nearby spur, the Suffolk advanced through Colleville-sur-Orne and overran a gun battery much damaged by the naval bombardment, but was halted at strong point HILLMAN half a mile beyond it. Here the headquarters of the *736th Regiment* was encased

AERIAL VIEW OF QUEEN SECTOR OF SWORD BEACH.   IMPERIAL WAR MUSEUM

in ferroconcrete bunkers behind numerous mines and barbed wire. Failing to penetrate these on first encounter, the Suffolk paused to mount a deliberate attack that delayed the advance until 2000. Meanwhile, HILLMAN's machine guns had inflicted considerable casualties on the 1st Battalion, the Royal Norfolk Regiment (Norfolk), a battalion of the 185th Brigade, which had landed behind the initial assault force.

The 185th Brigade was advancing to Caen. Because its tanks—the Shermans of the Staffordshire Yeomanry—were delayed on the crowded beach, the infantry marched on alone at noon. Fortunately the leaders—the 2d Battalion, the King's Shropshire Light Infantry (KSLI)—were overtaken in the afternoon, for soon after 1600, ninety tanks and two motorized infantry battalions of the *21st Panzer Division* began counterattacks, half of this force striking the foremost elements of the 185th Brigade at Biéville and Périers ridge. The Shermans, detachments of the 20th Anti-Tank Regiment, and the KSLI 6-pounders knocked out thirteen tanks with minor losses. The enemy withdrew. A fragment of the German battle group then penetrated down the western flank of the 3d Division to discover the gap between Sword and Juno beaches. Further attacks were then inhibited by air strikes on the *21st Panzer* and the erroneous belief of the divisional commander and staff that the air transport stream flying low across their front—destined, in fact, for the 6th Airborne Division—was about to land troops in the Caen area.

By nightfall, the whole of the 3d Division was ashore, including the attached 27th Armoured Brigade. The beach landing site was still a scene of confusion, but the 9th Brigade had deployed into the line on Périers ridge. The 185th Brigade had posts within five kilometers (three miles) of Caen and had cleared the Orne bridges. The remainder of Ouistreham had fallen to the 4th Commando and two French troops of the 10th, strongly supported by Royal Marine Centaurs and ten AVREs. The 41st Commando had captured half of Lion-sur-Mer.

Into this bridgehead had landed the 1st Special Service Brigade under Lord Lovat: the 3d, 6th, and 45th (Royal Marine) Commandos had marched across the Orne bridges to join the 6th Airborne Division, their arrival signaled by a tune on the bagpipes of the brigadier's piper.

In the next few days, the 3d Division struggled to advance on Caen. The 185th Brigade occupied Lébisey after several grievous mishaps and the 9th Brigade took Cambes. But there they were held, and there they themselves hung on under counterattacks by weighty enemy reinforcements in armor and infantry as a grand strategic maneuver developed on the hinge they provided.

[*See also* Task Force S *and articles on units mentioned herein.*]

BIBLIOGRAPHY

Belchem, David. *Victory in Normandy.* 1981.
Klee, Karl. *The Decisive Battles of World War II: The German View.* 1965.
McNish, Robin. *Iron Division: The History of the 3rd Division.* 1977.

ANTHONY FARRAR-HOCKLEY

BROADHURST, HARRY (1905–), British, air vice marshal, air officer commanding 83d Composite Group. Harry Broadhurst joined the Royal Air Force (RAF) in 1926 and, after service in India and in fighter squadrons in the United Kingdom, commanded Wittering during the Battle of Britain. Later, while in command of another fighter station, Hornchurch, he was selected to visit the United States where he met Generals Spaatz and Eaker, contacts that proved invaluable when the two air forces later operated together. In 1943, as air officer commanding Desert Air Force in North Africa under Air Marshal Coningham, he established a fine reputation as a commander of tactical air forces, and General Bernard L. Montgomery insisted that Broadhurst accompany him to northwest Europe as one of his tactical air commanders for Operation OVERLORD.

Broadhurst took over 83 Group in March 1944, bringing with him his private plane, a captured Fieseler Storch, and worked alongside Lt. Gen. Miles C. Dempsey in

HARRY BROADHURST.   IMPERIAL WAR MUSEUM

planning his group's close cooperation with the British Second Army. On D plus 4 he flew his own Spitfire across to Normandy; soon afterward he moved his headquarters to France. He remained in command of 83 Group until the end of the war. Such was Montgomery's confidence in Broadhurst that he often dealt directly with him on tactical air matters as the campaign progressed.

A brilliant pilot, a great leader, and an excellent planner, he remained in the RAF until 1961, completing his career by leading Bomber Command in the late 1950s when the V-Force was coming into operational service, and finally serving at Allied Air Forces Central Europe.

[*See also* 83d Composite Group.]

BIBLIOGRAPHY

Terraine, John. *The Right of the Line.* 1985.

HENRY PROBERT

BROOKE, ALAN (1883–1963), British, field marshal, chief of the Imperial General Staff. Born into a family of Irish Protestant soldiers, Brooke grew up in France before being commissioned into the Royal Artillery in 1902. Highly articulate, intelligent and professional, a natural leader, and moderately ambitious, he made a considerable reputation as an artillery officer during World War I, in which he came to appreciate the need to adopt mobile warfare. He developed the first British mobile division in 1937. When the Second World War began, his outstanding command of a corps in France and Belgium led to his becoming commander in chief of the United Kingdom Home Forces preparing in 1940 for a German invasion. The next year, he became chief of the Imperial (Army) General Staff just prior to the attack on Pearl Harbor and, shortly thereafter, chairman of the British Joint Chiefs of Staff.

As allies, America and Britain agreed that the combined forces should concentrate against Germany first, but Brooke urged that cooperation should begin in North Africa (GYMNAST) to clear the Mediterranean for shipping. All agreed that the cross-Channel invasion of northwestern Europe must follow. Gen. George Marshall favored immediate concentration of resources in the United Kingdom to land in France in 1942 (SLEDGEHAMMER), and when the arguments for GYMNAST prevailed, he pressed for the landings in 1943 (ROUNDUP).

As developments carried them through invasion of Sicily and Italy, Winston Churchill sought to avoid what he anticipated would be a "bloodbath" across the Channel. Though Brooke had no doubt that a break-in through Normandy (OVERLORD) had to be mounted, his support of Italian operations to pin down German formations

there suggested to American colleagues that his commitment to OVERLORD was halfhearted. This, combined with national considerations, led to rejection in Washington of Brooke as supreme commander of the Allied invasion of Europe. It was Brooke, however, who pressed adamantly for OVERLORD in 1944 when President Franklin D. Roosevelt, with scant resistance by his staff, ordered invasion of the Andaman Islands (BUCCANEER) as a sop to Chiang Kai-shek, an operation that would have used landing craft needed for OVERLORD. At the second Cairo conference in 1943, in the face of Brooke's unrelenting arguments, BUCCANEER was abandoned and resources for Italy agreed upon. As a quid pro quo he accepted the American proposal for an invasion of southern France—DRAGOON—following OVERLORD. His intervention subsequently modified the date and scope of DRAGOON.

By this time, Brooke and Marshall, originally strangers, had come to trust if not always to agree with one another. Both were direct in manner and upright in character. Despite considerable disappointment at the rejection of his nomination for the OVERLORD supreme command, he

ALAN BROOKE. NATIONAL ARCHIVES

unfailingly supported General Dwight D. Eisenhower in that appointment; though he regretted the latter's inexperience in the field, a diary entry in May 1944 noted that he was "a champion of inter-Allied cooperation."

As OVERLORD approached, he had again to dissuade Churchill from ventures elsewhere—Norway or Portugal, for example—in preference to the feared bloodbath in Normandy. On occasion, he was obliged to "tell off" General Bernard L. Montgomery, rebukes accepted meekly; Brooke was the only superior whom Montgomery wholly respected. Indeed, like General Marshall, Brooke held the wholehearted respect and affection of all those with whom he worked so long and effectively toward victory in the war.

Leaving the army in 1946, after forty-three years of service, he became a viscount—Lord Alanbrooke—and among other high honorary offices under the Crown, Lord High Constable of England. Widely valued for his quick intelligence and humanity, he joined the boards of a number of commercial companies and charities but made time for his two abiding interests, his family and birds, becoming an expert in bird photography. He died quietly at home in 1963.

BIBLIOGRAPHY

Bryant, Arthur. *Triumph in the West.* 1959.
Fraser, David. *Alanbrooke.* 1982.
Kennedy, John. *The Business of War.* 1957.

ANTHONY FARRAR-HOCKLEY

BROOKS, EDWARD H. (1893–1978), American major general, commander of the U.S. 2d Armored Division. Born in Concord, New Hampshire, on 25 April 1893, Edward H. Brooks entered the 1st Cavalry, Vermont National Guard, in 1915. In 1917 Brooks received a first lieutenant's commission in the regular army. During World War I he commanded a detachment of the 3d Field Artillery Brigade and participated in the Champagne-Marne, Aisne-Marne, Saint-Mihiel, and Meuse-Argonne campaigns. During the interwar years he graduated from the Field Artillery School and the Command and General Staff School, and taught military science at Harvard University. In 1937, as a major, he graduated from the Army War College in Washington, D.C. He joined the War Department General Staff as chief of the Statistics Branch in July 1939, receiving his lieutenant colonel's commission in that position. In 1941 Brooks became the artillery officer of the Armored Force and was given the temporary rank of brigadier general. He played a major role in the development of highly mobile armored artillery units for use in the army's newly evolving armored divisions. In July 1942 he assumed command of

the 11th Armored Division and the following month was promoted to major general (temporary). In April 1944 he took command of the 2d Armored Division in England.

During the critical weeks leading up to the Normandy invasion, General Brooks oversaw the preparations of the 2d Armored Division, which was scheduled to be one of the first follow-up divisions to land on Omaha Beach in order to help expand the beachhead. Departing England on 8 June, the division arrived off the coast of France the next day. Brooks landed on Omaha Beach on 11 June and immediately assumed command of the 2d. Elements of the division were dispatched to provide assistance to the 29th Infantry Division in securing a bridgehead over the Vire River, and patrols were sent out to reconnoiter the area.

Before dawn on 13 June Brooks received word that a German armored attack was expected in the vicinity of Carentan, a weak spot in the Allied line where the V Corps and VII Corps zones met. He immediately deployed elements of the 2d Armored Division to counter this threat. The Germans, expecting only infantry opposition, were caught off guard and routed by the American tanks. Over the next two days Brooks's troops played a pivital role in driving the Germans from Carentan, enabling the V Corps and VII Corps to be firmly linked.

In August 1944 General Brooks was awarded the Silver Star for gallantry in action. In October 1944 he was given command of the VI Corps, in which position he served during the remainder of the war in Europe. Highlights of Brooks's postwar career included tours of duty as deputy commander of the Seventh and Third armies; commanding general, U.S. Army in the Caribbean; and commander of the Second Army. Brooks retired on 30 April 1953 as a lieutenant general. He died on 10 October 1978.

[*See also* 2d Armored Division.]

BIBLIOGRAPHY

Brooks, Edward H. General Officer Biography files. Historical Records Branch, U.S. Army, Center of Military History, Washington, D.C.
Houston, Donald E. *Hell on Wheels: The 2d Armored Division.* 1977.
Trahan, E. A., ed. *A History of the Second United States Armored Division, 1940–1946.* 1946.

EDWARD N. BEDESSEM

BROWN, L. O. (1893-1978), British, air vice marshal, air officer commanding 84th Composite Group. Leslie Oswald Brown, born and brought up in South Africa, where he served initially in the Local Defence Force (Artillery), Brown joined the Royal Naval Air Service in 1915 and flew with distinction in the East

L. O. BROWN.   IMPERIAL WAR MUSEUM

African campaign. He continued on maritime air duties after the Royal Air Force (RAF) was formed, serving at Lee-on-Solent and Calshot, before spending several years in Iraq in the 1920s. During the 1930s he worked mainly with the army, partly in India, partly in command of an Army Cooperation Wing at Odiham. For the first years of World War II he was in the Middle East, where he commanded the handful of squadrons that tried to help the army counter Rommel's first advance in the Western Desert. He later headed the RAF in Palestine and Transjordan.

On returning home in 1943 he served at Army Cooperation Command and Fighter Command before taking over 84 Group on 19 November. He remained commander for exactly one year; working under Air Marshal Coningham, he directed the operations of his group from its headquarters at Cowley, near Oxford—and subsequently Goodwood Park—during the air campaign that preceded and accompanied the invasion. He moved across to France in August but, not in the best of health, left 84 Group in November. He was then appointed commandant of the School of Air Support, later to be renamed the School of Land/Air Warfare, and on retirement in 1948 he returned to South Africa.

[See also 84th Composite Group.]

BIBLIOGRAPHY

Wynn, Humphrey, and Susan Young. *Prelude to Overlord*. 1983.

HENRY PROBERT

BRYANT, CARLETON F. (1892-1987), American, rear admiral, commander, Naval Gunfire Support Group. Bryant graduated from the U.S. Naval Academy in 1914, 17th in a class of 250. His first duty (1914–1919) was on the battleship USS *Wyoming* and he also served on the battleship USS *Pennsylvania* and as commanding officer of the USS *Arkansas* (1941–1943). In Bryant's *Story of a Naval Officer's Lifetime in the U.S. Navy*, he observed that "I served . . . when battleships were in their prime and I am grateful for that privilege."

Bryant's involvement in World War II began even before 7 December 1941. As commanding officer of *Arkansas*, he commanded the first American troop convoy to Northern Ireland in September 1941. He became the innovative leading commander of fast troop convoys to the United Kingdom and North Africa. Bryant estimated that he had convoyed the astounding total of one million American servicemen without an enemy-caused casualty.

In May 1943 Bryant was promoted to rear admiral and made commander of Battleship Division 5. He continued to command fast troop convoys until the spring of 1944. Then he was ordered to Belfast Loch, Northern Ireland, to help plan the invasion of France as commander, Bombardment Group, Omaha Beach.

Bryant's D-day fleet comprised seventeen ships: two battleships, USS *Texas* (his flagship) and USS *Arkansas;* two British and two French light cruisers; and eight American and three British destroyers. These ships provided artillery support for the troops that landed on Omaha Beach.

Bryant's Group arrived about eight kilometers (five miles) offshore at 0130 on 6 June and at dawn began a one-hour bombardment. Enemy batteries on the cliffs above Omaha Beach were the main targets.

As the troops began going ashore none of the expected calls came in from the fire control officers who had accompanied the landing parties. It was learned later that nearly all the controllers had been killed. This severely hampered naval fire support. Nothing on the beach was moving, Bryant wrote: "You knew instinctively something was wrong. There was a gully up which our men . . . were to go, but nothing was going up it."

Finally, *Texas* was permitted to fire a few fourteen-inch shells (1,400 pounds each) up the gully. "They had an instant effect," Bryant noted, "as we could see Germans coming down . . . with hands up and our men began to move up."

Another D-day incident involved German use of a

church tower about three kilometers inland to direct fire at Omaha Beach. Bryant order a destroyer (USS *Emmons*) to eliminate the tower, which it did in a matter of seconds with three shots. On a postwar visit, Bryant found that the tower had been completely restored by the United States.

After D-day, the Bryant force had some slack days but on others "we had incessant calls for fire—one after another—troop concentrations or tanks. Several days we gave support fire continuously," Bryant recalled. His D-day involvement ended on 25 June when he commanded part of a force in the bombardment of Cherbourg.

Admiral Bryant's record as a commander of both gunfire support groups and fast troop convoys was unmatched. He provided outstanding leadership, which earned him a place as one of the top naval commanders of World War II.

Bryant returned to the United States in September 1944 to become commander, Atlantic Fleet Operational Training Command; part-time commander, Battleships and Cruisers; and commander, Amphibious Forces, Atlantic Fleet.

On 1 May 1946 Admiral Bryant retired and advanced to vice admiral on the retired list. He lived nineteen years in Santa Barbara, California, and then returned to Maine, his home state, where he died on 11 April 1987.

Admiral Bryant was given high marks by Samuel Eliot Morison in his *History of United States Naval Operations in World War II* both for his gunfire support roles and his convoy service. French Admiral Jaujard, who served under Bryant in the two French invasions, also praised him highly. There was fulsome praise about the navy's role from high-ranking army generals, such as "Our supporting naval gunfire got us in."

[*See also* Gunfire Support; Texas, USS; Western Task Force.]

BIBLIOGRAPHY

Bryant, Carleton F. *Story of a Naval Officer's Lifetime in the U.S. Navy.* 1974.
Morison, Samuel E. *The Invasion of France and Germany, 1944–1945.* Vol. 11 of *History of the United States Naval Operations in World War II.* 1957.

GORDON F. GRAHAM

BUCKNALL, G. C. (1894–1980), British, lieutenant general commanding British XXX Corps. Gerard Corfield Bucknall was born on 14 September 1894. Educated at Repton and Sandhurst, he was commissioned into the 1st Battalion of the Middlesex Regiment in 1914 and served throughout World War I, finally on the General Staff. He was wounded and was mentioned in dispatches. He held various commands in the 1920s and 1930s. When World War II came, after serving in the War Office as a staff colonel he went on to command the British 5th Division in Sicily and Italy in 1943.

By the eve of the Normandy invasion, Bucknall had been placed in command of XXX Corps, one of the four corps that made up the 21st Army Group's Second British Army, and one of the two British corps (the other being I Corps) that was assigned an assault role on D-day itself. Bucknall's elevation from divisional to corps command drew protests from Gen. Alan Brooke, chief of the Imperial General Staff, who intimated to General Bernard L. Montgomery that he regarded Bucknall as unsuitable for such an appointment. But Montgomery, impressed by Bucknall's performance in Sicily and Italy, expressed confidence in his corps commander.

Bucknall's XXX Corps failed to achieve its D-day objectives and then became stalled in the Seulles Valley between 9 and 11 June, though Lt. Gen. J. T. Crocker's I Corps likewise made insufficient progress by this time. Montgomery and Lt. Gen. Miles C. Dempsey, commander of the Second Army, were to develop real doubts about Bucknall's suitability as a corps commander as a result of his handling of XXX Corps during the battle of Villers-Bocage on 12–14 June. They felt he had not moved quickly enough to take

G. C. BUCKNALL.   IMPERIAL WAR MUSEUM

advantage of a gap in the German lines between Caumont and Villers-Bocage, and had not responded with sufficient vigor to the possibilities that emerged once the battle developed. Culpability, however, might also be laid at the door of the commanders of the XXX Corps formations involved, namely Brig. Robert ("Looney") Hinde of 22d Armoured Brigade and his superior, Maj. Gen. G. W. E. J. Erskine of 7th Armoured Division. Indeed, when Bucknall's corps was deemed to have shown insufficient drive after a subsequent offensive, Operation BLUECOAT of 30 July, Montgomery relieved all three of them of command, replacing Bucknall with Lt. Gen. Brian Horrocks.

After the war Bucknall became general officer commanding Northern Ireland, 1945–1947, and then retired shortly afterward, having served for nearly thirty-five years as an officer in the regular army. He was appointed lord lieutenant of Middlesex, 1963–1965, and assistant lieutenant for Greater London, 1965–1970. He died on 7 December 1980 at the age of eighty-six.

[*See also* Erskine, G. W. E. J.; 7th Armoured Division; XXX Corps.]

BIBLIOGRAPHY

Bucknall, G. C. Papers. The Imperial War Museum, London.
D'Este, Carlo. *Decision in Normandy: The Unwritten Story of Montgomery and the Allied Campaign.* 1983.
Ellis, L. F., et al. *The Battle of Normandy.* Vol. 1 of *Victory in the West.* 1962.
Hastings, Max. *Overlord: D-Day and the Battle for Normandy, 1944.* 1986.

FRANCIS TOASE

BULLEN-SMITH, D. C. (1898–1970), British, major general, commander of the 51st (Highland) Infantry Division.

As a young officer in the King's Own Scottish Borderers, Bullen-Smith had an excellent record in World War I. When British troops were back again in France in 1940, he was a staff officer in Maj. Gen. Bernard L. Montgomery's 3d Division, where he earned the high opinion of his commander. During the years following the retreat from Dunkirk, he served in the United Kingdom and became known as an outstanding trainer of troops. By 1943 he was commanding the 15th (Scottish) Infantry Division, which he turned into a first-class military formation. When Maj. Gen. Douglas M. Wimberley was brought home from Sicily to become commandant of the Staff College, Camberley, Bullen-Smith was chosen to take his place in command of the famous 51st (Highland) Division.

D. C. BULLEN-SMITH.   Pointing, with staff and G. H. A. MacMillan (left).   IMPERIAL WAR MUSEUM

To take over from Wimberley, a man of immense, if sometimes slightly eccentric, energy and well known to every man in the division, would have been a hard task for anyone. For Bullen-Smith, who was efficient but conventional, the chance of capturing the imagination of the Highlanders was virtually impossible. They were at the peak of their form after over a year of hard fighting, from the Battle of El Alamein to the conquest of Sicily, with victories all the way, and they were now given a new commander who had not been with them in any of the actions.

After their arrival back in Britain in November 1943, Bullen-Smith's task was to train the 51st to take part in the invasion of France. It was not easy to do this, as many key individuals were posted out to other duties, and there was a general feeling that as a battle-hardened formation the division "knew it all already." Furthermore his tendency to fuss over details that Wimberley had regarded as unimportant did not earn him respect.

In the invasion plan, the 51st was the reserve division in the I Corps, following the 3d British and 3d Canadian Divisions across the Channel. Bullen-Smith landed on D plus 1 to find that there had been considerable confusion in the way his leading 153d Brigade had been put ashore the previous afternoon, with the brigade commander arriving behind his battalions. It took until D plus 7 for the whole division to be assembled on French soil, by which time various elements of it had been put under command of the 6th Airborne Division and used in several scattered actions in which losses had been heavy.

By D plus 12 the division was in defensive positions east of the Orne River, eight kilometers (about five miles) northeast of Caen. It was still in this area, in which it had suffered many casualties in attacks by the Germans as well as in its own largely unsuccessful operations, when a month later Montgomery decided that the morale of the division was so low that Bullen-Smith had to be relieved of command. On 26 July he was ordered to return to Britain. His tragedy was that his name, unlike Wimberley's, had become synonymous with defeat, and lacking personal charisma, he was unable to inspire his division to overcome its difficulties.

[*See also* 51st (Highland) Infantry Division.]

BIBLIOGRAPHY

Hastings, Max. *Overlord.* 1984.
Salmond, J. B. *The History of the 51st Highland Division, 1939–1945.* 1953.

JOHN BAYNES

BULOLO, HMS. A passenger ship built in 1938 by Barclay, Curle of Kincaid for Burns, Philip & Co. and used in the Australian trade, *Bulolo* was converted into an armed merchant cruiser in September 1939, then into a Landing Ship Headquarters (Large)—LSH(L)—in the spring of 1942. Armed with four 4-inch guns, its weight was 6,257 tons

HMS *BULOLO.*   IMPERIAL WAR MUSEUM

and its speed 15 knots. Its crew of 264 was commanded by Acting Capt. C. A. Kershaw. It was at the capture of Algiers in November 1942, provided communication facilities for the Casablanca Conference in January 1943, and served at Anzio in January 1944. Returning to Britain only in mid-April 1944 to be fitted with additional communications equipment, it was available for training until the final dress rehearsal in early May. Of the four British LSH (L)s, three were deployed on D-day, *Lothian* being the reserve. They carried extensive communications and command facilities, acting as joint service command ships until a general headquarters could be set up ashore.

The flagship of Rear Adm. C. E. Douglas-Pennant for Task Force G, Gold Beach, *Bulolo* embarked Lt. Gen. G. C. Bucknall of XXX Corps with the 50th (Northumbrian) Division and No. 47 Royal Marine Commando. It con-

trolled all aspects of the assault, from landing craft to air cover and naval gunfire support. Anchoring at 0556, it shifted at 0624 under fire from the battery at Longues, which *Ajax* then neutralized; at 1730 it proceeded inshore to speed up the landing. At 0605 on 7 June *Bulolo* was hit by a 250-kilogram phosphorus bomb, with four killed; the bomb just missed the operations room. It left for Spithead on 27 June, general headquarters having been established ashore. On D-day *Bulolo* handled 3,219 signals; between D-day and D plus 20 it conveyed a total of 42,298. It was returned to its owners in 1946.

[*See also* Douglas-Pennant, C. E.; Task Force G.]

BIBLIOGRAPHY

London. Public Record Office. "Overlord Plans and Preparations." Cabinet Office Papers, CAB 44/242.
London. Public Record Office. Ship Log Books, HMS *Bulolo*, ADM 53/119055.

ANDREW LAMBERT

ALFRED BÜLOWIUS.   COURTESY OF ALFRED PRICE

BÜLOWIUS, ALFRED (1892–1968), German, brigadier general commanding *II Air Corps*, responsible for offensive air support for German ground forces in Normandy. Alfred Bülowius joined the Royal Prussian Army in 1912 and fought during World War I. He entered the new Luftwaffe in 1933. During the campaign in the West in 1940 and the Battle of Britain, he commanded a bomber unit. He then held a series of staff appointments, but in the spring of 1943 he was appointed to command *II Air Corps (Fliegerkorps II)*, comprising fighter-bomber and bomber units based in Italy.

In the spring of 1944 *II Air Corps* moved to southern France in preparation for the expected Allied invasion. Although Bülowius was conscientious and capable, following D-day he had to send inadequate forces to attack targets in the face of immensely strong defenses. The reinforcement of about 150 aircraft from home defense fighter units in Germany did little to increase the fighting power of *II Air Corps*, given the pilots' lack of training in fighter-bomber tactics.

On 12 June the *Third Air Force* headquarters ordered the home defense fighters employed as fighter-bombers to revert to air defense operations. That made *II Air Corps* virtually redundant, and its units were handed over to *II Fighter Corps*. For a couple of weeks Bülowius had no official position, then on 1 July he replaced Brig. Gen. Werner Junck as commander of *II Fighter Corps*. By that time this formation was also depleted, and the new commander was able to achieve little.

At the end of the war Bülowius, a lieutenant general, commanded German airfields in the Dresden area.

[*See also* II Air Corps.]

BIBLIOGRAPHY

Bruetting, Georg. *Das waren die deutschen Kampfflieger-Asse 1939–1945*. 1975.

United Kingdom. Air Ministry. *The Rise and Fall of the German Air Force, 1933 to 1945*. 1948.

ALFRED PRICE

BUTTS, JOHN E. (1923–1944), American, second lieutenant, platoon leader, Company E, 60th Infantry, U.S. 9th Infantry Division; Medal of Honor recipient. John E. Butts was one of five brothers who saw military service in World War II. He enlisted in 1939 and attended Officers Candidate School three years later. A second lieutenant at the age of nineteen, by the time he landed in Normandy Butts was a combat veteran, having fought with the 9th Infantry Division in North Africa and Sicily.

On D plus 4 the 9th Infantry Division began landing on Utah Beach, and by 14 June the 60th Infantry was leading the division in an attack west across the Cotentin Peninsula to isolate German forces in Cherbourg. Butts was wounded near the town of Orglandes on the first day of the attack, but he stayed with his platoon. Two days later, as the 9th Infantry Division forced its way across the Douve River, Butts was again wounded but refused medical evacuation.

A week later as Butts's regiment was moving toward Cherbourg, he led his platoon in an assault on Hill 180, a well-defended German position near Flotteman Hague. As the assault began, Butts received a third wound, but despite his injuries he rallied the platoon and directed one squad to make a flanking approach on the machine gun that was holding up the attack. Butts, described by his father as "fearless since childhood," then made a lone frontal assault toward the defenders. Hit by machine-gun fire almost immediately, he got within ten meters (thirty feet) of the German strongpoint and attacked it with hand grenades, silencing the machine gun.

His plan worked. The platoon captured the strong point, but it cost Butts his life. For his "superb courage, unflinching valor and inspiring actions" Butts received the Medal of Honor, posthumously.

BIBLIOGRAPHY

Obituary. *The Journal Record* (Medina, N.Y.), 23 July 1945.

U.S. Department of the Army, Public Information Division. *The Medal of Honor of the United States Army*. 1948.

CLAYTON R. NEWELL

CANADA. Canada went reluctantly but grimly resigned to war in September 1939. World War I, which ultimately cost the country 60,000 dead and 173,000 wounded, including 11,500 gas victims, had been an enormous sacrifice for a country of 8 million people. It also triggered the bitter conscription crisis of 1917 that set English-Canadians against French-Canadians. Unfortunately, as Canadians turned their backs on Europe, they encountered only disillusionment and uncertainty. The Great Depression that struck in October 1929 had shattered the export economy and thrown one-third of the labor force out of work by 1933. Mass emigration to the United States and a declining birthrate that reached a low in 1937 further sapped Canadian confidence. Not until 1938 did national revenue exceed that of 1929. In the eyes of many, it was because Canada had paid so dearly in World War I that it had been laid so low by the Depression.

The Depression nonetheless proved a political boon to the opposition Liberal party of W. L. Mackenzie King, which swept to power in 1935. King's policy of unity and liberty aimed to heal the rift between French and English Canada by remaining aloof from world affairs. Though neither isolationist nor anglophobic, King did harbor a neurotic suspicion of British imperialists, and he also recognized the domestic dangers of foreign involvements. When the Canadian representative at the League of Nations proposed cutting off oil supplies to Italy during its 1935 invasion of Ethiopia, King repudiated his initiative. The political reality was that Benito Mussolini had many admirers in Quebec, upon which constituency King's government was so largely dependent.

With Europe clearly on the path to war, the British commenced limited rearmament in 1935 and the next year announced a comprehensive armament program. While King established a Canadian Defence Committee in 1936, Canada commenced limited rearmament only in 1937.

At the Imperial Conference that year King embraced the appeasement stance of Prime Minister Neville Chamberlain and dodged all commitments. He refused to cooperate in military planning with the British, who wanted to develop war industries and identify sources of vital raw materials, and he even forbade Canadian senior officers from discussing measures for the defense of the Crown Colony of Newfoundland. In 1938 he rejected British overtures for a joint large-scale air training scheme. When Chamberlain finally abandoned appeasement in March 1939, King retained an apparently unshakable conviction of its efficacy.

As late as April 1939, only two months after Britain had reluctantly accepted a continental commitment, the King government established a series of defense service priorities that approximated those associated with Chamberlain's limited liability policy of December 1937. The development of the Royal Canadian Air Force (RCAF) was accorded primacy over the Royal Canadian Navy (RCN), which service was given priority over the army. By 1939–1940 RCAF appropriations constituted nearly half the total allocation for all three services and exceed those of the army by $8 million. By promising never to conscript for overseas service, King ensured that Canada remained reasonably united when war came. In a snap election called in March 1940, his government won a landslide victory.

On the advice of the general staff, which correctly gauged the mood of most of the Canadian people, the government authorized mobilization on 1 September 1939. When Britain declared war, King asked Chamberlain how the Dominion might lend assistance. Three days later the British government requested Canada to consider providing a token expeditionary force plus technical units and personnel for attachment to British formations. On 16 September, six days after Canada declared war, the government decided to dispatch one division overseas. Ten days

LT. GEN. HENRY D. G. CRERAR, COMMANDER OF THE FIRST
CANADIAN ARMY, AND GENERAL EISENHOWER.

later, however, Chamberlain made an additional appeal for Canada to participate in the British Commonwealth Air Training Plan (BCATP), a grand air training scheme intended to qualify annually 20,000 British, Canadian, Australian, and New Zealand air crew for service with the Royal Air Force. Not surprisingly, King expressed regret that this overture had not been made earlier so that Canada could have framed its war effort along this line instead of having to field expeditionary forces. He accordingly pressed the reluctant British for public acknowledgment that Canadian participation in the BCATP "would provide for more effective assistance toward ultimate victory than any other form of military cooperation."

In pursuing a policy of limited liability, however, King ensured that Canada was almost totally excluded from participation in the higher direction of the war. He recoiled from assuming a strategic voice and demonstrated scant interest in military affairs. Perhaps because of President Franklin D. Roosevelt's 1938 promise that

America "would not stand idly by" if Canada were threatened, he accepted without serious objection the U.S. decision not to allow Dominion representation during the 1941 Anglo-American military conversations. Canadian membership on the exclusive Anglo-American Combined Chiefs of Staff Committee was also denied by the Americans as it would have entailed giving similar status to Australia, France, and perhaps Brazil. In civilian board membership Canada fared better by promoting the "theory of functional representation," whereby size of contribution to the war effort in specific areas rather than overall power status determined the degree of representation. That Canada was the sole country apart from Britain and the United States to gain direct representation on the Combined Food Board and the Combined Production and Resources Board attested to its growing economic strength. No less significantly, however, it was not granted membership on the important Munitions Assignments Board. Neither was its prime minister informed beforehand of the date of D-day.

After the fall of France in June 1941 the Dominion became Britain's senior ally, and its army overseas swelled to army formation size. On 11 August 1941 the Canadian general staff estimated that there existed sufficient manpower for Canada to field an overseas "army" of two corps, each of one armored and two infantry divisions, for a war period of over six years. By the end of the war, in fact, the First Canadian Army comprised two national corps composed of three infantry divisions (each of three infantry brigades), two armored divisions (each of an armored and infantry brigade), two independent armored brigades, two "army groups" (brigades) of Royal Canadian Artillery, and ancillary troops. Total active strength in the meantime peaked at 495,804 men of all ranks, the RCAF at 215,200, and the RCN at 92,441. By the end of 1943 the Canadian army overseas had reached it greatest size as a force of over a quarter of a million men. Despite its name, however, the First Canadian Army was never able to operate entirely as a Canadian field force, for it required the permanent commitment of upwards of 9,000 men per division, contributed by the British War Office, to complete its rearward support services. As the Canadian army possessed no heavy artillery, this also had to be provided by the British.

In general, Canadian army organization, doctrine, and training conformed to that of the British army, with which Canadian troops acted "in combination" under terms of the Visiting Forces Act of 1933. In practice, both armies were integrated so closely that one Canadian overseas training school recorded that "there were not two armies, British and Canadian, but one." The formation structure of the Canadian army similarly reflected a regimental system of units, with the difference that the composition of expeditionary force divisions had been pre-determined so as to give proportional representation to the major territorial regions of Canada.

The Canadian army overseas was a virtually untrained citizen force of limited military proficiency. Raw recruits who required individual training made up more than half the 1st Canadian Infantry Division upon its arrival in the United Kingdom. Critical equipment shortages plagued the pace of training, which also suffered from the debilitating overlap that inevitably occurred between Canada and Britain. Largely because of instructor deficiencies and officer shortages, the army in England in August 1941 established its own Canadian Training School. The 1st Division, however, had more than three years in which to train before being committed to Sicily in June 1943. The 2d Canadian Infantry Division, which arrived in October 1940, passed little more than twenty-two months in Britain before its decimation on the beaches of Dieppe in August 1942; thereafter it enjoyed an equivalent period in which to recover for battle in Normandy. The 1st Canadian Army Tank Brigade (later 1st Canadian Armoured Brigade), which accompanied the 1st Division to Sicily, arrived in Britain in June 1941. The 3d Canadian Infantry Division sent over in the autumn of 1941 had more than

two and a half years in which to prepare. The 5th Canadian Armoured Division, complete by November 1941, trained for roughly eighteen months in England before departure for the Italian theater, and the 4th Canadian Armoured Division, which followed in the summer of 1942, passed a similar period prior to taking part in the Normandy campaign. The 2d Canadian Army Tank Brigade arrived overseas in June 1943, only ten months before its commitment to battle.

The dispatch of the 1st Canadian Infantry Division and 1st Canadian Army Tank Brigade to Sicily in July 1943 eroded the national component of the First Canadian Army and cast its future into doubt. Though such deployment aimed primarily at getting Canadian troops into action in response to mounting public pressure, the hope was momentarily entertained that they would return to leaven their battle experience among Canadian formations for the invasion of northwestern Europe. There is reason to believe that after the bloodbath of Dieppe, however, King viewed sending additional troops to the Mediterranean as a means of avoiding the heavy casualties anticipated for the Normandy assault. In any case, the Canadian government's action in sending the 5th Canadian Armoured Division and Headquarters I Canadian Corps to

CANADIAN TROOPS DISEMBARKING FROM LANDING CRAFT, JUNO BEACH.

Italy in December 1943, despite Eighth Army objections that it required neither an armored division nor an extra corps headquarters, largely squelched the idea of the First Canadian Army spearheading an invasion of Normandy. When Gen. Bernard L. Montgomery assumed command of the 21st Army Group in January 1944, he relegated it to a follow-up role. The 3d Canadian Division and 2d Canadian Armoured Brigade had meanwhile been selected for assault landing training with I British Corps. Neither reverted to Canadian command until 11 July 1944.

Since the Militia Act stipulated that no soldier could be compelled to serve continuously in the field for more than a year, volunteers were encouraged to enlist for the duration of the war on general service for overseas in the newly created Canadian Active Service Force. Once inducted, recruits underwent eight weeks basic training, followed by two to five months of specialist training. The Number 1 Training Brigade Group, established at Debert, Nova Scotia, later gave reinforcements four weeks of individual and collective training before proceeding overseas. After Dunkirk, however, the National Resources Mobilization Act of 21 June 1940 imposed conscription for home defense duty that, in effect, created two classes of soldier within the Canadian army. Although they both trained together from March 1941, differences in status invited comparison and criticism that inevitably translated into outright antagonism.

After Pearl Harbor, the Canadian government on 22 January 1942 announced its intention to seek through a national referendum a release from its commitment to not conscript for overseas service. In the meantime it moved to establish a 6th and an 8th Division for Pacific coast defense and a 7th Division for the Atlantic. When the national plebiscite was held on 27 April 1942, over 80 percent of English-Canadians granted approval. Seventy-three percent of Quebecois, on the other hand, refused to release King from his pledge. An equal percentage of military voters abroad also agreed with the introduction of compulsory overseas service. But overseas conscription was not immediately imposed. After the battles of Normandy and the Gothic Line in Italy, however, overseas casualties began to mount, and by November 1944, it was clear that the volunteer system could not produce replacements. Faced with the threat of mass resignations by his English-Canadian cabinet ministers, King reluctantly accepted conscription.

The Canadian field force sent overseas was in several respects a remarkable one. Though many of its soldiers did not see Canada for over five years, it never cracked in the field. Until the autumn of 1944 there was no system of rotational leave for the Canadian soldier overseas. When it did come into effect, eligibility was restricted to those with "five years satisfactory continuous service overseas." All told, over 11,000 Canadian soldiers fell in the liberation of Europe. Of the approximate 15,000 Canadians who landed in Normandy on D-day, 359 were killed and 715 were wounded. Total army casualties during the war numbered 75,596, including 22,917 dead. The RCN, which ended the war as the world's third largest navy, incurred 2,343 casualties, of whom 2,024 died. The RCAF, which finished the war as the fourth largest air force, suffered a total of 18,517 casualties, including 17,101 killed.

[See also King, W. L. Mackenzie; Royal Canadian Air Force; Royal Canadian Navy; 3d Infantry Division (Canadian).]

BIBLIOGRAPHY

Douglas, W. A. B., and Brereton Greenhous. *Out of the Shadows: Canada in the Second World War.* 1977.

Eayrs, James. *In Defence of Canada: Appeasement and Disarmament.* 1964.

Eayrs, James. *In Defence of Canada: From the Great War to the Great Depression.* 1964.

English, John A. *The Canadian Army and the Normandy Campaign: A Study of Failure in High Command.* 1991.

Granatstein, J. L. *Canada's War: The Politics of the Mackenzie King Government, 1939–1945.* 1975.

Granatstein, J. L., et al. *Twentieth Century Canada.* 2d ed. 1986.

Stacey, C. P. *Arms, Men and Governments: The War Policies of Canada, 1939–1945.* 1974.

Stacey, C. P. *Six Years of War: The Army in Canada, Britain and the Pacific.* Vol. 1 of *Official History of the Canadian Army in the Second World War.* 1966.

Stacey, C. P. *The Victory Campaign: The Operations in North-West Europe, 1944–1945.* Vol. 3 of *Official History of the Canadian Army in the Second World War.* 1966.

JOHN A. ENGLISH

CANADIAN BEACHES. *See* British Beaches, *article on* Juno Beach.

CANADIAN SHIPS. *See* Royal Canadian Navy.

CASS, E. E. E. (1898–1968) British, temporary brigadier, commander of British 8th Infantry Brigade, and from 13 to 23 June 1944, commander of the British 3d Infantry Division. Cass, originally of the King's Own Yorkshire Light Infantry, was made a temporary brigadier in August 1943, having held a substantive lieutenant colonelcy for a year. He served as commander of the 8th Brigade until 26 October 1944, when he was injured by a mine in Holland and evacuated the next day. In addition to the above decorations, Cass was awarded the U.S. Silver Star for his services in France in 1944. He left the army in 1948.

E. E. E. CASS.   Being decorated by Omar Bradley.
IMPERIAL WAR MUSEUM

Cass's record is similar to that of his divisional commander, Maj. Gen. Tom Rennie. Cass was a man of undeniable courage and he was also thorough in the planning and implementation of operations. However, he has been criticized for not maintaining the pace of his brigade's advance. One particular instance involved the strong point code-named HILLMAN which lay three-quarters of a mile southwest of Colleville, and two and a half miles southwest of the center of Queen Beach, between the planned lines of advance of the 2d King's Shropshire Light Infantry and the 1st Norfolks.

On D-day the strong point, held by the *736th Regiment*, slowed down the momentum of the 3d Infantry Division's attack, the maintenance of which was vital to the achievement of the 3d Infantry Division's ambitious objectives. The Norfolks' attempt to bypass the strong point during the morning and early afternoon of D-day resulted in their taking 150 casualties, and the delay prevented them from supporting the 2d Shropshires' advance. This enabled the Germans to reinforce Lébisey Wood, located on the ridge that dominated the approaches to Caen, which was only taken at great cost and with delays later. Cass ordered the 1st Suffolks to take HILLMAN, but their first attack in the early afternoon was repulsed, and the deliberate attack that followed took most of the afternoon to prepare. Final resistance was only ended at 2015.

Cass defended his decision to plan a deliberate attack on the grounds that the point was defended by steel and concrete structures, as well as by mines, and that further attempts to rush the position would merely have resulted in high casualties. Cass asserted that the order to the battalion's commanding officer to take the position before dark was made with the knowledge of these defenses, and in the belief that the Germans' holding on to the strong point was not hampering the advance of Allied forces on each flank, and thus that incurring heavy losses to take HILLMAN was unnecessary. However, the advances of the forces on the flanks were not as fast nor as extensive as they would have been, had HILLMAN been taken, but more importantly, the cost of these advances was high. Given these facts, it seems that HILLMAN could have been taken faster if there had been some impulse for speed from senior commanders such as Cass and Rennie.

Criticism of Cass's ability to maintain momentum should be kept in perspective. Despite the 8th Infantry Brigade's apparent inertia at times under his command, Cass should not be blamed for the static role which, after the first few days, enveloped the 3d Infantry Division, which Cass commanded temporarily between 13 and 23 June. This situation had begun to develop before his temporary command, due to more than just his brigade's inertia, and by then the opportunities to break out of this role were restricted. Cass showed later in the year that he was able to command in chaotic and fluid situations. He retired from the army in 1948 and died in 1968.

[*See also* 3d Infantry Division (British).]

BIBLIOGRAPHY

McNish, Robin. *Iron Division: The History of the 3rd Division.* 1978.
Wilmot, Chester. *The Struggle for Europe.* 1954.

TIM MUNDEN

CASUALTIES. [*This entry includes three articles:* Allied Casualties, French Casualties, *and* German Casualties.]

Allied Casualties

One item of particular concern for Allied invasion planners was the number of expected casualties. In addition to the requirement for medical treatment and evacuation, high casualty rates could jeopardize the invasion, as troops would have to be landed faster than they could be killed or disabled by the Germans, if they were to successfully break out of the beachhead. Based on experience in the Pacific and the Mediterranean, coupled with

CASUALTY EVACUATION BOATS.   In readiness at Omaha Beach on D-day.   NATIONAL ARCHIVES

intelligence on the strength of German positions in Normandy, planners estimated that initial landing divisions would take 15 percent casualties, with their regiments taking 25 percent casualties, 70 percent of those being wounded and 30 percent killed, captured, or missing. Of the wounded, not all would require hospitalization, for many would be lightly wounded and could be treated at a medical facility and returned to duty. In the days following the landings, divisional casualties would decrease to 8 percent per day, with regimental casualties falling to 15 percent per day, 75 percent of those being wounded and the other 25 percent killed, captured, or missing. Actual casualties, with some exceptions, fell well below expected rates.

Casualty figures for the first days following the landing vary from source to source. This presumably reflects problems in reporting casualties during the confusion following the landings. Personnel originally listed as missing, for example, were perhaps later found to have been killed or captured, or in some instances even serving with another unit. Adjustments to figures were made throughout. For this reason, all figures should be treated as close approximations.

Casualties for the U.S. First Army during the period 6 through 20 June 1944 amounted to some 24,162, of whom 3,082 were killed, 13,121 wounded, and 7,959 missing. British casualties for the same period totaled 13,572, of whom 1,842 were killed, 8,599 wounded, and 3,131 missing, while Canadian casualties totaled 2,815: 363 killed, 1,359 wounded, and 1,093 missing. Casualties in the British sector of the landing on D-day numbered about 3,000, nearly a third of them Canadian.

The heaviest casualties in the initial landings were in the American sector, primarily on Omaha Beach and in the 82d and 101st airborne divisions. From 6 to 10 June 1944, the 101st Airborne Division suffered 2,619 casualties out of an effective strength of 8,451, with 137 killed, 482 wounded, and 2,000 missing, while the 82d Airborne Division suffered 1,235 casualties out of an effective strength of 7,534: 89 killed, 936 wounded, 200 missing, and 10 known to be captured. By the time the two divisions were removed from the line for reconstitution, they had each suffered in excess of 50 percent casualties.

On Omaha Beach, casualties were heavy. The U.S. 1st Infantry Division suffered 1,638 casualties between D-day and D plus 4: 124 killed, 1,083 wounded, and 431 missing. The 29th Infantry Division's losses were even heavier: 280 killed, 1,027 wounded, 896 missing, and 7 known captured, for a total of 2,210 casualties. Nondivisional troops on Omaha suffered 148 killed, 656 wounded, and 569 missing, totaling 1,373 casualties.

In addition to combat losses, the forces committed in Normandy also suffered heavy attrition from disease and nonbattle injuries. In the U.S. First Army, for example, disease accounted for nearly 20 percent and nonbattle injuries (primarily recurrent malaria among troops who had originally been infected during operations in North Africa) for another 7.7 percent of all admissions to medical treatment facilities, including one patient admitted for combat stress for every 8.4 admitted for treatment of combat injuries.

The Allied armies suffered high casualty rates on the beaches of Normandy, but not high enough to prevent them from establishing a lodgment on the Continent. By comparison, in the American Civil War combined Union and Confederate losses during the Battle of Antietam totaled over 23,000 in a single day, while casualties at the Battle of Gettysburg totaled over 40,000 in three days of fighting.

[See also Medical Support, articles on American Medical Support and British Medical Support.]

BIBLIOGRAPHY

Ellis, L. F., et al. The Battle of Normandy. Vol. 1 of Victory in the West. 1962.
First United States Army Report of Operations, 20 October 1943–1 August 1944. 1944.

DONALD E. HALL

French Casualties

Until the landings, French casualties in Normandy were not unlike those in other regions of occupied France. Most of the losses came from executions of Resistance members, forced labor accidents, deaths among deportees in concentration and prisoner-of-war camps, and above all, Allied bombing. In spite of the many alerts—two or three a day—only fifty civilians died in air raids during April and May 1944. However, the Norman populace suffered losses of livestock commandeered by the occupying forces and the destruction of many buildings, especially along the coast, razed by German engineers to make way for pillboxes.

Beginning in June, and continuing as long as the battle waged in Normandy, the damage expanded to unreasonable and unanticipated proportions. Aerial bombing, together with shelling from warships, brought about appalling destruction, especially in areas such as Caen and Saint-Lô. Although some regions escaped serious damage—Churchill expressed pleasure on seeing the prosperous

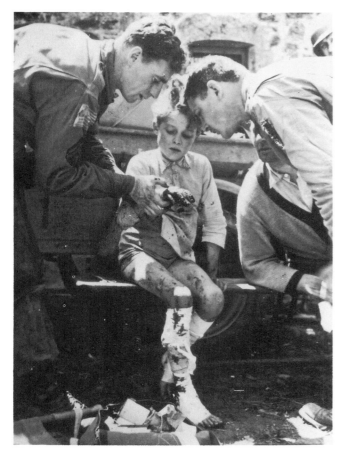

INJURED FRENCH BOY.   Attended by U.S. medics.
THE ROBERT HUNT LIBRARY, LONDON

Damage in Normandy

Buildings completely destroyed	120,000
Buildings damaged	270,000
Farmland temporarily unusable	118,000 acres
Factory space destroyed	16,000,000 sq. ft.

Adapted from Jean Quellien, *La Normandie au coeur de la guerre,* 1992, pp. 233–234

Destruction of a selection of Norman towns with prewar populations over 1,000 as estimated by the French Ministry of Reconstruction and City Planning in 1956

TOWN	PREWAR POPULATION	PERCENT OF DESTRUCTION
Villers-Bocage	1,202	86
Le Havre	165,067	82
Saint-Lô	10,985	77
Aunay-sur-Odon	1,676	74
Vire	5,786	73
Caen	61,334	73
Thury-Harcourt	1,008	71
Condé-sur-Noireau	4,800	70
Falaise	5,643	69
Colombelles	3,452	64
Évreux	19,305	58
Rouen	122,900	42

countryside when he visited Bayeux on 10 June—many villages and hamlets, like Sannerville, Saint-Martin-de-Fontenay, and Aunay-sur-Odon, were completely obliterated. The hard fighting around Villers-Bocage and Tilly-sur-Seulles (which changed hands twenty-three times) left the area in ruins, and the inhabitants, crouching in cellars and caves, in complete shock. Caen, the principal city of the department of Calvados, became an unsightly mass of rubble, with three-quarters of its buildings demolished. Many of Normandy's great abbeys and churches were shattered, and much of the countryside was reduced to wasteland.

How many people died or were wounded is difficult to estimate, because so many inhabitants left Normandy in a voluntary exodus estimated at from forty to sixty thousand, to which figure must be added several thousand forcibly deported to Germany. Approximately six thousand French Jews were deported; approximately one-half returned.

It is very difficult to obtain exact figures on the number of civilians killed during the battle of Normandy. Some estimates have been greatly exaggerated. Jean Quellien, of the University of Caen, is currently making an accurate survey of those killed (no adequate sources exist for those wounded) based on official records and other testimonies. This study will not be completed before the end of 1993.

On the basis of studies already done, Quellien estimates

THE DEVASTATION OF SAINT-LÔ.   THE ROBERT HUNT LIBRARY, LONDON

for the three departments that make up Lower Normandy:

Calvados:	between 7,000 and 8,000 killed
Manche:	between 4,000 and 5,000 killed
Orne:	between 1,500 and 2,000 killed

Unfortunately this inquiry does not cover Upper Normandy, especially the department of Seine-Inférieure, where the RAF raid of September 1944 destroyed Le Havre with possibly 2,000 or 3,000 civilians killed.

Members of the Norman Resistance who died—killed in action, shot after arrest, or perished in concentration camps—has been calculated at about 2,700. The numbers tabulated above cannot do justice to the sense of bereavement felt by a population whose families had been decimated, and whose everyday surroundings had included authentic architecture of the Middle Ages and Renaissance.

[*See also* France; French Resistance.]

BIBLIOGRAPHY

Aron, Robert. *France Reborn*. 1964.

Bédarida, François, ed. *Normandie 44: Du débarquement à la libération*. 1987.

Hastings, Max. *OVERLORD: D-Day and the Battle for Normandy*. 1984.

Quellien, Jean. *La Normandie au coeur de la guerre*. 1992.

ARTHUR L. FUNK

German Casualties

Casualties suffered by the German *Seventh Army* and by reserve units sent to defend Normandy cannot be established for the period from D-day to D plus 12 because of inadequate sources. From the German perspective, military events in Normandy occurred in four phases, each of which brought heavy losses. These were the battles on the beaches (6 to 11 June), the Allied breakthrough from the Cotentin Peninsula (8 to 27 July), the breakthrough at Avranches (27 July to 1 August), and the surrounding of the *Seventh Army* in the Falaise pocket (18 to 21 August). It is possible to give an inclusive account of German casualties from D-day to the end of the struggle for Normandy on 21 August, but casualties cannot be divided into dead, wounded, and missing.

Constant bombing attacks and rolling gunfire from naval armaments caused German casualties of between 4,000 and 9,000 men on 6 June. The *352d* and *716th* infantry divisions, stationed on the coast in the department of Calvados, were particularly affected, because they faced Omaha, Gold, Juno, and Sword landing zones. The *352d Infantry Division* was totally worn down during June; only 180 of the original 15,000 soldiers survived. The *716th Infantry Division* suffered a similar fate. With the fall of Cherbourg on 26 June, another 21,000 soldiers from the *709th Infantry Division* were lost, most of them captured. By 30 June, German losses had totaled 47,515.

At the beginning of July 1944 these losses continued with the battles of Caen and Saint-Lô so that, for example the *3d Parachute Division* lost 65 percent of its strength. By 12 July, German losses were already at 65,865 men. In combat against Operation GOODWOOD near Caen and against American attempts to break through German lines on the Cotentin Peninsula, losses rose to 114,000 dead and 41,000 prisoners by the end of July. In the battles around and in the Falaise pocket, which lasted until 21 August, the Wehrmacht lost another 90,000 men, including soldiers taken captive at the end. Thus some 250,000 soldiers were lost in immediate connection with the invasion in the West.

From the beaches of Calvados to Falaise, on the Cotentin Peninsula and in Brittany, and finally in the Falaise pocket, thirty-nine German divisions were destroyed. Most casualties were produced by grenades, shells, and shrapnels rather than by Allied small-arms fire. The highest mortality rate among the wounded came from head and abdominal injuries. It was not just the army that bore such terrible losses. Along with the infantry and panzer divisions SS panzer and panzer grenadier divisions suffered heavy casualties, as did the Luftwaffe with its air squadrons, field divisions, and parachute divisions. Their losses are included in the total of 250,000 casualties for the Supreme Command West.

BIBLIOGRAPHY

Guth, Ekkehart. *La Cambe: Deutscher Soldatenfriedhof in der Normandie.* 1985.

Ose, Dieter. *Entscheidung im Westen 1944.* 1982.

Zimmermann, Bodo. *Military Study T-121: Kampf in der Normandie.* 1948.

EKKEHART P. GUTH
Translated from German by Amy Hackett

CEMETERIES, MONUMENTS, AND MEMO-RIALS. [*This entry includes four articles that describe the cemeteries, monuments, and memorials dedicated to Allied and German soldiers who lost their lives in the Normandy campaign:*
American Cemeteries, Monuments, and Memorials
Commonwealth Cemeteries
British Monuments and Memorials
German Cemeteries, Monuments, and Memorials.]

American Cemeteries, Monuments, and Memorials

Although there are several cemeteries in France that are administered by the American Battle Monuments Commission (ABMC), the two most closely related to D-day are the Normandy Cemetery and the Brittany Cemetery. The Normandy Cemetery is situated on a cliff overlooking Omaha Beach and the English Channel, just east of Saint-Laurent-sur-Mer and northwest of Bayeux in Colleville-sur-Mer, 272 kilometers (170 miles) west of Paris. The cemetery site covers 172½ acres and contains the graves of 9,386 Americans, most of whom gave their lives in the landings and ensuing operations. On the walls of the semicircular garden, on the east side of the memorial, are inscribed the names of 1,557 missing

UTAH BEACH MEMORIAL.
AMERICAN BATTLE MONUMENTS COMMISSION, WASHINGTON, D.C.

Americans who rest in unknown graves.

The memorial consists of a semicircular colonnade with a loggia at each end containing large maps and narratives of the military operations; at the center is the bronze "Spirit of American Youth." Two orientation tables depict the landings in Normandy and the artificial harbor established there. To the west of the memorial are a reflecting pool, the burial area with its circular chapel, and granite statues representing the United States and France.

The Brittany Cemetery lies approximately 2½ kilometers (1½ miles) southeast of the village of Saint-James (Manche), France, 19 kilometers (12 miles) south of Avranches, and 22 kilometers (14 miles) north of Fougères. At this cemetery, covering 28 acres of farm country near the eastern edge of Brittany, rest 4,410 Americans, most of whom gave their lives in the Normandy and Brittany campaigns in 1944. Along the retaining wall of the memorial terrace are inscribed the names of 498 of the missing whose resting place "is known only to God."

The gray granite memorial, embellished with stained glass and sculpture, contains the chapel and two large operations maps with narratives and flags of the military services. The lookout platform of the tower affords a view of the burial area, as well as of the peaceful surrounding countryside.

There are two major monuments in the Normandy area that are administered by ABMC. The Pointe du Hoc Monument is located on a cliff 13 kilometers (8 miles) west of the Normandy American Cemetery overlooking Omaha Beach. It was erected by the French to honor elements of the 2d Ranger Battalion, which scaled the 100-foot cliff, seized the objective, and defended it successfully against determined German counterattacks at high cost. The monument consists of a simple granite pylon atop a concrete bunker with inscriptions in French and English on tablets at its base. It was officially turned over to the American government on 11 January 1979 for care and maintenance in perpetuity. This 30-acre battle-scarred area remains much as the Rangers left it on 8 June 1944.

VIEW OF NORMANDY CEMETERY FROM THE MEMORIAL.   Centered in the open arc of the memorial, foreground, is a 22-ft. bronze statue, "The Spirit of American Youth Rising from the Waves."

AMERICAN BATTLE MONUMENTS COMMISSION, WASHINGTON, D.C.

AERIAL VIEW OF BRITTANY CEMETERY.
AMERICAN BATTLE MONUMENTS COMMISSION, WASHINGTON, D.C.

The Utah Beach Monument is located approximately 3 kilometers (2 miles) northeast of Sainte-Marie-du-Mont (Manche), France. This monument commemorates the achievements of the American forces of the VII Corps, who fought in the liberation of the Cotentin Peninsula from 6 June to 1 July 1944. It consists of a red granite obelisk surrounded by a small, developed park overlooking the historic sand dunes of Utah Beach, one of the two American landing beaches during the Normandy invasion of June 1944.

BIBLIOGRAPHY

The American Battle Monuments Commission. "Brittany American Cemetery and Memorial." 1987.
The American Battle Monuments Commission. "Normandy American Cemetery and Memorial." 1987.
The American Battle Monuments Commission. "World War II Commemorative Program." N.d.

WILLIAM E. RYAN, JR.

Commonwealth Cemeteries

The positions of the Commonwealth war cemeteries in Normandy give an indication of the progress of the fighting. Near the British 50th Division beaches (Gold) is Ryes War Cemetery; near the 3d Canadian Division beaches (Juno), the Bény-sur-Mer Canadian War Cemetery; and near the 3d British Division beaches (Sword), the Douvres-la-Délivrande and Hermanville-sur-Mer war cemeteries. In the area of the 6th British Airborne Division paratrooper and glider landings across the Orne is the Ranville War Cemetery.

Away from the beachhead on the approaches to Caen are the Tilly-sur-Seulles, Jérusalem, Brouay, Fontenay-le-Pesnel, and Hottot-les-Bagues war cemeteries. The remaining sites mark the progress of fighting leading to the capture of Caen and the later stages of the Normandy campaign.

The Bayeux War Cemetery, the largest World War II Commonwealth site in France, contains over 4,500 buri-

BAYEUX MEMORIAL.   COMMONWEALTH WAR GRAVES COMMISSION, OTTAWA

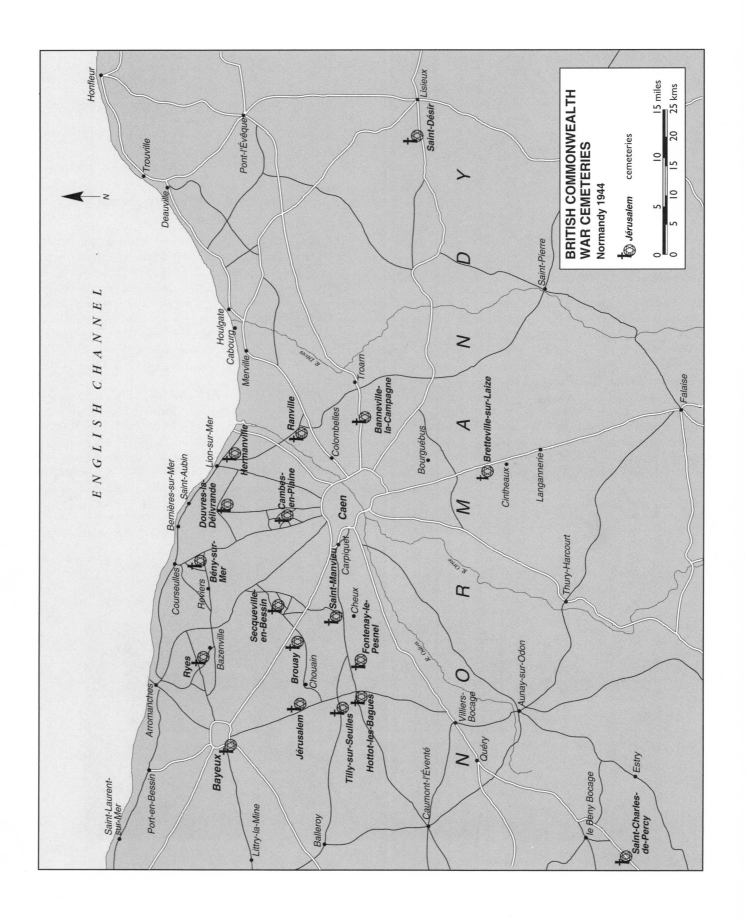

ENGLISH CHANNEL

N

BRITISH COMMONWEALTH
WAR CEMETERIES
Normandy 1944

Jérusalem   cemeteries

0   5   10   15 miles
0   5   10   15   20   25 kms

Honfleur

Trouville

Deauville

Pont-l'Évêque

Lisieux

Saint-Désir

Saint-Pierre

Houlgate
Cabourg

Merville

Troarn

R. Dives

N O R M A N D Y

Falaise

Ranville

Colombelles

Banneville-
la-Campagne

Bourguébus

Bretteville-sur-Laize

Langannerie

Cintheaux

Bernières-sur-Mer
Saint-Aubin

Lion-sur-Mer

Hermanville

Douvres-la-
Délivrande

Cambes-
en-Plaine

Caen

R. Orne

Thury-Harcourt

Courseulles

Reviers

Bény-sur-
Mer

Saint-Manvieu
Carpiquet

Cheux

Arromanches

Bazenville

Ryes

Secqueville-
en-Bessin

Brouay

Chouain

Fontenay-le-
Pesnel

R. Odon

Aunay-sur-Odon

Saint-Laurent-
sur-Mer

Port-en-Bessin

Bayeux

Jérusalem

Tilly-sur-Seulles

Hottot-les-Bagues

Villiers-
Bocage

Quéry

Caumont-l'Éventé

Littry-la-Mine

Balleroy

le Beny Bocage

Estry

Saint-Charles-
de-Percy

als brought in from the surrounding districts and hospitals. The Bayeux Memorial, located opposite the cemetery, was built by the Commonwealth War Graves Commission (CWGC). It honors by name over 1,800 members of the Commonwealth forces who fell in the Normandy invasion and the subsequent advance to the Seine and have no known grave. Most of the sites were opened by the assaulting units and formations, which gave the burials temporary marking. Records were maintained by the Graves Registration Units.

As after World War I, it was the policy of Australia, Britain, Canada, India, New Zealand, and South Africa not to repatriate the remains of those members of the Commonwealth forces who died in World War II. To ensure the permanent marking and maintenance of the graves, the erection of memorials to the missing, and the keeping of records, the Imperial (later Commonwealth) War Graves Commission had been established in 1917. Its duties were extended to cover those who died during World War II. The cemeteries and burial records were passed to the CWGC by the military authorities after the fighting ceased. The commission subsequently developed the cemeteries and continues to maintain them.

Use of the land in France occupied as Commonwealth war cemeteries was generously provided by the French government under the terms of the War Graves Agreement signed at Paris in 1951. The site of the Bayeux Memorial was provided in perpetuity by the municipality of Bayeux with the sanction of the French government.

BIBLIOGRAPHY

Commonwealth War Graves Commission. *The Bayeux Memorial Register*. Pt. 1 and 2 of *The War Dead of the Commonwealth*. 1955. Reprint, 1991.

Commonwealth War Graves Commission. *Bayeux War Cemetery*. Pt. 4 of *The War Dead of the Commonwealth*. 1955. Reprint, 1991.

Commonwealth War Graves Commission. *Normandy June–August 1944: Guide to the Commonwealth War Cemeteries and the Bayeux Memorial*. 1984.

S. MICHAEL NEWELL

British Monuments and Memorials

The manner in which a country commemorates great historical events often reflects the current values and attitudes of its society. Operation OVERLORD in general and D-day in particular are no exception to this observation. Probably the most novel and outstanding British memorial to the events surrounding and including 6 June 1944 is the Overlord Embroidery, now permanently on display in the D-Day Museum at Clarence Esplanade, Southsea,

Commonwealth War Cemeteries in Normandy

	IDENTIFIED	UNKNOWN
Banville-la-Campagne	2,030	140
Bayeux	3,805	338
Bény-sur-Mer (Canadian)	2,029	19
Bretteville-sur-Laize (Canadian)	2,870	87
Brouay	370	7
Cambes-en-Plaine	223	1
Douvres-la-Délivrande	879	63
Fontenay-le-Pesnel	452	8
Hermanville-sur-Mer	896	106
Hottot-les-Bagues	949	56
Jérusalem	46	1
Ranville	2,138	97
Ryes	594	58
Secqueville-en-Bessin	98	1
Saint-Charles-de-Percy	701	104
Saint-Désir	589	8
Saint-Manvieu	1,578	49
Tilly-sur-Seulles	945	45

NOTE: Additional burials will be found in over 75 church or communal cemeteries in Normandy; some of the cemeteries also contain the burials of Allied and German forces. Naval missing are commemorated on the appropriate naval memorials worldwide; air force missing are commemorated on the Runnymede Memorial in the United Kingdom. The Bayeux Memorial to the Missing identifies 1,803 of the Commonwealth forces missing.

near Portsmouth. It portrays the events of 1944 in a manner similar to that of the many centuries older Bayeux Tapestry, commemorating Duke William of Normandy's invasion of England in 1066. Designed by Sandra Lawrence and sewn by the Royal School of Needlework, it consists of thirty-four panels and measures 272 feet from end to end—about one-sixth longer than its famous predecessor at Bayeux. The Overlord Embroidery took five years to make and was completed in 1973.

Also in Portsmouth is the D-Day Window, unveiled by the Queen Mother in the cathedral on the fortieth anniversary of the invasion. It includes nineteen shields bearing the coats of arms of the various countries and services involved on that day. At nearby Southwick House (today a Royal Naval shore establishment, HMS *Dryad*), which in June 1944 was part of SHAEF headquarters, the map room still holds the wall-size display featuring the naval aspects of the invasion.

In Normandy there are many monuments and memorials to the British forces that took part in the attack. Disregarding the local museums and ubiquitous road and street names recalling British units, there is, for example, the moving British Memorial to the Missing at Bayeux, which bears the names of 1,803 British and

Commonwealth soldiers (besides 271 more from Commonwealth countries) who died during the Normandy invasion and for whom there are no known graves. This carries an apt Latin quotation, which translated reads: "We, once conquered by William, have now liberated the land of the conqueror."

Each beach, in turn, has its share of memorials. Thus, Gold Beach includes a plaque to No. 47 Royal Marine Commando placed upon a German blockhouse at Port-en-Bessin, while at Asnelles is the French Memorial to the 50th (Northumbrian) Division. In the town hall at Creully is a plaque to the BBC war correspondents. In the sector of Juno Beach, most memorials are dedicated to Canadian units and personnel, but farther east, in the Sword Beach area at Lagrune, stands a granite memorial to No. 48 Royal Marine Commando. At La Brèche is a Churchill petard tank commemorating the assault engineers of the 79th Armoured Division.

Finally, along the coastal strip, lies the area attacked by the British 6th Airborne Division. Pegasus Café is full of mementos to the glider-borne troops who took the famous bridge. At Ranville is a memorial to the 13th Parachute Battalion. At Amfreville stands another to the 1st Special Service Brigade, and not far away is another to No. 6 Commando. A memorial cairn commemorating No. 4 Commando stands at Hoger.

BIBLIOGRAPHY

Holt, Tonie, and Valmai Holt. *The Visitor's Guide to Normandy Landing Beaches*. 1989.
Jewell, B. *Conquest and Overlord*. 1981.

DAVID G. CHANDLER

German Cemeteries, Monuments, and Memorials

The largest German military cemetery in Normandy is La Cambe, located one kilometer west of that village in the Calvados department on the Bayeux–Isigny-sur-Mer–Carentan highway. Here, 21,222 German soldiers are buried.

During the course of the invasion, the American grave service set aside two large cemeteries in the La Cambe area for the German and American dead. When the war ended, other German dead were scattered among some 1,400 communities in the Calvados, Orne, and Manche departments. In 1945 the Americans established their own cemetery at Saint-Laurent-sur-Mer; German soldiers buried there were moved to La Cambe, which became solely a German cemetery. In 1956 the French government approved the expansion of La Cambe. An international youth camp, the first in France, helped to landscape the cemetery, which was dedicated on 21 September 1961. The cemetery is cared for by the German War Graves Commission (Volksbund Deutsche Kriegsgräberfürsorge), established in 1919. Financial support is shared by this private organization and the German government.

The landscape around La Cambe is characteristic of the bocage of Normandy, where thick hedgerows surround meadows and fields, creating rectangular patterns. The cemetery lies in one of these meadows and thus is somewhat shielded from the world outside.

An entry building with two sidewalls is made of unpolished granite and brick. The roof is of sheet copper; the windows are framed in oak and have bronze grating. Massive wooden doors are covered in cast bronze. The entry building contains three rooms: a central room opening onto the cemetery, a room containing lists of the dead, and a room with benches for rest and reflection.

At the center of La Cambe is an earthen barrow, surrounded at the base by a circular granite wall, where the unknown dead are buried. Atop the barrow is a granite cross, over four meters tall, flanked on each side by a figure. The cemetery contains forty-nine uniformly planted blocks, between which are paths. Groups of five crosses, each giving name, rank, and birth and death dates of the dead, are interspersed throughout the cemetery.

Several British military cemeteries in the Normandy region contain areas for the German dead. These cemeteries are laid out in the style of English lawns, with strips of briar roses and other low shrubs at the head of each row of graves. Of the ten British cemeteries, those with the largest number of German dead are at Cheux-Saint-Manvieu (11 kilometers, or 6.6 miles, west of Caen), with 556 German graves; Bayeux, with 466 German graves; Ryes-Bazenville (9.5 kilometers, or 5.7 miles, northeast of Bayeux), with 328 German graves; and Ranville (11 kilometers, or 6.6 miles, north of Caen), with 323 German graves. Finally, of the twenty-two Allied cemeteries located throughout Normandy, several contain German dead, primarily in the area between the British beachhead and the city of Caen.

BIBLIOGRAPHY

Volksbund Deutsche Kriegsgräberfürsorge. *Deutsche Kriegsgräber am Rande der Strassen: Frankreich, Belgien, Luxemburg und Niederlande*. 1991.
Volksbund Deutsche Kriegsgräberfürsorge. *La Cambe/Frankreich. Deutsche Soldatenfriedhöfe im Ausland*. N.d.

AMY HACKETT

CHAPLAINS. [*This entry includes separate discussions of American, British, and German chaplains at the time of the Normandy invasion.*]

American Chaplains

An estimated seventy Navy chaplains took part, either directly or indirectly, in the Normandy invasion. On 6 June 1944, there were forty-six serving at shore bases in Great Britain, fourteen on board transports and repair ships, while the remainder were aboard the warships of the Twelfth Fleet assembled for the invasion, but it was the Army chaplain who predominated on the Normandy battlefield.

The historical roots of the Army chaplaincy can be traced back to the early colonial period. During the American Revolution chaplains served in every major engagement, and since 1791 they have been a permanent component of the U.S. Army. In the summer of 1940 there were 137 chaplains in the Regular Army, with 157 reserve chaplains on active duty, and about 100 other reserve chaplains serving with the Civilian Conservation Corps.

By the summer of 1944 over 8,000 chaplains were serving on active duty, approximately 1,900 with the Army Air Forces. Led by Chief of Chaplains, Chaplain (Maj. Gen.) William R. Arnold, they were prepared to offer religious support and comfort to the American soldier on any battlefield at great personal risk. Although small in size the chaplain branch was third in combat deaths on a percentage basis, behind the air forces and the infantry. It was the chaplain "ministry of presence" and "be there" philosophy on the battlefield that led to this steep price. Normandy would prove no different.

The Army chaplains who landed in Normandy were under the overall direction of the Theater Chaplain, Chaplain (Col.) L. Curtis Tiernan, a Roman Catholic priest from Kansas City, Missouri. During World War I Father Tiernan had served with the 35th Infantry Division, Harry S. Truman's unit. The number of chaplains under

RELIGIOUS SERVICE.   Aboard a Coast Guard–manned assault transport shortly before invasion.   NATIONAL ARCHIVES

CATHOLIC CHAPLAIN.   Maj. Edward J. Waters celebrates Mass on a pier in Weymouth, England, on 6 June 1944.

NATIONAL ARCHIVES

Tiernan during the invasion fell short of the Army's needs. The ideal ratio was one chaplain for every 850 men, or one chaplain to each battalion. The ratio during D-day was approximately 1 to 1,100, slightly better than the 1 to 1,200 ratio in the American Expeditionary Force (AEF) during World War I. However, many units had no chaplain. To meet the shortfall the chaplaincy developed the concept of area coverage, which worked reasonably well. Almost 30 percent of the Army chaplains during the Normandy campaign were priests, a little over 2 percent were rabbis, and the balance were ministers.

The landings at Normandy were preceded by the dropping of American airborne forces, the 82d and the 101st Airborne Divisions. Fifteen chaplains were assigned to each of these divisions. Chaplain Francis L. Sampson, a Roman Catholic priest with the 101st, who was later to

become Chief of Chaplains during the Vietnam war, was captured but later freed in an American counterattack. Chaplain John Reuben Steel, a Methodist minister from Oklahoma was not so fortunate. Also with the 101st, he was killed on 6 June, the first chaplain to die in the campaign. Three more were dead by D plus 13.

On the beaches of Normandy, the experiences of a chaplain with an engineer special brigade were typical:

I landed from an LCI in ten feet of water and had to swim fifty yards before I touched bottom, and we waded through a hail of death to the shore. I was with my Combat Engineer Battalion that hit the coast at H-Hour plus thirty minutes. I spent the first hours ministering to the wounded while we were pinned down on the dune line until enemy resistance was further liquidated and a way opened to move off the beach to higher ground. Eighty-eights fell in our midst while digging in, killing and wounding men next to us. Work with the wounded and dying at the first aid stations, clearing stations, and evacuation points during the first few days has more than repaid for every sacrifice I have made and the toil of months of preparation for this task.

As more units arrived after the initial landings, consolidated the beachhead and moved inland, the number of chaplains on the ground increased. On D plus 5 Chaplain Tiernan arrived, and by D plus 11 there were approximately 375 chaplains ashore in Normandy. Later, General Eisenhower would look back on the role played by these chaplains during the invasion and say,

> The work of the Army chaplain has been of inestimable value to American forces in Europe. Their selflessness and unfailing devotion to the spiritual and material welfare of millions of Americans have won for them the admiration, respect, and affection of all commanders.

BIBLIOGRAPHY

"The Army Chaplain in the European Theater of Operations: Report of the General Board, U.S. Forces, European Theater." Study No. 68. U.S. Army Chaplain Center, Ft. Monmouth, N.J.

Gushwa, Robert L. *The Best and Worst of Times: The United States Army Chaplaincy, 1920–1945.* 1977.

WILLIAM J. HOURIHAN

British Chaplains

In Christ's Church, Portsdown, are two stained-glass windows showing the British beach landings on D-day and the Caen tank battle. These windows were given by the Second Army to commemorate the service held in the church, in strictest secrecy, prior to D-day, and attended by Gen. Miles C. Dempsey and his staff. It was typical of services held by all units, in places such as barracks and under the wings of gliders. The Reverend John Gwinnett with the 9th Battalion, Parachute Regiment, used as his text, "Fear knocked at the door, faith opened it and there was nothing there." (attribution unknown). Later he learned how many of his men relayed these words to their loved ones in their last letters home.

On the eve of the invasion new field communion sets were issued to replace the previous unsuitable model and two three-ton vehicles were converted into mobile churches, one of which was used by the Reverend Frederick L. Hughes, Bernard L. Montgomery's chaplain.

The initial four divisions involved in the landings and the airborne division had approximately fourteen chaplains each. In addition there were chaplains serving with the Royal Marine Commandos and eighteen chaplains in the bombardment ships and destroyers. Thomas Holland, a Roman Catholic chaplain and later bishop of Salford, won a Distinguished Service Cross with the men who manned small boats used as ferries. Geoffrey Harding, a Royal Air Force chaplain, landed on Omaha Beach on 7 June with a unit whose aim was to set up a radar station. Their specialist equipment was destroyed by heavy fire on landing, so he looked after American wounded for thirty-six hours and was awarded a Military Cross.

Chaplains accompanied the assault battalions. The 2d Battalion, East Yorkshire Regiment, on Queen Beach (part of Sword Beach), landed with each company carrying a black flag emblazoned with a white rose, made by the Ladies of Waterlooville Congregational Church through the good offices of their chaplain, the Reverend A. Price (a Congregationalist minister).

The earliest to arrive in France were the chaplains of the 6th Airborne; three were killed, including the chaplain of the Canadian Parachute Battalion, one was taken prisoner, and three were wounded. John Gwinnett, with the battalion that took the Merville battery, was awarded a Military Cross. The role these men served typified all chaplains. They brought in and looked after the wounded, they performed such services as were possible, and they buried the dead, collecting their effects and writing to the bereaved. This was an essential for reasons of hygiene and to fulfill the heartfelt need for the dead to be reverently buried. For example, the Reverend D. M. Nimmo, a Church of Scotland minister serving with the 2d Battalion, Oxfordshire and Buckinghamshire Light Infantry, buried three hundred men of both sides after the bitter fighting for Breville. The senior chaplain, George Hales, organized a cemetery outside the church at Ranville and another was sited at Hermanville, a mile inland from Queen Beach, which was to hold over six hundred bodies.

On 15 June 1944 the Reverend Frederick L. Hughes said on the BBC Home Service, "Many, many thousands of men went forth for righteousness' sake and for no other reason. The chaplains were asked, and strongly asked, to make our men as Christian as we could."

BIBLIOGRAPHY

Nightingale, P. R. *The East Yorkshire Regiment (Duke of York's Own) in the War, 1939–45.* 1952.

Smyth, John. *In This Sign Conquer.* 1968.

Taylor, Gordon. *The Sea Chaplains.* 1978.

P. R. C. ABRAM

German Chaplains

In the early years of the Third Reich, the German military chaplaincy remained virtually unchanged. After the introduction of universal compulsory military service in

1935, however, the possibilities for spiritual care within the military were gradually curtailed. The National Socialists increased their antichurch activities among the troops; at the same time, increasing indifference (especially among younger officers) was countered by cautious support for a chaplaincy by many officers.

In a 1939 directive, the Army High Command (Oberkommando des Heeres—OKH) suggested that, as part of the official Wehrmacht command structure, the field chaplaincy was an important means of strengthening the combat effectiveness of the army. At the outset of the war, both the German Catholic bishops and the ecclesiastical council of the Protestant church urged the discharge of soldierly duty for Führer and Reich.

Chaplain duties in the field army were carried out by civilian clerics, who were given the office of "military parson" (*Kriegspfarrer*) as civil servants within the Wehrmacht for the duration of the war, as well as by active-duty Wehrmacht chaplains. Military parsons wore the uniform of an active Wehrmacht civil servant along with the prescribed armband and a pectoral cross on a chain. Their immediate superior was the respective divisional commander or the highest officer to whose staff the chaplain was attached. Administratively they were responsible to Protestant or Catholic field bishops (*Feldbischöfe*).

In keeping with the military's largely functional understanding of religion, chaplains were to limit their wartime activities to direct encouragement before and after combat, consolation of the injured and ill, and ministrations to the dying. For this reason the Army High Command called for a field religious service oriented toward the spiritual needs of German soldiers, one that in particular served to foster and maintain internal combat readiness and that "in keeping with the internal unity of the troops" should "normally be for the entire military unit, not divided by denomination."

The opportunities for military chaplains to exercise denominational influence on soldiers conflicted with the totalitarian ambitions of the National Socialist German Workers Party, which wanted to abolish such influence as much as possible. Martin Bormann, in particular, espoused this cause and determined the approach to military chaplaincy during the war, while Hitler took a more dilatory stance. An initial step was the control of denominational literature intended for the troops. Censorship was increased during the course of the war, and in 1942 field bishops were informed that the Führer no longer wished the reprinting and continued distribution of writings from the Wehrmacht chaplaincy. In September 1942 Hermann Göring then issued a general ban on the distribution of religious literature in the Luftwaffe.

Further control was effected by an increased influence over the selection of chaplains, as the military agencies and the Reich ministry for church affairs, as well as party and Gestapo offices, gained a greater role. These tactics conformed to ever greater functional censorship, which took the form of suppressing the traditional wartime duties of the military chaplaincy. The apex was reached with the "Guidelines for the Exercise of Field Chaplaincy" of 24 May 1942: reduced to its basic message, the clergyman should henceforth simply be present for soldiers who expressly wanted him.

Further measures were directed in particular against the work of priest soldiers. As early as 1941, members of the Jesuit order, and in 1944 all Roman Catholic clergy, deacons, subdeacons, seminarians, and members of religious orders who were reserve officers were dismissed.

Despite all attempts to exclude the military chaplaincy during the war, or at least to greatly lessen its influence, German military chaplains nevertheless fulfilled their essential mission of ministering to spiritual needs; they thus gave comfort and support to countless soldiers in their most difficult hour, especially at the time of the invasion.

BIBLIOGRAPHY

Absolon, Rudolf. *Die Wehrmacht im Dritten Reich*. 2 vols. 1979–1988.

Güsgen, Johannes. *Die katholische Militärseelsorge in Deutschland zwischen 1920 und 1945*. 1989.

Messerschmidt, Manfred. "Aspekte der Militärseelsorgepolitik in nationalsozialistischer Zeit." *Militärgeschichtliche Mitteilungen (MGM)* 3 (1968): 63–105.

Messerschmidt, Manfred. "Zur Militärseelsorgepolitik im Zweiten Weltkrieg." *Militärgeschichtliche Mitteilungen (MGM)* 5 (1969): 37–85.

KARL DIEFENBACH
Translated from German by Amy Hackett

CHURCHILL, WINSTON (1874–1965), British prime minister and minister of defense. From the moment that France was overrun by the German Army in June 1940, Churchill was convinced that Germany could be driven out of its European conquests only by an amphibious cross-Channel landing; the British army had been driven back across the Channel from Dunkirk, and it would return across the Channel to reverse that defeat. Churchill was also convinced that Britain's military resources by themselves would never be sufficient for such a landing. Only if the United States, with its enormous potential manpower, air power, and shipping resources, including landing craft, were to enter the war would such a massive undertaking be possible.

Within three months of Adolph Hitler's declaration of war on the United States in December 1941, the question of the date by which such a cross-Channel landing would be possible was under discussion among the military, naval, and air chiefs in London and Washington. As a result, on 8 March 1942 President Franklin D. Roosevelt informed Churchill by telegram that, as a result of demands in the Pacific war zones, the American contribution to land operations on the continent of Europe in the summer 1942, the earliest possible date for some form of cross-Channel assault, would be "materially reduced." The shipping then available to the United States, Roosevelt pointed out, would allow only about 130,000 troops to be transported across the Atlantic by June 1942. Even with new naval construction, only 170,000 troops could be brought across by June 1943, and 270,000 by December 1943. Roosevelt added that the earliest possible date by which the "troop-carrying capacity" of the United States could reach 400,000, the minimum figure then envisaged for a major amphibious landing, was June 1944.

From the moment of Roosevelt's letter of 8 March 1942, Churchill set about making sure that the problems of sending at least 400,000 men across several hundred miles of water were examined and overcome. In a memorandum of 26 May 1942 he wrote about the specifications of the floating piers that would be essential to unload supplies from the landing ships once they had crossed the Channel: "They must float up and down with the tide. The anchor problem must be mastered. Let me have the best solution worked out. Don't argue the matter. The difficulties will argue for themselves."

Josef Stalin, the Soviet leader, who was extremely hard-pressed by Hitler's armies for the second summer in succession, was demanding a cross-Channel landing as soon as possible during the summer of 1942. Churchill first discussed the timing of the landing face to face with Roosevelt at Hyde Park on 20 June 1942, when, with the full backing of the British chiefs of staff, he stressed that "no responsible British military authority" could see any chance for a cross-Channel landing later that year. Some politicians in Britain, notably Lord Beaverbrook, the former minister of aircraft production, had taken up the Soviet call for a "Second Front Now." But once again it was lack of American resources that made any such assault impossible; according to Roosevelt's advisers, the United States could provide only

CHURCHILL AND EISENHOWER.   In England in the spring of 1944.   COURTESY DWIGHT D. EISENHOWER LIBRARY / U.S. ARMY

700 of the 5,700 combat aircraft then judged necessary to secure air mastery over the landing beaches.

The predominantly Canadian cross-Channel raid against Dieppe in August 1942, a small-scale raid designed to secure various technical and intelligence gains for the Allies, gave further guidance to the problems that would be faced by a large assault. Added to the experience at Dieppe was the unexpectedly strong German resistance to the Anglo-American forces in Tunisia at the end of 1942, a resistance that led to a feeling among Churchill's senior military advisers that the summer of 1944 (Roosevelt's original date) rather than 1943 (the Anglo-American hoped-for date) would be more realistic. Churchill did not want to delay the landing beyond 1943, however, and urged that major changes in the design of landing craft, thought necessary as a result of the Dieppe experience, should not be allowed to create overlong delays.

In the last months of 1942 Churchill was still seeking August or September 1943 as the date of the cross-Channel landing. At a staff conference on 16 December 1942, however, the three British chiefs of staff told him that it could not be done; that the rate and scale of the American troop buildup in Britain was inadequate for the task.

Supported by his foreign secretary, Anthony Eden, Churchill nevertheless pressed the chiefs of staff to make a 1943 cross-Channel landing the priority. The chiefs of staff were emphatic, however, that the American policymakers were no longer planning to have a large enough number of troops in Britain for the landing to be possible by then. Louis Mountbatten, shortly to be appointed head of Combined Operations, who had just returned from the United States, told Churchill and the chiefs of staff that, despite an agreement to the contrary, "the Americans were putting the good engines into their own landing-craft and fitting ours with the unsatisfactory type." Mountbatten also reported that many of the landing craft needed to transport the cross-Channel force were being diverted by the Americans to the Pacific. Thus Churchill learned that his hopes for a 1943 cross-Channel landing had been frustrated by the Americans.

The need to reach agreement on the date of the cross-Channel landing called for a further face-to-face meeting between Roosevelt and Churchill and their senior advisers. The meeting was held at Casablanca in January 1943; after eight days of intensive discussions centered upon the availability of men, aircraft, and landing craft, priority was given to further action in the Mediterranean in 1943, as opposed to a cross-Channel assault that year, for which the resources available to the Western Allies were judged insufficient. Indeed, in view of the general shortage of Allied shipping and escort vessels, it was also decided at Casablanca that the most realistic amphibious target in the Mediterranean, as soon as the still-resisting Germans had been driven out of Tunisia, was the island of Sicily, rather than the more heavily defended Italian mainland.

The Casablanca Conference set the summer of 1944 as the date of the cross-Channel assault, thereby reinstating Roosevelt's original date, as expressed to Churchill on 16 March 1942. In order to carry out a cross-Channel landing within eighteen months of Casablanca, it was agreed by the military experts at the conference that a total of 938,000 American troops would be assembled in Britain by the last day of 1943. This was more than twice the number of troops envisaged as necessary when the landings had been under discussion in early 1942, but by the beginning of 1943 the ability of the German army to resist had been made very clear indeed in Tunisia. If the December 1943 date for the arrival of the last of the American troops in Britain could be adhered to, these almost 1 million men would have five months' intensive training before the landings.

At the Quebec Conference in August 1943, when Churchill and Roosevelt met together with their respective chiefs of staff, it was confirmed that the primary Anglo-American effort in 1944 would be the cross-Channel landing. The aim of the landing would be not only to drive the Germans from northern France, but from there "to strike at the heart of Germany and destroy her military forces." It was agreed at Quebec that any conflict of priorities between operations in the Mediterranean and the Channel would be resolved in favor of the Channel. In deference to pressure from the American chiefs of staff, there would also be a landing in the south of France as a diversion to help the cross-Channel landings; the American chiefs of staff felt most strongly that such a landing would force the Germans to draw troops away from the Channel.

To enable supplies to be accumulated both for the cross-Channel landing and for the south of France diversion, it was agreed at Quebec that the advance in Italy would go no farther north than the Pisa-Ancona line; it would not seek to drive on to the top of the Adriatic or into southern Austria. Operations in the Balkans would be limited to sending air and sea supplies to the partisans and using minor commando forces.

In mid-October 1943, Churchill and the British chiefs of staff were excited by the prospect of a successful campaign in Italy, with Rome as its first objective as agreed at Quebec, and hoped to exploit any rapid success by further advances northward. They therefore proposed, as an alternative to the May 1944 date for OVERLORD, that Britain should first reinforce the Italian theater to the full and then seek victory over the Germans there during May and June and possibly July 1944. This would move the cross-Channel assault forward to July or August 1944.

To Anthony Eden, who was then in Moscow, Churchill explained the new plans in a telegram of 20 October 1943.

CHURCHILL VISITS THE BATTLEFRONT.   With Montgomery on 12 June 1944.   IMPERIAL WAR MUSEUM

Eden replied that the Russians would accept no cancellation or even postponement of OVERLORD, but Churchill persevered in his advocacy of the Mediterranean plan and of a two- to three-month OVERLORD delay. On 22 October 1943 he pointed out to Roosevelt that even two British divisions in Sicily, which could have joined the battle in Italy, were about to be transferred to Britain as part of the OVERLORD buildup. Yet these divisions would not be in action in northern France for at least six months, even under the May plan. Two days later Churchill telegraphed to Gen. George C. Marshall, the U.S. Army chief of staff: "I feel in my marrow the withdrawal of our 50th and 51st Divisions, our best, from the edge of the Battle of Rome in the interests of distant 'OVERLORD.' We are carrying out our contract, but I pray God it does not cost us dear."

These two British divisions were not the only ones being withdrawn on American insistence; two more were about to go, as well as four American divisions, these latter the best divisions in the Italian war zone. On 26 October 1943 Churchill wrote to Eden that the battle in Italy must be "nourished and fought until it is won." Only then would be the time for the cross-Channel landing. It should be made clear to Stalin, he added, that the assurances given about carrying out OVERLORD in May could well be "modified by the exigencies of battle in Italy."

Bitterly Churchill commented, "This is what happens when battles are governed by lawyers' agreements made in all good faith months before, and persisted in without regard to the ever-changing fortunes of war." Britain would do its "very best" for OVERLORD, but he added, "it is no use planning for defeat in the field in order to give temporary political satisfaction."

The British chiefs of staff agreed with Churchill and urged the American joint chiefs to give Italy priority until at least the capture of Rome, one of the Anglo-American objectives laid down at Quebec. British and American landing craft, which could have been used for an amphibious landing on the Italian coast near Rome, were about to leave the Mediterranean for Britain as part of the OVERLORD preparations. On 27 October Churchill told the war cabinet he would resign as prime minister if his request for "nourishing the battle" in Italy were refused by the Americans. He was supported in his Italian strategy by the chief of the imperial staff, Gen. Alan Brooke, who was also emphatic that sufficient forces must be sent to Italy to secure success there.

In order to calm Stalin, Churchill telegraphed to Eden on 29 October to stress that OVERLORD should not be abandoned, but that the retention of landing craft in the Mediterranean "in order not to lose the battle of Rome may cause a slight delay, perhaps till July." It was Gen. Dwight D. Eisenhower, the Supreme Allied Commander in Europe, who now intervened in the debate, arguing in support of Churchill that if the landing craft were withdrawn from Italy as planned, his own advance on Rome would be delayed until January or even February 1944. When Churchill asked Roosevelt to take Eisenhower's view into account, the American joint chiefs agreed that the landing craft due to leave Italy in mid-December could remain in Italy for one more month. But after that they would have to be transferred; OVERLORD must not be delayed beyond its agreed May date. The 50th and 51st divisions were to go back to Britain at once, as were two other British and four American divisions.

Henceforth there was to be no further diversionary plan. On 31 December 1943 Eisenhower, together with Gen. Bernard L. Montgomery, commander-designate of the British 21st Army Group, discussed details of the landings with Churchill, who was then at Marrakesh. Four days later Churchill telegraphed to Stalin that everything was going "full blast" for OVERLORD, and that Montgomery was full of zeal to engage the enemy and of confidence in the result." As commander of the victorious Eighth Army in North Africa, Montgomery was a symbol of British determination.

In January 1944 Churchill sent Col. John Bevan, the head of the London Controlling Section in charge of deception plans, to Moscow, together with his American opposite number, Lt. Col. William H. Baumer, to put to Stalin the need for various Soviet military deceptions designed to help OVERLORD. These included a spurious Soviet amphibious landing on the Black Sea shore of Romania and a Soviet offensive against northern Norway. After initial hesitation,

Stalin agreed to play his part, thus ensuring that as many as twenty German divisions would be kept away from the OVERLORD front. Churchill also presided at a weekly British war cabinet committee, the OVERLORD committee, whose task was to ensure that nothing was neglected or delayed. One of those present later recalled that as a result of Churchill's active participation, "difficulties which first appeared insuperable were overcome, and decisions were translated into immediate action."

Throughout the spring of 1944 Churchill also held regular meetings with Eisenhower and his chief of staff, Gen. Walter Bedell Smith. Together the three men examined every aspect of the landing preparations, including the initial airborne assault, the naval bombardment, and the air cover. On 7 April 1944, Churchill spoke to all the senior British and American officers involved in the planning. "Members of the audience who heard him on that day for the first time were tremendously impressed and inspired," wrote one British participant, Maj. Gen. John Kennedy, director of military operations at the War Office.

On 11 May 1944, as D-day drew nearer, Churchill went on a three-day tour of inspection of the assembled troops. On 15 May he spoke at a final briefing for senior officers. When, on 24 May, he was told of a shortage of naval pumping equipment needed to raise the concrete sections of the artificial harbor, a last-minute setback of serious dimensions, he at once suggested calling upon the pumping resources of the London Fire Brigade. This was done, and the crisis passed. On 5 June 1944 he telegraphed to Stalin: "Tonight we go. We are using 5,000 ships and have available 11,000 aircraft."

As the date of the landing drew near, Churchill's worries were of the casualties. "Do you realize that by the time you wake up in the morning, 20,000 men may have been killed?" he said to his wife during their final late-night vigil alone. "The actual death toll was 3,000. We had expected to lose 10,000 men," he confided to Stalin. Henceforth he was to monitor every aspect of the battle, visit the Normandy bridgehead three times, the first on D plus 6, and try to deal with a sudden new and frightening danger, the Flying Bomb. Starting on D plus 7 the new weapon claimed 2,752 civilian lives in Britain in the following four weeks—more than a third of the battle deaths in Normandy in the first month.

After Churchill's third visit to the battlefield, one British regimental commander wrote to him, "I would like to tell you how tremendously pleased, heartened and honoured every soldier was by your visit." This was not flattery; indeed, from the earliest inception of the Normandy landings, in their planning and their execution, despite the strategic debates between the British and Americans and the British search for victory in Italy, Churchill had been a crucial and constructive player,

deeply conscious that, though the risks would be high, it was through the beaches of Normandy that Germany's defeat would be made certain.

[*See also* Great Britain.]

BIBLIOGRAPHY
Churchill, Winston S. *The Second World War*. Vols. 2–5, 1949–1952.
Fergusson, Bernard, ed. *The Business of War: The War Narrative of Major-General Sir John Kennedy*. 1957.
Gilbert, Martin. *Road to Victory*. Vol. 7 of *Winston S. Churchill*. 1986.

MARTIN GILBERT

CLOSE AIR SUPPORT. Since 1919, the Royal Air Force (RAF) had justified its separate existence by a distinctive role: strategic bombing. The U.S. Air Corps, in contrast, was still part of the army, but anxiously seeking separation also. Both needed to relearn the value and techniques of army-air cooperation, "close support," regularly practiced in World War I.

For the RAF and the British Army the awakening came in 1940, when the world marveled at the dazzling joint performance of the German panzers (tanks) and Stuka dive bombers in the Battle of France. Suddenly close air support was seen to be a necessary mode of war. To handle it, the RAF created a new Army Cooperation Command, but this was not the answer.

The real answer emerged when battle was joined against the Italians in the western desert of Egypt and in East Africa. It then became clear that air cooperation with the army was not just a tiresome survivor of a forgotten war but, as in France, a present necessity. Another World War I lesson of these campaigns was the absolute need for air superiority over the battlefield.

A significant air-army conference in Cairo in July 1941, under the aegis of Air Chief Marshal Arthur Tedder, air officer commanding-in-chief (AOC-in-C) Middle East, defined direct air support as "that intended to have an immediate effect on current land or sea operations" and hammered out a technique for effecting it.

Conforming to this, under Air Vice Marshal Arthur Coningham, AOC Western Desert Air Force, army and air headquarters were located side by side and worked in a high degree of intimacy that was further enhanced when Lt. Gen. Bernard L. Montgomery became commander of the Eighth Army. It was Montgomery who later enunciated with characteristic clarity the principles of successful close air support:

The first and great principle of war is that you must first win your air battle before you fight your land and sea battle . . . .

PILOTS RETURNING FROM STRAFING MISSION.   U.S. Navy pilots who flew RAF Spitfire fighter aircraft over Normandy beachheads in June 1944. The aircraft are marked with the bold stripes signifying involvement in Operation OVERLORD.

NATIONAL ARCHIVES

The second great principle is that Army plus Air has to be so knitted that the two together form one entity. If you do that . . . nothing will be able to stand against it . . . .

The next principle is that . . . there are not two plans, Army and Air, but one plan, Army-Air, which is made . . . together . . . .

Next, the Army and Air Staff must sit together at the same headquarters. There must be between them complete mutual confidence and trust . . . . The Senior Air Staff Officer and the Chief of Staff have to be great friends.

While this immaculate conception was in practice, it worked admirably, causing *Africa Corps* commander Gen. Erwin Rommel to state that "anyone who has to fight, even with the most modern weapons, against an enemy in complete control of the air fights like a savage against modern European troops." The final stages of the campaign in Libya and Tunisia in 1943 displayed the truth of this judgment.

Thereafter, however, conflicts arose among the strong leading personalities. In Sicily and to a lesser extent in Italy, it became apparent that close liaison was a tender plant, very liable to wither without constant care. By D-day the rift between army and air had become serious, but Allied air superiority was so overwhelming that no grave damage ensued.

By the end of 6 June an Allied fighter control center was already functioning in the beachhead. Excellent teamwork between the U.S. Ninth Air Force and the RAF's Second Tactical Air Force (TAF) was established and became the hallmark of the campaign in Normandy. Using seaborne and then land-based control centers, the two air forces (impeded only by the weather of a conspicuously bad summer) proceeded to assert absolute authority over the beachheads: the battle in the air had been won before that on the ground began.

By the end of June thirty-one squadrons of the tactical forces were in France; every hour that weather permitted, the B-26s and A-20s of the U.S. IX Bomber Command, the Mitchells and Mosquitos of Second TAF, and the swarming P-47 Thunderbolts, P-38 Lightnings, and P-51 Mustangs of the IX and XIX Tactical Air Commands, with the rocket-firing Typhoons and Mustangs covered by Spitfire IX fighters of the RAF, struck at everything that moved in and behind the German lines. It was once more Rommel, reporting to Hitler's headquarters on 12 June, who summed up the meaning of "close support": "Our own operations are rendered extraordinarily difficult and in part impossible to carry out [owing largely to] the exceptionally strong and in some respects overwhelming superiority of the enemy air force."

[*See also* Air Superiority *and articles on units mentioned herein.*]

BIBLIOGRAPHY

Dean, Maurice. *The Royal Air Force and Two World Wars*. 1979.
Guedalla, Philip. *Middle East, 1940–42: A Study in Air Power*. 1944.
Saunders, Hilary St. G. *The Fight Is Won*. Vol. 3 of *The Royal Air Force, 1939–1945*. 1954. Official history.
Wilmot, Chester. *The Struggle for Europe*. 1954.

JOHN TERRAINE

CLOSE GUNFIRE SUPPORT. Support landing craft were originally studied by the Royal Navy, which armed LCAs (Landing Craft, Assault) to support landing troops. Wartime experience showed that air and naval bombardment, though essential to any landing, could not destroy beach defenses. While preparatory bombardment could keep an enemy from effective use of his weapons during the approach, it had to be lifted minutes before the first waves landed. This gave the defenders vital time to leave their bunkers and open fire. Landing forces had to include shallow-draft gun- and rocket-armed craft that could accompany them to the beach.

As with landing craft themselves, shortages of suitable support craft posed a continuing problem. The original plan allocated thirteen support craft to the entire operation, and not all of these would be available when needed. This was immediately seen to be inadequate, especially in view of a perceived shortage of bombardment ships. As planning and preparation went on, support craft received increasing attention to the degree that conflicting shipbuilding priorities and demands of the Mediterranean and Pacific theaters permitted. While OVERLORD was preparing, support craft conversion had to be reduced to ensure sufficient craft to lift the landing forces. The D-day naval forces finally included 290 support craft, 96 of which were allotted to the Western Task Force and 194 to the Eastern.

Some Utah Beach support craft were allocated to the Minesweeper Group; others formed the Support Craft Group. At Omaha Beach, these craft formed the Close Gunfire Support Group. Each of the two initial assault groups of Force G (Gold) and Force J (Juno) included one support squadron. Force S (Sword) had a single assault force with one support group.

The support craft included the following types:

LCF (Landing Craft, Flak); British LCTs with 2-pounder (40-mm) and 20-mm guns for defense against low-level air attack.

LBF (Landing Barge, Flak); commercial barges with light antiaircraft guns. Some had engines added.

LCG(L) (Landing Craft, Gun [Large]); British LCTs with 120-mm (4.7-inch) and 20-mm guns for use against shore defense. Adm. Bertram H. Ramsay, Allied naval commander, singled out the LCG(L) for "special mention" for its fire support and counterbattery work, noting that it had "proved a most valuable craft."

LCS(L) (Landing Craft, Support [Large]); British 47-foot LCS(L)(1) and 105-foot LCS(L)(2), and American 158-foot LCS(L)(3), mounting a light gun and automatic weapons.

LCS(M) (Landing Craft, Support [Medium]); British LCA with machine guns and smoke mortars or generators.

LCS(S) (Landing Craft, Support [Small]); American wooden motor boats with machine guns and smoke pots. Some carried 114-mm (4.5-inch) barrage rockets.

LCT(R) (Landing Craft, Tank [Rocket]); British LCT armed with 127-mm (5-inch) barrage rockets. Launchers were fixed in elevation, with a 3,200-meter (3,500-yard) range, and were aimed by positioning the craft itself. They required good training to use properly, but were judged very effective.

LCT(A) (Landing Craft, Tank [Armored]), LCT(HE) (Landing Craft, Tank [High Explosive]), and LCT(CB) (Landing Craft, Tank (Concrete Buster]), Normandy fire-support expedients. The LCT(A) had light armor added, with an elevated platform to let two of their embarked tanks—American Shermans with 75-mm guns, British Centaur IVs with 95-mm howitzers—or 105-mm self-propelled guns fire during the approach. The LCT(HE) was similar, but without armor. The LCT(CB) carried British Sherman VC Firefly tanks, armed with high-velocity 17-pounder (76.2-mm) guns for use against masonry fortifications.

LCA(HR) (Landing Craft, Assault [Hedgerow]). Unsuccessful British LCA firing Hedgerow (U.S. Hedgehog) impact-fuzed antisubmarine projectiles to explode minefields.

The last phase of the prelanding bombardment consisted of a heavy "drenching fire," first laid down by destroyers and support craft armed with guns and howitzers; this was lifted at signal as the first wave approached the beach. Attacks by some 1,600 medium and heavy bombers were timed to end within ten minutes of H-hour. During the final minutes before landing, massive salvos of 5-inch bombardment rockets from LCT(R)s, each of which could fire about a thousand rockets in 90 seconds, blanketed the beach defenses.

Close support fire worked well at Utah Beach, and at Gold, Juno, and Sword. Naval bombardment at Utah continued until the first wave was 700 yards from shore, and support craft kept the beach under automatic weapons fire until the landing craft were nearly ready to touch down. A strong point at Le Hamel, on the right flank of Gold Beach, unexpectedly survived the preliminary bombardment. Sited to enfilade the beach, and protected from seaward, it could not be hit by destroyer guns and had to be knocked out at short range by LCFs and LCGs of the support force. Canadians going ashore on Juno were met by heavy fire; bombardment ships lent their assistance, and support craft came within a thousand yards of the beach to deliver fire that helped the troops clear most of the defenses within an hour. In a freakish incident, a low-flying Typhoon fighter was destroyed as it flew through a salvo of rockets from an LCT(R).

At Omaha strong winds, heavy seas, and extensive beach obstacles submerged by an unexpectedly high tide complicated the run to shore, and defenses in the bluffs overlooking the beach made difficult targets. Fire support and troop movement were not as well integrated as at other beaches; supporting LCT(R)s were unable to approach the beach in line, and rocket fire was delivered piecemeal instead of simultaneously as planned. German fire was heavy, and the landing seemed, at first, to have been stopped at the water's edge. To avoid hitting their own troops, warships offshore were strictly ordered not to fire without clearance from shore fire-control parties, matters were stalemated until landing craft and support craft began to drive at high speed through the shallow-water obstacles and engage German gun positions with their own weapons. Destroyers then closed the beach to assist them. Shore fire-control parties began to establish communication, reinforcements started coming ashore, and troops began to push inland.

Admiral Kirk reported that "the work of gunfire support craft (LCG, etc.) before H-hour was . . . helpful and, in many cases, captains of these craft, acting on their own initiative, provided extremely valuable assistance after the landing, especially in the first bitter struggle to get across the Omaha beaches." Admiral Ramsay reported that "although the success of the assault . . . must be attributed in no small degree to a lack of determination on the part of the defenders, it was also largely due to the effect of the beach drenching fire during the final approach," and called the use of this supporting fire "fully justified." A 1945 British study concluded that "as a result of the drenching fire 10 to 20 percent of the enemy positions were put out of action. . . . The remaining enemy

weapons were not handled as effectively as might have been expected, probably in part due to the moral effect of our fire support."

Twenty-two British and six American close support craft were lost during June.

[*See also* Bombardment Ships.]

BIBLIOGRAPHY

Lenton, H. T., and J. J. Colledge. *British and Dominion Warships of World War II.* 1968.
U.S. Office of Naval Intelligence. *Allied Landing Craft of World War Two.* 1985. Reprint of wartime handbook of landing ships and craft.

JOHN C. REILLY, JR.

COASTAL COMMAND. One of the three front-line Royal Air Force (RAF) commands, along with Bomber and Fighter Command, Coastal Command was responsible for all shore-based operations over the sea. During World War II its major task was the defeat of the German attack on shipping, particularly in the North Atlantic. On 5 June 1944 the Command comprised 52 squadrons and 3 flights with 549 operational aircraft, and had 12 squadrons with 129 aircraft from the Fleet Air Arm, U.S. Navy, and Royal Canadian Air Force under its operational control. Its aircraft did not participate in the assault on D-day and did not come under the command of the Supreme Allied Commander.

VICKERS WELLINGTON XIV OF NO. 179 SQUADRON.   The retractable cylinder under the fuselage housed the Leigh Light, a searchlight used during the final stages of attack to illuminate a U-boat caught on the surface. This unit took part in the elaborate CORK patrol operation to prevent U-boats from entering the English Channel from the west during D-day and the following weeks.   COURTESY OF ALFRED PRICE

RAF BEAUFIGHTER.   Rockets hitting an armed merchant vessel off the northern coast of Holland.   IMPERIAL WAR MUSEUM

However, Coastal Command made a major contribution to the success of D-day; with the Royal Navy, it "held the ring" for the expedition.

In his report to the Commander in Chief, Allied Expeditionary Air Force, dated 1 March 1944, Air Chief Marshal W. Sholto Douglas outlined three main tasks:

1. To prevent the enemy U-boat flotilla from reaching the beachhead;
2. To prevent enemy light surface forces from interrupting the operation;
3. To interrupt enemy sea-based logistics where possible.

In the first role Coastal Command held a significant advantage, for the enemy had been decisively defeated in May 1943; U-boat losses had become so high (about fifty per month) that Grand Admiral Karl Dönitz called off the attack on Atlantic shipping. However, there were still approximately 420 U-boats available, many fitted with snorkels for submerged operations. The U-boats were based in the Bay of Biscay ports and Norway. Douglas anticipated 100 could be used on D-day for an all-out offensive in the Channel. Allied mines would seal off the Strait of Dover to the east, but Coastal Command had to close the western end of the Channel to U-boats. On 18

April plans were issued for a massive patrol system, codenamed CORK, to operate night and day over eleven distinct areas stretching out to the south coast of Ireland and the Biscay coast; the entire area was to be under constant surveillance. The object was to seal the western entrance to the Channel, driving off U-boats or forcing them to stay submerged, where their endurance was low. This role was given to No. 19 Group, based at Plymouth, comprising 19 squadrons of large maritime patrol aircraft—Liberators, Catalinas, Sunderlands, and Wellingtons—supported by four squadrons of Mosquitos, Beaufighters, and five Fleet Air Arm Avenger squadrons. This heavy concentration of aircraft in southwest England caused some logistics problems, but these had been resolved before D-day.

During the first three weeks of May intense patrolling forced the Bay of Biscay U-boats back to base, while the Norway flotilla, heading south on 16 May, was engaged en route by No. 18 Group, based in Scotland, losing 16 sunk and 12 damaged by the end of July; only a handful reached the Bay of Biscay ports. The Biscay boats remained in bombproof pens on D-day, leaving port only on the night of 6–7 June. During the period D-day to D plus 4, 36 Biscay boats were seen, 23 attacked, and 6 sunk, with 4 damaged and the remainder forced back.

The U-boats were defeated: 28 were sunk, 5 were "shared kills," and 29 more were damaged. Down to the American army breakout operation U-boats sank only 9 ships. But the cost was high; Coastal Command lost 60 aircraft, 38 by enemy action. In June there were 4,724 sorties, leading to 75 attacks.

Operations against enemy light surface forces, code-named CONEBO, were carried out by a reinforced No. 16 Group, with 10 squadrons, based at Chatham. There were over 100 E-boats (S-boats or *Schnellboote*—small, fast motor torpedo boats), 5 destroyers, and numerous light craft in the area, principally around Cherbourg and Le Havre. As the targets operated at night, they were suppressed by extensive patrolling, flare dropping, radar-equipped aircraft, and Beaufighter strikes at dusk and dawn off their bases. Heavy patrolling in May along the axes North Foreland to Calais, and Portland to Cherbourg, was stepped up for D-day, when 130 sorties were flown, with another 90 on D plus 1. During June there were 1,987 sorties, resulting in 400 attacks on 191 targets, 132 in the Channel. Although E-boats were a difficult target, they were kept under control.

The third task was restricted to an attack on German destroyers near the Gironde Estuary early in the invasion (later these ships were engaged by the Royal Navy off the Île de Batz, on the north coast of Brittany), and an operation on 15 June when two large supply ships were torpedoed off the Dutch coast by Beaufighters of No. 16 Group. The shift to strike warfare reflected the success of defensive operations.

In partnership with Royal Navy surface escorts, Coastal Command carried out its appointed task. If the bulk of this work was routine patrolling, it was routine that paved the way to success.

[*See also* Douglas, W. Sholto.]

BIBLIOGRAPHY

Royal Air Force. *The Liberation of North-West Europe.* Vol. 3 of *RAF Narrative.* 1957.

ANDREW LAMBERT

COASTAL DEFENSE. *See* Beach and Coastal Defenses.

COAST GUARD. The U.S. Coast Guard (USCG) is by law a military service and a branch of the armed forces at all times. On 1 November 1941, President Franklin D. Roosevelt issued Executive Order 8929, transferring the USCG from the U.S. Treasury to the U.S. Navy (USN). From late 1939 on, because the USN lacked ships, USCG cutters performed neutrality patrol and convoy escort duties in the Atlantic. The USCG also continued its weather patrol duties; played a significant role in the development of LORAN (long-range-aid-to-navigation),

COAST GUARD-MANNED LCVP.   Approaching landing beaches on 6 June 1944.   NATIONAL ARCHIVES

COAST GUARD LCIs.   A file of LCIs (Landing Craft, Infantry) moves across the English Channel, carrying barrage balloons as protection against low-flying German planes. Taken by a Coast Guard combat photographer, it was the first American photograph of the invasion to appear in London.   THE ROBERT HUNT LIBRARY, LONDON

the first virtually all-weather navigational system; and waged savage antisubmarine warfare in the North Atlantic while escorting convoys carrying American forces and supplies for the invasion of Europe. Its vessels also continued to respond to calls for rescues, often under enemy fire, saving 4,243 lives in the Atlantic theater.

The USCG manned 97 vessels on D-day, not counting the landing craft carried by their three attack troop transports. Individual Coast Guardsmen also served with USN crews on other ships. Six USCG officers participated in the construction of the artificial harbors, code-named MULBERRIES. For the crossing of the English Channel, the sixty fast, wooden-hulled cutters of USCG Rescue Flotilla 1, commanded by Lt. Comdr. Alexander V. Stewart, USCG Reserve (USCGR), sailed alongside the vessels loaded with soldiers.

This unique unit had been created at the suggestion of Roosevelt only weeks before D-day, in anticipation of heavy casualties. Rushed across the Atlantic and modified in England for rescue work, these 83-foot cutters were divided between the American and British beaches. Within mere minutes of H-hour, a rescue cutter picked up the first of the 450 survivors rescued on D-day.

In all, the rescue cutters saved 1,437 fighting men and one female nurse during the invasion. They dashed through deadly mine fields, underwater obstructions, barrages of shore batteries, strafing by airplanes, and naval, heavy, small-arms, and even friendly fire to aid endangered personnel, brought them to larger vessels, and then ran the dangerous gauntlet again to pick up more survivors. They often towed disabled landing craft to permit the unloading of their troops, tanks, artillery, and supplies on the beaches. In the following days, the 83-footers continued to shepherd the ships carrying troops and supplies to sustain the advance inland, ferried visitors, delivered mail, and performed other tasks.

At Utah Beach the attack troop transport *Joseph T. Dickman*, commanded by Capt. Raymond J. Mauerman, USCG, began unloading at 0305. Despite the loss of seven landing craft, it debarked 1,963 soldiers, 68 vehicles, and a considerable amount of explosives without losing a single soldier. The transport finished unloading at 1145, getting underway at 1438 with 153 wounded aboard.

The attack troop transport *Bayfield*, commanded by Capt. Lyndon Spencer, USCG, successfully landed soldiers and matériel on Utah Beach without loss, despite the swamping of three landing craft. Because this transport had been modified to function as a general command ship, it had been selected as the flagship for Rear Adm. Don P. Moon, USN, the naval assault force commander. As

LCVP.   Landing Craft, Vehicle and Personnel, from USS *Samuel Chase*.

such, *Bayfield* had to function as a supply, hospital, and accommodation ship, information center, and oiler. It also had aboard the senior U.S. Army commander, Maj. Gen. J. Lawton Collins, and his staff as well as the liaison officers for the U.S. Army Air Force. Coast Guardsmen on *Bayfield* operated forty-seven radio circuits to direct the operations of naval, army, and air forces. They even had pigeons aboard in case of a radio failure. Remaining on the scene until 25 June, the *Bayfield* treated hundreds of wounded and repaired several damaged landing craft.

The attack troop transport *Samuel Chase*, commanded by Capt. Edward E. Fritzche, USCG, began debarking infantrymen off Omaha Beach at 0530 and vehicles at 0800, and finished unloading—even three Piper Cub aircraft—by 1100. Six landing craft failed to return, having become casualties from gunfire, underwater obstacles, or swamping.

None of the ten USCG-manned 328-foot LSTs (Landing Ships, Tank)—six at the American and four at the British beaches—was lost, although several suffered damage, and casualties to their crews. After discharging their load in the initial assault, they crossed the English Channel many times, evacuating wounded to England and returning with reinforcements—personnel and vehicles, including freight cars. *LST-261* made the most trips—fifty-three.

USCG Flotilla 4, Capt. Miles H. Imlay, USCG, consist-

ed of twenty-four 158-foot LCI(L)s, or Landing Craft Infantry (Large). They assembled in the Channel ports with their particular task forces, accompanied them on the cross-Channel voyage, and went in with the troops at both Utah and Omaha beaches. The LCI(L)s successfully landed the troops in the face of heavy enemy fire, but four were lost to mines. The others survived to serve as fire fighting ships, tugs, channel guides, and ferries.

Originally scheduled to land on D-day, the approximately fifty members of the commando-trained USN Reconnaissance Party, commanded by Comdr. Quentin R. Walsh, USCG, with the mission of opening large seaports, did not come ashore until 10 June. During the capture of the important port of Cherbourg, the USCG commander took sixteen sailors, armed only with submachine guns and hand grenades, to reconnoiter the waterfront. Coming under fire, they killed several snipers and took over 400 Germans prisoner. Commander Walsh then bluffed the surrender of the 350-strong fanatical Nazi garrison of Fort du Homet, freeing 53 captured American paratroopers.

[*See also* Bayfield, USS.]

BIBLIOGRAPHY

Mercey, Arch A., and Lee Grove, eds. *Sea, Surf, and Hell: The U.S. Coast Guard in World War II.* 1945.

U.S. Coast Guard. *Landings in France*. 1946.
Willoughby, Malcolm F. *The U.S. Coast Guard in World War II*. 1957.

TRUMAN R. STROBRIDGE

COLE, ROBERT G. (1915–1944), American, lieutenant colonel, airborne battalion commander. Cole, the son of an army officer, graduated from West Point in 1939 and volunteered for the 101st Airborne Division in 1942. He jumped into Normandy on 6 June 1944 in command of a battalion of paratroopers.

On 11 June he led the final attack on Carentan. His battalion was stopped and forced to take cover by a withering combined-arms cross fire from mortars, machine guns, and artillery. "It looked like we couldn't go ahead because of the fire," Sgt. Roy Hendricks of the battalion said, "and we couldn't go to either side because of the flooded areas." Cole passed an order back through the ditches lining the road: "Fix bayonets. Load your guns; we're going to charge." He led the charge with drawn pistol. When a man fell beside him, Cole grabbed his rifle and using the bayonet rushed the German trench. His men followed.

"They charged like wild animals," a captured German told Reuter's correspondent Robert Reuben. "They screamed and shouted when they charged into our fire. It was unbelievable." The Germans surrendered.

Gen. Maxwell Taylor recommended the Medal of Honor for Cole, the only member of the 101st to be so honored in Normandy, but the recommendation had not been acted upon when Cole was killed in Holland, 18 September 1944. Walter Cronkite of the United Press described his death. Cole needed to put out recognition panels into an open area in the midst of a woods to guide fighter aircraft coming to provide support. "He knew the woods were filled with German snipers," Cronkite wrote. "So rather than order a man into the field to place the panels, Cole carried them himself. He was placing the last panel when a sniper's bullet got him."

In a handwritten letter to Cole's widow, Taylor said, "Bob was our ideal Airborne soldier. His courage was legendary and his hold on his rugged parachutists is an example which few other commanders ever attained." In his letter of condolence, General Dwight D. Eisenhower wrote, "He was one of our ablest and certainly one of our most gallant officers."

[*See also* 101st Airborne Division.]

BIBLIOGRAPHY

Rapport, Leonard, and Arthur Northwood. *Rendezvous with Destiny: A History of the 101st Airborne Division*. 1948.

STEPHEN E. AMBROSE

COLE-HAMILTON, J. B. (1894-1945), British, air vice marshal, air officer commanding 85th Composite Group. A former cadet from the Royal Naval Colleges at Osborne and Dartmouth, John Cole-Hamilton came to the Royal Naval Air Service in 1915 and spent the wartime years flying airships. During the 1920s and early 1930s he filled training appointments, commanded a squadron in India, held staff posts there and in the Air Ministry, and worked in army cooperation. After several more years in India, World War II brought him appointments as air officer commanding (AOC) 70 Group, where he was responsible for army cooperation training, then AOC Northern Ireland and AOC West Africa.

He took over as AOC 85 Group on 13 February 1944, charged with preparing his force to provide the night air defense and base support required by the RAF units that would be moving into France in June, and he commanded them from his headquarters at Hillingdon on D-day and over the following month. On 10 July he took over 10 Group, Air Defence of Great Britain, exchanging places with Air Vice Marshal Steele, and four months later he became AOC 11 Group. In 1945, he was taken ill and died in August.

[*See also* 85th Composite Group.]

J. B. COLE-HAMILTON.   IMPERIAL WAR MUSEUM

BIBLIOGRAPHY

Wynn, Humphrey, and Susan Young. *Prelude to Overlord*. 1983.

HENRY PROBERT

COLLINS, J. LAWTON (1896–1987), American, general, commander of the VII Corps. Joseph Collins was born in Algiers, Louisiana, on 1 May 1896. The son of an Irish immigrant, who had served in the Union Army, and Catherine Lawton, he attended local schools and Louisiana State University before entering the U.S. Military Academy at West Point in 1913. He graduated in the upper third of his class in April 1917, two weeks after the declaration of war against Germany. He requested assignment to the 22d Infantry Regiment stationed in New York City, which he expected would be one of the first units sent overseas. This was not to be, however; the 22d Infantry remained in the United States throughout the war.

In May 1919 Collins was ordered to join the Army of Occupation in Germany where he remained until the summer of 1921. For the next twelve years he was either a student or instructor at military schools. In 1933, now a major, he was assigned to the Philippines, first as a brigade executive officer and then as Operations and Intelligence officer of the Philippine Division.

Returning in 1936 Collins attended the Army Industrial College and then the Army War College, where, after graduation, he remained as an instructor. In June 1940, the War College closed with the approach of war and Collins, now a lieutenant colonel, was placed on temporary duty in the office of Gen. George C. Marshall, Chief of Staff of the Army.

In January 1941 Collins was promoted to colonel and assigned chief of staff of the VII Corps in Alabama. Three years later he would command the VII Corps when it landed on Utah Beach on D-day. Five days after Pearl Harbor he was on his way to California where he learned he was to be chief of staff of the Hawaiian Department. He arrived on 17 December 1941 and two months later was promoted to brigadier general, and then to major general in May 1942. Assigned that month to command the 25th Infantry Division, he trained it assiduously using the techniques he had learned during the Louisiana maneuvers of 1941. He prepared his unit for mobile warfare rather than for the static defense of Hawaii, which was its mission. The defeat of the Japanese at the Battle of Midway in June, however, eliminated the threat of invasion.

In November the 25th Division sailed for the South Pacific, where it relieved the 1st Marine Division on Guadalcanal. On 10 January 1943 the 25th Division started the attack, and in less than a month eliminated the Japanese forces on Guadalcanal. It was there that General

J. LAWTON COLLINS.   NATIONAL ARCHIVES

Collins received the nickname "Lightning Joe" from the lightning bolt on the shoulder patch of the 25th "Tropic Lightning" Division. After leading his division in the New Georgia campaign he was transferred to the European Theater of Operations and in February 1944 assumed command of the VII Corps in England. For the next four months he participated in the planning for the Allied landings in Normandy and intensified the training of the units assigned to the corps. This strenuous training included mock amphibious assaults on the southwest coast of England, one of which became overly realistic when German E-Boats penetrated the naval screen and sank several landing ships off Slapton Sands with the loss of some seven hundred soldiers and sailors.

On the evening of 5 June, General Collins sailed from Portsmouth on the command ship, USS *Bayfield*, with the commander of Task Force U, Rear Admiral Don P. Moon.

Bad weather on 5 June gave the Germans little reason to suspect an attack. The first clue the Germans had was the dropping of parachutists soon after 0130 hours on

6 June. The airdrop of the 82d and 101st airborne divisions was so badly scattered, however, that no pattern to the attack was discernible.

The 4th Infantry Division assaulted Utah Beach, on the west side of the Cotentin Peninsula, and after relatively light fighting pushed inland to the road center of Sainte-Mère-Église. Collins established his corps headquarters nearby and attacked rapidly to the north in an attempt to seize the port of Cherbourg. The push north ran into stiff resistance, however, and the hoped for rapid seizure of the major port was not possible.

The VII Corps then attacked to the south to link up with the V Corps in the Omaha bridgehead, then attacked to the east to seal off the Cotentin Peninsula. This was accomplished by the 9th Infantry Division on the night of 17–18 June and the Allied lodgment area was declared secure.

General Collins' drive and determination, his strong personality (he relieved one division commander), his ability to change plans promptly based on a changing situation and to inspire his subordinates contributed greatly to the rapid securing of the lodgment. He commanded the VII Corps with distinction for the remainder of the war in Europe and was preparing for the invasion of Japan when the war ended.

Assignments in Washington, D.C., followed: chief of Public Information of the Army, deputy chief of staff (promoted to general in January 1948), and vice chief of staff. On 16 August 1949 he became the eighteenth chief of staff of the U.S. Army. His four-year tenure as chief of staff, which included the Korean War, was marked by the great expansion of the army, the major increase in procurement of material and ammunition, and the disagreement between President Harry S Truman and General of the Army Douglas MacArthur.

At President Eisenhower's request, Collins remained on active duty as the U.S. Representative to the North Atlantic Treaty Organization's Standing Group and Military Committee, with a year and a half interlude as special representative of the United States in Vietnam. He retired from the Standing Group in March 1956 to become vice-chairman of the international division of the Charles Pfizer Company, until he retired in 1969.

Widely regarded in both U.S. and British military circles as the most aggressive and capable field commander in World War II, Collins led the breakout at Saint-Lô, stopped the German counterattack at Mortain, captured Aachen and Cologne, and led VII Corps in its envelopment of the Ruhr industrial area and its meeting with the Russians on the Elbe.

He was an educator, a diplomat, and a humanitarian in addition to being a superb soldier. He received many military and civilian decorations and awards including the *Laetare* Medal, four Distinguished Service Medals, two Silver Stars for gallantry in action, and many foreign decorations. He died at the age of ninety-two on 12 September 1987 and was buried in Arlington National Cemetery near Washington, D.C.

[*See also* VII Corps.]

BIBLIOGRAPHY

Collins, J. Lawton. *Lightning Joe: An Autobiography*. 1979.
Harrison, Gordon A. *Cross Channel Attack*. U.S. Army in World War II: The European Theater of Operations. 1951.
MacDonald, Charles B. *The Last Offensive*. U.S. Army in World War II: The European Theater of Operations. 1973.
Weigley, Russell F. *Eisenhower's Lieutenants: The Campaign of France and Germany, 1944–1945*. 1981.

JAMES LAWTON COLLINS, JR.

COMBINED OPERATIONS PILOTAGE PARTIES. These units were developed jointly by the Royal Navy and the British army, starting in the autumn of 1942, to make sure landing forces found the right beach. Combined Operations Pilotage Parties (COPP) were invented by Lt. Comdr. (eventually Capt.) Nigel Clogstoun-Willmott. He had observed variants of a mile in the chart readings around the island of Rhodes and resolved them by going to see for himself in a small boat, with Maj. Roger Courtney of the Special Boat Squadron (an offshoot of the Special Air Service).

Four of Clogstoun-Willmott's COPP assisted in securing correct landfalls for Operation TORCH at Algiers and Oran in November 1942. Combined Operations Headquarters, following Lord Louis Mountbatten's directions, then formalized COPP by creating a war establishment for them and settling Clogstoun-Willmott in a headquarters: the yacht club on Hayling Island, between Portsmouth and Chichester. There he trained his teams.

These were kept small—about ten members each—so that they could easily be sent anywhere by air. Each team, commanded by a naval lieutenant commander or lieutenant, comprised three naval officers (one for navigation, one for reconnaissance, and one for administration), an army captain (also for reconnaissance), a sergeant-bodyguard, three naval enlisted men as paddlers, and a mechanic.

They operated, out of small or midget submarines, from canoes. By incessant practice, they learned how to canoe quietly, how to get ashore from their canoes more quietly still, how to measure beach gradients using fishing lines and movable posts, and how to collect soil samples from beaches with augers. They were carefully trained in navigation, as well as in commando tactics with small arms and knives. They were never intended to go into combat, but if they did, they were formidable at close quarters. Clogstoun-Willmott developed suits for them of rubberized canvas, suitable for swimming under water. They carried flashlights, watches, and compasses waterproofed with periscope grease or held in condoms, as well as arms. Soon after the ballpoint pen was invented, they used them for making notes under water.

Parties successfully guided in both Lt. Gen. Miles C. Dempsey's and Gen. George S. Patton's forces for Operation HUSKY, the invasion of Sicily in July 1943, using infrared torches shining out to sea to guide the incoming landing craft. Others were used successfully for Operation AVALANCHE at Salerno in September.

By now COPP had arrived as a regular part of the British system for planning and mounting any large combined operation. Only secret planning staffs knew of their existence until landing craft navigators were told about them immediately before operations took place. They encountered the usual obstruction to anything new when they required special stores; Clogstoun-Willmott once had to convince the Third Sea Lord personally that his canoes must have brass anchors because iron ones would upset the compasses in their bows. As early as January 1944 COPP were investigating a beach in the Bay of the Seine, at Saint-Laurent-sur-Mer, later part of Omaha Beach. In April, a historian on General Dwight D. Eisenhower's intelligence staff recalled that in Roman times the coastline had been farther north and that the Romans had had peat bogs there. COPP had hurriedly to be sent, with extra-deep augers, to make sure the beaches would be safe for the transit of tanks.

American security staffs, worried that such expeditions would compromise security, made no use of COPP on D-day. The British had a COPP unit off Arromanches and another off Ouistreham in X-craft (midget submarines) that guided in their landing armadas precisely by a combination of light, radio, and sound signals.

BIBLIOGRAPHY

Dear, I. C. B. "On Hostile Shores." *The Elite* 11 (1987): 2441.

M. R. D. FOOT

COMMANDOS. British Commandos, like the U.S. Rangers, were conceived during the early days of World War II and named after the marauding bands of Boer commandos of South Africa. Initially composed of army volunteers, they raided enemy coasts. When Lord Mountbatten became chief of Combined Operations in 1941, he recommended that the mainly uncommitted Royal Marines Division should be retrained as commandos, a traditional sea-soldier role. The concept was that commando units should be used primarily for offensive operations and be lightly equipped, highly trained in individual battle skills, and exceptionally fit; when their tasks were completed, they would be relieved by regular

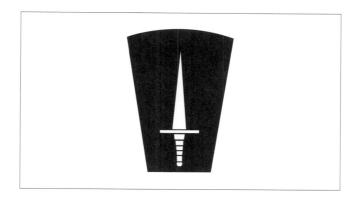

infantry. All ranks passed through the Commando Training Unit, Achnacarry, Scotland, as did many U.S. Rangers.

The British Commandos, formed from independent commando companies from 1940 onward, were divided almost equally between the army (Nos. 1 to 12, including No. 10 Inter-Allied Commando, all volunteer units) and later, from 1942, the Royal Marines (Nos. 40 to 48). Their task, similar to the U.S. Rangers, was initially that of raiding enemy-held coastlines and islands; they were smaller units (between 250 and 450 men) than infantry battalions, extremely adaptable, and mobile with a high proportion of commissioned and noncommissioned officers and automatic weapons. By 1944 Commandos had seen action in North Africa, Sicily, and Italy, raided the Lofoten Islands off the coast of Norway, Dieppe, and Saint-Nazaire, and conducted other smaller excursions.

For D-day, the Special Service Group under Maj. Gen. Robert G. Sturges, Royal Marines, consisted of the 1st and 4th special service brigades (totaling about 5,000 men) with the task of taking, protecting, and exploiting the left flank of the main invasion force. The 1st Special Service Brigade under Brig. Lord Lovat consisted of: No. 3 Commando (Lt. Col. Peter Young), which had previous battle experience at Dieppe and in Sicily: No. 4 Commando (Lt. Col. Robert Dawson), which had seen action at Vågø in the Faeroe Islands and Dieppe and had two troops of No. 10 Inter-Allied Commando attached; No. 6 Commando (Lt. Col. Derek Mills-Roberts), which had carried out many small raids and fought in North Africa; and No. 45 Royal Marine Commando (Lt. Col. Charles Ries), which was newly formed and comparatively inexperienced.

In the 4th Special Service Brigade, under Brig. B. W. Leicester, No. 41 Royal Marine Commando (Lt. Col. T. M. Gray) had seen action in Sicily and Italy, but No. 46 Marine Commando (Lt. Col. Campbell Hardy), No. 47 Royal Marine Commando (Lt. Col. C. F. Phillips), and No. 48 Royal Marine Commando (Lt. Col. J. L. Moulton) were all new to battle, having been re-formed as Commandos from Royal Marine battalions.

The 1st Special Service Brigade, on the extreme left of

ROYAL MARINE COMMANDOS.   Heavily laden Commandos moving inland from the area near Ouistreham to their first objective on 6 June 1944.   IMPERIAL WAR MUSEUM

Sword Beach, was ordered to land an hour after H-hour, pass through the 8th Brigade of the 3d British Division, and cut inland to link up before nightfall with the 6th Airborne Division, which had captured the bridges spanning the Orne River and the Caen Canal.

The 4th Special Service Brigade was more widely dispersed, with No. 41 Commando landing on Sword Beach to capture Lion-sur-Mer and No. 48 Commando on Juno Beach to take Saint-Aubin; No. 47 Commando had an independent role, landing on the right of Gold Beach under the XXX Corps at Le Hamel to capture Port-en-Bessin. No. 46 Commando landed on D plus 1 at Petit Enfer in support of the 3d Canadian Division to clear the Mue valley and take Le Hamel and Rots. The brigade regrouped at Douvres by D plus 4, having captured the radar station.

After D-day the Commandos fought as infantry for several weeks, mostly in defensive positions with vigorous patrolling, but because of their lack of a supply line they were highly dependent on army logistic support.

[See also 1st Special Service Brigade; 4th Special Service Brigade; Leicester, B. W.; Lovat, Lord.]

BIBLIOGRAPHY

Ladd, James D. *Commandos and Rangers of World War II.* 1978.
Ladd, James D. *The Royal Marines, 1919–1980.* 1980.
Saunders, Hilary St. G. *The Green Beret.* 1949.

DEREK OAKLEY

COMMUNICATION. The assault on the beaches of Normandy presented the greatest challenge to military communications in history. The Allies called upon every technique to coordinate their attack, from just developed multichannel radio relay to pigeons; the Germans needed responsive radar and communications nets to find the brunt of the attack and respond quickly.

During preinvasion preparations in England, the American and British communicators created a Combined Signal Board to integrate the planning of their army, navy, and air force communications. One of their primary tasks was allocating the distribution of radio frequencies to ensure that nets of adjacent units did not interfere with each other. Demand for frequencies was triple what was available in the bands used by Allied radios; heavy restrictions had to be placed on the numbers of nets, and crystals were being ground and changed right up to the week of the invasion.

For almost a year prior to the invasion, the Allies established nets with heavy dummy radio traffic. They wanted the enemy to perceive no increase in traffic as real communications increased during the weeks before the invasion. As the sea and air invasion forces crossed the Channel, strict radio silence was observed. Meanwhile radios were used by air and naval forces conducting feints toward Calais and Boulogne. Along with the use of metallic strips, called chaff, dropped into the sky to confuse German radars, radio countermeasures were important to the success of the deception strategy.

The Allied airborne drops on Normandy were guided by pathfinders who parachuted in several hours before the main assault. Having originally planned to use signal lights and electronic beacons to guide the airplanes and gliders with the main airborne force, the pathfinders were forced by the nearness of the enemy to forgo their lights and use only the electronic beacons that emitted a radio signal for the aircraft to home in on. The beacons worked well in helping the pilots find drop zones amid a dense cloud cover and German antiaircraft fire.

Once on the ground, the paratroopers faced the challenge of reassembling their units in terrain broken up by tall hedgerows. Lacking radios linking individuals or small teams, units regrouped in a haphazard and cautious fashion. Even then, control and coordination of tactical operations by the airborne units was always hampered by the scarcity of portable radios.

The Allied communicators assaulting the beaches of Normandy on the morning of 6 June faced a different challenge. Many had lost their radios or had them disabled when they waded through the rough surf. Once on the beach, they resorted to wire lines run between the command posts of the assaulting units. Eventually they were able to install small switchboards to make more efficient use of the wire network on the beaches. By 10 June, radios were collected into nets to support the Allied forces pushing inland.

Meanwhile the Germans were having difficulty coordinating a defense against the attacks. While they had the advantage of communications in place, many of their wire lines were cut by the French Resistance. Also, the Allied electronic deception had denied them preparation time.

Although the confusion and chaos of battle interfered with tactical communications, the Allies were able to establish most higher level communications according to plans. As soon as signal units reached the beach, they dispatched messenger pigeons back to headquarters units operating from ships offshore. Once the beach was secured, radios were landed to establish more dependable links, and within a few days two submarine cables were run from the command ships to shore units.

Since naval gunfire provided the primary artillery cover, communications between the beach and the ships were tactically critical. Forward observers used high-frequency (HF) radios to call in fire on German positions. Aircraft reconnaissance provided intelligence on targets farther behind the beach. As soon as the spotter planes returned to England, their photographs would be developed and sent by radio facsimile to naval gunfire ships and Allied artillery observers in Normandy.

While facsimile was a useful new development, the Normandy invasion witnessed the first use of a revolutionary communications technique just developed in the U.S. Army Signal Corps laboratories and rushed to England in time for the assault. Using radios in much higher frequencies (VHF) than current equipment, the army had developed a radio that would split its signal into four channels that could be fully integrated into a tactical wire network. Since it was untested outside the laboratory, two civilian technicians accompanied the equipment to install and operate it.

To supplement the high-frequency (HF) links from Normandy to England, the army installed the system across the Channel. While VHF signals are less susceptible to atmosphere interference, they are restricted to line of sight, so the signalmen had to install antennas on an old watchtower on the Isle of Wight that had been used to look for the approach of the Spanish Armada in 1588. On the afternoon of 8 June, the link was completed to a bluff overlooking Omaha Beach; a few hours later the first facsimile photos were being transmitted to the forward observers aiming Allied artillery at the German positions.

As the Allied armies pushed overland, they reverted to the more traditional communications tactics adopted in North Africa and Italy. But the communications used in the Normandy invasion laid the foundation for communications supporting large troop movements, called "force projection communications," as used over the next fifty years.

[See also Signal, articles on Allied Signal and German Signal.]

BIBLIOGRAPHY

Harris, Dixie R., and George R. Thompson. *The Signal Corps: The Outcome*. 1991.

JOHN D. BERGEN

CONINGHAM, ARTHUR (1895–1948), British (New Zealand), air marshal, air officer commanding

ARTHUR CONINGHAM. At left, with Air Vice Marshal Harry Broadhurst (center) and Air Chief Marshal Arthur Tedder (right), 29 June 1944.

IMPERIAL WAR MUSEUM

(AOC) Second Tactical Air Force (TAF). Coningham enlisted in the New Zealand Army in 1914 and transferred into the Royal Flying Corps in 1916; he was three times decorated for distinguished service on the Western front. He received a permanent commission in the Royal Air Force (RAF) in 1919.

War in 1939 found him in command of No. 4 Group, Bomber Command, which became the pioneer of the night operations soon adopted by the whole command's long-range force. In July 1941 he was transferred to the Middle East, where his new command was No. 204 Group, shortly to be renamed Air Headquarters, Western Desert, and later to go down in history as the Desert Air Force. At the time of Coningham's arrival both air and army were deeply concerned with what the army called "air support" and the RAF called "army cooperation." This had been highly successful against the Italians in north and east Africa, but when the Luftwaffe arrived with Rommel's *Africa Corps,* the picture changed: the early campaigns of 1941 had gone badly, and lack of cooperation was blamed.

Coningham threw all his vigorous energy and considerable talent into correcting this state of affairs and substantial progress was made, but army-air cooperation collapsed completely in the confusion following Rommel's 1942 offensive at Gazala. When Lt. Gen. Bernard L. Montgomery took command of the Eighth Army in August, one of his first steps was to place his headquarters beside Coningham's with senior officers sharing the same mess. In all the operations involved in the second El Alamein campaign, this top-level concord contributed greatly to decisive victory.

Unfortunately, at this juncture close support once more declined. The air commanders, Coningham and his superior, Air Chief Marshal Arthur Tedder, became critical of Montgomery's slow pursuit of Rommel and angry at the claims of his personal publicity. A rift developed between Montgomery and Coningham that was never healed.

On 21 January 1944 Coningham was appointed AOC Second TAF for Operation OVERLORD. It was written into the initial plan that Coningham would be the only air commander with whom Montgomery would have to deal, but Montgomery saw things differently. There was a sharp disagreement between them concerning the need to capture space for airfields, with Montgomery disconcertingly changing his opinion, to Coningham's disgust. Fortunately, the overwhelming weight of Allied air power prevented the worst effects of this retrogression.

Coningham's forces continued to give the armies vital support throughout the European campaign, during which he commanded some 1,800 aircraft and 100,000 men drawn from seven nations. An inspiring air commander, he died an airman's death in a crash in January 1948.

[*See also* Second Tactical Air Force.]

BIBLIOGRAPHY

Playfair, I. S. O., et al. *The Mediterranean and the Middle East.* Vol. 4, 1966. Official history.
Saunders, Hilary St. G. *The Fight Is Won.* Vol. 3 of *The Royal Air Force, 1939–1945.* 1975. Official history.
Tedder, Arthur. *With Prejudice: The War Memoirs of Marshal of the Royal Air Force Lord Tedder.* 1966.
Terraine, John. *A Time for Courage: The Royal Air Force in the European War, 1939–1945.* 1985.

JOHN TERRAINE

CONVOY COVER. The Allied troops that stormed the Norman coast on 6 June 1944 were ferried across the water by thousands of ships of every description, size, and function. Together, these ships represented the bulk of Allied naval assets, and military commanders put a premium on their protection. The original COSSAC Plan outlined the scope of air support for the invasion fleet, and as OVERLORD plans were fine-tuned in the spring of 1944, Air Chief Marshal Trafford Leigh-Mallory of the Allied Expeditionary Air Forces (AEAF) finalized the air cover blueprint. For the task, he drew upon 1,000 aircraft from the U.S. Eighth and Ninth Air Forces, the British Second Air Force, and British Coastal Command.

These air forces divided among them the major tasks of convoy cover. Coastal Command Spitfires and Hurricanes were responsible for the protection of ships as they assembled in English harbors. Two Ninth and four Eighth Air Force P-38 groups, their distinctive shape easy to identify from below, were assigned shipping route cover as the fleets

RAF SUPERMARINE SPITFIRE.   One of the best aircraft of World War II, it provided low cover to flotillas.

IMPERIAL WAR MUSEUM

steamed the short distance to Normandy. And once the flotilla reached the far shore, the Second Tactical and the Ninth Air Forces were to maintain beach protection, Spitfires providing low cover (3,000 to 5,000 feet altitude) and P-47s high cover (8,000 to 15,000 feet altitude). To avoid friendly fire, air plans prescribed safe distances between ships and aircraft, and strict limitations on night flight operations were enforced from the outset of OVERLORD.

Hurricanes were in the sky as the first ships left English harbors on 31 May. To avoid possible detection by German radar on the far shore, these planes flew below 5,000 feet. At 1600 on D minus 1 the first American P-38s gathered above the assembled navies in four-squadron units. Flying just under the cloud ceiling at 4,000 feet, each flight stayed over the ships ninety minutes as the Allies headed toward France. As 6 June dawned, over 300 British Spitfires and American P-47s patrolled the skies as beach cover, ranging from fifteen miles to seaward and five miles inland. Only over hotly contested Omaha Beach were the cover planes

pushed out of the air by intense Allied naval and air gunfire; the space there had simply become too crowded.

By every measure, the convoy cover operation was successful, if uneventful. Foreshadowing the air superiority the Allies enjoyed in France, few Luftwaffe planes appeared on the horizon. On D-day itself, just one flight of Focke-Wulf 190s came near the flotilla, and after dark the Luftwaffe mustered only sporadic attacks on shipping. Of these, a twenty-two plane raid did achieve direct hits, but the damage was slight; most forays were chased away by the American and British air umbrella. Friendly fire—which had caused casualties and considerable interservice tension in amphibious operations in the Mediterranean and marred the airborne operations in Normandy— was also negligible above the Channel. In all, only a handful of small mishaps blemished the entire convoy cover operation. If other segments of D-day proved problematic for the invaders, protecting the massive naval fleets went as well as war allows the plans of men to work.

BIBLIOGRAPHY

Fagg, John E. "Pre-Invasion Operations." In vol. 3 of *The Army Air Forces in World War II*, edited by Wesley Frank Craven and James Lea Cate. 1951.

George, Robert H. "Normandy." In vol. 3 of *The Army Air Forces in World War II*, edited by Wesley Frank Craven and James Lea Cate. 1951.

George, Robert H. *U.S. Air Forces Historical Study #36: Ninth Air Force, April 1944 to November 1944.* 1946.

THOMAS HUGHES

CORLETT, CHARLES (1889–1971), American, major general, commander of U.S. XIX Corps. It took Corlett two attempts to get into West Point, but in 1909 he succeeded. There, because he had grown up in Colorado, he acquired the nickname "Cowboy Pete." After graduation in 1913 he served in Alaska, California, New York, and Texas, but did not see combat in World War I. While in France as a signal corps staff officer, he contracted pneumonia and had to leave the army in 1919, but a year spent managing a cattle company in New Mexico improved his health enough to allow him to return to active duty.

Between the wars Corlett attended the Command and General Staff College and the Army War College, and served in various commands. As a brigadier general, in late 1941 he assumed command of Fort Greeley to prepare for the defense of Alaska. In August 1943 Corlett led the land forces in an unopposed amphibious landing at Kiska Island in the Aleutians, and in February 1944 he commanded the 7th Infantry Division in its successful assault landings on Kwajalein Atoll in the Pacific. Because of his experience in planning and conducting amphibious landings, Gen. George Marshall, the Army Chief of Staff, sent Corlett to England to command XIX Corps, which was scheduled to follow U.S. V Corps across Omaha Beach.

While familiarizing himself with the invasion planning, Corlett observed a VII Corps training exercise and expressed the opinion that the "troops were six months to a year behind the Pacific in amphibious technique." He advocated the use of amphibious tractors that could swim from the landing ships and cross the beaches to land the assault troops on high ground, a technique widely used in the Pacific. Corlett became upset when the American planners ignored his advice, apparently considering his experience in the Pacific theater inapplicable to D-day preparations. The British, however, being more interested in using mechanical devices in their landings, invited him to address a large audience of senior commanders and staff officers. Corlett also expressed concern that D-day planners had allocated inadequate ammunition. Although those concerns fell on deaf ears, Gen. Omar Bradley, the First Army commander in Normandy, later wrote that "we never had enough ammunition to shoot all we needed."

Corlett's XIX Corps became operational in Normandy on 14 June 1944 and assumed control of a sector between U.S. V and VII Corps. He commanded XIX corps through the Normandy campaign, leading it to the capture of Saint-Lô, but in October 1944 fatigue and poor health forced him to return to the United States. After a brief rest, he was selected to return to the Pacific as a corps commander, but the war ended before he could do so. He retired to his ranch in New Mexico in 1946 and died on 14 October 1971.

[*See also* XIX Corps.]

BIBLIOGRAPHY

Corlett, Charles H. *Cowboy Pete: The Autobiography of Major General Charles H. Corlett.* 1974.

CLAYTON R. NEWELL

CROCKER, J. T. (1896–1963), British, lieutenant general, commander of the I Corps. Coming from a poor west country family, John Tredinnick Crocker volunteered for service in World War I as a private in the Artists Rifles (28th London Regiment) in November 1915. Commissioned into the Machine Gun Corps in 1917, he subsequently served on the Western front, winning the Military Cross and the Distinguished Service Order. In 1919 he briefly left the army but rejoined a year later, transferring in 1922 to the Tank Corps—renamed the Royal Tank Corps in 1923 and the Royal Tank Regiment (RTR) in 1939.

Crocker was the highest-ranking British commander of World War II to come from the RTR, serving between the wars under such pioneers of armored warfare as George Lindsay, Charles Broad, and Percy C. S. Hobart. His career before World War II culminated in the post of chief staff officer (GSO1) of the new Mobile Division under Alan Brooke in 1938, and in May 1940 he commanded the 3d Armoured Brigade in action in France. As a successful commander, staff officer, and trainer of troops, Crocker received rapid promotion to lieutenant general over the next two years, commanding the IX Corps in Tunisia in March and April 1943.

In August 1943 Crocker took over the I Corps in Britain from Lt. Gen. G. C. Bucknall to prepare it for the liberation of France. Crocker's reputation was as a competent and utterly dependable soldier who understood the use of armor. He was a natural choice for training the British and Canadian armored brigade groups for D-day. In particular, Crocker encouraged wider use of the special armored vehicles of Hobart's 79th Armoured Division. In an Allied high command of powerful and

BIBLIOGRAPHY

Liddell Hart, B. H. *The Tanks.* 1959.
Macksey, Kenneth. *The Tank Pioneers.* 1981.

STEPHEN BADSEY

CZECHOSLOVAKIA. Except for individuals who served with forces of other nationalities, the Czechoslovak contribution to the Allied forces on D-day came entirely from the air. In 1938 Czechoslovakia had a population of about 14 million and the strongest armed forces in eastern Europe. The country was renamed Czecho-Slovakia after the Munich settlement of October 1938, as a result of which Slovakia gained limited independence. In March 1939 northern Czechoslovakia was occupied by Germany as the Protectorate of Bohemia and Moravia, and Slovakia became a nominally independent member of the Axis. Many of the Czechoslovaks who opposed Germany took service with the French forces, and then with the British after the collapse of France in May and June 1940.

The British formed four RAF squadrons of Czechoslovaks in 1940, all of which participated in D-day operations. Based at RAF Chailey in Sussex, southern England, 134 (Czechoslovak) Wing was led by Wing Commander J. Kowalski. It consisted of the 310, 312, and 313 (Czechoslovak) Squadrons flying Spitfire Mark IXs, and formed part of 84 Group under Second Tactical Air Force. The wing provided fighter support throughout the Normandy campaign, although it was transferred to the Air Defence of Great Britain in July 1944, and therefore did not move with Second Tactical Air Force to France. The fourth squadron was 311 (Czechoslovak) Squadron of 19 Group, RAF Coastal Command, flying Liberators. On and after D-day, 19 Group took part in Operation CORK, flying patrols over the Irish Sea and the Bay of Biscay to prevent German submarines from interfering with the Allied convoys.

In addition to those who formed the four Czechoslovak squadrons of the RAF, numerous Czechoslovak pilots and aircrew served with other RAF squadrons. Among these was Sgt. Josef Frantisek, one of the highest-ranking RAF aces, who flew with a Polish squadron.

The British also equipped and helped create 1st Armored Brigade of the Free Czechoslovak Army, which was commanded by Maj. Gen. A. Lisker in 1944 and landed in Normandy during the second half of the campaign. This brigade served with 21st Army Group until the end of the war in Europe, chiefly under First Canadian Army from September 1944 onward.

BIBLIOGRAPHY

Ready, J. Lee. *Forgotten Allies.* 1985.
Shores, Christopher. *2nd TAF.* 1970.

STEPHEN BADSEY

J. T. CROCKER (RIGHT) AND BERNARD L. MONTGOMERY. Observing shelling of German defenses in Caen area.
IMPERIAL WAR MUSEUM

willful personalities, Crocker was regarded as pleasantly modest and diffident for such a high-ranking officer and capable of working well with almost anybody.

Despite his being given the most important single corps commander's role for D-day, Crocker's unassuming competence has made him something of an invisible man in debates over the Normandy campaign. His role in directing the battle up to D plus 12 was necessarily restricted, and the controversy surrounding the I Corps's failure to take Caen has largely ignored him. Once the initial attempt to capture Caen had failed, Crocker's first priority was to secure the I Corps's lodgment area, which he did with great skill. Thereafter, he played only a subsidiary role in subsequent British offensives.

Crocker continued to command the I Corps throughout the campaign in northwestern Europe, usually as part of the Canadian First Army under Lt. Gen. Henry Crerar. Indeed, Crerar's brief attempt in July 1944 to dismiss Crocker was the only major controversy of his career. Crocker rose to the rank of full general after the war, receiving a knighthood and becoming colonel commandant of the RTR. He retired from his last post as adjutant general in 1953.

[*See also* I Corps.]

D

DALRYMPLE-HAMILTON, F. H. G. (1890–1977), British, vice admiral, commander of Naval Gunfire Support for the Eastern Task Force, commander of Fire Support Force E, Task Force J. Born in Scotland, Frederick

F. H. G. DALRYMPLE-HAMILTON.

H. G. Dalrymple-Hamilton entered the Royal Navy in 1905 and became a captain in 1931. He served as captain of Dartmouth Royal Naval College from 1936 to 1939. Captain of HMS *Rodney* from 1939 to 1941, he commanded his ship in the final engagement with the German battleship *Bismarck* on 25 May 1941, in which *Rodney* played the leading role. Promoted to rear admiral in 1941, he commanded in Iceland in 1941 and 1942. Navy secretary to the First Lord of the Admiralty in 1942, then vice admiral in 1944, he was appointed to command the 10th Cruiser Squadron. In March and April of 1944 his squadron escorted Arctic Convoy JW. 58. Arctic convoys were then suspended until mid-August, in favor of attacks on the battleship *Tirpitz* and other diversionary operations on the coast of Norway, as part of the Allied deception plan.

Force E, made up from Home Fleet units, assembled at Greenock, Scotland, and sailed on 3 June. The force comprised the flagship HMS *Belfast,* the light cruiser HMS *Diadem,* and fleet destroyers HMS *Faulknor, Fury, Kempenfelt, Venus,* and *Vigilant,* with the Canadian HMCS *Algonquin* and HMCS *Sioux;* in addition there were four Hunt-class destroyers, the French destroyer FFLN *La Combattante,* and the Norwegian destroyers HMNS *Stevenstone, Bleasdale,* and *Glaisdale.* Force E provided layered fire support for the landings on Juno Beach: the cruisers fired from 11 kilometers (12,000 yards) out; the fleet destroyers fired from the flank of the assault force; and the smaller Hunt-class destroyers operated as close to the shore as possible, engaging targets ahead of the assault troops. All the destroyers were firing directly at beach defense targets. The cruisers engaged targets in front of the 3d Canadian Division. The two cruisers in Force E each fired close to 2,000 main battery rounds between 6 and 14 June. They also provided fire support for operations against Caen. After the mining of *Scylla* on 23 June,

Admiral Dalrymple-Hamilton took temporary command of the Eastern Task Force until Rear Adm. Philip Vian established himself aboard *Hilary*. From 23 to 30 June Dalrymple-Hamilton was in command of all bombardment units in the Eastern Task Force Area.

In early August 1944 Dalrymple-Hamilton took command of successful operations in the Bay of Biscay against German shipping and submarines attempting to break out for Norway. From August 1944 through March 1945 he commanded Arctic convoy operations. On the night of 27–28 January 1945, with the cruisers *Diadem* and *Mauritius,* he engaged two German destroyers off Bergen, Norway, damaging both. Dalrymple-Hamilton subsequently served as vice admiral at Malta and Central Mediterranean (1945–1946), flag officer for Scotland and Northern Ireland (1946–1948), and admiral, Joint Services Mission to Washington (1948–1950). He retired in 1950 and died at home in Scotland in 1977. For Admiral Dalrymple-Hamilton, a fighting seaman with a string of successful actions to his name, most notably the sinking of the *Bismarck,* D-day was only one of the many highlights in an outstanding career.

[*See also* Belfast, HMS; Task Force J.]

BIBLIOGRAPHY

Roskill, S. W. *The Offensive.* Vol. 3, pt. 2, of *The War at Sea, 1939–1945.* 1961.
Who Was Who, 1970–1980.

ANDREW LAMBERT

D'ARGENLIEU, GEORGES THIERRY. *See* Thierry d'Argenlieu, Georges.

DAS REICH DIVISION. *See* 2d SS Panzer Division "Das Reich."

D-DAY AND NORMANDY FELLOWSHIP. *See* Associations and Organizations.

DECEPTION.
When the Allied authorities began to plan Operation OVERLORD, the Normandy landings, they accepted that they could not hope to conceal that the main Allied objective in 1944 was a cross-Channel invasion. In the second half of 1943, under plan COCKADE, they had simulated threats to Boulogne and Brittany and also to Norway, but the Germans had not been impressed. In plan JAEL, an early sketch for deception during 1944, they toyed with the opposite thesis that the Allies hoped to bring about Germany's collapse by bombing Germany and pursuing operations in Italy and the Balkans. But they abandoned JAEL at the end of 1943 because they believed that the Allied buildup in the United Kingdom would deprive this thesis of all credibility by spring. The plan BODYGUARD, which was adopted in January 1944, retained the JAEL thesis but introduced the need to concentrate on deceiving the Germans as to the time, place, and scale of OVERLORD: a cross-Channel assault, it suggested, would require fifty divisions, and even if the Allies could launch it in 1944, they would be unable to do so before late summer.

A detailed plan for OVERLORD called FORTITUDE, which was adopted on 23 February, took advantage of knowledge gleaned from Signals Intelligence (Sigint) and other intelligence that the Germans were giving priority to the threat to the Pas de Calais and exaggerating the number of Allied divisions in the United Kingdom. FORTITUDE was divided into two phases. Up to the actual D-day, FORTITUDE NORTH would suggest that landings in the Pas de Calais would not be made until July, after the Allies had carried out diversionary operations in northern Norway in conjunction with Soviet Russia and in southern Norway with assistance from Sweden; the landings would initially use six divisions and build up to fifty. After D-day, FORTITUDE SOUTH would stress that the landings in Normandy were a feint, the main assault force being held back for the descent on the Pas de Calais.

Supplementing FORTITUDE was the plan ZEPPELIN. This aimed to suggest that, as the Allies could not hope to carry out OVERLORD before late summer, if at all, they would meanwhile undertake large-scale operations in the Mediterranean toward the Balkans, initially from Italy and later through Crete and the Peloponnese. In May these projects gave way to the simulation of threats to southern France and Bordeaux.

The plans were implemented through bogus radio traffic, the display of dummy tanks, planes, and installations to mislead German aerial reconnaissance, and double agents who conveyed a skillfully orchestrated stream of false reports on Allied intentions and order of battle directly to the Abwehr, the intelligence directorate of the German Commander in Chief West. A considerable effort had to be made to support the information reaching the Germans through these channels with diplomatic initiatives and operational deception. Thus, actual requests for facilities were made to Sweden, Spain, and Turkey, while during the preliminary bombing campaign against communications, bases, and defenses in France and the Low Countries, the Allies attacked two targets outside the OVERLORD area for every one in it.

The plans depended for their credibility on the fact that, as the Allies knew from Sigint, the Germans were unable to check false reporting because of the poverty of their intelligence. In particular, they could not correct the greatly exaggerated notion of the Allied order of battle that deception had built up for them since 1942. The Germans believed that there were fifty-five divisions in the United Kingdom in January (actual: thirty-four) and seventy-nine in May (actual: fifty-two), and their estimates for the Mediterranean were almost equally inflated.

The deception program was not wholly successful. Of the several largely fictional army groups and armies in the United Kingdom and the Mediterranean to which the Germans gave credence, only the First U.S. Army Group (FUSAG), which they thought waited between the Thames and the Wash rivers under Gen. George S. Patton, Jr., seriously worried them. FUSAG was highly suitable for its fictional role. It had been set up as a skeleton headquarters in the U.K. in October 1943 with the intention that it should assume command of the American armies in France after the consolidation of the lodgment area. This task was transferred to Twelfth U.S. Army Group and FUSAG's fictional role was built up when Sigint revealed that the Germans had located FUSAG in the U.K. and were associating it with General Patton.

The German conviction that the Allies were bent on a cross-Channel invasion in 1944 was so unwavering that they discounted all suggestions that it might not take place that year and were unimpressed by the ZEPPELIN program. Despite FORTITUDE NORTH, they expected the Channel invasion at any time from April on, and concluded that the existing garrison in Norway would suffice against such diversion as the Allies might mount; but this threat may have delayed the withdrawal of troops to France, and U-boats were accumulated in southern Norway and deployed in a defensive patrol line there on D-day. As for FORTITUDE SOUTH, the German exaggeration of the scale of the forces available in the United Kingdom proved to be its Achilles' heel. Their detection of shipping concentrations on the southern coast of Britain and their perception that the Allies would have to seize a major port, Cherbourg or Le Havre, as soon as possible led them to suspect from early in May, a month before D-day, that landings would be made both in Normandy and the Pas de Calais.

In the third week in May, when Sigint revealed that the Germans were reinforcing Normandy, especially the Cotentin Peninsula, Sigint also disclosed that Adolf Hitler believed that the Allies would establish a bridgehead in Normandy or Brittany and carry out diversionary operations in Norway and the south of France before embarking on "the real second front" in the Pas de Calais. Other decrypts indicated, however, that the Germans nevertheless remained radically uncertain of the place, time, and scale of the invasion before D-day.

After D-day German efforts to contain the bridgehead were impeded by fear of "the real second front" until, from 16 June, D plus 10, the threat of actual disaster in Normandy began to override, though not yet to dispel, that misplaced but long-standing anxiety.

BIBLIOGRAPHY

Breuer, William B. *Hoodwinking Hitler: The Normandy Deception*. 1993.

Haswell, J. *The Intelligence and Deception of the D-day Landings*. 1979.

Hinsley, F. H. *British Intelligence in the Second World War*. Vol. 3, Part II, 1988.

Hinsley, F. H., and C. A. G. Simkins. *Security and Counterintelligence*. Vol. 4 of *British Intelligence in the Second World War*. 1990.

Howard, Michael. *Deception*. Vol. 5 of *British Intelligence in the Second World War*. 1990.

Masterman, J. C. *The Double Cross System*. 1968.

F. H. HINSLEY

DEFRANZO, ARTHUR F.

DEFRANZO, ARTHUR F. (1919–1944), American, staff sergeant, Medal of Honor recipient. Arthur F. DeFranzo was born in Saugus, Massachusetts, where he later entered the army. On 10 June 1944, near Vaubadon, Normandy, scouts from the 3d Battalion, 18th Infantry Regiment, U.S. 1st Division, were advancing across an open field when they came under intense enemy machine-gun fire. Staff Sergeant DeFranzo sustained a wound while rescuing an injured scout. Refusing medical attention, he led the attack on the enemy machine-gun positions, finally falling within a hundred yards of the positions. As his company closed up, DeFranzo, despite many severe wounds, got up and again led the attack. Wounded again, he managed to destroy the enemy emplacement with hand grenades before succumbing to his injuries. His extraordinary heroism and disregard of his own safety inspired his fellow soldiers to accomplish their mission. He received the Medal of Honor posthumously.

BIBLIOGRAPHY

U.S. Congress. Senate. Committee on Veterans' Affairs. *Medal of Honor Recipients, 1863–1978*. 96th Cong., 1st sess., 1979. S. Committee Print No. 3.

JOHN F. VOTAW

DE GAULLE, CHARLES (1890-1970), French, brigadier general, political leader. As head of the French Committee of National Liberation, General de Gaulle was in London during the Normandy landings. On 14 June 1944, he set foot on French soil for the first time in four years.

Charles de Gaulle graduated from Saint-Cyr, the French military academy, in 1912, served in World War I, and achieved notice in the 1930s with his writings on

DE GAULLE CELEBRATING THE LIBERATION OF PARIS.
Marching down the Champs-Élysées on 26 August 1944.
MUSÉE DE L'ORDRE DE LA LIBÉRATION, PARIS

leadership and his advocacy of mobile tank warfare. In 1940, commanding an armored division, Colonel de Gaulle skillfully deployed his tanks in an attempt to stop Guderian's advance north of Laon toward the Channel.

Promoted to brigadier general, de Gaulle became under secretary of state in the Ministry of Defense and, when the Germans marched into France, participated in a last-minute effort to ensure Anglo-French unity. The French surrender found de Gaulle in London, where on 18 June 1940 he made a famous appeal, calling on Frenchmen everywhere to continue the war.

Remaining in England, de Gaulle became leader of the Free French. He considered himself to be not the director of a movement but the head of a legitimate French government comparable to governments-in-exile of other occupied countries. Although this claim was endorsed by Prime Minister Winston Churchill, it was unacceptable to President Franklin D. Roosevelt, whose administration had not broken relations with Marshal Henri Philippe Pétain's Vichy regime.

In November 1942, when Anglo-American forces occupied French North Africa, Roosevelt bypassed de Gaulle and backed another French officer, Gen. Henri Giraud. In June 1943, however, the two French generals joined forces in Algiers and, as cochairmen, formed the French Committee of National Liberation. When General Giraud was pressed into retirement early in 1944, de Gaulle emerged as undisputed head of the French Committee.

In London in the spring of 1944, General Dwight D. Eisenhower, the Supreme Allied Commander, was preoccupied with plans for the Normandy assault. Eisenhower had a French unit under his command—Maj. Gen. Jacques Philippe Leclerc's 2d Armored Division—but he needed other kinds of French support, especially in areas behind the front, and he strongly advocated working with de Gaulle's representatives. Roosevelt reluctantly gave his approval, provided that cooperation did not develop on an exclusive basis and did not imply political recognition. Eisenhower had in fact already made contact with Gen. Pierre Koenig, de Gaulle's military delegate in London, but on 17 April, when for security reasons the British government suspended French communications to Algiers, de Gaulle ordered Koenig to break off relations. A diplomatic crisis loomed.

Prime Minister Churchill, convinced that French exclusion from D-day would constitute a major political blunder, sent his personal plane to Algiers so that de Gaulle could reach England in time for the landings. The French leader agreed to come on one condition: no political discussions.

De Gaulle arrived in London on 4 June. During his visit to Allied headquarters, he learned that Eisenhower planned to broadcast a message that had already been printed and distributed. De Gaulle noted that the text contained no mention of himself or the French Committee, and that Eisenhower was ordering all persons in France to continue in their present duties unless otherwise instructed. De Gaulle could well ask: "Instructed by whom?" By Vichy administrators? By an Allied military government?

De Gaulle also learned that the Allies planned to circulate a special invasion currency. Indignant at these developments, he forbade French liaison officers to disembark, and he insisted on broadcasting, *after* Eisenhower, a speech that would incorporate his own set of instructions. In this message de Gaulle enjoined all French citizens to cooperate with the Allied armies and to follow the instructions of *his* government and the French leaders *it* had authorized.

Shortly after the landing, the Allies enabled de Gaulle to visit the beachhead, and on 14 June he crossed the Channel on the French destroyer *La Combattante*. De Gaulle went to Bayeux, gave a speech that was enthusiastically received, and installed François Coulet, an experienced administrator, as regional prefect for Normandy. Replacing the Vichy authorities, Coulet exercised his powers with such competence that he assuaged many Allied concerns about a Gaullist administration.

A month after D-day, de Gaulle visited the United States, conferred with President Roosevelt, and paved the way for de facto recognition of his government, announced in August 1944 when Paris was liberated.

De Gaulle remained as head of the French government until January 1946. After twelve years in retirement, he returned to power in 1958 and, under France's new constitution, served as president of the Fifth Republic until 1969, a year before his death.

[*See also* France; French Resistance; Pétain, Henri Philippe Omer.]

BIBLIOGRAPHY

Cook, Don. *Charles de Gaulle: A Biography.* 1984.
de Gaulle, Charles. *Complete War Memoirs.* 3 vols. 1955–1960.
Lacouture, Jean. *Charles de Gaulle.* 1990.

ARTHUR L. FUNK

DE GLOPPER, CHARLES N. (?–1944), American, private first class, Medal of Honor recipient. Charles N. De Glopper was born in Grand Island, New York, where he entered the service. On 9 June 1944, he was advancing with the forward platoon of Company C, 325th Glider Infantry, 82d Airborne Division, to secure a bridgehead across the Merderet River at La Fière. The platoon had become cut off from the rest of the company and overwhelming German forces were in the process of flanking it. De Glopper volunteered to support the platoon while it withdrew. He walked into full view of the Germans, firing his automatic rifle. Wounded twice, he continued to fire until he was killed. His action allowed his comrades to fight from a better position, and they established the first bridgehead across the Merderet River, a very important tactical victory.

BIBLIOGRAPHY

U.S. Congress. Senate. Committee on Veterans' Affairs. *Medal of Honor Recipients, 1863–1978.* 96th Cong., 1st sess., 1979. S. Committee Print No. 3.

CHARLES E. SMITH

DE GUINGAND, FRANCIS W. (1900–1979), British, major general, chief of staff of the 21st Army Group. De Guingand was born in Acton, East London. Rejected by the Royal Navy because he was color-blind, he joined the army in 1918, was a prize cadet at the Royal Military Academy, Sandhurst, and was commissioned the into the West Yorkshire Regiment in 1919.

After a short time in India he was posted to Ireland, where he met Maj. Bernard L. Montgomery. They worked together there and later in York, and despite vast differences in temperament, got on well. Montgomery encouraged de Guingand, something of a playboy, to take his career more seriously. In 1933, on exercise near Alexandria, he acted as brigade major to Montgomery and impressed him. Next year Montgomery nominated him for Staff College.

By 1940 he was serving as a staff officer in Cairo. In 1942 he was made director of military intelligence, Middle East Command, with the rank of brigadier. When Montgomery arrived to take command of the Eighth Army, he immediately decided that he would have de Guingand as his chief of staff—a decision that neither of them ever regretted. They were together, as army commander and totally trusted chief of staff, for the rest of the war. De Guingand was generally known as "Freddie," and "Send for Freddie" became a famous and recurring cry of Montgomery's.

At Christmas 1943, when Montgomery was summoned from Italy to England to take command of the 21st Army Group, which was preparing to invade Normandy, he insisted on taking de Guingand and other key members of his Eighth Army staff with him. They had months of intense work as the complex forces were prepared and moved into position. Montgomery stuck to his rule of leaving all details in their care. De Guingand's quick and retentive mind, his diplomatic skills, and his capacity for sustained application proved invaluable.

When Montgomery sailed for the beaches with a small tactical headquarters, de Guingand stayed behind with most of the staff, keeping the flow of men and matériel moving smoothly, maintaining good relations with the navy and air force and the American high command. He was better at these things than his boss. He was rewarded at the end of June 1944 with a knighthood.

In the subsequent campaign across Europe he did all he could—and it grew increasingly difficult—to maintain a working cooperation between Montgomery and Eisenhower. It was all the more difficult because de Guingand suffered much ill health caused by overwork, and did not always agree with Montgomery's arguments and methods. Even so, after the war, when de Guingand was on sick leave, Montgomery wrote to him saying, "No commander can ever have had, or will ever have, a better Chief of Staff than you are."

De Guingand resigned from the army in 1946 and went to live in South Africa, where he made a successful career for himself as a businessman and influential figure in politics, and also wrote books. He died at Cannes in 1979.

[*See also* 21st Army Group.]

BIBLIOGRAPHY

de Guingand, Francis W. *Operation Victory.* 1947.

Montgomery, Bernard. *The Memoirs.* 1958.
Richardson, Charles. *Send for Freddie: The Story of Montgomery's Chief of Staff.* 1987.

ALAN HANKINSON

DEMPSEY, MILES C. (1896–1969), British, lieutenant general, commander British Second Army. Dempsey, who was commissioned into the Royal Berkshire Regiment in 1916, was awarded the Military Cross for gallantry on the Western front when only nineteen years old. In 1939 he went to France as commanding officer of the 1st Berkshire Regiment, and later commanded a brigade at Dunkirk for which he was awarded the Distinguished Service Order. He commanded both the 46th Infantry Division and the 42d Armoured Division in England and in 1942 went to Egypt to command XIII Corps and play an important part in the planning and execution of the Sicilian invasion. Sixteen days after the end in Sicily, his corps headed the invasion of Italy and thereafter played crucial parts in all the battles up to and including the capture of Cassino and the fall of Rome. At General Bernard L. Montgomery's insistence, Dempsey returned to England to plan for and train the Second Army for its task on the left flank of the 21st Army Group.

On D-day, the British XXX Corps on the right and the British I Corps on the left, with Commando units on each flank (British and Canadian infantry and armored brigades forming the main strike force and the British 6th Airborne Division on the extreme left), landed on Gold, Juno, and Sword beaches. By the end of the day, they held an area nineteen kilometers (twelve miles) wide and in places eight kilometers (five miles) deep, and were well across the main Bayeaux-Douvres road.

This striking success was in great part attributable to the use of the specialized armor—Flail, Crocodile, bridging, and amphibious tanks—to smash paths across the beaches, and of these Dempsey had from their inception been an ardent supporter. Though the Second Army failed to capture Caen on schedule, Dempsey then planned and conducted a series of furious battles that effectively tied down German panzer divisions until the American First Army on the right could break out to occupy the Cotentin Peninsula and then with the Third Army commence the gigantic sweep that ended in August on the Somme.

During the winter of 1944–1945, Dempsey's army fought its way up through Belgium and Holland and across the Rhine until by the time of the German capitulation it was across the Elbe. During the winter battles King George VI had visited the Second Army and bestowed a knighthood upon Dempsey, who by now had been promoted to general.

After the end of the war in Europe, Dempsey commanded the Fourteenth Army in Burma and was later appointed commander in chief of land forces in Southeast Asia. He resigned from the army in 1946 and devoted the rest of his life to his hobbies, music and horse racing.

[*See also* Second Army.]

BIBLIOGRAPHY

Keegan, John. *Six Armies in Normandy.* 1982.
Obituary. *Times* (London), 7 June 1969.

BARRIE PITT

MILES C. DEMPSEY.   Seated, with Maj. R. Priestley in Belgium, 31 December 1945.   IMPERIAL WAR MUSEUM

DEPOT SHIPS. *See* England, H. T.

DESTROYERS. In June 1944 the German Navy had five destroyers in French waters: *Z 23, Z 24, Z 32, Z 37,* and *ZH 1,* constituting the *8th Destroyer Flotilla* under Capt. Theodor Freiherr von Bechtolsheim. Commissioned in autumn 1940, *Z 23* and *Z 24* were Type 36A destroyers, with a standard displacement of 2,603 tons (full load 3,605 tons). *Z 32* (flagship) and *Z 37,* commissioned in the summer of 1942, were Type 36A(Mob) destroyers, with a standard displacement of 2,657 tons (full load 3,691 tons). The length of both types was 127.0 meters, the width 12.0 meters, and the maximum depth 4.65 meters. They were driven by turbines of 70,000 horsepower. Their designed speed was 36.0 knots and their range 2,500 or 2,950 miles at 19 knots. Their complement was 11 to 15 officers and 305

ZH 1.

to 321 men, depending on the antiaircraft armament and the inclusion of a flotilla commander and his staff. Their armament was five 15-cm guns, two in a twin turret forward and three in single mounts aft. The antiaircraft armament in 1944 was two twin 37-mm C30 guns, two quadruple 20-mm C38 sets, and from three to eight single 20-mm C38 guns. There were two sets of quadruple 53.3-cm torpedo tubes. Each ship was equipped with radar and radar detection equipment.

The fifth destroyer, *ZH 1*, the former Dutch destroyer *Gerard Callenburgh*, had been captured just after launching and completed for the German Navy; it was commissioned in October 1942. The standard displacement was 1,604 tons (full load 2,228 tons). Its length was 106.7 meters, the width 10.6 meters, and the maximum depth 3.52 meters. Geared turbines with 45,000 horsepower yielded a maximum designed speed of 36.0 knots. The range was 2,700 miles at 19 knots. The crew consisted of 12 officers and 218 men. The armament was five 12-cm guns in two twin mounts fore and aft, and one single mount superimposed aft. Antiaircraft armament consisted of two twin 37-mm C30 guns, and two twin and two single 20-mm C38 guns. There were two quadruple sets of 53.3-cm torpedo tubes. The vessel was equipped with radar and radar detection equipment.

Z 23 and *Z 37* were not operational, being under repair for earlier damage; the others lay in the Gironde Estuary. At 0650 on 6 June Adm. Theodor Krancke, the commander of Naval Group West, ordered the *8th Destroyer Flotilla* under Capt. Theodor von Bechtolsheim to Brest. *Z 24, Z 32*, and *ZH 1* departed at 1230. They were located by Allied air reconnaissance and attacked without great damage by British Beaufighters forty miles southwest of Saint-Nazaire. Arriving at Brest on 7 June, they were joined there by the fleet torpedo boat *T 24*. From signals intelligence (Sigint) the British learned that the four ships had been ordered to leave Brest at 1830 for Cherbourg; they also learned their course and speed. As a result, RAF Coastal Command reconnaissance planes helped the British 10th Destroyer Flotilla to intercept Bechtolsheim's flotilla north of the Île de Batz, off the northern coast of Brittany. The 10th Flotilla consisted of two sections: the destroyers *Ashanti, Haida* (Canadian), *Huron* (Canadian), and *Tartar* in the first, and *Blyskawica* (Polish), *Eskimo, Piorun* (Polish), and *Javelin* in the second.

At 0120 on 9 June both sides made radar contact. At 0127 the British ships opened fire, followed by the Germans. The torpedoes fired by both sides missed. In the battle *Tartar* was heavily hit and fires began to rage amidships (4 dead, 13 wounded). *Z 24* and *T 24* disengaged

Z 24 (ABOVE) AND *Z 32* (BELOW).

BIBLIOTHEK FÜR ZEITGESCHICHTE, STUTTGART

with damage. *Blyskawica*'s section soon lost contact with the two other ships of its group. The two Canadian destroyers pursued *Z 24* and *T 24*, but had to disengage when the German ships entered a British mine field and escaped to the southwest. *Ashanti*, going to *Tartar*'s assistance, made contact with *ZH 1*, which became unmaneuverable after hits to its machinery and was sunk by torpedoes at 0240 (33 dead), while *Ashanti* was lightly damaged. *Z 32* was located again by the two Canadian destroyers with radar, but they lost the ship when *Z 32* entered the British mine field from the west, trying to reach Cherbourg. Circumnavigating the minefield, *Haida* and *Huron* made contact again. In a running battle finally joined by ships of the other section, they forced *Z 32* onto the rocks of the Île de Batz (26 dead) at 0517, where it was finally destroyed by Beaufighters and the 12th Motor Torpedo Boat Flotilla.

Considering the British knowledge from Sigint about German operational intentions, the strength of the RAF Coastal Command's reconnaissance and attack squadrons, and the greatly superior Allied naval forces in the western Channel entrance, the *8th Destroyer Flotilla* had had no real chance to reach the approach routes of Allied landing forces inside the Channel. But since the destroyers were the only real fighting ships available except for the S-boats (*Schnellboote,* or small, fast, motor torpedo boats), they had to be sent into battle. Insufficient sea training because of a chronic oil shortage was one important reason why the ships achieved no real success before being sunk or put out of action.

[*See also* Bechtolsheim, Theodor.]

BIBLIOGRAPHY

Gröner, Erich. *Die deutschen Kriegsschiffe 1815–1945.* Edited by Dieter Jung and Martin Maass. Vol. 2, 1983.

Harnack, Wolfgang. *Zerstörer unter deutscher Flagge 1934–1945.* 1978.

Hinsley, F. H., et al. *British Intelligence in the Second World War.* Vol. 3, pt. 2, 1988.

Schull, Joseph. *The Far Distant Ships.* 1952.

JÜRGEN ROHWER

DEYO, MORTON L. (1887–1973), American, rear admiral, commander of Bombardment Group, Western Task Force. Morton L. Deyo graduated from the U.S. Naval Academy in 1911. During World War I he helped train destroyer crews and served in a troopship. After holding several staff positions and commands, Deyo became assistant hydrographer of the navy, responsible for charting and ocean surveying. He then served as aide to the Secretary of the Navy. In April 1941 he took command of a destroyer squadron and later escorted convoys to Britain.

After commanding the cruiser *Indianapolis* in the Aleutians and the Bering Sea, Deyo, promoted to rear admiral, became commander of destroyers, Atlantic Fleet. As planning for OVERLORD proceeded, he was ordered to England to command Bombardment Force A, the bombardment group of Assault Force U, the portion of the Western Task Force designated to land on Utah Beach.

Early on D-day Deyo, with his flag on the cruiser USS *Tuscaloosa,* deployed the U.S. battleship *Nevada* and British monitor *Erebus,* with five British and American cruisers, a Dutch gunboat, and ten destroyers and destroyer escorts, between the waiting transports and Utah Beach, while minesweepers cleared channels for the landing craft and support ships. Utah Beach was defended by fortified batteries armed with guns ranging from 75-mm to 170-mm; others inland mounted 105-mm to 210-mm guns, backed up by many mobile 88-mm guns.

H-hour at Utah Beach was set for 0630. At 0550 Deyo's warships were to begin attacking batteries and hitting the beaches with heavy fire. A German battery began to shoot at 0505. At 0525, 170-mm guns near Barfleur opened on minesweepers off the beaches; a British cruiser returned fire. Within minutes German shells were hitting near the Allied heavy ships. At 0536 Deyo ordered the bombardment to begin.

As the first landing craft closed the beaches, rocket-firing LCTs (Landing Craft, Tank) fired a barrage as LCGs (Landing Craft, Gun) laid down supporting fire from the flanks, and bombardment ships shifted fire to targets north and south of the landing beaches. The landing proceeded well in spite of German fire and reached its assigned objective line by the evening of D-day.

This success owed in no small measure to the quality of Deyo's fire support. In his report Rear Adm. Alan G. Kirk, commander of the Western Task Force, noted that "the performance of battleships, cruisers, and destroyers in support of the landing was magnificent" and called Deyo's bombardment plan "well designed and effective." "Naval guns," Kirk concluded, "lived up to our highest expectations."

On 15 June Admiral Kirk added Omaha Beach bombardment ships to Deyo's command. As the American Seventh Army advanced on Cherbourg, Deyo on 25 June bombarded the numerous German batteries at the northern end of the Cotentin Peninsula, thus hastening the surrender of Cherbourg.

On 15 August 1944 Deyo commanded a bombardment force in Operation DRAGOON, the landing in southern France. Later, as commander of Cruiser Division 13, supporting the Pacific Fleet's carrier striking force, he took part in the capture of Luzon, early air strikes against mainland Japan, and the assault on Iwo Jima.

In 1945 he commanded Task Force 54, the gunfire support force for the battle of Okinawa, through continuous

Japanese kamikaze attacks. When the war ended, he commanded landing forces in the early months of occupation of Japan. He retired from the navy in 1949 and died on 10 November 1973.

Admiral Deyo is remembered for his wartime contributions to the science of naval gunfire support to land forces, given to effect at Normandy and brought to a high degree in the long battle for Okinawa. The Spruance-class destroyer *Deyo* (DD 980) honors his memory.

[*See also* American Beaches, *article on* Utah Beach; Gunfire Support; Tuscaloosa, USS.]

BIBLIOGRAPHY

Deyo, Morton L. "Naval Guns at Normandy." In *The United States Navy in World War II,* edited by S. E. Smith. 1966.
Deyo Papers. Manuscript Division, Library of Congress, Washington, D.C.
Morison, Samuel Eliot. *The Invasion of France and Germany, 1944–1945.* Vol. 11 of *History of United States Naval Operations in World War II.* 1957. Reprint, 1988.

JOHN C. REILLY, JR.

DIESTEL, ERICH (1892–1973), German, lieutenant general, commander of the *346th Infantry Division.* Erich Diestel was born in Deutsch-Eylau on 8 November 1892. He was educated at various military schools, entered the service as a cadet in 1912, and was commissioned second lieutenant in the elite Brandenburg *35th Fusilier Regiment* on 18 August 1913. During World War I, Diestel fought on the Western front. He remained in the service after the war and was a major when Hitler came to power in 1933. In April 1937 he assumed command of the *I Battalion, 68th Infantry Regiment* in Brandenburg, and was promoted to lieutenant colonel later that year.

On 6 January 1940 Diestel assumed command of the *188th Infantry Regiment,* which he led later that year in the conquests of Luxembourg, Belgium and France, and on occupation duty in Poland (1940–1941). Promoted to colonel on 1 June 1940, he took part in Operation BARBAROSSA, the invasion of Russia in June 1941. Considered a highly competent infantry officer, he assumed command of the *101st Jäger (Light) Division* on 11 April 1942.

Diestel led the *101st Jäger* in the German victories at Iszum and Rostov, and took part in the capture of the Maikop oilfields. He was promoted to brigadier general on 1 August 1942, and was given command of the *346th Infantry Division,* then stationed at Bad Hersfeld in October. He was promoted to major general on 1 August 1943.

General Diestel's new command was a static nonmotorized unit that had recently been formed from elements of five other divisions from the *Fifteenth* and *Seventh* armies. Many of its men were *Osttruppen* (Eastern troops)

of questionable loyalty. The *346th* was stationed in the Saint-Malo sector of Brittany from November 1942 until the spring of 1944, when it was sent to Le Havre on the northern bank of the Seine. It was quickly thrown into the Normandy fighting, and took part in the battle east of the Orne, where it joined with *Battle Group Luck,* an element of *21st Panzer Division,* which successfully launched a spoiling attack against the British 51st (Highland) Division and 4th Armoured Brigade on 10 June. Its casualties were very heavy, however; by 13 June, it had lost more than half of its combat troops. Down to battle-group size, the *346th* nevertheless remained in the battle, and took part in the retreats across the Seine, northern France, and Belgium. It was part of the *Fifteenth Army* during the Battle of the Schelde, where it helped turn back an attempt by the Canadian 1st Army to break the Turnhout Canal line (near Antwerp) on 22 September, and it twice repulsed the Canadian 6th Infantry Brigade at Lochtenberg on 24 and 28 September. After the division successfully made its escape to the Netherlands, General Diestel was relieved of his command on 11 October, for reasons not made clear by the records. He seems to have been a competent divisional commander, especially in defense, and to have gotten the maximum effort out of troops that were considered marginal. In any case, he was replaced by Maj. Gen. Walter Steinmüller and was never reemployed.

[*See also* 346th Infantry Division.]

BIBLIOGRAPHY

Keilig, Wolf. *Die Generale des Heeres.* 1983.
Moulton, J. L. *The Battle for Antwerp.* 1978.
Tessin, Georg. *Verbände und Truppen der deutschen Wehrmacht und Waffen-SS, 1939–1945.* Vol. 9, 1974.

SAMUEL W. MITCHAM, JR.

DIETRICH, JOSEF ("SEPP") (1892–1966), German, SS Obergruppenführer (later Oberstgruppenführer), commander *I SS Panzer Corps.* Of Bavarian peasant origin, "Sepp" Dietrich fought throughout World War I, receiving decorations for bravery and rising to the rank of sergeant major. After the war he joined the Bavarian police and fought in Silesia as a member of the *Freikorps Oberland.* Dietrich joined the Nazi party and SS in 1928, receiving rapid promotion in the latter. He quickly came to Adolf Hitler's notice and was appointed to take command of his personal bodyguard unit. In March 1933 Hitler invited Dietrich to form the *Leibstandarte SS ("Adolf Hitler")* for the protection of the Reich Chancellery; this was the forerunner of the *Waffen SS.* Dietrich played a leading part in the June 1934 assassination operation (the Night of the Long Knives) that crushed the alleged Röhm putsch. This added to

JOSEF ("SEPP") DIETRICH.   NATIONAL ARCHIVES

his reputation for dependability, although he often clashed with Heinrich Himmler.

Dietrich led the *Leibstandarte* in the campaigns in Poland, the West, and Greece, where he was reprimanded for accepting the surrender of the Greek army on very generous terms. He remained in command of the *Leibstandarte* in Russia with continuing success, before leaving it in July 1943 to take over the newly formed *I SS Panzer Corps*. He then took his headquarters to Italy to secure the passes through the Alps. In January 1944 he moved his headquarters first to Belgium and in the spring to the Paris area, with the *12th SS Panzer Grenadier Division "Hitlerjugend"*, his only operational element, being deployed to Évreux in May.

On D-day, Dietrich was in Brussels visiting the *Leibstandarte*, which had been moved from Russia to join the *I SS Panzer Corps*. He immediately returned to Paris, while his staff prepared to deploy to Normandy. Commander in Chief West Gerd von Rundstedt ordered him to take the *Panzer Lehr Division*, based at Chartres, and the *21st Panzer Division* under command and, with the *12th SS Panzer Grenadier Division*, drive the Allies back into the sea. Allied air supremacy hindered the move of Dietrich's troops to the front, and his hopes of mounting a counterattack on D plus 1 were quickly dashed. With many of his radios destroyed, Dietrich also had difficulty establishing contact with the *Seventh Army*, under whose command he was. His attack was eventually mounted on D plus 2, but with only small elements of the *Panzer Lehr* and *21st Panzer* available, it failed in the face of overwhelming Allied firepower. Thereafter Dietrich was forced onto the defensive, inspiring his troops through frequent visits to the front line in the Caen area.

In July Dietrich successfully repulsed the British armored thrust east of Caen and for his efforts over the past few weeks was decorated and promoted to Oberstgruppenführer on 1 August. He was given temporary command of the *Fifth Panzer Army* (formerly *Panzer Group West*) and withdrew its remnants back across the Seine. In mid-September he returned to Germany to form the *Sixth Panzer Army*, which he led during the Ardennes counteroffensive. He then took it to Hungary, where, renamed the *Sixth SS Panzer Army*, it played the leading role in the disastrous Lake Balaton offensive in March 1945. He withdrew into Austria and eventually surrendered to the Americans.

After the war Dietrich was charged with complicity in the Malmédy massacre of U.S. troops and sentenced to life imprisonment. Paroled in October 1955, he was then tried by a German court for his part in the Night of the Long Knives in June 1934, in which he had led a squad which executed six prominent SA men. He received an eighteen-month sentence, but was released on medical grounds in February 1959. Dietrich had little intellect or understanding of strategy and was uncomfortable in senior command positions. Yet he did possess personal charisma, and his bravery, earthy humor, and loyalty to his men certainly inspired them.

[*See also* I SS Panzer Corps.]

BIBLIOGRAPHY

Messenger, Charles. *Hitler's Gladiator: The Life and Times of Oberstgruppenführer and Panzergeneral-Oberst der Waffen-SS Sepp Dietrich.* 1988.

Weingartner, James J. *Hitler's Guard: The Story of the Leibstandarte Adolf Hitler, 1933–1945.* 1974.

CHARLES MESSENGER

DOLLMANN, FRIEDRICH (1882–1944), German, colonel general, commander of the *Seventh Army*. Dollmann was born at Würzburg, Bavaria, on 2 February 1882, joined the army as a cadet in 1899, and was commissioned second lieutenant in the Bavarian *7th Field*

Artillery Regiment in 1901. He was a captain on the general staff when World War I broke out.

Dollmann showed great political adaptability throughout his career. There is little in his record to indicate why he advanced to the top rungs of the army in the next two decades, other than his skill at playing the political angles that exist in any army, but that proliferated in those of the Weimar Republic and Nazi Germany. Although not a Nazi, Dollmann recognized the way the political winds were blowing and was highly involved in fostering good relations between the Wehrmacht and the party. He openly blamed the officers' corps for the mistrust that existed between the party and the army, asserted that the officers' corps must accept the party's views without examination, demanded that officers' wives play active roles in the National Socialist League of Women, insisted that only "politically nonbiased" National Socialists be invited as speakers at service functions, and harangued his chaplains because their attitudes toward the Nazi movement were not sufficiently positive. In the meantime, Dollmann received rapid promotions, rising from colonel in 1932 to general of artillery in 1936. He assumed command of the *Seventh Army* on 25 August 1939, seven days before the outbreak of the war.

Dollmann's army did not participate in the Polish campaign and played only a minor role in the French campaign of 1940. He was nevertheless promoted to colonel general on 19 July 1940. He returned to occupation duty in France, where he and his army languished for the next four years. By 1944, Dollmann was almost an anachronism. He had failed to keep abreast of the developments in his field, had no understanding of panzer tactics and no grasp of the impact that Allied air superiority could have on tactical operations. In addition, he had grown fat during his years of occupation duty, and his health had deteriorated. But to his credit, he was now deeply troubled about the Nazis and their increasingly brutal methods and was ashamed of his previous support of the regime.

Prior to December 1943, Dollmann had believed that the proper strategy was to let the Allies land and advance inland and then defeat them in a blitzkrieg-like tank battle in the interior of France; consequently, he had done almost nothing to improve the coastal defenses in his sector. When Field Marshal Erwin Rommel took charge of *Army Group B*, Dollmann immediately adapted, and by February 1944, he was a firm advocate of Rommel's concept of operations—that the Allies should be defeated on the beaches. Four months of feverish activity could not make good four years of inactivity, however, and the *Seventh Army* was not ready when the Allies landed in Normandy on D-day.

Dollmann had scheduled a war game at Rennes for the morning of 6 June, and most of the key corps and divisional commanders were away from their posts. (In fact, so many German commanders were absent on 6 June that Adolf Hitler ordered an investigation to see if the British Secret Service had anything to do with it.) Rommel was also away from his post, and acting in his absence, Dollmann compounded the already serious situation by ordering the *Panzer Lehr* and *12th SS Panzer* divisions to the front in broad daylight. Making matters worse, he ordered the divisions to maintain radio silence—"As if radio silence could have stopped the fighter-bombers and reconnaissance planes from spotting us!" the disgusted *Lehr* divisional commander snapped later.

Dollmann's orders led to the complete disorganization of the *Panzer Lehr Division*, which lost forty loaded fuel trucks, eighty-four half-tracks, prime-movers (motorized or mechanized vehicles carrying heavy artillery), and self-propelled guns, and dozens of other vehicles. The *12th SS Panzer* suffered similar losses. Partly as a result, the Germans could not launch their armored counterattack until 9 June, at least two days too late to throw the Allies back into the sea. Rommel, meanwhile, returned on the night of 6 June, took the panzer divisions away from Dollmann, and placed the *Seventh Army* in charge of the somewhat less critical left flank of his defenses. For the next three weeks, an increasingly distressed Dollmann slowed but could not halt the progress of the invasion, while his divisions were ground to pieces in the process. The initial strategic objective of the invasion, the French port of Cherbourg, was cut off from the rest of the *Seventh Army* on 18 June and capitulated on 26 June.

Hitler was furious, and an investigation of the rapid fall of the fortress was launched. Accused of negligence, Dollmann was replaced by SS-Obergruppenführer Paul Hausser on 29 June. Dollmann, however, never knew he had been sacked. Worried and overworked, he had suffered a massive heart attack on the morning of the 29th and died shortly thereafter. Hitler authorized a laudatory obituary.

[*See also* Seventh Army.]

BIBLIOGRAPHY

Mitcham, Samuel W., Jr., and Gene Mueller. *Hitler's Commanders.* 1992.

O'Neill, Richard J. *The German Army and the Nazi Party, 1933–1939.* 1966.

Ruge, Friedrich. *Rommel in Normandy.* 1979.

SAMUEL W. MITCHAM, JR.

DÖNITZ, KARL (1891–1980), grand admiral, Commander in Chief of the German Navy. Karl Dönitz was born on 16 September 1891 in Berlin and entered the Imperial Navy in 1910. In 1914 he served as a lieutenant on the light cruiser *Breslau,* when this ship with the battlecruiser *Goeben* broke through to the Dardanelles. In

KARL DÖNITZ.

1916 he transferred to the submarine service. He participated in patrols with one of the most successful U-boats in the Mediterranean before becoming a U-boat commander in 1918. After returning from captivity he entered the postwar Reichsmarine and served with torpedo boats as a flotilla chief and later commanded the training cruiser *Emden.*

In 1935 he took command of the first new U-boat flotilla, *Weddigen,* then in January 1936 he became commander of submarines (*Führer der Unterseeboote, FdU*). Convinced of the potential offered by U-boats in a naval war against Great Britain, if they were given sufficient numbers and backup, between 1936 and 1939 he developed his "wolf pack" tactics, which he tested in Atlantic exercises. In 1939 Dönitz became admiral commanding U-boats (*Befehlshaber der Unterseeboote, BdU*).

When Hitler attacked Poland in September 1939, and Great Britain and France declared war, Dönitz had only a handful of U-boats capable of operating in the Atlantic. The real contest between convoys and his wolf packs began in the autumn of 1940. It was conducted from his shore headquarters by radio commands, based on the situation reports from his U-boats. Until mid-1941 the U-boats achieved great successes, but when the British decrypted the German radio signals from mid-1941 on,

their convoys were routed successfully around the U-boats. This first setback was only overcome by the very successful operations off the U.S. East Coast after the American entry into the war in December 1941. The culmination of the U-boat war came with the continuous convoy battles on the North Atlantic route from July 1942 to May 1943, when the U-boats experienced great successes, but then sudden defeat by the concentration of Allied ships and aircraft around the endangered convoys, which the timely decryption of the German radio signals made possible.

In January 1943 Dönitz became Commander in Chief of the German Navy as successor to Grand Admiral Erich Raeder. While Dönitz had so far concentrated all his energy only on the U-boat war, he now saw his task as leading the whole navy. He began by convincing Hitler not to give the Allies a bloodless victory by scrapping the big ships.

Despite the rising number of setbacks at sea, on land, and in the air, Dönitz, given the Allied demand for unconditional surrender and an ingrained tradition of loyalty to the government, saw no alternative to fighting to the bitter end. When the attempt to renew the convoy battles with new weapons failed in the autumn of 1943, he still continued the U-boat war so as to tie down Allied air and naval forces and prevent their use in an invasion against Fortress Europe. He at first hoped to get revolutionary new U-boat types ready in time to attack the convoys again, but Allied air raids delayed this effort. When the invasion started, Dönitz could only order the use of all available naval forces in the West to the limit of their capabilities—especially U-boats, but also S-boats, torpedo boats, and the few destroyers. His encouraging orders tried to bolster the morale of the crews.

In 1943 and 1944 Dönitz, trying to establish a close contact with Hitler, came to some extent under the influence of the dictator. Because he limited his activities to the command of the navy, he to a great extent closed his eyes to the areas outside of his responsibility. He won Hitler's confidence, which explains why in 1945 Dönitz, never a member of the Nazi party, was named by Hitler to be his successor as head of state. In this capacity he tried to save as many people as possible from the advancing Red Army, while initiating immediate negotiations with the Western Allies; within a week this led to the final surrender of Germany.

During the Nuremberg trials the accusation against the German conduct of the war at sea was not upheld in the final verdict, but Dönitz was sentenced to ten years in prison for accepting some of Hitler's criminal orders, like the order to shoot captured Soviet commissars and members of Allied commando units. After his release in 1956 he lived at Reinbek, near Hamburg, in close contact with his former U-boat men, receiving many historians from Germany and the former Allied countries, but not involving himself in politics. He died on 24 December 1980. His memoirs were reprinted several times and translated into English.

[See also Navy, article on German Navy.]

BIBLIOGRAPHY

Dönitz, Karl. *Memoirs: Ten Years and Twenty Days*. With an introduction and afterword by Jürgen Rohwer. Translated by R. H. Stevens in collaboration with David Woodward. 1990.
Fuehrer Conferences on Naval Affairs, 1939–1945. With a foreword by Jack P. Mallmann. 1990.
Salewski, Michael. *Die deutsche Seekriegsleitung 1935–1945*. 3 vols., 1970–1975.

JÜRGEN ROHWER

DOOLITTLE, JAMES (1896–), American, lieutenant general; commander, Eighth Air Force. Doolittle joined the Army Aviation Section in 1917 and served for thirteen years before returning to civilian life as a Shell Oil Company executive. In 1925 he received a Ph.D. in aeronautical engineering from the Massachusetts Institute of Technology. In the 1930s he helped develop the high-

JAMES DOOLITTLE.   NATIONAL ARCHIVES

octane aviation gasoline required by World War II era aircraft engines.

Doolittle returned to the air corps in 1940, and on 18 April 1942, he led the first bombing raid on Tokyo. He lost fifteen of sixteen B-25s but demonstrated great physical and moral courage by taking off from USS *Hornet* first (giving him the shortest take-off distance) and launching the raid 150 miles ahead of the planned location because the Japanese had spotted the task force. The raid earned him the Congressional Medal of Honor, promotion from lieutenant colonel to brigadier general, and command of the Twelfth Air Force, slated to support the invasion of North Africa on 8 November 1942. Throughout 1943 he served in the Mediterranean, commanding the Northwest African Strategic Air Forces in Tunisia, Sicily, and Italy. In December 1943 Gen. Henry H. Arnold, commander of the U.S. Army Air Forces (AAF), transferred him to Britain to command the AAF's largest air force, the Eighth. Doolittle served under the U.S. Strategic Air Forces (USSTAF) headed by Lt. Gen. Carl Spaatz.

Doolittle took over the force spearheading the American daylight precision strategic bombing of Germany. He found it recovering from earlier setbacks, but the arrival of long-range P-51 fighters and new drop tanks for his P-38s and P-47s enabled him to transform the situation. In late January 1944 he ordered his escort fighters to cease tying themselves to the bombers and to pursue and attack the Luftwaffe. The better-trained American pilots and their technologically superior aircraft smashed the Luftwaffe in a ten-week battle of attrition. In April 1944 the Eighth's fighters began low-level sweeps over Germany, attacking airfields and other targets of opportunity. Their successful operation enabled the bombers to strike any target in Germany. But at that point USSTAF came under General Dwight D. Eisenhower's control and became subject to the Transportation Plan, which called for heavy bomber strikes on French and Belgian rail-marshaling yards.

Spaatz gained permission to mount two missions against German synthetic oil production facilities, and the Eighth's raids of 12 and 28 May halved total production. During the six weeks before the Allied invasion of Normandy, the Eighth destroyed or damaged all twenty-three of its transportation targets. It attacked German airfields in early June. On D-day Doolittle observed the Eighth's mission against the beaches from his own P-38.

General Doolittle's greatest contribution to OVERLORD was his decision to change the tactics of the Eighth's fighters. The destruction of the Luftwaffe in the air and on the ground before the invasion rendered it unable to interfere on 6 June, greatly contributing to OVERLORD's success.

After Germany surrendered, Doolittle and the Eighth Air Force were transferred to Okinawa, but Japan surrendered before he began operations there. He reverted to reserve status in May 1946 and was promoted to general in April 1985.

[*See also* Eighth Air Force.]

BIBLIOGRAPHY

Doolittle, James H., and Carroll V. Glines. *I Could Never Be So Lucky Again*. 1991.
Thomas, Lowell, and Edward Jablonski. *Doolittle: A Biography*. 1976.

RICHARD G. DAVIS

DOUGLAS, W. SHOLTO (1893–1969), British, air chief marshal commanding Coastal Command. Sholto Douglas joined the Royal Horse Artillery in 1914, switching to the Royal Flying Corps in 1915. After a successful career as an observer, fighter pilot, flying trainer, and squadron leader, he retired from the Royal Air Force (RAF) in 1919. He rejoined in 1920, and after assignments as pupil and teacher at the Imperial Defence College and as air officer commanding in the Sudan, spent the period 1936 to 1940 at the Air Ministry.

In 1940 Douglas was deputy chief of the Air Staff and had a major role in the strategy of the Battle of Britain. In November 1940 he took over Fighter Command and dealt with German night bombing raids, then in 1941 switched his attention to offensive operations into France, to keep the Luftwaffe engaged away from the Soviet front. While serving in this capacity he was involved in the early stages of planning for the eventual invasion of northwest Europe. In late 1941 the British Chiefs of Staff Committee delegated the task of considering possible options to Lord Mountbatten, chief of Combined Operations, Douglas, and Gen. Bernard Paget, commander in chief of Home Forces. These three officers laid the foundations of the plan. Douglas coordinated the air cover for Mountbatten's costly Dieppe raid on 19 August 1942—one of the few successes of that unfortunate, if useful, operation.

In late 1942 Douglas was sent to Middle East Command, and in January 1944 returned home to take over Coastal Command. This appointment was a reflection of the high regard in which he was held by RAF high command. The new post brought Douglas back into the development of OVERLORD. Although he was not under the command of the Supreme Allied Commander, he was heavily involved in the planning process. In concert with the Royal Navy, Coastal Command provided theater

W. SHOLTO DOUGLAS.   At left in RAF Coastal Command headquarters operations room, 6 June 1944.

defense for the invasion, keeping German U-boats and S-boats occupied outside the invasion area. The measure of its success can be seen in the small number of ships lost to these forces. After the completion of OVERLORD, Douglas led Coastal Command in the war against the snorkel-equipped U-boats. After his time with Coastal Command had ended, Air Chief Marshal Charles Portal wrote to Douglas: "No-one in the whole of the RAF has given in fuller measure, personally or officially, the support without which I could not have carried on . . . you have done magnificently every job entrusted to you."

After the war he was air commander in chief in Germany, then British commander in Germany, a task that required him to confirm the sentences of the Nuremberg Trials. Retiring in 1947, he took his peerage as Lord Douglas of Kirtleside, and from 1949 to 1964 served as chairman of British European Airways, now part of the British Airways Group. He died in Northampton in 1969. In his history of the RAF Sir Maurice Dean observed that Douglas was "the complete professional, shrewd, capable, tough, experienced, intelligent; he served the RAF well."

[See also Coastal Command.]

BIBLIOGRAPHY

Dean, Maurice. *The RAF in Two World Wars*. 1979.
Probert, Henry. *High Commanders of the Royal Air Force*. 1991.

ANDREW LAMBERT

DOUGLAS-PENNANT, C. E. (1894–1961),

British, commodore of Task Force G for Gold Beach. Cyril Eustace Douglas-Pennant entered the Royal Navy in 1907 and served aboard destroyers in World War I. He had a staff appointment at Naval Staff College in 1937–1939. After the war he continued to serve in the Royal Navy and was appointed captain of the Reserve Fleet in 1939. He was promoted to commodore in the West Indies, serving from 1940 to 1942, and then served as Adm. Bertram H. Ramsay's chief of staff for the landings at North Africa, Sicily, and Salerno. He was appointed to Force G in January 1944, although the force was not formed until March. Part of this was caused by the late return of the flagship HMS *Bulolo* from the Mediterranean, but *Bulolo* was highly valued. Lt. Col. H. A. Pollock reported, "The experience gained by her ships' company of seamen, soldiers and airmen in these operations was of great value in ensuring that the Head Quarters communication organisation worked efficiently and smoothly" (Cabinet Office Papers, CAB 44/242).

Force G, based around Poole and Weymouth in Dorset, comprised the flagship and the force flagships HMS *Nith, Kingsmill,* and *Albrighton,* with associated landing ships and landing craft. Leading the thirteen convoys sailing westward round the Isle of Wight, Commodore Douglas-Pennant was co-located with his army opposite number, Maj. Gen. D. A. H. Graham. This facilitated the fullest cooperation, in the spirit of Admiral Ramsay's appreciation of the primacy of military problems in conducting amphibious operations.

On D-day Douglas-Pennant's flagship was forced to shift berth at 0624 under fire from the guns at Longues. H-hour was at 0725 on Gold Beach, ten minutes ahead of Juno Beach. Only after noon was the landing area entirely clear of enfilading fire from German strong points. The reserves were then landed. At 1730 the flagship moved inshore to speed up the landing process. In the face of a rough sea, the amphibious tanks for the center of the Gold area were put ashore directly, but this put them behind the slow-moving beach clearance parties and most were quickly knocked out. Because their radios went out of action during the landing, the troops ashore were unable to call for specific gunfire support and had to assault strong points without it. Fortunately the rest of Gold Beach proved rather easier. When Admiral Ramsay visited the beachhead on the 7th, meeting Douglas-Pennant ashore, Ramsay reported that "everything had gone like clockwork in the assault and the army on shore were doing excellently." This "cheered him up a lot" although the landing of vehicles was already twelve hours behind schedule. His flagship, *Bulolo,* was hit by a bomb on the 7th, although not disabled; it left for Spithead on the 27th.

Douglas-Pennant was promoted to rear admiral 7 July 1944. He was deputy chief of staff to Earl Mountbatten in the South East Asia Command; commandant of the Joint Services Staff College, 1947 to 1949; flag officer (air) in the Mediterranean, 1948 to 1950; and admiral, British Joint Services Mission in Washington, 1950 to 1952. He retired in 1953. An experienced and highly capable staff officer, Douglas-Pennant was also a first-class combat commander. He died in 1961.

[See also Bulolo, HMS; Task Force G.]

BIBLIOGRAPHY

London. Public Record Office. "Overlord Plans and Preparations." Cabinet Office Papers, CAB 44/242.
Roskill, Stephen W. *The Offensive.* Vol. 3, pt. 2, of *The War at Sea, 1939–1945.* 1961.

ANDREW LAMBERT

E

EAKER, IRA (1896–1987) American, lieutenant general, commander in chief of the Allied air forces in the Mediterranean. A Texas farm boy just finishing college and planning to be a lawyer, Eaker enlisted as a private in the army the day after the United States declared war on Germany in 1917. Commissioned a second lieutenant, he switched to the infant Army Air Corps. A few years later he was world-famous as a pilot and clearly marked for command distinction.

He was the first to fly coast to coast across the United States "blind"—that is, on instruments. More important, he was chief pilot of the *Question Mark's* flight in 1929, which droned over California for seven days, refueled by a hose from another plane, thus pioneering the technique of midair refueling.

Commanding *Question Mark* was Maj. Carl ("Tooey") Spaatz, a senior, lifelong teammate of Eaker's. Another friend was Col. Henry H. ("Hap") Arnold, with whom Eaker wrote three books on flying. When General Arnold became chief of the air corps in 1938, Colonel Spaatz was his operations officer and Lieutenant Colonel Eaker his executive. That one-two-three status held throughout their military careers. Thus, Spaatz was appointed commander of the Eighth Air Force in England but stayed in the States for six months organizing it while Eaker went abroad in February 1943 as Commander of the VIII Bomber Command to set up the Eighth's first headquarters.

Because Eaker was transferred to Italy in January 1944, he was distant from the D-day operation; he was in Moscow, having led the first shuttle mission of 150 B-17s from Italy. But his Fifteenth Air Force in Italy had a major impact on D-day by destroying most of the oil production at Ploesti in Romania and by flying eighteen joint missions with the Eighth from England against aircraft factories and synthetic oil refineries in southern Germany. Thus, the Luftwaffe was deprived of crucial oil.

Eaker and Spaatz also conferred regularly with General Dwight D. Eisenhower in England. Eisenhower's basic air plan was to cut German communications to Normandy, whereas Spaatz and Eaker favored concentrating on destruction of German oil. Eaker wrote Arnold in April 1944 after meeting with Eisenhower and Spaatz that "the communications plan had won out over the oil plan, but . . . all had firmly agreed that the German Air Force was to be an all-consuming first priority."

A year later, as the European war neared its end, Arnold had a heart attack, and Gen. George C. Marshall ordered Eaker home to be chief of air staff. It was Eaker who urged that the final air attack on Japan be commanded by Gen. Curtis LeMay and based in the Marianas instead of China. Spaatz went to the Pacific to secure LeMay's authority while Eaker remained in Washington as chief of air staff for Arnold, back briefly from the hospital.

Arnold retired in 1946, leaving Spaatz and Eaker to fight the battle for air force independence. It came in July 1947, and Eaker then retired. He accepted Howard Hughes's plea to salvage the failing Hughes Aircraft Company, which Eaker succeeded in doing. He then turned to full-time journalism, becoming, in Senator Barry Goldwater's words "one of our nation's most important military spokesmen." In 1977, he received the Wright Trophy "for 60 years of significant public service," and in 1985 Congress bestowed four-star rank on Eaker and James Doolittle. But Eaker's greatest honor was a Congressional Gold Medal as "Aviation Pioneer and Air Power Leader."

[*See also* Air Superiority; Eighth Air Force; Fifteenth Air Force; POINTBLANK.]

BIBLIOGRAPHY

Arnold, H. A., and Ira C. Eaker. *Army Flier.* 1942.
Arnold, H. A., and Ira C. Eaker. *This Flying Game.* 1936. Reprint, 1943.

Arnold, H. A., and Ira C. Eaker. *Winged Warfare*. 1941.
Coffey, Thomas A. *Decision over Schweinfurt*. 1977.
Parton, James. *"Air Force Spoken Here": General Ira Eaker and the Command of the Air*. 1946.

JAMES PARTON

EASTERN TASK FORCE. One of two naval task forces created for Operation NEPTUNE, the landing operations accompanying Operation OVERLORD, the British Eastern Task Force (ETF) was formed in January 1944 under Adm. Bertram H. Ramsay. The ETF was to transport three British and Canadian divisions in the eastern sector of the landing zone, a beachhead some forty-eight kilometers (thirty miles) wide between the Orne River on the east and the small harbor of Port-en-Bessin to the west. The beaches were code-named SWORD, JUNO, and GOLD from east to west. Rear Adm. Philip Vian took the seagoing command of the ETF, while Rear Adm. Arthur G. Talbot, Como. C. E. Douglas-Pennant, and Como. G. N. Oliver commanded the three assault areas. Each beachhead was divided into three sectors, each under a captain. Force S formed up seven months, Force J eighteen months, and Force G only two and a half months before the invasion. The first period was ideal, the second too long, and the last far too short for the most effective training. However, the changing size of the assault force, the pressure of operations in the Mediterranean, and the shortage of assault craft precluded a better balanced buildup. Follow-up Force L under Rear Adm. William E. Parry, with the 7th Armoured Division, was based at Tilbury and Felixstowe. All formations were under naval command while at sea. Ships were allocated to an assault force and were provided with details of their mission.

The ETF also had to cover the invasion shipping against land-based artillery, aircraft, mines, submarines, and surface ships, notably destroyers and E-boats. During the assault phase many escorts and minesweepers operating from British naval bases were placed under ETF command; when the army was established ashore, they reverted to their original command structure.

The assault required layered fire support to suppress defensive fire. Experience from earlier landings, particularly at Dieppe in 1942, demonstrated that shipping and troops would be vulnerable to artillery fire. Consequently the ETF included three support forces: Force D, Rear Adm. W. R. Patterson, Sword Beach; Force E, Rear Adm. F. H. G. Dalrymple-Hamilton, Juno Beach; and Force K, Capt. E. W. L. Longley-Cook, Gold Beach. The first of these, which covered the open eastern flank, had the greatest firepower: three battleships, one monitor, and five cruisers; the others were restricted to cruisers. The support forces trained and assembled in the Clyde and at Belfast,

joining the invasion force off the French coast. Each ship had a specific target among the fixed batteries, but would also engage targets of opportunity and support the army as it advanced inland. In addition there were a number of gun-armed landing craft to engage beach defenses, and rocket-armed landing craft for area saturation.

ETF assault shipping was based at Portsmouth, Newhaven, Shoreham, and Southampton. The forces assembled in the Solent, at Spithead. Force L assembled at Southend, Sheerness, and Harwich. The task force commander was responsible for establishing the timetable for the loading of the assault shipping.

The assault depended on the success of the Allied minesweeping effort in the Channel and at the beachhead. The assault forces used specially cleared and marked routes to approach the French coast. Ten routes were cleared through the German mine fields as the fleet advanced. After the assault the safe areas were extended. Ten percent of all mines cleared during the war were swept during Operation OVERLORD.

The assault was merely the opening move of the operation. To succeed, the Allies had to build up their strength ashore more quickly than the Germans could respond. "It is on the rapid follow up of reserves, and on the swift unloading of stores that the attack relies for the impetus which alone can sustain it," noted Admiral Ramsay. Force L began landing on the second tide of D-day. Thereafter the Build Up Control Organisation (BUCO) at Combined Headquarters controlled the turnaround and reloading of all tonnage. The unloading was controlled by the task force commander.

ETF assault ships began leaving Spithead and the Solent early on 5 June, under the command of Vian aboard the HMS *Scylla*. During the approach to the French coast the destroyer HMS *Wrestler* and one LCT (Landing Craft, Tank) were damaged by mines, and fifty small craft foundered. The invasion force was guided into the beachhead by the lights from midget submarines *X.20* and *X.23*. As the fire-support vessels came into action, in a chance encounter with German torpedo boats the Norwegian destroyer HMNS *Svenner* of Sword Force was torpedoed. Although a short, steep sea was running, the assault phase began on schedule, and all forces landed on the correct beach close to the timetable. Off Sword Beach one LCI (Landing Craft, Infantry) was hit, but otherwise there was little opposition. The supporting battleships and monitor engaged the heavy batteries east of the Orne River. By midafternoon the shipping off all three beachheads had moved inshore to speed up the landing operations. D-day proceeded much closer to the original plan than anyone at the headquarters of the Chief of Staff to the Supreme Allied Commander (COSSAC) had a right to hope. The ETF carried out its tasks with

Eastern Task Force
List of Ships and Commanders

Rear Adm. Philip Vian
Flagship *Scylla,* Capt. Douglas Brownrigg

Reserve: Cruiser *Sirius,* Capt. R. L. M. Edwards
Close Escort
    Corvettes *Alberni, Armeria, Mimico*
    22 antisubmarine trawlers
Reserve Minesweepers
    ANCXF, available to ETF or WTF: 102d and 205th
       Minesweeper Flotilla, 10 minesweepers each
    NCETF only: 143d Minesweeper Flotilla, 10
       minesweepers
Coastal Forces
    55th Motor Torpedo Boat Flotilla, 12 MTBs
    63d Motor Torpedo Boat Flotilla, 5 MTBs
    1st Coastal Forces Flotilla, 6 motor gunboats

Force S for Sword Beach
Rear Adm. Arthur G. Talbot
Flagship *Largs*

Force Flagships
Locust (Capt. W. R. C. Leggatt)
Dacres (Capt. R. Gotto)
Goathland (Capt. E. W. Bush)

Close Escort
Destroyer *Campbell*
Sloop *Stork*
Frigate *Torrington*
Corvettes *Clover, Lavender, Pennywort*
Marker beacon midget submarine *X 23* (Lt. G. B. Honour, RNVR)
Landing ship engineer, ex-seaplane carrier *Albatross* (Capt. D. S. McGrath, retired)

Minesweepers
1st Minesweeper Flotilla (Comdr. H. E. H. Nicholls, *Harrier*)
    9 minesweepers
15th Minesweeper Flotilla (Comdr. H. G. A. Lewis, *Fraserburgh*)
    8 minesweepers
40th Minesweeper Flotilla (Acting Comdr. L. C. Windsor, *Catherine*)
    7 minesweepers covering Force S bombardment units)

Motor Minesweepers
132d Motor Minesweeper Flotilla, 10 motor minesweepers

British Yard Minesweepers
165th British Yard Minesweeper Flotilla, 10 BYMS
8 danlayers (marking swept channels)
13th Motor Launch Flotilla (to support the minesweepers)

Force J for Juno Beach
Como. G. N. Oliver
Flagship *Hilary*

Force Flagships
Lawford (Capt. A. F. Pugsley)
Waveney (Capt. R. J. O. Otway-Ruthven)
Royal Ulsterman (Capt. A. B. Fanshawe)

Close Escort
Destroyers *Beagle, Versatile, Wrestler*
Corvettes *Clarkia, Petunia*
Marker beacon midget submarine *X 20* (Lt. K. R. Hudspeth, RANVR)

Minesweepers
7th Minesweeper Flotilla (Acting Comdr. G. Nelson, *Pelorus*)
    8 minesweepers
9th Minesweeper Flotilla (Comdr. R. W. D. Thompson, *Sidmouth*)
    8 minesweepers

British Yard Minesweepers
159th British Yard Minesweeper Flotilla, 10 BYMS
8 danlayers
20th Motor Launch Flotilla

Force G for Gold Beach
Como. C. E. Douglas-Pennant,
Flagship *Bulolo*

Force Flagships
Nith (Capt. J. B. Farquhar)
Kingsmill (Capt. F. A. Ballance)
Albrighton (Capt. G. V. Dolphin)

Close Escort
Sloops *Hind, Magpie, Redpole*
Corvette *Campanula*
Landing ship engineer, ex-minelayer *Adventure* (Acting Capt. A. M. Sheffield)

Minesweepers
6th Minesweeper Flotilla (Comdr. J. C. Richards, *Vestal*)
    8 minesweepers

18th Minesweeper Flotilla (Comdr. A. V. Walker, *Ready*)
8 minesweepers

British Yard Minesweepers
150th British Yard Minesweeper Flotilla
8 danlayers
7th Motor Launch Flotilla

Follow-up Force L
Rear Adm. W. Edward Parry
(headquarters ashore)

Destroyers
  Cotswold, 16th Destroyer Flotilla (Lt. Comdr. J. S. Whittle, RNVR)
  Vivacious, 21st Destroyer Flotilla (Lt. F. D. Cole)
Frigates
  Chelmer (Temporary Comdr. R. A. Cherry, RNVR)
  Halstead (Comdr. J. R. Westmacott)
Corvettes
  Clematis (Temporary Lt. R. H. Farrand, RNR)
  Godetia (Temporary Lt. M. A. F. Larose, RNR)
  Mignotte (Lt. H. H. Brown)
  Narcissus (Temporary Lt. Comdr. G. T. S. Clampit, RNR)
  Oxlip (Temporary Lt. J. K. Craig, RNVR)
3 ASW trawlers
49 LST
19 LCI(L)
53 LCT(3)

Invasion shipping in the Eastern Task Force comprised:
  37 LSI, 130 LST, 2 LSR, 1 LSD, 11 LCC, 116 LCI,
  39 LCI(S), 487 LCT, 66 LCS, 408 LCA, 73 LCS(S),
  90 LCP, and 10 LCP(S).
These were accompanied by the following inshore fire-support craft:
  16 LCG(L), 22 LCT(R), 14 LCS(L), 24 LCS(M),
  18 LCF, 45 LCA(H), and 103 LCT.

Fire Support Force D
Rear Adm. W. R. Patterson
Flagship *Mauritius*, Capt. W. W. Davis

Battleships
  Warspite (Capt. M. H. A. Kelsey); dedicated close escort, frigates *Holmes*, *Rowley*
  Ramillies (Capt. G. B. Middleton)
Monitor
  Roberts (Capt. R. C. C. Dunbar)
Cruisers
  Arethusa (Capt. H. Dalrymple-Smith)

Frobisher (Capt. J. F. W. Mudford)
Danae (J. R. S. Haines)
Dragon (Polish) (Comdr. Stanislaw Dzienisiewicz)
23d Destroyer Flotilla; leader *Saumarez* (Capt. P. G. L. Cazalet)
  Scorpion (Lt. Comdr. W. S. Clouston)
  Scourge (Lt. Comdr. G. I. M. Balfour)
  Serapis (Lt. Comdr. E. L. Jones)
  Swift (Lt. Comdr. J. R. Gower)
  Stord (Norwegian) (Lt. Comdr. Storheil)
  Svenner (Norwegian) (Lt. Comdr. Holther)
  Kelvin (Lt. Comdr. R. M. W. MacFadden)
  Impulsive (Lt. Comdr. P. Bekenn)
26th Destroyer Flotilla
  Verulam (Lt. Comdr. W. S. Thomas)
  Virago (Lt. Comdr. A. J. R. White)
16th Destroyer Flotilla: Hunt-class destroyers
  Slazak (Polish) (Comdr. Romuald Tyminski)
  Middleton (Lt. J. S. Cox)
  Eglinton (Lt. F. M. Graves)
Minesweepers: 115th Minesweeper Flotilla, 10 minesweepers

Force K
Capt. E. W. L. Longley-Cook
Flagship *Argonaut*

Cruisers
  Ajax (Capt. J. J. Weld)
  Orion (Capt. J. P. Garnall)
  Emerald (Capt. F. S. Wylie)
  Royal Netherlands Navy gunboat *Flores* (Lt. Comdr. G. Koudys)
25th Destroyer Flotilla; leader *Grenville* (Capt. H. P. Henderson)
  Ulster (Lt. Comdr. W. S. Donald)
  Ulysses (Lt. Comdr. R. J. Hanson)
  Undaunted (Lt. Comdr. A. A. MacKenzie, RNR)
  Undine (Comdr. T. C. Robinson)
  Urania (Lt. Comdr. D. H. P. Gardiner)
  Urchin (Lt. Comdr. D. N. R. Murdoch)
  Ursa (Comdr. D. B. Wyburd)
8th Destroyer Flotilla; *Jervis* (Lt. Comdr. R. P. Hill)
21st Destroyer Flotilla: Hunt-class destroyers
  Cattistock (Lt. R. G. D. Keddie)
  Cottesmore (Lt. W. D. O'Brien)
  Pytchley (Lt. Comdr. R. H. Hodgkinson)
  Krakowiak (Polish) (Lt. Comdr. Maracewicz)

Force E
Rear Adm. F. H. G. Dalrymple-Hamilton
Flagship *Belfast*, Capt. G. F. R. Parham

Cruiser *Diadem* (Capt. E. G. A. Clifford)
8th Destroyer Flotilla
    Faulknor (Comdr. C. F. H. Churchill)
    Fury (Lt. Comdr. R. F. Taylor)
26th Destroyer Flotilla; leader *Kempenfelt* (Capt. M. I.
    Power)
    Venus (Comdr. J. S. M. Richardson)
    Vigilant (Lt. Comdr. L. W. J. Argley)
    Algonquin (Canadian) (Lt. Comdr. D. W. Piers, RCN)
    Sioux (Canadian) (Lt. Comdr. E. E. G. Boak, RCN)
1st Destroyer Flotilla: Hunt-class destroyers
    Bleasdale (senior officer, Comdr. H. M. S. Munday)
    Stevenstone (Lt. H. McL. Duff-Still, RNVR)
    Glaisdale (Royal Norwegian Navy) (Lt. Comdr. Kjeholt)
    La Combattante (Free French Navy) (Capt. Patou)
    Blankney (Lt. B. H. Brown)

London. Public Record Office. Admiralty Staff History, Operation Neptune Appendix. ADM 234/367.

light losses. German war diaries attributed their failure to halt the landings primarily to heavy naval gunfire.

Rear Admiral Vian and his subordinates controlled the landing of men, vehicles, and supplies, while protecting the anchorage from air attack, minelaying raids, and surface ships. Nine vessels were sunk by mines, but only five were lost to air attack and none to submarines. Vian ordered the beaching of the LSTs (Landing Ships, Tank) on D plus 1, the unloading of tanks having fallen behind schedule. As German air and sea attacks became more frequent, the task of the ETF became one of protecting the beachhead, with a reduced role in support of operations ashore. The ETF was wound up in July, when Vian and the assault commanders returned to England.

Operation NEPTUNE reflected the experience of five years at war and several major amphibious operations. It left little to chance, carried a large measure of insurance against the unexpected, and resulted in an excellent operation of war. The ETF played a full part in that success, landing three divisions on D-day and supporting them during the critical buildup phase.

[See also British Beaches; Ramsay, Bertram H.; Task Force G; Task Force J; Task Force S; Vian, Philip.]

BIBLIOGRAPHY

Barnett, Corelli. *Engage the Enemy More Closely: The Royal Navy in the Second World War.* 1991.
Edwards, Kenneth. *Operation Neptune.* 1946.
London. Public Record Office. "Eastern Task Force: Assault Areas." Admiralty, ADM 199/1647.
London. Public Record Office. "Eastern Task Force: Plans and Orders." Admiralty, ADM 199/1562.

ANDREW LAMBERT

E-BOATS. *See* S-Boats.

EDDY, MANTON (1892–1962), American, major general, commander of the U.S. 9th Infantry Division. Commissioned in the Regular Army in 1913, Manton Sprague Eddy was a first lieutenant in the 39th Infantry when it sailed to France in 1918 as part of the 4th Division. During World War I he was wounded while commanding a machine gun company and after returning to duty became a battalion commander in the 4th Division. He ended his service in France in 1919, commanding the 1st Battalion of the Composite Regiment, General Pershing's personal escort.

Between the wars he spent most of his time as a student and teacher. He completed courses at the Infantry School at Fort Benning, Georgia, attended the Command and General Staff College at Fort Leavenworth, Kansas, served as Professor of Military Science and Tactics at the Riverside Military Academy in Gainesville, Georgia, and taught tactics at Fort Leavenworth. He also served in Hawaii as a staff officer for the assistant chief of operations for the Hawaiian Department. He gained additional staff experience as assistant chief of staff for intelligence in the III Corps area in Baltimore, Maryland.

In March 1942 Eddy was a brigadier general and assistant division commander of the 9th Infantry Division at Fort Bragg, North Carolina. He assumed command of the division three months later and led it through the campaigns in North Africa and Sicily. A big man, standing over six feet tall, with glasses and an inquisitive squint, he earned a reputation among the troops in Africa that war correspondent Ernie Pyle expressed as being "sort of old-shoe and easy to talk with and . . . we think he is a mighty good general." General Omar Bradley, Eddy's corps commander in the Mediterranean theater, pronounced him better balanced and more cooperative than any other division commander in North Africa and praised his tactical skills. Bradley summed up his evaluation by saying that although Eddy was "not timid, neither was he bold; Manton liked to count his steps carefully before he took them."

Eddy led the 9th Division ashore at Utah Beach on 10 June as part of the U.S. VII Corps. By 14 June he had his division racing across the Cotentin Peninsula to cut off the German defenders at Cherbourg. He reached the Atlantic on 18 June, and in one of the most remarkable tactical maneuvers of the war, he turned the entire division 90 degrees in less than twenty-two hours to launch an attack toward Cherbourg on 19 June. For his brave and aggressive leadership during the Cherbourg campaign Eddy received the Distinguished Service Cross.

In August 1944 Eddy assumed command of XII Corps and commanded it for the rest of the war. After the war he remained on active duty and in 1948 was promoted to lieutenant general and appointed commandant of the Command and General Staff College. From 1950 until his retirement in 1953 he commanded the U.S. Seventh Army in Europe. He died at Fort Benning, Georgia, on 10 April, 1962.

[See also 9th Division.]

BIBLIOGRAPHY

Eddy, Manton. Biographical summary. 18 August 1952. Department of Defense, Office of Public Information Press Branch.
Obituary. The New York Times, 12 April 1962.
Obituary. The Washington Post, 12 April 1962.

CLAYTON R. NEWELL

EDGAR, CAMPBELL D. (1889–1961), American, commodore, commander of Task Force 126 (Follow-up Force B). Born in Washington, D.C., the son of a U.S. Naval Academy graduate, Campbell Dallas Edgar himself graduated from the academy in 1912. He served at the U.S. naval occupation of Veracruz, Mexico, in 1914 and spent World War I aboard the convoy escort destroyer Sampson. Between the wars he rotated sea duty with tours as instructor at the Naval Academy and various engineering, communications, and logistics assignments. In November 1942 Edgar commanded Transport Division 8 in the Allied invasion of North Africa, drawing praise from army staff. In July 1943 he led Transport Division 11 in the invasion of Sicily with such skill that he was awarded the Legion of Merit. In September 1943 he repeated his performance during the Salerno landing as commander of Transport Division 3, winning a gold star in lieu of a second award. In November 1943 he was named as commodore, a traditional, temporary flag rank between captain and rear admiral, authorized for the duration of the war and often conferred on officers commanding large support units.

Appointed commander of Force B, in April 1944 Edgar established his headquarters ashore at Devonport, which allowed close coordination with both navy and army staff and greatly facilitated planning and training. His 135 ships and craft, divided into three convoys, were to land regimental combat teams of the U.S. 1st and 29th infantry divisions, engineer special brigade troops, beach battalions, and certain divisional, corps, and army troops at Omaha Beach to reinforce the initial landings—some 26,000 troops and 4,000 vehicles in all.

The first convoy of Force B to arrive sailed on 6 June, led by Edgar in destroyer escort USS Maloy, which also carried Maj. Gen. Charles H. Gerhardt, commander of the 29th. Though the convoy arrived as scheduled, its initial landings were postponed by one hour because of the chaotic situation on the beach. General Gerhardt went ashore soon thereafter, maintaining close contact with Edgar through the morning of 7 June to request landings of his regimental combat teams. Remaining in the assault area until 11 June, Edgar also coordinated the unloading of Force B's transports and ordered the detachment of ships with combat loads or tows for Utah Beach. He consulted with Adm. John L. Hall aboard USS Ancon, Adm. Alan G. Kirk aboard USS Augusta, and Adm. Don P. Moon aboard USS Bayfield. He was awarded a second gold star to his Legion of Merit for exceptional handling of his command.

Edgar led both a transport division and a beach assault group in Operation DRAGOON, the invasion of southern France in August 1944, adding a third gold star and a combat V for valor to his Legion of Merit. Later transferred to the Pacific, he held transport and training commands. Ordered to the San Francisco Naval Hospital in August 1946, he retired on 1 January 1947 as a "tombstone" rear admiral: all officers "specially commended before 1 January 1947 for performance of duty in actual combat" were promoted one grade upon retirement without ever having actually exercised that rank. He died at Fort Ord Military Hospital, California, on 24 June 1961.

[See also Maloy, USS; Task Force 126.]

BIBLIOGRAPHY

Commander Task Force 126 [C. D. Edgar]. Operation _____ [name not supplied]: Invasion of Northern France, June 6–11, 1944. Serial 299 of 22 June 1944. Operational Archives, Naval Historical Center, Washington, D.C.
Commander Task Group 126.4 [B. J. Skahill]. Narrative Report of Operations from 4 June through 17 June 1944. Serial 0020 of 1 August 1944. Operational Archives, Naval Historical Center, Washington, D.C.
Edgar, Campbell D. Flag officer file biography. Operational Archives, Naval Historical Center, Washington, D.C.
Morison, Samuel Eliot. The Invasion of France and Germany, 1944–1945. Vol. 11 of History of United States Naval Operations in World War II. 1957.
Reynolds, Clark G. Famous American Admirals. 1978.

STEVEN J. TIRONE

EHLERS, WALTER D. (1921–), American, staff sergeant; Medal of Honor recipient. Walter D. Ehlers and his brother Roland grew up on a farm near Fort Riley, then were inducted into the army at Manhattan, Kansas. They served side by side in the 1st Infantry Division through the North African and Sicilian campaigns, but were separated into different companies for the Normandy invasion; Walter survived, but Roland was killed in action on Omaha Beach.

Staff Sgt. Walter Ehlers distinguished himself by conspicuous gallantry in action near Goville, France, on 9 and 10 June 1944, while leading his squad from Company L, 18th Infantry Regiment, against heavily defended enemy strong points, personally attacking and destroying machine-gun and mortar crews that were bringing intense fire on his unit. After advancing deep into enemy territory the next day, Ehler's platoon was forced to withdraw. On more than one occasion he diverted enemy fire toward himself to allow members of his squad to withdraw. Although wounded himself, he rescued his wounded BAR (Browning Automatic Rifle) man, then returned under withering enemy fire to recover the man's weapon.

Promoted to lieutenant, Ehlers received the Medal of Honor in Paris in December 1944. After a brief furlough at home, he returned to his regiment to finish the war. After the war he served as a counselor for disabled veterans in California.

BIBLIOGRAPHY

Gallowary, Joseph L. "Medal of Honor: Profiles in Courage. Walter D. Ehlers, the Brother as Point Man." Special Report, *U.S. News & World Report*, 10 September 1990, 61–64.

Knickerbocker, H. R., et al. *Danger Forward: The Story of the First Division in World War II.* 1947.

U.S. Congress. Senate. Committee on Veterans' Affairs. *Medal of Honor Recipients, 1863–1978.* 96th Cong., 1st sess., 1979. S. Committee Print No. 3.

JOHN F. VOTAW

EIGHTH AIR FORCE. Created in January 1942 at Savannah, Georgia, the Eighth Air Force started to arrive in England in February and began operations against occupied France in August 1942. By the time of Operation OVERLORD, Lt. Gen. James Doolittle led the Eighth, which had become America's largest air force, comprising forty groups of B-17 and B-24 heavy bombers and sixteen groups of P-38, P-47, and P-51 fighters. The 2,800 bombers belonged to three bombardment divisions, and the 1,200 fighters served under VIII Fighter Command, headed by Maj. Gen. William Kepner. The Eighth Air Force also contained the VIII Service Command, which handled specialized air logistics and maintenance.

The U.S. Army Air Forces established the Eighth in England to prove its theories on the effectiveness of strategic daylight precision bombing. The Americans believed that unescorted, self-defending heavy bombers could penetrate into Germany and destroy its war industry.

B-24 LIBERATOR.   USAAF's Eighth Air Force attack on Luftwaffe base near Saint-Dizier, France, three months before D-day.

HULTON DEUTSCH

P-47D THUNDERBOLT.   82d Fighter Squadron, 78th Fighter Group, Eighth Air Force, with invasion markings.
COURTESY OF ALFRED PRICE

A series of setbacks in 1943, as the Germans built their air defenses faster than the Eighth could build its force, disproved the theory. But in January 1944 new long-range P-51 fighters and new drop tanks, extending the range of the P-38s and P-47s, arrived. This enabled the Eighth to start a campaign of attrition against the Luftwaffe fighter force. As the Eighth's bombers flew directly into Germany to strike the aircraft industry and other industrial facilities, their escort fighters fanned out to engage German fighters. The better-trained American pilots and their technologically superior aircraft overwhelmed their aerial opponents. In March the Eighth's fighters started descending to low altitudes to strafe airfields and other targets of opportunity during their return to base or later on planned sweeps. By mid-April the Eighth had attained daylight air superiority over Germany and occupied Europe. The German aircraft and pilots lost defending the Reich could not interfere with the invasion.

On 22 April the Eighth began participating in the Transportation Plan, an Allied air plan calling for a battle of attrition against German lines of communication in France and Belgium, particularly rail-marshaling yards.

The Eighth delivered thirteen thousand tons of bombs on the twenty-three rail centers assigned to it, destroying fifteen and severely damaging the remaining eight prior to D-day. On 9 May the Eighth commenced attacks on German airfields within 130 miles of Caen. That was supposed to erase any German range advantage over aircraft flying from southern England. The Eighth continued strategic missions as well, inaugurating a campaign against the German synthetic oil industry on 8 and 12 May. The initial raids halved German production, with severe long-term consequences for the Luftwaffe and German ground force mobility.

On 6 June the Eighth, serving under General Dwight D. Eisenhower's tactical air commander, Air Chief Marshal Trafford Leigh-Mallory, concentrated its entire force on the Normandy peninsula. As the empty troop carriers and night bombers withdrew, Eighth Air Force fighters began patrolling the outer perimeter of the operating area. They maintained the patrol until the assault troops hit the beaches, whereupon they moved to the area just in front of the troops to attack targets of opportunity. Four groups of the Eighth's P-38s provided an all-day air umbrella over the invasion convoys. The Eighth dis-

Eighth Air Force

1st Bomb Division (B-17s)
4 Combat Wings
  12 Bomb Groups

2d Bomb Division (B-24s)
5 Combat Wings
  14 Bomb Groups

3d Bomb Division (B-17s, B-24s)
5 Combat Wings
  14 Bomb Groups

VIII Fighter Command (P-38s, P-47s, P-51s)
3 Fighter Wings
  15 Fighter Groups

VIII Air Force Service Command
4 Strategic Air Depots

VIII Air Force Composite Command

8th Reconnaissance Wing (Provisional)

patched 1,805 heavy bombers to attack the beach defenses just before H-hour, and 1,074 of them, led by the 446th Bomb Group, located the target. Overcast covering the beaches compelled the bombardiers to resort to inaccurate radar bombing (H2X); this, and the natural tendency to release the bombs late in order to avoid hitting friendly troops, resulted in most of the 3,096 tons of bombs landing behind the defenses in swamps and flooded areas. An additional 380 bombers diverted to a secondary target, Argentan, and 37 of them dropped 109 tons of bombs. The Eighth staged a second mission in the afternoon, sending 782 bombers, 508 of which found their aim points, against Caen and transportation targets in a wide arc between Coutances and Lisieux. They

dropped a further 1,647 tons. The day cost the Eighth four heavy bombers and twenty-five fighters lost and thirty-two bombers and fourteen fighters damaged.

Although the Eighth Air Force's efforts on D-day itself helped secure the beachhead, the Eighth made its greatest contribution to the invasion in the skies over Germany, where it ruined the German day fighter force and killed or maimed many of Germany's experienced pilots. The Luftwaffe could mount barely one hundred sorties on the day of the invasion.

[*See also* Doolittle, James; VIII Air Force Service Command; VIII Fighter Command; Leigh-Mallory, Trafford; Railroads.]

BIBLIOGRAPHY

Freeman, Roger. *The Mighty Eighth*. 1970.
Freeman, Roger. *The Mighty Eighth War Diary*. 1981.
Hansell, Haywood S., Jr. *The Strategic Air War against Germany and Japan: A Memoir*. 1986.

RICHARD G. DAVIS

VIII AIR FORCE SERVICE COMMAND. This Eighth Air Force subordinate command responsible for logistics, personnel, maintenance, and repair arrived in England with the other elements of the Eighth Air Force and its first commander, Maj. Gen. Walter H. ("Tony") Frank, in July 1942. Frank established the service command headquarters at Bushy Park near London, also the site of Eighth Air Force headquarters. He immediately reached an agreement dividing duties with the U.S. Army Services of Supply (SOS), European Theater of Operations. The SOS retained overall control of construction, debarkation, and priority for shipping, which allowed it an important voice in determining the rate of growth of the Eighth Air Force, as well as the supply of items common to both the U.S. Army and the U.S. Army Air Forces (AAF). VIII Air Force Service Command controlled items of supply and maintenance peculiar to the AAF. For the remainder of the war the service command attempted to expand its responsibilities. In November 1942 Maj. Gen. Henry J. F. Miller replaced General Frank. He served in the post until October 1943, when Brig. Gen. Hugh J. Knerr succeeded him. On 6 January 1944 Knerr became deputy commanding general, administration, and commander of the Air Service Command (ASC), U.S. Strategic Air Forces in Europe (USSAFE, later USSTAF). He absorbed the former VIII Air Force Service Command Headquarters staff into his new command and created a new VIII Air Force Service Command out of the 8th Strategic Air Depot Area, Headquarters. Col. Donald R. Goodrich became the new commander of the service command.

The AAF's emphasis on fielding combat units at the expense of support units initially stunted the command's growth and efficiency—a situation that improved only in late 1943. The arrival of Lt. Gen. Carl Spaatz as AAF commander in Great Britain and his new headquarters, USSAFE (later USSTAF), which placed equal emphasis on operations and logistics, further rectified the situation. General Knerr, who had a genuine flair for supply work, controlled both the VIII and IX air force service commands. He placed them on an efficient footing, while eliminating duplication and competition.

In the five months before D-day the VIII Air Force Service Command found itself responsible for accommodating fourteen new heavy bomb groups and maintaining sustained operations on a far larger scale than before. Heavier operations required stocking and transporting immense amounts of fuel and bombs. During the week of 20–26 February 1944, for example, the Eighth Air Force dropped more bomb tonnage than it had in the entire first year of its existence. Heavy battle losses necessitated processing more replacement crews and aircraft and repairing battle damage. From 21 January to 30 April 1944, the Eighth Air Force dispatched 33,000 heavy bomber sorties that required the repair of 8,800 damaged aircraft. Without the efforts of the VIII Air Force Service Command, the effectiveness of the bombers preparing the way for D-day would have been drastically curtailed. [*See also* Goodrich, Donald.]

BIBLIOGRAPHY

Craven, Wesley Frank, and James Lea Cate, eds. *Europe: TORCH to POINTBLANK, August 1942 to December 1943.* Vol. 2 of *The Army Air Forces in World War II.* 1949.

Craven Wesley Frank, and James Lea Cate, eds. *Europe: ARGUMENT to V-E Day, January 1944 to May 1945.* Vol. 3 of *The Army Air Forces in World War II.* 1951.

RICHARD G. DAVIS

VIII CORPS (U.S.). VIII Corps was first organized in 1918 in France; it was demobilized the following year. The corps was activated for World War II at Fort Sam Houston, Texas, in 1940 as part of Third Army. In 1943 the corps headquarters moved to England to await further movement into Europe with Third Army. When Gen. Omar Bradley, First Army commander, requested a fourth corps for the invasion, VIII Corps received the mission.

VIII Corps did not participate in the D-day landings. Its first elements landed on Utah Beach on 14 June, and the headquarters became operational as part of First Army at noon the next day. Commanded by Maj. Gen. Troy H. Middleton, the corps was to organize defensive positions across the Cotentin Peninsula—the first step in organiz-

---

VIII Corps
Maj. Gen. Troy H. Middleton

15 June 1944

101st Airborne Division
Maj. Gen. Maxwell D. Taylor

19 June 1944

82d Airborne Division
Maj. Gen. Matthew B. Ridgway (to 27 August 1944)

90th Infantry Division
Maj. Gen. Eugene M. Landrum (to 30 July 1944)

101st Airborne Division
Maj. Gen. Maxwell D. Taylor

---

ing the southern flank of First Army in anticipation of securing the port city of Cherbourg. Initially, only 101st Airborne Division was attached to VIII Corps. On 18 June, when 9th Infantry Division reached the west coast of the peninsula at Barneville, the corps, still with only one division attached, held a sector of the front around Carentan between VII Corps and XIX Corps. The next day VIII Corps received 82d Airborne Division and 90th Infantry Division and assumed responsibility for a twenty-nine-kilometer (eighteen-mile) defensive line stretching across the peninsula from Carentan to the Bay of Biscay. While VIII Corps held the southern flank of First Army, VII Corps turned north to begin its attack on Cherbourg.

VIII Corps continued to fight as part of First Army through July 1944. When Third Army became operational in France on 1 August, the corps returned to its control. It remained under Middleton's command and stayed with Third Army until the end of the war in Europe. In July 1945 VIII Corps returned to the United States and was inactivated at Camp Gruber, Oklahoma, in December 1945. [*See also* Middleton, Troy H.]

BIBLIOGRAPHY

Harrison, Gordon A. *Cross-Channel Attack.* U.S. Army in World War II: The European Theater of Operations. 1951.

Wilson, John B. *Armies, Corps, Divisions, and Separate Brigades.* 1987.

CLAYTON R. NEWELL

VIII CORPS (BRITISH). The British VIII Corps started the war in a static role in southwestern England.

VIII Corps Headquarters
Lt. Gen. R. N. O'Connor
2d Household Cavalry Regiment
Lt. Col. H. Abel Smith

Guards Armoured Division
Maj. Gen. A. H. S. Adair

11th Armoured Division
Maj. Gen. G. P. B. Roberts

15th (Scottish) Infantry Division
Maj. Gen. G. H. A. Macmillan

6th Independent Tank Brigade
Brig. G. L. Verney

In June 1943 it was sent north to Yorkshire to be made into a largely armored formation and to be trained to take part in the invasion of Europe. Here it was organized into the form in which it in due course crossed the Channel.

The Eighth Army Group Royal Artillery was normally in support of the corps, whose total strength on D-day was just over 60,000 men, of whom 3,200 were officers.

Following the move north, three successive generals were in command before Lt. Gen. Richard N. O'Connor took over on 21 January 1944, only a month after returning to Britain following his escape from captivity as a prisoner of war in Italy. A major test exercise in February 1944 enabled the new commander to study his troops in the field before the corps started to move south in mid-April in preparation for the invasion. Corps headquarters were established near Crawley in Surrey, and the divisions were based at Eastbourne, Worthing, and Aldershot.

Given a follow-up role for the landings, the VIII Corps started to move slowly toward the coast only on 7 June, and it was not until the evening of 12 June, D plus 6, that the headquarters landed in Normandy in Riva-Bella, near the mouth of the Orne River. From there it moved to the area of Lantheuil, some ten kilometers (6 miles) northwest of Caen. It took some days for the whole corps to reach France: the 11th Armoured Division traveled from the Thames, around the coast of Kent, to disembark on 13 and 14 June.

As the weather deteriorated in the ensuing days, delays in the arrival of elements of the Guards Armoured and 15th (Scottish) Divisions grew worse, so that in the end the VIII Corps could not be committed to battle until D plus 20. But despite these holdups, soon after the headquarters arrived, planning began for what was intended to be its first action, code-named Operation DREADNOUGHT. The operation envisaged a breakout from the increasingly congested bridgehead to the east of the Orne River. The difficulties of forming up the corps in a suitable sector of the bridgehead, coupled with the strength of the enemy positions on its flank, convinced O'Connor that it was not a feasible operation. He was able to persuade General Bernard L. Montgomery that this was the case, and on 18 June, D plus 12, the plan was dropped.

The task of the VIII Corps was now switched to launching a major offensive across the Odon River southwest of Caen, to seize the high ground dominating the west bank of the Orne River. Given the code name EPSOM, this attack eventually started on 26 June and was the corps's first real taste of action in the Normandy campaign. Later it was involved in the major battles of GOODWOOD, east of Caen, and BLUECOAT, south from Caumont toward Vire, prior to the breakout of the Normandy beachhead. It suffered heavy casualties in all three engagements.

[*See also* O'Connor, Richard N.]

BIBLIOGRAPHY

D'Este, Carlo. *Decision in Normandy: The Unwritten Story of Montgomery and the Allied Campaign.* 1983.
Jackson, G. S. *Operations of Eighth Corps: Normandy to the River Rhine.* 1948.

JOHN BAYNES

VIII FIGHTER COMMAND. The VIII AF Fighter Command (FC) served in the European theater from May 1942 until its deactivation in March 1946. Initially under the leadership of Brig. Gen. "Monk" Hunter, the command's efforts to provide effective bomber escorts were frustrated by the diversion of aircraft and other resources to North Africa (and later to Italy), by the limited range of the Spitfires, and by the slow arrival of P-47 Thunderbolts. In August 1943 Maj. Gen. William E. Kepner took command, put combat-experienced pilots on his staff, and exerted pressure on the Air Technical Section to develop fuel tanks to provide the fighters with greater range. His priorities were to extend the range of the P-47s, to obtain more P-38 Lightnings, and to press for the earliest delivery of P-51s. Cardboard fuel tanks made by the British extended the combat radius of the P-47 from 280 kilometers (175 miles) to 725 kilometers (450 miles). As a time-saving measure, at Kepner's insistence P-38s were put together at the port and flown to their units. By December 1944 the first operations of the long-range P-51 Mustang marked the establishment of fighter reach sufficient to perform not only the escort role but also the attack missions later so vital to the so-called fourth task of the Air War Planning Documents: support for the land invasion of Europe.

By the spring of 1944, the VIII FC had placed fifteen battle-ready fighter groups at the disposal of its parent command, the Eighth Air Force. For D-day there were four P-38 groups, four P-47 groups, and seven groups flying the P-51. Comprising three squadrons each, the groups were nominally equipped with seventy-five fighters plus a 20-percent reserve. In fact, few groups ever had a full complement, but they were logistically healthy and well trained.

Kepner encouraged his tacticians and planners to experiment, and they did. For example, Col. Hub Zemke, when asked about the sudden increase of air victories in his 56th Fighter Group, explained that his fighters were now leaving the bombers to seek out German fighters. Eighth Air Force commander General Doolittle approved, and Kepner made such "sweeps" a standard escort tactic in all the groups. The longer range of their planes also gave the pilots fuel and time enough for targets of opportunity. In Col. Glen Duncan's 353d Fighter Group, pilots roared over German-controlled airfields at breakneck speed and treetop level, practicing their gunnery skills on everything in sight. While this activity was an unsanctioned "sport," Kepner told General Spaatz, commander of the U.S. Strategic Air Forces, "My fighters are doing some screwy things enroute and returning from the target, but I think they pay dividends." "Yes, Bill," Spaatz replied, "and as long as they do, you will have a job!" Kepner imposed methods on these activities by forming a strafe and dive-bomb training program at Metfield in southeastern England. After the program was disbanded in April 1944, VIII FC conducted extensive attacks, first in Germany, and by late May in occupied France. Employing literally hundreds of fighters per wave, Operations CHATTANOOGA CHOO-CHOO and JACKPOT were very successful in targeting rail yards and airfields, respectively. Command experience in this role peaked at exactly the right time, becoming the "bread and butter" of their invasion missions.

VIII FC was assigned three main missions in support of OVERLORD: to escort bombers and troop carriers, to protect Allied shipping, and to attack any air or ground movement toward the assault area. Early on D-day four groups of the command's P-38s established high-altitude air cover over the armada, while RAF Spitfires flew low cover beneath them. P-51s had the bulk of the escort duty, guarding the withdrawal of Ninth Air Force troop transports returning from their drop zones and RAF bombers from their predawn targets. The escorts also kept the skies clear for Eighth and Ninth air force bombers attacking targets throughout the day. P-51s and P-47s conducted an early morning sweep called Operation FULL HOUSE, then formed a screen east of the Channel traffic in an eighty-kilometer (fifty-mile) semicircle extending south of the invasion beaches, across the Cotentin Peninsula, and back to the Channel. This air umbrella remained in place from first light until they were relieved by other forces shortly before noon. No German aircraft got through it to the beach. Predominant D-day afternoon activity for VIII FC consisted of interdiction missions against road, rail, and barge movement. Code-named STUD and ROYAL FLUSH, these operations provided concentrated coverage over an area bounded by the Seine, the Loire, and a line from Paris to Orléans. The missions were split between those assigned specific targets, and armed reconnaissance missions that hunted targets of opportunity.

In the aggregate, VIII FC's tally for 6 June included 1,880 sorties flown in one of the most diverse fighter operations ever mounted by a single organization in a single day. Seventeen bridges, ten railroad marshaling yards, and eighty-five trains were attacked in addition to convoys, barges, tugboats, warehouses, radar towers, barracks, and even individual staff cars. Pilots claimed twenty-eight German aircraft destroyed and fourteen damaged. Twenty-five VIII FC planes were lost to all causes. The success of the first day, and of the days that followed, proved the efficacy of the command's training and aggressiveness.

Over the next twelve days, while ground elements solidified their initial hold on the coast, General Kepner's fighters devoted themselves to escort, counterair, and interdiction well inland of the invading force. German fighter opposition, although spotty, was occasionally intense. About 150 aircraft were encountered on 7 June, of which thirty-one were claimed by VIII FC. Another large engagement, with more than fifty adversaries, took place on 12 June. Eight P-47s were lost and five Messerschmitt BF-109s were downed. Although the missions of 9 June were canceled owing to bad weather, the interdiction effort between D-day and D plus 12 rendered German daytime movement virtually impossible. Every road bridge, rail yard, tunnel, and canal in the area was a potential target. Fighters even performed surveillance to look for signs of activity, and called out targets for other flights to attack when low fuel or lack of ammunition prevented them from doing the job themselves.

In OVERLORD's first twelve days, VIII FC flew nearly 12,000 sorties. They claimed 172 German aircraft destroyed and many more damaged. In attacks against hundreds of ground targets, they put more than 600 vehicles, 400 rail cars, and 40 locomotives out of action. These achievements, combined with the destruction of airfields, marshaling yards, ammunition dumps, bridges, and gun emplacements, constituted a major contribution to the Allied effort.

The work of VIII FC that preceded the invasion was as

important as what came after it. Every task they performed helped to isolate the battlefield, so the ground forces could establish and sustain a foothold on the Continent. In its escort role the command established air supremacy for subsequent land operations, while its bombing and strafing helped prevent the Germans from bringing reinforcements to the point of invasion.

[*See also* Eighth Air Force; Kepner, William.]

BIBLIOGRAPHY

Carter, Kit C., and Robert Mueller. *U.S. Army Air Forces in World War II: Combat Chronology, 1941–1945.* 1973. Reprint, 1991.

Fagg, John E. "Pre-Invasion Operations." In vol. 3 of *The Army Air Forces in World War II*, edited by Wesley Frank Craven and James Lea Cate. 1951.

Maurer, Maurer, ed. *Air Force Combat Units of World War II.* 1961. Reprint, 1984.

PAUL F. HENRY

85TH COMPOSITE GROUP.

85 (Base) Group was set up in December 1943 primarily as an air defense force to support the invasion, but it remained under the operational control of Air Defence of Great Britain until 17 August, when its headquarters moved from Hillingdon to Normandy. The group comprised fourteen squadrons of Mosquito night fighters, Spitfires, and Tempests, together with a reconnaissance wing and air spotting pool, and included Canadian, New Zealand, and Dutch units. Their tasks were to furnish air protection by night over the invasion buildup area, to provide a reserve of squadrons at readiness, to accommodate and administer all the RAF's base units in the captured areas, and to ensure their ground defense. Air Vice Marshal John Cole-Hamilton took command on 13 February 1944 and was succeeded by AVM C. R. Steele on 10 July.

Before D-day the squadrons were largely committed to defensive patrols, shipping and weather reconnaissance, and night intruder operations. On D-day and after they provided air defense cover over both the British and American sectors of the invasion front but encountered far less interference from the Luftwaffe than expected. They were consequently able to undertake many other types of operations: convoy patrol, attacks on enemy aircraft, laying mines and interfering with shipping, offensive sweeps against motor transport and trains, destruction of balloons, bomber escort, and weather reconnaissance, as well as sorties against flying bombs. On the ground a ground-controlled interception (GCI) unit reached Normandy on D-day, soon followed by repair and supply units, airfield construction formations, RAF regiment squadrons, and many other support organizations.

From then until the end of the war 85 Group provided the defense and backup services required by the large and ever-growing RAF forces deployed in northwest Europe.

[*See also* Cole-Hamilton, J. B.]

BIBLIOGRAPHY

Wynn, Humphrey, and Susan Young. *Prelude to Overlord.* 1983.

HENRY PROBERT

84TH COMPOSITE GROUP.

84 Group was established in June 1943 at Cowley, near Oxford, the second group formed specially to provide tactical air support for the army. Although initially located alongside Headquarters Second Army, in early 1944 it became associated with the First Canadian Army. Commanded from November 1943 by Air Vice Marshal L. O. Brown, it consisted by D-day of ten wings, its twenty-nine squadrons including four Polish, two Norwegian, three Czechoslovak, three French, one Belgian, and one New Zealand. Of these, fifteen flew the Spitfire, three the longer-range Mustang, and eight the Typhoon. There were also three reconnaissance squadrons, and two additional air observation squadrons flew the Auster.

Up to D-day, still operating as part of the Air Defence of Great Britain, the group's aircraft attacked V-weapon sites and airfields, and escorted Allied bombers in the assault on enemy communications. As the invasion approached, they struck the coastal radar stations. On D-day the Typhoons went into action just ahead of the main landings. The other squadrons joined in soon afterward, their targets being enemy guns, strong points, transport, armor, and radars; over 1,000 sorties were flown that day.

For the rest of June the group's aircraft averaged 500 sorties per day. While two Typhoon wings were soon based in Normandy, there were too few airfields for the others and most aircraft continued to operate from their bases in Sussex, using forward airstrips for refueling. On 6 August, however, 84 Group became fully operational in Normandy, and for the rest of the war— commanded from 10 November by AVM Edmund Hudleston—its main task was to support the Canadians.

[*See also* Brown, L. O.]

BIBLIOGRAPHY

Wynn, Humphrey, and Susan Young. *Prelude to Overlord.* 1983.

HENRY PROBERT

LXXXIV CORPS.

This German formation was responsible for defending the sector from Caen to the western side of the Cotentin Peninsula. As such, it had to bear the brunt of all the Allied landings on D-day.

LXXXIV Corps had originally been formed as *LX Corps Command* in late 1940 in France, but in the summer of 1942 it was upgraded to a full corps and designated *LXXXIV Corps*. In August 1943 Lt. Gen. Erich Marcks, who had earlier lost a leg on the Eastern front, took command. By early 1944 the corps was deployed to the sector that it would defend on D-day and had the following divisions assigned to it: *243d Infantry Division, 352d Infantry Division, 709th Static Division,* and *716th Static Division.* The corps headquarters was located just outside Saint-Lô.

As a result of Allied airborne landings, *LXXXIV Corps* was placed in the highest state of alert at 0215 on 6 June; *91st Air Landing Division*, a Seventh Army reserve unit located in the eastern part of the base of the Cotentin Peninsula, was placed under its command twenty minutes later. When the British began to storm ashore on Sword Beach at 0700, *Army Group B* also gave Marcks *21st Panzer Division*, which was then south of Caen. Since this represented his only means of counterattack, and communications with the panzer division were as yet nonexistent, Marcks hurried to the Caen area and personally led the leading elements of the division toward the beaches. Shortly after he left his headquarters, it was attacked by Allied aircraft. While he was able to stop the thrust on Caen by nightfall, Marcks could not prevent the British from establishing their beachheads. It was the same on the American beaches, where he had no mobile reserves available. The arrival, however, of Lt. Gen. Josef ("Sepp") Dietrich's *I SS Panzer Corps* headquarters and elements of *12th SS Panzer Grenadier Division* in the Caen area on the evening of D-day meant that on 7 June Marcks was able to hand this sector over to him. This included command of *21st Panzer Division* and *716th Static Division*.

During the next few days *LXXXIV Corps* tried, without success, to prevent the Allied beachheads from linking up, but its attention became increasingly concentrated on the Cotentin Peninsula. In spite of a desperate defense, the corps was unable to stop the Americans from cutting across its base and isolating Cherbourg. In the midst of this, on 12 June Marcks was killed by American fighter-bombers while on his way to organize a temporary garrison to hold Caumont, which fell early the following day. Lt. Gen. Wilhelm Fahrmbacher, then commanding *XXV Corps* in Brittany, was hastily summoned to take temporary command of *LXXXIV*. Three days later, on 15 June, Gen. Dietrich von Choltitz arrived from Italy to take over. He too could do nothing to prevent the loss of Cherbourg, which fell on 27 June.

Thereafter *LXXXIV Corps* held the extreme western sector of the German line with two panzer and four infantry divisions, all well under strength. It became deeply engaged in trying to hold back Gen. Omar Bradley's advance to Saint-Lô during the first part of July. With the American breakout from Saint-Lô, which began on 25 July, the corps was pressed back into what became the Falaise pocket. Von Choltitz was then ordered to go take command of Paris, which he later surrendered to the Allies. His successor in command of the corps, General Elfeldt, surrendered to the 1st Polish Armored Division in the Falaise pocket on 20 August; with that, *LXXXIV Corps* vanished from the German order of battle.

[*See also* Fahrmbacher, Wilhelm; Marcks, Erich; *and articles on units mentioned herein.*]

BIBLIOGRAPHY

Jacobsen, Otto. *Erich Marcks. Soldat und Gelehrter.* 1971.

CHARLES MESSENGER

82D AIRBORNE DIVISION.

In November 1943, COSSAC (Chief of Staff to the Supreme Allied Commander) began planning for Operation OVERLORD. A key element of the cross-Channel attack would be a predawn airborne assault including the British 6th Airborne Division on the Allied left flank, and two American airborne divisions, the 82d and the 101st, on the right. This would effectively isolate the beachheads, disrupting German communications, preventing German reinforcements from reaching the battlefield, and securing vital bridges, crossings, and exits from the beaches leading inland. Of the two American divisions, the 82d Airborne was the first such division in the U.S. Army and hence the most experienced at the time. In November 1943 the 82d was recalled from the Mediterranean, where the division's paratroopers had made night parachute assaults in Sicily and into the Allied beachhead near Salerno.

Prior to Normandy, the 82d was a "triangular" division containing three organic infantry regiments: two parachute, the 504th and 505th, and one glider infantry, the 325th. The 504th, however, had been retained in Italy for further fighting; when it rejoined the 82d in England in April 1944, it was in dire need of rest, refitting, and replacements, and in no condition to participate in the D-day operation. So the 507th and 508th parachute infantry regiments were attached to the 82d instead.

The division commander, Maj. Gen. Matthew B. Ridgway, was a highly capable, competent, and inspirational leader who had commanded the 82d from its inception as an airborne unit through all its earlier campaigns in North Africa, Sicily, and Italy. The 505th's former commander, Brig. Gen. James Gavin, was made assistant division commander in Italy and was a highly talented and charismatic leader; he also served on the COSSAC staff as senior airborne adviser.

AIRBORNE ASSAULT ON SAINTE-MÈRE-ÉGLISE.   This still from the movie *The Longest Day* dramatically depicts the night parachute drop of 5 June.

ARCHIVE PHOTOS, NEW YORK

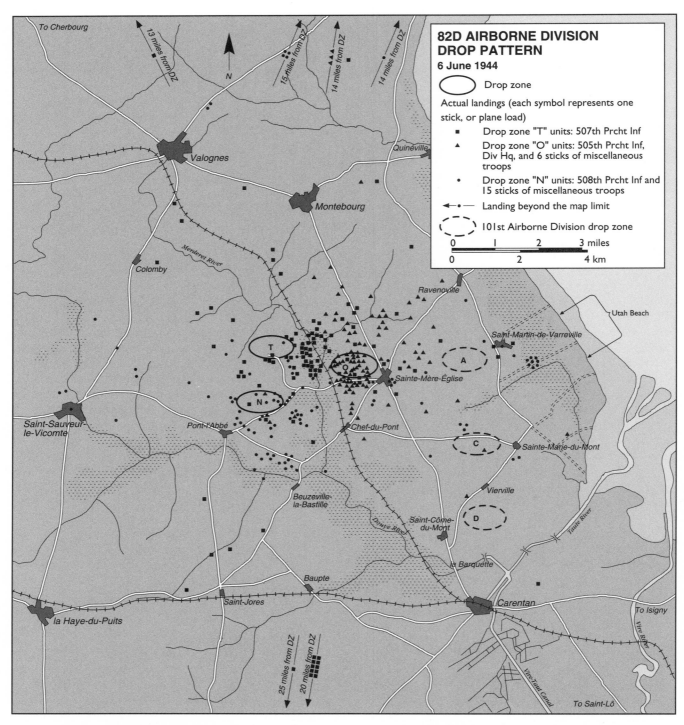

82D AIRBORNE DIVISION DROP PATTERN

6 June 1944

- ⬭ Drop zone

Actual landings (each symbol represents one stick, or plane load)

- ■ Drop zone "T" units: 507th Prcht Inf
- ▲ Drop zone "O" units: 505th Prcht Inf, Div Hq, and 6 sticks of miscellaneous troops
- • Drop zone "N" units: 508th Prcht Inf and 15 sticks of miscellaneous troops
- ←•— Landing beyond the map limit
- ⬭ (dashed) 101st Airborne Division drop zone

Upon reaching Great Britain, the 82d was stationed in the Leicester area, approximately 120 kilometers (seventy-five miles) northwest of London, and was soon heavily involved in an extensive training program preparing for its D-day mission. New replacements and the inexperienced 507th and 508th were forged into a team, benefiting from the 82d's combat experience. This team includ-ed the 52 Troop Carrier Wing of the Army Air Corps, which was paired with the 82d and would carry it to its drop zones in Normandy.

On 26 May 1944 the division's mission was changed from landing in the vicinity of Saint-Sauveur-le-Vicomte to the general area including Neuville-au-Plain, Sainte-Mère-Église, Chef-du-Pont, Étienneville, and Amfreville.

The division would land astride the Merderet River and seize, clear, and hold its area of operation. After destroying all crossings over the Douve River, the 82d was to be prepared to move west on order.

For the invasion, the division was organized into three echelon elements. Force A, the parachute assault element, had a total strength of 6,396 paratroopers. Force B, coming by glider, would have a strength of 3,871 glidermen. Finally the seaborne element, Force C, would depart England at 0645 with 1,712 soldiers. The 82d's strength for the invasion would be 11,979 men, including organic and attached troops.

Twenty-four hours prior to D-day the paratroopers of Force A were restricted to their seven assigned airfields in the Grantham-Cottesmore-Langar area, while the glidermen were held in the Aldermaston-Ramsberry-Merryfield area. Because of poor weather, the mission was postponed twenty-four hours. The first planes of Force A took off at 2315 on 5 June 1944, preceded by three regimental pathfinder teams who would land thirty minutes ahead of the main force to mark the drop zone.

Dropping down from 500 meters to 160 meters for the flight over the English Channel, the flight proceeded as planned. The route over England and the Channel was marked by lights and radio beacons. The C-47 aircraft crossed the Channel west of the invasion fleet, passing near the Channel Islands before turning east to make the final approach over the Cotentin Peninsula to the assigned drop zones. All was well until the aircraft encountered a dense cloud bank as they cleared the coastline. Fearing a collision, most of the aircraft took evasive action. After passing through the clouds, many pilots found they were off course and in many cases lost. Sporadic German antiaircraft fire added to the confusion, claiming several C-47s. Many of the aircraft were flying too fast and some too low, often giving the green-light jump signal over the wrong drop zones. Of the 6,396 paratroopers of the 82d who jumped, 272 or 4.24 percent were killed or injured as a result of the drop. The 505th generally landed in the vicinity of its drop zone, but the 507th and 508th were both widely scattered.

In spite of this, the 82d adapted to the situation and achieved all its primary objectives. The village of Sainte-Mère-Église was secured by dawn of 6 June, the first French village to be liberated. As an antiairborne effort, the Germans had flooded much of the adjoining area near the Merderet River. Nevertheless, by nightfall of 6 June approximately 30 percent of the division forces were under control, holding a line along the Merderet River from La Fière south to include the eastern end of the causeway over the river.

Throughout D plus 1, 7 June, the division continued to assemble, reorganize, and secure the area against severe German resistance. The German *91st Air Landing Division*

82d Airborne Division
Maj. Gen. Matthew B. Ridgway

Headquarters and Headquarters Company,
  82d Airborne Division
Headquarters and Headquarters Battery,
  82d Airborne Division Artillery
505th Parachute Infantry Regiment
507th Parachute Infantry Regiment
  Attached to division 14 Jan 1944
508th Parachute Infantry Regiment
  Attached to division 14 Jan 1944
325th Glider Infantry Regiment
456th Parachute Field Artillery Battalion
319th Glider Field Artillery Battalion
320th Glider Field Artillery Battalion
80th Antiaircraft Artillery Battalion (antitank)
307th Airborne Engineer Battalion
  (Companies A and B)

Also attached to the division were 307th Airborne Medical Company, 782d Airborne Ordnance Maintenance Company, 407th Airborne Quartermaster Company, 82d Signal Company, 82d Military Police and 82d Reconnaissance platoons, in addition to other units attached for the campaign.

was held west of the Merderet River and driven back in the north and northwest. Contact was made with elements of the U.S. 4th Infantry Division, which had met very light resistance landing on Utah Beach. The 325th Glider Infantry arrived by glider early in the morning to reinforce the division.

The 82d continued its attacks to the north, and along its southern flank to establish contact with the 101st Airborne Division. During the night of 7–8 June, it became evident to Ridgway that there were three isolated groups west of the Merderet River: a strong force from 2d Battalion, 508th, held high ground south of Gueutteville; elements of 2d Battalion, 507th, were north of Flaux; and about 425 troopers, mostly from the 507th, were west of

Amfreville. By D plus 3 the division gained a major bridgehead over the Merderet River and relieved two of the isolated groups and much of the third. Meanwhile the 82d's seaborne echelon, Force C, arrived in the division area.

On D plus 4 the U.S. 90th Infantry Division crossed the Merderet bridgehead and passed through the 82d to continue the attack to the west. Despite the scattered parachute drops and isolated groups, within four days the 82d had secured the Neuville-au-Plain–Sainte-Mère-Église–Chef-du-Pont area and established a firm bridgehead over the Merderet River. In the course of the fighting, the 82d had virtually destroyed the *91st Air Landing Division*.

Relieved at the Merderet bridgehead, the division continued to attack in the north against the *243d Division* on D plus 5, 6, and 7, frustrating German efforts to contain the assault from Utah Beach. On D plus 8 the 82d attacked alongside the U.S. 9th Infantry Division west toward Saint-Sauveur-le-Vicomte, through thick hedgerow country; considerable progress was made. Throughout D plus 9 and 10 the 82d continued its attack westward, protecting VII Corp's southern flank. Overcoming the *77th Division*, it established a firm bridgehead around Saint-Sauveur-le-Vicomte. Aware that the German forces west of the Douve River were in complete confusion, Ridgway ordered a battalion of the 505th to cross and establish a secure bridgehead for further operations. In three days of fierce hedgerow fighting, the 82d pushed steadily westward and made it possible for the 9th Infantry Division to pass through the Saint-Sauveur-le-Vicomte bridgehead on D plus 11 and 12 and drive to the sea, cutting off the Cotentin Peninsula.

The 82d Airborne Division continued to fight on the peninsula until relieved on D plus 32, 8 July 1944. Assembled in the U.S. First Army reserve until 11 July, the division moved to Utah Beach in preparation for its return to England.

In the 82d's after-action report for the Normandy campaign, General Ridgway summed up the division's outstanding performance: "33 days of action without relief, without replacements. Every mission accomplished. No ground gained ever relinquished."

Casualties of the 82d Airborne Division during the Normandy Campaign

Killed in action/ died of wounds	1,142	9.70%
Wounded in action	2,373	20.16%
Missing in action/missing	840	7.13%
Evacuated sick	377	3.20%
Evacuated injured	704	5.98%
Total casualties	5,436	46.18%
Committed strength	11,770*	

*Figure reflects soldiers organic to the 82d Airborne Division

[*See also* Airborne Forces; Gavin, James; Ridgway, Matthew B.]

BIBLIOGRAPHY

Crookenden, Napier. *Dropzone Normandy.* 1976.
Devlin, Gerard M. *Paratrooper!* 1979.
82d Airborne Division Headquarters. After-action Report. *Action in Normandy, France.* N.d.
Mrozek, Steven J. *The 82d Airborne Division, America's Guard of Honor.* 1987.
Warren, John C. *Airborne Operations in World War Two, European Theater.* U.S.A.F. Historical Study. 1956.

STEVEN J. MROZEK

LXXXVI CORPS. The *LXXXVI Corps* was formed by Commander in Chief West (OB West) headquarters and activated on 19 November 1942. Its home base was Lübeck, and its general headquarters units included the *180th Artillery Command*, the *431st Signal Battalion*, the *486th Supply Unit*, and the *LXXVI Corps Fortress Cadet Troop (Stammtruppe)*.

From December 1942 to June 1944 the *LXXXVI Corps*, as part of the *First Army*, garrisoned the area around Dax in southwestern France. On D-day its commander was Lt. Gen. Hans von Obstfelder, a capable but harsh officer who had commanded the *XXIX Corps* on the Eastern front.

On 16 June, Field Marshals Rommel and Rundstedt appealed to Hitler for reinforcements for the Normandy sector, but the Führer refused to move any of the infantry divisions of the *Fifteenth Army*; he did, however, order Rundstedt to move the headquarters of *LXXXVI Corps* to Normandy. The corps was assigned to Panzer Group West (later the *Fifth Panzer Army*) and ordered to contain the British bridgehead east of the Orne River and to cover the far right flank of the German front in Normandy. It was in position east of the Orne by 21 June. By 1 August it was directing the *346th* and *272d* infantry divisions and the remnants of the *711th Infantry Division*.

The *LXXVI Corps*'s mission was important, but strictly secondary in nature. It succeeded in limiting the British gains east of the Orne, and played a major role in defeating Montgomery's attempted breakout in the Caen sector on 18–19 July. Obstfelder's corps was too far to the northeast to be involved in the Falaise encirclement and, unlike most of the Wehrmacht, retreated in reasonably good order across the Seine with its divisions still intact. After various subsequent battles, the *LXXXVI Corps* surrendered to the British in northwest Germany at the end of the war.

[*See also* Obstfelder, Hans von.]

BIBLIOGRAPHY

McKee, Alexander. *Caen: Anvil of Victory.* 1964.

Tessin, Georg. *Verbände und Truppen der deutschen Wehrmacht und Waffen-SS im Zweiten Weltkrieg, 1939–1945.* Vol. 6, 1979.

SAMUEL W. MITCHAM, JR.

83D COMPOSITE GROUP.

83 Group was formed on 1 April 1943 at Redhill, Surrey, the first of several groups intended to provide tactical air support for the British army during the invasion. Commanded until March 1944 by Air Vice Marshal (AVM) William Dickson and thereafter by AVM Harry Broadhurst, by D-day it had some ten wings (one reconnaissance)—a total of twenty-nine squadrons, including fifteen Canadian and one Australian. Of these, thirteen operated the Spitfire, six the longer-range Mustang, and ten the Typhoon, whose armament of rockets, bombs, and cannons made it a highly effective ground-attack aircraft. There were also five air observation squadrons flying Austers.

Before the invasion, as well as practicing working with the army, this formidable force had carried out intensive fighter sweeps, attacks on V-1 construction sites, and reconnaissance. On D-day the Typhoons attacked just ahead of the main landings. By that first evening the Group Control Centre, previously at Uxbridge, was ashore and operating in Normandy; soon afterward the headquarters was established at Creully and some of its squadrons were flying from French soil, their initial tasks to prevent air interference, deny the German land forces freedom of movement, and give close support to the Second Army. On 10 June the Typhoons joined aircraft of 2 Group in attacking the German Panzer Group headquarters.

Since no higher RAF formation had yet arrived in Normandy, HQ 83 Group was at this stage controlling all RAF units ashore. Subsequently the group switched to its proper function of cooperating with Second Army, which it continued to support for the rest of the war, its squadrons moving forward closely behind the soldiers.

[*See also* Broadhurst, Harry.]

BIBLIOGRAPHY

Morgan, D. R. *No. 83 Group 1943/45.* 1957.
Wynn, Humphrey, and Susan Young. *Prelude to Overlord.* 1983.

HENRY PROBERT

REARMING A TYPHOON.   Ground crew loading rockets in France, 16 June 1944.

EISENHOWER, DWIGHT D.

EISENHOWER, DWIGHT D. (1890-1969), American, General of the Army; Supreme Commander, Allied Expeditionary Force. The meteoric rise of Dwight David Eisenhower from relative obscurity to the post of Supreme Commander, Allied Expeditionary Force, is among the most dramatic and notable aspects of the D-day saga. Skepticism about Eisenhower's fitness for command had dogged him since his appointment as Commanding General, European Theater of Operations (ETO), in June 1942. After all, this little-known American, nearly fifty-four years of age on D-day, had spent most of his career in training and staff assignments and had not commanded any unit larger than a battalion prior to America's entry into the war. How could such a man successfully direct a multinational force totaling more than 3.5 million combat and service troops, supported by 5,000 ships and an enormous air armada?

Born in Denison, Texas, on 14 October 1890, Dwight D. ("Ike") Eisenhower grew up in Abilene, Kansas. Bored with his job at the local creamery after graduation from high school, he went against the family's pacifist leanings and obtained a senatorial appointment to the United States Military Academy.

At West Point, Eisenhower distinguished himself chiefly as a promising football player, as a cheerleader and junior varsity coach, and for the number of personal conduct demerits he accumulated. But his academic record was solid: he ranked 65th of 170 graduates in the class of 1915.

Eisenhower spent World War I training troops for the Tank Corps and thus missed going to France. Promoted to major in 1920, in the peacetime army he remained at that rank for sixteen years. Nevertheless, the army still offered preferment to officers with persistence, intelligence, highly developed political skills, and a capacity to get along with peers and superiors—qualities with which Eisenhower was especially endowed. By the late 1920s he was marked as one of the most promising of the younger generation. Becoming a protégé of Gen. Fox Conner, who was an intimate of John J. Pershing and George C. Marshall, and helped by friends such as Leonard T. Gerow and George S. Patton, Jr., he graduated first in his class at the Command and General Staff School at Fort Leavenworth in 1925–1926. Early selection for the Army War College and a tour in the office of the assistant secretary of war led to seven years of service with another influential senior officer, Gen. Douglas MacArthur—first in the office of the chief of staff and then as MacArthur's deputy in the Philippines. In these posts Eisenhower acquired insights into the U.S. government's workings, the aplomb of a diplomat, and facility at dealing with easily ruffled egos. He was not tainted by the years with MacArthur, who had challenged Pershing and blocked Marshall's advancement.

Following Eisenhower's return to the United States in

EISENHOWER AND CHURCHILL.   Inspecting a special display of airborne equipment and supplies during a visit to an airborne division in England in March 1944.

December 1939, he spent an enjoyable and rewarding period as an infantry battalion commander in the 3d Division. During the army's expansion he served as chief of staff of the 3d Division and then of IX Corps. Outstanding ratings brought promotion to colonel in March 1941 and a posting as chief of staff of the Third Army. Eisenhower's meticulous planning of the Blue Force counterattack in the Louisiana maneuvers of 1941 earned him a first star and confirmed his standing among those to hold principal field commands, should America enter World War II.

Recalled to Washington just after Pearl Harbor, Eisenhower was assigned to the War Plans Division, War Department General Staff. As deputy chief of WPD, he worked closely with Chief of Staff Gen. George C. Marshall. Though they were never friends, in his frosty way Marshall demonstrated high regard by giving Eisenhower ever more responsibility. In early 1942 Eisenhower was promoted to major general and named to head the newly reorganized War Department command post, the Operations Division. This demanding job gave him an appreciation of the complexities of interservice rivalries and of organizing a modern military coalition. Eisenhower's unique breadth of experience made him Marshall's logical selection to replace Gen. James E. Chaney as the principal U.S. military representative to oversee BOLERO, the massive buildup of Allied forces in Britain.

In the spring of 1942 the Combined Chiefs of Staff (CCS) divided the world into several spheres of operation, subsequently termed "theaters" by Marshall. They ruled that the Pacific chain of command should go via the U.S. chiefs of staff, and that the chain of command in Southeast Asia and the Middle East should go through the British chiefs of staff. Only in Europe would the CCS claim a direct link to the theater commander. That common-sense principle was applied almost without exception for the duration of the war and greatly affected preparations for D-day.

This changed environment soon affected the American military representation in London. Though it was supposed to become American Expeditionary Force headquarters in Britain, the U.S. mission remained essentially General Chaney and a dozen or so officers, saddled with murky instructions and dependent upon the British for basic needs. Looking to create a unified headquarters, Marshall asked Eisenhower to draft the directive governing the future European Theater of Operations (ETO). A few weeks later, in June 1942, Eisenhower replaced Chaney and was designated as Commanding General, U.S. Army European Theater of Operations. With only modest modifications, the scheme of organization he had set down was to govern Allied command relationships in the North African, Mediterranean, and European theaters.

Historian Alfred D. Chandler later noted that Ike's responsibilities, embracing both Allied and combined forces, were the most convoluted and challenging of any field commander on either side in World War II. To keep air, naval, and army leaders representing several nations working effectively in harness demanded a high order of flexibility and willingness to innovate. Such questions as to whom did an individual seconded to a multinational command owe primary allegiance had to be confronted. The cooperative spirit manifested in AFHQ (Eisenhower's Allied Forces headquarters in North Africa) and to a lesser degree in MTO (Mediterranean Theater of Operations) and SHAEF (Supreme Headquarters Allied Expeditionary Force) stands as testimony to the strength of coalition loyalties. Still, combined command troubled Anglo-American relations throughout the war.

Eisenhower undertook the task of overseeing BOLERO, the buildup in Britain, and planning ROUNDUP, the invasion of northwest Europe being projected for 1943, fully assuming that Marshall would claim command of the Allied expeditionary forces and that he would likely return to Washington to become chief of staff. This scenario did not materialize because of the decision to launch TORCH, the Anglo-American invasion of North Africa in

the fall of 1942, and because of President Franklin D. Roosevelt's reluctance to lose Marshall's counsel in administering the American war effort. Ike, the stand-in, thus took center stage.

The diplomatic and military skills shown during his first months in London ensured that Eisenhower would command TORCH, the first major combined Allied operation of World War II. TORCH was also Eisenhower's first field command, and it proved a painful initiation. Conflicts between Vichy and Free French factions, and adverse political reaction in Washington and London, often overshadowed military operations. The U.S. Army's defects in training and inexperience led to a shocking defeat at Kasserine Pass in Tunisia in February 1943. Slow progress led Eisenhower to replace the II Corps commander, Maj. Gen. Lloyd R. Fredendall, with Eisenhower's friend George S. Patton, Jr., whom he could trust to lead from the front and to extract maximum effort from green troops. Eisenhower was then able to concentrate on building an efficient multinational staff at Allied Forces Headquarters in Algiers.

Postponement of the invasion of northwest Europe (now designated OVERLORD) until 1944 placed Eisenhower in command of the Mediterranean Theater of Operations. Willingness to delegate operational authority and to make ability and political necessity the chief criteria for command were hallmarks of Eisenhower's command style. Certainly, coordinating the invasions of Sicily and Italy, both of which produced serious disputes within the coalition, demanded Eisenhower's primary attention. From the British perspective, the division of responsibilities that evolved in 1943—with Eisenhower focusing on political issues and inter-Allied relations, while deputies (mostly British) took charge of military operations—was a necessary corrective to Ike's inadequacies as a battlefield commander. This arrangement continued through the Normandy invasion and the entire D plus 90 period. It left unanswered whether Ike could harness such disparate personalities as Patton and British general Bernard L. Montgomery.

Eisenhower's appointment to command of OVERLORD resulted from political calculation and chiefly reflected his value as a symbol of Anglo-American amity. When a U.S. proposal to have an overall commander for all of Europe was rejected by the British in late November 1943, and a compromise named an American to head OVERLORD, Eisenhower's stock soared. At Teheran in late 1943, the Soviets for the first time insisted that the OVERLORD timetable be honored. As proof of London and Washington's commitment to OVERLORD, Stalin demanded to be told who was to command the operation. That forced a wavering Roosevelt, strongly lobbied by Eisenhower's admirer, Winston Churchill, to decide. From Cairo he cabled Marshall that he had announced Eisenhower's appointment as Supreme Commander of the

DWIGHT D. EISENHOWER.   Center, observing armored maneuvers in England with Arthur Tedder (left) and Bernard L. Montgomery (right).

COURTESY DWIGHT D. EISENHOWER LIBRARY / U.S. ARMY

Allied Expeditionary Force. Disappointed but resigned, Marshall forwarded the message to Eisenhower on 7 December. It reached him after he had flown to Tunis to attend the president and had been stunned by FDR's greeting: "Well, Ike, you are going to command OVERLORD."

Though Eisenhower did not reach London until 16 January 1944, he immediately asserted control over all aspects of the forthcoming operation. Indeed, a letter to Marshall on 17 December 1943 set forth his agenda for success. The staff organization should emulate the arrangements effected in AFHQ and employ many of the same individuals: Air Marshal Arthur Tedder to oversee tactical air forces, West Point classmate Gen. Omar Bradley to command the U.S. First Army, and Patton to command the U.S. Third Army. He pressed for a single commander of ground forces during the invasion's critical first phase and desired that this individual (preferably Gen. Harold Alexander) be British.

The top echelon of the SHAEF staff—eventually totaling 16,000 persons sprawled across London and its environs—included most of Eisenhower's choices, though Montgomery was named assault phase commander and Air Marshal Trafford Leigh-Mallory, rather than Tedder, took charge of air operations. Pivotal was the appointment of Ike's longtime associate, Gen. Walter Bedell Smith, as chief of staff. SHAEF embodied Eisenhower's view of his func-tion as that of "chairman of the board." His management style, while sometimes producing ambiguity and mixed signals (such as occurred over the mission of the British and Canadian forces under Montgomery in the D plus 30 phase), raised morale and stimulated individual initiative among subordinates.

Eisenhower bore the ultimate responsibility for four key decisions affecting D-day operations. First was the choice between the Oil Plan and the Transportation Plan. Advocates of strategic bombing argued that any diversion from the air campaign against Germany would only post-pone victory. Ike, who viewed control over all air assets in the ETO as among his command prerogatives, pressed for use of heavy bombers to interdict German supply lines by pounding transportation targets. He won and the bombers played an important role in limiting the Wehrmacht's access to Normandy.

Second, Ike faced contrasting choices with regard to the location and makeup of the invasion. British planners urged a three-division assault in Normandy, where German defenses were weakest. Americans pushed for a broad-front, cross-Channel attack into the teeth of the German defens-es in the Pas de Calais. Eisenhower compromised. Opting for Normandy, he insisted on enlarging the assault phase of the operation to include five divisions landing along an extended front. This decision, reflecting Ike's innate cau-tion, strained Allied logistical capacity and gave greater importance to variables beyond SHAEF's control: the suc-cess of FORTITUDE, the Allied deception plan; the provi-sion of sufficient landing craft; and cooperation with French partisan groups and the Free French leader, Charles de Gaulle. Ike's cautious approach was justified by the total surprise achieved and the lessened casualties resulting, though some have argued that the logistical difficulties associated with the Normandy site delayed the Allied break-out and gave German forces an opportunity to regroup.

Eisenhower's third decision, dictated by the choice of Normandy, was to add U.S. paratroop divisions to the mix of invasion forces, so as to seize the beachhead approaches. Opponents argued that dropping light forces behind enemy lines would lead to a wholesale slaughter. Ike revealed how agonizing this decision had been by visiting the 101st Airborne Division as its men climbed aboard their planes and took off into the night.

Finally, Ike's most fateful decision of all was the "go" order for 6 June 1944. Bad weather in the Channel had led to one postponement. Another would compel a two-week delay and possibly rule out an invasion for several months. Would conditions make possible pivotal air operations and the deposit of 130,000 troops and their equipment on the far shore? Conscious that any military operation was a gamble, he accepted the risks and early on 5 June committed to D-day. Notably, he also scrawled a press release—accepting total responsibility for what had occurred—to be used if the invasion failed. Then, like all those who send men into battle, Ike waited.

The period of D-day to D plus 12, which saw the Normandy beachhead secured, both justified those decisions and offered unsettling glimpses of the difficulties that would attend the Allied effort to break out from Normandy. Eisenhower acted in those areas he found most congenial. Leaving operational decisions largely to subordinates, he dealt with the supply crisis and worked to smooth relations between SHAEF, the CCS, and the highest political authorities. Above all, he performed the role of cheerleader and public relations coordinator. Today an appreciation of how difficult it is to organize and sustain military coalitions, even successful ones, reaffirms the consensual judgment that Ike's effectiveness as coalition manager contributed significantly to the Allied triumph on D-day.

[See also Supreme Headquarters Allied Expeditionary Force (SHAEF).]

BIBLIOGRAPHY

Ambrose, Stephen E. *Eisenhower.* 1983.
Chandler, Alfred D., ed. *The Papers of Dwight D. Eisenhower.* Vol. 3, *The War Years.* 1970.
D'Este, Carlo. *Decision in Normandy.* 1983.
Eisenhower, David. *Eisenhower: At War, 1943–1945.* 1986.
Hamilton, Nigel, *Master of the Battlefield: Monty's War Years, 1942–1944.* 1983.
Pogue, Forrest. *The Supreme Command.* U.S. Army in World War II: The European Theater of Operations. 1954.

THEODORE A. WILSON

ELECTRONIC WARFARE. As part of the German West Wall defenses, no fewer than ninety-two radar sites had been erected along the north coasts of France and Belgium, positioned to give warning of the approach of Allied ships or aircraft. The sites were equipped with a menagerie of German ground radars: *Mammut, Wassermann,* and *Freya* early warning radars; *Seetakt* coast-watching radars; the *Giant Würzburg* for the control of night fighters; and the regular *Würzburg* to direct antiaircraft fire.

If the Allies were to achieve surprise, it was vitally important to knock out a large part of that network. During the softening-up operations the radar chain came under sustained attack, but for purposes of deception there were raids on three sites outside the area for each one attacked in Normandy.

The success of attacks depended on locating the radars accurately. A special ground direction-finding equipment, code-named Ping Pong, that could measure the bearing of a radar transmitter to a quarter of a degree, assisted in this. Three mobile Ping Pongs set up along the south coast of England took simultaneous bearings on individual radars along the north coast of France. The bearings were triangulated to find the radar's approximate position, and its exact location was confirmed by photographic reconnaissance.

Mosquitos, Spitfires, and Typhoons of the RAF Second Tactical Air Force flew more than two thousand sorties against the radar sites, using rockets and cannon. The cost was high, for many of the targets were well defended. By the evening of D plus 1 all but sixteen of the original ninety-two radar sites along the northern coasts of France and Belgium had been attacked. Most of the radars were put out of action, and in the invasion area proper no German radar remained fully operational.

As the invasion fleet headed for Normandy, two "ghost fleets" headed toward Le Havre and Boulogne. These "fleets" comprised no full-sized ships; the illusion was created by aircraft flying carefully planned patterns and releasing large quantities of chaff (aluminum foil) code-named Window. Operation TAXABLE, simulating an invasion force approaching Le Havre, was flown by eight Lancaster bombers of No. 617 Squadron RAF. The aircraft flew two waves with 3 kilometers (2 mi.) between aircraft in each wave and 13 kilometers (8 mi.) between each wave of four. Navigating alone in the darkness but maintaining formation with the others, each aircraft flew a series of oblongs 13 kilometers long and 3 kilometers wide. The aircraft released one bundle of chaff every five seconds, to produce a vast field of fluttering foil measuring 25 by 22 kilometers (16 by 14 mi.). At the end of each seven-minute orbit the aircraft edged 1.5 kilometers closer to the coast. Thus the vast radar reflector advanced toward France at 14 kilometers per hour (7.5 knots)—a realistic speed for an invasion fleet.

As this was happening another ghost fleet, Operation GLIMMER, headed for Boulogne. This illusion was created by six Stirling bombers of No. 218 Squadron RAF flying similar patterns and dropping chaff.

To add realism to these deceptions, other aircraft flew near the chaff-droppers, radiating noise-jamming on the German radar frequencies. But the positions of these aircraft were chosen so that radars watching the area would see the ghost fleet through the jamming.

The ghost fleets were but part of the huge electronic countermeasures operation mounted that night. Simultaneously, twenty-nine Stirling and Halifax bombers of Nos. 90, 138, 149, and 161 squadrons RAF staged fake airborne invasions—Operation TITANIC—in the Caen and Cap d'Antifer areas. These bombers also released large quantities of chaff, to increase the apparent size of the force as seen on German radar. Over the "dropping zones" the planes released dummy paratroops fitted with special fireworks, which exploded to give off the crackles and bangs of a ground battle in progress. To add further realism, the bombers dropped contingents of British Special Air Service men with orders to "make a lot of noise" when they reached the ground.

To prevent German night fighters from reaching the real dropping zones, twenty-nine Lancasters and Flying Fortresses of Nos. 101 and 214 squadrons RAF flew a communications jamming screen over eastern France. The aim was to ensure that German night fighters west of the screen received no assistance from their ground controllers in eastern France. These aircraft also released large quantities of chaff. The deception was successful. German night fighters arrived in the area to find the jamming on their communications channels so severe that they could receive no further instructions. They wandered around the chaff clouds looking for targets until shortage of fuel forced them to return to base. One Allied bomber was shot down but its crew survived. Meanwhile the armada of more than a thousand transport aircraft and gliders, laden with paratroops and equipment, delivered their loads and returned to England without the loss of a single plane to night-fighter attack.

More than two hundred warships and landing craft in the main invasion force carried radar-jamming transmitters. A powerhouse of jamming shimmered across the screen of the German radars that had survived the air attacks of the previous weeks. Only one radar observed the approach of the real invasion fleet, but such was the general chaos that night, its warning went unheeded.

The first report on the approach of the invasion fleet to be believed came from observation posts on the eastern side of the Cotentin Peninsula, where the unconcealable rumble of several hundred ships' engines could clearly be heard. No conceivable electronic countermeasures effort could have delayed German discovery of the invasion more than that.

From German records it is clear that the GLIMMER ghost fleet was reported by radar stations near Boulogne and an anti-invasion alert declared. Not until after daybreak on D-day, following a search of the area by reconnaissance planes and patrol boats, was the threat to Boulogne dismissed.

By extending the area of confusion and delaying an accurate appreciation of Allied movements and intentions, the electronic countermeasure operations materially assisted the landings and held down casualties. For the student of military history, the D-day deception operations provide an object lesson on what can be achieved if a carefully planned program of countermeasures is used to support a one-of-a-kind operation of the highest importance.

[*See also* Deception.]

BIBLIOGRAPHY

Jones, R. V. *Most Secret War.* 1978.
Price, Alfred. *The History of U.S. Electronic Warfare.* Vol. 1, 1984.
Price, Alfred. *Instruments of Darkness.* 1967.

ALFRED PRICE

11TH ARMOURED DIVISION. Widely considered one of the best British armored divisions of World War II, the 11th Armoured was originally formed in March 1941 in England by Maj. Gen. Percy C. S. Hobart, an outstanding trainer of armored forces. (It was he who designed the division's sign—a charging black bull on a yellow background.) Hobart left the division in October 1942 to command the 79th Armoured Division, which was to control all specialized armor used in northwestern Europe, handing the 11th over to Maj. Gen. Brocas Burrows. He in turn was replaced by Maj. Gen. G. P. B. ("Pip") Roberts at the end of 1943. Roberts led the division from then until the end of the war in Europe.

The 11th Armoured Division was based in the north of England and was to form part of the X Corps for

11th Armoured Division
Maj. Gen. G. P. B. Roberts

29th Armoured Division

23d Hussars
2d Fife and Forfar Yeomanry
3d Royal Tank Regiment
8th Battalion, The Rifle Brigade

159th Infantry Brigade

3d Battalion, The Monmouthshire Regiment
4th Battalion, The King's Shropshire Light Infantry
1st Battalion, The Herefordshire Regiment

Divisional Troops

2d Northamptonshire Yeomanry
13th Regiment, RHA
151st Field Regiment, RA
75th Anti-Tank Regiment, RA
58th Light Anti-Aircraft Regiment, RA
11th Armoured Divisional Engineers
11th Armoured Divisional Signals

OVERLORD, the Normandy invasion. As such it was part of the follow-up force behind the initial landings. In April 1944 the whole of the X Corps was moved down to the south of England, with the 11th Armoured Division being quartered at Aldershot, the traditional home of the British army, on the Surrey-Hampshire border. Here it carried out its final preparations.

The tank battalions were equipped with the Sherman tank, and the reconnaissance battalion with the Cromwell tank. The lorried infantry battalions were carried in trucks and also had eight 6-pounder antitank guns, eight medium machine guns, and six 3-inch mortars; the motor battalion was equipped with Bren gun carriers and halftracks. The Royal Horse Artillery Regiment had twenty-four self-propelled 25-pounder gun/howitzers, and the Field Regiment had the same number of towed 25-pounders. The Anti-Tank Regiment possessed forty-eight 17-pounder anti-tank guns, and the Light Anti-Aircraft Regiment fifty-four 40-mm Bofors antiaircraft guns. The total strength of the division was some fifteen thousand men and 306 tanks.

All the armored regiments and infantry battalions were from the Territorial Army and had spent the war training in England. The one exception was the 3d Royal Tank Regiment, part of the prewar Regular Army. It had already fought in France in 1940, where it distinguished itself in the defense of Calais, and throughout the campaign in North Africa. All regiments did, however, have a leavening of officers and noncommissioned officers who had seen some active service.

The division began to land in France on D plus 4 and was initially concentrated in the area of Creuilly, three kilometers (two miles) inland from Gold and Sword beaches. Its first action did not come until 26 June, when it took part in Operation EPSOM, Montgomery's plan to force crossings over the Odon and Orne rivers, and captured the vital Hill 112. Three weeks later it was the leading assault division in Operation GOODWOOD, the major thrust east of Caen, where it suffered 735 personnel casualties and the loss of 191 tanks in two days' fighting. The 11th Armoured Division was then switched to the extreme right flank of the 21st Army Group. Here it played a leading role in Operation BLUECOAT, designed to prevent the German armor's interfering with the American breakout from Saint-Lô. Acting as the flank guard, it quickly broke through the German defenses and could have gone on to capture the important communications center at Vire if this had not been in the U.S. 12th Army Group's sector.

Crossing the Seine on 28 August, the 11th Armoured Division took part in the dramatic thrust into Belgium, capturing Amiens and Antwerp in just one week. It then fought on the Maas and, reequipped with Comet tanks, crossed the Rhine and finished the war at Lübeck. During this last phase it liberated the concentration camp at Belsen. Disbanded shortly after the end of the war, the 11th Armoured Division re-formed in Germany in 1951 only to be disbanded finally six years later.

[See also Roberts, G. P. B.]

BIBLIOGRAPHY

A Short History of 11th Armoured Division. 1945.
Roberts, G. P. B. From the Desert to the Baltic. 1987.

CHARLES MESSENGER

EMBRY, BASIL (1902–1977), British, air vice marshal, air officer commanding 2d Composite Group. Basil Embry joined the Royal Air Force (RAF) in 1921, flew operationally in Iraq, served as an instructor at the Central Flying School, and spent several years on the Air Staff in India. During the early months of World War II he commanded 107 Squadron, equipped with Blenheim bombers, in 2 Group. After leading his squadron on many operations over Germany and Norway and then in the early weeks of the Battle of France, he was shot down while attacking German columns near Dunkirk on 27 May 1940. Although quickly taken prisoner, he managed to escape through France and Spain and was back in England two months later.

With a reputation for courage and intrepid leadership, he spent 1941 and 1942 commanding and directing night fighter operations before being appointed commander of 2 Group on 27 May 1943. Recognizing the need for his

BASIL EMBRY.   IMPERIAL WAR MUSEUM

medium bomber force to have its own distinctive role, he determined to train his squadrons to operate as well by night as by day, and to find and hit precision targets with great accuracy. Convinced that the only way to lead was by example, he often flew on operations himself, to the consternation of some of his superiors. By D-day he had made his group capable of undertaking the most dangerous and specialized missions. Consequently, when he attended the final preparatory conference of the Allied commanders at St. Paul's School on 15 May, he was confident that his squadrons could do whatever was asked of them.

The fruits of his work were amply demonstrated in the final weeks before and during the invasion, for he not only planned and directed the operations but also took part himself. He wanted to be in on the action, because he felt that he could command effectively only if he could speak from up-to-date experience. Throughout the campaign he led from the front, and went on doing so until the end of the war, flying for example on the famous raid against the Gestapo headquarters in Copenhagen in March 1945.

For such a man the constraints of high command in peacetime were bound to be irksome. As he moved through the posts of director general of Training and commander in chief of Fighter Command to that of commander in chief Allied Air Forces in Central Europe in the mid-1950s, he became increasingly outspoken in his criticisms of the defense structure. His RAF career thus ended a little early, in 1955, whereupon he turned much of his attention to the RAF Escaping Society, formed under his chairmanship primarily to assist the dependents of the many brave men and women of France and elsewhere who had lost their lives during the war helping airmen escape. This self-imposed task was totally in character for a man whose name, as Air Chief Marshal Sir Ralph Cochrane, one of his closest colleagues, wrote, would always be linked with the fighting traditions of the Royal Air Force.

[*See also* 2d Composite Group.]

BIBLIOGRAPHY

Bowyer, Michael J. F. *2 Group RAF–A Complete History*. 1974.
Embry, Basil. *Mission Completed*. 1957.

HENRY PROBERT

ENGINEERS. [*This entry includes three separate articles:*
American Engineers
British Engineers
German Engineers.]

AMERICAN ENGINEERS.   Laying out roads on soft sand for heavy vehicles, 6 June 1944.   COURTESY OF BARRY W. FOWLE

U.S. NAVAL DEMOLITIONS PERSONNEL.   Disarming German Goliaths, also known as Beetles, on Utah Beach, 11 June 1944. These miniature tanks carried 150 pounds of high explosives; they were steered and detonated by remote control.

NATIONAL ARCHIVES

American Engineers

The general plan for the engineers in Operation OVER-LORD called for the progressive development of the Omaha beachhead in three phases: the assault phase, the initial dump phase, and the beach maintenance dump phase. The first two phases would take place on D-day. During the assault phase, special engineer assault gapping teams would come ashore with the infantry and open fifty-yard-wide gaps in the barbed wire and obstacles lining the shore. Support teams would follow to widen the gaps, and command teams with additional demolitions would supervise and assist where needed. Once these engineer teams cleared the beach, they would be followed by engineer battalion beach groups to establish initial dumps of ammunition and fuel, clear the exits, and develop roads for the supported infantry units.

The Provisional Engineer Special Brigade Group, consisting of the 5th and 6th Special Brigades, provided landing support on Omaha Beach. On D-day it landed 34,250 men and 2,870 vehicles belonging to V Corps. Of these,

5,632 were engineers from the Provisional Engineer Special Brigade Group, with 315 vehicles. Approximately 2,500 other engineers also landed, members of corps and divisional units. Engineers made up approximately 25 percent of all the troops that landed on Omaha on D-day.

Omaha Beach was a 7,000-yard ribbon of sand with up to 200 feet exposed at high tide and as much as 400 yards showing at low tide. An eight-foot bank of coarse shingle (gravel) marked the seaward edge of the western part of the beach. The beach was backed with bluffs rising sharply from 100 to 170 feet in height. There were five designated exits leading through natural draws in the bluffs.

Generally, the obstacles on Omaha consisted of two bands, 50 to 75 yards wide, with about the same distance separating them. The outer line of obstacles, about 250 yards out from the high-water line, consisted of Element C, a gatelike structure of reinforced iron frames with iron supports, with a specially adapted waterproofed version of the powerfully lethal antitank Teller mine on the forward face, wooden ramps, and posts topped with Teller mines. The inner band combined wooden posts and ramp-style

MEMORIAL AT OMAHA BEACH TO UNITS OF 6TH ENGINEER SPECIAL BRIGADE. HULTON DEUTSCH

obstacles, antitank ditches, and impassable gravel and sand barred the tanks from moving until Pvt. Vinton Dove, a bulldozer operator from Company C, 37th Engineer Combat Battalion, assisted by his relief operator, Pvt. William J. Shoemaker, cleared a road through the shingle, removed the roadblock at E-1, and filled the antitank ditch, opening a path for the Sherman tanks. For their actions both men were awarded the Distinguished Service Cross.

Most of the 1st Engineer Special Brigade's assault teams on Utah touched down within one or two minutes of their scheduled time but, like the force at Omaha, they missed their intended assault area. They ran into only light opposing fire and few obstacles, and within five to eight minutes blew the first fifty-yard gaps in the barriers. Support teams found little work to do when they arrived a short time later, and by 0800 engineers had cleared the entire beach of enemy obstacles.

The only major difference between the obstacles on the two beaches was the absence of Teller mines at Utah, which allowed bulldozer work to proceed faster. Even so, the assault gapping teams lost 10 percent of naval combat demolition-unit personnel and more than 8 percent of army personnel to enemy fire.

Despite the doubts and fears of the early hours on Omaha, the invasion was successful. That success was in great part attributable to the efforts of the engineers. They contributed to the victory in their dual role as engineers and infantry. Without their effort in destroying obstacles on the beach, clearing mine fields, constructing exit roads off the beach, and fighting in the line as infantrymen, the invading force might not have held the beachhead and established the critical toehold in Nazi-occupied Europe.

[See also Beach and Coastal Defenses; Seabees.]

BIBLIOGRAPHY

Beck, Alfred M. U.S. Army in World War II. The Corps of Engineers: The War against Germany. 1985.
Heavey, William F. Down Ramp: The Story of the Army Amphibian Engineers. 1947.
U.S. Army, Center of Military History. Omaha Beachhead: 6 June–13 June 1944. 1945. Facsimile reprint, 1989.
U.S. Army, Center of Military History. Utah Beach to Cherbourg: 6–27 June 1944. Reprint, 1990.

BARRY W. FOWLE

British Engineers

The importance of engineers in the whole D-day operation may be judged from the fact that a major consideration in the selection of Normandy for the landings was the suitability of exits from the beaches there, and that of the Normandy countryside for the construction of airfields.

As early as December 1943 the engineer planning staff

obstacles backed by three staggered rows of steel hedgehogs (obstacles).

Landing with the 1,450 assault infantry during the first phase of the operation were gap assault teams consisting of 30 engineer officers and 516 enlisted men. Of that total, 11 officers and 115 enlisted men were U.S. Navy demolitions personnel. These assault gapping teams would blow holes in the obstacle lines on the beach. Of the personnel that made the initial landings at 0630 hours on 6 June 1944, engineers represented over one-third.

Similar operations were conducted on Utah Beach, where on the first day of the invasion the 1st Engineer Special Brigade put ashore some 20,000 troops and 1,700 vehicles of the VII Corps's 4th Infantry Division and supporting units.

For the first troops on Omaha, the early hours bordered on disaster. All landed 700 to 2,000 yards to the left of their assigned beaches because of the haze and strong shore currents. Devastating machine-gun fire raked the beaches. The engineers could not destroy many of the obstacles because the infantry took cover behind them and refused to move. All told, the Germans damaged about 60 percent of the equipment and wounded 34 percent of the attacking force.

Slowly, against stiff German opposition, the engineers began opening the exits. At Exit E-1 mines, barbed wire,

ROYAL ENGINEERS WIDENING AND REPAIRING ROADS.   Near Ver-sur-Mer.   IMPERIAL WAR MUSEUM

had doubts about the beaches' capacity to bear the passage of heavy guns and vehicles, particularly in the British and Canadian sectors. Despite the risk to secrecy if detected, a reconnaissance was ordered of a suspect area west of Ver-sur-Mer (Juno Beach). This was successfully carried out on New Year's Eve, when German vigilance would hopefully be relaxed, by Maj. Logan Scott-Bowden and Sgt. Bruce Ogden-Smith, who swam ashore from a small craft that had been towed across the Channel by a motor gunboat. They tested the beach and brought back soil samples that allayed anxieties.

A second reconnaissance was launched from 17 to 21 January when the same team were taken over in a midget submarine to the beach east of Vierville (Omaha Beach). By day, close inshore periscope reconnaissance revealed intense construction work on defenses. On two separate nights the soldiers swam ashore, evading alert sentries, to check the beach's bearing capacity, which was found to be generally sound.

The considerable allocation of engineer units to the assault divisions for D-day was as follows:

6 assault squadrons, one to each of the 6 initial landing brigades, amounting to 150 armored vehicles

9 field companies to work on beach maintenance

Standard field companies in each brigade, supported by divisional field park companies

2 field companies and a field park company to start work on Mulberry harbor

Corps and army units including armored bulldozers, allocated for special task such as bomb disposal, water supply, dumps of engineer stores, and the construction of an emergency landing strip for aircraft, completed by the evening of D-day

Field companies and assault squadrons contained about 250 men; field park companies rather less, but with more heavy equipment, bulldozers, etc. Each assault squadron manned twenty-six heavy Churchill tanks, reduced to twenty after D-day.

As in any major assault operation, the main engineer task was to open up routes for Allied troops through what had been German-occupied territory. It was to do this task on the beaches that the assault engineers were

GERMAN MINE FIELD.   HULTON DEUTSCH

created, because the problems there were different from normal land battlefields. Once the assault brigades moved inland, they faced the usual jobs, such as replacing demolished bridges and culverts and improving roads and tracks.

Because the need to open up routes inland was so critical, engineers landed early and came under fire from enemy defenses that had not yet been silenced. Inevitably, they took considerable casualties; after the landings all assault squadrons were forced to reorganize down from four troops to three.

The laying and lifting of mines was another important task. The standard German mine, well known to Allied forces from the North African campaign, was the Teller mine, a circular device about 30 centimeters (12 in.) across. As the invading forces approached the Normandy coast, Teller mines were plainly visible attached to metal stakes in the water, obviously designed to damage landing craft. Once landings had taken place, assault engineers removed some of these, but the main bulk were cleared by the beach group engineers who followed.

Extensive mine fields were located all along the front just inland from the beaches. These were marked with signs "Achtung, Minen" on their inland boundaries. Most contained Teller mines, but there were two surprises. First, some mines had special fuzes that detonated the explosive only after a second weight had come onto them.

This defeated the British Flail tanks, because the rotating flail formed only the first weight and its tracks formed the second, which detonated the mine. The second surprise was the new bar mine, a metal box about a meter (40 in.) in length able to cover a wider frontage than the Teller mine. A new danger in this was a booby-trap mechanism detonating the mine if an attempt was made to defuse it.

No description of the work of engineers in warfare is complete without reference to bridging. In World War II the invention of the Bailey Bridge had transformed this task by reducing the size of its parts to easily transportable panels. On D-day the first stocks of Bailey Bridge were landed against the likely eventuality that demolished bridges would be encountered. An example of its early use was at Graye-sur-Mer (Juno Beach), where an improvised bridge over a tank stuck in a large crater and blocking the main exit was replaced by a Bailey Bridge on D plus 1. At Courseulles the main bridge over the river Seulles was not sufficiently strong to take heavy tanks and had to be replaced by a Bailey. Gaps such as these could have held up Allied forces, if they had not been promptly dealt with.

No mention can be made of the essential work done by British engineers on D-day without including that of the Royal Canadian Engineers. Engineer support of First Canadian Army was to all intents identical to the support given by the Royal Engineers to the British army.

Finally, it must be emphasized that success in an operation as large and complex as the Normandy invasion depends on the close cooperation of all arms and services. Engineer plans depended on the requirements of other fighting forces; the ultimate success of the whole project indicates how well they cooperated with one another.

[*See also* Beach and Coastal Defenses.]

BIBLIOGRAPHY

de Guingand, Francis. *Operation Victory*. 1947.
Packenham-Walsh, R. P. *The Second World War, 1939–45; Military Engineering (Field)*. 1952.

A. E. YOUNGER

German Engineers

Overall plans for the defense of northern France were drawn up by the Inspectorate of Engineers (Inspectorate 5, Pionierabteilung) at Hitler's headquarters. Initially plans and calculations were presented to Hitler, who examined them to decide what was justified in terms of tactical values. The Führer set the priorities: first the major ports, Le Havre, Boulogne, Caen, and Cherbourg; next the heavy coastal batteries; then the sector of the *Fifteenth Army*, beginning just east of Caen, and including Boulogne; and finally, the sector of the *Seventh Army*, defending the area westward to the Atlantic. He also decided upon allocations of available cement: the major ports had the highest priority; the rest was divided among the branches of the Wehrmacht to complete their various construction projects. As for the engineers, in addition to the construction of defenses, they were limited to maintaining, where possible, the lines of communication.

Unfortunately for the Germans, much of this planning ultimately proved of little practical value. Since a decision was never definitively made between the two concepts of defense—Rundstedt's defense-in-depth plan and Rommel's linear plan to concentrate all defensive strength along the coast—many costly projects proved useless. Rundstedt thought that the Allies could be defeated in the open country of France, while Rommel thought that they would have to be defeated on the beaches. Actually, given the strength of the Allied invasion, the problem of defense in the West—linear versus defense in depth—was perhaps insoluble.

Under the command of Gen. Wilhelm Meise, Rommel's senior engineer officer, the major engineering task in

BELGIAN GATES.   COURTESY OF BARRY W. FOWLE

TELLER MINE.   On a pole at Utah Beach.

COURTESY OF BARRY W. FOWLE

preparation for the forthcoming battle for Normandy was the completion of the so-called Atlantic Wall, which included the emplacement of beach obstacles such as tetrahedra or hedgehogs, and Belgian Gates, barricade-like underwater obstacles—all interspersed with mines. The Germans began placing these obstacles near the high water mark, then extended them seaward. By the end of May these obstacles had not been extended below the 2.5-meter (8-foot) mark above high water because of chronic shortages of labor and matériel.

Rommel planned to supplement these obstacles by laying 50 million sea mines in the Channel and on the beaches. Between August 1943 and January 1944 sixteen mine fields, each about eight kilometers (5 miles) long, were put down between Boulogne and Cherbourg. They were supplemented by hasty mine fields emplaced offshore, immediately before the invasion was expected. From Zeebrugge in Belgium to Granville in France, thirty-six underwater mine fields were also planned. Finally, shallow-water mines were to be laid; a special seventy-kilogram (150-pound) concrete mine was developed for the purpose.

The accomplishment of these ambitious plans called for abundant labor, but labor had become increasingly scarce in the German Army. The famed Organization Todt was already fully engaged in fortifying what was Hitler's first priority—the major ports along the Channel and Atlantic coast. This work included the major U-boat bases and the vulnerable railways that served them.

Because many in the High Command expected the main Allied blow to fall in the *Fifteenth Army*'s sector, including the Pas de Calais area, it received priority in labor and matériel. The bulk of the remaining labor supply—the so-called *Freiwillige,* or volunteers, drawn from captured Russian personnel—were assigned to it. Consequently, the *Seventh Army* had to complete its defenses despite shortages of labor and matériel. Ironically it was in this army's sector that the main Allied landing took place.

The *Seventh Army* was not entirely neglected, however. In January 1944 its *LXXXIV Corps* received three engineer battalions, two for fortress construction and one for minelaying. In addition 2,850 men of the former French Labor Service were employed on a secondary defense line immediately behind the belt of coastal resistance points. As shortages became more acute, two East battalions, comprised of captured Russian soldiers, were attached.

The remaining source of labor for engineering tasks was combat troops. For example, a reserve battalion of the veteran *709th Infantry Division* was required to devote three days each week to labor duty at the expense of needed training. In February Rommel ordered that infantry in all *LXXXIV Corps* divisions were to engage in construction of defenses ordinarily performed by engineer troops. Only the *II Parachute Corps*'s *3d* and *5th* parachute divisions were to be exempt from engineering tasks.

In addition to preparation of defensive work in the coastal zones, Rommel ordered that all possible landing sites for gliders be made unusable through the installation of stakes interspersed with mines. Again, shortages of labor and matériel as well as time limited the effectiveness of these measures.

Some of the most elaborate defenses had been constructed around Cherbourg, which the Germans considered a major Allied objective. These defenses consisted of a belt of concrete and field fortifications dispersed in a semicircle on a collar of steep hills 6.5 to 9.7 kilometers (4 to 6 miles) from the port.

Here as elsewhere, efforts to construct major fortified strong points were hampered by a chronic shortage of cement, which was caused in turn by shortages of coal at the cement works. Movement of coal to the cement works was, in turn, limited by widespread destruction of the railways. Although army engineers labored day and night, they were unable to keep up with the rate of destruction caused by Allied bombers.

[*See also* Atlantic Wall; Beach and Coastal Defenses; Organization Todt.]

LONG-RANGE GUN BATTERY.   Built by German engineers.   HULTON DEUTSCH

CONCRETE DRAGON'S TEETH.   Tank obstacles built by French laborers.   THE ROBERT HUNT LIBRARY, LONDON

LAND MINES.   Being laid on an access route to Caen.   ARCHIVE PHOTOS, NEW YORK

STRINGING BARBED WIRE.   ARCHIVE PHOTOS, NEW YORK

BIBLIOGRAPHY

U.S. Army, Office of the Chief of Military History. "Army Group B Engineer Staff, 15 June–Sept. 1944." B-055. Captured Records Office, National Archives, Washington, D.C.
U.S. Army, Office of the Chief of Military History. "Representation of Engineer Interests." P-0410. Captured Records Office, National Archives, Washington, D.C.

ERNEST F. FISHER

ENGLAND. *See* Great Britain.

ENGLAND, H. T. (1884–1978), British, commodore commanding depot ships. Hugh Turnour England joined the Royal Navy in 1900 and served in the Boer War. He commanded a destroyer during the 1915 Dardanelles campaign and in the eastern Mediterranean, where he was severely wounded and mentioned in dispatches. He retired as a rear admiral in 1935. Recalled as a convoy commodore, he was principal sea transport officer, Middle East, from 1941 to 1943. England was convoy commander for Operation VIGOROUS, an Alexandria-to-Malta convoy in June 1942, and later commanded the flow convoy of invasion shipping for Operation HUSKY, the invasion of Sicily. His flagship was sunk 5 July 1943, but he resumed command and executed his mission.

England was appointed to Operation NEPTUNE in January 1944. As commodore of depot ships, he was responsible for the crews of the Ferry Service craft that were to land men and stores over open beaches for up to ninety days. In total, England commanded seven large depot ships and over seven hundred minor landing craft and vessels. Each sector was initially supported by a merchant ship, to be reinforced by an old cruiser once the latter's bombardment duties had ended.

England reached the beachhead late on D-day. His first three ships arrived early on D plus 2 with relief crews for the motor landing craft. England chose to shift his flag to the repair ship HMS *Albatross* until his designated flagship, the cruiser *Hawkins,* returned to the beachhead on D plus 5. The other two cruisers, *Frobisher* and *Danae,* reached the beachhead on D plus 11. The two large cruisers were also responsible for local air defense, while *Danae* serviced landing craft on the eastern flank of the beachhead. In total, the Ferry Service involved eight thousand men, but the command also maintained another seven thousand. On 16 June England left *Hawkins* temporarily for *Arethusa.* On 29 June he struck his pendant aboard *Hawkins* at Portsmouth. Adm. Philip Vian, commander of the Eastern Task Force, reported: "The government and ordering of the Ferry Service Crews presented him with a mass of problems, intricate and often minor, but in sum important to discipline and output, which he handled with characteristic energy and resolution."

Subsequently England was commodore at Hamburg and officer in charge of the postwar German minesweeping effort of 1945–1947. He never returned to the active list. One of many retired officers to serve in World War II, he was highly valued, notably by Vian, who referred to him as "that irrepressible warrior." Operation NEPTUNE exploited his talent and experience in handling merchant ships and seamen, always a difficult role for a naval officer, and earned him the highest praise.

[*See also* Hawkins, HMS.]

BIBLIOGRAPHY

London. Public Record Office. "Supply Organisation." Admiralty Records, ADM 199/1397.
London. Public Record Office. "Victualling Organisation." Admiralty Records, ADM 199/1643.
Vian, Philip. *Action This Day.* 1960.
Who Was Who, 1970–1980.

ANDREW LAMBERT

ERSKINE, G. W. E. J. (1899–1965), British, major general commanding the 7th Armoured Division. George Erskine was commissioned in the Kings Royal Rifle Corps just in time to take part in the closing stages of World War I. Between the wars he served at Regimental duty and on the Staff before becoming general staff officer I of 1st London Division. In World War II he commanded the 69th Infantry Brigade in North Africa in 1942 and then became chief of staff of XIII Corps. For a short period after the Battle of El Alamein, he acted as Eighth Army chief of staff to Gen. Bernard L. Montgomery, before assuming command of 7th Armoured Division in January 1943. He commanded it with distinction in Tunisia and Italy and brought it back to England in January 1944.

There was considerable resentment within 7th Armoured Division that it should be sent to Normandy ahead of formations that had seen no action at all. Nevertheless, its leading elements landed on 6 June and were followed next day by the rest of 22d Armoured Brigade. The division made only slow progress in the bocage to the south of Bayeux against stiff opposition. On 11 June Erskine was ordered by Gen. G. C. Bucknall, commander of the British XXX Corps, to advance on Villers-Bocage against the redoubtable *Panzer Lehr Division.* It was no task for an armored division, but 7th Armoured broke through to Villers only to have its advance guard wiped out in a tank ambush on the morning of the 13th. In heavy fighting Erskine's men held on to Villers until the evening, when the armor withdrew because Bucknall failed to reinforce it with additional infantry.

It was not Erskine's fault that his armored division was sent into unsuitable tank terrain, nor that his tanks were outclassed by Tiger tanks that played havoc at short range; the blame lay with Bucknall for committing it there insufficiently supported. But from this moment on the division's reputation suffered for being overcautious and lacking its previous celebrated prowess—an impression that Erskine was unable to dispel, partly because he had grown tired and cautious. Unfortunately, there was little time for remedial action before the exacting Operation GOOD-WOOD demanded the division's presence south of Caen on 18 July. Once again, 7th Armoured Division proved ineffective and Erskine, deemed in need of a rest, was removed from command during BLUECOAT, the British operation southeast of Caumont in late July. He was sent to head an Allied mission to Belgium.

After the war Erskine held several high military appointments, including commander in chief East Africa from 1953 to 1955, during the Mau Mau uprisings. He was knighted in 1953 and reached the rank of general.

[*See also* 7th Armoured Division.]

BIBLIOGRAPHY

Verney, G. L. *The Desert Rats.* 1954. Reprint, 1990.
Wilmot, Chester. *The Struggle for Europe.* 1954.

KENNETH MACKSEY

ESCORT SHIPS. The main types of specialized escort ships used to protect the assault and buildup convoys were escort destroyers, frigates, sloops, corvettes, and antisubmarine trawlers. The ships were deployed in two ways, as close escorts and in a western barrier.

Escort Destroyers were of three kinds:

1. Old British destroyers and destroyer leaders of World War I design, modified for escort duties. In some ships the forward boilers and funnel were removed to increase range. A 1,700-ton (load displacement) V- or W-class destroyer modified as a long-range escort would carry two single 4- or 4.7-inch and five 20-mm antiaircraft (AA) guns, a Hedgehog antisubmarine weapon, and 110 depth charges. Maximum speed would be 25 knots, compared to 34 knots when new. A similar short-range escort, specialized for use against S-boats, would retain its original speed and be armed with two single 4- or 4.7-inch guns, a twin 6-pounder gun mounting, three 2-pounder pom-poms, two 20-mm AA guns, three 21-inch torpedo tubes, and 20 depth charges. Different examples of former leaders (2,200 tons and all short-range escorts) were (anti–S-boat) *Mackay*, 2 single 4.7-inch guns, twin 6-pounder guns, one 3-inch and five 20-mm AA guns, six

21-inch torpedo tubes, and 70 depth charges; and (antisubmarine) *Keppel*, two 4.7-inch guns, one 3-inch and four 20-mm AA guns, six 21-inch torpedo tubes, one Hedgehog, and 88 depth charges. All were British and all were used for close escort.

2. Interwar British-designed 1,400-ton fleet destroyers with modified armament, three 4.7-inch guns, six 20-mm AA guns, four 21-inch torpedo tubes, one Hedgehog, and 125 depth charges. They retained their original speed of about 36 knots. Both British and Canadian, mostly used in the barrier patrol.

3. Hunt-class escort destroyers, normally displacing 1,450–1,600 tons and with a maximum speed of 27 knots. Armament was four or six 4-inch guns in twin mounting, a quadruple 2-pounder, six 20-mm AA guns, and often a single 2-pounder bow chaser. Up to 70 depth charges were carried, and some ships had two or three torpedo tubes. All four subtypes of this class were represented on D-day (including Norwegian and Free French vessels) and were used for other duties as well as escort.

Frigates were of two kinds: American-designed destroyer escorts (DEs) operated by the Royal Navy (RN) and U.S. Navy, and British-designed frigates built in Britain and Canada and operated by the RN, the Royal Canadian Navy, and the Free French. The American DEs (known as Captain-class frigates in the RN) displaced between 1,400 and 1,800 tons, depending on the power plant (diesel or steam turbine). The speeds of the respective types were 21 and 24 knots. Normal armament in British-operated ships (the vast majority) was three single 3-inch guns, up to fifteen 20-mm AA guns, one Hedgehog, and 160 depth charges. The River-class frigates displaced around 2,000 tons, had a speed of 21 knots, and were armed with two single 4-inch guns, up to ten 20-mm AA guns, one Hedgehog, and up to 200 depth charges. Both classes were used for both close escort and barrier patrol, most of the latter being Canadian. Also on barrier duty were two of the latest Loch-class frigates armed with the Squid antisubmarine weapon and a Colony-class frigate (an American River-class).

Sloops were all British and were almost all of the modified Black Swan type, of about 1,900 tons deep-load displacement, steam-turbine powered, with a maximum speed of almost 20 knots, and an armament of three twin 4-inch guns, one quadruple 2-pounder pom-pom, ten 20-mm AA guns, one Hedgehog, and 110 depth charges. They were used for both close escort and barrier patrol duties. Three prewar 1,500–1,600 ton sloops—*Scarborough, Rochester,* and *Londonderry*—escorted the Trinity House vessels and were used for laying and maintaining navigational markers.

Corvettes were deployed for close escort by the British, Canadians, Free French, Greeks, and Norwegians. There were 71 Flower-class corvettes, the most numerous single escort type. These 1,000-ton vessels were powered by a one-shaft, triple-expansion engine, had a maximum speed of 16 knots, and were armed with one single 4-inch gun, one 2-pounder, six 20-mm AA guns, one Hedgehog, and up to 72 depth charges.

Antisubmarine trawlers were of up to 1,200 tons deep displacement, were usually powered by a coal-fired, triple-expansion engine, and could travel at about 12 knots. Fifty-nine of varied types were available. Armament comprised a single 12-pounder or 4-inch gun, up to eight 20-mm AA guns, and up to 65 depth charges.

Three British escort carriers supported the barrier escort groups. Fleet destroyers also screened the assault, and American PC (patrol craft) boats and Coast Guard cutters contributed to the escort of the American convoys. The buildup convoys were escorted by a British system of escort groups: 101–108 (two escort destroyers or frigates and two corvettes plus one or two motor launches); 111–115 (five escort destroyers or sloops or frigates); 121–126 (1 or 2 corvettes and 1 or 2 MLs, motor launches); 131–144 (two larger escorts plus two trawlers or MLs); and 152–155 (3 corvettes or 6 corvettes or a frigate and 3 corvettes, plus a motor minesweeper or three trawlers). Other escorts were available to this organization but were not attached to specific groups.

[*See also* Navy, *article on* Allied Naval Forces; Eastern Task Force; Western Task Force.]

BIBLIOGRAPHY

Conway's All the World's Fighting Ships, 1922–1946. 1980.
Elliot, P. *Allied Escort Ships of World War Two.* 1977.
Lenton, H. T., and J. J. Colledge. *Warships of World War Two.* 1964.
Rohwer, Jürgen, and Gerhard Hümmelchen. *Chronology of the War at Sea, 1939–1945.* Translated by Derek Masters. 1992.

ERIC J. GROVE

F

FAHRMBACHER, WILHELM (1888–1970), German, lieutenant general commanding *LXXXIV Corps*. Wilhelm Fahrmbacher was commander of *5th Jäger Division* at the outbreak of war in 1939. As such, he did not take part in the Polish campaign, and his division played only a minor part in the campaign in France in the spring of 1940. Nonetheless, Fahrmbacher was promoted to lieutenant general (*General der Artillerie*) on 1 November 1940 and given command of *VII Corps*, which formed part of *Army Group Center* during the invasion of Russia in June 1941. Shortly after the German offensive came to a halt at the beginning of December, Fahrmbacher was transferred to France, where he took over *XXV Corps*.

In June 1944 Fahrmbacher's corps, together with *LXXIV Corps*, was part of *Seventh Army* and responsible for the defense of Brittany. On 12 June, however, Fahrmbacher was ordered to take temporary command of *LXXXIV Corps* as a result of the death in action of Gen. Erich Marcks. He was unable to prevent the Americans from securing the vital town of Caumont and advancing west along the base of Cotentin Peninsula. On 15 June, having been relieved by Gen. Dietrich von Choltitz, who had been ordered from Italy, Fahrmbacher returned to his own corps, which was not yet engaged in combat.

His moment came at the beginning of August, when Patton's U.S. Third Army broke out from Avranches and quickly drove *XXV Corps* back to the U-boat base of Lorient on the south coast of the Brittany peninsula. Here, behind strong defenses, Fahrmbacher resisted the initial American efforts to seize the port, which Hitler ordered to be held to the last man as a *Festung* (stronghold). To maintain the momentum of their drive eastward across France, the Americans decided to merely contain Lorient. Fahrmbacher continued to hold out and, indeed, did not surrender until the end of the war in Europe in May 1945. He died on 27 April 1970.

[*See also* LXXXIV Corps.]

CHARLES MESSENGER

WILHELM FAHRMBACHER.

FALLEY, WILHELM (1897–1944), German, major general, commander of the *91st Air Landing Division*. Falley was born in Metz, the capital of Lorraine (then part of Germany) on 25 September 1897. After being educated in various military schools, he entered the Imperial Army as a cadet in 1915 and was commissioned second lieutenant in the *93d Infantry Regiment* at the beginning of 1916.

After fighting in World War I, Falley remained in the Reichswehr during the Weimar era and in 1936 was a major and an instructor at the War School in Munich. Promoted to lieutenant colonel in 1939, he took command of the *I Battalion, 433d Infantry Regiment,* in the Königsbrück Maneuver Area when the war broke out. This regiment, a training unit, was not assigned to the *164th Infantry Division* until late 1939 and did not see action in either the Polish or French campaigns. Falley was nevertheless promoted to colonel in March 1941; he assumed command of the *4th Infantry Regiment* in East Prussia, a month later.

The famous *4th (Prussian) Infantry Regiment,* formed in Kolberg in 1921, had earned laurels in Poland, Belgium, and France. Falley had thus received a prize command, despite the fact that he had yet to see combat in World War II. Falley led his regiment with distinction at Dunaburg, Kholm, and in the Battle of the Demyansk Pocket, where the German *II Corps* was surrounded, or nearly surrounded, for an entire year. During this battle, Falley's regiment beat back repeated Russian attacks, and the colonel was decorated with the German Cross in Gold and the Knight's Cross. He was wounded in 1942 and, upon recovery, spent the next year on the staffs of the Infantry Schools at Döberitz and the military school at Posen.

Wilhelm Falley returned to active field command on 5 October 1943, when he assumed command of the *246th Infantry Division,* and was promoted to major general later that year. His new unit had been reduced by casualties to a battle group, but it remained in the line near Vitebsk and helped turn back a major Soviet offensive in the winter of 1943–1944. Falley was then transferred to France, where he assumed command of the *91st Air Landing Division* on 25 April 1944. He was promoted to major general on 1 May 1944.

Falley's new command was of higher quality than the average German infantry division in France and was specially trained to deal with Allied airborne attacks. The general continued training his unit until 5 June, when he left his headquarters (a château near Picauville) for Rennes, to attend Gen. Friedrich Dollmann's ill-fated war game. En route, he noticed that the Allied aerial bombardment had intensified to an unprecedented intensity. Suspecting that something exceptional was afoot, he ordered his driver to turn back. It was nearly dawn when, a short distance

from his headquarters, Falley heard the sound of machine guns. He went to investigate, and a few moments later was shot to death by an American paratrooper. The Normandy invasion had claimed its first German general.

Wilhelm Falley was an excellent tactical commander whose death was a major blow to the German Army on D-day. The *91st,* which might have taken energetic action against the American landings on 6 June, was left leaderless—and performed ineffectively—on the most important day in its history.

[*See also* 91st Air Landing Division.]

BIBLIOGRAPHY

Carell, Paul. *Invasion: They're Coming.* Translated by E. Osers. 1963. Paul Carell is the pseudonym used by Hans Karl Schmidt.
Keilig, Wolf. *Die Generale des Heeres.* 1983.
Tessin, Georg. *Verbände und Truppen der deutschen Wehrmacht und Waffen-SS im Zweiten Weltkrieg, 1939–1945.* Vol. 6, 1973.

SAMUEL W. MITCHAM, JR.

FALLSCHIRMJÄGER DIVISIONS. *See* 5th Parachute Division; 3d Parachute Division.

FAR SHORE SERVICE SHIPS. Allied invasion planners foresaw the danger of a postlanding stalemate in northern France. "You can almost always force an invasion," Gen. Omar Bradley said at the time, "but you can't always make it stick." Deception might give the assault the advantage of surprise but, once the Germans were sure of the direction of the invasion, they would make every effort to move up enough strength to defeat, or at least contain, it. The Allies would have to pour troops and supplies across the Channel in unprecedented volume to achieve the overwhelming strength they knew they would need to break out of the initial beachhead. As British Adm. Bertram H. Ramsay, commander of the Allied naval force, put it, "It is on the rapid follow-up of reserves, and on the swift unloading of stores, that the attack relies for the impetus which alone can sustain it."

This buildup, as the process was called, began as soon as the landing forces were ashore. To complicate matters, supply and reinforcement during the first weeks of the operation would have to come in over the landing beaches and through small ports. Cherbourg, the first major Channel port to fall, was not secured completely until 29 June; the first cargoes were landed there on 16 July, and the harbor was not entirely cleared until 21 September. Lacking large port facilities except for the artificial Mulberry harbors, invasion cargoes through the first weeks of OVERLORD would have to be unloaded and ferried ashore by small craft.

FAR SHORE SERVICE SHIPS.   An LCVP approaches two of USS *Bayfield*'s LCS(S)s. *LCT-533* is at right.   NATIONAL ARCHIVES

LCVP.   Landing Craft, Vehicle and Personnel, from USS *Thomas Jefferson*.   NATIONAL ARCHIVES

In planning the invasion, careful attention was given to the naval organization to be set up on the "Far Shore," as it was called, and to its relations with the landing forces. Rear Adm. J .W. Rivett-Carnac, Royal Navy (RN), was appointed flag officer, British Assault Area; Rear Adm. John Wilkes, U.S. Navy (USN), was later given command of the Western Task Force's service groups.

To organize the required crosss-Channel shuttle of ships and landing craft, two interservice organizations were set up. The Build Up Control Organization (BUCO) allocated available shipping to meet the armies' needs, while the Turn Round Control Organization (TURCO) saw to the movement of ships and cargoes between Britain and France. Each assault force commander had a senior officer afloat to oversee the work of ferry craft; another officer, ashore, was in charge of getting troops and supplies across the beaches to their destinations.

Each of the three British landing beaches was assigned two buildup squadrons of landing craft, one squadron each of LCMs (Landing Craft, Mechanized) and of LCVPs (Landing Craft, Vehicle and Personnel), with a Landing Barge Squadron. This latter unit included powered barges to ferry heavy equipment from landing ships; emergency repair craft to fight fires and patch damaged hulls; fuel and water tankers; and kitchen barges, equipped to feed hot meals to shuttle craft crews. The American beaches each had a Far Shore Service Group, with converted Liberty ships for crew accommodations and an ARL (Landing Craft Repair Ship), an LST (Landing Ship, Tank) converted to repair landing craft in an assault area). Service at Utah Beach was controlled from an LCH (Landing Craft, Headquarters), an LCI(L) (Landing Craft, Infantry [Large]) converted to a communications flagship for small craft. The Utah Beach group had LCMs and also Rhino ferries, pontoons assembled into 175-foot barges with detachable outboard motor units, which were used to carry up to forty vehicles from LSTs or cargo ships to beaches or Mulberry piers. Omaha Beach had these, as well as LCI(L)s, used as ferry control and local headquarters ships, LCTs (Landing Craft, Tank), and LCVPs. Both beach groups also had a British Landing Barge Squadron, made up of the same types of craft as those in the Eastern Task Force. A prominent share of work was given to the American DUKW, a 2.5-ton amphibious truck first used in the Sicily landings, and its British counterpart, the eight-wheeled Terrapin. Numbers of craft varied from beach to beach according to plan. Each of the five beach groups also had a number of British seagoing naval tugs, joined by three American tugs at Utah Beach, for salvage and rescue work.

As the buildup progressed, Rhino ferries proved better suited to unloading cargo ships in the Channel than did smaller landing craft, though their propulsion units were not powerful enough for rough open waters. Though Rhinos were intended for use with LSTs, this became unnecessary when it was found that LSTs could be beached without damage by the tides. LCTs were widely used, and British commanders found that the American DUKW, able to navigate in rough waters, was better suited to the job than their own Terrapin. They also thought the DUKW preferable to the LCM, which they deemed uneconomical in terms of the manpower needed to operate and maintain it. The American Omaha and Utah beach assault forces each had six Craft Recovery Units (CRU). Each CRU had three LCMs equipped with fire pumps and towing gear; two of the three craft carried a bulldozer to assist them in getting stranded landing craft off the beaches. Adm. Alan G. Kirk, USN, commander of the Western Task Force, complimented their "very useful service" in the assault and in the Channel storm of 19–21 June. He also found the British repair barges valuable for keeping landing craft operating through hard service. A number of LCP(L)s (Landing Craft, Personnel [Large]), 36-foot troop landing craft, had been fitted with smoke pots to screen the landing area against air attacks. When such attacks failed to materialize, the craft were used for offshore traffic control and messenger work, as were small support landing craft, LCS(S)s (Landing Craft, Support [Small]), after the assault. Admiral Kirk also praised the "yeoman's service" of LCVPs, used as taxis and utility boats.

On 7 June the first of the Gooseberries, chains of blockships to be sunk off the beachheads, arrived on station. By 10 June sixty of these ships had been sunk in five groups. As the buildup proceeded, these proved valuable as maintenance bases and weather shelters for the small ferry craft.

The operation order for the invasion prescribed convoy schedules for no more than the first four days of the operation. Admiral Ramsay realized that changes would be inevitable; further scheduling would have to be worked out as circumstances dictated. Events proved him right; German opposition, heavy weather, organizational problems, and the other disruptions inevitable in a military operation of this magnitude seriously affected matters in the first days of the buildup. Organizational problems were ironed out as time went on. The Channel storm of 19–21 June destroyed the American-sector Mulberry harbor; many small craft were lost or damaged. In spite of this, the tempo of unloading quickly resumed. By the end of June 621,986 troops, 95,750 vehicles of all types, and 217,624 tons of supplies had been delivered to the Far Shore. "This rate of reinforcement," Admiral Ramsay wrote, "undoubtedly met the requirements of the Ground Force and the Air Commanders-in-Chief and is, therefore, a cause of satisfaction."

[*See also* Artificial Harbors; Rivett-Carnac, J. W.; Wilkes, John.]

BIBLIOGRAPHY

Morison, Samuel Eliot. *The Invasion of France and Germany, 1944–1945*. Vol. 11 of *History of United States Naval Operations in World War II*. 1957. Reprint, 1988.
Roskill, Stephen W. *The Offensive*. Vol. 3, pt. 2, of *The War at Sea, 1939–1945*. 1961.
Schofield, B. B. *Operation Neptune*. 1974.

JOHN C. REILLY, JR.

FEUCHTINGER, EDGAR (1894–1958?), German, major general, commander of the *21st Panzer Division*. Feuchtinger was born in Metz on 9 November 1894. He joined the Imperial Army as a cadet in 1914 and was commissioned second lieutenant in the *14th Foot Artillery Regiment* in 1915. After seeing action in World War I, he remained in the service, mainly in the artillery, and, as a major, was given command of the *III Battalion, 26th Artillery Regiment*, in 1937.

When World War II broke out, Feuchtinger assumed command of the *227th Artillery Regiment* of the *227th Infantry Division* on the Eifel sector of the Western front. In 1940, he fought in the Netherlands, Belgium, and France. He was on occupation duty in northeastern France until October 1941, when his regiment was sent to the Eastern front. Feuchtinger took part in the battles around Wolchow and the siege of Leningrad until 16 August 1942, when apparently he was wounded; in any case, he saw no further active duty until July 1943, when he was named commander of the *21st Panzer Division*. He was promoted to brigadier general on 1 August 1943.

There is nothing in Feuchtinger's record to suggest that he was remotely qualified to command a panzer division; he owed his promotion solely to political considerations. During the 1930s, he had been in charge of organizing the military portions of the Reichsparteitage (National Party Day) at Nuremberg, where he had become friendly with Adolf Hitler and familiar with the Nazi party leadership; he had used these connections to obtain his command. Because he had no experience whatsoever in armored operations, he tended to leave the details of operations to his subordinates, who frequently had to fend for themselves. Feuchtinger was also known for his enjoyment of the finer things of life. During the decisive night of 5–6 June, when the Allied paratroopers landed in his sector, he was away from his post, partaking of the joys of Paris with his chief of operations. As a result, confusion reigned in the zone of the *21st Panzer Division* on D-day, and its counterattacks against both the invasion beaches and the airborne landings were late and ineffective.

Feuchtinger fought in the Caen sector during the Normandy campaign, where most of his division was destroyed. He escaped from the Falaise pocket with the survivors of his command and took part in the retreat to Germany. Despite his poor record as a divisional commander, he was promoted to major general on 1 August 1944. On Christmas Eve of that year, an order arrived at *21st Panzer Division* headquarters, requiring him to explain why he was not at his post on the night of 5–6 June. But once again, Feuchtinger was away. When his division was fighting against vastly superior Allied forces on the West Wall, he was at home in Germany—absent without leave!

Feuchtinger was relieved of his command in January 1945 and condemned by a court-martial in March. Owing to his Nazi party connections, however, he was not executed. Captured by the Americans at the end of the war, he returned after his release to Krefeld, where he earned a modest living until his death in the late 1950s. By any measure, he had been one of the least qualified and least successful of the German panzer commanders.

[*See also* 21st Panzer Division.]

BIBLIOGRAPHY

Keilig, Wolf. *Die Generale des Heeres*. 1983.
Luck, Hans von. *Panzer Commander*. 1989.

SAMUEL W. MITCHAM, JR.

FIFTEENTH AIR FORCE. On 1 November 1943 the U.S. Army Air Forces established the Fifteenth Air Force in the Mediterranean Theater of Operations, placing it under the theater commander, General Dwight D. Eisenhower, and the Mediterranean Allied Air Force (MAAF) commander, Lt. Gen. Carl Spaatz. Maj. Gen. James H. Doolittle was its initial chief, and at the same time was head of the Mediterranean Allied Strategic Air Force. In January 1944 Maj. Gen. Nathan Twining replaced General Doolittle. The new air force set up headquarters at Foggia, Italy, absorbing XII Bomber Command and its six heavy bomber groups. Plans provided for reinforcement within six months by fifteen additional heavy bombardment groups, giving it a total bomber complement half the size of the Eighth Air Force.

Both the British and Lt. Gen. Ira C. Eaker, the commander of AAF forces in Britain, strenuously objected to the creation of a strategic air force in Italy. They based their opposition on the premise that Italy could not supply an adequate logistical base for a large bomber force. They feared that diversion to Italy of groups scheduled for Britain would diminish American commitment to bomber operations based in Britain. General Eaker protested the weakening of his force and splitting of the American effort. However, Gen. Henry H. Arnold, AAF commander, General Spaatz, and General Doolittle

convinced the Combined Chiefs of Staff to approve the project by emphasizing the advantage of opening a second front against German air defenses; the supposedly superior operating weather in Italy; and the attainability of additional targets heretofore beyond the range of British-based bombers.

Of particular importance was the Romanian oil and industrial complex at Ploesti, the single most valuable target in Europe because it supplied a large percentage of German oil requirements. If Ploesti ceased to function, the Germans would be forced to rely on their fourteen synthetic oil plants, which presented a compact target highly vulnerable to American strategic bombing.

In January 1944 the AAF established the U.S. Strategic Air Forces in Europe (USSAFE, later USSTAF) as a headquarters with operational control over both U.S. strategic air forces, the Eighth and the Fifteenth. MAAF retained administrative control of the Fifteenth.

The Fifteenth's operations before D-day were dictated by General Spaatz's attritional struggle with the German fighter force, and his embroilment in the dispute within Allied headquarters between advocates of the Oil Plan, which would target the German oil industry, and advocates of the Transportation Plan, which would target the transportation network by which German forces would be rushed to the invasion area.

In January and February 1944 the Fifteenth attacked German aircraft industry targets in southern Germany, Austria, and the Balkan states. In Big Week (Operation ARGUMENT), the Eighth and Fifteenth conducted a combined assault on the German aircraft assembly industry, and suffered heavy casualties because of their comparative lack of long-range escort fighters. Operations in support of the Anzio beachhead on 19 February prevented the Fifteenth's participation in the first day of the operation.

In March the Fifteenth began to target rail marshaling yards in the Balkans. Air Chief Marshal Charles A. Portal,

chief of the Air Staff, RAF, continued to forbid the bombing of oil targets in the Balkans until June 1944. Nonetheless, by April the Fifteenth Air Force used the presence of marshaling yards at Ploesti to justify the bombing of the surrounding industrial complex.

In May the Fifteenth aided Operation OVERLORD by striking marshaling yards in southern Germany, Austria, and southern France as well as airfields in southern France, so as to slow air and ground reinforcement of German defenders. During D-day operations in June, when the Eighth Air Force tied much of its operations to the Normandy beachhead, the Fifteenth picked up the slack in the strategic bombing of Germany with raids on oil targets. German natural petroleum imports fell precipitously, with immediate consequences to the mobility of German land and air forces. Thus, although its distance from Normandy prevented the Fifteenth Air Force from making a direct contribution to the cross-Channel invasion, its bombing of strategic targets freed the Eighth to devote more effort to the beachheads. Reduced German fuel allotments, brought about in large measure by Fifteenth Air Force raids and incessant Allied fighter-bomber attacks, limited the German defenders' mobility so severely that they could not respond quickly enough to stop the decisive American breakthrough at Saint-Lô.

[See also Twining, Nathan.]

BIBLIOGRAPHY

Fifteenth Air Force. *The History of the Fifteenth Air Force.* A 6377. U.S. Air Force Historical Research Agency, Maxwell Air Force Base, Alabama. Microfilm.

RICHARD G. DAVIS

FIFTEENTH ARMY. The German *Fifteenth Army* was formed in France and activated on 15 January 1941. Its home base was Bayreuth, and its general headquarters units included the *509th Signal Regiment* and the *590th Army Supply Troop*. Its initial mission was to perform garrison duties in the West while the bulk of the Wehrmacht invaded the Soviet Union.

Headquarters, Fifteenth Army was transferred from the direct control of the Army High Command (Oberkommando des Heeres—OKH) to *Army Group D* (later Commander in Chief West—OB West—Headquarters) in April 1941 and took charge of the defensive sector in northern France and Belgium. Except for an occasional Allied coastal raid, the *Fifteenth Army* performed more or less routine occupation and garrison duties until the second half of 1943, when it became apparent that the Wehrmacht would have to face the Anglo-American cross-Channel invasion in 1944. It was then heavily reinforced and Gen. Hans von Salmuth, a veteran of the Eastern

Fifteenth Army
15 May 1944

LXXXIX Corps

165th Reserve Division
712th Infantry Division
48th Infantry Division

LXXXII Corps

18th Luftwaffe Field Division
47th Infantry Division
49th Infantry Division

LXVII Corps

344th Infantry Division
348th Infantry Division

LXXXI Corps

245th Infantry Division
17th Luftwaffe Field Division
711th Infantry Division

Army Reserve

19th Luftwaffe Field Division
182d Reserve Division
326th Infantry Division
346th Infantry Division
84th Infantry Division (in transit)
85th Infantry Division (in transit)
331st Infantry Division (in transit)

SOURCE: Kurt Mehner, comp. *Die geheimen Tagesberichte der deutschen Wehrmachtführung im Zweiten Weltkrieg, 1939–1945.* 1985.

front, was named its commander. Most of the German military leaders expected the Allies to land around the Pas de Calais, in the *Fifteenth Army*'s zone. According to the plan of Field Marshal Gerd von Rundstedt, Commander in Chief West, the Allied invasion would be slowed down and exhausted by the *Fifteenth Army*. Eisenhower would then be defeated in a major tank battle in the interior of France when Panzer Group West joined the battle.

The battle, of course, did not work out as Rundstedt planned. The Allies landed in Normandy, in the *Seventh Army*'s zone. Hitler, who had decided in April that the Allies would land in Normandy, now reversed himself and declared that the Normandy invasion was a diversion: the actual invasion would come in the *Fifteenth Army* zone after all. He stubbornly refused to allow Rundstedt or Rommel to transfer any divisions from the *Fifteenth Army* to Normandy; instead, he reinforced the *Seventh Army* with the bulk of his panzer divisions. The Normandy sector—excellent defensive terrain for infantry—

had a serious shortage of infantry throughout the battle. When the Allies broke out of Normandy and entered the area north of the Seine (excellent tank country), the panzer divisions were so badly depleted that they were unable to offer effective resistance. Eisenhower's forces overran France with relative ease and halted only because of supply and logistical difficulties.

The *Fifteenth Army* was trapped in eastern Belgium and southeastern Holland by the rapid Allied advance and only managed to escape because the Allies failed to cut its last possible line of retreat—something they easily could have done. They paid dearly for this mistake. Brilliantly led now by Lt. Gen. Gustav-Adolf von Zangen, the army made good its escape and played a significant role in defeating the Allied attempt to breach the Rhine defensive line via airborne assault. It fought well also against the Americans at Aachen, but was later surrounded by the Americans in the Ruhr pocket and surrendered on 18 April 1945.

[*See also* Salmuth, Hans von.]

BIBLIOGRAPHY

Mitcham, Samuel W., Jr. *Rommel's Last Battle: The Desert Fox and the Normandy Campaign.* 1983.
Tessin, George. *Verbände und Truppen der deutschen Wehrmacht und Waffen-SS im Zweiten Weltkrieg, 1939–1945.* Vol. 4, 1976.

SAMUEL W. MITCHAM, JR.

15TH (SCOTTISH) INFANTRY DIVISION. On 20 June 1943 the 15th (Scottish) Division was placed under command of the VIII Corps and for the next nine months trained hard for the invasion in Yorkshire and northeastern England before moving down to the south coast in April 1944. In August 1943 Maj. Gen. G. H. A. MacMillan was appointed to command the division, which had 790 officers and 15,000 men of other ranks.

Following the Guards and the 11th Armoured Divisions across the Channel, the division's progress was delayed by holdups at sea, culminating in the great storm of 19 to 22 June. In the end it was only just ready to go into action, three days later than planned, on 26 June, D plus 20, as the spearhead of the VIII Corps' first operation,

15th (Scottish) Infantry Division
Maj. Gen. G. H. A. MacMillan

44th (Lowland) Brigade
8th Royal Scots
6th Royal Scots Fusiliers
7th Kings Own Scottish Borderers

46th (Highland) Brigade
9th Cameronians (Scottish Rifles)
2d Glasgow Highlanders
7th Seaforth Highlanders

227th (Highland) Brigade
10th Highland Light Infantry
2d Gordon Highlanders
2d Argyll and Sutherland Highlanders

Divisional Troops
15th Reconnaissance Regiment, RAC
15th Divisional Engineers
15th Divisional Signals
15th Divisional Column, RASC
131st, 181st, and 190th Field
97th Anti-Tank and 119th Light A-A Regiments, RA
1st Middlesex Regiment (Machine Gun)

EPSOM. Although acquitting itself with distinction, the division suffered heavy casualties in this first experience of real warfare, losing 198 killed and 1,666 wounded and missing during the four days of the battle.

[*See also* MacMillan, G. H. A.]

BIBLIOGRAPHY

Jackson, G. S. *Operations of Eighth Corps: Normandy to the River Rhine.* 1948.
Martin, H. G. *The History of the 15th Scottish Division, 1939–1945.* 1948.

JOHN BAYNES

V CORPS. With the United States's entry into World War II, the American and British governments acted on the BOLERO plan to position U.S. troops in England. In conjunction with BOLERO, Operation MAGNET called for the deployment of American troops in Northern Ireland. Designated as the MAGNET force, V Corps's elements arrived in Belfast in January 1942 with the mission of receiving and training U.S. forces, and assisting in the defense of Northern Ireland.

V Corps transferred to England that November, but continued its training mission under the BOLERO concept. As the highest U.S. field headquarters in Britain at the time, the corps helped plan for the coming invasion of the continent. In June 1943 the European Theater of Operations, United States Army (ETOUSA), directed V Corps to develop a plan for U.S. forces to seize France's Brittany peninsula. The plan, Operation WADHAM, was a deception, under the larger COCKADE scheme, to trick the Germans into preparing for the pretended assault. ETOUSA, favorably impressed with V Corps's WADHAM plan, gave the corps another assignment: preliminary planning for Operation OVERLORD, the joint British and American invasion of the Continent. Maj. Gen. L. T. Gerow, a veteran planner from the War Department and former commander of the 29th Infantry Division, had assumed command of V Corps in mid-July 1943 and oversaw all the corps's invasion preparations.

After much debate, in January 1944 the invasion was set for the beginning of June, targeting the northwestern beaches of Normandy. The U.S. First Army, which now controlled the V and VII Corps, would strike at the areas around the Vire Estuary. Given the mission to secure a beachhead in the area between Port-en-Bessin and the Vire River, V Corps would assault and hold Omaha Beach. The 1st Infantry Division would lead the corps's assault force (Force O), comprising reinforced elements of the 16th, 18th, 115th, and 116th infantry regiments and the 2d and 5th Ranger battalions. Later that afternoon the 29th Division, with elements of the 26th and 175th infantry regiments, would also go ashore, and the 2d Infantry Division would land on D plus 1. Miscellaneous corps units would continue the buildup process beginning on D plus 2.

V Corps elements were to open the beach exits to facilitate more landings, and extend the beachhead toward the bocage, the hilly, wooded country to the south. The assault elements, however, faced great difficulties in their landings. Rough surf conditions carried landing craft away from their targets and, once ashore, soldiers could not identify their objectives. The air bombardment had done

V Corps
Maj. Gen. Leonard T. Gerow

1st Infantry Division
Maj. Gen. Clarence R. Huebner

2d Infantry Division
Maj. Gen. Walter M. Robertson

29th Infantry Division
Maj. Gen. Charles H. Gerhardt

Note: Additional antiaircraft artillery, cavalry, engineer, field artillery, medical, ordnance, quartermaster, and signal units were attached.

little to destroy the beach defenses, and the American soldiers faced heavy resistance from the *352d Division,* dug in to defend the beach. But corps units struggled inland, overcoming great obstacles, and reached their D-day objectives on D plus 2.

V Corps, including the newly landed 2d Armored Division, then advanced farther south toward the Cerisy Forest. On 10 June, V and VII Corps troops made contact at Auville-sur-le-Vey. Two days later, on D plus 6, the corps launched its drive toward Saint-Lô, an offensive that occupied it through the end of July. After a long, hard fight across Europe, from the breakout at Normandy, through Paris, on to the Siegfried Line and the Roer River dams, over the Rhine, and deep into the German heartland, V Corps troops ended the war with a V-E Day celebration in Czechoslovakia.

[*See also* Gerow, L. T.]

BIBLIOGRAPHY

Harrison, Gordon A. *Cross-Channel Attack.* U.S. Army in World War II: The European Theater of Operations. 1951.
Hill, John G. *V Corps Operations in the European Theater of Operations, 6 January 1942–9 May 1945.* 1945.
U.S. Army, Center of Military History. *Omaha Beachhead: 6 June–13 June 1944.* 1945. Facsimile reprint, 1989.
Wilson, John B. *Armies, Corps, Divisions and Separate Brigades.* 1987.

DONNA C. EVERETT

FIFTH PANZER ARMY. *See* Panzer Group West.

5TH PARACHUTE DIVISION. The German *5th Parachute Division (5. Fallschirmjägerdivision)* had been stationed around Reims since March 1944. Its cadres, including veterans from the Italian campaign, were to train new young recruits.

At the end of May 1944 the division moved into the

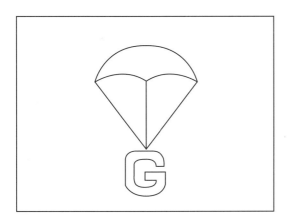

area of Saint-Lô–Reunes in Normandy to defend the coast and finish combat training. On D-day 95 percent of its weapons and equipment were available, but only 30 percent of its vehicles. Most of the young soldiers had not even completed the parachute training course. In early

---

5th Parachute Infantry Division
Division Headquarters
Commander Maj. Gen. Gustav Wilke

*13th Parachute Infantry Regiment
(Fallschirmjägerregiment 13)*
Three battalions, Lt. Col. Wolf Werner Graf v. d. Schulenburg

*14th Parachute Infantry Regiment
(Fallschirmjägerregiment 14)*
Three battalions, Maj. Herbert Noster

*15th Parachute Infantry Regiment
(Fallschirmjägerregiment 15)*
Three battalions, Col. Kurt Gröschke

*5th Parachute Artillery Regiment
(Fallschirm-Artillerieregiment 5)*
Three battalions, Colonel Winzer

*5th Parachute Antitank Battalion
(Fallschirm-Panzerjägerabteilung 5)*
Capt. Rolf Müller

*5th Parachute Engineer Battalion
(Fallschirm-Pionierbataillon 5)*
Capt. Gerhard Mertins

*5th Parachute Mortar Battalion
(Fallschirm-Granatwerferbataillon 5)*
Captain Maier

*5th Parachute Antiaircraft Artillery Battalion
(Fallschirm-Flak-Abteilung 5)*
Capt. Fritz Görtz

*5th Parachute Signal Battalion
(Fallschirm-Luftnachrichtenabteilung 5)*
Capt. Herbert Fock

*5th Parachute Field Replacement Battalion
(Fallschirm-Feldersatzbataillon 5)*
Captain Meyer

**Support and supply units
(*Versorgungstruppen/
5. Fallschirmjägerdivision*)**
Major Göner

June the division was moved to a position between Mont-Saint-Michel and Saint-Brieuc in Brittany with orders to prevent Allied landings, counterattack Allied forces, and defend its positions at any cost. On the left lay the *17th SS Panzer Grenadier Division*, and on the right the *Panzer Lehr Division*. The division command post was four kilometers south-southeast of Dinan, near Tressaint.

Since the Allies did not land in Brittany, the division was engaged piecemeal in Normandy. First to be moved to the invasion front was the *15th Parachute Infantry Regiment*. Because it was not yet combat-ready, it was reinforced with the experienced former cadre battalions of the *1st Parachute Division*, and fought together with the *5th Parachute Artillery Regiment* under tactical control of the *77th Infantry Division*. The *13th Parachute Infantry Regiment* was engaged with the *Panzer Lehr Division*; the *5th Parachute Engineer Battalion* with the *17th SS Panzer Grenadier Division*; and other units with the *12th SS Panzer Division "Hitlerjugend"* and *17th SS Panzer Grenadier Division* around Saint-Lô. There all units of the *5th Parachute Division* shared the fate of these other divisions, being captured by the Allies in the Falaise pocket after severe losses.

Between 15 June and 10 July 1944 the *5th Parachute Division* lost about 70 percent of its personnel (total strength 12,008 soldiers). The losses in late July 1944 were less: only 10 dead, 16 wounded, and 3 missing (although the losses of the *14th Parachute Infantry Regiment* are not available in the German records). Rebuilt from its remnants and replacement personnel in October 1944 in the Netherlands, the division fought again in the Battle of the Bulge in December 1944. After heavy losses in this battle, the rest of the division was taken prisoner in Germany in March and April 1945.

[*See also* II Parachute Corps; Wilke, Gustav.]

BIBLIOGRAPHY

Wilke, Gustav. *Bericht über 5. Fallschirmjägerdivision in der Normandie vom. 6.6–24.7.1944.* U.S. Army, Historical Division, MS B-820.
Der Deutsche Fallschirmjäger, no. 6 (1953): 11, and no. 7 (1953): 8.

FLORIAN BERBERICH

50TH (NORTHUMBRIAN) INFANTRY DIVISION.

"Fifty Div," as the Northumbrian Division had become known throughout the British Army after its magnificent performances at Gazala and El Alamein in North Africa in 1942, was on D-day allocated the British Second Army's western flank position. The division was directed to land on and secure the Jig and King sectors of Gold Beach between Le Hamel and La Rivière.

Once it was ashore, its right-hand brigade was directed to drive westward to capture Arromanches-les-Bains, releasing at the same time the 47th Royal Marine Commando, which was expected to reach Port-en-Bessin and there make contact with the American forces on the left-hand flank of Omaha Beach. The other three brigades of the division were ordered to drive south toward Bayeux on the right and Sainte-Croix-Grand-Tonne on the left, capturing Bayeux itself by the end of the day, and by nightfall holding a long stretch of the Bayeux-Caen road, with perhaps some country to the south of it as far as the railway line.

The division was commanded by Maj. Gen. D. A. H. Graham and consisted of four brigades. The two assault brigades would be the 231st on the right and the 69th on the left, with the 56th Brigade behind the 231st as the second wave, and the 151st on the left behind the 69th. Both assault brigades had field artillery units under command, and a battery of the Royal Marine Armoured Support Regiment was divided between the leading units of both brigades.

By tradition the men of the 50th Northumbrian Division came from the mining and shipbuilding towns of the Tyne and Tees area (their divisional sign was a Double T), and although after four years of war many of the original "Geordies"—as the native sons of the area are known—were gone (one complete brigade had been wiped out at Gazala), a spirit of dogged obstinacy still pervaded the division. No position they held would be easily yielded; no given objective would long evade them.

They were going to need all their determination, especially the battalions on their right flank. The long uncomfortable hours at sea had taken their toll in exhaustion and seasickness, yet some of them were singing on the last stretch into the Jig and King sectors, and an East York's bugler even sounded General Salute as they passed their command ship. But wind and tide had pushed them too far east, and the leading company of the 1st Hampshire Regiment landed near Les Roquettes where they immediately came under enfilade fire from Le Hamel. As the sea had been too rough to release the DD (Duplex Drive) tanks offshore and their half of the Royal Marine Support Battery had been either sunk or wiped out as they hit the beach, the infantry went in virtually unprotected with only their speed and training to carry them through. Almost unbelievably, they crossed the beach and reached Les Roquettes, where the other Hampshire companies quickly joined them.

They had by then lost both their commanding officer and the second in command; radio communication with headquarters was broken, so that they could not call for naval or field artillery support; and fire from Le Hamel grew ever stronger. But by 0730, sappers had cleared one lane across the beach and a few tanks and some guns were ashore and moving to their support, so the 1st

BREN GUNNER.   Of the 6th Durham Light Infantry.   IMPERIAL WAR MUSEUM

Hampshires drove forward to Asnelles-sur-Mer, intent on attacking Le Hamel from the south.

To their east, the Dorsets had been much more fortunate. Flail tanks of the Westminster Dragoons had landed successfully and were soon beating paths through the mine fields. Sappers worked fast to clear the beach obstacles, and the infantry poured ashore, reaching Les Roquettes hard on the heels of the Hampshires, and then drove south as far as Meuvaines, soon to become divisional headquarters. From there the Dorsets swung west along the road to Puits d'Hérode, aiming to bypass Le Hamel on their way toward Arromanches.

By now the battle for Le Hamel was growing in fury. The brigade's third battalion, the 2d Devons, had begun landing through uncleared beach obstacles and heavy small-arms fire about 0815. One company drove into Le Hamel and complemented the Hampshire's attack from the south; the others swung wide through Asnelles and then along the La Grond River to Ryes, thus to add to the threat to Arromanches.

Moreover, some three hundred men of the 47th Royal Marine Commando, despite having been forced in large measure to swim ashore with all their arms and equipment when three of their five landing craft were sunk, congregated on the Le Hamel beach behind the Devons.

They skirted Le Hamel and marched rapidly off across country behind Tracy-sur-Mer and Arromanches, aiming for Port-en-Bessin and junction with the U.S. forces.

Meanwhile the 69th Brigade had landed on King Beach in a positive copybook operation. Green Howards on the right and 5th East Yorkshires on the left flooded ashore between Hable de Heurtot and La Rivière. Sappers and beach clearance groups were already at work ahead of them, petard tanks were smashing strong points and pillboxes, and flail tanks were clearing paths through the mine fields. By early afternoon La Rivière, Mont-Fleury, and Ver-sur-Ver were taken. Prisoners were pouring back onto the beach, which was filling rapidly as more flail and crocodile tanks, self-propelled and antitank guns, Bren carriers, jeeps, machine guns, and mortars came ashore. Between 1100 and 1200 the second-wave brigades arrived—the 56th behind the 231st and the 151st behind the 69th—and only the superb beach organization and the opening of the chosen beach exits and the tracks leading to them prevented wide-scale congestion.

Thus by early afternoon of D-day, all four brigades of the 50th Division were ashore and pressing inland, with the two assault brigades out on the wings and the second wave between them—the 56th driving for Bayeux, the 151st on their left. By nightfall the Marine Commandos were at

50th (Northumbrian) Infantry Division
Maj. Gen. D. A. H. Graham

56th Brigade
2d South Wales Borderers
2d Gloucesters
2d Essex

151st Brigade
6th, 8th, and 9th Durham Light Infantry

231st Brigade
47th Royal Marine Commando
2d Devonshires
1st Hampshires
1st Dorsetshires
90th and 147th Field Regiment, RA

69th Brigade
5th East Yorkshires
6th and 7th The Green Howards
86th Field Regiment, RA

Divisional Troops
1st Nottinghamshire Yeomanry
4th/7th Dragoon Guards
1st Battalion Royal Marine Armoured Support
   Regiment
61st Reconnaissance Regiment, RAC
50th Divisional Engineers
50th Divisional Signals
74th and 124th Field, 102d Anti-Tank and 25th Light
   A-A Regiments, RA
2d Battalion The Cheshire Regiment (Machine Gun)

Point 72 just south of Port-en-Bessin, the 231st Brigade had taken the radar station at Arromanches, and the 56th Brigade had gone through La Rosière and was only two thousand yards short of Bayeux; the 151st Brigade had taken Esquay-sur-Seulles and the 69th Brigade, Coulombs, both only a mile from the Bayeux-Caen road. They came as near as any division did to attaining their D-day targets, now generally agreed to have been overly ambitious.

Consolidation was to occupy the next few days, though various small but important advances were made. Port-en-Bessin was occupied early on 7 June. The 56th Brigade entered Bayeux only hours afterward and over the next four days was to push farther south. On its right the Marine Commandos and the 231st Brigade cleared the ground out to the line of the Drôme River.

But it was the 69th Brigade that made the deepest penetration, crossing the Bayeux-Caen road on 7 June and then driving on toward the railway near Ducy-Sainte-Marguerite. Here the XXX Corps introduced a new element into the battle—the 8th Armoured Brigade augmented by the 50th Division's reconnaissance regiment and infantry companies from the Dorsets, temporarily detached from the 231st Brigade. On 8 June they burst out through the 69th Brigade line to reach Audrieu and then moved on to take Saint-Pierre and threaten Tilly-sur-Seulles.

By this time, the 7th Armoured Division had landed and moved close up behind the 151st Brigade, making ready to take further advantage not only of the firm base secured by the 50th but also of the deep penetration on the left flank from which they would mount an operation down toward Villers-Bocage.

[*See also* Graham, D. A. H.]

BIBLIOGRAPHY

Clay, E. W. *The Path of the 50th: The Story of the 50th (Northumbrian) Division in the Second World War.* 1950.

Ellis, L. F., et al. *The Battle of Normandy.* Vol. 1 of *Victory in the West.* 1962. Reprint, 1974.

BARRIE PITT

51ST (HIGHLAND) INFANTRY DIVISION.
Following the death or capture of two-thirds of the original 51st (Highland) Division in France in June 1940 at Saint-Valery-en-Caux, near Dieppe, a new formation with the same title was formed in the Scottish Highlands, based on the 9th (Scottish) Division and recruited from the same areas. Command was given to Maj. Gen. Douglas M. Wimberley, a fervent Scot known affectionately to his troops as "Tartan Tam."

In June 1942 the division sailed from Britain to the Middle East, where it joined the Eighth Army shortly before the arrival in Egypt of Lt. Gen. Bernard L. Montgomery, under whom it was to achieve an outstanding reputation as a fighting force. From the Battle of El Alamein in October 1942 to the end of the North African campaign in Tunisia in May 1943, the division suffered 5,400 casualties. Then came the short conquest of Sicily from 10 July to 16 August 1943, with a further 1,300 casualties, before the order came for the 51st to return to Britain to be trained for the invasion of France. In spite of their losses, the members of the division had been involved in a long string of victories during their fourteen

BLACK WATCH.   IMPERIAL WAR MUSEUM

GORDON HIGHLANDERS.   IMPERIAL WAR MUSEUM

months in the Mediterranean command, so that they returned home as battle-hardened veterans, feeling themselves fully a match for anyone.

A new commander of the division, Maj. Gen. D. C. Bullen-Smith, took over from Wimberley just before leaving for Sicily. On their return to Britain Bullen-Smith faced the difficult task of training a formation that did not know him and that considered itself so experienced as to need little guidance before going into action again.

In the invasion plan, the 51st was put under command of the I Corps and was given the follow-up position behind the 3d British and 3d Canadian divisions, which were to land first on Sword and Juno beaches, respectively.

Owing to problems at sea that built up behind the landings of the two assault divisions, the 51st was delivered to the beaches in piecemeal fashion. As soon as they appeared, individual units were used to plug gaps in the front or to carry out attacks on various enemy positions, without waiting for the whole division to assemble. On D plus 1, Bullen-Smith, the rest of the 153d, and some of the 152d Brigade landed. The 152d had all come in by D plus 3, and the next day the 154th began to arrive, though it was not complete until D plus 7.

The first action in which a unit of the division was involved was an unsuccessful attempt by the 5th Black Watch of 153d Brigade to take a radar station near Douvres on 7 June. Crossing some open ground, they were checked by murderous enemy fire and eventually ordered to withdraw. Following this the battalion was ordered to move east, crossing the Orne at Pegasus Bridge in support of the 6th Airborne Division. Gradually other elements of the division followed the same route. First came the 152d Brigade; then, the 154th. They moved south toward Colombelles and Hérouvillette.

On 13 June, D plus 7, the 5th Camerons and 2d Seaforth of the 152d Brigade were ordered to attack the villages of Sainte-Honorine and Demouville, which lie northeast and east of Caen. Neither battalion was able to achieve its objective, and the 5th Camerons suffered heavy losses. They later avenged their defeat by taking Sainte-Honorine on 22 June.

By D plus 12 the 51st Division was established in much the same area east of Caen, between the Orne and the railway line to Troarn. It was not a happy time. The defensive role in thick woods, being continually mortared and shelled by an unseen enemy, was a bitter contrast to the war of constant movement and advance in Africa and Sicily. There the division had always fought as a whole formation, but in Normandy battalions were sent hither and thither under different commands. In Africa and Sicily, briefing for operations had been extremely thorough, but in Normandy, problems in obtaining accurate information in the more confined terrain meant that troops were sent

51st (Highland) Infantry Division
Maj. Gen. D. C. Bullen-Smith

152d Brigade
2d and 5th Seaforth Highlanders
5th Cameron Highlanders

153d Brigade
5th Black Watch
1st and 5/7th Gordon Highlanders

154th Brigade
1st and 7th Black Watch
7th Argyll and Sutherland Highlanders

Divisional Troops
2d Derbyshire Yeomanry
51st Divisional Engineers
51st Divisional Signals
51st Divisional Column RASC
126th, 127th, and 128th Field
61st Anti-tank and 40th Light A-A Regiments, RA
1/7th Middlesex Regiment (Machine Gun)

into battle much less prepared. At times they were set tasks that could not be accomplished without greater strength. With the men lacking the leadership to help them overcome these difficulties, the division's morale sank so low that Bullen-Smith on 26 July was removed from command by Montgomery. He was replaced by Maj. Gen. T. G. Rennie from the 3d Division, who had earlier commanded the 5th Black Watch, and then the 154th Brigade in the 51st Division during its heyday in the Mediterranean. Under his leadership the division's good name was restored, and by mid-August it was earning praise for aggressive action in the battles culminating in the entry into Lisieux on 22 August.

[*See also* Bullen-Smith, D. C.]

BIBLIOGRAPHY

Belfield, E., and H. Essame. *The Battle for Normandy.* 1967.
Salmond, J. B. *The History of the 51st Highland Division, 1939–1945.* 1953.

JOHN BAYNES

FIGHTER BOMBER COMMAND. *See* Air Defence of Great Britain.

FIGHTER COMMAND. *See* Air Defence of Great Britain.

FILM. *For discussion of film documentation, see* Battlefield Film Footage.

FIREFIGHTING. *See* Salvage and Firefighting.

FIRST ARMY. Command of the U.S. First Army, the headquarters controlling all U.S. ground forces committed to the initial Normandy invasion, was vested in Lt. Gen. Omar Bradley. At the time of D-day his force included two corps and a total of nine divisions—six infantry, one armored, and two airborne.

The disposition of forces for invasion of the Normandy beaches put First Army on the right, with the British Second Army on its left. First Army had under command

OMAR BRADLEY.   On bridge of USS *Ancon.*
NATIONAL ARCHIVES

U.S. First Army		
V CORPS	VII CORPS	XIX CORPS*
1st Infantry Division	4th Infantry Division	3d Armored Division
2d Armored Division	9th Infantry Division	28th Infantry Division
2d Infantry Division	82d Airborne Division	30th Infantry Division
29th Infantry Division	90th Infantry Division	35th Infantry Division
	101st Airborne Division	

*XIX Corps became operational on 14 June 1944. On D-day to D plus 12, First Army consisted of two corps, the V and VII.

V Corps and VII Corps, assigned to assault Omaha and Utah beaches, respectively.

V Corps, commanded by Maj. Gen. Leonard T. Gerow, consisted of Maj. Gen. Clarence R. Huebner's 1st Infantry Division, the 29th Infantry Division under Maj. Gen. Charles H. Gerhardt, Maj. Gen. Walter M. Robertson's 2d Infantry Division, and the 2d Armored Division, commanded by Maj. Gen. Edward H. Brooks.

VII Corps, under Maj. Gen. J. Lawton Collins, included Maj. Gen. Raymond O. Barton's 4th Infantry Division, the 90th Infantry Division, initially—and briefly—under command of Brig. Gen. Jay W. MacKelvie, and the 9th Infantry Division, headed by Maj. Gen. Manton Eddy.

First Army also controlled the 82d Airborne Division, commanded by Maj. Gen. Matthew B. Ridgway, and the 101st Airborne Division under Maj. Gen. Maxwell D. Taylor. These units were to conduct parachute and glider assaults into the eastern half of the Cotentin Peninsula in the area between Sainte-Mère-Église and Carentan to seize control of the beach exits and establish an airhead from which VII Corps could push west and north.

First Army's initial mission was to push ashore on both sides of the Vire estuary, then thrust inland to capture the port of Cherbourg. After securing footholds ashore, elements of the two corps were to join up on the ground between the Vire and Taute rivers and continue the advance. Second priority was given to developing the beachhead south toward the village of Saint-Lô.

On Utah Beach there was surprisingly little enemy resistance, while the forces assaulting Omaha Beach ran into formidable obstacles and opposition, falling hours behind their planned timetable. Nevertheless, by the end of 6 June, First Army had moved ashore most of eight and one-third infantry regiments, a little less than planned. Army historians judged that "nowhere in First Army zone had initial objectives been fully achieved." By

7 June five divisions were ashore and operational, but all were seriously deficient in transport, tank support, artillery, and supplies, particularly ammunition.

During the next five days the attacking forces worked to join the several beachheads into a single, consolidated lodgment, then to expand that lodgment inland as rapidly as possible, linking up with the airborne divisions in the process. By 12 June the entire beachhead was continuous and secure, and the ultimate success of the landings seemed assured. "We would now force our way across the Cotentin," said Bradley, "then choke it off and capture the port of Cherbourg." The stage was being set for a breakout, but first would come six weeks of difficult fighting through the frustrating hedgerow country of Normandy.

[*See also* American Beaches; Bradley, Omar; *and articles on divisions mentioned herein.*]

BIBLIOGRAPHY

Bradley, Omar N., and Clay Blair. *A General's Life: An Autobiography.* 1983.
Bradley, Omar N. *A Soldier's Story.* 1951.
Colby, Elbridge. *First Army in Europe.* 1969.
Stamps, T. Dodson, and Vincent J. Esposito, eds. *Operations in the European Theaters.* Vol. 1 of *A Military History of World War II.* 1953.

LEWIS SORLEY

1ST BOMBARDMENT DIVISION. The division was established on 13 September 1943 by Eighth Air Force General Order 149. This regularized an organization that had informally come into existence in late November 1942. Throughout its history the bombardment division, one of three in the Eighth Air Force, was comprised solely of B-17 bombardment groups. It participated in all the major engagements of the Eighth Air Force, including the first and second Schweinfurt missions, the "Big Week" attack on German aircraft assembly plants, and the campaigns against the German synthetic oil industry and transportation system. During the OVERLORD campaign Maj. Gen. Robert B. Williams commanded the division, which he had led since July 1943.

On 6 June 1944 the division contained twelve bombardment groups: 91 BG, 92 BG, 303 BG, 305 BG, 306 BG, 351 BG, 379 BG, 381 BG, 384 BG, 398 BG, 401 BG, 457 BG. On D-day it attempted to bomb German defenses at the Allied invasion beaches in Normandy, but its bombardiers feared to drop too close to the invasion fleet and, as a consequence, released their bombs a few seconds too late, causing them to land in unoccupied areas beyond the German defenses. From 6 through 17 June the 1st Bombardment Division, and all the Eighth Air Force, bombed German rail targets, bridges, and air-

fields supporting the battlefield. On 18 June and at intermittent intervals afterward the division returned to the skies over Germany to strike strategic targets.

On 8 July (Operation CHARNWOOD) and 18 July (Operation GOODWOOD) the divisions joined the other bombardment divisions of the Eighth Air Force, the RAF Bomber Command, and Ninth Air Force medium bombers in attacks on German rear areas and frontline positions opposite General Bernard L. Montgomery's 21st Army Group. Although partially successful, these raids did not enable the British forces to break through the German defenses. On 24–25 July the division participated in Operation COBRA, a bombing raid near Saint-Lô. To avoid the American frontline troops, over half the division again released its bombs too late. Nonetheless, the bombing on 25 July shattered the German defenses, paving the way for the Allied breakout from the Normandy peninsula.

In August 1944 the Eighth Air Force reorganized by taking its fighter groups from direct control of VIII Fighter Command and attaching them to the bombardment divisions, so as to facilitate coordination of fighter escort and increase familiarization between specific bomber and fighter groups. As a result, the 1st Bombardment Division was redesignated the 1st Air Division.

[*See also* Eighth Air Force; Williams, Robert B.]

BIBLIOGRAPHY

Freeman, Roger. *The Mighty Eighth.* 1970.
Freeman, Roger. *The Mighty Eighth War Diary.* 1981.

RICHARD G. DAVIS

I CORPS. The British I Corps order of battle for Operation NEPTUNE comprised the 3d British, 3d Canadian, and 51st (Highland) infantry divisions, respectively supported by the 27th, 2d Canadian, and 4th armoured brigades, and the 1st and 4th Special Service brigades (Commandos). Corps troops were directly under command of the general officer commanding (GOC), Lt. Gen. J. T. Crocker, and included the Inns of Court Regiment R.A.C. (Armoured Car), the 62d Anti-Tank, 102d Light Anti-Aircraft, and 9th Survey regiments R.A., I Corps Troops Engineers, and I Corps Troops Signals. For the seaborne assault naval Force J transported the 3d Canadian Infantry Division and the 1st and 4th Special Service brigades, while Force S carried the 3d British Infantry Division. The 153d Brigade of the 51st (Highland) Division followed in Force L.

The I Corps had managed to fight its way out of the Dunkirk perimeter under the leadership of Maj. Gen. Harold Alexander. Early in 1943, when prospects of a return to the Continent began to look brighter, the corps (then commanded by Lt. Gen. F. E. Morgan) was ear-

marked as an assault formation. In May of the same year General Headquarters (GHQ) Home Forces specifically directed the new GOC, Lt. Gen. G. C. Bucknall, to train and equip his corps "to carry out seaborne assaults on the north east coast of France" and to study and report on the technique of the assault. Experimentation and exercises with landing craft, DD (Duplex Drive) amphibious tanks, and floating artillery fire thus continued to be conducted throughout 1943 under corps auspices.

The Normandy invasion plan developed by early 1944 called for the I Corps to land on two of five Allied assault areas: Juno, allocated to the 3d Canadian Infantry Division Group, and Sword, allocated to the 3d British Division Group. The 51st (Highland) Division and its supporting 4th Armoured Brigade were designated follow-up formations. The corps's D-day mission was to secure a lodgment fronting along the general line of Putot-en-Bessin to Caen. The 3d Canadian Division was to assault Mike and Nan beaches in the Juno area with two brigades, while the 3d British Division stormed Queen, in Sword, on a single brigade front so as to maximize power for a drive on Caen. The task of the 1st Special Service Brigade was to provide left flank protection for the corps sector.

Although the quick capture of Caen and neighboring Carpiquet airfield was a priority objective for the I Corps, Crocker realized that the *21st Panzer Division* stationed southeast of Caen was perfectly capable of intervening on D-day. The corps's plan in case Caen did not fall thus called for seizing the high ground to its north and masking the city for three to four days until the 51st (Highland) Division and 4th Armoured Brigade were available to participate in a concerted attack.

The I Corps sector received the brunt of panzer division counterattacks. The 3d British Division suffered the only major armored counterthrust on D-day, which, though staunchly repulsed, delayed the advance on Caen. The dash by *21st Panzer* elements to Lion-sur-Mer also exposed a serious two-mile-wide gap between the 3d Canadian and 3d British Divisions, a vulnerability

exacerbated by the continued resistance of German strong points near Douvres-la-Délivrande. On the afternoon of 7 June the 3d Canadian Division also received a rude shock when it was counterattacked and driven back by elements of the *12th SS Panzer Division* now coming into action.

More worrisome still, enemy attacks on the 6th British Airborne Division continued unabated east of the Orne for ground that, if lost by the Allies, would have given the Germans fire ascendancy over the Sword assault area, possibly jeopardizing the entire Normandy landing. In these circumstances Crocker correctly decided to give the highest priority to shoring up the airborne bridgehead across the Orne. In fact, although reinforced by the 1st Special Service Brigade, it would not have survived without the massed fire support of I Corps artillery. Crocker's decision to divert the reserve 9th Brigade from its original task of helping to take Caen and instead have it assist the 6th Airborne unfortunately constrained the operations of the 3d British Division. The I Corps sector was nonetheless consolidated on the evening of D plus 1 with the link-up of the 3d British and 3d Canadian divisions. As pressure continued to mount upon the 6th Airborne, which withstood repeated tank and infantry attacks between 10 and 12 June, the 51st (Highland) Division and 4th Armoured Brigade were correspondingly introduced into the Orne bridgehead to outflank Caen from the east. A counterattack by the *21st Panzer* on 13 June momentarily blunted the southward movement of the 51st Division, however.

On the same day, the unexpected appearance of the *2d Panzer* at Villers-Bocage caused General Bernard L. Montgomery to rethink his offensive priorities. He accordingly ordered the I Corps to assume an aggressive defensive posture in the Caen sector so as to permit the delivery of a massive blow by the XXX Corps in the Caumont area to the west. Over the next few days the I Corps repulsed a further attack on the airborne bridgehead and, by vigorous patrolling and active artillery fire, kept the bulk of the *21st* and *12th SS* panzer divisions pinned to their positions north and west of Caen. On 17 June, No. 41 Royal Marine Commando, directed by the I Corps and strongly supported by artillery and naval fire, liquidated the last German pocket near Douvres-la-Délivrande. By this time, too, elements of eight panzer divisions had also been drawn onto the Second Army front.

[*See also* Crocker, J. T.]

BIBLIOGRAPHY

Ellis, L. F., et al. *The Battle of Normandy.* Vol. 1 of *Victory in the West.* 1962.

Stacey, C. P. *The Victory Campaign: Operations in North West Europe, 1944–1945.* 1960.

JOHN A. ENGLISH

1ST INFANTRY DIVISION. The U.S. 1st Infantry Division, a regular army division with a distinguished battle history in World War I, was organized as a triangular infantry division with three infantry regiments in November 1939 at Fort Benning, Georgia. The authorized strength of the division in 1943–1944 was 14,253 men, not including attached units. The division underwent extensive training during maneuvers in North and South Carolina in November 1941, amphibious training at Virginia Beach, Virginia, in January 1942, and later in Scotland after arriving at the port of Gourock aboard the *Queen Mary* on 8 August 1942.

Following additional training in England, the division landed at Oran, Algeria, as part of Operation TORCH on 8 November 1942. After a short fight with French troops, the division moved eastward into Tunisia and fought in that campaign, then in July 1943 participated in the invasion of Sicily, Operation HUSKY.

Maj. Gen. Terry de la Mesa Allen had commanded the division through the campaigns in North Africa and Sicily, but he was replaced by Maj. Gen. Clarence R. Huebner on 7 August 1943. The relief of the division commander and his assistant, Brig. Gen. Theodore Roosevelt, Jr., initially was resented by many of the soldiers, who revered their leaders. Lt. Gen. Omar Bradley, commander of the U.S. First Army, took responsibility for the relief, citing Allen's unwillingness to be a team player and the division's

emulation of his feisty attitude, but recent scholarship has shown that the Bradley-Allen relationship was more complex. Huebner soon won the men of his division over with a combination of stiff discipline and fairness and became known to is officers as "the Coach."

In late October 1943 the division began its redeployment to the United Kingdom to prepare for the Normandy invasion.

On the eve of the cross-Channel attack, the 1st was the U.S. Army's most experienced, battle-tested infantry division. General Dwight D. Eisenhower and General Bradley believed that the division had to be an essential part of any successful amphibious invasion of Europe.

As part of Force O, the 1st Infantry Division was to make the U.S. V Corps's main effort on the Calvados coast of Normandy at Omaha Beach, between Port-en-Bessin and the Vire River. The division Field Order Number 35 for NEPTUNE was issued on 16 April, but many modifications were made up to the last possible moment. The division had participated in the extensive rehearsals at Slapton Sands in south Devonshire. The D-day forces comprising Force O numbered 34,142 men and 3,306 vehicles. Force B, the follow-up force scheduled to land later on D-day, totaled 25,117 men and 4,429 vehicles.

Reinforced with elements of the U.S 29th Infantry Division and additional artillery, armor, and engineer forces, the "Big Red One" landed at about 0630 on D-day with

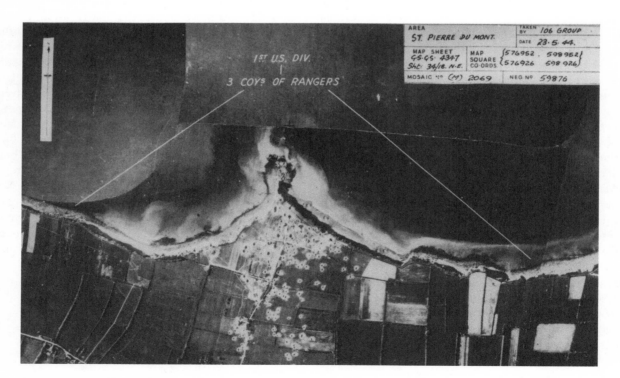

AERIAL VIEW.   Pointe du Hoc.

WOUNDED MEN OF THE 3D BATTALION, 16TH INFANTRY REGIMENT.   Receiving treatment after storming Omaha Beach.
NATIONAL ARCHIVES

the 116th Regimental Combat Team (RCT) of the 29th Division on the right on beach subsectors Dog Green, White, and Red, and Easy Green, and its own 16th RCT on the lest on beach subsectors Easy Red and Fox Green, each regiment with two battalions abreast and one in support. Two battalions of Rangers, formed in a provisional force, were assigned the bluffs on the right (west) end of the line in the 116th RCT's sector Charlie. Three companies of this Ranger force assaulted the cliffs at Pointe du Hoc, three miles west of the Omaha Beach sectors. DD (Duplex Drive) Sherman tanks that were to precede the 16th RCT to the beach either foundered in the rough water or had to be delivered directly on the beach. Tanks for support of the 116th RCT were delivered directly to shore by their landing craft. Many landing craft did not make it to their assigned beach sectors, unloading wherever they happened to land. Later waves, the 115th RCT (29th Division) and the 18th RCT (1st Division), were scheduled to allow a rapid buildup on the beach so that the two divisions could continue the attack abreast.

The Germans had prepared the beach defenses well; concrete reinforced pillboxes, underwater and beach obstacles, land mines, wire entanglements, and strong points were sited to provide the greatest interference. A reinforced battalion of about 1,000 soldiers from the *726th Infantry Regiment (716th Infantry Division)* manned the strong points

and beach defenses, with three additional battalions of divisional reserves farther inland. The *352d Infantry Division,* which Allied intelligence had placed near Saint-Lô, had moved forward in May to take over the Omaha Beach area, reinforcing the *726th Regiment.* The *352d* was an excellent fighting unit with experience on the Russian front. Although other German units capable of conducting a counterattack were available, the *352d's* commitment to the beach defense meant no serious German counterattack could be mounted in time as the Americans pushed inland.

Maj. Gen Huebner commanded the landing force; Brig. Gen. Norman D. Cota, the assistant division commander of the 29th, helped with the elements of this division that landed in the first waves. The 116th RCT was to capture Vierville-sur-Mer and push through the defenses, while the 16th RCT pushed east along the defenses. Company G, 2d Battalion, 16th Infantry, led the way off beach sector Easy Red, up a draw through a mine field to the bluffs beyond. The 16th RCT commander, Col. George A. Taylor, who had landed at 0815 saw men bunched up taking casualties from artillery and mortar fire. He exhorted his troops: "Two kinds of people are staying on this beach, the dead and those who are going to die—now let's get the hell out of here." In those first harrowing hours when the American infantrymen were clinging to Omaha Beach, General Bradley considered

1st Infantry Division
Maj. Gen. Clarence R. Huebner

16th Regimental Combat Team (RCT)

16th Infantry Regiment
7th Field Artillery Battalion
1st Engineer Combat Battalion (-)
1st Medical Battalion (-)
741st Tank Battalion (DD)
62d Armored Field Artillery Battalion
20th Engineer Combat Battalion
Additional attached units

18th Regimental Combat Team (RCT)

18th Infantry Regiment
32d Field Artillery Battalion
5th Field Artillery Battalion
Company B, 1st Engineer Combat Battalion
Companies B and D (-), 1st Medical Battalion
745th Tank Battalion
Additional attached units

26th Regimental Combat Team (RCT)

26th Infantry Regiment
33d Field Artillery Battalion
Company C, 1st Medical Battalion
1st Platoon, Company C, 1st Engineer Combat
  Battalion
Additional attached units

(-) Elements of the unit detached or not present

Note: Divisional troops included a headquarters company, military police platoon, ordnance company, quartermaster company, signal company, and other small units. As landing force commander for Omaha Beach, Maj. Gen. Huebner also commanded the 175th RCT and additional attached units from the 29th Division, the Engineer Special Brigade, and other units.

diverting the Omaha follow-up forces to the less-challenged Utah Beach. In his first book of memoirs, Bradley remembered his choice of the experienced 1st Infantry Division and concluded that it probably guaranteed the ultimate success of the invasion.

At about 1130, V Corps reported that the deadlock had been broken and the troop were moving inland, but on the beach the "Big Red One" still had plenty of resistance to deal with. General Huebner and his command group arrived at 1900 on Easy Red Beach and joined the division command post. By the evening of D-day, the bit of high ground near Vierville, Saint-Laurant, and Colleville were in Allied hands.

Driving south from the beachhead on 9 June, the 1st Infantry Division, now with the U.S. 2d Infantry Division on its right (west) flank, had reached Caumont and the Saint-Lô highway by 13 June. The Germans had managed to shift forces so that the division was facing elements of two divisions and three regiments. Five soldiers of the "Big Red One" received the Medal of Honor for acts of heroism during this first week of the invasion, during which the division sustained 1,744 casualties.

Following the breakout from the Normandy beachhead in early August, the 1st Infantry Division advanced east, passing south of Paris and then northeast through he World War I battlefield of Soissons, where the division had fought in 1918, and on through Belgium toward Aachen on the Siegfried Line. During the winter of 1944–1945 the 1st Infantry Division fought in the Huertgen Forest, then on the northern shoulder of the "Bulge" during the German counteroffensive in the Ardennes. Late it captured Bonn and continued the fight across the Rhine at Remagen in March 1945. Sprinting across Europe for the next two months, the division ended the war in Europe near Karlsbad, Czechoslovakia, on 8 May, the 443d day of combat in World War II for the "Big Red One."

[See also Barrett, Carlton W.; DeFranzo, Arthur F.; Ehlers, Walter D.; Huebner, Clarence R.; Monteith, Jimmie W., Jr.; Pinder, John J., Jr.; Rangers.]

BIBLIOGRAPHY

Bradley, Omar N. *A Soldiers Story.* 1951.
Bradley, Omar N., and Clay Blair. *A General's Life.* 1983.
D'Este, Carlo. *Decision In Normandy.* 1983.
D'Este, Carlo. *Bitter Victory: The Battle for Sicily, 1943.* 1988.
Harrison, Gordon A. *Cross-Channel Attack.* U.S. Army in World War II: The European Theater of Operations. 1951.
U.S. Army Center of Military History. *Omaha Beachhead: 6 June–13 June 1944.* 1945. Facsimile reprint, 1989.
Katcher, Philip. *US 1st Infantry Division, 1939–45.* 1978.
Knickerbocker, H. R., et al. *Danger Forward: The Story of the First Division in World War II.* 1947.

JOHN F. VOTAW

1ST SPECIAL SERVICE BRIGADE.

As part of the 3d British Division, the 1st Special Service Brigade under Brig. Lord Lovat was formed especially for Operation OVERLORD. It consisted of Nos. 3, 4, and 6 Army Commandos and No. 45 Royal Marine Commando, plus two troops of No. 10 Inter-Allied Commando, a total of over 2,500 men. Most of the Army Commandos had considerable previous battle experience, but No. 45 Royal Marine Commando was newly formed and comparatively inexperienced.

The 1st Special Service Brigade, on the extreme left of the invasion force, was landed on Sword Beach, mostly by LCIs and LCAs (Landing Craft, Infantry, and Landing Craft, Assault), and passed through the 8th Brigade of the 3d Division, who had landed an hour earlier at H-hour to secure the beachhead. Brig. Lord Lovat admitted later that the brigade rehearsal in the Moray Firth of Scotland had been disastrous, and this was aggravated on D-day by the poor showing of the 8th Brigade on the beaches, which left his brigade with more to do than expected. They suffered about sixty casualties, though this was, perhaps, lower than anticipated.

No. 4 Commando, with the two troops of No. 10 Inter-Allied Commando, mostly Frenchmen, landed at H plus 60 minutes at La Brèche and then advanced quickly about a mile east to Ouistreham to storm and silence the coastal gun battery there. No. 6 Commando and No. 45 Royal Marine Commando landed at H plus 90 minutes, followed shortly afterward by No. 3 Commando and advanced brigade headquarters. No. 6 took the lead, pushing swiftly southward and eastward to cross the bridges over the Caen Canal and the Orne River, which were already in the hands of the airborne forces who had been dropped during the night by glider and parachute. Here they linked up with the 5th Parachute Brigade, of the 6th Airborne Division, at Bénouville and Ranville. No. 3 Army and No. 45 Royal Marine Commandos soon followed them across the Orne, and No. 6 Commando, joined by the 9th Parachute Brigade, took the village of Le Plein after a sharp skirmish during the afternoon.

By nightfall on D-day the 1st Special Service Brigade, with the paratroopers, held a line of high ground running from Merville in the north to near Bréville in the south. By now No. 4 Commando, which had completed its task at Ouistreham, and brigade headquarters had joined them. The Germans counterattacked during the night, but the Commandos held their positions.

On D plus 1, No. 45 Royal Marine Commando attempted to take Franceville Plage on the coast to the east of the Orne Estuary but was driven back and all but surrounded. In the afternoon two troops of the No. 3 Commando tried to take the Merville battery, but after reaching the bunkers, they were driven back by self-propelled guns

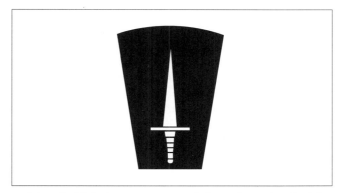

and lost half their troop strength in a fierce battle. The brigade was therefore forced to tighten its defensive perimeter amid the orchard and woods.

By D plus 3 the Commandos and airborne troops had been under almost constant bombardment from shells and mortar fire since they landed. Although their casualties had been lighter than expected on D-day, they now began to suffer badly. One troop of the No. 4 Commando was reduced to a mere fifteen men at one time. For the next three days probing patrols were sent out to determine the positions and strengths of the enemy, but the men were beginning to suffer from exhaustion, having had little sleep for nearly a week.

When German patrols from the *21st Panzer Division* tried to infiltrate through the British positions, the Commandos' fire discipline was superb, often delaying their fire until they were within twenty yards. On 10 June the brigade stood its ground against intense German pressure until the Germans were finally repulsed by No. 6 Commando in the evening. But the casualties had mounted. Two commanding officers had been wounded and evacuated, and two seconds-in-command and many of the senior troop commanders were either dead or out of action. An estimated 170 casualties were suffered in the first week, but the Germans had also taken heavy losses.

The Germans appreciated the strategic importance of containing the eastern flank, as their main armor was waiting farther south and east in the plains. Soon after D-day they had moved the *2d Panzer Division* and then the *1st* and *2d SS Panzer* divisions into the area around Caen. They tenaciously held on, denying the Allies the important city of Caen, which had been a target for D-day.

On 12 June, No. 6 Commando fought a gallant and prolonged action in the taking of Bréville, which the Black Watch had failed to capture the previous day. Brig. Lord Lovat was wounded that day and Derek Mills-Roberts, although himself wounded a few days earlier, assumed command. Lt. Col. Anthony D. Lewis took over the No. 6 Commando. The capture of Bréville was to prove a turning point in the battle for the eastern flank. It was the day the Germans lost the initiative, and the

Commandos once more took the offensive, harassing German positions mostly at night along the whole front. Strong fighting patrols were ordered to take prisoners with their smash-and-grab technique, and a coordinated sniping program was started, which required acute marksmanship, exceptional fieldcraft, and considerable patience, all part of the Commandos' makeup. Their hard training began to pay off.

The 4th Special Service Brigade, whose initial tasks had been successfully completed, moved in on 12 June with the No. 48 Royal Marine Commando, taking up positions around Salanelles. For the next few weeks the Commandos held their defensive positions on the high ground east of the Orne, a task not entirely suited to the Commandos' normal offensive techniques.

The 1st Special Service Brigade undoubtedly had one of the hardest of tasks, the holding of the vital left flank of the invading force, where German opposition was particularly strong. It was an easy area to defend, with its proliferation of hedgerows, small fields, woods, and orchards providing excellent cover for defensive positions and patrol infiltration. The superior quality of the Commandos, their enormous reserves of strength, and their individual battlefield skills were the deciding factors against a very determined enemy. Commandos were not trained to remain long in the fighting zone, and the lack of integrated fire support and a logistical backup was sorely felt at times. They had no previous experience of air support, but forward observation officers and forward bombardment officers attached to the Commandos controlled artillery and naval gunfire.

During the two and a half months the brigade remained in Normandy, it suffered casualties of 77 officers and 890 other ranks killed, missing, or wounded.

[See also Commandos; Lovat, Lord; 3d Infantry Division.]

BIBLIOGRAPHY

Ladd, James. *Commandos and Rangers of World War II.* 1978.
Lovat, Lord. *March Past.* 1978.
Saunders, Hilary St. G. *The Green Beret.* 1949.

DEREK OAKLEY

I SS PANZER CORPS. *I SS Panzer Corps* came into existence in the second half of 1943 and was deployed in the West as the reserve corps of the Armed Forces High Command (Oberkommando der Wehrmacht—OKW), directly subordinate to Hitler, an arrangement that led to confusion on D-day. It was intended to be a mobile armored fire brigade, its mission to engage antic-

JOSEF ("SEPP") DIETRICH (LEFT) WITH GERD VON RUNDSTEDT.   COURTESY OF CHARLES MESSENGER

ipated Allied landings on the coast of northwest Europe in *Army Group B*'s sector, from Antwerp to Cherbourg.

I SS Panzer Corps's commander was Oberstgruppenführer Josef ("Sepp") Dietrich, veteran commander of the *1st SS Panzer Division Leibstandarte SS "Adolf Hitler"*. Dietrich selected army Col. Fritz Kraemer as his chief of staff. The initial composition of the corps included the following powerful armored formations: *1st* and *12th SS Panzer* divisions, *17th SS Panzer Grenadier Division*, and the army's *Panzer Lehr Division*.

The Allied invasion came at a time when the corps had only the *12th SS Panzer Division "Hitlerjugend"* capable of taking action in the coming hours. When no orders from OKW were forthcoming, *Army Group B* assumed control of elements of this division in the invasion area at 0700, and ordered them to engage the Allies on the beach north of Caen. *1st SS* was refitting in Belgium. (Dietrich and Kraemer were at its headquarters in Brussels and left at once for the battle zone.) *17th SS*, deployed south of the Loire, was released from OKW Reserve and assigned to *LXXXIV Corps* of *Seventh Army*. *Panzer Lehr* was at Nogent-le-Rotrou, 140 kilometers (eighty-seven miles) away from the beach, and would require many hours to reach the front.

As the battle developed on 6 June the corps, subordinated to *Seventh Army*, assumed command of *12th SS*, *Panzer Lehr*, *21st Panzer Division*, and *716th Infantry Division*. *21st Panzer* was engaged in a dual role, supporting *716th Infantry Division*, which was being badly battered by British Second Army on the coast northeast of Caen, and attempting to join with *12th SS* in a drive to the sea east of the Orne River.

During the next forty-eight hours, unable to drive the invaders into the sea, the corps nevertheless conducted limited counterattacks against the British on both sides of the Orne River, north and northwest of Caen. By 9 June the corps had established a defensive line north of Caen that would not be cracked for a month.

By 11 June the corps's subordinate panzer divisions had experienced losses of more than 50 percent, and *716th Infantry Division* had been virtually destroyed.

From 12 through 18 June the corps absorbed the British Second Army's attacks on Caen, Villers-Bocage, and Tilly-sur-Seulles, skillfully committing its reshuffled elements in local offensive and defensive combined arms actions. Although Allied naval bombardment and air supremacy prevented the corps from launching a decisive counterattack, the defenders forced the Allies to fight a battle of attrition that was costly to both sides, thwarting Montgomery's plans to capture Caen on 6 June. The Germans would not be driven from the city until mid-July.

[*See also* Dietrich, Josef ("Sepp"), *and articles on units mentioned herein.*]

I SS Panzer Corps

Oberstgruppenführer Josef ("Sepp") Dietrich

SS Panzer Signal Battalion 101
SS Panzer Battalion 101 (heavy)
SS Panzer Artillery Battalion 101 and *Observer Battery 101 (heavy)* [formerly *SS Projector Battalion 101*]
SS Medical Battalion 101
SS Supply Battalion 101

12th SS Panzer Division
Brigadeführer Witt[1]
Standartenführer Meyer

21st Panzer Division
Maj. Gen. Edgar Feuchtinger

Panzer Lehr Division
Maj. Gen. Fritz Bayerlein

716th Infantry Division[2]
Maj. Gen. Wilhelm Richter

---

[1] Killed in action 14 June 1944
[2] Virtually decimated; removed from the front 9 June 1944

BIBLIOGRAPHY

D'Este, Carlo. *Decision in Normandy: The Unwritten Story of Montgomery and the Allied Campaign.* 1983.

Meyer, Hubert. *Kriegsgeschichte der 12. SS Panzer Division "Hitler Jugend".* Vols. 1–2. 1982. Reprint, 1987.

Ose, Dieter. *Entscheidung im Westen im 1944. Der Oberbefehlshaber West und die Abwehr der alliierten Invasion.* Vol. 22 of *Militärgeschichtliches Forschungsamt Beiträge zur Militär- und Kriegsgeschichte.* 1982.

Sauer, Robert J. "Germany's I SS Panzer Corps: Defensive Armored Operations in France, June–September 1944." Ph.D. diss., Boston College, 1992. Ann Arbor: University Microfilms, 1992.

Shulman, Milton. *Defeat in the West.* 1947. Rev. ed., 1986.

ROBERT J. SAUER

FLIEGERKORPS IX. *See* IX Air Corps.

FLIEGERKORPS II. *See* II Air Corps.

FLIEGERKORPS X. *See* X Air Corps.

FOLLOW-UP FORCE B. *See* Task Force 126.

FOLLOW-UP FORCE L. *See* Task Force L.

49TH (WEST RIDING) INFANTRY DIVISION. This British division was a territorial formation raised in the West Riding districts of the county of Yorkshire. It had the standard British triangular divisional composition: three infantry brigades, each of three battalions, with a field regiment of artillery in support of each brigade and the usual service units. The division served in the ill-fated 1940 Norwegian campaign and then formed part of the occupation forces in Iceland until relieved by the American army in 1941.

During the second week of April 1943, Maj. Gen. E. H. Barker, who was to lead the division in the Normandy battles, took over command. There were changes in organization and increases in strength, particularly of the antitank and machine-gun units. The order of battle for the campaign in Normandy was composed of the 146th, 147th, and 70th infantry brigades. Divisional strength was just over 18,000 men.

The 49th, forming part of the XXX Corps, was not chosen as one of the assault divisions for the invasion of Normandy but was scheduled to land on Gold Beach on 10 June (D plus 4). Bad weather delayed debarkation, so that it was not until 14 June that the division's final detachments entered the concentration area southwest of Creully. The 146th Brigade had, however, already reached the combat zone on 13 June, where it relieved a brigade of the 50th British (Northumbrian) Infantry Division near Cristot, some ten kilometers (about six miles) west of Caen. For ten days after D-day, its bridgehead remained territorially fairly constant. Thus the 49th spent its first days in the forward zone carrying out local attacks against panzer grenadiers and armor of the *12th SS Division "Hitlerjugend"* and preparing for its first set-piece battle, the capture of the village of Fontenay and the high ground to the south. When contact was lost with the *"Hitlerjugend"*, the 146th Brigade sent out patrols on 15 June to regain touch. The resistance the patrols met showed very clearly that the *12th SS* would fight hard to hold its perimeter.

As part of the operations to clear its front, the 146th Brigade attacked Cristot on 16 June, while the 147th Brigade mounted a mock assault in order to divert German attention away from that sector. The 146th Brigade's operation met no opposition. The *"Hitlerjugend"* had

MEN OF THE 49TH DIVISION.   Inspecting a German Panther tank, Model A, near the crossroads outside Bretteville in late June 1944.

IMPERIAL WAR MUSEUM

ANTITANK GUNNERS.   Of the Durham Light Infantry, with Tiger tank.   IMPERIAL WAR MUSEUM

been pulled back temporarily to a shorter perimeter.

The division resumed the attack on 17 June with the 70th Brigade coming out of reserve in order that the whole of the 49th could participate in the operation. The main weight was with the 147th Brigade whose 6th Battalion, Duke of Wellington's Regiment, attacked the thickly wooded Parc de Boislande. Meanwhile the 146th Brigade's 4th Battalion, Lincolnshire Regiment, advanced toward Les Hauts Vents, a fourth of a battalion of the King's Own Yorkshire Light Infantry attacked the wooded area southwest of Cristot, and the 70th Brigade's 11th Battalion, Royal Scots Fusiliers, combed the woods to the south of Brouay.

The barrage opened at 1500 on the Parc de Boislande sector and was followed by waves of the 8th Armoured Brigade's tanks and the 6th Battalion infantry. The attack struck the German main line where *"Hitlerjugend"* grenadiers attacked the tanks at close quarters, and others engaged the infantry in hand-to-hand fighting.

During the evening of 17 June, the Germans mounted a strong but unsuccessful counterattack to recapture the Parc de Boislande using the *3d Panzer Grenadier Battalion* with panzer support. The attack was renewed during the morning of the eighteenth and developed into bitter fighting between the *"Hitlerjugend"*, who were determined to take the Parc, and the Duke of Wellington's Regiment, who were equally determined not to relinquish their hold upon it. It was SS divisional headquarters that ordered the attack to be broken off. The grenadiers and panzers withdrew to their former positions. The British battalion that had borne the brunt of the fighting had lost 16 officers and 220 men in two days; no longer fit for active service, it was broken up. On the following day the 7th Battalion, Duke of Wellington's Regiment, fought its way through the Parc despite the fanatical resistance of the *12th SS*. While the Duke of Wellington's battalions were battling for the Parc, other battalions of the 49th Division were attempting without success to seize Cristot and Fontenay. Furious fighting marked the following days.

In the autumn the 49th crossed the Seine, passed through Belgium, and advanced toward Arnhem, where it held the line until the end of the war.

[*See also* Barker, E. H.]

49th (West Riding) Infantry Division
Maj. Gen. E. H. Barker

146th Infantry Brigade

4th Lincolns
1st/4th Kings Own Yorkshire Light Infantry
The Hallamshire Battalion of the Yorks and Lancs
  Regiment

149th Infantry Brigade

11th Royal Scots Fusiliers
6th Duke of Wellington's Regiment
7th Duke of Wellington's Regiment

70th Infantry Brigade

1st Tyneside Scottish
10th Durham Light Infantry
11th Durham Light Infantry

Divisional Troops

69th, 143d, and 185th Field Regiments, RA
Divisional Engineers (3 Field Companies and a Field
  Park Company)
55th Anti-Tank Regiment (Suffolk Yeomanry)
89th Light Anti-Aircraft Regiment
49th Reconnaissance Regiment
2d Kensington (Machine Gun)
49th Division Signals
49th Division Column RASC

BIBLIOGRAPHY

Belfield, E., and A. Essame. *The Battle for Normandy.* 1965
Ellis, L. F., et al. *The Battle of Normandy.* Vol. 1 of *Victory in the West.* 1962.
Headquarters, Second Army. *An Account of Operations of 2nd Army in Europe, 1944–45.* 1945.
Hughes, F. K. *A Short History of 49th (West Riding) Infantry Division, 1944–45.* 1958.
McKee, A. *Caen: Anvil of Victory.* 1964.

JAMES LUCAS

XLVII PANZER CORPS. This unit was formed at Hanover on 25 November 1940 as the *XLVII Motorized Corps.* Committed to the campaign against the Soviet Union from the first day of the invasion, it became a panzer corps on 21 June 1942. Its corps units included the *130th Artillery Command,* the *447th Signal Battalion (Corps),* the *447th Supply Troop (Corps),* and the *447th Eastern Battalion.* On 12 May 1944, it was ordered to move to Normandy, where it served as a liaison and training headquarters for several panzer divisions that were in the process of rebuilding.

The staff of the *XLVII Panzer Corps* made an effective and well-seasoned team. Its commander was Gen. Hans Freiherr von Funck, a veteran of three years on the Eastern front. The chief of staff was Col. Walther Reinhardt, a General Staff officer and veteran of the Russian campaign, who had joined the *XLVII* as chief of operations in 1942. The corps artillery was commanded by Col. Gunther Zugehor, a Knight's Cross holder; the supply troop was directed by Maj. Heinrich Baehr; and Maj. Richwein Froehlich was chief signal officer. The *447th Eastern Battalion,* which was made up mainly of Ukrainian "volunteers," was commanded by Count Jurgen von Rittberg, a reserve captain who spoke fluent Russian. They were used as outriders and headquarters guards.

The *XLVII Panzer Corps* was committed to the defense of Normandy on 10 June in the so-called Caumont Gap between the *Seventh Army* on the left and *Panzer Group West* on the right (i.e., between the *LXXXIV Corps* on the left and the *I SS Panzer Corps* on the right). The *XLVII Panzer* had only the *2d Panzer Division,* the *17th SS Panzer Reconnaissance Battalion,* and its own general headquarters units to plug the hole, and only part of the *2d Panzer* had arrived. The corps was facing attacks from the U.S. 1st Infantry Division on its left and the British 7th Armoured Division on its right. The *XLVII,* however, was able to conduct a skillful delaying action against the Americans, while the *2d Panzer* made a rapid march from the Abbeville-Amiens area and struck the 7th Armoured in the right flank and rear on 13 June, bringing its advance to a halt. By nightfall, the Germans had forced the British off Hill 174 (near Cahagnes) and were on the verge of cutting the road between Caumont and Amaye-sur-Orne. By the morning of the fourteenth, the 7th Armoured was under attack from three sides, and during the day, the *XLVII Panzer Corps* was reinforced with strong battle groups of panzer grenadiers from the *2d SS Panzer Division "Das Reich,"* which quickly joined the battle against the Americans west of Caumont. That night, under cover of a Royal Air Force raid, the 7th Armoured pulled back seven miles. The first Allied attempt to encircle Caen had failed.

There were no further major offensives in the Caumont sector. Shortly thereafter, a regiment from the *III Antiaircraft Corps* was attached to Funck's command, and about two weeks after D-day, the *276th Infantry Division* reinforced the *XLVII Panzer Corps,* bringing further security to the sector.

The *XLVII Panzer Corps* escaped the Falaise pocket and the retreat from France. It fought in the Battle of the Bulge and surrendered in the Ruhr pocket in April 1945. Its last commander was Gen. Heinrich von Lüttwitz, who had commanded the *2d Panzer Division* at Caumont.

[*See also* Funck, Hans von.]

BIBLIOGRAPHY

Geyr von Schweppenburg, Leo. "Pz. Grp. West (Mid. 43–5 Jul. 44)." Office of the Chief of Military History, MS B-466. Report dated 14 Apr. 1947. U.S. Army Military History Institute, Carlisle Barracks, Pa.

McKee, Alexander. *Caen: Anvil of Victory.* 1964.

Stauffenberg, Friedrich von. "Panzer Commanders of the Western Front." Manuscript in the possession of the author.

SAMUEL W. MITCHAM, JR.

43D (WESSEX) INFANTRY DIVISION.

This British division was a territorial formation composed of units drawn from the southwestern counties of England. It had the standard British triangular composition: three infantry brigades, each of three battalions, together with artillery and service units. At full strength the division numbered 18,400 men. The division was to have landed on Juno Beach and was then to have moved toward Second Army's perimeter so that Second Army could open the offensive to take Caen.

The 43d was scheduled to complete its debarkation during the second week of June, but bad weather in the English Channel so delayed the turn-round of shipping that it was not until 24 June that the whole division had landed and concentrated north of Bayeux. Upon arrival, the 43d had already suffered casualties. A sea mine exploded under *Derry Cunihy,* the ship carrying the divisional reconnaissance regiment, and 180 men were lost and 150 were wounded.

On 6 August, the division captured Mont Pinçon, the most important tactical feature in Normandy, and later that month it crossed the Seine. Advancing through Belgium it entered Holland and fought its way forward

43d (Wessex) Infantry Division
Maj. Gen. G. I. Thomas

129th Infantry Brigade
4th Somerset Light Infantry
4th Wiltshire Regiment
5th Wiltshire Regiment

130th Infantry Brigade
7th Royal Hampshire Regiment
4th Dorsetshire Regiment
5th Dorsetshire Regiment

214th Infantry Brigade
7th Somerset Light Infantry
1st Worcestershire Regiment
5th Duke of Cornwall's Light Infantry

Divisional Troops
94th, 112th, 179th Field Regiments, RA
Divisional Engineers (3 Field Companies and a Field Park Company)
59th Anti-Tank Regiment
110th Light Anti-Aircraft Regiment
43d Reconnaissance Regiment
8th Middlesex (Machine Gun)
43d Wessex Divisional Signals
43d Wessex Division Column RASC

toward Arnhem. The 43d then swung eastward into Germany and after operations in the Roer River area reached and crossed the Rhine. The end of the war saw the Wessex Division fighting in the Bremen area of northern Germany.

[*See also* Thomas, G. I.]

BIBLIOGRAPHY

Ellis, L. F., et al. *The Battle of Normandy.* Vol. 1 of *Victory in the West.* 1962.

Essame, A. *The 43rd (Wessex) Division at War, 1944–1945.* 1952.

McKee, A. *Caen: Anvil of Victory.* 1964.

JAMES LUCAS

4TH INFANTRY DIVISION.

Maj. Gen. Raymond O. Barton commanded the U.S. 4th Infantry Division. By the time of the Normandy landings, he had been with the division for four years, beginning as its chief of staff in 1940. In June 1942 he took command, organizing and training the division for war, and in January 1944 brought it to England to conduct final preparations for the invasion.

TORQUAY, SOUTHWESTERN ENGLAND.   4th Division marching to its ships, 3 June 1944.

THE ROBERT HUNT LIBRARY, LONDON

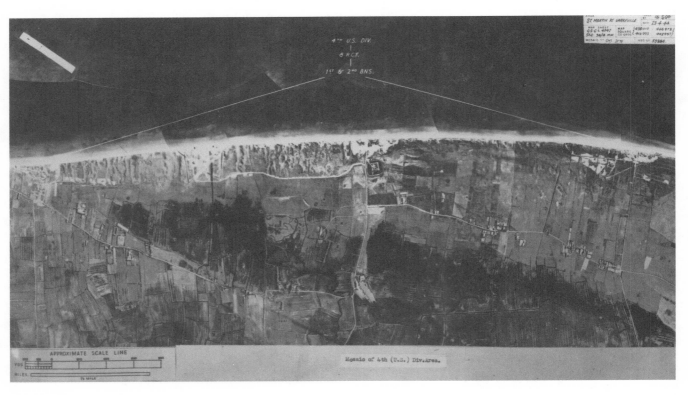

AERIAL VIEW.   4th Division landing area.

IMPERIAL WAR MUSEUM

8TH INFANTRY REGIMENT.   Commanded by Col. James A. Van Fleet, moving inland with full equipment.
THE ROBERT HUNT LIBRARY, LONDON

The division, which Gen. Omar Bradley praised as "superbly trained," consisted of more than 18,000 soldiers. It was built around three infantry regiments backed up by four battalions of artillery and supported by the usual cavalry, engineer, signal, medical, ordnance, quartermaster, and military police elements. In addition to small arms and mortars, the infantry was equipped with a number of 57-mm antitank guns.

The division, as part of Maj. Gen. J. Lawton Collins's VII Corps, was assigned to conduct the initial D-day landings on Utah Beach. Because of constricted conditions in the landing area, it would attack in a column of regiments. The 8th Infantry, commanded by Col. James A. Van Fleet, was to conduct the initial assault, reinforced with an attached battalion of the 22d Infantry. Its mission was to occupy the high ground along the road running between Sainte-Marie-du-Mont and Les Forges, then push westward across the Merderet River.

The 22d, under Col. Hervery A. Tribolet, was to land at H plus 85 minutes with its remaining two battalions, then move north to seize the causeway that spanned the inundated ground at Les Dunes de Varreville. From there it would continue northwest to capture Quinéville and occupy the surrounding high ground.

Finally the 12th Infantry, under Col. Russell P. ("Red") Reeder, would come ashore at H plus 4 and advance to seize the high ground between Emondeville and the Merderet River, along with a crossing of the Merderet at Port-Brehay. On D-day the 4th Division also had attached one regiment, the 359th Infantry, of the 90th Infantry Division, the first follow-on division in its sector.

The 4th Division had surprisingly little difficulty in the initial assault, taking only light casualties and quickly gaining a lodgment. It turned out that by fortuitous error the entire force had been landed some 1,830 meters (2,000 yards) south of the intended beach, where much stronger defenses would have been encountered. Brig. Gen. Theodore Roosevelt, Jr., a "spare" brigadier with the 4th Division, had volunteered to lead the first wave of the assault force. His actions that day, improvising and leading an attack out of the unexpected locale, won him a Medal of Honor.

After gaining the beaches, the 4th Division's lead regiment crossed the flooded areas on existing causeways and moved west to establish contact with the airborne units. Follow-on forces attacked northwest to enlarge the beachhead. By dusk most of the division had gotten ashore and pushed some 6 to 11 kilometers (4 to 7 miles) inland. At the end of D-day virtually the entire division had landed, and Colonel Reeder's 12th Infantry was the farthest inland of any unit on the ground. These advances had been achieved economically, for D-day casualties in the division were, as West Point's history text put it, "astonishingly low," totaling 197 men, 60 of whom had been lost at sea.

The next day the 4th Division broke through to the important road junction at Sainte-Mère-Église, relieving

4th Infantry Division
Maj. Gen. Raymond O. Barton

8th Infantry Regiment
12th Infantry Regiment
22d Infantry Regiment

HHB (Headquarters and Headquarters Battery) Division Artillery
20th Field Artillery Battalion
29th Field Artillery Battalion
42d Field Artillery Battalion
44th Field Artillery Battalion

4th Reconnaissance Troop
4th Engineer Combat Battalion
4th Medical Battalion
704th Ordnance Light Maintenance Company

Note: Divisional troops included a headquarters company, military police platoon, quartermaster company, signal company, and other small units. Following 9 June 1944 various tank destroyer battalions were attached to the division.

elements of the 82d Airborne Division, and by 9 June it had advanced about 4.8 kilometers (3 miles) toward Cherbourg, which it had been ordered to seize. In contrast to the relative ease of the landings, beyond the beachhead the defenders put up stiff resistance. In the next three days of very hard fighting, the division captured several enemy forts blocking its advance and approached the ridgeline through Montebourg-Quinéville, where it again encountered determined defenses as the German *91st, 243d,* and *709th* divisions were ordered to stop its drive on Cherbourg.

The 4th Infantry Division had been the first unit to cross the Normandy beaches. It subsequently fought its way to Cherbourg, then wheeled and punched through the hedgerow country south of Carentan, playing a key role in the Normandy breakthrough. It was also the first American unit to enter Paris. At the war's end Gen. George S. Patton, Jr., wrote to General Barton that "no American division in France has excelled the magnificent record of the 4th Infantry Division, which has been almost continuously in action since it fought its way ashore on the 6th day of last June."

[*See also* Barton, Raymond O.; Roosevelt, Theodore, Jr.]

BIBLIOGRAPHY

Army Navy Publishing Company. *A Pictorial Record of the 4th Infantry Division.* 1946.
Harrison, Gordon A. *Cross-Channel Attack.* U.S. Army in World War II: The European Theater of Operations. 1951.
Stamps, T. Dodson, and Vincent J. Esposito, eds. *Operations in the European Theaters.* Vol. 1 of *A Military History of World War II.* 1953.
Stars & Stripes. *Famous Fourth: The Story of the 4th Infantry Division.* 1945.

LEWIS SORLEY

4TH SPECIAL SERVICE BRIGADE. The 4th Special Service (later Commando) Brigade was formed in September 1943, when the British Commandos were reorganized under the umbrella of the Special Service Group. In March 1944 the brigade, then stationed in Kent in the southeast corner of England, came under command of the 21st Army Group for OVERLORD, the Normandy invasion. The Commandos themselves were made up of two types, Army Commandos, which were the original Commandos formed from volunteers in the summer of 1940, and Royal Marine Commandos, which were created from battalions of the Royal Marine Division. The latter was not established until February 1942, but eight were in existence by the end of March 1944. The 4th Special Service Brigade was commanded by a Royal Marine officer, Brig. B. W. Leicester, and consisted of four Royal Marine Commando units—No. 41 (formed in October 1942), Nos. 46 and 47 (formed in August 1943), and No. 48, which was not formed until March 1944. Of these only No. 41 had seen action, taking part in the Sicilian and Italian landings before returning to Britain in November 1943.

Each Commando unit was organized into five troops and a heavy weapons troop. Each of the former consisted of 60 men and was made up of a troop HQ and two sections. The heavy weapons troop had three-inch mortars and medium machine guns. In all, the Commando unit consisted of just under 450 men. Every one had graduated from the Commando Basic Training Centre at Achnacarry in the Highlands of Scotland, a physically and mentally demanding course including instruction in demolitions, unarmed and armed close combat, fieldcraft, and amphibious operations.

The main objective of the 4th Special Service Brigade on D-day was the radar station at Douvres, which was situated one mile inland and midway between Juno and Sword beaches. The plan was for two Commando units to land simultaneously on separate beaches, clear the coastline between Juno and Sword, and then turn inland to Douvres. The men of No. 41 Royal Marine Commando were put ashore three hundred yards west of their allotted beach at the western end of Juno, but quickly reoriented themselves and began to advance westward; they were held up by strong German opposition in Luc-sur-Mer. The men of No. 48, which landed with Brigade HQ on the eastern end of Sword, had more serious problems, some of their landing craft hitting underwater obstacles and all meeting heavy fire from the shore. Nevertheless, they got ashore and then turned eastward for the linkup with No. 41. But they also became embroiled in a battle among the houses of the village of Langrune, which continued until nightfall. Thus the linkup was not achieved.

No. 47 Royal Marine Commando was given a totally different task. This was to land with the 231st Independent Infantry Brigade on the west end of Gold Beach and then turn westward to seize Port-en-Bessin, which lay on the coast midway between Gold and Omaha. They, too, initially headed for the wrong beach and had four out of their fourteen landing craft sunk by German guns as they moved parallel to the shore to the correct beach. This resulted in the loss of much equipment as well as seventy-two men being posted as missing, although some rejoined a few days later. Consequently, it took time to organize the unit after landing. The delay caused by this and by German opposition as the men advanced toward their objective meant that they, too, were unable to secure it before nightfall, halting on a small hill just short of the little port. As for No. 46, its members had trained for a cliff assault to seize either the Houlgate or the Bénerville coastal batteries. But both had been successfully neutralized by naval gunfire, and hence the unit experienced a frustrating D-day as a reserve.

On D plus 1, Nos. 41 and 48 renewed their efforts against Luc-sur-Mer and Langrune and eventually, with the help of infantry and tanks, managed to subdue them. Port-en-Bessin was also secured in the afternoon by No. 47, supported by artillery and naval gunfire. When No. 46 finally landed, its men were ordered to capture a strongpoint at Petit Enfer, two miles east of Langrune, which they did with the help of naval gunfire, artillery, and tanks, and then linked up with No. 41. The brigade now turned inland toward Douvres, but Lt. Gen. J. T. Crocker, commanding the I Corps, decided not to assault it until his strength was sufficient to avoid needless casualties. Thus, leaving No. 41 to contain it, the remainder of

STORMING ASHORE.   The men at center are carrying a miniature motorcycle, probably for use by a signals dispatch rider.   IMPERIAL WAR MUSEUM

the brigade was able to pause in order to recuperate. Douvres was eventually to fall to No. 41 on 15 June.

Meanwhile, on the night of 11–12 June, Brigade HQ, with Nos. 47 and 48, was switched to the Allied left flank to bolster the 6th Airborne Division and the 1st Special Service Brigade, and No. 46 was loaned to the 9th Canadian Brigade for the clearance of the valley of the Mue River, which ran northwest of Caen between Barbière and Rots. Faced with elements of the *12th SS Panzer Division "Hitlerjugend,"* but supported by tanks, No. 46 had an extremely successful day on 11 June, capturing the villages of Le Hamel and Rots at a cost of sixty casualties.

Then Nos. 41 and 46 rejoined the brigade, which remained, under command of the 6th Airborne Division, guarding the Allied left flank for the next two months, with much of their time being taken up by aggressive patrolling in order to dissuade the Germans from attacking. The 4th Special Service Brigade then took part in the closing up to the Seine and the breakout across it. The men spent September containing the German garrison of Dunkirk, which held firm until the end of the war, and then moved to Ostend. In November, with No. 4 Commando having replaced No. 46, which returned to England, the brigade played the leading role in the assault on Walcheren at the mouth of the Scheldt, and thereafter, retitled the 4th Commando Brigade, it fought under Canadian command in Holland.

At war's end it spent a few months in Germany before being withdrawn to England in November 1945. Before this, No. 4 Commando had been disbanded in line with the decision to hand the Commando role over to the Royal Marines, and the three Royal Marine Commando units in the brigade were disbanded in February 1946 as part of the postwar reductions.

[*See also* Commandos; Leicester, B. W.]

BIBLIOGRAPHY

Ladd, James. *Commandos and Rangers of World War II.* 1978.
Messenger, Charles. *The Commandos, 1940–1946.* 1985, 1991.
Saunders, Hilary St. George. *The Green Beret: The Story of the Commandos, 1940–45.* 1949.
Young, Peter. *Storm from the Sea.* 1956.

CHARLES MESSENGER

FRANCE. By D-day, Nazi Germany occupied all of metropolitan France. The colonial empire and fleet were in the hands of either Gen. Charles de Gaulle's Free French or the Allies. More than 2 million French were prisoners of war or forced laborers in Germany. The French economy was being drained at a greater rate than that of any other occupied country. Civilians, especially in urban areas, suffered malnutrition and deprivation as well as punitive acts by the Nazis.

The Nazi blitzkrieg of May 1940 resulted in a rapid defeat, and the so-called armistice of June 1940 divided France into two parts: an occupied zone of the entire

PIERRE LAVAL.   A member of the Vichy cabinet, Laval fled to Germany upon the liberation of France. After the war he was tried in France, found guilty, and executed.

NATIONAL ARCHIVES

JEAN MOULIN.   One of the organizers of the Maquis, Moulin was arrested and killed in 1943.

MUSÉE DE L'ORDRE DE LA LIBÉRATION, PARIS

Atlantic coast plus all lands north of the Loire River, and an unoccupied southern sector under the Vichy regime headed by Marshal Henri Philippe Pétain. The Allied landings in North Africa in November 1942 provoked the Germans to extend their control over Vichy as well. Vying with Vichy for the French people's loyalty and support were the Resistance groups and de Gaulle's Free French movement based at first in London and then in Algiers.

On 10 July 1940, the discredited, disoriented, and disillusioned Parliament of the Third Republic voted overwhelmingly (569–80) to name Pétain head of state and authorize him to draft a new constitution. Seated in Vichy, Pétain and his coterie proceeded to do so. Outright fascists, more frequently found in occupied France, were vocal but few. More common in Vichy were traditionalists, conservatives, and opportunists.

Pétain proposed a "National Revolution," with the slogan *Travail, Famille, Patrie* replacing *Liberté, Egalité, Fraternité.* The roots were more native French than derivative of Nazi or Italian Fascist models, although they shared anti-Communist, antiparliamentarian, anti–trade union, and anti-Semitic biases. The Vichy regime stressed a rule by local notables and businessmen within state-regulated agencies. Youths, veterans, and others were encouraged to join patriotic organizations under Vichy auspices. Although it never went so far as to reestablish the Catholic church, the regime did favor the church with subsidies and a greater role in state functions and education. Improved state-church relations were set back, however by Vichy's treatment of the Jews. After 1942, when Vichy, on its own initiative or at the Nazis' behest, began rounding up Jews, many Catholic clergy and laypersons objected and sheltered thousands of Jews from deportation and a Final Solution.

The Vichy regime's policies were formulated by Pétain and his constantly changing cabinet, Pierre Laval being the most notable member. The laws and edicts were implemented by a purged civil service and officials (prefects) often carried over from the Third Republic. Rules were unevenly enforced by the 100,000-man Armistice army, the existing police forces, and a newly established and more ruthless militia. Communists, Jews, Freemasons, and resisters were ferreted out, tortured, and killed in the increasingly oppressive police state.

Living conditions in all of France had grievously deteriorated by 1944. Occupation costs, forced credits from the Bank of France, and outright confiscation and looting had reduced France to near-starvation. William L. Shirer in *The Rise and Fall of the Third Reich* (1961) cites the enormous drain of natural resources, livestock, finished goods, and even ten thousand carloads of art works. Production in French enterprises was directed to German war needs rather than local use. The population of large cities suffered the most, though the rural inhabitants were usually able to subsist unless German troops raided their farms.

After the war, Vichy officialdom claimed it had acted as the shield for France while de Gaulle's Free France was designated the sword. Vichy, however, shielded little and collaborated more. Pétain's ministers, and Laval in particular, often preceded or exceeded the Germans in anti-Semitic programs, forced labor allocations, and punishment of resisters and Communists. Collaboration by the French populace included a wide range of activities—from selling a loaf of bread to a German soldier or wining, dining, or sleeping with a Nazi to converting a factory to production for enemy use. Illustrative of the last activity was Louis Renault's retooling his auto plant outside Paris to build tanks for the German army. (Renault paid the price by dying in prison in 1946 while awaiting trial for

CHARLES DE GAULLE.   Speaking from the balcony of Cherbourg City Hall, 20 August 1944.

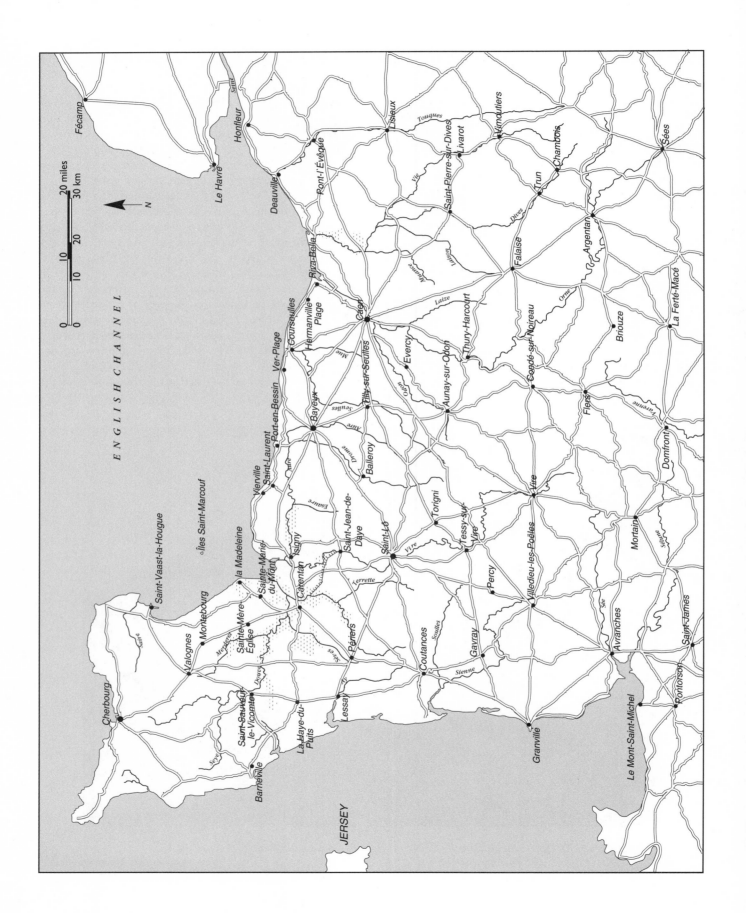

GERMAN SURRENDER OF PARIS.   Dietrich von Choltitz, German commanding officer in Paris, 25 August 1944, refused to carry out Hitler's order to burn the city.

NATIONAL ARCHIVES

treason.) The ethical and practical dilemma of the French in deciding whether to collaborate or resist is stunningly portrayed in Marcel Ophul's film *The Sorrow and the Pity*.

Acts of resistance to Vichy and the occupiers varied as widely as collaboration—from failing to yield the sidewalk to a German officer to writing or distributing clandestine anti-Nazi literature to enlisting in underground military groups and destroying enemy installations. As a movement, the Resistance began slowly and incohesively after 1940. The best-organized element, the Communist party, surfaced only after the Nazis attacked the Soviets in June 1941. To avoid Vichy and Nazi forced labor policies, tens of thousands of young men joined the Resistance by fleeing into the scrubland (maquis) of southern France.

Between 1940 and 1944 Charles de Gaulle had progressed from being a lone, self-exiled voice in London to achieving leadership of a provisional government in Algiers with control over Free French armed forces and the Resistance movement. Subsidized sparingly by Prime Minister Winston Churchill in London in 1940, de Gaulle at first attracted only a trickle of followers. Among them was Gen. Jacques Philippe Leclerc (né Jacques Philippe de Hauteclocque), a vibrant armored division commander. After the Allied landings in North Africa in November 1942, swelling numbers flocked to de Gaulle in Algeria, notably Gen. Jean de Lattre de Tassigny. The latter had served Pétain as head of the Armistice army, but defected and

escaped to Algiers with his family after the Nazis occupied the Vichy zone in 1942. He built up and led the Second French Army to invade southern France in August 1944.

In Algiers, de Gaulle established his leadership over the provisional government not only by eliminating such rivals as the American-supported Gen. Henri Giraud but also by uniting the disparate Resistance groups in metropolitan France. The non-Communist elements were easiest to assimilate through the efforts of Jean Moulin, who was betrayed, tortured, and killed in 1943. The "nonpolitical" Resistance, comprising thousands of armed young men in the Maquis, was also subsumed under the Free French banner. The Communists were more balky but at least gave lip service to de Gaulle by D-day. On the diplomatic front, however, he failed to obtain recognition as representative of French sovereignty by the Allies until after D-day. The stumbling block was the American president's suspicion of the general's colonial stance and alleged Napoleonic ambitions. De Gaulle was barred from the detailed planning for D-day and was invited by Churchill only on D minus 2 to be briefed in London. A mere 200 French troops crossed with the British and Canadians. Three French fighter groups and four bomber groups contributed one hundred of the three thousand Allied aircraft in the D-day activities. De Gaulle himself did not visit the Normandy front until D plus 8.

In anticipation of the landing, Vichy shared with the

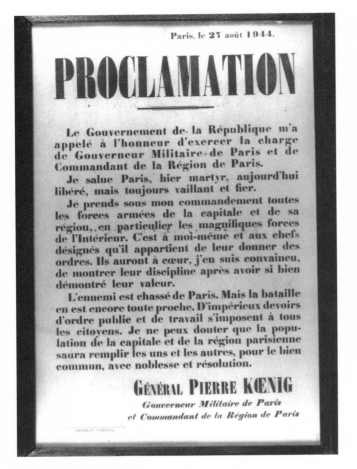

Paris, le 27 août 1944.

PROCLAMATION

Le Gouvernement de la République m'a appelé à l'honneur d'exercer la charge de Gouverneur Militaire de Paris et de Commandant de la Région de Paris.

Je salue Paris, hier martyr, aujourd'hui libéré, mais toujours vaillant et fier.

Je prends sous mon commandement toutes les forces armées de la capitale et de sa région, en particulier les magnifiques forces de l'Intérieur. C'est à moi-même et aux chefs désignés qu'il appartient de leur donner des ordres. Ils auront à cœur, j'en suis convaincu, de montrer leur discipline après avoir si bien démontré leur valeur.

L'ennemi est chassé de Paris. Mais la bataille en est encore toute proche. D'impérieux devoirs d'ordre public et de travail s'imposent à tous les citoyens. Je ne peux douter que la population de la capitale et de la région parisienne saura remplir les uns et les autres, pour le bien commun, avec noblesse et résolution.

GÉNÉRAL PIERRE KŒNIG

*Gouverneur Militaire de Paris
et Commandant de la Région de Paris*

KOENIG'S PROCLAMATION. Issued 27 August 1944. The proclamation reads: The government of the Republic has named me to exercise the office of military governor of Paris and of commandant of the Paris region. I salute Paris, yesterday a martyr, today liberated, but always valiant and proud. I take under my command all the armed forces of the capital and its region, in particular the magnificent [French] Forces of the Interior. It rests with me and with designated commanders to give them their orders. They will have the mettle, I am convinced, to demonstrate their discipline after they have so well demonstrated their valor. The enemy is driven from Paris. But the battle is still quite close. The pressing duties of public order and of work are imposed on all citizens. I cannot doubt that the population of the capital and of the Paris region will discharge both, for the common good, with nobility and resolution. MUSÉE DE L'ORDRE DE LA LIBÉRATION, PARIS

Free French the fear of a Communist takeover or of Allied military government rule in the liberated areas. Pétain instructed all administrative personnel to remain at their posts and maintain order as the Germans retreated. The officials were to adopt a policy of neutrality vis-à-vis Nazis, Allies, and Free French. De Gaulle, on the other hand, planned to replace the Vichy prefects with his own appointees and to frustrate any attempt by Communist resisters or the Allied military to establish their own administration in the liberated territories.

And so it transpired. De Gaulle's civil emissaries began arriving in France on 8 June. Centered in Bayeux, they worked with the Vichy subprefect to shelter and provide for the local populace, help with provisions and hospital space for the Allies, and keep up the functioning of the public utilities to the best of their ability as the battles raged around them. By 14 June, the Vichy official was replaced and de Gaulle's appointees assumed responsibility with the tacit permission of the British commanders. The massive destruction of many Norman towns obviously prevented a return to normalcy, but the citizenry enjoyed the services of the same baker, butcher, postman, policeman as in previous times. De Gaulle's personal appearance in Bayeux on 14 June signaled his success in asserting French sovereignty over its own territory.

Elsewhere in France, the Resistance had responded to a D minus 1 coded call over BBC, ordered by SHAEF, for a general uprising to weaken and confuse the Germans as to the exact site of the landings. Beyond the range of Allied ground support, the Resistance suffered severe losses from German reprisals, but did inflict damage upon the infrastructure, hampering Nazi units from easy deployment to Normandy.

D-day marked the beginning of the liberation of France, but the French would experience many months of misery and devastation before the Germans were removed completely from their soil.

[*See also* de Gaulle, Charles; French Resistance; Pétain, Henri Philippe Omer.]

BIBLIOGRAPHY

Aron, Robert. *France Reborn: The History of the Liberation*. 1964.
de Gaulle, Charles. *War Memoirs of Charles de Gaulle*. 1960.
Kedward, H. R. *In Search of the Maquis: Rural Resistance in Southern France, 1942–1944*. 1993.
Paxton, Robert. *Vichy France: Old Guard and New Order, 1940–1944*. 1972.
Warner, Geoffrey. *Pierre Laval and the Eclipse of France, 1931–1945*. 1968.

DONALD J. HARVEY

FRANZO, ARTHUR F. DE *See* DeFranzo, Arthur F.

FRASER, SIMON. *See* Lovat, Lord.

FRENCH RESISTANCE. The French Resistance, in its broadest sense, comprised the dedicated minority that undertook to harass the German occupiers of France, to

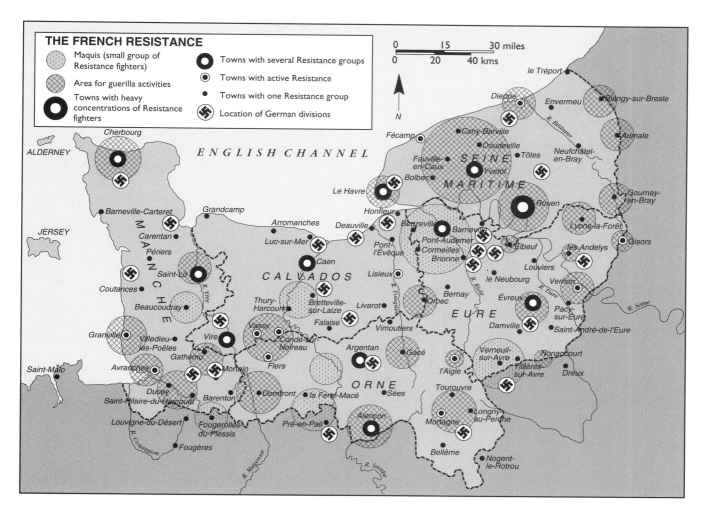

THE FRENCH RESISTANCE

- Maquis (small group of Resistance fighters)
- Area for guerilla activities
- Towns with heavy concentrations of Resistance fighters
- Towns with several Resistance groups
- Towns with active Resistance
- Towns with one Resistance group
- Location of German divisions

undermine Marshal Henri Philippe Pétain's collaborationist government at Vichy, to help in the liberation of France, and (for most members) after 1943, to install Charles de Gaulle as head of a French provisional government.

Of all Resistance activity the best known, because it directly affected the Normandy landings, was that of the French Forces of the Interior (FFI), or, to use a popular term, the Maquis. The Maquis (a Corsican term referring to the brush in which outlaws could hide) consisted of small guerrilla bands, ten to several hundred, living off the land. Armed with guns and explosives parachuted from England, they continually sabotaged railroads, highways, power lines, and telephone cables, and ambushed German convoys whenever possible.

In two Normandy coastline departments, Calvados and Manche, many Maquis encampments and resistance groups stood by in readiness for the eventuality of an Allied landing. Although all were affiliated with the FFI, most of them belonged to an assortment of Resistance movements such as the OCM (Organisation Civile et Militaire), the ORA (Organisation de Résistance de l'Armée), the pro-Com-

munist FTP (Francs-Tireurs et Partisans), and Libération-Nord, to name but a few of those especially active in Normandy. Possible 3,000 insurgents stood ready in these departments, many of them armed from stocks of weapons parachuted to them by the British Special Operations Executive (SOE). The Maquis, on orders from London, carried out specific missions identified by code—for example, GREEN (VERT) for railroad sabotage and TORTOISE (TORTUE) for attacks on vehicles on highways. A special phrase, such as "beware the bullfighter" (*méfiez-vous du toréador*), transmitted by the British Broadcasting Corporation, would inform a particular Resistance group of the desired action.

Resistance in the coastal departments faced unusual difficulties. The shores were off-limits to French citizens, and the Germans had deported many of the inhabitants: in some areas the occupation troops outnumbered the French. Furthermore, a diligent Gestapo had infiltrated so many Resistance organizations that by D-day many leaders and all-important clandestine radio operators had been arrested, executed, or forced out of the area. Messages sometimes reached England by carrier pigeon.

PIERRE BOURGOIN.   Legendary commandant of the French Special Air Service.

Nevertheless, when BBC action signals went out on 5 June, the Maquis, already alerted, did their utmost to carry out orders. In the Calvados department, the FFI blew up eight bridges, destroyed over a hundred vehicles, and cut innumerable railway lines. To the north of Utah Beach, the departmental FFI chief Yves Gresselin harassed the Germans south of Cherbourg. In the days following, the FFI could relax in some areas quickly liberated—such as Bayeux—but had to concede that the heavy bombardments at Saint-Lô and Caen rendered guerrilla actions impossible.

It was different story in the departments behind German lines. On 5 June Allied headquarters asked the FFI to hinder movements of the *275th Division,* stationed at Redon, 200 kilometers (125 miles) southwest of Normandy. In response the Maquis cut six out of seven strategic railway lines. Attacks by guerrillas and air force bombing postponed the division's arrival at Saint-Lô until 11 June. The Maquis also played an important role in delaying the march of a more powerful force, "*Das Reich,*" the *2d SS Panzer Division,* quartered over 700 kilometers (450 miles) from the front. Assaults by the FFI, coordinated by SOE agents and augmented by air force bombs,

inflicted 4,000 casualties and lengthened what could have been a three-day march into a nightmare of twelve. The delayed arrival of "*Das Reich*" certainly diminished German effectiveness, but the cost to France was heavy—one of the war's worst atrocities, the destruction of Oradour-sur-Glane and most of its inhabitants on 10 June, was committed by the frustrated Germans during the march.

In those Normandy departments, Orne and Eure, situated beyond the D-day battle zone, the Maquis persevered in exploits to block German deployments. Especially in the Eure department Marcel Baudot, the departmental chief, had banded the various Resistance groups together, and in coordinated efforts they felled trees across highways, blew up bridges and railway lines, sabotaged military equipment, cut telephone cables and power lines, and provided tactical intelligence to the Allied commands.

The Maquis assisted the D-day landings not only in Normandy but throughout France in actions that interfered with German reinforcements. They did this because on 5 June the BBC, under instructions from SHAEF (Supreme Headquarters Allied Expeditionary Force), called for a national insurrection, encouraging the FFI all over France to begin offensive operations. Then, as response to the insurrection order had generated devastating reprisals, it was revoked on 10 June; but as the cancellation could not halt operations already begun, the order resulted in heavy Resistance casualties.

One area, adjacent to Normandy, provided noteworthy help to the Allies in the week after D-day. This was Brittany, a 150-mile-long peninsula lying south and west of Normandy that served as the base for the German *XXV Corps.* These troops guarded the important U-boat pens at Brest, and unless blocked they could pose a serious threat to the flank of the Allied advance. Officers of General Eisenhower's Special Force Headquarters (staffed by SOE and OSS personnel) believed that the 20,000 lightly armed men of the Breton Resistance could hold the Germans, and they obtained the Supreme Allied Commander's approval for dispatch of supplies and agents. On the eve of D-day the first elements of a French Special Air Service (SAS) contingent dropped into Brittany, followed on 10 June by their leader, the legendary one-armed commandant Pierre Bourgoin, who rallied thousands of Bretons to fight the occupiers. Allied agents and matériel followed, and until the Allied Brittany campaign got under way in August, the Breton Resistance kept the Nazi occupation forces off balance. During the American army's sweep into Brittany the Resistance performed in spectacular fashion and was singled out by Eisenhower for special mention.

While guerrilla and sabotage actions made specific tangible contributions to D-day, other Resistance operations rendered significant though indirect assistance. For example, escape chains had helped many an Allied airman shot down over occupied territory to return to England by means of an "underground railroad." And during the Normandy landings the Resistance helped paratroopers who landed by error outside their designated drop zone.

The Resistance also provided invaluable intelligence both before and during the landing. One of France's most celebrated secret agents, Gilbert Renault-Roulier, known as Rémy, brought to London all kinds of information useful to the OVERLORD planners. Another Frenchman in Normandy obtained precise data on German installations and plotted them on a fifty-foot map. The map arrived at Allied headquarters two months before D-day. In May 1944, 3,700 secret reports reached England from Resistance intelligence networks.

Effective as the Resistance was, it might have made more of a contribution if it had been unified. Heroic efforts had been made in this direction, and General de Gaulle's capable emissary, Jean Moulin, who had helped bring three southern groups together as the MUR (Mouvements Unis de la Résistance), almost succeeded in fusing all the movements and political parties. In May 1943 he established the National Council of the Resistance (CNR), whose sixteen members, representing all factions including the Communist-dominated Front National, agreed at their first meeting to support de Gaulle. But a month later Moulin was arrested (and later beaten to death), and under his successor, Georges Bidault, the CNR tended to develop policies that, though representing the concerns of the interior Resistance, occasionally conflicted with those of de Gaulle and his Algiers-based Committee of National Liberation.

A parallel effort was made to unify the Resistance military groups—the French Forces of the Interior (FFI)—under Gen. Pierre Koenig, named by de Gaulle as FFI commander and also as his representative at SHAEF. Koenig's status, however, remained unclear because President Franklin D. Roosevelt refused to recognize de Gaulle as head of a French provisional government. On D-day Koenig was still negotiating with Eisenhower, and not until 17 June was his status clarified as being "similar to that of any Allied Commander serving directly under SHAEF."

During the eleven weeks that elapsed between D-day and de Gaulle's assumption of power in Paris, the Maquis continued to help as Allied regular armies broke out of Normandy and pushed the Germans back to the Rhine. For the British and Americans, the Resistance had provided invaluable military assistance; for the French it had demonstrated that honor, courage, and tenacity were qualities not lacking among the people who had suffered so grievous a defeat in 1940.

[See also France; Office of Strategic Services (OSS); 2d SS Panzer Division "Das Reich"; Special Operations.]

BIBLIOGRAPHY

Aron, Robert. *France Reborn.* 1964.
Funk, Arthur Layton. *Charles de Gaulle: The Crucial Years, 1943–1944.* 1959.
Miller, Russell, and Time-Life Editors. *The Resistance.* 1979.
Schoenbrun, David. *Soldiers of the Night: The Story of the French Resistance.* 1980.
Sweets, John. *The Politics of Resistance in France.* 1976.

ARTHUR L. FUNK

FRENCH SHIPS. Originally the Allied command had planned that only the light French ships of the Naval Forces of Great Britain (NFGB) would take part in Operation OVERLORD. But Rear Adm. André-Georges Lemonnier, general chief of staff of the French Navy in Algiers, arranged for the participation of two light cruisers, *Montcalm* and *Georges Leygues,* backed up by another cruiser, *Duquesne.* After coming from the Mediterranean, the ships, under the command of Rear Adm. Robert Jaujard, went on exercises off the coasts of Scotland and Ireland before heading to the landing zone on the eve of 6 June.

Until 10 June, the main activity of *Georges Leygues* and *Montcalm* was providing covering fire within the Bombardment Group of Rear Adm. Carleton F. Bryant of the Western Task Force. Both ships operated off Port-en-Bessin at the eastern tip of Omaha Beach. Their targets were coastal batteries, such as one in Longues, and German troops massed farther inland. After exhausting their 152-mm ammunition, both cruisers remained in the landing zone to provide antiaircraft support. On 15 June they returned to Great Britain and from there sailed to the Mediterranean where they took part in the landing at Provence.

Within the Eastern Task Force, the French destroyer *La Combattante* operated off the coast of Courseulles-sur-Mer in conjunction with four British destroyers. On 6 June, it successfully attacked several German light batteries, but did not escape damage. After running aground, it returned on the same evening to Portsmouth, England, where it was repaired. It then headed back to the French coast on 14 June, carrying on board Gen. Charles de Gaulle who landed at Courseulles, his first return to France since 17 June 1940.

French participation also included the frigates and corvettes of the NFGB, which were responsible until 19 June for escorting convoys through the English Channel. The corvettes *Aconit* and *Renoncule* operated in the Utah zone; the frigates *L'Escarmouche, L'Aventure,* and *Roselys* in the Omaha zone; and *Surprise, Découverte,* and *Commandant d'Etiennes d'Orves* in the Gold zone. From Cowes the submarine chasers *Calais, Paimpol, Audierne,* and *Dielette* also escorted other ships to Port-en-Bessin and Courseulles. The old battleship *Courbet* was towed across the English Channel and sunk off Ouistreham to act as a breakwater to facilitate the construction of an artificial harbor at Arromanches.

[*See also* Jaujard, Robert; Montcalm.]

BIBLIOGRAPHY

Auphan, Paul, and Jacques Mordal. *The French Navy in World War II.* 1959.
Jaujard, Robert. *Croiseurs en action.* 1959.
Jaujard, Robert. *Paisible Normandie.* 1954.

PHILIPPE MASSON
Translated from French by Marie-Josée Schorp

FUNCK, HANS VON

FUNCK, HANS VON (1891–1979), German, general, commander of the *XLVII Panzer Corps.* Hans Emil Richard, Freiherr von Funck, was born on the family estate near Aachen on 23 December 1891. He volunteered for active duty with the *2d Dragoon Regiment* when World War I broke out and spent most of the war on the Eastern front. He was commissioned a second lieutenant in 1915 and was selected for the new German army after the armistice. He was promoted to first lieutenant in 1923.

Baron von Funck was one of the pioneers in the movement to mechanize the German Army, commanding a motorized machine-gun squadron as early as 1919. He worked for Oswald Lutz, the first general of mobile troops, and Col. Heinz Guderian, the "father" of the blitzkrieg, in the 1920s and 1930s, and served as a liaison officer to Francisco Franco and the *Condor Legion* in the Spanish civil war. By the outbreak of World War II, Funck was a colonel, serving as military attaché to Lisbon. After the Polish campaign, he was given command of the *5th Panzer Regiment,* which he led with distinction in France. He briefly commanded the *3d Panzer Brigade* and the *5th Light Division* (1940–1941) before being named commander of the *7th Panzer Division.* He again distinguished himself on the Eastern front and was named acting commander of the *XXIII Corps* on 7 December 1943. Promoted to general on 1 March 1944, he assumed command of the *XLVII Panzer Corps* four days later.

On 12 May 1944, Wehrmacht High Command ordered Funck's headquarters to Normandy, where it initially served as an intermediate headquarters for several panzer divisions rebuilding in France. On 9 June, after Allied bombers knocked out the headquarters of *Panzer Group West,* Funck put his staff at the disposal of Gen. Leo Geyr von Schweppenburg. The following day, the *XLVII Panzer Corps* was inserted in the line between the left flank of the *I SS Panzer Corps* and the right flank of the *LXXXIV Corps* in order to plug the Caumont gap. Initially the *XLVII Panzer* controlled only the reconnaissance battalion of the *17th SS Panzer Grenadier Division,* the *2d Panzer Division,* and its own corps units; nevertheless, Funck was able to launch an effective counterattack against the British 7th Armoured Division (on his right flank) on 13 June while simultaneously holding the U.S. 1st Infantry Division to minor gains on his left. By 15 June, the Caumont gap had been closed.

Funck continued to hold his lines until 2 August, when, on orders from Adolf Hitler, he was instructed to direct an attack against Allied forces at Mortain and Avranches with every available panzer unit. This attack failed on 7 August. Funck later directed the remnants of his corps in the retreat from France, but was relieved of his command on 4 September on orders from Hitler, who held him partly responsible for the failure of the Mortain-Avranches attacks. Hitler also disapproved of Funck's divorce and some derogatory remarks he had made in early 1941 about the German-Italian alliance. Germany thus lost one of its most experienced panzer leaders and an excellent corps commander.

Funck managed to secure a minor appointment (as commander of *Reserve Panzer Headquarters XII* in the Wiesbaden area) in October but was forced into retirement by Gen. Wilhelm Burgdorf, chief of the Army Personnel Office, in January 1945. He was captured by the Russians at the end of the war. Repatriated to West Germany in 1955, he died on 14 February 1979.

[*See also* XLVII Panzer Corps.]

BIBLIOGRAPHY

Harrison, Gordon A. *Cross-Channel Attack.* U. S. Army in World War II: The European Theater of Operations. 1951.
Stauffenberg, Friedrich von. "Panzer Commanders of the Western Front." Papers in the possession of the author.

SAMUEL W. MITCHAM, JR.

G

GALE, RICHARD N. (1896–1982), British, major general, commander of British 6th Airborne Division. Richard Gale was commissioned into the Worcestershire Regiment in 1915, transferred to the Machine Gun Corps on the Western front in 1916, and there won the Military Cross. Between the wars he spent eighteen years at regimental duty, and by September 1939 he was a major on the staff of the War Office in London. From December 1940 to July 1941 he commanded an infantry battalion and in September of 1941 took over command, as a brigadier, of the newly raised 1st Parachute Brigade. By 1943 he was a major general and director of air at the War Office, and in April of that year he was ordered to raise and command the 6th Airborne Division.

Gale at once initiated a vigorous training program based on the assumptions that his division of one glider and two parachute brigades would be called upon to silence coastal batteries, seize ground overlooking the landing beaches, and delay the approach of enemy reserves. By June 1944 he had succeeded in producing a highly trained division and a close-knit family of men in hard physical condition. His orders for D-day included the capture intact of the bridges over the Caen Canal and the Orne River near Bénouville, the destruction of the coastal battery at Merville, and the delay of enemy reserves approaching from the east and southeast.

At 0050 hours on 6 June both the parachute brigades landed and were followed at 2100 hours by the glider brigade. Well before the seaborne landings the two bridges had been captured intact, the battery at Merville had been silenced, and the bridges over the Dives River blown. Gale himself, with a small staff, landed in the first glider lift at 0300 hours and by 0600 had established his headquarters in the Château de Heaume at Ranville. By the end of the first week's fighting, the division had achieved all its objectives and the left flank of the Allied bridgehead was secure.

The 6th Airborne Division returned to England in September 1944, and Gale was appointed commander of the I British Airborne Corps and in December 1944 deputy commander of the First Allied Airborne Army. After World War II he held a succession of senior appointments in the British army, until in 1952 he took over command of the Army of the Rhine and the NATO Northern Army Group. From 1957 to 1960 he was deputy supreme Allied commander, Europe.

R. N. GALE.   IMPERIAL WAR MUSEUM

His British honors included the Order of the Bath, the Order of the British Empire, the Distinguished Service Order, and the Military Cross. He was a commander of the United States Legion of Merit and of the French Legion of Honor and held the French Croix de Guerre with Palm. He died in London on 29 July 1982.

Richard Gale had a forceful, robust personality and a deep understanding of soldiers. Steeped in military history, he was a real professional, and these qualities made him an excellent trainer of troops. His success in preparing his division for D-day and in leading them through the first days and weeks of fierce fighting made a valuable contribution to the campaign by ensuring the security of the Allies' left flank.

[*See also* 6th Airborne Division.]

BIBLIOGRAPHY

Gale, R. N. *With the 6th Airborne Division in Normandy.* 1948.
Gale, Richard. *Call to Arms.* 1968.

NAPIER CROOKENDEN

GAULLE, CHARLES DE See de Gaulle, Charles.

GAVIN, JAMES (1907–1990), American, brigadier general, assistant division commander of the 82d Airborne Division, and senior airborne adviser COSSAC (Chief of Staff to the Supreme Allied Commander). James Maurice Gavin was born on 22 March 1907 in Brooklyn, New York. He joined the army at the age of seventeen and later won appointment to the U.S. Military Academy, and was commissioned second lieutenant in 1929. Gavin attended Parachute School at Fort Benning, Georgia, in August 1941 and was given command of the 505th Parachute Infantry Regiment in July 1942. Deployed with the 82d Airborne Division, his command participated in the North African, Sicily, and Salerno campaigns. Gavin was appointed assistant division commander in October 1943, and was assigned to COSSAC in November 1943. He commanded the division's parachute assault echelon (Force A) on D-day. He parachuted into Normandy with the 508th Parachute Infantry Regiment and landed about two miles north of the La Fière Bridge on the western side of the flooded Merderet River. Being unable to secure the La Fière Bridge from the west side with his band of over 150 men, Gavin crossed over to the east side and made contact with additional troops. He organized attacks aimed at capturing the La Fière Bridge and the bridge near Chef-du-Pont several miles south. The Chef-du-Pont Bridge was taken on 6 June, while the La Fière Bridge was finally captured on 9 June. During the fighting,

JAMES GAVIN.   COURTESY OF STEVEN J. MROZEK

Gavin established his command post a short distance east of La Fière.

Gavin assumed command of the 82d Airborne Division on 15 August 1944 at age thirty-seven, the youngest American division commander in World War II, and he commanded it for the duration of the war. He was later promoted to lieutenant general, and retired from the Army in 1958 after thirty-three years of service.

[*See also* Airborne Forces; 82d Airborne Division.]

BIBLIOGRAPHY

Gavin, James M. *Airborne Warfare.* 1947.
Gavin, James M. *On to Berlin.* 1978.

STEVEN J. MROZEK

GEORGE VI (1895–1952), king of Great Britain. Known as "Bertie" within the royal family, Prince Albert Frederick Arthur was the second son of King George V and Queen Mary. He became an officer in the Royal Navy in 1913 after training at Britannia Royal Naval College, Dartmouth. Very shy as a boy, he suffered all his life from a speech impediment.

In 1916 he served aboard HMS *Collingwood* at the Battle of Jutland and later was trained to fly in the infant Royal

KING GEORGE VI. With Adm. Harold R. Stark at Red Cross Club in London. NATIONAL ARCHIVES

Air Force at Cranwell. In 1920 he was created Duke of York and performed sterling services for the Boys' Club movement and carried out many other public duties. In 1923 he married Elizabeth Bowes-Lyon; in 1926 Princess Elizabeth (Queen Elizabeth II) was born and four years later Princess Margaret Rose. In 1936 he unexpectedly succeeded to the throne upon the abdication of his elder brother, Edward VIII, and undertook a number of overseas tours, including one to Canada and the United States in mid-1939 as war clouds gathered over Europe.

During the London Blitz George VI earned the affection of his people by refusing to move his family or himself from the twice-bombed Buckingham Palace. His tours of the devastated East End of London helped maintain national morale, as did his frequent visits to the armed forces at home and journeys to North Africa, Malta, and Italy. His public broadcasts were much admired, and few realized his great nervousness on these occasions.

Probably his most significant contribution to the war effort was his close relationship with Winston Churchill, the British prime minister, whom he was constitutionally empowered to consult, advise, and (if necessary) warn. King George attended a top secret preinvasion briefing at St. Paul's School on 15 May and briefly addressed the assembled commanders. Just before D-day he restrained his forceful premier from watching the operation from a

naval vessel only by threatening to do so himself. On 16 June King George visited the troops in Normandy (Churchill had preceded him four days earlier). A dumbfounded assistant provost-marshal received an order from the British Second Army headquarters "to clear the road: the King is coming" and managed to perform this not inconsiderable feat despite the complexities involved.

Following the Allied victory, King George continued to lead and inspire his people through the difficult postwar period. By 1950 his health was declining, and on 6 February 1952 he died—deeply mourned and regarded as the exemplar of a man and king whose life was selflessly devoted to performing his royal duty.

[*See also* Great Britain.]

BIBLIOGRAPHY

Judd, Denis. *King George VI*. 1982.
Wheeler-Bennett, John. *George VI: His Life and Reign*. 1958.

DAVID G. CHANDLER

GERHARDT, CHARLES H. (1895–1976), American, major general, commander of the U.S. 29th Infantry Division. The son of a career army officer, Gerhardt attended the U.S. Military Academy from 1913 to 1917, graduating 50th in a class of 139. Upon America's entry into World War I, Gerhardt joined the 3d Cavalry in Texas, and accompanied that regiment to France. He soon departed, however, to act as an aide to the commander of the 89th Division, with which he participated in the Saint-Mihiel and Meuse-Argonne offensives.

Upon America's entry into World War II, Gerhardt commanded the 51st Cavalry Brigade in Texas, but was soon promoted to commanding general of the 91st Infantry Division in Oregon. In July 1943 Gerhardt departed for England to assume command of the 29th Infantry Division, one of the first U.S. Army divisions to be shipped across the Atlantic during the war.

Gerhardt was directed to train the 29th for amphibious operations in preparation for the upcoming invasion of Europe. Furthermore, he was ordered "to correct the situation of too many 29th Division men in the guardhouse." The 29th was a National Guard division from Maryland and Virginia, and its citizen-soldiers were wary of their new general. Gerhardt quickly established a rigorous code of discipline and instilled an aggressive spirit among his men. Two of Gerhardt's enduring legacies were the divisional battle cry, "Twenty-nine, let's go!" and the infamous chin strap rule, which specified that helmet chin straps must never be left dangling and must always be hooked underneath the chin.

Gerhardt insisted that "this war is won at battalion level," and drove home his point one day at a meeting

CHARLES H. GERHARDT. At right, with Dwight D. Eisenhower. NATIONAL ARCHIVES

with his battalion commanders. "A year from today, one out of every three of you will be dead," he said, "and the toll will be higher if senior commanders don't know their stuff and don't get out of their chairs!"

In Operation OVERLORD, the 29th Division, along with the 1st Division, was to assault Omaha Beach on D-day and then push inland to capture the city of Saint-Lô by D plus 9 (15 June). Gerhardt came ashore on the night of 6 June and established his command post a few hundred yards from the water's edge. By 9 June, Gerhardt had successfully carried out his mission to link up with VII Corps troops from the Utah beachhead. The German resistance stiffened about ten kilometers (6.2 miles) north of Saint-Lô, however, as German reinforcements arrived from Brittany. Gerhardt directed a series of costly attacks toward Saint-Lô from 12 to 18 June, but failed to take the city. Saint-Lô finally fell to the 29th Division on 18 July.

Gerhardt, known as Uncle Charlie to his men, commanded the 29th for the rest of the war. Although his sternness was legendary, the 29ers recognized that he was more demanding of officers than he was of enlisted men. In his jeep "Vixen Tor," accompanied by his dog "D-Day," Gerhardt usually visited at least two frontline battalions each day to check on the welfare of his troops.

After the war, Gerhardt became the American military attaché to Brazil. He died in 1976 in Winter Park, Florida, and was buried in Arlington National Cemetery.

[*See also* 29th Infantry Division.]

BIBLIOGRAPHY

Balkoski, Joseph. *Beyond the Beachhead: The 29th Infantry Division in Normandy*. 1989.
Ewing, Joseph. *Twenty-Nine, Let's Go!* 1948.
Gerhardt, Charles H. "Memoirs." 1964. U.S. Army Military Institute, Carlisle Barracks, Pa.

JOSEPH M. BALKOSKI

GERMANY. "The onset of the invasion is widely experienced as a deliverance from unbearable tension and oppressive uncertainty. It constitutes almost the only subject of conversation. Everything else totally recedes" (Boberach, *Meldungen aus dem Reich*, p. 511). This report of the Security Service (Sicherheitsdienst—SD) aptly captured the mood among the German populace, which during the afternoon of 6 June 1944 learned through the mass media (radio, newspapers, posters) that the Allied invasion had begun. Reich press chief Otto Dietrich expressed a widespread opinion when he declared on 6 June: "This morning our adversaries in the West have, at Moscow's demand, begun the bloody sacrificial path that they had long avoided. The often heralded attack on the freedom of Europe by the Western helpers of Bolshevism has begun. We will give them a warm reception. Germany is conscious of the importance of this hour. It will fight with all its force and with passionate resolve to safeguard Europe, its culture, and the life of its peoples from the onslaught of barbarism." (*Keesings Archiv der Gegenwart*, 1944, p. 6403). The day before, Propaganda Minister Joseph Goebbels had publicly announced: "The German nation listens only to one sole command, and that is the command of the Führer."

There is no question that on 6 June the mass of the German populace was convinced that the hour of decision of the entire war had arrived. For the last time during World War II, hope flared that the Third Reich would finally win the war within a foreseeable time. In 1942 Hitler himself had declared that the Allies would not last even nine hours on the European continent. SD reports from the first days of June made it clear that the majority of the population remained convinced of Hitler's genius and the ideas of national socialism. Even the prior year's military reverses had led to no basic change of opinion. Hitler's rule on 6 June 1944 was as uncontested as ever. The German opposition movement, culminating in the assassination attempt against Hitler on 20 July of that year, found no widespread echo; rather, Germans succumbed to Goebbels's propaganda, which skillfully exploited Allied bombing of Ger-

ALBERT SPEER.   Reich minister for armaments and war production from 1942 to 1945, Speer controlled almost all aspects of German production toward the end of the war. While serving twenty years in Spandau Prison, he wrote his best-selling memoir, *Inside the Third Reich*.   NATIONAL ARCHIVES

man cities. In May 1944 the air war had left 7,152 dead and 15,231 injured among German civilians; 7,289 buildings had been totally destroyed and 9,417 heavily damaged. In June, air attacks killed 5,914 civilians, although a decrease in the intensity of this bombing had accompanied the invasion. Propaganda exploitation of the attacks extended to the suggestion by Martin Bormann, head of the Party Chancellery, that downed Allied pilots be lynched when captured. Although this occurred only in isolated instances, Allied air operations—designated as "terror attacks" in the summer of 1944—produced a reaction of defiance that stiffened as the Third Reich leadership announced the imminent deployment of "wonder weapons" to wreak vengeance against Great Britain in particular. The first use of six Fi 103 (V-1) flying bombs was made public on 17 June. Subsequent propaganda suggested that these first in a series of "V-weapons" could have a decisive effect on the war's outcome, as was widely believed in June and July. In fact, the five hundred flying bombs launched by 18 June had no strategic result at all.

The solemn but tranquil bearing of the German populace was also attributable to the relatively smooth supply of foodstuffs. In May 1944, the daily ration was 1,930 calories per person, so that no German had to starve. The comparison was often made to the catastrophic situation in 1917 and 1918, to the advantage of the regime. Propaganda was silent on the fact that these provisions were possible only through relentless exploitation of the occupied countries (in the Netherlands there was indeed starvation). On the other hand, discontent did surface among workers; once the sixty-hour week had become customary, officials attempted to increase it to seventy-two hours, causing a rapid increase in illness and absenteeism among factory workers.

The Reich's economic strength and arms production was based on the labor of 29 million German civilian workers and 7.1 million foreign workers (alien laborers and prisoners of war) (Blaich, *Wirtschaft und Rüstung im "Dritten Reich"*, p. 105). The labor force included 14.2 million German men and 14.8 million German women. By the end of May 1944 a total of 12.4 million men had been called to the Wehrmacht; subtracting the cumulative casualties, the Wehrmacht then had 9.1 million men at its disposal. Some 400,000 concentration-camp prisoners were working in German armament installations in the fall of 1944. "Thus in September 1944 some 33% of all employees and workers in the German economy belonged to the categories 'foreign civilian worker,' 'prisoner of war,' or 'concentration camp prisoner'" (Herbert, *Europa und der "Reichseinsatz"*, p. 7). In spite of this economic irrationality, Jews and Soviet prisoners of war were subjected to extermination through labor. Some 3.5 million of the total 5.7 million Russian prisoners of war died in POW camps by the end of the war. The organized mass murder of European Jews intensified in the first half of 1944. By 17 June, 437,402 Hungarian Jews had been deported to Auschwitz, and by 27 July, some 400,000 had been gassed (Schumann, *Deutschland im Zweiten Weltkrieg*, vol. 5, p. 238).

The increased labor shortage in the first half of 1944 led to the fourth so-called Sauckel Action, Labor Minister Fritz Sauckel's attempt to obtain 885,000 workers from France. Eventually only 36,000 to 50,000 workers left France for the Reich. At this point internal French resistance to these efforts had stiffened considerably.

What the mass of the German populace actually knew about the extermination of Jews is still debated, but it was no secret that Jews were being transported "to the East." Every criticism, every opposition was relentlessly persecuted by the SD and the Gestapo. In the first half of 1944 a total of 256,892 persons were arrested and 2,607 death sentences were carried out. In June 1944 German prisons held 190,500 persons. The National Socialist system of terror functioned smoothly in the weeks of the invasion; spying among the populace was extensive and

SIGNING OF UNCONDITIONAL SURRENDER.   Seated left to right: Col. Gen. Stumpf, Field Marshal Wilhelm Keitel, and Admiral of the Fleet Hans Georg von Friedeburg 9 May 1945, at Karlshorst, a district in Berlin.   NATIONAL ARCHIVES

effective. The terror was softened with "social policy" measures: the party knew enough to help the victims of bombing; large numbers of women and children were sent from the endangered cities to the "safe" countryside; the number of National Socialist schooling and morale-building events was increased; and the idea of the "Volk community" was kept alive through rigorous suppression of black market and profiteering, as well as a plethora of "happy" entertainment films. The "German Week-in-Review," a short film, in particular, suggested that the Reich's military and strategic situation was serious but by no means hopeless. Propaganda pointed out that the Reich's production of armaments was growing steadily, so that collapse of the economy or the arms industry was impossible. In fact, Germany's arms production reached its high point in the period from June to September 1944, despite the loss of important arms production areas such as the Crimea and the Ukraine. Thus Armaments Minister Albert Speer on 9 June spoke of an "arms miracle" to

representatives of Rhenish-Westphalian industry (Boeleke, *Deutschlands Rüstung im Zweiten Weltkrieg*, p. 360). Propaganda immediately picked it up.

Of course there was no "miracle"; the success was due to rigorous exploitation of the resources of all countries and regions under German domination, and to the reorganization achieved by Speer after he succeeded Fritz Todt as minister for arms and war production in February 1942. In June 1944 German production of weapons and war matériel was 34 percent over the figure for 1943, and in July it was 45 percent higher, although monthly average production in basic raw materials—lignite, coal, iron ore, raw steel, rolling-mill products, and fuels—increased only insignificantly. Moreover, German production of synthetic fuels came to a near collapse after 12 May 1944, when the U.S. Army Air Force began its Oil Plan attacks on the most important hydrogenation plants, which were converting coal into synthetic oil by combining it with hydrogen. Speer's efforts to clear away bottlenecks in the German fuels industry through a targeted rebuilding of hydrogenation facilities (the Geilenberg Program) was as desperate as it was finally in vain. Speer's hydrogenation memo of 30 June 1944 established that "total production in the month of July was only 53,000 t[ons] of aviation fuel," while 195,000 tons had been consumed in May. Against this background, the absolute production figures of Germany's aircraft industry meant little. In 1944 Germany produced 28,926 fighter planes (1940: 3,106), 6,468 bombers (1940: 763), and a total of 39,807 aircraft (1940: 10,826). The June 1944 production was 2,449 fighters, 703 bombers, and a total of 3,248 aircraft. Production figures for tanks were no less impressive: 1944 production of all panzer types was 548,575; in June alone, 49,898. For numerous other areas of weapons and munitions production, June and July 1944 marked an absolute high point, notably for U-boats and small fighting ships.

The Speer ministry's assumption of responsibility for aircraft production and the creation of a "fighter staff" under the minister and general for aircraft ordnance, Erhard Milch, contributed significantly to the rationalization and efficiency of the Luftwaffe. While the German armaments industry lost its initial scientific and technological advantage between 1940 and 1944, technical innovations in individual areas were achieved. Most spectacular, aside from the A 4 (V-2) rocket, was the Me 262 jet fighter. However, because Hitler favored the bomber version of the Me 262, holding to his command that it be produced exclusively as a bomber, a turnaround in the strategic air war was not to be expected. This ultimately also thwarted the intended resumption of naval warfare in the Atlantic with the new XXI- and XXIII-model U-boats.

As the invasion began on 6 June, Germany's military empire was all in all still fully functional. Nevertheless, the strategic and, even more, the political situation of Hitler's Reich was already hopeless. Even with the continuation of June's production figures, the burgeoning military potential of the Allies could not be matched or surpassed. Until 6 June there had been no breach of a front so dramatic as to be felt as a catastrophe; but with the Allied landings in North Africa, then in Sicily and Italy, and the systematic forward push of the Red Army after the late fall of 1942, it was only a matter of time until the Third Reich must collapse.

In the first days of June 1944 the military command was focused primarily on Italy. Against intense resistance, the Allied attack slowly but systematically proceeded. The fall of Rome on 5 June was especially irritating to the Germans, even if propaganda insisted that defense of the Holy City had been forsworn in deference to its "cultural treasures."

What was brewing in the central sector of the Eastern front since spring was intentionally withheld from the populace. The Soviet offensive, which began on 22 June, within a few weeks would lead to the collapse of Heeresgruppe Mitte (Army Group Center) and the loss of twenty-five divisions. But in the daily Wehrmacht reports and the terse commentaries of the controlled press, the talk was always about local battles, so that readers received the impression of a stable central front. The Soviet offensive against the Karelian Isthmus, which led to the rapid collapse of Finnish resistance, was not suppressed in the official reportage, but its importance was systematically downplayed. It was to be expected that the military occupation of Hungary by German troops on 4 May was reported as a "concentration of forces"; the Germans hardly acknowledged the inevitable collapse of German rule in all of southeastern Europe.

Daily reports from the invasion front gave Germans a picture of hard-fought but ultimately victorious battles. Only with the cutting off of the Cotentin Peninsula and the fall of Cherbourg was there a clearcut turnaround of the popular mood. According to an SD report: "The enthusiasm of the first days after the beginning of the invasion and the retribution [against the Allies] suffers a rapid slackening off everywhere. The initial great happiness and hope that the military situation would decisively change and that it would 'again go forward with us' has given way to very sober and skeptical reflections" (Steinert, *Hitlers Krieg und die Deutschen*, p. 464).

Meanwhile, triggered not least by the unexpectedly rapid success of the Normandy invasion, the conspiratorial circle around Col. Claus Schenk Count von Stauffenberg decided to act quickly. Especially given the start of the Soviet offensive on 22 June, there was no other choice. Stauffenberg secured the agreement of his coconspirators, who already had the Gestapo on their heels (on 5 July trade union leader Julius Leber was arrested). Forever memorable are the words of Brig. Gen. Henning von Tresckow: "The assassination attempt must succeed, cost what it may. If it does not succeed, one must still act in Berlin. For it is no longer a matter of practical ends, rather that the German opposition, before the world and before history, has dared to make the decisive move. Compared to this, nothing else matters."

[*See also* Hitler, Adolf; Propaganda, *article on* Geman Propaganda.]

BIBLIOGRAPHY

Blaich, Fritz. *Wirtschaft und Rüstung im "Dritten Reich."* 1987.

Boberach, Heinz, ed. *Meldungen aus dem Reich: Auswahl aus den geheimen Lageberichten des Sicherheitsdienstes der SS 1939–1944.* 1965.

Boelcke, Willi A., ed. *Hitlers Konferenzen mit Albert Speer 1942–1945.* 1969.

Herbert, Ulrich, ed. *Europa und der "Reicheinsatz." Ausländische Zivilarbeiter, Kriegsgefangene und KZ-Häftlinge in Deutschland 1938–1945.* 1991.

Roon, Gevan. *Widerstand im Dritten Reich.* 1979.

Schumann, Wolfgang, ed. *Der Zusammenbruch der Defensivstrategie des Hitlerfaschismus an allen Fronten.* Vol. 5 of *Deutschland im Zweiten Weltkrieg.* 1984.

Steinert, Marlis. *Hitlers Krieg und die Deutschen.* 1970.

MICHAEL SALEWSKI

GEROW, L. T. (1888–1982), American, major general, commander of U.S. V Corps. As an honors graduate from the Virginia Military Institute, Leonard T. Gerow received his commission in the regular army as a second lieutenant of infantry in 1911. A captain, in 1918 he was sent to France, where he worked with the Signal Corps.

In the 1920s and 1930s he held a series of staff positions and graduated from the Army War College and other army training schools. In December 1940 Gerow, now a brigadier general, was acting chief of staff of the War Plans Division, while also serving as the chief of staff of the 2d Division. He became a major general in February 1942 and assumed command of the 29th Infantry Division.

In October 1942 his division deployed to England as part of the buildup of U.S. forces there. In July 1943 Gerow assumed command of V Corps, then the highest U.S. field command in England. As commander of the ranking U.S. tactical headquarters in the country, Gerow and his skill as a war planner were put to use in the OVERLORD planning from the beginning.

Although the actions in Normandy were Gerow's first large-scale combat operation, Gen. Omar Bradley, commander of the U.S. First Army, expressed confidence in his corps commander's abilities. The two had attended the Infantry School at Fort Benning together and Bradley valued Gerow's conscientious and stable character. Bradley was also aware that Gerow, because of his long-term work on the plan, possessed an extensive understanding of OVERLORD's operations and goals.

V Corps's primary mission was the capture and enlargement of the Omaha beachhead. The corps assault force, led by the 1st Infantry Division, faced stiff resistance and was pinned down on the beach for hours. Unknown to Allied intelligence, the Germans had moved the *352d Division* from Saint-Lô to the coast, and this division kept V Corps from its D-day objectives. Offshore, Gerow waited for news of this troops' progress, but communications were difficult. By midafternoon the Americans on Omaha were making progress opening the beach exits, but operations were well behind schedule. Gerow took the corps headquarters ashore that evening to try to restore order on the beach and allow the second assault wave to land the following day.

L. T. GEROW.   NATIONAL ARCHIVES

Once ashore Gerow spent much of his time traveling between his subordinate units' command posts. V Corps continued its struggles and reached its objectives on D plus 2. Gerow observed his troops' progress firsthand, urging them on to their mission goals, and setting new goals as they pushed farther inland. Gerow then led his men south, enlarging their foothold and seizing new ground in preparation for the breakout and the drive across Europe.

Gerow commanded V Corps during the Normandy landings, the breakout across northern France, the liberation of Paris, and the penetration of the Siegfried Line. In January 1945 he was promoted to lieutenant general and took command of the Fifteenth Army. In October 1945 he became commandant of the Command and General Staff School. Three years later he retired after thirty-nine years of service. He was temporarily recalled to active duty in 1951 to serve on the Army Logistical Support Panel of the Office of the Chief, Army Field Forces. In 1954, while still in retirement, Gerow was advanced to the rank of general. He died on 19 May 1982.

[*See also* American Beaches, *article on* Omaha Beach; V Corps.]

BIBLIOGRAPHY

Berlin, Robert H. *U.S. Army World War II Corps Commanders: A Composite Biography.* 1989.

Bradley, Omar N. *A Soldier's Story.* 1951.

Pogue, Forrest C. *The Supreme Command.* U.S. Army in World War II: The European Theater of Operations. 1954.

Weigley, Russell F. *Eisenhower's Lieutenants.* 1981.

DONNA C. EVERETT

GEYR, LEO (1886–1974), German, commanding general of *Panzer Group West.* Leo Geyr Freiherr (Baron) von Schweppenburg, born in Potsdam on 2 March 1886, came from an old military family. Geyr joined the *2d Württemberg Dragoons No. 26* (Stuttgart) in 1904; the next year he made lieutenant. In 1911 he was appointed to the War Academy. Except for a brief tour as battalion leader in 1917, Geyr spend World War I in General Staff positions. During the Weimar years he held various staff and command positions, and in 1928 spent time in the Soviet Union gathering information to be used in the buildup of Germany's panzer forces.

After 1933 Geyr represented Germany as military attaché in London, Brussels, and The Hague. As a military diplomat he was one of the sharpest critics of Hitler's foreign policy, notably the invasion of the demilitarized Rhineland in March 1936. After his service abroad, which gained him respect for his social skills and manners, in

LEO GEYR FREIHERR VON SCHWEPPENBURG.
THE ROBERT HUNT LIBRARY, LONDON

October 1937 as a major general he assumed command of the *3d Panzer Division,* which he led in the Polish campaign in 1939. Here his unconventional training methods proved themselves, as did his confident command style, which more than once led to friction with his superiors, especially Gen. Heinz Guderian. In the French campaign of 1940, Geyr was commanding general of the *XXIV Army Corps.* Until the fall of 1942, he commanded panzer troops in the Russian campaign. Despite illness, Geyr was named general of *Panzer Troops West,* a unit created in July 1943; in January 1944 the *Panzer Group West* was established.

Anticipating an Allied invasion of the Continent, Geyr vehemently and abrasively argued for a mobile defense force comprising panzer and panzer grenadier divisions; however, he did not anticipate the effectiveness of Allied air power. Headquartered in Paris until 6 June, *Panzer Group West* by 8 June was moving east of the Orne River toward Tilly. On 10 and 11 June its staff was nearly totally destroyed by bombing attacks, denying Geyr decisive participation in the defense of the West. Although Geyr was not seriously injured, the psychological impact rendered him ineffective in the field. An improvised staff did not come together again until the end of June.

In early July Geyr was transferred to the reserve command, then in August he was made inspector of the *Replacement Army*'s (*Ersatzheer*'s) panzer troops, in which capacity he used his talents as an instructor. He also acted according to the principle that as many soldiers as possible should be brought home intact from a war that had long since been lost.

POSSIBLE ATTACK OF 13 JUNE (*see overleaf*). Writing for the U.S. Army's Office of the Chief of Military History while a prisoner of war in 1947, Gen. Leo Geyr von Schweppenburg asserted that a better strategy could have been adopted on 13 June by concentrating three powerful forces for a single, coordinated offensive against the Allied center. The map illustrating this strategy was drafted by an American lieutenant in consultation with General Geyr. Geyr suggested concentrating the *17th SS Panzer Grenadier Division* and the motorized elements of the *3d Parachute Division* on the left; the panzer grenadier regiments of the *2d Panzer Division* and an armored battle group of the *21st Panzer Division* in the center; and the *Panzer Lehr Division,* reinforced with elements of the *12th Panzer Division,* on the right. Such an attack, Geyr suggested, might have succeeded in breaking through the American line and reaching the sea, recapturing Bayeux in the process.

Given the Allies' overwhelming aerial superiority, it is highly doubtful that such powerful German forces could have been assembled for Geyr's proposed offensive. Had he been given permission to launch his offensive and been able to somehow assemble the forces earmarked for this strike, Geyr's offensive might have seriously disrupted the Allied invasion.

COURTESY OF SAMUEL W. MITCHAM, JR.

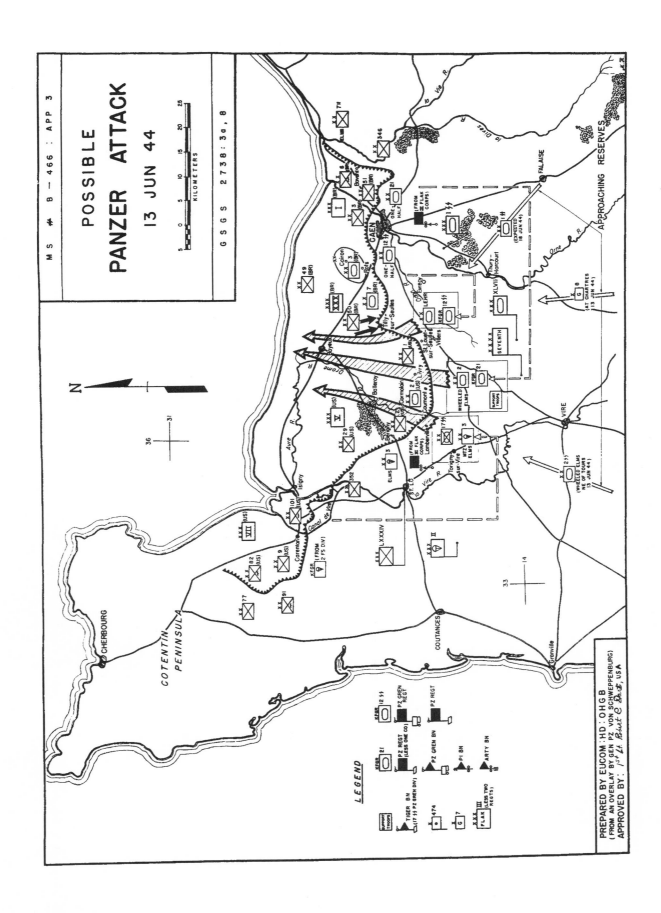

POSSIBLE
PANZER ATTACK
13 JUN 44

MS # B-466 : APP 3

KILOMETERS

GSGS 2738 : 3a, 8

N

CHERBOURG

COTENTIN
PENINSULA

CAEN

FALAISE

VIRE

COUTANCES

Granville

APPROACHING RESERVES

LEGEND

PREPARED BY EUCOM : HD : OH G B
(FROM AN OVERLAY BY GEN PZ VON SCHWEPPENBURG)
APPROVED BY:

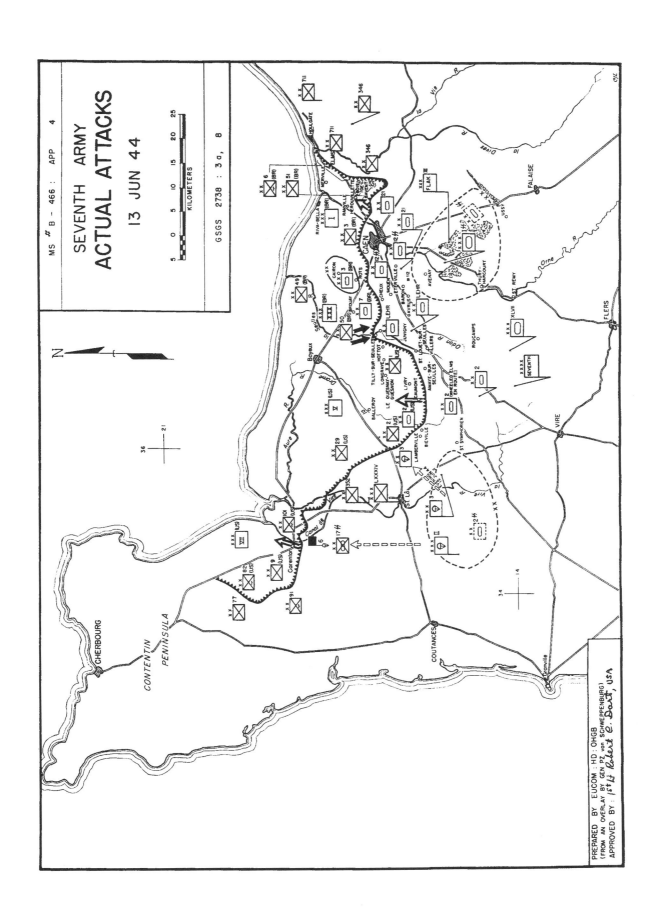

SEVENTH ARMY
ACTUAL ATTACKS
13 JUN 44

MS # B - 466 : APP 4

GSGS 2738 : 3 a, 8

KILOMETERS

5   0   5   10   15   20   25

N

CHERBOURG

CONTENTIN PENINSULA

COUTANCES

Granville

VIRE

FLERS

FALAISE

CAEN

Bayeux

St.LÔ

Carentan

PREPARED BY EUCOM : HD : OHGB
(FROM AN OVERLAY BY GEN PZ von SCHWEPPENBURG)
APPROVED BY : 1st Lt Robert C. Bart, USA

After internment as an American prisoner of war, Geyr utilized his established foreign connections to make himself a critical, relentless writer on military issues. He followed the buildup of West Germany's Bundeswehr with considerable attention and skepticism because of what he perceived as an unfortunate General Staff mentality alienated from the troops. His critique did not gain him appreciable influence. Geyr died in Irschenhausen on 27 January 1974.

[*See also* Panzer Group West.]

BIBLIOGRAPHY

Guderian, Heinz. *Erinnerungen eines Soldaten.* 1951.

Ose, Dieter. *Entscheidung im Westen: Der Oberbefehlshaber West und die Abwehr der alliierten Invasion.* Beiträge zur Militär- und Kriegsgeschichte. 1982.

Speidel, Hans. *Invasion 1944: Ein Beitrag zu Rommels und des Reiches Schicksal.* 1949.

GEORG MEYER
Translated from German by Amy Hackett

GLIDERS. Both American and British glider units were selected to spearhead the Allied invasion of France in June 1944. Their task was to land in conjunction with parachute troops at opposite ends of the sixty-mile-wide Normandy beachhead to seize key terrain and disrupt German defenses. During this crucial mission all British gliders were to operate under the command of the Royal Air Force's 38 Group, while American gliders would be controlled by the U.S. IX Troop Carrier Command.

The British utilized two types of gliders in Normandy. The Horsa Mark II had a wing span of 88 feet, was 68 feet long, and carried 28 fully armed troops plus a pilot and copilot. In lieu of an equivalent weight of combat troops, the Horsa could carry two jeeps, or one jeep and a 75-mm howitzer plus ammunition and crew, or a mixed load of ammunition and supplies weighing 7,380 pounds.

The second type of British glider was the Hamilcar, the largest wooden aircraft built during World War II. This giant glider had a wing span of 110 feet and measured 68.5 feet in length. Flown by two pilots who sat in tandem and were protected from the front and sides by bulletproof glass and from below by armor plating, the Hamilcar was originally conceived as a transport for a Tetrach Mark IV tank and crew. Other typical loads consisted of 40 troops, or two armored scout cars, or a 25-pound gun with tractor. When empty, the Hamilcar weighed in at an amazing 18,000 pounds, yet it could easily carry an additional 17,500 pounds of cargo or personnel.

WRECKED HORSAS.   On the bank of the Caen Canal, 8 June 1944.

WRECKED HORSA.   Dead American soldiers beside the glider that delivered them to Normandy.   HULTON DEUTSCH

BRITISH HAMILCAR.   With its front swung open to unload a Tetrarch tank.   IMPERIAL WAR MUSEUM

LANDING ZONES.   The bocage of the Normandy countryside necessitated extremely small landing zones.

The American Waco CG-4A glider was the primary means of transportation for the glider infantry regiments of both the U.S. 82d and 101st airborne divisions. Designed for two pilots who sat side by side, the CG-4A had a wing span of 83 feet and measured 48 feet in length. Its wings and tail assembly were made of wood, but the fuselage consisted only of welded steel tubing covered by stretched canvas. The floor in the troop and cargo compartment was made of honeycombed plywood, which let the glider carry 13 troops. Other load variations ranged from one jeep and driver to one 75-mm howitzer plus a crew of three, or 4,060 pounds of mixed cargo.

Just as British glider pilots had flown American CG-4A gliders during the invasion of Sicily, some American pilots would be flying British Horsas during Operation OVERLORD. This was at the request of the Americans, who needed the larger Horsas to deliver heavy-caliber howitzers and antitank guns to repulse German counterattacks.

The first Allied glider mission of the Normandy campaign began at 2303 on 5 June, when six Horsas loaded with British troops took to the air behind their Halifax tow ships from Tarrant Rushton, southwest of London on the Salisbury Plain, bound for a pair of bridges over the Caen Canal and Orne River in France. Upon their arrival above the objectives, the glider pilots found the bridges partially obscured by ground haze. Nevertheless, they skillfully guided their Horsas down to the landing zones in total darkness. Five minutes after touchdown, both bridges were in British hands.

A second landing of British glider troops occurred at 0300 on 6 June, when 68 Horsas (one of which carried Maj. Gen. R. N. Gale, commanding the British 6th Airborne Division) and 4 Hamilcars landed near Ranville. One hour later 52 American CG-4As began landing near Hiesville. Riding in the lead glider was Brig. Gen. Donald F. Pratt, assistant division commander of the 101st Airborne Division. When the lead glider touched down on the dew-covered grass of the landing zone, it skidded out of control and crashed, killing Pratt and the copilot.

Misdropped paratroopers were still roaming the Norman countryside when at 0420 one Horsa containing British troops landed within fifty yards of the Merville battery. Moments later the glider troopers were busy providing covering fire for Lt. Col. Terrance Otway's 9th Parachute Battalion, which successfully stormed the battery.

Succeeding Allied glider landing missions took place throughout the remainder of D-day and on into D plus 1. All told, the Allies landed some 850 gliders in Normandy, the majority of them during total darkness. Because of the ruggedness of the landing zones—most of which were quite small and strewn with obstacles—a great many gliders sustained considerable damage upon landing and had to be scrapped. A total of 25 American and 34 British glider pilots were killed in Normandy. Sixty-five glider pilots were wounded and 162 others were seriously injured during crash landings. A total of 53 glider pilots were listed as prisoners of war.

Despite relatively high casualty rates among pilots and passengers, the glider assault landings contributed greatly to the overall success of OVERLORD's opening phase.

[See also Airborne Forces; 82d Airborne Division; 101st Airborne Division; 6th Airborne Division.]

BIBLIOGRAPHY

Devlin, Gerard M. *Paratrooper! The Saga of U.S. Army and Marine Parachute and Glider Combat Troops during World War II.* 1978.
Devlin, Gerard M. *Silent Wings: The Saga of U.S. Army and Marine Combat Glider Pilots during World War II.* 1983.
Harrison, Gordon A. *Cross-Channel Attack.* U.S. Army in World War II: The European Theater of Operations. 1951.
Liddell Hart, B. H. *History of the Second World War.* 1970.
United Kingdom. Ministry of Information. *By Air to Battle.* 1945.
Warren, John G. *U.S. Air Force Historical Study No. 97: Airborne Operations in World War II, European Theater.* 1956.

GERARD M. DEVLIN

GOLD BEACH. *See* British Beaches, *article on* Gold Beach.

GOODRICH, DONALD (1894–1945), American, brigadier general, commander VIII Air Force Service Command. Donald R. Goodrich joined the Aviation Section of the Army Signal Corps in 1917. Throughout his military career he occupied staff and administrative posts. From 1938 to 1940 he was assistant chief of the Personnel Division, Planning Group Office, of the chief of the Air Corps (OCAC), and liaison officer to the adjutant general's office. From 1940 to 1942 he served as executive officer, Military Personnel Division, OCAC, and in 1942–1943, now a colonel, he commanded the 3d Air Service Area Command, in Atlanta, Georgia. In March 1943 he became chief of staff of VIII Air Force Service Command and assumed command of the 8th Strategic Air Depot Area in August.

In January 1944 Lt. Gen. Carl Spaatz established the headquarters of the U.S. Strategic Air Forces in Europe (USSAFE, later USSTAF) at Bushy Park near London. USSTAF had administrative and logistical control of the Eighth and Ninth air forces. Spaatz appointed Brig. Gen. Hugh J. Knerr as his deputy for administration and commanding general of Air Service Command, USSTAF. Knerr absorbed the former VIII Air Force Service Command Headquarters into his new functions and redesignated

Goodrich's organization as the new VIII Air Force Service Command. In February 1944 the War Department recognized this action by promoting Goodrich to brigadier general and officially making him head of the VIII Air Force Service Command. He held that post until January 1945, when he returned to the United States.

During his tenure in VIII Air Force Service Command, Goodrich presided over the servicing of the large number of fighter and bomber groups that reinforced the Eighth Air Force before D-day and preparing airfields to receive new units. During the five months before the invasion, the Eighth Air Force engaged in a campaign of attrition against the Luftwaffe that involved heavy damage to U.S. aircraft; large loss of aircraft, requiring preparation of replacement aircraft and air crews; and expenditure of vast quantities of aviation gasoline, bombs, ammunition, and stores of all types. As the chief administrative officer of the Eighth Air Force, Goodrich made a significant contribution in maintaining that force's rate of operations and combat capability. This in turn greatly assisted the successful operations of the Eighth Air Force in bombing German lines of communication, destroying the Luftwaffe fighter force, and aiding the ground forces during the Normandy campaign.

[See also VIII Air Force Service Command.]

BIBLIOGRAPHY

Craven, Wesley Frank, and James Lea Cate, eds. *Europe: ARGUMENT to V-E Day, January 1944 to May 1945.* Vol. 3 of *The Army Air Forces in World War II.* 1951.

Goldberg, Alfred. "Air Logistics in the ETO." In vol. 2 of *The Army Air Forces in World War II*, edited by Wesley Frank Craven and James Lea Cate. 1949.

RICHARD G. DAVIS

GOOSEBERRIES. *See* Artificial Harbors.

GRAHAM, D. A. H. (1893–1971), British, major general, commander 50th (Northumbrian) Infantry Division. Shortly after the outbreak of World War I, Graham was commissioned into the Cameronians (Scottish Rifles) and sent to France. By 1916 he had been promoted to captain and by the end of the war had been awarded the Military Cross and the French Croix de Guerre. Between the wars he progressed steadily up the ranks of regimental promotion and between 1936 and 1939 served in Palestine.

Graham was thus well placed to move to North Africa when Italy declared war, and he played a distinguished part in the desert campaign during which he was appointed commander of the Order of the British Empire and won the Distinguished Service Order and bar before being given command of the 56th (London) Infantry Division. He was wounded at Salerno, but after convalesence and a return to England he took command of the 50th Division in time to train it for D-day.

He landed shortly after noon on D-day and took his headquarters organization to Meuvaines, where they remained until the 7th Armoured Division could release him to move closer up behind his forward units.

By the end of the war, Graham had added another Croix de Guerre to his list of decorations, together with the Legion of Merit (Commander) and the French Legion of Honor (Officer), and had been made a Commander of the Bath.

Douglas Graham was the epitome of the Lowland Scottish Covenanters from whom the Cameronians sprang; like them, he took a tough, independent approach toward military problems. He was never impressed by intellectual or specialized staff training, but was cast in the finest tradition of regimental officers. His firm religious convictions lent him an indomitable courage, which made him an ideal leader during the crucial months of the bitter battles that followed the breakout from the bridgehead up to the assault across the Rhine.

Perhaps the period of his military service that gave him the greatest satisfaction was his time as colonel of the Cameronians from 1954 to 1958. He retired in 1947 and lived in Breckin, Angus, until his death in 1971.

[See also 50th (Northumbrian) Infantry Division.]

BIBLIOGRAPHY

Clay, E. W. *The Path of the 50th: The Story of the 50th (Northumbrian) Division in the Second World War.* 1950.

Obituary. *Times* (London), 30 September 1971.

Sixsmith, E. K. G. Letter. *Times* (London), 4 October 1971.

BARRIE PITT

GREAT BRITAIN. The high degree of Allied cooperation achieved for the D-day landings renders discussion of any one country's achievements in isolation potentially misleading. Much of the success of the Allied effort, however, was undeniably due to the United Kingdom of Great Britain and Northern Ireland. Britain provided for D-day the base and infrastructure from which the landings were mounted, crucial intelligence and support services, the bulk of the naval forces and about half the ground and air forces, and most of the senior Allied commanders.

Britain at War. Although rightly subject to revisionist questioning, the wartime propaganda image of a politically and socially united Britain remains essentially the correct one. Despite its high and complex levels of stratification,

CHURCHILL WITH ROYAL FAMILY.   From left to right: Princess Elizabeth, Queen Mary, Winston Churchill, King George VI, and Princess Margaret.

British society showed remarkable cohesion and resilience, and opposition to the war, whether expressed by conscientious objection (under 3 percent of those conscripted in 1944), politically motivated strikes, or by-elections (based on the 1939 electoral register), remained negligible. The coalition government of Winston Churchill may have been unrepresentative by 1944 (having been formed in 1940 largely from a House of Commons based on the 1935 general election), but evidence from opinion polls suggests that from late 1942 onward it held the support of at least 70 percent of the electorate. The general election victory in July 1945 of a Labour party committed to social reform and equality reaffirmed, rather than contradicted, the values for which most people believed they were fighting the war. Similarly, the British tolerated with remarkably little friction, and often welcomed, the extensive numbers of American military personnel who arrived from January 1942 onward, and their relations with all the Dominion and Allied forces involved in Operation OVERLORD were generally good. Long British experience of coalition warfare also contributed significantly to the unity of command established for D-day.

Britain was the only country to fight against Germany from the start of the Second World War until its end, and by 1944 it had endured five years in the front line. With the exception of the Channel Islands, no part of the United Kingdom was ever occupied by enemy forces. But a sustained campaign of naval blockade claimed the lives of 35,000 British merchant seamen, and air raids accounted for some 60,000 civilian deaths and 235,000 injuries.

Of these, some 9,000 of the dead came in the Little Blitz, the Luftwaffe offensive against London and the English Channel ports that began in January 1944, supplemented by the first V-1 Flying Bomb attacks on 12 June (D plus 6) and the first V-2 rockets in September.

Insofar as it is possible to generalize about a population of 49 million people, the British in June 1944 were war-weary in the literal sense. Few seem to have doubted that the war would be won, but a mood of indifference and exhaustion was evident after five years of danger and austerity, compounded by an average working week of 51.2 hours for men (48.6 hours for the total work force), plus compulsory fire-watching, civil defense, or Home Guard duties. During 1944 a disturbing 3,696 working days were lost from strikes of a predominantly nonpolitical nature (compared to 1,832 days in 1943), and the government took elaborate precautions to ensure that industrial disputes did not disrupt the execution of OVERLORD. In the event, these precautions proved completely unnecessary, as the civilian workers at over twenty British ports provided vital support for the Allied landings.

Britain's War Effort. Although in 1939 Britain with its global empire still ranked as a great power, its economic position had slipped to about fourth in the world behind the United States, the Soviet Union, and Germany. British economic and social planning for war started as early as 1936, with partial implementation in 1939 and the full move to a war command economy in 1941. For the remaining years of the war, over half the national income was devoted to war expenditure (a feat equaled among the allies only by New Zealand after 1942 and Canada after 1943), and it is probable that no other single belligerent organized its society and economy for war to the same extent as Britain.

Military conscription (called National Service) was introduced in May 1939 just before the outbreak of war and was significantly broadened in 1941, even including the limited conscription of women for the first time in any nation. By June 1944, some 4.967 million of an available work force of 22.008 million, or 22 percent, were serving in the armed forces or auxiliary services (such as the Home Guard and Royal Observer Corps), and a further 7.25 million, or 33 percent, were in civilian war employment (including 3.8 million employed in the manufacture of military equipment and supplies).

This level of commitment to the war effort was achieved by a dilution of the traditional work force approximately equal to the size of the armed forces, so that the total civilian work force barely declined from its prewar level. The number of women engaged in work outside the home increased by 42 percent from prewar levels to 7.1 million, including 500,000 women in the armed forces, 300,000 in the Civil Service, and 200,000 in the Women's Land Army. Real wages rose significantly faster than real prices between 1939 and 1944, but under wartime conditions the actual standard of living could hardly be said to have risen, and consumer spending fell by about 20 percent. Strict rationing (introduced at the start of the war), the winning of the Battle of the Atlantic, and an increase in land under cultivation by 40 percent from prewar levels to 14.5 million acres meant that by 1944 there was no doubt that Britain could be fed. Housing was seen as the most pressing problem: in addition to 300,000 substandard homes in 1941, air raids destroyed or damaged 4.5 million buildings during the war, a full third of them in the Little Blitz.

British productivity in traditional heavy industries such as mining, engineering, and aircraft production was low. Together with conscription and dilution this had produced a serious manpower shortage in industry by October 1943, when conscription was extended to include civilian labor, with limited numbers of conscripts (known as "Bevin Boys" after Minister of Labour Ernest Bevin) being sent to coal mines. The same problem was evident in munitions production, which peaked in the first quarter of 1943 and had dropped back by D-day to 1942 levels. Britain provided only 60 percent of the munitions it required during the war, and the rest of the empire a further 15 percent (largely from Canada, India, and Australia). The balance came from the United States as Lend-Lease, which beginning in March 1941 was confirmed by the Anglo-American Mutual Aid Agreement of February 1942 and provided Britain with $27.025 billion (£5.405 billion) of war matériel. Net U.S. aid to Britain during the war has been estimated at $19 billion, with a further $3.725 billion from Canada.

A major historical dispute exists concerning whether Britain's economic performance during World War II presaged (or even precipitated) its decline after 1945. It seems fair to conclude that although the transition to a command economy strained Britain's resources, it had by 1944 coped with its problems more successfully than its chief enemy, Germany, as well as having proved strategically more sophisticated. Although, for example, Germany outproduced Britain in combat aircraft in 1944, Britain outproduced Germany in airframe weight, building heavy bombers to attack Germany rather than the fighters to defend against them. Nevertheless, in 1944, Britain's loss of status as a great power and its economic dependence on the United States were undeniable facts. It is dramatic but essentially true to say that Britain intentionally sacrificed itself, economically and politically, in order to defeat Nazi Germany.

The British Armed Forces. Although by 1944 its position within the Big Three had slipped to that of third among equals beside the United States and the Soviet Union, Britain was able to capitalize on its stronger position early in the war, on its possession of intelligence sources such as Ultra (the top secret method of breaking the most important German radio codes), on its traditional coalition skills, and on its being host nation for OVERLORD to achieve a level of importance for its armed forces on D-day probably exceeding its real political and military strength. Although the Supreme Allied Commander for OVERLORD was inevitably an American, General Dwight D. Eisenhower, the remaining higher command posts were held by British officers: Air Chief Marshal Arthur Tedder as Deputy Supreme Allied Commander; Admiral Bertram H. Ramsay as Allied Naval Commander in Chief Expeditionary Force; Air Chief Marshal Trafford Leigh-Mallory as Air Commander in Chief Allied Expeditionary Force; and General Bernard L. Montgomery as general officer commanding the 21st Army Group and effective Allied commander for the landings.

The Royal Navy in World War II was, as it had been for centuries, Britain's senior service, with a long-established high reputation. In June 1944 it numbered 778,000 personnel, with about 9,500 vessels including landing craft. Of these, some 958 naval combatant vessels were assigned by the Royal Navy and Royal Canadian Navy to the D-day operation, including 63 warships with the Eastern and Western Naval Task Forces off the D-day beaches. Royal Navy ships, together with those of the Royal Canadian Navy and the smaller European Allies under British control, provided 83.5 percent of the naval combatant vessels for D-day. In terms of personnel, 112,824

Royal Navy sailors were employed on D-day (not including the Fleet Air Arm or the Royal Marine Commandos of the 1st and 4th Special Service Brigades, who served alongside the Army Commandos but like all Royal Marines counted as part of the Royal Navy). The Eastern Task Force under Rear Adm. Philip Vian, responsible for the British and Canadian beaches (Gold, Sword, and Juno), successfully landed 53,815 British and 21,400 Canadian troops on D-day, together with over 6,000 vehicles and 4,300 tons of supplies.

The Royal Air Force in June 1944 numbered 1,002,000 personnel, but the nature of air power makes its actual contribution to D-day much harder to quantify. In total, 5,656 RAF sorties were flown in direct support of the D-day landings, but virtually the whole RAF strength in Britain, including Bomber Command, Coastal Command, and Airborne and Transport Command, also contributed directly or indirectly. The RAF commitment to the Allied Expeditionary Air Force (AEAF) under Leigh-Mallory consisted of the Second Tactical Air Force and the Air Defence of Great Britain (formerly Fighter Command). The RAF was much less specifically British than the Royal Navy and British army forces involved on D-day, with more than a third of its AEAF squadrons recruited from the empire or from countries occupied by Germany and numerous individuals from the same countries serving with British squadrons. The RAF, as the world's oldest independent air force, particularly treasured its separate existence. Although the British coordination of air power with ground forces had advanced considerably since the start of the war, it was still not without its problems.

The British Army in June 1944 numbered 2.27 million personnel. Of these, 61,715 troops landed on D-day (in the equivalent of five divisions) at Gold and Sword beaches, on the airborne landing zones south and east of Sword Beach, and at Juno Beach together with the Canadians, who also formed part of the British Second Army under Lt. Gen. Miles C. Dempsey. Purely British losses for D-day are estimated at 2,700 troops. By 16 June (D plus 10) the British Second Army had landed elements of a further five divisions and in all 279,000 troops, 46,000 vehicles, and 95,000 tons of supplies.

Much controversy surrounds the performance of the British army on D-day and later in Normandy. By 1944 it had overcome most of the problems associated with the transition from its imperial policing role before the war and had lost much of its earlier amateurism. Generally, the artillery and engineers were excellent and the infantry formidable in defense, but problems existed in coordinating armor with other arms. There is evidence that, like Britain itself, much of the British army was suffering from war-weariness and that overcaution existed at all levels. The judgment of their peers was that the British in 1944 were steady but slow, very hard to beat but reluctant to take risks to win.

[See also British Beaches; Churchill, Winston; and biographies of numerous figures mentioned herein.]

BIBLIOGRAPHY

Barnett, Correlli. *The Audit of War.* 1986.
Calder, Angus. *The People's War.* 1971.
French, David. *The British Way in Warfare, 1688–2000.* 1990.
Pelling, Henry. *Britain and the Second World War.* 1970.

STEPHEN BADSEY

GREECE. The contribution of Greece and the Royal Hellenic armed forces to D-day was understandably small and chiefly naval, coming from a country with a long tradition of seamanship and one of Europe's largest merchant marine fleets, but whose interests lay in the Mediterranean and the Balkans rather than in northwestern Europe. Greek involvement in World War II began in October 1940 with a declaration of war by Italy. The Greeks repelled the Italian invaders, but in April 1941 German and other Axis troops overran and occupied both Yugoslavia and Greece, and Crete a month later. Supported by the British, King George II of the Hellenes established a government-in-exile in Egypt, and for the remainder of the war Greek land, naval, and air forces fought alongside the British, largely in the Mediterranean theater.

On D-day Greek nationals served as individual combatants with British forces, as merchant mariners, or with smaller vessels such as landing ships. The only fighting units of the Royal Hellenic Navy involved in action on D-day were the sister ships *Kriezis* and *Tompazis*, both Flower-class corvettes of 950 tons, built by the British at the start of the war and transferred to the Royal Hellenic Navy in 1943. As with most European Allied forces, both ships served under British command as part of the Eastern Task Force, escorting convoys to the British and Canadian landing beaches.

Other than as individual pilots in RAF squadrons, Greeks played no further significant part in the Normandy invasion. Greece itself was liberated when the Germans withdrew their occupation forces in October 1944.

BIBLIOGRAPHY

Elliot, Peter. *Allied Escort Ships of World War II.* 1979.
Ready, J. Lee. *Forgotten Allies.* 1985.

STEPHEN BADSEY

GROUND TRAINING. Although practical training for the D-day invasion could be carried out on friendly beaches with profiles and layouts similar to those in France, there was no way to duplicate the appearance of the terrain as seen either from the air or sea. Synthetic training aids were needed to familiarize not only those in the airborne and seaborne assaults with the terrain they would encounter, but also those units with special tasks such as the seizure of the Pegasus Bridge, destruction of the Merville battery, and the clearance of the underwater and beach obstacles.

The extensive collection of visual information of the French coast included holiday snapshots, topographical postcards, and reconnaissance photographs that had been collected over a long period of time. Large-scale maps of the landing areas were augmented by high-resolution and large-scale oblique and vertical photographs.

Probably the most useful aids, however, were sand tables and terrain models which could be up to 3.6 meters (12 feet) on a side (13.4 square meters or 144 square feet). Sand tables used sand about 0.3 meters (1 foot) deep to produce a simple three-dimensional large-scale model. Terrain models were much more realistic. On a prepared base, a ground plan was drawn from maps or photographic projections, and contours were cut from the correct thickness card to provide heights. This framework was then covered by a "skin" of vertical photographs joined together and applied wet. Teams of modelmakers who were artists, engravers, and illustrators added construction features such as embankments and cuttings. They used both vertical and oblique photographs to model houses, factories, bridges, trees, and hedges. Color was added to increase the realism, and the models were used for specific briefings and were filmed from various angles under different light conditions to simulate an approach from some distance away.

Copies of the models were made from the originals by using a three-dimensional plaster mold. Of the ninety-seven original models made for this operation, none is known to exist today.

BIBLIOGRAPHY

Johnson, Garry, and Dunphie Christopher. *Brightly Shone the Dawn*. 1980.
Powys-Lybbe, Ursula. *The Eye of Intelligence*. 1983.

FREDERICK SOWREY

GUINGAND, FRANCIS W. DE *See* de Guingand, Francis W.

GUNFIRE SUPPORT. *See* Bombardment Ships; Close Gunfire Support.

H

HALL, JOHN L. (1891-1978), American, rear admiral, commander, Assault Force O. Born in Williamsburg, Virginia, John Lesslie Hall, Jr., graduated from the U.S. Naval Academy in 1913. He had a routine naval career until the United States entered World War II. Hall's duties then revolved around a relatively unknown form of warfare—amphibious operations.

Promoted to rear admiral, Hall was chief of staff to the commander of the Western Naval Task Force for the invasion of French Morocco in November 1942. Hall soon became commander of the Eighth Amphibious Force and was responsible for American amphibious training for future Mediterranean operations. Subsequently he commanded naval task forces at Gela, Sicily, and at Salerno. In both these operations naval gunfire, heavily stressed by Hall, played a pivotal role in hotly contested Allied victories. Through these three operations and his training command, Hall was at the center of perfecting the doctrines and practices of modern amphibious assaults.

In November 1943 Hall became commander of the Eleventh Amphibious Force at Plymouth, England, which rigorously trained U.S. sailors, soldiers, ships, and craft for the Allied invasion of Normandy. On 5 June 1944 Hall, as commander of Assault Force O, sailed for France in the amphibious command ship USS *Ancon*. His 691 ships and craft had to land elements of Maj. Gen. Leonard T. Gerow's U.S. V Corps on Omaha Beach in the Vierville-Colleville sector. Heavily fortified with natural and man-made obstacles, these beaches were the most formidable of the five Allied target areas.

Early on D-day, 6 June, Hall's ships opened fire and knocked out numerous enemy guns, tanks, and troops. Hall directed assault waves to the beaches, where they encountered withering fire. Throughout most of the day naval ships, sometimes closing to 720 meters (800 yards), provided the only real gunfire support for the soldiers pinned down on the beach. The effectiveness of naval gunfire prevented defeat at Omaha, and soon the troops moved inland.

While his ships continued their fire support of the troops, Hall also supervised the buildup of vast quantities of men and matériel. To speed unloading, Hall utilized a "drying out" technique that he had tried in the Mediterranean, allowing LSTs (Landing Ships, Tank), and later British coasters, to run directly onshore to unload. From D-day to D plus 12, Hall's force put ashore 191,629 men, 26,237 vehicles, and 66,977 tons of supplies.

JOHN L. HALL. COURTESY OF SUSAN H. GODSON

He remained in the assault area until 27 June (D plus 21). His Eleventh Amphibious force continued the buildup in the Bay of the Seine and by 6 August had landed more than two million troops, 400,000 vehicles, and millions of tons of supplies.

In late 1944 Hall went to the Pacific as commander, Amphibious Group 12. He commanded the Southern Attack Force during the invasion of Okinawa in April 1945. After the war he became a vice admiral and held various high naval commands until he retired in 1953. He died in 1978 in Scottsdale, Arizona, and was buried in Arlington National Cemetery.

[*See also* Ancon, USS.]

BIBLIOGRAPHY

Commander Assault Force "0" [J. L. Hall, Jr.]. Action Report: Assault on the Vierville-Colleville Sector, Coast of Normandy, serial 00876 of 27 July 1944. Operational Archives, Naval Historical Center, Washington, D.C.

Commander Assault Force "0" [J. L. Hall, Jr.]. Recording of Unloading, serial 00807 of 9 July 1944. Operational Archives, Naval Historical Center, Washington, D.C.

Godson, Susan H. *Viking Assault: Admiral John Lesslie Hall, Jr., and Amphibious Warfare.* 1982.

Godson, Susan H. "Virginia's Amphibious Admiral: John Lesslie Hall, Jr." *Virginia Cavalcade* 31 (1982): 132–143.

Hall, John Lesslie, Jr. Papers. College of William and Mary, Williamsburg, Va.

Morison, Samuel Eliot, *The Invasion of France and Germany: 1944–1945.* Vol. 11 of *History of United States Naval Operations in World War II.* 1957.

SUSAN H. GODSON

HARRIS, ARTHUR (1892–1984), British, air chief marshal; commander in chief of Bomber Command. Having flown as a fighter pilot in World War I, Harris commanded bomber squadrons in the 1920s, served at the Army Staff College, and was Deputy Director of Plans, Air Ministry, in the mid-1930s. He later led two of the groups in Bomber Command and in 1941 served as Deputy Chief of Air Staff and head of the RAF Delegation in Washington. He was appointed commander in chief of Bomber Command in February 1942.

Harris's main task was to direct the RAF's strategic bombing offensive against Germany. While sometimes required to switch his bombers to other objectives such as U-boat bases, he always resisted such diversions, firmly believing that his aircraft could best contribute to Germany's defeat by direct attack. Throughout 1942 and 1943 he conducted a night-bombing campaign that caused great damage to German cities and industries, imposing increasing strain on the German economy.

In January 1944, however, when it became clear that

ARTHUR HARRIS.   IMPERIAL WAR MUSEUM

Bomber Command, together with the U.S. Strategic Air Forces, was to be placed at General Dwight D. Eisenhower's disposal for OVERLORD, he protested strongly at what he saw as the abandonment of the air offensive against Germany, which he—like U.S. Gen. Carl Spaatz—firmly believed could force Germany's surrender on its own, if properly applied. In his judgment the only efficient support that Bomber Command could provide was to intensify its attacks on German industry. To substitute gun emplacements, beach defenses, communications, and supply dumps as targets would be an irremediable error; his force had not been equipped or trained for such tasks.

Harris's objections were overruled and he was allotted a major role in the Transportation Plan, designed to cut the German rail communications in France before D-day. Although doubtful that the necessary precision could be achieved and worried about causing heavy French casualties, he spared no effort to ensure that Bomber Command would execute its mission effectively. He personally attended Eisenhower's weekly meetings from early May onward, and attached senior members of his staff to the Supreme Commander's headquarters. The success of the Transportation Plan owed much to Harris's personal drive—and exceeded his expectations. Then, during the actual invasion, he ensured that the full weight of his bomber force was applied to the selected targets. Harris would later tell Eisenhower of the honor and delight of serving under him, and Eisenhower told Gen. George Marshall: "Harris actually proved to be one of the most effective members of my team: he met every request."

Harris has been much criticized—often unfairly—over the conduct of the strategic bombing campaign, and throughout his long retirement years after 1945 he never ceased to defend the reputation of his command and the men he led. Singled-minded, utterly determined, convinced of the rightness of his opinions, he could often be difficult, but as a leader prepared to take responsibility and make decisions, none could surpass him.

[*See also* Bomber Command.]

BIBLIOGRAPHY

Harris, Arthur. *Bomber Offensive.* 1947
Probert, Henry. *High Commanders of the RAF.* 1991.
Saward, Dudley. *Bomber Harris.* 1984.

HENRY PROBERT

HAWKINS, HMS.

HAWKINS, HMS. A Hawkins-class cruiser with a weight of 9,500 tons and a speed of 29 knots, *Hawkins* was armed with seven 7.5-inch and four 4-inch guns. Designed in 1916, it was built at Chatham Dockyard and completed in 1919. Its crew of 749 was commanded by Capt. J. W. Josselyn. Employed in the Indian Ocean, in February 1941 it supported the British offensive from Kenya into Italian Somaliland and later captured five Italian merchant ships.

Recalled to Britain in March 1944, *Hawkins* was fitted with enhanced radar and close-range antiaircraft armament. As part of Task Force 125, it was attached to Rear Adm. Morton L. Deyo's Bombardment Group, providing fire support for Utah Beach. The new crew worked up quickly in May and June on the coast of Northern Ireland to provide the additional fire support needed when the operation was increased to a five-division landing. Positioned to the southeast of the fire-support area, *Hawkins* opened fire at 0538 and engaged Target 16, a battery of four 155-mm guns two miles southwest of Grandcamp, across the Carentan estuary, securing several hits. It shifted to Target 5, the guns at Pointe du Hoc, at 0600 and ceased fire at 0640, then later fired on local targets and field guns. Targets 16 and 5 were neutralized by repeated hits. On the 7th it was assigned to Omaha Beach sector and engaged battlefield targets and batteries. Captain Josselyn was impressed with the crew. During the night of 7–8 June, the Luftwaffe's first attack on the Utah beachhead area almost hit *Hawkins*. On 8 June *Hawkins* fired in support of the advance of U.S. VII Corps. It returned to Portsmouth on 13 June, landed part of its crew, then returned as the flagship of Como. H. T. England (commodore, depot ships). Withdrawn into reserve on 29 June, *Hawkins* arrived at Rosyth, Scotland, on 31 June and saw no further service. It was broken up in 1947.

[*See also* Bombardment Ships; England, H. T.; Task Force 125; Western Task Force.]

BIBLIOGRAPHY

London. Public Record Office. Ship Log Books, HMS *Hawkins*, ADM 53/119542.
Raven, Alan, and John Roberts. *British Cruisers of World War Two.* 1980.

ANDREW LAMBERT

HELLMICH, HEINZ

HELLMICH, HEINZ (1890–1944), German, major general, commander of the *243d Infantry Division* and *Battle Group Hellmich.* Hellmich was born in Karlsruhe on 9 June 1890. He entered the Imperial Army as a cadet in the fall of 1908 and was commissioned second lieutenant in the *136th Infantry Regiment* on 22 March 1910. Hellmich fought in World War I, remained in the service, and was a major when Adolf Hitler came to power in 1933.

A highly competent and professional officer with no affiliation to the Nazi party, Hellmich was rapidly promoted to lieutenant colonel (1934), colonel (1936), and brigadier general (1939). He held various General Staff posts in the 1930s, including a tour of special duty as an Army General Staff officer attached to the Luftwaffe and as a branch chief at the Air Ministry. Upon the outbreak of World War II, he was named quartermaster general of the newly activated *Seventh Army*, which served on the West Wall in 1939. In October of that year he was named quartermaster general of *Army Group B.*

Clearly earmarked for greater things, Hellmich was named commander of the Berlin-Brandenburg *23d Infantry Division* on 1 June 1940. This elite unit was the heir to the traditions of the old Imperial Guards and was considered a prized command. Sent to East Prussia in September 1940, it crossed the border into the Soviet Union on 22 June 1941.

Hellmich skillfully led his division in the battles of Bialystok and Minsk, the siege of Mogilev, and the battle for Smolensk. It pushed on to the gates of Moscow in December 1941. Hellmich, meanwhile, was promoted to major general on 1 September.

The *23d Infantry* was caught in the Soviet winter offensive of 1941–1942. By January 1942 it was reduced by casualties and frostbite to a strength of barely 1,000 infantrymen, and its nine infantry battalions were consolidated into three. Most of the artillery was lost because the horses that transported it died in the subzero temperatures. Hellmich's nerves and health collapsed and he had to be sent back to Germany on 17 January, ruining a heretofore promising career.

Hellmich returned to duty on 1 April 1942, as commander of the *141st Mobilization* (later *Replacement*) *Division* at Insterburg, East Prussia—a definite step down from his previous assignments. On 15 December he was named inspector of *Osttruppen* (Eastern troops). He was not given another combat unit until 10 January 1944, when he assumed command of the *243d Infantry Division* on the Cotentin Peninsula. He supervised its reorganization into a limited attack division and was involved in the Normandy campaign from the beginning. As part of *Group Schlieben*, Hellmich did an excellent job of halting the American advance in the Montebourg-Quinéville sector from 9 to 13 June. Then Gen. Karl Wilhelm von Schlieben ordered him to defend the western Cotentin, where he had the almost hopeless task of blocking the American advance to the sea. *Battle Group Hellmich* consisted of elements of his own *243d Infantry Division* and the *77th Infantry Division*, which was only just arriving in the Cotentin. General Hellmich was in the process of trying to organize his command and halt the U.S. VII Corps on 16 June when his vehicle was strafed by an Allied fighter-bomber. The general was struck by a 20-mm shell and killed instantly. His death robbed the Germans of whatever very slim chance they had of preventing the Americans from isolating the Cherbourg fortifications.

[*See also* 243d Infantry Division.]

BIBLIOGRAPHY

Keilig, Wolf. *Die Generale des Heeres*. 1983.
Mitcham, Samuel W., Jr. *Rommel's Last Battle: The Desert Fox and the Normandy Campaign*. 1983.
Seaton, Albert. *The Battle of Moscow*. 1971.

SAMUEL W. MITCHAM, JR.

HENNECKE, WALTER (1898–1984), rear admiral, commander, Normandy Coast. Walter Hennecke was born on 23 May 1898 in Betheln, near Hannover. He joined the Imperial Navy in October 1915 and was promoted to lieutenant in December 1917. Entering the Weimar Republic's navy after the war, he served on various ships and for a time as an instructor at the Naval Artillery School in Kiel-Wik.

In July 1940 Hennecke returned to the Naval Artillery School, first as a commander and later as a captain, and concurrently commanded the training ship *Schleswig-Holstein*. In April 1943 he became naval commander for Normandy with headquarters in Cherbourg, his port at the time of the invasion. On 1 March 1944 he was made rear admiral. Hennecke was captured by American forces when the harbor fell on 27 June 1944. (The day before he had been awarded the Knight's Cross of the Iron Cross.) He lived in Hamburg after his release as a prisoner of war in April 1947. He died on 1 January 1984 in Bad Lippspringe.

BIBLIOGRAPHY

Hildebrand, Hans H., and Ernest Henriot. *Deutschlands Admirale*. Vol. 2, 1990.

GERHARD HÜMMELCHEN

HIGHLAND DIVISION. *See* 51st (Highland) Infantry Division.

HILARY, HMS. Built in 1931 by Cammell, Laird of Birkenhead as a passenger liner for the Booth Line, *Hilary* was converted to an ocean boarding vessel serving from 1940 to 1942. It was rehired in March 1943 and converted to a Landing Ship Headquarters (Large)—LSH(L). Its weight was 7,403 tons and its speed 14 knots; as armament it had only light antiaircraft guns. Its crew of 313 was commanded by Acting Capt. J. F. Paget. *Hilary* served in Operation HUSKY (the Sicily invasion) in July 1943 as the flagship of Rear Adm. Philip Vian, and in Operation AVALANCHE (the Salerno invasion) on 9 September 1943 as the flagship of Como. G. N. Oliver.

Hilary became the D-day flagship of Como. G. N. Oliver, commanding Force J. An experienced amphibious command ship, *Hilary*, with its combined services personnel and commodore, proved invaluable. All three LSH(L)s (*Hilary, Bulolo*, and *Largs*) were practiced and professional ships, which went a long way toward ensuring that all went smoothly. In addition *Hilary* carried the headquarters and elements of the 3d Canadian Division, under Maj. Gen. R. F. L. Keller, and No. 48 Royal Marine Commando to land on Juno Beach. With naval and military commanders co-located, and liaison officers aboard, the LSH(L)s were the only ships with a complete picture of the assault phase.

In position by 0558 *Hilary* moved inshore during the evening to speed up landing. *Hilary* suffered near hits by bombs during the night of 12–13 June and dragged its anchors during the great gale of 19–20 June, when it was in some danger. It became the flagship of Eastern Task Force at 0800 on 23 June, when Rear Admiral Vian raised his flag on it after *Scylla* had been mined. Commodore Oliver and his staff returned to England at this time.

Hilary left the assault area with Vian on the 30th, the official end of Operation NEPTUNE. *Hilary* returned to mercantile service in March 1946.

[*See also* Eastern Task Force; Oliver, G. N.; Task Force J.]

BIBLIOGRAPHY

Roskill, Stephen W. *The Offensive*. Vol. 3, pt. 2, of *The War at Sea, 1939–1945*. 1960.
Schofield, B. B. *Operation Neptune*. 1974.

ANDREW LAMBERT

HILL, RODERIC M.

HILL, RODERIC M. (1894-1954), British air marshal, commander of the Air Defence of Great Britain. Roderic Hill had been a pilot with the Royal Flying Corps, but from the 1920s until 1943 he specialized almost exclusively in experimental flying and technical support. Given this narrow background, it is somewhat surprising that in July 1943 he was appointed to command No. 12 Group, responsible for the air defense of the British Midlands. Only four months later he moved a step higher and took over Fighter Command, by now renamed the Air Defence of Great Britain, with responsibility for defending the whole country from German attack by air while the Allied invasion of Europe was being planned. This was a crucial task, since it meant protecting the massive buildup of forces in the United Kingdom from attack by the Luftwaffe and by the expected V-1 bombs.

The only protracted night attack by the Luftwaffe was the "little blitz" of London in early 1944. The first V-1 attacks came seven days after D-day, and almost one month later Hill ordered a complete redeployment of his defenses. This decision proved to be very successful and he was knighted for his efforts.

At the end of the war Hill joined the Air Council of the Royal Air Force, where he held two successive posts before retiring in 1948 with the rank of air chief marshal. He died six years later after holding the appointment of vice-chancellor of London University.

The academic position suited Hill's talents well, as had his posts in the support echelons of the RAF, where his sensitive nature was of little consequence. But he lacked the broad vision and the sure touch essential to high operational command. He fulfilled his task with distinction in leading the air defense of Britain at an important time.

[*See also* Air Defence of Great Britain.]

BIBLIOGRAPHY

Hill, Prudence. *To Know the Sky: The Life of Air Chief Marshal Sir Roderic Hill*. 1962.
Saunders, Hilary St. G. *The Fight Is Won*. Vol. 3 of *The Royal Air Force, 1939–1945*. 1954.

MICHAEL ARMITAGE

RODERIC M. HILL.   IMPERIAL WAR MUSEUM

HITLER, ADOLF

HITLER, ADOLF (1889–1945), German, Führer and Commander in Chief of the German armed forces. Born at Braunau in northern Austria on the German border, Hitler, the son of a customs official, spent the years before World War I living a penurious bohemian existence in Vienna and Munich. On the outbreak of war he joined the Bavarian infantry as a volunteer and was sent to the Western front. During the next four years he won four decorations for bravery, was wounded and gassed, and rose to the rank of corporal. It was his experience as an army political officer in the aftermath of the 1919 Bavarian civil war that set him on the path of national socialism. As leader of the National Socialist party, he assumed total power in Germany fourteen years later.

When Hitler became chancellor of Germany in January 1933, he was determined to restore the country's greatness. To do this, he had to throw off the shackles of the 1919 Treaty of Versailles and rebuild the armed forces. Such a policy was welcomed by the military, but Hitler's rapid expansion plans put almost intolerable strains on the armed forces' structure. This, together with Hitler's ever more aggressive foreign policy, caused some generals to have increasing doubts. Hitler's answer was to engineer their removal and replace them with such men as Wilhelm Keitel and Walter von Brauchitsch, who would not stand in his way. In addition, in 1937 he made himself commander in chief of the armed forces.

ADOLF HITLER.

The dazzling success enjoyed by German arms during the blitzkrieg campaigns of 1939–1941 served both to increase the Wehrmacht's confidence in their leader and to reinforce Hitler's belief in his own infallibility. This was reflected in his growing interference with operations on the Eastern front. Here, at the end of 1941, he decreed that there should be no voluntary surrender of ground, which led to the dismissal of Brauchitsch, the army's commander in chief, and Field Marshal Gerd von Rundstedt, commanding *Army Group C*. Nowhere would the results of this policy be better displayed than in the debacle at Stalingrad during the winter of 1942–1943.

Because the bulk of the German forces were engaged on the Eastern front from June 1941 onward, this theater preoccupied Hitler more than any other. Consequently, the allocation of resources to the other theaters, especially the West, was neglected. While work had begun to construct fortifications, the so-called Atlantic Wall, on the French Atlantic and Channel coasts, the number and quality of troops in France remained low. Indeed, it became little more than a convalescent home where divisions shattered on the Eastern front could rebuild their strength. The failure of the German offensive at Kursk in July 1943, after which the Germans were definitely on the defensive in Russia, and the 1943 Allied landings in Sicily and Italy, caused Hitler gradually to pay more attention to the West, something for which Rundstedt, Commander in Chief West, had long been agitating. The upshot was Hitler's Directive No. 51 of 3 November 1943, stating that the greatest danger to the Reich was now Anglo-American landings on the Continent mounted from Britain; therefore the defenses in the West must be strengthened, and more mobile formations, antitank weapons, and artillery sent to that theater. Three days later he sent Field Marshal Erwin Rommel on a tour of inspection of the coasts of Denmark, the Low Countries, and France. Rommel's belief that the battle must be fought on the beaches, not least because Allied air power would make the quick deployment of German reserves very difficult, accorded well with Hitler's policy of never surrendering ground. Hitler also overemphasized the significance of the Dieppe raid of August 1942, disastrous for the Allies, in demonstrating the ability of coastal defenses to repulse an amphibious attack. Consequently, he fully supported Rommel's recommendations for strengthening the defenses. He also concurred with the view of Rommel and Rundstedt that the most likely point of attack was between Boulogne and the Seine River.

The argument between Panzer commander Lt. Gen. Leo Geyr von Schweppenburg, Rommel, and his superior, Rundstedt, over the deployment of the mobile reserves, revealed a different characteristic of Hitler as military commander. Rundstedt had compromised by giving Rommel some of the mobile divisions for deployment close to the coast while retaining the remainder as a central reserve under Geyr, but at the end of April 1944 Hitler, now believing that the landings could also take place on the Normandy coast, ordered that the reserve not be moved without his permission. This meant that Rundstedt had lost virtually all control over his mobile reserves. This only added to his frustration since Hitler, who operated a "divide and rule" policy in all aspects of the Third Reich, had allowed Rundstedt only limited military powers, with merely partial control over the naval and Luftwaffe elements in his theater, and none over the SS and SD. Hitler's overall control was such that Rundstedt remarked to Geyr that he even needed Hitler's permission to change the guard posts outside his headquarters.

Hitler, like his generals, expected the invasion in May, so when the danger period passed there was a slight relaxation. Indeed, he decamped from Berlin to his Alpine retreat at Berchtesgaden. On the night 5–6 June he went to bed with a sleeping draught. Such fear of him was instilled in his staff that they dared not wake him when news of the invasion came through. Even when he was up and dressed, he was more concerned to drive for an hour to Klessheim Castle to greet the Hungarian dictator, Adm. Miklos Horthy, who had come on a state visit: Field Marshal Wilhelm Keitel and Gen. Albert Jodl had to go there as well, in order to brief him and pass on Rundstedt's request for the mobile reserves to be released to him. Consequently, not until midafternoon was consent given to deploy some of the mobile formations to Normandy. By then it was too late: the Allies were firmly established ashore.

During the next few days Hitler sent a stream of orders demanding that the invader be thrown back into the sea, especially from 8 June onward, when he concluded that there would not be additional landings north of the Seine River. Allied air power, however, and the French Resistance hindered the move of the mobile reserves to Normandy; as a result, they were committed to battle piecemeal and unable to push the Allied forces back. Such was the pressure inflicted by the latter that the panzer divisions found themselves holding the line. Rundstedt and Rommel remonstrated with the Wehrmacht High Command (Oberkommando der Wehrmacht, or OKW) that the only way that a counterstroke could succeed was to send infantry reinforcements to relieve the armor, and to withdraw to a more defensible line. They also demanded freedom to conduct the campaign without interference. Hitler would have none of it, but did agree to come to France to hear the field marshals' views in person. They met at Margival near Soissons on 17 June, but Hitler ignored what they had to say and launched into a long diatribe on how the so-called "miracle weapons"—V-weapons and jet bombers—would restore

ADOLF HITLER.   LIBRARY OF CONGRESS

German fortunes. That evening a defective V-1 crashed close to Margival, and Hitler and his entourage scurried back to Berchtesgaden without informing Rundstedt or Rommel. He then ordered Rundstedt to mount a counterstroke designed to split the U.S. First Army from the British Second, even specifying the divisions that were to take part. Rundstedt protested that it would take some two weeks before this could be mounted, because of the difficulties in disengaging the armor and concentrating it. Hitler then demanded a counterattack against the American forces besieging Cherbourg, but this was preempted by Montgomery's offensive near Caen at the end of June (EPSOM). In any event, the field marshals pointed out to Hitler that Cherbourg could not hold out and that the crucial sector was Caen, which was under constant pressure. Hitler disagreed and once more demanded an attack against the Americans.

Totally exasperated, Rundstedt and Rommel reiterated their demands for the right to withdraw their forces to more favorable terrain. The result was a summons from Hitler on the evening of 27 June for both to meet him at Berchtesgaden in forty-eight hours, laying down that they must travel the six hundred miles by road. This conference consisted largely of one of Hitler's monologues, again on the "miracle weapons," but also resulted in the decision

to replace Rundstedt by Field Marshal Hans von Kluge, although Rundstedt himself was not told of this until the day before the latter arrived to relieve him. On their return to their respective headquarters, Rundstedt and Rommel were met with orders from OKW for an immediate counterstroke against the EPSOM attack. Rundstedt replied that it was essential to withdraw the *I SS Panzer Corps* and *21st Panzer Division* from the Caen area to put them out of range of Allied naval gunfire and not run the risk of being encircled. The immediate OKW response was that there were to be no withdrawals. This was the final straw for Rundstedt, who was now thankful to be relieved of his command.

After this, Hitler's attention turned elsewhere. The Soviet summer offensive had torn a great hole in *Army Group Center* and he moved to his eastern headquarters, the Wolf's Lair at Rastenburg in East Prussia. There, on 20 July, he survived the attempt against his life, which merely increased his distrust of his generals. The Allies now broke out of the Normandy bridgehead and for a time it looked as though nothing could stop them from entering Germany. One facet of Hitler's strategy halted them: his orders that the French ports be turned into *Festungen* (strongholds) and hold out to the last man. Since this made the Allies continue to rely on resupply through the beachhead, their ever stretching lines of communication eventually forced a halt, allowing the Germans to recover. This meant a slow, slogging approach to and penetration of the West Wall, guarding the Franco-German frontier, during the autumn.

Hitler's final flourish in the West, the Ardennes counteroffensive of December, was too ambitious in scope to achieve its aim, although it initially caught the Allies off balance and delayed a further advance for six weeks, while costing the Germans irreplaceable men and equipment. Thereafter Hitler retired to the unreal world of the *Führerbunker* in Berlin, seldom venturing out. As a last desperate measure, he ordered a scorched-earth policy to be carried out, but this was circumvented by his minister for armaments and war production, Albert Speer. He now resolved to die with his people in Berlin, but even then continued to believe that the Russians could be thrown back. Eventually, on 30 April 1945, he committed suicide as the final Soviet offensive across the Oder River closed in on the center of the capital.

Hitler was widely read in military history, and it was this, together with his own experience as a frontline soldier, that gave him confidence in his own military judgment. During the early part of the war, his intuition and his remarkable ability to absorb technical detail often worked well for him. As the tide turned against Germany, Hitler became increasingly blinkered in his outlook, binding his generals in ever tighter subservience, which robbed them

of any freedom of action; he refused to heed their advice, and those who objected were simply retired. By the end he had entered a fantasy world totally divorced from the reality of the ever larger catastrophe engulfing his country.
[*See also* Germany.]

BIBLIOGRAPHY

Bullock, Alan. *Hitler: A Study in Tyranny.* Rev. ed., 1965.
Keegan, John. *The Mask of Command.* 1987.
Messenger, Charles. *The Last Prussian: A Biography of Field Marshal Gerd von Rundstedt, 1875–1953.* 1991.
Wilmot, Chester. *The Struggle for Europe.* 1952.

CHARLES MESSENGER

HITLERJUGEND DIVISION. *See* 12th SS Panzer Division "Hitlerjugend."

HOBART, PERCY C. S. (1865–1957), British, major general, commander of the 79th Armoured Division. Hobo, as Hobart was known, was commissioned a royal engineer in the Indian army in 1906. He fought in France, Mesopotamia, and Palestine, was twice decorated, and after the First World War qualified at the Army Staff College. A brilliant staff officer, he transferred to the Royal Tank Corps, eventually becoming a ruthless, controversial inspector of the corps and commander of the 1st Tank Brigade, heavily engaged in the struggle for modernization and mechanization of the British army. In 1938 he formed in Egypt what was to be the famous 7th Armoured Division. Sacked in 1939 for his revolutionary ideas, he was recalled to active service to form in 1941 the 11th Armoured Division and in 1942 the 79th Armoured Division. He was knighted in 1943 for his services to armored developments.

In March 1943 the Chief of the Imperial General Staff (CIGS), Gen. Alan Brooke, made Hobart responsible for the development of specialized armor to spearhead the invasion of Europe. Using a reorganized 79th Armoured Division, he trained and developed a doctrine for the units, which were to be equipped with amphibious Duplex Drive (DD) Sherman tanks; Sherman Crab minesweeping flail tanks; Churchill AVRE (Armoured Vehicle Royal Engineer) tanks equipped with a spigot mortar to project petards and such devices as fascines and small box-girder bridges for crossing obstacles and Bobbin carpet layers for crossing soft beaches; so-called Canal Defence Light (CDL) Grant tanks with powerful searchlights for night operations; and Churchill Crocodile flamethrower tanks. Eventually all except the CDL Grant tanks played key roles on the British beaches in subduing the German defenses before the infantry landed. The

PERCY C. S. HOBART.   IMPERIAL WAR MUSEUM

Americans, however, adopted only the Duplex Drive Sherman tank and suffered unnecessarily heavy losses on Omaha Beach when only two tanks managed to struggle ashore in the rough seas.

Hobart and his headquarters arrived in Normandy on D plus 2. Henceforward, as Special Armoured Adviser to his brother-in-law, General Bernard L. Montgomery, he not only played a significant part in developing the use of specialized armor in land battles but also influenced the conduct of the campaign as a whole. The 79th Armoured Division's so-called "Funnies," such as the Crocodile tank, were in the lead in Normandy and later in clearing the Channel ports and the approaches to Antwerp, and crossing the Rhine and Elbe rivers.

After the war Hobart became representative colonel commander of the Royal Tank Regiment and lieutenant governor of the Royal Hospital, Chelsea.
[*See also* 79th Armoured Division.]

BIBLIOGRAPHY

The History of 79th Armoured Division. 1946.
Macksey, Kenneth. *Armoured Crusader: General Sir Percy Hobart.* 1967.

KENNETH MACKSEY

HOBBS, LELAND

HOBBS, LELAND (1892–1966), American, major general commanding 30th Infantry Division. Graduating from West Point in 1915, Leland S. Hobbs was commissioned in the infantry. He saw early service in skirmishes with Mexican bandits along the Texas border, then in Europe during the last days of World War I. During the interwar years he had troop duty, served as an instructor at West Point, and attended many military schools, including the Army War College.

In September 1942 he was assigned as commanding general, 30th Infantry Division, the outfit he would organize and train, then lead in battle through five campaigns in Europe. Composed of National Guard units from North and South Carolina, Georgia, and Tennessee, the "Old Hickory Division" proved to be a hard-fighting and reliable outfit.

In the invasion landings, on the night of 13–14 June, Hobbs took his troops ashore across Omaha Beach with the intention of driving the enemy from an area south of the Carentan-Isigny railroad between the Canal de Vire et Taute and the Vire River. There, said the official history, "in the great Allied victory in the breakout battle of Normandy, the 30th Infantry Division received the brunt of a powerful enemy counterattack." It was, said historian Martin Blumenson, "the first large-scale German counterattack launched after the Allied invasion of Normandy." Hobbs had assumed responsibility for the Mortain area—where the German counterattack by the *XLVII Panzer Corps* was concentrated—in the dark of night only four hours before the Germans hit. During the attack, elements of the division were isolated by superior enemy forces, but held their position and, after six days of heavy fighting, prevailed. Later General Bradley wrote of that battle that "it was to cost the enemy an Army and gain us France."

Subsequently Hobbs led his forces in a rapid series of offensives across France, Belgium, and Holland, a total of 282 combat days, culminating at war's end in what was described by *The New York Times* as "a triumphant meeting at the Elbe with Soviet troops."

In a battlefield dispatch for the Associated Press, correspondent Wes Gallagher dubbed the 30th Infantry "the American Army's work horse division." Subsequently S. L. A. Marshall, the historian of the European Theater of Operations, was asked by General Eisenhower to rate the various divisions in terms of their worthiness for presidential unit citations. The 30th Infantry Division, under Hobbs, was one of five infantry divisions he placed in the first category, those which had "performed the most efficient and consistent battle service."

And, Marshall added, "We picked the 30th Division No. 1 on the list of first category divisions" based on the consensus view of some thirty-five historical officers. "We were especially impressed with the fact that it had con-sistently achieved results without undue wastage of its men," he said. "We felt that the 30th was the outstanding infantry division of the ETO." Hobbs was awarded the Distinguished Service Medal for his World War II service, along with two Silver Stars and three Bronze Star medals. He led from the front.

Following World War II General Hobbs served successfully as commanding general of the IX Corps in the Far East Command; as chief of the Joint U.S. Military Assistance Group to the Philippines; and as deputy commanding general of the First Army from 1951 until his retirement in 1953. He died in Washington, D.C., on 6 March 1966.

[*See also* 30th Infantry Division.]

BIBLIOGRAPHY

Blumenson, Martin. *Breakout and Pursuit.* U.S. Army in World War II: The European Theater of Operations. 1961.

Hewitt, Robert L. *Work Horse of the Western Front: The Story of the 30th Infantry Division.* 1946. Reprint, 1980.

LEWIS SORLEY

HODGES, COURTNEY H.

HODGES, COURTNEY H. (1887–1966), American, lieutenant general, deputy commander of the U.S. First Army. Hodges entered West Point in 1904 to pursue his childhood dream of becoming a soldier. He failed mathematics in his first year and returned home to Georgia. In 1906 he enlisted in the 17th Infantry Regiment, serving as a private until he earned his officer's commission in a competitive examination in 1909.

In 1918 Hodges served with the 6th Infantry Regiment in France, where he rose to the rank of lieutenant colonel and earned the Distinguished Service Cross and the Silver Star for his "fearlessness and courage" in combat. Returning to the United States in 1920, Hodges attended the Field Artillery School, the Command and General Staff College, and the Army War College. His subsequent experience in teaching and training soldiers helped him lay a firm foundation for the techniques of training infantry that would be followed during the army's rapid World War II expansion.

In 1941 Gen. George Marshall, Army Chief of Staff, summoned Hodges to Washington to become chief of infantry and receive a promotion to major general. After briefly commanding the Replacement and School Command of the Army Ground Forces, he activated X Corps in Texas as part of the Third Army. He was promoted to lieutenant general and assumed command of that army in February 1943 and a year later preceded it to England to complete plans for the invasion.

In England Hodges became Gen. Omar Bradley's deputy and was responsible for preinvasion training for the U.S. First Army. A slender man of medium height,

COURTNEY H. HODGES.   NATIONAL ARCHIVES

with a small mustache, he looked more like a successful businessman than a military commander. He had a reputation for painstaking attention to detail. Bradley termed him "a military technician" with "faultless techniques and tactical knowledge." His supervision of the tactical preparations allowed Bradley to focus on plans for the army group he would eventually command in France. During the first weeks after D-day Hodges spent most of his time with the corps and division commanders, becoming acquainted with the tactical situation and preparing to take command of the First Army.

In August 1944, after Operation COBRA, the Allied breakout from the Normandy beachheads, Bradley moved to command the 12th Army Group, and Hodges assumed command of the First Army. He commanded the army until the end of the war in Europe, gaining reputation as a quiet, competent commander who shied away from publicity. He was promoted to general in April 1945. After the German surrender in May 1945, Hodges traveled to the Pacific theater of operations in anticipation of the First Army's employment there. When the war ended before his army was needed, Hodges returned to the United States and commanded the First Army until his retirement in 1949.

[*See also* First Army.]

BIBLIOGRAPHY

MacDonald, Charles B. "A Personal Tribute." *The Voice* 1 (1966): 2, 7.
Murray, G. Patrick. "Courtney Hodges: Modest Star of WWII." *American History Illustrated* 7 (1973): 12–25.
Stone, Richard G. "Hodges, Courtney." In *Dictionary of American Military Biography*, vol. 2, pp. 481–484.

CLAYTON R. NEWELL

HODGES, JAMES P. (1894–), American, major general, commander 2d Bombardment Division, Eighth Air Force. Hodges joined the Aviation Section of the Army Signal Corps in 1917 but did not receive a posting to France. He served in the War Department general staff 1938–1940, and in September 1942 took command of the 2d Bombardment Wing (subsequently 2d Bombardment Division), Eighth Air Force. He became a brigadier general in 1942, and a major general in 1944. In August 1944 he left the Eighth Air Force to become the assistant chief of staff for intelligence (A-2), Army Air Forces Staff. He held that post until July 1945.

As the commander of the Eighth Air Force's B-24s, Hodges confronted a formidable task. The aircraft's longer range and lower combat ceiling, as compared to the B-17, meant higher losses to German flak and deeper missions into enemy territory, which increased the exposure time to enemy countermeasures. Larger losses, and assignment to an aircraft of possibly lesser performance, depressed B-24 crew morale. Furthermore, in May 1943 the Combined Chiefs of Staff decided upon Operation TIDALWAVE, a B-24 attack on the Ploesti oil complex in Romania, slated for the summer of 1943. The operation diverted four of Hodges's B-24 groups for a considerable time and inflicted heavy damage on them.

For the first eight months of 1944, Hodges's command never finished first in Eighth Air Force bombing accuracy and finished last five times. His groups also led the Eighth Air Force in numbers of aircraft and air crew interning themselves in Sweden and Switzerland. In June and July 1944, 43 of 78 crews interned belonged to the 2d Bombardment Division. The entire division was also involved in two ineffective operations in direct support of Allied ground forces in July 1944. On 18 July, in support of General Bernard L. Montgomery's Operation GOODWOOD, the division dropped 76,000 fragmentation bombs on German positions, but the British reported ineffective results. On both days of Operation COBRA, many squadrons of the division bombed short (13 of 45 squadrons on the second day, in spite of warnings), causing hundreds of American casualties and a great deal of embarrassment for the Army Air Forces.

Taken as a whole the division had not achieved the level of accomplishment of the remainder of the Eighth Air Force. In August 1944 Maj. Gen. William E. Kepner took over Hodges's command. Hodges returned to Washington, D.C., as chief of intelligence and never received another combat assignment. He retired from the service in September 1951.

[*See also* Eighth Air Force; 2d Bombardment Division.]

BIBLIOGRAPHY

Craven, Wesley Frank, and James Lea Cate, eds. *Europe: ARGU-MENT to V-E Day, January 1944 to May 1945*. Vol. 3 of *The Army Air Forces in World War II*. 1951.
Davis, Richard. *Carl A. Spaatz and the Air War in Europe, 1940–1945*. 1993.

RICHARD G. DAVIS

HOFFMANN, HEINRICH (1910–), German, commander of the *5th Torpedo Boat Flotilla*. Heinrich Hoffmann was born on 17 August 1910 in Bottrop, Westphalia. He joined the German Navy in 1928, beginning his career as a noncommissioned officer. Promoted to lieutenant in 1936, then to first lieutenant in 1938, he became watch officer with the *6th Torpedo Boat Flotilla*. During the first years of World War II Hoffmann served in turn on several torpedo boats, the last of which he commanded. Promoted to commander, in November 1943 he became chief of the *5th Torpedo Boat Flotilla*, which on D-day consisted of five boats. Only *T 28, Möwe,* and *Jaguar* were battle-ready.

On the evening of 6 June 1944 Hoffmann led his three boats in an attack from Le Havre on the far superior Force S, part of the British Eastern Task Force. In this engagement off Sword Beach the German torpedoes went between the battleships *Warspite* and *Ramillies,* missed the headquarters ship *Largs,* and sank the Norwegian destroyer *Svenner*. On the next two nights the three torpedo boats again put to sea, and on 8–9 June engaged the British 55th Motor Torpedo Boat Flotilla. During the night of 9–10 June they engaged the Norwegian destroyer *Glaisdale,* the British destroyer *Ursa,* and the Polish destroyer *Krakowiak*. Only *T 28* and *Möwe* were involved in the flotilla's last engagement on the night of 12–13 June, when, having engaged the British destroyers *Stord* and *Scorpion* with no result, they returned to Le Havre. *Falke, Jaguar,* and *Möwe* were sunk during the British air attack on that port on the evening of 14 June. Only *T 28* remained; after 21 July, proceeding in stages, it managed to escape back to Germany. *T 24,* which was also part of the flotilla, remained with the *8th Destroyer Flotilla* in Brest. Along with the destroyer *Z 24,* it fell victim to British bombers in the Le Verdon roadstead on 24 August.

HEINRICH HOFFMAN.

BIBLIOTHEK FÜR ZEITGESCHICHTE, STUTTGART

In November 1944 Hoffmann, who had been awarded the Knight's Cross and Oak Leaf Cluster, became commander of the navy's small craft training division, where he remained until war's end. He was accepted into the West German navy as a commander in 1956 and was promoted to captain in May 1960. Retired in 1968, he lives in Schiffdorf near Bremerhaven.

[*See also* Torpedo Boats.]

BIBLIOGRAPHY

Rohwer, Jürgen, and Gerhard Hümmelchen. *Chronology of the War at Sea, 1939–1945*. Translated by Derek Masters. 1992.

GERHARD HÜMMELCHEN

HOGE, W. M. (1894–1979), American, brigadier general, commander, 1st Engineer Special Brigade Group (Provisional). Born in Booneville, Missouri, on 13 January 1894, William Morris Hoge graduated from the U.S. Military Academy in 1916 and was commissioned into the Corps of Engineers. Hoge served briefly in Texas with the 1st Engineers, then went to France with the 7th Engineers, doing both construction and combat engineering. After returning in July 1919, Hoge spent most of the interwar years either in military schools, training, or in civil works assignments with the Corps of Engineers. In February 1942 Hoge was given responsibility for building the Alaska Highway. Then, in October 1943, he was sent to England as commander of the 5th Engineer Special Brigade.

Because the Omaha Beach operations were so extensive that they required the deployment of the 5th and 6th engineer special brigades along with the 11th Port Headquarters, the 1st Engineer Special Brigade Group (Provisional) was activated to control and coordinate those units. On 8 March 1944 Hoge took command of the group. His principal concerns were close cooperation with the U.S. Navy and preparation for the assault and logistical work of D-day and the following weeks.

On D-day Hoge came ashore shortly after 1500 and set up a command post in a concrete pillbox just west of Exit E-1 on Omaha Beach. From there, he assumed responsibility for engineer command on Omaha. Keeping track of his engineers in his head and making quick decisions without paperwork, Hoge kept men and supplies moving across the beach while under fire. Hoge was wounded there, but remained in charge of the beachhead until 26 June. On 1 July, Hoge assumed command of the 16th Major Port, responsible for the rehabilitation and operation of ports in support of the VIII corps on the Brittany peninsula.

Hoge later requested combat assignments. He fought in the Battle of the Bulge and later participated in the capture of the Ludendorff Railroad Bridge over the Rhine at Remagen. After several postwar commands, Hoge retired with the rank of general in 1955. Hoge died at Fort Leavenworth, Kansas, 20 October 1979 at age 85.

[See also American Beaches, article on Omaha Beach; Engineers, article on American Engineers; Shore Party.]

BIBLIOGRAPHY

Beck, Alfred M., Abe Bortz, Charles W. Lynch, et al. *The Technical Services, The Corps of Engineers: The War against Germany*. U.S. Army in World War II. 1985.

Fowle, Barry W., ed. *Builders and Fighters: U.S. Army Engineers in World War II*. 1992.

Hoge, William M. *Engineer Memoirs: General William M. Hoge, US Army*. 1993.

MARTIN K. GORDON

HOLLE, ALEXANDER (1898–),

German, major general, commander of *X Air Corps (Fliegerkorps X)*, responsible for specialized antishipping bomber units employed against the Allied invasion. Alexander Holle joined the German Army in 1915 as an infantryman and fought in the battle of Verdun. After gaining his commission he served as an observer in balloons on the Western front; three times his balloon was shot down in flames, and each time he escaped by parachute. After the war he remained in the army and was one of the thirty-six German officers permitted to receive pilot training under the terms of the Paris Air Agreement.

When the new Luftwaffe was formed, he transferred to it and served as a staff officer in Spain with the *Condor Legion*. Later he commanded a squadron of the then new Stuka dive bombers. During the Polish campaign he was chief of staff of *IV Air Corps*. In 1941 he was appointed *Fliegerführer Nord*, responsible for the direction of the torpedo-bomber and reconnaissance units based in Norway operating against Allied convoys sailing round the north of that country to the Soviet Union. In recognition of the success of his work, in February 1943 he was awarded the Knight's Cross.

By the summer of 1943 he was one of the acknowledged specialists in antishipping operations, and therefore was appointed commander of *X Air Corps*, based in southern France. He held that position until July 1944, when the formation was disbanded.

[See also X Air Corps.]

BIBLIOGRAPHY

United Kingdom. Air Ministry. Intelligence Summary.

ALFRED PRICE

HOLLINGHURST, L. N. (1895–1971).

British, air vice marshal, air officer commanding, No. 38 Group, Allied Expeditionary Air Force. As air officer commanding (AOC), a post he held from the formation of No. 38 Group in October 1943, Hollinghurst was a tough commander—described as "a hard, red-faced professional airman with a strong character and considerable powers of leadership"—but he was admired by both soldiers and airmen, whom he criticized indiscriminately when he considered criticism justified. He led from the front, and was aboard the leading pathfinder Albemarle when it took off for Normandy at 2303 on 5 June 1944, carrying paratroops who were to prepare and illuminate a landing zone. His "original and inspired methods of training" paid off in the good results achieved by his squadrons in Operation OVERLORD.

When appointed to command No. 38 Group, which spearheaded the airborne forces in the Allied invasion of Normandy, Hollinghurst had experienced air operations on the Western front in 1918 (when he was awarded the Distinguished Flying Cross) and on the northwest frontier of India in the early 1920s and 1929–1934, when he commanded an army cooperation squadron. In between these

L. N. HOLLINGHURST.   IMPERIAL WAR MUSEUM

tours he was on the staff of the RAF College, Cranwell, and took the staff college course.

He relinquished command of No. 38 Group in October 1944 when posted to BAFSEA (British Air Forces, South-East Asia). He was knighted in 1948 (Knight Commander of the Order of the British Empire [Military]) and appointed successively air member for Supply and Organisation on the Air Force Board, inspector general, and finally—as Air Chief Marshal Sir Leslie Hollinghurst—air member for Personnel until his retirement from the RAF in 1952. He died in 1971, just after attending the annual pilgrimage of D-day veterans to Normandy on 6 and 7 June.

[*See also* Transport Command.]

BIBLIOGRAPHY

Crookenden, N. "The Airborne Forces." In *75 Eventful Years: A Tribute to the Royal Air Force, 1918–1993.* 1993.

Hollinghurst, L. N. Air Ministry Record of Service. RAF Personnel Management Centre, Gloucester.

HUMPHREY WYNN

HOLLIS, STANLEY ELTON (1921–1972), British,
company sergeant major, 6th Battalion. The only award of the Victoria Cross made on D-day went to CSM Stanley Hollis of D Company, 6th Battalion, The Green Howards, near the Mont-Fleury battery on the King sector of Gold Beach, the area stormed by the 50th (Northumbrian) Division at 0745.

The official citation (dated 17 August 1944) records how, when his company commander, Maj. R. Lofthouse, realized that his men had inadvertently missed two German pillboxes that were threatening D Company's rear, Hollis and Lofthouse (who received a Military Cross for his part in the ensuing action) went back to clear them. When they were within twenty yards of one of the positions, a German machine gun opened up from a weapon slit, whereupon Hollis rushed forward, threw in a grenade, and raked the interior with his Sten gun, killing two Germans and taking a number of prisoners. This action permitted his battalion to open the main exit from Gold Beach.

Later on the sixth a German field gun, backed by machine guns, held up D Company in the village of Crépon. When their attack was delayed, Hollis pushed forward with a Piat (Projector, Infantry, Anti-Tank) to a house within 45-meter (50-yard) range. Despite his suffering a cheek-graze from a sniper's bullet and the house itself receiving a direct hit, Hollis led his men to an alternate position from which they watched the German piece destroyed. Realizing that two of his men were left behind, trapped by fire in the gradually disintegrating house, Hollis volunteered to return. Firing a Bren gun out in the open with utter disregard for his own safety and under heavy fire, he distracted the enemy's attention long enough to permit his men to escape. "It was largely through his heroism and resource," the citation ends, "that the Company's objectives were gained and casualties were not heavier, and by his bravery he saved the lives of many of his men."

Hollis was a native of Middlesborough in England. He joined the 6th (Territorial Army) Battalion of his regiment and served with them in the 1940 Dunkirk campaign and in Sicily and then in northwestern Europe. After he was wounded in September 1944, his active wartime career came to an end, although he remained in the Territorial Army until 1949. The postwar years brought him mixed fortunes, but he eventually became landlord of two public houses (pubs) in North Ormesby and Liverton Mines in turn. Over the years he participated in many Camberley Staff College battlefield tours to the Gold Beach area. He died on 8 February 1972. When his Victoria Cross was sold by his widow in 1983, it fetched the then record sum of 32,000 pounds sterling.

BIBLIOGRAPHY

Powell, Geoffrey. *The History of the Green Howards: 300 Years of Service.* 1992.

Smyth, John. *The Story of the Victoria Cross.* 1963.

DAVID G. CHANDLER

HORSES. The German army of World War II was not the highly mechanized force many people have conceived it to be. Of the fifty-eight German divisions that were deployed in the West, only ten (17 percent) were panzer or panzer grenadier—that is, divisions that employed tanks and other armored vehicles and motor vehicles for transport. The vast majority of German infantry divisions in the West relied on horses for transport.

The Germans used different types of horses for various tasks. The light, hardy Russian panje horses, employed in large numbers, were suitable for pulling light wooden carts carrying supplies. For hauling artillery, larger and heavier draft horses were needed. These animals, which also provided the tractive power on European farms, were required in large numbers. Six horses were needed to haul one 105-mm artillery piece, with the gun and limber being driven as a single unit and weighing a total of four tons. Thus, a single 105-mm artillery battalion of twelve guns would require a minimum of seventy-two horses just for the guns. A 150-mm artillery battalion required a far larger number of horses; it took eight to draw the reserve ammunition cart of one gun alone. Vehicles of the infantry regiments and supply elements were also drawn largely by horses. Thus, by 1944, the average high-grade German infantry division (one able to undertake offensive operations) required between three thousand and four thousand horses to move.

The most critical item for any army employing horses in large numbers is fodder. A small Russian panje horse might need twelve pounds of fodder a day, and a large draft horse could require as much as twenty pounds. Since infantry divisions were stationed in static positions along the coast, fodder had to be shipped to them by rail. As a ton of fodder (an amount sufficient to feed a hundred draft horses for one day) takes up five hundred cubic feet of space, a great deal of valuable rail transport space was consumed in shipping fodder, instead of fuel and ammunition, to units. The disruption of the rail system in France by Allied aerial operations created tremendous difficulties for infantry units in this regard, even in areas well away from the projected invasion sectors.

The German army developed a large and complex veterinary organization to care for its horses. All German army personnel who dealt with horses were trained in elementary veterinary care. Seriously sick or wounded horses were sent to the divisional horse hospital, which could handle up to 500 horses at one time, and any overflow went to an army horse hospital (a field army normally had three), which could handle up to 550. Once a horse was fit for duty, it was taken to an army horse park, from which horses were drawn as replacements.

German infantry units in France often obtained horses for transport locally. The *276th Infantry Division*, assembling in southern France in early 1944, had no trouble acquiring horses in the area, but the *711th Infantry Division*, organized in Normandy in the spring of 1943, still lacked horses when it left its coastal position to move to the front in 1944. The *711th* experienced trouble because it was assembling in an area of France that had been under German occupation since 1940. The German army had impressed large numbers of horses for the invasion of the Soviet Union and again in 1942 to replace the losses suffered in 1941. The *276th*, in contrast, drew its horses from southern France, which had not been occupied until 1942 and thus had not been subjected to heavy impressment of horses.

The D-day invasion and the campaign in Normandy presented German infantry divisions with a peculiar set of problems owing to their dependence on horses. With the rail system rendered largely inoperative, infantry divisions had to march to the front overland. Since the Allies had complete control of the air, divisions could move only at night, when horses usually sleep. Although the animal's sleeping pattern can be altered, the rest obtained under those circumstances was not adequate, and the horses suffered accordingly. Some divisions, while moving to the front, were able to make use of prepared depots along their line of march, where they could obtain fodder or replacements for horses too sick or exhausted to continue.

Although the divisions that were defending the Normandy beaches on D-day, such as the *352d* and *716th*, suffered heavy losses in horses almost immediately, infantry divisions that moved into the area of operations after the invasion suffered relatively light losses. The *243d Infantry Division*, for example, reported losing a mere nine horses to enemy action between 10 June and 13 June. Green fodder was abundant in the Normandy countryside, and the warm, sunny weather relieved German units of having to deal with outbreaks of disease or problems arising from exposure to the elements.

The most important factor operating in the German army's favor in regard to horses was that, with the exception of the advance to Cherbourg, the front during June was static. This prevented the Allies from exploiting the German army's greatest weakness, its operational and strategic immobility derived from its reliance on thousands of horses for transport. That changed, however, when Operation COBRA finally ruptured the German front and restored mobility to Allied operations.

BIBLIOGRAPHY

DiNardo, R. L. *Mechanized Juggernaut or Military Anachronism? Horses and the German Army of World War II.* 1991.

R. L. DiNardo

CLARENCE R. HUEBNER   At right, with (from left) Lt. Gen. Omar Bradley, Rear Adm. John L. Hall, Maj. Gen. Leonard T. Gerow.
NATIONAL ARCHIVES

HUEBNER, CLARENCE R. (1888–1972), American, major general, commander of the 1st Infantry Division. Clarence Ralph Huebner was born on 24 November 1888 in Bushton, Kansas, and died on 23 September 1972 at Walter Reed Hospital in Washington, D.C. This very active life, which began on a large wheat farm and ended in a military hospital, included more than forty years of distinguished military service. In World War I Huebner commanded units within the 28th Infantry Regiment, rising in rank from captain to lieutenant colonel and receiving two Distinguished Service Crosses and the Distinguished Service Medal. After typical training and school assignments during the interwar period, he served at the War Department and the Services of Supply prior to his assignment to the European Theater of Operations in April 1943.

On 7 August 1943, following the invasion of Sicily, Maj. Gen. Huebner took command of the 1st Infantry Division, succeeding another legendary soldier, Maj. Gen. Terry de la Mesa Allen. The "Big Red One" left Sicily on 23 October 1943 en route to Great Britain to prepare for the Normandy invasion. As the division trained for the

ordeal ahead, Huebner, now fifty-five years old, suffered from abdominal pains and bursitis that he thought might prevent him from leading his division ashore. "The Coach," as he was known to his officers, held his personal ailments in check and put his division through rigorous training. He insisted that each battalion commander be familiar with the terrain assigned to the other battalion commanders, so that a last-minute change in the alignment of units would not jeopardize the success of the landings. This foresight was typical of Huebner's style of command.

On D-day the assistant division commander, Brig. Gen. Willard G. Wyman, commanded the troops ashore on Omaha Beach, while Huebner and his staff waited aboard the USS *Ancon*. At 1429 Wyman notified Huebner that the situation was difficult, information limited, and progress slow. The division commander was eager to get ashore. A soldier who was present on *Ancon* recalled that all the officers went in one landing craft with Huebner, and all the enlisted men from the headquarters in a second craft. The command group departed the *Ancon* at 1700 and landed on Easy Red Beach at 1900. After struggling through the surf under small-arms fire, Huebner joined Wyman at the division command post. As noted later in his Distinguished Service Medal citation, Huebner's "organizing ability, foresight, indomitable determination and inspiring leadership" were the exact qualities needed to get his division out of the beachhead and moving inland."

Although a stern disciplinarian, Huebner had a sharp sense of humor. He appreciated good soldiers. He had a cavalier attitude toward danger and death; after the war he told Arthur L. Chaitt, long-time executive director of the Society of the First Division, "Hell, Art, any of us who lived a day after May 8, 1945 [V-E Day], have been on borrowed time." Anyone who came in contact with him remembered the encounter and usually was richer for the experience. His chief of staff, Stanhope Mason, recalled, "His logic, [and] his common sense, were extraordinarily good [and] his tactical judgment was almost infallible." Omar Bradley remembered Huebner's strict adherence to discipline and his tendency to speak frankly from the early days of his divisional command on Sicily.

Bradley's decision to put the "Big Red One" in the vanguard at Omaha Beach was personally difficult because he suspected the assault would be particularly arduous. But he knew that he needed an experienced division to go in first with the green troops.

General Huebner took command of the U.S. V Corps in January 1945 and led it to the end of the war in Europe. Following peacetime assignments, he retired as a lieutenant general on 30 November 1950. He was remembered at his funeral in 1972 by an old soldier: "They buried the Army today."

[*See also* 1st Infantry Division.]

BIBLIOGRAPHY

Blumenson, Martin, and James L. Stokesbury. *Masters of the Art of Command.* 1975.

Bradley, Omar N., and Clay Blair. *A General's Life: An Autobiography.* 1983.

Chaitt, Arthur L. "Clarence R. Huebner: Lieutenant General, U.S.A. (Retired), 1888–1972." *Bridgehead Sentinel,* Spring 1973, 1–23.

JOHN F. VOTAW

I

INFANTRY WEAPONS AND EQUIPMENT.

[*This entry includes two articles:* Allied Infantry Weapons and Equipment *and* German Infantry Weapons and Equipment.]

Allied Infantry Weapons and Equipment

The weapons carried ashore by the Allied infantry on D-day showed relatively little advance over those used at the outbreak of war. The basic infantry weapon, the rifle, reflected a divergence of opinion between the British and Americans, in that as far back as 1936 the U.S. Army had settled upon a semiautomatic weapon, the .30-inch M1 Garand, whereas the British (in common with every other combatant) stayed with the bolt-action magazine rifle, in their case in the .303-inch Lee-Enfield, which had been continuously in service since the turn of the century. However, the success of the Garand rifle in the field was sufficient to move every other nation in that direction, and by 1944 the Allied troops were likely to encounter such weapons in German hands.

Perhaps the most innovative change in infantry arms was the wide adoption of the submachine gun, a weapon scarcely known in prewar military circles. The submachine gun, firing pistol ammunition, was an effective and convenient way of giving men the maximum firepower, but to have the greatest effect the weapon needed to be distributed generously. This, in turn, demanded cheap and rapid production, and though both the U.S. and British armies had begun the war using the expensive and heavy Thompson gun, by 1944 the cheap but equally effective Sten and M3 "grease gun" were issued by the tens of thousands.

For close-quarter fighting, hand grenades were widely issued. The basic hand grenades were elderly designs: the British 36M originally appeared in 1918, while the U.S. M1 was actually a French design adopted in 1917. But a variety of specialized grenades had appeared during the war years, notably ones with white phosphorus to give concealing smoke as well as incendiary effects, and blast grenades that disoriented the victim while the thrower rushed in to take advantage of the shock effect. Rifle grenades, to be projected from various forms of muzzle adapter, were designed and approved but in fact saw relatively little use; most soldiers felt that using them was liable to affect the accuracy of their rifle and therefore avoided them.

In the contemporary tactical doctrine, the pivot of

VICKERS MEDIUM MACHINE GUN.   Being used by gun crew of the 50th (Northumbrian) Infantry Division to support an attack.   IMPERIAL WAR MUSEUM

AMERICAN GARAND RIFLES.   Although American enlisted men were issued the M1 Garand rifle (left), officers were issued the lighter 30-caliber carbine (right). The carbine was light and handy, but did not have the long-range accuracy of the M1.

THE ROBERT HUNT LIBRARY, LONDON (LEFT) / NATIONAL ARCHIVES (RIGHT)

maneuver for the infantry section was the light machine gun, and here too the armies differed. Britain and the Commonwealth troops used the excellent Bren gun, designed in Czechoslovakia. With a quick-change barrel and a 30-round magazine, this had a rate of fire of about 500 rounds per minute and could keep up a harassing fire while the rifleman maneuvered. The U.S. Army, on the other hand, had committed itself to the Browning automatic rifle, a fixed-barrel weapon with a 20-shot magazine and a rate varying between 350 and 550 rounds per minute. It was lighter than the Bren, but less efficient at its basic task. The medium machine guns used by both armies were those of World War I—the British Vickers and the American Browning M1917; both were tripod-mounted, water-cooled, belt-fed weapons that could keep up a heavy rate of fire for hours, if necessary. The Americans had, though, discovered that the Browning air-cooled machine guns, developed for aircraft use, were perfectly

adequate for ground use also, and by 1944 the cumbersome M1917 was gradually being replaced by the more convenient M1918 air-cooled version.

Among the major threats to the infantry was the tank, and by 1944 the earlier antitank rifles had been abandoned in favor of shaped-charge projectiles. The U.S. Army used the rocket launcher M9—more familiarly known as the "bazooka"—to launch a 2.36-inch caliber 3.4-pound rocket to an effective range of about 250 yards. The British had the "Projector, Infantry, Anti-Tank," or PIAT, a cumbersome device that used a heavy steel spigot to launch a 3-pound projectile to 100 yards. Both missiles could penetrate 75 to 80 millimeters of armor, so if the infantryman could stalk his prey so as to get a shot at the rear of the tank, where the armor was thinnest, either weapon was effective.

Heavier support came from the infantry's mortars. These fell into two groups: the light models used by the

BRITISH .303-INCH LEE-ENFIELD RIFLE.   This bolt-action .303-in. rifle served the British Army well from 1895 to 1954. The rifles shown here are of World War I type, with 19-in. sword bayonets. By 1944 many troops carried a later model rifle that used a 9-in. spike bayonet.   IMPERIAL WAR MUSEUM

infantry platoon, exemplified by the U.K. 2-inch and U.S. 60-mm weapons; and the medium mortars operated by the infantry company and exemplified by the U.K. 3-inch and U.S. 81-mm models. The British 2-inch mortar was little more than a grenade thrower, firing a 2.25-pound bomb to 500 yards and being aimed entirely by eye. The American 60-mm was a more formidable weapon, firing a 3-pound bomb to almost 2,000 yards and employing proper sighting apparatus to aim it. The U.S. 81-mm fired a 7-pound bomb to 3,290 yards, while the U.K. 3-inch fired a 10-pound bomb to 2,800 yards, which gave a useful radius of action around the company area. Both countries used heavier (4.2-inch) mortars, but these were manned by specialist troops and not infantry.

But perhaps the most useful weapon in the infantry-man's hands was the portable radio. Perfected since the outbreak of war, radios light enough for the infantryman to carry had given a new dimension to tactical control, allowing higher commanders to know what junior for-

mations were doing, and giving the infantryman the ability to call for supporting artillery fire, air strikes, or tank support when the situation demanded. Because of this ability to call on supporting arms, the concept of the infantry-manned cannon found little application in the Allied doctrines; it had been tried in North Africa but abandoned because of the ease with which heavy support could be provided on call.

An exception to this view was made in the case of anti-tank artillery. It was accepted that tanks could appear almost anywhere, and not necessarily where the specialist artillery-manned antitank guns were deployed. As a result of war experience, infantry companies were given the lighter antitank guns for their immediate protection. The U.S. 37-mm and British 40-mm 2-pounder were the first issue, but by 1944 both these weapons had been outstripped by tank design, and the infantry of both Allied armies now used the same gun, the British 6-pounder, under slightly differing nomenclature, the Americans calling it the 57-mm

BRITISH BREN GUN.   Probably the best light machine gun of the war. Based on a Czech design that was modified to accept British .303 ammunition, it fired about 500 rounds per minute and had a quick-change barrel to avoid overheating. (The gunner pictured here, A. J. Bull, is writing a poem.)   IMPERIAL WAR MUSEUM

THOMPSON SUBMACHINE GUN.   British Commandos land from folding boats in a training exercise. Most are armed with the Thompson submachine gun, though the man at the left is carrying a Vickers medium machine gun.   IMPERIAL WAR MUSEUM

AMERICAN 50-CALIBER BROWNING HEAVY MACHINE GUN.   Intended as an air defense weapon on vehicles, it was not widely issued to infantry units as a ground gun. Its long-range destructive effect, however, was too valuable to be ignored when field strong points were encountered.   HULTON DEUTSCH

AMERICAN 81-MM M1 MORTAR.   The standard American infantry company support weapon.   HULTON DEUTSCH

BRITISH 4.2-INCH MORTAR.   The Cheshire Regiment supports an attack of the 50th Division with a 4.2-in. mortar, assigned to infantry battalions for heavy support. It fired 20-lb. high-explosive (HE) or smoke bombs to a range of 3,300 yards.   IMPERIAL WAR MUSEUM

BRITISH 6-POUNDER ANTITANK GUN.   The Green Howards of the 50th Division wait in ambush. By D-day this antitank gun was provided with new "discarding sabot" projectiles. In U.S. service, this gun was known as the 57-mm M1.

IMPERIAL WAR MUSEUM

BRITISH INFANTRY GEAR.   Not everything the infantry carries is a weapon: shown is pickax handle (helve), shovel, gas mask (left hip), and entrenching tool in a canvas case. Elsewhere are stowed rations, drinking water, first-aid dressings, and a change of clothing.   IMPERIAL WAR MUSEUM

Gun M1. As the British title implied, this fired a 6-pound steel shot that could pierce 75 millimeters of armor at 1,000 yards and a striking angle of 30 degrees. Improved types of armor-defeating projectiles had been developed, so that troops going ashore on D-day had available the new armor-piercing discarding sabot shot, capable of penetrating 146 millimeters of armor at 1,000 yards.

The only item of equipment not commonly held by both U.K. and U.S. troops was the flamethrower; in the British army this was an infantry weapon, whereas the U.S. Army issued it to specialist engineer units. The British Lifebuoy flamethrower was worn on the back, carried sufficient fuel for eight or ten shots, and had a range of little more than 50 yards. Nevertheless, it was a highly effective weapon against strong points, though the operator had to have a heavily armed protection party to enable him to get close to his target.

Perhaps the one piece of equipment unique to D-day was the life preserver, an inflatable belt worn by many of the landing infantry in case their landing craft could not reach the beach.

BIBLIOGRAPHY

Hogg, Ian V. *Infantry Weapons of World War Two.* 1977.
Hogg, Ian V., and John Weeks. *Military Small Arms of the 20th Century.* 1992.
Young, Peter, ed. *The Almanac of World War II.* 1981.

IAN V. HOGG

German Infantry Weapons and Equipment

The German infantry units facing the Allies in Normandy in June 1944 had a wide variety of each type of infantry weapon, some tailor-made for different types of unit, and others captured arms. This was symptomatic both of an inefficient weapons procurement system that allowed too wide a variety of weapons to be developed simultaneously, and of the strains on Germany's war industry partially resulting from that system.

The infantryman's basic weapons, the rifle, appeared in a number of guises. The standard German caliber was 7.92 mm (0.31 in.), and the main weapon was the Karabiner 98K, the last in a long line of Mausers, and a modified version of the bolt-action rifle with which the infantry had fought World War I. It had a five-round magazine, weighed 3.9 kg (8 lb., 9 oz.), and had an overall length of 1,107.5 mm (43.6 in.). Many of the paratroops had the heavier FG42, which had a 20-round magazine and was normally semiautomatic, being gas-operated, but did have an automatic setting as well. Its main drawback was its relative inaccuracy, in spite of its pistol grip combined with a conventional butt. There were also a number of Czech and Hungarian weapons rebored to 7.92

GERMAN MG34 MACHINE GUN.

mm caliber, and a plethora of other captured weapons used by troops on the lines of communication.

The other significant German small arm was the machine pistol, which the Western Allies popularly termed the "Schmeisser," after the leading German designer of machine pistols, and categorized as a submachine gun. Their caliber was 9 mm (0.35 in.); army units generally used the MP40, with a 32-round magazine and a rate of fire of 500 rounds per minute. The Waffen SS, however, also used the MP35, again with a 32-round magazine, but which had a higher rate of fire at 650 rounds per minute.

The two most common machine guns were the MG34 and MG42. The former, a redesign by Mauserwerke of the Swiss Solothurn MG30, had entered German Army service in 1936. Its rate of fire was 900 rounds per minute, using either belt ammunition or a 75-round drum magazine. It was the first general-purpose machine gun (*Maschinengewehr*). With a bipod, it was employed as a squad weapon, but it could also provide sustained fire as a medium machine gun if mounted on a tripod. Perhaps its only drawback was the fact that the engineering tolerances were very tight, making it expensive to produce. The later MG42, which entered service in 1942, was also a general-purpose weapon, but it had the highest rate of fire,

CAPTURED GERMAN MG42 MACHINE GUN.   IMPERIAL WAR MUSEUM

1,200 rounds per minute, of any machine gun employed during the war, and used only belt ammunition. When the German army was re-formed as part of NATO in the mid-1950s, manufacture of the MG42 recommenced, its caliber altered to the standard NATO 7.62 mm (0.3 in.). Luftwaffe field divisions, however, used the MG15, also a derivative of the Solothurn MG30, but originally designed as an aircraft-mounted weapon. With a length of 133 cm (52.5 in.) and weighing 12.7 kg (28 lb.) when empty, it was somewhat cumbersome as a light machine gun, although very accurate. A number of models based on the highly successful Czech Brno design, from which the British Bren gun was derived, and some French types were also in use, mainly by the static divisions on the coast.

The mortar (*Granatwerfer*) in use at platoon level during the early part of the war was the Granatwerfer (GrW) 36, a 50-mm (1.97-in.) calibered weapon. It had an effective range of 500 meters (547 yards) and a rate of fire of forty bombs per minute. Its effectiveness proved to be disappointing, however, and by 1944 it had been largely replaced by a variant of the 81.4-mm (3.2-in.) GrW34. Nevertheless, there were still some in use in the lower-grade divi-

sions in Normandy. The GrW34 was, however, the main battalion mortar and fired a number of different types of bomb. The range of this mortar was 2,400 meters (2,625 yd.), and 15 bombs per minute could be fired. The mortar in general use at lower levels in Normandy was a lightweight version of the GrW34 originally designed for airborne troops and known as the *Stummelwerfer*. This had a shorter barrel, giving a range of 1,100 meters (1,200 yd.), but at 28 kilograms (62 lb.) it was exactly half the weight of the standard GrW34. At regimental level the Germans also employed infantry guns, called *Geschütze,* usually of 75-mm (2.96-in.) caliber, but also 105-mm (4.14-in.) and 150-mm (5.91-in.) as well, although the last was mainly used on the Eastern front. The typical maximum range was 5,000 meters (5,500 yd.). By 1944, however, for reasons of cost and simplicity of manufacture, infantry guns had been replaced in a number of formations by the 120-mm (4.73-in.) GrW42, adapted from a Russian model, with a range of 6,050 meters (6,616 yd.).

In terms of antitank weapons, the German infantry relied primarily on three types of gun. The first was the 50-mm (2-in.) Panzerabwehrkanone (PAK) 38, which had

CAPTURED GERMAN GRANATWERFER (GRW) 34 8-CM (81-MM) MORTAR.   This medium mortar was equivalent to the American 81-mm M1 mortar.   IMPERIAL WAR MUSEUM

entered service in late 1940 and fired a solid shot that could penetrate 47 mm (1.85 in.) of vertical armor at 1,200 meters (1,300 yd.). While ineffective at this range against Allied tanks in Normandy, which generally had thicker armor, the PAK38 was still effective at the much shorter ranges at which antitank engagements usually took place in the Normandy bocage. More powerful, but very similar in appearance, was the 75-mm (2.96-in.) PAK40, which could penetrate 83 mm (3.27 in.) of armor at 2,500 meters (2,700 yd.), although it was somewhat bulky and, with its towing tractor, was difficult to bring into action covertly. Often, therefore, deployment had to be by night. Finally there was the powerful 88-mm PAK43, which could penetrate 159 mm (6.3 in.) of armor at 2,500 meters (2,700 yd.), and was much feared by Allied tank crews. All

three types fired high-explosive as well as antitank rounds.

The infantry also had a hand-held rocket-firing weapon, the Panzerfaust 30, whose hollow-charge warhead could penetrate 140 mm (5.516 in.) of armor at 30 meters (32 yd.), the maximum range at which it could be fired with accuracy. Also available was the Panzerschreck 43. This was based on the American bazooka, numbers of which had been captured in Tunisia in early 1943, and fired an 88-mm (3.46-in.) electrically detonated rocket. The weapon had an effective range of 150 meters (184 yd.). A major disadvantage was the sheet of flame produced on firing, which meant that the firer had to wear protective clothing. Later in 1944 it would be replaced by the improved Panzerschreck 54, which had a shield to protect the firer.

GERMAN STICK GRENADES BEING ASSEMBLED.   BIBLIOTHEK FÜR ZEITGESCHICHTE, STUTTGART

As for hand grenades, the infantry had two basic types, the Steilhandgranate 39 or stick grenade, and the Eihandgranate 39 or egg grenade. They also had an ingenious magnetic antitank grenade, the Heft Hohladunggranate 3 KG, which could be stuck on a tank's armor and was used successfully against a number of British and U.S. tanks in Normandy. Finally, the German infantry had a wide range of rifle grenades, high-explosive, antitank, illuminating, and smoke.

Increasing strains on the war economy necessitated the introduction of a new field uniform in 1943. Although superficially it looked the same as its predecessor, the Model 1936, its tendency to crease badly was indicative of inferior cloth, with a large percentage of wool being replaced by rayon. Likewise the traditional high boot (*Marschstiefel*) had begun to give way to ankle boots worn with canvas gaiters . Also, a cheaper method of steel helmet manufacture was introduced in 1943, giving the helmet a slightly sharper appearance than its predecessor. The paratroops, though, had their own dis-

tinctive helmet without a rim, and also fought in their parachute smocks. Otherwise, the field cap or *Einheitsfeldmütze* was standard in action. The infantryman's personal equipment remained leather, however, including the familiar three-strap yoke with metal rings to which items could be attached. Camouflage uniform was also worn, that of the Waffen SS having a distinctive mottled appearance. The infantry divisions, especially those manning the coastal defenses, still relied heavily on horse-drawn transport; only the panzer grenadier formations were totally motorized.

BIBLIOGRAPHY

Davis, Brian L. *German Uniforms and Insignia, 1933–1945*. 1971.

Gander, Terry, and Peter Chamberlain. *Small Arms, Artillery, and Special Weapons of the Third Reich: An Encyclopedic Survey*. 1978.

Hogg, Ian V. *The Encyclopedia of Infantry Weapons of World War II*. 1977.

CHARLES MESSENGER

PANZERFAUST.   A hand-held, one-shot, antitank weapon. The man on the left carries a Model 98 Mauser bolt-action rifle.

INTELLIGENCE. In the six months before D-day the Allies enjoyed a double advantage in intelligence. Their own was so comprehensive that they could be reasonably confident that no substantial change in Germany's dispositions and expectations of Allied intentions would escape their notice. Because their sources included Signals Intelligence (Sigint), they knew that, on the other hand, Germany's intelligence was poor—that it was virtually unable to carry out air reconnaissance over the United Kingdom, that all its agents in Britain were under British control, and that it was decrypting no Allied signals.

After the landings, the value of these advantages was somewhat reduced. Apart from the fact that Sigint, on account of decryption delays, was usually less useful during operations than it was for planning and strategy, the Allies obtained no Sigint about the German army, as distinct from the navy and the air force, from 6 June until the morning of 8 June, D plus 2.

The Planning Stage

Intelligence made two contributions to Allied planning. First, a mass of information on the topography and the defenses of the entire French coast, accumulated over the previous two years, determined the initial recommendation by Chief of Staff to the Supreme Allied Commander (COSSAC) that the landings should be made between the Vire and Dives rivers. Second, the revision in January 1944 of COSSAC's initial plan—by which the assault area was extended from forty kilometers (twenty-five miles) to nearly eighty kilometers (fifty miles), the seaborne assault raised from three to five divisions, and the rate of reinforcement and supply accelerated—was undertaken because intelligence showed that from the autumn of 1943 Germany was intensifying its coastal defenses and increasing the army formations it kept in France.

Most of this intelligence came from agents and the Resistance movements and from aerial photographic reconnaissance. But Sigint, as yet confined to decrypts of telegrams from the Japanese embassy in Berlin, was invaluable from November on. Some decrypts gave details of every element in the coastal defense system in France, from the heaviest batteries down to grenade throwers, with comments on how "enormously" they had improved since February. Others listed the divisions by type under each of the subordinate commanders under Commander in Chief West (Oberbefehlshaber West—OB West) and disclosed that they were about to be reinforced by three reserve panzer divisions from Germany, two parachute divisions from Italy, and a number of infantry divisions.

Aerial reconnaissance, now supplemented by daily sorties by U.S. Air Force Lightnings flying at very low altitude and improved by the introduction of oblique photography, continued to be the main source of intelligence on German coastal defense measures. The Allies used their detailed knowledge to develop specialized craft and equipment for destroying the worst of the hazards—the underwater obstacles that appeared near the beaches after February—and to settle in advance where every assault craft would land and every ship in the bombarding force would take up station. Agents and the Resistance supplied an increasing amount of intelligence on the German army's order of battle. From spring on, they were sending reports on troop movements and locations in France and the Low Countries at the rate of 150 a day.

The significant development, however, was an increase in Sigint. This took place when the German army and air force, which unlike the navy had hitherto confined their communications to land lines, gradually reverted to radio. From the end of February the Government Code and Cypher School at Bletchley Park (a requisitioned country house in Buckinghamshire) read the new air force Enigma keys regularly and the new army keys occasionally. In March it solved the non-Morse cipher link that had recently been opened between Berlin and OB West. At the same time, the naval Enigma keys and the ciphers used by the Japanese in Berlin, which had long been read regularly, became more illuminating as the Germans prepared to meet an invasion.

On Germany's coastal defenses and, above all, on its army order of battle, Sigint's precision and reliability helped eliminate inaccuracy and resolve inconsistency in the evidence provided by the other sources. On other subjects, Sigint provided evidence that could have been obtained from no other source. These concerned the army's chain of command and its discussions about how to counter the landings, the anti-invasion plans of the navy and the air force, and Germany's estimates regarding the place and time of the invasion.

German Strategy. In March, when other sources began to report that trained and equipped infantry was moving closer to the coast, the Japanese decrypts disclosed that, following disagreements as to whether to aim to defeat the invasion on the beaches or to allow the invasion force to move inland before destroying it, the Germans had decided under pressure from Field Marshal Erwin Rommel to hold the coast "absolutely." They had therefore released offensive infantry divisions to the armies and were keeping only the armored formations in reserve under Field Marshal Gerd von Rundstedt, Commander in Chief West.

By the end of March the Enigma had confirmed that Rommel commanded *Army Group B,* with the *Fifteenth* and *Seventh* armies, and revealed that *Panzer Group West* had been set up to command the armored formations. But the German decrypts were not precise about the control of the armor; this in fact reflected disagreement between Rommel, who wanted all of it under his command, and Rundstedt, who insisted on retaining some of it in a central reserve. In April the decrypts disclosed that four of the armored divisions had been place in OKW reserve, but left some doubt as to whether *Army Group B* and the remaining armor were under the control of OB West. In May they reported that *Army Group G* had been set up to command the *First* and *Nineteenth* armies in the south and southwest. Thereafter, the Allies assumed, correctly, that *Army Groups B* and *G* and *Panzer Group West* were all directly subordinated to Rundstedt.

German Army Order of Battle. Among other preconditions for the success of the assault, COSSAC's initial plan had stipulated that the number of full-strength, first-quality German divisions in France and the Low Countries should not exceed twelve on D-day and that they should be so located that the number deployed in the assault area would not exceed three on D-day, five by D plus 2, and nine by D plus 9. After the plan was revised, the Allies accepted that some small but unspecified increase in these figures could be tolerated. The greatest test for Allied intelligence in the long interval from February to the beginning of June was whether it would detect the extent to which these upper limits were being exceeded. It did so.

It traced the increase in the total number German divisions in the West from an estimated forty-four (actually forty-eight) in January to an estimated fifty-nine or sixty (actually fifty-eight plus two still arriving) on 4–5 June.

It enabled the Allies to calculate by 1 March that the total would include between sixteen and twenty offensive divisions, seven of them infantry, by D-day. By 1 May it had identified and located most of the offensive infantry divisions and all eight of the panzer divisions that were then in the West (*2d, 9th, 10th, 21st,* and *116th Panzer; 2d* and *12th SS Panzer; 17th SS Panzer-Grenadier*) and had disclosed that *1st SS Panzer* and *Panzer Lehr* divisions were arriving and had given their location. In the light of this intelligence and of Sigint about the state of many of the divisions, the Allies estimated on 20 May that the landing would be opposed by the equivalent of between twelve and sixteen first-quality, full-strength divisions, as compared with the twelve stipulated by COSSAC, and that the rate of buildup of first-quality opposition would be correspondingly higher than COSSAC had stipulated—three divisions on D-day, six to seven on D plus 2, and eleven to fourteen on D plus 9.

This estimate took account of the discovery that *21st Panzer* had recently moved to Caen from Rennes and been replaced there by the newly formed *5th Parachute Division*. It was decided that no further revision of Allied plans was necessary. Between 24 and 27 May, however, Sigint revealed that the Germans were bringing the *91st Infantry Division* and several nondivisional formations from Germany into the Cotentin Peninsula to guard against airborne attacks, The decrypts gave full details of the consequent redisposition of all forces in the Cotentin. This intelligence enabled the U.S. First Army to make last-minute changes in its plan for dropping the 82d and 101st airborne divisions and to advance by a month the follow-up by the 79th Division at Utah Beach. But it put back by over a week the date set for the capture of Cherbourg.

The fact that the expected level of early German opposition exceeded COSSAC's limits was offset by another consideration. It had been stipulated that, as a further precondition of success, Germany should not be able to transfer more than fifteen first-quality divisions to Normandy from other fronts by D plus 60. By 13 May the Allies had concluded that the Germans would be able to move only between five and seven from Scandinavia, Italy, and the Balkans in this period, that a further six might be brought from those fronts if the situation became critical, and that none would come from the Soviet fronts. Such calculations were necessarily less precise than estimates of immediate order of battle, but they were based on comprehensive Sigint coverage since the summer of 1942 of the situation on these fronts and the state of the German divisions there. This established that the German army lacked significant reserves.

Germany's Naval Preparations. The naval Enigma established the extent and whereabouts of Germany's defensive mine laying and the anti-invasion preparations of the U-boat command.

With some assistance from aerial photographic reconnaissance, the decrypts established that except on the banks south of Saint-Vaast, across the boat lane selected for the approach of the assault force at Utah Beach, no inshore mine laying had taken place. (But the air force Enigma revealed on 30 May that the air force was about to rectify this omission.) Naval decrypts enabled the Admiralty to establish the exact southern limits of the deep-water minefield the Germans laid in the Bay of the Seine between 17 and 23 May and showed that the area of mine-free waters

available to the assault forces had not changed by D-day.

From early in April Sigint established that U-boats were being withheld from the Atlantic in order to accumulate an anti-invasion force. The Allies exploited this knowledge by increasing the size and frequency of convoys in preparation for OVERLORD and reducing convoy escort forces to meet the heavy demand for naval support for the landing. In May Sigint disclosed the intentions of the U-boat command for the deployment of such U-boats as were in Bay of Biscay ports on D-day. They would sail in the evening, those without a snorkel to wait in a line between specified points in the bay, and the others deployed to operational areas in the Channel. The number of U-boats that would be involved remained uncertain—the Admiralty's estimate of 70 by D-day proved to be nearly twice the actual figure—but the Allies concentrated intense antisubmarine patrols against these operational areas and waiting positions from D-day.

German Air Force. The Allies knew by the spring of 1944 that, having defeated the German fighter forces over Germany, they would have air superiority over the beaches and in France. But Sigint revealed an increase in German strength in the West from the end of April and indicated that it reflected a deliberate conservation policy and an intensive repairs program. Between 30 April and 5 June, Allied estimates of nominal frontline strength available to the *Third Air Force* (*Luftflotte 3*) changed; the original estimate of 750 aircraft on D-day rising to 1,200 by D plus 4 was increased to 1,105 rising to 1,600 by D plus 4. The *Third Air Force*'s actual nominal strength on 30 May was 891, and it rose to 1,300 by D plus 10.

On the other hand, the Allies recognized that projections of the nominal strength of the German air force exaggerated the actual strength it would have on D-day. They knew from Sigint, prisoners, and actual operational performance that the German air force as a whole was suffering from lack of training and shortage of pilots, that its bomber arm and especially its potentially formidable antishipping force had been weakened by its concentration on the development of its fighter arms, and that despite this concentration there was a shortage of close-support aircraft.

On 6 May decrypts disclosed the German plans for delaying the bringing up of air reinforcements to the invasion area until the last minute and for assembling them at selected airfields in the vicinity of Paris, Brussels, and Marseilles before deploying them to forward bases, many of which had ceased to be used. Thirty-four of these reception and forward bases, most of them within 130 miles of Caen, were attacked between 11 May and the beginning of June as part of the preliminary Allied air offensive.

Intelligence on German Expectations. German and Japanese decrypts showed that the Germans had no doubt as of February that the Allies would carry out a cross-

Channel invasion, together with diversionary landings in the south of France, in 1944; that they were inclined to believe that it would not take place before June; and that they were radically uncertain as to where, between the Pas de Calais and the Bay of Biscay, the main blow would fall. As for the scale of the undertaking, they had reports that the Allies had assembled between seventy-five and eight-five divisions in the United Kingdom and were associating part of the buildup with rumors that Gen. George S. Patton, Jr., had arrived to take command of the First U.S. Army Group (FUSAG) with two armies.

In the middle of April Sigint revealed that the German army and naval authorities had recently concluded that the Allies would probably invade within the next four weeks. They had been alerted chiefly by the increase in Allied bombing against communications and the introduction since the beginning of the month of Allied security measures—the closing of coastal zones and the stoppage of travel in, and mail from, the United Kingdom. On 20 April a naval Enigma decrypt informed all ranks that the invasion in western France was to be expected at any time, and on 27 April an army decrypt announced that leaves had been canceled throughout OB West command the previous day. The alert lasted until 6 May, when the Japanese embassy, in a signal decrypted on 11 May, reported that the Germans had concluded that the landings had been postponed for two or three weeks.

In decrypts obtained on 8 May the *Third Air Force* reported its belief, in the light of the pattern of Allied bombing, that the Allies intended to land between Le Havre and Cherbourg. Allied alarm at this intelligence was only partly dispelled by a signal from OB West issued on 8 May and decrypted on 13 May; this announced that the most threatened sector was from Boulogne as far as Normandy inclusive, but added that Rundstedt was bringing reinforcements into Normandy and Brittany, as being likely areas for strong airborne attacks. On 27 May a decrypt showed that the *Third Air Force* still believed that the Allies would land in the Dieppe and Bay of the Seine areas. On the same day Adolf Hitler told the Japanese ambassador that the Allies had assembled eighty divisions and would carry out diversionary operations in Norway, Denmark, and the south of France and establish a bridgehead in Normandy or Brittany before embarking on the "real second front" in the Pas de Calais; the ambassador's report was decrypted on 1 June. Although still somewhat disturbing, this intelligence persuaded the Allied authorities that the Germans remained radically uncertain of OVERLORD's destination.

The Assault

The decrypt of a message issued by OB West on 8 May stated that, though invasion did not yet appear to be imminent, it could come at any time when the Allies could count on "a series of days of continuous fine weather." On 5 June—in a message the Allies did not decrypt—Rundstedt repeated that "as yet there is no immediate prospect of the invasion." He was no doubt influenced by the bad weather that had persuaded Gen. Dwight D. Eisenhower to postpone the landings for twenty-four hours, to 6 June.

Land Operations. The effects of the bad weather in delaying breakout from the beaches were compounded by two inaccuracies in the Allied reconstruction of the German army's order of battle. This had assumed, in the absence of detailed evidence about its locations, that the *21st Panzer Division* would attack as a whole division from southeast of Caen. Except that its tanks were in a lay-back position, it was in fact widely dispersed around the approaches to the town, where its resistance played a large part in denying the Allies the capture of Caen and Bayeux on D-day. At Gold and Omaha beaches considerable delay in moving inland was imposed by the *352d Infantry Division;* the Allies had failed to detect that it had been moved close to the coast.

The Allies ceased to be able to read Rundstedt's non-Morse link just before D-day, and no Enigma decrypt bearing on the ground fighting was obtained until Bletchley broke a new army–air force liaison key on the morning of 8 June. But aerial reconnaissance and field Sigint (the interception of tactical signals) tracked the arrival of *21st Panzer*'s tanks for the thrust to the coast it made on D-day, and the approach of the *12th SS Panzer* and *Panzer Lehr* divisions was detected by aerial reconnaissance and the Resistance. Their arrival was more delayed—by Hitler and by Allied bombing—than the Allies had allowed for. The delay forced the Germans to divert the *Panzer Lehr* and *12th SS Panzer* divisions to halt the Allied advances from Juno and Gold beaches at Villers-Bocage and thwarted their plan for counterattack in force in the Caen sector. The earliest decrypts disclosed that they had ordered this on 7 June and again on 8 June. Their prospects of reviving it were reduced when on 10 June the headquarters of *Panzer Group West* was destroyed by Allied bombers after Sigint had located it at La Caine. On 11 June Rundstedt and Rommel advised Hitler that they must remain on the defensive until reinforcements enabled them to release armored divisions from the line.

The departure from their base areas of almost all further German reinforcements was detected by reconnaissance and the Resistance, and their approach was delayed by bombing and road and rail disruptions. Enigma decrypts confirmed most of the arrivals and gave the positions they were taking up in the effort to hold a line. By the evening of 15 June the Allies knew that, whereas they had expected that the Germans would assemble twenty-five divisions by D plus 10, including nine armored, the actual number was six armored, one parachute, and elements of eleven infantry. On the strength of battlefield contacts and Sigint, they estimated that in armored content the six armored were the equivalent of only four divisions and that some of the eleven infantry formations were only brigade groups. No further arrivals had been detected by 18 June, and though intelligence was then giving notice that considerable reinforcements were beginning to move, it was clear that few could arrive soon.

On 10 June decrypts showed that *II Parachute Corps* with *17th SS Panzer Grenadier* and *3d Parachute* divisions and infantry divisions from Saint-Nazaire and Lorient were ordered to the Saint-Lô area to counter the U.S. threat from Carentan. On 12 June they disclosed that the *2d Panzer Division* from beyond the Seine was assembling south of Falaise; the Allies expected it would go into action in the Caen sector, but Sigint had established by 14 June that it had filled the gap in the line in the Balleroy area south of Bayeux, between the *Panzer Lehr* on its right and the *3d Parachute* on its left, where the Germans had initially hoped to use the *II Parachute Corps*. On the other hand, no source had detected the arrival of *Heavy Panzerabteilung 101,* the formation that checked the 7th Armoured Division at Villers-Bocage on 13 June, though Sigint had indicated that it would be encountered.

The Allies did not receive much tactical intelligence during the fighting. The Germans made little use of field ciphers, and the Enigma decrypts were usually obtained too late to be operationally valuable. On 12 June, however, decrypted orders to *17th SS Panzer Grenadier* to recapture Carentan from the south and west, the fact that its attack had been delayed, and the time chosen for the delayed operation early on 13 June reached the U.S. VII Corps in time for it to redeploy and repulse the attack.

Deterioration in the German position in the Saint-Lô area sucked in the next panzer division to arrive. The Enigma, the Resistance, and aerial reconnaissance had tracked the approach of the *2d SS Panzer Division* from Toulouse since 11 June. On 17 June a decrypt disclosed that on 15 June it had been placed under the *XLVII Panzer Corps* with the *2d Panzer*. But on 18 June decrypts disclosed that it had left that corps and was assembling south of Saint-Lô.

On 17 and 18 June intelligence from Enigma and the Resistance warned of movements from Holland, Belgium, Germany, and eastern and southern France. It reflected Hitler's decision of 16 June—which was not decrypted— that Rundstedt must take the risk of weakening other fronts so that the armored divisions in the line could be relieved by infantry and used in a massive counterattack with four other panzer divisions now being brought up— *2d SS Panzer* and *9th* and *10th SS Panzer* from the Eastern front, and *1st SS Panzer* from Belgium. Except for *2d SS Panzer* and *353d Infantry* from Brittany, identified

at Saint-Lô on 18 June, the Allies knew by evening that none of the new arrivals was imminent. But they recognized that the Germans might be reconsidering their earlier conclusion that the Allies intended to carry out further landings. Enigma decrypts and decrypts of signals from the Japanese embassy in Berlin had provided frequent references to this German anxiety, particularly in relation to the Pas de Calais, since D-day.

Naval and Air Operations. Intensive antisubmarine patrols prevented all but two U-boats from operating in the Channel before 18 June. The patrols obtained no immediate help from intelligence: Sigint did not disclose U-boat positions. But it showed that, of about sixteen U-boats ordered into the Channel by 12 June, all had been sunk or forced back to port by 18 June, and that no others reached the area until 25 June. More serious opposition was encountered from E-boats and torpedo boats; though Enigma gave details of their mine laying and attacks on convoys, it was rarely obtained in time to be operationally valuable. But their activities were greatly reduced by heavy Bomber Command raids on their bases at Le Havre on 14 June and Boulogne on 15 June. On 9 June the Germans dispatched from Brest to the Bay of the Seine three destroyers and one torpedo boat—their only serviceable surface ships in the Bay of Biscay. This force was intercepted and destroyed after the Enigma passed along its route and time of departure.

Advance notice from the Enigma of the arrival of air force reinforcements from the morning of D-day assisted the Allied attacks on their airfields and transit depots, and on the aircraft themselves as they flew in. Partly because of this and partly because of low serviceability, opposition from German bombers and antishipping units was far less than the Allies had expected. Sigint disclosed that the German air force, acknowledging the ineffectiveness of its attacks, confined itself to mine laying increasingly from 10 June and almost exclusively from 14 June. Carried out by individual low-flying aircraft, which were difficult to detect, and using new oyster mines, which were difficult to sweep, this greatly exceeded the mine laying by E-boats, and its effect in slowing the Allied rate of buildup remained a serious problem until the end of June.

[See also French Resistance.]

BIBLIOGRAPHY

Beesly, Patrick. *Very Special Intelligence*. 1977.
Bennett, Ralph. *Ultra in the West*. 1979.
Foot, M. R. D. *S.O.E. in France*. 1976.
Hinsley, F. H. *British Intelligence in the Second World War*. Vol. 3, Part II, 1988.
Jones, R. V. *Most Secret War*. 1978.
Lewin, R. *Ultra Goes to War*. 1978.

F. H. HINSLEY

INTERDICTION OPERATIONS. The planners of OVERLORD originally envisioned a brief interdiction campaign to isolate the Cotentin Peninsula chiefly through the destruction of bridges. Early in 1944 the British scientist Solly Zuckerman urged what became known as the Transportation Plan. He contended that the destruction of 101 rail centers over a period of ninety days with 45,000 tons of bombs would create a "railway desert" in France by destroying maintenance facilities and deranging the complex processes upon which railroads depend. By 1 February Zuckerman had won the backing of both the air commander in chief for OVERLORD, Air Chief Marshal Trafford Leigh-Mallory, and the Supreme Allied Commander, General Dwight D. Eisenhower. The Transportation Plan was designed to complement rather than replace tactical interdiction within the lodgment area at the time of invasion.

The Transportation Plan did not begin in earnest until early May, the chief reason for delay being Prime Minister Winston Churchill's reservations about possible casualties among French civilians. In all, Allied planes dropped 71,000 tons of bombs on eighty rail centers before D-day. After 10 May the Transportation Plan was, at the insistence of SHAEF's G-2 (Intelligence), supplemented by the bombing of bridges over the principal rivers of northwestern France. Wide-ranging armed reconnaissance began on 20 May, when Allied fighters began to strafe trains throughout France and even in Germany. By D-day overall French rail traffic was 40 percent of what it had been on 1 March—and even less in and around Normandy. The several forms of attack were mutually reinforcing, but attacks on rail centers were the most effective. By D-day the Germans had—albeit with difficulty—stocked their forward positions with prescribed amounts of food and ammunition. But work on the fortifications of the Atlantic Wall lagged badly because the state of the railroads hindered shipment of the large quantities of cement required.

On D-day, the need for strategic deception past, Allied aircraft downed all the major bridges over the Seine,

BOMBING OF SEINE BRIDGES.

including all the railroad bridges. Those over the Loire resisted destruction, but this profited the Germans little because armed reconnaissance made it impossible to move trains within the area defined by the Seine and the Loire. Even road travel was hazardous by day, as shown by the sever punishment suffered by the *Panzer Lehr* and *12th SS Panzer* divisions as they struggled to reach the front on D-day. (Interdiction was not, however, the reason for their failure to reach the front on 6 June. As weather hindered Allied tactical aircraft until late afternoon, they might have reached the fight in time to make a difference had Adolf Hitler not dithered about releasing them until 1600.)

Throughout the battle for Normandy the Germans were poorly supplied, and at times they had to surrender positions for want of ammunition. But the most significant effect of interdiction was that it reduced their schedule for concentrating their forces to a shambles. By 18 June, the *Seventh Army* had been reinforced by only five divisions. According to German mobilization plans, it should have received seventeen within several days of the Allied landing.

[*See also* Air Strategy, *article on* Allied Air Strategy; Railroads.]

BIBLIOGRAPHY

Mark, Eduard. *Aerial Interdiction: Air Power and the Ground Battle in Three American Wars.* 1993.

EDUARD MARK

J

JAGDKORPS II. *See* II Fighter Corps.

JAUJARD, ROBERT (1896–1977), French, rear admiral, commander of the French 4th Cruiser Division. Born on 6 March 1896 in Saint-Martin de Saint-Maixent, Jaujard joined the navy as an ordinary seaman in September 1914, a year before his admission to the naval academy. As a midshipman he served in World War I on several major ships. He was promoted to lieutenant in January 1921 and assigned to the staff headquarters of the naval division of the Far East. After returning to France in 1925, Jaujard served on the battleship *Lorraine* before taking command of the oil tanker *Var*. In 1927–1928, he became navigation officer on *Jeanne d'Arc* and then on the armored cruiser *Edgar Quinet*. Promoted to lieutenant commander in 1931, he was appointed second in command of the cruiser *Foch*. After commanding the torpedo boat *Fortune* (1934–1935), he served as chief of maintenance and safety on the battleship *Dunkerque* when its construction was completed.

Named a commander in 1939, Jaujard served as commander of the destroyer *Vauquelin* in the Mediterranean and then as second in command of the cruiser *Algérie*. In June 1940, after Italy entered the war, he took part in the shelling of Vado in the vicinity of Genoa. Joining the French Free Forces, he was promoted to captain in July 1941. After Operation TORCH, the Allied invasion of North Africa in 1942, he was placed in command of the light cruiser *Georges Leygues*. After the ship was overhauled and modernized in the United States, he sailed on patrol missions in the Atlantic from Dakar to Freetown, at one point intercepting and sinking the German auxiliary cruiser *Portland*. Jaujard was then placed in charge of the navy in Algiers and was promoted to rear admiral in March 1944. As commander of the 4th Division cruisers *Georges Leygues* and *Montcalm,* he took part in Operation OVERLORD. Both ships were part of Rear Adm. Carleton F. Bryant's Bombardment Group in Task Force 124, the Assault Force for Omaha Beach. After the war, Jaujard told historian Samuel Eliot Morison, "You may well imagine what emotion was aroused when we were ordered to bombard our homeland!"

He also served during DRAGOON, the invasion of the southern coast of France in August 1944, and in the Mediterranean. Appointed a vice admiral in 1946, Jaujard became chief of staff before ending his career as an admiral in central Europe with NATO in 1951. He left active duty in April 1956 and died in Toulon on 25 January 1977.

[*See also* French Ships; Montcalm.]

BIBLIOGRAPHY

Jaujard, Robert. *Cape sur la Provence*. 1954.
Jaujard, Robert. *Croiseurs en action*. 1959.
Jaujard, Robert. *Paisible Normandie*. 1954.
Morison, Samuel Eliot. *The Invasion of France and Germany: 1944–1945*. Vol. 11 of *History of U.S. Naval Operations in World War II*. 1957.

PHILIPPE MASSON
Translated from French by Marie-Josée Schorp

JODL, ALFRED (1890-1946), German, general of artillery, chief of operations of the Wehrmacht High Command. The son of a retired Bavarian artillery captain, Jodl followed in his father's footsteps, joining a field artillery regiment as an officer cadet. Commissioned in 1912, he served throughout World War I and was selected to remain in Germany's 100,000-man postwar army. When Hitler came to power in 1933, Jodl was a major in the Operations Branch of the Army High Command, and two years later moved to the Armed Forces Office,

ALFRED JODL.   BIBLIOTHEK FÜR ZEITGESCHICHTE, STUTTGART

which in early 1938 became the Wehrmacht High Command (Oberkommando der Wehrmacht—OKW). A short spell in a field command followed. Then, just before the invasion of Poland, he was summoned back to Berlin by Field Marshal Wilhelm Keitel, chief of the OKW, to head its Operations Branch, a post he would occupy for the rest of the war.

Jodl soon found that the OKW had no executive powers and merely acted as a filter of reports to, and orders from, Hitler. The only exception to this was during the Norwegian campaign of April 1940, when Jodl was given a relatively free hand to coordinate the army, navy, and Luftwaffe. Matters became even worse at the end of 1941, when Hitler took personal command of the army, giving total responsibility for operations on the Eastern front to the Army High Command (Oberkommando des Heeres—OKH), and leaving other theaters of war, of which the only active one at that time was North Africa, to the OKW. Even so, for much of the time OKW was based at

Hitler's so-called Wolf's Lair at Rastenburg in East Prussia, and Jodl did become involved in Eastern front affairs. After the failure of the German offensive at Kursk in July 1943, to which Jodl had been vehemently opposed, and the resulting realization that Germany was now on the defensive, Hitler's attention began to turn to the West and the threat of Allied invasion.

In January 1944 Jodl was sent to inspect the Atlantic and Channel defenses. His report on their poor state reinforced the one that Field Marshal Erwin Rommel had drawn up the previous month for the Commander in Chief West, Field Marshal Gerd von Rundstedt. Jodl's report and Rommel's agitation did help to provide the necessary resources to improve the situation, but, unlike Hitler, Jodl remained convinced that fixed defenses alone would not stop the Allies, and that strong mobile reserves were crucial. Thus he persuaded Hitler to send more armored divisions to the West.

In the spring of 1944 OKW moved back to Berlin in expectation of the cross-Channel attack, but D-day found it temporarily shifted to Hitler's Alpine retreat at Berchtesgaden. It was Jodl who had to explain by telephone to Rundstedt's chief of staff, Gen. Gunther Blumentritt, who was demanding the release of the OKW reserve mobile divisions, that Hitler had gone to bed with a sleeping draught and could not be disturbed. Even when he woke up, Keitel and Jodl were unable to discuss the situation with him immediately, but had to drive for an hour to Klessheim Castle, where Hitler was receiving Adm. Miklos Horthy, the Hungarian dictator, on a state visit. Jodl briefed Hitler in a side room, but only that afternoon was Rundstedt told that he could have the *12th* and *17th* SS panzer grenadier divisions and the *Panzer Lehr Division*.

On 8 June Jodl concluded that, contrary to his previous view, the Normandy landings were the main Allied effort and there would not be others elsewhere, but Rommel, not yet convinced, refused for a time to deploy the two panzer divisions positioned north of the Seine River. However, Jodl could do nothing to persuade Hitler that his ban on voluntary withdrawals was merely preventing the reformation of a strong armored reserve for counterattacks. When Rundstedt and Rommel remonstrated in person with Hitler at Margival on 17 June, and again at Berchtesgaden on the 29th, Jodl was present merely as a mute witness.

In truth, Jodl had become almost intoxicated in his belief that Hitler was infallible. He had told a conference of Gauleiters in November 1943: "I must testify that he is the soul not only of the political but also of the military conduct of the war, and that the force of his willpower and the creative riches of his thought animate and hold together the whole of the Wehrmacht." The failure of the attempted assassination of Hitler at the Wolf's Lair on 20

July 1944, in which Jodl received minor head injuries, merely reinforced this conviction; he even advocated that the General Staff be done away with as an institution, since it could not be trusted. The end of the war found Jodl in Schleswig-Holstein with Hitler's successor as Führer, Grand Adm. Karl Dönitz. It was Jodl who signed the documents of the German surrender to the Western Allies at Reims on 8 May 1945. Arrested two weeks later, together with Dönitz and the remaining Nazi hierarchy, Jodl later stood trial before the International Military Tribunal at Nuremberg, was found guilty of war crimes and crimes against humanity for his part in passing on Hitler's orders, and was sentenced to death and hanged.

There is no doubt but that Jodl was a highly competent staff officer, but he fell too much under Hitler's spell and lost his objectivity. For this, he paid the ultimate penalty.

BIBLIOGRAPHY

Barnett, Correlli, ed. *Hitler's Generals*. 1989.
Brett-Smith, Richard. *Hitler's Generals*. 1976.
Jodl, Luise Katherine. *Jenseits des Endes: Leben und Sterben des Generaloberst Alfred Jodl*. 1976.

CHARLES MESSENGER

JUNCK, WERNER (1895–1976), German, brigadier general commanding *II Fighter Corps*, responsible for providing air defense for German forces in northern France. Werner Junck flew as a fighter pilot in the Imperial Air Service during World War I and was credited with five victories. He entered the new Luftwaffe in 1934. In April 1938 he was appointed commander of *Fighter Wing 53* and held that post until October 1939. He then became inspecting officer for the fighter force (*Inspekteur der Jagdflieger*), and in 1941 commanded the small Luftwaffe contingent sent to Iraq to support the unsuccessful uprising against the British. Thereafter he commanded the *3d Fighter Division (Jagdivision 3)* with headquarters at Metz in France, providing day and night fighter defense of the area.

Shortly before the invasion Junck was appointed commander of *II Fighter Corps (Jagdkorps II)*, with responsibility for single-seat day-fighter units based in France and Belgium. On D-day and D plus 1 the corps was able to achieve little, until home air defense units flown in from Germany were ready to resume action. For a few days thereafter the corps fought hard, but then the superior fighting power of the Allied air forces began to tell. The formation suffered heavy attrition in the grim daily battles and could provide little protection for the sorely tried German ground forces. Junck's reputation suffered accordingly, and on 1 July Alfred Bülowius replaced him as commander of *II Fighter Corps*.

[*See also* II Fighter Corps.]

BIBLIOGRAPHY

Obermaier, Ernst. *Die Ritterkreuzträger der Luftwaffe, Jagdflieger 1939–1945*. 1966.
United Kingdom. Air Ministry. *The Rise and Fall of the German Air Force, 1933 to 1945*. 1948.

ALFRED PRICE

JUNO BEACH. See British Beaches, *article on* Juno Beach.

K

KEITEL, WILHELM (1882–1946), German, field marshal, chief of staff of the Wehrmacht High Command. Wilhelm Keitel, son of a Lower Saxon estate owner, was born in Helmscherode on 22 September 1882. He had a lifelong passion for rural life, agriculture, and hunting. In 1901 he joined the *46th Field Artillery Regiment,* and after peacetime service as a recruit instructor served as a battery commander on the Western front in World War I, then in the spring of 1915 was posted to the General Staff as a captain. After service as a General Staff officer with the *19th Reserve Infantry Division* in the West, in December 1917 he was posted to Flanders.

Keitel was imbued with the ethos of uncritical and faithful service and the unquestioning fulfillment of duty; indeed, he was later known as "Lakeitel" (*Lakei* = "lackey"). But he also had organizational talents. Except for a brief tour as divisional commander of the *6th Artillery Regiment,* he spent the years 1925 to 1933 in the Armed Forces Ministry, where he rose to department chief of the Organization Office (T 2). His responsibilities in T 2—organization, expansion of the army, covert mobilization, and defense preparations on the eastern borders—suited his abilities and his willingness to work hard. He lacked qualifications and training for operational assignments.

In October 1933 Keitel was made infantry commander for Military District III in Potsdam, responsible for mobilization and training. Although he had decided to leave active service, after temporary duty with a new division in Liegnitz, Keitel was given command of the new *22d Infantry Division* in Bremen, an assignment that occupied him fully. Often in touch with Werner von Blomberg, who was named armed forces minister in January 1933 (war minister after 1935), in October 1935 Keitel succeeded Gen. Walter von Reichenau as head of the ministry's Wehrmacht Office. He now had responsibility over departments for home defense, foreign matters, domestic affairs (welfare), legal affairs, counterespionage, budget, and military staff. It thus fell to him to deal with frictions that soon developed between the War Ministry and the Army High Command and General Staff, a feud primarily concerning the army's traditional control over the military command structure. Keitel, who in 1936 had been promoted to general, sought to make the war minister effectively supreme commander of the Wehrmacht. He was supported above all by Col. Alfred Jodl, chief of the home defense division.

When Blomberg fell from power in February 1938 and the position of war minister was abolished, Keitel assumed ministerial duties with the imprecise designation "chief

WILHELM KEITEL.   Being congratulated by Adolf Hitler on Keitel's sixtieth birthday.

of the Wehrmacht High Command" (*Chef Oberkommando der Wehrmacht*), yet without exercising the real functions of a commander in chief, not to mention influence over military operations. At the beginning of the invasion Keitel was an obstacle to making quick military decisions. His elevation to field marshal after the fall of France in 1940 was largely a matter of protocol, after Göring's machinations had resulted in Erhard Milch's being given that rank as state secretary in the Reich Air Ministry.

Keitel's proximity to Hitler and his unconditional and unquestioning dedication to duty increasingly enmeshed him in the Führer's criminal war and made him, too, responsible for the extension of National Socialist tyranny to the Wehrmacht. He was found guilty of war crimes and crimes against humanity by the International Military Tribunal at Nuremberg and was hanged there on 16 October 1946.

BIBLIOGRAPHY

Görlitz, Walter, ed. *Generalfeldmarschall Keitel, Verbrecher oder Offizier? Erinnerungen, Briefe, Dokumente des chefs OKW.* 1961.

GEORG MEYER
Translated from German by Amy Hackett

KELLER, R. F. L. (1900–1954), Canadian, general-officer-commanding, 3d Canadian Infantry Division. Born in Tetbury, Gloucestershire, England, Keller immigrated with his family to Kelowna, British Columbia, where he attended Chesterfield School. Upon graduation from the Royal Military College of Canada (RMC) in 1920, Keller was commissioned into the Princess Patricia's Canadian Light Infantry (PPCLI). Breveted captain in 1925, he returned to RMC as superintendent of physical and weapons training from 1928 to 1932. Here, the big-boned and red-headed Keller earned the nickname "Captain Blood" and began to acquire a reputation as a physically hard, tough-talking officer. From 1934 to 1936 he attended Staff College, Camberley.

Employed as general staff officer, second grade, Military District No. 12 on the outbreak of war, Keller in November 1939 was appointed brigade major, 2d Canadian Infantry Brigade, and sailed with that formation to Britain in December. On the promotion of his brigadier, George R. Pearkes, to command the 1st Canadian Infantry Division in July 1940, Keller accompanied him as general staff officer, first grade, or principal staff officer with the rank of lieutenant colonel. Appointed to command the PPCLI in June 1941, Keller was made a brigadier only six weeks later and given command of the 1st Canadian Infantry Brigade. On promotion to major general in the fall of 1942, he took over the 3d Canadian Infantry Division.

This appointment no doubt reflected Lt. Gen. H. D. G.

R. F. L. KELLER.   IMPERIAL WAR MUSEUM

Crerar's great confidence in Keller's "two-fisted and competent" field leadership. Indeed, Crerar considered him corps commander material as late as May 1944. Others, among them subordinates as well as superiors, clearly did not share this opinion. General-Officer-Commanding-in-Chief, 1st British Corps, Lt. Gen. J. T. Crocker, eventually felt moved to report to General-Officer-Commanding-in-Chief, Second British Army, Lt. Gen. M. C. Dempsey, that Keller "was not really fit temperamentally and perhaps physically (he is a man who has the appearance of having lived pretty well) for such a responsible command." While Crocker acknowledged that Keller deserved "some credit" for the 3d Canadian Division having "carried out its D-day tasks with great enthusiasm and considerable success," he went on to charge that, with the exception of the 7th Brigade, Keller's division had "lapsed into a very nervy state" after "the excitement of the initial [assault] phase had passed." The jumpiness of the division, in Crocker's view, "was a reflection of the state of its Commander," who "was obviously not standing up to the strain and showed signs of fatigue and nervousness (one might almost say fright) which were patent for all to see."

Dempsey concurred in this assessment, but refrained from recommending Keller's removal because he was

Canadian. In a subsequent letter to Crerar, General Bernard L. Montgomery offered his opinion that Keller "was not good enough to command a Canadian division." When finally confronted with these allegations by Lt. Gen. G. G. Simonds, Keller admitted that "his health was not good enough to stand the heavy strain and asked that he be medically boarded (examined by a medical board) as he felt that he would be found to be unfit." For reasons related to maintaining the morale of the 3d Division, Simonds did not immediately relieve Keller, who remained popular with the rank and file, but it is almost certain he would have done so at the appropriate time. Fortunately perhaps for Keller's reputation, Simonds was spared from taking such drastic action by the U.S. Army Air Forces. On 8 August 1944 several bombers of the Eighth Air Force mistakenly attacked Keller's headquarters, nearly killing him. Rendered unconscious for a week, he was later invalided back to England and released from the service in 1946.

Keller died in London on 21 June 1954 after being stricken with a heart attack at Caen while en route to the tenth anniversary ceremonies of the D-day landing. He was buried with full military honors in Kelowna, British Columbia.

[*See also* 3d Canadian Infantry Division.]

BIBLIOGRAPHY

English, John A. *The Canadian Army and the Normandy Campaign: A Study of Failure in High Command.* 1991.

JOHN A. ENGLISH

KEPNER, WILLIAM (1893–1982), American, major general, U.S. Army Air Forces; commander, VIII Fighter Command. A wounded and decorated company commander during World War I, Kepner began his aviation career in 1920 at the Army Balloon School. He graduated from the Air Corps Tactical School in 1936, and in the years preceding World War II commanded the 8th Pursuit Group, the 1st Air Support Command, and the IV Fighter Command.

Promoted to general in 1942, he took over VIII Fighter Command in late August 1943 with orders from Gen. Henry ("Hap") Arnold to provide long-range fighter escort for the bombers of Eighth Air Force, a task he accomplished by finding sources of external fuel tanks for his P-47s, and by expeditiously equipping eleven units with more capable P-38s and P-51s. Of more immediate significance for D-day preparations, Kepner encouraged tactical innovation. He implemented the 56th Group's "roving" escort methods across his command, allowing fighters to seek out opposing aircraft at extended distances from the bombers they were protecting. He also sanctioned airfield attacks that were being conducted by

353d Group pilots looking for excitement during their escort runs. Kepner capitalized on their ideas and created a central training program in strafe and dive-bomb techniques that proved crucial to VIII Fighter Command's successful support of the invasion.

From the "Ajax" control center at Bushey Hall, Watford, northwest of London, Kepner and his planners conceived and directed nearly 2,000 D-day escort, patrol, counterair, and interdiction missions. By D plus 12 the total approached 12,000 sorties, all flown to provide ship cover, protect bombers, destroy aircraft, knock out airfields, and interdict road, rail, and canal traffic. The success of this effort reflected Kepner's abiding belief in structured training, and fulfilled his prediction that the winning side would be the one quickest to challenge traditional tactical ideas.

Kepner went on to command 2d Bombardment Division, and then Eighth Air Force until its transfer to the Pacific. After the war he was the senior air force commander at the Bikini and Eniwetok atomic tests. His last assignment was as commander in chief of Alaskan Air Command. He retired with three-star rank in 1953, and remained a board member and consultant in aerospace virtually until his death in 1982 in Orlando, Florida.

[*See also* VIII Fighter Command.]

BIBLIOGRAPHY

Kepner Document Collection. U.S. Air Force Historical Research Agency, Maxwell Air Force Base, Alabama.

PAUL F. HENRY

KING, W. L. MACKENZIE (1874–1950), Canadian, prime minister of Canada. Born in Berlin (Kitchener after 1916), Ontario, King studied at the University of Toronto, the University of Chicago, and Harvard, specializing in economics, social work, and labor relations.

Elected to Parliament as a Liberal member in 1908, King became Canada's first minister of Labor in 1909. On the eve of the Great War he accepted an invitation from the Rockefeller Foundation to direct its Department of Industrial Relations, where he earned a reputation as a labor conciliator. In the election of 1917, King again ran for Parliament as one of the few English-Canadians who openly aligned with Wilfrid Laurier against conscription. Though King was defeated, his stance made him acceptable to French-Canadian Liberals whose support guaranteed the success of his unity bid for party leadership on the death of Laurier in 1919.

As prime minister, King catered to Quebec for pragmatic reasons related to strengthening national unity and retaining political power. A master of prevarication and ambiguity, he was suspicious of British imperialists, but personally revered the Crown and displayed a profound respect for British Liberal statesmen. Although not an emotional nationalist, he persistently sought autonomy for Canada. At the Imperial Conference of 1923 he successfully resisted British efforts to impose a common foreign policy on the empire. Another such conference in 1926, which reflected King's influence, recognized the dominions as equal members of the British Commonwealth, a status formalized by the 1931 Statute of Westminster. King's insistence that Canada could be committed only by its own Parliament, however, translated into a policy of no foreign involvements. As late as 1937, he refused to agree to defense pledges in advance, to the extent that British planners interpreted his policy of "calculated confusion" as meaning they could no longer count on Canada.

Although King dreaded British participation in European war for the divisive effect it would have upon Canadian unity, he is credited with bringing a united Canada into the war in 1939. In a 1937 visit to Adolf Hitler (whom he likened to Joan of Arc), King apparently indicated that Canada would respond if Britain were threatened. His clearly preferred military policy, however, was for Canada to concentrate on industrial production and air, naval, and garrison forces rather than a large army almost certain to require conscription for sustainment. When pressured to introduce compulsory overseas service after Japan's entry into the war, King held a national plebiscite in which he asked to be released from his earlier promise not to introduce such conscription. Although he won his release handily, Quebec's disenchantment was such that he subsequently adopted the policy of "not necessarily conscription, but conscription if necessary." Indeed, King stood his ground on this issue—or dragged his feet, depending on one's point of view—until the fall of 1944 when critical troop shortages in fighting formations could no longer be met by the volunteer system. Faced with the prospect of either ordering conscripts overseas or seeing his government break up, he chose the former alternative.

W. L. MACKENZIE KING.   Middle, flanked by Franklin D. Roosevelt (left) and Winston Churchill (right). King hosted two conferences in Quebec in 1943 and 1944.

As a war leader the same age as Winston Churchill, King was dull, uninspiring, and boringly verbose. His main concerns, to perhaps the detriment of Canada's role, were almost entirely domestic. Canadians accordingly embraced Britain's prime minister and America's president as their real leaders. Although by no means pacifistic, King abhorred war and distrusted military men. Unlike Prime Minister Robert Borden who had constantly visited wounded soldiers during World War I, King stayed away from hospitals. Canadian fighting men, in turn, detested the prime minister. They not only booed him publicly during his 1941 visit to England but cost him his electoral seat in the 1945 election, in which the service vote was counted separately. King's Liberal party nonetheless squeaked to victory with 127 seats out of 245, including 53 from Quebec. The solid-bloc Quebecois once again provided the foundation of King's power, as it always had.

King retired in 1948 and died on 22 July 1950.

[See also Canada.]

BIBLIOGRAPHY

Dawson, R. MacGregor, and Blair H. Neatby. *William Lyon Mackenzie King*. 3 vols. 1958, 1963, 1976.

English, John, and J. O. Stubbs, eds. *Mackenzie King: Widening the Debate*. 1978.

Granatstein, J. L. *Mackenzie King: His Life and World*. 1977.

Stacy, C. P. *A Very Double Life: The Private World of Mackenzie King*. 1976.

JOHN A. ENGLISH

KIRK, ALAN G. (1888–1963), American, rear admiral, commander, Western Task Force. Alan Goodrich Kirk graduated from the U.S. Naval Academy in 1909 and served in the Atlantic and the Far East. During World War I he directed ordnance testing, later serving in gunnery billets and as naval aide to Presidents Wilson and Harding. He attended the Naval War College before joining its staff. After senior command and staff tours afloat, he became naval attaché in London from 1939 to 1941.

Kirk directed the Office of Naval Intelligence from March to October 1941. He commanded a destroyer squadron and a transport division in the Atlantic before returning to duty as naval attaché to Great Britain and chief of staff to Adm. Harold Stark, commander, U.S. Naval Forces Europe. Kirk took command of the Amphibious Force, Atlantic Fleet, in February 1943 and organized its training program. In July 1943 he commanded the naval force that landed Lt. Gen. Omar Bradley and the 45th Infantry Division on Sicily. The Sicily landings went well; the British and American navies and land forces worked cordially together. Historian Samuel Eliot Morison praised the "intelligence in planning and suppleness in execution" of Kirk and the other naval commanders.

Kirk arrived in London in mid-November 1943 to prepare for OVERLORD as commander, Western Task Force. Historian Thomas B. Buell remarks that Kirk's previous experience seemed to make him a natural choice to command the American landing force and to work with the British. Admiral Stark wrote to Adm. Ernest J. King, Commander in Chief, U.S. Fleet, that "bad feelings" between Kirk and Adm. Bertram H. Ramsay, commander of the Allied naval task force, made matters risky. King chose to leave Kirk in place, and his confidence proved to be justified; though British and American approaches to planning and operations differed significantly, this did not prevent fruitful cooperation.

Allocation of landing craft and gunfire support ships led to Anglo-American disputes. Gen. George Marshall and Admiral King sent senior officers to London in February 1944 to confer with Kirk and other top army and navy planners. The landing-craft question was resolved, but fire support was still at issue. Admiral King felt that the British could provide all the fire support needed, but the Royal Navy's resources did not permit this. Kirk had asked King for American gunfire ships, but without result until, at this conference, Rear Adm. John L. Hall, commander of Assault Force O, pointedly complained about the lack of gunfire support. King's representative rebuked Hall for his bluntness, but obtained three battleships and two destroyer squadrons for Kirk's task force.

As D-day approached, Kirk and his staff completed the operation plan for the Western Task Force and directed the preparation of his ships. On 6 June he commanded the western landings from the cruiser *Augusta*, establishing sea defense sectors off Utah and Omaha beaches to guard against German counterattack. After the initial landings he organized the reinforcement, supply, and gunfire support of the American beachheads through the fall of Cherbourg on 26 and 27 June. Kirk later told Samuel Eliot Morison that General Bradley developed such a liking for naval gunfire that Kirk had to warn him that too much firing was wearing out the rifling of guns that would soon be needed in southern France. Comdr. Kenneth Edwards, Royal Navy, wrote that "it would have been difficult to find an American officer more suited" to command of the Western Task Force. "Rear Admiral Kirk was a professional sailor and a gunnery specialist; he had greater experience than any other American naval officer both of British naval methods and of actual invasion." Though there were differences among British and American naval commanders, "their very smallness in relation to the gigantic enterprise of the invasion . . . is a measure of the accord that existed."

The Western Task Force was dissolved a month after D-day. Kirk became commander, U.S. Naval Forces,

ALAN G. KIRK.   On the deck of the USS *Augusta,* 6 June 1944. Front from left to right: Kirk, Omar Bradley, Arthur D. Struble, and Hugh Keen.

France. Working directly under General Dwight D. Eisenhower, he oversaw the flow of supplies across the Channel to the Allied armies, and commanded naval forces operating against German-held pockets along the French coast. When Admiral Ramsay was killed in an aircraft accident on 2 January 1945, Kirk became temporary Allied Naval Commander, Expeditionary Force, until Vice Adm. Harold Burrough, RN, could assume the post. As Allied forces reached the Rhine, Kirk organized the amphibious operation that carried assault troops across that river. Kirk returned to the United States with Eisenhower after V-E Day and was promoted to vice admiral.

After brief service with the General Board, the navy's planning group, Kirk retired in March 1946. He served in a number of diplomatic posts before his death in 1963. The frigate *Kirk* (FF 1087) was named in his honor.

[*See also* American Beaches, *articles on* Omaha Beach *and* Utah Beach; Augusta, USS; Western Task Force.]

BIBLIOGRAPHY

Buell, Thomas B. *Master of Sea Power: A Biography of Fleet Admiral Ernest J. King.* 1980.

Edwards, Kenneth. *Operation Neptune.* 1946.

Kirk Papers. Manuscript Division, Library of Congress, Washington, D.C.

Morison, Samuel Eliot. *The Invasion of France and Germany, 1944–1945.* Vol. 11 of *History of United States Naval Operations in World War II.* 1957.

Morison, Samuel Eliot. *Sicily–Salerno–Anzio.* Vol. 9 of *History of United States Naval Operations in World War II.* 1954.

JOHN C. REILLY, JR.

KLOSTERKEMPER, BERNHARD (1897–1962),
German, colonel commanding the *920th Grenadier Regiment*. Klosterkemper was a prewar regular soldier who by June 1944 commanded one of the three grenadier regiments in *243d Infantry Division*, which was deployed in the Cotentin Peninsula. Here his regiment fought against the paratroops of the U.S. 82d and 101st airborne divisions, and then in the desperate attempt to prevent the Americans from cutting off the northern part of the peninsula. When his divisional commander, Lt. Gen. Heinz Hellmich, was killed during an air attack on 16 June, Klosterkemper took command of what remained of the division. Half of these remnants were cut off when the Americans reached the west coast of the peninsula on 18 June; Klosterkemper then took over the remains of the *91st Air Landing Division* as well. In early July the *91st Division* was given back its separate identity, but Klosterkemper continued to lead the weakened *243d Division* for the next few weeks. Only after the final Allied breakout were its remnants withdrawn.

The division was then broken up and Klosterkemper, still a colonel, was sent in the autumn to command the *180th Infantry Division*, which had been hastily sent from Germany to Holland in September 1944 to counter an Allied airborne assault. Klosterkemper, promoted to major general on 1 December, led the division against Montgomery's 21st Army Group during the bitter fighting of the winter of 1944–1945 as the Allies approached the Rhine. After the Allies crossed the Rhine, the *180th Division* was trapped with the remains of Field Marshal Walter Model's *Army Group B*. Klosterkemper and his surviving men surrendered to the Americans on 18 April. He died on 19 July 1962 in Bremen.

[*See also* 243d Division.]

CHARLES MESSENGER

KNERR, HUGH J. (1887–1971), American, major
general, deputy commanding general, administration, U.S. Strategic Air Forces (USSTAF). Hugh Knerr was intelligent and acerbic, and did not suffer fools. He had a passionate, uncompromising belief in air power. His early love for aviation began in childhood when he performed odd jobs in the Wright Brothers Bicycle Shop. He graduated from Annapolis in 1908, but found his desire for an aviation assignment frustrated. He transferred to the Signal Corps Aviation Section, earning his wings in 1917, but an assignment to Hawaii prevented his participation in combat during World War I. For the next twenty years his championship of air power created enemies within the air corps, on the army staff, and in the Navy Department. In the late 1920s he commanded bombardment units and in the following decade held important positions in the air material command. In 1935 he became chief of staff, GHQ Air Force, and cemented his relationship with Lt. Gen. Frank M. Andrews, commander of GHQ Air Force. He retired on disability in 1939.

The War Department recalled Lieutenant Colenel Knerr to active duty in October 1942 and soon put his logistics skills to use. By May 1943 Knerr received promotion to brigadier general and a posting to the Eighth Air Force. In October 1943 he became commander of the VIII Air Force Service Command. He reorganized the command and prepared to handle an influx of numerous new fighter and bomber groups, with supporting personnel.

When Lt. Gen. Carl Spaatz established Headquarters, U.S. Strategic Air Forces in Europe (USSAFE, later USSTAF) in early January 1944, Knerr convinced him to adopt a unique double-deputy system that recognized the equality of operations and logistics and the dual nature of USSTAF's responsibilities. It had operational control of the Eighth and Fifteenth air forces and administrative control of the Eighth and Ninth. Spaatz appointed Knerr deputy commanding general, administration, which placed Knerr in charge of setting policy regarding all administration and logistics problems for all U.S. Army air forces participating in OVERLORD. At the same time Knerr became commander of the Air Service Command, USSTAF, which placed him in direct control of both the VIII and IX air force service commands. This position enabled Knerr to prevent duplication and competition between the administrative functions of those two air forces.

Three months later the administration of the Fifteenth Air Force in Italy came under Knerr's purview as well. In March 1944 Knerr was promoted to major general.

The placing of the vital administrative functions under a single hand went far to ensure the maximum efficiency of American air support on D-day and in further operations in Normandy. Without efficient air power OVERLORD might have failed or been a far more bloody success.

[*See also* Air Service Command; U.S. Strategic Air Forces (USSTAF).]

BIBLIOGRAPHY

Craven, Wesley Frank, and James Lea Cate, eds. *Europe: ARGUMENT to V-E Day, January 1944 to May 1945.* Vol. 3 of *The Army Air Forces in World War II.* 1951.

Green, Murray. "Hugh J. Knerr: The Pen and the Sword." In *Makers of the United States Air Force*, edited by John L. Frisbee. 1987.

RICHARD G. DAVIS

KRAISS, DIETRICH (1889–1944), German, major
general, commander of the *352d Infantry Division*. Kraiss

was born in Stuttgart on 16 November 1889. After graduating from a cadet academy, he was commissioned a lieutenant in 1909 and fought in World War I as a company commander. Transferred from the Imperial Army into the army of the Weimar Republic as a professional officer, he had advanced to colonel by 1937 and assumed command of the newly formed *90th Infantry Regiment*, with which he began World War II. As regimental commander he participated in the Polish and French campaigns. After promotion to brigadier general on 1 February 1941, Kraiss took command of the *169th Infantry Division*, which he led into the campaign against the Soviet Union. For his accomplishments, he received the Knight's Cross (27 July 1942) and promotion to major general (1 October 1942).

On 6 November 1943 Kraiss became commander of the newly formed *352d Infantry Division* in Normandy. He brought to bear the extensive experience of his military life; within a few months he commanded a combat-ready division. He emphasized training in close quarters with tanks, expansion of the coastal fortifications, and the training of young recruits, his particular interest.

On 6 June 1944, Kraiss was at his divisional headquarters near Littry. Thus he immediately alerted his troops and ordered the first defensive measures. But his strategy to oppose an Allied landing was not limited to defensive maneuvers; rather it included effective counterattacks. On the day of the invasion he repeatedly ordered his regiments out from their positions in order to throw back the Allied assaults. The troops engaged the Allies but were not strong enough to push their counterassault to the sea. On D-day the general at times directed the defense from a forward position, visited the regimental command posts, and conferred with his commanders. He immediately utilized every force available to him, throwing engineers, his field replacement battalion, and an antiaircraft regiment into the battle to prevent a U.S. breakthrough.

When the balance of the first day of fighting was drawn that night, Kraiss reported the current situation to his commanding general, Lt. Gen. Erich Marcks, praising the heroic coastal defense and the resolute counterassault by a battalion. He announced continued tenacious resistance for the next day, but also pointed out the urgent need for new forces.

Kraiss and his division, however, remained largely without substantive reinforcements and his ammunition situation became ever more critical. Kraiss had to improvise. Although his soldiers delayed the advance of the increasingly strong Allied forces, the worsening situation forced the general to withdraw both wings of his division in risky breakout maneuvers on 8 June. Though this ran contrary to the Führer's commands, the corps commander supported Kraiss's actions in the absolutely critical situation. Kraiss thus succeeded in preventing the destruction of the *352d Infantry Division* and preserving the unit's structure.

From 10 June to 18 June, Kraiss's command was oriented toward further shortening his division's front, collecting and marshaling his troops, and deploying them in new formations in a line some twenty kilometers (twelve miles) back from the coast for a concentrated defense. In this precarious situation Kraiss displayed both personal bravery and a clear sense of what the situation required. Thus the *352d Infantry Division* held until new forces (infantry, tanks, and artillery) arrived, and the U.S. advance was halted before Saint-Lô.

Kraiss commanded his division until 2 August 1944, when he was severely wounded in combat and died near Saint-Lô. He received a posthumous Oak Leaf Cluster for his Knight's Cross. Even today, he is remembered—in the words of the former commander of the *II Parachute Corps*, Col. Ernst Blauensteiner—as an "incredibly brave and circumspect troop commander." Kraiss was buried in the German Military Cemetery, Mont-de-Huisnes.

[*See also* 352d Infantry Division.]

BIBLIOGRAPHY

Keilig, Wolf. *Die Generale des Heeres*. 1983.
Lenfeld, Erwin, and Franz Thomas. *Die Eichen Laubträge, 1940–1945*. 1983.

GÜNTER HILLER
Translated from German by Amy Hackett

KRANCKE, THEODOR (1893–1973), admiral, Commander in Chief of Naval Group Command West. Theodor Krancke was born on 30 March 1893 at Magdeburg. He entered the Imperial Navy in 1912, serving in several ships during World War I, then joined the postwar Reichsmarine, the navy of the Weimar Republic. From October 1937 to August 1939 he was commander of the Naval Academy, and then up to June 1940 held some important staff positions. In October 1940 he took the pocket battleship *Admiral Scheer* on an extended raider cruise into the Atlantic, attacking the convoy HX.84 and sinking the armed merchant cruiser *Jervis Bay;* he then went into the South Atlantic and the Indian Ocean, returning to Germany on 1 April 1941, after sinking 17 ships totaling 113,233 tons. From June 1941 to September 1942 he was chief of the Quartermaster Division in the Naval Staff and, up to March 1943, navy representative in Hitler's headquarters. In April 1943 he took over as Commander in Chief of Naval Group Command West.

Krancke's command consisted of the surface vessels available in French and Belgian ports, divided into offensive forces such as destroyers, torpedo boats, and S-boats

THEODOR KRANCKE. At right.

(*Schnellboote,* called E-boats by the Allies), and defensive forces that included mine destruction vessels (*Sperrbrecher*), minesweepers, patrol boats (*Vorpostenboote*), submarine chasers (*U-bootjäger*), and gun carriers (*Artillerie-Fähren*), all organized into divisions and flotillas. Also under him were the commanders of the naval shore defense forces and installations, the naval fortresses, the harbor captains, and the other land-based naval units.

Krancke was subordinate to the Commander in Chief of the Navy, Grand Admiral Karl Dönitz, and had to work in close coordination with the Commander in Chief West, Field Marshal Gerd von Rundstedt. While the Wehrmacht High Command (Oberkommando der Wehrmacht, or OKW) and Rundstedt expected the invasion in the Somme River region, held by the *Fifteenth Army,* Krancke shared the opinion of the commander of *Army Group B,* Field Marshal Erwin Rommel, that the invasion might come more to the west, where the Cotentin Peninsula gave some cover against the western winds and seas. Also, like Rommel, he thought that the invasion should be checked at the coast and therefore tried to strengthen the shore defenses with offshore mine fields.

In early June Krancke, like most of the German commanders, did not expect the invasion during the next few days or weeks. Only when German radar stations reported strong contacts at sea at 0309 on 6 June, did Krancke order naval forces to reconnoiter the approach routes; they were, however, intercepted by the Allied covering forces. After Krancke reported the start of the invasion, the Commander in Chief West and the OKW delayed the necessary orders for countermeasures for some hours because of doubts about the real situation. During the following days the superiority of the Allied air and naval forces was so great that the available German naval forces could do no great harm to the invasion.

After the retreat from western Europe, Krancke in April 1945 became commander in chief of Naval Command Norway, a post that he held until the end of the war. He surrendered with his command in Oslo. Released from captivity in 1947, he lived in retirement at Wentorf, near Hamburg, until his death on 18 June 1973.

[*See also* Navy, *article on* German Navy; Western Defense Force.]

BIBLIOGRAPHY

Krancke, Theodor. "Invasionsabwehrmaßnahmen der Kriegsmarine im Kanalgebiet 1944." *Marine-Rundschau* 66 (1969): 170–187.

JÜRGEN ROHWER

KRIEGSMARINE. *See* Navy, *article on* German Navy.

L

LAMMERDING, HEINZ (1905–1971), German, Brigadeführer commander of the *2d SS Panzer Division "Das Reich"*. Lammerding graduated from two universities with engineering degrees. These gained him employment in the head office of the army's Training Department and then with several Pioneer units of the Nazi party's SA (*Sturmabteilung*). He progressed to the SA Pioneer School at Hoxter where he held a staff appointment with the Engineering Inspectorate. On 1 April 1935, Lammerding joined the Pioneer branch of the SS *Verfügungstruppen* (paramilitary police formations) with the rank of lieutenant, and by the outbreak of war he had been promoted to captain and was a lecturer in the SS Officers' School in Braunschweig.

In mid-October 1939, Lammerding took over the *SS Death's Head (Totenkopf) Division*'s *Pioneer Battalion*, which he led during the 1940 campaign in France. For his performance in that campaign, during which he played a distinctive role in repelling a British armored attack near Arras, and for other acts of bravery, he was awarded the Second and First Classes of the Iron Cross—one of the first soldiers of *Totenkopf* to gain the latter award.

As divisional Ia (chief assistant, operations) on the Eastern front, Lammerding played a prominent role in the battles to smash the Stalin line during the autumn of 1941. Then, in the early part of 1942, his skill as a staff officer helped defeat the Soviet forces that had encircled German units at Demyansk. Now a lieutenant colonel, he was given command of *Totenkopf*'s motorcycle battalion in August 1942 and led it in the battles around Kharkov in the winter of 1942–1943; for his part in those operations he was awarded the German Cross in Gold.

Lammerding then spent a brief period as Ia with the *II SS Panzer Corps* before becoming chief of staff to the commander of antipartisan units. In December 1943, he was given command of *Battle Group "Das Reich"* and a month later took over the *SS Division "Das Reich"*. Although the bulk of the division was sent to refit in southern France, Lammerding stayed with the battle group until March 1944. In April of that year he was awarded the Knight's Cross of the Iron Cross for his success as commander of the battle group and was promoted to the rank of Brigadeführer.

Battle Group "Das Reich" joined the main body of the division in France where Lammerding supervised its conversion to panzer division status. On D plus 1 the *2d SS* moved from Toulouse in southern France toward Normandy, and as its commander Lammerding was technically responsible for the reprisals for partisan activity carried out at Oradour-sur-Glane during that move (over six hundred French civilians killed). He was wounded on 26 July 1944, returned to command the division again in November, and led it during the Battle of the Bulge. He then became Ia to Heinrich Himmler and occupied that post until the end of hostilities.

In the war crimes trials held after the war in France, Lammerding was tried in absentia by a court and condemned to death for the reprisals at Oradour-sur-Glane, but the German government refused to extradite him. He died of cancer in January 1971.

[*See also* 2d SS Panzer Division "Das Reich."]

BIBLIOGRAPHY

Weidinger, O. *Division "Das Reich."* 6 vols.
Yerger, M. *Das Reich.* Vol. 1 of *Knights of Steel.* 1989.

JAMES LUCAS

LANDING SHIPS. There were two main families of landing ship used in Normandy, the LSI (Landing Ship, Infantry) and the LST (Landing Ship, Tank). The first tank landing craft (LCTs) developed by the British in

LST 21.   Unloading British tanks and trucks onto a Rhino ferry, 6 June 1944.

1940 were too small for all but short sea operations; Churchill demanded something bigger. In order to produce such vessels as rapidly as possible, three shallow-draft tankers constructed for use on the Maracaibo River in Venezuela were taken in hand for conversion. Their bows were cut away, and a new section with a bow door hinged at the bottom was built on. A 68-foot-long double ramp allowed the tanks or other vehicles to drive on and off. All three vessels were used in Normandy in Assault Convoy L3, alongside fifteen American LSTs. The three ships were HMS *Bachaquero* and *Misoa,* both 6,455 GRT (gross registered tons) and built in 1937, and HMS *Tasajera,* 5,679 GRT, built in 1938. The first two could make 10 knots, and the third 8.5. Carrying capacity was eighteen 40-ton tanks, or twenty-two 25-ton tanks, or thirty-three motor vehicles, along with about 200 troops. They were armed with 4-inch smoke mortars and up to twenty-six 20-mm antiaircraft guns; *Bachaquero* also carried three 2-pounder pompoms. *Misoa* was also used as a coastal forces depot ship off the beaches.

The main type of LST used in Normandy was LST(2), mass-produced in the United States for service with the Royal Navy (RN) and with the U.S.

Navy (USN). Its origins were in the "Atlantic tank landing craft" as they were originally designated, planned in 1941 to be able to cross the Atlantic under their own power, so as to supplement the smaller TLCs built in the United Kingdom and thus meet an invasion requirement of over two thousand such vessels. The LSTs were designed by John C. Niedermair of the U.S. Navy's Bureau of Ships with liquid ballast tanks to allow deep draft for ocean voyages and shallow draft for beaching. The design was kept as simple as possible, with the minimum number of pieces of standardized plates welded together. Two General Motors 12-567 V-12 diesel engines of standard railway-locomotive type provided power through twin screws. Dimensions were overall length 99.9 meters (327.75 ft.), and width 15.5 meters (50.1 ft.). Displacement in the light condition was 1,475 tons with a draft of 0.76 meters (2.5 ft.) forward, and 1.86 meters (6.1 ft.) aft. The load displacement for beaching was 2,100 tons with drafts of 0.95 meters (3.1 ft.) forward and 12.8 meters (9.5 ft.) aft. For ocean passage, load displacement was 3,800 tons with draft of 2.2 meters (7.1 ft.) forward and 4.1 meters (13.5 ft.) aft. Maximum speed was 11.5 knots with an economical cruising speed of 8.75 knots.

The designed load was 20 Sherman tanks or up to about 120 small vehicles plus 177 troops. The average vehicle load was 70, if no tanks were carried. Tanks could only be carried on the 70-meter (231-ft.) tank deck, but lighter equipment such as guns or vehicles could be carried on the upper deck also. Other than weight, the only constraint was the size of the vehicle elevator that lowered the upper deck loads to the tank deck: 7.2 x 4.1 x 3.2 meters (23.5 x 13.5 x 10.5 ft.) The ship was loaded and unloaded through the double bow doors and bow loading ramp. The ship could be beached or loads could be disembarked onto Rhino pontoon ferries, which some LSTs towed in the initial assault convoys. Disembarkation by pontoon ferry overcame two problems: the very flat Normandy beaches, and the danger to the relatively big ships as they sat high and dry at low tide in the early stages of the invasion. LSTs also carried a pair of small landing craft on davits on each side of the after superstructure, and some of those in the reinforcing convoys towed barges. Some LSTs were equipped with medical parties to act as forward mobile hospitals carrying operations out on the tank deck; these ships were also used to evacuate wounded.

Some 59 Royal Navy LST(2)s were used in NEPTUNE: *LST 8, 9, 11, 62, 63, 65, 80, 159, 160, 162–165, 180, 198–200, 214, 215, 237–239, 301–304, 319–324, 361, 363–368, 402–406, 408–410, 412, 413, 415, 416, 419–421, 423, 425, 427, 428,* and *430.* Armament in RN service was usually one 12-pounder AA gun aft and six 20-mm AA guns.

British LST(2)s were numbered in series with LST(2)s retained by the U.S. Navy, which nicknamed them "Large Slow Targets." American LST(2)s were armed with up to seven 40-mm and twelve 20-mm AA guns. 174 American LSTs were involved in the Normandy landings: *LST 1, 2, 5–7, 16, 17, 21, 25, 27, 28, 30, 44, 46, 47–61, 72, 73, 75, 133, 134, 137–139, 157, 175, 176, 197, 208, 209, 212, 229, 230, 261–264, 266, 279, 280–288, 290–295, 306–312, 314–317, 325–327, 331, 332, 335–338, 344–347, 350–352, 355–357, 359, 360, 369–386, 388, 389, 391–393, 400, 493–506, 508–512, 515–517, 519–524, 527–530, 532–543, 548, 550, 682,* and *980–983.*

LST(2)s were disposed approximately as follows (the sources are contradictory):

Eastern Naval Task Force: 127, made up of Force S, with 22 RN; Force J, 22 RN; Force G, 23 USN; Force L (follow-up), 15 RN, 45 USN. Western Naval Task Force: 106, made up of Force O, 25 USN; Force U, 30 USN; Force B (follow-up), 51 USN.

No British LSTs were lost, but five American ships were sunk off Normandy. *LST 314* and *LST 316* were sunk by torpedoes from S-boats on 9 June; *LST 496* was mined off Omaha on 11 June; *LST 499* was mined on 8 June; and *LST 523* was mined on 19 June.

LST UNLOADS TANK OF 2D ARMORED DIVISION OF THE FRENCH ARMY.   Under Gen. Jacques Philippe Leclerc, the division landed in Normandy in mid-August 1944.
IMPERIAL WAR MUSEUM

LSTs were used to tow pieces of the Mulberry harbor across the Channel. The first LSTs began to return to Britain from the morning of D plus 1 on, and thereafter worked a shuttle service from British ports to the beaches to supply the armies ashore. One British LST, *416,* made as many as twenty-eight cross-Channel runs between D-day and the end of September, presaging the roll-on/roll-off ferry services of today that are the direct descendants of these pioneering ships.

[*See also* Amphibious Assault Training; Assault Ships.]

BIBLIOGRAPHY

Barger, Mel. *Large Slow Target.* Vol. 1, 1987.
Conway's All the World's Fighting Ships, 1922–1946. 1980.
Dictionary of American Naval Fighting Ships. Vol. 7, 1981.
MacDermott, Brian. *Ships with No Name.* 1992.

ERIC J. GROVE

LANDRUM, EUGENE M. (1891–1967), American, commanding general, U.S. 90th Infantry Division.

Eugene M. Landrum was born in Florida on 6 February 1891. In World War I he enlisted in the army and was commissioned a second lieutenant. He served with the U.S. expeditionary force to Russia in 1919, and thereafter attended various U.S. Army military schools. Early in World War II he served in the Alaskan Defense Command and then, promoted to major general, became commander of the 87th Infantry Division in October 1943.

General Landrum assumed command of the 90th Infantry Division in Normandy after the relief of Gen. Jay W. MacKelvie on 12 June 1944 (D plus 6). Landrum had been assigned deputy corps commander of U.S. VII Corps to provide, if necessary, a combat veteran to take over a division with failing leadership. Taking command of the 90th in the midst of its first week of combat in the hedgerows, Landrum could do little to change the course of the division's first battle. Its role was to protect the flanks and rear of VII Corps 15–18 June (D plus 9 to D plus 12), and his presence was barely felt.

During the relative calm after the first costly battles, Landrum visited the various units in an effort to reinspire them after their heavy earlier losses. Both physically and personally, Landrum was unimpressive. He was short, chubby, and unathletic, had a round face and a prominent nose; he wore an oversized overcoat and usually carried a cane. Pessimistic in outlook, he had no command presence, no personal magnetism, and no combat drive; his talks were usually bland, although they did convey some hope that things might get better. Despite these negative characteristics, on 3 July he directed the 90th Division in a costly yet successful attack on Mont Castre, the most important terrain feature still in German hands on the Cotentin Peninsula. He commanded most of this attack from a cellar in the Château Francquetot, never visiting his troops in the field. Later, in an effort to tidy up the battlefield in preparation for Operation COBRA, U.S. First Army's forthcoming attack to break out of the hedgerow country, Landrum on 22 July ordered a limited attack on a narrow front against the "Island" on the Sèves River, which resulted in 231 men and 14 officers of the 1st Battalion, 358th Infantry, surrendering to the *6th Parachute Regiment.*

Landrum's command was marked by his controversial relief of both Col. Clark Fales, an admired commander of the 359th Infantry, and his assistant division commander, Brig. Gen. Sam Williams, a superb leader and inspirational commander.

In sum, Landrum's failure to understand the problems of hedgerow combat, his failure to motivate by example, and his apparent attempts to blame subordinates for his own shortcomings severely undermined the confidence of his subordinates and superiors. He was relieved of command on 28 July 1944 and was succeeded by Gen. Raymond S. McLain.

Landrum became commander of the Infantry Replacement Training Center at Camp Maxey, Texas, in October 1944. He died on 24 July 1967.

[*See also* 90th Infantry Division.]

BIBLIOGRAPHY

Colby, John. *War from the Ground Up: The 90th Division in World War II.* 1991.

FRANK NORRIS, ORWIN TALBOTT, and
EAMES YATES

LARGS, HMS. Built in 1938 by Chantiers et Atlantique of Provence as the passenger liner *Charles Plumier,* it was commissioned as a French armed merchant cruiser in 1939 and was seized off Gibraltar by the Royal Navy on 22 November 1940. Renamed *Largs,* it served as an ocean boarding vessel in 1941–1942, then in early 1942 was converted into a Landing Ship, Headquarters (Large)—LSH(L). Its weight was 5,850 tons and its speed 17 knots. *Larg's* crew of 284 was commanded by Capt. H. S. Allen. In November 1942 it was the flagship of Rear Adm. Thomas Troubridge for Operation TORCH, the landings at Oran, and then the flagship of Adm. Rhoderick McGrigor for Operation CORKSCREW, the capture of Pantelleria, an island off Sicily, on 11–12 June 1943, and for Operation HUSKY, the Sicily landings, in July 1943.

Largs was the flagship of Force S, Rear Adm. A. G. Talbot, for D-day. It embarked the headquarters of British I Corps, Gen. J. T. Crocker, and elements of the British 3d Division for Sword Beach. It was almost hit by torpedoes from German torpedo boats at 0525 on D-day, when a torpedo sank the Norwegian destroyer *Svenner.* Approaching the beachhead, it landed Admiral Talbot briefly in the afternoon. This pattern was repeated on many of the subsequent days, when the admiral spent much of his time ashore. *Largs* suffered near misses from bombs on 12 June, and was withdrawn from Operation NEPTUNE on 30 June 1944, when floating command was no longer required.

Largs served as the flagship of Adm. John Cunningham for Operation DRAGOON, the Allied landings in the south of France on 15 August 1944, and as the flagship of Rear Adm. B. C. S. Martin for Operation DRACULA, the landings at Rangoon, Burma, on 1 May 1945. It was returned to French government service under its original name in 1945.

[*See also* Talbot, Arthur G.]

BIBLIOGRAPHY

Chalmers, W. S. *Full Cycle: The Biography of Admiral Sir Bertram Home Ramsay.* 1959.

Roskill, Stephen W. *The Offensive*. Vol. 3, pt. 2 of *The War at Sea, 1939–1945*. 1960.

ANDREW LAMBERT

LEATHAM, RALPH

LEATHAM, RALPH (1886–1954), British, admiral, commander in chief at Plymouth. Leatham entered the Royal Navy in 1900, became a torpedo specialist, then commanded the First Battle Squadron in 1938 and 1939. During the war he was vice admiral commander in chief East Indies, then served in the Mediterranean in 1942 and 1943.

From 1942 to 1945 Leatham was commander in chief at Plymouth, a major base for Operation NEPTUNE housing one of the COREP (Coordination of Repairs) Committees charge with streamlining the repair of landing craft and other assault vessels. This involved coordinating all shipyard facilities in the command area, naval and mercantile, public and private, to keep the invasion shipping in action. It also involved the recovery of damaged craft and oversight of the scale of invasion shipping and of estimated damage. Plymouth also served as the amphibious training center for the U.S. Navy's Force U (TF 125), commanded by Rear Adm. John L. Hall, in October 1943, and for Rear Adm. John Wilkes's command from January 1944. The American installations at Plymouth included a maintenance and repair facility with 1,500 officers and men. Although senior to Adm. Bertram H. Ramsay on the Navy List, Leatham and the other port admirals willingly placed themselves under Ramsay's command as Allied Naval Commander, Expeditionary Force (ANCXF). This relieved Ramsay and his staff of the administrative burden of assembling and supporting the invasion armada. Ramsay took command of the shipping only when the invasion forces were about to sail.

During Operation NEPTUNE Plymouth controlled nine antisubmarine escort groups, to provide distant cover to the assault and followup shipping, and acted as base for the destroyers and coastal craft covering the western flank of the invasion from the threat posed by German submarines, destroyers, and S-Boats based on the Atlantic coast. This threat was largely neutralized early on 9 June when the 10th Destroyer Flotilla, eight ships under Captain B. Jones, HMS *Tartar,* engaged four German destroyers to the west of Cherbourg, sinking *ZH1* and *Z32*. Leatham controlled the escort groups operating between the base and the beachhead and was also responsible for the reloading, turnaround, and convoying of all Plymouth shipping. Air and naval forces accounted for the majority of the submarines that attempted to break into the assault area. After the great gale of the 19th, Leatham organized special teams to recover and repair damaged vessels. From 27 June he resumed responsibility for all shipping in the Plymouth sector of the English Channel, on the withdrawal of the Eastern and Western task forces.

Leatham retired in February 1946 and served as governor of Bermuda, 1946–1949. He demonstrated all the attributes required for senior command afloat. His contribution to NEPTUNE may have been remote from the landings, but it was nonetheless critical.

BIBLIOGRAPHY

Morison, Samuel E. *The Invasion of France and Germany, 1944–1945*. Vol. 11 of *History of United States Naval Operations in World War II*. 1957.

ANDREW LAMBERT

LEICESTER, B. W.

LEICESTER, B. W. (1901–1977), British, brigadier, commander of the 4th Special Service Brigade. Bernard W. ("Jumbo") Leicester joined the Royal Marines Light Infantry in 1918, spending his early service at sea and qualifying in physical training. In 1929 he volunteered for the Sudan Defence Force, and two of his five years there were spent in the Camel Corps, an appointment that was to influence his military philosophy.

Soon after attending the Army Staff College, Camberley, he gained the coveted appointment of brigade major of the 9th Infantry Brigade. At the outbreak of World War II he went with this brigade to France, subsequently becoming brigade major of the 102d Royal Marine Brigade in 1940. In December 1941 he became GSO 1 (general staff officer, grade 1) of the Royal Marines Division and then commanding officer of the 1st Royal Marine Battalion. He had foreseen the need for a new role for the Royal Marines and came to the conclusion that they should expand their shipborne role into a combined/joint operations role. He fell out with many of his seniors over his desire to see a major change in direction for his corps. He believed that the Commando concept could be achieved by any troops who were highly motivated, professional, and preferably volunteers, and he became heavily involved in developing military operational procedures and the Commando role.

His prewar experience of practical soldiering stood him in good stead, and he was impatient for the Royal Marine battalions to be retrained as Commandos. Thus he was pleased to be given the job of forming and commanding the 4th Special Service Brigade. His task in converting a mixture of regular and conscript marines into a Commando force competing with the all-volunteer Army Commandos was immense, but he achieved this by personal example, his refusal to allow circumstances to ruffle him, and his profound professional knowledge.

His 4th Special Service Brigade, consisting of Nos. 41,

46, 47, and 48 Royal Marine Commandos, landed across a ten-mile front in support of the 3d Canadian Division. Headquarters and No. 48 Commando landed at Saint-Aubin from H plus 45 minutes to H plus 60 with Leicester and his command post landing with the 8th Canadian Infantry Brigade at Bernières-sur-Mer. His four Commando units fought individual engagements, regrouping again by D plus 4 after clearing the Mue valley and capturing the radar station at Douvres. The brigade then moved to support the 1st Special Service Brigade east of the Orne. The ferocity of the battles fought is reflected in the casualty figures of 136 officers and marines of the 4th Special Service Brigade killed and more than twice that number wounded between D-day and D plus 10. Indeed the No. 48 Royal Marine Commando was down to 223 men at the end of D-day, half its strength.

First and foremost, Leicester was a leader of men, and he lived to command. His principal wartime action came later in the successful amphibious assault on Walcheren in Holland on 1 November 1944 after the 4th Special Service Brigade had regrouped. He subsequently became the first head of the combined operations division in the Southeast

Asia Command under Mountbatten and after the war went to the Pentagon as chief of Combined Operations from 1947 to 1949. He later returned to the Sudan, serving as deputy commander of British troops in the Sudan and Eritrea from 1950 to 1954.

[*See also* Commandos; 4th Special Service Brigade.]

BIBLIOGRAPHY

Ladd, James. *Commandos and Rangers of World War II.* 1978.
Leicester, B. W. Papers. Royal Marines Museum Archives, Eastney, Southsea, Hampshire, England.

DEREK OAKLEY

LEIGH-MALLORY, TRAFFORD

LEIGH-MALLORY, TRAFFORD (1892–1944), British, Air Chief Marshal, commander in chief, Allied Expeditionary Air Force (AEAF). Trafford L. Leigh-Mallory was commissioned in the infantry in 1914 and transferred in 1916 into the Royal Flying Corps, later the Royal Air Force (RAF). After World War I he received a permanent RAF commission. In 1921 he joined the School of Army Cooperation, becoming commandant, from

TRAFFORD LEIGH-MALLORY.   Addressing crews of a glider pilot regiment.   IMPERIAL WAR MUSEUM

1927 to 1930, a period when this activity was falling out of favor in the RAF. In 1937 he became air officer commanding (AOC) No. 12 Group, Fighter Command.

In the Battle of Britain in 1940 he was involved in serious controversy over tactics, arguing that prohibitive losses could be inflicted on the Luftwaffe by attacking the Germans with "big wings" (three to five squadrons) as they returned from raids on Britain. This contradicted Fighter Command doctrine as propounded by Air Chief Marshal Hugh Dowding, which insisted that the prime duty of the command was to prevent the Luftwaffe from ever reaching its targets. The disagreement was fundamental, and exacerbated by sharp personality conflicts, sometimes provoked by Leigh-Mallory's bluff and forceful manner.

The Battle of Britain was nevertheless won by Dowding's system of tight control based on radar intelligence and the brilliant defensive tactics of Air Vice Marshal Keith Park, AOC No. 11 Group. Yet Dowding and Park were removed, Leigh-Mallory replacing Park in December 1940. During 1941 Leigh-Mallory vigorously pressed costly offensive air operations against German-held territory; in November 1942 he was promoted to AOC Fighter Command.

Early in 1943 it became apparent that progress with OVERLORD planning required the expert cooperation of a responsible air officer. It was the view of the Combined Chiefs of Staff (CCOS) that the most important element of the air contribution to OVERLORD would be protection of the beachheads by asserting air superiority; the AOC Fighter Command thus seemed to be a correct choice as Allied air commander, and this was confirmed at the QUADRANT conference at Quebec in August. In November Leigh-Mallory received his directive from the Combined Chiefs as commander in chief, AEAF. This defined his command of the Allied tactical air forces, but, significantly, it left undecided his authority over the strategic bomber forces that formed a major part of Allied air power.

By January 1944, when the senior commanders were taking up their posts, it became apparent, in the words of the deputy supreme Allied commander, Air Chief Marshal Arthur Tedder, "that the scale of air effort needed before and after the 'Overlord' landings would be far beyond the capacity of [tactical] forces alone to provide. The Strategic Air Forces must be brought in" (*With Prejudice*, 1966, p. 504). This, however, raised serious difficulties with the commanders of those forces, who believed that their own bombing offensives could win the war without the need for OVERLORD, and who were averse to taking orders from Leigh-Mallory.

An impossible situation thus arose, accentuated by the arrival of thoroughly experienced tactical air commanders from the Mediterranean. Leigh-Mallory retained his title of C-in-C, AEAF, but control of air strategy was increasingly exercised by Tedder. Leigh-Mallory's loyally conceived attempts to help the ground troops by direct support with heavy bombers were a failure, disappointing the army and annoying other airmen, who saw them as a misuse of air power. But his Transportation Plan for destroying German communications and isolating the battlefield (interdiction) proved a valuable contribution to victory.

As the Allies advanced out of Normandy, Leigh-Mallory's lonely role further diminished. In October 1944 he was appointed air commander, South East Asia Command, but on his way to assume this post he was killed in an air crash on 14 November.

[*See also* Air Force, *article on* Allied Expeditionary Air Force; Tedder, Arthur.]

BIBLIOGRAPHY

D'Este, Carlo. *Decision in Normandy: The Unwritten Story of Montgomery and the Allied Campaign.* 1983.

Terraine, John. *A Time for Courage: The Royal Air Force in the European War, 1939–1945.* 1985.

Webster, Charles, and Noble Frankland. *The Strategic Air Offensive against Germany, 1939–1945.* Vol. 3, 1961. Official history.

JOHN TERRAINE

LEMAY, CURTIS E. (1906–1990), American, major general, commander of the 3d Air Division, U.S. Eighth Air Force. LeMay was born on 15 November 1906 in Cleveland, Ohio, of French-Canadian descent. His military career began as an R.O.T.C. student at Ohio State University in 1924. Appointed a second lieutenant in the field artillery in 1928, he resigned his commission to enter flying training as an enlisted cadet, graduating in 1929; he was recommissioned a second lieutenant in the Air Corps of the Regular Army in January 1930. He flew pursuit (fighter) aircraft until January 1937, when he transferred to B-17s with the 2d Bomb Group at Langley Field, Virginia. His self-taught skills as a navigator led to his participation in a demonstration flight of six B-17s to South America and in the famous B-17 interception of the Italian luxury liner *Rex* seven hundred miles east of New York City (both in 1938). LeMay was promoted to captain in January 1940 and major in March 1941, when he received his first command assignment, the 34th Bomb Group. Promoted to lieutenant colonel in January 1942 and colonel in March, he took command of the 305th Bomb Group in June. This was the organization he led to England in October 1942, and in which he earned his reputation as both an innovative tactician and the most effective combat air commander in the European theater.

LeMay's most important innovations lay in convincing his aircrews that evasive action on the bomb run was not necessary, and in devising the eighteen-ship "combat box" formation, with the aircraft stacked at three different altitudes to provide overlapping fields of fire against enemy fighters. Both changes were soon adopted throughout the Eighth Air Force, and LeMay himself continued, whenever possible, to fly in the lead aircraft of his group. In June 1943 he was commander of the 3d Bomb (later Air) Division, eventually comprising fourteen bomb groups. On 17 August 1943 he led the famed shuttle mission against the Messerschmitt complex at Regensburg, Germany, landing in North Africa. A month later he was advanced to brigadier general and on 2 March 1944, to major general, becoming at age thirty-seven the youngest in the U.S. Army. From then until mid-June he remained commander of the 3d Air Division, which, along with the rest of the Eighth Air Force, devoted the majority of its efforts during May and June to preparing the way for the invasion. LeMay's principal contribution to D-day was in a sense indirect; it lay in the leading role he played in the attainment of such air superiority over Western Europe that the Luftwaffe failed to contest the landings.

Shortly after D-day LeMay was sent to the Pacific, where he commanded the B-29 assault on Japan. His postwar career was unparalleled. Recalled from running the Berlin airlift in 1948, he commanded the Strategic Air Command for nine years, from 1948 to 1957. By then a senior four-star general, he became vice chief of staff, U.S. Air Force (1957–1961), and finally chief of staff, U.S. Air Force (1961–1965). Following his retirement in February 1965, he remained quietly active in air force affairs until his sudden death from heart failure in early October 1990, on the eve of his eighty-fourth birthday.

[See also Eighth Air Force.]

BIBLIOGRAPHY

Coffey, Thomas M. *Iron Eagle: The Turbulent Life of General Curtis LeMay.* 1986.
LeMay, Curtis E., with MacKinlay Kantor. *Mission with LeMay.* 1965.

DAVID MACISAAC

LONGLEY-COOK, E. W. L. (1898–1983), British, captain commanding Fire Support Force K, Task Force G, Gold Beach. A midshipman in 1914, Eric William Longley-Cook served at the Dardanelles in 1915. Commanding the cruiser HMS *Argonaut* (1942–1945), he served in the Home Fleet on Arctic Convoy escort, and as part of Force H in the TORCH landings in North Africa, and at the Salerno landings in September 1943.

Longley-Cook was under the administrative command of the 10th Cruiser Squadron until Force K reached the beachhead, when he came under the orders of Como.

C. E. Douglas-Pennant, Gold Beach. Force K comprised the cruisers HMS *Argonaut, Ajax, Orion,* and *Emerald,* the Dutch gunboat *Flores,* and the fleet destroyers HMS *Grenville, Ulster, Ulysses, Undaunted, Undine, Urania, Urchin, Ursa,* and *Jervis,* and the Hunt-class destroyers HMS *Cattistock, Cottesmore,* and *Pytchley,* with the Polish *Krakowiak.* Force K proved particularly effective in dealing with the German antishipping batteries; *Argonaut* engaged the Vaux-sur-Aure battery and then defensive strong points on the beachhead. The naval historian Capt. Stephen Roskill notes that "return fire from the German batteries was negligible"; only when the troops left the beach did they encounter serious opposition. In addition *Argonaut* served as radar control ship for both Eastern and Western task forces, and as night surface cover to the northwest of the landing area. There was initial difficulty in contacting the air spotter. From the tenth, *Argonaut* moved into the Juno Beach area, for lack of targets. Up to D plus 14 *Argonaut* fired 1,921 5.25-inch rounds, and a further 1,899 down to its withdrawal on D plus 26. Of the total of 4,394 rounds fired, only 684 were used against aircraft. After the mining of *Scylla* on 23 June, Longley-Cook took command of the night surface patrols. On 25–26 June *Argonaut* provided fire support for the Caen offensive.

On 27 June Force K was broken up and placed under Rear Adm. J. W. Rivett-Carnac. Subsequently many ships were withdrawn from the area. On the 30th *Argonaut* was hit by a 155-mm shell that passed through the quarter deck without exploding. In his final report Longley-Cook dwelt on the performance of the guns, fire control, and radar. He was impressed with the surface fire control, but found the antiaircraft control inadequate, and that for the light antiaircraft guns "useless." *Argonaut* formed part of Task Force 87 for the DRAGOON landings in the south of France on 15 August, and in September and October took part in the reoccupation of Greece and the Aegean Islands. In early 1945 Longley-Cook served as temporary chief of staff to Vice Adm. Bernard Rawlings, the afloat commander of the British Pacific Fleet aboard HMS *King George V.*

Longley-Cook returned home to serve as director of plans in 1945, as captain of HMS *Duke of York* in 1948, and as director of naval intelligence (DNI) from 1948 to 1951. He retired as vice admiral in 1951 and became the director of the Fairfield Shipbuilding and Engineering Company. He was an outstanding gunnery specialist with a range of talents, as exemplified by his appointment as DNI.

[See also Ajax, HMS; Task Force G.]

BIBLIOGRAPHY

Roskill, Stephen W. *The Offensive.* Vol. 3, pt. 2, of *The War at Sea, 1939–1945.* 1960.

ANDREW LAMBERT

LOVAT, LORD (1911–), British, brigadier, commander of the 1st Special Service Brigade. Simon ("Shimi") Fraser, educated at Ampleforth College and Magdalene College, Oxford, succeeded his father to the title as the seventeenth Baron Lovat in 1933 and became the twenty-fifth chief of the Scottish clan Fraser. He started military service as a cadet in the Oxford University Cavalry Squadron, described as a *corps élite*, and was commissioned into the Scots Guards in 1932.

His father, the sixteenth baron, had raised the Lovat Scouts in 1899 for service in the Boer War. The spirit of irregular soldiering appealed to the young Lovat, and he joined the Lovat Scouts as soon as war broke out in 1939, thirsting after adventure. When the Commandos were formed in 1940 he was one of the first to volunteer.

He first saw action with No. 4 Commando in the successful raid in the Lofoten Islands off the coast of Norway in March 1941 and led a sharp incursion on the French coast a year later. By August 1942 he had been promoted to lieutenant colonel in charge of the No. 4 Commando at Dieppe, about which he later said, "The raid itself was a disaster, and the changed plan nothing short of suicidal." His leadership and skill, however, were inspiring, and the raid provided lessons that were to save many lives in Normandy.

For Operation OVERLORD Lovat was promoted to raise and command the 1st Special Service Brigade. He was delighted to have Nos. 3, 4, and 6 Army Commandos, but expressed doubts about the quality of the newly formed No. 45 Royal Marine Commando of mixed conscripts and regulars. He quickly appreciated the strategic importance of his task of holding the left flank of the invasion force. His plan was based on the 8th Brigade landing first on Queen Beach (a sector of Sword) and successfully securing a beachhead so that his lightly equipped, highly mobile Commandos could move swiftly inland to cross the Orne River and join up with airborne forces that had been dropped during the night.

Generally the landing went according to plan, although his Commandos spent longer on the beaches than envisaged before striking inland. They joined up with the airborne forces and established defensive positions on the high ground east of the Orne. Lovat came ashore in the early afternoon of D-day, being proceeded by a lone bagpiper. His philosophy of Commandos being an offensive force had to be tempered during the next few days as the brigade defended stoutly against strong German opposition. Lovat, however, urged the Commandos to carry out intensive patrolling, which slowly wrested the initiative from the Germans by D plus 6.

Lovat was severely wounded during the No. 6 Commando's battle for Bréville Wood on 12 June, and he was evacuated, handing over command to Derek Mills-

LORD LOVAT.   Right, with Bertram Ramsay.
IMPERIAL WAR MUSEUM

Roberts. His inspiring leadership and careful planning had ensured that the 1st Special Brigade achieved all that was expected of them against fierce opposition.

After the war Lord Lovat became under secretary of state for foreign affairs in 1945, subsequently returning to Scotland to develop his Highland estates.

[*See also* Commandos; 1st Special Service Brigade.]

BIBLIOGRAPHY

Lovat, Lord. *March Past*. 1978.
Saunders, Hilary St. G. *The Green Beret*. 1949.

DEREK OAKLEY

LUFTFLOTTE 3. *See* Third Air Force.

LUFTLANDE DIVISION. *See* 91st Air Landing Division.

LUFTWAFFE. *See* Air Force, *article on* German Air Force.

LÜTTWITZ, HEINRICH VON (1896–1969), German, major general, commander of the *2d Panzer Division*. Lüttwitz came from an old Prussian military family. He served in World War I after joining the army as a cadet in August 1914. A cavalryman at heart who enjoyed fast maneuvering, he commanded a battalion of cavalry in the 1930s. Freiherr von Lüttwitz was wont to sport a monocle and was rather sturdily built. He could be a very demanding, severe, and ruthless man.

From being a newly promoted lieutenant colonel and battalion commander at the beginning of the war, Lüttwitz rose to divisional commander within a short time. He was severely injured on the second day of the Polish campaign but was able to return to active duty as regimental commander in July 1940. He was given the *20th Panzer Division* in October 1942 and commanded it on the Eastern front until May 1943. Lüttwitz assumed command of the *2d Panzer Division*, then re-forming near Amiens, in February 1944.

Lüttwitz's division was alerted on 6 June, but it was not until the ninth that he was ordered to move toward the Normandy invasion front. Lüttwitz trusted his subordinates sufficiently to risk splitting the division up into small units, making Allied air reconnaissance that much more difficult. The gamble paid off. His units got to the front almost unscathed, albeit at the price of arriving piecemeal and late. The divisional headquarters were established at Lignou, south of Briouze. Because of the late arrival of his armored units, Lüttwitz could not engage in the mobile combat he preferred. Instead, his division had to try to contain British attacks south of Caumont. It held the area for over a week, repelling several minor British assaults and giving way only after coming under extremely heavy air attacks and fire from Allied artillery.

After the attempted overthrow of the Nazi regime in July 1944, Lüttwitz, together with many other generals from the nobility, came under suspicion. SS Oberstgruppenführer "Sepp" Dietrich intervened personally on behalf of Lüttwitz, who had not been involved in the conspiracy. Therefore, Lüttwitz was still in command of the division when it was virtually annihilated in the Falaise pocket, and he was severely injured again. Even so, it was largely due to his skill and energy that any units got out at all. After a speedy recovery, he was given command of the *XLVII Panzer Corps* in September 1944 and took part in the Ardennes offensive.

Lüttwitz, who was promoted to lieutenant general in November 1944, was decorated with the Swords to the Oak Leaves of the Knight's Cross by Grand Admiral Karl Dönitz on 9 May 1945 (he had received the Oak Leaves in February 1944 while in command of the *2d Panzer Division*). Lüttwitz was taken prisoner by the Americans at the beginning of April 1945 and was released in July 1947. He never joined the Bundeswehr (the army of the Federal Republic of Germany) and he died in Neuburg an der Donau in September 1969.

[*See also* 2d Panzer Division.]

BIBLIOGRAPHY

Keilig, Wolf. *Das deutsche Heer 1939–1945. Gliederung, Einsatz, Stellenbesetzung, Abschnitt 211: Die Generalität des Heeres im 2. Weltkrieg 1939–1945 (Truppenoffiziere).* 1956–1970.

Lenfeld, Erwin, and Franz Thomas. *Die Eichenlaubträger 1940–1945.* 1983.

WINFRIED HEINEMANN

M

MCEWEN, CLIFFORD M. (1896–1967), Canadian, air vice marshal, air officer commanding Six (RCAF) Group, Bomber Command. Born in Griswold, Manitoba, a University of Saskatchewan graduate, he enlisted in the Canadian Army in 1916, transferring to the Royal Flying Corps in June 1917. In October 1917 he joined Twenty-Eight Squadron and proceeded with it to the Italian front. There McEwen scored twenty-two victories, winning several decorations. After demobilization in 1919 McEwen flew aerial photographic surveys for Canadian government departments until re-enlisting in the newly established Royal Canadian Air Force (RCAF) in 1924. With the inauguration of the British Commonwealth Air Training Plan in 1939, he commanded Number Three Training Command until March 1941, then headed Number One Group, Eastern Air Command, before proceeding overseas in 1942. On 29 February 1944 he assumed command of the RCAF's Six Group, the only non-British unit in RAF Bomber Command.

Although good-natured, McEwen (nicknamed "Black Mike" because of his swarthy complexion) was also a strict disciplinarian. Aware of Six Group's substandard record during its first operational year, he initiated rigorous drill, navigation, and bombing and fighter affiliation exercises for all squadrons. Despite regulations forbidding senior officers from flying operationally, McEwen carried out seven officially recorded sorties, and at least as many more unofficially. Through the changes he instituted, and by his example, he transformed a group characterized by uncertain morale and indifferent performance into one of Bomber Command's most efficient units. On D-day under McEwen's direction, Six Group carried out 230 sorties in support of the Normandy landings. Between 7 and 16–17 June, when the group resumed its strategic role with a raid on Sterkrade in Germany, its squadrons successfully attacked railway transportation targets in northern France.

McEwen continued to plan and oversee Six Group operations until the war's end, when Six Group was disbanded and withdrawn to Canada. Following retirement from the RCAF in April 1946, he became a consultant to aircraft manufacturers and became a director of Trans-Canada Airlines (now Air Canada), thus continuing his long association with Canadian aviation.

[*See also* Bomber Command; Royal Canadian Air Force; Six Group.]

BIBLIOGRAPHY

Carter, William. *Anglo-Canadian Wartime Relations, 1939–1945: RAF Bomber Command and No. 6 (Canadian) Group.* 1991.
Cosgrove, Edmund. *Canada's Fighting Pilots.* 1965.
Douglas, W. A. B. *The Creation of a National Air Force.* Vol. 2 of *The Official History of the Royal Canadian Air Force.* 1986.
Dunmore, Spencer, and William Carter. *Reap the Whirlwind: The Untold Story of 6 Group, Canada's Bomber Force of World War II.* 1991.
Wise, S. F. *Canadian Airmen and the First World War.* Vol. 1 of *The Official History of the Royal Canadian Air Force.* 1980.

WILLIAM RODNEY

MACKELVIE, JAY W. (1890–1985), American, commanding general, U.S. 90th Infantry Division. Jay W. MacKelvie was born in Esmond, South Dakota, on 23 September 1890. He enlisted in the army in World War I, was commissioned a second lieutenant in the cavalry, and participated in the Saint-Mihiel offensive in 1918. Between the wars he was a student and instructor at various army schools, and after lengthy service with the War Department General Staff became artillery commander of the 85th Infantry Division in April 1942. In January 1944, after the 90th Infantry Division had arrived at Fort Dix, New Jersey, to prepare for early movement overseas, MacKelvie relieved Maj. Gen. Henry Terrell, who had commanded the division since its activation on 25 March 1942.

At Fort Dix General MacKelvie quickly gained a reputation as a stickler for protocol, concentrating not on combat readiness but on disciplinary statistics (i.e., venereal disease and AWOL rates). He remained aloof from his personal staff and his major subordinate commanders.

Once in England he showed poor judgment by relieving Col. John Sheehy, the experienced and much-admired commander of the 357th Infantry Regiment, replacing him with Col. P. D. Ginder, a bombastic officer who was ruinous to the 357th in combat and was himself relieved on his third day of combat command (12 June). Perhaps most damaging to the men of the division was MacKelvie's preinvasion pep talk, personally delivered to each unit. Read in an uncertain voice, ineptly phrased, and filled with clichés such as "don't fire 'til you see the whites of their eyes," the talk damaged confidence in his leadership and generally lowered morale.

During the 90th Division's entry into combat, on arriving off Utah Beach on D plus 2 MacKelvie showed personal timidity by requiring his aides to secure him with a safety rope as he climbed down the debarkation ladder of the transport. Once ashore he consistently ignored the advice not only of his staff, but also of his two superb assistants, Brig. Gen. Sam Williams (assistant division commander) and Brig. Gen. John Devine (division artillery commander). He nitpicked important division attack orders to achieve "perfection" and thus delayed the receipt of the orders by his troops. This resulted in piecemeal, uncoordinated, and very costly actions that caused unnecessary casualties and further damaged unit morale and confidence. Early on 12 June, for instance, MacKelvie traveled to the 357th Infantry command post, discovered that the troops were not attacking, and loudly criticized the regimental and battalion commanders for their failures. While this was going on, a runner arrived with the very order that MacKelvie was castigating his subordinates for not executing. Even so, he did not delay the execution time for the order. Later that day the VII Corps commander, Gen. J. Lawton Collins, relieved MacKelvie. This action was warranted by every reasonable criterion.

MacKelvie lasted in combat only four days. While his tenure was brief, his impact on his inexperienced division was most damaging. Never was a single, well-coordinated attack launched. Instead the division's strength was dissipated in hurried, fragmentary attacks that had no chance of success against the stout, seasoned German defense of the *91st Air Landing Division* and *5th Parachute Division* in that difficult hedgerow country.

MacKelvie became commander of the 80th Infantry Division artillery in September 1944. In June 1945 he returned to the United States to command the V Corps artillery at Fort Jackson, South Carolina. He died on 5 December 1985.

[*See also* 90th Infantry Division.]

BIBLIOGRAPHY

Colby, John. *War from the Ground Up: The 90th Division in World War II.* 1991.

FRANK NORRIS, ORWIN TALBOTT, and
EAMES YATES

MACMILLAN, G. H. A. (1897–1986), British, major general, commander of the 15th (Scottish) Infantry Division. MacMillan was known throughout the army as "the Babe" because of his youthful appearance when he was a young officer in the Argyll and Sutherland Highlanders. He was commanding a brigade in Sicily in the 51st (Highland) Division when ordered home to take over the 15th (Scottish) Division in August 1943. Inspired by his leadership and training, the division was to earn a reputation throughout the campaign in northwestern Europe as one of the best divisions in the British Second Army.

As part of the VIII Corps, MacMillan's division was a reserve formation for the landings in Normandy. Not all its men arrived on French soil until 23 June, D plus 17, some units having been delayed even more than anticipated by the storms in the Channel from 19 to 22 June.

MacMillan led his division with skill in the VIII Corps's first battle during Operation EPSOM (26 to 30 June), aimed to form a bridgehead over the Odon River west of Caen. His division was the leading element of the corps and bore the brunt of the fighting and the casualties. He himself was wounded on 4 August while advancing south from Caumont toward Vire during BLUECOAT, another VIII Corps operation. By November 1944 he was back in Europe commanding the 49th West Riding Division. In March 1945 he returned to the 51st (Highland) Division to assume command following the death of Maj. Gen. T. G. Rennie.

[*See also* 15th (Scottish) Infantry Division.]

BIBLIOGRAPHY

Baynes, John. *The Forgotten Victor: General Sir O'Connor, KT, GCB, DSO, MC.* 1989.
Martin, H. G. *The History of the 15th Scottish Division, 1939–1945.* 1948.

JOHN BAYNES

MCNAIR, LESLEY J. (1883–1944), American, general, commander, U.S. Army ground forces. Lesley J. McNair was born on 23 May 1883 in Verndale, Minnesota. He entered the U.S. Military Academy at West Point in 1900, graduated in the top 10 percent of his 1904 class, and was commissioned a second lieutenant in the Artillery Corps.

Prior to World War I he served mainly with the 4th Field Artillery. He participated in the Funston Expedition to Vera Cruz, Mexico (1914), in the Punitive Expedition into Mexico (1916–1917), and went to France with the 1st Infantry Division in 1917. He then served in Gen. John J. Pershing's General Headquarters (GHQ), American Expeditionary Force (AEF). In October 1918 at age thirty-five, he became the youngest brigadier general in the AEF. For his work as senior artillery officer in the GHQ Training Section of the AEF, he was awarded the first of three Distinguished Service Medals.

Between the world wars he served at military schools and on staff assignments. As war loomed, Gen. George C. Marshall, U.S. Army Chief of Staff, who recognized McNair's special abilities and experience in organizing and training, made him commandant of the Command and Staff School at Fort Leavenworth, Kansas, with a directive to bring the old-fashioned curriculum up to date. This he did, but Marshall soon assigned him a much more important task: supervising the organization and training of all the field forces within the United States. It was under McNair's command that a handful of regulars, a smattering of national guardsmen, and millions of raw recruits were transformed into the greatest army the United States had ever fielded. The success of the American arms in World War II was due in large part to General McNair's insistence on realistic training.

Never one to spend much time in his headquarters, he visited his troops frequently. He was wounded in North Africa while observing combat there. In July 1944 he went to England on temporary duty to take the place of Gen. George S. Patton, Jr., as the commander of the mythical First Army Group, which was intended to make the Germans believe the Allies' main landings would be in the Pas de Calais. Later he visited the front to see combat at close range and on 25 July 1944 was killed near Saint-Lô by American bombs, which fell short during the preparatory strikes for the breakout from the lodgment area of the VII Corps. He was the first three-star U.S. Army general to die in combat. He was promoted posthumously to full general.

BIBLIOGRAPHY

Greenfield, Kent Roberts, Robert R. Palmer, and Bell I. Wiley. *The Army Ground Forces: The Organization of Ground Combat Troops.* U.S. Army in World War II: The European Theater of Operations. 1947.

Palmer, Robert R., Bell I. Wiley, and William R. Keast. *The Army Ground Forces: The Procurement and Training of Ground Combat Troops.* U.S. Army in World War II: The European Theater of Operations. 1948.

Whitaker, John T. "Lieutenant General Lesley James McNair." In *These Are the Generals.* 1943.

JAMES LAWTON COLLINS, JR.

MAHLMANN, PAUL (1892–1963), German, major general commanding the *353d Infantry Division.* Paul Mahlmann, a pastor's son, was born on 10 December 1892 near Erfurt in Gispersleben, Saxony. He entered the German army as a cadet in 1907 and in January 1914 became a lieutenant in the *98th Infantry Regiment* at Metz. During World War I he served as a platoon and company commander, then as a battalion and regiment adjutant, and in 1917 was promoted to first lieutenant. At the war's end Mahlmann became adjutant of his peacetime unit, then in April 1919 joined the *Freikorps* of Gen. Georg Maercker, which put down Sparticist revolts in central Germany and protected the Weimar National Assembly. In the mid-1920s Mahlmann was involved primarily in troop-level staff work. After a tour as company commander with the *16th Infantry Regiment,* he resigned as a captain in 1925, but returned to active duty in February 1934 and in May was promoted to major.

At the outbreak of war, Mahlmann, now a colonel, commanded the *181st Infantry Regiment.* A division commander, in November 1941 he was awarded the German Cross in gold. During 1942 Mahlmann commanded two recruiting centers for officer candidates. Then, until early September 1943, he commanded first the *147th Reserve Division* and then the *39th Infantry Division.* Assigned to command the newly organized *353d Infantry Division,* in June 1944 he was promoted to major general. This division fought in Brittany in June and July 1944 with the LXXIV and then the LXXXIV Corps. In August he led his division out of the Falaise pocket, with about half the survivors escaping capture. Ill at the war's end, Mahlmann was an American prisoner of war from April 1945 to mid-1947. Before and after a term in the U.S. Army Labor Service from 1950 to 1952, he was active as a journalist. He died in Munich in 1963.

[See also 353d Infantry Division.]

BIBLIOGRAPHY

Ose, Dieter. *Entscheidung im Westen: Der Oberbefehlshaber West und die Abwehr der alliierten Invasion.* Beiträge zur Militär- und Kriegsgeschichte. 1982.

GEORGE MEYER
Translated from German by Amy Hackett

MALOY, USS. *Maloy* (DE-791) was the flagship of Como. Campbell D. Edgar, commander of Task Force 126, Follow-up Force B, and headquarters ship for Maj. Gen. Charles H. Gerhardt, commander of the U.S. 29th

Infantry Division. Built in 1943 and named for a Navy Cross winner killed at Guadalcanal, *Maloy* was a Buckley-class destroyer escort. Specifically designed for antisubmarine warfare, it lacked the speed and firepower of a destroyer, but was highly maneuverable and carried submarine detection gear and a heavy battery of depth charge projectors, including a forward-firing Hedgehog. The 306-foot vessel also mounted three 21-inch torpedo tubes, and three 3-inch, four quad-mounted 1.1-inch, and eight 20-mm guns. It carried a crew of 186.

Under Lt. Cmdr. Frederic D. Kellogg, *Maloy* sailed from Plymouth on 6 June and arrived with its convoy off Omaha Beach at H plus nine, as scheduled. As command ship, it coordinated Force B's initial landings, which were postponed by one hour because of the chaotic situation on the beach. General Gerhardt went ashore at 1705, maintaining close contact with *Maloy* through the morning of 7 June to request landings of his regimental combat teams. *Maloy* also controlled the unloading of Force B's transports and conveyed Commodore Edgar to shipboard meetings with Admirals Kirk, Hall, and Moon. It participated in numerous antiaircraft barrages, with mixed outcomes: on the night of 6 June *Maloy* shot down a Dornier Do 217, later rescuing its pilot, but on 9 June it lost four wounded, most likely by 20-mm fire from nearby ships in the crowded anchorage. On 11 June, with the dissolution of Force B, *Maloy* sailed for Portland, England.

For the rest of the war, *Maloy* patrolled the Normandy coast and the German-held Channel Islands, hunting submarines and raiding shipping in conjunction with American PT boats. Awarded one battle star, it served until its decommissioning in 1965 and was later scrapped.

[*See also* Edgar, Campbell D.]

BIBLIOGRAPHY

Commander Task Force 126 [C. D. Edgar]. Operation _____ [name not supplied]: Invasion of Northern France, June 6–11, 1944. Serial 299 of 22 June 1944. Operational Archives, Naval Historical Center, Washington, D.C.

Maloy, USS. Revised Form for Reporting A.A. Action by Surface Ships. Operational Archives, Naval Historical Center, Washington, D.C.

Mooney, James L. ed. *Dictionary of American Naval Fighting Ships*. Vol. 4, 1969.

STEVEN J. TIRONE

MAQUIS. *See* French Resistance.

MARCKS, ERICH (1891–1944), German, lieutenant general commanding the *LXXXIV Corps*. Erich Marcks was born on 6 June 1891 in Schöneberg in the Mark

ERICH MARCKS.   BIBLIOTHEK FÜR ZEITGESCHICHTE, STUTTGART

Brandenburg (now Berlin-Schöneberg). Both his parents were Prussians, but his mother came from an aristocratic officer family, and his father from a Huguenot family in Magdeburg. The senior Marcks, also Erich, was a professor in modern history and a prominent Bismarck scholar at the University of Berlin and elsewhere. The son graduated from secondary school, then studied law and philosophy in Freiburg.

In December 1911 Marcks became a lieutenant in the *9th Field Artillery Regiment*, with which he fought in World War I until he received severe facial injuries. Thereafter he was active mainly as an adjutant until 1917, when he was transferred to the General Staff. There, a captain, he first became involved with issues of military policy, and also met Maj. Kurt von Schleicher, who later played an important role in the Reichswehr and finally became chancellor of the terminal Weimar Republic.

After the war was lost, Marcks served in various paramilitary *Freikorps* protecting the new democratic government against unrest. He then entered the new Reichswehr, where he worked on basic issues in the Armed Forces Ministry under Schleicher and served with several units. In

1929 Marcks returned to the Armed Forces Ministry as head of the press section, and in 1932 became civilian press chief with the rank of ministerial director under Chancellor Franz von Papen, behind whom Schleicher pulled the strings. Marcks retained this post under Schleicher's two-month turn as chancellor, which failed to prevent Hitler's seizure of power in 1933. (Schleicher himself was murdered by the Nazis during the "Röhm Putsch" in 1934.)

Marcks rejoined the army as a major in April 1933. His republican past kept him from employment in a ministry or central General Staff position, but he rose within the troop structure and staffs. From 1933 to 1935 he was a battalion commander in Münster, then in 1935 became chief of the *VIII Army Corps* general staff in Breslau; as a brigadier general, he participated with this unit in the Polish campaign in 1939. In July 1940 Marcks was assigned to draw up deployment plans for an attack on the Soviet Union (Operation BARBAROSSA). The commanding officer of the *101st Jäger Division* after December 1940, in June 1941 he was seriously wounded on the fifth day of the invasion, losing his left leg. Promoted to major general, in March 1942 he was given the first of several army commands in France. In August 1943 he was assigned to the *LXXXIV Corps* in Normandy, with headquarters at Saint-Lô. This corps was responsible for some 400 kilometers (240 miles) of coastline on the Cotentin Peninsula from the Orne Estuary near Caen to the Gulf of Saint-Malo—the Allied landing zone on 6 June 1944.

In the great war game of Field Marshal Gerd von Rundstedt, Commander in Chief West, in February 1944 Marcks, playing the role of the Allies, projected an invasion on the Calvados coast, where it later in fact occurred. Because of Germany's military weaknesses, he argued for emptying southern France of troops in order to conserve forces, and then abandoning the rigid coastal defense plan to concentrate counterattack units between the Brittany and Cotentin peninsulas. This went against Hitler's orders, so he could not prevail. But he complied with, and carried out to the letter, the pioneer- and technology-based static-defense tactics of Field Marshal Erwin Rommel, his superior, commander of *Army Group B*. He got along well with Rommel, who was a difficult commander.

On 6 June Marcks's corps stood in the center of the landing operation. The resources available to him did not allow him to push the Allied armies back to the ocean. The only armored unit in his region was the *21st Panzer Division*, which after some delay was placed under his command. He personally led the only direct counterattack, by the *192d Panzer Regiment* from northwest of Caen toward the beach at Luc-sur-mer, which had to be broken off at the onset of darkness. While the *1st SS Panzer Corps* was being inserted into the right wing of the *LXXXIV Army Corps* to no avail, Marcks concentrated on fighting the Americans on both sides of the Vire Estuary. The lack of reserve forces made any operational counterattacks impossible; only a cordoning off could be attempted. On one of his customary visits to the frontline, Marcks, who never spared himself, was fatally wounded by a low-flying air attack on 12 June near Saint-Lô.

[*See also* LXXXIV Corps.]

BIBLIOGRAPHY

Jacobsen, Otto. *Erich Marcks. Soldat und Gelehrter.* 1971.
Marcks, Erich. Papers. File 6/269. Bundesarchiv-Militärarchiv, Freiburg, Germany.

REINHARD STUMPF

MARSHALL, GEORGE (1880–1959), American general, Chief of Staff of the U.S. Army. Born on 31 December 1880 in Uniontown, Pennsylvania, George Catlett Marshall graduated from Virginia Military Institute and took his oath as second lieutenant of infantry on 3 February 1902. He served in the Philippines and Oklahoma Territory, and studied and taught at Fort Leavenworth.

In World War I Marshall went to Europe as a planning officer of the 1st Infantry Division, the first American

GEORGE MARSHALL.   NATIONAL ARCHIVES

division to be sent to France, and was chief of operations of the U.S. First Army in planning the final operations of the war. His postwar career included tours of duty in China and Europe, five years as chief of instruction at the Army Infantry School, Fort Benning, assignments with the National Guard and Civilian Conservation Corps, and a short stint as chief of war plans in the War Department, then as deputy chief of staff. He became chief of staff a few hours after Hitler invaded Poland in September 1939.

As head of the U.S. Army and its air forces during World War II, Marshall increased the forces from 200,000 to more than 8.3 million, directing their arming, equipping, and training. As a member of the U.S. Joint Chiefs of Staff, he met with Franklin D. Roosevelt, Winston Churchill, and the Allied chiefs of staff to devise the strategy of the war. As executive of the Joint Chiefs, he issued directives for the use of American troops in Europe under General Dwight D. Eisenhower.

Marshall was the strongest proponent of the cross-Channel strategy to defeat Germany, leading American opposition to peripheral approaches favored by the British. He lost to the British as regards the invasions of North Africa, Sicily, and Italy, but at the Teheran Conference in 1943 he won his battle for the cross-Channel attack.

At the Allied Conference in Quebec in August 1943 (QUADRANT), Roosevelt had indicated that he wanted Marshall to command the Allied forces in the invasion. But at Cairo in late 1943, increasingly aware of his dependence on Marshall's counsel, he hedged on his commitment by asking Marshall what command he wanted. When Marshall replied that his wishes should not be considered, Roosevelt remarked that he could not sleep at night with Marshall out of Washington. The command was then given to Eisenhower.

Marshall could be content. The forces that he had built would be commanded by many who bore his mark, including his own former chief of war plans, Eisenhower, whom he had sent to London in 1942 and a former member of his office staff, Walter Bedell Smith, whom he had picked as Eisenhower's chief of staff. More than 160 future generals had been at Fort Benning while Marshall was assistant commandant there, including three key men at Normandy: Omar Bradley, commander of the U.S. First Army; J. Lawton Collins, commander of the U.S. VII Corps; and Matthew Ridgway, commander of the 82d Airborne Division.

After receiving word from Eisenhower that the invasion would go ahead and that paratroopers would leave the United Kingdom at 2300 on 5 June, Marshall passed that information to Henry Stimson, Secretary of War. As reports continued to come in from Eisenhower, Marshall left for England on the morning of 8 June after attending dinner at the White House the evening before. Marshall took an overnight train with Churchill and others from London to Portsmouth, where they were met by Eisenhower. On the destroyer USS *Thompson*, then a submarine chaser and finally a DUKW amphibious truck, Marshall finally set foot on Omaha Beach.

As victory in Europe became certain, Eisenhower wrote, on 8 May 1945, "Our army and our people have never been so deeply indebted to any other soldier." Churchill said of Marshall, "He is the true organizer of victory." He became general of the army on 16 December 1944, a rank that was made permanent in 1949.

On 19 November Marshall submitted his resignation. A week later President Harry S. Truman read the citation for Marshall's second Oak Leaf Cluster: "In a war unparalleled in magnitude and in horror, millions of Americans gave their country outstanding service. General of the Army George C. Marshall gave it victory."

Marshall then spent a year trying to secure a truce between warring Nationalist and Communist Chinese. He served as secretary of state from January 1947 to early 1949. In 1950, after serving as president of the American Red Cross, Marshall accepted Truman's offer of the secretaryship of the Department of Defense, but retired again in September 1951. He had been savagely attacked by Sen. Joseph R. McCarthy before his retirement. He was awarded the Nobel Prize for Peace in 1953.

Marshall died on 16 October 1959 and was buried at Arlington National Cemetery.

[See also Roosevelt, Franklin D.]

BIBLIOGRAPHY

Bland, Larry, ed. *Papers of George C. Marshall*. 3 vols. 1981–.

Marshall, George C. *Memoirs of My Service in the World War*. 1976.

Pogue, Forrest C. *George C. Marshall*. 4 vols. 1963–1987.

Pogue, Forrest C. *The Supreme Command*. U.S. Army in World War II: The European Theater of Operations. 1954.

FORREST C. POGUE

MAUCHENHEIM, THEODOR FREIHERR VON. See Bechtolsheim, Theodor.

MAURITIUS, HMS.

A Colony-class light cruiser with a weight of 8,000 tons and a speed of 30 knots, and armed with twelve 6-inch and eight 4-inch guns, *Mauritius* was built by Swan Hunter, Wallsend and completed in 1941. *Mauritius* served with the Eastern Fleet in 1941 and 1942, then supported Operation HUSKY, the Sicily landings, on 8 July 1943, and Operation BAYTOWN, the Calabrian landings, on 31 August 1943. After serving at Salerno and Anzio, *Mauritius* was recalled from the

Mediterranean in May 1944 to be fitted with a Type 650 missile jammer. As part of Task Force S, *Mauritius* was to provide fire support for Sword Beach. It was the flagship of Fire Support Force D (Rear Adm. W. R. Patterson) and the 2d Cruiser Squadron.

Arriving off Ouistreham at 0515 on 6 June, *Mauritius* engaged enemy small craft, sinking one trawler. Its main role on D-day was to support the British 6th Airborne Division east of the Orne River, with whom it proved difficult to establish contact. This formation later recorded that without naval gunfire support over a period of several days, they would have been wiped out. At 1725 *Mauritius* fired on batteries at Houlgate, and subsequently on troop concentrations and armored forces. Just missed by bombs at 0025 on 13 June, it sustained slight damage. On 13–15 June it took part in the attack on Caen and Cuverville, then later supported the attack on Caen up to 21 June. On 18 June bombs fell close astern. Rear Admiral Patterson struck his flag on the 21st at Portsmouth. With Rear Adm. J. W. Rivett-Carnac's Bombardment Force in July, *Mauritius* supported the Anglo-Canadian advance on Caen. On 14–15 and 22–23 August it engaged German convoys escaping from the Bay of Biscay. It then rejoined the Home Fleet and on 28 January 1945 engaged German destroyers off Bergen. It was broken up in 1961.

[*See also* Eastern Task Force; Patterson, W. R.; Task Force S.]

BIBLIOGRAPHY

London. Public Record Office. Ship Log Books, HMS *Mauritius*, ADM 53/119862-3.
Raven, Alan, and John Roberts. *British Cruisers of World War Two*. 1980.

ANDREW LAMBERT

MC-. *Names beginning with this prefix are alphabetized as if spelled Mac.*

MEDALS. [*This entry includes separate discussions of Allied and German medals.*]

Allied Medals

The Medal of Honor and Victoria Cross are the premier military decorations for heroism and bravery of the United States and Great Britain, respectively. A number of American, British, and Commonwealth soldiers received their nation's highest award for unmitigated gallantry in Normandy.

Shortly after the outbreak of the American Civil War (1861–1865), the need to recognize soldiers who had distinguished themselves in battle became evident. The best precedent in American history for honoring soldiers had been the creation of the Purple Heart by General George Washington in 1782, as a decoration for "singular meritorious action." Three soldiers were awarded the Purple Heart in 1783. In 1847, during the war with Mexico, the Certificate of Merit, signed by the president but without an accompanying medal, was authorized for award to deserving soldiers.

The Medal of Honor for U.S. Navy and Marine Corps enlisted men was approved by President Abraham Lincoln on 21 December 1861, and for U.S. Army soldiers on 12 July 1862. This law was amended on 3 March 1863 and made retroactive to the beginning of the Civil War to make officers eligible for the award. On 25 March 1863 the first Medals of Honor were awarded "in the name of the Congress of the United States"; as a result, this decoration has been erroneously called the "Congressional Medal of Honor." The Medal of Honor is awarded for bravery in action involving actual conflict with the enemy, and then only to those who distinguish themselves by conspicuous gallantry, intrepidity, or self-sacrifice "above and beyond the call of duty."

As of 1993, 3,408 Medals of Honor had been awarded. Of these awards, 293 were awarded to U.S. Army soldiers during World War II, including ten in Normandy from D-day to D plus 12. The heavy involvement of the U.S. Army in Normandy and the ferocity of the fighting there is indicated by the fact that eight of those ten Medals of Honor were awarded posthumously.

Great Britain had no recognized gallantry medal prior to the Crimean War (1854–1856), when individual acts of heroism seemed to make such an award necessary. Queen Victoria, at the suggestion of the Prince Consort, instituted by royal warrant on 29 January 1856 the decoration that bears her name. The queen's interest in the award was clearly shown when she personally invested 62 of the 111 Crimean War recipients at a parade held on 26 June in Hyde Park. Upon its institution, the Victoria Cross was unique in that "neither rank, nor long service, nor wounds, nor any other circumstances or condition whatsoever, save the merit of conspicuous bravery," served as the criteria for its award. Deserving individuals were selected by ballot from among those present in a unit that had been engaged in an action of outstanding gallantry.

The Victoria Cross, of which some 1,351 (and three bars, or second awards) had been awarded as of 1993, was traditionally made from bronze of cannons captured in the Crimea. One hundred eighty-two Victoria Crosses (83 of them posthumously) were awarded during World War II. Two were awarded for gallantry in action in Normandy from D-day to D plus 12: one to a member of the Green Howards, and the second, posthumously, to a Royal

Canadian Air Force warrant officer.

Other decorations were awarded to soldiers in Normandy for extraordinary heroism that was not thought to justify their nation's highest honor. U.S. soldiers, including officers, were also eligible, in descending order of precedence, for the Distinguished Service Cross, Silver Star, and Bronze Star Medal. The reinstituted Purple Heart was awarded to those killed or wounded by enemy action. British and Commonwealth officers could receive the Distinguished Service Order (generally field-grade officers) and the Military Cross (usually company-grade officers); other ranks could be awarded the Distinguished Conduct Medal and the Military Medal.

Medal of Honor Winners, D-day to D plus 12 (asterisk indicates posthumous award):

1. Barrett, Carlton W. Private, U.S. Army, 18th Infantry Regiment, 1st Infantry Division. 6 June 1944, near Saint-Laurent-sur-Mer.
* 2. Butts, John E. Second lieutenant, U.S. Army, E Company, 60th Infantry Regiment, 9th Infantry Division. 14, 16, 23 June 1944, Normandy.
* 3. Cole, Robert G. Lieutenant colonel, U.S. Army, 101st Airborne Division. 11 June 1944, Carentan.
* 4. DeFranzo, Arthur F. Staff sergeant, U.S. Army, 1st Infantry Division. 10 June 1944, Vaubadon.
* 5. DeGlopper, Charles N. Private first class, U.S. Army, C Company, 325th Glider Infantry Regiment, 82d Airborne Division. 9 June 1944, Merderet River at La Fière.
6. Ehlers, Walter D. Staff sergeant, U.S. Army, 18th Infantry Regiment, 1st Infantry Division. 9–10 June 1944, Goville.
* 7. Monteith, Jimmie W., Jr. First lieutenant, U.S. Army, 16th Infantry Regiment, 1st Infantry Division. 6 June 1944, Colleville-sur-Mer.
* 8. Peregory, Frank D. Technical sergeant, U.S. Army, K Company, 116th Infantry Regiment, 29th Infantry Division. 8 June 1944, Grandcamp.
* 9. Pinder, John J., Jr. Technical sergeant, U.S. Army, 16th Infantry Regiment, 1st Infantry Division. 6 June 1944, Colleville-sur-Mer.
* 10. Roosevelt, Theodore, Jr. Brigadier general, U.S. Army, 4th Infantry Division. 6 June 1944, Normandy.

Victoria Cross Winners, D-day to D plus 12:

1. Hollis, Stanley E. Company sergeant-major, The Green Howards (Alexandra Princess of Wales's Own Yorkshire Regiment). 6 June 1944, Normandy.

* 2. Mynarski, Andrew C. Warrant Officer II, No. 419 Squadron, Royal Canadian Air Force. 12 June 1944, near Cambrai.

[*See articles on medal winners listed herein.*]

BIBLIOGRAPHY

Dorling, H. Tapprell. *Ribbons and Medals*. 1916. Reprinted, 1974.
Kerrigan, Evans. *American Medals and Decorations*. 1990.
Lucas-Phillips, C. E. *Victoria Cross Battles of the Second World War*. 1973.
McDowell, Charles P. *Military and Naval Decorations of the United States*. 1984.
Register of the Victoria Cross. 1981.
Smyth, John. *The Story of the Victoria Cross*. 1963.
U.S. Congress. Senate. Committee on Veterans' Affairs. *Medal of Honor Recipients, 1863–1978*. 96th Cong., 1st sess., 1979. S. Committee Print No. 3.

HAROLD E. RAUGH, JR.

German Medals

The Iron Cross (*Eisernes Kreuz*) was established in March 1813 by King Friedrich Wilhelm III of Prussia to recognize acts of bravery in the German Wars of Liberation (1813–1815). Limited originally to Prussian recipients, the Iron Cross was reestablished and made open to all Germans at the outbreak of the Franco-Prussian in 1870 and was again reinstituted at the outbreak of World War I. The award consisted of four levels of distinction: Second Class, First Class, Grand Cross, and Breast Star, the latter being awarded only twice, to Field Marshal Prince Blücher von Wahlstatt in 1815 and to Field Marshal Paul von Hindenburg in 1918.

On 1 September 1939 Adolf Hitler reestablished the decoration of the Iron Cross and added an additional level of distinction, the Knight's Cross (*Ritterkreuz*) of the Iron Cross, which fell between the Iron Cross First Class and the Grand Cross (the latter awarded only to Reichsmarschall Hermann Goering in 1940). By the time of the Normandy invasion, Hitler had added three additional levels of distinction to the Knight's Cross, consisting in ascending order of the Knight's Cross with Oak Leaves (3 June 1940), the Knight's Cross with Oak Leaves and Swords (21 June 1941), and the Knight's Cross with Oak Leaves, Swords, and Diamonds (15 July 1941). During the war, awards of the varying degrees of Iron Cross ranged from an estimated three million recipients of the Iron Cross Second Class to 159 winners of the Knight's Cross with Oak Leaves and Swords, and a mere twenty-seven winners of the Knight's Cross with Oak Leaves, Swords, and Diamonds.

It is impossible to determine with any degree of accuracy the number of awards given during the period 6 to

U.S. ARMY MEDICS.   Giving emergency care on Utah Beach on D-day.   HULTON DEUTSCH

18 June 1944, as approval and formal bestowing of awards were often months late in coming. Nevertheless, the summer of 1944 brought a dramatic increase in the awarding of Knight's Crosses of all levels. Among those recipients of the Knight's Cross with Oak Leaves and Swords whose awards were clearly linked to the opening phases of the Normandy campaign were the Tiger tank ace SS Obersturmführer Michael Wittmann, for his action at Villers-Bocage, and Maj. Gen. Fritz Bayerlein, for his leadership of the *Panzer Lehr Division*. The only Diamond recipient from the opening phases of the campaign was SS Obergruppenführer Joseph ("Sepp") Dietrich, in recognition of his leadership of the *1st SS Panzer Corps* at Caen.

BIBLIOGRAPHY

Sawicki, James A. *Nazi Decorations and Medals, 1933–1945.* 1958.
Williamson, Gordon. *Nights of the Iron Cross: A History, 1939–1945.* 1987.

CHARLES S. THOMAS

MEDICAL SUPPORT. [*This entry includes separate discussions of American, British, and German medical support during the Normandy invasion.*]

American Medical Support

Health services support for the Normandy landings was the single greatest challenge to face the U.S. Army Medical Department in its entire history. Planning for support of the operation began almost as soon as planning for the invasion itself, and continued until the landings began.

During the landings, medical support was brought ashore in echelons corresponding to the number and type of troops landed. Landing with the initial assault forces were the companies' combat medics, followed shortly thereafter by their supporting battalion aid stations. About two hours later they were joined by their regimental aid stations and a medical collecting company from the divisional medical battalion supporting that regiment. As the separate regimental beachheads consolidated into divisional beachheads, a medical collecting company from the engineer special brigade supporting the landing arrived and began receiving patients from the divisional collecting companies. This allowed the clearing companies from the divisional medical battalions to move directly inland and establish themselves, rather than setting up on the beaches and moving again a short time later. Finally, the hospitals, ambulance companies, and other medical units of the corps and First Army's medical support system landed and became operational.

While this system was developing over the beachheads, the medical clearing companies of the 82d and 101st airborne divisions landed by glider and began operation in their divisional airheads, assisted by teams of surgeons from the First Army's auxiliary surgical group who had landed with them. Unlike the system on the beaches, which focused on treating patients and evacuating them, the medical companies of the airborne divisions treated their patients and held them until the divisions landing on the beaches linked up with them, at which time these patients, too, were evacuated.

The navy had the responsibility for providing all medical care up to the high water mark on the beach, and for receiving patients from the army, although the army was also responsible for loading patients on returning landing craft. The primary means of moving patients by sea were the LSTs (Landing Ships, Tank). Since the medical accommodations aboard LSTs were austere, 100 of them were modified to provide a small operating facility at the back of the tank deck, and special brackets were mounted on the bulkheads of that deck to allow them to transport up to 147 patients on litters. Each of these modified LSTs was provided with two physicians and thirty medics, most on loan from the Third Army.

Once the LSTs returned to England, patients were unloaded by army units, usually ones on loan to the Services of Supply from the Third Army, and were moved to field medical facilities near the ports. There they were examined, provided additional treatment if necessary, and then sent to general or station hospitals farther inland. To make the best use of limited assets, physicians in some medical specialties had been moved between facilities to create specialty centers; patients arriving from France were sent to the facility that could best care for their injuries. Similar field medical units were established near

REGIMENTAL AID POST.   IMPERIAL WAR MUSEUM

A MAKESHIFT HOSPITAL IN NORMANDY.   IMPERIAL WAR MUSEUM

the major airfields in England, so that once air evacuation from France began, patients arriving at the airfields were handled in a similar manner.

One area of special concern was resupplying the medics on the beachhead. To ensure that they had sufficient medical supplies in the initial landings, each of the first 200 LSTs to land was provided with a special package of high-demand medical supplies such as litters, blankets, plasma, and field dressings. The crews of the LSTs would dump the packages on the beachhead, where medics had easy access to them. As the beaches became secure and combat moved inland, teams from the medical depot companies collected the supplies that remained, which then served as their initial depot stockage.

As the beachheads stabilized, the first hospitals began to come ashore. The first to arrive was the 42d Field Hospital, landing on Utah Beach late in the day on D plus 2 and becoming operational on D plus 4. The first hospital to land on Omaha was the 13th Field Hospital. Originally scheduled to land on D-day, it finally came ashore on D plus 2 and became operational on D plus 3. Airfields in the beachhead were rapidly secured, and the first patients to be evacuated by air left for England on D plus 4, ten

days ahead of schedule. The number of patients moved by air rapidly increased, and by the end of July 1944 virtually every patient transported from the Continent to Great Britain would be flown.

By the end of June, the medical force that began as a few medics wading ashore with the first wave had grown to a force of some 30,760 personnel: 1,994 physicians, 705 nurses, 458 dentists, 10 veterinarians, 493 Medical Administrative Corps officers, 6 Sanitary Corps officers, 64 warrant officers, 27,029 enlisted personnel, and a lone hospital dietician. Together they operated 10,111 beds in 17 hospitals, along with their associated evacuation, preventive medicine, medical logistics, and command and control facilities.

BIBLIOGRAPHY

Cosmos, Graham A., and Albert E. Cowdrey. *The Medical Department: Medical Service in the European Theater of Operations.* 1992.

Dowling, George B. *Special Report to the Chief of the Bureau of Medicine and Surgery, U.S. Navy, of United States Naval Medical Service in the Invasion of Normandy, 6 June 1944.* 1945.

DONALD E. HALL

REGIMENTAL AID POST.   After battle at Lingevres, British troops and German prisoners receiving treatment.

IMPERIAL WAR MUSEUM

British Medical Support

The medical services of the British forces in Normandy performed an essential role in receiving and treating casualties and evacuating the more serious cases to be treated in Britain. The army's medical support was mostly provided by the Royal Army Medical Corps (RAMC), which together with specialized branches formed Army Medical Services (AMS). The Royal Air Force (RAF) and Royal Navy had their own medical services, which cooperated closely with those of the army, as did the Canadian medical services.

British medical arrangements in Normandy benefited greatly from experience gained in previous campaigns. Extensive preparations had begun in 1942. Allocated to the invasion were medical units of various kinds. On the eve of D-day it was estimated that they would have to handle 6,900 cases from British and Canadian forces in the initial phase of the operation.

On D-day and in the initial period of the invasion it was planned that all casualties were to be evacuated to Britain except those whose lives would be endangered by such a move. Emergency surgery would be carried out by advance medical units that would land with the assault troops. When the medical infrastructure in Normandy was sufficiently developed, casualties requiring a maximum of seven days' treatment would be retained in the beachhead. Gradually, as more hospital beds became available, fewer and fewer casualties would be evacuated across the Channel.

Thus speedy evacuation of casualties was a key principle of British medical planning for D-day. As it was believed that the use of large hospital ships would be too dangerous in Channel waters, casualties were mainly to be carried in hospital carriers and suitably modified LSTs (Landing Ships, Tank) that, when equipped with stretcher racks, could transport three hundred patients. Amphibious lorries were to be employed to ferry patients from the beaches to the LST. The exact number of transports available for casualty evacuation was the subject of a bureaucratic struggle, and the medical authorities lost the battle to have a precise number of LSTs dedicated to this duty. It was planned, however, that a maximum of two hundred patients could be evacuated by air beginning on D plus 9.

On arrival at the ports of Southampton, Portsmouth, and Gosport, casualties were fed into the medical system, being sent by road or by ambulance train to hospitals. Hospitals were divided into three categories: seven coastal or port hospitals (total of 1,200 beds) for the most serious cases; thirteen transit hospitals (6,550 beds), which equated to the Casualty Clearing Station (CCS); and the heart of the system, ninety-seven home-base hospitals (50,000 beds, 23,000 available on D-day). Ordinary military hospitals in Britain could find only 16,800 hospital beds. Others were provided by civilian hospitals under the Emergency Medical Services scheme.

The first British medical units to land in Normandy were those of the 6th Airborne Division. A small number of medical personnel were among the coup de main party at Pegasus Bridge, and the 225th Parachute Field Ambulance (FA) landed at 0100 hours, their main dressing station (MDS) being established at 0300 hours. The 224th Parachute FA arrived a few hours later. The glider-borne 195th Air Landing FA, complete with three jeeps and trailer, arrived at 2100 on 6 June. By 20 June the division's RAMC troops had suffered 128 casualties and treated over 3,000 casualties at MDSs.

The beach groups of the British assault divisions included an integral medical organization of two field dressing stations (FDS), two field surgical units (FSU), and one field transfusion unit (FTU), in addition to surgical teams. Apart from one sector of the 50th Division's front, at Le Hamel, FDSs were in operation only ninety minutes after

WOUNDED OUTSIDE HOSPITAL.   HULTON DEUTSCH

Some other aspects of British medical support can be briefly mentioned. Blood transfusion, the responsibility of the FTU, was of vital importance: sixty-three pints of blood were, on average, needed for every one hundred wounded. The nurses of Queen Alexandra's Imperial Military Nursing Service did sterling work, as did the Army Dental Corps, who deployed one dentist for every three thousand soldiers. Psychiatric cases, who by D plus 9 accounted for 13 percent of all casualties, were handled by the Army Psychiatric Service, being treated at corps and army exhaustion centers prior to evacuation.

It is generally agreed that faith in medical arrangements is an important factor in military morale. The success of British medical support can thus be seen to have contributed greatly to the Allied victory.

[See also Casualties, article on Allied Casualties.]

BIBLIOGRAPHY

The Administrative History of the Operations of 21 Army Group on the Continent of Europe, 6 June 1944–8 May 1945. 1945.

Crew, F. A. E. North-West Europe. Vol. 4 of The Army Medical Services, Campaigns. 1962.

McLaughlin, Redmond. The Royal Army Medical Corps. 1972.

G. D. SHEFFIELD

German Medical Support

The defense of Normandy was the assignment of the Seventh Army. On D-day it consisted of three stationary (nonmotorized) infantry divisions, the 352d, 716th, and 709th, and the mobile 91st Parachute Division and 21st Panzer Division. In line with German regulations, all had equivalent systems for the care and transport of casualties.

The system employed on the Normandy battlefield had proven itself earlier in the war. It consisted of an evacuation chain reaching from the battlefield to a military hospital in the homeland. After the wounded soldier had been treated with basic first aid in the coastal zone, he was removed by company stretcher-bearers to a casualty station with other wounded. From there the wounded were taken to the battalion field dispensary (Truppenverbandplatz, TVP) two to three kilometers behind the front lines, where the first and thus most important medical help was given. The dispensary provided the lowest level of medical care, under the battalion medical officer and his medical assistant. Because of the proximity of the battlefield, this treatment was limited to examining, changing, and improving bandages and slings; stopping bleeding; administering drugs to improve circulation and relieve pain; and injecting antitetanus serum.

The primary task of the field dispensary was, however, to make it possible to move the wounded to one of the medical facilities far behind the lines where serious

---

the first assault troops splashed ashore. The prebattle estimates of casualties proved to be pessimistic. In total, British and Canadian casualties on D-day amounted to about 4,300 dead, wounded, or missing. The 3d Division, for example, who fielded 1,154 RAMC personnel in the initial wave, evacuated 272 casualties on D-day, 844 on D plus 1, and 543 on D plus 2.

As the beachhead began to expand, the normal medical infrastructure for a land campaign was established. A wounded soldier would be passed through the regimental aid post to the casualty-collecting post and then back to another unit farther in the rear. The CCSs, set up by D plus 2, handled serious cases, while the FDSs treated the sick and lightly wounded. Eventually, the casualty would be passed to a general hospital or evacuated via a casualty evacuation post (CEP), the central CEP (one FTU, two FDSs, and two FSUs with accommodations for 1,500 casualties) being located at Courseulles. On 10 June the first of seven general hospitals was established in Normandy.

The first two days of the operation were marked by heavy seas, which posed problems for evacuation of casualties, leading to the decision to beach LSTs to allow the direct transfer of patients. After this, the evacuation procedure generally worked well. An unexpected bonus was the beginning of the air evacuation service on 13 June, rather earlier than had been expected. Casualties were flown to airfields on Salisbury Plain, where the RAF medical services established casualty reception centers. By 26 July, 38,581 patients had been evacuated by sea and 7,719 by air.

wounds could be treated. This was the task of the medical company that was part of every division. With its personnel and equipment, this company set up the main dispensary (*Hauptverbandplatz, HVP*). The medical companies of the stationary divisions defending Normandy in the first days of the invasion were either equipped with horse-drawn transport or had motorized ambulances. The personnel strength of one of these medical companies was some 160 men. Each company had three trains: a stretcher train, a dispensary train, and a supply train to reinforce or relieve the other trains. The dispensary lay six to ten kilometers behind the front and received the wounded sent from the battalion field dispensary. The value of the main dispensary was that it could provide every type of critical surgical aid, and above all, life-saving operations. There were dentists and a field pharmacist, as well as two surgery tents, and other tents for the severely and less critically wounded. Two surgery teams were always ready to operate. Basically, however, even the main dispensaries were only a link in the medical service's evacuation chain.

The next level of care was also organized within the division. This was a field hospital (*Feldlazarett, FL*), in which care for the wounded and ill was provided under conditions similar to those in a good civilian district hospital. It could provide even the difficult surgical procedures necessitated by abdominal wounds. These hospitals had staffs of seventy-six. Usually located fifteen to twenty kilometers from the coast, they were housed in solid buildings and could care for 200 patients.

The largest medical installation for the *Seventh Army* was the Military Hospital (*Kriegslazarett, KLZ*) in the École Militaire in Paris, with 5,000 beds and divisions for all medical specializations. The hospital also had a group of consulting physicians consisting of three surgeons, one internist, one hygienist, one neurologist, and one pathologist. They supported their fellow specialists, but, being eminent authorities recruited from the universities, also went to the field hospitals to treat unusual cases. The Military Hospital was the highest medical institution outside the German Reich. From there, wounded were moved directly to a specialized or military hospital in the homeland.

The evacuation chain proved its worth in the battles for Normandy. The *Seventh Army*'s medical services succeeded in transporting all the movable wounded to Paris. This accomplishment cannot be evaluated too highly, since normal transport with hospital trains was impossible because Allied bombings had destroyed the railroads and German supply lines were under constant attack. The ambulances of the dispensaries and field hospitals and the ambulance divisions of the Military Hospital, supplemented by rebuilt motor vehicles and buses, accomplished this mission under cover of night.

German medical care in Normandy was not without problems. Penicillin was not available in the field or in Germany; at this stage of the war, blood plasma was no longer available in sufficient quantity. Only a limited number of convalescents returned to the Normandy front, because the two and a half months that elapsed between the invasion and the German retreat rarely allowed a soldier to recover and be redeployed there.

BIBLIOGRAPHY

Dankert, D. "Der deutsche und der alliierte Sanitätsdienst während des II. Weltkrieges unter besonderer Berücksichtigung der Invasion 1944." In *Wehrmedizinische Monatsschrift*, no. 2 (1983).

Haubenreisser, G. "Der Sanitätsdienst während der Invasion." In *Geschichte des Oberbefehlshabers West*. (Military Study T-121, part B I.)

EKKEHART GUTH

MEINDL, EUGEN (1892–1951), German, lieutenant general commanding the *II Parachute Corps*. Eugen Meindl was born on 16 July 1892 in Donaueschingen in Baden. His father was a forestry official of the prince of Fürstenberg; his family was Catholic. After graduating from secondary school, he joined the *67th Field Artillery Regiment* in Hagenau (then in German Alsace) as a cadet. Promoted to lieutenant in February 1914, in World War I he fought with his regiment as a platoon and battery commander and regimental adjutant. He ended the war as a first lieutenant and adjutant in the *52d Artillery Detachment*.

In 1919 Meindl transferred into the Reichswehr, the army of the Weimar Republic, where he was deployed primarily with the *5th Artillery Regiment*. In 1935, as a major, he was a battalion commander in his regiment. In November 1938, after Austria's annexation, he was posted to the *112th Mountain Artillery Regiment* in Graz. As a colonel, he participated with this unit in the Polish campaign. During the invasion of Norway he made a parachute jump over Narvik, although he had not had parachute training. In November 1940 Meindl transferred to the Luftwaffe, becoming commanding officer of the *Airborne Storm Regiment* in the parachute troops. Now a brigadier general, he jumped with this regiment over Malemes, Crete, in May 1941, and was seriously wounded.

In the winter of 1941–1942 Meindl created the first Luftwaffe field division, the *Group Meindl*, out of dispensable air force personnel. As part of *Army Group Center* they were supposed to relieve overextended army units on the Eastern front. In October 1942 he became commanding general of the *XIII Air Corps*, the staff responsible for creating and organizing some twenty-two Luft-

EUGEN MEINDL.   At right.   BIBLIOTHEK FÜR ZEITGESCHICHTE, STUTTGART

waffe field divisions that fought with the army but remained under the command of Hermann Göring as commander in chief of the Luftwaffe. Because of their motley composition and inadequate training, these divisions, which owed their creation to Göring, did not acquit themselves well. Meindl was promoted to major general in February 1943. In November he was given command of the *II Parachute Corps (II Fallschirmkorps),* which served first in Italy and then in France.

Meindl commanded the *3d* and *5th* parachute divisions in Brittany after 12 May 1944; his corps functioned as reserves of the Commander in Chief West. After the invasion began, on 12 June an army group under Gen. Erich Marcks was to be formed from the *LXXXIV Army Corps* and the *II Parachute Corps,* which was moved onto the Cotentin Peninsula to form a line facing the American, and the western half of the British, bridgeheads. Because Marcks was killed that same day, the *II Parachute Corps* was placed directly under the *Seventh Army.* In hard combat the corps—in concert with the *LXXXIV Army Corps*—managed to halt the advance of the U.S. V Corps at Saint-Lô until 20 July. It then fought in a stage-by-stage retreat until, on 27 and 28 July, the Allies achieved a breakthrough into central France.

The *II Parachute Corps* pulled back eastward, then regrouped at Rouen in late August after the Allied breakout from the Falaise pocket. In September they were deployed as part of the *1st Parachute Army* against the British at Cleve and Nijmegen on the German-Dutch border. Until February 1945 Meindl fought at Venlo and Roermund, then until March defended the Wesel bridgehead on the lower Rhine. On 8 May he surrendered in Schleswig-Holstein, and was a British prisoner of war until 1947. Meindl died in Munich on 24 January 1951.

[*See also* 5th Parachute Division; II Parachute Corps; 3d Parachute Division.]

BIBLIOGRAPHY

Meindl, Eugen. Papers. File 6/274. Bundesarchiv-Militärarchiv, Freiburg, Germany.
Winterstein, Ernst Martin, and Hans Jacobs. *General Meindl und seine Fallschirmjäger. Vom Sturmregiment zum II. Fallschirmjägerkorps 1940–1945.* 1974.

REINHARD STUMPF

MEMORIALS.   *See* Cemeteries, Monuments, and Memorials.

MEYER, KURT (1910–1961), German, SS Standartenführer, commander *25th SS Panzer Grenadier Regiment* and later, SS Brigadeführer, *12th SS Panzer Division.* "Panzer" Meyer was one of the outstanding members of the Waffen SS, displaying a high degree of toughness, bravery, and military skill. Son of a laborer, he worked as a miner before becoming a policeman in 1929. He became a member of the Nazi party in 1930 and shortly afterward joined the SS, then a very small body compared with Adolf Hitler's other paramilitary organization, the SA. Promoted to officer rank in July 1932, Meyer was transferred to Hitler's personal bodyguard, the *Leibstandarte SS "Adolf Hitler"*, in early 1934. During the Polish campaign he commanded the *Leibstandarte*'s antitank company and then took over its motorcycle company for the campaign in the West. Meyer's reputation was made in Greece in April 1941, where, commanding the *Leibstandarte*'s reconnaissance battalion, he stormed and seized the Klissura Pass, for which he was later awarded the Knight's Cross. Meyer continued to lead his reconnaissance battalion in Russia, earning the Oak Leaves to the Knight's Cross for his part in the recapture of Kharkov in February 1943.

In July 1943 he was transferred from the *Leibstandarte* and promoted to regimental commander in the *12th SS Panzer Grenadier Division "Hitlerjugend"*, which was then forming. His now extensive combat experience and zeal contributed much to welding this division of young extremists into a first-class fighting formation. On D-day itself, Meyer's regiment spearheaded the division's deployment from Évreux to Normandy and it was he who persuaded Lt. Gen. Edgar Feuchtinger, the indecisive commander of the *21st Panzer Division*, that they should both

KURT MEYER.   BIBLIOTHEK FÜR ZEITGESCHICHTE, STUTTGART

attack the 3d Canadian Division on D plus 1 and drive it back into the sea. This was not successful, but it did stop the advance on Caen. Throughout the next few days Meyer's men were engaged in bitter fighting against the 3d Canadian Infantry Division, inspired by his personal example. When Fritz Witt, Meyer's divisional commander, was killed on 13 June, Meyer took his place, making him the youngest divisional commander in the whole of the Wehrmacht. For the next two months he continued to conduct a bitter, prolonged resistance to Canadian attempts to secure Caen and thereafter to seal the Falaise pocket. For this Meyer was awarded the Swords to the Knight's Cross. In the process his division was destroyed, and he himself escaped from the Falaise pocket on his own, only to be captured by the British near Namur in Belgium at the beginning of September.

After the war Meyer was charged by the Canadians with the murder of some of their men whom his division had captured during the early days of the fighting in Normandy. In December 1945, he was sentenced to death, the first German war criminal to be so sentenced, although this was reduced to life imprisonment on appeal. Released in 1954, he became an active member of the Waffen SS Old Comrades Association and wrote his memoirs before dying at a relatively young age. Meyer never renounced his National Socialist beliefs, remaining proud of everything that the Waffen SS had stood for.

[*See also* 12th SS Panzer Division "Hitlerjugend."]

BIBLIOGRAPHY

Meyer, Kurt. *Grenadiere*. 1957.

CHARLES MESSENGER

MIDDLETON, TROY H. (1889–1976), American, major general, commander of the U.S. VIII Corps. In 1910, after graduating from the Mississippi Agriculture and Mechanical College, Middleton enlisted in the regular army. In World War I he became the youngest colonel in the American Expeditionary Forces, commanded the 29th and the 47th infantry regiments, and earned decorations for tactical skill and bravery. In the 1920s he graduated from the Infantry Advanced Course, the Command and General Staff College, and the Army War College. In 1930 he became professor of military science and tactics at Louisiana State University in Baton Rouge. After serving six years in the Philippine Islands with the inspector general, in 1937 he retired with the rank of colonel to become dean of administration at Louisiana State University.

Middleton volunteered for active duty in January 1941. By October 1942 he was a major general commanding the 45th Infantry Division, which he led during the cam-

TROY H. MIDDLETON.   On USS *Ancon*.

paigns in Sicily and Italy, gaining a reputation of responding well under pressure and making the best use of available forces. In January 1944 he left the division because of an arthritic disability in his knees and ended up in Walter Reed Hospital.

This incapacity would have ended his military service, had not General Dwight D. Eisenhower, Supreme Allied Commander, told Gen. George Marshall, Army Chief of Staff; "I don't give a damn about his knees, I want his head and his heart. And I'll take him into battle on a litter if we have to." Arriving in England in March to replace an officer removed because the Third Army commander, George S. Patton, Jr., wanted only combat-experienced corps commanders under him, Middleton assumed command of U.S. VIII Corps, which was scheduled to follow VII Corps across Utah Beach. Middleton took his corps across the Channel on 13 June and arrived in France the next day. For the next two months VIII Corps fought as part of Gen. Omar Bradley's First Army. In August, when the Third Army headquarters arrived in France, Middleton and the VIII Corps returned to Patton's command.

His performance as a corps commander in Europe received high praise; Patton said of him after the Battle of the Bulge that his "decision to hold Bastogne was a stroke of genius." Middleton retired in August 1945 as a lieutenant general, after commanding VIII Corps during the Allied sweep across France. He returned to Louisiana State University to become president.

BIBLIOGRAPHY

Lowenthal, Mark M. "Middleton, Troy H." In *Dictionary of American Military Biography*, vol. 2, pp. 765–767.
Price, Frank James. *Troy H. Middleton: A Biography*. 1974.

CLAYTON R. NEWELL

MILLS-ROBERTS, DEREK (1908–1990), British, brigadier, commander of No. 6 Commando (until 13 June 1944), then commander of 1st Special Service Brigade. Derek Mills-Roberts was educated at Liverpool College and was a contemporary and close friend of Lord Lovat at Oxford University. He trained as solicitor before the war and was subsequently commissioned into the Irish Guards. He saw action with his battalion in Norway, but after their return he volunteered for the Commandos.

As a major he became second-in-command to Lord Lovat in No. 4 Commando and led half the unit into a fierce action at Dieppe in August 1942. A fearless soldier and excellent leader, he devised a number of experimental techniques that were highly successful.

On promotion to lieutenant colonel, he commanded No. 6 Commando in Tunisia, where he won the Distinguished Service Order for a dawn raid against the *Hermann Göring Jäger Division*. On D-day his No. 6 Commando landed at H plus 90 and led the push south and east across the Orne River and Caen Canal to establish a bridgehead with the British 6th Airborne Division on the eastern flank of the Allied front.

He was slightly wounded on 12 June during the prolonged battle of Bréville Wood, a turning point in wrenching the initiative from the Germans; the following day he took over the 1st Commando Brigade from Lord Lovat, who had been severely wounded and evacuated. His brigade's vigorous sniping and patrolling kept the Germans guessing. For seven days he commanded the brigade as a lieutenant colonel before being promoted to brigadier, and subsequently led the 1st Special Service Brigade triumphantly across Europe to the Baltic at the head of the British 21st Army Group, finally accepting the surrender of Field Marshal Erhard Milch.

[*See also* Commandos; 1st Special Service Brigade.]

BIBLIOGRAPHY

Lovat, Lord. *March Past*. 1978.
Mills-Roberts, Derek. *Clash by Night*. 1956.
Saunders, Hilary St. G. *The Green Beret*. 1949.

DEREK OAKLEY

MINESWEEPER SHIPS.

MINESWEEPER SHIPS. [*This entry includes separate discussions of Allied minesweepers and German fleet minesweepers. For discussion of German motor minesweepers, see R-Boats; for discussion of German mine destruction vessels and auxiliary minesweepers, see Auxiliary Warships. For analysis of minesweeping operations in the Normandy invasion, see Mine Warfare.*]

Allied Minesweepers

The minesweeping groups clearing the way for the assault waves were assigned to the individual attack forces. Force U (Utah Beach) had 16 British fleet minesweepers; Force O (Omaha) had 17 British and 11 American fleet minesweepers, and 20 British and 18 American motor minesweepers; Force G (Gold) had 16 British fleet and 10 British motor minesweepers; Force J (Juno) had 16 British fleet and 10 British motor minesweepers; and Force S (Sword) had 24 British fleet and 30 British motor minesweepers.

Fleet Minesweepers. Prewar seagoing minesweepers were steel ships equipped to sweep contact mines. This general type continued to be designed into World War II, and such war-built minesweepers as the Algerine and Raven classes did worthy service. Degaussing, or counteracting a ship's natural magnetism by passing electrical current through cables around the hull, was originally thought sufficient protection from magnetic mines. Wartime experience dictated better protection; this, and the need to use wooden shipbuilding capacity, led to the wood-hulled motor minesweepers.

The British Hunt class, also called the Town class, were World War I coal-burners nicknamed "Smokey Joes." Nine British Hunts were in the Western Task Force.

The British Halcyon class were minesweeping sloops. Similar to sloops—small antisubmarine escort ships—of the 1930s, they carried depth charges and could double in the escort role. They were built to sweep moored mines, using steel wires armed with cutters to sever the mines' anchor cables. Their ample size (245 feet long) allowed the addition of heavy electrical cables, used to create an artificial magnetic field to detonate magnetic mines, and "hammer boxes" or powered noisemakers used to trigger acoustic mines. Nine Halcyons were in the Eastern Task Force.

The British Bangor class were built early in the war as 162-foot Halcyons. Like them, they were designed for moored sweeping. Their smaller size made influence sweep gear a problem, and later fleet sweepers were enlarged with this in mind. Sixteen British Bangors were in the Eastern Task Force; thirteen British and fifteen Canadian were in the Western.

The British 225-foot Algerine class incorporated early war experience and proved highly satisfactory for moored and influence sweeping. Twenty-five Algerines were in

MOTOR MINESWEEPERS (YMS).   Detonating mines off Utah Beach on D-day.   NATIONAL ARCHIVES

USS TIDE.   Part of the minesweeper group of Task Force 125, it struck a mine off Utah Beach and later sank while under tow. USS *Pheasant,* also a minesweeper, stands off to the right.   NATIONAL ARCHIVES

the Eastern Task Force.

The American Raven class has been called "undoubtedly the outstanding fleet sweeper design of the war" by Peter Elliott in *Allied Minesweeping in World War II* (1979). These 221-footers fell between the successful Halcyon and Algerine classes in size, and were liked for their handiness and eighteen-knot speed. Some were built for the Royal Navy, which called them the Catherine class. Eleven Ravens were in the Western Task Force, and twelve Catherines in the Eastern.

Coastal Minesweepers. The introduction of influence mines, and the foreseen need for amphibious assault sweeping, led to the development of mass-producible diesel sweepers designed to combat moored and influence mines. British and Americans alike called them "motor minesweepers," abbreviated MMS in the Royal Navy and YMS in the U.S. Navy. Many MMS and YMS were transferred to Dominion or Allied navies.

Motor minesweepers (MMS) were Admiralty-designed 119- and 140-footers resembling trawlers, fitted to sweep influence mines. Thirty MMS were in the Eastern Task Force, and thirty-one in the Western.

Motor minesweepers (YMS) were 136-footers fitted for moored and influence sweeping. Built in large numbers, they proved useful and set a pattern for postwar minecraft. Twenty-one American and ten British YMS were in the Western Task Force, with thirty British YMS in the Eastern.

Motor Launches. 112-foot Fairmile B-class launches were fitted with light moored sweep gear and sent ahead of the lead ship of each minesweeping group during the approach to the landing beaches. Twenty Fairmiles were in the Eastern Task Force, and sixteen in the Western.

Danlayers. Mine clearance demands precise navigation and careful marking of swept areas. Twenty-five converted trawlers, with thirteen war-built naval trawlers and eight fleet sweepers, were used to plant temporary dan buoys to mark the limits of the assault channels for the landing craft that followed.

BIBLIOGRAPHY

Elliott, Peter. *Allied Minesweeping in World War 2.* 1979.

Lenton, H. T. *American Gunboats and Minesweepers*. 1974.

Lenton, H. T., and J. J. Colledge. *British and Dominion Warships of World War II*. 1968.

JOHN C. REILLY, JR.

German Minesweepers

In addition to motor minesweepers (*Räumboote,* or R-boats) and auxiliary minesweepers, the German Navy in France had seven flotillas of fleet minesweepers (*Minensuchboote*) belonging to two types.

Type 35 had a displacement of 682–685 tons standard and 874–908 full load. The length was between 68.1 and 71 meters, the width 8.7 to 9.2 meters, and the maximum depth 2.65 meters. The vessels were driven by triple-expansion engines and oil-fired boilers. They had 3,500–3,700 horsepower and a maximum speed of 18.2 knots. The crew consisted of 3 to 5 officers and 81 to 90 men, depending on the antiaircraft (AA) armament and the inclusion of a flotilla staff. The armament was two 10.5-cm guns, and two 37-mm, one quadruple 20-mm, and two single or twin 20-mm AA guns. They could lay 30 mines.

Type 40 had a displacement of 543 tons standard and 775 tons full load. The length was 62.3 meters, the width 8.9 meters, the maximum depth 2.8 meters. They were driven by triple-expansion machines and coal-fired boilers. They had 2,400 horsepower and a maximum speed of 16.8 knots. The crew in 1944 consisted of 5 officers and 65 men. The armament was one 10.5-cm gun, and one 37-mm, one quadruple 20-mm, and up to three 20-mm single AA guns. They had no minelaying capacity.

Three flotillas belonged to the *3d Defense Division* in the area of Brest. On D-day the *2d Flotilla* at Bénodet had five Type-35 boats: *M 9, M 12, M 21, M 25,* and *M 38. M 13* had been sunk on 31 May by a German mine in the Gironde Estuary after a steering failure; the others were being used in the Bay of Biscay to escort U-boats. They survived the war in the besieged fortress of Lorient, were captured by the Americans, and then were given to the French Navy, which used them up to 1960. Only *M 25,* unable to reach Lorient, had to be scuttled in September 1944. The *6th Flotilla* at Concarneau had six Type-35 boats: *M 83, M 84, M 85, M 133, M 155,* and *M 206. M 39* had been sunk on 24 May northwest of Ouistreham by British motor torpedo boats. *M 83* was sunk on 14 June

M 432.

and others were lost in the Saint-Malo area or at Le Havre, but two survived. The *24th Flotilla* had eight Type-40 boats: *M 343, M 402, M 412, M 422, M 432, M 442, M 452,* and *M 475.* They operated in the Channel Islands area and were involved in a battle on 14 June off Jersey with the British destroyer *Ashanti,* the Polish destroyer *Piorun,* and British motor torpedo boats (MTBs); *M 83* (*6th Flotilla*) was sunk by an 'MTB torpedo, and *M 343* by destroyer gunfire, while *M 412, M 422, M 432, M 442, M 452,* and *Piorun* were damaged. *M 402* was lost during the Allied air raid on Le Havre on 15 June.

Four flotillas belonged to the *4th Defense Division* in the Bay of Biscay: the *8th Flotilla* with four Type-35 and four Type-40 boats at Royan; the *10th Flotilla* with seven Type-40 boats at Paimboeuf; the *26th Flotilla* with eight Type-40 boats at Couëron; and the *28th Flotilla* with six Type-40 boats at Pauillac. They operated only in the Bay of Biscay area to escort U-boats and other vessels.

The fleet minesweepers were efficient in their main task, the sweeping of mines, and could defend themselves and their escorted vessels against moderate air attacks, but they were unable to fight destroyers or heavier ships with any chance of success. Consequently, they could only be used for escort operations in the area west of the Cotentin Peninsula and in the Bay of Biscay. Some were sunk by Allied cruisers and destroyers, others by air attacks. After the Allied breakthrough at Avranches, some of these vessels became the backbone of the German defense of the Channel Islands, which were never attacked by the Allies. Four boats of the *24th Flotilla* participated in the commando strike against Granville on 8–9 March 1945.

BIBLIOGRAPHY

Gröner, Erich. *Die deutschen Kriegsschiffe 1815–1945.* Edited by Dieter Jung and Martin Maass. Vol. 2, 1983.
Rohwer, Jürgen, and Gerhard Hümmelchen. *Chronology of the War at Sea, 1939–1945.* Translated by Derek Masters. 1992.

JÜRGEN ROHWER

MINE WARFARE. Mines are shallow-water weapons and, in any amphibious operation, mine countermeasures must inevitably play a major role. In the Normandy operation minelaying and minesweeping were major concerns of German and Allied planners and operating forces alike.

A moored contact mine floats beneath the surface. When a ship strikes one of its protruding horns, an electrical circuit fires the mine. Influence mines, introduced during World War II, are bottom-planted in shallow water. They include magnetic mines triggered by a ship's magnetic field, and acoustic mines set off by engine and propeller noise. By 1943 the Germans had also developed pressure mines, actuated by the change in water pressure as a ship

passes. An influence mine can have a ship counter that controls the number of looks (actuations of the firing mechanism) needed to fire the mine; a certain number of ships can pass without harm before a final look triggers it. A combination mechanism, requiring two or three influences, is harder to sweep. German minefields included magnetic-acoustic mines; pressure-acoustic and pressure-magnetic mines were used after D-day. In early 1944 the Germans planted mines from the Pas de Calais to Cherbourg. Contact mines were laid in deep water, while influence mines protected the beaches. Aggressive Allied operations hindered German minelaying in the months before OVERLORD, but could not eliminate it. Intelligence thought contact mines the principal concern, but landing forces found influence mines to be the real threat.

Area Z, the rendezvous area southeast of the Isle of Wight where assault convoys from British ports were to converge and turn southward toward Normandy, was swept under tight security before D-day. On 4 June the American fleet sweeper *Osprey* struck a newly laid mine and became the first mine fatality of the invasion. Minesweeping groups led the way for the landing forces. They cleared contact mines in the Spout (the cross-Channel convoy route to the landing beaches) and marked the channels with buoys, working with difficulty in strong cross-currents. As the sweepers closed the beachhead area, some diverged to sweep channels for bombardment ships or clear areas for deep-draft transports and cargo ships, while others continued to the landing beaches. During the approach a British destroyer was damaged by a mine, and an LCT was sunk. As the assault sweeps were completed, minesweepers began to widen the channels and enlarge the swept areas inshore to allow shipping to approach the beachhead. Thereafter all swept channels had to be reswept daily to forestall German minelaying.

During the night of 6–7 June German surface craft planted mines off Cherbourg, in the Seine Estuary, and in the Pas de Calais (the Strait of Dover) where the main Allied effort was still expected. As the landings proceeded, pressure mines were laid in growing numbers—after 9 June, by planes as well as ships. At this time they could not be swept, though efforts were made to simulate a ship's pressure wave. Some success was had in actuating the pressure side of pressure-combination mines and then quickly subjecting them to a magnetic or acoustic sweep. After examining a pressure mine dropped ashore, the Admiralty set speed limits for ships to minimize pressure fluctuation. This slowed movement but reduced casualties.

In the first two weeks of operations most Allied mine casualties were American. Off Utah Beach influence mines, with ship counters, were not exploded by assault sweeping and sank a destroyer, four landing craft, and a fire-support craft on D-day. Between 6 and 15 June four

American destroyers and two minesweepers were sunk; twenty-five other ships and craft were damaged. American losses then declined, while British casualties rose considerably. Between 22 and 29 June nine British ships were lost; eight others were damaged, including Eastern Task Force commander Adm. Philip Vian's flagship, the cruiser HMS *Scylla*. Strict enforcement of speed directives helped protect ships from pressure mines, while energetic minesweeping made good progress against others. By early July mines were no longer a serious danger

As Allied forces closed in on Cherbourg, British and American sweepers again cleared the way for bombardment ships under heavy fire.

Rear Adm. Alan G. Kirk, commander of the Western Task Force, reported that "minesweeping was the keystone of the arch in this operation. All . . . waters were suitable for mining, and . . . plans of unprecedented complexity were required. The performance of minesweepers can only be described as magnificent. . . . An equally high standard was maintained in the unremitting daily labor of sweeping the assault area during the build-up phase." In a conference at his headquarters on 1 July, Hitler told Admiral Dönitz that "we have got to lay more mines and still more mines in the Bay of the Seine with the tenacity of a bulldog." By then it was too late.

[*See also* Minesweeper Ships.]

BIBLIOGRAPHY

Elliott, Peter. *Allied Minesweeping in World War 2*. 1979.
Lott, Arnold S. *Most Dangerous Sea: A History of Mine Warfare and an Account of U.S. Navy Mine Warfare Operations in World War II and Korea*. 1959.
Melia, Tamara M. *"Damn the Torpedoes": A Short History of U.S. Naval Mine Countermeasures, 1777–1991*. 1991.

JOHN C. REILLY, JR.

MONTCALM. A French light cruiser of the La Galissonnière class, *Montcalm* was the flagship of Rear Adm. Robert Jaujard. Built in the shipyard of La Seyne, it was launched on 26 October 1936 and entered active duty on 9 December 1937. It had a displacement of 7,720 tons, was 179.5 meters long (about 589 ft), 17.48 meters wide (about 57 ft.), and drew an average of 5.08 meters (16 ft., 7 in.) of water. Its 88,000 horsepower engine produced a top speed of 30 knots, and it had a range of 4,600 nautical miles when averaging 18 knots.

It was originally fitted with nine 152-mm guns in three

MONTCALM.

triple turrets, eight 90-mm guns in four double mounts, and a limited antiaircraft battery of a few 37-mm guns and some heavy machine guns. It could also accommodate four planes protected in a hangar, launched by catapult, and retrieved by a landing ramp attached to the stern. A 105-mm (4-in.) outer armored layer and a 38-mm (1.5-in.) armored layer on the deck protected the ship. Its crew numbered thirty-two officers and 732 seamen.

Montcalm took part in the campaign in Norway in the spring of 1940. In September 1940, *Montcalm* was involved in the failed Operation MENACE when Royal Navy ships escorting some French ships carrying General de Gaulle and Free French troops landed at Dakar, the capital of French West Africa. Between February and June 1943, after France reentered the war, it was overhauled and modernized in a shipyard in Philadelphia, receiving two radars. The plane section was discarded, and the antiaircraft battery was drastically reinforced with twenty-four 40-mm guns in quadruple mounts, and sixteen 20-mm guns.

After more patrols in the Atlantic from Dakar and Freeport in North Africa, *Montcalm* (with Capt. Édouard de V. Deprey in command) joined *Georges Leygues* (with Capt. Joseph de V. Laurin in command) in England to participate in Operation OVERLORD under the command of Rear Adm. Robert Jaujard and took part in some exercises off the coasts of Scotland and Ireland. At dawn on 6 June, it was east of Port-en-Bessin, off Omaha Beach. As part of the Bombardment Group of Rear Adm. Carleton F. Bryant along with the American battleship *Arkansas* and *Georges Leygues,* following cues from its shore fire-support party, it engaged the coastal battery of Longues and various targets along the beaches of Saint-Laurent. During the next four days, *Montcalm* tackled various targets within the range of its guns (22,000 meters, 13.8 miles) until it exhausted all its ammunition—eight hundred and forty-three 152-mm (6-in.) shells. It fired on crossroads, troop concentrations, and ammunition dumps. Between 10 and 15 June, it remained in the area to offer antiaircraft support before returning to Milford Haven, Wales, and then to the Mediterranean, where it took part with *Georges Leygues* in Operation DRAGOON, the Allied invasion of the southern coast of France in August 1944.

[*See also* French Ships; Jaujard, Robert.]

BIBLIOGRAPHY

Morison, Samuel Eliot. *The Invasion of France and Germany: 1944–1945.* Vol. 11 of *History of U.S. Naval Operations in World War II.* 1957.

PHILLIPE MASSON
Translated from French by Marie-Josée Schorp

MONTEITH, JIMMIE W., JR. (1917–1944), American, first lieutenant; Medal of Honor recipient. Jimmie W. Monteith, Jr., was born on 1 July 1917 in Low Moor, Virginia. He entered the army in Richmond, Virginia, in October 1941, after two years at Virginia Polytechnic Institute. Graduating from infantry officer candidate school in June 1942, he immediately joined Company L, 3d Battalion, 16th Infantry Regiment, of the 1st Infantry Division.

On 6 June 1944, First Lieutenant Monteith distinguished himself by conspicuous gallantry and intrepidity above and beyond the call of duty near Colleville-sur-Mer, Normandy. Landing with the initial assault waves on Omaha Beach under heavy enemy fire, he organized his men and led them in an assault across open ground to the safety of a cliff. He then returned under withering enemy artillery and machine-gun fire and led two tanks through a mine field into firing positions. He then directed the tanks' fire, destroying several enemy positions. Returning to his company, he led his men in a successful attack, then repeatedly ignored his own safety to consolidate his defenses. While leading the defense of his unit position, he was killed in action. He was awarded the Medal of Honor posthumously for his personal heroism, gallantry, and intrepid leadership under fire.

BIBLIOGRAPHY

U.S. Congress. Senate. Committee on Veterans' Affairs. *Medal of Honor Recipients, 1863–1978.* 96th Cong., 1st sess., 1979. S. Committee Print No. 3.

JOHN F. VOTAW

MONTGOMERY, BERNARD L. (1887–1976), British, general, commander of 21st Army Group. Montgomery was one of the most dynamic and controversial senior commanders of World War II. As a soldier he was either worshiped or despised by most of his contemporaries; few regarded him dispassionately, and the controversies associated with his name continue to exercise both scholars and military men. A great executive general, "Monty" was not a notable originator of military concepts, but he rapidly developed a unique command style that inspired the citizen-soldiery of the British armies and made him a popular idol to the British population. At the same time his supreme self-confidence in his undeniably impressive martial talents made him a prima donna whose tactless and abrasive characteristics all too frequently aggravated his superiors and equals, particularly the Americans. However, he retained the full confidence and unswerving support of both Winston Churchill and the Chief of the Imperial General Staff (CIGS), Gen. Alan Brooke, and ended the war a field marshal. Subsequently he was made a viscount.

BERNARD L. MONTGOMERY.   NATIONAL ARCHIVES

Born the son of a bishop, Montgomery was educated at St. Paul's School in London before being commissioned into the Royal Warwickshire Regiment from Sandhurst in 1908. He proved a headstrong subaltern, albeit a man of sober inclination (he was strongly against both drinking and smoking during all his lifetime). He was severely wounded in 1914, but after recovery successfully held a series of staff appointments and rose to the rank of lieutenant colonel and battalion commander by the end of World War I. In 1940 he commanded the British 3d Division in the short Dunkirk campaign before coming to the notice of Winston Churchill while in charge of anti-invasion preparations in southeast England. It was on the

prime minister's insistence that in August 1942 he assumed command of the "brave but baffled" British Eighth Army in Egypt. He took immediate steps to improve its morale, and subsequently halted Field Marshal Erwin Rommel at Alam Halfa and then decisively defeated him at El Alamein—two victories that firmly established his reputation as a general and won the acclaim of the British people. El Alamein was Britain's first major land victory in the war, and together with Stalingrad became regarded as a vital turning point in the struggle against the Axis powers.

Unfortunately, Montgomery soon developed a poor opinion of his American allies, whom he regarded as amateurs, during the campaign in northwest Africa that followed, and then added to this prejudice an intense antipathy toward Lt. Gen. George S. Patton, Jr., while sharing the conquest of Sicily with the U.S. Seventh Army in July 1943. With Montgomery first impressions died hard, and these exaggerated views persisted to the war's end and beyond. Subsequent to the success in Sicily, the early stages of the Italian campaign proved too slow for Montgomery's taste, and at year's end he was delighted to accept command of the land forces massing in England for the invasion phase of the impending Second Front, scheduled at that stage for May 1944. Although they would have preferred Gen. Harold Alexander as field commander in northwest Europe, the Americans concurred in Montgomery's appointment; the post of Supreme Commander was allocated to General Dwight D. Eisenhower.

Montgomery's view of Chief of Staff to the Supreme Allied Command's (COSSAC's) preliminary plan for the invasion of Normandy was critical. Within less than a day of becoming privy to its proposals at Marrakesh (where Churchill was convalescing after a serious illness), he wrote a strong memorandum to the prime minister arguing that the frontage of the attack should be doubled to 80 kilometers (50 miles), citing the beach congestion that had occurred in Sicily to support his arguments. He won the point, but did not receive support for his suggestion that a preliminary assault on the Channel Isles should be mounted to provoke a decisive air battle with the Luftwaffe.

On 2 January 1944 Montgomery returned to London. He was fifty-six years old, at a peak of physical fitness, and wholly convinced of his ability to win. His incisive mind tore apart Gen. Frederick Morgan's proposals for the invasion, and a greatly changed concept was the result that began to emerge. Five beaches instead of COSSAC's suggested three along an 80-kilometer (50-mile) sector of coast; eight assault brigades (five of them British and Canadian); two complete airborne divisions instead of two brigades to seize the flanks (on D-day there would in fact be three thus employed); and commensurately larger air and naval lift and support. These were, he argued, the minimum requirement to breach the German defenses, which were daily becoming stronger under the direction of Rommel, now commander of *Army Group B* under Field Marshal Gerd von Rundstedt, Commander in Chief West. Nobody could accuse Montgomery of doing things by halves.

The increases envisaged in shipping and aircraft left the Allied planning staffs at Supreme Headquarters, Allied Expeditionary Force (SHAEF), aghast, and Gen. Omar Bradley (commander U.S. First Army) disliked Montgomery's domineering attitude. But when General Eisenhower reached London for the conference called for 21 January he generally approved Montgomery's suggestions, and it was agreed that the date for Operation OVERLORD should be postponed until early June to facilitate the extra preparations required. Montgomery was quite aware of the shortage of time (largely due to the last-minute announcements of the senior appointments), and proceeded to cut many an administrative Gordian knot by appealing directly to Sir James Grigg, Secretary of State for War. Although Montgomery's suggestion to abandon Operation ANVIL on the Italian front was defeated, he succeeded in having more LSTs (Landing Ships, Tank) transferred back to England in preparation for D-day. Ably supported by his hand-picked and trusted staff team (headed by Maj. Gen. Francis de Guingand as chief of staff, Brig.

Bill Williams as chief intelligence officer, and Brig. Charles Richardson as senior planner), Montgomery settled into a pattern. He held weekly conferences and in his own spare time visited units and factories throughout the country, using his charisma to raise morale.

On 7 April the full invasion plan was revealed to a select audience at a top secret briefing held at St. Paul's School. Much stress was laid upon German defenses and reinforcement capacities, using the invaluable information supplied by Ultra, and on the means to be used to conceal Allied intentions (Operation FORTITUDE). Montgomery was in good form, speaking clearly and decisively, but had unwillingly to concede the American insistence that clear Allied target phase-lines up to D plus 90 (by which time the Seine should have been reached) must be set. At the second and last such briefing on 15 May (attended by King George VI), Montgomery again stressed the importance of gaining initial success ("Rommel will try to defeat us on the beaches") on D-day, and on the need for Allied armored columns to penetrate deep inland on the first day to disrupt enemy counterstroke plans. He stressed the significance of reinforcing the bridgehead rapidly, for by D plus 5 the worst-case scenario envisaged a major German counterattack by twenty-four divisions against a possible Allied eighteen divisions ashore.

Thus Montgomery played a prominent role in the plan-

BERNARD L. MONTGOMERY.   Montgomery (left), Miles C. Dempsey (center), and Omar Bradley (right), 10 June 1944.   IMPERIAL WAR MUSEUM

ning of Operation OVERLORD from early January to early June 1944. By the end of May, HQ 21st Army Group was established just north of Portsmouth. D-day was set for 5 June, but on 2 June a great Channel gale blew up, causing a major crisis. Should the invasion be postponed until the end of June when tide and moon conditions would once more be favorable? Montgomery spoke strongly of the need to go whatever the weather, earning Air Marshal Arthur Tedder's lasting enmity by discounting his objections. In the end, after agreeing to a one-day postponement to 6 June, Eisenhower decided that Operation OVERLORD should proceed on that date, trusting a single meteorologist's estimate that a two-day pause in the gale over the vital period was possible. Fortunately it proved to be correct.

Montgomery spent D-day at Southwick House reading the early reports. The next morning he was off the beaches aboard a Royal Navy destroyer. After paying a visit to Bradley aboard USS *Augusta*, he returned to his own vessel to meet Gen. Sir Miles Dempsey, commander of British Second Army, to learn of progress on Gold, Juno, and Sword beaches. It was clear that the initial landings had been a success, although the Americans had achieved less at Omaha Beach than had been hoped, and Second Army had failed to reach Caen. Nevertheless, the overall position was reassuring in most respects. The German coastal defenses had not proved as formidable as expected in most sectors, and the preliminary air and naval bombardments had neutralized many enemy positions. Montgomery was particularly relieved to learn that only twenty Allied aircraft had been lost during the airdrops (despite the fears of the senior airmen that losses would be crippling) and that the airborne forces had succeeded in their tasks on the flanks of the beachhead. His eventual insistence (despite the senior airmen's advice) that three airborne divisions (two American and one British) were required in the assault phase had proved correct. The American airborne divisions were only half the strength of the British division on D-day.

His faith in Gen. Percy C. S. Hobart's special armor (or Funnies) had also been proved correct. Although many DD (Duplex Drive) amphibious tanks had foundered in rough water offshore, enough had reached the beaches to give immediate fire support to the first waves of assault infantry, and the flail tanks and mortar tanks had proved especially effective against mine fields and concrete bunkers, respectively, on the British and Canadian beaches. Although all American commanders used DD Shermans, some had declined the offer of the other types of British special beach-clearing equipment, and its absence had been sorely felt at Omaha on 6 June.

Montgomery's hopes and inspirational ideas had not all been fully realized, however. Owing to congestion on the beaches and nearby roads, the deep inland thrusts he ordered had failed to materialize. A handful of Canadian tanks from Juno Beach had in fact reached the Caen-Bayeux main road almost within range of Carpiquet airfield as early as 1000 on 6 June, but, finding themselves unsupported, had fallen back. British 3d Division likewise had failed to reach Caen from Sword, and only reached the 6th Airborne Division's positions at Bénouville, about five kilometers (three miles) from Caen, by late evening. This disappointment was in no small measure due to the afternoon counterattack by the *21st Panzer Division* from the Caen area. One German tank group had actually fought its way briefly to the cliff tops near Lion-sur-Mer despite the antitank precautions taken to meet such an anticipated development in British Second Army's plans. The German unit subsequently withdrew during the night. But all in all Montgomery had good reason for satisfaction. As he informed de Guingand early on 8 June, "I am very well satisfied with the general situation." Surprise had been achieved for the assault phase and an initial lodgment had been effected.

On 8 June Montgomery landed in Normandy and moved to Creully, where his tactical headquarters had been established, and where it remained until 22 June. His camouflaged caravans were placed in an orchard. His main headquarters was still in England, but senior staff officers flew over daily to consult with their chief. At Creully he soon established his routine. Each day he visited his commanders in forward areas, and then returned to his caravans and map room late in the afternoon to receive the reports of his liaison officers. These handpicked young men were an essential part of his command system, serving as his eyes and ears throughout the bridgehead area. Every evening he sent a situation report to the Chief of the Imperial General Staff. It has been suggested that by living in relative isolation from his senior commanders Montgomery contributed to the criticism he would soon attract from his allies.

Indeed, Montgomery set himself to keep VIP visits from England to a minimum. Grigg, a firm ally and friend, was always welcome, and, rather less so, Winston Churchill and King George VI. Others were asked to keep away.

There was less friction between Montgomery and Bradley and other Americans during the first weeks in Normandy than has sometimes been claimed. Of this period Omar Bradley wrote that he "could not have wanted a more tolerant or judicious commander." The main stresses and criticisms would center around the evolution of the strategy for the breakout from Normandy. This remains a contentious issue, but on balance it would appear that Montgomery's claim is correct, that from the first his overall intention was to use the Caen area as a magnet to attract the redoubtable German armor to the eastern end of the bridgehead, and thus facilitate the American First Army's breakout farther to the west. There would later be even more Anglo-American dissent and friction, centering around Montgomery, as how best the war in western Europe could be finally won. There is no denying that Montgomery was often vain, outspoken, and supremely self-confident. Scornful of dissent or criticism, forever stridently insisting that he alone knew what was best, there is small wonder that he became increasingly unpopular with Eisenhower and Bradley as the months passed. But General Montgomery's contributions to both the planning and execution of Operation OVERLORD, and his direction of the fighting during the first weeks of the battle of Normandy, although far from faultless, were nonetheless of central importance. On 18 June, despite the great and damaging gale in the Channel, SHAEF deemed the Allied bridgehead secure. And in that achievement Bernard Law Montgomery had played a truly vital part.

Montgomery was promoted to the rank of field marshal on 1 September 1944 and remained in command of 21st Army Group to the end of the war. In later years he became Chief of the Imperial General Staff (1946–1948) and then deputy commander of NATO (1951–1958). He died at Isington Mill, Hampshire, on 24 March 1976.

[See also Churchill, Winston; Great Britain; 21st Army Group.]

BIBLIOGRAPHY

Lamb, Richard. *Montgomery in Europe, 1943–45: Success or Failure?* 1983.

Hamilton, Nigel. *Monty: Master of the Battlefield, 1942–44.* 1983.

Montgomery, Bernard L. *Normandy to the Baltic.* 1947.

Wilmot, Chester. *The Struggle for Europe.* 1954.

DAVID G. CHANDLER

MONUMENTS. See Cemeteries, Monuments, and Memorials.

MOON, DON P. (1894–1944), American, rear admiral, commander of Assault Force U (Task Force 125). Graduating fourth in the 1916 class at Annapolis, Moon spent most of his early career working with ordnance. His thesis at the University of Chicago in 1921 on problems in direction fire was tested by the navy and led to improvements in major-caliber gunnery. During the interwar period, he rotated tours aboard battleships and destroyers with assignments to the Naval Proving Ground, the Naval Gun Factory, and the Naval War College. In December 1941, Moon assumed command of Destroyer Squadron 8 and led it ably in the defense of Convoy PQ-17 and during Operation TORCH, the Allied invasion of French North Africa in November 1942. Staff duty in Washington followed.

When the planners of the Normandy invasion (OVERLORD) broadened the invasion front in January 1944, Moon was named to head Task Force 125, Assault Force U, to execute the landings on Utah Beach. Moon established his headquarters in Plymouth on 6 March; vessels assigned to his force continued to arrive, often with largely untrained crews, up to the end of May. Fortunately, Moon worked well with Maj. Gen. J. Lawton Collins, the commander of the VII Corps, although that army officer became concerned about Moon's "overly cautious" nature and his propensity for overwork.

During the training exercises, code-named TIGER, Moon's Force U on 28 April suffered E-boat attacks that sank two landing ships and killed 197 sailors and 441 soldiers(the casualty figures initially reported in 1944)—a greater loss than Force U experienced on Utah Beach on D-day. After its initial start on 3 June was aborted by bad weather, Assault Force U sailed in earnest on 5 June with Moon and Collins in the attack transport *Bayfield*. Their twelve convoys carried the U.S. 4th Infantry Division and other elements of the VII Corps.

Almost exactly on schedule, Moon's flagship anchored thirteen miles off the Cotentin Peninsula, and the first five assault waves went ashore with little opposition. But the loss of the destroyer *Corry* and several lesser vessels to mines, coupled with reports of heavy German resistance, led Moon to hold up the landing of the seven following waves. When he considered suspending the operation altogether, Collins protested vehemently and successfully. On 7 June, with the 4th Division driving inland from Utah Beach, Moon moved *Bayfield* to an anchorage five miles offshore and pushed supplies and reinforcements to Collins's troops. Moon ultimately reported that there was "little to write about the assault," except that it went "essentially according to plan." But the invading forces did suffer losses, for German mines and gunfire by 15 June had sunk four destroyers (*Corry*, *Glennon*, *Meredith*, and *Rich*) and two minesweepers (*Osprey* and *Tide*) from Moon's command. Twenty-five more vessels in Force U suffered damage.

Moon in late June went to the Mediterranean to head units scheduled to take part in Operation DRAGOON, the landing in southern France. Moon, who had been working without letup, became deeply pessimistic about the prospects of the assault. On 5 August, the despondent and exhausted officer committed suicide. For his service in Operation OVERLORD, Moon received the Legion of Merit and the army's Distinguished Service Medal.

[See also Task Force 125; Bayfield, USS.]

BIBLIOGRAPHY

Collins, J. Lawton. *Lightning Joe: An Autobiography.* 1979.
Morison, Samuel Eliot. *The Invasion of France and Germany, 1944–1945.* Vol. 11 of *History of United States Naval Operations in World War II.* 1957. Reprint, 1988. (Morison dedicated this volume to Rear Admiral Moon.)

MALCOLM MUIR, JR.

MORGAN, FREDERICK

MORGAN, FREDERICK (1894–1967), British, lieutenant general, Chief of Staff to the Supreme Allied Commander. Morgan was born in Kent, England. Educated at Clifton College and the Royal Military Academy, Woolwich, he was commissioned into the Royal Artillery in 1913. He was twice mentioned in dispatches in France in World War I and later served with the Canadian Corps. He went to the Quetta Staff College and was chief of staff of the 3d Division when World War II broke out. He commanded the Support Group of 1st Armoured Division in May 1940, and later commanded 55th Division and then the I Corps.

In March 1943 he was given his greatest test as Chief of Staff to the Supreme Allied Commander (COSSAC) for the invasion of Europe, although at that time no Supreme Commander had been appointed. He was first told to prepare a plan to attack the heart of Germany with one hundred Allied divisions. Accordingly he assembled a tri-service Anglo-American staff at Norfolk House in St. James's Square, London. But the enormity of the task was not realized until Eisenhower and his deputy commanders were appointed early in 1944. There were serious shortages of landing craft, other ships, and transport aircraft. After lengthy arguments with those who wanted major landings in the south of France, he managed to get enough landing craft for D-day; this was a major factor in determining the date of the invasion.

Morgan selected the landing beaches, but no harbor would be available for a rapid buildup once the troops were ashore. Accordingly he perfected a plan to take a floating harbor across the Channel. Slowly the mass of data and detail was put together in preparation for the most ambitious assault landing ever attempted in the history of war. Part of OVERLORD was a huge deception plan to convince the Germans that the real attack would come across the Straits of Dover.

Before the invasion Morgan was replaced as COSSAC to become deputy chief of staff to Eisenhower, in which capacity he served until the end of the war. He soon fell out with Bernard L. Montgomery, who wrote in his memoirs: "Morgan considered Eisenhower was a God; since I had discarded many of his plans he placed me at the other end of the celestial ladder." But Morgan's plan for OVERLORD remained essentially intact, even though much was changed as more resources became available and the deputy commanders were appointed. He overcame enormous intelligence, operational, and logistical problems and, by his drive and energy, forced the plan forward to fruition.

In September 1945 Morgan was appointed to the United Nations Relief and Rehabilitation Administration (UNRRA) as chief of operations in Germany, and worked to help the millions of displaced persons in Europe. Later he stated publicly that UNRRA was being used as a cover for Soviet agents; although history was to prove him right, he lost his job. In 1951 he became controller of atomic energy in London and witnessed Britain's first atomic explosion at Monte Bello in October 1952. He received many decorations.

[*See also* Deception; Intelligence; Supreme Headquarters Allied Expeditionary Force (SHAEF).]

BIBLIOGRAPHY

"Obituary to Lieutenant General Sir Frederick Morgan KCB." *Regimental News Royal Artillery*, April 1967.
The Royal Artillery Commemoration Book, 1939–1945. 1950.

MARTIN FARNDALE

MULBERRIES. *See* Artificial Harbors.

MUSÉE DE L'ORDRE DE LA LIBÉRATION.

The Museum of the Order of the Liberation occupies a building on the Boulevard Latour-Maubourg in Paris, inconspicuously located on a street adjacent to the grander home of the Hôtel des Invalides. It was originally intended as a memorial to the recipients of the Croix de la Libération (Liberation Cross), created by Gen. Charles de Gaulle in November 1940 "to reward the persons of military and civilian groups who have distinguished themselves in an exceptional manner in liberating France and her Empire." As of 23 January 1946, this honor had been awarded to five cities, eighteen units, and 1,036 civilian and military persons.

In 1943, de Gaulle created the Médaille de la Résistance (Resistance Medal) to "recognize the remarkable acts of honor and courage that, in France, in the Empire, and beyond, contributed to the resistance of the French people against the enemy and their accomplices since June 18, 1940." Eventually, 48,000 medals were awarded (as of March 1947).

In 1967, the Museum of the Order of the Liberation was installed in its present home, which was designed over two hundred years earlier by Robert de Cotte for the officers of the king. The exhibits on the first floor contain thousands of documents and photos of the Free French and the Resistance, and items such as uniforms, forged

PHOTO MURAL AT MUSEUM.   Sabotage of the rail line: while resistance fighter #1 places an explosive charge, his comrades #2, #3, #4, and #5 cover him in all directions with their machine pistols.

MUSÉE DE L'ORDRE DE LA LIBÉRATION, PARIS

identification papers, and equipment used in blowing up trains. The second floor is dedicated to the men, women, and children deported to Buchenwald, Dachau, and other Nazi concentration camps. The museum also contains many items relating to de Gaulle, including personal papers, photographs, and medals.

CHARLES E. SMITH

MUSEUMS. The commemoration of D-day in museums is comprehensive on both sides of the English Channel. In London, where most of the planning took place, the Imperial War Museum devotes much space to the subject, including Montgomery's two headquarters caravans. In mid-Thames, opposite the Tower of London, HMS *Sheffield* (the 11,500-ton cruiser commissioned in 1938 that gave fire support off Juno Beach on 6 June 1944) swings at anchor, a floating museum. At Hendon, the RAF Museum contains many aircraft of the period, as does the IWM Air Museum at Duxford, east of London.

Portsmouth and the surrounding area, scene of intensive preinvasion activity, has many special collections. Eisenhower's main pre–D-day headquarters, Southwick House

(visitation only by arrangement), still contains the giant situation map left just as it was on D-day. Near the shore in Portsmouth itself, near Southsea Castle, is the D-Day Museum. In addition to a wealth of fascinating relics and audiovisual presentations, this museum houses the famous Overlord Embroidery, which depicts the Allied preparations for, and mounting of, D-day. Two hundred seventy feet in length, comprising thirty-four panels, it took the Royal School of Needlework five years to complete. This balances the even more famous Bayeux Tapestry, also done in needlework, which depicts Duke William's invasion of England in 1066 and is on display at Bayeux in Normandy.

Crossing the Channel to France, the visitor has a wealth of museums to choose from. In May 1945 the Comité du Débarquement was set up to preserve the major sites and memories of June 1944. The Committee set up ten significant monuments at important places and numerous museums. The largest, outside Caen, is Le Mémorial: Un Musée pour la Paix, built partly on top of the German area HQ bunker. This museum covers all of World War II, and ends with an idealistic (if somewhat hopeful) section, the Nobel Peace Prize Gallery, which pleads for a peaceful world from 1945. As at Portsmouth, many vehicles and weapons are on display. Audiovisual and computerized displays are employed to bring out the story of the liberation of France.

Near Arromanches on the coast is the site of Port Winston [Churchill], one of the two floating Mulberry harbors that were constructed after D-day. The visitor can still see the remains of the artificial harbor's breakwaters out to sea. This Mulberry was damaged by a severe gale on 19 June 1944 that completely destroyed its U.S. counterpart off Omaha Beach. The Exposition Permanente du Débarquement contains many models of the complete Port Winston and vehicles and weapons involved in the invasion and shows a useful film. In nearby Bayeux, close to the impressive Commonwealth War Graves Commission Cemetery, is the Musée-Memorial de la Bataille de Normandie, 1944. Opened in 1987, it covers the entire Normandy campaign from the landings to the breakout. A selection of tanks and tank destroyers are arrayed outside.

The airborne and glider-borne aspects of D-day are commemorated in three museums. In England, the Paratroop Museum at Aldershot pays major attention to both D-day and Arnhem (September 1944). Outside stands a Douglas Dakota, the vital maid-of-all-work transport aircraft of the World War II on the Allied side. In France at Bénouville is the British Airborne Museum, dedicated to the British 6th Airborne Division. Nearby are Pegasus Bridge and the sites of the crashed gliders from which paratroopers took the vital bridge and freed the café owned by the Gondrieu family, the first house to be liberated in the early hours of 6 June. The café contains many mementos, plaques, and souvenirs; the nearby museum, designed by François Carpenter (who also planned the Arnhem and Sainte-Mère-Église museums) and paid for by the Syndicat Comité du Débarquement, opened in June 1974 and well rewards a visit.

The U.S. 82d and 101st airborne divisions are suitably commemorated in the Musée de Troupes Aéroportées at Sainte-Mère-Église, the town so strongly contested by both sides on the western flank of the invasion area. It was opened by Generals Matthew B. Ridgway and Maxwell Taylor in June 1964. The main building, innovatively designed in the shape of a parachute, contains a U.S. glider as an important part of its contents. There is also a rubber doll (or *Gummipuppe,* a one-third size dummy paratrooper) hanging from the roof. These were dropped in hundreds to confuse the German defenders during the early hours of 6 June 1944. Outside is a DC-3 (Dakota) transport aircraft.

Other museums of the group are to be found at Sainte-Marie-du-Mont, Vierville-sur-Mer, Surrain, Tilly-sur-Seulles, Ouistreham, Pourville, L'Aigle, and Merville-Franceville-Plage, not to overlook Cherbourg and more distant Dieppe, scene of the failed Anglo-Canadian raid in

divisional strength on 19 August 1942. Massive German gun emplacements are to be found at Longues-sur-Mer and Pointe du Hoc.

In the United States the National D-Day Museum, conceived by historian Stephen E. Ambrose, will be located at the University of New Orleans on the shore of Lake Pontchartrain. The U.S. Congress has appropriated $4 million to the museum, which is expected to cost $12 million.

As a military museum, it will preserve, maintain, and make available for further study the records, artifacts, exhibits, and first-hand accounts of the participants in the invasion. It will honor those individuals and units who fought and died in the greatest amphibious operation in history.

As an educational museum, it will provide the public with an accessible, comprehensive resource for understanding the events surrounding the D-day invasion as well as its legacy and its implications for American and world history. The museum will also focus on the issues of peace, the aftermath of World War II, public policy decision making, and international cooperation.

The National D-Day Museum will chronicle the role of American industry in producing the incredible numbers of landing craft, planes, ships, guns, tanks, and so much more, as well as provide a legacy of records, artifacts, and oral histories of the actual participants of the invasion. Displays will highlight the way in which industry geared up for the war, how the matériel was brought across the Atlantic, and how the battle was fought. The paratroopers at Saint-Mère-Église, the Rangers at Pointe du Hoc, the first wave at Omaha Beach, and the role of the navy and air force will be shown in state-of-the-art displays, backed up by audio, video, and documentary material.

BIBLIOGRAPHY

Tanter, J., and M. Chauvet. *Guide des musées du débarquement.*

DAVID G. CHANDLER

MYNARSKI, ANDREW CHARLES (1916–1944), Canadian, pilot officer, recipient of Victoria Cross. Born and raised in Winnipeg, Manitoba, Mynarski worked as a furrier before enlisting in the Royal Canadian Air Force (RCAF) on 29 September 1941. He was mid-upper gunner in Flying Officer Arthur de Breyne's Lancaster aircraft crew operating in No. 419 (Moose) Squadron, RCAF, from Middleton St. George, Yorkshire, as part of Six Group of RAF Bomber Command. Very early on D-day, as part of a partially successful Six Group effort against German coastal defenses, 419 Squadron attacked coastal guns at Longues, near Arromanches, in Normandy. Flying home, de Breyne and his crew viewed

the awesome invasion fleet. After participating in three invasion diversion/support raids on bridges, crossroads, and marshaling yards, this crew took part in a raid against Cambrai on the night of 12–13 June. German night fighters appeared in force. De Breyne's aircraft, KB726, was hit by a JU 88 during the approach near Amiens, as the Lancaster was descending to bomb at 2,000 feet. In the doomed aircraft the rear gunner, Pat Brophy, was trapped. Observing this, Mynarski, who had a clear chance to jump free, crawled through fire to attempt a rescue. He failed to budge the turret and eventually jumped, with his clothing on fire, saluting Brophy, whom he thought doomed. Mynarski himself died of his injuries on the ground. Almost miraculously, the rear gunner was freed on impact and flung free. He survived along with the rest of the crew. Mynarski was awarded Canada's first Victoria Cross in Bomber Command on 11 October 1946. This unassuming and gallant young man represents many thousands of his fellow Canadian aircrew whose stories will never be told. The records state, "Everybody liked him."

[*See also* Royal Canadian Air Force.]

DONALD M. SCHURMAN

N

NAVAL BASES. The availability of adequate base facilities was critical for Operation OVERLORD. In view of the size and nature of the operation, and in particular the sheer number of vessels in the assault phase, existing naval bases and civil ports were inadequate. To preserve a degree of surprise, the operation required a short sea crossing; only the south coast, therefore, was suitable for the assault phase. In consequence it was necessary to combine existing installations with new facilities. The entire effort came under the control of the naval bases, and more directly under the port admirals. A wealth of new facilities, particularly loading hards, moorings, slipways, and storage areas, were built along the south coast. Facilities east of Southampton were used by the British, those to the west by the Americans; Southampton was shared.

Established centuries before, the main British naval bases in the area, Plymouth and Portsmouth, had been developed during the wars between Britain and France. As a result they were ideally placed for operations in the English Channel. Portsmouth, with major anchorages at Spithead and the Solent, and sheltered by the Isle of Wight, was the assembly area for the Eastern Task Force, while Plymouth hosted the Western Task Force. Further afield Chatham, Sheerness, and Milford Haven supported the follow-up forces. Shipping was loaded at every available port along the south coast before assembling for the operation. Moving the ships from their loading point to the assembly area created an additional escort task. At this stage it was essential to deny the enemy air reconnaissance over the bases, so as to preserve tactical surprise. This involved a large air operation; 171 squadrons of Allied fighters were assigned to Operation OVERLORD.

In addition to the assault shipping, the escort and minesweeping forces also required bases, and these had to be found as close to Portsmouth and Plymouth as possible: Chatham, Dover, Portsmouth, Portland, Plymouth,

Dartmouth, Falmouth, and Milford Haven were all used. The bombardment groups were assembled at Belfast and on the Clyde River, Scotland, well away from the assault shipping. Once the operation began, however, they would require base facilities at Portsmouth and Plymouth for reloading and refueling. The lengthier process of replacing worn guns was left to Rosyth in Scotland.

Along the banks of the Thames, the construction and movement of the caissons for Mulberry harbors created a new task for Chatham Dockyard. Once the operation opened, the Build Up Control Organisation (BUCO) at Combined Headquarters controlled the reloading, while the Turn Round Control Organisations at Chatham, Portsmouth, and Plymouth were responsible for ships' refueling and stores, and their dispatch back to the beachhead. The two major bases also exercised local control of repair, salvage, and tugs.

Naval bases played a major role in the preparation and support of Operation NEPTUNE. They handled the administrative, technical, and logistic support of the largest amphibious force ever assembled, and ensured the smooth running of the operation under Adm. Bertram H. Ramsay's master plan.

BIBLIOGRAPHY

Edwards, Kenneth. *Operation Neptune*. 1946.
Roskill, Stephen W. *The Offensive*. Vol. 3, pt. 2, of *The War at Sea, 1939–1945*. 1960.

ANDREW LAMBERT

NAVAL SUPPLY. The object of Operation NEPTUNE was to secure a bridgehead on the coast of France; until this had been extended to include a rear area safe from enemy artillery, with airfields and large supply dumps, the armies would depend on naval support. Thus the naval responsibility did not end with landing the troops.

For their tasks off the beachhead, naval forces required their own logistic support: large ships able to return to bases in Britain, and small craft employed for inshore support, unloading, and medical evacuation. The importance of supply, both to the smooth functioning of the operation and to the morale of naval personnel, was widely recognized. Detailed planning was in place by November 1943. The instructions to the depot ships under Como. H. T. England stressed the need to deliver food and mail to the Ferry Service vessels off the beachhead. The local naval units were supported from their own depot ships, with dedicated ammunition carriers, galley barges, and water carriers. The postoperation analysis was critical of the late arrival of the depot ships, and their subsequent delay in becoming operational. Inevitably, the delivery of mail did not match up to expectations.

The home ports assigned to the bombarding squadrons were prepared for the rapid turnaround of large warships, particularly the resupply of ammunition and fuel. Other tasks were more complex. The battleship HMS *Warspite* was sent to Rosyth, Scotland, to have its 15-inch guns changed, and was mined off Harwich; swift repair work was necessary. The turnaround of craft from the home ports was complicated by the need to evacuate the wounded, as well as increasingly large numbers of prisoners, starting with seven hundred of the latter on D plus 1.

The level of supplies required off the beachhead can be gauged from the amount of fresh stores sent in the first two weeks, as shown below, in tons:

Week ending	Potatoes	Meat	Bread	Vegetables
10 June 1944	446	98	61	51
17 June 1944	400	106	62	49

Stores had been built up ashore, both at the naval victualing yards in Portsmouth and Plymouth, and in dispersed inland sites, against the danger of enemy action. Arrangements had been made with the Ministry of Food for access to civilian stocks. In the event, the main shortfall came in bread and baking capacity; to remedy it, a large mobile bakery unit was deployed at Plymouth.

The task of unloading was formidable. During the first week a daily average of arrivals included 25 Liberty ships, 38 coasters, 9 troopships, 40 LSTs, 75 LCTs, and 20 LCI (L)s. Between D plus 1 and D plus 24, 4,257 ships and vessels arrived off the beachhead; most required unloading. Around the 20th there was some anxiety over the levels of naval stores in the British Assault Area, as demand had exceeded estimates, but this problem was resolved. Even after the capture of Cherbourg and Le Havre, Adm. Bertram H. Ramsay insisted on retaining the cross-Channel convoy organization, which, he argued, provided the best system for giving notice of intended cargoes, so that unloading capacity could be provided. Beach-based logistics remained a feature of British army operations long into the autumn, and that required a large naval presence.

BIBLIOGRAPHY

Schofield, Brian. *Operation Neptune*. 1974.

ANDREW LAMBERT

NAVY. [*This entry includes separate discussions of Allied and German naval forces.*]

Allied Naval Forces

The naval forces for Operation NEPTUNE (the code name for the naval component of Operation OVERLORD) were commanded by British Adm. Bertram H. Ramsay. As Allied Naval Commander in Chief, Expeditionary Force, Ramsay was responsible for all direct naval aspects of the invasion. Admiral Ramsay had been appointed to this position in June 1942, months before detailed planning for the operation was begun. After undertaking a variety of other tasks during 1942 and 1943, he eventually returned to his OVERLORD duties in October of that year.

Directly under Admiral Ramsay in the chain of command were U.S. Rear Admiral Alan G. Kirk, commander, Western Task Force, and British Rear Adm. Philip L. Vian, commander, Eastern Task Force. Kirk joined the NEPTUNE organization in mid-November 1943. Vian took on the Eastern Task Force assignment in January 1944, following the expansion of the landings from the planned three-division, 48-kilometer-wide (30-mile-wide) assault to the five-division, 80-kilometer-wide (50-mile-wide) one. Under Kirk's and Vian's task force commands were arrayed officers in command of assault forces for each landing beach and for the follow-on forces.

The naval vessels comprising the NEPTUNE force included warships and landing ships and craft from a number of different navies; not only from Great Britain, Canada, and the United States, but also from the navies-in-exile of France, the Netherlands, Norway, Poland, and Greece. In all, the Allied warships assembled for Operation NEPTUNE numbered 1,213 ships, including seven battleships, two monitors, twenty-three cruisers (two of them French and one Polish), three gunboats (two of them Dutch), eighty fleet destroyers (two of them Norwegian and two Polish), and seventy-one corvettes (three of them French, two Greek, and three Norwegian). In terms of overall composition by national origin, the combatant ships were 79 percent British and Canadian, 16.5 percent American, and 4.5 percent French, Dutch, or other Allies. The landing ships

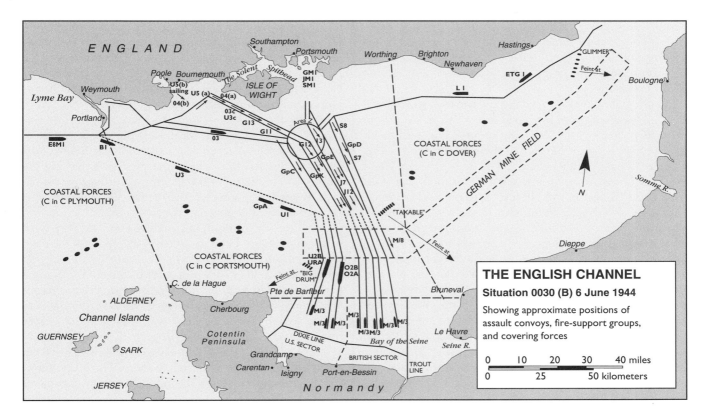

THE ENGLISH CHANNEL

Situation 0030 (B) 6 June 1944

Showing approximate positions of assault convoys, fire-support groups, and covering forces

0   10   20   30   40 miles

0   25   50 kilometers

and craft for NEPTUNE numbered 4,126. These consisted of a wide variety of specialized types developed for assault landings during the previous several years, among them, the LSH (Landing Ship, Headquarters), LCF (Landing Craft, Flak), and LCT(R) (Landing Craft, Tank [Rocket]) types.

The warships assigned to NEPTUNE were a mixture of old and modern combatants. The battleships and monitors, whose job it was to provide the heaviest weight of bombardment against German gun emplacements and other targets along the coast of northern France, were aging behemoths in 1944. They included the British battleships HMS *Warspite*, which had participated in the Battle of Jutland in 1916, and the USS *Arkansas*, the oldest active battleship in the U.S. Navy. As heavy bombardment ships, however, they were highly effective, being superb gun platforms capable of lobbing 12-, 14-, or 15-inch shells many thousands of meters inland. On the other hand, many of the smaller warships, including destroyers and minesweepers, were modern vessels.

As stated in Admiral Ramsay's Naval Operation Orders, the object of Operation NEPTUNE was "to carry out an operation from the United Kingdom to secure a lodgement on the Continent from which further offensive operations can be developed." Accomplishing this mission required an initial assault from landing ships and craft on a five-division front between Ouistreham and Varreville in the Bay of the Seine (the area along the French coast of Normandy between the Orne River in the east and the area of the Cotentin Peninsula just northward from the mouth of the Vire River in the west). This territory was divided into five beach landing areas, codenamed (from east to west) Sword, Juno, Gold, Omaha, and Utah. The first three beaches were assigned to Admiral Vian's British-dominated Eastern Task Force. The other two were the responsibility of Admiral Kirk's largely American-manned Western Task Force. The dividing line on the Normandy beaches between the Eastern and Western task forces was set at the town of Port-en-Bessin.

From the Allies' perspective, the Germans defending the coast of northern France benefited from two major advantages: the weakness of the assaulting force during the landing period; and the slow rate of buildup achievable using sea communications, compared to that achievable with land communications. As Allied naval planners saw it, however, these advantages could be countered by the effective employment of naval gunfire and air superiority.

On 5 June 1944, the hundreds of ships taking part in Operation NEPTUNE began heading to sea from the assembly ports on Britain's Channel coast. They sailed in their separate convoys toward a rendezvous point designated Area Z, southeast of the Isle of Wight. From there, they moved southeast into the northern end of the Spout, the series of ten mine-swept channels (two lanes for each of the five assault forces) through the German mine fields laid in the middle of the English Channel. Their passage to France was protected by covering forces arrayed far to the east and west of their route, including antisubmarine escort carriers, destroyer groups, and British Coastal Command patrol aircraft.

Despite heavy weather, the assault convoys all reached their allotted sectors of the Normandy coast before dawn on 6 June. Just before 0530, the bombardment ships of Vian's Eastern Task Force began their prearranged firing against German coastal defenses. The ships of Kirk's Western Task Force had been instructed to withhold their fire until 0550 (H-hour minus 40 minutes), but as shots from German guns began ranging ever closer to the anchored ships, the American gunfire support commanders gave orders to begin the firing a few minutes early.

The landings were staggered in order to take tidal variations into account. H-hour for the Utah landing was set for 0630, an hour earlier than on the British front. Two hours before, U.S. Rangers had seized the unoccupied Saint Marcouf Islands, situated seaward of the landing beaches. At Utah, the assault forces landed slightly to the south of the designated beaches, which proved fortuitous, however, since it allowed the assaulting troops to avoid many of the heavier beach defenses. Beach obstacles were destroyed quickly or sidestepped. As a result, the U.S. 4th Division advanced rapidly inland, and the unloading program proceeded according to plan.

The landings of Omaha began at 0635. Here, things did not go smoothly. The wind and rough seas at Omaha swamped some of the special craft designed to breach the obstacles planted offshore and at the beach line by the Germans. This greatly hindered the underwater demolition teams in clearing paths through the thickly planted obstacles. Instead of the expected sixteen lanes, they were able to clear only five before the assault waves began arriving. As a result, landing craft began piling up around the entrances to the few open lanes, easy targets for the waiting German gunners. It was not until just before noon that the first organized units from the U.S. 1st and 29th divisions began crossing the beach line, and it was 1300 before a general advance began in that sector.

Overall, the landings in the British sector were more successful. At Sword the assault began at 0730. Although heavy seas caused similar problems with the clearing of beach obstacles, there was little initial German opposition. Thus, the entire assault brigade of the British 3d Division was ashore by 0943, only minutes behind schedule. Thereafter, however, the going got much heavier, as severe fighting broke out on the beaches.

At Juno, the landings (originally scheduled to begin at 0735) were postponed for ten minutes; even then, the initial assault forces were delayed. The higher-than-expected tide at the beaches meant that the landing craft were forced to ground among the obstacles, rather than ahead of them. Here, effective naval gunfire support aided the assault by keeping German defensive fire to a minimum before the landing craft touched down. Despite some holdups, by early afternoon, the entire Canadian 3d Division was ashore and pressing southward toward its objectives.

H-hour at Gold was 0725. In this area too, the tide was higher than anticipated. Moreover, the beach obstacles were far more numerous than expected. The beach clearing was slow to start, and in the process of getting the troops ashore, many of the landing craft became casualties. By nightfall, however, the British 50th Division had secured a firm lodgment in the Gold area.

Casualties to the warships involved in NEPTUNE were surprisingly light. In all, from 6 to 30 June 1944, the navy lost twenty-four combatants (the majority to German mines), and another fifty-nine were damaged. In the same period, thirty-five Allied merchant ships and auxiliaries were sunk and sixty-one damaged. As expected, however, the losses of landing craft were much higher; more than 700 were lost or damaged.

In every regard, the Allied navy carried out Operation NEPTUNE with great skill and courage. The amphibious capabilities provided by the naval forces employed in OVERLORD enabled the Allied armies to land on the coast of France in the face of German resistance, overcome the enemy's initial defenses, expand the individual beachheads into a firm lodgment, and build up the combat forces quickly enough to enable the armies to move over to the offensive within a few weeks, all the while keeping them supplied across open beaches.

[*See also* Eastern Task Force; Kirk, Alan G.; Vian, Philip; Western Task Force]

BIBLIOGRAPHY

Ellis, L. F., et al. *The Battle of Normandy*. Vol. 1 of *Victory in the West*. 1962.

Morison, Samuel Eliot. *The Invasion of France and Germany, 1944–1945*. Vol. 11 of *History of United States Naval Operations in World War II*. 1957

Roskill, S. W. *The Offensive*. Vol. 3, pt. 2, of *The War at Sea, 1939–1945*. 1961.

Roskill, S. W. *White Ensign: The British Navy at War, 1939–1945*. 1960.

Schofield, Brian B. *Operation Neptune*. No. 10 of *Sea Battle in Close Up*. 1974.

JEFFREY G. BARLOW

German Navy

To understand the role of the German Navy in the defense against the invasion, it is necessary to describe its responsibilities in connection with the other services. The

UJ 1401.   Submarine Chaser.

Commander in Chief West, Field Marshal Gerd von Rund-stedt, commanded all shore-based forces in France including the naval shore forces. Adm. Theodor Krancke, Commander in Chief Naval Group Command West, was responsible for tasks oriented to the sea, like the firing of naval coastal artillery, radar that was directed at the sea's surface, naval communications, and naval surface forces. The U-boats remained under operational control of the U-boat commander, Grand Admiral Karl Dönitz (also Commander in Chief of the Navy). Dönitz delegated the daily control of operations to Rear Adm. Eberhard Godt, chief of the Second Department of the 2d Naval Staff, U-boat Operations, in Berlin. The commander of U-boats West, Capt. Hands-Rudolf Rösing, was responsible only for the administration of the bases and flotillas in France; he had no operational control.

Up to the actual moment of the invasion, the main tasks of the navy were to attack Allied shipping with U-boats and S-boats (*Schnellboote*—small, fast motor torpedo boats), and to defend and minesweep the German sea lines of communications, including routes for U-boats going out or coming back. Other tasks were reconnaissance and the laying of mine fields against the possible invasion. In the event of an invasion all forces were to be used to the very limit of their capabilities.

In June 1944 Krancke had the following naval forces under his command:

For offensive operations:

5 destroyers of the *8th Flotilla*, of which two were out of service owing to heavy damage or repairs

2 torpedo boats of the *4th Flotilla* (two others had been lost in April 1944 in actions with Allied destroyers) and 4 torpedo boats of the *5th Flotilla*, two of which were damaged

44 S-boats of the *2d* and *8th* flotillas in Ostend, the *4th Flotilla* in Boulogne, and the *5th* and *9th* flotillas in Cherbourg (29 of these boats were operational on 6 June)

For defensive operations, under the commander of the Western Defense Force, Rear Adm. Erich Alfred Breuning:

18 Type-35 and 33 Type-40 fleet minesweepers (*Minensuchboote*) of the *2d, 6th*, and *24th* flotillas with the *3d Defense Division* in the western Channel, and of the *8th, 10th, 26th*, and *28th* flotillas in the Bay of Biscay

53 R-boats (motor minesweepers, or *Räumboote*) of the *2d Flotilla* at Dunkirk, the *4th Flotilla* at Boulogne, the *8th Flotilla* at Bruges, the *10th Flotilla* at Le Havre, and the *14th Flotilla* at Dieppe

22 big and medium mine destruction vessels (*Sperrbrecher*) of the *2d Flotilla* at Royan and the *6th* at Concarneau

In addition there were many auxiliary minesweepers (former trawlers, whalers, luggers, etc.) of the *36th Flotilla* at Ostend, the *38th Flotilla* at Le Havre, the

KARL DÖNITZ.   Center, with Erich Raeder (left) and Adolf Hitler, greeting the crew of *U 29,* October 1939.

BIBLIOTHEK FÜR ZEITGESCHICHTE, STUTTGART

40th and *46th* flotillas in the western Channel, and the *42d* and *44th* flotillas in the Bay of Biscay (each flotilla had between 12 and 20 operational vessels).

15 auxiliary submarine chasers (*U-bootjäger;* former whalers) of the *14th Flotilla* in the Bay of Biscay

Auxiliary patrol boats (*Vorpostenboote*): former trawlers, and newly built luggers, or *Kriegsfischkutter,* of the *2d Flotilla* in Saint-Malo, the *4th, 6th*, and *7th* flotillas in the Bay of Biscay, and the *15th* and *18th* flotillas at Le Havre

Seagoing barges (*Marine-Fähr-Prähme,* or *MFP*), similar to Allied LCTs (Landing Craft, Tank), rebuilt into the heavily armed gun carriers (*Artillerie-Fähren,* or *AF*) of the *2d Flotilla* between Boulogne and Fécamp, and the *6th Flotilla* in the Bay of the Seine

Actually available and operational in the area from Boulogne to Cherbourg on 6 June were 3 torpedo boats, 1 minesweeper, 29 S-boats, 36 R-boats, about 35 auxiliary minesweepers and patrol boats, 11 gun carriers, and 3 minelaying *MFP*s.

One important defense measure was the laying of mine fields. Because of the strong currents and the heavy tides in the Channel area, however, the fields soon lost their effectiveness, so the decision was made to lay mine fields with time limits on the firing devices, so as to clear the area after a certain time for the laying of new mines. In shallow waters ground mines were used, and in deeper areas mines of the anchored type. From January to March 1944, eighteen fields were laid in the Channel area, of which only nine were still active on 6 June. In April Field Marshal Erwin Rommel, commander in chief of *Army Group B,* asked that some "blitz barrages" be laid immediately; 1,061 such mines were laid up to 1 May. In addition, special coastal mines were laid on the mud flats below the high-water mark to hit beaching landing craft. But the supply of mines was impeded by Allied bomb damage both to production sites in Germany and to the transportation system in France.

The navy operated a number of coastal batteries, some armed with German guns, and some with guns captured from French arsenals. Because the Wehrmacht High Command (OKW) and the Commander in Chief West expected the invasion in the Somme River area and the Pas de Calais, the heaviest batteries were located there. In the Bay of the Seine area and on the Cotentin Peninsula there were heavy batteries with three 21-cm guns at Marcouf and three 17-cm guns near Barfleur, and medium batteries with four 15- or 15.5-cm guns near Le Havre, at Honfleur, Villerville, Bénerville, Houlgate, Ouistreham, Longues, the Pointe du Hoc, Morsalines, and Gatteville. Light batteries with four to six 10.5- or 12-cm guns were at Villerville, Ver-sur-Mer, Sainte-Madeleine, Azeville, Quinéville, and Barfleur.

Because of the unfavorable weather conditions, the invasion was not expected during the night of 5–6 June. At 2230 on 5 June the commander of the *Fifteenth Army,* Col. Gen. Hans von Salmuth, ordered a standby for action, following the interception of the code word for the French Resistance sent from London. At 0130 on 6 June the first reports of parachute landings came in. Radar station reports of a great number of echoes on the screens were first interpreted as a possible jamming operation by the British. At 0309 the radar station at Port-en-Bessin reported ten large vessels anchored and unloading. Then Naval Group Command West gave the alarm: "Big enemy landing Bay of the Seine." Orders were given for the three torpedo boats at Le Havre to attack, for the *15th Patrol Flotilla* to reconnoiter the area, and the *6th Gun Carrier Flotilla* to open fire on the landing craft. They came under heavy fire, and patrol boat *V 1509* was the first German vessel lost. The S-boats from Cherbourg had to return because of the heavy sea.

From 0309 on, Naval Group Command West was of the opinion that the operations in the Bay of the Seine were the main Allied invasion. The Commander in Chief West, Field Marshal von Rundstedt, and at first also *Army Group B,* waited for more evidence, fearing this might be a feint to cover a main landing farther to the east. When Rundstedt at 0700 finally requested the release of the armored forces held in reserve, Hitler did not allow it, because of continuing doubt about the location of the main landing. Only at 1100, when the BBC announced the invasion in Normandy, were the first orders to the armored groups sent out. So the Allies secured the first beachheads, supported by the intense gunfire of battleships, monitors, cruisers, and destroyers trying to silence German coastal batteries. The German naval forces could not prevent the landings; they could only try to attack the flanks of the invasion forces with torpedo boats from Le Havre and S-boats from Cherbourg.

In the days that followed, Admiral Krancke tried to bring in destroyers from the Bay of Biscay and S-boats from Dutch bases. The German naval forces had no real chance to prevent or simply harass the Allied invasion. The superiority of the Allied air and naval forces was so great that the few German units capable of offensive action rarely got close enough to the landing forces to fire their torpedoes or guns.

German vessels lost from 6 to 13 June were as follows: by gunfire: the patrol boat *V 1509,* the destroyers *ZH 1* and *Z 32,* and the minesweeper *M 343*; by action with Allied motor torpedo boats: the minesweeper *M 83,* the patrol boats *V 1314, V 2020,* and *V 2021,* and the S-boat *S 136*; by mines: the S-boats *S 139* and *S 140*; by air attacks: the motor minesweepers *R 221* and *R 97,* the gun carrier *AF 15,* and the S-boats *S 178, S 189,* and *S 197*; and by scuttling: the gun carriers *AF 62, AF 64, AF 67,* and *AF 72,* the submarine chaser *UJ 1401,* and the patrol boat *V 206.* During the heavy RAF Bomber Command attacks on Le Havre and Boulogne on 14–15 and 15–16 June, 3 torpedo boats, 15 S-boats, 1 minesweeper, 2 escorts, 8 R-boats, 3 gun carriers, 9 auxiliary minesweepers, 10 auxiliary patrol boats, and 3 depot vessels were destroyed.

German torpedo boats sank the Norwegian destroyer *Svenner,* and German S-boats sank the destroyer USS *Nelson,* 4 LSTs, 1 LCI, 2 LCTs, 1 MTB, 1 tug, and 3 freighters. German mines destroyed the Allied destroyers, frigates, and minesweepers USS *Osprey,* HMS *Wrestler,* USS *Corry,* USS *Tide,* and USS *Rich.* Bombs or gunfire damaged the destroyer USS *Meredith* and sank the destroyer USS *Glennon.* German gunfire damaged the French destroyer *Mistral* beyond repair, and air attacks sank the frigate HMS *Lawford* and the destroyer HMS *Boadicea.*

[*See also* Dönitz, Karl; Krancke, Theodor; Western Defense Force.]

BIBLIOGRAPHY

Adams, H. H., E. B. Potter, and J. Rohwer. "Von der Normandie zur Elbe." In *Seemacht. Von der Antike bis zur Gegenwart,* edited by E. B. Potter, C. W. Nimitz, and J. Rohwer. 1982.

Krancke, Theodor. "Invasionsabwehrmaßnahmen der Kriegsmarine im Kanalgebiet 1944." *Marine-Rundschau* 66 (1969): 170–187.

Rohwer, Jürgen, and Gerhard Hümmelchen. *Chronology of the War at Sea, 1939–1945.* Translated by Derek Masters. 1992.

JÜRGEN ROHWER

NETHERLANDS. The Netherlands was invaded by German forces on 10 May 1940, as part of the German offensive in western Europe. After four days of fighting, the Dutch capitulated. Their resistance had enabled Queen Wilhelmina, the royal family, and the government to escape to Great Britain. Few Dutch army troops managed to escape, though several hundred army and army air corps personnel did reach England. The Royal Netherlands Navy, on the other hand, was able to remove its units, including submarines, naval aircraft, and most of its personnel, to British ports and airfields. The main force of the fleet, however, was assigned to the Netherland East Indies, now Indonesia.

Dutch forces in Britain on the eve of Operation

PRINCE BERNHARD.   Queen Wilhelmina's son-in-law helped organize Dutch resistance. Here he presents the order of Orange-Nassau to four members of the U.S. Ninth Army for their service in liberating the Netherlands.

NATIONAL ARCHIVES

OVERLORD included the Royal Netherlands brigade Princess Irene, Commando Unit No. 2 Troop (a part of No. 10 [Interallied] Commando), and several squadrons with the Royal Air Force. The Princess Irene Brigade was put ashore in Normandy in August 1944 to take part in the campaign up to the capitulation of Germany. Commando Unit No. 2 fought later on the Continent.

The Dutch contributed three squadrons to the RAF: No. 320; No. 321, which was combined with No. 320 in 1941; and No. 322. Dozens of Dutch air corps personnel were assigned to various other RAF squadrons. Squadrons 320 and 322 were not deployed as a part of OVERLORD but took part in the subsequent campaign in Normandy. On 10 June 1944, seventeen B-25 Mitchell bombers of Squadron 320 attacked the headquarters of a German armored division near La Caine; the commanding officer and several members of his staff were killed.

The cruiser HNMS *Sumatra* and the gunboats HNMS *Soemba* and *Flores* participated in OVERLORD. The obsolete *Sumatra*, its armament dismantled, was sailed to the coast of Normandy and scuttled near the shore on 9 June as a breakwater for the artificial harbor constructed there.

Flores and *Soemba*, both built in 1926, had shown the value of their 15-cm (6-inch) guns during the Italian campaign. *Soemba* served in Rear Adm. Morton L. Deyo's Bombardment Group at Utah Beach. The vessel stood by to support the daring attack of American Ranger units on the Pointe du Hoc stronghold, but was deployed to shell two inland targets and an antiaircraft battery east of Pointe du Hoc. On 10, 11, and 12 June *Soemba* attacked enemy batteries selected by the ship's commander, then late on 12 June was withdrawn to Plymouth. *Flores* served in Capt. E. W. L. Longley-Cook's Fire Support Group at Gold Beach. On D-day it used up half its ammunition. It was engaged in these operations up to August, taking two breaks, one to take on ammunition 17–19 June and one for repairs 30 June–21 July. During these operations it was attacked on several occasions by medium-sized enemy coastal batteries.

Dutch forces suffered no losses in OVERLORD.

BIBLIOGRAPHY

Bosscher, Philip M. *De Koninklijke Marine in de Tweede Wereldoorlog*. 3 vols. 1984–1990.
Geldhof, Nico. *70 jaar Marineluchtvaartdienst*. 1987.
de Jong, Louis. *Het Koninkrijk der Nederlanden in de Tweede Wereldoorlog*. 13 vols. 1969–1991.

C. M. SCHULTEN

NEWMAN, JAMES (1896–1959), American, brigadier general, commander of the IX Engineer Command. Newman, who commanded the Ninth Air Force's engineer units during the D-day operations, was responsible for building airfields in the American sector of the Normandy beachhead. He was a highly experienced civil engineer with extensive experience in airfield construction. He graduated from West Point in 1918 and was commissioned in the Corps of Engineers. After receiving a B.S. degree in Civil Engineering from M.I.T. in 1921, he spent most of the interwar period involved in major construction projects such as the Florida ship canal.

Newman began his association with airfield engineering as director for construction of the Washington, D.C., National Airport in 1939–1940. As district engineer at Wright Field, Ohio, in 1940, he built both Wright and Patterson air bases. His reputation as a civil engineer was such that, between 1940 and 1942, he was given the task of supervising construction of more than two hundred airfields for the Army Air Forces' flight training program.

After arriving in England in November 1943, Newman assumed command of the Ninth Air Force engineer units in January 1944. In March these units were reorganized as the IX Engineer Command. As with most of the other senior Army Air Forces commanders, his primary duty before D-day was in organizing and training units. He was fortunate in receiving relatively well-trained men before D-day, but he ensured that they received additional training by building airfields and facilities for the Eighth Air Force.

The IX Engineer Command units came ashore on D-day. Within the first week of the landing, several airstrips were in operation in the American sector, and Newman had established a forward headquarters for his engineers. His ability to organize and deploy his units effectively meant that the very ambitious airfield construction schedule planned before D-day was met and even exceeded.

General Newman's reputation as one of the best civil engineers in the army and a man who could manage large projects was enhanced by his performance during the D-day campaign. By May 1945 his command had assisted Allied air operations on the Continent by building and repairing hundreds of airfields for the Army Air Forces. He retired from the army in 1946 and died in 1959.

[*See also* IX Engineer Command.]

BIBLIOGRAPHY

Ninth Air Force. Operation Records. USAF Historical Research Agency, Maxwell Air Force Base, Alabama.

JAMES S. CORUM

NEW ZEALAND. By June 1944 nearly 200,000 of New Zealand's 1.6 million people were in the armed forces, with some 100,000 serving abroad. Although New Zealand was maintaining a division in Italy and a division in the southwest Pacific, more than one third of New Zealand's overseas manpower, about 35,000 men, were serving in Great Britain. Of these, about 30,000 were in the RAF or in the six squadrons designated Royal New Zealand Air Force (RNZAF), while just under 4,000 of the Royal New Zealand Naval Volunteer Reserve (RNZNVR) were in the Royal Navy. Because New Zealanders were found in virtually every ship of the Royal Navy and every squadron of the Royal Air Force, this article will treat only those ships and squadrons commanded and manned substantially by New Zealanders.

Junior officers of the RNZNVR commanded scores of landing craft on D-day. Among the more notable exploits were Lt. D. J. M. Glover's and Lt. J. F. Ingham's handling of their landing craft, *LCI(S) 516* and *LCI(L) 110,* respectively, under heavy fire while negotiating mines and underwater obstacles in order to put Commandos ashore at Ouistreham, Sword Beach. Both officers were subsequently awarded the Distinguished Service Cross (DSC). On the beach Lt. R. Crammond's work as naval liaison officer with the Commandos earned him a mention in dispatches (m.i.d.) and a Croix de Guerre. Offshore, flotillas of New Zealand–manned motor torpedo boats engaged in running fights for the first few nights with German E-boats. Lt. N. Watson, commanding *MTB 453,* and Lt. C. J. Wright, commanding *MTB 454,* engaged E-boats in six separate night engagements; both were awarded the DSC.

RNZAF fighter and bomber squadrons took part in every phase of the operation. During May and early June,

the Tempests of No. 486 Squadron and the Mosquito Intruders of No. 487 Squadron attacked the railway system of northern France. On D-day No. 489 Squadron's Beaufighters patrolled along the invasion coast and in the week after the landing carried out 34 separate attacks on E-boats and R-boats. The Spitfires of No. 485 Squadron helped maintain aerial superiority over the beachhead during the day, shooting down two JU 88s over Omaha Beach at 1500 on 6 June, and in the following week shot down another seven German fighters, including four rocket-firing FW 190s. After dusk the Mosquito night fighters of No. 488 Squadron took over patrol work and intercepted several Luftwaffe raids against the beachhead, the Mosquito pilots claiming in the first week to have shot down twenty German bombers. Meanwhile No. 75 Squadron's Lancasters had bombed Ouistreham on the night of 5–6 June, and carried out subsequent raids in the Normandy area on four of the six succeeding nights.

BIBLIOGRAPHY

Mitchell, A. W. *New Zealanders in the Air War.* 1945.
Waters, S. D. *The Royal New Zealand Navy.* 1956.

DUNCAN ANDERSON

XIX CORPS. The XIX Corps was constituted in 1942 at Camp Polk, Louisiana. In 1944, after being reorganized and redesignated, the corps received its first combat assignment as one of the follow-on formations for the Allied landings at Normandy. Commanded by Maj. Gen. Charles Corlett, a combat veteran from the Pacific, the XIX Corps began landing in Normandy on D plus 6, its mission to deepen the area where the U.S. V and VII corps had joined forces. The corps headquarters became operational in France on 14 June and assumed responsibility for a sector between the V and VII corps.

The XIX Corps began its first limited-objective attacks the next day with the 29th Division, assigned from V Corps, and the 30th Division, which was still landing its forces and concentrating them between the Vire and Taute rivers. By the evening of 15 June the attack had secured positions along the north side of the Vire-Taute Canal. General Corlett ordered the 30th Division to act

---

XIX Corps
Maj. Gen. Charles Corlett

29th Infantry Division
Maj. Gen. Charles H. Gerhardt

30th Infantry Division
Maj. Gen. Leland S. Hobbs

---

defensively along the canal while the 29th Division continued the attack toward Saint-Lô. After attacks on three successive days (16, 17, and 18 June) that went virtually nowhere, the corps front settled into a stalemate for the rest of the month.

Forces assigned to XIX Corps finally captured Saint-Lô in mid-July. The corps fought across France as part of the U.S. First Army until the war ended in Europe. The XIX Corps was disbanded in France in September 1945.

[See also Corlett, Charles.]

BIBLIOGRAPHY

Harrison, Gordon A. Cross-Channel Attack. U.S. Army in World War II: The European Theater of Operations. 1951.
Wilson, John B. Armies, Corps, Divisions, and Separate Brigades. 1987.

CLAYTON R. NEWELL

XIX TACTICAL AIR COMMAND.

XIX Tactical Air Command (TAC) formed part of the U.S. Ninth (Tactical) Air Force. It was activated in February 1944 under the command of Brig. Gen. Otto ("Opie") Weyland as the XIX Air Support Command and was redesignated XIX TAC on 18 April 1944. In its formative stages XIX TAC worked under the tutelage of U.S. IX Fighter Command, which had responsibility for giving new fighter groups six weeks of in-theater training.

In theory the U.S. Army Air Forces provided one numbered air force to work with each American army group. Ninth Air Force headquarters would work directly with the U.S. Twelfth Army Group, commanded by Lt. Gen. Omar Bradley. Ninth Air Force headquarters retained control of IX Bomber Command, because the medium bombers had the range to support the entire army group and could therefore be quickly allocated as needed. According to American air support doctrine, each U.S. army was supported by a tactical air command consisting of fighter-bombers having the range to cover its frontage, and tactical air reconnaissance units. IX TAC supported U.S. First Army, which commanded all American ground troops during the Normandy invasion and breakout; XIX TAC would support U.S. Third Army, commanded by Lt. Gen. George S. Patton, Jr.; XXIX TAC would assist U.S. Ninth Army. The function of each TAC was to provide close air support (the direct application of airborne firepower to the battlefield), air interdiction (the strafing and bombing of lines of communication, supply, and units in the enemy's rear areas), aerial photographic reconnaissance, and, if necessary, protection from and suppression of enemy air operations.

In February and March 1944 Ninth Air Force fighters were heavily involved in long-range strategic escort duties for Eighth Air Force missions penetrating into Germany. This led to a dispute between Air Chief Marshal Trafford Leigh-Mallory, commanding the tactical air forces of Eisenhower's Allied Expeditionary Air Force (AEAF), who wanted to free the Ninth Air Force's fighters to begin training for the invasion, and Gen. Carl A. Spaatz, commander of U.S. Strategic Air Forces (USSTAF), who needed the fighters to kill Germans pilots over Germany. Spaatz retained the fighters until mid-March, when the needs of the Transportation Plan, which called for interdiction of German lines of communication in Belgium and France, required the fighters' services. In the meantime, both XIX TAC and Third Army headquarters echelons began working with each other in February 1944; by the time both units became operational on 1 August 1944, they had established an excellent working relationship.

XIX TAC began operations by assuming command of veteran groups formerly assigned to IX TAC. When XIX TAC became operational, it divided its headquarters into advanced and rear echelons. At the advanced section, which consisted of operations, intelligence, and signal personnel with a small detachment of administrative officers, General Weyland planned and directed operations. The advanced section moved often and was never more than forty-eight hours behind the Third Army command post. An "X-ray" section of XIX TAC chief of staff and two or three assistants stayed with the Third Army command post at all times to maintain personal liaison. The rear section, which performed the administrative functions of the command, located itself near the attached air units, where it could deal with their logistical, personnel, and administrative needs. It moved far less frequently than the advanced section.

The Third Army/XIX TAC collaboration formed the most effective and successful American air-ground team in World War II. The volatile Patton pronounced his relationship with the soft-spoken but firm Weyland as "love at first sight" and after the war called Weyland "the best damned general in the Air Force." The two generals worked closely together for nine months. TAC covered Third Army's 500-mile-long open flank along the Loire River during the race from Normandy to the German border, assisted Patton's counterattack during the Battle of the Bulge, and helped open the way for Third Army in its final drive deep into the Third Reich.

[See also Weyland, Otto.]

BIBLIOGRAPHY

Craven, Wesley Frank, and James Lea Cate, eds. Europe: Argument to V-E Day, January 1944 to May 1945. Vol. 3 of The Army Air Forces in World War II. 1951.
Ninth Air Force. Condensed Analysis of the Ninth Air Force in the European Theater of Operations. 1946. Reprint, 1984.

Spires, David N. *Air Power for Patton's Army: The XIX Tactical Air Command in the Second World War.* Forthcoming late 1993.

RICHARD G. DAVIS

90TH INFANTRY DIVISION.

The U.S. 90th Infantry Division arrived in England in April 1944. Its headquarters was in Birmingham; it was commanded by Brig. Gen. Jay W. MacKelvie.

Invasion plans called for the 1st and 3d battalions, 359th Infantry, to land on Utah Beach with the U.S. 4th Infantry Division as its reserve on 6 June (D-day), to be followed by the 2d Battalion and Regimental Headquarters on D plus 1. The ship carrying the latter group, USS *Susan B. Anthony*, struck a mine off the beach and sank in about two hours. All the troops were saved, however, and the entire regiment was then attached to the 4th Division. Remaining combat elements of the 90th Division landed on 8 June, and the entire division was ashore by the 9th. The original plan called for the entire division to attack northward along the coast on the 4th Division's right toward the port of Cherbourg. Because the battle shaped up differently than had been expected, the 90th was assigned a new mission—to attack due west to cut the Cotentin Peninsula and isolate Cherbourg.

Early on 10 June (D plus 4) the division attacked with two regiments abreast across the Merderet River. The 358th, on the left, jumped off at 0400 at Chef-du-Pont and was stopped by stiff resistance west of Picauville. The 357th attacked on the right at 0515 across the causeway at La Fière and was also stopped short of Amfreville by day's end. The attacks resumed on 11 June, with the 359th Infantry rejoining the division late in the day and being inserted into the middle of the line near Picauville. On that day Amfreville fell to the 357th Infantry. On 12 June, with the help of massed artillery and an air strike, Pont-l'Abbé was overrun by the 358th Infantry; on 15 June Gourbesville finally succumbed to the 357th Infantry. Also on 12 June (D plus 6), the 90th

Division commander, Brigadier General MacKelvie, was replaced by reason of incompetence; Maj. Gen. Eugene M. Landrum succeeded him.

On 14 June VII Corps ordered the 82d Airborne Division and the 9th Infantry Division to pass through the 90th to continue the corps attack westward, while the 90th protected the corps's right flank between Terre de Beauville, northwest of Golleville, and Montebourg station near Le Ham.

As the division was being passed through, the 359th Infantry began to advance to the northwest toward Golleville in the western portion of the new objective. Meanwhile the 358th, prepositioned near Gourbesville, began its northward advance to Le Ham to occupy the eastern half of the division's new objective. On 17 June the division occupied its objective and on the 18 June (D plus 12) the 357th Infantry, assembled after the Gourbesville fight, was motorized and moved westward to defensive positions formerly occupied by the 9th Division between Portbail and Saint-Sauveur-de-Pierre-Pont.

The early combat record of the 90th Division was dismal and costly; it had taken heavy losses and had frequently failed to seize objectives. It is estimated that during the month of June the division suffered more than 2,800 wounded and injured, and another 800 to 1,000 dead. Most of these casualties took place in the eight days from 10 to 17 June.

The infantry units suffered the heaviest losses, including two regimental commanders killed, one wounded, and one relieved for cause—all within the same period. More shocking were the losses in the rifle companies.

Gen. Omar Bradley called the 90th a "problem division" and ascribed its failure to poor training. His First Army staff recommended that the division be broken up and used as replacements. Actually the problems of the 90th stemmed, not from poor training, but from inept leadership at the division, regimental, and battalion levels of command. Another serious failure can be attributed to the Allies' lack of foresight as to the magnitude of the problems of hedgerow fighting.

The 90th avoided breakup for two reasons. First, it had two high-quality brigadier generals (Sam T. Williams, assistant division commander, and John M. Devine, division artillery commander) who compensated for the poor leadership by the division commanders. Second, the young division staff put forth an excellent effort.

Credit must also be given to Gens. Raymond S. McLain and James A. Van Fleet, who followed MacKelvie and Landrum. These two exceptional leaders encouraged a remarkable group of young, courageous junior officers to fill the voids of command; by the war's end, these officers were commanding the same regiments and battalions that were so badly led in the hedgerows of Normandy. Generals

Eisenhower and Patton later designated the division as one of the very best in the theater.

[*See also* Landrum, Eugene M.; MacKelvie, Jay W.]

BIBLIOGRAPHY

Bradley, Omar N. *A Soldier's Story.* 1951.
Colby, John. *War from the Ground Up: The 90th Division in World War II.* 1991.
U.S. Army, Center of Military History. *Utah Beach to Cherbourg: 6–27 June 1944.* 1948. Reprint, 1990.

FRANK NORRIS, ORWIN TALBOTT, and

EAMES YATES

91ST AIR LANDING DIVISION. The *91st Air Landing (Luftlande) Division* was responsible for the defense of the southern part of the western coast of the Cotentin Peninsula, its eastern boundary being the Merderet River, and to act as a reserve in the event of landings on the east coast. It was under command of the German *Seventh Army.* The *91st* was a Category 25 division, raised in early 1944 from elements of the *Replacement Army (Ersatzheer)* on a reduced establishment of just two three-battalion infantry regiments, a fusilier company to act as its reconnaissance element, and an artillery regiment with one heavy battalion (twelve 155-mm guns) and two 105-mm battalions, each also with twelve guns. Its actual order of battle was as follows: *1057th Grenadier Regiment, 1058th Grenadier Regiment, 91st Fusilier Company, 191st Artillery Regiment, 191st Antitank Battalion, 191st Engineer Battalion,* and *191st Signal Battalion.*

Although designated an air landing division, the *91st* never fought as such, but received special training in countering Allied airborne landings. It deployed to the Cotentin Peninsula in late May 1944. Resisting airborne landings was to be its first task on D-day, when it faced elements of the U.S. 82d Airborne Division, who dropped west of the Merderet River, and of the 101st Airborne in the Sainte-Mère-Église area. The *91st* suffered an early blow when the divisional commander, Gen. Wilhelm Falley, was killed in his car by American paratroops while returning from the *Seventh Army* war games at Rennes. Nevertheless, its two infantry regiments were quickly sent into action. The *1058th Regiment* moved on Sainte-Mère-Église from the north, while the *1057th Regiment* was deployed to counter the landings on the Merderet itself. Additional support was given by the *6th Parachute Regiment,* the advance portion of the *2d Parachute Division,* which began to sweep northward from Carentan and was temporarily placed under the operational control of the *91st Division.* Lack of armor and artillery meant, however, that they were unable to prevent the American paratroopers from consolidating their positions.

With the Utah beachhead secured and linkup with the 82d and 101st airborne divisions achieved, the Americans now began to attack westward with a view to cutting off the northern part of the Cotentin Peninsula. For a time the *91st Division* was able to prevent the U.S. 90th Division from advancing west of the Merderet, but its casualties were mounting, and by the end of 10 June its strength had fallen from 10,555 men at the outset to 6,596. Eventually, increasing American pressure and the *91st*'s depleted strength allowed the Americans to achieve their aim, and they reached the west coast of the peninsula on 18 June. The remnants of the *91st Division* now found themselves facing north in the area of La Haye-du-Puits while the battle for Cherbourg was fought out. During this time the *91st* was combined with the *243d Infantry Division* under Col. Bernard Klosterkemper. In early July it regained its separate identity under Col. Bernard Koenig, but before the month was out SS Oberstgruppenführer Paul Hausser, now commanding the German *Seventh Army,* was listing the division as practically destroyed. It was therefore pulled out of the line just before the Allied breakout from Saint-Lô and reinforced by two battalions before being sent back into combat again. It was deployed to Rennes, where it found itself in the path of Patton's Third Army and was driven out of the town after a daylong fight on 3 August. The division was then withdrawn to the West Wall, or Siegfried Line. In autumn 1944 it combined with the *275th* and *344th* divisions to form the *344th Volksgrenadier Division,* which fought in the Huertgen Forest in November 1944, prior to being sent to the Eastern front in early 1945, finishing the war in Czechoslovakia.

[*See also* Falley, Wilhelm.]

BIBLIOGRAPHY

Carell, Paul. *Invasion: They're Coming.* Translated by E. Osers. 1963. Paul Carell is the pseudonym used by Hans Karl Schmidt.
Mitcham, Samuel. *Hitler's Legions: German Army Order of Battle in World War II.* 1985.

CHARLES MESSENGER

IX AIR CORPS. Subordinated to the German *Third Air Force,* IX Air Corps (Fliegerkorps IX) controlled the conventional medium bomber force. Commanded by Brig. Gen. Dietrich Peltz, it operated from bases in northern France, Holland, and Belgium, with headquarters in Beauvais, France. At the beginning of June 1944 it possessed 261 twin-engined bombers: Junkers Ju 88s, Ju 188s, and Dornier Do 217s. The number of bombers did not redress IX Air Corps's deep-seated weaknesses, however. The aircraft were not equipped for antishipping

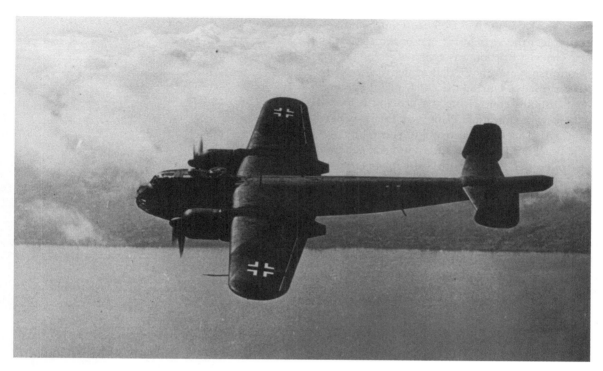

DORNIER DO 217.

strikes, nor were their crews trained for this type of operation. Most of the units had been in action almost continuously during the previous year and had suffered heavy losses. Now their serviceability rates were poor and they were woefully short of experienced crews.

From the start it was clear that the strength of the Allied air defenses over the beachhead area would restrict *IX Air Corps* to night operations. On the evening following D-day it mounted 130 sorties against Allied shipping. The corps received a reinforcement of ninety bombers after D-day, and during subsequent nights it flew an average of sixty to seventy sorties, weather permitting. Because of the shortcomings already mentioned, however, the direct attacks on shipping were uniformly unsuccessful.

From 12 June on, *IX Air Corps* shifted to laying mines in shallow waters off the landing area, maintaining the same nightly weight of attack. The weapon used, the newly developed Oyster mine, was detonated by the reduction in hydrostatic pressure at the sea bed as a ship passed over it. Extremely difficult to sweep, these mines sank several Allied ships. The weapon could be rendered ineffective if ships reduced speed to a minimum while passing through shallow water, and for a while the mining campaign caused considerable inconvenience and delayed the buildup of Allied forces ashore. Yet while these operations were not and could not be decisive, it was probably the only way that *IX Air Corps* could be used to any effect.

[*See also* Peltz, Dietrich.]

BIBLIOGRAPHY

Dierich, Wolfgang. *Die Verbände der Luftwaffe.* 1976.
Price, Alfred. *The Last Year of the Luftwaffe.* 1991.

ALFRED PRICE

IX AIR DEFENSE COMMAND. The IX Air Defense Command was activated on 30 March 1944 with Brig. Gen. William L. Richardson as the commander. It consisted of two antiaircraft brigades which, by D-day, controlled eleven battalions. The 71st Fighter Wing, two night fighter squadrons, and several communication and support units constituted the rest of the command. At its peak, in the summer of 1944, the IX Air Defense Command comprised more than 5,200 men.

The IX Air Defense Command was the only unit of its type in the Army Air Forces in World War II. It was created as a test of new doctrine and as an attempt to create a more economical air defense organization. The U.S. Ninth Air Force staff conceived of the IX Air Defense Command as a means of providing unified antiaircraft defense in the rear area. The air force commanders and Gen. Omar Bradley approved the concept of a unified air defense organization, but General Dwight D. Eisenhower decided that antiaircraft battalions would not be permanently assigned to the IX Air Defense Command, but only placed under its operational control.

Each brigade of the IX Air Defense Command was assigned to protect the airfields of one of the tactical air commands. The 51st Brigade was assigned to the IX Tactical Air Command, and the 52d Brigade, to the XXIX Tactical Air Command. During the D-day planning, there were several disputes concerning the use and responsibilities of the new organization. Plans were finally worked out for the IX Air Defense Command to control its own sector of the beachhead. Coordination was arranged with the Royal Air Force's 85th Group, which operated air defense in the British sector.

Elements of the IX Air Defense Command, notably a radar unit for night fighter control, landed on D-day. During the following days, more units arrived. The advanced headquarters of the IX Air Defense Command was established at Ecrammeville on 20 June 1944. In the first days of the campaign, antiaircraft defense was the responsibility of the First Army's antiaircraft units, but as the Allies advanced and the beachhead expanded, the IX Air Defense Command took over the rear area defense.

The Allied air superiority over France in the summer of 1944 made an antiaircraft defense against the Luftwaffe almost superfluous. During the Normandy campaign, U.S. antiaircraft gunners claimed ninety-six German aircraft, certainly an exaggeration. In fact, in the weeks after D-day, Allied antiaircraft units were as dangerous to Allied aircraft as to the Luftwaffe. There were dozens of instances of Allied antiaircraft firing on, and shooting down, Allied aircraft. The air defense system during the Normandy campaign was complex, and the gunners were still learning their trade.

In time, however, the IX Air Defense Command became an effective organization. The high point of its service came in late 1944, when it performed effectively in defending Antwerp against V-1 missile attacks.

[See also Richardson, William L.]

BIBLIOGRAPHY

Kohn, Richard H., and Joseph P. Hanrahan, eds. *Condensed Analysis of the Ninth Air Force in the European Theater of Operations.* Reprint, 1984.
Werrell, Kenneth P. *Archie, Flak, AAA, and SAM.* 1988.

JAMES S. CORUM

NINTH AIR FORCE. During the D-day campaign and in the advance across Europe, the mission of the U.S. Ninth Air Force was to provide tactical air support for the U.S. ground armies. The Ninth Air Force, with more than 2,500 combat aircraft in June 1944, played a decisive role in the Allied success on D-day by ensuring Allied air superiority and crippling German transportation before and during the campaign.

LEWIS H. BRERETON. Right, with Arthur Coningham.
IMPERIAL WAR MUSEUM

The Ninth Air Force, constituted in the Middle East in November 1942, moved to England in September 1943. As of October, the Ninth had only 38,457 men assigned to it. Its major units consisted of only a headquarters, four medium bomber groups, one troop carrier group, a reconnaissance group, and a few service units. By D-day, the Ninth had expanded to eleven light and medium bomber groups, each with eighty-five aircraft; eighteen fighter and fighter-bomber groups; fourteen troop carrier groups; and some night fighter and reconnaissance squadrons. Commanded by Lt. Gen. Lewis H. Brereton, the whole force had grown to 172,000 men.

In the weeks before D-day, the Ninth Air Force switched from its mission of supporting the strategic bombing campaign of Germany and began a carefully coordinated bombing program designed to shatter the northern French transportation network and isolate the invasion area from German reinforcement and supplies. In May 1944, the Ninth

Ninth Air Force
Lt. Gen. Lewis H. Brereton

IX Air Defense Command
Brig. Gen. William L. Richardson

IX Air Force Service Command
Brig. Gen. Myron Wood

IX Bomber Command
Maj. Gen. Samuel E. Anderson

IX Engineer Command
Brig. Gen. James Newman

IX Fighter Command
Maj. Gen. Elwood R. Quesada

XIX Tactical Air Command *
Maj. Gen. Otto Weyland

IX Tactical Air Command
Maj. Gen. Elwood R. Quesada

IX Troop Carrier Command
Maj. Gen. Paul L. Williams

* Added on 1 August 1944

Air Force flew over 34,000 sorties, including 12,000 bomber runs that dropped 20,000 tons of bombs. Most of this effort was directed to the destruction of French railyards and bridges. German defense positions along the entire Channel were repeatedly attacked by bombers and fighter-bombers. Between 1 May and 5 June, thirty-six German airfields from France to Holland were attacked; most were hit more than once. Although the Luftwaffe had already lost control of the air, the Ninth Air Force's attacks helped ensure the total air superiority of the Allies on 6 June.

During D-day and the three weeks following, the Ninth

Air Force made a maximum effort. The bomber and fighter-bomber force dropped 24,000 tons of bombs in June. The Ninth as a whole flew almost 47,000 combat sorties that month, a total exceeded only in March 1945. Although the Luftwaffe was scarcely to be found in the air, the American losses to flak were heavy. In June, the bomber force lost 12.5 percent of its aircraft, and the fighter force over a quarter of its planes, in combat and to accidents.

The sixth of June, and the days that followed, found the Ninth Air Force constantly over the Normandy battlefields attacking German fortifications, headquarters, vehicles, and troop concentrations. The IX Fighter Command devoted over 1,000 sorties to fly cover over the beachheads and convoys, although the Luftwaffe was in no condition to contest the beachhead.

The Ninth Air Force would later become an effective force for close air support of ground troops, but during D-day it was only moderately effective in that role. The techniques of forward air control would need to be worked out in the following months. The Ninth Air Force

GERMAN TANKS UNDER AIR ATTACK.   Fighter-bombers of the U.S. Air Force destroyed almost 400 German tanks during the first week of the invasion.

nevertheless made a decisive contribution toward the success of the Allied landings by its attacks on the Wehrmacht's transportation lines.

[See also Brereton, Lewis H., and articles on the units mentioned herein.]

BIBLIOGRAPHY

Goldberg, Alfred. "The Ninth Air Force." In vol. 3 of The Army Air Forces in World War II, edited by Wesley Frank Craven and James Lea Cate. 1951.
Kohn, Richard H., and Joseph P. Hanrahan, eds. Condensed Analysis of the Ninth Air Force in the European Theater of Operations. Reprint, 1984.
Rust, Kerm. The 9th Air Force in World War II. 1967.

JAMES S. CORUM

IX AIR FORCE SERVICE COMMAND. The IX Air Force Service Command (AFSC) was responsible for the logistics support of the U.S. Ninth Air Force. The effective accomplishment of its mission was characteristic of the industrial and managerial capability that America brought to the war effort. The IX AFSC, more than 62,000 men strong at its peak, was the largest command of the Ninth Air Force by July 1944.

The IX AFSC was formed in October 1943 around a nucleus provided by the Eighth Air Force service units. The IX AFSC was responsible for the Ninth Air Force's aircraft maintenance, repair, and salvage, as well as all classes of supply, including munitions and aviation fuel. The IX AFSC was initially organized by Maj. Gen. J. F. Miller, who turned over command to Brig. Gen. Myron Wood in May 1944.

Simply organizing and training the IX AFSC before D-day was a major accomplishment of the Army Air Forces. When it was activated in October 1943, the IX AFSC had only 6,300 men, and the army personnel command in the United States was unable to send enough complete units overseas to man it. Thus, the IX AFSC, which at its peak comprised 439 units, had to activate and fill over 200 units with more soldiers sent from the United States. Since many of the replacements were only partially trained, the IX AFSC was faced with the daunting task of training thousands of soldiers, in both its own and in the Royal Air Force's technical schools.

The IX AFSC had over fifty types of units, most of which belonged to the thirteen air depot groups or the twenty-three service groups. Unlike the Eighth Air Force, which operated from fixed bases in England, the support units of the Ninth Air Force had to be sufficiently mobile to supply and maintain air groups operating from advanced airfields, constantly moving forward in support of the ground armies. It was one of the more difficult logistics missions undertaken by the Army Air Forces.

Depot and ordnance units of the IX AFSC landed on D-day, and an advanced headquarters was established on D plus 2. Throughout the Normandy and European campaigns, the IX AFSC kept the Ninth Air Force units supplied with enormous amounts of gas and munitions—during June and July 1944, more than 200,000 gallons of aviation fuel per day, and overall in the course of the war, over 241 million gallons of aviation gas, mostly to units operating from forward airfields. The maintenance groups of the IX AFSC kept the Ninth Air Force combat aircraft more than 70 percent operational during the summer of 1944.

From October 1943 to May 1945, the IX AFSC repaired 15,952 aircraft, modified 5,427, assembled 1,775, and salvaged 2,133. Logistical units such as the IX AFSC played a major role in Allied domination of European skies.

[See also Wood, Myron.]

BIBLIOGRAPHY

Goldberg, Alfred. "The AAF's Logistical Organization." In vol. 6 of The Army Air Forces in World War II, edited by Wesley Frank Craven and James Lea Cate. 1951.
Kohn, Richard H., and Joseph P. Hanrahan, eds. Condensed Analysis of the Ninth Air Force in the European Theater of Operations. Reprint, 1984.

JAMES S. CORUM

IX BOMBER COMMAND. On 16 October 1943 the U.S. Army Air Forces (AAF) reestablished the Ninth Air Force in Britain, after transferring it from the Middle East, to serve as the tactical air force to support American invasion forces. It came under operational control of the Allied Expeditionary Air Force (AEAF), which oversaw Anglo-American tactical aviation, and was under General Dwight D. Eisenhower's direct command. IX Bomber Command, under Brig. Gen. Samuel E. Anderson, absorbed the Eighth Air Force's 3d Bombardment Wing (Medium) of four medium bomber groups, equipped with B-26 aircraft. These aircraft had the same Norden bombsight as, and were faster than, the heavy B-17 and B-24 bombers. The B-26s operated at altitudes of 3,050–3,660 meters (10–12,000 feet) while the heavy bombers operated at altitudes of 6,100 meters (20,000 feet) or higher. The lower operational altitude exposed the B-26s to heavier losses from German antiaircraft artillery (flak) and from German fighters, which had improved performance at lower altitudes. Initially these medium bomber units formed the Ninth Air Force's only operational formations. In February and March 1944 four more medium groups of B-26s and three light groups of A-20s joined the command, making it the largest tactical bomber command ever assembled by the AAF. This gave American air commanders the flexibility to either mass force for concentrated attacks or parcel it out to tactical air commands.

General Anderson formed three wings: the 97th Wing for the light groups and the 98th and 99th wings for the mediums. The command continued operations to support Eighth Air Force heavy bombers, which were striking strategic targets in Germany, by staging harassing attacks on German airfields in France, and Ninth Air Force fighters continued to escort heavy bombers on their missions. These support operations delayed training and preparation of IX Bomber Command for the invasion until approximately 1 April, a delay that soured relations between American bomber leader Lt. Gen. Carl Spaatz, who had administrative control of the Ninth Air Force, and the commander of the AEAF, Air Chief Marshal Trafford Leigh-Mallory. Another diversion of the command's effort, which continued from its inception through July 1944, was the bombing of German V-1 sites in the Pas de Calais area, which were under construction or, from 13 June onwards, in use. General Spaatz objected to the campaign against the V-1 sites as a waste of assets (the Germans appeared to use the sites as flak traps), claiming that they were being used against a target of value more to British internal politics than to the military.

As the time for the invasion approached, the command concentrated on its primary preinvasion mission: interdicting German lines of communication in France and Belgium. Plans specified attritional attacks on the rail system, especially marshaling yards and other supporting rail facilities. Shortly before the invasion the command devoted its attention to a campaign of precision attacks against large German anti-invasion guns that were in use or under construction on the French coast. The Allies carefully planned the attacks so as not to reveal the actual invasion site. On D-day the command contained the 409th, 410th, and 416th light bombardment groups and the 322d, 323d, 344th, 386th, 387th, 391st, 394th, and 397th medium bombardment groups. By the end of the war ten of those eleven groups had earned Presidential Unit Citations, America's most prestigious unit award.

Rather than cancel the 6 June missions because of low cloud cover, General Anderson obtained permission to attack at 3,500 feet, striking outlying targets at 0500 and Utah Beach, with 278 aircraft and 550 tons of bombs, at 0605. Their performance exceeded the accuracy of the Eighth Air Force's heavy bombers, whose bombs fell far over their targets. Forty-three percent of the command's bombs fell within 300 feet of the aiming point (Craven and Cate, p. 192). For the campaign's duration the command launched interdiction attacks against lines of communications and missions in direct support of ground oper-

ations, such as Operations CHARNWOOD and GOODWOOD. On 25 July 380 medium bombers supported Operation COBRA, which assisted the American Saint-Lô breakout. Forty-two of its bombers misidentified their target and dropped within American lines, causing casualties and confusion, but not significant delay in the ground assault. Short bombs on 25 July, either from the command or the Eighth Air Force, killed American Lt. Gen. Lesley J. McNair, on tour of the battlefield before assuming command of an army. General McNair was the highest-ranking Allied officer to die in the campaign. The effective overall performance of the command demonstrated the necessity of having bomber aircraft assigned to supporting ground forces.
[See also Anderson, Samuel E.]

BIBLIOGRAPHY

Craven, Wesley Frank, and James Lea Cate, eds. Europe: ARGUMENT to V-E Day, January 1944 to May 1945. Vol. 3 of The Army Air Forces in World War II. 1951.
U.S. Ninth Air Force. Condensed Analysis of the Ninth Air Force in the European Theater of Operations. 1984.

RICHARD G. DAVIS

IX ENGINEER COMMAND. The IX Engineer Command was activated on 30 March 1944 under Brig. Gen. James Newman. It was the only organization of its type in the Army Air Forces in World War II. The IX Engineer Command consisted of engineer and support units able to build airfields from scratch or repair former German airfields as fast as the ground troops could capture them.

Assigned to the Ninth Air Force, the IX Engineer Command was created from four regiments of aviation engineers, which in turn commanded twenty-five engineer aviation battalions. Three airborne engineer battalions, capable of supporting parachute and glider troops, were also assigned to the unit. By D-day, the IX Engineer Command totaled over 17,000 men, and this strength was maintained until war's end.

The IX Engineer Command was a highly mobile force that practiced for the European campaign by building airfields in Britain. The D-day planners insisted on a heavy schedule of airfield construction and repair from the first day of the invasion, so that the Ninth Air Force fighter and fighter-bomber units could move their operations to the Continent as rapidly as possible. The closer to the front that aircraft could operate, the faster the reaction time for close air support and the higher the aircraft sortie rate. An effective network of forward airfields meant a doubling of the Ninth Air Force's tactical airpower, as well as improving the chances for damaged aircraft to land safely.

AERIAL VIEW OF ONE OF THE FIRST AMERICAN AIRFIELDS IN FRANCE.   Constructed by the IX Engineer Command.
THE ROBERT HUNT LIBRARY, LONDON

Elements of the IX Engineer Command landed with the U.S. forces on D-day, and an emergency airstrip near Omaha Beach was completed by 2145 hours. Elsewhere within the beachhead on D-day, the IX Engineer Command began construction of two more airfields. From then on, the aviation engineers usually kept ahead of their planned construction schedule. In good weather, a battalion of engineers needed ten days to complete an advanced airfield suitable for full fighter group operations, complete with a 5,000-foot-long runway. Various types of steel mesh laid over sod or earth provided the usual surface.

By 30 June 1944, the IX Engineer Command had completed nine airfields in Normandy, most with 5,000-foot-runways, and seven more airfields were under construction. During the Normandy campaign, most of the Ninth Air Force moved to the Continent, and by late July 1944, thirteen fighter-bomber groups and one reconnaissance group were operating from airfields built in France.

The airfields of the IX Engineer Command not only enabled U.S. troops to enjoy effective air support, but also made aerial supply and medical evacuation more efficient. Even in June 1944, large numbers of American wounded—

19,490 men—were evacuated by air. The evacuation system doubtless saved thousands of American lives.

[*See also* Newman, James.]

BILIOGRAPHY

Fagg, John E. "The Aviation Engineers in Africa and Europe." In vol. 7 of *The Army Air Forces in World War II*, edited by Wesley Frank Craven and James Lea Cate. 1958.

Goldberg, Alfred. "The Ninth Air Force." In vol. 3 of *The Army Air Forces in World War II*, edited by Wesley Frank Craven and James Lea Cate. 1951.

Kohn, Richard H., and Joseph P. Hanrahan, eds. *Condensed Analysis of the Ninth Air Force in the European Theater of Operations*. Reprint, 1984.

JAMES S. CORUM

IX FIGHTER COMMAND. The U.S. IX Fighter Command (FC) was activated on 17 October 1943 in England, and in the preparatory phases of OVERLORD exercised administrative control over the U.S. Ninth Air Force's fighter-bombers. Under its commander, Brig. Gen. Elwood R. Quesada, the command was responsible for the training of fighter-bomber groups then arriving from the United States, although the IX and XIX tactical air commands (TACs) retained operational control over the aircraft. Within the overall scheme of the Allied invasion, the fighter-bombers were to provide tactical or close support of American invasion forces on D-day. At the outset, military planners intended to deactivate the IX Fighter Command once the TACs became fully operational, but decided in February 1944 to retain the command and promote Quesada to major general to preserve organizational parity with the British Second Tactical Air Force in the months leading to 6 June 1944.

Training the fighter-bombers for their assigned D-day tasks— convoy cover, interdiction or isolation of the battle area, and close support of assault troops on the American beaches— proved a comprehensive task. Fresh from the United States, the aircraft crews needed to learn tactical air theory. Drawing upon Allied experience in Italy, the Command's staff officers regularly lectured airmen on the tactics and techniques of close air support. In the spring of 1944 the training program also required participation in combat exercises for D-day, but poor weather and escort missions into Germany with U.S. Eighth Air Force bombers precluded perfect attendance at such maneuvers. Nonetheless, the command did manage to join a number of preinvasion rehearsals, including DUCK, KNOCKOUT, and BUNSEN. From this uneven participation, Quesada and his staff came to two major conclusions: effective close air support demanded flexible tables of organization and was only as good as the communications between air and ground units.

Accordingly Quesada, who also commanded the IX TAC, and the XIX TAC commander, Brig. Gen. Otto Weyland, adopted a command structure whereby the more established IX TAC exercised operational control of all Ninth Air Force fighter-bombers in the initial stages of OVERLORD. In addition IX Fighter Command's signals officer, Col. Blair Garland, established a complicated system of communications and signals centered around a command post in Uxbridge, England. By D-day, ship-to-shore, point-to-point, and ground-to-air signals were available on each of three headquarters ships scheduled to accompany the initial American invasion force. And finally, to foster the effective support of ground troops and to identify enemy aircraft, IX Fighter Command pioneered the use of Microwave Early Warning Radar (MEW) as an offensive tool.

Both the IX Fighter Command's size and training responsibility steadily increased throughout the spring of 1944. The command's first fighter-bomber group arrived in early December 1943; four more came in February, three in March, four in April, and the last seven in May 1944. By 6 June, the command included five combat wings, nineteen groups, approximately 36,000 troops, and some 1,600 P-38, P-47, and P-51 aircraft. The command's role diminished, however, as the training neared completion and the two TACs exerted more operational control over the groups. Beginning in mid-April, the fighter-bombers engaged more and more in actual missions preparatory to the Allied assault, and the importance of the training command decreased.

After D-day the IX Fighter Command played a modest role in the employment of tactical aircraft over Normandy. Although carried on as a headquarters and technically still the administrative center for the Ninth Air Force's tactical air commands, the unit increasingly resembled a small paper organization. In midsummer 1944 the IX Fighter Command had only 177 officers and 338 enlisted men, responsible for little more than feeding pilots and ground crews. Despite this, in the months before D-day, the IX Fighter Command had played a critical part in forming an American tactical air force and developing trained crews and aircraft for effective close air support of American troops in Normandy.

[*See also* Close Air Support; Interdiction Operations; XIX Tactical Air Command; Ninth Air Force; IX Tactical Air Command; Quesada, Elwood R.]

BIBLIOGRAPHY

Goldberg, Alfred. "The Ninth Air Force." In vol. 3 of *The Army Air Forces in World War II*, edited by Wesley Frank Craven and James Lea Cate. 1951.
Kohn, Richard, and Joseph Hanrahan, eds. *Condensed Analysis of the Ninth Air Force in the European Theater of Operations.* 1946. Reprint, 1984.

THOMAS HUGHES

9TH INFANTRY DIVISION.

The 9th Infantry Division was the last regular army division to be activated for World War I; when the war ended four months later, the division was disbanded. In August 1940 at Fort Bragg, North Carolina, the division was once again activated for war. Under Maj. Gen. Manton Eddy soldiers of the 9th spent the summer of 1942 on the Chesapeake Bay learning amphibious warfare, then sailed across the Atlantic to assault the shores of North Africa on the morning of 8 November 1942. The fighting in North Africa ended in May 1943, and after a couple of months of rest and training the division went to Sicily, where it fought until August 1943.

In November the 9th Infantry Division moved to England to prepare for the invasion of Normandy. As one of only two divisions with combat experience (the 1st Infantry Division was the other), it crossed the English Channel and began landing on Utah Beach on 10 June as part of the U.S. VII Corps. The 39th Infantry Regiment landed first and, supported by the division's 34th and 60th field artillery battalions, became the division's first combined arms team to see action in France when it was attached to the 4th Infantry Division on 12 June. On 14 June the 9th led the VII Corps drive across the Cotentin Peninsula to trap the German forces defending Cherbourg. The division entered the center of the corps front with the 90th Infantry Division on its right flank and the 82d Airborne Division on its left. The 60th Infantry Regiment led the attack along the narrow division front. On 15 June the front widened enough to allow the 47th Infantry to join the attack on the right flank of the 60th. The 39th Infantry returned to the division on the same day and the 359th, a regiment of the 90th Infantry Division, also joined the Ninth Division's "Old Reliables" in the attack. The 47th and 60th led the advance east across the Douve River, and by late evening on 17 June the first elements of the division reached the Atlantic. They completed the mission of sealing the peninsula early on 18 June with the 47th at Port Bail and the 60th at Barneville-sur-Mer.

In crossing the peninsula the 9th Infantry Division had moved twelve and a half miles in two days, the fastest advance of the campaign. General Eddy and his veterans were given little time to rest, however, as they were ordered to reorient their attack north toward Cherbourg on 19 June as the left flank of a three-division attack by VII Corps. The success they had in turning the entire division 90 degrees in less than twenty-two hours ranks as one of the major tactical achievements of the entire war. General Omar Bradley, commander of the First Army in Normandy, considered it "an unbelievably swift change in direction" and credited the maneuver with catching the German forces defending Cherbourg off balance.

The U.S. war reporter Ernie Pyle wrote that the 9th "performed like a beautiful machine in the Cherbourg campaign." One of the reasons the division met with such great success was its continuity of command. For two years Eddy led the 9th: he trained it and led it in combat. In August 1944 he took command of XII Corps, but he had left his mark. The division continued to fight with distinction across France and into Germany until the end of the war.

[See also Eddy, Manton.]

BIBLIOGRAPHY

Henry, Thomas R. "The Avenging Ghosts of the 9th." *Saturday Evening Post* 219 (6 July 1946): 24–25.

Mittelman, Joseph B. *Eight Stars to Victory: A History of the Veteran Ninth Infantry Division.* 1948.

U.S. Army, Center of Military History. *Utah Beach to Cherbourg: 6–27 June 1944.* 1948. Reprint, 1990.

Wilson, John B. *Armies, Corps, Divisions, and Separate Brigades.* 1987.

CLAYTON R. NEWELL

9th Infantry Division
Maj. Gen. Manton S. Eddy (to 18 August 1944)

Organic units

39th Infantry Regiment
47th Infantry Regiment
60th Infantry Regiment
9th Reconnaissance Troop (Mech)
9th Medical Battalion
15th Engineer Combat Battalion

9th Division Artillery

26th Field Artillery Battalion (105 Howitzer)
60th Field Artillery Battalion (105 Howitzer)
84th Field Artillery Battalion (105 Howitzer)
34th Field Artillery Battalion (155 Howitzer)

Special Troops

709th Ordnance Light Maintenance Company
9th Quartermaster Company
9th Signal Company
Military Police Platoon
Headquarters Company
Band

IX TACTICAL AIR COMMAND. The IX Tactical Air Command (TAC) was a major subordinate headquarters of the U.S. Ninth Air Force. Activated on 17 October 1943, it was the oldest and largest of the American TACs exercising operational control over Ninth Air Force fighter-bombers in Operation OVERLORD. From D-day to D plus 12, the IX TAC provided tactical or close air support for the American invasion forces. Together with its sister organization, the XIX TAC, the IX TAC controlled a total of nineteen groups and over 1,600 P-38, P-47, and P-51 aircraft in the skies over Omaha and Utah beaches. Within weeks of the Allied invasion, IX TAC had established itself as a flexible and innovative unit eager to assist Lt. Gen. Omar Bradley's ground troops in their march through Normandy and beyond.

Throughout the spring of 1944, the IX TAC built

strength in numbers and experience in the air. Its first fighter-bomber group had arrived from the United States in early December 1943; over the following months the command received an additional eleven groups. Although the IX Fighter Command retained administrative command over the aircraft, the IX TAC gradually exerted more control as operational missions replaced training maneuvers. Beginning in late March 1944, the command turned its attention to Normandy. The 67th Reconnaissance Group flew daily patrols that delivered thousands of pictures of German beach defenses to Allied ground planners. At the same time, in a bid to isolate the Normandy area, IX TAC fighter-bombers cut rail lines leading into western France, attacked German marshaling areas, and harassed operations at nearby enemy airfields. In the two months before 6 June, the IX TAC flew over 20,000 sorties in direct preparation for D-day.

By 1 June the IX TAC's twelve fighter-bomber groups were stationed in the Hampshire area of southern England, close enough to France to maintain thirty minutes over the fighting zone. For D-day the IX TAC, which had temporary control over XIX TAC aircraft for the invasion, supplied five P-47 groups for high-altitude cover over the beach area and two P-38 groups to help protect the invasion armada. Two additional P-38 groups and four P-47 groups attacked German gun emplacements at H-hour and furnished direct fire support of ground forces thereafter as requested. The remaining groups were held in readiness as part of a reserve strike force.

The reserve groups were called into action early, at about H plus 3. When German resistance on Omaha Beach proved greater than expected, IX TAC commander Maj. Gen. Elwood R. Quesada bypassed the regular communications structure in Uxbridge and instructed his representative aboard the headquarters ship USS *Ancon* to direct aircraft to various targets behind the beach. Relying on radio-equipped air-support parties already on the beach, communications officers directed wave after wave of fighter-bombers at German emplacements impeding the Allied advance. This system guided 1,431 sorties the first day, and with additional naval bombardment helped the infantry secure a firm beachhead by evening.

From D-day onward the the IX TAC built a reputation as an effective provider of close air support. A makeshift airfield immediately behind Omaha Beach was constructed within thirty-six hours of H-hour; by eliminating the need to return to England to refuel, it allowed aircraft to increase their time over battle areas. Building on the critical requirements of communications, the command operated the first cross-Channel radio phone on D plus 2. The next day the 70th Fighter-Bomber Wing established headquarters on the Continent to coordinate air

activities. On D plus 4 the IX TAC published its first continental telephone directory, which included direct land line links to various ground units. On 8 June Quesada established an advance headquarters in Normandy immediately adjacent to General Bradley's command post near Au Gay, and in the following days the two men worked in close association to ensure air support for infantry troops in the tough bocage country.

The slow fighting in Normandy throughout June put a high premium on the mobility and firepower of fighter-bombers, and the IX TAC flew numerous missions in support of ground troops. From D-day to D plus 12, the IX TAC flew 13,283 sorties and dropped 3,345 tons of bombs on German fortified positions, railroad lines, bridges, marshaling areas, and ammunition dumps. Allied control of the air over Normandy precluded any sustained German challenges to the fighter-bombers, and the IX TAC suffered negligible casualties. In fact, the only serious threat to airborne craft came from friendly fire: both air and ground crews proved unable to consistently identify each other in the heat of battle. These errors never reached epidemic proportions, but the mistakes continued to dog air-ground relations throughout the summer campaign. Nonetheless, by the time other TACs were activated on the Continent, Bradley's First Army and the IX TAC had worked out the essential doctrine and technique of close air support followed for the balance of the European fighting.

[*See also* Aerial Reconnaissance; Close Air Support; Ninth Air Force; Quesada, Elwood R.; Railroads.]

BIBLIOGRAPHY

Craven, Wesley Frank, and James Lea Cate, eds. *The Army Air Forces in World War II.* Vol. 3, 1951.
Hastings, Max. *Overlord: D-Day and the Battle for Normandy.* 1984.
Kohn, Richard, and Joseph Hanrahan, eds. *Condensed Analysis of the Ninth Air Force in the European Theater of Operations.* 1946. Reprint, 1984.

THOMAS HUGHES

IX TROOP CARRIER COMMAND. The IX Troop Carrier Command (TCC) and RAF Troop Carrier Command were the principal air transport organizations of the Allied Expeditionary Force. The invasion plans called for IX TCC to carry portions of the American 82d and 101st airborne divisions, the first American soldiers to land in France, to drop zones behind German defenses on the Normandy beaches on the night of 5–6 June. During the remainder of the day the IX TCC would tow glider infantry and follow-on echelons to support the original drops. IX TCC belonged to the

AMERICAN WACOS AND THEIR C-47 TUG PLANES OF THE IX TROOP CARRIER COMMAND.   Arriving over the perilously small and hedgerow-enclosed landing zones near Sainte-Mère-Église on D-day.

IMPERIAL WAR MUSEUM

U.S. Ninth Air Force, the American component of Air Chief Marshal Trafford Leigh-Mallory's Allied Expeditionary Air Force.

Ninth Air Force activated IX TCC on 16 October 1943; by February 1944 it consisted of two troop carrier wings and five troop carrier groups for a total of 353 aircraft. The next month another wing and nine more groups joined and by May the command totaled three wings, fourteen groups, and 1,226 C-47 and C-53 type aircraft. Under its experienced commander, Maj. Gen. Paul

Williams, IX TCC conducted intensive training with the airborne forces, holding thirty-eight wing and three command exercises, as well as a full-scale rehearsal on 12 May. Individual groups also conducted extensive training in night flying, drop procedures, and night location techniques. Air Marshal Leigh-Mallory feared that the planned drops would end in a catastrophe and strenuously recommended cancellation of airborne operations to General Dwight D. Eisenhower, who, after some soul searching, decided that the airborne drops were crucial to the success of the invasion and on 30 May ordered them to proceed.

On the night of 5–6 June, flying with no ground air control or airborne radar, 900 transports and 100 gliders, carrying 17,000 soldiers and their equipment and escorted by RAF night fighters and intruders (night attack aircraft), formed up over England and headed for drop zones in Normandy. RAF Stirling Bombers dropped Window (strips of metal foil designed to mislead German radar) so as to divert attention southward.

The Germans subjected all but the lead aircraft to heavy antiaircraft fire while fog and clouds further disrupted formations. As a result the main drops, from 0016 to 0404 on 6 June, were scattered, with both regiments of the 82d Airborne and 4,100 of the 101st Airborne's 6,600 troops thrown in disarray. For the day IX TCC flew 1,606 sorties, towed 512 gliders, and lost 41 aircraft and 9 gliders.

Without the airborne landing, which confused the Germans and delayed reinforcements, the Utah Beach landings might not have succeeded. On 9 June the command consisted of 50th, 52d, and 53d Troop Carrier wings, and Troop Carrier Groups 61, 313 through 316, and 434 through 442. IX TCC continued to support the airborne troops with supplies and reinforcements until the paratroop units were withdrawn. It also evacuated casualties from Normandy to England. On 10 July two-thirds of IX TCC were transferred to the Mediterranean to assist in the invasion of southern France. The loss of their gasoline transport capacity would be keenly felt in the race across France. When it returned in September, IX TCC became part of the First Allied Airborne Army.

[See also Williams, Paul.]

BIBLIOGRAPHY

Craven, Wesley Frank, and James Lea Cate, eds. *Europe: ARGU-MENT to V-E Day, January 1944 to May 1945*. Vol. 3 of *The Army Air Forces in World War II*. 1951.
Ninth Air Force. *Condensed Analysis of the Ninth Air Force in the European Theater of Operations*. 1946. Reprint, 1984.

RICHARD G. DAVIS

NORMANDY FELLOWSHIP. *See* Associations and Organizations.

NORMANDY FOUNDATION. *See* Associations and Organizations.

NORMANDY VETERANS' ASSOCIATION. *See* Associations and Organizations.

NORTHUMBRIAN DIVISION. *See* 50th (Northumbrian) Infantry Division.

NORWAY. Tragedy marred the opening of Norway's contribution to the D-day assault. The brand-new fleet destroyer *Svenner*, on its first combat mission, became the first naval casualty of the day. *Svenner*, together with its sister ship *Stord*, formed part of Bombardment Force D of the Eastern Task Force, with Sword Beach north of Caen as the target area. While the ships were waiting at dawn for minesweepers to clear the approach channel to Sword Beach, three German torpedo boats from Le Havre attacked the assembled force under cover of a smoke screen laid by Allied vessels. At 0530 a torpedo from one of the German boats hit *Svenner* midship between the boiler rooms. It went down within fifteen minutes, and one officer and thirty-three crew members went down with it.

Svenner was one of ten warships of the Royal Norwegian Navy in exile—three destroyers, three corvettes, three motor launches, and one patrol vessel—that went into action on D-day. The other vessels went unharmed until D plus 17, when a Norwegian Hunt-class destroyer, *Glaisdale*, hit a mine in the approaches to Caen. There were no casualties, but the ship was heavily damaged and had to be towed back to Britain, where it was laid up for the remainder of the war.

The other aspect of Norway's maritime contribution to Operation NEPTUNE (code name for naval operations on D-day) was on the transport side. Forty-three ships of the Norwegian merchant navy, the third largest Allied merchant fleet, were engaged in the transport of troops and supplies, six of them on D-day itself. Two older cargo ships were among those sunk off the beach to serve as wave breakers for the landing craft.

In the air the main Norwegian contribution was through 132 (N) (Norwegian) Wing, part of the Allied Second Tactical Air Force, which had been organized for the invasion. Two of the wing's four squadrons came from the Royal Norwegian Air Force; the other two were assigned to it from the British Royal Air Force. The plan was for the wing to move to an airfield near Caen on D plus 10, but fierce German resistance in that area meant that the wing continued to operate from airfields near Bognor Regis on the English side of the Channel until mid-August. The main mission of the wing's Spitfires, modified for fighter-bomber operations, was to provide tactical support for the First Canadian Army and the Second British Army.

Owing to the total lack of German air activity during the first week, casualties were light and partly caused by friendly fire. The first serious encounter with the German Luftwaffe occurred on 15 June, when three of the wing's squadrons engaged a formation of FW 190 and Me 109 aircraft near Évreux. Eight German planes were shot down and ten damaged, with only one Norwegian aircraft lost and three damaged. Even so, the fighting spirit shown by the German pilots proved that the Luftwaffe was still a force to be reckoned with.

BIBLIOGRAPHY

Andenaes, J., O. Riste, and M. Skodvin. *Norway and the Second World War.* 4th ed., 1989.

Mehre, Helge. *Spitfire: En beretning om den 132. norske jagerving i den 2. verdenskrig.* 1982.

Steen, Erik A. *Norges sjøkrig.* Vol. 6, pt. 2, 1969.

OLAV RISTE

O

OBSTFELDER, HANS VON (1886–1976), German, general of the infantry commanding the *LXXXVI Corps*. Hans von Obstfelder, son of a pastor and superintendent in the Protestant church, was born in Steinbach-Hallenberg, near Kassel, on 6 September 1886. In 1905 he entered an infantry regiment as a cadet. Promoted to lieutenant in 1906, in 1911 he became battalion adjutant in his regiment. In 1913 he was posted to the War Academy, where in February 1914 he was made a first lieutenant. With the outbreak of World War I he became adjutant of a reserve infantry regiment and then of a division, and was promoted to captain. From August 1916 to the end of the war and into the buildup of the new Weimar Republic army, he was assigned to the General Staff. After holding various military posts in the 1920s and early 1930s, he was promoted to colonel in 1933. With the post-1935 remilitarization, Obstfelder was made commander of the *28th Infantry Division*. After further promotions, in World War II he became a major general commanding the *XXIX Corps*, which he led in the Russian campaign from 1941 to 1943.

Obstfelder then commanded the *LXXXVI Corps* from August 1943 until November 1944. From May to June 1944 it was attached to the *First Army, Army Group G*, stationed in the Dax region of southwestern France. In July 1944 the corps was attached to *Panzer Group West, Army Group B*, in Normandy.

In November 1944 Obstfelder was awarded the Knight's Cross with Swords and Oak Leaf Cluster. Until the end of the war he served as commander in chief in turn of the *First, Nineteenth*, and *Seventh* armies, leaving no doubt of his determination to follow orders to hold out to the end. He died in Wiesbaden on 20 December 1976.

[*See also* LXXXVI Corps.]

GEORG MEYER
Translated from German by Amy Hackett

O'CONNOR, RICHARD N. (1889–1981), British, lieutenant general, commander of VIII Corps. Commissioned into The Cameronians (Scottish Rifles) in 1909, O'Connor was marked out from the start as an officer of unusual promise. In World War I he was heavily decorated, serving both as a brigade major and battalion commander on the Western front and in Italy. Rapid promotion between the wars found him in Palestine at the age of fifty as an unusually young major general for those days. By 10 June 1940 he was in Egypt commanding a force, later designated the XIII Corps, composed of the 7th Armoured Division and the 4th Indian Infantry Division. Here they faced the Italian *Tenth Army*, against which O'Connor launched Operation COMPASS on 9 December. By 10 February 1941, in Britain's first victory of the war, the Italian army had been virtually destroyed.

O'Connor returned to Cairo to be honored with a knighthood, but was recalled to the desert when Field Marshal Erwin Rommel invaded Cyrenaica in April 1941. Captured in an unfortunate muddle while attempting to help his successor, Lt. Gen. Philip Neame, he was sent to Italy as a prisoner of war. Nearly three years later, after his third escape attempt succeeded, O'Connor arrived back in Britain on Christmas Day 1943. A month later, after being interviewed by Gen. Alan Brooke, the chief of the Imperial General Staff, he was appointed to take command of the VIII Corps on 21 January 1944.

Having kept himself physically fit and as mentally alert as possible during his period in captivity, O'Connor was in unexpectedly good shape after his ordeal. But he had a great deal to catch up on in respect to the latest techniques in warfare, and something of the driving force that had so inspired his troops during COMPASS had left him. He remained a good, sound commander, but the spark of genius had dimmed.

After three months getting to know the formations in the

RICHARD N. O'CONNOR.   Right, with G. H. A. MacMillan at the 15th (Scottish) Infantry Division games at Brighton in May 1944.   COURTESY OF JOHN BAYNES

VIII Corps in Yorkshire, O'Connor moved south with his headquarters in April 1944 and settled at North Priory near Crawley in Sussex. Since the corps was not part of the first wave in the invasion, he did not cross to France until 10 June, D plus 4. The next day the bulk of his own staff crossed, and he met them at Riva-Bella near the mouth of the Orne River. With his headquarters then established at Lantheuil, about ten kilometers (6 miles) from Caen, he was forced to wait for some days for all the components of his corps to arrive. While he was waiting, plans were made for a possible operation code-named DREADNOUGHT, which General Bernard L. Montgomery wished to launch in order to make a breakout from the increasingly congested bridgehead to the east of the Orne. After O'Connor had explained the difficulties of DREADNOUGHT on 18 June, D plus 12, Montgomery informed him by letter the next day that he had told Gen. Miles C. Dempsey "to chuck it; VIII Corps instead to deliver its blow on the Evrecy flank."

Owing to the late arrival in Normandy of much of the corps, the Évrecy operation, code-named EPSOM, could not begin until 26 June. O'Connor remained in command for all the Normandy battles and took the VIII Corps into Holland as far as the Maas River. Here, on 2 December, he

said sad good-bye to all units of the corps on posting to India as commander in chief of the Eastern Command. He later reflected: "It was no doubt a young man's war, and perhaps I was getting too old for the job."

[See also VIII Corps.]

BIBLIOGRAPHY

Baynes, John. *The Forgotten Victor: General Sir O'Connor, KT, GCB, DSO, MC.* 1989.

Jackson, G. S. *Operations of Eighth Corps: Normandy to the River Rhine.* 1948.

JOHN BAYNES

OFFICE OF STRATEGIC SERVICES (OSS). By D-day, 6 June 1944, the Office of Strategic Services (OSS) under Gen. William J. Donovan had been in existence only two years. President Franklin D. Roosevelt had given Donovan a peacetime task of creating a central intelligence system, and on 13 June 1942 the president signed the military order that designated the birth of OSS. With prospects of involving the fledgling intelligence service in the Allied drive through Europe, Donovan and David Kirkpatrick Este Bruce, chief of OSS/London, requested British intelligence to open its doors to the untested American agency. Although the original OVERLORD planners for the Normandy invasion had contemplated keeping intelligence separate from military activities, Special Operations (SO/London), a closely controlled unit of OSS, began collaborating in 1943 with the British Special Operations Executive (SOE), which was devoted to sabotage behind enemy lines in France.

In May 1944, SO/London, SOE, and the Free French formed a tripartite staff to operate directly under General Dwight D. Eisenhower's Supreme Headquarters Allied Expeditionary Force (SHAEF). Col. Joseph P. Haskell, chief of SO/London, assigned three Americans, including John A. Bross, to serve as apprentices to SOE. Bross later became a high official in the CIA. The role of SO in OVERLORD before the landings was to supply the French forces with guns and ammunition and assist in sabotage, especially against French railroads.

This was the opportunity that Donovan had sought. He boarded the U.S. cruiser *Tuscaloosa* with David Bruce on D-day. After watching the landings, he went ashore at Utah Beach on 7 and 8 June. He had established the four field OSS groups that were operating inland in support of the Allied armies. They included SO/London, the Jedburghs, the Operational Group (OG), and Secret Intelligence (SI). Elements of SI, stationed at the Washington headquarters, were espionage experts and furnished secret agent reports for the benefit of groups in the field.

The first tripartite SO/SOE team, code-named UNION,

WILLIAM DONOVAN.   NATIONAL ARCHIVES

command that five hundred well-camouflaged German Tiger tanks (Mark VI) of the *2d Panzer Division* were preparing to move toward Clermont on the left flank of the British Second Army. In the morning, realizing that the tanks had been discovered, the Germans withdrew them.

The Jedburghs were tripartite teams, supplementary to the SO units, usually made up of two officers (one American or British and one French) and a radio operator. They wore army uniforms and had military ranks and serial numbers. Most served in division or army headquarters in the field in France, with the mission of collecting local intelligence, acting as guides, and organizing intelligence activities behind the lines.

Between June and September 1944 eighty-seven Jedburgh teams were operating in French combat zones. Eighteen French Special Airborne Service (SAS) teams dropped into France on the night of 8–9 June 1944. In Brittany, the Jedburghs, working with units of SAS teams, trained and organized twenty thousand French Maquis, who cut rail tracks, making them permanently unusable to the German armies. They derailed trains, destroyed engines, and ambushed German troop movements. As a result when George S. Patton, Jr.'s Third Army dashed from the U.S. right flank to secure the Breton ports, his troops were unopposed.

William Colby, former director of U.S. Central Intelligence, wrote of his service in the Jedburgh team BRUCE assigned to coordinate its activities with Patton's Third Army as it turned away from Brittany and crossed central France to Metz on the Moselle River. In a ceaseless series of hit-and-run raids the BRUCE team, acting with a Maquis network, blew up bridges, ambushed patrols, attacked depots, blocked roads, and cut rail lines. With little opposition, Patton's army made the long march to Metz on 1 September, six days after Paris fell.

To support the Maquis in confronting the Germans, the Americans organized special units, OGs, who were administratively separated from the British and consisted of four officers and thirty enlisted men, very heavily armed. One of these groups from the OSS base in London and seven from Algiers parachuted into Brittany and the Rhone valley. In size and scope, they were paramilitary units, similar to the British commandos and capable of guerrilla warfare, ambushing German columns, and destroying major supply lines. They cut eleven power and communications cables and demolished thirty-two bridges on key railway lines and highways. In the course of these efforts, they captured and held 10,000 German prisoners, wounded 467, and killed 461.

The SI was the only group Donovan determined would not collaborate or integrate with its British counterpart, the SIS. The SI needed the experience of SIS, but while cooperating, insisted on retaining its independence. Though not a smooth relationship, in the end it worked well.

had parachuted behind enemy lines into the Rhone valley on 6 January 1944. By the end of the year, SO/SOE teams, including eighty-five OSS officers and men augmented by the Jedburghs, had organized, armed, and trained 300,000 of Charles de Gaulle's Resistance forces—the Maquis—and provided then with communications equipment. With SO/SOE ground and air support, they formed strong bands to conduct guerrilla warfare against the German military forces in the hilly wooded areas of central and southern France. On 11 April 1944, another SO/SOE team, code-named BEGGAR, consisting of one SO officer and two enlisted men, parachuted into France to organize and direct French Resistance in the area north and west of Paris. By 31 August, after recruiting more than 90 enlisted men, this team had trained and equipped 505 Maquis guerrillas with carbines, bazookas, clothing, shoes, and medicine supplied by OSS. Combined deliveries of these essentials by SO and SOE operatives amounted to ten thousand tons before and shortly after D-day. In a rendezvous with the Maquis, BEGGAR alerted the OVERLORD

HOMING PIGEON. Airdropped to the Maquis, who used them to carry emergency messages back to the OSS.
MUSÉE DE L'ORDRE DE LA LIBÉRATION, PARIS

Between 9 April and 31 August SI/London dispatched twenty-six two-man teams to France. One of these teams sent in early to support the D-day assault was code-named VITRAIL, a joint SI/SIS project. It succeeded beyond expectations. On D-day it reported it had located the German *Panzer Lehr Division* on maneuvers in Tilly-sur-Seulles southwest of Caen, poised to take part in a bold drive to the Normandy coast. The attack never materialized because the VITRAIL intelligence report put the Allies on alert and the *Panzer Lehr Division* remained in position on the defensive for about a week. In estimating the value of this mission, an officer of General Bernard L. Montgomery's 21st Army Group said, "This piece of information alone was sufficient to justify all the work that had been put into the joint . . . project."

The work of OSS's Research and Analysis Branch in Washington provided more and more information for the field units. William L. Langer, chief of the branch, said that Donovan concentrated on the war effort, yet never lost his interest in research and analysis. It was then that the branch first began to make careful target studies, providing plans for sabotaging enemy installations and research studies to assist French Resistance groups.

Five hundred OSS officers and enlisted men in the field, assisting the French Resistance forces, made at least one thousand cuts of rail lines and roads. The most notable success before D-day, according to U.S. Army records, was the sabotage of roads that delayed the German *2d SS Panzer Division* from reaching the OVERLORD landing area. Even the SHAEF commanders finally had to admit that intelligence was not separate from the forces of war.

To celebrate victory Donovan flew to London, while David Bruce marched into Paris with the American troops on 25 August, the day the city fell.

[*See also* French Resistance; Special Operations.]

BIBLIOGRAPHY

Cline, Ray S. *Secrets, Spies, and Scholars: Blueprint of the Essential CIA.* 1976.

Colby, William. *Honorable Men: My Life in the CIA.* 1978.

Harrison, Gordon A. *Cross-Channel Attack.* U.S. Army in World War II: The European Theater of Operations. 1951.

Lankford, Nelson D., ed. *OSS against the Reich: The World War II Diaries of Colonel David K. E. Bruce.* 1991.

Macksey, Kenneth. *The Partisans of Europe in the Second World War.* 1975.

Roosevelt, Kermit, ed. *The Overseas Targets: War Report of the OSS.* Vol. 2, 1976.

RAY S. CLINE

OLIVER, G. N. (1898–1980), British commodore, naval commander, Task Force J, Eastern Task Force. Geoffrey Oliver entered the Royal Navy (RN) in 1915 from Rugby School as a "special entry" cadet and served at sea from 1916 on in the battleship *Iron Duke* and then the battle cruiser *Renown.* He attended Cambridge University, then became a gunnery specialist after returning to the navy in 1921. His interwar service was varied, with periods in the Admiralty and in charge of the Gunnery School's experimental section, as well as sea duty as a cruiser and battleship gunnery officer and in command of a destroyer division in the Mediterranean Fleet.

In 1940–1941 Oliver commanded the new light cruiser *Hermione* in the Atlantic and the eastern Mediterranean until it was torpedoed and sunk. As senior officer, Inshore Squadron, Oliver provided seaward support to the British Eighth Army as it advanced from El Alamein to Tunis in 1942–1943. He took no part in the invasion of Sicily, but was chosen to lead a composite British and American navy force at the Salerno landings in September 1943.

In February 1944 Oliver was appointed commodore 1st class, as senior officer, Task Force J. Oliver continued the planning and training program with 3d Canadian Division and No. 48 Royal Marine Commando, which would be landed in the Courseulles sector supported by Bombarding Force E, all directed by Oliver from HMS *Hilary*. The assault on 6 June went according to plan, although beach obstructions in the Juno sector caused more damage to landing craft than elsewhere, and the port of Courseulles was in use by barges and minor craft by D plus 2, greatly speeding the buildup of this beachhead.

After the initial phase, the assault force commanders became responsible for the reception and berthing of ships in their anchorages, for the shuttle service between the ships and the beaches, and for sailing minor warships, the shuttle convoys, and the ambulance ships (hospital carriers) to England, all in addition to the defense of their sectors. Coordination was achieved by a daily meeting at 1830 with Rear Adm. Philip Vian, commander of the Eastern Task Force. On 24 June, with the establishment ashore of a naval officer-in-charge, Juno Sector, Oliver withdrew with his staff. Only in his sector had the assault and buildup gone entirely to plan.

Commodore Oliver went on to command an escort carrier squadron in the Mediterranean and East Indies, being promoted to rear admiral shortly before V-J Day. After the war his appointments included commander in chief of the East Indies and Nore stations, before his final retirement as a full admiral in December 1955.

[*See also* Eastern Task Force; Hilary, HMS; Task Force J.]

BIBLIOGRAPHY

Schofield, B. B. *Operation Neptune*. 1974.
Vian, Philip. *Action This Day*. 1960.

DAVID BROWN

OMAHA BEACH. *See* American Beaches, *article on* Omaha Beach.

101ST AIRBORNE DIVISION. The 101st Airborne Division played a central role in the Normandy cross-Channel landing. Along with its companion unit, the U.S. 82d Airborne Division, and the British 6th Airborne Division, it was to be the initial large-scale assault force on the ground in Normandy on 6 June 1944. The entire D-day invasion plan was linked to the success of the 101st Airborne drop.

The activation of the division on 16 August 1941 represented a new concept in American military strategy. Brig. Gen. William C. Lee, known as the "father of American airborne troops," was the first to command the unit; in his initial speech to the men, he observed, "The 101st has no history, but it has a rendezvous with destiny." Taken ill in the spring of 1944, he was replaced by Brig. Gen. Maxwell Taylor, who then commanded the 101st

101st Airborne Division
Brig. Gen. Maxwell Taylor

Division Headquarters
Headquarters Company
Military Police Platoon
326th Airborne Engineer Battalion
326th Airborne Medical Company
101st Airborne Signal Company
426th Airborne Quartermaster Company
801st Airborne Ordinance Maintenance Company

327th Glider Infantry Regiment
  (includes 1st Battalion, 401st Glider Infantry
  Regiment)
501st Parachute Infantry Regiment
502d Parachute Infantry Regiment
506th Parachute Infantry Regiment

101st Airborne Division Artillery Headquarters and
  Headquarters Battery
321st Glider Field Artillery Battalion
907th Glider Field Artillery Battalion
377th Parachute Field Artillery Battalion
81st Airborne Antiaircraft Battalion

---

during the invasion. Following the parachutists' tradition of having all officers—including those of flag rank—and enlisted men jump into a combat zone, General Taylor made what was only the third jump of his life in the early hours of the assault.

The division was in the vanguard of the D-day assault. Its mission was to parachute into the interior of the Cotentin Peninsula and prevent German troops from aiding those confronting the main Allied landing force on Utah Beach. In addition, it was to secure several roads for the main force to use as it drove inland from the beachhead.

EISENHOWER CHATTING WITH PARATROOPERS.   In this often reprinted picture, it is usually recorded that Dwight D. Eisenhower was giving the Order of the Day to members of the 502d Parachute Regiment, 101st Airborne Division, at Greenham Common airfield in England on 5 June 1944, just before they boarded for the first assault of the Normandy invasion. Eisenhower is talking to Lt. Wallace C. Strobel, the jump master of Company E; it was Strobel's twenty-second birthday. Strobel reports that Eisenhower simply asked, "What's your name, lieutenant?" and "Where are you from?" A version of this photo was used on the stamp issued in October 1990 to mark the centenary of Eisenhower's birth.   NATIONAL ARCHIVES

The organization of the 101st was shaped around the mission to be accomplished. During the period of preparation in England, the "All American Screaming Eagles," as they were known, operated under U.S. First Army command, but once they were on the ground in Normandy, control shifted to U.S. VII Corps. Seventeen units made up the full division.

An assessment of the division's D-day activities may be reviewed within the several stages of the assault. The initial boarding of the C-47 planes, CG4 Waco gliders, and Horsa gliders took place at various airfields in southwestern England. Flight crews were drawn from the 50th and 53d troop carrier wings of the IX Troop Carrier Command. Each aircraft held approximately eighteen

men. The flights were arranged into twenty serials of about forty planes each. Launch times and estimated jump times were staggered. Pathfinder flights preceded this armada, to illuminate and set up radar equipment at drop zones and landing sites.

The pathfinder flights commenced around 2150 on 5 June and covered the 136 miles from England to the drop zone in fifty-four minutes. The C-47s needed fifty-eight minutes for the flight, while the gliders took seventy-one. The main force of 490 C-47s with 6,600 paratroopers aboard was airborne by 2330. They crossed the English Channel in a southerly direction at 500 feet, banked southeasterly just north of Guernsey and Jersey, then climbed to 1,500 feet on reaching the coast of the Cotentin Peninsula. Thereafter,

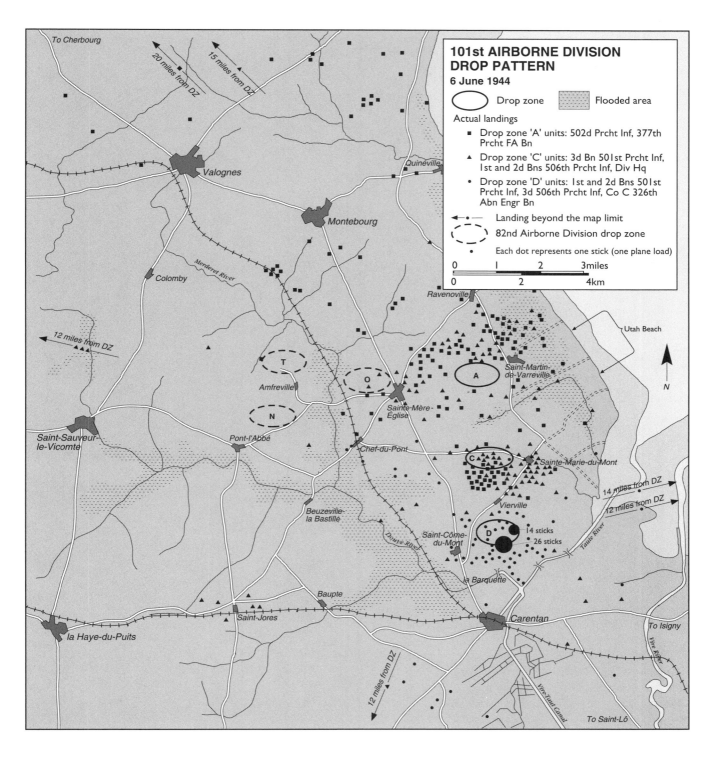

101st AIRBORNE DIVISION DROP PATTERN
6 June 1944

⬭ Drop zone   ▨ Flooded area

Actual landings

■ Drop zone 'A' units: 502d Prcht Inf, 377th Prcht FA Bn

▲ Drop zone 'C' units: 3d Bn 501st Prcht Inf, 1st and 2d Bns 506th Prcht Inf, Div Hq

● Drop zone 'D' units: 1st and 2d Bns 501st Prcht Inf, 3d 506th Prcht Inf, Co C 326th Abn Engr Bn

←·—·— Landing beyond the map limit

⬭ 82nd Airborne Division drop zone

• Each dot represents one stick (one plane load)

heading in an easterly direction toward Utah Beach, they descended to 700 feet for the drop.

About 4,600 of the paratroopers landed within the region bordered by the Douve River, Sainte-Mère-Église, and Ravenoville. Those landing outside this zone were almost all captured or killed. In the early morning hours following the landing, a considerable amount of time was spent trying to group the widely scattered units into fighting forces. Estimates indicate that of the 6,600 men dropped, only about 2,500 had assembled by the end of the first day.

Despite the disorganizing effect of the drop, the division proceeded to take its primary objective, the region

SITTING ON A CAPTURED JEEP IN CARENTAN.   Men of the 101st Airborne Division in Carentan, 12 June 1944. Carentan was one of the first French cities to fall to the Allied invasion force.

THE ROBERT HUNT LIBRARY, LONDON

west of Utah Beach between Pouppeville and Saint-Martin-de-Varreville. This assured beach landing troops access to exit roads leading to German units and other targets farther inland. Indeed, so dispersed were the landings that German efforts to confront the invaders were proportionally diffused. Though fighting was fierce and casualties high, by D plus 1, with two of their three division commanders absent, and unable to establish effective communications between frontline units, the Germans could not execute a focused counterattack against the initial airborne assault.

The costs were high. During the month of June, the division suffered 4,670 casualties. Hardest hit were the parachute and glider infantry battalions, which accounted for the vast majority of losses. Yet through valiant sacrifice and unparalleled personal courage, the mission was accomplished. The division continued its ground combat role without relief until early July, only to be reassigned later in the year to Belgium, where it would make its famous stand at Bastogne.

[See also Airborne Forces; Taylor, Maxwell.]

BIBLIOGRAPHY

Harrison, Gordon A. Cross-Channel Attack. U.S. Army in World War II: European Theater of Operations. 1951.
Huston, James A. Out of the Blue: U.S. Army Airborne Operations in World War II. 1972.
Keegan, John. Six Armies in Normandy. 1982.
Marshall, S. L. A. Nightdrop: The American Airborne Invasion of Normandy. 1962.
Rapport, Leonard, and Arthur Northwood, Jr. Rendezvous with Destiny: A History of the 101st Airborne Division. 1948.

DONALD E. BAIN

ORDNANCE. For discussion of Allied supplies, see Quartermaster and Ordnance Corps. For discussion of German supplies, see Supply Corps.

ORGANIZATION TODT. This important noncombatant construction organization, a branch of the

Nazi party, had originally been organized by and named after Dr. Fritz Todt. Todt and Dr. Ludwig Troost were the architects chosen by Hitler to design the great public monuments that were to glorify the Third Reich. After Troost's death, Hitler selected Albert Speer, a youthful and talented student of Troost, to take over the latter's tasks in partnership with Todt.

In 1940 Todt became Hitler's minister for armaments and munitions, in addition to his work as chief of road-building (the autobahns), waterways, and utilities. In the Nazi hierarchy, Todt wore the uniform of a Luftwaffe major general. In Reichsmarschall Hermann Göring's Four-Year Plan, Todt therefore became subordinate to Göring, who never let him forget it.

As head of the German building industry, Todt in 1938 had created Organization Todt (OT), a vast organization of uniformed construction battalions. Under Todt's leadership Organization Todt built the formidable West Wall along the Franco-German frontier and, after the fall of France, the U-boat bunkers along the Atlantic coast. Still later it built military roads in the occupied areas of Russia, and in occupied Europe from Norway to southern France.

In the winter of 1942 Todt died in an airplane crash after visiting Hitler's East Prussian headquarters. Within

hours of his death, Hitler called young Albert Speer into conference and appointed him as successor to Todt in all his duties. Göring had always regarded Todt as a potential rival, for many aspects of the Reichsmarschall's Four-Year Plan, formed in 1936 to create sufficiency in raw materials, conflicted with Todt's plans. After Todt's death, Göring's animosity transferred to Speer. Even without Göring's cooperation, Speer remained confident that Hitler would support Speer's control of OT's many large-scale construction projects and German industry.

Many of Speer's concepts for the wartime organization of German production were derived, by Speer's own admission, from the brilliant Jewish financier Walter Rathenau, who had organized German industry and conservation of raw materials during World War I. Rathenau's concepts had been transmitted first to Todt and then to Speer through a lengthy memorandum composed by an elderly coworker of Rathenau. Throughout the Third Reich this technocrat continued to work out of an attic office, first in Todt's ministry and then in Speer's.

Though not considered combatants, members of the OT were older workers who belonged to the Nazi party and wore a brown uniform with a swastika armband. After several OT workers were killed while working on a bunker during the Canadian raid on Dieppe, Speer recommended to Hitler that they no longer wear the armband. Hitler, however, refused this request. For his part, Speer tried to ignore the party and its demands in the interest of overall efficiency.

After the cancellation of Operation SEELÖWE (SEA LION) (the planned invasion of England), Hitler had directed Organization Todt to begin construction of bombproof U-boat pens along the French coast, especially at Brest, Lorient, and Saint-Nazaire. For a time this project absorbed most of the labor and matériel available for the construction of fortifications in the West.

By the eve of D-day, Allied bombing had so devastated French railways as to force the withdrawal of 18,000 OT men from Atlantic Wall construction tasks, to try to keep the railways running so as to bring men to the Atlantic front. Previously, on 8 May, OKW had approved the withdrawal of an additional 10,000 OT men. Following a conference with Hitler, Speer agreed that OT's main task in the West should henceforth be maintenance of the French railways, but ultimately this proved to be impossible. Thereafter OT no longer had anything to do with the Atlantic Wall, which in any case by early June had been decisively penetrated by the Allied armies.

[See also Atlantic Wall.]

BATTERY TODT.   One of the batteries on the coast of the English Channel was named for and dedicated to Dr. Fritz Todt.   THE ROBERT HUNT LIBRARY, LONDON

BIBLIOGRAPHY

Harrison, Gordon A. *Cross-Channel Attack*. U.S. Army in World War II: The European Theater of Operations. 1951.

MacDonald, Charles B. *The Mighty Endeavor: The American War in Europe*. 1969.

Speer, Albert. *Erinnerungen*. 1969.

ERNEST F. FISHER

OSS. *See* Office of Strategic Services (OSS).

OSTENDORFF, WERNER (1903–1945), German, Gruppenführer, commander of the *17th SS Panzer Grenadier Division*. Ostendorff served with the *1st Infantry Regiment* and then transferred to the Deutscher Luftsportverband (German Air Sports Organization), the cover name for the illegal Luftwaffe. In that organization he qualified as a pilot and was commissioned.

Ostendorff changed services again and on 1 October 1935 joined the SS. In April 1938, he took over the *4th Company* of the SS *"Der Führer" Regiment* and led it until June 1939. Shortly before the outbreak of World War II he was sent as an observer on the staff of *Panzer Division "Kempf"*, a formation composed of both army and SS units. Ostendorff was subsequently selected for General Staff training.

When the *SS Verfügungs Division* was created in October 1939, he led the group formed to undertake the raising of the new division, and when it became operational, he was appointed to the post of Ia (chief assistant, operations), which he held until 26 June 1942. By that time the *SS Verfügungs Division* had been renamed *"Das Reich"*. SS Oberstgruppenführer Paul Hausser's selection of Ostendorff for this post was a testimony to his skill as a staff officer.

In the Battles of the Yelnya Bend, Ostendorff frequently led attacks and counterattacks to beat back the Red Army's assaults, many of which ended in hand-to-hand fighting. For his superior performance in the Yelnya Bend battles, Ostendorff was awarded the Knight's Cross of the Iron Cross on 13 September 1941. During this time, Ostendorff was also commanding a battle group that bore his name. This was later renamed *Battle Group "Das Reich"*. That formation held the flank of the German *Ninth Army* near Rzhev, and his successful leadership brought the award of the German Cross in Gold on 25 June 1942.

Now promoted to the tank of Brigadeführer, Ostendorff was chosen, again by Hausser, to be chief of general staff of the *II SS Panzer Corps* when this unit was raised during May 1942. In this post Ostendorff tried in vain to persuade Hausser to obey Adolf Hitler's uncompromising order to defend Kharkov to the last. Hausser refused to accept his advice, but despite that difference of opinion

Ostendorff continued to serve as chief of staff until after the Battle of Kursk in July 1943. Four months later, Ostendorff, now holding the rank of Gruppenführer, took command of the newly raised *17th SS Panzer Grenadier Division "Götz von Berlichingen"*, and at forty years of age was among the youngest divisional commanders in the German armed forces.

Although he was faced with great shortages of equipment, lacked armored fighting vehicles, and had insufficient soft-skin transport, Ostendorff's tireless energy and enthusiasm brought his division to combat-readiness shortly before the Allies invaded Normandy. His division was located south of the Loire, between Tours and Nantes. When the invasion was announced Ostendorff immediately carried out fresh reconnaissance of the routes the *17th SS* would follow once it was ordered into action. His immaculate planning, clear orders, and careful attention to detail enabled his division, led by its spearhead reconnaissance battalion, to cross the Loire and advance toward Carentan. The division marched from positions south of the Loire to Bayeux and was then directed to the Saint-Lô sector, where it came under command of the *II Parachute Corps*. During the fighting in Normandy, Ostendorff, who was usually to be found in the front line, was wounded. Before he returned to the division he was again employed as Ia and this time to the Reichsführer SS, Heinrich Himmler, who had been given temporary command of *Army Group "Upper Rhine"*. Ostendorff's quiet but firm personality was of great help to the SS leader in mastering the complex duties of army group commander. When Himmler took over *Army Group "Vistula"* Ostendorff returned to the *"Götz von Berlichingen" Division* in October 1944 and in November was wounded for a second time.

Promotion to Obergruppenführer came in December 1944, and during February 1945 he took over command of the *2d SS Panzer Division "Das Reich"*. In the fighting around Stuhlweissenburg in Hungary during the early spring of 1945, he was wounded again, this time so severely that he died on 1 May 1945 in a hospital in Austria. Ostendorff was posthumously awarded the Oak Leaves to the Knight's Cross on 6 May 1945.

[*See also* 17th SS Panzer Grenadier Division.]

BIBLIOGRAPHY

Kleitmann, K. G. *Die Waffen SS: Eine Dokumentation*. 1965.

Kratschmer, E. G. *Die Ritterkreuzträger der Waffen SS*. 1982.

Stoker, H. J. *Die eiserne Faust: Bildband und Chronik der 17 SS Panzergrenadier Division*. 1966.

Tessin, Georg. *Verbände und Trupppen der deutschen Wehrmacht und Waffen-SS im Zweiten Weltkrieg, 1939–1945*. 1973–1980.

JAMES LUCAS

P

PANZER GROUP WEST. The German *Panzer Group West* was created in France on 24 January 1944, under the command of Gen. Leo Geyr von Schweppenburg, to control Germany's strategic mobile reserves in the West. Its organic general headquarters (GHQ) units included the *309th Higher Artillery Command*, a rear-area command, a signal battalion, and a few miscellaneous and supply units. Initially it was charged with training the ten panzer divisions in the West (including the SS divisions), and it performed this task very well. Compulsory night problems were held three days a week, special training was conducted in hedgerow fighting, and demonstration battalions schooled in British combat methods engaged in war games against German mobile forces. One day a week was set aside as *Fliegertag* (aviation day) for training against air attacks.

Geyr von Schweppenburg was a highly intelligent and experienced tank officer who, however, did not as yet fully appreciate the dominating effect Allied aerial forces would have on the battlefields of the Western front. He and Field Marshal Erwin Rommel sharply disagreed as to how Germany should use its mobile reserves. Rommel felt that an Allied landing had to be prevented at any cost; Geyr maintained that it was impossible to prevent a landing and that the panzer divisions should be held in reserve, to crush the Allies when they advanced into the interior of France. The result was a compromise dictated by Adolf Hitler that satisfied neither side. The *2d, 21st,* and *116th Panzer* divisions were transferred from the control of *Panzer Group West* to *Army Group B* (Rommel); the *9th, 11th,* and *2d SS Panzer* divisions were transferred to the soon-to-be activated *Army Group G* (Col. Gen. Johannes Blaskowitz); and Geyr was allowed to retain only four mobile divisions: the *1st SS Panzer, 12th SS Panzer, 17th SS Panzer Grenadier,* and *Panzer Lehr.*

On the morning of 7 June, *Panzer Group West* was ordered to take charge of the sector on both sides of the Orne River up to Tilly-sur-Seulles and to counterattack the Allied invasion forces north of Caen. It initially controlled only the *21st Panzer, 12th SS Panzer,* and *Panzer Lehr* divisions, as well as the remnants of the nearly destroyed *716th Infantry Division.* The initial attack was repulsed on 9 June in inconclusive fighting. Geyr regrouped and was preparing to launch another attack during the night of 10–11 June; that afternoon, however, his command post near La Caine was subjected to several hours of Allied saturating bombing raids and strafing attacks. Geyr was only slightly wounded, but his entire operations staff was killed, as was his chief of staff, Maj. Gen. Sigismund-Hellmut Ritter und Elder von Dawans. The bulk of the group's vehicles and almost all the technical equipment of its signal battalion were also destroyed. *Headquarters, Panzer Group West* had to be withdrawn from the battle that evening, and the *I SS Panzer Corps* took over its sector. The group headquarters was rebuilt in Paris and did not return to the battle until 1700 on 28 June.

Panzer Group West was redesignated *Fifth Panzer Army* on 5 August. It was mauled during the Falaise encirclement, but was rebuilt and fought in almost all the major battles on the Western front until it was destroyed in the Ruhr pocket in April 1945.

[*See also* Geyr, Leo.]

BIBLIOGRAPHY

Geyr von Schweppenburg, Leo. "Pz. Grp. West (Mid 43–5 Jul. 44)." Office of the Chief of Military History, MS B-019 (Change 2). Report dated 14 Apr. 1947. U.S. Army Military History Institute, Carlisle Barracks, Pa.

Knesebeck, Goetz Lothar von dem, ed. "Report of General von Geyr (12–15 Jun. 44)." Translated by Alexander Rosenwald, Office of the Chief of Military History, MS B-019. Report dated 8 May 1946. U.S. Army Military History Institute, Carlisle Barracks, Pa.

Mitcham, Samuel W., Jr. *Rommel's Last Battle: The Desert Fox and the Normandy Campaign*. 1983.

SAMUEL W. MITCHAM, JR.

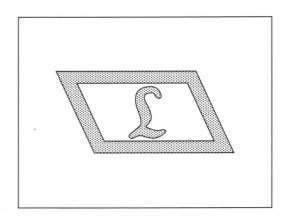

PANZER LEHR DIVISION.

The *Panzer Lehr Division* was formed as an elite outfit consisting of units that had formerly belonged to the various armor schools. The suggestion to concentrate these units into a fighting division had come from Col. Gen. Heinz Guderian himself, who also saw to it that one of his closest colleagues, Brig. Gen. Fritz Bayerlein, was put in charge of it.

Set up in January 1944, the division was equipped with the best material available, including the latest model tanks, mostly Panzer V (Panther). It was allotted special strength authorizations, but because of incipient shortages, the authorizations were never realized. Often new equipment was issued before it had been fully tested, which led to a high percentage of failures.

Personnel, coming as it did from combat schools, was usually experienced and of superior quality. On the other hand, its experience had generally been gathered on the Eastern front, where fighting conditions were somewhat different. In particular, most officers and men had never known combat in the face of Allied air supremacy.

The division consisted of two armored infantry regiments, the *901st* and *902d Panzer Grenadier Lehr* regiments, as well as one armored regiment, the *130th Panzer Lehr Regiment*, and one armored artillery regiment, the *130th Panzer Artillery Regiment*. These were supported by a variety of other units, including the *130th Antitank Battalion (Panzerjäger Lehr Abteilung 130)*, the *130th Armored Reconnaissance Battalion (Panzeraufklärungs Lehr Abteilung 130)*, and the *130th Engineer Battalion (Panzer Pionierbataillon 130)*. Authorized personnel strength was 449 officers and 14,185 men. In May 1944 the division was up to full personnel strength, although a lack of noncommissioned officers had to be compensated for by senior privates. It had 183 tanks, 58 antitank guns (some of them self-propelled), and 53 artillery pieces.

After a brief interlude in Hungary, the division was transferred to the area around Chartres–Le Mans–Orléans, where it was held in readiness to oppose possible airborne operations against Paris. At 1700 on 6 June 1944 it was placed under the *I SS Panzer Corps*, commanded by SS Obergruppenführer Josef ("Sepp") Dietrich, and ordered to move toward the coast, 130 kilometers (80 miles) away. However, it did not reach the sector west of Caen allotted to it until the evening of 8 June. During the overland move, the division was subjected to constant heavy bombing attacks that caused severe losses.

Together with the *21st Panzer Division* and the *12th SS Panzer Division*, the *Panzer Lehr Division* was ordered to counterattack around Saint-Aubin, Vauvres, and Creully and throw the Allied forces west of Caen back into the sea. However, when the division arrived in the assigned area, it found that some of the ground had already been taken by the 8th Armoured Brigade. Nevertheless, the division attacked on the morning of 9 June. The open left flank was guarded by the reconnaissance battalion. The left wing of the attack force was formed by one tank battalion and one infantry battalion. The right wing consisted of the entire *901st Panzer Grenadier Lehr Regiment*, reinforced by the antitank battalion. After some ground had been gained, Brigadier General Bayerlein himself had to cancel the attack because of British pressure on his right wing. Later in the day the division held the eastern suburbs of Tilly against a battalion-size British tank attack.

The following day, 10 June, the *Panzer Lehr Division* attacked elements of the British 7th Armoured Division, pre-empting a British strike toward Villers-Bocage. However, the German attack did not gain much ground either, mostly because of the intervention of heavy naval guns.

On 11 June it had to be conceded that the attempt to repel the invasion forces immediately had failed. Together with the entire *I SS Panzer Corps*, the division had to take up defensive positions. Its main task now was to defend Tilly against the 7th Armoured Division's attacks. The major problem was that its left flank was largely in the open and could only be supervised intermittently by the armored reconnaissance battalion. The left wing was now held by the tank regiment and the *902d Panzer Grenadier Regiment*, while the *901st Regiment* and one battalion of the tank regiment made up the right or eastern wing. Each sector was allotted two artillery battalions.

The division managed to hold its positions even when British attacks on 11 June were again supported by naval artillery. But on 13 June the British found their way around the division's left flank and captured Villers-Bocage until a hasty counterattack restored the situation.

When the British 7th Armoured Division was pulled

PANZER IV FROM THE *PANZER LEHR REGIMENT*. Dug in and used essentially as a pillbox, it was captured by the British.   IMPERIAL WAR MUSEUM

out of the line on 15 June, *Panzer Lehr Division* had hardly any fight left either. However, it was able to shorten its front line when the *2d Panzer Division* appeared on its left. Losses for the entire month of June amounted to 490 dead, 1,809 wounded, and 673 missing—altogether, some 18 percent of the division's strength. The division was involved in almost continuous fighting during the withdrawal to the German border. After a short spell to recover, it took part in the Ardennes offensive in December. In April 1945, it was taken prisoner by the 99th U.S. Infantry Division around Winterberg in the Ruhr pocket.

[*See also* Bayerlein, Fritz.]

BIBLIOGRAPHY

Ose, Dieter. *Entscheidung im Westen 1944: Der Oberbefehlshaber West und die Abwehr der alliierten Invasion.* 1982.

Ritgen, Helmut. *Die Geschichte der Panzer-Lehr-Division im Westen 1944–1945.* 1979.

WINFRIED HEINEMANN

PARATROOPERS. *See* Airborne Forces.

PARRY, W. EDWARD (1893–1972), British rear admiral, naval commander, Task Force L (Follow-Up Force L). Edward Parry came, on his mother's side, from a long line of distinguished naval officers, the Fremantles having provided four generations of admirals, Parry's uncle being the last. Parry himself entered the Royal Navy (RN) in 1905 and passed out of Dartmouth at the head of his term. He qualified as a torpedo officer during World War I and served thereafter with the Grand Fleet in the light cruiser *Birmingham*. Between the wars he held staff appointments ashore and afloat. In command of the light cruiser *Achilles*, in December 1939, in company with the cruisers *Exeter* and *Ajax*, he intercepted the German pocket battleship *Admiral Graf von Spee* and drove it into the River Plate, where it was later scuttled. Parry was subsequently appointed as the principal naval adviser to New Zealand, and as such was largely responsible for creating and organizing a separate Royal New Zealand Navy. After commanding the Home Fleet battle cruiser *Renown* in 1942–1943, he was promoted to rear admiral, representing the fifth successive generation of his family to reach flag rank.

In early 1944 Parry was appointed to command

Follow-Up Force L, the fourth British assault group, which formed and trained in the Thames Estuary area, based on Harwich, Southend, and Sheerness. Unlike the other assault group commanders, he did not exercise command afloat, for Force L's military units were to be landed over the Gold beaches, and the amphibious ships (U.S. as well as RN), transports, and coasters came under the control of Como. C. E. Douglas-Pennant on arrival in the Force G area. Carrying the British 7th Armoured Division and units from other formations, including the headquarters of 21st Army Group, Force L sailed in six convoys, the first group leaving the Thames on 5 June and arriving off Asnelles in time for the afternoon high tide on D-day, having lost a U.S. Navy LST (Landing Ship, Tank) to a mine. Thereafter, the remainder of Force L's groups arrived on schedule, the last reaching the anchorage twenty-four hours after the assault had begun.

Once unloading was completed, the ships of Force L were allocated to the cross-Channel shuttle service for the buildup phase. The only ships to return to the Thames for further loads were two dozen U.S. LSTs, the others using south coast ports to supply the U.S. and British areas on demand. With the dispersal of his force, Rear Admiral Parry was effectively left without a command after D plus 1; he was subsequently transferred to the staff of Adm. Bertram H. Ramsay, Allied Naval Commander, Expeditionary Force, where he remained until the end of the war in Europe.

Parry became deputy head of the naval division of the Allied Control Commission in Berlin, returning to London in July 1946 to become director of Naval Intelligence. This was followed by promotion to vice admiral and three years as chief of staff of the Royal Indian Navy, which he guided to independence, as he had done in New Zealand. On return to Britain in 1952, Parry, who had been created a Knight Commander of the Bath in 1950, was promoted to admiral on his retirement.

[See also British Beaches, article on Gold Beach; Douglas-Pennant, C. E.; Task Force L.]

BIBLIOGRAPHY

Barnett, Corelli. *Engage the Enemy More Closely: The Royal Navy in the Second World War.* 1991.
Roskill, Stephen W. *The Offensive.* Vol. 3, pt. 2, of *The War at Sea, 1939–1945.* 1961.

DAVID BROWN

PATHFINDERS. The seaborne assault of Operation OVERLORD relied on airborne forces being dropped to protect its flanks. To protect the west flank, the U.S. 82d and 101st airborne divisions parachuted onto drop zones (DZs) and used gliders to land on landing zones (LZs) near Sainte-Mère-Église, while the east flank was pro-

tected by the British 6th Airborne Division, which landed between Cabourg and the Orne River. The pathfinders preceded the main airborne assault by about thirty minutes to mark the DZs and LZs visually with small flare-paths, illuminated "Ts," and electronically with Eureka beacons.

Virtual air superiority had been achieved over the invasion area and the American IX Troop Carrier Command allocated twenty aircraft to mark their six DZs and to position aids for the first glider missions. The approach from the west across the Cotentin Peninsula made best use of the navigational aid transmitted from stations in England, but low cloud hampered visual identification on the final approach to the DZs. The drop was made at 0016 hours; two aircraft were right on target, and the remainder were sufficiently close to achieve their objective.

The 6th Airborne Division pathfinders from 22d Independent Parachute Company, flown by No. 38 Group Royal Air Force, approached from the east directly over the sea and made their drop at 0020 hours accompanied by a glider-borne force of 200 men from the Oxfordshire and Buckinghamshire Light Infantry and the Royal Engineers, whose task was to seize and hold two bridges over the Orne River and Caen Canal, the latter renamed Pegasus Bridge. This coup de main operation was very successful, and the pathfinders marked the DZs with only half the planned marker force.

Despite the accuracy of the pathfinders, the main force was not so successful. The difficulties caused by flak, low clouds, and errors in map reading at night resulted in the main force being widely scattered. Fortunately, this unintentional dispersion of the main force made it difficult for the German defenders to make tactical sense of the attack, and therefore the Germans failed to make a rapid response where it was needed.

The complex assault plan conceived by Adm. Bertram Ramsey required very accurate navigation to the beaches. Many vessels were fitted with Gee, a navigational aid carried by aircraft or ships based on radio transmissions from ground stations. D-day provided the first operational use of the Decca navigator, a later and more accurate system; nineteen preproduction sets were fitted in key craft. German mine fields lay in the path of the invasion fleet, and to provide a safe approach, two channels, each 3.2 kilometers (2 miles) wide, were swept for every one of the five assault forces. Motor launches marked the beginning of the swept channels, and the edges were indicated by dan buoys made more conspicuous by lights or flags.

In the British sector, two midget submarines lay on the bottom for two days and nights before surfacing to mark the inshore edges of the assault lane with blinking lights.

BRITISH PATHFINDERS SYNCHRONIZING THEIR WATCHES BEFORE EMPLANING.   These troops were among the first to land.   IMPERIAL WAR MUSEUM

BIBLIOGRAPHY

Barnett, Corelli. *Engage the Enemy More Closely.* 1991.
Eisenhower Foundation. *D-Day.* 1971.
Johnson, Garry, and Christopher Dunphie. *Brightly Shone the Dawn.* 1980.
Tugwell, Michael. *Airborne to Battle.* 1971.
Warren, John C. *Airborne Operations in World War II: European Theatre.* 1950.

FREDERICK SOWREY

PATTERSON, W. R. (1894–1954), British, rear admiral, commander of Bombarding Force D. Wilfrid Patterson joined the Royal Navy as a cadet in 1906 and served in Grand Fleet destroyers during World War I. Specializing as a gunnery officer immediately after the war, he was promoted to captain in 1933, following which he commanded a sloop on the China Station, a training cruiser in home waters, and a Royal Australian Navy heavy cruiser, HMAS *Canberra*. He returned from the last in 1940 to assume command of the new battleship *King George V*, in which he achieved the professional gunnery officer's ultimate ambition by taking part in the destruc-

tion by gunfire of the German battleship *Bismarck* in May 1941. Patterson was later in the year appointed chief of staff to the British Admiralty Delegation in Washington, a particularly important post on the eve of the U.S. entry into the war.

Promoted to rear admiral in July 1942, Patterson returned to Britain in March 1943 to become assistant chief of naval staff (weapons). One of his responsibilities was for the development of the Mulberry harbor scheme, but when he was selected as one of the Operation NEPTUNE commanders, it was for a task in his own specialization. Bombarding Force D, formed from Home Fleet ships to provide bombardment support for Task Force S, the assault force for Sword Beach, had begun live training with the assault force in the Moray Firth in March 1944. On 14 May 1944 Patterson moved to the light cruiser HMS *Mauritius* as flag officer, 2d Cruiser Squadron, and commander of Force D.

Patterson's force comprised two old battleships, a monitor, five light cruisers, nine fleet destroyers, and three Hunt-class escort destroyers, plus fifteen close-support landing craft. For the assault, the battleships and monitor were to neutralize the coast defenses to the east of Sword Beach, while the cruisers neutralized batteries to

British 3d Infantry Division's front and the destroyers and close-support craft engaged the beach defenses prior to landing and, in the case of flanking defenses, until they were overrun.

The heavy ships reached their positions without interference on D-day and had just opened fire, when three German torpedo boats attacked from the east through a smoke screen laid by Allied aircraft to mask the transports' lowering position from the shore batteries. The attack was beaten off by Force D, assisted by the Eastern Task Force flagship, HMS *Scylla*, but the Norwegian destroyer *Svenner* was torpedoed and sunk during the skirmish. The initial bombardment of the defenses was so successful that there was a lull after the first phase, although this was partly due to casualties among the army forward observation teams. Once communications were established between the frontline units and the bombardment control team in the Sword headquarters ship, HMS *Largs*, the warships could begin effective gunfire support of the British 3d Infantry Division. During the twenty-four days that Force D operated, half the cruisers' missions were fired against tanks, infantry concentrations, and motor transport targets.

The force was less successful against German defenses to the east of the Orne River, where mobile batteries were brought up into prepared positions. The ships were unable to neutralize these guns or to prevent the deployment of additional batteries, and were not assisted by the British divisional or corps artillery. The port of Ouistreham was thus largely unusable and unloading over the beaches became increasingly hazardous, personnel disembarkation being halted on 15 June and stores traffic on 25 June. Four days later, on 29 June, Sword Beach was abandoned altogether. Force D had already been disbanded as a unit on 22 June, when Admiral Patterson had withdrawn and Rear Adm. F. H. G. Dalrymple-Hamilton assumed control of all bombarding forces..

Patterson, appointed a Commander of the Bath for his contribution to NEPTUNE, commanded the 5th Cruiser Squadron in the Bay of Bengal during the last months of the war. Promoted to vice admiral in March 1946, he was knighted later in the year and was appointed admiral commanding reserves in 1947. This was his last naval post; he retired in 1950, after promotion to admiral.

[*See also* Bombardment Ships; Mauritius, HMS; Task Force S.]

BIBLIOGRAPHY

Barnett, Correlli. *Engage the Enemy More Closely: The Royal Navy in the Second World War.* 1991.
Roskill, Stephen W. *The Offensive.* Vol. 3, pt. 2, of *The War at Sea, 1939–1945.* 1961.

DAVID BROWN

PATTON, GEORGE S., JR. (1885–1945), American, lieutenant general, commanding general, Third Army. Born in California, a graduate of the U.S. Military Academy in 1909, and a cavalryman, Patton saw action with Pershing's punitive expedition in Mexico in 1916. In France in 1917, he was the first officer transferred into the Tank Corps. He trained his tank brigade and then, as colonel, led it in the Saint-Mihiel and Meuse-Argonne operations until he was wounded. He received the Distinguished Service Cross for gallantry.

A graduate of the Command and General Staff College and of the Army War College, Patton became the 2d Armored Division brigade commander in 1940. As the division's commander and a major general, he participated in the Tennessee, Carolina, and Louisiana-Texas maneuvers of 1941. Named commanding general of the I Armored Corps in 1942, he opened and directed the Desert Training Center in the southwestern United States.

Patton commanded the Western Task Force in the invasion of North Africa in November 1942, took his troops ashore in French Morocco, and obtained French surrender after three days of battle. After the devastating American defeat at Kasserine Pass in February 1943, Patton took

GEORGE S. PATTON, JR. Left, with Louis Mountbatten.
NATIONAL ARCHIVES

command of the II Corps in Tunisia, restored its fighting spirit, and led it in successful offensive actions.

Promoted to lieutenant general in March 1943 and appointed commanding general of the Seventh Army, Patton invaded Sicily in July, seized Palermo, and then captured Messina to close out the campaign. Visiting hospitals to cheer the wounded, Patton, in two incidents a week apart, slapped two soldiers suffering from combat exhaustion because he thought them to be malingering. For his outbursts, he was denied command of the U.S. army group to be activated for the campaign in northwestern Europe.

Instead, Patton received command of the Third Army in England early in 1944. In addition to preparing his troops for combat, Patton contributed, simply by his presence, to a vast deception program named FORTITUDE, a large-scale measure designed to make the Germans believe that Patton, whom the Germans regarded as the best American battlefield general, would lead the main invasion forces across the Channel at its narrowest point, from Dover to Pas de Calais. The deception, which included dummy installations and communications, plus the manipulation of agents, succeeded beyond expectation.

Patton himself arrived in France on 6 July. His army became operational on 1 August. Although his name and army remained unmentioned and received no publicity during the first fifteen days of the month in order to maintain the FORTITUDE deception, Patton exploited the local breakthrough created by the U.S. First Army into a theaterwide breakout that ended early in September because of gasoline shortages. Some of Patton's units raced westward to Brest; others streamed eastward and were the first to cross the Seine River, moving well into Lorraine.

In December, during the German Ardennes counteroffensive, Patton turned his army north and rescued the men surrounded at Bastogne. Promoted to general in April 1945, he entered Czechoslovakia and captured Pilsen.

Patton headed the occupation forces in Bavaria and then commanded the Fifteenth Army. Injured in an automobile accident in December, he died after eleven days in the hospital. His fame rests on his audacity and will power, and the unceasing pressure he exerted against the enemy.

[*See also* Deception.]

BIBLIOGRAPHY

Blumenson, Martin. *Patton: The Man behind the Legend, 1885–1945.* 1985.
Blumenson, Martin. *The Patton Papers.* 2 vols. 1972, 1974.

MARTIN BLUMENSON

PELTZ, DIETRICH (1914–), German, brigadier general, commander of *IX Air Corps,* responsible for con-

DIETRICH PELTZ. BIBLIOTHEK FÜR ZEITGESCHICHTE, STUTTGART

ventional twin-engined bomber units employed against the Allied invasion. Dietrich Peltz joined the Luftwaffe in 1935. During the campaigns in Poland in 1939 and in the West in 1940, he commanded a squadron *(Staffel)* of Junkers Ju 87 Stuka dive bombers. In the Battle of Britain he flew Junkers Ju 88s with *Bomber Wing (Geschwader) 77,* and in the spring of 1941 he was appointed a group *(Gruppe)* commander. In September 1942 he took command of *1st Group, Bomber Wing 66,* a Ju 88 unit active over the Mediterranean. In the following December he was appointed inspector of bomber units *(Inspekteur der Kampfflieger)* and in March 1943 took command of operations against England *(Angriffsführer England)* and was promoted to colonel. In September he also became commander of *IX Air Corps,* with headquarters in Beauvais, France. Between then and May 1944, with limited forces, his attacks on Britain tied down many squadrons of RAF fighters and a large antiaircraft organization. Despite imaginative tactics, his force suffered heavy losses.

Following D-day, the bombers of *IX Air Corps* engaged in nightly attacks against the lodgment area and shipping off the coast. Owing to the lack of suitable equipment and specialized training for antishipping attacks, however, the force was ineffective in direct attacks on Allied vessels. The formation then moved to laying mines in shallow water off the coast; these measures took a toll of vessels passing through the area, but were not decisive. Given the huge disparity between Peltz's forces and those confronting him, it was probably the only way that *IX Air Corps* could be employed to any effect.

During the German offensive in the Ardennes in December 1944 Peltz commanded *II Fighter Corps*, which provided air support for that operation.

[*See also* IX Air Corps.]

BIBLIOGRAPHY

Brütting, Georg. *Das waren die deutschen Kampfflieger-Asse 1939–1945.* 1975.
Price, Alfred. *Blitz on Britain.* 1976.

ALFRED PRICE

PEREGORY, FRANK D.

PEREGORY, FRANK D. (1915–1944), American, Medal of Honor winner, technical sergeant, 29th Infantry Division. A native of Esmont, Virginia, Peregory joined the Virginia National Guard unit from Charlottesville, known as the Monticello Guard (Company K, 116th Infantry Regiment, 29th Division), in 1931 at the age of sixteen.

On D-day, Sergeant Peregory landed on Omaha Beach with Company K at 0720 hours (H plus 50 minutes). On 8 June the 116th Infantry Regiment moved westward out of the beachhead toward the port of Grandcamp, which was held by a powerful German rear guard. An attack by elements of the 2d and 5th Ranger battalions in early afternoon had failed to dislodge the Germans. Following bombardment of the German position by the British cruiser *Glasgow*, Companies K and L of the 116th attempted another assault, but were pinned down by German fire from an entrenched position atop a hill just east of the town. Peregory rose and rushed toward the German strong point, firing his M1 and hurling hand grenades. His amazed comrades saw him jump into an enemy trench, and emerge moments later with three German prisoners. Handing the prisoners over to a guard, he resumed his one-man attack. "After what seemed like an eternity," a witness recalled, "he again emerged from the trench, this time with thirty-two German prisoners." As German fire slackened, Company K rose, overran the German strong point, and moved into Grandcamp.

For his deeds at Grandcamp, Sergeant Peregory was awarded the Medal of Honor, one of only two members of the 29th Division to receive that award during World War II. Peregory never knew of the honor, however; he was killed in action near Saint-Lô just six days later.

BIBLIOGRAPHY

Balkoski, Joseph. *Beyond the Beachhead: The 29th Infantry Division in Normandy.* 1989.
Branham, Felix P. "Frank D. Peregory: Medal of Honor." *Twenty-Niner Newsletter* 35, no. 2 (July 1991): 15.
Ewing, Joseph. *Twenty-Nine, Let's Go!* 1948.

JOSEPH M. BALKOSKI

PÉTAIN, HENRI PHILIPPE OMER (1856–1951), French marshal, Vichy head of state. Pétain was born into a landed family in the Calais area. In 1876 he entered military school at Saint-Cyr and by the early 1900s was lieutenant colonel at the École de Guerre. There he preached against the prevailing concept of the *offensive à l'outrance*. An infantry commander in 1914–1915, Colonel Pétain became the hero of Verdun in 1916, and his popularity swelled when he quelled the French mutinies in 1917 by humane reform instead of rigid repression.

After the war, Marshal Pétain served briefly as minister of war in 1934 and as ambassador to Franco's Spain in 1939.

PÉTAIN'S D-DAY PRONOUNCEMENT.
THE ROBERT HUNT LIBRARY, LONDON

His chief contribution, however, was in framing the French defensive strategy and the Maginot Line. Tanks and airplanes were valuable to him only as adjuncts to the infantry and not in mass formations—a severe deficiency for the French facing Nazi panzers and the Luftwaffe in 1940.

Following the debacle of 1940, the eighty-four-year-old Pétain entered the cabinet and was voted by Parliament to be head of state at Vichy. His regime was more traditionalist and conservative than precisely fascist. To its discredit, it collaborated with the Nazis in persecuting the Jews and imposing forced labor on the French.

On D-day, Pétain feared an ensuing chaos and civil war in which the Communists would seize power. He advised his officials to pursue a policy of neutrality and even cooperation with the other opposing forces in order to maintain order. In August, the Nazis forcibly removed him to Germany, where he remained until the Allies arrived in April 1945. A French court sentenced him to death, but President Charles de Gaulle commuted the sentence to life imprisonment. The marshal died in exile on the Île d'Yeu in 1951.

[*See also* France.]

BIBLIOGRAPHY

Paxton, Robert. *Vichy France: Old Guard and New Order, 1940–1944.* 1972.
Speers, Edward. *Two Men Who Loved France.* 1966.
Warner, Geoffrey. *Pierre Laval and the Eclipse of France, 1931–1945.* 1968.

DONALD J. HARVEY

RUDOLPH PETERSEN.

BIBLIOTHEK FÜR ZEITGESCHICHTE, STUTTGART

PETERSEN, RUDOLF (1905–1983), German, commander of S-boats (*Schnellboote*). Rudolf Petersen was born on 15 June 1905 in Atzerballig bei Alsen. He joined the German Navy in 1925 and in October 1929 was made lieutenant. After serving on various ships, in 1935 he was posted to the S-boat force, which was then being created. After service in the Baltic training battalion (*Schiffsstammabteilung*) in Stralsund, in August 1938 he took command of the newly formed *2d S-Boat Flotilla*, with which he fought in the North Sea, Norway, and the Baltic from 1939 to 1941. After the conclusion of S-boat deployment in the Baltic, in October 1941 Petersen became naval staff officer on special assignment on the staff of the commander of torpedo boats, to whom the S-boats were subordinate.

In April 1942 the position commander of S-boats was created and given to Petersen. In this capacity he directed S-boat operations in the West from headquarters in Scheveningen, Holland. In March 1943 he was promoted to commander. The S-boats operating in the Mediterranean and in the Black Sea were organized under his command, but were operationally under local naval commanders. During the Normandy invasion, ancillary command posts were set up in Le Havre, then Ostende–De Hann, and finally Den Helder; five flotillas of S-boats were deployed with limited success. Petersen was promoted to captain (1 March) and then to commodore (1 October) in 1944 and was awarded the Knight's Cross with Oak Leaf Cluster of the Iron Cross. After the war he lived in Flensburg-Mürwik, where he died on 2 January 1983.

[*See also* S-Boats.]

BIBLIOGRAPHY

Lohmann, Walter, and Hans H. Hildebrand. *Die deutsche Kriegsmarine 1939–1945.* 1956–1964.

GERHARD HÜMMELCHEN

PINDER, JOHN J., JR. (1921–1944), American, technician fifth grade; Medal of Honor recipient. John Pinder was born on 7 June 1921 in McKees Rocks, Pennsylvania, and entered the service in Burgettstown,

Pennsylvania. He was assigned to the headquarters and headquarters company, 16th Infantry Regiment, 1st Infantry Division. Near Colleville-sur-Mer, Normandy, Technician Fifth Grade Pinder struggled ashore on 6 June 1944 in waist-deep water carrying a heavy radio, when he was gravely wounded. He persisted with his mission and delivered the radio, refused medical attention, then returned to the surf and intense enemy fire three times to salvage urgently needed radio equipment. On the last trip he was wounded in the legs by machine-gun fire, but he still managed to put his radio into operation on the beach. While doing so, he was hit for the third time and killed. His courage was an inspiration to his fellow soldiers. For these acts of heroism, he received the Medal of Honor posthumously.

BIBLIOGRAPHY

U.S. Congress. Senate. Committee on Veterans' Affairs. *Medal of Honor Recipients, 1863–1978.* 96th Cong., 1st sess., 1979. S. Committee Print No. 3.

JOHN F. VOTAW

PLANNING. [*This entry includes separate discussions of Allied and German planning prior to the Normandy invasion.*]

Allied Planning

The planning for D-day can be traced back to the aftermath of the evacuation of Dunkirk, May–June 1940. The Combined Operations Staff was established to conduct commando raids and study the problems of amphibious warfare. In 1941 Louis Mountbatten, newly appointed chief of combined operations, was instructed by Winston Churchill to prepare for the invasion of Europe. Staff members did not prepare a formal plan, but they uncovered some practical lessons, identified two possible landing sites, and developed ideas into feasible proposals. Britain, however, lacked the strength to invade the Continent alone; it would require the drive and resources of a new ally—the United States—to make invasion planning more than just talk.

A cross-Channel invasion became likely after the Arcadia Conference in Washington (December 1941–January 1942). The Allies agreed that the primary task was the defeat of Germany. Gen. George C. Marshall, the U.S. Chief of Staff, flew to Britain in April to propose an early opening of the second front. The British appeared to accede to the Marshall memorandum, assuming they could restrain their enthusiastic ally, but Russian pressure led to a firm American commitment to open the second front in 1942. News of this projected operation (SLEDGEHAMMER) forced the British to send Mountbatten to Washington to

Allied Conferences and the Second Front in 1943

CONFERENCE	CODE NAME	DATE	DECISION
Casablanca	ANFA	Jan.	COSSAC to be established
Washington	TRIDENT	May	Date set for D-day (May 1944)
Quebec	QUADRANT	Aug.	COSSAC plan approved, Mulberry project approved
Teheran	EUREKA	Nov.	Firm commitment to OVERLORD
Cairo	SEXTANT	Dec.	Eisenhower to be Commander in Chief

tell the Americans a cross-Channel invasion was not possible in 1942. The Americans, with some justice, suspected the British were lukewarm about invading France, and some even believed that Britain's Mediterranean strategy was motivated by imperial interests. Without continual American pressure D-day would not have been launched, but British caution prevented a premature attempt to invade France and gave the Allied planners time to consider the operation thoroughly.

Throughout 1943 U.S. military power grew, and having become the senior partner, the Americans were able to persuade the British to commit themselves to a cross-Channel invasion in 1944. In April 1943 Lt. Gen. Frederick Morgan was appointed Chief of Staff to the Supreme Allied Commander (designated COSSAC). Morgan's organization was responsible for turning ideas into a firm proposal for opening the second front, and having won the approval of the conference in Quebec (QUADRANT) in August, they produced a detailed operational plan for Operation OVERLORD.

Initially COSSAC had to answer the question of whether a landing could succeed. They calculated that a first wave of three divisions and two airborne divisions—which would stretch available resources to the limit— could succeed, provided that no more than three German divisions were in the immediate vicinity of the landing site. Having decided that a cross-Channel invasion was feasible, COSSAC proceeded to consider landing sites, and after a weekend conference at Largs in Scotland, they selected western Normandy. This decision partly reflected the broad vision that COSSAC had of the invasion, looking beyond the problems of the landing to the subsequent campaign and placing a high value on the early occupation of ports. Normandy also offered the Allies greater opportunities to achieve surprise, which Morgan believed was a necessary condition for success. His staff contributed to the Allied deception plan by working with other organizations to ensure that activities like bombing did not give the game away, and in 1943 they organized Operation STARKEY, a dress rehearsal for a landing in the Pas de Calais.

Besides achieving surprise, COSSAC's other major concern was the rate at which Allied forces could be built up. The bloody failure of the 1942 Dieppe raid, in which the Canadian attackers suffered a casualty rate of over 60 percent, convinced the planners that a port could not be seized in the initial assault. One of Normandy's advantages was access to Cherbourg and the ports of Brittany, but COSSAC felt it was dangerous to depend on the early capture of a working port and strongly backed the Mulberry harbor project. Like many of the ideas fostered by COSSAC, the notion of building an artificial harbor predated the organization, but it was COSSAC that won the resources for the project sufficiently early for it to contribute to the success of D-day.

The planners examined both the big questions and the minutiae. For instance, patches of clay at the landing site, which would make it hard to move vehicles up the beaches, might have been overlooked by a less meticulous planning organization, but COSSAC's awareness of the problem led to the development of Bobbin mats, which enabled vehicles to cross the patches.

Dwight D. Eisenhower was appointed Supreme Commander Allied Expeditionary Force on 6 December 1943, heralding the demise of COSSAC, which became Supreme Headquarters Allied Expeditionary Force (SHAEF). Eisenhower and General Bernard L. Montgomery (who as commander of the British 21st Army Group was ground forces commander for D-day) argued for a month's delay to increase the strength of the first wave. In January 1944 the new command team demanded and got a first wave of five divisions rather than three and three airborne divisions to protect the flanks of the beachhead.

With these extra resources Montgomery put the finishing touches to COSSAC's plan, and on 7 April he briefed senior Allied commanders. Brushing aside fears that the landing area would stretch Allied resources, Montgomery planned to assault on a front of more than eighty kilometers (fifty miles). He hoped to be able to take Caen quickly and press south in the east, while in the west the landing on Utah Beach would place the Americans north of the coastal marshes, ensuring the early fall of Cherbourg.

Montgomery, correctly anticipating that Field Marshal Erwin Rommel would attempt to eliminate the Allies in the beachhead rather than fight an in-depth mobile defense, planned to combine Allied firepower and rapid penetration of British armored formations to frustrate Rommel's intent. Offensive action by the British in the east was intended to protect the Americans in the west, facilitating a rapid seizure of ports and then a wide sweep toward the Loire River.

Sadly the success of the Allied planning for D-day has been obscured by the controversy created by Montgomery's claim that "I never once had cause or reason to alter my master plan." Not only was Montgomery's claim demonstrably untrue, but it also gave a very misleading idea of what good planning strives to achieve. The immense effort put into planning D-day was not expected to produce an operation that ran like clockwork; but it did give a competent commander (and Montgomery was one despite his arrogance) the ability to improvise successfully without disrupting the overall coherence of the operation. The potential for utter disaster on 6 June was immense, and those who planned D-day played a major role in ensuring its success.

BIBLIOGRAPHY

D'Este, Carlo. *Decision in Normandy: The Unwritten Story of Montgomery and the Allied Campaign.* 1983.
Morgan, Frederick. *Overture to Normandy.* 1950.

SEAN MCKNIGHT

German Planning

Preparations to defend western Europe against an Allied landing were primarily determined by the following factors: development of the overall military situation, the probable intentions of the Allies, and the situation in the occupied territories.

Although the German occupation policy in western Europe was somewhat more moderate than in eastern Europe, it offered the western countries little for the future. Indeed, German policy imposed a pervasive and precisely functioning repressive regime. It is no wonder that collaboration was rare and that resistance movements flourished. Even before the invasion this was an incalculable advantage for the Allies. Many living in the occupied countries risked their lives to pass on military secrets to the British and Americans. For this reason, the staff of the Commander in Chief West, Field Marshal Gerd von Rundstedt, did not expect cooperation from the people in the occupied countries. On the other hand, they did not anticipate any great insurrection when the Allies landed.

The transportation infrastructure of western Europe, with its dense network of efficient rail lines, highways, and waterways, initially facilitated German military goals, although Allied bomber squadrons increasingly destroyed bridges and transportation junctions. In May 1944 thousands of trains were stuck in Belgium and eastern France, unable to travel westward to carry supplies and reinforcements to the invasion area.

When, where, and in what strength would the Allies land? German commanders and intelligence services posed this question shortly after the Battle of Britain was lost in

1940. Reliable intelligence on the Allies was not easy for Rundstedt's staff to obtain, because there were no central authorities or offices to review, compare, and analyze reports. Thus it is not surprising that Allied strength in Great Britain was routinely exaggerated and that as early as February 1943 Rundstedt warned his divisions of an immediate large-scale invasion. In May 1944 the Germans suspected the presence in England of some seventy-five to eighty divisions, approximately twice the number of divisions actually present. The Germans gave credibility to similarly exaggerated reports from North Africa.

Thus it was thought that Allied invasions could occur anywhere from Norway to Turkey. The Germans expected the main landing at the narrowest point in the Channel (the Pas de Calais) because they erroneously believed that a strong army group in southeastern England under Gen. George S. Patton, Jr., was preparing for the assault. Moreover, they knew that the Americans and British were capable of diversionary operations elsewhere. This view was based on the assumption that the Allies intended to push forward with their main forces into the Ruhr Valley as quickly as possible. Since this was the opinion of Hitler, the Wehrmacht command, Rundstedt, and Field Marshal Erwin Rommel (supreme commander of all land forces between Brittany and Holland), most of the German forces in the West were concentrated between the Seine and the Netherlands.

On the other hand, the Naval Command West in France did not believe that the Allies would attack precisely at the center of German strength, and also questioned reports about Patton's army group in southeastern England. The Third Air Command (Luftflottenkommando 3) in Paris did not follow the official line either. The Luftwaffe officers thought that, after Allied bombers destroyed all the bridges across the Seine from Mantes downstream, an Allied landing between Le Havre and Cherbourg would be more likely. Fortunately for the Allies, Rommel, Rundstedt, and Hitler did not give much credence to these views.

Until the fall of 1943 Hitler and his generals paid primary attention to the Eastern front. Thereafter they made an Allied invasion their highest priority, for it became clear that the war would be decided in the West. The German beach and coastal defenses were impressive: 12,250 defense installations were built, 500,000 barricades were erected along the coast, and 6.5 million mines were laid. Again fortunately for the Allies, most of the installations were located between Le Havre and Holland, not in the eventual landing zone between Le Havre and Cherbourg.

In June 1944 General Rundstedt had available sixty divisions, including ten panzer divisions, although combat in the Soviet Union and Italy had absorbed more and more of Germany's resources. While the motorized, infantry, and parachute divisions were of high quality, units of lesser quality were often deployed directly on the coast. Frequently armed with captured weapons and inadequate motor vehicles, they were unsuited for mobile warfare. At the beginning of June 1944, the Luftwaffe in the West had 891 aircraft, but only 650 were ready for action. Thus it was hopelessly inferior to the Allied air forces. The navy was in a similar situation, since nearly all its larger ships had been ordered to Norway or back to Germany because of enemy air superiority.

The weakness of air and naval forces prevented the Germans from engaging the Allies in the English staging areas or even on the Atlantic, well before they reached the coast. Aside from vague hopes for the effectiveness of the V-1 and V-2 weapons, the only remaining alternative was to strike the Allies after they landed. Whenever it became clear where the main Allied landing site was, Rundstedt's staff would have to decide how to deploy the motorized divisions most effectively. A month-long argument finally ended in a compromise: some panzer divisions would be deployed immediately behind the Atlantic Wall in order to engage rapidly, while the rest would be grouped around Paris as a reserve force, to be deployed from there when the main Allied landing was unquestionably in progress.

In Normandy, the eventual landing zone, there was only one panzer division, south of Caen. Two other divisions were some 100–130 kilometers (60–80 miles) away, northwest of Orléans. Rundstedt had deployed all the other panzer divisions north of the Seine or in southern France.

The Wehrmacht troops in the West had lost the élan of earlier years; military setbacks and Allied superiority in matériel inevitably affected morale. Moreover, capture by the Allies inspired no great fear because it was known that the British and Americans treated their prisoners much better than the Russians did. Thus the will to hold out and sacrifice oneself, as the German military leadership constantly demanded, was lacking. German propaganda tried to counteract this by emphasizing that Allied bombing attacks on German cities were aimed at defenseless women and children, and that it was a life-and-death matter for the German soldier to defend his homeland.

It is questionable whether such arguments fell on fertile ground. Even so, German divisions that had fought well in the past and whose personnel remained intact would provide dogged resistance to the Allies. However, few such divisions still existed in the West. Many formations had been recruited from diverse units and thus rarely shared common battle experiences from the past.

In the summer of 1944 German soldiers in the West—like those elsewhere—placed their hopes in the secret weapons that Hitler had announced and that they hoped would turn the war in their favor. Until those weapons could be deployed, they had to hold firm.

Hitler's circle and Rommel and the other generals awaited the landing with considerable confidence. They believed that their plans encompassed everything possible to hand the Allies a conclusive military defeat.

[*See also* Deception; Intelligence.]

BIBLIOGRAPHY

Ose, Dieter. *Entscheidung im Westen 1944. Der Oberbefehlshaber West und die Abwehr der alliierten Invasion.* Vol. 22 of *Militärgeschichtliches Forschungsamt Beiträge zur Militär- und Kriegsgeschichte.* 1982.
Wegmüller, Hans. *Die Abwehr der Invasion. Die Konzeption des Oberbefehlshabers West 1940–1944.* 1979.
Wilt, Alan F. *War from the Top: German and British Military Decision Making during World War II.* 1990.

DETLEF VOGEL
Translated from German by Amy Hackett

PLUTO. For a fighting force relying on mechanized mobility and air power, readily available fuel supplies are essential, and as early as 1942 the problems of supplying fuel during the Allied invasion of continental Europe were being considered.

Laying fuel pipelines under water was quickly shown to be feasible, and the concept of a Pipe Line Under The Ocean (PLUTO) proved an irresistible acronym for the planners.

The final design was of 7.6-centimeter (three-inch) diameter steel pipe welded into single continuous runs of more than fifty kilometers (thirty miles) in length, and rolled onto huge floating drums—"HMS Conundrums"—for laying. Looking like huge cotton reels, the Conundrums were some twenty-seven meters (ninety feet) long and fifteen meters (fifty feet) in diameter, and when fully wound weighed about as much as a destroyer. U.K.-mainland connections to the Channel pumping stations on the Isle of Wight allowed fuel to be landed at Liverpool and piped straight to the depots at Cherbourg.

However, PLUTO was unable to support the early D-day operations because the first line (BAMBI) could not be deployed until Cherbourg had been taken and the hostile mine fields around the Cotentin Peninsula cleared. By the time the first pumping operations commenced on 18 September, the Allied armies were hundreds of miles away, rapidly sweeping through Belgium. Although a second pipeline (DUMBO) was also laid from Dungeness, England, to Boulogne, the opening of the port of Ostend, Belgium, on 20 September allowed bulk discharge of tankers to provide a more local resource. Nonetheless, more than one half million kiloliters (112 million imperial gallons) of

DRUMS BEING TOWED ACROSS THE CHANNEL.   IMPERIAL WAR MUSEUM

fuel were eventually pumped through the PLUTO system.

BIBLIOGRAPHY

Ellis, L. F. *The Defeat of Germany.* Vol. 2 of *Victory in the West.* 1968.
Journal of the Royal Army Service Corps, July 1945.

GEOFFREY WOOTTEN

POINTBLANK.

POINTBLANK was the code name for the around-the-clock Combined Bomber Offensive approved at the Casablanca Conference in February 1943—Americans would attack by day, British at night. Target priority was given jointly to U-boats and the Luftwaffe, with operational choice left to the two commanders, Maj. Gen. Ira Eaker of the U.S. Eighth Air Force and Air Chief Marshal Arthur Harris of the Royal Air Force Bomber Command.

The U-boat threat was soon resolved through increased convoy protection by very long-range B-24s. Harris then reverted to his strategy of smashing German cities, of which he had a hit list of thirty-five, with several thousand bombers on hand. "If you can't hit the works," said he, "hit the workers."

Eaker's choice was more complex. His force was still very small throughout 1942—at most a hundred bombers per raid. Meanwhile, a Committee of Operations Analysts concluded that "German industry may well be paralyzed by the destruction of not more than sixty targets." It specified the ball-bearing industry, concentrated in tiny Schweinfurt, as particularly vulnerable.

A joint AAF-RAF team in England expanded the target list to seventy-six, with the German fighter force first, U-boats second, and ball-bearings third. The team also specified that U.S. forces needed 800 heavy bombers by July 1943, 1,192 by October, and 2,702 thereafter.

Promised these forces, Eaker in August ordered twin attacks by 230 bombers on the Schweinfurt ball-bearing works and 146 on the nearby factory at Regensburg, source of 43 percent of Luftwaffe fighters, both far

RAF BOMBERS ATTACKING BOULOGNE HARBOR.   Bombs hit the S-boat and R-boat pens and dock (left) and the artillery arsenal (right), September 1943.

IMPERIAL WAR MUSEUM

MAIN OBJECTIVES OF
"BIG WEEK" OPERATIONS
20–25 February 1944

beyond American fighter range. Bombing results were superb, but losses were heavy—sixty bombers downed (20 percent). Undaunted, Eaker sent 261 bombers to Schweinfurt in October, again losing 20 percent but causing great damage. Bad weather intervened until January 1944, while Albert Speer, Adolf Hitler's armaments minister, dispersed the ball-bearing machinery. After the war, Speer said: "If you had repeated your bombing attacks

and destroyed our ball-bearing industry, the war would have been over a year earlier."

Meanwhile, the Eighth's bomber strength lagged behind promises. When the second Schweinfurt mission went out, the Eighth mustered 911 bombers versus 1,246 promised and 825 crews versus 1,039 promised. Lacking entirely were fighters able to accompany bombers all the way.

In January 1944, Maj. Gen. James Doolittle succeeded

Eaker as commander of the Eighth Air Force, and Eaker became commander in chief of the Allied air forces in the Mediterranean, comprising four air forces—two American and two British. The American Fifteenth (strategic) would cooperate with the Eighth in joint attacks in southern Germany and also hit targets out of reach from England, notably the Ploesti oil fields in Romania and adjacent sources of both natural and synthetic oil.

At last the superb P-51 fighter, which could go the distance with the bombers, became available in quantity for both theaters, and bad weather over southern Germany finally broke in February 1944 for five days (the famous "Big Week"). The Eighth and Fifteenth air forces smashed most of Germany's fighter factories and destroyed large numbers of Luftwaffe planes.

But the death blow to the Luftwaffe came when Doolittle sent the Eighth to hit the thirteen synthetic oil plants clustered in southern Germany. Desperately trying to protect these vital targets, the Luftwaffe lost 1,432 fighters in February, 2,012 in March, 2,540 in April, and 2,461 in May. Nonetheless, Luftwaffe strength continued to grow from assembly plants cleverly dispersed in caves and forest nooks by Speer. It was the dearth of oil that prevented the Luftwaffe from defending Normandy. A year later, Speer testified that "the oil campaign was the decisive battle of the war."

[See also Air Strategy, article on Allied Air Strategy; Air Superiority; Bomber Command; Eaker, Ira; Eighth Air Force; Harris, Arthur.]

BIBLIOGRAPHY

Craven, Wesley F., and James Lea Cate. *The Army Air Forces in World War II*. Vols. 2 and 3. 1949, 1951.
Parton, James. *"Air Force Spoken Here": General Ira Eaker and the Command of the Air*. 1986.
The United States Strategic Bombing Surveys. 1945. Reprint, 1987.
Webster, Charles, and Frankland Noble. *The Strategic Air Offensive against Germany, 1939–1945*. 4 vols. 1961.

JAMES PARTON

POLAND. Poland's hope that the Soviet Union would respond if Poland were attacked was shattered when Germany and the Soviet Union signed a nonaggression pact on 23 August 1939. This pact secretly awarded western Poland to the Germans and eastern Poland to the Soviets. On 1 September 1939 Germany attacked Poland; the Soviets moved in later. Some of the Polish military escaped to France and, after the fall of France in June 1940, went to England, where a Polish government-in-exile was established.

Shortly after the Soviet Union was invaded by Germany in June 1941, the Polish government-in-exile and the Sovi-

et Union signed an agreement whereby Poles taken as prisoners of war by the Soviets in 1939 were allowed to enter the Polish army. One and a half million Polish soldiers had been held in Soviet camps.

The Polish armed forces in Great Britain were eager to take part in the OVERLORD operation from the very start and Polish aircraft and ships did so. Indeed, the 131st Wing of the 84th RAF Group, commanded by Air Vice Marshal L. O. Brown and composed of the 302d, 308th, and 317th squadrons equipped with Mustang fighters, was entirely Polish. As for heavy bombers, Poles manned the Lancasters of the 300th Squadron, belonging to the I Group of Air Vice Marshal E. A. B. Rice, part of the famed Bomber Command of Air Chief Marshal A. T. Harris. Also participating in D-day was the Polish destroyer *Krakowiak,* armed with six 4-inch guns, which belonged to the bombarding force of the Eastern Task Force.

Waiting also in Great Britain were Polish army units. The most important was the 1st Polish Armored Division, commanded by Maj. Gen. S. Maczek, with the 10th, 12th, and 31st Armored Brigades. Other units were also ready, including the 1st Airborne Brigade, the 3d Infantry Brigade, and the 10th Battalion of Dragoons. These units were almost totally composed of veterans who had seen fighting from the start of the war, some of whom had been released from prisoner-of-war camps by agreement with the Soviets. While waiting, they completed their armament and training, preparing for the day when Polish soldiers would fight on the Western front, as they were already fighting in Italy. They were not used in the D-day landings, but in August 1944 the 1st Armored Division, as part of the Canadian First Army, fought in Normandy on the bloody hills of Bourguébus, southeast of Caen. A month later the 1st Airborne Brigade took part in the appalling Allied defeat at Arnhem.

[See also Polish Ships.]

BIBLIOGRAPHY

Anders, Wladyslaw. *An Army in Exile*. 1949.
Stacey, Charles P. *The Victory Campaign*. 1960.

RAIMONDO LURAGHI

POLISH SHIPS. It was appropriate that Poland, whose invasion sparked the war, was represented in the Allied invasion. Five ships of the Polish navy, among them the destroyer *Blyskawica,* which had escaped from Gdynia before the actual outbreak of war, and eight Polish-flagged merchant ships took part in Operation NEPTUNE.

The light cruiser *Dragon* (Comdr. Stanislaw Dzienisiewicz) and the Hunt-class escort destroyer *Krakowiak* (Lt. Comdr. W. Maracewicz) were attached to Force D, which supported the assault on the Ouistreham beaches. Both were involved in bombardments in the Houlgate area on D-day and D plus 1; *Dragon* was credited with destroying a 4.1-inch battery and remained in the area to provide support. *Krakowiak*'s sister ship *Slazak* (Comdr. Romuald Tyminski) formed part of Force K, covering the Arromanches area, where on D-day it took part in close-range bombardment to silence beach defenses. The three ships remained in the Eastern Task Force area after the assault phase, providing counterbattery fire on the eastern flank by day and anti–E-boat patrols around the anchorages by night. On 10 and 11 June *Krakowiak* helped break up an E-boat minelaying operation.

Periodically, the ships returned to Portsmouth to replenish fuel, ammunition, and stores, or for repairs. They were usually attached to convoys whose escorts they reinforced; on one of *Slazak*'s return passages it served as escort for the damaged light cruiser HMS *Scylla*. Shortly before dawn on 8 July *Dragon,* which had just returned from Portsmouth, was torpedoed off Ouistreham by a Biber-class midget submarine. Too damaged to return to England, on 11 July the old cruiser was beached off Arromanches as part of the Gooseberry harbor.

The destroyers *Blyskawica* (Comdr. Konrad Namiesniowski) and *Piorun* (Lt. Comdr. Tadeusz Gorazdowski) operated from Plymouth with the Royal Navy's 10th Destroyer Flotilla during NEPTUNE, assigned to protect assault areas and resupply convoys from interdiction by considerable German surface forces based in the Bay of Biscay. The 10th Flotilla's first test came on the night of 8–9 June in a naval battle off the Île de Batz that ended with the sinking of the German destroyer *ZH 1,* the loss by grounding of *Z 32,* and serious damage to two other German ships. On 13–14 June *Piorun* and HMS *Ashanti* intercepted a group of German minesweepers transporting torpedoes to the E-boat base at Cherbourg and in a running battle off the Channel Islands sank *M 83* and *M 343* and damaged four of their sister ships. These actions ended any attempt by the German Navy to use ships larger than motor torpedo boats in the Channel. After Cherbourg's capture in late June, the 10th Flotilla was employed offensively, seeking out enemy shipping to the south of Brest.

Two Polish merchant ships, *Kmicic* and *Kordecki,* were in the second resupply convoy to arrive off Omaha Beach, and a third, *Poznan,* was in the second convoy into the Arromanches anchorage. They were preceded by *Modlin,* which made its way to the Arromanches area to be scuttled as a blockship for the Mulberry harbor. Four other Polish ships—the coasters *Chorzow, Katowice, Narocz,* and *Wilno*—took part in the Allied buildup in the weeks that followed.

[See also Eastern Task Force; Poland.]

BIBLIOGRAPHY

Brown, David. *Warship Losses of World War Two*. 1990.
London. Public Record Office. Admiralty War Diary, 1–16 June 1944. ADM 199/2295.
London. Public Record Office. Naval Staff History, "Operation NEPTUNE: Landings in Normandy." ADM 234/42. 1947.

TADEUSZ PANECKI

POLITICAL-MILITARY RELATIONS.

The Grand Alliance shared a fundamental objective, the destruction of the Axis, but variant political objectives of member nations led to disparate strategic ideas. The United States fought to foster a just and lasting peace that would preserve the future for democracy. Great Britain shared this objective but also hoped to preserve its far-flung empire. The Soviet Union wanted to regain territories lost during the two world wars and to improve its security vis-à-vis potential enemies, especially in Europe. It also wished to foster international communism. These differing goals led to controversies over the means of defeating the Axis.

Discussion of coalition strategy began before the Soviet Union and the United States became belligerents. Secret military conversations between the United States, Britain, and Canada (January–March 1941) culminated in the ABC-1 Staff Agreement, which endorsed the strategic premise of "Germany first." It was agreed that the defeat of Germany would ensure the defeat of the other Axis nations. Because limited resources would preclude simultaneous all-out efforts in the European and Pacific theaters, operations against Germany must receive priority. The Soviet Union adopted the same view after the German attack of June 1941. Concentrating their power on the Eastern front, the Russians remained neutral in the Pacific war.

The "Germany first" principle did not settle the question of how to encompass the defeat of the Nazis. Premier Josef Stalin of the Soviet Union called vigorously for a significant second front in Western Europe that would relieve pressure on the Red Army. Both Prime Minister Winston Churchill of Britain and President Franklin D. Roosevelt of the United States favored a second front at the earliest opportunity, but they entertained different views on its timing and location.

The United States pressed for the earliest possible attack on Fortress Europe (Festung Europa) across the English Channel. Roosevelt and his principal military advisers, Gen. George C. Marshall and Adm. Ernest J. King, believed that a cross-Channel attack was the quickest and easiest method of destroying Hitler's Germany. This route posed the least difficult logistical problems. Memories of World War I, when the United States concentrated its forces in France and helped force a decision on the Western front, strengthened the American commitment to a cross-Channel attack. This view received strong support from Moscow.

Great Britain, however, preferred to conduct operations in the Mediterranean and to attack northward through the Balkans against what Churchill called "the soft underbelly of Europe." This peripheral strategy reflected preoccupation with the preservation of imperial communications east of Suez, fear of a stalemate in France like that of 1914–1918 when Britain had experienced unacceptable losses, and the lack of sufficient resources, especially landing craft.

This difference in strategic design engendered a long Anglo-American controversy. As soon as the United States entered the war, it began planning for a cross-Channel attack against Germany in 1943, using Britain as a base, and its civilian and military leadership incessantly urged this course on Churchill and his advisers. The British counseled delay, urging as initial steps the bombing of Germany, encouragement of internal subversion in that nation, aid to the Soviet Union, strenuous antisubmarine warfare in the Atlantic to maintain maritime communications to the European theater, and, above all, operations in the Mediterranean. A cross-Channel attack would come when these activities had weakened Germany sufficiently to ensure an Anglo-American success.

During 1942, British ideas prevailed. Roosevelt felt compelled to launch an early attack against the Axis powers, but he soon recognized the impracticality of an early cross-Channel operation. Overruling his military advisers, he reluctantly agreed to TORCH, an Anglo-American assault on North Africa in November 1942. This decision irritated Moscow because it might not force sufficient diversions of German resources from the Eastern front. To propitiate Stalin, Roosevelt and Churchill pledged at the Casablanca Conference in January 1943 to require the unconditional surrender of the Axis nations, despite the possibility that this policy might strengthen the enemy's resolve and prolong hostilities. Also at Casablanca, Churchill obtained American acquiescence in an attack on Sicily, hoping to force Italy out of the war. Mediterranean commitments later expanded when, after seizing Sicily, Anglo-American forces invaded Italy. In return for the decision to continue operations in the Mediterranean, Roosevelt gained agreement for a cross-Channel attack in 1944.

During 1943, at a series of Anglo-American meetings—TRIDENT in Washington during May, QUADRANT in Quebec during August, and SEXTANT in Cairo in December—the United States pressed for the operation eventually named OVERLORD. At the first wartime meeting of Churchill, Roosevelt, and Stalin, at the Teheran Conference, 28 November to 1 December, the grand Alliance committed itself definitively to a cross-Channel attack in 1944.

During the early months of 1944, Anglo-American leaders considered plans for an attack on southern France to support TORCH. American planners maintained that this operation, code-named ANVIL, would divert some German forces from the Channel and cut off their retreat eastward. The British instead favored attacks against the Balkans and Rhodes. The decision to mount ANVIL demonstrated the growing influence of the Americans, a reflection of their expanding contributions during 1943 and after. Throughout the debate over the cross-Channel operation, the United States sought to divert some resources to the Pacific, sometimes successfully. The possibility that Roosevelt might drastically modify his commitment to priority for Europe if planning for the cross-Channel attack did not develop satisfactorily limited British bargaining power. So did Russian support for American desires. Churchill and his advisers never attempted to prevent OVERLORD; they sought to delay it in favor of Mediterranean projects that they deemed desirable preliminaries to victory and that they thought likely to preserve the empire.

Operation OVERLORD led to the decisive defeat of Germany, but not before lengthy and sometimes acrimonious debates took place within the Grand Alliance about its feasibility and timing, a product of diverse political aims and of constraints on resources. It is impossible to decide whether Britain's strategy might have produced more favorable results than that of the United States.

Military and civil authorities within each nation of the Grand Alliance were usually in accord on strategy, a circumstance that produced generally smooth civilian-military relations at the national level. On occasion, however, civilian leadership overruled recommendations from military authorities in favor of alternative military designs that seemed either desirable or unavoidable, particularly to accommodate given political objectives. Both Roosevelt and Churchill followed this course at various times during disputations about the timing and character of OVERLORD.

[See also Great Britain; United States of America; and biographies of Churchill, Roosevelt, and Stalin.]

BIBLIOGRAPHY

Leighton, Richard M., and Robert W. Coakley. *Global Logistics and Strategy, 1943–1945.* 1969.

Leighton, Richard M., and Robert W. Coakley. *Logistics and Strategy, 1940–1943.* 1955.

Matloff, Maurice. *Strategic Planning for Coalition Warfare, 1943–1944.* 1959.

Matloff, Maurice, and Edwin M. Snell. *Strategic Planning for Coalition Warfare, 1941–1942.* 1953.

Wilmot, Chester. *The Struggle for Europe.* 1952.

DAVID F. TRASK

PORTAL, CHARLES (1893–1971), British, air chief marshal, chief of the Air Staff. Charles Portal entered the army at the outbreak of World War I and later transferred to the flying service, where he carried out reconnaissance and bombing missions, and was decorated for bravery. With this distinguished record he decided on a career in the recently formed Royal Air Force. Appointments on the staff and in command of flying units followed and in 1937 Portal went to the Air Ministry as director of organisation involved in the expansion to meet the threat from Nazi Germany. As air member for personnel in 1939 he was involved in training, and his move to Bomber Command in April 1940 and to chief of the Air Staff in October was a natural progression.

From October 1940 until the end of the war, Portal was responsible for the performance of the Royal Air Force and provided advice on all air matters to the government. He strongly supported the strategic bomber offensive and the need for an amphibious invasion of the Continent. He regarded both as essential, and one the prerequisite for the other. Bomber Command by night and the Eighth Air Force by day mounted round-the-clock destruction of industrial areas and pinpoint targets, thus reducing Germany's ability to wage war and stretching its air defenses and its technology to the limit. The importance of Portal's contributions to these achievements and his support for the preparations for D-day cannot be overstated.

Together with his army and naval colleagues he formed the Chiefs of Staff Committee that provided collective military advice. Portal served on the committee for five years, longer than any of his fellow chiefs, and attended almost 2,000 meetings. Following the entry of the United States into the war, they joined with their American counterparts as the Combined Chiefs of Staff serving both the U.S. president and the British prime minister.

The Chiefs of Staff did not fight the war in the detailed sense. Their task was to issue directives to commanders on the agreed strategy and within the allotted resources, and to provide the support for successful completion. To arrive at this workable strategy needed collective agreement. Portal was noted for his ability to defuse a confrontation, not by compromise but by step-by-step persuasion shorn of histrionics. General Eisenhower describe him as a man dedicated to cooperation, and General Marshal was impressed by Portal's judgment.

Winston Churchill's leadership needed the checks and balances of an analytical and determined military mind, which Portal provided. Both men respected each other's great qualities, and the firm personal friendship that developed enabled Portal to support his chosen commanders when under criticism. An example was Air Marshal Tedder, who did not have Churchill's full confidence when commanding the Royal Air Force in the Western Desert

CHARLES PORTAL.   Right, with Alan Brooke.
NATIONAL ARCHIVES

campaigns of 1941–1942. Portal's support and friendship enabled Tedder to maintain the momentum of command appointments, including his successful relationship with Eisenhower, that were so crucial for D-day and beyond. Tedder's Transportation Plan to isolate the coastal strip of France prior to the invasion by concentrated bombing of the railway network was not initially favored by Portal. However, after his reservations were overcome, he was convinced of its value, and he accepted that the control he exercised on behalf of the Combined Chiefs of Staff over Anglo-American strategic bomber forces in Europe should pass to the Supreme Allied Commander for the period of the invasion.

After victory, Portal was honored by a peerage and awards from the grateful nations of the alliance. With the emergence of the Cold War the British government embarked on the production of fissionable material, both for peaceful purposes and the manufacture of the atomic bomb. On leaving the Royal Air Force, Portal agreed to coordinate this work, which resulted in the development of a British nuclear deterrent. He retired from government service in 1951 and was active in business, banking, and the aircraft industry until his death twenty years later.

[*See also* Air Force, *article on* Allied Expeditionary Air Force.]

BIBLIOGRAPHY

Churchill, Winston S. *The Second World War*. 1952.
Richards, Denis. *Portal of Hungerford*. 1977.
Terraine, John. *The Right of the Line*. 1985.
Probert, Henry. *High Commanders of the Royal Air Force*. 1991.

FREDERICK SOWREY

PRELUDE. Prior to D-day, a number of military themes of World War II stand out. One was the ability of the Allies—at first the British and then, in 1941, the Soviets and the Americans—to withstand the initial onslaught of Germany and its Axis partners, Italy and Japan, during the early phases of the war. Having held on, the Allies by late 1942 had proceeded to wrest the initiative from the Axis and started launching a number of offensives on a worldwide scale. As a result, the Axis powers, much against their inclinations, were forced to assume primarily a defensive orientation for the remainder of the conflict. Another significant theme was the Anglo-American buildup of their naval and air forces, so that by the time they mounted the Normandy invasion on 6 June 1944, their air and sea superiority were virtually complete.

Although the British and the United States and their allies did not launch D-day until the later stages of the war, its genesis occurred early on. Nine months after the war began, in May and June 1940, Germany overran France and the Low Countries. As related to D-day, the Battle of France had a number of repercussions. Western Europe was now under German control. Britain had lost its foremost ally and had been driven off the Continent. Italy had seen the campaign as a propitious moment to enter the conflict on Germany's side, thus expanding Britain's military commitments in the Mediterranean and in northern and eastern Africa.

These results put the British at a grave disadvantage, but rather than attempting to return immediately to Western Europe, they had to content themselves during the next twelve months with trying to survive. Even survival was not an easy task. The Royal Air Force's Fighter Command was able to fend off the vaunted Luftwaffe from securing control of the air, thereby preventing a German-planned invasion of the British Isles, and British ground and air forces also scored successes against Italian units in the Mediterranean and Africa. But the British could not stop the Germans from spreading their tentacles into the Balkans and North Africa in the spring of 1941.

Having assembled three huge army groups with 148 divisions, 3,350 tanks, and 2,713 aircraft, Adolf Hitler and his military commanders on 22 June 1941 made the fatal mistake of attacking the Soviet Union. Great Britain at once joined hands with the Soviets, and in spite of horrendous losses and against Western expectations, the Red Army held on. Germany's decision to invade Soviet territory had an important impact on the British, for the respite allowed them to concentrate on keeping open the Atlantic lifeline, building up their Bomber Command, and strengthening their Western Desert Force (later Eighth Army) and air force in Africa instead of having to face a German amphibious assault from across the Channel.

In December 1941, Hitler made another mistake. He went along with Japan's decision to attack American territory and declared war against the United States. The Japanese might have bombed Pearl Harbor in any event, but their action brought the Allies together into a coalition that far outstripped the Axis in economic productivity, although not necessarily in military capabilities.

Nevertheless, Allied economic superiority was not as evident at the time as its appears in retrospect. Over the winter, Soviet armies pushed back the Wehrmacht before Moscow, and the British Eighth Army successfully counterattacked in Libya, but then the Germans and their allies regained the initiative and, during the summer, made large-scale advances in southern Russia and into Egypt. The Axis once again seemed invincible.

But the Allies had not been idle. Toward the end of 1941, President Franklin D. Roosevelt and Prime Minister Winston Churchill and their military advisers had met in Washington at the first of many wartime conferences. At the meeting, they reaffirmed, in spite of Pearl Harbor and Japanese expansion into the Pacific and Southeast Asia, their previously agreed-upon "Germany first" strategy. The Soviet Union, which was not at war with Japan, was, of course, elated with the decision, but its leader, Stalin, continued to press for an immediate second front in Western Europe to relieve some of the pressure on Soviet troops.

Even though both the United States and the British were sympathetic to Stalin's plight, the second front issue further shows the contrast between the British and American ways of conducting war. Great Britain, because of its experiences in World War I and during the first twenty-eight months of World War II, tended to view the conflict realistically, but overestimated the difficulties involved. Consequently, it wanted to avoid major combat with the Wehrmacht on the Continent until operations on the periphery and bombing attacks against industrial targets had weakened the Germans substantially. A weakened Germany would ensure a successful invasion. The United States, because of its vast personnel and economic resources, tended to view the war optimistically, but underestimated the difficulties. Its desire was to meet the Germans directly in battle, preferably in France, and defeat them as rapidly as possible. Although this difference in U.S. and British thinking did not stand in the way of

CASABLANCA CONFERENCE, JANUARY 1943.   From left to right, seated: Gen. George Marshall, Franklin D. Roosevelt, Adm. Ernest King; standing: Harry Hopkins (special adviser to President Roosevelt), Lt. Gen. Henry ("Hap") Arnold, Gen. Brehon Somervell (principal logistics adviser to General Marshall), W. Averill Harriman (ambassador to Russia).   LIBRARY OF CONGRESS

launching Operation OVERLORD, it did determine its timing. As for the Soviets, direct Western assistance to them remained confined to sending equipment and goods via Murmansk to the north, the Persian corridor to the south, and Siberia to the east.

During the first half of 1942, the Western Allies, and especially the Americans, became so concerned about the fate of the Soviet Union that they planned a small operation, SLEDGEHAMMER, against France's western coast to siphon off German divisions from the east. But by June, the

British had become convinced that they had insufficient forces available in the United Kingdom to establish even a beachhead in France that could withstand the Germans deployed there (a judgment confirmed by the failure of the Dieppe raid in August). And since Britain and its Canadian partner were to provide the troops for SLEDGEHAMMER, their refusal to go ahead proved decisive.

Still, the Allies wanted some way to put additional pressure on the Axis and to introduce American soldiers into combat in the European arena. This led them to resurrect

HITLER'S WOLFSSCHLUCHT (WOLF'S GORGE) HEADQUARTERS AT BRÛLY-DE-PESCHES, BELGIUM, JUNE 1940. Left to right: Alfred Jodl, Adolf Hitler, Wilhelm Keitel, and Erich Raeder (Commander in Chief of the German Navy until January 1943). LIBRARY OF CONGRESS

plans for an assault against northwest Africa, which was under the German-backed Vichy French government. During July 1942, after an extended debate, the British got the Americans to go along, and in November, the Allies undertook Operation TORCH. Allied troops under the overall command of Lt. Gen. Dwight D. Eisenhower landed along the Moroccan and Algerian coasts and soon moved inland. Two weeks earlier, General Bernard L. Montgomery's Eighth Army had undertaken an offensive against Field Marshal Erwin Rommel's *Africa Corps* and Italian troops at El Alamein in Egypt. Thereafter, the Allies ran into such stiff opposition from the Wehrmacht in Tunisia that not until May 1943 did they clear North Africa of Axis forces. But the operations signaled that the Anglo-Americans had gained the initiative in the West. At the same time, the Red Army turned back the German *Sixth Army* at Stalingrad and *Army Group A* in the Caucasus and thus assumed the initiative in the East. In Churchill's memorable phrase, the "tide had turned" in favor of the Allies.

But the TORCH decision, though probably correct, had grave implications for any possible Western undertaking in 1943. Although the Americans and to a lesser extent the British continued to hope that a cross-Channel operation might be executed, events in the Mediterranean, plus a lack of certain equipment, especially landing craft,

led to its being pushed back, much to Stalin's displeasure, into 1944. For 1943, operations in the Mediterranean became the preferred strategy.

This strategy—for the British, though not for the Americans—took shape at Casablanca in January 1943. By the time the conference was over, Roosevelt and Churchill and their advisers had rendered a number of important decisions, including taking steps to defeat the German U-boat menace in the Atlantic, intensify their strategic bombing offensive against the German homeland, and undertake operations against the Japanese. But their primary concern was where to strike the Axis next in a European land campaign. They resolved to continue their buildup in Great Britain for a landing in France, perhaps even in 1943, but only if conditions, such as an unlikely German collapse, warranted such a move. Meanwhile, they decided that once they had defeated the Axis in North Africa, they would invade the island of Sicily, presumably during the summer months. The British and Americans stipulated nothing beyond Sicily, although both were well aware that other operations, such as an invasion of the Italian mainland, were possible options.

From this point on, Anglo-American plans and operations worked in tandem. They thrashed out their differences and then proposed plans that they duly executed while working out new plans. Yet, throughout the remainder of 1943, the two partners remained suspicious of each other. The Americans felt uneasy about Britain's Mediterranean strategy and even suspected that the latter wanted to undertake operations in the Balkans and to avoid a cross-Channel assault altogether. Britain, for its part, believed that the United States might well be trying to shift its primary focus from Europe to the Pacific. Therefore, while each side realized the necessity of getting along with its most important ally, each also wanted to make sure that its top strategic priorities were adhered to. In May, the Americans finally received a definite commitment from the British for a Western invasion; in August, the United States had the decision reaffirmed and, in November, had it reaffirmed again at the three-power conference at Teheran. The Western Allies set the target date for some time in May 1944 with the coast of Normandy as the landing site. The British insisted upon the invasion of Italy, and the Americans agreed, provided that Britain undertake no further major operations in the Mediterranean area. Both partners were at times frustrated with all the give-and-take, but they were undoubtedly satisfied with the results.

Operationally, on 10 July, Lt. Gen. George S. Patton, Jr.'s U.S. Seventh Army, Montgomery's British Eighth Army, and their supporting air forces launched an invasion of Sicily and captured it in thirty-nine days, although 135,000 Axis soldiers managed to get away to the mainland. In September, the Allies undertook a series of amphibious land-

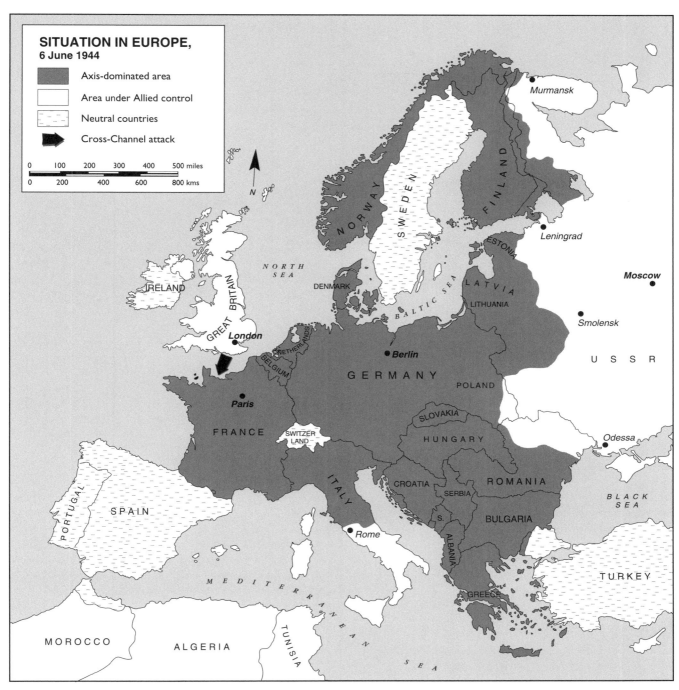

SITUATION IN EUROPE,
6 June 1944

- Axis-dominated area
- Area under Allied control
- Neutral countries
- Cross-Channel attack

ings against the Italian peninsula itself, but tenacious German defensive fighting, especially at Salerno from Field Marshal Albert Kesselring's *Army Group South*, slowed the operations to a crawl, despite the overthrow of dictator Benito Mussolini and the new Italian government's decision to exit from the war. At the onset of winter, the Germans held Lt. Gen. Mark Clark's U.S. Fifth Army and Montgomery's British and Commonwealth army at bay north of Naples.

With the Normandy campaign in the offing, however, the principal British and American land theater was soon to shift from Italy to Western Europe. Throughout the spring of 1944, the Allies had to make adjustments, including the postponement of the proposed invasion of southern France, an operation designed to support OVERLORD. But even though Germany had built up its armies and fortifications in the West, it was still about to experience the full force of Allied military strength along the Normandy coast.

British and American experience before D-day had

Nazi warplanes over Paris.

helped them a great deal. It had demonstrated to them the importance of using effectively their air, land, and sea capabilities; of having allies and treating them with respect even when they disagreed; and of taking advantage of their economic superiority. These factors helped shape the contours of future military campaigns as well as ensure D-day's success.

[*See also* Planning, *article on* Allied Planning.]

BIBLIOGRAPHY

Harrison, Gordon A. *Cross-Channel Attack.* U.S. Army in World War II: The European Theater of Operations. 1951.
Hastings, Max. *OVERLORD: D-Day, June 6, 1944.* 1984.
Keegan, John. *Six Armies in Normandy: From D-Day to the Liberation of Paris, June 6th–August 25th, 1944.* 1982.

ALAN F. WILT

PRISONERS. In making plans for Operation OVERLORD, the Allied staffs paid special attention to the subject of prisoners of war. As in every operation, there was a requirement to dispose of and elicit information from prisoners. Ground forces were briefed that German prisoners would be a prime means of discovering details of formations reinforcing the bridgehead battle. Interrogation centers and camps were prepared in England and Scotland. On the other hand, it was vital that Allied servicemen with knowledge of the date, site, and other details of the landings should not be taken prisoner in advance.

In theory, prisoners taken on either side should have been protected from interrogation by their captor. The Geneva Convention, initiated in 1864 to protect those deemed defenseless on the battlefield, was developed by the Hague Land Warfare Convention of 1907, and revised in Geneva again in 1929. The final document included clauses to safeguard the rights of military captives. Britain, France, Germany, and the United States were signatories. As a consequence, there was agreement between the warring powers in northwestern Europe that the only information that should be demanded of a prisoner of war was his full name, service number, and date of birth. However, there was nothing to prevent a captor from seeking information by moral persuasion or ruse, practices that were widespread on both sides. By the summer of

1944, however, it was known in Britain that the German authorities had found a way to circumvent the Convention on the protection of prisoners of war.

From 18 October 1942, by Hitler's special order,

all enemies on commando type missions, even if they are in uniform, armed or unarmed, in battle or in flight, are to be slaughtered to the last man. If it should be necessary initially to spare one man or two for interrogation, then they are to be shot immediately after this is completed.

Another protective provision of the Convention was subverted by Himmler in August 1943, when he reminded the civil police publicly that it was not their duty to intervene "in altercations between the German people and landed English and American terror pilots." This was an incitement to lynch aircrew brought down over enemy territory. The German intelligence service protested that this action would prevent it from gaining important information, and so the police and military were again ordered to protect captives. Even so, the severity of air attacks thereafter prompted a major German propaganda campaign that accused Allied aircrew of attacking the civil populace preferentially. Field Marshal Göring called for

OSTTRUPPEN. Some of the first soldiers captured by the Allies were *Osttruppen* (Eastern troops). Seen here en route to Britain, they are guarded by a Coast Guardsman and a Marine.
NATIONAL ARCHIVES

PRISONER OF WAR ENCLOSURE. German soldiers on Utah Beach on D-day. NATIONAL ARCHIVES

CAPTURED GERMAN TROOPS BEING SEARCHED.
NATIONAL ARCHIVES

the execution of Allied airmen making "emergency landings" after such acts. On 6 June 1944, the advantages and disadvantages of restraint were being debated.

Following the landings, Wehrmacht High command (Oberkommando der Wehrmacht—OKW) reiterated Hitler's orders concerning "commando type" forces:

All members of terror and sabotage units found outside the immediate combat area, who include fundamentally all parachutists, are to be killed in combat. In special cases they are to be turned over to the Sicherdienst [the security service].

This background convinced the Allied senior commanders that the enemy would be ready to use inhuman means to obtain information from captives. Special security arrangements, beyond those in force for the assembly and briefing of the assault echelons, were provided for two groups at manifest risk: aircrew and part of the air/sea rescue force; and those engaged in late reconnaissance and clearance of the selected beaches. Information about the landings was withheld from the former, who were engaged in interdiction, strategic bombing, air defense, and recovery, until the combined operation was launched. The latter were briefed to tell a common story in the event they were captured and tortured.

The Allied escape and evasion organization in London instructed all aircrew on a day-to-day basis on options for recovery through the expanding bridgehead.

Shortly after the landings, Hitler gave fresh warnings that aircrew shot down might be executed as war criminals, and further passed instructions to Allied prisoners in camps that he was aware of "Anglo-American instructions" to them to escape and "to act like gangsters." Those who attempted to escape would be shot.

Paradoxically, most airmen taken prisoner immediately before and after D-day discovered that physical coercion was used only in the very early stages of capture, but that it had been abandoned at the principal interrogation center at Oberursel, near Frankfurt, partly due to intervention of the Protecting Power, Switzerland, and partly to the discovery that the threat of force was more effective that the action. The landing operations swelled the number of prisoners arriving at Oberursel by about 1,000 because a number of airborne troops were included with aircrew. Others were sent to the Hamburg and Munich areas and newly established centers in northern France and Holland, staffed by interrogators from Oberursel.

The Allies lost almost 1,700 prisoners between 6 and 18 June. Aircrew apart, the airborne forces were most exposed to capture in the opening hours. A variety of prisoners were taken from those infantry, armored reconnaissance, artillery, and engineer units that thrust most boldly forward from the beaches. A quarter of these managed to escape before being moved behind the German army group rear boundary. Some, who fell into the hands of SS units, were murdered.

The number of German prisoners taken during the same period exceeded 6,000. They were interrogated briefly in brigade, divisional, and later corps temporary barbed wire cages before being sent in landing ships across the Channel. By the time they reached a British port, officers had been segregated from other ranks. Those thought to possess special information were sent to the "London Cage," the greater number passing to Edinburgh, Scotland, and four locations in northern England: Catterick, the racetrack at Doncaster, Loughboro, and the football stadium at Preston.

The German archives disclose that by June they had obtained accurate details of the land forces ashore on D-day from prisoners. Most of this information was gained from those questioned within a few hours of capture.

A mass of information flowed in from German prisoners, much of it already well known. Of greater value were documents captured in formation headquarters, and weapons and equipment.

Among the unluckiest of those taken prisoner was a German corporal due to go on leave from a beach regiment on 4 June whose departure was delayed due to food poisoning. Similarly, a British sailor, whose landing craft was destroyed on the beach, moved inland with his army passengers and was snatched away within minutes by a German detachment on the outskirts of a village.

BIBLIOGRAPHY

Foot, M. R. D. *MI9, Escape and Evasion, 1939–45*.
Foy, David A. *For You the War is Over*. 1981.
Langley, J. M., and A. J. Barker. *Behind Barbed Wire*. 1974.
U.S. War Department Military Intelligence Service. *American Prisoners of War in Germany*. 1944.

ANTHONY FARRAR-HOCKLEY

PROPAGANDA.

PROPAGANDA. [*This entry includes separate discussions of Allied and German propaganda.*]

Allied Propaganda

Propaganda may be defined as the attempt to persuade its target audience to think and behave in a way desired by the source.

By 1944, the Allies had developed significant and well-established propaganda machinery to influence both civilian and military morale. It was based on what the Americans termed a Strategy of Truth, in that it often spread truth, but with certain information omitted. For the invasion of Europe, it was essential to ensure that the overall propaganda campaign was carefully coordinated to serve as an auxiliary to the military effort and, to this end, the Psychological Warfare Division (PWD) was established at SHAEF, which drew heavily upon the experience of the British Ministry of Information (MoI) and Political Warfare Executive (PWE), and on the American Office of War Information (OWI) and the Office of Strategic Services (OSS).

The PWD's charter defined psychological warfare as "the dissemination of propaganda designed to undermine the enemy's will to resist, demoralize his forces and sustain the morale of our supporters." Strategic propaganda, the task of the OWI and MoI, gradually gave way in significance during Operation OVERLORD to tactical or combat propaganda (with PWE/OSS staff and ideas feeding the PWD) and consolidation propaganda directed specifically to the military situation after the invasion had been completed. The "Standing Directive for Psychological Warfare against Members of the German Armed Forces," issued secretly in June 1944, pointed out that such activity was not a magic substitute for physical battle, but an auxiliary to it. "By attacking the fighting morale of the enemy, it aims at: (a) reducing the cost of the physical battle, and (b) rendering the enemy easier to handle after surrender."

During the buildup for D-day, the Allies concentrated their efforts on a wide psychological front designed to aid the military operation before, during, and after the invasion. It was essential to prevent information about when and where the invasion would occur from entering the public domain. In terms of positive output, however, this

---

EINE MINUTE

die Dir das Leben retten kann.

Lies die folgenden 6 Punkte gründlich und aufmerksam! Sie können für Dich den Unterschied zwischen Tod und Leben bedeuten.

1. Tapferkeit allein kann in diesen Materialschlachten den Mangel an Panzern, Flugzeugen und Artillerie nicht wettmachen.

2. Mit dem Fehlschlag im Westen und dem Zusammenbruch im Osten ist die Entscheidung gefallen: Deutschland hat den Krieg verloren.

3. Du stehst keinen Barbaren gegenüber, die am Töten etwa Vergnügen finden, sondern Soldaten, die Dein Leben schonen wollen.

4. Wir können aber nur diejenigen schonen, die uns nicht durch nutzlosen Widerstand zwingen, unsere Waffen gegen sie einzusetzen.

5. Es liegt an Dir, uns durch Hochheben der Hände, Schwenken eines Taschentuchs usw. deutlich Deine Absicht zu verstehen zu geben.

6. Kriegsgefangene werden fair und anständig behandelt, ohne Schikane—wie es Soldaten gebührt, die tapfer gekämpft haben.

Die Entscheidung musst Du selber treffen. Sollst Du aber in eine verzweifelte Lage geraten, so erwäge, was Du gelesen hast.

ONE MINUTE

that may save your life.

Read the following six points carefully and thoroughly. They may mean the difference between life and death.

1. In a battle of arms, valor alone cannot offset inferiority in tanks, planes, and artillery.

2. With failure in the West and breakthrough in the East, the verdict has been determined: Germany has lost the war.

3. You are not facing barbarians who delight in killing, but soldiers who would spare your life if possible.

4. But we can only spare those who do not force us, by senseless resistance, to use our weapons against them.

5. It is up to you to show us your intention by raising your arms, waving a handkerchief, etc., in an unmistakable manner.

6. Prisoners of war will be treated decently and fairly as becomes soldiers who have fought bravely.

You must decide for yourself. But in the event that you should find yourself in a desperate situation, remember what you have read.

RE-CREATION AND TRANSLATION OF TACTICAL PROPAGANDA LEAFLET.   Designed for distribution in areas of strong resistance, this leaflet's avoidance of a political message and its simple soldier-to-soldier appeal contributed to its effectiveness.

COURTESY OF PHILIP M. TAYLOR

**FLOW CHART OF
LEAFLET OPERATIONS**

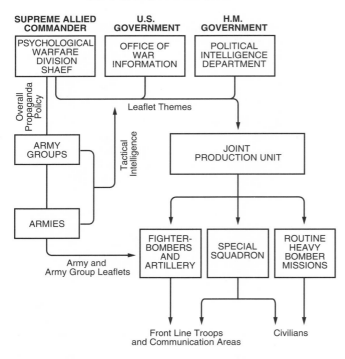

troops), of which 250,000–750,000 were dropped nightly by the U.S. Air Force over targets identified by 21st Army Group. This was largely "gray" propaganda (or "dirty white" as Delmer called it) in that it gave no indication of its origin. Distribution began a month before D-day in preparation for Operation OVERLORD. It was a joint PWE/OSS operation and the paper combined accurate, up-to-the-minute military news gained from all possible sources with international and German home news. Third, irregular medium-wave talks were directed at opposition groups within the SS. Finally, forged documents and subversive leaflets were distributed in Germany and in occupied countries, by balloon and by agents, to promote defeatism and subversive activity such as sabotage and passive resistance.

The aim of all this activity was "to concentrate the attention of the German solder on the enemy within (i.e., the Party authorities) rather than on the enemy without." As an adjunct to military operations, the purpose was to keep in the forefront of the minds of German soldiers the military disasters on the Eastern front, the growing weakness of German war production under the stress of Allied bombing and blockade, the impotence of the Luftwaffe, and the breakdown of authority and corresponding rise of law defiance. Psychological warriors also cooperated in the deception campaign that accompanied OVERLORD, Operation FORTITUDE.

After the landings, the campaign shifted to illustrating the hopelessness of Germany's continuation of the war. The soldiers were informed that they were being sacrificed needlessly and were being let down by their leaders. Interservice rivalry was also exploited, as were the quarrels Field Marshal Erwin Rommel had with Field Marshal Gerd von Rundstedt and Gen. Friedrich Dollmann. A principal aim was to divide the German army from the Nazi leadership, although this could only be done through black activity, given that white propaganda policy had been defined (and constrained) largely by the call for unconditional surrender.

Evaluation of the effectiveness of this activity is among the most difficult of tasks, but it is known that Joseph Goebbels, minister of propaganda, and other Nazi party officials were particularly worried about the leaflets. A German civil court in Innsbruck in October 1944 even ordered the death sentence for anyone caught reading or distributing Allied leaflets, while Foreign Secretary Anthony Eden informed the House of Commons that 77 percent of the prisoners taken during the invasion claimed to have read them. Subsequently, a report from the U.S. Third Army noted that "prisoners taken during the operation against the Ardennes salient all claimed to have been deeply impressed by the leaflets."

By themselves, words cannot win wars. But in critical

consisted principally of lowering enemy morale, raising morale in occupied countries, and sowing seeds of confusion about Allied dispositions and about enemy intentions and capabilities.

The principal weapons in this campaign were radio and leaflets, both "white" (overt, attributable, Allied-sponsored propaganda) and "black" (which seeks to falsify its origin, usually by purporting to originate from an enemy source). The white campaign consisted mainly of BBC broadcasts and leaflets dropped by the Royal Air Force and the U.S. Eighth Air Force; a total of 3.24 billion leaflets were dropped throughout the entire operation. In addition, the Fifth Army Combat Propaganda Team possessed radio and leaflet-shell distribution equipment.

The black, or covert, campaign was conducted chiefly by four means. First there was the radio program *Soldatensender Calais angeschlossen der Deutsche Kurzwellensender Atlantik* (The soldier's Calais broadcast in association with the German Atlantic shortwave broadcasting station), which broadcast news bulletins and entertainment designed for the German troops. Although it purported to be a German soldiers' station located in France, it was in fact run by Sefton Delmer at the PWE in Britain and transmitted in both short and medium wave (the latter made possible by the acquisition in 1942 of the powerful Aspidistra transmitter). The second method used to influence German troop morale was the production of a daily newspaper, *Nachrichten für die Truppe* (News for the

military situations, they can sow seeds of doubt that can affect morale. During the Normandy landings, a war of nerves was conducted in an attempt to save lives, not just Allied but also, through inducements to surrender, German as well. Psychological warfare proved to be a low-cost/high-return combat weapon that was worth trying, especially against a generation of German soldiers who had been indoctrinated by a decade of Nazi propaganda.

BIBLIOGRAPHY

Cruikshank, Charles. *The Fourth Arm: Psychological Warfare, 1938–1945.* 1977.

Delmer, Sefton. *Black Boomerang.* 1962.

Howe, Ellic. *The Black Game: British Subversive Operations against the Germans during the Second World War.* 1982.

Lerner, Daniel. *Psychological Warfare against Nazi Germany.* 1949.

PHILIP M. TAYLOR

German Propaganda

Anticipating an Allied invasion in the West, Joseph Goebbels launched two major propaganda campaigns in 1943. The first one was called *Vergeltung* (retaliation). Its idea was to reassure the German people that the Third Reich was developing powerful new weapons that would cause great destruction in enemy lands. Goebbels hoped that the Americans and British would fear a destructive retaliation by secret weapons and hence decrease their bombing raids. The Allies, however, had actually increased bombing sorties throughout 1943. Consequently, the retaliation propaganda program was dropped by early 1944; it was resurrected in July 1944, after the V-1 rockets were finally launched against England.

Interestingly, the retaliation campaign did not mention invasion. While German leadership knew that the western Allies were planning an invasion, they were reluctant to use it in propaganda, fearing widespread defeatism as many believed had occurred in 1918. Invasion was mentioned, though, in connection with the mighty Atlantic Wall that Hitler ordered to be constructed to thwart an Allied invasion of western Europe. At a conference on 29 September 1943, Hitler stated that strong defenses along the French coast would have the same psychological effect on the enemy that Germany's fortified West Wall had on French Premier Édouard Daladier during the Czech crisis in 1938: a strong deterrent, which would force the Allies to forgo a landing. German civilians read stories of the construction of the Atlantic Wall, with pictures of large artillery guns being put in concrete bunkers. Goebbels believed his propaganda efforts might dissuade the Allies from invading "Fortress Europe." While the talk of secret weapons and the impregnable Atlantic Wall were important pieces of his

propaganda campaign, Goebbels put special importance on the specter of Bolshevism.

The second and most successful major propaganda campaign was initiated by Goebbels as a vehicle to describe the demands of total war. Labeled "strength through fear," it promoted two general themes: first, the horror of the atrocities that would be committed against the German people by victorious Allies; second, the danger of Bolshevism spreading throughout Germany and Europe. Goebbels believed that the evil specter of Bolshevism would both divide the Allies and bolster German resistance. Banners displayed throughout Germany read "Victory—or Bolshevistic Chaos!" The German people were constantly told of barbarities committed by the communists.

In regard to a possible invasion by the Western Allies, Goebbels created an image of destruction and horrible deeds that the Allies would inflict upon a defeated Germany. At this point Nazi leadership was willing to mention the possibility of an Allied invasion, hoping to strengthen the German people's will to resist. This propaganda barrage was aimed at soldiers at the front as well as German civilians. Vicious stories were told about American gangsters, zoot-suiters, and "Mexicans and

JOSEPH GOEBBELS.   The master propagandist of Hitler's Germany.   NATIONAL ARCHIVES

Negroes." American plane crews who piloted the bombers were labeled *Luftgangster* (air gangsters) who carried out *Terrorangriffe* (terror attacks) against the German people. Such invectives appeared confirmed when, in December 1943, an American plane was shot down with the nickname, inscribed on its side by the crew, of "Murder, Inc." This, declared Goebbels, proved that American gangsters were responsible for the bombing raids on German homes! Such propaganda did improve German morale, and any harsh comments made by the Allies concerning the future of Germany were fully exploited.

An example of exploiting Allied threats for propaganda purposes was Goebbels's use of Sir Robert Vansittart's remarks to the House of Lords that Germany must be totally crushed and that all Germans must suffer for the war they had unleashed. Goebbels immediately pounced on Vansittart's comments, telling the German people that they must resist the Western Allies, for defeat would mean certain destruction of the Fatherland and terrible suffering thereafter. The "strength through fear" campaign proved to be very successful in bolstering morale both on the home front and among Germans serving throughout Europe. After all, what German would want to live as a slave under the rule of alien powers? Would it not be better to meet a stoic death in resisting the enemy, whether Bolshevist, American, or British? Supportive articles appeared weekly in *Das Reich* and other Propaganda Ministry publications.

Although successful in improving German morale, Goebbels was anxious regarding the impending invasion of France. Constant references to such an event, part of the "fear" element, wore on everyone's nerves. The propagandists, acting on advice from the Wehrmacht, assumed the invasion would occur in early 1944. When it did not occur in March, or even April, the Reich Propaganda Ministry decided not to use the word "invasion" and on 25 May ordered the press not to refer to it. Hitler, meanwhile, recognizing both the deterioration on the Eastern front and the importance of bolstering the morale on the home front and among the troops, ordered a new slogan: "German Wonder Weapons," inspired by the spectacular achievements of Albert Speer's armaments industry. At a conference on 22 to 23 May 1944 Hitler stated that the statistical accomplishments of Speer's ministry could form the basis of a new propaganda effort.

The tension broke when the Allies finally invaded on 6 June 1944, although Goebbels's anxiety increased when he heard nothing from Hitler or the military for several days. Goebbels's first priority was to calm the German public, which he attempted by claiming that because the Allies landed in large numbers, they would be dealt a decisive defeat by the German Army! In reality, of course, the landing was successful and a bridgehead was soon established. The success caught the Reich Propaganda Minister off guard, and following D-day Goebbels and his staff scrambled to come up with a new propaganda line. The one that remained was the fear of Bolshevism, which was spread by means that included dropping leaflets on American and British soldiers accusing them of being Bolshevist lackeys. In fact, the ministry was unprepared to deal with the success of the landing and the subsequent breakout into western France.

BIBLIOGRAPHY

Baird, Jay W. *The Mythical World of Nazi War Propaganda, 1937–1945*. 1974.

Balfour, Michael. *Propaganda in War, 1939–1945*. 1979.

Boelcke, Wilhelm. *Deutschlands Rüstung im Zweiten Weltkrieg: Hitlers Konferenzen mit Albert Speer, 1942–1945*. 1969.

Bramsted, Ernest K. *Goebbels and National Socialist Propaganda, 1922–1945*. 1965.

The Goebbels Diaries. 1948.

Heiber, Helmut. *Goebbels*. Translated by John K. Dickinson. 1972.

Herzstein, Robert E. *The War That Hitler Won: Goebbels and the Nazi Media Campaign*. 1987.

Speer, Albert. *Inside the Third Reich: Memoirs*. Translated by Richard and Clara Winston. 1970.

GENE MUELLER

QUARTERMASTER AND ORDNANCE
CORPS. Logistics was a dominating factor in the origins, planning, and execution of the Normandy invasion. In supplying the American and British troops on the beachhead and battlefront, the operations of the quartermaster and ordnance corps and other maintenance elements closely reflected the character of the combat campaign they supported. Although a year of combat experience in the Mediterranean meant that planning was not conducted in a logistical vacuum, no amphibious assault had ever been larger or more complex.

As the forces on the eve of the landing finalized their requirements and completed the buildup, the principal expectation at Supreme Headquarters in London was for heavily contested landings in the assault phase and a slow but steady rate of advance to the Seine thereafter.

Preparations. For the supply and service elements—the U.S. Army Quartermaster Corps and the Royal Army Service Corps—the chief preoccupations on the eve of the landing were amassing food and fuel reserves at the English points of embarkation; packaging those commodities in such a way as to assure ease of handling and safety in the course of the crossing and landing; and finally, assuring that daily requirements were met and a reserve accumulated on the Continent. Since there were pronounced differences between the American and British supply systems, the two national armies assigned to the assault, the U.S. First Army and the British Second Army, were given responsibility for their own sustainment.

Where subsistence was concerned, each American soldier was to carry one D ration (basically three four-ounce chocolate bars) and one K ration when disembarking, while each assaulting element was to carry three C or K rations for its members. No unit was to draw subsistence until its third day ashore. British and Canadian troops were similarly supplied, with tins of self-heating soup

and cocoa for the crossing and the early hours on the beachhead, and twenty-four-hour rations intended for consumption the day after the landing. Clothing and personal equipment were also quartermaster items, and both armies, learning from excessive issue in the Mediterranean, kept individual allowances frugal.

Fuel was considered a long-term problem and enjoyed a preeminence in the planning and preparation phases matched only by concern for the Normandy ports. The difficulty was estimating consumption requirements, both before and after installation of a pipeline on the Continent. Early in the operation, quartermaster units were expected to decant gasoline into five-gallon jerricans and move it forward as dry cargo to the combat units. This immediately raised questions about how many cans the manufacturers, predominantly British, would need to produce. American requirements alone were estimated at 15.5 million cans, a figure that the chief American quartermaster in the theater, Maj. Gen. Robert M. Littlejohn, noted several months later, was "so accurate that it has been astounding."

Three activities rounded out the period of preparation, and all were the technical province of men in the ordnance service of the invading force—the U.S. Army Ordnance Corps and the Royal Army Ordnance Corps. One was equipping the armies as they reached their staging sites in southern England, and making recommendations on extra weapons and vehicles and special equipment such as beach packs. A second was assuring that equipment and vehicles were waterproofed for the sea voyage and assault, a problem the British had been working on continually since 1942. A third concern was ammunition, the central combat consumable of every army. In establishing the basic loads for the forces and determining the theater level of supply, the watchword of the planning boards was plainly abundance. For instance, although beach capacity in Normandy was expected to be limited in the early days, every assault division was authorized quantities beyond basic loads, if they could furnish the transport. To this problem the two-and-a-half-ton amphibian truck, the famous DUKW of World War II, provided the answer.

One task remained, prestowage in strict accord with the OVERLORD supply plan—filling coasters, landing craft, and motor transport ships—sufficient for the first eight days (90,000 tons for the U.S. First Army alone). Nothing was to be left to chance, even if preloading, advance scheduling, and preset priorities for the beaches imposed rigidity on the whole supply movement scheme. Although arrangements were made for special delivery of urgently needed items by reserved shipping and by air—notably rations, ammunition, and engineer equipment—such procedures did not dispel all worries. No one doubted that immediate requirements would be met, but there seemed, by common consent, to be no margin of safety.

The Far Shore. No sooner had the invasion commenced on 6 June than concise plans for organization of the assault beaches dissipated under heavy surf and enemy resistance. Both in the British sector at Sword, Juno, and Gold, and in the American sector chiefly at Omaha, difficulties resulting from wreckage along the shore and poorly coordinated ship-to-shore operations put the logistic unloading operation immediately behind schedule. Some gains were made when the navy lifted its previous objections and permitted the beaching of its landing ships after high tide for direct discharge as the waters receded. But the ground forces adhered for too long to the priority unloading plan, with the result that a shipping backlog quickly developed. Ammunition shortages threatened soon after, until the navy on 10 June insisted on scrapping the scheme.

All the beach organizing groups were spearheaded by the engineers, to whom small ordnance and quartermaster (or service) elements were attached. By the end of the first day, landing groups under fire had formed emergency dumps and makeshift transfer points in small fields just clear of the assault areas, chiefly for ammunition and medical stores, although little segregation of supplies was initially possible. Except at bloody Omaha, they had also taken the critical next stop of dispatching small reconnaissance parties to search for potential sites farther inland for beach maintenance area dumps to hold supplies to sustain the forces for the first four weeks. A week into the invasion the inland dumps began to operate, including an ammunition point belatedly established at Formigny on Omaha. As the emergency supply phase ended in Normandy, the two armies took control of the inland dumps from the beach engineers.

By D plus 10, the limiting factor in the supply buildup was the arrival of ships. Both armies by then had about

Allied Landings, 6–16 June, Inclusive

	MEN	VEHICLES	STORES (IN LONG TONS)
American	278,000	35,000	88,000
British	279,000	46,000	95,000
Total	557,000	81,000	183,000

seven days' supply of rations, and gasoline enough to travel 240 kilometers (150 miles), with more offshore. Infantry and artillery ammunition was also accumulating rapidly, although there were already signs of heavy use in the hedgerow fighting, especially hand grenades and mortar rounds. The totals were impressive, yet complacency was plainly not called for. On the American beaches, for instance, the vehicles available represented 66 percent of the planned buildup, and the supplies on hand about 68 percent. If deliveries to the troops were satisfactory, this was owing chiefly to the shallowness of the lodgment and the absence of the Luftwaffe. Meanwhile congestion on the beaches was growing, foreshadowing difficulties for the supply base when the breakout occurred.

[*See also* Naval Supply; PLUTO.]

BIBLIOGRAPHY

Mayo, Lida. *The Ordnance Department: On Beachhead and Battlefront.* The U.S. Army in World War II. 1968.

Ross, William F., and Charles F. Romanus. *The Quartermaster Corps: Operations in the War against Germany.* The U.S. Army in World War II. 1965.

Wilson, H. W. *Administrative Planning, The Second World War, 1939–1945: Army.* 1952.

Wilson, H. W. *Ordnance Services, The Second World War, 1939–1945: Army.* 1950.

JOEL D. MEYERSON

QUESADA, ELWOOD R.

QUESADA, ELWOOD R. (1904–), American, major general, commander of IX Fighter Command and IX Tactical Air Command. Born in Washington, D.C., Elwood "Pete" Quesada enlisted in the U.S. Army in 1924 and received his wings and commission in 1926. Recognized as a superior pilot from the outset, he spent much of his prewar service as flying officer to senior military officials, including Gen. George Marshall. Quesada joined the fighting in North Africa in January 1943, where he became the deputy commander of the Northwest African Coastal Air Force. In October 1943 he was transferred to England and the Ninth Air Force to begin preparations for D-day, when he would be responsible for the tactical or close air support of Lt. Gen. Omar Bradley's U.S. First Army assault troops on Omaha and Utah beaches.

Quesada assumed command of the IX Fighter Command and the IX Tactical Air Command on 17 October 1943. Throughout the spring of 1944, he directed the training and operations of fighter-bomber groups then arriving from the United States. As a field commander Quesada played no central role in the overall planning for D-day, but was often called upon to judge the feasibility of various air support proposals. He soon earned a reputation as a forceful and innovative officer willing to try anything to ensure effective support of infantry and armored forces. By 6 June his 1,600 P-38, P-47, and P-51 aircraft had tasks including convoy cover, interdiction, and close support of assault troops in the U.S. invasion zone.

Quesada spent D-day at his communications center in Uxbridge, England. By 0900 he was diverting airborne groups from convoy cover to German strong points behind Omaha Beach. With this help from the air and additional naval bombardment, assault troops there secured a foothold in the sand by nightfall. Anxious to command from the field, Quesada landed his P-38 in a makeshift field overlooking Omaha Beach at 0900 on D plus 1; he did not spend a night outside France until after the occupation of Paris. Quesada's airmen opened the first Allied airfield in Normandy on D plus 1, established an advanced headquarters on D plus 2, and had moved an entire fighter-bomber wing to the Continent by D plus 5. The sur- prisingly tough bocage fighting put a premium on the mobility and firepower of Quesada's aircraft, and he and Bradley continually sought ways to aid the infantry advance. In the following weeks the two men worked out many of the basic tenets of close air support that would guide U.S. forces for the rest of the European fighting. By the war's end he was perhaps the U.S. Army Air Force's foremost expert on air-ground battlefield cooperation.

After the war Quesada's expertise earned him the command of the U.S. Air Force's Tactical Air Command. But the air force's growing emphasis on strategic bombardment in the Cold War era, coupled with Quesada's sometimes abrasive personality, stalled the general's career. Frustrated, he retired as a three-star general in 1951 at the age of forty-seven.

[See also Close Air Support; Ninth Air Force; IX Fighter Command; IX Tactical Air Command.]

BIBLIOGRAPHY

Craven, Wesley Frank, and James Lea Cate, eds. *The Army Air Forces in World War II.* Vol. 3, 1951.

Hastings, Max. *Overlord: D-day and the Battle for Normandy.* 1984.

Schlight, John. "Elwood R. Quesada: Tac Air Comes of Age." In *Makers of the U.S. Air Force,* edited by John Frisbee. 1989.

THOMAS HUGHES

R

RADAR. *See* Electronic Warfare.

RAF. *See* Air Force, *article on* Allied Expeditionary Air Force.

RAILROADS. The extremely dense and closely integrated rail networks of Belgium and northwest France were the main conduits for supplies and reinforcements to the Wehrmacht in the Normandy invasion area. Since June 1942, the Reich Transportation Ministry in Berlin had coordinated them with the very highly developed sections of the German National Railway (Deutsche Reichsbahn) in the Rhineland and the Saar regions of western Germany. Reichsbahn officials supervised operations in the occupied countries, but trains were run by locals. A heavy volume of military and industrial traffic moved between the occupied areas and Germany. During 1943, Germany had increased its exploitation of the economies of western Europe and had become more reliant than ever on the French National Railway (SNCF) and the Belgian National Railway (SNCB). By January 1944, 85 percent of all rail traffic in France served German purposes, two-fifths of this for the Wehrmacht.

Anticipating an invasion, the Wehrmacht transport chief and the Reichsbahn created a reserve of 484 trains with about 20,000 cars in eastern France and the western sections of the Reich. At the appropriate moment, this reserve would be used to rush reinforcements and supplies to the landing area. They also designated German railroaders who would be sent into the occupied territories at short notice to ensure smooth operations. However, coordination between the railways and the military was not always the best. Reichsbahn operating personnel resented the Wehrmacht's intervention in train movements and its imposition of military discipline. At the same time the French and Belgian railroaders cooperated with their German overseers only reluctantly and occasionally sabotaged trains or simply stayed away from work.

Long before the invasion the Allies began attempting to disrupt the railroads of occupied Europe. Especially during 1943, the French Maquis cut track, blasted bridges and tunnels, and ambushed Reichsbahn personnel in ever increasing numbers. From March 1944 on, however, these blows were overshadowed by Allied air attacks on marshaling yards and locomotive sheds. The Transportation Plan issued by Air Marshal Arthur Tedder on 19 April targeted seventy-four railway centers in France, Belgium, and western Germany for destruction by bombing. Locations were selected so as not to give away the planned site of the landings. Later Tedder ordered attacks on bridges and a coordinated program of strafing locomotives to complement the rail-center strikes. Tedder stressed that the objective of the campaign was not to block particular lines (interdiction), but to reduce the railroads' ability to generate and move traffic coherently. This would be achieved by disrupting the locomotive-servicing, engineering, marshaling, and traffic control organizations clustered in rail centers.

The OVERLORD transportation bombing campaign began with an order on 4 March 1944 by Charles Portal, chief of the Air Staff, to the RAF Bomber Command to demonstrate that it could destroy marshaling yards in night attacks. The raids, flown beginning 6 March against six targets in France, were completely successful. Bomber Command executed its segment of the plan in earnest beginning in mid-April, with the U.S. Eighth Air Force following later in May. They were joined by the U.S. Fifteenth Air Force and by the fighters and medium bombers of the Allied Expeditionary Air Force. By D-day, 101 rail targets had been hit with 67,416 tons of bombs.

Bomber Command made the greatest contribution by striking 37 targets with 45,830 tons of explosives and incendiaries. Most objectives were in France and Belgium, but five important marshaling yards in western Germany were also attacked.

The Reichsbahn sensed the increased pressure immediately and reacted by increasing flak protection for its trains, by placing more of its personnel in key operating positions in the SNCF and SNCB, and by sending locomotives, freight cars, and engine repair crews into France and Belgium. Ten thousand Organization Todt construction workers were removed from military projects to repair rail yards, in addition to 15,700 German troops. The

Wehrmacht also began drafting more French and Belgian civilians into this difficult work and slashed all nonessential traffic, hoping to save precious car space for itself. Nevertheless, by the beginning of May about 1,700 trains were backed up in the bombed areas. From mid-May on, supply trains could not be run systematically west of the line Brussels-Paris-Orleans. Not only did the military suffer, but the French economy was weakened by a major coal shortage that closed factories and cut utility service.

These problems reverberated back into Germany. The Reichsbahn's Saarbrücken region was choked with cars that could not be sent into France and by thousands of damaged cars that it could not repair. Indeed, instead of the

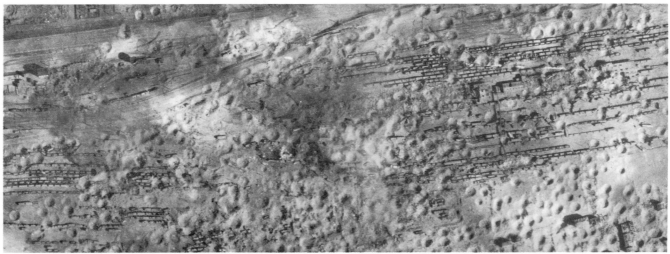

RAILWAY YARDS AT JUVISY-SUR-ORGE, SOUTH OF PARIS.   Top: Before the bombing of 18–19 April 1944.

IMPERIAL WAR MUSEUM

Bottom: The attack by Lancasters and Halifaxes of Bomber Command was extremely effective. Note the destruction of workshops, repair depots, signaling apparatus, roundhouses, and rolling stock.

IMPERIAL WAR MUSEUM

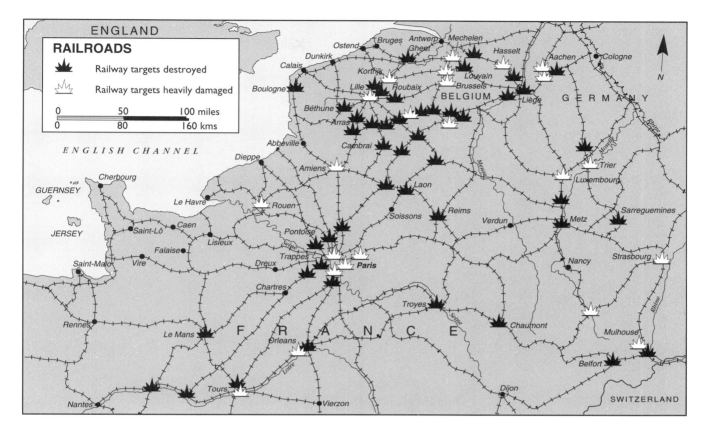

RAILROADS

⬛ Railway targets destroyed

⬜ Railway targets heavily damaged

100 military supply trains needed daily, only 32 moved from Germany into France in late May. On 20 May, only 40 percent of the locomotives in the SNCF's strategically important northern region were serviceable, owing primarily to the decline of its maintenance organization caused by bombing. In the western region containing the invasion area, only half as many cars were in circulation as compared to 6 March. Overall, by 26 May the SNCF carried 45 percent less freight than in January 1944.

When the Allied armies landed in Normandy, the French and Belgian railways were in a state of near paralysis. The SNCF was operating at only 10 percent of its normal capacity. German units such as the *9th* and *10th SS Panzer* divisions, transferred from Poland, were forced to detrain hundreds of kilometers from the beachhead and make the trip by road to their deployment areas, subject to constant harassment from Allied fighter-bombers and saboteurs. Coming from the north, the *1st SS Panzer Division* struggled for seven days to cover the 300 kilometers (186 miles) from Louvain, Belgium, to Paris, ordinarily a single day's journey by train, because all three rail routes had been blocked by bombing.

In sum, the German-controlled railways of northwest Europe were unable to provide the Wehrmacht with the logistical support or strategic maneuverability that it so badly needed. Reichsbahn officials attributed this pri-

marily to the destruction of marshaling yards and locomotive sheds by bombing. They considered air attacks on bridges and moving trains, and sabotage by the Resistance, less dangerous, though still troublesome.

[*See also* Air Strategy, *article on* Allied Air Strategy.]

BIBLIOGRAPHY

Kreidler, Eugen. *Die Eisenbahnen im Machtbereich der Achsenmächte während des Zweiten Weltkrieges*. 1975.

Schramm, Percy Ernst, ed. *Kriegstagebuch des Oberkommandos der Wehrmacht*. Vol. 7, 1982.

Tedder, Arthur. *With Prejudice: The War Memoirs of Marshal of the Royal Air Force Lord Tedder*. 1966.

Webster, Charles, and Noble Frankland. *The Strategic Air Offensive against Germany, 1939–1945*. Vol. 3, 1961. Official history.

ALFRED C. MIERZEJEWSKI

RAMSAY, BERTRAM H. (1883–1945), British, admiral, Allied Naval Commander, Expeditionary Force. Bertram Home Ramsay entered the Royal Navy in 1898. He specialized in staff work from 1913 on. Promoted to rear admiral in 1935, he retired after a disagreement with his commander in chief on the role of staff. Returning to the service, he commanded the Dunkirk evacuation in 1940. Ramsay planned Operation TORCH (the North

BERTRAM H. RAMSAY.   Left, with Dwight D. Eisenhower and Bernard L. Montgomery aboard HMS *Apollo*.

IMPERIAL WAR MUSEUM

African landings, November 1942), and served as naval commander of the Eastern Task Force for Operation HUSKY (the Sicily invasion, July 1943), which he also planned.

Returning to Britain in July 1943, Ramsay began work on NEPTUNE. At Churchill's insistence, he was appointed Allied Naval Commander, Expeditionary Force (ANCXF) and served from 19 July 1943 until his death on 2 January 1945. Ramsay had to mount the largest seaborne invasion ever and support an Allied army of well over one million men. By adopting the use of artificial harbors, he eliminated the need to capture a major port during the assault phase. Ramsay left the daily administration to the local commanders in chief, concentrating on planning. He summed up his philosophy of combined operations thus: "It is important that the military plan for the subsequent land campaign should be worked out first, and that the assaults should be solely designed to position our forces for the commencement of this. A sound military plan subsequent to the assaults must be the basis of the whole operational plan." He retained the flexibility to take account of major naval problems. His relations with the Western Task Force commander, Rear Adm. Alan G. Kirk, USN, were far from ideal, for Ramsay was not impressed with Kirk, who he believed was unduly influenced by

his chief of staff and at times either hysterical or rude. He personally selected Rear Adm. Philip Vian for the Eastern Task Force. Subordinates found him demanding, and some USN officers considered his detailed planning excessive. However, his work stood the test of war.

The plan for NEPTUNE, issued on 2 March 1944, began with minelaying off the enemy ports from D minus 45, while the loading of assault forces commenced on D minus 21. Ramsay exercised command from Southwick Park, north of Portsmouth. He visited the beachhead on D plus 1 with Eisenhower and found the situation satisfactory, despite the problems inevitable in any operation of war. "One can honestly say that the naval side of this great operation, so far as it has gone, has been very successful, and for this I am most grateful to Providence, to my staff for their excellent planning and meticulous care of details, and to all those to whom the actual carrying out of my orders was entrusted." He accompanied the king to Montgomery's headquarters on the 16th, and inspected the artificial harbor on the 18th. On 24 June he inspected the damage caused by the great gale, which his COREP (Coordination of Repairs) organization was in the process of repairing.

Ramsay shifted his headquarters to France on 10 September 1944. He planned the amphibious assault on Walcheren, which opened the Scheldt estuary, vital for the advance into Germany. He was killed in an air crash on 2 January 1945. From Dunkirk to Walcheren, he played a major part in the Allies' final victory. He was one of the great admirals.

[*See also* Eastern Task Force; Navy, *article on* Allied Naval Forces; Western Task Force.]

BIBLIOGRAPHY

Barnett, Corelli. *Engage the Enemy More Closely.* 1990.
Chalmers, W. S. *Full Cycle: The Biography of Admiral Sir Bertram Home Ramsay.* 1959.
Edwards, Kenneth. *Operation Neptune.* 1946.

ANDREW LAMBERT

RANGERS. In a mission vital to successful landings on Omaha Beach, U.S. Army Rangers attacked German fortifications on Pointe du Hoc on 6 June 1944. Situated between Omaha and Utah beaches, Pointe du Hoc was six thousand meters (3.7 miles) west of Vierville. Protected by rocky cliffs rising thirty meters (100 feet) above a narrow beach covered by enfilading machine-gun fire, a German battery located on the commanding bluffs of Pointe du Hoc dominated the proposed landing areas for American forces. The *726th Infantry Regiment*'s six-gun battery of 155-mm howitzers could reach the transport areas, approach lanes, and landing sites of V and VII Corps on Omaha and Utah beaches. Needing troops capable of scaling the cliffs, conducting shock attacks, and moving inland quickly, American invasion planners assigned the task to the elite Ranger battalions then training in England.

Two Ranger battalions were available in 1944 for the invasion. Both the 2d and 5th Ranger battalions had been activated in summer 1943 at Camp Forrest, Tennessee. Organized with a headquarters company and six rifle companies amounting to 566 men, and armed with an assortment of automatic weapons, light machine guns, bazookas, and 60-mm mortars, the Rangers trained specifically for long-distance speed-marches, amphibious raids, assaults on key fortified objectives, and independent, small-unit missions. As they completed initial training in the United States, both battalions deployed to England and Scotland where they practiced cliff ascents, amphibious assaults, and attacks against fortified positions. On 9 May Lt. Col. James E. Rudder assumed command of the Provisional Ranger Group, composed of both battalions.

The Rangers' D-day missions were to seize and neutralize the guns on Pointe du Hoc, sever the Vierville-Grandcamp road, and attack emplacements on Pointe de la Percée. To accomplish these assignments, Rudder divid-

ed his units into three elements. Composed of Companies D, E, F of the 2d Ranger Battalion, Force A conducted the main attack on Pointe du Hoc at H-hour (0630). Lt. Col. Maxwell Schneider's 5th Ranger Battalion and the 2d Battalion's Companies A and B constituted Force C, reinforcements that waited offshore until Rudder signaled that initial objectives were secure. If he had not received the proper signal by H plus 30, Schneider was to land his element behind the 116th Infantry on Omaha Dog Green Beach and proceed overland through Pointe de la Percée to attack Pointe du Hoc. The bluffs of Pointe de la Percée, two thousand meters (1.25 miles) northwest of Vierville, marked the western extremity of Omaha Beach. Company C, 2d Ranger Battalion, received the independent mission at Pointe de la Percée.

Rough seas, poor navigation, and German fire caused Rudder's Ranger Force A to land forty minutes late, disrupting planned Ranger actions for the next two days. Despite their late start, small Ranger teams used rocket-propelled grapnel hooks attached to climbing ropes and portable extension ladders to scale the cliffs within ten minutes after landing. They met only scattered German resistance and quickly swept over the Pointe in search of the battery. When they found empty gun emplacements, the Rangers continued their advance to the Vierville-Grandcamp road. The Rangers later discovered four unmounted 155-mm guns and destroyed them with incendiary grenades. Rudder's men set up a defensive perimeter around the highway and fought off three fierce counterattacks from elements of the German *914th Infantry Regiment* while waiting for reinforcements. During the next two days, casualties reduced Ranger Force A from 225 men to 90 effectives.

The other two Ranger forces also encountered difficulties. Suffering over 50 percent casualties (38 of 64 men), Company C, 2d Ranger Battalion, slowly made its way across the beach below Pointe de la Percée, climbed the cliffs—at times using bayonets to cut handholds—and cleared German positions on the heights before proceeding overland toward Pointe du Hoc. When he failed to receive the appropriate code word from Rudder's Rangers, Schneider waited an additional fifteen minutes, then directed Ranger Force C to Dog White Beach. Under heavy German fire the Rangers made their way to a

seawall where they huddled for protection. Brig. Gen. Norman Cota, assistant division commander of the 29th Infantry Division, appeared and demanded to know which unit it was. When he learned the Rangers were present, Cota forcefully yelled at them to "lead the way" off the beach. Spurred to action, Ranger Force C spearheaded the advance off the beach and captured Vierville by evening. Two days later, Schneider's Rangers relieved Force A on Pointe du Hoc.

The Ranger battalions earned Presidential Unit Citations for their D-day achievements but only at great human cost. In spite of heavy casualties and an unsuccessful attempt by Rudder to have them evacuated to Great Britain for reorganization and retraining, the Rangers remained in France and joined in the fighting in the hedgerows of Normandy. The 5th Battalion captured coastal defenses at Grandcamp on D plus 4, while the 2d Battalion reorganized, patrolled, and guarded prisoners for most of June. Both units participated in the capture of Brest in August. The Rangers further distinguished themselves during the Siegfried Line campaign in late 1944 when the 2d Rangers Battalion seized critical terrain in the Huertgen Forest and the 5th Ranger Battalion conducted a deep infiltration attack to sever German lines of communication along the Irsch-Zerf road, before redeploying to the United Sates and disbanding in October 1945.

CLIFFS OF POINTE DU HOC.   Top: Showing the ladders used to climb the cliffs.   THE ROBERT HUNT LIBRARY, LONDON
Bottom: A section collapsed by bombardment formed the mound from which the Rangers made their assault.

ARCHIVE PHOTOS, NEW YORK

BIBLIOGRAPHY

Black, Robert W. *Rangers in World War II*. 1991.
Harrison, Gordon. *Cross-Channel Attack*. U.S. Army in World War II: The European Theater of Operations. 1951.
U.S. War Department, Historical Section. *Small Unit Actions*. 1946. Reprint, 1986.

DAVID R. GRAY

R-BOATS. R-boats (*Räumboote*) were German motor minesweepers, smaller than fleet minesweepers (*Minensuchboote*), that were designed for inshore service. Fifty to sixty R-boats were available to oppose the invasion. R-boats were used for a range of duties other than the minesweeping for which they had been designed. They were used offensively as minelayers, as tugs for the Linse explosive motorboats, and as motor gunboats in support of S-boats (*Schnellboote*, small, fast motor torpedo boats). They were also used as coastal escorts.

There were at least three classes of R-boats. Those built by Abeking and Rasmussen of Lemwerder between 1940 and 1943 (*R 43* to *R 129*) displaced 125 tons, were 37 meters (124 ft.) long, 5.8 meters (19 ft.) wide, and drew 1.4 meters (4.5 ft.). Twin diesels, either 6-cylinder units (*R 43* to *R 48*) or 8-cylinder engines of 1,800 horsepower (hp), gave a maximum speed of 20 knots. Voith-Schneider propellers were fitted that gave excellent maneuverability and a tight turning circle, but at some cost in speed. Range was 900 nautical miles at 15 knots. Boats built over the same period by Burmeister at Burg Lesum and Swinemunde (*R 151* to *R 217*) were only 35.4 meters (116.25 ft.) long and 5.6 meters (18.25 ft.) wide; draught was similar. Twin supercharged diesels and conventional screws gave a higher maximum speed of 23.5 knots and range at 15 knots of 1,100 nautical miles. There were also examples of the enlarged Burmeister type (*R 218* to *R 300*) built from 1943 on. These displaced 148 tons, were 39.2 meters (128.5 ft.) long, 5.7 meters (18.75 ft.) wide, and 1.5 meters (5 ft.) in draught. Twin diesels of 2,550 hp drove these larger boats at 22.5 knots. Range at 15 knots was 1,000 nautical miles.

The original armament had comprised a 20-mm gun forward and aft, but by 1944 the boats normally carried four gun mountings, a 37-mm aft, two 20-mm singles or twins amidships, and a 20-mm single or twin forward. In addition, boats were being fitted with a tubular launcher for 86-mm rockets. This fired explosive wire or illuminating rockets against surface or air targets. The normal maximum load of mines was ten, but the larger boats could carry twelve.

The boats were of steel-light alloy-mahogony composite

R 49.

construction and were flush-decked with a speedboatlike foreship. The boats manufactured by the Abeking and Rasmussen Company had nine watertight compartments, the others eight. Original complement was one officer and twenty-eight or twenty-nine men, but this increased to two officers and thirty-six to thirty-eight men.

In addition to the German-built boats, there was a captured vessel, *RA 9*, the former Royal Navy motor launch *ML 306*, commissioned in 1941 and captured in the Saint-Nazaire raid. A standard Fairmile Type B motor launch of 82 tons maximum displacement, it was built of mahogany with a round bilge. Its 1,290-hp twin Hall-Scott petrol engines gave a maximum speed of 20 knots. Range at 15 knots was 990 nautical miles. The Germans rearmed it like a normal R-boat with a 37-mm gun and three single 20-mm guns. Its complement was seventeen.

Fourteen R-boats were lost in connection with the Normandy landings between 6 and 16 June, and eleven were damaged, ten and seven respectively in heavy air attacks on Le Havre and Boulogne. Those sunk were *R 50*, *R 51*, *R 92*, *R 96*, *R 97*, *R 100*, *R 117*, *R 125*, *R 129*, *R 182*, *R 221*, *R 232*, *R 237*, and *RA 9*. *R 49* was badly damaged by British motor torpedo boats on a minelaying sortie from Le Havre by the *4th Motor Minesweeper Flotilla* on the night of D-day.

[*See also* Minesweeper Ships, *article on* German Minesweepers; Navy, *article on* German Navy.]

BIBLIOGRAPHY

Groner, E., D. Jung, and M. Maass. *U-Boats and Minor War Vessels.* Vol. 2 of *German Warships, 1815–1945.* 1991.
Rohwer, Jürgen, and Gerhard Hümmelchen. *Chronology of the War at Sea, 1939–1945.* Translated by Derek Masters. 1992.

ERIC J. GROVE

RCAF. *See* Royal Canadian Air Force.

RCN. *See* Royal Canadian Navy.

RECONNAISSANCE. *See* Aerial Reconnaissance.

REICHERT, JOSEF (1891–1970), German, major general commanding the *711th Static Division.* Josef Reichert, the son of a customs official, was born in Burgfeld, Bavaria, on 13 December 1891. In 1910 he joined the Royal Bavarian army as a cadet in the *21st Infantry Regiment.* A battalion commander in World War I, in October 1918 he was captured by the French. Released in 1920, he was accepted into the Reichswehr,

the army of the Weimar Republic. After holding various military posts in the 1920s and 1930s, in November 1938, now a colonel, he became commander of the *6th Infantry Regiment.*

As divisional commander, Reichert rose from brigadier general to major general between September 1941 and September 1943. In April 1943 he was given command of the *711th Static Division.* The division was decimated in the Normandy battles, then re-formed in Holland between September and December 1944 and reorganized as a field division. Severely injured in an automobile accident on 14 April 1945, he later became an American prisoner of war from May 1945 to July 1947. He died in Gauting on 15 March 1970.

[*See also* 711th Static Division.]

GEORG MEYER
Translated from German by Amy Hackett

RENNIE, T. G. (1900–1945), British, major general, commander of the British 3d Infantry Division. Tom G. Rennie was born in Foochow, China, and educated at Loretto, before going to the Royal Military Academy at Sandhurst. He joined the Black Watch in 1919, became adjutant of the 2d Battalion, and attended Staff College in 1933–1934. From 1939 to December 1942, Rennie served with the 51st (Highland) Division. In June 1940 he was taken prisoner at Saint-Valery, France, but escaped within ten days. Between 1941 and 1942 he commanded the Black Watch, winning a Distinguished Service Order at El Alamein in 1942, and going on to fight in Sicily. Between 1942 and 1943 he commanded a brigade of the Highland Division before becoming commander of the 3d British Infantry Division on 12 December 1943. He fractured his arm when his jeep hit a mine on 13 June 1944, and he returned to the United Kingdom on 18 June. He returned to the Continent in September 1944 as commander of the 51st (Highland) Division, and was killed by mortar fire while crossing the Rhine on 24 March 1945.

Although he ceased to be commander of the 3d Infantry Division on D plus 7, Rennie had been responsible for the training of the division, and has been criticized for failing to train his formation in the speedy exploitation of opportunities, and for failing to ensure that exploitation himself. An example of this concerns the strong point code-named HILLMAN. This was located 2½ miles southwest of the middle of Queen Beach and ¾ of a mile southwest of Colville, on the planned line of advance of the 2d Shropshires and the 1st Norfolks. The failure to take it until the evening of D-day caused high casualties to 8th Infantry Brigade troops and delays in

T. G. RENNIE.   IMPERIAL WAR MUSEUM

the 3d Infantry Division's advance, which enabled the Germans to strengthen their defenses located in the approaches to Caen, the division's ambitious D-day objective. After the *736th Regiment* repulsed an attack, Rennie took the time to prepare a deliberate assault, which broke up the momentum of the advance. Rennie bears some blame, for his order to the commanding officer of the 1st Suffolks was merely to take the point before dark, a strange order since the division was ordered to take Caen or be in a position covering it by dark.

Although Rennie was in part responsible for the delay, the division was also hampered by factors beyond Rennie's control such as the weather. In addition, his units, who on the whole had not been in combat for some years, bore the brunt of the counterattacks by high-caliber German forces, and eventually won, despite high losses.

[*See also* 3d Infantry Division (British).]

BIBLIOGRAPHY

McNish, Robin. *Iron Division: The History of the 3rd Division.* 1978.
Wilmot, Chester. *The Struggle for Europe.* 1954.

TIM MUNDEN

RESISTANCE. *See* French Resistance.

RESOURCES, ALLIED AND GERMAN COMPARED.

In a famous passage in his history *The Second World War* (1950), Winston Churchill wrote that after the entry of the United States into the war the defeat of Germany, Italy, and Japan was "merely the proper application of overwhelming force." By 1944 the combined Allied strength against Germany was three to four times greater than anything the Germans could have achieved. Germany also suffered from considerable shortages in the material resources with which industrialized war was waged. In World War II a list of over thirty "strategic materials" was identified, without which modern societies and their armed forces could not function. Germany was self-sufficient in only four of these, while the Allies between them had access to sufficient stocks of all but one vital commodity, rubber.

Germany had overland access at reasonably short distances to the material wealth of Europe and the western Soviet Union. By 1942 the Germans were demanding approximately three-quarters of the goods and services of all the conquered countries of Europe, which between them contributed the equivalent of a further 14 percent of Germany's gross domestic product directly to the German war effort between 1940 and 1944. But Germany had severe difficulty in reaching resources outside Europe. The Allied position was the exact opposite, with comparatively easy access to very substantial resources in either their own territory or lands under their political control, but problems in translating this potential strength into forces on the battlefield because of the distances involved. German grand strategy throughout the war showed a preoccupation with acquiring further resources, reflected in such decisions as the push for the Caucasus oil fields of the southern Soviet Union in 1942, while the Allies' grand strategy was driven more by the need to expand industrial output and to create a global transport system, enabling them to exploit their tremendous potential.

Population and Agriculture. In 1941 the populations of the major belligerents in the European war were approximately as follows:

Germany	69,500,000
Canada	1,130,000
Great Britain	49,000,000
Soviet Union	170,500,000
United States	131,409,000
Allied total	352,039,000

Differences in levels of education and workforce skills between the belligerents, or differences in the quality of troops and fighting skills, were not sufficiently marked to offset the impact of these figures. Great Britain and the

United States had only relative difficulties in finding sufficient numbers of skilled workers for their expanding industries. Germany suffered from a marked labor shortage, partly offset by the seven million workers from occupied countries who had arrived in the Third Reich by 1944, their status varying from that of genuine volunteers to outright slavery. By D-day, about 40 percent of Allied prisoners of war (largely those from the Soviet Union) were also working directly or indirectly in German arms production.

The United States and Canada were net food exporters, particularly of wheat, and suffered no major food problems. Although always a net food importer, Great Britain could just about feed itself by rationing and increased agricultural production, as long as it also had access to overseas supplies. Prewar Germany was self-sufficient only in potatoes, and occupied Europe could not feed itself. Germany was fed at ration rates by progressively depriving the occupied countries through a system of quotas, fixed prices, and rationing that amounted to 25 million metric tons of food extracted from occupied Europe by 1944.

As a by-product of the food shortage, Germany also suffered shortages in animal fats, leather, and wool that were partly reduced by the invention of artificial substitutes by the German chemical industry. The Germans also managed to synthesize artificial fertilizers from nitrogen after the Allies cut off their supplies of nitrates from South America.

Fuels. The basic fuels for industrialized societies in the 1940s were bituminous coal and crude oil. In 1944 the Allies controlled or produced about 66 percent of the world's coal. Germany and occupied Europe had considerable coal reserves, but production was hampered by passive resistance in the occupied countries. Estimated coal production for the major belligerents between 1939 and 1945 is as follows:

Germany	2,420,300,000 metric tons
Canada	101,900,000 metric tons
Great Britain	1,441,200,000 metric tons
Soviet Union	590,800,000 metric tons
United States	2,149,700,000 metric tons
Allied total	4,283,600,000 metric tons

Apart from its obvious use as fuel for power stations, furnaces, and domestic purposes, coal was also used in the manufacture of explosives, synthetic rubber, medicines including aspirin and the sulfa drugs, and methane gas. The Germans also put considerable effort into converting coal into synthetic oil by combining it with hydrogen.

Petroleum oils and gasoline were the single biggest German deficiency during the war, a fact that at times formed the basis for both German and Allied strategies. In 1944 the world's major oil fields were in Texas, Venezuela, and the Soviet Union, with the oil wealth of the Middle East still largely unexploited, and the Allies controlled about 85 percent of the world's oil output. The only source of oil to which the Germans had access was the Ploesti oil fields in Romania. The estimates of oil either produced or imported by the major belligerents between 1939 and 1945 reflects this Allied advantage:

Germany	45,000,000 metric tons
Canada	8,400,000 metric tons
Great Britain	90,800,000 metric tons
Soviet Union	110,600,000 metric tons
United States	833,200,000 metric tons
Allied total	1,043,000,000 metric tons

From 1943 onward the Ploesti oil fields were subject to a bombing campaign by the U.S. Fifteenth Air Force, while German synthetic oil plants formed a major target for U.S. Eighth Air Force bombers.

Metals. The standard measure of industrialization in the 1940s was the level of production of iron ore and crude steel. In these the Allies had a significant, but not overwhelming, advantage over Germany, which imported over two-thirds of its iron ore, mainly from neutral Sweden. Iron ore production between 1939 and 1945 is estimated as follows:

Germany	240,700,000 metric tons
Canada	3,600,000 metric tons
Great Britain	119,300,000 metric tons
Soviet Union	71,300,000 metric tons
United States	396,900,000 metric tons
Allied total	591,100,000 metric tons

The figures for crude steel, which was produced by recycling scrap metal as well as directly from iron ore, are as follows for the period between 1939 and 1945:

Germany	159,900,000 metric tons
Canada	16,400,000 metric tons
Great Britain	88,500,000 metric tons
Soviet Union	57,700,000 metric tons
United States	334,500,000 metric tons
Allied total	497,100,000 metric tons

Aluminum, produced from bauxite but also obtained from recycling scrap metal, was most commonly used in aircraft and engine parts. German potential reserves of bauxite and aluminum scrap within Europe during World War II were fractionally greater than those available to the Allies. Nevertheless, Allied superiority over Germany in aluminum production between 1939 and 1945 almost equaled that in steel, although on a smaller scale:

Germany	2,142,300 metric tons
Great Britain	236,500 metric tons
Soviet Union	283,000 metric tons
United States	4,123,200 metric tons
Allied total	4,642,700 metric tons

The largest deposits of bauxite then known lay in Dutch and British Guiana (modern Surinam and Guyana respectively), beyond German reach, although the world's largest producer of bauxite was actually France.

Of the less important industrial metals, Germany during the war could obtain only 70 percent of its zinc requirements (chiefly from France and Sweden), 40 percent of its lead requirements, and 10 percent of its copper requirements. The Allies suffered no significant shortages in these metals, with the largest deposits being found in Australia and Mexico, the United States, and Canada respectively. One important, but not vital, Allied shortage was in tin, owing to the Japanese occupation in 1942 of British Malaya and the Dutch East Indies (parts of modern Malaysia and Indonesia respectively), where most of the world's reserves lay. However, the near impossibility of transporting bulk products from Japan to Germany meant that the Germans also suffered a shortage of tin.

A major German problem was a shortage in ferroalloys, the comparatively rare metals essential for improving the hardness, lightness, or quality of steel for specialized machinery and weapons. Canada by itself produced almost all the world's nickel. China and the American continent supplied most of the world's tungsten (from wolfram ore) and antimony. The Allies controlled most of the world's chrome, either producing it themselves or obtaining it from neutral Turkey, and most of the world's manganese, together with such rare metals as molybdenum, vanadium, and platinum, and the micas (naturally occurring silicates of aluminum) used in electrical equipment. In South Africa the Allies also controlled the main source of the world's gold and diamonds, which had important industrial applications apart from their commercial value.

Rubber and Sulfur. The Japanese occupation of British Malaya and the Dutch East Indies also cut the Allies off from almost all the world's rubber, giving the Axis a theoretical advantage in this crucial commodity. Throughout the war, rubber tires for vehicles were strictly rationed by the Allies. But again, it was virtually impossible for Japan to supply Germany with rubber. Commercial rubber also needed to be vulcanized by the addition of sulfur. The world's largest sulfur deposits were found in the United States, and although Italy had substantial sulfur deposits, Germany suffered once more from a serious shortage. Both sides managed to produce synthetic rubber substitutes during the war.

This total massive disparity in resources between the Allies and Germany has led historians to a degree of economic determinism in their view of World War II. As long as the three major Allies remained at war, and as long as they committed no major political or strategic blunders, then, without a miracle, the defeat of Germany was indeed inevitable. By D-day most senior German officers had also accepted this view, and regarded the war as virtually already lost.

BIBLIOGRAPHY

Calvocoressi, Peter, and Guy Wint. *Total War*. 1972.
Ellis, John. *Brute Force*. 1990.
Kennedy, Paul. *The Rise and Fall of the Great Powers*. 1988.

STEPHEN BADSEY

RICHARDSON, WILLIAM (1901–1973), American, brigadier general; commander of the IX Air Defense Command. General Richardson commanded the IX Air Defense Command of the Ninth Air Force from its activation in December 1943 until the end of the war. During the D-day Campaign, the IX Air Defense Command was responsible for the defense of the Ninth Air Force's airfields and for the U.S. Army rear area in Normandy.

Richardson graduated from West Point in 1924, and was commissioned in the Coast Artillery, the branch of the army responsible for antiaircraft artillery. During the prewar period, he specialized in antiaircraft defense. After attending the army's advanced antiaircraft school at Fort Monroe, Virginia, he served with the 60th Antiaircraft Regiment in the Philippines. The army, recognizing his technical competence, assigned him to the Army General Staff in 1941 to help plan for the expansion of the antiaircraft force and to advise on the development of its equipment.

In 1942, Richardson was ordered to England and assigned as the antiaircraft officer for the Eighth Air Force. As such, he was responsible for the defense of Eighth Air Force airfields and installations. Richardson, primarily concerned with training soldiers and organizing antiaircraft units, worked closely with the British forces and studied their air defense methods. He arranged for American soldiers to be sent to British antiaircraft schools, and also set up an antiaircraft gunnery school for the U.S. troops stationed in Britain.

In February 1943, Richardson returned to the United States to assume command of the 51st Coast Artillery Brigade (Antiaircraft). In late 1943, he directed the combined training of air and antiaircraft units on the U.S. West Coast. In December 1943, he returned to England to activate the IX Air Defense Command, which included his own 51st Antiaircraft Artillery Brigade as one of its two principal units.

Richardson was a particularly effective trainer and organizer, and his strong technical understanding enabled him to organize units to employ new radar and communications effectively. Before D-day, he trained his forces in his concepts of antiaircraft defense, stressing that units must be highly mobile and operate as closely as possible behind the frontline units. His preinvasion training program emphasized developing cooperation and coordination of the air and ground antiaircraft forces.

By D-day, the IX Air Defense Command was ready and able to defend the Allied forces from heavy Luftwaffe attacks. But the Army Air Forces' preinvasion campaign to sweep the Luftwaffe from French skies was so successful that General Richardson's forces were almost superfluous during and after D-day. Later in 1944, however, the IX Air Defense Command performed effectively in defending the Allied ports in northern Europe against German V-1 missile attacks.

After the war, Richardson transferred from the army to the air force, where he spent the next nine years in guided-missile development and testing. He retired as a major general in 1954.

[*See also* IX Air Defense Command.]

BIBLIOGRAPHY

Kohn, Richard H., and Joseph P. Hanrahan, eds. *Condensed Analysis of the Ninth Air Force in the European Theater of Operations*. Reprint, 1984.

JAMES S. CORUM

RICHTER, WILHELM (1892–1971), German, major general, commander of the *716th Infantry Division*.

Wilhelm Richter was born in Hirschberg on 17 September 1892. He joined the Imperial Army as a cadet in 1913 and was commissioned second lieutenant in the *55th Field Artillery Regiment* on 18 June 1914. He fought in World War I and remained in the army during the Weimar era. A major when Hitler came to power in 1933, Richter was promoted quickly during the Wehrmacht's rapid expansion phase. A full colonel by 1937, he assumed command of the *30th Artillery Regiment* at Rendsburg on 1 April 1939. As part of the *30th Infantry Division,* Richter fought in Poland, Belgium, and Flanders (1939–1940) and took part in the drive on Leningrad in 1941. On 1 Octo-

ber he was named leader of the *35th Artillery Command,* which was part of the *XLI Motorized* (later *Panzer*) *Corps.* Richter led this unit in the final stages of the advance on Moscow, in the subsequent retreat, at Velish, in the defensive battles of the Rzhev salient, at Bryansk, Orel, and in the Rzhev salient again in late 1942.

Richter attended the divisional commanders' course in January 1943, then continued his training as the deputy commander of a Luftwaffe field division from 1 February to 30 March 1943. On 1 March he was promoted to brigadier general and one month later assumed command of the *716th Infantry Division* in Normandy. It mustered about 10,000 men and consisted of two static grenadier regiments, an artillery regiment, and a few divisional and attached units. His primary mission was to defend a thirty-four-kilometer-long (twenty-one-mile-long) coastal sector north of Caen from Allied amphibious attack—a frontage that was much too long. Richter complained that his defensive positions lacked depth, but he was unable to rectify the situation with his limited resources.

After engaging British airborne troops during the night of 5–6 June, the *716th Division* was struck by the full weight of the Allied air and sea bombardments on the morning of 6 June, during which most of its artillery regiment was destroyed. The *716th* then absorbed the brunt of the attacks of the British Second Army. Richter's "Eastern" battalions (the *439th, 441st,* and *642d*) collapsed almost immediately, but his German units fought well and were largely responsible for preventing General Montgomery from capturing Caen. The division was smashed in the process, however, and by 11 June had suffered more than 6,000 casualties.

The remnants of the *716th Infantry* remained in the line until around 11 June. It was then withdrawn to rebuild at Perpignan on the Mediterranean coast, but was caught up in the Allied invasion of southern France instead. It was re-formed and reinforced in Alsace that fall. Richter's performance as a divisional commander, however, had obviously been judged as inadequate by Berlin, and he was relieved of his command in September. He never received another important assignment. In November 1944 he was recalled to active duty as a deputy commander of an infantry division—a definite demotion. He gave up this job on 25 December 1944, and was again unemployed until 1 February 1945, when he assumed command of the *14th Luftwaffe Field Division.* This two-regiment static unit was on coastal defense and occupation duty in north-central Norway, an inactive sector. He was still there when the war ended.

After two years in prisoner-of-war camps, Wilhelm Richter retired to Rendsburg, the former home base of his regiment. He died there on 4 February 1971.

[*See also* 716th Infantry Division.]

BIBLIOGRAPHY

Keilig, Wolf. *Die Generale des Heeres.* 1983.

Mehner, Kurt, ed. *Die Geheimen Tagesberichte der deutsche Wehrmachtführung im Zweiten Weltkrieg, 1939–1945.* Vol. 12. 1984.

Tessin, Georg. *Verbände und Truppen der deutschen Wehrmacht und Waffen-SS im Zweiten Weltkrieg, 1939–1945.* Vol. 12, 1975.

SAMUEL W. MITCHAM, JR.

RIDGWAY, MATTHEW B.

RIDGWAY, MATTHEW B. (1895–1993), American, major general, commander of the 82d Airborne Division. Matthew Bunker Ridgway was born on 3 March 1895 at Fort Monroe, Virginia. Ridgway entered the U.S. Military Academy and graduated in April 1917. From June 1917 to March 1942, Ridgway held duty assignments all over the world including China, the Philippines, Nicaragua, West Point, and Fort Benning, Georgia. He also graduated from the Command and General Staff School, held various staff positions, and attended the Army War College. Assigned to the War Plans Division of the War Department General Staff, he remained in this post until January 1942.

On 26 June 1942 Ridgway became commanding general of the 82d Infantry Division, soon redesignated the 82d Airborne. In April 1943 he led the division to North Africa, where he was responsible for planning and executing the first large-scale airborne assault in the history of the U.S. Army in the invasion of Sicily in July. He then led the 82d in Italy from September to November 1943. Instead of riding a glider into Normandy as planned, Ridgway decided two days prior to the invasion to parachute in with the main assault force. He jumped in with the 2d Battalion of the 505th Parachute Infantry, landing in a pasture west of Sainte-Mère-Église. Throughout the early critical days of the invasion, Ridgway was constantly on the move from his small command post in an orchard near where he landed to the points where the fighting raged most heavily.

In August 1944 Ridgway was selected to command the XVIII Airborne Corps, in which capacity he directed operations in the Ardennes campaign, the crossing of the Rhine, the Ruhr pocket, the crossing of the Elbe, and the advance to junction with Russian forces on 2 May 1945.

Following World War II General Ridgway was appointed deputy supreme Allied commander, Mediterranean. He became the U.S. representative on the Military Staff Committee of the United Nations, then commander in chief of the U.S. Caribbean command in Panama. He assumed command of the U.S. Eighth Army in Korea on 26 December 1950 at the height of the Korean War. Following President Truman's dismissal of General of the

MATTHEW B. RIDGWAY.   In 1952.   NATIONAL ARCHIVES

Army Douglas MacArthur in 1951, Ridgway was appointed Supreme Allied Commander in Korea on 11 April. Now a four-star general, in May 1952 he succeeded Dwight D. Eisenhower as Supreme Commander of the Allied Powers in Europe. He became chief of staff of the U.S. Army on 15 August 1953. After more than thirty-eight years of military service, he retired on 30 June 1955 to his home at Fox Chapel, Pennsylvania. He died there on 26 July 1993.

[*See also* Airborne Forces; 82d Airborne Division.]

BIBLIOGRAPHY

Blair, Clay. *Ridgway's Paratroopers.* 1985.

Ridgway, Matthew B. A brief personal biography and résumé. 1973. Private collection.

Ridgway, Matthew B. *Soldier: The Memoirs of Matthew B. Ridgway.* 1956.

STEVEN J. MROZEK

RITCHIE, N. M.

RITCHIE, N. M. (1897–1983), British, lieutenant general, commander of British XII Corps. Neil Methuen Ritchie was born in British Guiana, where his father managed a sugar plantation. He was sent back to England, first to Lancing College and later to the Royal Military College, Sandhurst. Commissioned into the Black

N. M. RITCHIE.   Right, with Miles C. Dempsey (left) and Richard N. O'Connor (center).   IMPERIAL WAR MUSEUM

Watch in 1914, he joined their 1st Battalion in France in 1915. Later he served with the 2d Battalion in Mesopotamia, earning two decorations.

After the war he went to Staff College, then rose steadily to reach the rank of brigadier general by 1939. He was on the staff of II Corps in France, and after Dunkirk was given the job of re-forming the 51st (Highland) Division. In 1941 he was sent to Cairo as Gen. Claude Auchinleck's deputy chief of staff. Toward the end of that year, when Rommel had forced the Eighth Army back in disarray, Ritchie was made its commander.

It was the key moment of his career, his first command in twenty years. He had many admirable qualities, but his thinking was neither fast nor imaginative, and he was painfully aware that his commanding officer, Auchinleck, was breathing over his shoulder. Rommel's brilliant offensive in May–June 1942 drove the Eighth Army back into Egypt in confusion, with the loss of many tanks. Tobruk fell, and on 25 June Ritchie was dismissed. Ritchie bounced back remarkably, returning to Britain to take charge of the 52d (Lowland) Division.

At the beginning of 1944 he was made a temporary lieutenant general and given command of XII Corps, which was training for the Normandy invasion. XII Corps was not part of the initial landings, but the corps headquarters was established in Normandy by the end of June. The corps was in action on 15–16 July in a night attack on Évrecy, near Caen, using a technique called "Movement Light" involving the reflection of searchlights from a cloudy sky. It also participated in Operation GOODWOOD, the attack to break out of Normandy, and later in the fighting at the Falaise pocket.

Ritchie and his corps were never given a leading role to play, but for the rest of the campaign in Europe they were kept actively and efficiently engaged all the way to the crossing of the Rhine and the final advance to the Elbe.

After the war he was appointed general officer commanding in chief, Scottish Command, then commander in chief of Far East Land Forces. He was knighted and received many other honors. When he retired in 1951, he went to live in Canada and launched a successful career in business. He died in 1983.

BIBLIOGRAPHY

Barnett, Correlli. *The Desert Generals*. 1960.
D'Este, Carlo. *Decision in Normandy: The Unwritten Story of Montgomery and the Allied Campaign*. 1983.

ALAN HANKINSON

RIVETT-CARNAC, J. W. (1891–1970), British, rear admiral, British Assault Area. James William Rivett-Carnac served in the Royal Navy in World War I. He was commander of HMS *Kent* under Capt. Bertram Ramsay, captain of the HMS *Rodney* (1941–1943), and in September 1943, as a rear admiral in Force H, supported the Salerno landing.

Rivett-Carnac was appointed to Operation NEPTUNE in January 1944, initially as the shore-based deputy for Rear Adm. Philip Vian, commander of the Eastern Task Force, with the subsequent responsibility of taking over as commander of the invasion forces once a shore headquarters had been established. He was responsible to Vian for the Ferry Service, which would land the men and stores over the open beaches after the assault phase; for the repair, salvage, and refueling of landing craft; for interservice cooperation on all issues involving shore defense; for the establishment of a shore headquarters; and for the administration of the Gooseberry and Mulberry units (the artificial harbors). In addition he would assume command, should Vian be disabled.

Initially Rivett-Carnac hoisted his flag aboard the large ex-mercantile minelayer HMS *Southern Prince,* Acting Capt. R. H. F. de Salis. After the mining of the cruiser *Scylla,* Vian's flagship, on 22 June, he took control of all coastal forces in Eastern Task Force Area. On 24 June he established headquarters ashore at Courseulles, and on the 30th replaced Vian as flag officer British Assault Area, with control over all naval assets. At first his major role was the direction of fire support, but in July, as German countermeasures developed, he had to deal with increasing levels of air attack, submersible assault craft (known as human torpedoes), and miniature submarines. He moved his headquarters to Rouen on 14 September after the capture of Le Havre ended the need to land supplies at the original beachhead. He hauled down his flag on 31 December 1944, at which time British Assault Area Command ceased to exist.

Rivett-Carnac became rear admiral, flag ashore, and then vice admiral with the British Pacific Fleet aboard HMS *Beaconsfield.* He retired in 1947. He was a capable and professional administrator who made a major contribution to the smooth running of the campaign from D-day to the end of 1944. His control of fire support during the critical battles for Caen was a major contribution to the success of the British Army.

[*See also* Eastern Task Force; Navy, *article on* Allied Naval Forces.]

BIBLIOGRAPHY

Vian, Philip. *Action This Day.* 1960.

ANDREW LAMBERT

ROBERTS, G. P. B. ("PIP") (1906–), British, major general, commander of the 11th Armoured Division. One of the finest British armored commanders of World War II, "Pip" Roberts was commissioned into the Royal Tank Corps in 1926. He served throughout the campaign in North Africa, on the staff of the 7th Armoured Division, 4th Armoured Brigade, and XXX Corps, and as commander of the 3d Royal Tank Regiment. From August 1942, he was an armored brigade commander, especially making his name during the Battle of Alam Halfa. Awarded four decorations for bravery, Roberts was recalled to England at the end of the Tunisian campaign and took command of the 11th Armoured Division in December 1943. As such he was the youngest divisional commander in the British army. Roberts landed in Normandy on D plus 5 and spent the next few days seeing his division ashore and preparing it for its first action, which was to be EPSOM, the offensive near Caen.

Roberts led his division with much verve throughout the whole of the campaign in northwestern Europe and was made a Commander of the Order of the Bath; he also received the French Legion of Honor and Croix de Guerre.

After the war Roberts commanded the 7th Armoured Division in Germany and was director of the Royal Armoured Corps before retiring in 1949 to become a businessman. A very popular commander and much admired by Bernard L. Montgomery, Roberts achieved much of his success by always positioning himself well forward so that he could react quickly to any given situation. He also laid much stress on accurate tank gunnery and close cooperation between tanks and infantry.

[*See also* 11th Armoured Division.]

BIBLIOGRAPHY

Liddell Hart, B. H. *The Tanks: The History of the Royal Tank Regiment, 1914–1945.* Vol. 2, 1959.
Roberts, G. P. B. *From the Desert to the Baltic.* 1987.

CHARLES MESSENGER

ROBERTSON, WALTER M. (1888–1954), American, major general, commander of the U.S. 2d Infantry Division. Walter Melville ("Robby") Robertson was born 15 June 1888 in Nelson County, Virginia, and graduated from the U.S. Military Academy in 1912. He then joined Company M, 1st Infantry, at Schofield Barracks, Hawaii. Robertson trained troops in the United States during World War I and did not reach France until 1919, when he served as a camp inspector at the port of Brest. During the 1920s and 1930s he taught at the Army War College, commanded troops in the Philippines, and served in various staff posts. Promoted to lieutenant colonel in 1935, Robertson was on the War Department General Staff for four years and then joined the 2d Division at Fort Sam Houston, Texas, in 1940. He commanded both the 9th and the 23d infantry regiments before he succeeded John C. H. Lee as commander of the division in May 1942. He trained the division in the United States, took it overseas to Northern Ireland in October 1943, and led it until the end of the war in Europe.

Slim, balding, and bespectacled, Robertson appeared more a scholar than a warrior, but he showed in Normandy that looks can be deceiving. He and the 2d Division, part of the V Corps supporting the 1st and 29th divisions, landed at Omaha Beach between D plus 1 and D plus 3. From 8 to 10 June, with his division not yet fully ashore, Robertson took Trévières and pressed beyond the Cerisy Forest. From 10 to 18 June he continued to attack stubbornly in the hedgerows approaching Hill 192, which covered the Bayeux–Saint-Lô road. Heavy casualties and slow going after the initial surge past Trévières and the Cerisy Forest revealed deficiencies in the division's combined arms training, and when action shifted away from the V Corps front toward Cherbourg, Robertson reorganized his command structure. He also began intensive regimental, company, and small unit exercises involving close tank and artillery cooperation, which proved effective when the division attacked Hill 192 again on 11 July.

After the Normandy breakout Robertson and his division were transferred to Troy H. Middleton's VIII Corps for the attack on Brest. His division was recuperating in the Ardennes when it was replaced by the ill-fated 106th Division and ordered to rejoin the V Corps in the Monschau Corridor for the attack on the Roer dams. His great moment came in December 1944 when he defended the Elsenborn Ridge during the German counteroffensive in the Ardennes.

Robertson was an outstanding trainer and a conscientious combat commander. In July 1945 he succeeded Wade H. Haislip as commander of the XV Corps and in 1946 and 1947 served as an American delegate to the Allied Control Mission in Bulgaria. His last assignment was as commanding general of the Sixth Army. Awarded the Distinguished Service Medal, the Distinguished Service Cross, the Silver Star, and the Legion of Merit, Robertson retired on 30 June 1950 to become director of civilian defense for the state of California. He died in San Francisco 22 November 1954.

[*See also* 2d Infantry Division.]

BIBLIOGRAPHY

Combat History of the 2d Infantry Division in World War II. 1946.
Cullum's Biographical Register of the Officers and Graduates of the United States Military Academy at West Point, New York. Supplement, vols. 6–9. 1920–1950.
"Obituary of Walter M. Robertson." *Assembly: The Magazine of the West Point Alumni Association* 14 (July 1955): 76.

DANIEL R. BEAVER

ROMMEL, ERWIN (1891–1944), German, field marshal, commander in chief, *Army Group B*. Erwin Rommel was born on 15 November 1891 in Heidenheim, a small town east of Stuttgart in Württemberg. He came from a family of teachers, married the daughter of a teacher, and was himself successful as a military instructor in the army. Rommel's mother, Helene Luz, was the daughter of a high government official who, as was customary in Württemberg, had been awarded a personal title of nobility. Thus Rommel's background was clearly at odds with that of the stereotypical German general: he came from the educated bourgeoisie, not from an officer family or the old nobility; he was a Swabian from Württemberg and thus a South German, not a Prussian; and he was not one of the older generation of high Wehrmacht officers born in the 1880s, but of a younger generation. Field Marshal Gerd von Rundstedt, sixteen years his senior, who did exemplify the classic Prussian general, jokingly called him the "Boy Marshal" (*Marschall Bubi*).

In 1907 Rommel's family moved from Heidenheim to neighboring Aalen. There and in the larger town of Schwäbisch-Hall, Rommel attended elementary and secondary school. In 1910 he joined a Württemberg infantry regiment as a cadet. In 1911 and 1912 he trained as an officer at the military academy in Danzig. When war broke out in 1914, Lieutenant Rommel went into battle with his regiment, and took part in the first encounters on the Western front; within three weeks he was wounded near Varennes. After a long stay in a military hospital in Germany, he returned to his regiment as a company commander, fighting with them at the Somme and in the Argonne. In October 1915 he was transferred as a first lieutenant to a new elite troop, the *Württemberg Mountain Battalion,* which he led in the Vosges, the Carpathian Mountains, and finally in the Eastern Alps. In 1916, during the Battle of Caporetto in Italy, his mountain combat group breached the Italian fortification system and captured over nine thousand prisoners. In December 1917 Rommel received Germany's highest award for bravery, *Pour le mérite*. His superior called him "a commander of genius whom his troops followed with blind trust anywhere."

Although not on the General Staff, in 1919 Captain Rommel was accepted into the Reichswehr, the small professional army allowed the Weimar Republic under the Versailles Treaty. A company commander in the 1920s, he became an instructor in tactics at the Dresden school for infantry officers in 1929, and from 1935 to 1938 was head of the War College in Potsdam. After Austria's absorption into the German Reich in 1938, Rommel, now a colonel, commanded the officer training school in Vienna's Neustadt.

Like most of his comrades, Rommel was apolitical, that is, unreflectively loyal with a basically conservative nation-

ERWIN ROMMEL.

al outlook formed during the imperial era. He welcomed Hitler's reintroduction of compulsory military service and his enlargement of the army, which in 1935 was pointedly renamed the Wehrmacht. But Rommel remained cool toward the National Socialist party; at his request, he was relieved of the auxiliary responsibility of organizing the Hitler Youth for premilitary instruction. Yet it was decisive for his career that in 1936 he came to Hitler's attention as the Führer's escort for the Berlin Olympic Games. Hitler requested that in the event of mobilization Rommel be put in command of his headquarters; it was in this capacity that he served in 1938 and 1939. On 1 August 1939 Rommel was promoted to brigadier general.

Rommel also owed his command of a panzer division to Hitler's personal intervention. This was an exceptional assignment since Rommel, an infantry officer, had no experience with modern panzer weapons. Nonetheless, Hitler's decision was astute, as the French campaign of 1940 demonstrated. At the head of his *7th Panzer Division,* soon known as the "Ghost Division," Rommel pushed through the Ardennes to the Maas River, crossed it, and advanced to the Atlantic after fighting off a British tank attack. His flexible and energetic leadership established his new reputation as a panzer commander.

In late 1940 and early 1941, when Italy's Libyan colony was threatened by a British offensive, Hitler sent a German panzer unit to North Africa in support of his ally. He named Rommel, now a major general, as commander of the *Africa Corps*. Formally, he was subordinate to Benito Mussolini, the Italian Duce, but he had been given far-reaching authority by Hitler. In March 1941 he began an offensive with German and Italian troops that by mid-April reached the Egyptian border. In November 1941 a British counteroffensive forced him back to his starting point in Libya, but on 21 January 1942 he again seized the initiative in a surprise attack that drove the British back into Egypt and made him the youngest field marshal in the German army. Now at the apex of his career, with Hitler's and Mussolini's approval he stormed eastward deep into Egypt, but was stopped by the British at El Alamein. There, at the end of July, a tenacious war of position developed in which Rommel, who suffered from inadequate reinforcements, in the long run was inevitably defeated. On 4 November 1942 General Bernard L. Montgomery broke through Rommel's position at El Alamein. Hitler's "no retreat" order could not stop events, but it finally broke the relationship of trust between Rommel and Hitler that up till then had withstood the general's military doubts. In a dramatic and dazzling 2,000-kilometer retreat, Rommel led the bulk of his army across Libya to Tunisia, where in late February 1943 he won a spectacular victory against the U.S. II Corps at Kasserine Pass. Given Allied superiority, the battles in Tunisia quickly came to an end. Rommel was flown out on 9 March, long before the final German and Italian surrender there in May. Hitler awarded him the Knight's Cross of the Iron Cross with oak leaf cluster, swords and diamonds, the sixth soldier to receive what was then Germany's highest military decoration.

ROMMEL REVIEWING TROOPS.

BIBLIOTHEK FÜR ZEITGESCHICHTE, STUTTGART

With the North African campaign concluded, it was foreseeable that the Allies would next focus on Sicily and the Italian mainland, trying to draw Germany's most important ally to their side. To meet this military and political threat, Hitler called Rommel to his headquarters in early May and assigned him to form a working staff for the new *Army Group B,* which would lead the German troops in Italy. But after Italy's change of side became known, Field Marshal Albert Kesselring was given the supreme command there. On 5 November 1943 Rommel was ordered to inspect Germany's defensive capacity on the western European coast from the Spanish border to Norway and then work out defense plans. In December he set up headquarters in Fontainebleau, later moving to La Roche-Guyon, on the Seine northwest of Paris. As inspector of the Atlantic Wall, Rommel remained even later directly under the Wehrmacht High Command (Oberkommando der Wehrmacht—OKW). In addition, on 1 January 1944 he received operational command over eventual landing sites in northern France, Belgium, and the Netherlands, commanding the *Seventh* and *Fifteenth* armies, and Wehrmacht troops in the Netherlands.

Rommel devoted himself with great energy to building up the coastal fortifications; his African experience with mine warfare and with the effects of Allied bombardments proved useful here. A master in mobile warfare, Rommel's tragedy was that his ultimately decisive battles were those of stationary war and siege: El Alamein in 1942 and Normandy in 1944. He was particularly concerned with securing the coastal plain (for example, through using "Rommel asparagus," obstacles to thwart glider landings). As supreme commander of *Army Group B* he argued for massing all available panzer divisions in order to counteract the landing without a long march. Like Montgomery at Alam Halfa in September 1942, he wanted to strengthen his defensive front through entrenched panzers. But Gerd von Rundstedt, Commander in Chief West, persevered in what had become classic German doctrine in panzer warfare: he wanted to form a "great mass of panzers" in the hinterland under a separate command staff responsible to him (*Panzer Group*

West under Lt. Gen. Leo Geyr von Schweppenburg). Remaining beyond the fire zone of the Allies' naval artillery, they would "deliver the decisive operational blow" (Ose, p. 49). Because the *6th Panzer Division* in northern France could not be deployed for twenty-four to forty-eight hours, and because Allied air mastery severely hindered nighttime movements, the decisive panzer battle that was hoped for, and that would be sought even after a successful Allied landing, had hardly any prospect of success. Furthermore, Hitler tied most panzer divisions to his personal command as an OKW reserve; as a result, events on D-day developed differently than the German command intended.

The Germans did not expect an invasion on 6 June 1944. Rommel was at home in Herrlingen, near Ulm. Informed of the invasion by telephone, he reached Reims by afternoon, where he gave the order to throw the *21st Panzer Division* into battle. Though stationed right on the coast, it had not yet been deployed by the army group's chief of staff, Lt. Gen. Hans Speidel, because the situation long remained unclear, and the High Command expected the main landing in the Pas de Calais. In the night of 6 June Rommel arrived at his headquarters and took command. His beach barriers proved inadequate in the face of the Allied landing as superiority in matériel overwhelmed the operational and tactical planning of the German staff. Allied firepower (naval armament and bombardment) permitted little but tactical countermeasures. Rommel was on the move without pause, visiting troops and staffs in advanced positions and coordinating their actions. Because five Allied bridgeheads had already been established by the evening of 6 June, it was necessary that they be cordoned off and isolated. On 11 June Rommel wanted to shift his focus westward to the Cotentin Peninsula, in order to protect Cherbourg harbor. But the next day Hitler ordered successive attacks on the Vire and Orne river bridgeheads in order to destroy them. In reality, the German leadership had by this point lost the initiative; defensive tactics were all that was left. The Allies' great offensive began on 18 July at Caen, starting the breakout from the landing zone. The day before, as Rommel was returning to La Roche-Guyon from the headquarters of *Panzer Group West,* his car was hit by the cannon of a British Spitfire, severely injuring him. He was taken to a hospital in France, and on 8 August returned to Herrlingen.

Thus Rommel missed further combat in the West, as well as the conspiracy of 20 July 1944. On that day Col. Claus Count Schenk von Stauffenberg brought a bomb to the Führer's headquarters in East Prussia; its explosion was to set off a coup attempt, which however was defeated the same day. Rommel's chief of staff, Maj. Gen. Hans Speidel, was involved in the plot, many of whose participants had hoped for the cooperation of the popular field marshal. Stauffenberg's cousin, Lt. Col. Caesar von

Hofacker, had sounded Rommel out; Rommel's answer is not known, but Rommel was not informed about the assassination attempt itself. He no doubt hoped to come to terms with his old adversary Montgomery, now leading the British 21st Army Group in France. Verbally and in a letter of 15 July, Rommel had attempted to win Hitler over to negotiations, but he always met with abrupt rejections. Hitler's court took prompt action against the conspirators; most were executed, and Rommel himself came under suspicion. On 14 October 1944, when two generals appeared at Rommel's house in Herrlingen and offered him the alternatives of poisoning himself or facing the Nazi tribunal, he chose the former. Rommel received a state funeral, at which Field Marshal von Rundstedt delivered the eulogy. The cause of death was kept secret. In this shabby way Hitler had rid himself of his most prominent military leader.

[*See also* Army Group B.]

BIBLIOGRAPHY

Irving, David. *The Trial of the Fox: The Life of Field Marshal Erwin Rommel.* 1977.
Liddell Hart, B. H., ed. *The Rommel Papers.* 1953.
Ose, Dieter. *Entscheidung im Westen 1944.* 1982.
Rommel, Erwin. Personal Papers (File 6/15). Bundesarchiv–Militärarchiv, Freiburg, Germany.
Ruge, Friedrich. *Rommel und die Invasion.* 1959.
Stumpf, Reinhard. *Die Wehrmacht-Elite.* 1982.
Wegmüller, Hans. *Die Abwehr der Invasion.* 1979.

REINHARD STUMPF
Translated from German by Amy Hackett

ROOSEVELT, FRANKLIN DELANO (1882–1945), American, president of the United States. Roosevelt served as a member of the New York State legislature, assistant secretary of the navy during World War I, governor of New York from 1929 to 1932, and president from 1933 until his death. He was the first president to be elected four times, and also the last, since the Constitution now includes a two-term limit.

In the judgment of many historians, OVERLORD owed more to Roosevelt than to any other man. Gen. George C. Marshall, the Army's chief of staff, with the support of Secretary of War Henry L. Stimson, championed it vigorously, but Prime Minister Winston S. Churchill of Great Britain put many obstacles in its path. Although British historians maintain that Churchill strongly favored the cross-Channel attack, and he put himself on record many times to this effect, Churchill devoted a large part of his diplomacy to fostering operations that would have postponed OVERLORD.

As a result, American planners believed that Churchill's

real intent was to mount the cross-Channel assault, if at all, only after Russian successes had taken the risk out of it. That explained to them why Churchill repeatedly insisted that the best place for the Allies to fight was in the Mediterranean, even after the grueling Italian campaign had demonstrated that the northern Mediterranean coast was anything but the "soft underbelly" of Europe. In the face of his energetic and repeated efforts to delay or derail OVERLORD, a weaker American president might well have given way.

Fortunately for the Allied cause, Roosevelt accepted Marshall's argument that the quickest road to victory in Europe began at the Channel coast of France. American planners were agreed that the war could not be won without invading Germany itself and that operations in the Mediterranean would only delay coming to grips with the core of German strength. Even so, in 1942 FDR sided with Churchill, who wanted to take North Africa before, or probably instead of, attacking German forces in France. Although Marshall opposed operation TORCH as a wasteful diversion, politically there was no getting around it—as even Marshall would concede many years later.

Roosevelt's problem was that Americans were much angrier with Japan than with Germany. At the time of the American entry into the war, Germany had done little damage to the United States, whereas the Japanese had bombed Hawaii and seized many American possessions. A Gallup poll released on 20 December 1944 found that 13 percent of respondents favored exterminating the entire Japanese population. Another, released on 10 June 1945, after the Nazi death camps had been photographed by newsreel cameras and shown in movie theaters, found that 82 percent of Americans believed the Japanese were more "cruel at heart" than the Germans. These powerful emotions, tinged in some degree by racial animosity, put immense pressure on Roosevelt to concentrate the war effort on Japan. To compound his difficulties, army planners were working on a cross-Channel attack, code-named ROUNDUP, that would not take place until May 1943. Marshall did advance Operation SLEDGEHAMMER, an ill-considered emergency plan to land a few divisions in France during 1942 to take some of the heat off Russia. But even if executed, which fortunately it was not, the troops involved would have been largely British.

If all went as the U.S. Army proposed, therefore, American soldiers would sit out the first eighteen months of the war against Germany, during which time public opinion might force Roosevelt to move instead against Japan. However, Roosevelt was committed to beating Germany first, a strategy arrived at in secret talks between British and American military representatives while the United States had still been neutral. To protect that strategy, he decided that Americans had to engage German ground forces

at the earliest possible date. Accordingly, on 25 July 1942 FDR ordered his military chiefs to plan for an invasion of North Africa by 30 October.

Operation TORCH could not be launched until 8 November, and progressed sluggishly after that because Hitler decided to hold North Africa and poured men into Tunisia. Thus when Roosevelt and Churchill met at Casablanca with their chiefs of staff in January 1943, the cross-Channel operation was receding into the future. Marshall fought hard for a cross-Channel attack (ROUNDUP) at Casablanca, but, as he had feared, the North African campaign took too long and was not finished until after ROUNDUP's target date had passed. Further, the great Allied buildup in Africa made an invasion of Sicily inevitable, as the men and machines assembled at such great cost could not be allowed to remain idle. Sicily was so close to the mainland that Italy also would be invaded, from sheer momentum as much as a desire to knock Italy out of the war. Contrary to Churchill's wishes, though, there would be no further large-scale operations in the Mediterranean.

At the next Big Two summit meeting, the Trident Conference in Washington that began on 12 May 1943, FDR and his chiefs insisted that the cross-Channel attack had to be the next big step after Italy and that it must take place in 1944, not 1945 or even 1946 (as suggested by General Alan Brooke, chief of the Imperial General Staff and, after Churchill, the most formidable Briton). With the Americans united against them, the British backed down, accepting 1 May 1944 as the date for D-day of what was now code-named OVERLORD. This British retreat was less than it seemed, for Churchill had many arrows left in his quiver and would shoot them all at OVERLORD before he was finished.

At the November Sextant Conference in Cairo just before Teheran, the British argued that Operation BUCCANEER, a proposal to invade the Andaman Islands off Burma, must inevitably delay OVERLORD. Then when the Big Three met for the first time at the Teheran Conference during November–December 1943, Churchill spent days arguing for more peripheral campaigns. Finally, on 30 November, worn down by the resistance of Roosevelt and Soviet dictator Josef Stalin, and with the British chiefs having agreed to it, Churchill once again accepted OVERLORD. Stalin then ensured its success by promising to launch a Soviet offensive timed to prevent Germany from reinforcing its French garrison with troops withdrawn from the Eastern front (an offensive that actually began on 23 June—late, but not fatally so).

On 5 December in Cairo, Roosevelt made what has been deemed one of his most important and best decisions of the war: General Dwight D. Eisenhower would command OVERLORD. General Marshall, who very much

FRANKLIN D. ROOSEVELT.

wanted the job, was the sentimental favorite of most American leaders. He had built the U.S. Army up from scratch and deserved the opportunity to lead it in its greatest battles. According to Marshall, Roosevelt in breaking the news to him said: "I feel I could not sleep at night with you out of the country." This was tactful, and perhaps true as well, but in the view of many historians, Roosevelt judged Eisenhower to be better qualified to lead the most critical Allied attack of the war. Marshall, though a brilliant staff officer, had never commanded troops in battle, while Eisenhower was a veteran of three amphibious invasions. His unique experience and growing skill were significant Allied assets. Of major importance was the fact that he was liked and trusted by the British, an essential requirement for combined operations.

Sentiment aside, it made little sense to put the untried Marshall in charge of OVERLORD. Nor was there much to be said for making Eisenhower chief of staff, which was to have been his job when Marshall left it, since the army was already being led by the greatest chief in history. Keeping the right men in the right jobs was Roosevelt's second most important contribution to OVERLORD, and may have been a crucial one, since Marshall's inexperience would have added additional risk to an operation that was by its very nature hazardous. Roosevelt took the prudent course and history would justify it.

Subsequently Roosevelt's main task would be to keep Churchill from putting off OVERLORD for the sake of various Mediterranean schemes that he persisted in promoting. As the campaign in Italy bogged down, Churchill railed against the "tyranny" of OVERLORD, since the troops being sent to England to prepare for it would, to his mind, be better employed in the Italian campaign—which he apparently hoped would make OVERLORD unnecessary. Roosevelt bent over backward to accommodate Churchill. When Allied planners proposed to outflank the German Gustav Line by landing behind it in Anzio, there were too few LSTs (Landing Ships, Tank) available to ensure success. Roosevelt arranged for fifty-six LSTs, scheduled for Britain and OVERLORD, to be kept in the Mediterranean. This made it possible to invade Anzio on 22 January 1944, but prompt German counterattacks bottled up the American troops. Anzio became another stalemate leading to renewed British demands.

Churchill began insisting that Operation ANVIL, landings on the Mediterranean coast of France in support of OVERLORD, be canceled or put off. In this, too, he would fail. Roosevelt had promised Stalin, who regarded ANVIL as an essential complement to OVERLORD, that the French Riviera would be invaded. Eisenhower, worried about supplying the Allied armies in France, wanted its southern ports. But there were still not enough LSTs to go around, so it was finally decided that ANVIL would have to wait until landing ships could be released from OVERLORD and sent to Italy to pick up the assault troops.

Another of Roosevelt's contributions to victory was the tactical bombing of French rail and road targets in preparation for OVERLORD. Inevitably, French civilians would be killed as a result of these sorties. Although most Free French leaders accepted them as part of the price of liberation, Churchill and his advisers were afraid that French resentment over these casualties would become a serious problem. On this issue Roosevelt remained adamant, informing Churchill on 11 May 1944 that he would not support any limitations on the military that would jeopardize OVERLORD or cause additional Allied losses. He was vindicated here as well, since French civilian casualties proved to be much lower than Churchill feared, while the bombing itself was sensationally effective. There was no French backlash afterward.

In one area, which turned out to have no military significance, Roosevelt met defeat. FDR disliked Charles de Gaulle, the leader of the Free French, and insisted that until elections were held, Eisenhower should govern liberated France. The British Foreign Office strongly opposed the decision, feeling that de Gaulle would take charge in any case, but Churchill, having fought Roosevelt on so many matters, declined to make an issue of it. All the fuss was for nothing. While de Gaulle was given no part to play in OVERLORD, he could not be kept from visiting Normandy on D plus 6. He was rapturously received by the populace and left behind one of his officers to look after civil affairs. No more was heard of AMGOT (Allied Military Government for Occupied Territory), which Roosevelt had intended to rule France.

After D-day Roosevelt's main task was to keep ANVIL, renamed DRAGOON, on schedule. This he did, though of all his struggles with Churchill, preserving the timetable for DRAGOON was one of the hardest. Numerous messages passed between them for weeks after D-day, the prime minister using every argument he could muster to block, or at least minimize, DRAGOON for the sake of operations in Italy. Not until after 1 July 1944, when Churchill made his last attack on DRAGOON, did Britain finally give way. DRAGOON took place on 15 August and contributed significantly to the Allied victory in France.

Roosevelt was felled at his desk in the "little White House" in Warm Springs, Georgia, at 1315 on 12 April 1945. He was pronounced dead of a massive cerebral hemorrhage at 1535. Though he did not live to see it, he knew at the time of his death that victory in Europe was near. OVERLORD had done its work, and so too had Roosevelt by making the great venture possible.

[See also Planning, article on Allied Planning; United States of America.]

BIBLIOGRAPHY

Burns, James MacGregor. *Roosevelt: The Soldier of Freedom, 1940–1945.* 1970.
Greenfield, Kent R. *American Strategy in World War II: A Reconsideration.* 1963.
Kimball, Warren F., ed. *Churchill and Roosevelt: The Complete Correspondence.* 1984.

WILLIAM O'NEILL

ROOSEVELT, THEODORE, JR.

(1887–1944), American, brigadier general, attached to the U.S. 4th Infantry Division. Although the son of the 26th president of the United States was born frail and slight with poor eyesight, he fought with the 26th Infantry, a regiment in the 1st Division, in World War I and was twice wounded in action. Between the wars he returned to an active civilian life writing books, leading museum expeditions to Asia, and playing an active role in politics.

In 1941 he returned to active duty with the 26th Infantry. In the invasions of North Africa and Sicily he was the assistant division commander of the 1st Infantry Division and accompanied the first wave of the assault

GRAVE OF THEODORE ROOSEVELT, JR.
AMERICAN BATTLE MONUMENTS COMMISSION, WASHINGTON, D.C.

troops carrying only a cane and a .45-caliber pistol. His enthusiasm and powerful voice, described as "a bellow only a few decibels higher than a moose call" were well known to the troops.

Roosevelt left the 1st Division in Sicily and made his third amphibious assault landing in the French invasion of Corsica. On D-day, attached to the 4th Infantry Division, he made his fourth assault landing, but only after repeated requests to the division commander. In his written request he argued that his experience would steady the troops "to know that I am with them," and in the event his words proved prophetic. Although the lead regiment of the division landed 1.8 kilometers (2,000 yards) south of the planned assault area, Roosevelt, landing in the first wave, set an example of coolness under fire and drew on his considerable amphibious experience to improvise an attack inland. His leadership contributed directly to the division's success on Utah Beach, and earned him a Medal of Honor. He remained the 4th Division's assistant division commander until he died of a heart attack on 12 July 1944, the day before Eisenhower had agreed to give him command of the 90th Infantry Division.

BIBLIOGRAPHY

Hamilton, Maxwell. "Junior In Name Only." *The Retired Officer* (June 1981): 28–32.
U.S. Department of the Army, Public Information Division. *The Medal of Honor of the United States Army.* 1948.

CLAYTON R. NEWELL

RÖSING, HANS RUDOLF

(1905–), German, commander of U-Boats West. Hans Rösing was born on 28 September 1905 in Wilhelmshaven. He joined the German Navy in 1924 and was promoted to lieutenant in October 1928. After serving in various posts he transferred to the U-boat force as it was being built up, and took command of *U 11* in September 1935. In December 1938 he was promoted to commander (*Korvettenkapitän*) and to chief officer of the *5th U-Boat Flotilla "Emsmann,"* and in January 1940 to chief of the *7th U-Boat Flotilla.* As commanding officer of *U 48,* Rösing sank twelve Allied merchant ships (60,702 gross register tons) in the Atlantic between June and August 1940. After serving as liaison officer to the commander of Italian submarines in Bordeaux, he briefly commanded the *3d U-Boat Flotilla* in 1941, and then in August became chief of the Central Division on the staff of the commander in chief of U-boats.

In July 1942 Rösing took over as commander of U-Boats West, in which post he remained until the war's end. One week before D-day he was promoted to captain. He commanded all of the submarines stationed in western France. On 6 June 1944 he sent seventeen U-boats from Brest, fourteen from Saint-Nazaire, four from La Pallice, and one from Lorient to engage the invading naval force. Most of his U-Boats had no snorkel and were unable to reach the invasion area.

Captured by the British, Rösing returned from prisoner-of-war internment in November 1946. He joined the West German navy in 1956 as head of the ship construction section on the naval command staff in Bonn. As flotilla admiral, in November 1957 he became commanding officer of the Naval Section Command North. He was promoted to rear admiral in April 1962 and made commander in chief of Military Sector I in Kiel. He retired in September 1965 and has since lived in Kiel.

[See also U-Boats.]

BIBLIOGRAPHY

Lohmann, Walter, and Hans H. Hildebrand. *Die deutsche Kriegsmarine 1939–1945*. 1956–1964.

Rohwer, Jürgen. *Axis Submarine Successes, 1939–1945*. 1983.

Rohwer, Jürgen, and Gerhard Hümmelchen. *Chronology of the War at Sea, 1939–1945*. Translated by Derek Masters. 1992.

GERHARD HÜMMELCHEN

ROYAL AUSTRALIAN AIR FORCE.

The major contribution made by the Royal Australian Air Force (RAAF) to D-day came from the 2,802 aircrew engaged in operations. About one-third of those aircrew flew with the ten RAAF squadrons in the United Kingdom, while the remainder served with Royal Air Force (RAF) units. All came under RAF control. Australian crews were employed predominantly in Bomber Command but also flew with Fighter, Coastal, and Transport Commands and the 2d Tactical Air Force. Aircraft types flown included Lancasters, Halifaxes, Mosquitos, Mitchells, Bostons, Wellingtons, Liberators, Stirlings, Beaufighters, Mustangs, Spitfires, Typhoons, Tempests, Sunderlands, and Dakotas.

RAAF units and pilots were involved in the full range of air warfare activities, from control of the air to strategic and tactical interdiction and support for surface forces. For example, of the 1,136 Bomber Command aircraft committed to the final preinvasion strikes on enemy shore batteries, 168 (14.8 percent) came from RAAF squadrons or were flown by RAAF pilots. No. 10 Squadron set a monthly record in June for a Sunderland unit, flying 92 sorties involving 1,146 hours on maritime patrols. During an attack on a German E-boat base at Le Havre, Squadron Leader D. J. Shannon (one of the heroes of the Dam Busters raid) shared the target-marking duties with Wing Commander Leonard Cheshire. RAAF Mosquito night fighter crews enjoyed considerable success against Luftwaffe bombers. During the actual landings, thirteen Halifaxes from No. 466 Squadron bombed an enemy battery at Maisy, which threatened both Omaha and Utah beaches, while twenty-eight Lancasters from Nos. 463 and 467 squadrons were part of a force that attacked the Pointe du Hoc battery on the shore of Omaha Beach.

The Australian involvement was not limited to combat operations. A small but useful input to the planning of Operation OVERLORD was made by men like the noted air power scholar Air Commodore E. G. Kingston-McCloughery, who was chairman of the Allied Expeditionary Air Force (AEAF) Bombing Committee, and Air Commodore F. M. Bladin, who planned airborne operations with No. 38 Group RAF.

BIBLIOGRAPHY

Herington, John. *Air Power over Europe, 1944–1945*. 1963.

McCarthy, John. *A Last Call of Empire: Australian Aircrew, Britain and the Empire Air Training Scheme*. 1988.

ALAN STEPHENS

ROYAL CANADIAN AIR FORCE.

At the end of May 1944 the RCAF Overseas consisted of forty-one squadrons and 53,816 personnel, of which some 24,000 air and ground crews were on duty with Royal Air Force (RAF) units. The bulk of the overseas force, thirty-seven squadrons, was dispersed throughout the British Isles. Its battle order on 6 June 1944 included fifteen squadrons in Bomber Command, eighteen in Second Tactical Air Force (Second TAF), four in Coastal Command, and two in Air Defence of Great Britain (ADGB), formerly Fighter Command.

Of the Canadian units directly involved in Operation OVERLORD, Six Group, the only non-British unit in RAF Bomber Command, had Halifax- and Lancaster-equipped squadrons located in Durham and Yorkshire counties, and with a strength of over 17,000 personnel, constituted the largest component of the RCAF Overseas. Four RCAF wings (Numbers 126, 127, and 144, each composed of three squadrons flying Spitfire Vs and IXs, and Number 143, with three Typhoon squadrons), together with three Mustang and Spitfire squadrons that made up Number Thirty-Nine Reconnaissance Wing, formed the backbone of Second TAF's 83d Composite Group. In addition, during OVERLORD's assault, one Beaufighter night-fighter squadron from Number Ten Group, and one Mosquito night-fighter unit from Number Eleven Group, ADGB, came under Second TAF's control for daylight operations, as did one Eleven Group Mosquito intruder squadron.

Supplementing and complementing the RCAF units designated for operations over and around the invasion area, four Canadian Coastal Command squadrons flying Albacores, Beaufighters, Cansos, Sunderlands, and Wellingtons from bases in Scotland, the Shetland Isles, and southwest England undertook "cork" patrols to bottle up German surface and underwater naval vessels and prevent them from interfering with the D-day convoys. Thus on 6 June RCAF Coastal Beaufighters attacked three destroyers that left Brest in an attempt to reach the English Channel and the Allied invasion fleet. Driven back by the Beaufighters, the same vessels again attempted to reach the Normandy area on 8–9 June only to be sighted by Coastal Command aircraft, intercepted by Allied naval forces, and sunk in concert with the Canadian Beaufighters.

Throughout the invasion week RCAF Sunderland anti-submarine patrols covered the Bay of Biscay's upper reaches and Channel approaches, while Cansos (the RCAF designation for Consolidated PBY5 Catalina flying boats), operating from Scotland, patrolled northern waters to prevent German naval units from leaving Norwegian ports for the North Sea and the English Channel. By D plus 4 Coastal Command aircraft, including RCAF planes, sighted thirty-eight and attacked twenty-five U-boats, many of which were heading for the invasion area. As a result of such peripheral operations, coupled with the Allied air umbrella over the invasion armada, convoys reached the Normandy beachheads with little interference.

On 5 and 6 June the bombers of Six Group, in direct support of the landings, carried out 230 sorties (out of a total of over 1,200 flown that day by Bomber Command) against the rail crossings at Coutances and Condé-sur-Noireau in the invasion area. Over the next week the group attacked such diversified targets as marshaling yards and strong points at Achères, Arras, Cambrai, Mayenne, Saint-Pol, Tours, and Rennes. Within three days of the landings, such Six Group and Bomber Command attacks virtually paralyzed German troop and supply movements over the railway network serving northern France.

Initially, losses during Six Group's operations were light, but they increased rapidly as German defenses improved. On 12–13 June, out of eighty-nine Six Group aircraft dispatched against the Arras marshaling yard, six fell to German night fighters, the Luftwaffe's most proficient element. In that operation Pilot Officer Andrew Charles Mynarski won the RCAF's second Victoria Cross. That same night nine out of ninety-two of the group's aircraft were downed attacking the Cambrai railway junction. Indeed, before Six Group reverted to its strategic role by attacking Sterkrade in Germany on 16–17 June and subsequent attacks upon V-1 Flying Bomb sites, out of a total of twenty-three aircraft lost during some 2,400 sorties flown that month, fifteen were downed between 5–6 and 12–13 June.

Over Normandy beachheads, while RCAF reconnaissance Mustangs and Spitfires covered the battle area on high and low photographic missions, the three Canadian fighter wings patrolled the invasion area between Cher-bourg and Le Havre. Despite little Luftwaffe opposition on D-day, the Canadian squadrons claimed thirteen enemy destroyed, one possibly destroyed, and four damaged against the loss of three Spitfires on 7 June. Simultaneously, RCAF Typhoons provided direct support to Allied ground forces with bombing and rocket attacks against German strong points, bridges, supply dumps, tanks, and motorized columns attempting to reach the beachheads. On 10 June Number 144 Wing's Spitfires began using the landing strip laid down at Sainte-Croix-sur-Mer as a refueling station, before transferring from England to the newly constructed forward operational bases in Normandy.

From the moment OVERLORD began, RCAF Beaufighter and Mosquito ADGB night-fighter squadrons patrolled over the Allied armadas from dusk to dawn. Initially, operations during the first four nights (5–8 June) resulted in few encounters with German aircraft, and only one was claimed as probably destroyed. That situation changed dramatically as the Luftwaffe's response to the Allied assault increased, and over the following four nights fifteen enemy aircraft were shot down before the Canadian squadrons were reassigned to Channel patrols in response to the V-1 Flying Bombs that began falling upon London on 13 June.

In contrast to the night fighters' carefully delineated operational sectors during OVERLORD, the RCAF intruder squadron's Mosquitos were allowed to range freely within a wide area encompassed by an arc stretching from Brest to Laon. There they strafed trains and motorized columns, attacked bridges, flak positions, and airdromes, and destroyed six aircraft in combat before also being redeployed to take part in the campaign against the V-1 "buzz bombs."

With the successful consolidation of the beachheads into a major bridgehead, RCAF squadrons, like their Allied counterparts, revised their roles in preparation for the battle for France. Their actions during the invasion's initial phase had contributed significantly to OVERLORD's success and confirmed Canada's major role in the creation and direction of the British Commonwealth Air Training Plan.

[See also Air Defence of Great Britain; Bomber Command; Coastal Command; 83d Composite Group; Mynarski, Andrew Charles; Second Tactical Air Force; Six Group.]

BIBLIOGRAPHY

Anon. The Fifth Year. Vol. 2 of The R.C.A.F. Overseas. 1945.

Carter, William. Anglo-Canadian Wartime Relations, 1939–1945: RAF Bomber Command and No. 6 (Canadian) Group. 1991.

Dunmore, Spencer, and William Carter. Reap the Whirlwind: The Untold Story of 6 Group, Canada's Bomber Force of World War II. 1991.

Webster, Charles, and Noble Frankland. The Strategic Air Offensive against Germany, 1939–1945. 4 vols. 1961.

WILLIAM RODNEY

ROYAL CANADIAN NAVY. For the invasion of Europe the Royal Canadian Navy (RCN) loaned the Admiralty 126 of its fighting ships, including 44 landing craft, about a third of its total strength, and 9,780 of its approximately 30,000 seagoing personnel. The size of this contribution was remarkable because the RCN, since its formation in May 1910, had survived twenty-five years of penury before a modest buildup in the late 1930s. In 1939 the fleet had consisted of six destroyers, five elderly minesweepers, and about 1,500 personnel. No other navy had expanded so rapidly in proportion to its prewar size (about sixtyfold).

Assigned to the Allied invasion fleet was the 31st Minesweeping Flotilla, consisting of ten Canadian Bangor-class minesweepers (HMCS *Caraquet, Blairmore, Cowichan, Fort William, Malpeque, Milltown, Minas, Wasaga, Bayfield, Mulgrave*) under Lt. Comdr. A. H. G. ("Tony") Storrs, RCNR. Six other "Bangors" scattered among the 4th (HMCS *Thunder*), 14th (HMCS *Georgian, Guysborough, Kenora,* and *Yegreville*), and 16th (HMCS *Kenso*) flotillas worked with the Western Task Force. All other Canadian ships formed part of the Eastern Task Force and the covering forces. An RCN beach commando unit trained for, but did not take part in, the D-day landings.

The LSI(M)s (Landing Ships, Infantry [Medium]) *Prince Henry* and *Prince David* carried fourteen LCAs (Landing Craft, Assault). Three Canadian flotillas of LCI(L)s (Landing Craft, Infantry [Large]) sailed from Southampton: the 260th and 262d with Force J, and the 264th, supplemented by three American LCIs, with Force G. All told, Canadian LCAs and LCI(L)s landed 5,396 troops, of whom about 63 percent were Canadian, the rest British. The V-class destroyers HMCS *Algonquin* and *Sioux* formed part of the gunfire support force.

The other ships directly assigned to the Eastern Task Force were fifteen corvettes escorting blockships, piers and barges, and assault forces destined for both Eastern and Western Task Force areas. On 31 May, sailing from Oban, Scotland, HMCS *Trentonian* and HMCS *Nasturtium* escorted the first section of "corncobs" (blockships to provide shelter from gales while the Mulberry harbors were being prepared). This section consisted of twenty-four ships bound for the eastern area; HMCS *Mayflower* and *Drumheller* took the next section of sixteen American ships to the western area; and HMCS *Rimouski* and *Louisbourg* took the remaining twenty ships, which were split between the two areas. HMCS *Camrose, Baddeck, Prescott, Alberni, Mimico, Lunenburg,* and *Calgary* provided additional escort to various tows from the south coast of England on 6, 7, and 8 June.

Covering forces on D-day included the Tribal-class destroyers *Haida* and *Huron* with the 10th Destroyer Flotilla on the western flank; five frigates with the 6th Escort Group (HMCS *Waskesiu, Outremont, Cape Breton, Grou,* and *Teme*), and six with the 9th Escort Group (HMCS *Matane, Swansea, Stormont, Port Colborne, St. John, Meon*), allocated to antisubmarine patrols 130 miles or so west of Land's End; five River-class destroyers with the 11th Escort Group (HMCS *Ottawa, Kootenay, Chaudiere, St. Laurent, Gatineau*), and four with the 12th Escort Group (HMCS *Qu'Appelle, Saskatchewan, Skeena, Restigouche*), allocated to inshore antisubmarine patrols; and two MTB flotillas, the 29th (six British Power Boat "shorts," stripped on this occasion of their torpedo tubes), and the 65th (seven Fairmile D's).

In the buildup that followed the landings, Canadian LCIs ferried 6,181 troops to Normandy between 6 and 18 June. Canadian corvettes continued to escort towed barges and piers, LSTs (Landing Ships, Tank), and transports. Another seven corvettes from Milford Haven, HMCS *Lindsay, Summerside, Moosejaw, Port Arthur, Woodstock, Regina,* and *Kitchener,* now contributed to the overall effort by escorting a series of coaster convoys to and from the assault areas. Of the remainder of the forces allocated to Operation NEPTUNE, *Haida,* Comdr. H. B. ("Harry") DeWolf, and *Huron,* Lt. Comdr. H. S. Rayner, particularly distinguished themselves on 9 June in the engagement with German surface forces off the Île de Batz.

Official Canadian naval opinion at the time was that "the RCN's invasion operations marked the culmination of the wartime growth of Canada's navy . . . representing the cream of the R.C.N." Great pride was taken in the ability to make a contribution "greater than that of all the other Allies combined," with the exception of the Royal Navy and the U.S. Navy. If that contribution was no more than 4 percent of the whole naval effort, it was because the RCN was continuing to carry on its "acknowledged role as guardian of the North Atlantic convoys." Postwar scholarship has shown that emphasis on the invasion operations was a calculated objective on the part of the Canadian naval establishment, achieved against some objections by the Admiralty, and to some degree at the expense of escort groups in the Western Local and Mid-Ocean Escort Forces. Whatever the merits of Canadian wartime naval policy, the battle honor "Normandy" is an important element of the Canadian naval tradition.

[*See also* Canada; Eastern Task Force; Western Task Force.]

BIBLIOGRAPHY

German, Tony. *The Sea Is at Our Gates: The History of the Canadian Navy.* 1990.
Law, C. A. *White Plumes Astern.* 1990.
Schull, Joseph. *The Far Distant Ships: An Official Account of Canadian Naval Operations in the Second World War.* Rev. ed., 1987.
Sclater, William. *Haida.* N.d. [1946].

W. A. B. DOUGLAS

ROYAL MARINE COMMANDOS. *See* Commandos; 1st Special Service Brigade; 4th Special Service Brigade.

RUGE, FRIEDRICH (1894–1985), German, vice admiral, *Army Group B*. Friedrich Otto Ruge was born on 24 December 1894 in Leipzig. He entered the Imperial Navy in April 1914, serving on torpedo boats and then as commander of a destroyer with the German squadron interned at Scapa Flow in 1919. In 1920 he entered the new German Navy, serving on minesweepers and later as an expert in the mine-testing command *(Sperrversuchskommando)*. Ruge's command of English enabled him to serve frequently as a liaison officer with visiting British and American warships. In the 1930s he served with the Baltic defense installations, then in 1938 became commander for minesweepers *(Führer der Minensuchboote)*.

At the outset of World War II Ruge, now a captain, saw combat with minesweepers first in the Gulf of Danzig, then in the April 1940 occupation of Denmark. He was posted to Paris in 1940, and in 1943, now a rear admiral, was sent to Italy to reorganize the protection of supply transports to North Africa. After the loss of Tunisia in 1943, Ruge became commander in chief of Germany's naval command in Italy, a post he held until 10 August 1943.

Ruge's next command was as admiral with *Army Group B* under Field Marshal Erwin Rommel, who was given command of German forces in Holland, Belgium, and northern France. As naval adviser Ruge concerned himself with the construction of coastal defense installations in preparation for the anticipated Allied invasion. To be closer to the probable landing zone, Rommel moved his headquarters from Fontainebleau to La Roche-Guyon, near Mantes on the Seine, in March 1944. Rommel and Ruge were unsuccessful in their efforts to persuade Adm. Theodor Krancke, commander of Naval Group Command West, to mine the Bay of the Seine—with far-reaching consequences. After Rommel's serious injury from strafing by a British fighter in July 1944, Ruge was transferred to Berlin, where he became chief of the Office for Naval Construction on 1 November 1944. His primary assignment was to facilitate production of the new Type XXI U-boat. He remained in this position until the end of the war, when he was interned by the British until November 1946.

Ruge then became a translator and English instructor and worked with the Naval Historical Team in Bremerhaven. In 1951 he published his first book, *Entscheidung im Pazifik* (Decision in the Pacific). With the creation of the West German navy, Ruge became head of Department VII (Navy) in the Defense Ministry in March 1956; after June 1957 he served as naval inspector. After retiring in 1961, he published numerous works on naval history and related subjects.

[*See also* Army Group B.]

BIBLIOGRAPHY

Ruge, Friedrich. *In vier Marinen*. 1979.
Ruge, Friedrich. *Rommel und die Invasion*. 1959.

GERHARD HÜMMELCHEN

FRIEDRICH RUGE.   Right, with Erwin Rommel.
BIBLIOTHEK FÜR ZEITGESCHICHTE, STUTTGART

RUNDSTEDT, GERD VON (1875–1953), German, field marshal, Commander in Chief West. Born into an ancient aristocratic Prussian family with a strong military tradition, Rundstedt showed early promise as a soldier and became a member of the General Staff. In World War I he served on both the Eastern and Western fronts and was chief of staff of an army corps at the end of the war, being twice recommended for Prussia's highest military award. After the war he was rapidly promoted; by the time Adolf Hitler came to power he was a general of infantry in charge of the prestigious *Group Command 1* based in Berlin, a post he held from 1932 to 1938. After taking part in the occupation of the Sudetenland in October 1938, he was retired at his own request.

In May 1939 Rundstedt was recalled to head a small staff charged with planning the invasion of Poland. After a brief spell as Commander in Chief East, he was appointed to command *Army Group A* for the invasion of France and the Low Countries. Promoted to field marshal in July 1940, he was given command of the ground forces in Hitler's planned invasion of Britain; when this was postponed, he became Oberbefehlshaber West (Commander in Chief West). He then commanded *Army Group South* in

GERD VON RUNDSTEDT.   Left, with Adolf Hitler.

the invasion of Russia, but was removed in December 1941 after a disagreement with Hitler.

Rundstedt was recalled to active duty in March 1942 as Commander in Chief West once more. Hitler's "divide and rule" policy, however, meant that Rundstedt , to his frustration, had direct authority only for defending the coast of occupied western Europe against invasion. A further problem was the low quality of troops assigned to him, with better formations being constantly moved to combat crises in other theaters. Matters improved when Hitler issued his Directive No. 51 in November 1943 and gave greater priority to the defense of the West. Even so, Rundstedt was suspicious of Erwin Rommel's appointment as commander in chief of *Army Group B,* since he did not consider him suited to such a high command. The main point of issue between the two was the location of the panzer reserves, but, in fact, the argument was more between Rommel and Leo Geyr von Schweppenburg, who commanded them under the umbrella of *Panzer Group West.* Although Rundstedt 's compromise solution of allotting some armor to Rommel to deploy close to the coast satisfied neither Rommel nor Geyr, Rundstedt and Rommel did make good their differences before the invasion took place.

Rundstedt kept an open mind regarding where the invasion would take place, believing that it could come anywhere between Boulogne and Normandy. Like the other German commanders, he thought that it would be mounted in May and was taken by surprise when OVERLORD began, having been about to set out from his headquarters in Paris on an inspection of the southwestern part of the Cotentin Peninsula. He was content to give Rommel a free hand over the conduct of operations and devoted much of D-day to persuading Armed Forces High Command (Oberkommando der Wehrmacht—OKW) to release *Panzer Group West* to him. He was not prepared, however, to allow Rommel to use the two panzer divisions positioned north of the Seine, for fear that the main invasion was still to come. It soon became clear to both Rundstedt and Rommel that, having failed to prevent the Allies from establishing a beachhead, it was imperative to withdraw from Normandy to a more defendable line. They argued this to Hitler at Margival, near Soissons, on 17 June, but Hitler refused to listen. Rundstedt continued to pressure OKW over withdrawing his forces, so much so that on 3 July he was replaced by the more pliable Field Marshal Hans Günther von Kluge.

Once more, Rundstedt 's retirement did not last long. Hitler ordered him to preside over the court of honor set

GERD VON RUNDSTEDT.

up after the July 1944 bomb plot and then, on 1 September, to resume as Commander in Chief West. As such he was theoretically responsible for the conduct of the Ardennes counteroffensive in December, but his involvement was minimal. Eventually, having conducted a skillful withdrawal to the Rhine, he was sacked for a third time, after the U.S. capture of the Remagen Bridge on 7 March 1945.

Held as a prisoner of war at war's end, Rundstedt was charged with war crimes in August 1948. Ill health prevented his being tried, and he was released in May 1949 to live out his years in poverty. Regarded by both Eisenhower and Montgomery as the best of the German commanders, Rundstedt was, in truth, well past his prime by 1942. Never an original thinker, as he was the first to admit, he was a pragmatist, possessed of much common sense, and a believer in decentralized command. His strength lay in his adherence to the Prussian military code of duty, honor, and loyalty, which also made him incapable of actively opposing Hitler and his regime.

BIBLIOGRAPHY

Blumentritt, Günther. *Von Rundstedt: The Soldier and the Man*. 1952.

Messenger, Charles. *The Last Prussian: A Biography of Field Marshal Gerd von Rundstedt, 1875–1953*. 1991.

CHARLES MESSENGER

S

SALMUTH, HANS VON (1888–1962), German, general, commander of the *Fifteenth Army.* Hans von Salmuth was born in Metz, then a German garrison town, on 29 November 1888. He entered the Imperial Army as an officer-cadet in 1907 and was commissioned second lieutenant in 1909. He served in World War I as a battalion executive officer and then as a General Staff officer. He was captain when he joined the Reichsheer, the 100,000-man army of the Weimar Republic, in 1919. Thereafter he alternated between field and General Staff assignments. A lieutenant general by 1940, he assumed command of the *XXX Corps* on 10 May 1941 and led it in the southern sector of the Eastern front.

Salmuth distinguished himself as an infantry commander on the Russian front, but also helped the SS massacre Soviet Jews, ordered that every civilian found with arms in his area of operation be shot immediately, transported slave laborers to Germany, authorized the execution by hanging of persons "strongly suspected" of sabotage, and ordered that ten hostages be shot for each German or Romanian solder killed by partisans. However, he disapproved of Hitler's infamous Commissars' Order (the order to shoot Stalin's political officers, even after they had surrendered) and instructed his subordinates not to obey it.

Salmuth led the *Second Army* in the disastrous Stalingrad campaign of 1942, and by launching a brilliant breakout against vastly superior Soviet forces successfully escaped encirclement with his battered army intact. For this success he was relieved of his command on 4 February 1943, for having violated Hitler's senseless orders against voluntarily giving up territory. This act earned the Nazis Salmuth's undying hatred.

Hitler and the Nazis then realized that they had made a mistake and allowed Salmuth to return to active duty on 1 August 1943 as commander of the *Fifteenth Army* in northern France. Salmuth disagreed with Field Marshal Erwin Rommel's theories of defense and especially with his massive minelaying program, and tended to agree with the defensive strategy advocated by Gerd von Rundstedt and Geyr von Schweppenburg. After a harsh dressing down by Rommel, however, he made significant progress in fortifying his zone of operations. But the Allies landed in the zone of the *Seventh Army,* so that Salmuth and his *Fifteenth Army* did not participate in the Normandy campaign.

Salmuth was relieved of his command on 25 August 1944, because of his anti-Nazi attitudes and the fact that he had been in contact with the conspirators who tried to kill Hitler on 20 July but had not reported them. He was tried as a war criminal by the U.S. Military Tribunal at Nuremberg and was sentenced to twenty years imprisonment in 1948. This sentence was commuted to twelve years in 1951, and Salmuth secured an early release in 1953. He retired to Wiesbaden and died in Heidelberg on 1 January 1962.

[*See also* Fifteenth Army.]

BIBLIOGRAPHY

Keilig, Wolf. *Die Generale des Heeres.* 1983.
Reitlinger, Gerald. *The Final Solution: The Attempt to Exterminate the Jews of Europe, 1939–1945.* 1953.
The High Command Case. Vols. 10 and 11 of *Trials of the War Criminals before the Nuremberg Military Tribunals.* 1951.

SAMUEL W. MITCHAM, JR.

SALVAGE AND FIREFIGHTING. The principal salvage officer for Operation NEPTUNE was Como. Thomas McKenzie, Royal Navy Reserve, a member of the staff of Adm. Bertram H. Ramsay, naval commander in chief of the Allied Expeditionary Force. McKenzie's deputy was Como. William A. Sullivan, U.S. Navy, who commanded Task Group 122.2, the Salvage and Firefighting Group. The joint British-American effort was in two stages: combat salvage and firefighting while the invasion was in progress, and harbor clearance in the aftermath. In fact, the firefighting requirements were minimal because the operation was markedly different from the Pacific theater, where Japanese aerial attacks on warships led to numerous shipboard fires. In Normandy the principal threat came from mines; the only ship that required substantial firefighting was the U.S. transport *Susan B. Anthony*, which sank rapidly after being mined on 7 June. A fleet tug kept the transport's fires under control long enough for the crew and troops to be rescued by small craft.

The salvage vessels under Commodore Sullivan's command included the British wreck dispersal vessels *Marie, Admiral Sir John Lawford, Thehana, Help,* and *Abigail;* the U.S. salvage vessels *Brant, Diver,* and *Swivel;* the U.S. auxiliary tugs *Pinto, Arikara, Kiowa,* and *Bannock;* and various small craft. The wreck dispersal vessels were equipped with explosives for breaking up obstacles, and some had horns on their bows so they could lift up and carry away sections of damaged ships.

During the assault itself, the salvage vessels were hampered by the firing of German guns ashore on the Normandy beaches. For example, the U.S. destroyer *Corry* was damaged when it struck a mine while in its shore bombardment station off Utah Beach on 6 June. German batteries, whose firing had contributed to its striking a mine, subjected the destroyer to a further shelling that prevented salvage vessels from rescuing it and it sank. On D-day itself more than a dozen LCTs (Landing Craft, Tank) and a number of LCIs (Landing Craft, Infantry) were also lost because of mines, and many other landing craft were damaged. Because of the shallowness of the water at the shoreline, fleet tugs were unable to effect rescues of damaged landing craft. Those craft that were able to retract and reach deeper water on their own received emergency repairs from the offshore tugs.

In some cases landing craft repair was accomplished on the beaches by shore party members, even while they were still under gunfire from the Germans. To aid in the work, Sullivan sent ashore salvage personnel and supplies so that makeshift repairs could be accomplished on the beach. Then the craft were removed beyond the range of enemy artillery, so more durable repairs could be accomplished alongside fleet tugs by shipboard personnel.

Once the salvage work was done during the invasion and its immediate aftermath, attention turned to moving cargo ashore on a regular basis. Artificial harbors were the initial solution, but they were so badly damaged by the severe storm that struck Normandy on 18 and 19 June that salvage workers had the additional problem of clearing away the wrecked harbor components.

With those cargo-handling facilities unavailable, the focus then shifted to the recently captured harbor at Cherbourg, and the clearance by the salvage teams of sufficient lanes for ships to enter and dock. The harbor was obstructed by ships and concrete barges that had been deliberately sunk by the Germans and by some four hundred mines. Eventually the mines were neutralized and wreckage cleared away by heavy-lift ships and by the refloating of wrecks with compressed air. Within two months after Cherbourg had been occupied, the Allies were able to move nine thousand tons of cargo a day through the port in support of their fast-moving armies ashore.

BIBLIOGRAPHY

Bartholomew, C. A. *Mud, Muscle, and Miracles: Marine Salvage in the United States Navy.* 1990.

Mason, John T. *The Atlantic War Remembered: An Oral History Collection.* 1990.

PAUL STILLWELL

S-BOATS. Called E-boats by the Allies, *Schnellboote* (or S-boats) were small, fast motor torpedo boats—as such, Germany's only offensive surface naval weapons that, under cover of night, could be a threat to Allied shipping. In mid-1944 the German Navy had little else to offer in the entire Western theater to counter the anticipated Allied invasion of western France. The disparity in strength was so enormous that the few destroyers, torpedo boats, and S-boats could at most interrupt the invasion for a few days, but not seriously jeopardize it.

Five flotillas of S-boats were available. Under the command of Capt. Rudolf Petersen, commander of *Schnellboote* in Schweningen, Germany, they were attached to Naval Group Command West in Paris, under Adm. Theodor Krancke:

> *8th Schnellboote Flotilla* (Ijmuiden, Holland), under Comdr. Felix Zymalkowski: *S 83, S 117, S 127, S 132.* (*S 64, S 67, S 85* had just been transferred to the S-boat Training Division.)
>
> *2d Schnellboote Flotilla* (Ostend, Belgium), under Comdr. Hermann Opdenhoff: *S 177, S178, S 179, S 181, S 189.* (*S 176, S 180, S 182, S 190* were not fully operational.)
>
> *4th Schnellboote Flotilla* (Boulogne, France), under Lt. Comdr. Kurt Fimmen: *S 169, S 171–175, S 187, S 188.*
>
> *5th Schnellboote Flotilla* (Cherbourg, France), under Lt. Comdr. Kurt Johannsen: *S 84, S 100, S 136, S 138, S 139, S 140, S 142.* (*S 112, S 143* were not fully operational.)
>
> *9th Schnellboote Flotilla* (Cherbourg, France), under Lt. Comdr. Götz Baron von Mirbach: *S 130, S 144, S 145, S 146, S 150, S 167, S 168.*

S 130.

S 132.

This came to thirty-one battle-ready and six conditionally battle-ready boats.

As the first reports of paratroop landings west of Cotentin and the Seine bight arrived in the early morning of 6 June 1944, at 0300 hours Group West ordered reconnaissance thrusts by the flotillas in the Channel zone, all of which reported nothing.

On the night of 6–7 June all available S-boats were deployed. The *5th Schnellboote Flotilla* lost *S 139* and *S 140* to mines. Nearly every night, as far as weather permitted, the S-boats went to sea. They nearly always encountered superior forces—destroyers, frigates, machine gun boats—that prevented most of them from even approaching the landing fleet and supply convoys. Their successes thus remained limited, although they were considerably exaggerated on the German side, thus giving the leadership the illusion of greater effectiveness. In June 1944 they torpedoed the U.S. destroyers *Meredith* (later sunk) and *Nelson*, as well as the British frigate *Halstead* and *LST 538*. They sank the landing craft *LCT 875, LCI 105, LST 376,* and *LST 314*; the freighters *Dungrange* (621 gross registered tons [GRT]), *Ashanti* (534 GRT), and *Brackenfield* (657 GRT), all carrying munitions and gasoline; the tugboats *Partridge* and *Sesame*; and *MGB 17, MTB 448,* and an element for an artificial harbor. Beyond this, the S-boats dropped sixty-eight mines. On the night of 22–23 June the boats *S 130, S 145,* and *S 168* transported artillery ammunition and twenty-four army officers from Saint-Malo to Cherbourg.

During these operations the flotillas lost the following boats: *S 139* and *S 140* to mines on 7 June; *S 136* in battle on 11 June; and *S 178, S 179,* and *S 189* to fighter-bombers on 13 June. A British air attack on Le Havre on the evening of 14 June was catastrophic; besides many other ships, three torpedo boats and fourteen S-boats were destroyed: *S 84, S 100, S 138, S 142–144, S 146, S 150, S 169, S 171–173, S 187,* and *S 188*. Thereafter, there were only thirteen battle-ready S-boats in the western zone. These were the only craft that might possibly reach the Seine bight. On 23 June, *S 190* was sunk in combat.

As reinforcement, on 26 June the *6th Schnellboote Flotilla* (Comdr. Albrecht Übermaier) arrived from the Baltic in Ijmuiden, on the Dutch coast, north of The Hague, with *S 29, S 76, S 90, S 91, S 97, S 114, S 132,* and *S 135*. By the end of June 1944 there were twenty-three S-boats in the west, of which only fifteen were fully battle-ready. But military conditions had further deteriorated against a superior adversary, and any further successes were only pinpricks incapable of affecting Allied operations. Nor was this changed by the use of new, more effective torpedoes such as T-5 (*Zaunkönig* or Wren) and FAT (*Flächenabsuchende Torpedos* or surface-seeking torpedoes). The supply of torpedoes could not keep pace with their use,

S 142.

S 29.

especially when, early on the morning of 6 July, the torpedo assembly and maintenance facility at Le Havre was blown up with forty-one assembled weapons, presumably as a result of sabotage.

In July 1944 the S-boats were able to torpedo only the British frigate *Trollope*. It was towed into port, but written off as a constructive total loss. One of the few successes of the period was achieved on 31 July at 0122 by *S 91, S 97,* and *S 114* of the *6th Schnellboote Flotilla* in an attack on a convoy east of Eastbourne, on the southeast coast of England. With six FAT, they sank the British freighter *Samwake* (7,219 GRT) and torpedoed four more ships totaling 26,699 gross registered tons.

Even the use of the long-range T-3D torpedoes did not improve the success of the S-boats. In engagements between 4 and 15 August 1944, the boats launched eighty-four T-3Ds, but hit only the old British cruiser *Frobisher,* the minesweeper *Vestal,* the freighter *Iddesleigh* (5,205 tons), and the tender *Albatross.*

[*See also* Petersen, Rudolf; Western Defense Force.]

BIBLIOGRAPHY

Rohwer, Jürgen, and Gerhard Hümmelchen. *Chronology of the War at Sea, 1939–1945.* Translated by Derek Masters. 1992.

GERHARD HÜMMELCHEN

SCHIMPF, RICHARD (1897–1972), German, major general, commander of the *3d Parachute Division.* Born 16 May 1897 in Eggenfelden, Bavaria, Schimpf entered the Bavarian army on 11 February 1915 as a cadet and was promoted thirteen months later to second lieutenant. Taken into the Reichswehr, he served until 1925 as a platoon commander. In 1925, now a first lieutenant, he was trained as a civilian pilot and entered general staff training, then still secret. From September 1929 to September 1930 he received training as a military pilot at Lipetsk, one of Germany's secret training centers in the Soviet Union. He then studied at the Berlin Technical University and graduated as an engineer. Promoted to captain, Schimpf was slated for a career in the new German air force (the Luftwaffe) to which he transferred in February 1935. He initially served as a reconnaissance squadron commander and, after promotion to major, as division chief of Air Photography and Geodetic Affairs in the Air Ministry. In 1937, now a lieutenant colonel, he served with the *Condor Legion* in the Spanish civil war.

On 1 September 1938 Schimpf was appointed to the Luftwaffe General Staff and entered World War II first as general staff officer and then as a colonel in the headquarters of the air force general attached to *Army Group A* in the Western theater. After another short engagement in the Air

RICHARD SCHIMPF.
BIBLIOTHEK FÜR ZEITGESCHICHTE, STUTTGART

Ministry, he served after November 1940 as chief of staff of the *4th Air Fleet* and, from February 1941 to September 1942, as chief of staff of several Luftwaffe territorial commands in the Eastern theater. In September 1942 he was named commander of the *21st Luftwaffe Field Division,* the former *Luftwaffe Division Meindl.* In October 1943, after becoming a major general, he was transferred to the commanders' reserve of the Luftwaffe High Command.

After February 1944 Schimpf commanded the *3d Parachute Division* and received favorable mention in the *Wehrmachtsbericht* (Daily Army Report) of 19 June for his performance during the Normandy Invasion. On 20 August 1944 he was seriously wounded in the Falaise pocket. His men brought him out in a repaired armored personnel carrier during the breakout of parts of the *3d* and *5th* parachute divisions. After his recovery, Schimpf returned to his division, which had been rebuilt in the Netherlands. On 8 March 1945 he surrendered the town of Bad Godesberg and the remnants of his division to the Americans to avoid further senseless destruction.

Schimpf was released from American captivity in December 1947, after which he worked as a civilian engineer. From October 1957 until his retirement in July 1962, he served as a major general in the Bundeswehr as commander of the III Territorial Defense District at Düsseldorf. After his retirement, he taught military technical affairs at the Technical University of Aachen. He died on 30 December 1972.

Richard Schimpf was one of the volunteer officers of World War I who were carefully trained by the Reichswehr in military, aeronautical, and technical capacities for the rapid construction of the German air force from 1935 to 1939. As a result of this training, Schimpf, who was awarded the Iron Cross, the German Cross in Gold, and the Knight's Cross over the years, succeeded as a pilot, as a general staff officer, and as a vital commander of a parachute infantry division.

[*See also* 3d Parachute Division.]

BIBLIOGRAPHY

Schimpf, Richard. Personnel records. Bundesarchiv-Militärarchiv, Freiburg, Germany.

Thomas, Franz, and Günter Wegmann. "Fallschirmjäger." Part 2 of *Die Ritterkreuzträger der deutschen Wehrmacht, 1939–1945.* 1986.

FLORIAN BERBERICH

SCHLIEBEN, KARL-WILHELM VON (1894–1964), German, major general commanding the *709th Static Division.*

Karl-Wilhelm von Schlieben, son of a Prussian army officer, was born in Eisenach on 30 October 1894. He enlisted in the *3d Berlin Foot Guard Regiment* at the outbreak of war in August 1914. (His father, a major, was killed in November.) Schlieben was promoted to lieutenant in early 1915. After the war he served in infantry and cavalry regiments as adjutant and squadron chief, and was made cavalry captain in 1929. During the 1930s he continued to serve as adjutant. From 1940 to 1942 he commanded a rifle regiment within a panzer division, being promoted to colonel in 1941. In 1943 he rose to brigadier general and was made commander of the *18th Panzer Division,* deployed in the central sector of the Eastern front.

In December 1943 Schlieben was given command of the *709th Static Division* in France. Promoted to major general in May 1944, he led this division (within the *LXXXIV Army Corps*) in heavy fighting on the Cotentin Peninsula. The inadequacies in matériel and personnel of these units soon became apparent. In light of increasing Anglo-American superiority, disagreements arose over the direction of German defense forces between the Commander in Chief West and *Army Group B* and the Wehrmacht High Command; Hitler himself intervened.

On 21 June 1944, the Führer made Schlieben "commandant and defender of Cherbourg," which had now been cut off by the Americans; Hitler enjoined him to follow the example set by Prussia's General Gneisenau, who during the War of Liberation against Napoleon had held out in the fort of Kolberg (1807–1808). But Schlieben had been given command of a makeshift combat group *(Group Schlieben)* made up of remnants of his own division, parts of the *91st Airborne Division,* the *243d* and *77th* infantry divisions, Reich Labor Service workers, overage antiaircraft personnel, and naval personnel. His battle-weary and underequipped troops were not up to this assignment, as Schlieben dutifully and repeatedly reported. Reinforcements proved as illusory as the buildup of an orderly defense. Ordered by Hitler to "fight to the last cartridge" so as to deny Cherbourg harbor to the Allies as a supply base, Schlieben initially rejected two demands to surrender from the commander of the U.S. VII Corps, Lt. Gen. J. Lawton Collins, before capitulating on 25–26 June. Taken prisoner by the Americans, he was interned in Great Britain until October 1947. Although Cherbourg harbor remained unusable by the Allies until September 1944, and his behavior was militarily correct under the hopeless circumstances, Schlieben was not spared criticism at the time. He died in Giessen on 18 June 1964.

[*See also* 709th Static Division.]

BIBLIOGRAPHY

Ose, Dieter. *Entscheidung im Westen: Der Oberbefehlshaber West und die Abwehr der alliierten Invasion.* Beiträge zur Militär- und Kriegsgeschichte. 1982.

GEORG MEYER
Translated from German by Amy Hackett

SCHMIDT, HANS (1895–?), German, major general, commander of the *275th Infantry Division.* Schmidt was born in Bayreuth on 14 March 1895. He entered the Imperial Army as a cadet in August 1914. Commissioned second lieutenant in the *7th Bavarian Infantry Regiment* in 1915, he fought on the Western front in World War I. He remained in the German army and was a major when Hitler came to power in 1933.

In October 1935, Schmidt was named commander of the *3d Battalion, 41st Infantry Regiment,* in Amberg. Promoted to lieutenant colonel at the beginning of 1938, he was given command of the *46th Replacement-Training Regiment* in his hometown of Bayreuth. Prior to the invasion of France, Schmidt was named commander of the *245th Infantry Regiment,* which was then forming in the Grafenwöhr Maneuver Area. He led this regiment (part of the *88th Infantry Division*) in the last stages of the Battle of France, but saw little or no action. He was promoted to full colonel in November 1940.

After the fall of France, the *245th Infantry* returned to northern Bavaria until February 1941, when it returned to France on garrison duty before being sent to the Eastern front. Schmidt led his regiment in the battles of Kharkov, Kursk (1942), and Voronezh, and took part in the drive on Stalingrad. He was named commander of the *68th Infantry Division* on 24 January 1943, though he was only a colonel. He was promoted to brigadier general on 1 April and to major general only six months later.

Schmidt proved to be an excellent divisional commander, but he could not prevent his division from being smashed in the retreats across southern Russia in 1943. After the battle for Kiev, the *68th Infantry* was down to battle-group strength. Schmidt, meanwhile, was returned to France, where he assumed command of the newly organized *275th Infantry Division* on 10 December 1943. He trained his division well. The mobile elements of the *275th* (dubbed *Battle Group Heinz*) fought very well in the Normandy campaign. Schmidt and the nonmotorized parts of the *275th,* however, did not arrive in Normandy until the second half of July, just in time to be overwhelmed in Operation COBRA, when the Americans finally broke the Normandy stalemate.

Schmidt escaped the Falaise encirclement with only 800 men. By 10 September he had been reinforced to a strength of 5,000 men: mostly former Luftwaffe personnel, security troops (older men), and local defense troops. Although severely wounded, Schmidt remained in command of his division and in the Huertgen Forest took full advantage of the excellent defensive terrain to decimate several U.S. divisions in heavy fighting between September and December 1944. Schmidt thereby prevented the Americans from disrupting Hitler's plans for launching the Ardennes offensive; however, Schmidt's own division was virtually wiped out in the process, and the general himself was again seriously wounded in the last days of the battle.

Schmidt resumed command of the *275th Infantry Division* during the last days of the war and fought his last battles in Czechoslovakia. Schmidt was an outstanding divisional commander with a talent for getting the most out of his troops, many of whom were considered marginal.

[*See also* 275th Infantry Division.]

BIBLIOGRAPHY

Keilig, Wolf. *Die Generale des Heeres.* 1983.
MacDonald, Charles B. *The Battle of the Huertgen Forest.* 1963.
MacDonald, Charles B. *The Siegfried Line Campaign.* U.S. Army in World War II: The European Theater of Operations. 1961.
U.S. Army. "Battle of Schmidt." Lesson 2 in *Winning the Land Battle: Introduction and Fundamentals.* 1977.

SAMUEL W. MITCHAM, JR.

SCHWEPPENBURG, LEO GEYR FREI-HERR VON. *See* Geyr, Leo.

SCOTTISH DIVISION. *See* 15th (Scottish) Infantry Division.

SCYLLA, HMS. A Dido-class light cruiser with a weight of 7,000 tons and a speed of 32 knots, *Scylla* was designed for antiaircraft and surface fire, with five dual-purpose twin 5.25-inch turrets. It was built by Scott of Greenock and completed in 1942. Owing to a shortage of 5.25-inch turrets it was completed with eight 4.5-inch guns, and was nicknamed the "Toothless Terror" from its underarmed appearance in contrast to other ships of its class. It had no dedicated surface fire control. *Scylla* served in Arctic and home waters in 1942 and in 1943 under Capt. I. W. Browning. In September 1943 it was at Salerno as part of Rear Adm. Philip Vian's Escort Carrier Task Force. It was refitted in October 1943–April 1944 as an escort carrier squadron flagship, with Type 650 missile-jamming equipment installed. Unlike other ships of its class, it had space for extra staff and communications facilities. Assigned as a flagship on 8 March 1944, *Scylla* was unsuitable for fire support but possessed good communications facilities. It hoisted Rear Admiral Vian's flag, Eastern Task Force, on 3 June.

On D-day *Scylla* had no specific bombardment target. Arriving off Ouistreham, it fired on shore positions at 0531, anchored one hour later, and ceased fire at 0729. After closing on Sword Beach it fired briefly on shore defenses there and later at Arromanches. Vian kept moving between Sword and Juno beaches. *Scylla* controlled night patrols against E-boats and air attack, acting as depot ship for the motor torpedo boats, normally from a position off Sword Beach. It suffered near misses from bombs on D-day, but was visited by Admiral Ramsay and General Eisenhower on D plus 1. On 22 June it used a Type 650 radio-jamming device to decoy a radio-guided bomb. Mined at 2256 on 23 June, while patrolling the northeast corner of the British Assault Area, it was badly damaged; towed to Portsmouth, it was never repaired. It was demolished in 1950.

[*See also* Eastern Task Force; Vian, Philip.]

BIBLIOGRAPHY

London. Public Record Office. Ship Log Books, HMS *Scylla,* ADM 53/120451.
Vian, Philip. *Action This Day.* 1960.

ANDREW LAMBERT

HMS *SCYLLA.*

IMPERIAL WAR MUSEUM

SEABEES. U.S. Navy Seabees—their name derived from "CBs," the abbreviation for "construction battalions"—played a pivotal role in the landings in Normandy, first clearing beach obstacles for the initial assault, then building artificial harbors and transporting men and equipment to the beaches.

The first Seabees ashore in Normandy were members of Naval Combat Demolition Units. They landed at H-hour and began blasting corridors through the beach obstacles so that the first assault wave could land. They performed this important mission under heavy German fire and suffered very high casualties.

Clearing beach obstacles was, however, only the begin-

ning of Seabee involvement in Normandy. Moving large numbers and amounts of troops, equipment, and supplies from transports and LSTs (Landing Ships, Tank) offshore to the beaches in a short period of time was critical to the success of the landings. To effect this goal, the Allies built great breakwaters and artificial harbors off the invasion beaches to provide protected anchorages for cargo ships, LSTs, and small craft. Multispan Whale bridges, pontoon Rhino ferries, sunken pontoon causeways, and LCTs (Landing Craft, Tank) were used to convey equipment, matériel, and troops ashore from vessels moored within the artificial harbors.

During the preparations for D-day, the Seabees were

SEABEE BULLDOZER.   On a Rhino ferry, off Normandy beaches on D-day.

responsible for constructing causeways, ferries, and all other assemblies and craft made of pontoons. On 5 June they manned these pontoon assemblies, as well as the artificial harbor Phoenix caissons, the pier heads, and Whale bridge trains while these facilities were being towed across the English Channel. On 6 and 7 June the Seabees arrived in strength and began installation of the artificial harbor facilities and pontoon causeways on Omaha and Utah beaches. Men and equipment began to move ashore almost immediately. By midnight 6 June, 175 vehicles had been unloaded from LSTs on Utah Beach. All this was done in the face of sporadic German air attacks and shelling by 88-mm guns.

The Seabee unit responsible for these far-shore activities was the 25th Naval Construction Regiment, commanded by Capt. Clyde Coryell, Civil Engineer Corps (CEC), USN. The regiment comprised Naval Construc-

tion Battalions 28, 69, 81, 108, 111, 114, and 146; Naval Construction Battalion (Special) 30; and Construction Battalion Detachment 1006. (The last two units were respectively a stevedore battalion and a pontoon-specialist detachment.) All told, nearly 10,000 Seabees were involved in supporting the Normandy landings.

Operations continued at breakneck speed until 19 June, when a gale struck the landing beaches. The storm raged for two days, destroying or severely damaging most of the artificial harbor structures and halting landing operations. Following the storm the Seabees immediately went to work, clearing the beaches of wrecked small craft and broached Rhino ferries. On 22 June, the first day after the storm, the Rhino ferries were back in operation on Utah Beach.

In addition to unloading 5,286 vehicles on Utah Beach and 16,000 vehicles on Omaha Beach, the Seabees also

MOVING TROOPS AND EQUIPMENT ON RHINO FERRIES. struction Regiment. Assembled and operated by Seabees from the 25th Naval Construction Regiment.
NATIONAL ARCHIVES

SEABEE BULLDOZER.   Building a sand causeway to the ramp of a Rhino ferry.   National Archives

constructed and operated a 6,000-man camp at Omaha Beach and a 1,500-man camp at Utah Beach. These camps primarily housed Seabees and other U.S. Navy personnel involved in beach operations.

Following the Normandy landings, Seabees of the 25th Regiment moved on to Cherbourg and Le Havre and had the ports there back in operation by mid-October 1944. Thus Navy Seabees not only played a critical role on Normandy beaches, but also reopened major French seaports to assure an uninterrupted flow of men and supplies for the advancing Allied armies.

BIBLIOGRAPHY

U.S. Navy, Bureau of Yards and Docks. *Building the Navy's Bases in World War II: History of the Bureau of Yards and Docks and Civil Engineer Corps, 1940–1946.* Vol. 2, 1947.

U.S. Navy. Citation and supporting documentation for award of the Navy Cross to Ensign Lawrence S. Karnowski, CEC, USNR, officer-in-charge of Naval Combat Demolition Unit 45.

U.S. Navy. Report of Activities of Twenty-Fifth U.S. Naval Construction Regiment (30 November 1944). Prepared by Lcdr. (later Capt.) Palmer W. Roberts, CEC, USN, executive officer of the 25th Naval Construction Regiment.

U.S. Navy. Report on the employment of Naval Combat Demolition Units in Operation NEPTUNE. Prepared by Maj. R. R. Fairbairn, Royal Engineers, and Lt. J. G. J. E. Martin, USNR, Eleventh Amphibious Group (received 20 July 1944).

Vincent A. Transano

II AIR CORPS. Subordinated to the *Third Air Force, II Air Corps (Fliegerkorps II)* controlled the ground attack and tactical reconnaissance units earmarked to support the German Army following D-day. Commanded by Brig.

FOCKE-WULFE FW 190F.   With four 50-kg (110-lb.) bombs under the wings.   COURTESY OF ALFRED PRICE

Gen. Alfred Bülowius, the corps moved from Italy to southern France in the spring of 1944 as part of anti-invasion preparations. Owing to the insatiable demands of the Eastern front, the expected reinforcement of fighter-bomber units failed to materialize, so that at the beginning of June 1944 *II Air Corps* possessed only two such groups with a total of 67 aircraft. Both units were equipped with the Focke-Wulf FW 190F, a fighter-bomber variant of the famous aircraft with additional armor around the cockpit, and provision to carry bomb racks under the fuselage and wings. The tactical reconnaissance force comprised a single group (*Gruppe*) with 42 Messerschmitt Bf 109s. In addition, the corps included two groups with fifty-two Junkers Ju 88 long-range fighters assigned to protect U-boats passing through the Bay of Biscay; these unwieldy machines were extremely vulnerable to attack if they encountered Allied single-seat fighters, however, and were withdrawn soon after D-day. The *II Air Corps* was also assigned several of the home defense fighter units that transferred from Germany to France after the invasion began, for use as fighter-bombers.

On the morning of D-day the fighter-bomber units began moving to forward bases within range of the landing area. What then happened is exemplified by the story of one of these units, *3d Group* of *Ground Attack Wing (Geschwader) 4*, initially with one squadron (*Staffel*) of Focke-Wulf FW 190s near Saint-Quentin and two in the south of France.

On the morning of D-day the headquarters unit of *3d Group* and two squadrons left for the assigned forward operating base at Laval and the remaining squadron left for Tours. As usual during rapid operational deployments of this type, each Focke-Wulf carried a mechanic in the rear fuselage to help get the aircraft ready for action as soon as possible after its arrival. To reduce the likelihood of their encountering enemy fighters, the aircraft flying from Saint-Quentin made a wide detour south of Paris and remained at low altitude. In spite of these precautions several Focke-Wulfs were intercepted by Mustangs and Thunderbolts, which shot down five of them, killing eight out of the ten men on board. Because the mechanic had no way of abandoning the aircraft in flight, pilots often stayed with their aircraft after it had been hit rather than bail out and leave the mechanic to face certain death.

During the late afternoon *3d Group* mounted three attacks against the landing area near the mouth of the Orne River, with a total of thirteen aircraft. Allied fighters drove off one raiding force, and the other two carried out fleeting attacks that allowed their pilots no time to assess the damage caused.

On D plus 1 the group sent twenty-four Focke-Wulfs to attack British troops coming ashore near the mouth of the Orne. Again, the defensive fighter patrols forced most of the German planes to jettison their bombs short of the target and abandon the attack. Also that morning, Mustangs attacked the airfield at Laval, shooting down one Focke-Wulf and destroying four more on the ground. That evening, Mustangs shot down another Focke-Wulf near the airfield.

With the influx of home defense fighter units from Germany, *II Air Corps* took control of about 150 of these aircraft for use as fighter-bombers. The pilots had little or no training for the specialized ground attack mission, however, and were able to achieve little.

On D plus 2, *3d Group* attempted to mount three separate operations against the British troops landing near Riva-Bella and Bénouville. Allied fighters caused one of the attacks to be abandoned, and the other two achieved no observable result; one pilot was lost. On D plus 3 an early morning attack on the beachhead had to be abandoned, but a dusk attack on troops coming ashore at Riva-Bella appeared to be more successful. That night a large force of RAF bombers struck the airfield at Laval, destroying several aircraft and cratering the runway; repairs took two days. Early on the 12th four of the surviving aircraft attempted a low-level attack on British troops coming ashore at Riva-Bella, but the fighter-bombers were intercepted on the way in and forced to jettison their bombs.

Later that day the group received orders to drop supply containers to German forces cut off at Douvres, north of Caen. As the Focke-Wulfs were about to take

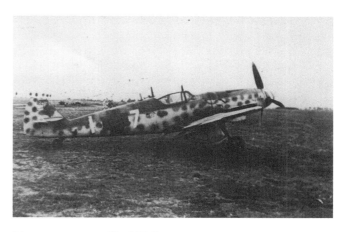

MESSERSCHMITT BF 109G. COURTESY OF ALFRED PRICE

off, eight Allied fighters strafed the airfield, destroying all four of them as well as two Messerschmitt Bf 109s that were airborne in the area. Following these losses the group suspended operations pending the arrival of replacement aircraft.

Throughout the Normandy campaign Allied army commanders enjoyed frequent and comprehensive aerial photographic coverage of the enemy-occupied areas in front of them. In sharp contrast, German field commanders often received no warning of the approach of Allied

JUNKERS JU 88S. ARCHIVE PHOTOS / DEUTSCHE PRESS

forces until the leading units came within view of their forward positions.

The sole German tactical reconnaissance unit was *Short-Range Reconnaissance Group 13 (Nahaufklärungsgruppe 13)*, with forty-two aircraft but only thirty-three qualified pilots on D-day. The unit was equipped with Messerschmitt Bf 109s modified to carry a vertical camera in the rear fuselage, and with the cannon armament removed and the gun ports faired over to increase their speed. Usually these aircraft operated in pairs, with one conducting the reconnaissance while the other kept watch for enemy fighters. Such was the strength of the Allied defenses, however, that the pilots invariably became involved in a grim battles for survival that left them little opportunity to carry out their primary role.

Following strong representations from the hard-pressed German army commanders for better protection from Allied bombers and fighter-bombers, on 12 June the *Third Air Force* headquarters ordered fighters from home defense units to cease fighter-bomber operations and revert to air defense. With that move, *II Air Corps* was disbanded and its units were incorporated into *II Fighter Corps*.

[See also Bülowius, Alfred.]

BIBLIOGRAPHY

Dierich, Wolfgang. *Die Verbände der Luftwaffe*. 1976.
Price, Alfred. *The Last Year of the Luftwaffe*. 1991.
III Gruppe, Schlachtgeschwader *4. War Diary*. 1944. Bundesarchiv-Militärarchiv, Freiburg, Germany.
United Kingdom. Air Ministry. *The Rise and Fall of the German Air Force, 1933 to 1945*. 1948.

ALFRED PRICE

2D ARMORED DIVISION. Activated at Fort Benning, Georgia, on 15 July 1940, the 2d Armored Division spent its early days developing and testing armored tactics and doctrines. It participated in army maneuvers in 1941, and in August 1942 trained for amphibious warfare off the Carolina coast. The division gained valuable combat experience in assault landing techniques during its participation in the invasions of North Africa and Sicily, and in late November 1943 arrived in England to begin training for the Normandy invasion.

The philosophy behind the 2d Armored Division's structure was signified by its nickname, "Hell on Wheels." Organized into two combat commands and the division reserve, the division was designed to couple massive firepower with the ability to maneuver quickly to wherever that firepower was needed. Total strength was 14,620 men.

On 7 June 1944, under the command of Maj. Gen. Edward H. Brooks, the division assembled at Southampton and Weymouth to begin loading onto landing craft for the trip across the English Channel. Assigned to V Corps, the division was to be one of the early follow-up divisions onto Omaha Beach to assist in expanding the beachhead once the leading assault divisions had assured an Allied foothold. It was the first armored division to land in France.

A small advance party of the division arrived on Omaha Beach on 7 June, one day before the bulk of the division sailed from England. The Channel crossing for the main force went fairly well, although one LST (Landing Ship, Tank) was sunk by a mine, costing the division thirty-one tanks, several other vehicles, and the lives of seven soldiers.

Arriving off Omaha Beach about midday 9 June, the main body of the division began disembarking immediately. Because it arrived at an established beachhead, the 2d Armored Division's unloading operations went very smoothly. After being dewaterproofed and otherwise prepared for combat, the vehicles were moved to an assembly area near Mosles.

As the division landed, tactical missions were assigned to some of its units. By the afternoon of 11 June the 3d Battalion, 41st Armored Infantry, had assisted the 29th Infantry Division in securing a bridgehead over the Vire River near Auville-sur-le-Vey, and divisional reconnaissance elements had established contact with friendly forces on the corps flanks.

On 12 June the division completed its disembarkation and in the first hours of the 13th, received its most important mission yet. U.S. First Army had intelligence indicating the Germans were planning an armored counterattack to drive a wedge between the V Corps and VII Corps, which were tenuously linked between the towns of Carentan and Isigny. Elements of Combat Command A were sent to assist in defending against this counterattack, which was expected to occur near dawn.

At 0630, as these units were preparing to launch a preemptive attack south from Auville, their mission was suddenly changed. The Germans had struck Carentan, a few kilometers west of Auville. The 101st Airborne Division, which was holding Carentan a few kilometers west of Auville, was being counterattacked by German armor of the *17th SS Panzer Grenadier Division* and was ill equipped to counter the tanks. Combat Command A raced toward Carentan to assist the paratroopers. Unaware that U.S. armor was in the area, the Germans were taken by surprise and, despite determined resistance, were repulsed with over 500 killed. The 2d Armored Division dead numbered only two officers and six enlisted men. On the 14th the battle continued with similar results. Despite the difficulties of operating armored vehicles among the hedgerows in the area, Carentan was cleared and the link between the V Corps and VII Corps beachheads was solidified.

2d Armored Division
Maj. Gen. Edward H. Brooks

Combat Command A

Headquarters, Combat Command A
66th Armor
41st Armored Infantry (-)
14th Armored Field Artillery Battalion
Company A, 17th Armored Engineer Battalion
Company A, 48th Armored Medical Battalion
Company A, 2d Armored Ordnance Maintenance Battalion
Detachment, Company B, 2d Armored Division Supply Battalion

Combat Command B

Headquarters, Combat Command B
67th Armor
1st Battalion, 41st Armored Infantry
78th Armored Field Artillery Battalion
Company B, 17th Armored Engineer Battalion
Company B, 48th Armored Medical Battalion
Company B, 2d Armored Ordnance Maintenance Battalion
Detachment, Company A, 2d Armored Division Supply Battalion

Division Reserve

Headquarters Company, 2d Armored Division
Headquarters, Division Artillery
195th Antiaircraft Artillery Automatic Weapons Battalion
92d Armored Field Artillery Battalion (-)
702d Tank Destroyer Battalion
82d Reconnaissance Battalion
142d Armored Signal Company
Detachment F, 165th Signal Photo Company
Military Police Platoon, Service Company
1st Platoon, 608th Quartermaster Company
Maintenance, medical, engineer, and supply battalions (-)

(-) Elements of the unit detached or not present

On 15 June elements of the division became engaged in a fierce battle along the Carentan-Périers road. Once more German losses far outnumbered those of the 2d Armored Division. As the division's reputation spread, "Hell on Wheels" became known within the Wehrmacht as "Roosevelt's Butchers."

Late on the 15th the division was placed in reserve and for several days executed local security missions around Balleroy and performed maintenance on its tanks and equipment. As German resistance faltered all along the line during the following weeks, the 2d Armored Division raced across France. Later it spearheaded the drive into Germany and received the distinction of being the first U.S. division to enter Berlin.

[*See also* Brooks, Edward H.]

BIBLIOGRAPHY

Houston, Donald E. *Hell on Wheels: The 2d Armored Division.* 1977.
Trahan, E. A., ed. *A History of the Second United States Armored Division, 1940–1946.* 1946.
Wilson, John B. *Armies, Corps, Divisions, and Separate Brigades.* 1987.

EDWARD N. BEDESSEM

SECOND ARMY. The British Second Army, commanded by Lt. Gen. Miles C. Dempsey, formed the left flank of the 21st Army Group with the D-day tasks of capturing the landing beaches Gold, Juno, and Sword, and then driving inland to cross the Bayeux-Caen road and occupy both towns. At the eastern end of its perimeter it was to attempt to reach Cabourg and the line of the Dives River as far south as Bures, and at the western end, to link with the U.S. First Army at Port-en-Bessin.

Although the Second Army did not reach the main objectives of Caen on the left or the link with Omaha Beach on the right by nightfall, nevertheless considerable gains had been won. The specialized armor of the 79th Armoured Division had cleared nineteen lanes across Gold and Juno beaches and three across Sword Beach during the first five hours; through these had flooded the Sherman tanks of five British and Canadian armored brigades, supported by the infantry of four divisions.

On the eastern flank two brigades of the British 6th Airborne Division had captured vital bridges over the Orne River and the Caen Canal, where within hours they were joined by commando units that had landed around Ouistrehem. On the western flank Royal Marine Commandos had reached the Port-en-Bessin–Bayeux road. Between them, the XXX Corps across Gold Beach and the I Corps across Juno had by nightfall on D-day established a beachhead nineteen kilometers (twelve miles)

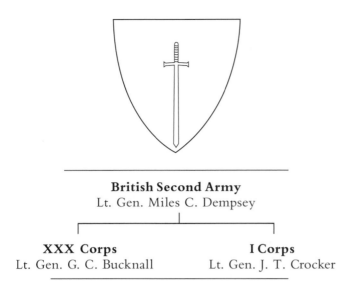

British Second Army
Lt. Gen. Miles C. Dempsey

XXX Corps
Lt. Gen. G. C. Bucknall

I Corps
Lt. Gen. J. T. Crocker

wide on the coast and in places eight kilometers (five miles) deep, with the Sword beachhead to the east, nine kilometers by seven. Forward units on Juno and Sword were some seven kilometers short of Caen.

All bridgeheads were linked by the evening of 10 June. By this time it was becoming evident that the Germans' main intentions were to contain the eastern end of the perimeter until substantial reinforcements could arrive, at the same time holding fast to the vital road and communication center of Caen.

This situation, however, did not unduly affect the overall plan. In order to tie down the German forces, especially panzer formations, in this area to allow the U.S. First Army time and space in which to break out across the Cotentin Peninsula and capture Cherbourg, the Second Army now began a series of furious attacks. Involved were not only the four infantry divisions and their supporting armor that had come ashore on D-day but also the 7th Armoured Division, the 51st (Highland) Infantry Division, and the 49th Infantry Division, all of which had followed during the first week. Moreover, VIII Corps began arriving on 15 June, its leading formation the 11th Armoured Division.

There was little attempt by these forces to gain ground, though the 7th Armoured Division did drive south and into Villers-Bocage, but they attained their objective of pinning down four panzer divisions and their supporting German infantry east of Caumont, away from the inter-army boundary and the vital launching area for the U.S. First Army breakout. Plans had been laid for a heavy Second Army attack actually to capture Caen on D plus 12, but furious gales unexpectedly raged in the Channel and severely damaged the vital prefabricated Mulberry harbors, thus disrupting all arrangements for the next five days.

[*See also* Dempsey, Miles C.; I Corps; XXX Corps.]

BIBLIOGRAPHY

Keegan, John. *Six Armies in Normandy.* 1982.
Montgomery of Alamein. *Normandy to the Baltic.* 1947.

BARRIE PIT

2D BOMBARDMENT DIVISION. The division was established on 13 September 1943 by Eighth Air Force General Order 149. This regularized an organization that had informally come into existence in late November 1942. Throughout its history the bombardment division, one of three in the Eighth Air Force, was the only one normally comprised of B-24 bombardment groups. It participated in most of the the major engagements of the Eighth Air Force, including the "Big Week" attack on German aircraft assembly plants, and the campaigns against the German synthetic oil industry and transportation system. During the OVERLORD campaign Maj. Gen. James P. Hodges commanded the division. By 6 June the division had fourteen bombardment groups (44 BG, 93 BG, 389 BG, 392 BG, 445 BG, 446 BG, 448 BG, 453 BG, 458 BG, 466 BG, 467 BG, 489 BG, 491 BG, 492 BG). On D-day the division attempted to bomb German defenses at the Allied invasion beaches in Normandy, but its bombardiers feared to drop too close to the invasion fleet; consequently, they released their bombs a few seconds late, causing them to land in areas beyond the German defenses. On 8 July (Operation CHARNWOOD) and 18 July (Operation GOODWOOD), the division participated in attacks on German frontline and rear positions opposite General Bernard L. Montgomery's 21st Army Group. Although partially successful, these raids did not enable the British forces to break through the German defenses. On 24–25 July the division participated in the Operation COBRA bombing near Saint-Lô. On both days a few units of the division dropped short, sending bombs into American troops and causing hundreds of casualties. Thirteen of its forty-five squadrons released too soon on 25 July. Nonetheless, the 25 July bombing shattered the German defenses, paving the way for the Allied breakout from the Normandy peninsula.

Although many B-24 crews admired their aircraft, some questioned it. This doubtful attitude may have affected the division's performance. During the first eight months of 1944, Eighth Air Force records reveal that the 2d Bombardment Division consistently finished last in bombing accuracy. It also suffered a higher loss rate to flak, because of the lower combat altitude of the B-24 as compared to the B-17. Possible poor morale revealed itself in another statistic: in June and July 1944, seventy-eight Eighth Air Force bombers and crews interned themselves in Switzerland or Sweden. This represented a tiny fraction of all sorties, but the 2d Bombardment Division contributed forty-three of the crews, more than the other divisions combined. Shortly after COBRA, Hodges returned to Washington for a desk job on the air staff; he never received another combat assignment.

In August 1944 the Eighth Air Force reorganized by attaching its fighter groups directly to the bombardment divisions, which facilitated coordination of fighter escort and increased familiarization between specific bomber and fighter groups. This change resulted in the redesignation of the 2d Bombardment Division as the 2d Air Division.

[See also Eighth Air Force; Hodges, James P.]

BIBLIOGRAPHY

Davis, Richard. *Carl A. Spaatz and the Air War in Europe, 1940–1945.* 1993.
Freeman, Roger. *The Mighty Eighth War Diary.* 1981.

RICHARD G. DAVIS

2D COMPOSITE GROUP. 2 Group was formed in the late 1930s to operate the medium bomber squadrons of Bomber Command. Early in the war, equipped mainly with the Bristol Blenheim, it took part in all the campaigns in northwest Europe, including the Battle of France and the assault on the German invasion barges during the Battle of Britain. By mid-1943, when the group was transferred to the newly formed Second Tactical Air Force, its nine squadrons were operating Boston, Ventura, and Mitchell medium bombers. Since its prime task would be to contribute to OVERLORD, its commander, Air Vice Marshal Basil Embry, insisted on perfecting his crews' ability to strike accurately at precision targets such as factories, power stations, bridges, headquarters, radars, and gun positions. The group was also expanded and reequipped, and by June 1944 comprised six Mosquito squadrons, four Mitchell, and two Boston; French, Polish, Dutch, Australian, and New Zealand squadrons were included. All were based in Hampshire, Surrey, and Kent, and controlled from Headquarters 2 Group at Mongewell Park in Berkshire.

During the winter of 1943–1944 the group's capabilities had been developed mainly through attacks on German V-weapon sites and also in special raids on such targets as the Amiens prison and the Gestapo headquarters in The Hague. They then joined in the preinvasion Transportation Plan, bombing the French railways. The role allocated to them for D-day reflected not only their precision bombing skills but also their ability to operate at night. The operation order required all the Mosquito and Mitchell squadrons to seek to delay German road and rail movement on the night of 5–6 June: the Mosquitos were

to patrol over specific areas behind the British and American fronts and attack opportunity targets; the Mitchells were to bomb specific objectives. The Bostons, lacking radar navigational aids, were to provide smoke screens for the landing forces at first light.

All went according to plan on the invasion night, and after resting during the day 2 Group's squadrons were out in force again on the next two nights against German road traffic that was attempting to reach the battle area, and against point targets. Then bad weather intervened, limiting the offensive to rail communications. On 10 June, alerted by an Ultra decrypt, the Mitchell squadrons joined 83 Group's Typhoons in a highly successful attack on Gen. Leo Geyr von Schweppenburg's Panzer Group Headquarters south of Caen, killing among others the chief of staff. The night operations against road communications were then resumed, together with daylight attacks on German armored columns and fuel supplies. On 14 June, however, the opening of the German V-weapon campaign caused the medium bombers to be switched back to attacks on the launching sites.

For the rest of the war 2 Group's bombers, operating mainly from continental bases, continued to provide close support for the Allied armies, as well as being on call for the pinpoint attacks on special targets that had become their particular hallmark.

[See also Embry, Basil.]

BIBLIOGRAPHY

Bowyer, Michael J. F. *2 Group RAF—A Complete History.* 1974.
Wynn, Humphrey, and Susan Young. *Prelude to Overlord.* 1983.

HENRY PROBERT

II FIGHTER CORPS. Subordinated to the *Third Air Force, II Fighter Corps (Jagdkorps II)* controlled the activities of all single-seat day fighter units based in northern France operating in the fighter (as distinct from the fighter-bomber) role. On D-day it was commanded by Brig. Gen. Werner Junck. Initially this force comprised six groups (*Gruppen*) with 168 Messerschmitt Bf 109s and FW 190s, reinforced by more than 200 fighters from home air defense units by dusk on D plus 2, and a further hundred by D plus 4. In northern France, however, the home defense fighter units were launched into a type of battle for which they were quite unprepared. In Germany they had been accustomed to operating from well-stocked permanent airfields, with radar ground control to direct their activities. In France the fighter units often had to operate from forward landing grounds with minimal facilities and little or no radar assistance. The story of one of the home defense units, *1st Group (Gruppe) of Fighter Wing (Geschwader) 1,* illustrates their plight.

On the afternoon of D-day *1st Group* moved with thirty-one FW 190s to Le Mans, where it arrived on D plus 1. That day it flew two missions, escorting fighter-bombers attacking targets in the beachhead. Several Junkers Ju 52 transports had been allocated to *1st Group* to fly in key personnel and important items of equipment, but one of these aircraft was shot down by Allied fighters and all on board were killed. The road convoy carrying the rest of the ground staff would take a further three days to reach Le Mans.

On D plus 3 almost every serviceable aircraft of the group was fitted with a 250-kg (550-lb.) bomb for an attack on shipping off the coast (for these operations the unit operated under the control of *II Air Corps*). None of the pilots had previous experience in fighter-bomber operations, however, and from Allied records it is known that no ship was hit. All the Focke-Wulfs returned, though some had battle damage. A repeat operation on the following day was similarly unsuccessful. Yet the unit's luck held and again there were no losses, though one pilot suffered injuries when he made a belly landing on his return.

On the next day, 10 June, more than a hundred Royal Air Force heavy bombers attacked the airfield at Le Mans. The operations room, three hangers, and several buildings were demolished, and craters pockmarked the landing field. About half of *1st Group*'s Focke-Wulfs were destroyed or damaged. The survivors were flown to a field landing ground near Alençon.

On the evening of 13 June the group mounted a patrol in the Saint-Lô area with thirteen FW 190s and became embroiled in a dogfight with Thunderbolts. Two American fighters were claimed shot down, the group's first announced aerial victories during the campaign. But two German pilots were wounded and a third had to make a belly landing in his damaged fighter. On the 14th the groups flew two patrols to protect German troops without encountering Allied aircraft.

During a patrol on the following day, the 15th, the unit was again in action against Thunderbolts near Saint-Lô. This time it claimed the destruction of three American fighters and a small spotter plane (probably a Piper Cub). Three FW 190s were also shot down, however, and two of their pilots were killed.

On the 16th *1st Group* again tangled with Allied fighters near Caen, losing two aircraft shot down and one pilot killed. The unit claimed to have shot down six Spitfires during the action, but this finds no confirmation in Allied records. Probably their opponents came from the Australian No. 453 Squadron, which claimed two Me 109s shot down and two probably shot down in that area without loss to itself. The group lost two more pilots in combat against Thunderbolts near Argentan on the following day, bringing to nine the cumulative losses in pilots killed or wounded during the previous eight days, or more than one quarter of its strength on D-day. Replacement aircraft were easy to get but replacement pilots were not, and when the latter arrived at frontline units they were usually woefully undertrained for fighter-to-fighter combat.

JUNKERS JU 52.

The problems facing *1st Group* were repeated in many of the units sent to reinforce *II Fighter Corps* following D-day. Some suffered heavier losses, a few escaped more lightly, but the force as a whole was steadily worn away. Although the German fighter pilots fought bravely and sometimes with success over Normandy, they were quite unable to provide adequate air protection for sorely tried German ground forces. The latter had an aircraft recognition catchphrase that illustrated their plight: "If the aircraft above us were camouflaged, they were British. If they were silver, they were American. And if they weren't there at all, they were German!"

[*See also* Junck, Werner.]

BIBLIOGRAPHY

Mombeek, Eric. *The History of Jagdgeschwader 1*. 1992.
Price, Alfred. *The Last Year of the Luftwaffe*. 1991.
United Kingdom. Air Ministry. *The Rise and Fall of the German Air Force, 1933 to 1945*. 1948.

ALFRED PRICE

2D INFANTRY DIVISION. The 2d Infantry Division was among the oldest divisional organizations in the U.S. Army. The division was organized during World War I in France where, with its famous Marine Brigade, it forged an outstanding combat record. During the late 1930s it was used to develop the characteristic American triangular division organization used in World War II. The division trained at Fort Sam Houston, Texas, and Camp McCoy, Wisconsin, and in October 1943 sailed for Northern Ireland. From May 1942 until the end of hostilities in Europe it was commanded by Maj. Gen. Walter M.

HEADING INLAND.   Men of the 2d Infantry Division move out from Omaha Beach on D-day.

THE ROBERT HUNT LIBRARY, LONDON

2d Infantry Division
Maj. Gen. Walter M. Robertson

Organic Combat Elements

9th Infantry Regiment
23d Infantry Regiment
38th Infantry Regiment
12th Field Artillery
15th Field Artillery
37th Field Artillery
38th Field Artillery

Important Divisional Troops

2d Combat Engineers
2d Reconnaissance Troop
2d Medical Battalion
2d Signal Company

Significant Attached Units

612th Tank Destroyer Battalion
635th Tank Destroyer Battalion
741st Tank Battalion
747th Tank Battalion

Robertson. Assigned to the V Corps of the First Army, the 2d Division was selected along with the 2d Armored Division to support the 1st and 29th divisions in the assault on Omaha Beach.

The division embarked for Normandy from ports on the Bristol Channel and began to unload on D plus 2. The 9th Infantry Regiment (Col. Chester J. Hirschfelder) landed on the evening of 7 June. As it came ashore it was ordered to clean up pockets of enemy resistance near the beach. It was followed by the 38th Infantry (Col. Walter A. Elliot) and the 23d Infantry (Col. Hurley E. Fuller), and by the evening of 8 June the division had most of its

infantry strength ashore. On the morning of 9 June the division, still without all its ancillary units, received its baptism by fire. With the 15th and 38th field artillery battalions in support, it was inserted on a five-thousand-yard front to the north of the little French village of Trévières between the 1st and 29th divisions to secure the remaining D-day objectives and press inland.

Shortly after noon, the 9th (on the left) and the 38th Infantry Regiment (on the right) launched an attack to envelop Trévières and capture the critical high ground around the Cerisy Forest. Supported by armor from the 747th Tank Battalion and self-propelled guns from the 635th Tank Destroyer Battalion, the attack began shortly after noon. On the left, the 9th attempted to cut the road from Trévières to Rubercy. German fire slowed its 1st Battalion when it attempted to cross the Aure River. Its 2d Battalion did not reach the line of departure until dark. Held up by fire from its own artillery, which inflicted heavy losses, it finally reached the Trévières-Rubercy road at 2400 on 9 June. The 3d Battalion met resistance at Haut-Hamea but was approaching Rubercy by 2300.

On the right, the 39th Infantry Regiment attempted to flank Trévières, and by 2200 its 2d Battalion was fighting in the streets of the town. Its 3d Battalion, supported by accurate artillery fire, got around the town toward dawn, and on the morning of 10 June, German resistance began to give way. By 0845 the division was pressing toward the Cerisy Forest. The forest was virtually undefended, and the division secured most of its objectives by 2200.

The next day, 11 June, was relatively quiet. On the left, the 9th organized its positions after its successful advance, while on the right, the 38th Infantry Regiment secured the crossroads at Haute-Litée. The 23d moved into reserve behind the 38th. On 12 June, the 9th, supporting the 1st Division around Caumont, secured the Litteau Ridge at the edge of the Cerisy Forest. There were only scattered German formations in front of them in the Caumont Gap, but no one knew that at that time.

Meanwhile, the 38th and 23d regiments, whose objective was the high ground called Hill 192 beyond the forest covering the road from Bayeux to Saint-Lô, ran into difficulty. The division had already met the noxious Norman bocage with its forbidding checkerboard hedgerows and sunken roads, and more of the same lay ahead. The 23d passed through the 38th, and its 1st Battalion crossed the Elle River, fighting slowly across the hedgerows toward the little town of Bérigny. Its 2d Battalion struck hard along the Bayeux–Saint-Lô road, while its 3d Battalion attacked through the Cerisy Forest. German observation posts on Hill 192 gave enemy forces substantial advantage, and the attack stalled after small gains. On the morning of 13 June the 38th replaced the 23d and pushed toward Hill 192. The attack again bogged down in the bocage, and at a little after noon on 13 June action was temporarily suspended.

On 16 June the division attacked Hill 192 again. The 9th took heavy casualties, and the 23d, equally hard hit, made little progress. The 38th managed to get within 630 meters (700 yards) of the crest of the hill, but losses were so great that the 2d Combat Engineer Battalion was committed to strengthen the regiment's depleted ranks. On the evening of 18 June the division, following orders from V Corps, suspended offensive operations as the thrust of the battle shifted toward the Cotentin Peninsula and Cherbourg.

During its first ten days of battle the 2d Division had proved itself. From 8 to 10 June, without all its support units, it pressed beyond most of its objectives. From 10 to 18 June it attacked stubbornly in the hedgerows approaching Hill 192. Although some opposing units that it encountered, the *716th Division,* for example, were not of high quality, the *352d Division,* the *30th Mobile Brigade,* and those elements of the *17th Panzer Grenadier Division* and the *3d Parachute Division* that it fought contained some of the best German troops in Normandy. During the battle the 2d Division suffered over sixteen hundred casualties and became, in the words of its commanding general, a "spearhead shock" force that would show its fortitude later at Brest, in the Monschau Corridor, and at Elseborn Ridge in the Ardennes.

[*See also* V Corps; Robertson, Walter M.]

BIBLIOGRAPHY

Combat History of the 2nd Infantry Division in World War II. 1946.

Harrison, Gordon A. *Cross-Channel Attack.* U.S. Army In World War II: The European Theater of Operations. 1951.

U.S. Army, Center of Military History. *Omaha Beachhead: 6 June–13 June 1944.* 1945. Facsimile reprint, 1989.

DANIEL R. BEAVER

2D PANZER DIVISION.

The *2d Panzer Division* was formed in Würzburg in 1935 as one of the very first panzer divisions under Col. Heinz Guderian. It took part in the invasion of Poland, was part of Guderian's armored force during the campaign in France, and fought briefly in Greece before seeing action on the Eastern front from October 1941 until December 1943. Early in 1944 it was transferred to France for replenishment, and was allotted an area around Amiens. In February 1944 Maj. Gen. Heinrich von Lüttwitz assumed command. The division was to be a part of *Army Group B*'s reserve, but a reserve that Rommel could not deploy without prior permission from the Army High Command (Oberkommando des Heeres—OKH).

It has been alleged that the division was held in readiness in order to assist with the planned putsch against Hitler, its purported role being to crush any Nazi resistance to the overthrow in Paris. The assumption is that without this unofficial task the division would have been deployed farther west, enabling it to reach the invasion beaches sooner. However, as the German commanders were never sure about where the invasion would be launched and could therefore not deploy their forces in advance anyway, this allegation must be dismissed as an intended slight against those officers who sought to overthrow Hitler.

In June 1944 the division consisted of two armored infantry regiments (*2d* and *304th* panzer grenadier regiments as well as one tank regiment (the *3d Panzer Regiment*) with two battalions, one equipped with Panzer IV tanks, the other with Panzer V (Panthers). They were supported by the *2d Armored Reconnaissance Battalion, 74th Artillery Regiment,* an army air defense battalion, an engineer battalion, and the usual divisional supply units.

It took until 9 June 1944 for the division's marching orders to arrive. The wheeled components were divided into two separate columns of about equal strength, each centered around an armored infantry regiment. All tracked vehicles were supposed to be moved by rail. Since all bridges across the Seine below Paris had been destroyed by Allied air raids, the division had to detour through Paris, divided up into single units of no more than company size to escape air attacks. Despite all these hindrances, the advance elements of the armored reconnaissance battalion reached the invasion front early on 12 June. Still without tanks, the division was to close the gap between the *3d Parachute Division* on its left and the *Panzer Lehr Division* on its right. Contact was established with the *Panzer Lehr Division* on the 13th. This was none too soon, for when the *2d Panzer Grenadier Regiment,* supported by a battalion of artillery, advanced on Villers-Bocage, it arrived just in time to repel a British attack that threatened to turn the *Panzer Lehr Division*'s left flank. The German units found that the dense bocage offered excellent opportunities for close-range antitank combat, thus offsetting their lack of tanks.

The division's tanks had had to be unloaded east of Paris and moved by road. This required great caution, owing to Allied aerial surveillance of all major roads, which led to further delay. Therefore it was still only the two armored infantry regiments that established a coherent, if thinly manned, front line south of Caumont. However, the division's left wing was still very much exposed, and a continuous front line with the *3d Parachute Division* was established only on 15 June. The *2d Panzer Division*'s tanks began to arrive on 18 June; prior to that, no division-sized attacks were planned. As a consequence, the front line remained fairly stable; the *2d Panzer Division* succeeded only in driving the Allies out of the Bois de Saint-Germain.

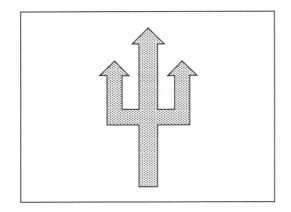

The *2d Panzer Division* was virtually annihilated during the fighting in Normandy in August. However, it was reconstituted in November with a new complement. It took part in the Ardennes offensive in December 1944 and then withdrew across the Rhine into central Germany, where it was taken prisoner by the Americans.

The division's deployment in Normandy is a good example of how many German units were thrown into the front line piecemeal. This resulted from two circumstances: uncertainty as to whether there would be another invasion, and Allied air supremacy.

[*See also* Lüttwitz, Heinrich von.]

BIBLIOGRAPHY

Steinzer, Franz. *Die 2. Panzer-Division 1935–1945: Bewaffnung, Einsätze, Männer.* 1977.
Strauss, Franz-Josef. *Geschichte der 2. (Wiener) Panzerdivision.* 1977.

WINFRIED HEINEMANN

II PARACHUTE CORPS. On Hitler's order in November 1939 Capt. Walter Koch formed from some units of the German parachute and air force the so-called *Glider Assault Group Koch,* which, landing with gliders on 10 May 1940, captured the Belgian fort Eben-Emael and three bridges over the Albert Canal. As a result, Koch's battalion-sized unit was enlarged to a glider assault regiment under Col. Eugen Meindl. Partly glider-borne and partly airborne, this regiment participated successfully in the battle of Crete in May 1941. Thereafter the regiment was never again employed as a whole; its four battalions served as cadres for new parachute infantry regiments.

The regiment's headquarters served on the Eastern front during the winter of 1941–1942. From it, during the following winter, was formed the headquarters of the *XIII Air Corps* (*XIII Fliegerkorps*), having as its mission to set up, equip, and train air force field divisions. This task

accomplished, *XIII Air Corps Headquarters* returned to the parachute forces under the name of *II Parachute Corps* (*II Fallschirmkorps*) and became responsible for organizing and training the *3d* and *5th* parachute divisions (*3* and *5 Fallschirmjägerdivision*) in northern France. Besides these two divisions, the following units belonged to II Parachute Corps:

> *Headquarters, 12th Parachute Artillery Command (Fallschirm-Artilleriekommandeur 12)*
> *12th Parachute Signal Battalion (Fallschirm-Luftnachrichtenabteilunq 12):* Lt. Col. Herbert Flesch
> *12th Parachute Reconnaissance Battalion (Fallschirmaufklärungsabteilung 12):* four companies, Capt. Bodo Göttsche
> *12th Parachute Assault Gun Brigade (Fallschirm-Sturmgeschützbrigade 12):* three companies, 27 assault guns, three 7.5-cm guns, three 10.5-cm howitzers, Capt. Günther Gersteuer
> *12th Parachute Machine-gun Battalion (Fallschirm-Maschinengewehrbataillon 12)*
> *Support and supply units (Fallschirm-Nachschubeinheiten 12)*
> *12th Parachute Training and Replacement Regiment (Fallschirmjäger-Ausbildungs und Ersatzregiment 12)*

The *12th Parachute Artillery Regiment (Fallschirm-Artillerieregiment 12)* and *12th Parachute Antiaircraft Artillery Regiment (Fallschirm-Flak-Abteilung 12),* with three battalions each, were set up in Germany but never joined *II Parachute Corps.* Commanding *II Parachute Corps* was Lt. Gen. Eugen Meindl. During the Allied invasion *II Parachute Corps* was under the tactical control of the *Seventh Army.*

On 6 June 1944 the *II Parachute Corps,* including the *3d Parachute Division,* was ordered to Normandy to counterattack a reported Allied air landing near Coutances. As soon as this report proved false, the *II Parachute Corps* was ordered to counterattack in the area of Saint-Lô with *3d Parachute Division,* along with the *352d Infantry Division* and (still absent) *17th SS Panzer Grenadier Division,* and push the invaders back to the Channel. With its headquarters at Les Cheris, 10 kilometers (6 miles) southeast of Avranches, the *II Parachute Corps* was under the tactical control of *LXXXIV Army Corps.*

Overwhelming Allied superiority did not allow a counterattack and forced *II Parachute Corps* onto the defensive. The units of *II Parachute Corps* were nearly annihilated in the Falaise pocket in August 1944.

In June 1944 the corps units of *II Parachute Corps* lost 65 dead, 258 wounded, and 25 missing, mostly in the *12th Parachute Reconnaissance Battalion.* While most of the survivors of the Falaise battle were taken prisoner, some succeeded in breaking out of the pocket and continued to resist the Allied invasion all the way to the West Wall (Siegfried Line) along Germany's western frontier. In

October 1944 *II Parachute Corps* was rebuilt, but never again was it brought into action as a whole. The reconstituted *3d* and *5th* parachute divisions were involved in the Battle of the Bulge. Their last remnants were captured in the Ruhr pocket in April 1945.

[*See also* 5th Parachute Division; Meindl, Eugen; 3d Parachute Division.]

BIBLIOGRAPHY

Blauensteiner, Ernst. "Normandy, 6th to 24th June 1944." U.S. Army, Historical Division, MS B-261.

Blauensteiner, Ernst. "II Parachute Corps." U.S. Army, Historical Division, MS B-240.

Winterstein, Ernst Martin, and Hans Jacobs. *General Meindl und seine Fallschirmjäger.* 1969.

FLORIAN BERBERICH

2D SS PANZER DIVISION "DAS REICH".

Logically, this division should have been numbered 1, because it was the first SS division to be created. But when the *Leibstandarte SS "Adolf Hitler"* regiment became a division, that bodyguard formation took the premier number. The genesis of the *2d SS Division* was the Nazi party's need to have absolutely loyal political formations available to support the national police forces in the event of a revolution against Hitler's government. Thus was created in October 1939 the motorized *SS Verfügungs Division,* concentrating paramilitary police units of the SS. Under that name it fought in the western and Balkan campaigns.

It was during the 1941–1942 winter battles around Moscow that the division, now named *"Das Reich",* demonstrated fighting qualities that raised it to the status of an elite unit. Those qualities were the product of the tough, realistic methods of battle training designed by Felix Steiner, first commander of the division's *"Deutschland"* regiment. His method of teaching and the standards he demanded inculcated all ranks with such a ruthless and aggressive spirit that a small unit of Steiner-trained men was considered equivalent in fighting power to a much larger-sized standard formation. Small wonder then that units of *"Das Reich" Division* were frequently detached from the main body and employed as battle groups to support a defense that was wavering or to spearhead a crucial offensive. As a consequence the *2d SS Division* was seldom able to fight as a complete body.

Its officers took Steiner's concepts with them when they were posted to other divisions, so that by 1944, most Waffen SS units fought according to those principles. Several officers of *"Das Reich"* went on to attain high-ranking positions in the Waffen SS. Two became army commanders, several rose to lead corps, and others either led *"Das Reich"* or some other SS division. The division comman-

der, Heinz Lammerding, was chief of staff of *Army Group "Vistula"* in 1945. At a lower level the division included men of such outstanding fighting ability as the tank ace Erich Barkmann.

In January 1944, the division, now named *2d SS Panzer Division "Das Reich",* was posted from Russia to Montauban in southern France to be re-formed after the heavy losses it had incurred. Between March 1944 and D-day it lost one hundred men killed or kidnapped and as many wounded in partisan attacks. On 6 June, *"Das Reich" Division* was brought to alarm status. Because its units had not yet received their full quota of vehicles, they commandeered civilian trucks to increase their mobility. The divisional order of battle was a panzer regiment, two panzer grenadier regiments—*"Der Führer"* and *"Deutschland"*—an artillery regiment, motorcycle and armored car battalions and the usual supporting services. Its strength as of 1 June 1944 was 20,184 men.

The first elements of *"Das Reich"* began their march from Toulouse in southern France to the invasion area on 7 June. Two things connected with that movement are notable. One is the "retaliatory measure" (*Vergeltungsmassnahme*) taken by one of its units against the village of Oradour-sur-Glane in reprisal for partisan activity. Over six hundred French civilians were killed. The second was the belief that partisan attacks played a significant part in delaying the division's advance and thus prevented its early participation in the beachhead battle. Otto Weidinger's history of *"Das Reich" Division* refutes this, pointing out that it went into the army reserve when it finally reached Normandy—implying that there was not the urgency that was claimed.

The first elements of the division reached the concentration area south of Domfront, having lost sixteen trucks to attacks by Allied fighter bombers. Although *"Das Reich"* had still not completed its grouping by 18 June, some of its units were detached to support neighboring formations, particularly the *3d Parachute Division* and the army's *2d Panzer Division.* The *2d SS Panzer Division "Das Reich",* therefore, did not operate as a complete formation in the

Normandy fighting between 6 and 18 June. In July a battle group action was fought at Saint-Lô, and in the first week of August, the division participated in the German counteroffensive at Mortain. Later that month it played a prominent part in mounting counterattacks to hold open the shoulders of the collapsing Falaise pocket so as to allow the trapped German units to escape across the Seine.

"Das Reich" participated in the Battle of the Bulge and in fighting in Hungary. The end of the war saw remnants of the division serving in eastern Germany, Austria, and Czechoslovakia.

[*See also* Lammerding, Heinz.]

BIBLIOGRAPHY

Ellis, L. F., et al. *The Battle of Normandy.* Vol. 1 of *Victory in the West.* 1962.
Weidinger, O. *Division "Das Reich".* 6 vols.
Weidinger, O. *Tulle and Oradour. A Franco-German Tragedy.* 1985.
Yerger, M. *Knights of Steel.* Vol. 1, *"Das Reich".* 1989.

JAMES LUCAS

SECOND TACTICAL AIR FORCE. The Royal Air Force (RAF) Second Tactical Air Force (TAF) was formed on 1 June 1943 in preparation for Operation OVERLORD, planned for May 1944. Its models were the Desert Air Force of 1941–1942 fame and the Anglo-American North African Tactical Air Force in Tunisia. It therefore had, from the first, a light- and medium-bomber ingredient, No. 2 Group of the RAF's Bomber Command.

Nevertheless, since the air contribution to OVERLORD was envisaged at that time as a chiefly fighter commitment, and fighters were to constitute the main strength of the new TAF, No. 2 Group initially formed part of Fighter Command under Air Marshal Trafford Leigh-Mallory, who was also designated as commander of the Allied Expeditionary Air Force (AEAF).

This organization was established in November 1943, its hard core being the two tactical air forces: the U.S. Ninth Air Force under Maj. Gen. Lewis H. Brereton, and Second TAF under Air Marshal Arthur Coningham. These two formations worked in close and profitable cooperation throughout the campaign in northwest Europe.

The composition of Second TAF for D-day, 6 June 1944, was as follows:

No. 2 Group, Bomber command: 12 squadrons
No. 83 Composite Group: four Royal Canadian Air Force (RCAF) reconnaissance squadrons; twenty-five

AIR AND GROUND CREWS.   Arthur Coningham addressing the Second Tactical Air Force, 1944.

IMPERIAL WAR MUSEUM

RAF, RCAF, Royal Australian Air Force (RAAF) fighter and fighter-bomber squadrons; five Air Observation Post squadrons; group total, 34 squadrons

No. 84 Composite Group: three RAF reconnaissance squadrons; twenty-six RAF, Royal New Zealand Air Force (RNZAF), Polish, Norwegian, Czech, Belgian, Free French air force squadrons; two Air Observation Post squadrons; group total, 31 squadrons

No. 85 Base Group: twelve RAF, RCAF, RNZAF day- and night-fighter squadrons; three RAF photo-reconnaissance squadrons; six and a half Fleet Air Arm and RAF air spotting pool squadrons; group total, $21^1/_2$ squadrons

Second TAF total, $98^1/_2$ squadrons (initial establishment, 1,576 aircraft)

The work of Second TAF began long before 6 June. The reconnaissance squadrons maintained an unceasing surveillance program at all levels from zero feet to 40,000, while disguising their true targets with innumerable deception flights. In the two weeks before D-day, one mobile field photographic section alone made over 120,000 prints for the army. The medium bombers made a vigorous contribution to Leigh-Mallory's Transportation Plan, directed against German communications. Rocket-firing Typhoons already had a great reputation as "train-busters" and took a leading part in attacking locomotives and rolling stock. Second TAF also won public acclaim by pinpoint attacks on headquarters and on Gestapo prisons holding French Resistance members. Less publicized but immensely important targets were radar stations and Luftwaffe airfields.

On D-day itself, supported by squadrons of the Air Defence of Great Britain, the tactical forces set up what has been called "virtually an air umbrella stretching from England to the beaches." From the first, the Allies enjoyed complete air superiority, deploying no fewer than 5,400 fighters—one of the most important single factors in the success of the invasion.

By nightfall on 6 June No. 83 Group's control center was ashore and operating night-fighter control over the beachhead. It was shortly followed by the Ninth Air Force fighter control squadron, the two centers operating, in Coningham's words, as "effective parts of a single machine thanks to excellent teamwork" between British and Americans. By 8 June two emergency landing strips had been created in the beachhead, and on 10 June No. 144 Wing became the first RAF unit to operate from French soil in the campaign.

It had been laid down in the plans that the early seizure of good airfield areas was a prime objective, but stubborn German ground resistance prevented this for some weeks. Yet the tactical air forces operated successfully from the first, harrying German reinforcements trying to approach the beachheads. On 7 June, Second TAF caught the crack *Panzer Lehr Division* moving by daylight and destroyed 130 trucks and tankers, 5 tanks, and 84 self-propelled guns and half-tracks before it even reached the battlefield. Three days later, rocket-firing Typhoons of No. 83 Group and Dutch Air Force and RAF Mitchells of No. 2 Group attacked the headquarters of *Panzer Group West,* uncamouflaged in an orchard. Maj. Gen. Sigismund-Hellmut Ritter und Elder von Dawans, the *Panzer Group's* chief of staff, was killed, and most of the officers were killed or wounded and the wireless cars destroyed, along with much of the transport.

The German Air Force had been rendered impotent, and soon the last offensive of the German Army would be smashed by the pulverizing power of "cab-ranks" of rocket-firing fighters and fighter-bombers poised over the panzers and displaying air history in the making. As the campaign in Normandy drew to an end, the pilots of the Second TAF and the Ninth Air Force turned a serious German defeat into an utter rout.

[*See also* Air Force, *article on* Allied Expeditionary Air Force; Close Air Support; Coningham, Arthur.]

BIBLIOGRAPHY

Ellis, L. F., et al. *The Battle of Normandy.* Vol. 1 of *Victory in the West.* 1962. Official history.

Saunders, Hilary St. G. *The Fight Is Won.* Vol. 3 of *The Royal Air Force, 1939–1945.* 1975. Official history.

Terraine, John. *A Time for Courage: The Royal Air Force in the European War, 1939–1945.* 1985.

Wilmot, Chester. *The Struggle for Europe.* 1954.

JOHN TERRAINE

711TH STATIC DIVISION. On D-day the *711th Division,* the most westerly of the formations of the German *Fifteenth Army,* was responsible for the defense of the Norman coast between the Dives River and Honfleur, a frontage of almost thirty miles. It had originally been formed in April 1941 in Germany as a Category 15 division, which meant that it was tailored for static defense in occupied Europe. As such, it lacked medium mortars and antitank and infantry guns, and was made up largely of Class II reservists, men born between 1901 and 1913 who had undergone no military training prior to the outbreak of war. Its order of battle consisted of the *731st* and *744th* infantry regiments, each with three battalions, and the *711th Artillery Battalion* (twelve 105-mm guns) and *711th Engineer* and *711th Signal* companies. In December 1941 the division moved to France. Initially deployed on the demarcation line between the occupied North and Vichy France, it later served on the Atlantic

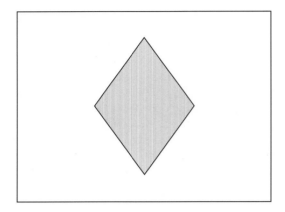

coast. In early 1943 it was switched to the sector that it would defend on D-day, and in April Gen. Josef Reichert became its commander, a position he would hold for the remainder of the war.

The division's task was to defeat any amphibious landing on the beaches themselves: to this end its battle positions consisted of concrete strong points, a forward line dominating the shoreline, a support line one mile inland, and a rear position some ten miles from the coast. In addition, strong points were constructed on the riverbanks within its sector. By the spring of 1944 the division's firepower had been considerably enhanced. Its artillery was reinforced by four four-gun batteries of French 105-mm howitzers, and it had also received two antitank and two mortar companies, as well as a number of 20-mm antiaircraft guns. In addition, the *1255th Coastal Artillery Battalion,* with 38 French 100-mm and 150-mm guns, was to be controlled by the division once a landing took place. A gradual transfer of men to the Eastern front in exchange for frostbite casualties also meant that some 20 percent of the manpower had seen combat; however, one complete battalion of the *731st Regiment* had been exchanged for one of ethnic Russians of doubtful loyalty.

The first indication that the invasion was about to take place came at 0100 on 6 June, when men of the British 6th Airborne Division dropped close to the divisional headquarters at Pont-l'Évêque, ten miles south of Deauville. Reichert promptly alerted his men, who began to occupy their strong points, and informed *LXXXI Corps* headquarters at Rouen and the *716th Division* on his left. He also sent out parties to hunt down invading paratroops. His prompt action was not, however, sufficient to prevent three bridges over the Dives, at Robehomme, Bures, and Troarn, from being destroyed by the paratroops. When daylight came the division's forward positions were subjected to naval bombardment, but casualties were few and damage slight. Once it became clear that there were no amphibious landings east of the Orne River, Reichert continued to clear his area of parties of

paratroops, a task which was completed by nightfall.

On the night of 6–7 June Reichert was told that he would receive a regiment from the *346th Division* on his right, and that he was to destroy the bridge over the Orne at Bénouville and prevent the Allies from advancing eastward. This regiment arrived on the afternoon of the 7th. In the meantime, the *711th Division* captured Varaville, on the Cabourg–Bénouville road, as a preliminary. The main attack was launched at 1600 hours, but got no further than Bréville because of mounting opposition. Thereafter, the remainder of the *346th Division,* supported by elements of the *21st Panzer Division,* and with the *744th Regiment* under command, were thrown against the bridgehead east of the Orne, again without success. The *711th Division* reverted to its original task of static defense and was not further involved in active operations. Even so, it had to hand over many of its supporting weapons and two infantry battalions, all of which suffered severely during the next few weeks.

In August 1944 the division was withdrawn to Holland to refit; in the autumn it took part in the battles around the Schelde River. In December it was transferred to the Eastern front. Eventually, in May 1945, the division was trapped in a pocket near Prague and forced to surrender to the Russians.

[*See also* Reichert, Josef.]

BIBLIOGRAPHY

Mitcham, Samuel. *Hitler's Legions: German Army Order of Battle, World War II.* 1985.

Reichert, Josef. "Anti-Invasion: The Normandy Battles from the Enemy Side." *Royal Armoured Corps Journal,* Spring 1950, 4–14.

CHARLES MESSENGER

709TH INFANTRY DIVISION.

The German *709th Infantry Division* was activated in Butzbach (Military District IX), in the 15th wave of mobilization on 2 May 1941. It initially consisted of two infantry regiments, the *729th* and *739th,* each of which had three battalions. The *729th* was formed from the *9th* and *15th* infantry replacement regiments (at Marburg and Kassel, respectively), while the *739th* was created from the *214th* and *251st* infantry replacement regiments (at Aschaffenburg and Friedberg). It also included the *669th Artillery Battalion* (three batteries) and the *709th Divisional Supply Unit.* Its soldiers were older troops from Hesse and Thuringia.

The *709th,* a static division, was transferred to Brittany in June 1941, where each regiment received a machine gun company. In December 1942 it was transferred to Normandy, where it became part of the *LXXXIV Corps* and the garrison for the city of Cherbourg. Its infantry regiments were concurrently redesignated grenadier regiments. It underwent several organizational changes in the last half of 1943. In October it received a third regiment, the *919th Grenadier,* which was not a static unit. Its artillery unit received a battalion each from the *242d* and *266th* artillery regiments and was upgraded and redesignated the *1709th Artillery Regiment* in December. The division also received a major influx of *Osttruppen* (Eastern troops), mainly from Soviet Georgia, and both the *729th* and *739th* grenadier regiments had four battalions by the beginning of 1944.

Although its structure changed considerably, the *709th Infantry Division* remained an overage unit. In 1944 its average soldier was 36 years old. Its personnel constantly changed and many of its men were only partially trained in 1944. The overall quality of the division in 1944 was considered to be lower than it had been in 1942.

Its commander on D-day was Lt. Gen. Karl Wilhelm von Schlieben, who had previously commanded the *18th Panzer Division* on the Eastern front. When the Allies landed, the *709th* was deployed along or near the eastern coast of the Cotentin Peninsula, from Cherbourg to Carentan. Only one of its 42 planned coastal defense positions was fully completed.

At 0200 on 6 June, the *III Battalion* of the *919th Grenadier Regiment* became heavily engaged with elements of the U.S. 101st Airborne Division east of Montebourg in one of the first engagements on D-day. At 0300, the *709th Division* was ordered to counterattack the American paratroopers. On the morning of D-day, the *II Battalion* of the *191st Artillery Regiment* (which had been attached to the *709th* for coastal defense purposes) was overrun and largely destroyed by the U.S. 506th Parachute Infantry Regiment; it was finished off by elements of the U.S. 4th Infantry Division later that day.

The *709th Division*'s response to the Allied airborne and seaborne landings was sluggish on the morning of D-day, largely because General Schlieben was attending the *Seventh Army*'s war games at Rennes when the invasion struck and could not get back to his headquarters near Valognes until noon. He was unable to contact all of his units, including the *I Battalion, 919th Grenadier Regiment,* which was fighting in the Utah Beach area. In addition, the division was scattered along fifty miles of coastline and had been pounded by the initial Allied bombardment. Schlieben personally directed a counterattack against the American paratroopers at Sainte-Mère-Église on the night of 6–7 June, using the assault gun and engineer battalions of his own division, part of the *6th Parachute Regiment,* the *100th Panzer Replacement Battalion,* and strong elements of the *91st Air Landing Division* (leaderless since the death of Gen. Wilhelm Falley), but time did not allow him to form up the disorganized *709th* and commit it to combat as a single unit. In addi-

709th Infantry Division

729th Grenadier Regiment
I, II, III, IV (East) Battalions

739th Grenadier Regiment
I (East) II, III, IV (East) Battalions

919th Grenadier Regiment
I, II, III Battalions

1709th Artillery Regiment
I, II, III Battalions

Divisional Troops
*2d Battalion, 191st Artillery Regiment**
709th Antitank Battalion
709th Engineer Battalion
709th Signal Company
709th Divisional Supply Unit

*On D-day this battalion, which was organic to the 91st Air Landing Division, was temporarily attached to the 709th Division to defend the coast near Sainte-Marie-du-Mont.

tion, many of the Eastern troops either ran away or surrendered as soon as the opportunity presented itself, confirming a remark Schlieben made earlier: "We are asking rather a lot if we expect Russians to fight in France for Germany against Americans" (Carell, *Invasion: They're Coming,* p. 91). German elements of the division, however, did perform credibly in the hedgerow fighting around Montebourg, where the U.S. VII Corps was checked for three days, and the *919th Grenadier Regiment* fought particularly well.

When Gen. J. Lawton Collins broke through farther south and cut the Cotentin Peninsula at its base, the *709th* was cut off at the Cherbourg fortifications, along with elements of three other divisions. It fell back into the fortress, but German resistance quickly deteriorated, and Schlieben surrendered the garrison on 30 June, earning Hitler's censure. The *709th Infantry Division* had ceased to exist.

[*See also* Schlieben, Karl Wilhelm von.]

BIBLIOGRAPHY

Breuer, William B. *Hitler's Fortress Cherbourg.* 1984.

Carell, Paul. *Invasion: They're Coming.* Translated by E. Osers. 1963. Paul Carell is the pseudonym used by Hans Karl Schmidt.

Tessin, Georg. *Verbände und Truppen der deutschen Wehrmacht und Waffen-SS im Zweiten Weltkrieg, 1939–1945.* Vol. 12, 1975.

U.S. Army Military Intelligence Service. "Order of Battle of the German Army, 1944." 1944.

SAMUEL W. MITCHAM, JR.

716TH INFANTRY DIVISION. The German *716th Infantry Division* was a static (nonmotorized) unit, formed in Bielefeld from previously existing replacement (*Ersatz*) units in Military District VI. Its soldiers were older men from the Rhineland and Westphalia. Initially it consisted of the *726th Infantry Regiment* (formed in Bielefeld from elements of the *166th Replacement Division*), the *736th Infantry Regiment* (formed from elements of the *156th Replacement Division* in Cologne), the *656th Artillery Battalion* (three batteries), and the *716th Divisional Supply Unit.* Initially, both infantry regiments had three battalions.

The division was activated on 2 May 1941. After performing coastal defense duties in Normandy, it was posted to Soissons and then Belgium before returning to the Caen sector of Normandy in June 1942, where it remained until D-day. The structure of the unit, however, changed considerably. Most of its older soldiers were replaced by younger men, many of them veterans who had been wounded on the Eastern front. In early 1944 it received an additional artillery battalion, *II/656th* (created in Military District VI), and the *656th Artillery Battalion* was upgraded and redesignated the *1716th Artillery Regiment.* It also received the *439th* and *642d East* battalions, made up of *Osttruppen* (Eastern troops) from the Soviet Union; they were attached to the *726th* and *736th Grenadier* (formerly infantry) regiments and acted as the fourth battalion for these units.

On 1 April 1943 the division's initial commander, Col. Otto Matterstock, was succeeded by Brig. Gen. Wilhelm Richter, who led it until September 1944. His primary mission was to defend a 21-mile-long coastal sector north of Caen from Allied amphibious attack. A reasonably good division could only be expected to hold six miles of frontage against a determined attack. Although he managed to construct forty to fifty fortified centers of resistance, General Richter complained that they were beaded along the coast like a string of pearls. The division's fortified sector had a hard crust but lacked depth beyond the coast.

A few weeks prior to D-day, the *I* and *III* battalions of the *726th Grenadier Regiment,* along with the regimental headquarters, were attached to the *352d Infantry Division.* The *II/726th Grenadier* became the divisional reserve, and the division's other five infantry battalions came under the command of Colonel Krug's *736th Grenadier Regiment.* The *441st East Battalion* (about 1,000 men) was attached to the division as well and was charged with the task of defending the strong point at La Rivière, near the *716th's* juncture with the *352d Infantry Division.* The units of the *716th Division* were partially intermixed with the forward elements of the *21st Panzer Division,* a condition that became much more pronounced as D-day progressed.

After engaging troops of the British 6th Airborne Division during the night of 5–6 June, the *716th Division* was struck by the full weight of the Allied air and sea bombardments on the morning of 6 June, during which the *1716th Artillery Regiment* was practically destroyed; then the division absorbed the brunt of the attacks of the British Second Army. Early in the day, the *441st East Battalion* collapsed completely, exposing Bayeux to British attack. The British did not immediately exploit the gap in the German lines, but the collapse of the *441st East* forced Gen. Erich Marcks, the commander of the *LXXXIV Corps,* to commit part of his reserve (*Battle Group Meyer,* which consisted of the *II/915th Infantry Regiment* and the *352d Füsilier Battalion* of the *352d Division*) prematurely and at the wrong location. Bayeux fell the next day, *Battle Group Meyer* was destroyed, and the left wing of the *716th Infantry Division* collapsed. By 10 June the gap in the German lines (called the Caumont Gap) was ten miles wide.

Meanwhile, on Richter's right flank, the grenadier battalions of the *716th Infantry Division* put up a very effective defense on or near the Atlantic coast. Using tactics they perfected in Russia, the grenadiers let the Allied tanks pass without firing upon them; then they emerged to ambush the infantry and support units. The Allied spearheads (the Canadian 3d and British 3d Infantry Divisions, with the British 8th and 27th Armoured Brigades attached) were thus forced to halt and dispatch tanks to their rear, significantly delaying their progress. Major Lehman, the commander of the *II Battalion, 726th Grenadier Regiment,* rallied his command after the initial Allied armored wave had passed and then ambushed elements of the Canadian 3d Division near Juno Beach. He then made a determined stand at the hill of Sainte-Croix, along the main route of Allied advance, and the Canadians had to recall their tanks to deal with it. At 1548 Lehman signaled that he was fighting hand to hand inside the command post. Then there was silence. Major Lehman

was dead and the *II/726th* had been destroyed, but the Allied advance had been significantly delayed. Such incidents were representative of the *716th Division*'s defensive actions on D-day. The *II/736th Grenadier Regiment* defended Tailleville in a similar manner, and the *III/736th Grenadier* launched a counterattack into the rear of the British 3d Infantry Division and retook the village of Lion-sur-Mer, on the very edge of Sword Beach.

While Colonel Krug's grenadiers engaged the British and Canadians from the rear, two panzer grenadier battalions and an assault gun battalion from the *21st Panzer Division* were attached to the *716th,* allowing General Richter to delay them frontally until the rest of the *21st Panzer Division* could mount a counterattack. The truly heroic efforts of the *716th Infantry Division* prevented General Montgomery from capturing Caen on D-day, as he had planned, and enabled Field Marshal Rommel and the other German commanders to stalemate the Allies in the hedgerow country of Normandy. Instead of gaining the thirty-two miles he intended to gain on 6 June, Montgomery did not even gain ten miles. In the process, however, most of the *716th Division* was hopelessly cut off behind British lines, where it was destroyed, strong point by strong point. Krug's command post was overrun on the morning of 7 June, and the colonel was captured, but isolated pockets of resistance continued to fight for days, and some of those cut off actually managed to work their way back to German lines again.

On 7 June, the *I* and *III* battalions of the *726th Grenadier Regiment* (temporarily under the command of the *352d Infantry Division*) were involved in the unsuccessful attack on Bayeux. Later that day, the regiment (along with the *30th Mobile Brigade*) was trapped between the British 50th and the U.S. 1st infantry divisions, but it fought well and succeeded in preventing the British and American bridgeheads from linking up until 8 June. That night, the *726th* was able to infiltrate through Allied lines and successfully extricate itself from the trap. By 10 June, the *726th Grenadier* was down to a strength of only a few hundred

men; shortly thereafter, it was withdrawn from the battle and sent to reunite with the rest of the *716th Division.*

The *716th Infantry* was practically destroyed on D-day, even though it remained in the line until around 11 June. It was then withdrawn to rebuild at Perpignan near the Mediterranean coast, but was caught up in the Allied invasion of southern France instead. It was re-formed and reinforced in Alsace that fall, but had only 4,546 men at the beginning of 1945. It was virtually destroyed in the Colmar pocket in February, although remnants of the division continued fighting until the end of the war, when it surrendered to the Americans.

[*See also* Richter, Wilhelm.]

BIBLIOGRAPHY

Harrison, Gordon A. *Cross-Channel Attack.* U.S. Army in World War II: The European Theater of Operations. 1951.

Mitcham, Samuel W. *Hitler's Legions: The German Army Order of Battle, World War II.* 1985.

Mitcham, Samuel W. *Rommel's Last Battle: The Desert Fox and the Normandy Campaign.* 1983.

Tessin, Georg. *Verbände und Truppen der deutschen Wehrmacht und Waffen-SS im Zweiten Weltkrieg, 1939–1945.* Vol. 12, 1975.

SAMUEL W. MITCHAM, JR.

17TH SS PANZER GRENADIER DIVISION.

This German division was raised on 3 October 1943 in response to the demand from Adolf Hitler's headquarters for a new formation that was to bear the name of the German knight Götz von Berlichingen, and that, together with the new *10th SS Panzer Division "Frundsberg"* (another heroic figure), would form the so-called *"Landsknecht"* Corps.

The order of battle for the *17th SS Division* was for two regiments of grenadiers, the *37th* and *38th,* each composed of three motorized battalions, an artillery regiment, and the usual services. The growing shortages in manpower in Germany slowed the raising of the division, but as of 1 June 1944, its strength was 17,321 men of all ranks. Although deficient in weapons and equipment, the *17th* was considered ready to undertake operations. In that respect the U.S. official history *Cross-Channel Attack* records that the division was so poorly outfitted that four of its six grenadier battalions had only improvised transport, some of which was Italian in origin, and that the two grenadier battalions were mounted on bicycles. The panzer battalion had no tanks, but there were thirty-seven self-propelled guns on establishment.

The *"Götz von Berlichingen"* Division formed part of the high command reserve but once released began its move toward the beachhead led by the reconnaissance battalion,

which reached the Tessy area during 8 June. Some bicycle-mounted grenadier units took so long to reach the combat zone that they were effectively out of the battle until the second half of the month.

The reconnaissance battalion took up position in the sector held by the German *352d Division,* in the Trévières-Littry area, and one of its patrols, sent out on 10 June, clashed with units of the British 7th Armoured Division. The main force of the *17th SS Division,* suffering from the fuel shortages that bedeviled German operations on every front, was stranded in and around Vers with the result that by 11 June, only advance parties had reached the designated divisional assembly area to the southwest of Carentan.

Fuel supplies rushed to the division made some units mobile, and the advance continued to a point north of Périers, where the German *6th Parachute Infantry (Fallschirmjäger) Regiment* was holding the line. On 11 June, the commander of the *"Götz von Berlichingen" Division,* Werner Ostendorff, went forward to contact Col. August von der Heydte, the paratroop regiment's commander, in Carentan, where a fierce battle was raging. Allied superiority on the ground and in the air soon forced the *6th Fallschirmjäger Regiment* out of the town. That seriously depleted regiment was then placed under the command of the *"Götz von Berlichingen" Division.* It is interesting to note that the veteran soldier Heydte had a low opinion of the *17th SS.* In his memoir *Muss ich sterben will ich fallen,* he records how its Ia (chief assistant, operations) dismissed demands for closer liaison with the remark, "We don't do things that way," and later how SS officers gave conflicting orders. For their part the senior commanders of the *17th* tried in vain to have Heydte court-martialed for giving up Carentan.

It was very clear that the German forces in that sector would be unable to undertake a concerted attack to recapture the town, for even as late as 12 June, the *17th SS Division* had control of only two-thirds of its effectives. A check showed that there was a serious shortage of ammu-

nition for the heavy weapons whose fire was needed to support the panzer grenadier and paratroop assaults. The attack set for 13 June, which was already encountering difficulties, had these compounded when the promised Luftwaffe support was canceled without warning. Under a very meager covering barrage of artillery, the men of the *"Götz von Berlichingen"* opened their first attack against two American airborne divisions (82d and 101st) as well as the 2d Armoured Division.

The ground across which the German units advanced was swamp covered with bushes, and the whole area was defended tenaciously by the American troops. Fighting continued for weeks with few advances made by the panzer grenadiers, who were then forced onto the defensive. On 16 June, Ostendorff was badly wounded. He was replaced by Standartenführer Otto Baum, who led the division from 16 June to 30 July. On 18 June, the *17th SS,* holding the Périers-Neumesnil sector, was relieved from the line by the *353d Division.*

After service in Normandy, near Metz, and on other sectors of the Western front, the *"Götz von Berlichingen" Division* finished the war in southern Germany and Austria.

[*See also* Ostendorff, Werner.]

BIBLIOGRAPHY

Blumenson, Martin. *Breakout and Pursuit.* 1961.

Covington, H. *A Fighting Heart: The Unofficial History of 82d Airborne Division.* 1949.

Harrison, Gordon A. *Cross-Channel Attack.* U.S. Army in World War II: The European Theater of Operations. 1951.

Rapport, L., and A. Northwood. *Rendezvous with Destiny: A History of 101st Airborne Division.* 1948.

Stoker, H. J. *Die eiserne Faust: Bildband und Chronik der 17 SS Panzergrenadier Division, Götz von Berlichingen.* 1966.

JAMES LUCAS

7TH ARMOURED DIVISION. The British 7th Armoured Division was formed in February 1940 in the Western Desert, acquiring shortly afterward the jerboa or desert rat as its divisional insignia. As part of the Western Desert Force, which was expanded and rechristened as the Eighth Army in the autumn of 1941, the Desert Rats fought in virtually all the great battles of the desert war in 1941 and 1942, then in the Tunisian campaign and the invasion of Italy in 1943.

At the end of 1943, 7th Armoured Division sailed for Britain to prepare for the invasion of Normandy, together with the 51st (Highland) Division, with which it had served since the second Battle of El Alamein. In Britain the division was re-equipped and reorganized with more light and medium tanks than the other two British armored divisions intended for Normandy, so as to be available as a pursuit force if the chance arose. The Desert Rats were to go to Normandy under the command of Maj. Gen. G. W. E. J. ("Bobby") Erskine, forming part of Lt. Gen. G. C. Bucknall's XXX Corps, one of four corps making up the Second British Army and one of the two British corps that were to attack on D-day itself.

7th Armoured Division had gained fame and glory in the Western Desert, but in Normandy, far from pursuing a retreating enemy across the desert, it faced a determined and resourceful foe in unfamiliar terrain offering advantages to the defender. It also went into battle there with equipment that was new to it, and arguably inferior to that used by the enemy. Moreover, like the corps of which it formed a part (and for that matter, like several other formations of Second British Army), 7th Armoured Division was by this time somewhat battle-weary, leading to suspicions at 21st Army Group that the division was "sticky" (reluctant to push ahead in the face of opposition), or even resting on its laurels.

This suspicion was borne out within a few days of D-day. The 7th Armoured Division had begun to come ashore in strength on D plus 1, following up XXX Corps's lead division, the 50th (Northumbrian) Division, on Gold Beach and then moving inland toward Bayeux and the Seulles Valley, preparatory to a drive toward Mont Pinçon. This move inland, already delayed by poor weather, beachhead congestion, and stiff resistance, was at first hesitant and then, at Villers-Bocage on 12–14 June, faltering. Finding the route due south through Tilly-sur-Seulles to Villers-Bocage blocked by the enemy, XXX Corps ordered 7th Armoured Division to outflank the defenders to the west through a gap in the German lines between Villers-Bocage and Caumont. The division made this move on 12–13 June, but its spearhead brigade, 22d Armoured Brigade under Brig. Robert ("Looney") Hinde, was mauled by a small number of German Panzer VI Tiger tanks at Villers-Bocage and then isolated by German countermoves. 22d Armoured Brigade might have held on if adequately reinforced, but when the corps commander's attempt to drive due south from Tilly-sur-Seulles failed, he ordered the brigade's withdrawal. The culpability for the debacle at Villers-Bocage rested primarily with 7th Armoured Division, which had missed an opportunity to turn the German defenses (if indeed this had been the intention of higher headquarters), rather than with XXX Corps.

The Desert Rats had little chance to redeem themselves during Operation GOODWOOD, a massive armored offensive east of Caen on 18–20 July; they had just begun to enter the fray when the offensive ground to a halt. Doubts as to the division's drive hardened, and when it made little progress at the start of Operation BLUECOAT on 30 July, Lt. Gen. Miles Dempsey (commander of the

7th Armoured Division
Maj. Gen. G. W. E. J. Erskine

22d Armoured Brigade
1st Royal Tank Regiment
5th Royal Tank Regiment
4th County of London Yeomanry
5th Royal Inniskilling Dragoon Guards

131st (Queens) Brigade
Queens Royal Regiment
  1/5th Battalion
  1/6th Battalion
  1/7th Battalion
Royal Northumberland Fusiliers
  No. 3 Support Company

Divisional Troops
8th Hussars
11th Hussars
Divisional Signals

Royal Artillery
3d Royal Horse Artillery
5th Royal Horse Artillery
15th Light Antiaircraft Regiment
65th Antitank Regiment

Royal Engineers
4th Field Squadron
621st Field Squadron
143d Field Park Squadron

Second Army) removed about one hundred of its officers, including Hinde and Erskine, who was replaced by Maj. Gen. G. L. Verney. Whether the Desert Rats' subsequent progress can be attributed primarily to this shakeup or to collapsing German resistance remains a debatable point, but once out of Normandy the division achieved a whirlwind advance of 350 kilometers (220 miles) in only six days from the Seine into northern France and Belgium.

[See also Erskine, G. W. E. J.; XXX Corps.]

BIBLIOGRAPHY

D'Este, Carlo. *Decision in Normandy: The Unwritten Story of Montgomery and the Allied Campaign.* 1983.

Ellis, L. F., et al. *The Battle of Normandy.* Vol. 1 of *Victory in the West.* 1962.

Forty, G. *The Desert Rats at War.* 1977.

Hastings, Max. *Overlord: D-Day and the Battle for Normandy, 1944.* 1984.

Neillands, R. *The Desert Rats: 7th Armoured Division, 1940–1945.* 1991.

Verney, G. L. *The Desert Rats: A History of 7th Armoured Division.* 1954.

FRANCIS TOASE

SEVENTH ARMY. Activated at Stuttgart on 25 August 1939, the German *Seventh Army* was under the command of Col. Gen. Friedrich Dollmann, who led it until his death on 29 June 1944. It occupied a sector on the West Wall (1939–1940), played a relatively minor role in the French campaign (1940), and then occupied a sector on the Atlantic Wall (1940–1944). The D-day landings took place in the zone of its *LXXXIV Corps* on 6 June 1944.

Because many in the German High Command expected the landings to come in the zone of the *Fifteenth Army*, the *Seventh Army* prior to D-day consisted mainly of units of poor to indifferent quality. Of the forty-two infantry battalions in the *LXXXIV Corps*, for example, eight were

---

Seventh Army
15 April 1944

LXXXIV Corps

716th Infantry Division (Bo.)
352d Infantry Division
709th Infantry Division (Bo.)
243d Infantry Division
319th Infantry Division (Bo.)
77th Infantry Division (en route)

LXXIV Corps

721st Infantry Division
266th Infantry Division (Bo.)

XXV Corps

343d Infantry Division (Bo.)
265th Infantry Division (Bo.)
275th Infantry Division (en route)
353d Infantry Division

(Bo.) Bodenständige (static) divisions

SOURCE: *Die geheimen Tagesberichte der deutschen Wehrmachtführung im Zweiten Weltkrieg, 1939–1945.* Vol. 10, *1. März 1944–31. August 1944* (Osnabrück: Biblio Verlag, 1985), pp. 498–499.

Seventh Army
15 May 1944

LXXXIV Corps

716th Infantry Division (Bo.)
352d Infantry Division
709th Infantry Division (Bo.)
243d Infantry Division
319th Infantry Division (Bo.)

LXXIV Corps

77th Infantry Division
266th Infantry Division (Bo.)

XXV Corps

343d Infantry Division (Bo.)
265th Infantry Division (Bo.)
275th Infantry Division
353d Infantry Division

Army Reserve

II Parachute Corps
  2d Parachute Division
  3d Parachute Division
  5th Parachute Division
91st Air Landing Division

(Bo.) Bodenständige (static) divisions

SOURCES: *Die geheimen Tagesberichte der deutschen Wehrmachtführung im Zweiten Weltkrieg, 1939–1945.* Vol. 10, *1. März 1944–31. August 1944* (Osnabrück: Biblio Verlag, 1985), p. 501; Georg Tessin, *Verbände und Truppen der deutschen Wehrmacht und Waffen SS im Zweiten Weltkrieg, 1939–1945.* Vol. 3, *Die Landstreitkräfte 6–14* (Osnabrück: Biblio Verlag, 1974), p. 51.

composed almost entirely of *Osttruppen*: anti-Communist citizens of the Soviet Union who were enlisted to fight against Moscow. Generally these men were former prisoners of war who were often unreliable in combat. In May 1944, the *Seventh Army* alone had twenty-three "Eastern" battalions, about a sixth of the total infantry strength of the army. Other units were made up of *volksdeutsche*: ethnic German troops drawn from territories integrated into the Reich. Most of these were from former Polish regions, and their morale and fighting abilities were considered lower than those of German troops. In addition, between 1940 and December 1943, the *Seventh Army* did little to improve its coastal defenses, and its antiairborne and antilanding defenses were far from complete on D-day.

The *Seventh Army* was significantly reinforced in the spring of 1944 but performed poorly on D-day. It was taken by surprise, and (unlike the *Fifteenth Army*) it did not put its subordinate units on alert until 0215 on 6 June. Its countermeasures against the airborne landings were ineffective, its use of armor was poor, and its overall reaction

---

Seventh Army
15 June 1944

I SS Panzer Corps

21st Panzer Division (-)
12th SS Panzer Division
Panzer Lehr Division
243d Infantry Division
716th Infantry Division (Bo.)

LXXXIV Corps

II Parachute Corps
  Elements, 2d Panzer Division
  3d Parachute Division
  352d Infantry Division (+ KG 275)
  6th Parachute Regiment
  KG 265
  17th SS Panzer Grenadier Division (-)
KG Hellmich
  243d Infantry Division
  91st Air Landing Division
  77th Infantry Division
  709th Infantry Division (Bo.)
  752d Infantry Regiment
319th Infantry Division (Bo.)**

LXXIV Corps

266th Infantry Division (Bo.)
353d Infantry Division *

XXV Corps

265th Infantry Division (Bo.)
275th Infantry Division *
343d Infantry Division (Bo.)
2d Parachute Division *

Army Reserve

XXXXVII Panzer Corps
5th Parachute Division
Elements, 17th SS Panzer Grenadier Division *

(Bo.)	*Bodenständige* (static) divisions
(-)	Elements of the unit detached or not present
*	In transit
**	Stationed on the Channel Islands and not engaged in the Normandy campaign
KG	*Kampfgruppe* (Battle Group; approximately regimental strength)

SOURCE: *Die geheimen Tagesberichte der deutschen Wehrmachtführung im Zweiten Weltkrieg, 1939–1945.* Vol. 10, *1 März 1944–31. August 1944* (Osnabrück: Biblio Verlag, 1985), p. 503.

---

to the invasion was sluggish. At nightfall on D-day, four of the five Allied beachheads were secure. On 7 June, Field Marshal Gerd von Rundstedt decided to entrust the decisive armored counterattack to Gen. Leo Geyr von Schwep-penburg's *Panzer Group West*, and the *Seventh Army* was relegated to the left (western) flank of the invasion front (although Geyr was nominally subordiate to the *Seventh Army*). *Headquarters, Panzer Group West*, however, was bombed out on 10 June, and the *Seventh Army* again assumed command of the entire invasion front.

Although it managed to hold Caen against repeated British attacks, the *Seventh Army* was not able to prevent the U.S. VII Corps from cutting the Cotentin Peninsula in two, nor was it able to prevent the fall of Cherbourg. It then conducted an effective delaying action in hedgerow country, north of Caen and Saint-Lô, in the second half of June.

The *Seventh Army*'s organic general headquarters (GHQ) units included the *550th Rear Area Command (Korück 550),* the *551st Army Supply Command (Armee-Nachschub-Führer 551),* the *558th Army Signal Regiment,* and the *319th Higher Artillery Command.* These units were largely destroyed during the Falaise encirclement and in the retreat across the Seine. The army, however, was rebuilt in September 1944 and continued to fight on the Western front until the end of the war.

[*See also* Dollmann, Friedrich.]

BIBLIOGRAPHY

Harrison, Gordon A. *Cross-Channel Attack*. U.S. Army in World War II: The European Theater of Operations. 1951.

Tessin, Georg. *Verbände und Truppen der deutschen Wehrmacht und Waffen SS im Zweiten Weltkrieg, 1939–1945*. Vol. 3, 1974.

SAMUEL W. MITCHAM, JR.

VII CORPS. Activated at Fort McClellan, Alabama, on 25 November 1940, the U.S. Army VII Corps arrived in England in October 1943 and began preparation for its landing at Utah Beach on D-day. On 14 February 1944, Maj. Gen. J. Lawton Collins arrived from the Pacific to take command of VII Corps, made up of six divisions.

Extensive training preceded the operation, including the disastrous amphibious rehearsal at Slapton Sands on the English coast where German E-boats destroyed several American landing craft with an estimated loss of over 700 dead.

The 82d and 101st airborne divisions remained under the First U.S. Army commanded by Lt. Gen. Omar Bradley until they dropped on Normandy. Generals Bradley and Collins and their staffs worked together throughout these preparations. General Collins also worked closely with Rear Adm. Don P. Moon, whose Naval Task Force U (TF 125) would take the D-day forces to Normandy and provide fire support and beach clearance in the process. The Ninth Air Force supported the undertaking with preinvasion bombardment and tactical support during and after the landing.

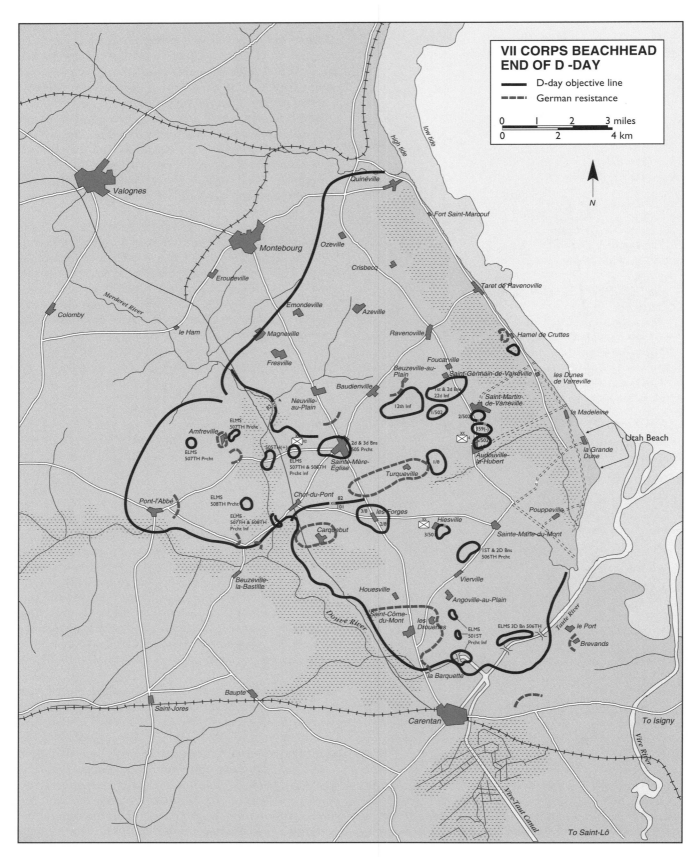

VII CORPS BEACHHEAD
END OF D-DAY

— D-day objective line
--- German resistance

0   1   2   3 miles
0   2   4 km

N

Valognes

Montebourg

Quinéville

Fort Saint-Marcouf

Ozeville

Eroudeville

Crisbecq

Taret de Ravenoville

Colomby

Merderet River

Emondeville

Azeville

le Ham

Magneville

Ravenoville

Hamel de Cruttes

Fresville

Foucarville

Beuzeville-au-Plain

Saint-Germain-de-Varréville

les Dunes de Varreville

Baudienville

Neuville-au-Plain

12th Inf

1st & 2d Bns 22d Inf

Saint-Martin-de-Varreville

la Madeleine

ELMS 507TH Prcht

1/502

2/502

Amfreville

1/502

359(-)

la Grande Dune

Utah Beach

ELMS 507TH Prcht

505TH(+)

82

2d & 3d Bns 505 Prcht

3/502

Audouville-la-Hubert

ELMS 507TH & 508TH Prcht Inf

Sainte-Mère-Eglise

1/8

Turqueville

Pont-l'Abbé

ELMS 508TH Prcht

Chef-du-Pont

82

101

3/8

les Forges

Hiesville

Pouppeville

ELMS 507TH & 508TH Prcht Inf

Carquebut

2/8

3/50

Sainte-Marie-du-Mont

1ST & 2D Bns 506TH Prcht

Beuzeville-la-Bastille

Houesville

Vierville

Angoville-au-Plain

Saint-Côme-du-Mont

les Droueries

ELMS 501ST Prcht Inf

ELMS 3D Bn 506TH

le Port

Brevands

Taute River

Douve River

la Barquette

Baupte

Saint-Jores

Carentan

To Isigny

Vire River

Vire-Taute Canal

To Saint-Lô

high tide

low tide

510

VII Corps
Maj. Gen. J. Lawton Collins

4th Infantry Division
Maj. Gen. Raymond O. Barton

9th Infantry Division
Maj. Gen. Manton S. Eddy

79th Infantry Division
Maj. Gen. Ira T. Wyche

82d Airborne Division
Maj. Gen. Matthew B. Ridgway

90th Infantry Division
Maj. Gen. Jay W. MacKelvie

101st Airborne Division
Maj. Gen. Maxwell D. Taylor

The German defense in Normandy had been dictated by Field Marshal Erwin Rommel, who placed his forces near the coast, dotted the shoreline with man-made obstacles, and inundated the low-lying terrain. Utah Beach was on the east side of the Cotentin Peninsula, where the landscape was crosshatched with bocage—the trees and brush that delineated the area's small, irregular fields.

In addition to a successful D-day landing, VII Corps had two principal missions: to link up with the U.S. Army V Corps, which was to land on Omaha Beach immediately to the east; to drive to the tip of the Cotentin Peninsula to the west and take the port of Cherbourg, thereby ensuring a stable port to support subsequent operations.

Bad weather caused a one-day delay in the launching of Operation OVERLORD. Early on 6 June the 82d and 101st airborne divisions, commanded by Maj. Gen. Matthew B. Ridgway and Maj. Gen. Maxwell D. Taylor, respectively, dropped in the areas behind Utah Beach. The 101st Division secured the terrain to the southeast while the 82d Division captured the town of Sainte-Mère-Église. In both cases the paratroopers were quite scattered, although Ridgway's forces were more dispersed.

Maj. Gen. Raymond O. Barton's 4th Infantry Division stormed Utah Beach at 0630 on D-day. It had abundant support—engineers, artillery, and other units. Admiral Moon's task force consisted of 875 vessels.

Enemy opposition was amazingly light. Even so, a number of factors caused the lead battalion to land 2,000 meters south of its objective. As luck would have it, this new area was less strongly defended than the original objective. Brig. Gen. Theodore Roosevelt, Jr., who came ashore in the initial assault, led the troops to a causeway that took them off the beach.

D-day losses on the beach were light: the 4th Infantry Division had a total of only 197 casualties. But the 101st Airborne Division lost 1,240 men and the 82d, 1,259.

The linkup with V Corps took place on 14 June when the 101st Airborne captured Carentan. The drive on Cherbourg was more difficult. Progress was so slow that General Bradley ordered General Collins to cut off the peninsula so that the Germans could neither escape from nor reinforce Cherbourg. Finally, on 27 June the VII captured the German-occupied port, completing its initial mission.

[*See also* Collins, J. Lawton, *and articles on the six divisions and their commanders.*]

BIBLIOGRAPHY

Collins, J. Lawton. *Lightning Joe: An Autobiography.* 1974.
Harrison, Gordon A. *Cross-Channel Attack.* U.S. Army in World War II: The European Theater of Operations. 1951.
U.S. Army, Center of Military History. *Utah Beach to Cherbourg, 6–27 June 1944.* 1948. Reprint, 1990.

BROOKS KLEBER

79TH ARMOURED DIVISION. 79th Armoured Division was formed as a normal armored division in October 1942. In April 1943 its commander, Maj. Gen. Percy C. S. Hobart, was charged with training its regiments in new pieces of equipment that were coming into service as a result of war experience, and which would be required in the early stages of a major landing in Europe. For example, chains had been fixed to rotating axles in front of tanks in the Western Desert to detonate antitank mines, thereby clearing routes through extensive mine fields. Again, in the disastrous seaborne raid on the French port of Dieppe, it was found that tanks could not leave the beach on which they landed because of obstacles. To overcome this, assault engineer units were formed to lead future landings in special tanks designed to overcome obstacles that limited the movement of normal tanks.

Another significant development was the DD (Duplex Drive) tank. It could be propelled either by normal tracks on land or by a propeller mounted at the rear in water. A canvas screen mounted around the main body of the tank could be raised to provide flotation. This became a critical weapon on the beaches as it enabled high-velocity firepower to be brought to bear in the early stage against the enormous defensive works that had been built by the Germans.

Another development was the flame-throwing tank, code-named Crocodile, which towed an armored trailer of fuel and could project a jet of flame against enemy defenses. Crocodiles were not used in the initial landings but became valuable farther inland. Another, the CDL tank, projected a very bright beam of light to blind defensive positions in night attacks.

This collection of specialized armor was dubbed the "Funnies" by the army. Of them all, however, the AVRE (Assault Vehicle Royal Engineers) required far the most development work before D-day. AVREs were based on the standard Churchill tank of about 40 tons. Instead of the usual gun, they were armed with the Petard, which could throw an 18-kilogram (40-pound) bomb a distance of 75 meters (80 yards); its purpose was to destroy concrete.

AVREs were modified to operate seven types of specialized equipment, each designed to deal with a specific type of obstacle, including some natural hazards such as soft ground and sand dunes. First in importance were the assault bridges to span 9-meter (30-foot) gaps; then fascines, which were bundles about 2.4 meters (8 feet) in diameter of chestnut palings or lengths of pipe, designed to be tipped into antitank ditches to enable armor to cross; snakes, up to 122 meters (400 feet) of 7.6-centimeter (3-inch) pipe filled with explosive to be pushed in front of an AVRE and detonated to explode the mines. Each AVRE carried twenty-four General Wade charges, which were arch-shaped blocks of explosive weighing about 13.6 kilograms (30 pounds) and used for destroying concrete.

The experimentation required to develop these devices, and the training needed for the personnel to use them, involved intense activity before D-day. Tests, exercises, and demonstrations were carried out, shrouded in secrecy and often resulting in failure. But by constant trial and error, the squadrons gradually became effective.

The first production AVREs were not received until the beginning of April 1944. In mid-May the laborious task of water-proofing them was started. On 6 June four squadrons of 5th and two of 6th Assault Engineer regiments landed at H-hour, supported by Flail tanks of 22d Dragoons and Westminster Dragoons. Together they opened exits from all the British and Canadian beaches.

AVREs and Flail tanks, and later Crocodiles, were in great demand immediately after the landings both to clear up pockets of enemy resistance, such as the heavily defended radar station at Douvres-la-Délivrande, and to advance progress toward the capture of Caen, and, after the fall of Caen, toward Falaise. They were involved in the crossings of the Orne and Laison rivers and played major parts in the capture of the Channel ports of Le Havre and Boulogne.

British (4/7 Dragoon Guards, 13/18 Hussars, 15/19 Hussars, 1 East Riding Yeomanry, Notts Yeomanry, and Staffordshire Yeomanry), Canadian (1st Hussars and Fort Garry Horse), and American (70th, 741st, and 743d tank battalions) units were all trained in the handling of DD tanks by 79th Armoured Division and played a notable part in the success of D-day.

Later in the campaign, as the need to attack heavy defenses from the sea decreased, 33d Armoured Brigade and two regiments of the Assault Engineers took over Buffaloes (the code name for Landing Vehicles, Tracked, which had been developed by the U.S. Marine Corps). These highly mobile, lightly armored vehicles were decisive in assaults across the Schelde River to open up the port of Antwerp, and in assaults across the Rhine.

MINESWEEPING FLAIL TANK.   A British Flail (or Crab) moves toward the front.   IMPERIAL WAR MUSEUM

79th Armoured Division
Maj. Gen. Percy C. S. Hobart

30th Armoured Brigade (Flails)
22d Dragoons
1st Lothian and Border Horse
2d County of London Yeomanry (Westminster
 Dragoons)

31st Armoured Brigade (Crocodiles)
1st Fife and Forfar Yeomanry
7th Royal Tanks
141st Regiment Royal Armoured Corps
49th Armoured Personnel Carrier Regiment (CDLs)
1st Canadian Armoured Personnel Carrier Regiment

33d Armoured Brigade (Buffaloes)
1st Northamptonshire Yeomanry
1st East Riding Yeomanry
4th Royal Tanks
11th Royal Tanks

1st Assault Brigade (AVREs and Buffaloes)
5th Assault Regiment
6th Assault Regiment
42d Assault Regiment

79th Armoured Division never fought independently. Its units were put under command of whatever brigade or division was launching an attack, with the task of breaking through the initial enemy defenses in order to create a gap that the main force could pass through.

[See also Hobart, Percy C. S.]

BIBLIOGRAPHY

A.R.E.: The Story of 1st Assault Brigade Royal Engineers. 1945.
The Story of 79th Armoured Division. 1945.

A. E. YOUNGER

79TH INFANTRY DIVISION. The 79th Infantry Division was initially organized in 1917, after the U.S. entry into World War I. Reaching France in July 1918, it saw brief action in Lorraine in mid-September and then fought in the Meuse-Argonne offensive from late that month until the armistice on 11 November. Demobilized in 1919, it was subsequently assigned to the Organized Reserves (essentially as a "paper" division). Early in World War II the division was reactivated on 15 June 1942 at Camp Pickett, Virginia, under the command of Maj. Gen. Ira T. Wyche and trained in the United States. Organized and equipped as a standard triangular infantry division of about 14,000 men, it sailed from Boston on 7 April 1944 and reached the United Kingdom ten days later, undergoing final precombat training in the weeks before D-day.

The 79th Division did not participate in the initial D-day landings but came ashore one week later. It was part of the U.S. VII Corps of Maj. Gen. J. Lawton Collins in Lt. Gen. Omar Bradley's U.S. First Army. Collins's corps was charged with landing on Utah Beach on the east coast of the Cotentin Peninsula, securing that large arm of land, and capturing the key port of Cherbourg at its northern tip.

General Wyche and advance elements of the 79th Division began landing on 12 June; the remainder of the unit followed during the next two days. VII Corps troops had secured the area around the Utah beachhead and linked up at Carentan, to the south, with American forces pushing west from Omaha Beach. While the 79th Division prepared to join the attack, on 17 June VII Corps successfully completed its drive across the neck of the Cotentin Peninsula, blocking any possible German effort to reinforce the now-isolated port of Cherbourg. There were still, however, some 40,000 defenders in that city, dug in behind concrete and field fortifications in dominating hill positions, and Maj. Gen. Karl Wilhelm von Schlieben, the garrison commander of the *709th Static Division*, was under direct orders from Hitler to fight to the end. Nevertheless, by 19 June General Collins was ready to begin his drive on Cherbourg, using the 79th Division to replace the U.S. 90th Division, whose progress had been slowed.

From an east-west line across the peninsula, Collins attacked north that morning with three divisions. In the center was the 79th, pushing off across the high ground west and northwest of Valogne, with the 9th and 4th divisions on its left and right. Continuing the attack that night and the next day, Wyche's division moved forward rapidly and reached the outer defenses of Cherbourg itself, with the 9th and 4th divisions making similar gains on its flanks. By day's end on 21 June all three divisions were in a tight arc against the powerful fortifications of Cherbourg. The importance of the early capture of that port was reemphasized by a violent storm that had raged since the 19th, crippling Allied landing vessels and halting all unloading along the beaches. On 22 June the three American divisions began their final assault on Cherbourg, supported by

79th Infantry Division
Maj. Gen. Ira T. Wyche

313th Infantry Regiment
314th Infantry Regiment
315th Infantry Regiment
310th Field Artillery Battalion
311th Field Artillery Battalion
312th Field Artillery Battalion
904th Field Artillery Battalion
304th Engineer Battalion
304th Medical Battalion
79th Reconnaissance Troop
79th Signal Company
779th Ordnance Company
79th Quartermaster Company

punishing air attacks on the German defenses, against stubborn resistance. On 25 June, after a heavy naval bombardment, 79th Division troops seized the old French fortress of Fort du Roule and were the first to enter the city of Cherbourg. By the following night all three American divisions were well into the city and General von Schlieben and other senior commanders had been captured. By 29 June Cherbourg was completely in American hands.

The 79th Division had suffered 2,376 casualties: 240 killed, 1,896 wounded, and 240 missing. But it had acquitted itself well in its first experience in combat. It would continue to do so in future battles in France and Germany until the end of the war.

[See also Wyche, Ira T.]

BIBLIOGRAPHY

Army and Navy Publishing Co. *The Cross of Lorraine: A Combat History of the 79th Infantry Division, June 1942–December 1945*. 1946.

Harrison, Gordon A. *Cross-Channel Attack*. U.S. Army in World War II: The European Theater of Operations. 1951.

U.S. Army, Center of Military History. *Utah Beach to Cherbourg: 6–27 June 1944*. 1948. Reprint, 1990.

STANLEY L. FALK

77TH INFANTRY DIVISION. On 15 January 1944, at Muensingen, the German *364th Infantry Division* was combined with the remnants of the *355th Infantry Division* to form the *77th Infantry Division*. The *355th*, which consisted mainly of Württemberger reservists, had been formed in France in February 1943 and had been smashed in the Kharkov and Krivoy Rog battles on the Russian front. The *364th Infantry* had been formed in Poland in late 1943 but had never seen combat.

The new division hardly fit the definition of an elite unit. It was understrength and had only two infantry regiments (the *1049th* and *1050th Grenadiers*) instead of the normal three. Its artillery regiment (the *177th*) was very weak, and it had no engineer battalion and few reconnaissance forces. Its *177th Antitank Battalion* comprised only two companies, and the entire division was short on trained officers, noncommissioned officers, and equipment of every description. Moreover, a high proportion of the division's men were Volksdeutsche (ethnic Germans from the occupied territories), Polish, or former Soviet citizens (mainly Tatars from the Volga region), whose loyalty to the Third Reich was questionable at best.

The *77th* was sent to France in February and was initially assigned the task of defending Caen. In April 1944, however, a highly dissatisfied Field Marshal Erwin Rommel inspected the division and concluded that it was not good enough to defend such a potentially important sector. He replaced it with the *21st Panzer,* assigned the *77th* a new commander, Maj. Gen. Rudolf Stegmann, and sent it to the less threatened Saint-Malo–Saint-Brieuc sector in Brittany.

The *77th Infantry* was placed on alert on D-day, but *Army Group B* delayed its move because of erroneous reports of Allied paratroop landings in Brittany. On the morning of 7 June, however, Rommel ordered that it be used to reinforce *Group Schlieben,* which had been assigned the task of holding the southern approaches to Cherbourg. The division started its move late (at 1500 hours), but then marched as rapidly as could be expected, since it had virtually no motorized transport and was under constant harassment by Allied fighter-bombers. Friedrich Dollman, commander of the *Seventh Army,* was very much concerned that it would not arrive in time to prevent the collapse of Maj. Gen. Karl Wilhelm von Schlieben's line. But its vanguard arrived at the front on 10 June and much of the division was in position the following day, defending in the hedgerow country on both sides of the Merderet River. Here it fought very well, checking much stronger elements of the U.S. VII Corps and preventing the Americans from outflanking Montebourg, a major junction on the road to Cherbourg. A much-relieved Dollman signaled Rommel on 11 June that he was satisfied that the situation was well in hand in this sector.

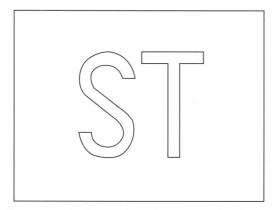

Dollmann's relief was short-lived. South of the *77th Infantry,* the *100th Panzer Replacement Battalion,* which consisted mainly of non-German personnel, broke and ran at its first contact with the Americans. Gen. J. Lawton Collins quickly committed the U.S. 9th Infantry and 82d Airborne divisions to the attack along the Pont-l'Abbé–Saint-Sauveur-le-Vicomte road, taking full advantage of the hole in the German line. At 0505 hours on 18 June, his spearheads reached the sea near Barneville, isolating *Group Schlieben* in the northern part of the Cotentin Peninsula.

By this time, Rommel had ordered the *77th Infantry* to break out in the direction of Saint-Lô, but Adolf Hitler countermanded these instructions and ordered Stegmann to hold his present positions at all costs. With elements of the VII Corps already working their way north (i.e., behind) his division, Stegmann chose to obey Rommel instead of Hitler. He formed his division in column formation and attempted to break out on 18 June. Much of the division was already in heavy combat against the U.S. 9th Infantry Division, however, and could not disengage. One major column, consisting of the *177th Artillery Regiment* and the bulk of the division's transport, was caught on the road and destroyed by the U.S. 60th Field Artillery Regiment, and Stegmann was killed by a fighter-bomber. Command of the division devolved on Colonel of Reserves Bernard Bacherer, who found a corridor between the U.S. VII and VIII corps during the night of 18–19 June, overran an American infantry battalion, and made his way back to German lines with 1,500 men.

Despite the fact that it had lost three-quarters of its strength, the *77th* remained in the line until September, when it was surrounded and finally destroyed at Dinard by VII Corps.

[*See also* Stegmann, Rudolf.]

BIBLIOGRAPHY

Carell, Paul. *Invasion: They're Coming.* Translated by E. Osers. 1963. Paul Carell is the pseudonym used by Hans Karl Schmidt.
Harrison, Gordon A. *Cross-Channel Attack.* U.S. Army in World War II: The European Theater of Operations. 1951.
Mitcham, Samuel W., Jr. *Hitler's Legions: The German Army Order of Battle, World War II.* 1985.
Tessin, Georg. *Verbände und Truppen der deutschen Wehrmacht und Waffen-SS im Zweiten Weltkrieg, 1939–1945.* Vol. 6, 1979.

SAMUEL W. MITCHAM, JR.

SHAEF. *See* Supreme Headquarters Allied Expeditionary Force (SHAEF).

SHORE PARTY. The shore party was a logical offshoot of the development of amphibious warfare. By 1934 the U.S. Marine Corps had established the need in an assault landing for special units to mark the beaches for the flow of traffic, set up supply dumps, evacuate casualties, and repair boats. Later study of amphibious assaults by the U.S. Army Engineers emphasized a role for the shore party to construct emergency roads, remove obstacles, and provide hasty defensive works. Thus the shore party, composed largely of army engineers, was patterned after the Marines' concept but operated independently of the U.S. Navy. In 1941 an army engineer committee of three, including one Marine Corps representative, studied British, German, and Japanese landing tactics, but found little that could help the committee develop the concept of the shore party except U.S. Marine Corps doctrine and experience.

After numerous training exercises and discussions about responsibilities for amphibious ship-to-shore and shore-to-shore assaults, the U.S. Army received control of the beaches in the shore-to-shore assault that became the D-day landings. The U.S. Army structure that evolved was the engineer amphibian (renamed special) brigade, which included an engineer shore regiment. These brigades were trained and equipped to carry out all communications zone functions within their geographic areas. Their D-day beach maintenance areas included the adjacent hinterland to a depth of 6.5 kilometers (4 miles). Their missions included traffic control, road construction and maintenance, security from ground and air attack, discipline, police, and the logistics responsibilities of cargo handling, mine removal, and movement of supplies across beaches to dump areas.

The 1st Engineer Special Brigade Group (Provisional) under Brig. Gen. W. M. Hoge consisted of the 5th and 6th engineer special brigades, which were activated specifically for cargo handling and related functions and provided support for V Corps on Omaha Beach. The 1st Engineer Special Brigade under Brig. Gen. James E. Wharton provided the support for VII Corps on Utah Beach. Typically, the brigades included medical, quartermaster, and truck battalions along with amphibian truck, ordnance, and chemical decontamination companies. Their equipment included DUKWs (amphibious trucks), D-7 and D-8 angle dozers, power cranes, motorized road graders, tractors, and trailers. A naval beach battalion was attached to each of the special brigades for ship-to-shore communications (radio, flag, and blinker), small-craft repair, hydrographic surveys, and casualty evacuation. Rough seas, unexpectedly heavy enemy resistance on Omaha, bad weather, delays in opening the ports, and expanding demands all contributed to an increase in the movement of supplies across the beaches beyond what had been planned.

On D-day, the brigade group of 34,250 men and 2,870 vehicles landed on Omaha, the larger of the two operations. The 37th Engineer Combat Battalion, landing at 0700, was the first brigade unit ashore. Intending to erect beach markers and to organize the beach for the following waves, its men instead moved to the attack, using bangalore torpedoes to blow apart German wire entanglements. The 348th followed. Under enemy fire, they cleared obstacles and prepared paths and road exits out of the congested waterfront area. On Utah the 1st Brigade landed some 20,000 troops and 1,700 vehicles the first day. Combat both as infantry and as engineers followed, but over the following days the shore regiments cleared the beaches, moved supplies to the front, took care of the wounded, removed enemy obstacles, and kept the U.S. First Army moving forward. With the landing over, the brigades either went on to prepare for landings in the Pacific or became conventional engineer units performing combat and support functions in Europe.

[See also American Beaches, articles on Omaha Beach and Utah Beach; Engineers, article on American Engineers; Hoge, W. M.; Wharton, James E.]

BIBLIOGRAPHY

Cole, Blanche D., Jean E. Keith, and Herbert H. Rosenthal. *The Technical Services, The Corps of Engineers: Troops and Equipment.* The United States Army in World War II. 1958.

Fowle, Barry W., ed. *Builders and Fighters: U.S. Army Engineers in World War II.* 1992.

Heavy, William F. *Down Ramp! The Story of the Army Amphibian Engineers.* 1947.

MARTIN K. GORDON

SIGNAL. [*This entry includes separate discussions of Allied and German signal corps.*]

Allied Signal

In addition to creating, maintaining, and operating Allied signal communications during the D-day operation, the Allied signal elements created and maintained an electronic deception, convincing the Germans that the actual point of the Allied invasion of the continent was to be the Pas de Calais area, and that Normandy was simply a diversion.

Prior to D-day Allied forces in England had assembled a vast and sophisticated network of signal communications unrivaled in the history of warfare. As the invasion date approached, U.S. signalmen for the European Theater of Operations (ETO) had completed radio facilities to serve the needs of the tactical forces. These facilities provided one voice and three radioteletype channels to the United States.

Signal equipment for all ETO units was provided by the Supply Division, ETO-USA. Through its various branches this division planned the ETO signal supply program. Consequently, Supreme Headquarters Allied Expeditionary Force (SHAEF) was well supplied with radio facilities prior to D-day.

The most difficult task confronting signal planners was to develop a workable plan of frequency allocation. This task was more difficult for the Allies than for the Germans because of the larger naval, air, ground, and service forces in a combined operation. Moreover, several nations were involved, which meant that different types of transmissions and different frequency bands of the transmitters had to be considered.

At the tactical level the Allies prepared large quantities of short- and medium-range radio sets for combat use by battalions, companies, and platoons. Thousands of sets were waterproofed and supplied with fresh and fully charged batteries. The Allies also had on hand thousands of miles of assault and field wire, enough for the five ground divisions and three airborne divisions that took part in the D-day assault, and sufficient for the total of sixteen divisions that would be operating in Normandy by D plus 5. There also had to be enough field signal equipment for the million men expected to be in France within three weeks, with plenty more to compensate for anticipated battle losses.

Allied armies in Normandy also required heavy-duty communications lines back to England. For that, submarine cables as well as radio sets that operated on very high frequency (VHF) were provided. The British also supplied cable ships and radio ships and most of the initial supply of VHF radios. Several British AM multichannel VHF systems were established on the Isle of Wight to link up with companion sets whose crews closely followed the assault units to the high ground beyond the beaches. Meanwhile the cable ships stood by to unreel their coils between Southbourne and the Normandy beach near Longues as soon as the enemy had been pushed back from the coast and the sea lanes swept free of mines.

During the night of 5–6 June 1944 the Allied armada

moved across the Channel under complete radio silence. As the naval force moved out, vast air fleets of the troop carrier commands flew toward France. In spite of the darkness and radio silence, a U.S. Microwave Early Warning (MEW) Radar station at Start Point in Devon, England, observed the entire crossing throughout the night.

Five and a half hours before the beach assault began, twenty pathfinder aircraft from the IX Troop Carrier Command took off for Normandy guided by British Gee navigational aids and using ASV (air–to–surface vessel) radars such as SCR-717 to scan the terrain below. The pathfinder paratroopers carried Eureka Beacons (AN/PPN-1) and signal lights to mark the designated drop zones for the troop carrier aircraft that would follow. Unfortunately, clouds and ground fog obscured the landscape, and many pathfinders were unable to locate all of the areas chosen for drop zones. Nevertheless, some pathfinders landed safely and set out signal lights and switched on their Eurekas. In two zones west of the Merderet River, the proximity of German units prevented the pathfinders from showing their lights; they used the Eurekas instead. Half an hour later, when aircraft of the Troop Carrier Command approached with the main paratrooper force, their Rebeccas (AN/APN-2's) interrogated and received pulsed responses from the Eurekas on the ground, thus guiding the pilots to the drop zones.

Although hostile antiaircraft fire scattered the troop carriers' tight formations, the aircraft landed their paratroopers exactly on three drop zones. Ninety-five percent of all the airborne troops dropped used information from the AN-APN-2 beacons; 25 percent dropped were guided by radar alone with no help at all from signal lights.

All the American Rebecca-Eureka radar beacons had functioned properly; only one Rebecca had not. The Germans failed to jam the sets, but if they had, the Allies were prepared with an alternate device that used microwaves, since the pathfinders carried with them a number of the very new radar beacons (AN/UPW). These radar devices made the Normandy landings more accurate than previous airborne operations in Sicily and at Salerno.

The first U.S. Signal Corps troops to land in France were twenty-eight men of the 101st Airborne Signal Company who had jumped with the division headquarters group and troops of the 3d Battalion of the 501st Parachute Infantry Regiment. Of the twenty-eight, twenty-one landed in the designated zone, the remaining seven landed about forty kilometers (twenty-five miles) away. The men managed to recover only four of the twenty-seven equipment bundles, but fortunately for them there were two radios.

Additional signalmen of the 101st had remodeled one of the powerful long-range SCR-499s by mounting it in a quarter-ton trailer that could be towed by a jeep. Although the glider with the SCR-499 landed safely, despite enemy fire, the jeep-carrying glider crashed. The signalmen unloaded their radio, hailed a passing jeep, and towed the set to the spot near Hiesville designated as the division headquarters. At about 1800 hours on 6 June the troopers sent their first radio signal to England. This SCR-499 served for the first week of the invasion as the only link to England for the two airborne divisions.

The D-day experience of the 82d Airborne Division's signal company was less fortunate. Dropping by parachute in the vicinity of Sainte-Mère-Église or coming in by glider, the company lost many men and much equipment. The radio section was seriously hampered—of six high-powered sets sent into the combat zone, only one survived the glider crash landings. Likewise, of thirteen low-powered sets, only one survived those landings. In the first days following the invasion, a small wire platoon of thirteen men struggled heroically to provide wire communications to four regiments and twenty other units, besides operating switchboards at division headquarters. The magnitude of the task can be measured by realizing that ordinarily a wire platoon that serves a three-regiment division numbers ninety-four officers and men.

As for ground troops, when the men of the U.S. V Corps came ashore at Omaha Beach on D-day, they ran into fire from the German *352d Infantry Division*. Equipment losses were heavy. For example, the 116th Infantry Regiment lost 75 percent of its radio sets that morning, and command and control necessarily suffered.

The 2d Platoon of the 284th Joint Assault Signal Company (JASCO) landed with elements of the 37th Engineer Combat Battalion at Omaha Beach during the first hour of the assault. Despite losing most of their vehicles, the men managed to get most of their hand-carried communications equipment ashore and turned it over to infantry and shore fire-control parties that had lost their own equipment. With the remaining wire equipment, the JASCO men, still under fire, set up a skeletal wire system on the beach. Until noon on D-day this system was the only communications system on that beach.

At Utah Beach the landing was much easier. There the 286th Joint Assault Signal Company landed quickly and soon had wire communications functioning satisfactorily. However, failure to get an SCR-193 ashore left a gap in radio communications between the shore and the VII Corps headquarters ship, USS *Bayfield,* a gap the U.S. Navy fortunately closed. The main problem that remained was to connect the forces on the two beaches—Omaha and Utah. This was accomplished initially by radio, then completed by laying spiral-four cable.

Despite all obstacles, men and equipment reached the beaches and beyond. The various networks quickly became operational. These included army, corps, and division commands, point-to-point radio nets, separate regimental combat teams, radioteletype and wire teletype, radio nets for army corps radio intelligence, and a cross-Channel net used jointly by the army and signal intelligence service (ETOUSA).

Meanwhile both the British and American versions of a new and very significant innovation—multichannel radio relay—maintained heavy traffic loads. The equipment had been installed and put into operation much sooner than the cable. Moreover, it remained unaffected by storms and hazards of the sea.

Facsimile transmissions, too, received high praise. Photo reconnaissance planes took pictures and flew them back to England to be developed. Seven minutes after they were put on the facsimile machine, they were received at Omaha Beach and rushed to the gun control officer. American gunners had a continuing picture of German gun emplacements, tanks, and other targets concealed behind hedgerows, buildings, and terrain. Facsimile equipment also transmitted typewritten material, line drawings, and photographs with equal ease. Tactical field radio equipment had been successfully integrated with wire line and terminal equipment to form a system comparable in reliability and traffic capacity to all wire systems.

[See also Communication.]

BIBLIOGRAPHY

Thompson, George Raynor, and Dixie R. Harris. *The Signal Corps: The Outcome (Mid-1943 through 1945)*. 1966.
U.S. Army, Office of the Chief of Military History. "Cobra and Mortain." A-894. Captured Records Office, National Archives, Washington, D.C.

ERNEST F. FISHER

German Signal

The German *Signal Group (Amtsgruppe Nachrichtenwesen)* was formed in December 1943 with the expansion of *Inspectorate 7, Signal Branch (Nachrichtengrät-Abteilung)*. In 1940, shortly after the defeat of France, the Germans had begun work on an underground cable that paralleled the Channel coast and linked major ports and submarine bases. The cable, 1,672 kilometers (1,036 miles) in length, extended from Belgium to Boulogne in France. Beyond that point it was completed only piecemeal to the Atlantic coast. *"Gut erkundet, ist halb verlegt"* (well reconnoitered, is half laid) was an apt motto for the *Signal Corps (Fernmeldetruppe)* cable builders' most significant achievement in the West.

Completed in 1943, the cable had only a short useful life, because when the Allies came ashore in June 1944, military operations quickly made it useless. Thereafter the German army often relied upon the French domestic telephone network for communications. Unfortunately for the Germans, it had been allowed to deteriorate considerably during the occupation and was frequently sabotaged by the Resistance. This left the German field army more and more dependent upon mobile radio communications units attached to every headquarters from army group to division. The number of vans in each unit numbered from ten to twenty, depending upon the size of the headquarters.

Companies, battalions, and regiments were linked with one another and higher headquarters by their own organic radio equipment. Before D-day, all units in the West were tied together by a well-designed radio network, but German signal communications were among the invasion's first casualties. Thousands of low-flying Allied aircraft sought out and destroyed even carefully concealed radio vans. Officer couriers and messengers were driven off the roads of Normandy by daylight. Soon virtually all tactical movements by German forces were impossible during daylight hours. For example, Lt. Gen. Leo Geyr von Schweppenburg lost 75 percent of his radio vans to low-flying aircraft early in the invasion. The *I SS Panzer Corps* commander, Joseph ("Sepp") Dietrich, suffered similar losses, so that only four of twenty radio vans remained operational.

Allied airborne troops scattered over the countryside also made communications difficult among the widely dispersed German units. On 7 June Maj. Gen. Karl Wilhelm von Schlieben, commander of the *709th Infantry Division,* lost contact with two of his battalions, one in the Utah Beach area and the other near Turqueville. Also the *LXXXIV Corps* could no longer control or coordinate the actions of three divisions on the Cotentin Peninsula, which contributed to the failure of the German counterattack there.

Senior German commanders such as Lt. Gen. Erich Marcks and even Field Marshal Erwin Rommel had no choice but to race from unit to unit in order to maintain control of their subordinate commands. This practice, however, was costly: Marcks was killed in an air attack on 12 June, and Rommel was gravely injured when his car was attacked by low-flying aircraft. The lack of Luftwaffe forces in the skies above France severely inhibited German communications in the West after D-day. This in turn made tactical coordination of units much more difficult.

BIBLIOGRAPHY

Irving, David. *The Trail of the Fox: The Search for the True Field Marshal Rommel.* 1977.
U.S. Army, Office of the Chief of Military History. "Signal Communication in the West." P-112. Captured Records Office, National Archives, Washington, D.C.
U.S. Army, Office of the Chief of Military History. "Signal Communications." B-146. Captured Records Office, National Archives, Washington, D.C.
U.S. Army, Office of the Chief of Military History. "Wire Communications in the West, Organization and OKW Communications Net." C-002. Captured Records Office, National Archives, Washington, D.C.

ERNEST F. FISHER

SIX GROUP. Number Six (RCAF) Group was the only non-British unit in RAF Bomber Command during World War II. Its establishment on 25 October 1942 stemmed from Article Fifteen of the British Commonwealth Air Training Plan agreement between Canada and Great Britain signed on 17 December 1939, which provided for the eventual consolidation of the Dominion's aircrew serving abroad into Canadian squadrons and, ultimately, into higher echelons of wings and groups.

Although unique, Six Group was an integral part of Bomber Command, which determined strategy, issued operational orders, and provided logistical support. To facilitate its deployment, Six Group took over stations in Durham and Yorkshire counties formerly occupied by Four Group of Bomber Command. Like Four Group units, the Canadian squadrons were equipped with Handley Page Halifax aircraft.

When Six Group became operational on 1 January 1943, it consisted of eight squadrons (three in Durham, five in Yorkshire) and almost 9,000 personnel, of which only 46 percent were Canadian. On 31 May 1945 the group boasted fifteen squadrons equipped with Halifax and Lancaster aircraft, and over 17,000 personnel, of which 95 percent were Canadian. Out of over 1,200 Bomber Command sorties on D-day, Six Group contributed 230 directed against rail crossings at Coutance and Condé-sur-Noireau in the invasion area. Between 7 and 16 June the group attacked marshaling yards and strong points at Achères, Arras, Cambrai, Mayenne, Saint-Pol, Tours, and Rennes, operations intended to paralyze German troop and supply movements over the railway network serving northern France. With its attack on Sterkrade in Germany on 16 and 17 June, Six group reverted to its strategic bombing role. During hostilities Six Group squadrons carried out over 40,000 operations, dropped and laid 126,122 tons of bombs and mines, experienced 1,312 attacks by enemy aircraft, shot down 116, claimed 24 others as probably destroyed, and won 2,230 awards for gallantry. It also lost 814 aircraft and some 5,700 airmen, of whom 4,292 were killed. During the last days of the war Six Group dropped food supplies to Dutch civilians in The Hague and Rotterdam, and afterward, in operation EXODUS, flew 4,329 liberated prisoners of war to Britain.

[See also Bomber Command; McEwen, Clifford M.]

BIBLIOGRAPHY

Anon. *The Fifth Year.* Vol. 2 of *The R.C.A.F. Overseas.* 1945.
Carter, William. *Anglo-Canadian Wartime Relations, 1939–1945: RAF Bomber Command and No. 6 (Canadian) Group.* 1991.
Dunmore, Spencer, and William Carter. *Reap the Whirlwind: The Untold Story of 6 Group, Canada's Bomber Force of World War II.* 1991.
Hatch, F. J. *The Aerodrome of Democracy: Canada and the British Commonwealth Air Training Plan, 1939–1945.* Department of National Defence, Directorate of History, Monography Series No. 1. 1983.
Saunders, Hilary St. G. *The Fight Is Won.* Vol. 3 of *The Royal Air Force, 1939–1945.* 1954.
Webster, Charles, and Noble Frankland. *The Strategic Air Offensive against Germany, 1939–1945.* 4 vols. 1961.

WILLIAM RODNEY

6TH AIRBORNE DIVISION. On 23 April 1943 Maj. Gen. R. N. Gale was ordered to raise Britain's 6th Airborne Division on Salisbury Plain in England. Through 1943 the division formed up with two parachute brigades, an air-landing brigade, and supporting armor, artillery, engineer, and logistic units. In July the 1st Canadian Parachute Battalion joined the division.

Organization and Planning. The parachute brigades contained three battalions apiece, each with three companies and a jumping strength of six hundred men. In the air-landing brigade were three infantry battalions, each of one thousand men in four rifle companies and a strong support company, flying to battle in thirty-man Horsa gliders. There was only one regiment of artillery of three batteries, armed with the American 75-mm pack howitzer. To remedy this lack of firepower, artillery forward observation parties from units landing by sea with the 3d British Division and I Corps accompanied the airborne units. From its formation the division trained vigorously for three main tasks—silencing a coastal battery, denying ground overlooking the landing beaches to the German army, and delaying the approach of German reserves.

On 17 February 1944 General Gale received orders to protect the left flank of the Allied seaborne landings by the capture intact of the two bridges over the Orne River and the Caen Canal near Bénouville; the destruction of the coastal battery at Merville; and the delay of German forces moving from the east and southeast, including the destruction of the bridges over the Dives River. He allotted the capture of the Orne and Canal bridges to Brig. Nigel Poett's 5th Parachute Brigade with a company of six platoons from the glider-borne 2d Battalion, Oxfordshire and Buckinghamshire Light Infantry. To Brig. James Hill and his 3d Parachute Brigade went the other two primary tasks. The destruction of the Merville battery was assigned to the 9th Battalion and the destruction of the Dives bridges and delaying the approach of German reinforcements were allotted to the 8th and 1st Canadian battalions. There was insufficient aircraft to land the division in one lift, and the 6th Airlanding Brigade was to land at 2100 on D-day to defend the southern flank.

D-Day Operations. On 5 June 1944 six Halifax bombers of the Royal Air Force, towing six Horsa gliders, took off at 2256 from RAF Tarrant Rushton. At 0015 on 6 June at five thousand feet over Cabourg the gliders were released from their tugs and began their eight-kilometer (five-mile) glide to the bridges. Five minutes later three gliders crash-landed within thirty yards of the Canal bridge, and the three infantry platoons scrambled out and rushed the bridge defenses. Their accompanying engineers dismantled the bridge demolition charges, and fifteen minutes later the bridge was captured at a cost of one officer killed and four men wounded. Two other gliders landed near the Orne River bridge, which was undefended. The sixth glider landed seven miles away near the Dives River. At 0300 the 7th Parachute Battalion crossed the Canal bridge and for the rest of D-day fought off a series of attacks by elements of the German *716th Division*.

At 0050 the 9th Parachute Battalion dropped near Varaville, but the men were widely scattered. By 0250 only 150 out of 600 jumpers had reached the rendezvous; nevertheless, the commanding officer gave the order to advance. Between 0030 and 0040 a hundred Lancaster bombers of the Royal Air Force attacked the battery with 4,000 pound bombs, most of which fell south of the target. At 0430, as the battalion prepared to attack, two of the three Horsa gliders scheduled to crash-land among the battery case-mates appeared overhead. One disappeared into the darkness, and the second, under fire from the battery, crashed in an orchard to the rear of the battalion. The assault went in, and all four casemates were captured. The guns were silenced, but attempts to destroy them permanently were ineffective. The battalion, now some 80 men strong, moved off at 0600 to their next task of clearing Le Plein.

The 8th and 1st Canadian battalions with their supporting engineers blew the Dives River bridges and occupied defensive positions around Le Mesnil and in the Bois de Bavent. At 0300 General Gale, his tactical headquarters, and the first antitank guns landed by glider.

Between 2051 and 2123, 248 gliders reached their landing zones, bringing in two air-landing battalions, 1st Royal Ulster Rifles and the main body of 2d Oxfordshire and Buckinghamshire, the Armored Reconnaissance Regiment, a company of the 12th (Battalion) Devonshire Regiment, a battery of the 53d Light Regiment, and the 6th Airlanding Brigade Headquarters. Only ten gliders failed to arrive.

At noon on D-day the 1st Commando Brigade crossed the Canal bridge and came under command of the 6th Airborne Division. They held the northern sector of the division's bridgehead from Sallenelles to Amfreville until the advance on 17 August. The main body of the 12th

6TH AIRBORNE DIVISION.   Struggling to load a 75-mm antitank gun aboard a Normandy-bound Horsa glider.
IMPERIAL WAR MUSEUM

Devons landed by sea and rejoined the air-landing brigade on D plus one.

Operations after D-day. The 6th Airlanding Brigade took over the defense of Longueval, Le Bas de Ranville, and Hérouvillette. Its assaults on Sainte-Honorine-la-Chardonnerette and Escoville failed, and for the next week it was attacked by the *125th Panzer Grenadier Division* and one panzer battalion of the *21st Panzer Division,* supported by the *200th Assault Gun Battalion.* On 13 June the brigade was relieved by the British 51st (Highland) Division and moved up the eastern flank.

On 10 June the 5th Parachute Brigade, in divisional reserve, counterattacked and destroyed an attempt by a battalion of the German *857th Grenadier Regiment* to attack the Canal and Orne bridges from Bréville. The 3d Parachute Brigade continued to hold the Bois de Bavent ridge with the 9th Battalion now around the Château Saint-Côme, the 1st Canadian Battalion around Le Mesnil, and the 8th Battalion still in the Bois de Bavent. From 8 June to 12 June the German *857th Grenadier Regiment* made a series of attacks on the Château Saint-Côme, where the 9th Battalion was reinforced on 10 June by the 5th (Battalion) Black Watch. On 11 June the Black Watch attacked Bréville but was driven back with severe losses. The next morning a renewed German attack went in against the 9th Parachute and Black Watch battalions around Saint-Côme and was held only after fierce close-range fighting.

At 1700 on this same day, 12 June, General Gale decided to close this last gap in his perimeter by an immediate attack on Bréville. his only reserves were three hundred men of the 12th Parachute Battalion, a company of the 12th Devons, a squadron of Sherman tanks from the 13/18th Hussars, and the guns of the 51st (Highland) Division. The attack went in at 2200. There were heavy losses on both sides from artillery fire, but by midnight Bréville was in British hands. The 6th Airborne Division bridgehead was complete, and the Allied left flank remained secure.

The division had carried out all its tasks successfully at a cost of 4,457 casualties, of whom 821 were killed, 2,709 wounded, and 927 missing. Only about half of this last number were prisoners of war. There were few if any battle exhaustion casualties, and the division remained an excellent fighting unit until the end of the war in Europe.

[*See also* Gale, Richard N.; Gliders.]

BIBLIOGRAPHY

Crookenden, Napier. *Drop Zone Normandy.* 1976.
Gale, R. N. *With the Sixth Airborne Division in Normandy.* 1948.
Harclerode, Peter. *"Go To It": The Illustrated History of the 6th Airborne Division.* 1990.
United Kingdom. Air Ministry. *The Second World War, 1939–1945: Airborne Forces.* 1951.
United Kingdom. War Office. *The Second World War, 1939–1945: Airborne Forces.* 1951.

NAPIER CROOKENDEN

SMITH, WALTER BEDELL (1895–1961), American, major general, chief of staff of General Eisenhower's Supreme Headquarters Allied Expeditionary Force (SHAEF). Smith joined the U.S. National Guard at the age of sixteen and continued serving despite his father's ill health, which forced him to quit school to support his family. Soon after the United States entered World War I, Sergeant Smith attended one of the newly created officer training schools and was commissioned lieutenant of infantry in the fall of 1917. Assigned to the 4th Division and sent to France in 1918, his experience as a platoon leader lasted fewer than 24 hours, when he was wounded. That fall he was one of a small group of officers rotated back to Washington for service on the War Department General Staff. When the war ended a few months later, he passed an examination to become a regular army lieutenant.

In the post–World War I army, Smith advanced because of his competence as an officer and his outstanding performance in the army schools: Infantry School, Command and General Staff School, and Army War College. Most important, at Infantry School he strongly impressed one of his instructors, Omar N. Bradley, and also the director of instruction, George C. Marshall. Eight years later Marshall was chief of staff and Bradley, in Marshall's secretariat, recommended that Smith be added to the staff. Less than a year later Smith became secretary, General Staff. With Marshall's backing he served as secretary of the Joint Chiefs of Staff, secretary of the Combined Chiefs of Staff, and was also Marshall's liaison to the White House. He had been made brigadier general in February 1942.

In the summer of 1942, when Eisenhower was in England organizing his Allied command for the North African invasion, Marshall sent Smith to London to become chief of staff of the new command. Smith proved so effective in this position that Eisenhower, when he was selected commander of Supreme Headquarters Allied Expeditionary Force, sent Smith from Africa to London to organize SHAEF. In the months before D-day, Smith played a major role in creating the combined British and American staff to coordinate the Allied invasion in northwest Europe. Driving them as hard as he would later in the hectic fighting of 1944–1945, Smith lived on his nerves and on the forbearance of hard-driven subordinates, colleagues, and superiors. He was an excellent complement to the affable Eisenhower. He was made major general in December 1942.

As chief of staff for SHAEF, Smith was present and supported Eisenhower at the meeting of top-ranking British and American officers where Eisenhower decided that D-day would be 6 June 1944. General Montgomery had been chosen by Eisenhower to command the Allied forces in the opening days of the invasion and Smith had no direct role during this period. Montgomery proved cautious in developing the battle, and Smith was one of the British and American officers who urged Eisenhower to pressure Montgomery to be more aggressive in action.

Eisenhower assumed more active control of operations after 1 September 1944 and Smith's role increased. At the close of the war in Europe Eisenhower placed Smith and British Maj. Gen. Kenneth Strong, who spoke German, in charge of the German capitulation arrangements. Smith firmly refused to allow the Germans to surrender on the Western front while continuing to fight the Russians in the East. He witnessed the unconditional German surrender and then escorted the enemy representatives to meet Eisenhower. On 13 February 1944 he was made lieutenant general.

After Japan had surrendered, Truman appointed Smith ambassador to Russia, a post he held from 1946 to 1949. In 1949 Smith became commander of the U.S. First Army in Governor's Island, New York, and he received the fourth star of a full general in 1951. Seven months later Truman asked him to become head of the Central Intelligence Agency. When Eisenhower became president, he moved Smith to the State Department. He resigned this position in October 1954 and became wealthy as a businessman before his death in 1961.

Irascible, brutal in manner, impatient, and fiercely demanding, "Ike's hatchet man" won acceptance only because he demonstrated that he expected no more of others then he did of himself.

BIBLIOGRAPHY

Crosswell, D. K. R. *The Chief of Staff: The Military Career of General Walter Bedell Smith*. 1991.

Eisenhower, Dwight D. *Crusade in Europe*. 1949.

Pogue, Forrest C. *The Supreme Command*. U.S. Army in World War II: The European Theater of Operations. 1954.

FORREST C. POGUE

WALTER BEDELL SMITH.   Standing, far right. With him, left to right: (standing) Omar Bradley, Bertram H. Ramsay, Trafford Leigh-Mallory; (seated) Arthur Tedder, Dwight D. Eisenhower, Bernard L. Montgomery.   NATIONAL ARCHIVES

SPAATZ, CARL (1891–1974). American, lieutenant general; commanding general, U.S. Strategic Air Forces (USSTAF). Spaatz graduated from West Point in 1914 and during much of World War I commanded a training center in France. In September 1918 he transferred to the front and shot down three German aircraft. Between the world wars he served in operational, command, and staff assignments. Spaatz testified at Brig. Gen. William ("Billy") Mitchell's court-martial in 1924. Spaatz supported Mitchell's radical airpower theories and his contention that the army had badly managed its air arm. Spaatz flew in the pioneer *Question Mark* endurance and air-to-air refueling flight in 1929. In the 1930s he attended the Army Command and Staff School and served with the first operational B-17 bombers. He also befriended Lt. Col. Henry H. Arnold, who subsequently commanded the U.S. Army Air Forces (AAF) in World War II.

In the summer of 1940 Colonel Spaatz observed the Battle of Britain and familiarized himself with the Royal Air Force and its leadership. Upon returning to the United States, he helped prepare the air corps for modern warfare. He took the Eighth Air Force to Britain in the summer of 1942 and in late December Lt. Gen. Dwight D. Eisenhower, commander of the Anglo-American forces in North Africa, requested Spaatz's transfer to the Mediterranean, where he served for the following year. General Spaatz commanded the Northwest African Air Forces and became a close friend of General Eisenhower. In December 1943 General Arnold ordered Spaatz to London to command the U.S. Strategic Air Forces in Europe (USSAFE), which had operational control of the American Eighth Air Force, based in Britain, and the Fifteenth Air Force, based in Italy, and administrative control of the Eighth and Ninth Air Forces, both in Britain. Redesignated U.S. Strategic Air Forces (USSTAF), it was independent of Eisenhower's command.

Spaatz balanced two objectives. He had to conduct the American daylight precision strategic bombing campaign against the German war economy. If he failed, Germany might prolong the war and the AAF might never become an independent air force. But he had also pledged his assistance to Eisenhower for the invasion of the Continent at the appropriate time. If that operation failed, Spaatz wanted no blame attached to the AAF. During the first third of 1944 Spaatz engaged in a two-front conflict, one a battle of attrition against the Luftwaffe and the other a struggle against plans pulling his forces from Germany and committing them to the invasion. The arrival of long-range P-51 fighters and new drop tanks for his P-38s and P-47s enabled Spaatz to attack the Luftwaffe directly. He allowed the Eighth's commander, Lt. Gen. James Doolittle, to free the fighters from escort duty in order to pursue the Germans. By mid-April the Eighth had crushed German aerial opposition and attained air

CARL SPAATZ.   NATIONAL ARCHIVES

superiority. It began to send its fighters on low-altitude raids, strafing airfields and other targets.

By March 1944 the Eighth could bomb any target in Germany with acceptable losses. Spaatz hoped to capitalize on his operational freedom by attacking German synthetic oil industry facilities. Lack of oil would hamstring the Luftwaffe and the German army. This plan, however, countered a transportation plan developed by Eisenhower's tactical air commander, Air Chief Marshal Trafford Leigh-Mallory. The transportation plan required half of the Eighth's heavy bombers to begin attritional attacks on German lines of communication in Belgium and France, particularly rail-marshaling yards, sixty days before the invasion. Spaatz objected to this threat to nullify his gains over Germany by using his bombers on lower-priority targets. But on 25 March, Eisenhower chose the transportation plan, and, a few days later he gained direction of USSTAF's operations.

Nonetheless, Spaatz delayed hitting transportation plan targets until 22 April, by which time he had persuaded Eisenhower to permit two raids on synthetic oil facilities. The raids, on 12 and 28 May, halved total German production, but occurred too late to affect the invasion. The Eighth also struck and destroyed or damaged all twenty-three of its transportation targets. On 6 June the Eighth attacked the beaches and transportation targets in Normandy. Its fighters provided ground support and air cover for the invasion fleet and beachhead.

General Spaatz accomplished the difficult task of maintaining the AAF strategic bombing campaign while assisting OVERLORD. His excellent personal relations with many of the other senior officers in Britain helped him convince them that he was sincere in his intent to meet both of his tasks. Without his insistence on engaging and destroying the Luftwaffe over Germany, that force might have significantly hindered the invasion.

After Germany's surrender Spaatz transferred to the Pacific theater where he assumed command of the U.S. Strategic Air Force, Pacific. He gave the direct orders for the atomic bomb drops on Japan. After the war he succeeded Arnold as commander of the AAF and in September 1947 he became the first chief of staff of the USAF. He retired to private life as a consulting journalist to *Newsweek* in April 1948.

[*See also* U.S. Strategic Air Forces (USSTAF).]

BIBLIOGRAPHY

Davis, Richard G. *Spaatz and the Air War over Europe, 1940–1945*. 1993.
Mets, David R. *Master of Airpower: General Carl A. Spaatz*. 1988.

RICHARD G. DAVIS

SPECIAL OPERATIONS. Four years' preparation bore fruit on D-day. Winston Churchill had been urging raids on the northern coasts of France since the summer of 1940, when he had originated both the commandos and the Special Operations Executive (SOE), a new secret service devoted to subversion and sabotage.

The sabotage effort can be dated back in principle to Charles de Gaulle's appeal of 18 June 1940, from which the Free French movement originated, and to 22 July 1940, when the British war cabinet approved the founding of SOE. After four years' trial and error, SOE had over forty networks in France (called circuits in English, *réseaux* in French) of saboteurs, armed and waiting on orders to act, in its F (independent French) Section, which came, through several intermediate commanders, under the Combined Chiefs of Staff. The Gaullists had more numerous and more diffuse groupings, also waiting on orders, in this case from General de Gaulle, in SOE's RF (or Gaullist) Section. The F and RF Sections between them planned to make 1,050 rail cuts on the eve of D-day, for which warning orders went out by coded BBC messages on 1 June and action orders at 2115 on 5 June: 950 of these cuts were successfully carried out that night. This made the railways all but unusable to the Germans for the transport of ammunition, food, and reinforcements. They were compelled

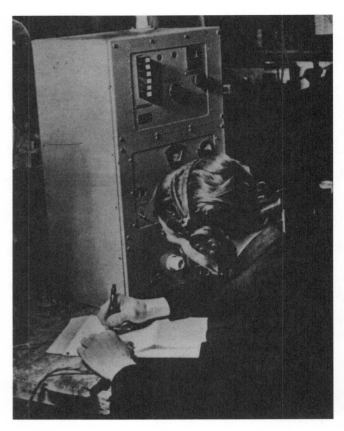

HIDDEN SHORTWAVE TRANSMITTER IN FRANCE. Used by the Resistance to maintain contact with England.
THE ROBERT HUNT LIBRARY, LONDON

to send convoys on the roads, thus depleting their scarce gasoline stocks and providing targets both for the Allied air forces and for ambush parties mounted by members of the local Resistance. These men often carried weapons flown in by the Royal Air Force on SOE's instructions and sometimes acted on SOE organizers' advice about tactics.

Expert groups under F Section's guidance also tackled telephone sabotage, attacking cables in remote spots rather than damaging exchanges, which the Allies hoped soon to be using themselves, and, when possible, ambushing repair parties, aiming to kill their German escorts and to persuade their French technicians to join the Resistance. Most long-distance telephone service in France was thereafter either unavailable or subject to tiresome delays, thus forcing the Germans to make more use of radios, which in turn provided more raw material for decipherment and fresh, up-to-date intelligence.

A third large section of SOE, AMF, operated from Algiers under Anglo-American command, cooperating with General de Gaulle. AMF organized circuits into southern France to support the impending landing on the Riviera; some of these circuits also played a substantial part in making the Germans' rear areas dangerous to them. Between them, these three SOE sections put some 1,600 agents into France during the war, about a quarter of whom fell into enemy hands with horrible results.

Further stiffening was provided by the Special Air Service (SAS) Brigade, founded in North Africa in October 1941 by David Stirling, then a junior Scots Guards officer. By spring 1944 it had expanded from a few dozen men to a brigade of two British and two French units—each about 400 strong—with an independent Belgian company and a special "Phantom" signals company. All had been trained as parachutists and saboteurs; they rivaled the commandos and rangers for toughness and enterprise. One of the British units was commanded by R. B. ("Paddy") Mayne, who, in a single night, had destroyed forty-seven enemy aircraft with his own hands in North Africa.

Two small SAS parties created Operation TITANIC on the eve of D-day, each dropping with 500 dummy parachutists (supposed to explode on arrival) to simulate a major airborne landing. One of these parties, southeast of Isigny, combined with stray drops from the 82d and 101st airborne divisions to give the acting commander of the German division behind Omaha Beach such a fright that he woke his reserve regiment at 0300 hours and had it search the woods southeast of Isigny all the morning of 6 June, instead of being on hand to counterattack on the beach.

The advance guard of one of the French SAS battalions dropped into south Brittany at about midnight that night. Eighteen small follow-up parties on 8–9 June put the Breton railways out of action, thus providing plenty of targets for the Allied air forces when German reinforcements for Normandy had to approach by road. This Breton expedition was invaluable. With Jedburgh help, it armed some thirty thousand members of the local Resistance, who seized every German-garrisoned village in the peninsula, on a signal sent over the BBC, to coincide with Gen. George S. Patton's breakthrough at Avranches.

Other SAS advance parties on 5–6 June set up Operation BULBASKET to block the Paris-Bordeaux railway line near Poitiers and to hamper German movements across Poitou; Operation HOUNDSWORTH in the Forêt du Morvan in northern Burgundy, which became a sharp thorn in the Germans' side; and Operation GAIN, which laid nighttime ambushes on the roads southwest of Paris. As OVERLORD developed, the whole brigade was deployed—all in uniform—with the effect of providing a steel core for dozens of Maquis (French Resistance) groups.

All over France, the same aim was pursued by the Jedburgh teams, organized jointly by SOE, by its U.S. equivalent, the Office of Strategic Services (OSS), and by the Free French. Each of these teams had three members, usually one from each of the three nationalities; one of the three was a radio operator. All were highly trained and motivated. Eighty teams were in France by the end of June, most of them arriving on D-day or a day or two later (including five in Brittany). All came in uniform, though some found it prudent to change quickly into plain clothes to avoid Gestapo attention.

Almost always, Jedburgh teams parachuted in to reception parties arranged for them by SOE agents who had already prepared a task for them. Some of the agents had been operating under cover for over two years. Among them were women—in SOE's longer-term circuits, not in the Jedburgh parties—who suffered even heavier casualties than men.

The F and AMF teams remained available to carry out any directives they might get from the Allied high command; General Dwight D. Eisenhower had a special forces team at his elbow, headed by Col. Robin Brook, to advise him what could and could not be done and to initiate action. Eisenhower's staff had hoped for a bonus from the Resistance; they got a much larger one than they expected. He said later that the Resistance was worth five or six divisions to him.

The RF teams, besides helping in the arming of Resistance members and in demolitions, were preparing the Gaullists' seizure of power, achieved on the spot, village by village.

One example can indicate the sort of influence a well-placed agent could exert. The *2d SS Panzer Division* was at Montauban, north of Toulouse, on 6 June. It was ordered to Normandy on the seventh and might have been expected on the ninth, D plus 3. But its tank transporters' axles had been doctored with abrasive grease parachuted in by SOE on the orders of Tony Brooks, a twenty-two-year-old English F Section agent; this sabotage was often carried out by two French sisters, the elder of them just sixteen. None of the tanks could be moved more than five kilometer (three miles) out of Montauban by rail. Constantly harassed by SOE-inspired ambushes on the way north, the division did not reach Normandy until D plus 17.

The air crews and sailors who took these special forces to work performed more or less routine tasks. Everyone in special forces was a volunteer.

[*See also* French Resistance; Office of Strategic Services (OSS); Railroads.]

BIBLIOGRAPHY

Foot, M. R. D. *SOE in France*. 1968.
Strawson, John. *A History of the SAS Regiment*. 1984.

M. R. D. FOOT

SPEIDEL, HANS (1897–1984), German, chief of general staff of *Army Group B*. Speidel was born into a nonmilitary bourgeois family in Württemberg. He joined the

HANS SPEIDEL.   Left, with Adolf Hitler.
THE ROBERT HUNT LIBRARY, LONDON

army in November 1914 and was commissioned a year later. He was trained as a general staff officer and was one of the very few officers to receive a doctorate (in history). At the beginning of World War II, Speidel was a lieutenant colonel and operations officer in an infantry division. After June 1940, he held numerous appointments as chief of general staff to command authorities, first in France and then on the Eastern front. Speidel rose to brigadier general in January 1943 and to major general in January 1944. For his excellent service on the Eastern front, he received the Knight's Cross in 1944. Field Marshal Erwin Rommel picked him as his chief of general staff for *Army Group B* in the spring of 1944 not only because of his brilliant reputation as a staff worker but also because Speidel—like Rommel—was a Swabian. In fact, the two had met during World War I and had served in the same regiment for a short time during the interwar period.

Speidel was an intellectual, bespectacled, quiet, and efficient. He loved the arts, balancing his commander in chief's purely military tastes, as Rommel himself would admit. He was also given to vanity, however, and to many he appeared self-centered.

Unlike the Anglo-American system, the German military command structure at the time did not provide for deputy commanders. In the absence of the commander, the chief of staff assumed day-to-day responsibilities, even issuing orders to those subordinate commanders who were his superiors in rank. Rommel, who usually led from the front and was therefore away from his headquarters for most of the day, always took great pains to

pick capable chiefs of staff, knowing the responsibility they would have to assume. During the period immediately before the Normandy invasion, while Rommel traveled widely around the French countryside, inspecting, exhorting, and admonishing the German forces, Speidel was left to "mind the shop." Only early in the mornings and late in the evenings would he see Rommel. To the end, Rommel was very pleased with Speidel's style of operating headquarters.

Speidel was involved in the conspiracy against Adolf Hitler, although in not nearly as central a role as he himself would claim after the war. The degree to which he seriously attempted to involve Rommel is not known. It has been contended in recent years that Speidel's suggestions for deploying *Army Group B*'s divisions (in particular the *2d* and *116th* panzer divisions) were influenced by his desire to have reliable troops ready for an attempted coup d'état rather than for the Allied invasion. The evidence, however, remains inconclusive, with reliable witnesses testifying to the contrary.

On 6 June 1944, Rommel was away in Germany, celebrating his wife's fiftieth birthday, and Speidel was in charge at *Army Group B*'s headquarters at La Roche–Guyon, west of Paris. Speidel did not take intelligence warnings about an impending invasion very seriously, nor was he inclined to believe that the first incoming reports of airborne landings heralded more than a local raid. Only at about 0900, when the *Seventh Army* reported large-scale amphibious landings on the beaches, did Speidel alert Rommel and ask him to come back. Even then, Speidel did not rule out the possibility of another invasion in the Pas de Calais area, nor would he and Rommel do so for another week. As a consequence, Speidel did not move reinforcements south from the *Fifteenth Army* on 6 June. In addition, the OKW was reluctant to release its armored reserves, delaying the deployment of the *Panzer Lehr Division* and others.

Early in the evening, Rommel arrived back at his headquarters and assumed responsibility, although it remains doubtful if his presence would have greatly altered the course of events. Rommel himself was convinced that he would have obtained the release of the reserve divisions sooner, but that was hindsight. Nor is there any reason to believe that Rommel would have alerted his subordinate units sooner.

Speidel remained chief of *Army Group B*'s general staff until he was arrested for his involvement in the conspiracy against Hitler in the early days of September. He was cleared by an army court of inquiry, which probably saved him from execution, but he remained a prisoner until liberated by French troops in the spring of 1945. Unlike Rommel, Speidel survived.

Speidel after the war served as the chief military negotiator in the European Defense Community talks in 1952–1953 and was commissioned into the Bundeswehr as lieutenant general in 1955. After promotion to full general in 1957, he became the first German to hold the post of commander of Allied Land Forces Central Europe (LANDCENT) in Fontainebleau, France. He retired in 1963 and died in 1984.

[*See also* Rommel, Erwin.]

BIBLIOGRAPHY

Irving, David. *The Trail of the Fox: The Search for the True Field Marshal Rommel.* 1977.
Speidel, Hans. *Aus unserer Zeit: Erinnerungen.* 1977.

WINFRIED HEINEMANN

SPERRLE, HUGO (1885–1953), German, field marshal, commander of the *Third Air Force,* responsible for air operations from bases in France, Holland, and Belgium. Hugo Sperrle joined the Imperial Army in 1903 as an infantryman. During World War I he served as an observer in the Imperial Flying Service, and rose to command the flying units attached to the *Seventh Army.* After the war he remained in the army until 1935, then moved to the newly formed Luftwaffe. In the following

HUGO SPERRLE.   NATIONAL ARCHIVES

year, with the rank of brigadier general, he was appointed commander of the *Condor Legion,* the contingent of German air units that fought alongside Gen. Francisco Franco's forces in the Spanish Civil War. Early in 1938 he was appointed commander of *Luftwaffengruppe 3,* later renamed the *Third Air Force (Luftflotte 3).*

With headquarters in Paris, Sperrle commanded the *Third Air Force* during the spectacular blitzkrieg in the West in the spring of 1940, and during the daylight and night attacks of the Battle of Britain. In the spring of 1941 flying units were transferred east in preparation for the attack on the Soviet Union, and the fighting strength of the *Third Air Force* waned. Nevertheless, Sperrle maintained a steady pressure on the British Isles with his small bomber force, tying down many squadrons of RAF fighters and a large antiaircraft organization that might otherwise have been used in other theaters of the conflict.

Following D-day the *Third Air Force* was overwhelmed by the Allied air forces arrayed against it, and Sperrle was able to do little to influence events. Hitler blamed him for the Luftwaffe's failure to achieve more, though given the disparity in forces it is unlikely that another commander could have done better. In August 1944 Sperrle was transferred to the reserve. After the war he was tried at Nuremberg for war crimes, but was acquitted.

[*See also* Third Air Force.]

BIBLIOGRAPHY

Price, Alfred. *The Last Year of the Luftwaffe.* 1991.
Suchenwirth, Richard. *The Development of the German Air Force, 1919–1939.* 1968.

ALFRED PRICE

STALIN, JOSEF (1879–1953), Soviet, marshal of the Soviet Union, chairman of the Council of People's Commissars and the State Committee of Defense, Supreme Commander in Chief of the Soviet Armed Forces. Stalin called for a second front and proposed northern France as the site on 18 July 1941 in his first wartime letter to Prime Minister Winston Churchill. Thereafter, until a second front came into being, he regarded the British and Americans as in default on their obligations to the Soviet Union. His own commitment to the two-front strategy fluctuated. It hit a low point in the winter of 1941–1942 when a Soviet victory appeared to be in sight and peaked during the second German summer offensive. By the time of the Teheran Conference with Churchill and President Franklin D. Roosevelt in late November 1943, his armies were completing a year of almost uninterrupted successes, his confidence was running high, and he was determined to extract the maximum political and territorial profit from the Axis defeat.

JOSEF STALIN.   With Winston Churchill at Yalta, 1945.
NATIONAL ARCHIVES

The chiefs of the British and American military missions in Moscow, Lt. Gen. Giffard Martel and Maj. Gen. John R. Deane, had briefed the Soviet Supreme Command on the OVERLORD plan in October 1943, but Roosevelt and Churchill arrived at Teheran unprepared to state positively when or whether the plan would be executed. In the first session, Roosevelt leaned toward implementing OVERLORD in May 1944, but Churchill maintained that so early a date would be premature. He argued that it would sacrifice opportunities still available in the Mediterranean, such as landings in southern France or on the Yugoslavian coast at the head of the Adriatic Sea. Roosevelt and Churchill appeared satisfied to have stated the problem, but Stalin insisted on their deciding on the spot to implement OVERLORD in May 1944 because, he said, his forces could then plan simultaneous supporting operations to tie down the Germans on the Eastern front. He insisted also on a decision for a landing in southern France; when his requirements were met, he agreed to give help in the deception operations for OVERLORD. The southern France landing was the crux of what Stalin later called "the Teheran Plan." It ensured him against the venture into Yugoslavia, which he believed was conceived to block him in the Balkan area.

In February 1944, the Soviet General Staff gave a mixed response to the BODYGUARD deception plan, under which it was requested to feign threats to the Petsamo area in northern Finland and to the Bulgarian Black Sea coast. It accepted the Petsamo assignment at once but argued for four weeks that it could not even simulate a threat against Bulgaria, with which the Soviet Union was not formally at war. In May, the deputy chief of the General Staff told General Deane that ships and troops were being concentrated in the Kola Inlet, east of Petsamo, and air and sea reconnaissance was being conducted along the Arctic coast. The requirements for a threat to Bulgaria, he added, should be regarded as having been met by a Soviet advance to the Romanian border completed in April. The only tangible evidence Deane had of Soviet engagement in the deception were some misleading leaks in the Moscow newspapers.

Roosevelt and Churchill informed Stalin on 18 April that D-day would be 31 May, plus or minus a few days, and Stalin replied that to give "maximum assistance," his armies would open an offensive "at the same time." Deane believed that the General Staff, which always reflected Stalin's judgments on such matters, regarded the date all along as a probable deception designed to cover a nefarious Anglo-American enterprise like a strike into the Balkans.

On 6 June, Stalin congratulated Churchill and Roosevelt on OVERLORD, adding that "as agreed at Teheran," the Soviet forces would begin an offensive "in an important sector of their front" by mid-June. On the ninth, he told Churchill that the Soviet offensive would start the next day on the Leningrad front. Churchill welcomed the news and passed it immediately to Roosevelt and General Dwight D. Eisenhower. There were no German troops on the Leningrad front, however. The offensive was directed exclusively against the Finnish army. Stalin was following a summer agenda he had devised with no particular reference to the Teheran agreements. On 22 June, after the Normandy beachhead was solidly established and was tying down the German forces in western Europe, he passed to the second phase, a massive 130-division assault on the center of the German Eastern front. His most positive contribution to OVERLORD was his mitigating his allies' concern over a danger that did not materialize but might have impaired their decision-making process.

[See also Planning, article on Allied Planning.]

BIBLIOGRAPHY

Deane, John R. *The Strange Alliance: The Story of Our Efforts at Wartime Co-operation with Russia.* 1947.

Feis, Herbert. *Churchill, Roosevelt, Stalin: The War They Waged and the Peace They Sought.* 1957.

EARL F. ZIEMKE

STARK, HAROLD R. (1880–1972), American, admiral, chief of naval operations then commander, U.S. Naval Forces Europe. After graduating from the U.S. Naval Academy in 1903, Stark served on a wide variety of ships. During World War I he commanded a flotilla of destroyers on the long voyage from Manila to Gibraltar and then served on the staff of U.S. Adm. William S. Sims in London. As a young officer Stark met Franklin D. Roosevelt, then assistant secretary of the navy. They remained friends until Roosevelt's death in 1945.

Stark resigned as chief of naval operations in 1942. Roosevelt then sent him to London as commander of U.S. Naval Forces, Europe. In that capacity Stark was the administrative commander for the logistics buildup and amphibious training for all naval forces involved in Operation OVERLORD. With the creation of the Twelfth Fleet in 1943, he became the operational commander of these forces.

Following the decision by Roosevelt and Churchill in 1943 to make a cross-Channel landing on the French coast, Stark was put in charge of the myriad details attendant upon the necessary buildup and preparations for such an ambitious undertaking. Numerous bases were established in Scotland and England for training men for the maintenance and repair of landing craft and other equipment, and extensive storage facilities for supplies of all sorts and description were established. In 1943 additional facilities were established along the south coast of England and the Admiralty turned over the Royal Naval College at Dartmouth to the U.S. Navy. Over 125,000 men and 3,000 ships and landing craft were under Stark's command.

Because the landing site on the French coast was open, exposed to tides and currents, and without port facilities, it was necessary to prepare artificial harbors in the United Kingdom; these were to be towed across the English Channel and then sunk to make a temporary harbor on the French coast so that men, ammunition, food, and other supplies could be sent to the invading armies. Commander Naval Forces Europe (COMNAVEU) was in charge of these complex preparations. When French ports were finally liberated after D-day, COMNAVEU and its subordinate commands were responsible for making them operational in the shortest period of time.

The invading American and British armies did not just appear on the Normandy beaches. The U.S. Navy and the Royal Navy transported them, their supplies, and equipment. The success of this indispensable logistics support can be attributed to Stark's leadership and the efficiency of his command.

Stark returned to the United Sates in August 1945. He remained on active duty until the spring of 1946, when the congressional investigation into the attack on Pearl Harbor concluded. In 1946 Oxford University awarded him an honorary degree; later, he served with distinc-

HAROLD R. STARK.

tion as a trustee of Wilkes College, Wilkes Barre, Pennsylvania. He died in August 1972 in Washington, D.C.

[*See also* Navy, *article on* Allied Naval Forces.]

BIBLIOGRAPHY

Simpson, B. Mitchell, III. *Admiral Harold R. Stark: Architect of Victory, 1939–1945.* 1989.
Stark, Harold R. Official Papers. Naval Historical Center, Washington, D.C.

B. MITCHELL SIMPSON III

STEGMANN, RUDOLF (1894–1944), German, brigadier general, commander of the *77th Infantry Division*. One of the few German heroes of the Cherbourg debacle, Stegmann was born in East Prussia and joined the Imperial Army in 1912. He was commissioned a second lieutenant in the *141st Infantry Regiment* in 1914, fought on both the Eastern and Western fronts in World War I, and remained in the German army during the era of the Weimar Republic. He was a major when Adolf Hitler assumed power in 1933.

Stegmann was associated with the infantry or motorized infantry throughout his career. He commanded a motorized battalion in Poland, led the *14th Motorized Regiment* in France and Russia (1940–1942), and commanded the *2d Panzer Grenadier Brigade* and *36th Panzer Grenadier* (later *Infantry) Division* on the Eastern front (1942–1944). He was seriously wounded in the successful defensive battles around Bobruisk in the Soviet Union and did not return to active duty until 1 May 1944, when he assumed command of the *77th Infantry Division* in the Saint-Malo–Saint-Brieuc sector of Brittany.

The *77th Infantry* was an understrength, nonmotorized division made up largely of Volksdeutsche (ethnic Germans from eastern European countries), Poles, and Tatars from the Volga region, whose loyalty to the Third Reich was questionable at best. Stegmann was nevertheless able to transform it into a reasonably good combat division. It was placed on alert on D-day but not used due to erroneous reports of Allied airborne landings in Brittany. Ordered on 7 June to reinforce *Group Schlieben* west of Sainte-Mère-Église, it marched to the battlefield on foot and first engaged the Americans on 10 June, when it defended hedgerow country on both sides of the Merderet River and successfully prevented much stronger elements of the U.S. VII Corps from outflanking the critical position of Montebourg, a major road junction on the road to Cherbourg, and temporarily prevented the collapse of *Group Schlieben*. South of Stegmann's positions, however, the VII Corps under Gen. J. Lawton Collins broke through and reached the coast near Barneville on the morning of 18 June, cutting off *Group Schlieben* in the northern part of the Cotentin Peninsula.

In the meantime, Stegmann successfully held up the advance of the U.S. 90th Infantry Division, proving that he could get the maximum combat effort from a division previously considered unreliable. On 18 June, Field Marshal Erwin Rommel authorized the *77th Infantry* to break out to the south, but Hitler countermanded the order. Stegmann's division broke out anyway. Whether this move was initiated or even authorized by Gen. Friedrich Dollmann is still the subject of debate; Dollmann denied it at the time, and his chief of staff unquestionably denied Stegmann permission on the evening of 16 June. In any case, Stegmann was the man who acted. He began thinning out his line and tried to break out in five columns on the afternoon of 17 June, although some elements of the division were too heavily engaged against U.S. troops to disengage. One major column, which included the division's artillery and most of its transport, was destroyed by an American artillery regiment, and some of the other columns were scattered.

About 1,500 badly needed infantrymen reached safety on 20 June after overrunning part of the U.S. 47th Infantry Regiment and taking 250 prisoners. Stegmann was not with them, however. He had been killed near the village of Bricquebec, when his car was spotted by an American pilot, who dived to almost ground level and opened up on it at close range. The general's body was riddled with 20-mm shells, one of which struck him in the head. He was succeeded by Colonel of Reserves Bernard Bacherer.

Although Stegmann was credited with saving the remnants of the *77th Infantry Division,* had he lived, he might well have been court-martialed for disobeying the Führer's orders. Ironically, Stegmann was posthumously promoted to lieutenant general, effective 1 June 1944.

[*See also* 77th Infantry Division.]

BIBLIOGRAPHY

Keilig, Wolf. *Die Generale des Heeres*. 1983.
Mitcham, Samuel W., Jr., and Gene Mueller. *Hitler's Commanders*. 1992.

SAMUEL W. MITCHAM, JR.

SUPREME HEADQUARTERS ALLIED EXPEDITIONARY FORCE (SHAEF).

General Dwight D. Eisenhower assumed command of the Allied Expeditionary Force on 15 January 1944. By that date, the interim planning organization serving the Chief of Staff to the Supreme Allied Commander (COSSAC) had expired, though the greater part of its membership formed the basis of the emergent SHAEF.

COSSAC had been predominantly a British headquarters. SHAEF was based on the American command and staff system but was not simply a U.S. organization to which other nationalities were attached. This was due in part to Eisenhower's unique experience as an international tri-service supreme commander in North Africa, in which he had personally ordered the subordination of national propensities to Allied interests and set an example by firing American officers who failed to meet this requirement. It was due also to the inclusion of a substantial British element in senior and other posts together with Canadian and French members of the staff.

Eisenhower brought with him as his chief of staff Lt. Gen. Walter Bedell Smith, with whom he had established an excellent working relationship in Algiers, but the three deputy chiefs were British and included Lt. Gen. Frederick Morgan, the former COSSAC. The deputy supreme commander was British Air Chief Marshal Arthur Tedder, former air commander in chief in the Mediterranean. While Eisenhower would doubtless have been replaced by another American, if he had been killed or otherwise incapacitated, Tedder would have served in his place pending that appointment; there was no plan to bring in any other senior American soldier on an interim basis.

The balance of nationalities was preserved among the assistant chiefs of staff, American officers filling the G1

(Personnel), G3 (Operations), and G4 (Supply) posts, and the British those in the G2 (Intelligence) and G5 (Civil Affairs) posts. The G2 division would in any case have fallen necessarily to an American or British officer, because these two nationalities alone were partners in the signals intelligence organization (Sigint), the knowledge of which was closely reserved. Two senior political advisers were appointed to the staff, one American and one British. SHAEF military liaison missions were established to the Allied governments involved in northwest Europe. However, as neither President Roosevelt nor Prime Minister Churchill was ready to accord political status to General de Gaulle, Maj. Gen. John T. Lewis, head of the mission to France, was instructed to wait for the emergence of a popular and legitimate government in France following its liberation. A French general officer, nominated by Gen. Charles de Gaulle, led a French liaison mission to the Supreme Commander.

Arrangements were not quite as straightforward as indicated. There was no ground force commander in chief; Eisenhower decided that this duty, essentially coordination of the army group operations, should fall directly to him. It was manifest, however, that he would not have time to direct in detail the planning and break-in operation. He instructed British General Bernard L. Montgomery to command all ground forces until the United

States deployed an army group headquarters in France. Headquarters of the British 21st Army Group conveniently linked in with SHAEF and the headquarters of the naval and air commanders in chief.

Some adjustments were also made in the direction of the air forces. Tactical air operations were directed by SHAEF through the air commander in chief, but strategic, or long-range, bomber operations were directed by the Combined Chiefs of Staff. From 14 April on it was agreed that this latter direction should fall to Eisenhower, and the requisite orders be issued by SHAEF "until OVERLORD is established on the Continent." Within the headquarters, Air Chief Marshal Tedder was to coordinate all air operations, a useful employment of the deputy, whose role would otherwise be limited. But this sensible arrangement actually transformed the system. Progressively, Tedder functioned as the air commander in chief, and as a consequence the latter post, originally held by Air Chief Marshal Trafford Leigh-Mallory, was later abolished.

Another aspect not apparent from the organizational chart concerned the scope of the intelligence staff. It was decided at an early stage of planning that appropriate Sigint information should be sent directly to all commanders in chief from the decrypt centers to avoid delay in passage. This meant that SHAEF would not be employed as a channeling agency and, concomitantly, that its own Sigint staff would be solely responsible for providing this material for the Supreme Commander and his immediate subordinates. This was in accord with a greater principle that the SHAEF intelligence staff should "neither procure intelligence for itself nor attempt to appreciate operational intelligence." Their task would be to digest what came up to them and relate it to what came down; major assessments would stem from Washington and London. Yet it was apparent by February 1944 that this was not working. Daily demands were being made on the SHAEF intelligence division for planning purposes, so it began to function as a theater intelligence staff and continued to do so when operations began in June. The penalty was a doubling of its numbers.

SHAEF formed up in Bushy Park on the outskirts of London. Without disrupting its immense burden of work, General Bedell Smith divided staff, communications, security, and domestic elements among three echelons. The Forward Echelon was the smallest, designed to provide the Supreme Allied Commander with the information he needed to make decisions and the means to convey them to those who would ensure their execution. The Main Headquarters would provide the center to which all information would flow and from which executive orders would, with certain exceptions, be issued; it would thus contain the joint intelligence and joint operations centers, the joint planning staff, and the greater share of radio and telephone communications. The Rear Headquarters

Supreme Headquarters, Allied Expeditionary Force, 6 June 1944

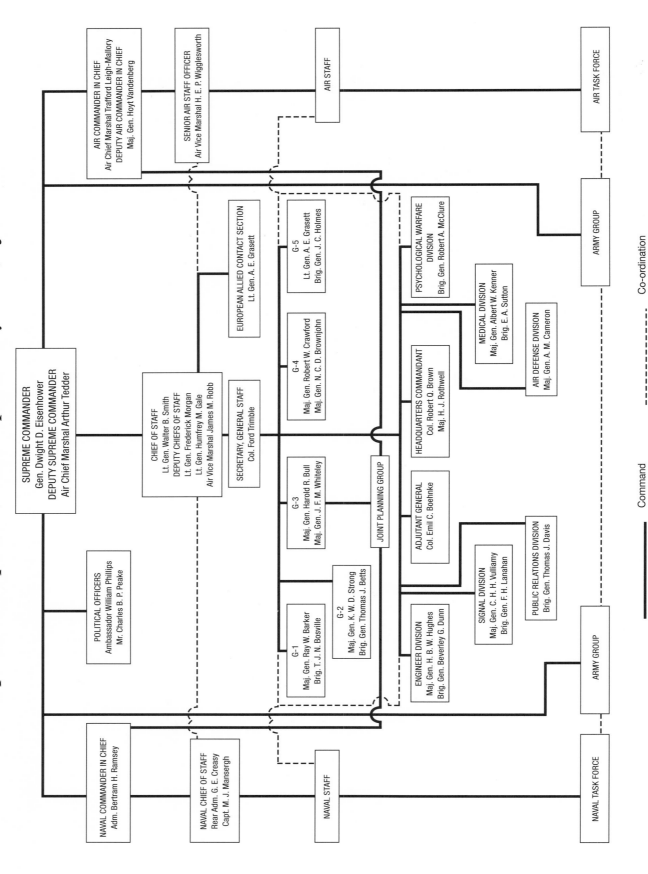

SUPREME COMMANDER
Gen. Dwight D. Eisenhower
DEPUTY SUPREME COMMANDER
Air Chief Marshal Arthur Tedder

AIR COMMANDER IN CHIEF
Air Chief Marshal Trafford Leigh-Mallory
DEPUTY AIR COMMANDER IN CHIEF
Maj. Gen. Hoyt Vandenberg

SENIOR AIR STAFF OFFICER
Air Vice Marshal H. E. P. Wigglesworth

AIR STAFF

AIR TASK FORCE

POLITICAL OFFICERS
Ambassador William Phillips
Mr. Charles B. P. Peake

CHIEF OF STAFF
Lt. Gen. Walter B. Smith
DEPUTY CHIEFS OF STAFF
Lt. Gen. Frederick Morgan
Lt. Gen. Humfrey M. Gale
Air Vice Marshal James M. Robb

SECRETARY, GENERAL STAFF
Col. Ford Trimble

EUROPEAN ALLIED CONTACT SECTION
Lt. Gen. A. E. Grasett

G-5
Lt. Gen. A. E. Grasett
Brig. Gen. J. C. Holmes

G-4
Maj. Gen. Robert W. Crawford
Maj. Gen. N. C. D. Brownjohn

G-3
Maj. Gen. Harold R. Bull
Maj. Gen. J. F. M. Whiteley

G-2
Maj. Gen. K. W. D. Strong
Brig. Gen. Thomas J. Betts

G-1
Maj. Gen. Ray W. Barker
Brig. T. J. N. Bosville

JOINT PLANNING GROUP

PSYCHOLOGICAL WARFARE DIVISION
Brig. Gen. Robert A. McClure

MEDICAL DIVISION
Maj. Gen. Albert W. Kenner
Brig. E. A. Sutton

AIR DEFENSE DIVISION
Maj. Gen. A. M. Cameron

HEADQUARTERS COMMANDANT
Col. Robert Q. Brown
Maj. H. J. Rothwell

ADJUTANT GENERAL
Col. Emil C. Boehnke

SIGNAL DIVISION
Maj. Gen. C. H. H. Vulliamy
Brig. Gen. F. H. Lanahan

PUBLIC RELATIONS DIVISION
Brig. Gen. Thomas J. Davis

ENGINEER DIVISION
Maj. Gen. H. B. W. Hughes
Brig. Gen. Beverley G. Dunn

ARMY GROUP

ARMY GROUP

NAVAL COMMANDER IN CHIEF
Adm. Bertram H. Ramsey

NAVAL CHIEF OF STAFF
Rear Adm. G. E. Creasy
Capt. M. J. Mansergh

NAVAL STAFF

NAVAL TASK FORCE

———— Command

- - - - Co-ordination

provided the principal working headquarters for the administrative and logistic staffs, as also for those engaged in civil affairs, the military government of the operational areas in Europe.

Involved from his arrival in Britain in frequent political and military consultations in London, Eisenhower was also obliged to maintain a personal office and living quarters there in Belgrave and St. James's squares. In April it became necessary to establish a temporary command post in the Portsmouth area, site of the combined headquarters for the three commanders in chief, so as to control the assault across the Normandy beaches. SHAEF Forward provided the necessary facilities, including proximity to a site for Eisenhower's personal aircraft.

Portsmouth was the SHAEF site closest to France until the end of June 1944. By that date SHAEF had drawn together as a working entity; Eisenhower's requirement for devotion to the Allied as distinct from national interest so militated. Where there were instances to the contrary, they were the exception. And although this huge body—almost twenty thousand strong, exceeding a division in strength with all its organic units—was, like all superior headquarters, often derided by those under its control, it nevertheless coordinated effectively the naval, air, and ground onslaught upon the German defenses in the greatest of all amphibious operations.

[*See also* Bedell Smith, Walter; Eisenhower, Dwight D.; Morgan, Frederick; Tedder, Arthur.]

BIBLIOGRAPHY

Harrison, Gordon A. *Cross-Channel Attack*. U.S. Army in World War II: The European Theater of Operations. 1951.

Hinsley, F. H., et al. *British Intelligence in the Second World War*. Vol. 3, pt. 2, 1988.

Morgan, Frederick. *Overture to Overlord*. 1950.

Pogue, Forrest C. *The Supreme Command*. U.S. Army in World War II: The European Theater of Operations. 1954.

ANTHONY FARRAR-HOCKLEY

SWORD BEACH. *See* British Beaches, *article on* Sword Beach.

T

TALBOT, ARTHUR G. (1892–1960), British, rear admiral commanding Assault Force S supporting the landings on Sword Beach. Arthur George Talbot entered the Royal Navy in 1905 and served as a lieutenant in World War I. As director of the Admiralty Anti-Submarine Warfare Division in 1939–1940, he was sent to sea for providing Churchill with accurate estimates of U-boat losses, in place of the inflated figures the First Lord of the Admiralty preferred. Knighted in 1940, he saw action as captain in turn of the aircraft carriers *Furious, Illustrious*, and *Formidable* from 1940 to 1943. Though he was promoted to rear admiral in 1943, this experience did not make him a natural choice for an amphibious task force command.

Force S, formed in November 1943, trained in the Moray Firth in Scotland. It was assigned to the eastern end of the assault area. On D-day Admiral Talbot's flagship *Largs* acted as headquarters to the British I Corps under Lt. Gen. J. T. Crocker, comprising the 3d Infantry Division and 27th Armoured Brigade.

At 0525 on D-day, as Force S approached the beachhead, *Largs* was almost torpedoed. The DD (Duplex Drive) tanks were launched closer inshore than planned and arrived late, some being swamped by passing LCTs. The assault force was ashore by 0943, only eighteen minutes late. In his report Talbot commented on the poor German response in the Sword Beach area: "The air was full of our bombers and fighters, and of the noise and smoke of our bombardments. The enemy was obviously stunned by the sheer weight of support we were meting out." He also praised the resolve and courage of the sailors and soldiers, most of whom were going into action for the first time. Talbot himself landed on Sword Beach at 1535 on D-day, where he found twenty-four landing craft stranded and much congestion on the beach. Additional working parties were then landed to clear extra exits from the beachhead.

As the operation progressed Talbot spent much time ashore, often distributing bread to the troops. During D plus 4 he insisted on altering the position of the Gooseberry blockships off Ouistreham so as to give greater protection from the northwest at the expense of the northeast, a decision that he regretted when the great gale of the 19th came in from the northeast. As the other beaches were improved, Sword was closed down, since it was impossible to silence the German artillery. Talbot was withdrawn with the other task force commanders at the end of June.

ARTHUR G. TALBOT.   IMPERIAL WAR MUSEUM

Later Talbot went to the Pacific as rear admiral commanding Force X, the amphibious assault component of the Pacific Fleet, an unwanted task that proved doubly unfortunate: his flagship HMS *Lothian* suffered a mutiny, and his forces were used only as transports. He would have had a major role in the amphibious attack on Japan.

After World War II Admiral Talbot was chairman of a committee on equipment for saving life at sea, and from 1946 to 1948 headed the British naval mission to Greece. He retired in 1948. A stern disciplinarian with a voice to match, Talbot was known to the lower deck as "Noisy."

[*See also* Largs, HMS; Task Force S.]

BIBLIOGRAPHY

Glennon, W. *Mutiny in Force X.* 1988.
Roskill, S. W. *The War at Sea, 1939–1945.* 1954–1961.

ANDREW LAMBERT

TASK FORCE, EASTERN. *See* Eastern Task Force.

TASK FORCE, WESTERN. *See* Western Task Force.

TASK FORCE 124. Task Force 124 (TF 124, Assault Force O, assigned to Omaha Beach) was commanded by Rear Adm. John L. Hall, flying his flag aboard the amphibious command ship USS *Ancon.* Having less far to steam than Task Force 125 (Utah Beach), his ships sailed from Portland, Weymouth, and Poole beginning at 1600 on 5 June 1944. They carried the assault elements of V Corps (Maj. Gen. Leonard Gerow). Their attached Bombardment Force C (Rear Adm. Carleton F. Bryant, USN) preceded the two convoys, one fast and one slow, that made up TF 124. Led by the battleship USS *Arkansas,* the bombardment force included two Free French cruisers, *Montcalm* and *Georges Leygues,* eight U.S. destroyers, and three British Hunt-class destroyers. British and Canadian minesweepers swept the approach to Omaha Beach by shortly after midnight. Despite some confusion en route, all the ships reached their proper stations on time early on 6 June. The bombarding ships took up their position around 0220, and the transports anchored at 0250.

Allied photo interpreters believed that there were 155-mm batteries on Pointe du Hoc and near Port-en-Bessin. This belief led Admiral Hall and Maj. Gen. Clarence R. Huebner, the commander of the first wave, to have the transports anchor and begin unloading eighteen kilometers (eleven miles) offshore in the open waters, out of range of the big batteries. This meant that the landing craft had to negotiate unexpectedly rough seas that further prolonged their journey to shore, exposing them to intensive German fire.

The army had not wanted the bombardment force to open fire until daylight, but German batteries opened up on *Arkansas* at first light, 0530, an hour before H-hour. *Arkansas* and the destroyers immediately responded. The prelanding bombardment by the heavy ships, however, focused on what was believed to be the major battery atop Pointe du Hoc. Unfortunately, the Germans had relocated the guns, so *Arkansas* wasted most of its rounds. This bombardment continued until 0555.

The actual landing nearly failed. The long passage in high seas caused the successive waves of landing craft to get separated and lose formation. The defenses at Omaha Beach were the most formidable encountered anywhere on D-day. Photo interpreters had failed to detect the presence of gun emplacements dug into the bluffs to enfilade the entire length of the beach. Protected from offshore observation and from gunfire by three-foot concrete shields, these guns wreaked havoc with the landing craft.

The shore fire-control parties had not established themselves ashore, so ships depended on what they could see for themselves. The big ships, firing on prearranged targets with the aid of Spitfire spotting, helped seal off the landing zones, but the troops on the beach initially made little progress and lost heavily. By 0950 the situation ashore was sufficiently desperate for Admiral Bryant to order all destroyers to maneuver as close to shore as possible. Thus eight U.S. destroyers and three British Hunt-class destroyers, whose even shallower draft permitted them to get as close as five kilometers (5,000 yards) to shore, went inshore of the heavier ships. Firing on targets of opportunity, they quickly established their dominance of the beachhead and provided the necessary covering fire that enabled the troops to begin moving inland.

By noon, the landing forces had secured an initial foothold on Omaha Beach, and Force B, the second contingent, was able to land. The bombardment now shifted to inland targets. Aided by spotters, the battleship USS *Texas* broke up two German columns near Longueville and Formigny, several miles inland, on D-day. *Arkansas* destroyed a train at La Plaise and also hit a battery southeast of Trévières on the next day. Naval gunfire from the big ships detonated several large mine fields ashore that the Germans had hoped would delay any breakthrough.

On 7 June, the cruiser HMS *Glasgow* fired thirteen times in response to calls to attack German batteries, vehicle convoys, or troop concentrations. By 8 June ships from TF 124 were firing at targets eleven to thirteen kilometers (seven to eight miles) inland, but by now the battle was moving beyond the range of all but the heavy armament of the battleships. On 9 June USS *Ellyson* provided the last destroyer fire support in the Omaha sector.

The initial errors of anchoring far offshore and the mistaken concentration on Pointe du Hoc, combined with the brevity of the firing, reduced the effectiveness of the overall bombardment. The subsequent close support provided by the destroyers saved the day.

[See also American Beaches, article on Omaha Beach; Ancon, USS; Hall, John L.; Task Force 126; Western Task Force.]

BIBLIOGRAPHY

Barnett, Correlli. *Engage the Enemy More Closely: The Royal Navy in the Second World War.* 1991.

Ellis, L. F., et al. *The Battle of Normandy.* Vol. 1 of *Victory in the West.* 1962.

Morison, Samuel E. *The Invasion of France and Germany, 1944–1945.* Vol. 11 of *History of United States Naval Operations in World War Two.* 1957.

Ramsay, Bertram H. "The Assault Phase of the Normandy Landings." Dispatch dated 16 October 1944, printed in *The London Gazette,* 30 October 1947.

Roskill, Stephen W. *The Offensive.* Vol. 3, pt. 2, of *The War at Sea, 1939–1945.* 1961.

MARK JACOBSEN

TASK FORCE 125. Rear Adm. Don P. Moon, USN, commanded Task Force 125 (TF 125, Assault Force U), responsible for supporting the landings on Utah Beach and transporting the U.S. 4th Infantry Division (Maj. Gen. J. Lawton Collins). Moon flew his flag aboard the attack transport USS *Bayfield.* Owing to the length of the passage from the originating ports in Devonshire, the lead elements of Admiral Moon's force sortied from Dartmouth, Salcombe, Torbay, and Brixham late in the afternoon of 3 June 1944. At noon that day, its three minesweeping groups had sailed from Channel ports. They cleared a channel, but in the process lost one minesweeper, USS *Osprey,* which hit a mine and sank shortly after 1815 on 5 June.

When General Dwight D. Eisenhower postponed OVERLORD by twenty-four hours, the convoys already at sea reversed course and returned to the sheltered waters of Weymouth Bay, while those that had not yet sailed stood by. The gunfire support ships of Bombardment Force A (Rear Adm. Morton L. Deyo, USN) had sailed from Northern Ireland late on 2 June. They reversed course and steamed north in the Irish Sea on 4 June before returning to their original course that evening. One slow convoy of 128 LCTs (Force U2A) missed the signal and at 0900 on 4 June was still on course some forty kilometers (twenty-five miles) south of the Isle of Wight and approaching the range of German radar. A naval aircraft and two destroy-ers sent from Portsmouth overtook it and ordered it to return to Weymouth Bay to anchor and refuel.

Most of Force U was able to return, but some ships were unable to make their way through the head sea and spent the next day in the Channel. Throughout 4 June, while commanders debated the wisdom of sailing in the face of uncertain weather, they faced the added dilemma of whether to order Force U to return to its original Devonshire ports and re-form. Had Eisenhower and Rear Adm. Alan G. Kirk, commanding the Western Task Force, done so, they would have had to postpone OVERLORD until the next moon period. In the end, Admiral Kirk recommended that Force U proceed.

Admiral Moon left Portland harbor a second time at 0930 on 5 June and was joined en route off St. Alban's Head by the rest of TF 125 and the bombarding ships. The bombardment group, commanded by Rear Adm. Morton L. Deyo, USN, positioned itself between the transports and the shore, ready to protect the force if necessary and to cover the minesweepers that were still clearing channels in the mine fields. There were an estimated twenty German batteries (110 guns) in the Utah sector, ranging from 75-mm field pieces to 210-mm rifles. Since the heavy ships could not maneuver in the narrow swept channels to which they had been assigned, Rear Admiral Deyo directed them to anchor in their assigned channels beginning at 0140 on 6 June. He wanted a short but intense bombardment that would begin only at H-hour minus 40 minutes. The battleships and cruisers of TF 125 dropped anchor some eleven kilometers (11,000 yards) off the beaches, with destroyers anchored five kilometers (5,000 yards) out.

The Germans commenced firing at first light. Although the bombardment was scheduled to begin a bit later, Admiral Deyo authorized his ships to fire at 0536. At about 0620, German batteries hit the destroyer USS *Corry,* which then struck a mine while maneuvering. Nearly cut in two, it quickly sank.

Following H-hour, the U.S. battleship *Nevada,* and heavy cruisers *Tuscaloosa* and *Quincy,* and the British light cruiser *Black Prince* and monitor *Erebus,* bombarded German heavy batteries north of the beachhead near Saint-Vaast-la-Hougue for fifty minutes. Thereafter, they joined the British light cruiser *Enterprise* and the eight destroyers in responding to targets of opportunity and answering requests for fire support on Utah Beach.

The shore fire-control parties at Utah Beach enabled ships to provide more effective gunfire support in the days that followed. Aided by spotting aircraft and firing from twenty-five kilometers (23,500 yards), *Nevada* destroyed or immobilized some ninety tanks and twenty trucks 1.3 kilometers (one mile) west of Montebourg on 6 June. On 7 June, *Nevada* destroyed a 155-mm battery near Saint-Vaast. On 8 and 9 June, naval gunfire concentrated on deep-support missions. Cruisers USS *Tuscaloosa,* HMS *Hawkins,* and HMS *Enterprise* answered numerous calls for fire support at ranges up to sixteen kilometers (ten miles). The destroyers directed their fire at troop concentrations, coastal batteries, or pillboxes not yet overrun by troops.

[See also Bayfield, USS; Moon, Don P.; American Beaches, *article on* Utah Beach; Western Task Force.]

BIBLIOGRAPHY

Morison, Samuel E. *The Invasion of France and Germany, 1944–1945.* Vol. 11 of *History of Unites States Naval Operations in World War Two.* 1957.

Ramsay, Bertram H. "The Assault Phase of the Normandy Landings." Dispatch dated 16 October 1944, printed in *The London Gazette,* 30 October 1947.

Roskill, Stephen W. *The Offensive.* Vol. 3, pt. 2, of *The War at Sea, 1939–1945.* 1961.

MARK JACOBSEN

TASK FORCE 126. Task Force 126 (Follow-up Force B), commanded by Como. Campbell D. Edgar aboard his flagship, destroyer escort USS *Maloy,* was assigned to reinforce the initial landings at Omaha Beach. Its 135 ships and craft, divided into three convoys, carried regimental combat teams of the U.S. 1st and 29th infantry divisions, engineer special brigade troops, beach battalions, and certain divisional, corps, and army troops, as well as Maj. Gen. Charles H. Gerhardt, commander of the 29th, and Lt. Gen. Courtney H. Hodges, deputy commander of the U.S. First Army.

The first convoy of Force B, slow convoy B-1, sailed from Plymouth on 4 June, but was recalled when Operation OVERLORD was postponed by twenty-four hours. B-1 and the second slow convoy, B-3, departed on 5 June. B-3 was joined by nine LSTs of convoy U-4, Assault Force U, the combined group being redesignated convoy ECL-1. Fast convoy B-2, led by Edgar in USS *Maloy,* sortied on 6 June and anchored as scheduled off Omaha Beach at H plus nine, with B-1 arriving one hour later. However, their initial landings were postponed by one hour because of the chaotic situation on the beach. General Gerhardt went ashore soon thereafter, maintaining close contact with Edgar through the morning of 7 June to request landings of his regimental combat teams. Troops were debarked throughout the night.

Task Force 126, coming as it did after the bulk of initial fighting, saw little combat. Most of what it did see took place on the night of 6–7 June, when one of its escorts, destroyer USS *Hambleton,* repeatedly intercepted and jammed strong enemy radio-controlled bomb signals, and the flagship *Maloy* shot down a Dornier Do 217, later rescuing its pilot. However, the task force's USCG sea res-cue cutters were kept busy dealing with the aftermath of the assault, as when cutter *No. 29* rescued twelve men from the torpedoed British *LCT 715.* The crowded anchorage itself proved dangerous: on 9 June *Maloy* lost four wounded during an antiaircraft barrage, most likely by 20-mm fire from nearby ships. The task force's only ship loss was escort corvette HMS *Boadicea.*

ECL-1 arrived on the morning of 7 June, its arrival timed to coincide with the flood tide so that its landing craft could run onto the beach. This technique, known as "drying out," greatly speeded unloading, allowing vehicles to be driven off vessels directly ashore. Commodore Edgar noted that though the landing of troops went essentially as planned, the considerable delay in removing beach obstacles and preparing beach exits for vehicles substantially hindered their unloading. Despite these difficulties, Force B rapidly unloaded massive amounts of personnel and matériel—in all some 26,000 troops, 4,000 vehicles, and fifty-four sections of pontoon causeway for the artificial harbor Mulberry A. On 11 June, its mission completed, Task Force 126 was dissolved.

[See also American Beaches, *article on* Omaha Beach; Edgar, Campbell D.; Maloy, USS; Task Force 124; Western Task Force.]

BIBLIOGRAPHY

Commander Task Force 126 [C. D. Edgar]. Operation _____ [name not supplied]: Invasion of Northern France, June 6–11, 1944. Serial 299 of 22 June 1944. Operational Archives, Naval Historical Center, Washington, D.C.

Commander Task Group 126.4 [B. J. Skahill]. Narrative Report of Operations from 4 June through 17 June 1944. Serial 0020 of 1 August 1944. Operational Archives, Naval Historical Center, Washington, D.C.

Morison, Samuel Eliot. *The Invasion of France and Germany, 1944–1945.* Vol. 11 of *History of United States Naval Operations in World War II.* 1957.

STEVEN J. TIRONE

TASK FORCE G. As a component of the British Eastern Task Force (ETF), Task Force G was organized to land at Gold Beach. Its organization was as follows:

Force G Flagship HMS *Bulolo,* 50th (Northumbrian) Division and No. 47 Royal Marine Commando, Como. C. E. Douglas-Pennant

Assault Force G1, Flagship HMS *Nith,* 231st Infantry Brigade Group, Capt. J. W. Farquhar

Assault Force G2, Flagship HMS *Kingsmill,* 69th Infantry Brigade Group, Capt. E. A. Balance

Reserve Force G3, Flagship HMS *Albrighton,* 56th and 151st Infantry Brigade Groups, Capt. G. V. M. Dolphin

Force G was not formed until 1 March, at Weymouth, to add the fifth division that Montgomery had requested for the assault. Consequently it was less well prepared than the other ETF forces, not least because HMS *Bulolo* did not arrive until 17 April. The final rehearsal, Exercise FABIUS, was carried out at Hayling Island between 2 and 6 May. Force G assembled at Southampton.

Fire support was provided by Force K, flagship *Argonaut*, Capt. E. W. L. Longley-Cook, cruisers HMS *Ajax, Orion,* and *Emerald;* the Dutch gunboat *Flores;* the fleet destroyers HMS *Grenville, Jervis, Ulster, Ulysses, Undaunted, Undine, Urania, Urchin,* and *Ursa;* the Hunt-class destroyers HMS *Cattistock, Cottesmore,* and *Pytchley* with the Polish *Krakowiak*. These were accompanied by the following fire-support craft: three LCG(L)s, eight LCT(R)s, four LCS(L)s, seven LCFs, and three regiments of self-propelled artillery in sixteen LCT(A)s, in an assault group of 243 ships.

Gold Beach was divided into four sectors: How, Item, Jig, and King. The most formidable defenses were the four 5.9-inch guns at Longues, overlooking How sector.

The assault force reached the lowering position, some 10.8 kilometers (6.7 miles) offshore, at 0455–0456. Their landing was preceded by Force K, which opened fire at 0545 and suppressed the shore defenses covering the anchorage. *Bulolo* had been forced to move from its anchorage by the guns at Longues, but these were knocked out by *Ajax*. The Northumbrian Division was soon ashore, although the DD (Duplex Drive) tanks could not be launched because of the high state of the sea, and high tide hampered clearance work on beach obstacles. There were 2,500 obstacles on the 6 kilometers (3.75 miles) of Gold Beach that held up and damaged landing craft, leaving them exposed to enfilading fire, which was not suppressed until noon. At Le Hamel the strong point held out until 1600. The commando attack on Port-en-Bessin was held up until the middle of the following day, but by early afternoon the two reserve brigades, which had begun landing around 1100, were ashore. Gold Beach was securely held by the end of the day. Arromanches, one of the sites selected for the Mulberry harbors, was taken at 2100 with fire support from the ETF flagship *Scylla*. The beach officer for Gold was Capt. G. V. M. Dolphin.

At 0600 on D plus 1 the *Bulolo* was hit by a 250-kilogram (550-pound) phosphorus bomb that killed four men; but this and other raids were more of a nuisance than a threat to the operation. By 29 June the Mulberry harbor was in use despite the great gale of 19 June.

On 27 June *Bulolo* left for Spithead and Force G was dismantled as part of the change in the command structure.

[See also British Beaches, *article on* Gold Beach; Bulolo, HMS; Douglas-Pennant, C. E.]

BIBLIOGRAPHY

Edwards, Kenneth. *Operation Neptune*. 1946.

ANDREW LAMBERT

TASK FORCE J. As a component of the British Eastern Task Force (ETF), Task Force J was created for the landing at Juno Beach. Its organization was as follows:

Force J Flagship HMS *Hilary,* 3d (Canadian) Division and No. 48 Royal Marine Commando, Como. G. N. Oliver

Assault Force J1, Flagship HMS *Lawford,* 7th (Canadian) Infantry Brigade, Capt. A. F. Pugsley

Assault Force J2, Flagship HMS *Waveney,* 8th (Canadian) Infantry Brigade, Capt. R. J. O. Otway-Ruthven

Reserve Group J3, Flagship HMS *Royal Ulsterman,* 9th (Canadian) Infantry Brigade, Capt. A. B. Fanshawe

Force J formed at Southampton eighteen months before the invasion, and was almost stale by 6 June 1944. Force J began to assemble around the Isle of Wight on 26 April 1944. The rehearsal was conducted in Bracklesham Bay 2–6 May. The force sailed in thirteen convoys, J1 to J13; the first two contained the assault elements: the 3d (Canadian) Infantry Division and 2d Canadian Armored Brigade. Juno Beach was 7.3 kilometers (4.5 miles) long, extended from Ver to Lagrune, and was divided into three sectors: Love, Mike, and Nan.

The Fire Support Force E comprised the flagship HMS *Belfast,* Rear Adm. F. H. G. Dalrymple-Hamilton; cruiser HMS *Diadem;* fleet destroyers HMS *Faulknor, Fury, Kempenfelt, Venus,* and *Vigilant* with the Canadian *Algonquin* and *Sioux;* the Norwegian Hunt-class destroyers *Stevenstone, Bleasdale,* and *Glaisdale* with the French *La Combattante*. The support group included seven LCG(L)s, eight LCRs, six LSL(L)s, and six LCFs. There were four regiments of self-propelled artillery in eight LCT(A)s and eight LCTs (explosive) with assault convoys J1 and J2. The major batteries in the Juno area were neutralized by fire support and captured.

The invasion shipping arrived off Juno Beach at 0558 on D-day. H-hour was set between 0735 and 0745. Navigational errors in J1 and reports of dangerous shoals delayed H-hour by ten minutes, leaving the landing craft to beach among the defenses. Force J elected not to launch their DD (Duplex Drive) tanks due to poor weather, although J1 launched some about one kilometer (about 1,000 yards) out. Despite landing among the obstacles, J1 and J2 quickly secured their landing area with inshore fire support. No. 48 Royal Marine Commando, entrusted with beach clearance and establishing links with Sword Beach, suffered badly in the wooden LCIs, but the targets were finally secured the following day.

At 1915 the shipping had moved inshore to speed up landings, and by day's end 3,200 vehicles and 2,500 tons of stores had been landed. Elements of Force L arrived off the beachhead shortly after 1800 with 7th Armoured Division and part of 51st (Highland) Division. From D plus 2 the small port of Courseulles, largely undamaged, was open and could handle 1,000 tons per day; by D plus 4 two 213-meter (700-foot) pontoons were discharging LSTs at low water. The beach officer for Juno was Capt. C. D. Maud.

By D plus 16 the Mulberry harbor permitted Commodore Oliver to "rest" areas of the beach in rotation, as the weight of traffic was rapidly "wearing it out." HMS *Lawford* was bombed and sunk on the night of 8–9 June. On 16 June King George VI, with Admiral Ramsay and the First Sea Lord, Adm. Andrew Browne Cunningham, landed on Juno Beach. Following this, the HMS *Fury* was mined and driven ashore by a gale, and on 23 June HMS *Hilary* became ETF flagship after the *Scylla* was mined. Force J was dismantled in late June.

[*See also* British Beaches, *article on* Juno Beach; Hilary, HMS; Oliver, G. N.]

BIBLIOGRAPHY

Schofield, B. B. *Operation Neptune.* 1974.
Vian, Philip. *Action This Day.* 1960.

ANDREW LAMBERT

TASK FORCE L. Follow-up Force L, commanded by Rear Adm. W. Edward Parry, RN, from headquarters ashore at Harwich, was assigned to reinforce the initial landings at Gold Beach. Its Royal Navy and U.S. Navy ships and craft, divided into five convoys, embarked the British 7th Armoured and the 3d (Canadian) and 51st (Highland) Infantry divisions, the 22d Armoured Brigade, support units of the I and XXX corps, and 21st Army Group headquarters.

Loaded at Felixstowe and Tilbury, Force L assembled for the passage in the Thames Estuary at Harwich, Southend, and Sheerness. The first convoy, L-1, left the Thames on 5 June and arrived on D-day in time for the afternoon high tide, having lost a U.S. Navy LST (Landing Ship, Tank) en route to a mine. Its thirteen remaining LSTs began debarking the 3d (Canadian) and 51st (Highland) divisions and 21st Army Group headquarters shortly thereafter. Force L's other convoys arrived on schedule and without further loss on the night of 6 June and the morning of 7 June; the last, L-5, was accompanied by two Mulberry (artificial harbor) control ships and was joined by six landing craft from Force S.

Once unloading was completed, Force L was disband-ed and its ships were allocated to the cross-Channel shuttle service for the buildup phase.

[*See also* British Beaches, *article on* Gold Beach; Eastern Task Force; Parry, W. Edward; Task Force G.]

BIBLIOGRAPHY

London. Public Record Office. "Admiralty Staff History, Operation Neptune Appendix." ADM 234/367.

DAVID BROWN

TASK FORCE S. As a component of the British Eastern Task Force (ETF), Task Force S was created for the landing at Sword Beach. Its organization was as follows:

Force S Flagship HMS *Largs,* Rear Adm. A. G. Talbot, 3d (British) Infantry Division
Assault Force S1, Flagship HMS *Locust,* 9th Infantry Brigade, Capt. W. R. C. Leggatt
Assault Force S3, Flagship HMS *Goathland,* 8th Infantry Brigade, Capt. E. W. Bush
Intermediate Group S2, Flagship HMS *Dacres,* 185th Infantry Brigade, Capt. R. Gotto

Force S formed seven months before D-day, an ideal training period, and trained on the Moray Firth before assembling around Portsmouth and Spithead. Its task was to land the 3d British Infantry Division and the 27th Armoured Brigade, and build up the beachhead. The final exercise was carried out at Littlehampton on 2–6 May.

Sword Beach extended 9.7 kilometers (6 miles) east from Aubin-sur-Mer to the estuary of the Orne River, on the west of which lay the Caen Canal. It was subdivided into four areas: Oboe, Peter, Queen, and Roger; only Queen was used for the assault landings. The anchorage was within range of three German 16-inch guns sited north of Le Havre, but these were disabled before D-day. There were, however, many 11- and 6-inch guns in the same area, although the beach defenses were less formidable than those in the other sectors.

Force S sailed from Spithead at 0945 on 5 June and rendezvoused with Force D off the Isle of Wight.

Fire Support Force D had been strengthened to cope with the heavy shore batteries. It comprised the flagship HMS *Mauritius,* Rear Adm. W. R. Patterson; the battleships HMS *Warspite* and *Ramillies;* the monitor HMS *Roberts;* the cruisers HMS *Arethusa, Frobisher, Danae,* and the Polish *Dragon;* the destroyers HMS *Saumarez,* 23d Flotilla, *Scorpion, Scourge, Serapis, Swift, Stord,* the Norwegian destroyer *Svenner,* and HMS *Verulam, Virago,* and *Kelvin;* the Hunt-class destroyers *Slazak* (Polish) and HMS *Middleton* and *Eglinton.* These were accompanied by the fire-support craft: three LCG(L)s, five LCT(R)s, three LCS(L)s, and four LCFs. The assault shipping, in convoys

S1 and S3, carried eight regiments of self-propelled artillery in eight LCT(A)s.

Force S, joined by the ETF flagship *Scylla,* was the only group to encounter the enemy at sea, losing *Svenner* to German torpedo boats at 0530. German batteries set fire to one LSI, which was abandoned, before *Warspite* subdued them. The mine clearing and DD (Duplex Drive) tanks of the assault wave, guided by the midget submarine *X23,* reached the beach around 0730. Here, as elsewhere, obstructions proved a major problem until they were cleared at low water. The assault group completed its landing at 0943, only eighteen minutes later than planned. The intermediate brigade followed soon after, but subsequent forces were delayed by increasing congestion on the beach. The beach officer for Sword was Capt. W. R. C. Leggatt.

Bombed on the first afternoon, Sword Beach was never entirely safe from German shellfire, and after heavy damage on 15 and 16 June, notably to HMS *Locust,* landing craft were not allowed to remain on the beach. After 23 June the beach was restricted to coasters. Depot ships and coasters moved to Juno and Gold. On 24 June the destroyer HMS *Swift* was mined and sunk. The port of Ouistreham was secured and opened. Sword was abandoned on 1 July, and Force S was dismantled at the end of June.

[*See also* British Beaches, *article on* Sword Beach; Largs, HMS; Talbot, Arthur G.]

BIBLIOGRAPHY

Barnett, Correlli. *Engage the Enemy More Closely: The Royal Navy in the Second World War.* 1991.
Chalmers, W. S. *Full Cycle: The Biography of Admiral Sir Bertram Ramsay.* 1959.

ANDREW LAMBERT

TAYLOR, MAXWELL (1901–1987), American,

major general, commander of the U.S. 101st Airborne Division. Maxwell D. Taylor graduated from West Point in 1922, was commissioned first in the engineers and subsequently in the field artillery. He spent thirteen of the interwar years in schools, either as teacher or student, culminating in his graduation from the Army War College in 1940.

In July 1942 he was appointed chief of staff of the 82d Division, and assisted Gen. Matthew B. Ridgway in converting the division to airborne. Subsequently as a brigadier general and division artillery commander he accompanied the division to North Africa, and later participated in the invasion of Sicily in July 1943. In September he entered Italy behind German lines on a secret nighttime trip to assess the ability of the Italians to support an American airborne drop in the vicinity of Rome. Taylor determined the landing would be a disaster and

MAXWELL TAYLOR.   NATIONAL ARCHIVES

on his advice General Eisenhower canceled it. Later Eisenhower, writing about Taylor's mission, said, "The risks he ran were greater than I asked any other agent or emissary to undertake during the war."

In March 1944 Taylor assumed command of the 101st Airborne Division in England when Maj. Gen. Bill Lee, the father of American parachute operations and the 101st's commander, suffered a heart attack. From then until the Normandy invasion Taylor supervised the division's intense preparations for combat, in the course of which he was promoted to major general.

The 101st dropped into Normandy on D-day and Taylor became the first American general to fight in France in World War II. The 101st had a threefold mission: capture the four exits from Utah Beach, protect the southern flank of the VII Corps advance, and destroy the bridges over the Douve River north of Carentan.

After a couple of days of intense but scattered fighting, clearing out patches of German resistance, Taylor perceived that his main mission was the capture of Carentan, an important communications link between VII Corps's widely scattered objectives, Cherbourg in the north and Saint-Lô in the south. He launched a successful attack on Carentan on 9 June, but the force was counterattacked on 12 June by the *17th Panzer Division.* This was thrown back with the assistance of elements of the American 2d Armored Division the following day. At this point the 101st had achieved its objective, and had made a major contribution to the success of OVERLORD.

By mid-July the 101st was back in England, and subsequently participated in the airborne invasion of Holland (Operation MARKET GARDEN) in September, and later the campaigns of the Ardennes-Alsace during the final stages of the war.

After the war Taylor was appointed superintendent of West Point, assumed command in combat of the U.S. Eighth Army in Korea in February 1953, and served as Chief of Staff, United States Army, from 1955 to 1959 during the Eisenhower presidency. At the end of this tour Taylor authored *The Uncertain Trumpet,* a book critical of the Eisenhower defense strategy (the New Look), as he retired from the army.

After less than two years of civilian endeavors he was recalled by President John F. Kennedy to be his military representative. Subsequently Taylor served as chairman of the Joint Chiefs of Staff from 1962 to 1964. Thereafter, he was ambassador to Vietnam from 1964 to 1965 and subsequently special consultant on Vietnam to President Lyndon Johnson from 1965 to 1969.

After he retired he published his memoirs, *Swords and Plowshares,* in 1972. Taylor died on 19 April 1987 and was buried in Arlington National Cemetery.

[*See also* 101st Airborne Division.]

BIBLIOGRAPHY

Blair, Clay. *Ridgway's Paratroopers.* 1985.
Kinnard, Douglas. *The Certain Trumpet.* 1991.

DOUGLAS KINNARD

TEDDER, ARTHUR

TEDDER, ARTHUR (1890–1967), British, air chief marshal, Deputy Supreme Allied Commander. Tedder was unusual among senior D-day commanders of any nationality in that he was a university graduate who had published a book and had no decorations for gallantry despite long, hard service in World War I. Even so, his capacity for command enabled him to rise swiftly through Royal Air Force ranks after that war. He specialized in the development, production, and armament of aircraft, in professional training for all ranks, and in the teaching of military history to selected officers.

As late as November 1940, Tedder's talents and experience seemed to fit him for an unsung place in Britain's war effort as a "nuts and bolts man"—which is how Prime Minister Winston Churchill then regarded him. Churchill vetoed his posting to Cairo as deputy air commander and agreed to it only when the officer chosen in his stead was captured en route.

Tedder met General Dwight D. Eisenhower in December 1942, forming a partnership that grew into a lifelong friendship. Acutely aware that national rivalries might wreck the Allied coalition, they shared a determination to submerge them under a wash of official goodwill. By December 1943, their achievements in battles and conferences had prepared them well for command of OVERLORD.

The question arose of how air power—specifically, four-engined strategic bombers—could best assist that venture. The British bomber commander, Air Chief Marshal Arthur Harris, preferred to continue his destruction of German cities, hoping to win the war before the invasion could begin, whereas the American bomber commander, Carl A. Spaatz, wanted to employ his forces against Germany's aircraft and oil industries and the aircraft defending them.

Tedder, supported by Eisenhower, successfully urged a prolonged, systematic attack on the numerous railroads serving the invasion area. It would be easy for the Germans to move in reinforcements quickly if they had the use of railroads. Therefore, if the Allies were not to be swept back into the sea, the German buildup must be delayed and disorganized. Churchill, fearing the political consequences if civilian casualties resulting from the attacks on railroads were heavy, sought President Franklin D. Roosevelt's help in canceling the plan, but Roosevelt supported the field commanders. In the event, although casualties proved far lighter than even Tedder had feared, his standing with Churchill was harmed by the long, bitter arguments.

In advocating railroad targets, Tedder was influenced by his knowledge of the success achieved by Allied bombers against such targets in Sicily and southern Italy and by the advice of British railroad executives. The task of preparing the detailed Transportation Plan was the work of Solly Zuckerman, Tedder's chief scientific adviser. They considered it the most effective means not only of safeguarding the Normandy landings but also of helping soldiers win the war.

Entwined with the arguments over the employment of air forces were arguments over their command. Here again, Tedder had the necessary "patience, tact, cunning and political sense" (in Zuckerman's words) to get most of what he wanted: in particular, a way through—or around—Air Chief Marshal Trafford Leigh-Mallory, who occupied a position in the hierarchy (commander of the air forces assigned to OVERLORD) made only barely tenable by the reluctance of his fellow commanders, British or American, to accept his authority. Consequently, Leigh-Mallory drew closer to General Bernard L. Montgomery, the British ground force commander who was even more unpopular in American circles.

Eisenhower and Tedder believed that the invasion might

ARTHUR TEDDER.   Right, with Bernard L. Montgomery (left) and Dwight D. Eisenhower (center).

fail unless Allied air superiority were fully exploited. They therefore agreed in rejecting Leigh-Mallory's advice to cancel airborne operations in the Cotentin Peninsula to support the American landing on Utah Beach, and in rejecting Montgomery's willingness to begin the invasion on 5 June despite poor flying weather. Although Tedder's eloquently blunt opposition to both Leigh-Mallory and Montgomery was ill-received in Whitehall and in the War Office, it enhanced his credit in Washington and with American commanders. From D-day onward, Tedder became increasingly critical of Montgomery's conduct and urged Eisenhower to seek his dismissal. Though sorely tempted on occasion, Eisenhower refused.

Promoted to five-star rank after the war, Tedder was raised to the peerage and appointed chief of the air staff, a position he held for four critical years (1946–1949) that saw the RAF reshaped and adapted to a cold war role. Tedder then spent another critical year in Washington (1950–1951) heading the British Joint Services Mission and representing Britain on NATO's military committee before "retiring" to several demanding civilian occupations.

[See also Air Strategy; Air Superiority; Railroads; Supreme Headquarters Allied Expeditionary Force.]

BIBLIOGRAPHY

Mierzejewski, Alfred C. The Collapse of the German War Economy, 1944–1945: Allied Air Power and the German National Railway. 1988.
Tedder, Arthur. With Prejudice: The War Memoirs of Marshal of the Royal Air Force Lord Tedder, GCB. 1966.
Zuckerman, Solly. From Apes to Warlords. 1978.
Zuckerman, Solly. Six Men Out of the Ordinary. 1992.

VINCENT ORANGE

TENNANT, WILLIAM G. (1890–1963), British, rear admiral, in command of the planning, preparation, towing, and placement of the artificial harbors for Operation NEPTUNE, the naval operations of the Normandy invasion. Entering the Royal Navy as a cadet at the age of fifteen, Tennant specialized in navigation and served aboard battleships, cruisers, and destroyers through World War I and the interwar years. Appointed chief staff officer to the First Sea Lord at the outbreak of war, in May 1940 he was sent to Dunkirk to organize the evacuation of the British Army and succeeded in extricating almost

GOOSEBERRY HARBOR.   Built of American Liberty ships, deliberately scuttled.   THE ROBERT HUNT LIBRARY, LONDON

two hundred thousand troops. Given command of the battle cruiser *Repulse,* he survived its sinking by Japanese aircraft off Malaya. Promoted to rear admiral in 1942, he commanded a cruiser squadron until 1943.

Put in charge of the Mulberry caissons in January 1943, from the outset Tennant doubted their ability to resist even moderate storms and recognized that they would take more than two weeks to complete. He proposed that additional breakwaters (codenamed Gooseberries) for sheltering small craft be created off all five landing beaches from blockships sunk bow to stern. Initially, the Admiralty objected to giving up ships so vehemently that Tennant's deputy remarked, "We came here to get a Gooseberry and all we seem to have got is a raspberry!" The Combined Chiefs of Staff intervened and fifty-nine ships were provided. Throughout April into late May, Tennant also dealt with the raising of Mulberry caissons that had been stored underwater and had stuck in the mud of the sea floor.

On D plus 1 the towing and assembly of the two Mulberries began and proceeded essentially according to Tennant's schedule. By D plus 5 the Gooseberry harbors were

in place and by 19 June the Mulberries were 90 percent complete; however, a three-day storm that began that night wrecked the American and heavily damaged the British Mulberry and sank or damaged hundreds of craft. The Gooseberries prevented a greater disaster and afterward allowed continued unloading of supplies, vindicating Tennant's judgment.

Tennant, promoted to acting vice admiral for his services in the invasion, held various fleet commands for the rest of the war and afterward. Confirmed as vice admiral in July 1945 and promoted to admiral in October 1948, he retired in August 1949. Admiral Tennant died in Worcester Royal Infirmary on 26 July 1963.

[*See also* Artificial Harbors.]

BIBLIOGRAPHY

Barnett, Corelli. *Engage the Enemy More Closely: The Royal Navy in the Second World War.* 1991.
Hartcup, Guy. *Code-Name Mulberry.* 1977.
Obituary. *The Times* (London), July 27, 1963.

STEVEN J. TIRONE

X AIR CORPS. Commanded by Maj. Gen. Alexander Holle and based in the south of France, at the beginning of June *X Air Corps (Fliegerkorps X)* comprised the specialized antishipping units assigned to the German *Third Air Force*. The most formidable part of the force was the four squadrons with 136 Heinkel He 177, Dornier Do 217, and Focke-Wulf FW 200 bombers modified to carry radio-controlled guided missiles. Two types of guided weapon were available, the Henschel Hs 293 glider bomb and the Fritz-X guided bomb. The principle of operation of both weapons was that now known as radio command-to-line-of-sight (CLOS).

The Hs 293 resembled a small aircraft with a wing span of 3.1 meters (10 ft., 3.5 in.). Fitted with a 500-kilogram (1,100-lb.) warhead in the nose, the weapon was intended for use against unarmored ships. After launch, a rocket motor accelerated the missile to a maximum speed of about 600 kilometers per hour (375 mph). When the fuel was exhausted, the missile coasted on to the target. The glider bomb carried a flare in the tail, and during this phase of the flight the observer in the aircraft operated a joystick controller linked to a radio transmitter to steer the missile, so that the flare appeared to be superimposed on the target until the weapon impacted. The glider bomb had a maximum effective range of about 8 kilometers (5 mi.). Its minimum range, governed by the distance covered during acceleration and the time needed to bring the weapon under control and for the corrections to take effect, was about 4 kilometers (2.5 mi.).

The Fritz-X was a free-fall weapon weighing 1,400 kilograms (3,100 lb.) intended for use against armored ships. Shaped like a regular bomb, the missile was fitted with fixed cruciform wings midway along the body and movable control surfaces at the tail. It too carried a flare in the tail and employed a radio-command guidance system similar to that used by the Hs 293. If the Fritz-X was released from altitudes around 6,000 meters (about 20,000 ft.), it would achieve an impact velocity sufficient to penetrate the deck armor of a battleship.

Supplementing the missile carriers were four squadrons with 136 Junkers Ju 88 torpedo bombers belonging to *2d Air Division*, a formation subordinated to *X Air Corps* and also based in the south of France. The most effective direct-attack torpedo employed by the Luftwaffe was the Italian F5W, which had a running speed of 40 knots over 3,400 meters; alternatively, it could be preset to run at 44 knots over a shorter distance. The optimum release altitude for the weapon was 100 meters plus or minus 20 meters (250–380 ft.). After release, the weapon was stabilized in flight by a wooden box tail with gyroscopically controlled rudders and elevators that broke away on impact with the sea. The other main type of weapon available was the LT 350 circling torpedo, suitable for use in anchorages where several ships were present. The LT 350 could be released from almost any altitude; however, since it descended by parachute, the greater the release altitude, the greater the chance of its coming down outside the target area. On entering the water the weapon shed its parachute, the motor started, and the torpedo began its underwater run following the pattern programmed into the weapon before it was loaded on the aircraft.

With the onset of darkness on 6 June, *X Air Corps* launched about forty missile carriers and torpedo bombers to attack the concentration of Allied shipping off

HENSCHEL HS 293 RADIO-CONTROLLED GLIDER BOMB (MOUNTED FOR MUSEUM DISPLAY). COURTESY OF ALFRED PRICE

the beachhead. Those bombers that reached the beachhead area encountered such a violent reception that in many cases attacks had to be broken off prematurely. Escort vessels in the area added to the raiders' problems by laying smoke screens and jamming on the aircraft radars and the missile radio control channels.

The aircraft with Hs 293 glider bombs ran in to attack at altitudes of around 1,500 meters (5,000 ft.). Unless there were clear moonlight conditions, it was necessary for other planes to drop flares to illuminate the targets. Given the strength of the defenses, such attacks usually had to be carried out in great haste, and with so many ships in the area it was difficult to coordinate the activities of the flare droppers and attack planes. As a result, often the ships illuminated were too far away from the planes, and by the time the latter had maneuvered into position to deliver their attack, the flares had gone out. Because of the missile's 4-kilometer (2.5 mi.) minimum launch range, under operational conditions it was necessary to acquire the target initially at about twice that distance on radar or visually, so as to give time to align the aircraft on the target before missile launch. With the combination of darkness, radar jamming, and smoke screens laid by the escorting ships, such ideal conditions were rare and the effectiveness of the glider bombs was reduced accordingly.

Attacks with Fritz-X were usually carried out at last light, and for accurate guidance the weapon required a clear sky of at least 3,000 meters (about 9,500 ft.) to surface. Used earlier over the Mediterranean by day, the weapon had been very effective; but during night attacks over the English Channel it scored few hits (possibly only one during the period under review).

When the torpedo bombers launched a direct attack at night, their usual tactic was to send in separate illuminator aircraft to release strings of flares along one side of the group of ships at a predetermined time. As they did so, the attacking aircraft ran in from the opposite side of the ships, ready to aim their torpedoes at the vessels thus silhouetted. These attacks suffered similar problems of coordination as did those using glider bombs, however. An additional hazard facing torpedo bombers carrying straight-running weapons, which had to descend below 120 meters (400 ft.) to launch their torpedos, was the large number of barrage balloons flying from transport ships in the area.

In combination, these factors prevented the loss of any Allied ships during the night of 6–7 June.

The only reinforcement to reach X Air Corps following D-day was forty-five Ju 88 torpedo bombers drawn from a group (Gruppe) of Bomber Wing (Geschwader) 77 that had been in the process of reforming, and from training units.

Adding to the many problems facing X Air Corps was the constant harassment around its bases in the south of France from partisan units. For several days the air base at Mont-de-Marsan, south of Bordeaux, was cut off completely, until German troops mounted a relief operation to clear a road into the area.

X Air Corps smashed itself against the powerful defenses protecting the concentrations of Allied shipping and achieved few successes. For example, the 3d Group of Bomber Wing 100 operated missile-carrying Dornier Do 217s from Blagnac and Francazal airfields near Toulouse. At the end of May the unit possessed thirty aircraft and seventeen combat-ready crews. During operations between D-day and D plus 11 the unit lost ten aircraft and eight crews. On the night of 10–11 June alone the unit lost three crews, one of them in particularly painful circumstances. As it neared its base after a grueling action over the landing area, the Dornier was shot down by German antiaircraft gunners. The crewmen bailed out of the stricken aircraft, but soon after landing, three of them were captured by partisans and shot.

During the two weeks following the invasion only two Allied ships were sunk and seven damaged in air attacks using conventional bombs or guided missiles; a further three ships were sunk and two were damaged by air-dropped torpedoes. The Royal Navy destroyer HMS Onslow had a lucky escape on 18 June, when an air-dropped torpedo struck it on the starboard side but failed to explode.

[See also Holle, Alexander; Third Air Force.]

BIBLIOGRAPHY

Balke, Ulf. Kampfgeschwader 100 Wiking. 1981.
Dierich, Wolfgang. Die Verbände der Luftwaffe. 1976.
Price, Alfred. The Last Year of the Luftwaffe. 1991.
United Kingdom. Air Ministry. The Rise and Fall of the German Air Force, 1933 to 1945. 1948.

ALFRED PRICE

TEXAS, USS. At Normandy this old battleship (displacement 31,924 tons; dimensions 573 x 95 x 28 feet; crew 1,290) carried ten 14-inch, six 5-inch, and almost one hundred antiaircraft guns. Built at Newport News, Texas was launched on 18 May 1912, served in the 1914 blockade of Vera Cruz, and reinforced the Grand Fleet in 1918. Overhauled between the wars, Texas supported Operation TORCH, the Allied landings in North Africa in November 1942, and escorted convoys until April 1944, when it arrived in Britain as Rear Adm. Carleton F. Bryant's flagship for Force C, the bombardment group supporting the Omaha Beach landings.

Beginning with an 0550 bombardment of Pointe du Hoc, Texas made five shoots before noon on 6 June 1944. It helped clear the German defenders from the Vierville exit to the beach and gave effective support to American troops near Longueville and Formigny. On 7 and 8 June

on 15 June by flooding its starboard antitorpedo blisters. The commander of Assault Force O for Omaha Beach, Rear Adm. John L. Hall, Jr., concluded: "The support of the 14-inch guns of *Texas* was invaluable."

On 25 June *Texas* was slightly damaged by two 11-inch shells while helping to silence Battery Hamburg near Cherbourg. In August 1944 it supported the Allied landings in southern France, prior to participating in the Iwo Jima and Okinawa campaigns in the Pacific. Decommissioned in 1948, the battleship became a Texas state memorial at Houston, where it remains.

[*See also* Bryant, Carleton F.]

BIBLIOGRAPHY

Morison, Samuel Eliot. *The Invasion of France and Germany, 1944–1945*. Vol. 11 of *History of United States Naval Operations in World War II*. 1957. Reprint, 1988.
U.S. Navy. Action Report, U.S.S. *Texas* (BB-35), 28 June 1944. Naval Historical Center, Washington, D.C.

MALCOLM MUIR, JR.

THIERRY D'ARGENLIEU, GEORGES (1889–1964), French, rear admiral, commander of Free French naval forces on D-day. Born into a naval family in Brest, Thierry d'Argenlieu became a midshipman in 1909, and

USS *TEXAS*.   NATIONAL ARCHIVES

Texas fired so frequently on enemy troop concentrations at Trévières and Isigny that it had to return to England on 9 June to replenish its magazines. Back on line on 11 June, the battleship supported lead elements of V Corps, gaining additional range for its 14-inch guns

USS *TEXAS* CREW MEMBERS.   Inspecting a damaged pillbox at Pointe du Hoc. The covered body of a Ranger killed in the assault is at lower right.   NATIONAL ARCHIVES

GEORGES THIERRY D'ARGENLIEU.
MUSÉE DE L'ORDRE DE LA LIBÉRATION, PARIS

two years later was promoted to ensign, seeing service in Morocco. During World War I he served on torpedo boats and a cruiser in the Mediterranean, and as commander was given his first ship, a patrol vessel. He then left the French Navy in September 1919 to follow a religious avocation.

As a reservist, Thierry d'Argenlieu was mobilized in 1939 and served on the naval staff at Cherbourg. He had recently been appointed lieutenant commander in the reserves when he was taken prisoner of war in June 1940. Escaping en route to Germany, he made his way to London, where he was promoted to commander and appointed chief of staff to the newly formed Free French navy. He was badly wounded during Operation MENACE, the attempted Allied amphibious landing at Dakar, French West Africa, in September 1940. After commanding the Free French in Equatorial Africa, he led a mission to Canada and then was made Free French high commissioner in the Pacific. As acting rear admiral, he was recalled to London in December 1942.

In July 1943 Thierry d'Argenlieu became chief of the Free French Naval Mission to Great Britain. In this post he commanded a considerable force of naval vessels deployed in support of the landings at Utah, Omaha, and Gold beaches—namely the destroyer *La Combattante,* eight frigates and corvettes, and six submarine chasers. After the war he served as a controversial high commissioner in Indochina, becoming a full admiral in June 1946. He retired in 1947.

[*See also* French Ships.]

DAVID G. CHANDLER

THIRD AIR FORCE. On D-day the Luftwaffe was divided into seven regional air forces (*Luftflotten*), each controlling the combat flying units based in a defined geographical area. The *Third Air Force (Luftflotte 3),* covering France, Holland, and Belgium, was responsible for air attacks to counter the Allied invasion. Its commander was Field Marshal Hugo Sperrle.

Sperrle's main antishipping force was *X Air Corps, (Fliegerkorps X),* commanded by Maj. Gen. Alexander Holle and based in the south of France. The most formidable part of the force was made up of four groups (*Gruppen*) with 136 Heinkel He 177, Dornier Do 217, and Focke-Wulf FW 200 bombers modified to carry radio-controlled guided missiles. Supplementing these were four groups with 125 Junkers Ju 88 torpedo bombers. In addition to these specialized antishipping units, the *Third Air Force* possessed 189 twin-engined bombers grouped within *IX Air Corps* intended for use in attacks on the lodgment area and shipping off the coast.

Considering the magnitude of the task ahead, the antishipping and bomber units attached to the *Third Air Force* were grossly inadequate. Yet in fact these elements made up the strongest part of Sperrle's force. At the beginning of June his single-engined day-fighter force, *II Fighter Corps,* possessed only 168 Messerschmitt Bf 109 and Focke-Wulf FW 190 fighters. Similarly weak was *II Air Corps,* responsible for air support for the army, with only sixty-seven Focke-Wulf FW 190F fighter-bombers plus a tactical reconnaissance unit with forty-two Messerschmitt Bf 109s. This formation also possessed fifty-two Junkers

MESSERSCHMITT ME 410.

COURTESY OF BILL YENNE

DORNIER DO 217.

COURTESY OF ALFRED PRICE

Ju 88 long-range fighters assigned to protect U-boats passing through the Bay of Biscay, though these unwieldy aircraft would be extremely vulnerable if they encountered Allied single-seat fighters.

During the Allied aerial bombardment in the months preceding D-day, the main airfields in northern France came under systematic attack. To safeguard the flying units, the latter had been withdrawn to safer areas to the south and east, with the exception of a few fighter units.

The Luftwaffe had elaborate plans for the transfer of these units, as well as home defense fighter groups in Germany, to northern France as soon as the invasion began. To that end several forward landing grounds had been prestocked with fuel and munitions, so that in theory the incoming units would be able to go into action immediately on arrival. This shift of home defense units would leave the homeland almost bereft of fighter protection, but it was anticipated (correctly) that in the weeks immediately following the landings the Allied heavy bomber forces would concentrate on attacking targets in the support of the land battle.

With long-range reconnaissance aircraft, night fighters, and other types, the *Third Air Force* possessed 952 combat aircraft at the beginning of June 1944. Nearly every unit had taken a battering during the previous six months, and it showed. Average unit serviceability was below 50 percent and all were short of experienced crews.

The Allied airborne and seaborne landings on D-day took the *Third Air Force* by surprise. Weather conditions led to the assumption that a seaborne invasion was unlikely that night; no reconnaissance aircraft was in position to observe the approach of the huge invasion armada and initially there was no reaction from the defenses. Throughout the day the troops coming ashore enjoyed the protection of powerful fighter patrols flying in relays from airfields in southern England, and the *Third Air Force* was unable to mount effective attacks during the critical period following the initial landings. The total Luftwaffe effort during the daylight hours amounted to about a hundred sorties, mostly by fighters and fighter-reconnaissance aircraft.

The beginning of the invasion triggered the mass transfer to northern France of combat units from the south and east of France, and also from Germany. In the face of the Allied air opposition, however, parts of the carefully laid plan went awry. In many cases the airfields assigned to the incoming units had been bombed, so that the newcomers had to land at other hastily chosen landing grounds. The signals network broke down, adding to the confusion. Key personnel were flown to France by Junkers Ju 52 transports, but most of the ground staff went by rail; because of the disruption of the French rail network, many of them spent more than a week in transit.

With the onset of darkness *X Air Corps* launched about forty missile carriers and torpedo bombers to attack the concentrations of Allied shipping off the beachhead. Conventional bombers of *IX Air Corps* were also active that night. During their approach flights the attackers suffered casualties not only from Allied night fighters, but also from German flak units long accustomed to regarding any aircraft as hostile. Owing to the strength of the Allied defenses, no ships were lost to air attack that night.

On D plus 1 the reinforcement fighter units began arriving in northern France, and on D plus 2 the Luftwaffe flew more than 500 sorties of all types over the battle area—far fewer than what the opposing air forces

Third Air Force
Headquarters, Paris
Field Marshal Hugo Sperrle

X Air Corps (Fliegerkorps X)
Missile-carrying bombers
Maj. Gen. Alexander Holle

IX Air Corps (Fliegerkorps IX)
Conventional bombers
Maj. Gen. Dietrich Peltz

II Fighter Corps (Jagdkorps II)
Air defense
Maj. Gen. Werner Junck

II Air Corps (Fliegerkorps II)
Air support, tactical reconnaissance
Maj. Gen. Alfred Bülowius

flew. German losses were high, and in the days to follow the number of sorties declined steadily. This, and the continual harassment suffered by the German crews throughout every phase of their missions, meant that their ground troops received little air cover during the hard-fought initial actions to contain the Allied bridgeheads.

Following the invasion the antishipping units of *X Air Corps* smashed themselves vainly against the powerful defenses protecting the concentrations of shipping off the coast, causing minimal damage among the latter. The conventional bombers of *IX Air Corps* were even less successful and soon gave up their attempts to bomb the ships. Instead they resorted to sowing the newly developed Oyster pressure mines in shallow water off the coast. Although the mines caused considerable inconvenience and delayed the Allied buildup ashore, the effects were not decisive.

A major problem facing German ground force commanders throughout this period was the almost complete lack of effective air reconnaissance on the positions and movements of Allied forces. *II Air Corps*, with only forty-two tactical reconnaissance fighters on D-day, was quite unable to meet the demands placed on it. Given the strength of the defenses protecting Allied ground and naval forces, the German long-range reconnaissance force, comprising sixty Junkers Ju 88s, Ju 188s, and Messerschmitt Me 410s, was restricted to night photographic missions. The normal tactic was for the aircraft to fly over the target area at maximum speed at altitudes around 6,000 meters (19,000 ft.), releasing up to ten photo-flash bombs at 10-second intervals. The bombs were fitted with barometric fuzes set to ignite at

about 1,300 meters (4,000 ft.) above the surface, and produced a flash of 6 million candlepower lasting one-third of a second. At the start of the run the shutters of both cameras were held open. The flash triggered a photoelectric cell that closed the shutters four seconds later, wound on the film in each camera, and reopened the shutters. This process was repeated as the remaining flash bombs ignited in turn. By the end of the run the defenses would be thoroughly alerted and the German crew would dive away and retire from the scene as fast as possible. Night photographs provided considerably less information than those taken during the day, however, and these methods gave only a fragmentary picture of the Allied dispositions.

During the twelve-day period following D-day, the *Third Air Force* proved unable to oppose the Allied landings effectively or give air support or air cover for German operations on land or at sea. Neither quantitatively nor qualitatively was the force a match for the Allied forces opposing it.

[*See also* Sperrle, Hugo.]

BIBLIOGRAPHY
Balke, Ulf. *Kampfgeschwader 100 Wiking.* 1981.
Dierich, Wolfgang. *Die Verbände der Luftwaffe.* 1976.
Price, Alfred. *The Last Year of the Luftwaffe.* 1991.
United Kingdom. Air Ministry. *The Rise and Fall of the German Air Force, 1933 to 1945.* 1948.

ALFRED PRICE

3D BOMBARDMENT DIVISION. The division was established on 13 September 1943 by Eighth Air Force General Order 149. This regularized an already existing organization set up in November 1942. Unlike the other bombardment divisions, the 3d had both B-17s and B-24s. On 6 June it had five B-24 groups (34 BG, 486 BG, 487 BG, 490 BG, and 493 BG) and nine B-17 groups (94 BG, 95 BG, 96 BG, 100 BG, 385 BG, 388 BG, 390 BG, 447 BG, and 452 BG). It participated in all major engagements of the Eighth Air Force, including the first and second Schweinfurt missions, the "Big Week" attack on German aircraft assembly plants, and the campaigns against the German synthetic oil industry and transportation system. As part of the first Schweinfurt mission in August 1943 it flew a unique "shuttle mission," taking off from its bases in England, bombing the target, and continuing on to American airfields in North Africa. During the OVERLORD campaign the redoubtable Brig. Gen. Curtis LeMay commanded the division.

On 6 June the division attempted to bomb German defenses at the Allied invasion beaches in Normandy, but its bombardiers feared to drop too close to the invasion fleet and as a consequence released their bombs too late, causing them to land in unoccupied areas beyond the German defenses. Two weeks later, on 21 June 1944, the division sent 114 B-17s and 70 P-51s on a shuttle mission to Poltava airfield in the Soviet Union as part of Operation FRANTIC. The Soviets and Americans had prepared this and other bases in order to mount strategic bombing attacks on Germany from the east as well as the west and south. Unfortunately that same evening, in one of its last effective offensive actions, the Luftwaffe attacked the field and destroyed or damaged 69 B-17s and 15 P-51s. The German attack extinguished the enthusiasm of both the United States and the U.S.S.R. for the project, which died by mid-September 1944.

On 8 July (Operation CHARNWOOD) and 18 July (Operation GOODWOOD) the division participated, with the other bombardment divisions of the Eighth Air Force, the RAF Bomber Command, and Ninth Air Force medium bombers, in attacks on German frontline positions opposite General Bernard L. Montgomery's 21st Army Group. Although partially successful, these raids did not enable the British forces to break through the German defenses. On 24–25 July the division participated in the Operation COBRA bombing near Saint-Lô. The Eighth Air Force bombing on 25 July shattered the German defenses and paved the way for the Allied breakout from the Normandy peninsula.

In August 1944 the Eighth Air Force reorganized by taking its fighter groups from direct control of VIII Fighter Command and attaching them to the bombardment divisions, to facilitate coordination of fighter escort and to increase familiarization between specific bomber and fighter groups. As a result, the 3d Bombardment Division was redesignated as the 3d Air Division.

[See also Eighth Air Force; LeMay, Curtis E.]

BIBLIOGRAPHY

Craven, Wesley Frank, and James Lea Cate, eds. *Europe: ARGUMENT to V-E Day, January 1944 to May 1945*. Vol. 3 of *The Army Air Forces in World War II*. 1951.
Freeman, Roger A. *Mighty Eighth War Manual*. 1984.

RICHARD G. DAVIS

3D INFANTRY DIVISION (BRITISH).

Part of Lt. Gen. J. T. Crocker's British I Corps, 3d Infantry Division played a central role in the Second British Army's mission, which was to protect the flank of the invading force, the most vulnerable part of the force during the beach assault phase.

Crocker, in accordance with General Bernard L. Montgomery's wishes, ordered that before dark on D-day Caen should either have been captured, or contained by the division's brigades located northwest of Bénouville and northwest of Caen. This was a difficult, even unrealistic, goal because not only was the division the farthest force from its objective and assumed to be the focus of any counterattack, it also was to land after the other divisions in I Corps and on the most exposed beaches, where the Germans would most easily be able to call up reserves. In the event, owing to rocks and the tide, the division had to land one and a half hours after dawn, allowing the German forces time to prepare. Naturally, the Germans also realized the importance of the city and had planned a resolute defense.

3d Infantry Division had been commanded by Maj. Gen. T. G. Rennie since December 1943, but he was injured by a mine on 13 June and was evacuated to England. Brigadier E. E. E. Cass of 8th Brigade took over until 23 June, when Maj. Gen. L. G. Whistler relieved him. The division's infantry brigades were 8th, 185th, and 9th, and it was supported by 27th Armoured Brigade, formations that had spent the previous years in the United Kingdom and consequently were less seasoned than those who had spent that time in combat.

The division landed just west of the Orne River on Queen Beach, in Sword area, the first units landing at 0725. 8th Brigade rapidly forced exits from Queen White, but the advance from Hermanville was halted by the 88-mm guns of *21st Panzer Division*. Progress was slower on Queen Red, where fierce opposition was encountered. By 1130 185th Brigade was ashore, but the reserve 9th Brigade could not complete its landings until midafternoon. With *21st Panzer Division* between 185th Brigade and Canadian 3d Division, Rennie and Crocker decided to secure the British flank instead of trying to reach Caen. Thus, 9th Brigade was ordered to Pegasus Bridge to reinforce the 6th Airborne Division and strengthen the Orne bridges against attack from the west. However, before the brigade commander, Brigadier Cunningham, could give the orders, he was injured, which caused a delay that was compounded by the absence of his second in command.

Once ashore, 185th Brigade was to spearhead the drive for Caen by capitalizing on the shock already achieved. The 2d Battalion, the King's Shropshire Light Infantry (KSLI), riding on tanks of the Straffordshire Yeomanry, were to move down the main Hermanville-Caen road, while the 2d Warwickshire Regiment and 1st Norfolk Regiment cleared their flanks. This was delayed for several reasons: the Yeomanry's tanks and the infantry's heavy weapons were still on the beach, the congestion there magnified by winds and tide that rapidly reduced the size of the beach; also 8th Brigade had not yet taken the Périers ridge (the intended launch point for 185th Brigade's attack) or the strategic point HILLMAN southwest of Colville, which lay in the path of the main advance and was held by the German *736th Regiment*. The momentum of the attack thus slowed and HILLMAN was not taken until 2000 hours.

THE KING'S SHROPSHIRE LIGHT INFANTRY.   With captured Germans.   IMPERIAL WAR MUSEUM

The KSLI and their Yeomanry armor eventually secured Biéville at 1600 hours, when signs of the *21st Panzer Division* counterattack were discerned. The only armored counterattack of D-day, it had insufficient infantry support to capitalize on the gap between 3d Canadian and 3d British divisions. One company of the KSLI pushed toward Lébisey, but on meeting stiff resistance, they withdrew and dug in for the night.

By the end of D-day Caen had not been taken, nor were the brigades in a position to contain the city. During the night, *21st Panzer Division* reinforced the Lébisey–La Londe ridge that dominated the approaches to Caen, and which was only taken at great cost later.

The next day the division moved slightly closer to Caen. 185th and 9th brigades pushed for the city from the left and right flanks. The Warwicks became entangled in Lébisey Wood, and took heavy casualties. The Norfolks moved in to extricate them, and both withdrew. This additional delay in the advance meant that any support of the 2d KSLI at Biéville was impossible, and the battalions of 185th Brigade remained in these locations until just before the city fell the next month.

9th Brigade's battalions followed a similar pattern; the unsuccessful attack on Cambes, begun on 7 June, on the axis Périers–Mathieu–Le Mesnil, resulted in heavy losses

to the Royal Ulster Rifles (RUR). The battle continued on 9 June, and by the time A Company of the RUR had taken the objective all the platoon commanders had been killed or wounded, and only one sergeant and one lance sergeant remained. The King's Own Scottish Borderers reinforced them, and 9th Brigade remained at this position until the first week of July.

8th Brigade's battalions reached Le Londel, Le Mesnil, and the surrounding woods on 9 June, and despite violent encounters, they too remained largely unmoved until after 22 June. The division remained static on the line Blainville-Cambes. German counterattacks rarely cost the division ground, although they did result in casualties.

The division played a vital part in taking Caen in July 1944. Following the air bombardment of the city the previous day, 3d Infantry Division attacked from the left flank of I Corps on 8 July. By dark its leading brigade had reached the northern outskirts of the city, and the next day, along with Canadian forces, its patrols entered Caen.

There can be no doubt as to the courage of members of 3d Infantry Division from Rennie, whose frequenting of forward positions resulted in his injury on 13 June, down. Criticism has been made about the failure of the formation's commanders to maintain the pace of the attack and to coordinate the various battalions' activities in the most

3d Infantry Division
Maj. Gen. T. G. Rennie (until 13 June 1944)
Brig. E. E. E. Cass (acting)
Maj. Gen. L. G. Whistler (from 23 June 1944)

8th Brigade

1st Battalion, Suffolk Regiment
2d Battalion, The East Yorkshire Regiment
1st Battalion, The South Lancashire Regiment

9th Brigade

2d Battalion, The Lincolnshire Regiment
1st Battalion, The King's Own Scottish Borderers
2d Battalion, The Royal Ulster Rifles

185th Brigade

2d Battalion, The Royal Warwickshire Regiment
1st Battalion, The Royal Norfolk Regiment
2d Battalion, The King's Shropshire Light Infantry

Divisional Troops

3d Reconnaissance Regiment RAC
3d Divisional Engineers
3d Divisional Signals
7th, 33d, and 76th Field, 20th Anti-Tank, and 92d
   Light Anti-Aircraft Regiments RA
2d Battalion, The Middlesex Regiment (Machine Gun)

efficacious way, but it seems not wholly justified. There were opportunities that, if seized, could have averted the static situation that developed. The area of Colville and the strong points HILLMAN and MORRIS had been saturated by artillery on D-day morning, to the extent that 1st Special Service Brigade Commandos and some engineers were able to move through it to reach the Orne at 1330. But divisional infantry reached Bénouville via that area only eight hours later. Similarly, the important Périers ridge failed to be seized on the morning of D-day because a resolute attempt was not made. The initial fighting in Lébisey Wood would have been more promising, if it too had not been hampered by the absence of speed, the absence of adequate and coordinated support (particularly tanks), and the limited deployment of battalions. Even the seizure of all such opportunities, however, would not have guaranteed that Caen would have fallen much sooner. The weather hindered speed on D-day, and the night gave *21st Panzer Division* and *12th SS Panzer Division* time to dig in on good defensive ground. Ultimately however, British 3d Infantry Division fulfilled its role. The flank was held successfully and significant German forces were tied up; thus in fundamental respects, the division's role may be termed a success.

[*See also* Cass, E. E. E.; Rennie, T. G.]

BIBLIOGRAPHY

Ellis, L. F., et al. *The Battle of Normandy*. Vol. 1 of *Victory in the West*. 1962.
London. Public Record Office. 8th Brigade War Diary. WO 171/611.
London. Public Record Office. 9th Brigade War Diary. WO 171/616.
London. Public Record Office. 185th Brigade War Diary. WO 171/702.
London. Public Record Office. 3d British Division War Diaries. WO 171/410–414.
McNish, Robin. *Iron Division: The History of the Third Division.* 1978.
Wilmot, Chester. *The Struggle for Europe.* 1954.

TIM MUNDEN

3D INFANTRY DIVISION (CANADIAN). This division, commanded by Maj. Gen. R. F. L. Keller, was, with its three infantry brigades, structured for what General Bernard L. Montgomery called the decisive "fight to kill"; in his view, there was simply no substitute for the "power of the well-trained Inf[antry] Div[ision]" of three infantry brigades.

The brigades of the 3d Infantry Division, numbered 7 through 9, each consisted of a headquarters and three infantry battalions whose selection, by design, reflected both Canadian geography and regimental tradition. Individual battalions consisted of a headquarters, four rifle companies of three platoons each, and a support company that included a carrier platoon (with thirteen Bren carriers), a mortar platoon (with six 3-inch tubes), an antitank platoon (with six 6-pounders), and an assault pioneer platoon.

The field regiments were specially equipped with American 105-mm self-propelled Priests. The antitank regiment consisted of four batteries, each of twelve 17-pounders organized in three troops of four guns. The light antiaircraft regiment similarly disposed three batteries, each of eighteen 40-mm Bofors organized in three troops of six guns. The reconnaissance regiment, the 7th Reconnaissance Regiment (17th Duke of York's Royal

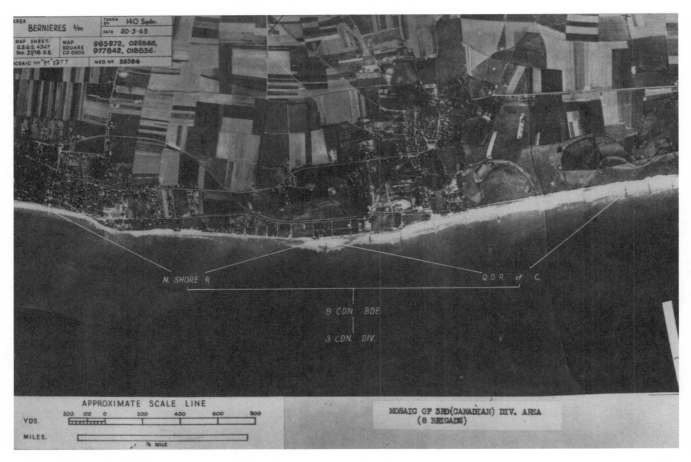

ASSIGNED BEACH AREAS.   IMPERIAL WAR MUSEUM

Canadian Hussars), comprised a headquarters squadron that included a mortar troop (with six 3-inch tubes), an antitank troop (with six 6-pounders), and three squadrons, each composed of three reconnaissance troops and one assault troop. The divisional engineers consisted of the 6th, 16th, and 18th field companies and the 3d Field Park Company. The divisional machine-gun battalion, the Cameron Highlanders of Ottawa (M.G.), fielded three machine-gun companies, each of three platoons of four medium Vickers .303 machine guns, and a heavy mortar company of three heavy mortar platoons, each of four 4.2-inch mortars. The division was additionally supported by four Royal Canadian Army Service Corps transport companies and Numbers 14, 22, and 23 field ambulances. All told, Keller commanded about 18,000 soldiers.

The 2d Armoured Brigade, assigned as intimate support for the 3d Division in its assault, was roughly 3,500 strong. It consisted of a headquarters and three armored regiments: the 6th Armoured Regiment (1st Hussars), the 10th Armoured Regiment (The Fort Garry Horse), and the 27th Armoured Regiment (The Sherbrooke Fusiliers). Each armored regiment comprised a headquarters (four

tanks), headquarters squadron, and three tank squadrons of a headquarters (three tanks) and four troops of four tanks each, one of which was a Firefly Vc. The Firefly, rushed into production for D-day, was a British-modified Sherman that mounted a 17-pounder gun capable of penetrating the frontal armor of any German panzer. In fact, the brigade had converted from Rams to Shermans only in May. Assault regiments equipped with DD (Duplex Drive) tanks had also secretly trained under the auspices of the 79th Division.

Since July 1943, when they were selected for the OVER-LORD assault, both Canadian formations had undergone intense training in combined operations along the Scottish coast. Brigade groups had also trained in the Portsmouth area with Force J, the same naval task force that had lifted Canadian troops to Dieppe. From 30 January 1944, when the 3d Division Group came under the actual command of the British I Corps, attention focused on collective divisional assault training and full-dress rehearsals for Operation NEPTUNE. The "joint fire plan," which included 105-mm Priests firing a beach barrage from landing craft, received emphasis throughout.

3d Canadian Infantry Division

7th Infantry Brigade

The Royal Winnipeg Rifles
The Regina Rifle Regiment
The Canadian Scottish Regiment

8th Infantry Brigade

The Queen's Own Rifles of Canada
Le Régiment de la Chaudière
The North Shore (New Brunswick) Regiment

9th Infantry Brigade

The Highland Light Infantry of Canada
The Stormont, Dundas, and Glengarry Highlanders
The North Nova Scotia Highlanders

Divisional Troops

17th Duke of York's Reconnaissance Regiment
3d Divisional Engineers
3d Divisional Signals
3d Divisional Column, RCASC[1]
12th, 13th, 14th, 19th Field (SP)
3d Anti-Tank Regiment, RCA[2]
4th Light AA Regiment, RCA[2]
The Cameron Highlanders of Ottawa (MG)[3]

[1] Royal Canadian Army Service Corps
[2] Royal Canadian Artillery
[3] Machine Gun

The task of the 3d Canadian Division Group was to secure the Juno assault area and advance inland to the railway line connecting Caen and Bayeux, the respective objectives of the 3d British and 50th (Northumbrian) infantry divisions. The Canadian attack was to be carried out with the 7th Canadian Infantry Brigade Group, under Brig. H. W. Foster, on the right, and the 8th Brigade Group, under Brig. K. G. Blackader, on the left. Their immediate beachhead objective, known as "Yew," ran just forward of the villages of Graye-sur-Mer, Courseulles-sur-Mer, Bernières, and the western outskirts of Saint-Aubin-sur-Mer. The intermediate divisional objective to be taken in the second phase, "Elm," ran through Creully, Pierrepont, and Colomby-sur-Thaon. The reserve formation, the 9th Brigade Group commanded by Brig. D. G. Cunning-

ham, was then to land, preferably on the left if the situation allowed, and advance on Carpiquet in conjunction with the 7th Brigade to capture the final objective, "Oak," along the Caen-Bayeux railway line. The plan stressed that infantry brigades were to reorganize rapidly, digging in to repulse counterattacks, leaving the 2d Armoured Brigade to concentrate as a mobile reserve.

At 0745 hours on D-day the first Canadian assault troops stormed ashore, the DD tanks of the 1st Hussars followed by the Regina Rifles on "Nan Green," and the Royal Winnipeg Rifles with an attached company of the Canadian Scottish on "Mike Red" and "Mike Green" beaches. After some severe fighting the Winnipegs pushed inland quickly, consolidating in and around Creully by 1700 hours. At the same time, the Reginas began to advance southward from Reviers; by 2000 hours they were on "Elm." To the east on "Nan White," where tank support was late, the Queen's Own Rifles began to suffer the greatest number of casualties of any Canadian unit on D-day in a sharp fight for Bernières. They nonetheless managed to reach Anisy that afternoon. In the meantime on "Nan Red," the North Shores supported by Fort Garry Horse and engineer tanks pushed through to Tailleville by 2010 hours.

The deployment of reserves did little to improve the gains of the assault units. Within the 7th Brigade, the Canadian Scottish passed through the Winnipegs toward Pierrepont. Having encountered little or no opposition, they could have gone farther, but they were ordered by brigade headquarters to consolidate in that vicinity. In the 8th Brigade sector, the Chaudières meanwhile pushed on through Bény-sur-Mer and Basly to the area of Colomby-sur-Thaon. Keller's decision to land the 9th Brigade behind the congested 8th Brigade unfortunately delayed its forward movement. Not until 1820 hours were the North Novas and Sherbrooke tanks, which together constituted the brigade advanced guard, able to leave their assembly areas to pass through the Queen's Own and Chaudières and resume the advance southward. When their vanguard ran into resistance at Villons-les-Buissons, it became evident that they would not reach objective "Oak" before dark. They were therefore ordered to dig in on "Elm" for the night and form a firm base while there was still light. Notwithstanding such caution, the 3d Canadian Division advanced farther inland than any other Allied division on D-day.

The next day, on discovering that there was no enemy of consequence to its front, the 7th Brigade dashed for its final objectives. By noon, both leading units were on them, the Winnipegs in Putot-en-Bessin and the Reginas in Bretteville-l'Orgueilleuse and Norrey-en-Bessin, with the Canadian Scottish following in reserve. On the 9th Brigade front the advanced guard of the North Novas and Sherbrookes again led off, but after fighting through Buron and Authie by early afternoon they were strongly counterattacked. In what may have been an ambush, the *25th Panzer Grenadier Regiment* of the *12th SS Panzer Division* launched three infantry battalions supported by artillery and a battalion of Mark IV tanks against the left flank of the 9th Brigade. This reverse, which saw the Canadians thrown out of Authie and Buron, might have been avoided had the 3d Division's artillery been within range, as it probably should have been, beach congestion aside. As it was, the ground lost by the 9th Brigade within sight of its final objective, the Carpiquet airfield, was not to be recovered for a full month. The next morning Lt. Gen. M. C. Dempsey visited Keller to impress upon him "the importance of getting his artillery and armor properly under control."

On the morning of 8 June the *2d Battalion, 26th Panzer Grenadier Regiment,* also attacked the Royal Winnipeg Rifles occupying Putot-en-Bessin. Believing themselves surrounded by panzers and superior enemy forces, three companies of Winnipegs attempted to withdraw under cover of smoke, suffering heavy casualties. In fact, no German tanks participated in this attack, though it does appear that British armor of the 24th Lancers did counterattack from the northwest. The Germans attacked with but three panzer grenadier companies, infiltrating between Winnipeg subunits. Significantly, each SS company possessed on average two to three MG42 general-purpose machine guns per section as compared to one Bren in each Canadian equivalent. That evening, however, the Canadian Scottish supported by a squadron of tanks and two artillery field regiments counterattacked behind a creeping barrage to retrieve the situation. The entire affair cost the Canadians over four hundred casualties, forty-five of them murdered by the SS after being taken prisoner.

At the time of the Canadian Scottish counterattack, the *12th SS* commenced another attack against the Reginas in Bretteville-l'Orgueilleuse and Norrey-en-Bessin. While part of the Regina's position was overrun in the first shock, the Germans were eventually repulsed. When the 2d Canadian Armoured Brigade launched the 1st Hussars and Queen's Own toward Le Mesnil–Patry on 11 June, they were badly mauled. This action was the last major Canadian operation in the month of June, and it marked the end of a phase for the 3d Canadian Infantry Division Group. Total Canadian casualties to this point amounted to 196 officers and 2,635 other ranks, slightly more than a third of whom were dead.

[*See also* I Corps; Keller, R. F. L.]

BIBLIOGRAPHY

Roy, R. H. *1944: The Canadians in Normandy.* 1984.
Stacey, C. P. *The Victory Campaign: The Operations in North West Europe, 1944–1945.* 1960.

JOHN A. ENGLISH

3D PARACHUTE DIVISION. The German *3d Parachute Division (3. Fallschirmjägerdivision)* had been stationed in the Reims area in France since February 1944. Two parachute battalions, veterans from Italy and the Eastern front, and parts of a glider-borne instruction battalion served as cadres for forming three new regiments.

Under the command of Maj. Gen. Richard Schimpf, experienced cadres had trained the young volunteers, aged twenty-one to twenty-two years, whose morale was excellent. In January 1944 the division moved from the Reims region to the Monts d'Arrée, approximately fifty kilometers (thirty miles) east of Brest in Brittany. Under tactical control of *XXV Army Corps*, the division had orders to counterattack any Allied parachute attacks, besides completing its own training.

By D-day the personnel buildup and training were finished, but the division had only 70 percent of its weapons. Above all it lacked machine guns and antitank weapons. It had sufficient ammunition for three to six days, but only 40 percent of its trucks and not enough gasoline even for them.

On 7 June 1944 the *3d Parachute Division* was ordered to move as soon as possible into the region of Avranches, in Normandy, using all available trucks, with the bulk of the division following on foot. Because the available trucks could transport only one-third of the division, the rest were transported on hired horse-drawn carriers. The motorized advanced units of the division got the mission to counterattack along the northern edge of the Cerisy Forest, to prevent further Allied advances south from Bayeux. During the night of 17–18 June, most of the division reached the area of Saint-Lô.

Since 10 June the motorized advance party of the *3d Parachute Division* (one mixed regiment) had been defending the sector Saint-Germain-d'Elle–Bérigny–Couvains. They had not always had close contact with their neighbors, the *352d Infantry Division* on their left and the *17th SS Panzer Grenadier Division* on their right. Division headquarters was three kilometers northeast of Torigni-sur-Vire and east of Chapelle-du-Fest. From 14 to 17 June the division successfully repelled all Allied attacks on both sides of the road from Bayeux to Saint-Lô, and repeatedly launched counterattacks.

An Allied fighter-bomber attack forced the division headquarters to move into an area two kilometers east of Condé-sur-Vire. Meanwhile the division, with nearly all units assembled, was to defend a forward line of defense twenty-four kilometers (fifteen miles) long under all circumstances. The *8th Parachute Regiment* held the right, the *5th Parachute Regiment* the center, and the *9th Parachute Regiment* the left. Division reserves were the *3d Parachute Engineer Battalion* and one company from each battalion of the engaged regiments. On 11 June 1944 the division repulsed successfully, but with heavy losses, an

3d Parachute Division
Division headquarters,
Commander Maj. Gen. Richard Schimpf

5th Parachute Infantry Regiment (Fallschirmjäger-regiment 5)
Three battalions, Maj. Karl Heinz Becker

8th Parachute Infantry Regiment (Fallschirmjäger-regiment 8)
Three battalions, Col. Ernst Liebach

9th Parachute Infantry Regiment (Fallschirmjäger-regiment 9)
Three battalions, Maj. Kurt Stephani

3d Parachute Antitank Battalion (Fallschirm-Panzerjägerabteilung 3)
Captain Persch

3d Parachute Antiaircraft Artillery Battalion (Fallschirm-Flak-Abteilung 3)
Major Müller

3d Parachute Mortar Battalion (Fallschirm-Granatwerferbataillon 3)
Not yet combat-ready on D-day

3d Parachute Artillery Battalion (Fallschirm-Artillerieabteilung 3)
On D-day being enlarged to a regiment,
Captain Fleischmann

3d Parachute Engineer Battalion (Fallschirm-Pionierbataillon 3)
Maj. Karl Heinz Beth

3d Parachute Signal Battalion (Fallschirm-Luftnachrichtenabteilung 3)
Capt. Kurt Hölzner

3d Parachute Medical Battalion (Fallschirm-Sanitätsabteilung 3)
Lieutenant Colonel Wichert

Support and supply units (Versorgungstruppen/3.Fallschirmjägerdivision)
Lieutenant Colonel Diesterhöft

Allied attack toward Saint-Lô, which finally fell on 19 July.

After the Allied breakthrough the bulk of the weakened division was involved in the German retreat from Normandy and was caught in the Falaise pocket. In June 1944 the *3d Parachute Division* lost 436 dead, 1,513 wounded, and 136 missing, or about 17 percent of its strength. Only parts of the division succeeded in breaking out, taking their seriously wounded commander with them, and joined the retreat to the West Wall (Siegfried Line). After a fresh buildup in the Netherlands, the division fought in the Battle of the Bulge in December 1944, but could not repeat the former combat performance so feared and respected by the Allies. In April 1945 the remnants of the division were caught in the Ruhr pocket and surrendered.
[*See also* Schimpf, Richard; II Parachute Corps.]

BIBLIOGRAPHY

Der Deutsche Fallschirmjäger, no. 3 (1952): 12; no. 1 (1953): 6–7; no. 1 (1980): 20–21; no. 3 (1982): 19–20.
Schimpf, Richard. *Die Kämpfe der 3. Fallschirmjäger Division in Frankreich Juni–August 1944.* U.S. Army, Historical Division, MS B-541.

FLORIAN BERBERICH

XXX CORPS. The British XXX Corps was formed in the autumn of 1941 as one of two corps (the other being XIII Corps) making up the newly established Eighth Army, an expanded and rechristened Western Desert Force. XXX Corps took part in most of the battles of the desert war in 1941–1942, and in the Tunisian campaign of 1943. By early 1944 the corps had been earmarked as one of the four corps that would make up the 21st Army Group's Second British Army, and one of the two British corps (the other being I Corps) that were to attack on D-day itself. The commander selected to lead it in Normandy was Lt. Gen. G. C. Bucknall, former commander of 5th Division in Sicily and Italy.

A veteran formation by the time of OVERLORD, on D-day XXX Corps was to establish itself on Gold Beach and then move quickly inland to Bayeux and toward Villers-Bocage, preparatory to a drive toward Mont Pinçon. In practice XXX Corps, like I Corps on its left, found these objectives unrealistic: congestion on the beaches and stiff resistance from the hamlets inland caused delays, so that the 50th (Northumbrian) Division and 7th Armoured Division had advanced only seven to nine kilometers by dusk on D-day, still some five kilometers short of Bayeux. The corps's infantry and armor began to make some progress on the morning of 7 June, taking Bayeux and moving south into the Seulles Valley toward Tilly-sur-Seulles, Seulles, and Longues. But the corps then faltered, as German resistance stiffened on 9–10 June, and it failed to exploit a gap in

XXX Corps
Lt. Gen. G. C. Bucknall

50th (Northumbrian) Division
Maj. Gen. Douglas Graham

7th Armoured Division
Maj. Gen. G. W. E. J. Erskine

49th (West Riding) Division
Maj. Gen. E. H. Barker

Plus 56th Infantry Brigade, 8th Armoured Brigade,
units of 79th Armoured Division, and corps troops

the German lines between Caumont and Villers-Bocage during the following days, resulting in a debacle at Villers-Bocage on 12–14 June, when the 22d Armoured Brigade was assaulted by German tanks and forced to withdraw.

If the failure at Villers-Bocage gave rise to accusations that XXX Corps now lacked the initiative it had displayed in North Africa, its performance at the start of subsequent offensives confirmed this impression. In early August Montgomery relieved three top commanders of their commands: the corps commander, Bucknall; Gen. G. W. E. J. Erskine of 7th Armoured Division; and Brig. Robert Hinde of 22d Armoured Brigade. The corps then improved in performance, though the extent to which this can be attributed to a change of command as opposed to the collapse of German resistance remains a moot point. Either way, under Lt. Gen. Brian Horrocks, XXX Corps advanced all the way to Brussels by 3 September and to the Elbe River by the end of the war in Europe.

[*See also* Bucknall, G. C.; Erskine, G. W. E. J.; 7th Armoured Division.]

BIBLIOGRAPHY

D'Este, Carlo. *Decision in Normandy: The Unwritten Story of Montgomery and the Allied Campaign.* 1983.
Ellis, L. F., et al. *The Battle of Normandy.* Vol. 1 of *Victory in the West.* 1962.
Hastings, Max. *Overlord: D-Day and the Battle for Normandy, 1944.* 1984.
Horrocks, Brian. *Corps Commander.* 1977.

FRANCIS TOASE

30TH INFANTRY DIVISION. The 30th Division, later designated the 30th Infantry Division, was federalized with other National Guard divisions as part of the United States' preparation against the threat of war in Europe. Inducted in September 1940, "Old Hickory," as the division was known because of its origins in Tennessee and the Carolinas, assembled for training at Fort Jackson, South Carolina. In the spring of 1942 the division was reorganized under the Army Ground Force's triangular concept, reducing the size of the division to approximately 15,500 men to facilitate command and control. The reorganization cut the number of infantry regiments from four to three and the amount of organic field artillery; the organization and size of divisional support troops also changed. With the reorganization complete, the 30th Infantry Division's maneuver elements consisted of 117th, 118th, and 120th infantry.

Federal service changed the nature of the National Guard divisions. No longer regionally based, the divisions received volunteers, draftees, reservists, and regulars to serve with their guardsmen. Frequently providing cadre for other units, the 30th routinely traded trained personnel for untrained recruits. During August 1942 the 118th Infantry and 197th Field Artillery Battalion transferred overseas to become a separate regimental combat team. The 119th Infantry and the 115th Field Artillery Battalion arrived as replacements, but in September the division loaned the 117th Infantry to the Infantry School at Fort Benning until February 1943.

"Old Hickory" continued to train until it received orders for transfer overseas. On 12 February 1944 the division left Boston for England aboard three troopships. The soldiers spent the spring on the southern coast training and polishing their amphibious skills for the coming invasion.

The Normandy assault plans called for the 30th Infantry Division, operating under the XIX Corps, to come ashore on Omaha Beach and advance inland. The division's first unit ashore was the 230th Field Artillery Battalion, which was alerted on 8 June for early transport. The battalion landed two days later, temporarily augmenting the 29th Infantry Division since that division's 111th Field Artillery Battalion had lost its guns during the Omaha landings. The 230th served with the 29th Division until the morning of 14 June.

On D plus 8, as the rest of the 30th Infantry Division prepared to come ashore at Omaha, the Allied beachhead was still precarious. With the junction between Omaha and Utah threatened, the XIX Corps' mission changed from breakout to strengthening defensive positions. In order to strengthen the Allied foothold and prevent the isolation of either American beach, the corps directed the 30th Infantry Division to secure the northern bank of the Vire-Taute Canal.

During the evening of 13–14 June, divisional elements waded ashore on Omaha Beach. The landing was marred when the LST carrying the division's 113th Field Artillery Battalion struck a mine, killing several soldiers. A combat team organized around the 120th Infantry was ordered to seize the Vire-Taute Canal. The 1st and 2d battalions jumped off at 0800 on 15 June, pushing south toward the village of Montmartin-en-Graignes. As they crossed railroad tracks north of the town, the soldiers encountered determined resistance. After a heated exchange, the 2d Battalion cleared the position and advanced to Montmartin-en-Graignes. The 1st Battalion passed through the 2d Battalion to push southeast toward La Ray on the Vire River. The next morning, minus a small mop-up force at La Ray, the 1st Battalion advanced farther south toward the canal's junction with the river.

The 3d Battalion also moved south on 15 June, operating in the regiment's western sector. Halted by fierce opposition at the village of La Compte, the battalion requested armored support. A tank platoon, together with a reinforced infantry platoon, eliminated the German resistance. Battalion troops proceeded to the highway bridge that spanned the canal, but they arrived too late, for the bridge was already destroyed. The battalion assumed positions along the canal and repulsed a German counterattack during the night.

While the 120th fought its way south, other divisional elements came ashore to join the battle. The 117th took positions near the town of Airel, while the 119th engaged German troops at La Meuffe. The 30th Infantry Division now occupied defensive positions from the beachhead to the Vire-Taute Canal. The situation at Omaha Beach stabilized and the serious threat to the beachhead was eliminated. The 30th went on to the fighting around Saint-Lô, and later at Mortain it withstood the brunt of a German offensive designed to contain the Allies in Normandy. The 30th, however, held its ground, and the Allies recovered within a week to break the offensive and continue the drive across Europe.

[See also Hobbs, Leland.]

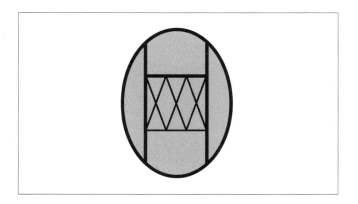

BIBLIOGRAPHY

Hewitt, Robert L. *Work Horse of the Western Front: The Story of the 30th Infantry Division*. 1946.
"The 'Old Hickory' Division: A Condensed History of the 30th Infantry Division." *National Guardsmen* 2 (August 1948): 18–19.
Wilson, John B. *Armies, Corps, Divisions, and Separate Brigades*. 1987.

DONNA C. EVERETT

THOMAS, G. I. (1893–1972), British, major general, commander of the 43d (Wessex) Infantry Division. Thomas graduated from the Royal Military Academy in 1912 and joined the Royal Artillery. During World War I he served on the Western front, was wounded, and won the Distinguished Service Order and the Military Cross. He was seconded to the War Office and remained there until November 1917, the first of many staff postings.

Promotions came steadily, and on 9 March 1942, with the rank of major general, Thomas took over command of the 43d Division, which he led during the campaign in northwestern Europe. Although General Thomas knew that his division would not make the assault landing, he nevertheless trained his men hard, impressing upon them that sweat in training saves blood in battle. In the United Kingdom on the eve of D-day, Thomas briefed his officers on the divisional task in Operation OVERLORD and a week later, in the evening of 12 June, his division was placed on six-hours notice to move. Thomas filled that week of waiting attending conferences where officers returning from Normandy reported on conditions in the beachhead, the ability of the German defenders, and local topography. Thomas also visited every one of his units before they and he set sail for the battlefront.

Of Thomas the divisional history recorded that "he impressed his own personality and ideas on those under his command . . . and those above him, with . . . incisive effect." In 1945 he took over the I Corps in the British Zone of Occupation and subsequently held administrative posts including quartermaster general to the forces. He retired from the army in 1952 and died on 29 August 1972.

[See also 43d (Wessex) Infantry Division.]

BIBLIOGRAPHY

Ellis, L. F., et al. *The Battle of Normandy*. Vol. 1 of *Victory in the West*. 1962.
Essame, A. *The 43rd (Wessex) Division at War, 1944–45*. 1952.
Headquarters, Second Army. *An Account of Operations of Second Army in Europe, 1944–45*. 1945.

JAMES LUCAS

352D INFANTRY DIVISION. The German *352d Infantry Division* was formed in November 1943 and was first deployed in the vicinity of Saint-Lô in Normandy, the headquarters of the *LXXXIV Army Corps*, under which the division was organized as part of the *Seventh Army*. Under the command of Maj. Gen. Dietrich Kraiss, the division quickly developed into a combat-ready unit. By February 1944 it had attained a strength of over 12,000 men, mostly combat-tested soldiers, who were joined by young recruits born in 1926.

In March 1944 the *352d Infantry Division* was moved to the Normandy coast and deployed in direct coastal defense. By 19 March the division had taken over the Bayeux Coastal Defense Sector, extending from the mouth of the Vire River to Asnelles; it immediately went to work extending the fifty-seven kilometers (about thirty-four miles) of coastal defense installations.

The division included the *914th Grenadier Regiment* (Lt. Col. Ernst Heyna), the *915th Grenadier Regiment* (Lt. Col. Karl Meyer), the *916th Grenadier Regiment* (Col. Ernst Goth), and the attached *726th Grenadier Regiment* (Colonel Korfes). The four artillery units of the *352d Artillery Regiment* (Lt. Col. Karl-Wilhelm Ocker) were deployed inland. Also available were the *352d Division Fusilier Battalion*, the *352d Antitank Battalion* (with antitank, antiaircraft, and assault weapons), the *352d Engineer Battalion*, and the *352d Field Replacement Battalion*.

On 6 June 1944 the *352d Infantry Division* confronted the American landing at Omaha Beach and part of the British assault at Gold Beach. Remarkably, the division's presence immediately inside the coastal defenses was kept secret from the Allies until shortly before D-day. Even before sunrise on 6 June, the division's mobile assault troops, the *915th Grenadier Regiment* and the *352d Division Fusilier Battalion*, were deployed as a reserve corps against U.S. paratroop landings near Brévands on the Vire River. In the course of the day, however, they were thrown against the British incursion on the eastern divisional border and were almost totally destroyed; the commanding officer fell in battle.

The Omaha Beach landing operation proceeded dramatically, as this was the division's defensive center. The *916th Grenadier Regiment* fought from well-constructed fortified coastal installations with a system of overlapping machine-gun and mortar fire, as well as artillery fire zones. The first waves of the invading U.S. V Corps established a hold with great difficulty, being pinned down for a long time by German fire. The U.S. operations command considered breaking off the Omaha landing operation at this point, but further troops and matériel were landed. In the course of the morning U.S. forces occupied the coastline at several points and attained the heights behind the beach, achieving a breakthrough between Vierville and Colleville-sur-Mer.

The *916th Grenadier Regiment* was reinforced by the *2d Battalion* of the *915th Grenadier Regiment*, and engineer units and antiaircraft detachments. They did not succeed in their objective of pushing the Americans back into the sea, but merely cordoned off the landing zone temporarily. In the left divisional sector the U.S. paratroop landing was encountered near Brévands, a Ranger attack was met at Pointe du Hoc, and further invasion efforts were repelled on the eastern mouth of the Vire. In the right divisional sector the *726th Grenadier Regiment* was severely threatened by the British incursion near the contiguous *716th Infantry Division*. The *915th Grenadier Regiment* counteroffensive did not succeed. The German defenses were quickly unhinged, and British troops proceeded toward Bayeux.

By evening the U.S. Omaha landing could be counted a success. The *352d Infantry Division* had lost approximately 1,200 men; the U.S. troops in this zone had lost at least twice as many.

In the following days the division could only delay the Allied advance. The right divisional wing had been decimated and remained so, and the commander of the *726th Grenadier Regiment* was taken prisoner. On 8 June Bayeux was lost. British troops advanced far into the hinterland, until stopped by the rapidly advancing *Panzer Lehr Division* and *2d Panzer Division*. On the Vire River the left wing of the *352d Infantry Division* was withdrawn, and the *914th Grenadier Regiment* escaped the threatened encirclement by breaking through to the south. Isigny fell on 9 June. U.S. troops crossed the Vire, and the meeting of troops from the Utah and Omaha beachheads could no longer be prevented.

In the center of the division's defensive front, dogged fighting continued. Colonel Goth's *916th Grenadier Regiment* energetically defended the villages of Formigny and Trévières against the 1st Infantry Division. Here, too, the front line had to be withdrawn because of a threat to the flank. The front was shortened and combat strength regained. The *352d Infantry Division* remained capable of carrying out its offensive and defensive duties. Orders from above kept the coastal forces in place until they were either killed or captured. By 10 June the division had established a new defensive position on the Elle River, and the divisional headquarters were moved to Le Mesnil-Rouxelin, near Saint-Lô.

More combat-ready troops arrived as reinforcements: aside from the already deployed *30th Schnelle Brigade* and the *Panzer Reconnaissance Unit* of the *17th SS Panzer Grenadier Division*, the motorized advance commando of the *3d Parachute Division* arrived from Brittany. After 10 June this part of the *3d Parachute Division* was deployed on the defensive front along the southern edge of the Cerisy Forest, protecting the *352d Infantry Division*'s exposed right flank.

On 12 June the *352d* was placed under the *II Parachute Corps*. From 13 to 18 June heavy combat took place in the Elle sector against the U.S. 29th Infantry Division, which succeeded in bridging the river. Fierce battles occurred around Couvains and Villiers-Fossard. As the engagement developed, the *914th Grenadier Regiment* had to abandon its very extended frontal arch on the Vire. After 16 June the *Böhm Group* of the *353d Infantry Division* was deployed in the eastern zone and able to engage in combat.

Thus an effective defensive front was developed north and northeast of Saint-Lô. Massive German artillery tenaciously supported the defense. In the *352d Infantry Division*'s zone the defenses had been augmented considerably by 18 June and the front lines stabilized.

On 11 July the U.S. XIX Corps began massive attacks north of Saint-Lô. After heavy combat on the outskirts, the 29th Infantry Division seized the city on 18 July. After the major U.S. breakthrough on the Cotentin Peninsula from 25 July on, the *352d Infantry Division* also had to withdraw. The remnants of the division were attached to the *XLVII Panzer Corps* and were deployed with the *2d Panzer Division*.

In battles during the retreat in August 1944, the *352d Infantry Division* defended positions at Rambouillet and south of Paris. The division was then finally withdrawn from the front and dissolved. During the autumn of 1944 it was reorganized as the *352d Volks Grenadier Division* and redeployed in the Reich's last battles in late 1944 and 1945.

[*See also* Kraiss, Dietrich.]

BIBLIOGRAPHY

Carell, Paul. *Invasion: They're Coming.* Translated by E. Osers. 1963. Paul Carell is the pseudonym used by Hans Karl Schmidt.
Hayn, Friedrich. *Die Invasion.* 1954.
Klapdor, Ewald. *Die Entscheidung–Invasion 1944.* 1984.
Ose, Dieter. *Entscheidung im Westen 1944.* 1982.

GÜNTER HILLERS

353D INFANTRY DIVISION. The German *353d Infantry Division* was activated in Brittany on 5 November 1943. It was formed mostly around cadres from the *328th Infantry Division*, which had been smashed on the southern sector of the Eastern front during the summer and autumn of 1943. Its commander from November 1943 until 15 February 1945 was Maj. Gen. Paul Mahlmann, who was promoted to lieutenant general on 1 June. The division consisted of the *941st, 942d* and *943d Grenadier* regiments, the *353d Artillery Regiment,* the *353d Fusilier Battalion,* the *353d Antitank Battalion,* the *353d Engineer Battalion,* and the *353d Signal Battalion.* Most of its men came from Military District II (Pomerania and Mecklenburg).

Unlike many of the other divisions of the *Seventh Army,* the *353d* was classified as an attack (i.e., nonstatic) division by early 1944. Because it was made up largely of veterans from the Eastern front, it was of higher quality than the average German infantry division in France in 1944. The division was stationed near Brest on D-day and on 10 June was ordered to proceed to Saint-Lô, where it became part of Gen. Eugen Meindl's *II Parachute Corps.* Its approach march was slowed by Allied fighter-bombers, and the first elements of the division (two battalions of Colonel Boehm's *943d Grenadier Regiment,* plus part of the fusilier battalion) did not arrive in Normandy until 16 June. It was committed to the battle of the Villiers-Fossard salient on 17 June, where it held numerically superior elements of the U.S. 29th Infantry Division to minor gains for three days. It then made a successful withdrawal, knocking out at least four American tanks in the process. During the next ten days the rest of the division came up and occupied Montgardon Ridge, west of Saint-Lô. The Americans, who were focused on the capture of Cherbourg, put little pressure on the *353d* during this period.

From 3 to 7 July, the *353d* held Montgardon Ridge and the high ground around La Haye-du-Puits against attacks by the U.S. VIII Corps. It was finally forced to give up the ridge, but prevented the Americans from advancing beyond it, and inflicted more than 1,000 casualties on the U.S. 79th Infantry Division on 7 July alone.

The *353d Infantry* was gradually battered to pieces in the hedgerow fighting around Saint-Lô. One of its battle groups (which was attached to the *3d Parachute Division* in early July with 1,000 men) fell to a strength of 180 by 11 July. In mid-July, the depleted division was withdrawn from the line and placed in *LXXXIV Corps* reserve. After the Allied heavy bombers destroyed the *Panzer Lehr Division* in Operation COBRA, the *353d* was thrown into the breach almost immediately but was unable to restore the front. Part of the division was overrun near Marigny by the U.S. 4th Infantry Division on 26 July. Despite the fact that it fought well in all its battles, the *353d* was now

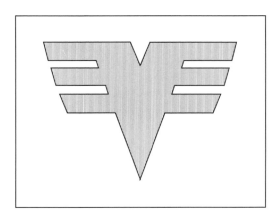

down to regimental strength and was no longer able to check the highly mobile U.S. infantry and armored divisions. It nevertheless remained in the line, was trapped in the Falaise pocket, and was largely destroyed in the subsequent breakout. The divisional headquarters gave up the few troop units it had left in September and was sent to the rear. During the battle for Aachen it took charge of several poor quality units, but then was returned to Germany, where it was completely rebuilt, mainly with security or local defense troops, older men, and former Luftwaffe personnel. It never regained its former quality.

The *353d* fought in the battles of the Siegfried Line from 1944 to 1945 and was destroyed in the Ruhr pocket. Its survivors ended up in American captivity.

[*See also* Mahlmann, Paul; II Parachute Corps.]

BIBLIOGRAPHY

Blumenson, Martin. *Breakout and Pursuit.* U.S. Army in World War II: The European Theater of Operations. 1960.
Harrison, Gordon A. *Cross-Channel Attack.* U.S. Army in World War II: The European Theater of Operations. 1951.
Tessin, Georg. *Verbände und Truppen der deutschen Wehrmacht und Waffen-SS im Zweiten Weltkrieg, 1939–1945.* Vol. 9, 1974.
U.S. Military Intelligence Service. *Order of Battle of the German Army, 1945.* 1945.

SAMUEL W. MITCHAM, JR.

346TH INFANTRY DIVISION. The *346th Infantry Division* was activated at Bad Hersfeld in Military District IX on 21 September 1942. Its soldiers came from the *257th, 319th* and *320th* infantry divisions of the *Seventh Army,* the *304th* and *332d* infantry divisions of the *Fifteenth Army,* and replacement troops from Military Districts VI and IX. A static division, it consisted of the *857th* and *858th* Fortress infantry regiments (three battalions each), the *346th Artillery Regiment* (two battalions), and the *1346th Divisional Supply Unit.* Many of its men were *Osttruppen* (Eastern troops), whose loyalty to the Third Reich was questionable at best. The *346th* was stationed in the Saint-Malo sector of Brittany from November 1942 until the spring of 1944, when it was sent to Le Havre on the northern bank of the Seine. During that time the *I Battalion, 857th Fortress Infantry Regiment,* was taken away and replaced by the unreliable *630th East Battalion;* however, it also gained a third artillery battalion, as well as the *346th Antitank, Engineer,* and *Signal* battalions. Its commander at this time was Maj. Gen. Erich Diestel.

The *346th Division* was thrown into the Normandy fighting on 9 June and took part in the battle east of the Orne, where it joined with *Battle Group Luck (Kampf-*

gruppe Luck) of the *21st Panzer Division* in launching a successful spoiling attack against the British 51st (Highland) Division and 4th Armoured Brigade on 10 June. Its casualties were very heavy, however; by 13 June, it had lost more than half its combat troops, and its rifle companies had been reduced to a strength of 35 to 60 men each. Down to battle-group size, the *346th* nevertheless remained in the battle east of the Orne. By 15 July, it had only six operational antitank weapons left.

After the Falaise debacle, the *346th* took part in the retreats across the Seine, northern France, and Belgium, and was part of the *Fifteenth Army* during the Battle of the Schelde, where it helped turn back an attempt by the Canadian 1st Army to break the Turnhout Canal line (near Antwerp) on 22 September, and twice repulsed the Canadian 6th Infantry Brigade at Lochtenberg on 24 and 28 September. It successfully made its escape to the Netherlands, where it was rebuilt in December. It added a third regiment (the *1018th Grenadier*) and absorbed remnants of the *70th, 331st,* and *334th* infantry divisions and the *16th Luftwaffe Field Division.* It returned to the front in January 1945, and fought in eastern Holland for the rest of the war, surrendering to the British north of Arnhem in May 1945.

[*See also* Diestel, Erich.]

BIBLIOGRAPHY

Mitcham, Samuel W., Jr. *Hitler's Legions: The German Army Order of Battle, World War II.* 1985.
Tessin, Georg. *Verbände und Truppen der deutschen Wehrmacht und Waffen-SS, 1939–1945.* 15 vols. 1973–1980.

SAMUEL W. MITCHAM, JR.

TORPEDO BOATS. The German Navy had a traditional predilection for small torpedo boats rather than proper destroyers. It had been limited to such vessels by the Treaty of Versailles (1919) but after treaty restrictions lapsed, continued to build them in addition to destroyers for shorter-range operations. The *5th Torpedo Boat Flotilla* based at Le Havre on D-day consisted of four 1920s-vintage vessels, *Mowe, Kondor, Falke,* and *Jaguar,* and the newer and larger fleet torpedo boat *T 28.* Both *Kondor* and *Falke* were damaged on the night of 23–24 May on passage to Le Havre, when their sister *Greif* was sunk. Another larger boat, *T 24,* the last survivor of the *4th Flotilla,* was attached to the *8th Destroyer Flotilla* when it moved to Brest on 6 June. Details of the three classes represented above are as follows:

Type 23: *Mowe, Kondor, Falke.* Displacement 924 tons standard, 1,290 tons deep load; length overall 87.7 meters (281.2 ft.), width 8.43 meters (27.7 ft.), maximum draught 3.65 meters (12 ft.); twin-shaft, geared turbines,

MOWE, 1943.   BIBLIOTHEK FÜR ZEITGESCHICHTE, STUTTGART

T 28.   BIBLIOTHEK FÜR ZEITGESCHICHTE, STUTTGART

TORPEDO BOAT OF THE JAGUAR CLASS, TYPE 24.
BIBLIOTHEK FÜR ZEITGESCHICHTE, STUTTGART

23,000 horsepower (hp), 33 knots. Three 105-mm (4.1-in.) guns, one forward, two aft; six 533-mm (21-in.) torpedo tubes in two triple mountings amidships; and six 20-mm antiaircraft (AA) guns (one quadruple and one single mount); thirty mines; complement 127. *Mowe* was built 1924–1927, the other two 1925–1928, all at Wilhelmshaven naval dockyard. These ships were a direct development of World War I ships armed with 1916-pattern L/45 guns; the forward of the two aft 4.1s had no shield.

Type 24: *Jaguar.* Displacement 933 tons standard, 1,320 tons deep load; length overall 92.6 meters (303.8 ft.), width 8.65 meters (28.3 ft.), maximum draught 3.52 meters (11.5 ft.); twin-shaft, geared turbines, 25,500 hp, 35 knots. Three 105-mm (4.1-in.) guns, one forward, two aft; six 533-mm (21-in.) torpedo tubes in two triple mountings amidships; and four 20-mm AA guns (four single mount); thirty mines; complement 127. It was built 1927–1929 at Wilhelmshaven naval dockyard. The guns were model SK C/28 in 30-degree LC/28 mountings, rare weapons for which it was hard to find ammunition.

Type 39: *T 24* and *T 28.* Displacement 1,294 tons standard, 1,754 tons deep load; length overall 102 meters (334.7 ft.), width 10 meters (32.8 ft.), maximum draught 3.22 meters (10.6 ft.); twin-shaft, geared turbines,

32,560 hp, 34 knots although 30 knots was more normal. Four 105-mm (4.1-in.) guns, one forward, one fore of the after funnel, and two aft; six 533-mm (21-in.) torpedo tubes in two triple mountings amidships; four 37-mm AA guns and six (*T 24*) or seven (*T 28*) 20-mm AA (one quadruple and two or three single mount); four depth-charge throwers and 32 depth charges; up to 60 mines; complement 206. Built in 1942 and 1942–1943 respectively by the Schiehau Company at Elbing, these were modern ships, classified as fleet torpedo boats, with dual-purpose guns and sonar.

Mowe, Jaguar, and *T 28* made repeated nocturnal sorties following the landings, sinking the Norwegian destroyer *Svenner* on the night of D-day. On the night of 8–9 June they were held off by British motor torpedo boats and on 9–10 and 12–13 June engaged destroyers inconclusively. *Mowe, Falke,* and *Jaguar* were sunk in the air raid on Le Havre on the night of 14–15 June. *T 28* managed to return to Germany and served in the French Navy after the war. *Kondor* was finished off by bombing at Le Havre on 28 June. *T 24* got away from the engagement between the *8th German* and the 10th British destroyer flotillas on the night of 8–9 June, but was finally sunk by air attack on 24 August near Bordeaux.

[*See also* Navy, *article on* German Navy.]

BIBLIOGRAPHY

Groner, E., D. Jung, and M. Maass. *Major Surface Vessels.* Vol. 1 of *German Warships, 1815–1914.* 1990.
Rohwer, Jürgen, and Gerhard Hümmelchen. *Chronology of the War at Sea, 1939–1945.* Translated by Derek Masters. 1992.
Whitley, M. J. *German Destroyers of World War II.* 2d ed. 1992.

ERIC J. GROVE

TOURS. See Battlefield Tours.

TRACKED VEHICLES. See Armor and Tracked Vehicles.

TRAINING. See Amphibious Assault Training; Ground Training.

TRANSPORTATION PLAN. See Interdiction Operations.

TRANSPORT COMMAND. A major facet of air operations in support of the Allied invasion of Normandy in June 1944 was the use of airborne forces—landed by parachute or in gliders—to capture key points in the rear of the German defenses. This use had been tried in the July 1943 invasion of Sicily—Operation HUSKY—with mixed success, British Albemarles and Halifaxes and U.S. C-47s taking part. For various reasons, American losses were heavy. Nevertheless when Operation OVERLORD came to be planned, the Chief of Staff to the Supreme Allied Commander (COSSAC) included airborne forces in the order of battle.

The Royal Air Force (RAF) had formed Transport Command on 25 March 1943 to take over ferry and transport roles; in Operation HUSKY, its first experience of battle, its No. 38 Wing squadrons had acquitted themselves well. Halifaxes of No. 295 Squadron had towed Horsa gliders from Britain to North Africa, a 1,400-mile flight including the dangerous Bay of Biscay crossing; only 2 out of 25 Halifax/Horsa combinations were lost. Albemarles of No. 296 Squadron also flew out: 25 of them took part in Operation LADBROOKE on 9 July 1943, when 137 aircraft/glider units began the invasion of Sicily. Halifaxes and Albemarles participated in subsequent airborne operations over the island, earning commendations from Brig. Gen. Ray Dunn, commanding the 51st Troop Carrier Wing, U.S. Army Air Forces (USAAF), and from Lt. Gen. Carl Spaatz, commanding the Northwest African Air Forces.

It was therefore not surprising that No. 38 Wing should have been upgraded to group status on 11 October 1943, with ten squadrons and a forceful air officer commanding (AOC), Air Vice Marshal L. N. Hollinghurst. No. 38 Group led the airborne forces landings in Europe on 5/6 June 1944 with its Albemarle, Stirling, and Halifax squadrons supporting an airborne corps that had begun to form in Britain after the fall of France in 1940.

Shortly after the creation of No. 38 Group another group, No. 46, was formed in Transport Command under Air Vice Marshal Arthur Fiddament for transport support operations, with five squadrons of Dakotas towing Horsa gliders. These two groups and the three troop carrier wings (50, 52, and 53) of IX Troop Carrier Command, U.S. Ninth Air Force, spearheaded the Normandy invasion.

The 15 RAF squadrons and 15 USAAF groups of the airborne forces were based on twenty-two airfields. From their inception in early 1944, they took part in tough exercises with their army components—the British 6th Airborne Division, the U.S. 82d and 101st airborne divisions, and Canadian and Polish paratroops. The 6th Division was to land east of Caen, and the 82d and 101st at the eastern end of the Cotentin Peninsula. Big parachute and glider exercises were mounted during February and March; No. 38 Group aircrew gained experience of flying over enemy territory by carrying out Special Air Service (SAS) operations: some 200 were flown over France during May. On the 21st of that month, when the last large-scale exercise

before D-day was held, 74 Horsa gliders were put down by night in 12½ minutes on a small landing zone (though enemy defenses against such landings—forests of poles and extensive flooding— could not be realistically simulated).

The role of the No. 46 Group Dakotas, also taking part in the airborne invasion, was somewhat different from that of No. 38 Group's aircraft: they were to bring medical supplies, armament, aircraft spares, vehicles, bombs, and personnel to the forward areas. Harrow high-wing, fixed-undercarriage aircraft (nicknamed "Sparrows") were also to be used after D-day for casualty evacuation, their short take-off and landing (STOL) capabilities making them suitable for operations into improvised airstrips.

In Operation NEPTUNE, on the night of 5–6 June 1944, some 1,100 transport aircraft of Nos. 38 and 46 groups and IX Troop Carrier Command carried some 17,000 airborne (glider and parachute) forces across the English Channel as the vanguard of the Allied armies in Operation OVERLORD. The AOC of No. 38 Group, Air Vice Marshal L. N. Hollinghurst, led his forces from the front, flying in the lead Albemarle of a pathfinder force that was to prepare and light up a landing zone.

The creation of Transport Command some fifteen months earlier, with the lift of airborne forces as one of its roles, had been well justified. As an official history put it, "after two days' fighting the 6th Airborne Division had gained all its objectives except for a small section on the coast near Franceville." Surprise and disruption of the enemy had been achieved.

In the days following D-day, Dakotas of No. 46 Group and Stirlings and Halifaxes of No. 38 Group carried out resupply operations: the Dakotas dropped food, ammunition, radio sets, explosives, medical stores, and petrol, and the four-engined aircraft containers, jeeps, and six-pound guns, in Operation ROB ROY, which continued until 10 June.

The ultimate decision to deploy airborne forces in Operation OVERLORD had rested with the Supreme Allied Commander, General Dwight D. Eisenhower. Though he had instituted an Airborne Air Planning Committee on which the AOCs of Nos. 38 and 46 groups, the U.S. IX Troop Carrier Command, and the U.S. Army were represented in November 1943, the Commander in Chief, Allied Expeditionary Air Force, Air Chief Marshal Trafford Leigh-Mallory, under whose command the airborne forces lay, had misgivings about committing them. He doubted their ability to muster their numbers effectively once they had been dropped or landed, and feared unnecessary casualties.

In the event, despite some navigational and recognition errors, poor weather, and the hazard of friendly fire, many objectives were successfully seized, like a swing bridge over the Caen Canal (Pegasus Bridge), the target for six Horsa gliders, one of which landed within fifty yards of it. Clearly, the difficult and dangerous exercises mounted before the invasion had paid off. Operation NEPTUNE, as the naval and airborne phase—the first ever on such a large scale—of Operation OVERLORD was called, had been successful, despite many unpredictable factors like weather and human reaction under the stress of conflict. From D-day until the end of June 1944—twenty-four days—aircraft of No. 38 Group made twenty-six supply-dropping sorties, while those of No. 46 Group reverted to their transport role.

Transport Command's formation in 1943 had recognized existing reinforcement and transport operations: the supply of aircraft to operational areas, across the Atlantic and Africa and to India, and transport routes eastward and westward from the United Kingdom. The invasion of Sicily and then of mainland Europe brought it into battle over Normandy and later over Arnhem and across the Rhine, flying unarmed aircraft into enemy defenses. This passive heroism was epitomized in the command's motto (approved in 1943), *Ferio feriendo,* "I strike by carrying."

[*See also* Airborne Forces; Gliders; Hollinghurst, L. N.; IX Troop Carrier Command.]

BIBLIOGRAPHY

Craven, Wesley Frank, and James Lea Cate, eds. *Europe: ARGUMENT to V-E Day, January 1944 to May 1945.* Vol. 3 of *The Army Air Forces in World War II.* 1951.
Saunders, Hilary St. G. *The Fight is Won.* Vol. 3 of *The Royal Air Force, 1939–1945.* 1954.
Wynn, Humphrey, and Susan Young. *Prelude to Overlord.* 1983.

HUMPHREY WYNN

TUSCALOOSA, USS. A heavy cruiser of the New Orleans class, the USS *Tuscaloosa* was 588 feet long and 62 feet wide, and had a standard displacement of 9,975 tons. It was armed with nine 8-inch guns and eight 5-inch antiaircraft guns. Commissioned in August 1934, the *Tuscaloosa* performed a variety of roles in the early part of World War II, including operations with the British Home Fleet and support of the invasion of North Africa in November 1942.

In Normandy the *Tuscaloosa* was flagship for Rear Adm. Morton L. Deyo, commander of Force A, the shore bombardment group for the landings on Utah Beach. In June 1944 the *Tuscaloosa* had a crew of approximately 1,050 men and was commanded by Capt. John B. W. Waller. The ship was to provide accommodations and communications facilities for Admiral Deyo and his staff, and to use its guns for gunfire support of troops ashore.

Off Utah Beach the ship joined a fire-support line about 11,000 yards offshore. With it were the cruiser USS

Quincy and battleship USS *Nevada*; additional cruisers were in the vicinity, and a line of destroyers about 5,000 yards off the beach. Ranged against the American ships were nearly thirty German batteries, comprising more than one hundred individual guns. The American heavy ships anchored, because the narrowness of the channels swept of mines limited their ability to maneuver.

Admiral Deyo ordered the prelanding shore bombardment to begin earlier than scheduled, because the German batteries had already begun firing at the Allied ships offshore. At 0536 the *Tuscaloosa* unleashed the 8-inch guns of its main battery and then opened up shortly afterward with its 5-inch guns. The first wave of assault troops landed on schedule at H-hour, 0630. During the remainder of D-day, the heavy cruiser continued to fire at coast defense batteries, artillery positions, troop concentrations, and motor transport.

The *Tuscaloosa* continued to support Allied troops until leaving for England on 9 June to replenish ammunition. Returning to France, it continued on station in the fire-support area until 21 June. Subsequently it provided fire support for the land attacks on Cherbourg in late June and the invasion of southern France (DRAGOON) in mid-August 1944.

[*See also* Deyo, Morton L.]

BIBLIOGRAPHY

Dictionary of American Naval Fighting Ships. Vol. 7, 1981.
Morison, Samuel Eliot. *The Invasion of France and Germany, 1944–1945.* Vol. 11 of *History of United States Naval Operations in World War II.* 1957. Reprint, 1988.
Smith, S. E. *The United States Navy in World War II.* 1966.

PAUL STILWELL

12TH SS PANZER DIVISION "HITLER-JUGEND." This was the first SS formation to go into action against the Allies in Normandy. Its young soldiers, recruited primarily from the Hitler Youth organization, fought ruthlessly in infantry combat and in close-quarter actions against tanks, gaining a fearsome reputation among the Canadian and British soldiers against whom they battled.

First conceived in June 1943 as a panzer grenadier formation, *"Hitlerjugend"* was raised to panzer division status in October of that year. On 1 June 1944, the order of battle was the *12th Panzer Regiment,* the *25th* and *26th Panzer Grenadier* regiments, an artillery regiment, a reconnaissance, an antiaircraft and an antitank battalion, and the usual service detachments. Divisional strength of 20,540 was slightly higher than called for, owing to the very large numbers of young men who had volunteered to serve in this elite formation. The divisional

commander, Gruppenführer Fritz Witt, laid great emphasis in training his men on field exercises during which live ammunition was used. Little time was given to barrack square drill.

At 1430 on 6 June 1944, *"Hitlerjugend"* was released from reserve and ordered by the German *Seventh Army* to collaborate with the *21st Panzer* and *Panzer Lehr* divisions in an attack at 1600 on the following day. The army's plan to drive the invading Allied forces into the sea was unrealizable, however. The *21st* was already locked in defensive battle, *Panzer Lehr* would not be able to reach the battlefield in time, and *"Hitlerjugend"* had not yet been fully concentrated. The *Seventh Army's* massive counterblow was thus reduced to one launched by only the formations of the *12th SS* that were immediately available: the *25th Panzer Grenadier Regiment,* its *2d Panzer Battalion,* and its *3d Artillery Battalion.*

Sturmbannführer Kurt ("Panzer") Meyer, commanding the *25th Regiment,* aware that the *Panzer Lehr* was not yet covering his regiment's left flank, placed a strong group—his *3d Panzer Grenadier Battalion,* antitank and flak detachments, and a battalion each of the reconnaissance and panzer—on that wing. Their double task was to protect the exposed flank and to defend the important Carpiquet airfield. On the right wing, at Cambes, the *1st Battalion* was in touch with the *21st Panzer Division,* thus covering the regimental right flank, and the *2d Battalion* held the center.

Canadian armor and infantry thrusts that threatened to outflank the *2d Battalion* forced Meyer to bring forward the designated time of attack to 1400, and although the *1st* and *2d* battalions made initial gains, the regiment lacked the strength to carry out the *Seventh Army's* orders. The division aborted the attack, and the battalions then went over to an aggressive defensive posture.

The attack by the *25th Panzer Grenadier Regiment* created a strong perimeter, and there can be no doubt that it played a crucial part in preventing the British Second Army from capturing Caen as early as 7 June. Over the following days the remaining divisional formations

reached the combat zone and were immediately committed to battle. The point of maximum effort for *"Hitlerjugend"* then swung from the *25th Regiment* on the right flank to the *26th Regiment* on the left, but panzer and grenadier assaults failed either to extend the divisional perimeter or to capture Bayeux. The bitter fighting in and around tactically important villages was frequently hand to hand, and the whole divisional sector was smothered daily by Allied artillery fire. On 14 June, a barrage fell upon Witt's headquarters and killed him. He was succeeded as divisional commander by Meyer.

When an Allied offensive opening on 15 June eventually forced *Panzer Lehr* (on the left wing of *"Hitlerjugend"*) to give ground, the division pulled back its own left flank at Boislande to avoid being outflanked. Although heavy casualties had reduced the strength of the battalions, the survivors were determined to hold the divisional perimeter. But Allied pressure was too strong. The attacks finally drove the SS out of the villages they had captured during the first days. The fighting for Caen died away on 18 June, and in the short lull that followed both sides regrouped, ready to resume the struggle for the ruined city.

Although up to 16 June 1944, *"Hitlerjugend"* had lost 403 men of all ranks killed, 847 wounded, and 63 missing, no replacements had been received. The self-sacrifice of the young men of the division had played a prominent part in the German army's defensive success in Normandy between 6 and 18 June. The *12th SS Panzer Division* subsequently demonstrated the same spirit in the Battle of the Bulge and in the last offensives of the war in Hungary and in Austria.

[*See also* Meyer, Kurt; Witt, Fritz.]

PANZER IV, MAKE H.   West of Caen, June 1944.
THE ROBERT HUNT LIBRARY, LONDON

BIBLIOGRAPHY

Ellis, L. F., et al. *The Battle of Normandy*. Vol. 1 of *Victory in the West*. 1962.

Klietmann, K. G. *Die Waffen SS: Eine Dokumentation*. 1965.

Kratschmer, E. G. *Die Ritterkreuzträger der Waffen SS*. 1982.

Meyer, H. *Kriegsgeschichte der 12te SS Panzer Division "Hitlerjugend."* 1982.

Tessin, Georg. *Verbände und Truppen der deutschen Wehrmacht und Waffen-SS im Zweiten Weltkrieg, 1939–1945*. 1973–1980.

JAMES LUCAS

21ST ARMY GROUP. The original plan of the Chief of Staff to the Supreme Allied Commander (COSSAC) had of necessity been limited to an initial assault on the French coast by three seaborne and two airborne divisions, together hardly exceeding the paper establishment of a single corps. Once the various commanders had been chosen and discussions between them initiated, however, the necessity for a larger assault force landing on a wider front was recognized. Soon after General Bernard L. Montgomery arrived from Italy, the projected force had been increased to five seaborne divisions, two of which would be American, and three airborne, with two of those also American.

General Montgomery's appointment at this time (January 1944) was as commander in chief of the 21st Army Group. The group had been set up in July 1943 under the command of Gen. Bernard Paget, who since late 1941 had been commander in chief of Home Forces. He had thoroughly reorganized the infantry training of the

BERNARD L. MONTGOMERY WITH SOME OF HIS COMMANDERS, 24 JUNE 1944.   From left to right: (front row) G. I. Thomas (43d Div.), G. C. Bucknall (XXX Corps), H. D. G. Crerar (First Canadian Army), Bernard L. Montgomery (21st Army Group), Miles C. Dempsey (Second Army), Harry Broadhurst (83d Composite Group, RAF), N. M. Ritchie (XII Corps); (second row) D. C. Bullen-Smith (51st Div.), R. F. L. Keller (3d Div., Canadian), D. A. H. Graham (50th Div.), G. P. B. Roberts (11th Armoured Div.), Richard N. O'Connor (VIII Corps), E. H. Barker (49th Inf. Div.), J. T. Crocker (I Corps); (rear row) G. H. A. Macmillan (15th Div.), R. N. Gale (6th Airborne Div.), and G. W. E. J. Erskine (7th Armoured Div.).   IMPERIAL WAR MUSEUM

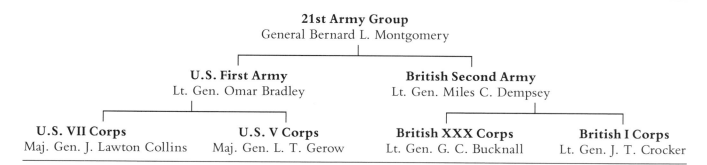

21st Army Group
General Bernard L. Montgomery

U.S. First Army
Lt. Gen. Omar Bradley

British Second Army
Lt. Gen. Miles C. Dempsey

U.S. VII Corps
Maj. Gen. J. Lawton Collins

U.S. V Corps
Maj. Gen. L. T. Gerow

British XXX Corps
Lt. Gen. G. C. Bucknall

British I Corps
Lt. Gen. J. T. Crocker

British army along modern and realistic lines, gaining an excellent reputation as a trainer of troops.

Shortly after the formation of the 21st Army Group, which initially consisted of only those British and Canadian divisions selected to take part in Operation OVERLORD, it was decided that its commander in chief should be "jointly responsible" with the naval and air force commanders for the planning and execution of the operation including the capture of the lodgment area, "until such time as the Supreme Allied Commander allocated an area of responsibility for the First American Army Group." Thus the U.S. First Army came under command of the 21st Army Group, and for a time it seemed that General Paget would command both the British and American forces during the opening phase of the assault.

Paget, however, whatever his reputation throughout the army, was hardly known to the British or American public, and not known at all to General Dwight D. Eisenhower. Not surprisingly, in so vast and crucial an operation as OVERLORD, General Eisenhower preferred to have as his overall land forces commander someone with whom he had already established a sound working relationship. To Paget's intense disappointment, he was appointed commander in chief, Middle East, at the end of 1943, and General Montgomery took his place.

Montgomery's headquarters, by a piece of fortuitous coincidence, were in St. Paul's School, Hammersmith, where he had been a pupil for five years before going to Sandhurst in 1907. Despite the considerable increase in the size of the 21st Army Group shortly after he took command, he decided only to expand the headquarters and to change neither its location nor its title.

Thus the 21st Army Group, now with the U.S. First Army and the British Second Army as its constituent parts, became a military reality, eventually comprising five seaborne divisions, three airborne divisions, four armored brigades, a host of shore groups and beach parties, and a minimum of eighteen follow-up divisions. It says a great deal for the spirit of cooperation insisted upon by Eisenhower that a senior American commander, Gen. Omar Bradley, would willingly and loyally accept subordination to a British commander, even for the limited period before breakout from the lodgment area would give him independence from it.
[*See also* First Army; Second Army.]

BIBLIOGRAPHY

Ellis, L. F., et al. *The Battle of Normandy.* Vol. 1 of *Victory in the West.* 1962. Reprint, 1974.
Thompson, R. W. *The Price of Victory.* 1960.

BARRIE PITT

21ST PANZER DIVISION. The original *21st Panzer Division* was destroyed in Tunisia in May 1943, and on 15 July a new division was formed at Rennes, France, under the general supervision of the *Seventh Army.* Its men came from *Africa Corps* veterans who had escaped the disaster in Tunisia, veterans of the Eastern front, the *931st Mobile Brigade,* and miscellaneous units in the zone of the *Seventh Army,* including *Panzer Company Paris* and the panzer company of the *LXXXI Corps.* "The Division was reorganized . . . with undesirable personnel from a large number of divisions," Gen. Leo Geyr von Schweppenburg noted later. "Even very thorough and experienced training could never overcome this basic fault."

The *21st Panzer* consisted of the *100th Panzer Regiment,* the *125th Panzer Grenadier Regiment,* and the *192d Panzer Grenadier Regiment,* all of which had only two battalions, instead of the normal three. The division also included the *155th Panzer Artillery Regiment* (three battalions), the *220th Panzer Engineer Battalion,* and the *305th Army Antiaircraft Artillery Battalion.* Much of the division was equipped with captured French vehicles and obsolete weapons; in fact, of the ten panzer and panzer grenadier divisions in the West, the *21st Panzer* was the only one rated as unfit for service in Russia.

In the early spring of 1944, when the Eastern front seemed on the verge of collapse, the *21st Panzer* was transferred to Hungary. It was sent back to France in late April, where it was essentially split up and placed in several assembly areas on either side of the Orne River, with its artillery stationed on the coast.

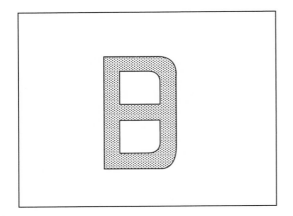

The *21st Panzer* was commanded by Brig. Gen. Edgar Feuchtinger, a less than competent officer. In late May, Field Marshal Erwin Rommel inspected the division and found mine fields still surrounded by barbed wire and labeled as such, and French civilians wandering freely about, despite orders he had given to the contrary. Some of Feuchtinger's subordinates were hardly better. A few weeks before the invasion, Rommel appeared at the headquarters of the *100th Panzer Regiment* at Falaise at 0800 one morning and found no one there with any authority. Half an hour later the regimental commander, Col. Hermann von Oppeln-Bronikowski, showed up—drunk. Why Rommel did not relieve him from duty on the spot is a minor mystery. On the other hand, Colonels Hans von Luck and Josef Rauch, the commanders of the panzer grenadier regiments, demonstrated consistent talent for their jobs.

On the morning of D-day, Feuchtinger was away from his post, and command paralysis gripped the *21st Panzer*. As early as 0120 Maj. Gen. Wilhelm Richter, the commander of the *716th Infantry Division,* tried to get the division to attack the British 6th Airborne Division's bridgehead east of the Orne, but Feuchtinger did not decide to move against the paratroopers until 0630, and the movement did not begin until 0800. Shortly before noon, however, Gen. Erich Marcks, the commander of the *LXXXIV Corps,* reversed this order and instructed the *21st Panzer* to counterattack the British and Canadians, who were now advancing on Caen. Luck's *125th Panzer Grenadier Regiment* (reinforced with a tank company) was left behind to contain the paratroopers.

As a result of these delays, the *21st Panzer* had to make a long approach march in full daylight, with a significantly diminished cloud cover. It was pounded by Allied fighter-bombers. The division had less than sixty operational tanks left when it counterattacked against the British I Corps at Biéville and Périers late that afternoon. Completely outclassed by the British weapons, it lost sixteen tanks in a matter of minutes—most of them before they could get within range of their opponents.

Meanwhile, the *I Battalion* of Colonel Rauch's *192d Panzer Grenadier Regiment* was lucky enough to strike directly between Sword and Juno beaches and penetrated to the coast at 2000 hours without doing any real damage. At 2300, however, a misdirected Allied glider lift convinced Feuchtinger that the Allies were trying to cut the battalion off with paratroopers, so he hastily retreated. Col. Bodo Zimmermann of the OB West staff accused Feuchtinger of taking to his heels, which seems to have been an accurate assessment.

The *21st Panzer* defended positions north of Caen on 7 and 8 June and took part in General Geyr's unsuccessful counterattack on 9 June. Thereafter it took no further part in offensive operations, although its grenadiers continued to fight doggedly until the end of the campaign. It was largely destroyed in the fighting around Caen in June and July. Partly rebuilt in September, the *21st Panzer Division* fought in the Siegfried Line campaign and was sent to the East in early 1945. Most of its survivors were captured by the Russians at the end of the war.

[*See also* Feuchtinger, Edgar.]

BIBLIOGRAPHY

Carell, Paul. *Invasion: They're Coming.* Translated by E. Osers. 1963. Paul Carell is the pseudonym used by Hans Karl Schmidt.

Geyr von Schweppenburg, Leo. "Pz. Grp. West (Mid. 43–5 Jul. 44)." Office of the Chief of Military History, MS B-466. Report dated 14 Apr. 1947. U.S. Army Military History Institute, Carlisle Barracks, Pa.

Mitcham, Samuel W., Jr. *Rommel's Last Battle: The Desert Fox and the Normandy Campaign.* 1983.

Tessin, Georg. *Verbände und Truppen der deutschen Wehrmacht und Waffen-SS im Zweiten Weltkrieg, 1939–1945.* Vol. 12, 1975.

SAMUEL W. MITCHAM, JR.

29TH INFANTRY DIVISION.

The 29th Infantry Division, a National Guard division, was called into federal service on 3 February 1941, more than ten months before the Japanese attack on Pearl Harbor. The 29th was first formed in World War I, when it was shipped to France and fought in the Meuse-Argonne offensive in 1918. The 29th component units had even older lineages. The 116th Infantry, which originated as a Virginia militia unit in 1741, gained immortality in the Civil War as Stonewall Jackson's legendary "Stonewall Brigade," and the 175th Infantry, known as "The Dandy Fifth of Maryland," was raised in 1774. The 29th's regional roots earned it the nickname "The Blue and Gray Division" because its components had fought on opposing sides in the Civil War. Even on the eve of D-day, the 29th maintained a distinctive regional flavor because many of the draftees who joined the division after mobilization were drawn from Maryland, Virginia, and Pennsylvania.

The 29th was one of the first U.S. Army divisions to be shipped to Europe in World War II, reaching Britain in October 1942. Indeed, it trained in England for so long that it gained the derisive nickname "England's Own."

The 29th Infantry Division played a major role on D-day, undertaking a successful amphibious assault against the German defenders of the *352d Division* on Omaha Beach. Prior to D-day the 29th Division had been assigned to the U.S. First Army's V Corps, which planned the Omaha landing. Maj. Gen. Leonard T. Gerow, the V Corps commander, had in fact commanded the 29th Division for sixteen months, relinquishing command to Maj. Gen. Charles H. Gerhardt in July 1943. For the D-day assault, Omaha Beach was divided into two sectors: the 1st Infantry Division was to assault the eastern half, the 29th Infantry Division the western half. Operation OVER-LORD called for the 29th Division to first establish a firm foothold at Omaha and then expand the beachhead as rapidly as possible southward toward the key Norman city of Saint-Lô, a D plus 9 (15 June) objective.

The 29th Division was organized as a normal U.S. Army infantry division, consisting of three infantry regiments (115th, 116th, 175th), three 105-mm artillery battalions (110th, 111th, 224th), a 155-mm artillery battalion (227th), an engineer battalion (121st), a medical battalion (104th), and support units. Generally the 29th's three infantry regiments trained and fought as regimental combat teams (RCT), each of which consisted of a single infantry regiment plus an attached artillery battalion, medical company, and engineer company.

The 116th RCT was the 29th Division's first-wave assault force on D-day. The 116th, which had been the first U.S. Army regiment to undertake amphibious training at the U.S. Army Assault Training Center in England, had practiced seaborne invasions for almost a year prior to Operation OVERLORD. On D-day, the 29th was slightly over its prescribed strength of 14,281 men because the 116th RCT had been reinforced prior to the invasion by 500 "over-strength men" in expectation of high casualties on the beach. For the landings, the 116th was reconfigured as an assault regiment. As such, rifle

29TH INFANTRY DIVISION COMMANDERS.   Left to right: Charles Corlett (XIX Corps commanding general), Charles Gerhardt (29th Div. commanding general), Edward McDaniel (29th Div. chief of staff), William Witte (29th Div. G-3).

NATIONAL ARCHIVES

29th Infantry Division
Maj. Gen. Charles H. Gerhardt

29th Division HQ Company

115th Infantry Regiment ("1st Maryland")
1st Battalion
2d Battalion
3d Battalion

116th Infantry Regiment ("The Stonewall Brigade")
1st Battalion
2d Battalion
3d Battalion

175th Infantry Regiment ("5th Maryland")
1st Battalion
2d Battalion
3d Battalion

Each regiment also had a headquarters company, a service company, a cannon company, and an antitank company. Divisional troops included a signal company, military police platoon, quartermaster company and band (all 29th Division), and the 729th Ordnance Company; 110th, 111th, 224th, and 227th Field Artillery battalions (105-mm); 121st Engineer Battalion; 104th Medical Battalion.

companies were organized into six thirty-one–man boat teams, each of which occupied a single landing craft. A boat team was led by one officer and contained flamethrower, mortar, wire-cutting, bazooka, and demolition teams in addition to riflemen.

On D-day, the 29th's Omaha Beach assault began disastrously when the 116th's four first-wave assault companies came ashore at H-hour (0630 hours) and were met by withering German fire from the bluffs behind the beach. Inspired by Brig. Gen. Norman Cota, the 29th's assistant commander, and Col. Charles Canham, commanding officer of the 116th, small groups of 29ers bravely ascended the bluffs and penetrated the German defenses by about 1030 hours. The 115th RCT, scheduled to land soon after the 116th, could not do so because German coastal obstacles in that sector had not been cleared due to heavy German fire. Instead the 115th landed in the 1st Division sector shortly before 1200 and pushed inland on the 116th's

left. The beachhead had been secured, but at a cost of nearly 1,000 29th Division casualties, 850 of whom were members of the 116th.

From D plus 1 to D plus 5, the 29th pushed out of its beachhead against disorganized German resistance. The 175th RCT, which landed on 7 June, attacked westward, captured the key bridge over the Vire River at Isigny and linked up with VII Corps forces from the Utah beachhead on 10 June. Meanwhile the 116th cleared the coastal sector west of Omaha, relieved the beleaguered Rangers at Pointe du Hoc, and liberated the port of Grandcamp on 8 June. The 115th advanced south of the flooded Aure River valley toward Saint-Lô, but its 2d Battalion ran into a German ambush shortly after midnight on 10 June near the village of Le Carrefour and was routed.

On the arrival of reinforcements from Brittany, including the powerful *3d Parachute Division*, German resistance stiffened about ten kilometers (6.2 miles) north of the city along a placid stream known as the Elle. Attacks across the Elle on 12 and 13 June made little headway toward Saint-Lô and cost the division 600 men. Another major attack toward Saint-Lô on 16 June made good progress at first, but was halted by German counterattacks five kilometers (3.1 miles) from the city. For the 29th, no day of fighting in Normandy was more fierce than 18 June. On a minor elevation known as Hill 108, the 1st Battalion, 175th Infantry, held off German attacks all day at a cost of more than 40 percent of its men. The unit won a Distinguished Unit Citation for the action, and in regimental lore the site would forever be known as "Purple Heart Hill."

From D-day to D plus 12 (18 June), the 29th Division suffered approximately 3,500 casualties, or about one-quarter of its strength. Nearly 1,000 of these men were killed.

The 29th remained in the line opposite Saint-Lô for another month, finally liberating the city on 18 July after a fierce seven-day battle. Subsequently the division participated in the Normandy breakout, the Brest campaign, the Rhineland battles, and the final conquest of Germany.

[See also Gerhardt, Charles H.]

BIBLIOGRAPHY

Balkoski, Joseph. *Beyond the Beachhead: The 29th Infantry Division in Normandy.* 1989.
Balkoski, Joseph, and Arthur Plaut. *The 115th Infantry Regiment in World War II.* 1948.
Brewer, James. *History of the 175th Infantry.* 1955.
Ewing, Joseph. *Twenty-Nine, Let's Go!* 1948.

JOSEPH M. BALKOSKI

TWINING, NATHAN F. (1897–1982), American, major general, commander of the U.S. Fifteenth Air

Force. Following family tradition, Nathan Farragut Twining began military service in 1915 with the Oregon National Guard. He graduated from West Point in November 1918, too late for World War I, and secured a transfer to the U.S. Army Air Service in 1923. In 1942 he served in the Solomon Islands as commander of the U.S. Thirteenth Air Force and later directed Allied air operations there. At the end of 1943 General Twining was sent to the Mediterranean to command the newly formed U.S. Fifteenth Air Force.

Promoted to major general while in the South Pacific, Twining arrived in Italy on 1 January 1944 to direct the Fifteenth and serve as head of the Mediterranean Allied Strategic Air Forces. From captured Italian airfields at Bari and Foggia, Twining's Fifteenth supported the Allied Combined Bomber Offensive, coded POINTBLANK, against German industry, including oil refineries, and the Luftwaffe. These missions were to support the planned cross-Channel invasion by diminishing German industrial output and reducing the number of aircraft that would threaten Allied landings.

Bad weather and lack of critical equipment forced Twining to divert his air force to the stalled Italian ground campaign until the third week of February 1944. Clear weather on 22 February allowed him to dispatch his bombers and a small number of long-range escort fighters to participate in air operation ARGUMENT, later called BIG WEEK, which killed more German fighter pilots than could be replaced. Although Twining's force lost heavily during BIG WEEK, the effort had won the Allies virtual command of the air. He recalled later that after ARGUMENT "we could roam the skies practically at will."

Because the Fifteenth lacked enough escort fighters, it could not continue its effort to completely destroy the Luftwaffe. Until mid-April 1944, Twining directed his air force again to the Italian campaign, in which it did not do well. As a result of that poor performance, he improved training and brought its strength up to authorized levels so that he could send it to attack the rail yards and oil refineries at Ploesti, Romania.

On 15 April General Eisenhower temporarily assumed control of the U.S. Strategic Air Forces, which included the Fifteenth. Eisenhower ordered bombing of communication and transportation targets that the Germans could use to funnel reinforcements and supplies into the D-day invasion area in Normandy, or into southern France to opposed the later Allied assault there in support of the cross-Channel landings. Twining ordered his air force to bomb railroad marshaling yards and Luftwaffe airfields in Italy and the Balkans. His most important targets were German coastal batteries, airdromes, and railways in southern France.

Just before D-day Twining directed his air force to shut-

NATHAN F. TWINING.   NATIONAL ARCHIVES

tle-bomb through Soviet territory. The Fifteenth's bombers were to fly nearly to their range limits, bomb German factories and refineries, and then go to Soviet airfields and refuel before returning to Italy. The intent was to distract the Germans on the eve of D-day by demonstrating that no target, regardless how deep within the Reich, was safe from aerial assault. Shuttle-bombing enjoyed only mixed results, owing largely to increasingly difficult Soviet relations.

After D-day Twining concentrated on German crude-oil production around Ploesti, which his air force had destroyed by August 1944, albeit at a high cost in men and machines. For the remainder of the war in Europe, he aided Allied operations in the Mediterranean and Soviet efforts in the Balkans by bombing transportation and oil targets. He emerged from the war in Europe as one of the most experienced and successful bomber commanders.

Twining later commanded the U.S. Twentieth Air Force in the closing days of the Pacific war. His postwar assignments included vice chief and then chief of staff to the U.S. Air Force; finally, he was the first air general to be Chairman of the Joint Chiefs of Staff.

[See also Fifteenth Air Force.]

BIBLIOGRAPHY

Craven, Wesley F., and James L. Cate, eds. *Europe: Argument to V-E Day.* Vol. 3 of *The Army Air Forces in World War II.* 1951. Reprint, 1983.

McCarley, J. Britt. "General Nathan Farragut Twining: The Making of a Disciple of American Strategic Air Power, 1897–1953." Ph.D. diss., Temple University, 1989.

Twining, Nathan F. Interviews 634, 635, 636, and 808. 1965–1973. Albert F. Simpson Historical Research Center, Maxwell Air Force Base, Alabama.

Twining, Nathan F. Interviews. 1967. Oral History Research Office, Columbia University.

J. BRITT MCCARLEY

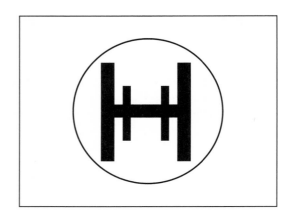

243D INFANTRY DIVISION. The *243d Infantry Division* was formed in the Dollersheim Maneuver Area of northeastern Austria as *Division B,* using cadres from the *387th Infantry Division,* a unit which had seen considerable action on the Eastern front. Initially a static division, it consisted of the *920th, 921st,* and *922d* grenadier regiments (three battalions each), the *243d Artillery Regiment* (three battalions), the *243d Fusilier Battalion,* the *243d Engineer Battalion* (two companies), the *243d Signal Battalion,* and the *243d Divisional Supply Unit.* The *243d* was sent to Normandy in September, and the following month *III Battalion* of the *920th Grenadier* was sent to the Crimea in southern Russia as a reserve unit.

In January 1944 the entire division was reorganized; it was reduced to six infantry battalions. Four of the remaining infantry battalions were equipped with bicycles, and the division was upgraded to a limited attack unit. (German divisions were categorized based on their mobility and the types of missions they could conduct: full attack, limited attack, full defense, or limited defense.) The *243d* also added the *243d Antitank Battalion.* According to the plan, the divisional artillery regiment, the supply troops, the antitank battalion, and two infantry battalions were supposed to be motorized, but only six infantry companies had been equipped with trucks by D-day, and one of these had subsequently been dissolved. Apparently none of the other units had received its motorized vehicles when the Allies landed in Normandy, and the artillery was horse-drawn.

The *243d Infantry Division* was defending the Carentan-Montebourg-Bricquebec-Lessay sector on D-day, and was in action from the beginning. It was, however, scattered over too wide an area to be committed as a unit, or even to maintain unit integrity. A good example of the hopelessly confused mixing of German units occurred at dawn on 7 June, when the *III Battalion, 243d Artillery Regiment (243d Division),* along with the *456th* and *457th* motorized artillery battalions (from the *Seventh Army*'s reserve),

joined the battle of Saint-Mère-Église, firing in support of the *1058th Grenadier Regiment* (from the *91st Air Landing Division*), the *709th Antitank Battalion* (from the *709th Infantry Division*), the *Seventh Army Storm Battalion* (from the *Seventh Army* reserve), and elements of the *6th Parachute Regiment,* all under Gen. Karl Wilhelm von Schlieben, commander of the *709th Infantry Division.* The *III/243d Artillery* rejoined its parent unit; later it attached itself to the *77th Infantry Division* and successfully passed through American lines near Barneville-sur-Mer during the night of 17–18 June, avoiding entrapment in Cherbourg. In the period of 6 to 18 June, it lost only four guns.

On 7 June Schlieben placed the *922d Grenadier Regiment* under the control of Col. Helmuth Rohrbach of the *709th Division.* (*Battle Group Rohrbach* included the colonel's own *729th Grenadier Regiment.*) Most of the remainder of the *243d Infantry Division* was involved in the defense of the Montebourg-Quinéville sector; it was slowly pushed back from 9 to 13 June, but generally held its lines in heavy fighting against repeated American attacks. After 13 June most of the division was shifted west, in a vain attempt to prevent the Americans from penetrating to the west coast of the Cotentin Peninsula. From 10 to 16 June, the divisional headquarters operated under the name *Battle Group Hellmich,* after the divisional commander, Lt. Gen. Heinz Hellmich. He was killed on 16 June. The Americans reached the coast two days later. The *243d Division* lost much of its cohesion during the subsequent retreat from the western Cotentin and the Montebourg line to Cherbourg (18–21 June). On 20 June, it was down to regimental size, its morale had flagged, and its combat value was rated very low.

Lt. Col. Franz Müller, the commander of the *922d Grenadier Regiment,* assumed command of the remnants of the *243d Infantry Division* (now dubbed *Battle Group Müller*) and led them in the fight for Cherbourg. Two days later, however, General Schlieben, the fortress commander, signaled Field Marshal Rommel that the leaderless remnants of the *243d* and *77th* infantry divisions were more of a burden than a help. In any case, *Battle Group Müller* defended the western side of the Cherbourg fortifications from Vanville to Sainte-Croix-Hague, and was destroyed by the time Cherbourg completely surrendered on 29 June. The small remnants of the *243d Infantry Division* that had escaped encirclement in the fortress were absorbed by the *182d Reserve Division*. The *243d Division* had ceased to exist.

[*See also* Hellmich, Heinz.]

BIBLIOGRAPHY

Harrison, Gordon A. *Cross-Channel Attack.* U.S. Army in World War II: The European Theater of Operations. 1951.

Tessin, Georg. *Verbände und Truppen der deutschen Wehrmacht und Waffen-SS im Zweiten Weltkrieg, 1939–1945.* 15 vols. 1973–1980.

U.S. Military Intelligence Service. *Order of Battle of the German Army, 1944.* 1944.

SAMUEL W. MITCHAM, JR.

275TH INFANTRY DIVISION. The German *275th Infantry Division* was formed in Saint-Lô in December 1943, mainly from the remnants of the recently disbanded *223d Infantry Division,* which had been largely destroyed on the southern sector of the Eastern front. The cadres used to form its divisional staff came from the *352d Infantry Division.* Sent to Brittany in February, by mid-month it consisted of the divisional staff, one regimental staff, one artillery unit, two battalions of "old men," and very little else. Over the next few weeks it absorbed three reserve grenadier battalions from Poland, the *234th, 425th,* and *475th,* and the *190th Reserve Battalion,* which was transferred from the *158th Reserve Division,* then on garrison duty in southern France. It also received an artillery battalion from the *94th Infantry Division,* then in Italy, and two infantry battalions from the *102d Infantry Division,* then serving on the Russian front. By D-day, the *275th Infantry Division* consisted of the *983d, 984th,* and *985th* grenadier regiments (two battalions each), the *275th Fusilier Battalion,* the *275th Antitank Battalion,* the *275th Engineer Battalion,* the *275th Signal Battalion,* and the *275th Divisional Supply Unit.* Unlike most divisions of its type, the *275th* was partially motorized in the spring of 1944. Its commander was Maj. Gen. Hans Schmidt.

According to the German plan, the motorized elements of the *275th Infantry* were to be committed separately from the rest of the division if the Allied landings took place outside Brittany. These forces, dubbed *Battle Group Heinz (Kampfgruppe Heinz),* consisted of the *984th Grenadier Regiment,* the *275th Fusilier Battalion,* a three-battery artillery battalion, and an antiaircraft battery. On D-day, the *Angers Engineer Battalion* (which consisted of the

staff, instructors, and students of the *7th Army Engineer School* at Angers) was attached to *Battle Group Heinz.*

When the battle group was alerted on the morning of 6 June, it was less than 200 kilometers (120 miles) from Saint-Lô by rail. Under normal conditions, this trip would have taken less than a day. Due to heavy Allied air attacks, however, the last train did not leave Brittany until 8 June. Almost all of the battle group's motorized vehicles were destroyed by Allied fighter-bombers at Fougères on 9 June, and the battle group suffered heavy casualties. Then it was ordered to detrain and proceed to the front the best way it could. Using bicycles, the fusilier battalion and the *II/984th Grenadier* arrived in its assembly areas (in the rear of the *17th SS Panzer Grenadier Division*) on the evening of 11 June. The *I/984th* arrived on foot on 13 June. The problems of this battle group were typical of German units attempting to reach the front in June 1944.

Battle Group Heinz was attached to the *17th SS Panzer Grenadier Division* and was sent into battle southeast of Carentan, where it inflicted severe casualties on the U.S. 175th Infantry Regiment of the 29th Infantry Division. The battle group fought very well and remained under operational control of the *17th SS* until 7 July, when it suffered very heavy casualties while fighting the U.S. 30th Infantry and 3d Armored Divisions between the Vire River and Saint-Lô. In the process, however, it significantly delayed the American advance and prevented a genuine breakthrough until the *Panzer Lehr Division* arrived to reinforce the wavering German line. The battle group was down to a strength of 450 men on 11 July, and not all of these were members of the *275th Infantry.*

Meanwhile, the nonmotorized elements of the *275th Infantry Division* arrived in Normandy during the second and third weeks of July and went into reserve behind the *Panzer Lehr Division. Battle Group Heinz* was destroyed during Operation COBRA on 25 July, and one of the remaining grenadier regiments was reduced to a strength of 200 men by the massive Allied bombing attack and the subsequent American ground advance. The *275th*

Artillery Regiment was cut off on 27 July, and lost almost all of its heavy equipment. That evening, the divisional command post was overrun.

The *275th Infantry Division* was practically destroyed in the Normandy campaign and the subsequent breakout from the Falaise pocket. By the end of August, it was down to a strength of 800 men. By 10 September, however, it had absorbed the survivors of the *353d Infantry Division* and a few local defense battalions, and had a total strength of five thousand men, thirteen 105-mm howitzers, one 210-mm howitzer, and six assault guns. It then fought in its most famous engagement—the battle in the Huertgen Forest—where it decimated, in succession, the U.S. 9th, 28th, and 4th infantry divisions, Combat Command R of the 5th Armored Division, the famous U.S. 1st Infantry Division, and the elite 2d Ranger Battalion in heavy fighting between September and December 1944. It was practically annihilated in the process. Its few sur-

vivors were transferred to the *344th Infantry Division,* and the divisional headquarters was sent back to Germany, where it organized a new *275th Infantry Division*. It was sent to the Eastern front and ended the war in Czecho-slovakia.

[*See also* Schmidt, Hans.]

BIBLIOGRAPHY

Blumenson, Martin. *Breakout and Pursuit*. U.S. Army in World War II: The European Theater of Operations. 1960.

Harrison, Gordon A. *Cross-Channel Attack*. U.S. Army in World War II: The European Theater of Operations. 1951.

Tessin, Georg. *Verbände und Truppen der deutschen Wehrmacht und Waffen-SS im Zweiten Weltkrieg, 1939–1945*. Vol. 8, 1979.

U.S. Military Intelligence Service. "Order of Battle of the German Army, 1945." 1945.

SAMUEL W. MITCHAM, JR.

U, V

U-BOATS. In the spring of 1944, in anticipation of the Allied invasion, the Commander in Chief of the German Navy and commander of U-boats (*Unterseeboote*), Grand Admiral Karl Dönitz, ordered the buildup in French bases of the U-boat group *Landwirt*. For combat operations against the invasion fleet in the Channel area, only the medium U-boats of Type VII C could be used. They displaced 769 tons on the surface and 871 tons submerged. Their length was 67.1 meters, their width 6.2 meters, and their maximum depth 4.7 meters. On the surface they were driven by two diesel motors of 1,600 horsepower each; submerged, by two electric motors of 375 horsepower each. They could reach 17.0 knots on the surface and about 7.0 knots submerged. Their range was 8,500 miles at 10 knots on the surface, and 130 miles at 2 knots submerged. Their complement in 1944 was 4 officers and 45 to 50 men. Their armament consisted of four 53.3-cm torpedo tubes at the bow and one at the stern. They could load up to 14 torpedoes by using the outboard stowage tubes, but in 1944 the normal load, only inside the boat, comprised three Gnat (*Zaunkönig*) homing torpedoes, and five LUT torpedoes, running according to a set program, in the bow, and two Gnats at the stern. For air defense they had one 37-mm M42U and two twin 20-mm 38MII guns. They were equipped with a radar FuMO 61, and a radar observation set FuMB 26.

In early June the group *Landwirt* consisted of nine boats, eight in Brest and one in La Pallice, with snorkels (tubes to be raised above the surface to circulate air in a submerged U-boat, so as to recharge the diesel engines' electric batteries). Also, there were ten boats without snorkels in Brest, three in Lorient, fourteen in Saint-Nazaire, and three in La Pallice. An additional seven boats were being outfitted with snorkels. Simultaneously the group *Mitte* had been built up in Norwegian ports. Seven of its snorkel boats and four others had departed for France (one was lost); seven

U 275.

snorkel and twenty-two other boats waited in their bases.

When the invasion started on 6 June, seventeen boats set out from Brest, fourteen from Saint-Nazaire, four from La Pallice, and one from Lorient. This force included all the snorkel boats, which were ordered into the Channel to attack the invasion forces at all costs. The boats without snorkels were to try to enter the Channel.

The U-boats had to force the barrier of three destroyer

and seven frigate escort groups with three attached escort carriers. From 6 June on, four to six frigate groups and the carriers operated west of the Channel and the Bay of Biscay, while two destroyer groups patrolled the western entrance to the Channel. In addition the area was covered by continuous day and night patrols of the shore-based, reinforced No. 19 Group of the RAF Coastal Command.

The U-boats suffered considerable damage. On 7 June *U 970* was sunk by Sunderland R of No. 228 Squadron RAF. Wellington G of No. 179 Squadron RAF damaged *U 415*, and Liberator L of No. 53 Squadron RAF damaged *U 963* and *U 256*, though one of these boats shot down Liberator B of No. 53 Squadron RAF. On 7 June *U 989* was damaged by the Canadian Wellington C of No. 407 Squadron RCAF and Liberator M of No. 224 Squadron RAF, which were both shot down by the U-boat. *U 212** (asterisk indicates a snorkel boat) was damaged by Mosquitos O and L of No. 248 Squadron RAF. The damaged boats had to return to base.

On 8 June Liberator G of No. 224 Squadron RAF sank *U 629* and *U 373*, and Halifax F of No. 502 Squadron RAF damaged *U 413*. On 9 June *U 740* was sunk by Liberator V of No. 120 Squadron RAF. Since it had been impossible for nonsnorkel boats to enter the Channel, those still operational (*U 228, U 255, U 260, U 262, U 270, U 281, U 333, U 382, U 437, U 445, U 608, U 650, U 714, U 758, U 766, U 981, U 985*, and *U 993*) were stationed in a patrol line to cover the Bay of Biscay until 15 June.

Of the snorkel boats, *U 212** had to return to base twice, but the others persisted in their effort to pass into the Channel, augmented by the snorkel boats from Norway (*U 671*, U 767*, U 971*, U 988**, and *U 1191**). On 7 and 8 June *U 984*, U 621**, and *U 953** fired four, two, and four Gnat torpedoes respectively at the destroyers *Qu'Appelle, Restigouche, Saskatchewan,* and *Skeena* of the Canadian 12th Escort Group, all of which detonated prematurely in the ships' wakes. On 9 June *U 764** fired four Gnats at destroyers without a hit, and by 11 June *U 621*, U 269**, and *U 275** had all attacked destroyers unsuccessfully. *U 821** was sunk in an attack by Mosquitos T, S, W, and V of No. 248 Squadron RAF (of which one was lost) and Liberator K of No. 206 Squadron RAF.

On 11 June Sunderland U of No. 228 Squadron RAF damaged *U 333* in the Bay of Biscay but was shot down in return. On 12 June Liberator S of No. 224 Squadron RAF damaged *U 441** but was also shot down. On 13 June *U 270* shot down Liberator C of No. 53 Squadron RAF in the Bay of Biscay and was then damaged by Wellington Y of No. 172 Squadron RAF.

On 14 June the first snorkel U-boats reached the shipping lanes, simultaneously with Allied support groups that had been relocated into the Channel following decrypts of German radio signals. On 14 June *U 984**

missed a search group, but on 15 June *U 621** sank the landing ship *LST 280*, and *U 767** sank the frigate HMS *Mourne*, while *U 764** torpedoed the frigate HMS *Blackwood* beyond repair. On 18 June *U 621** missed two U.S. battleships with a salvo, while British destroyers *Fame, Inconstant,* and *Havelock* sank *U 767**, and Wellington A of No. 304 Polish Squadron RAF sank *U 441**.

Between June and August 1944 snorkel boats sank seven escorts, three landing ships, and thirteen transports, and damaged one escort and six transports, against the loss of eighteen snorkel U-boats.

[*See also* Dönitz, Karl.]

BIBLIOGRAPHY

Gröner, Erich. *Die deutschen Kriegsschiffe 1815–1945.* Edited by Dieter Jung and Martin Maass. Vol. 3, 1985.

Ministry of Defense (Navy). *The U-Boat War in the Atlantic, 1939–1945.* Vol. 3 of *German Naval History.* 1989.

Rohwer, Jürgen. "Les Sous-marins allemands contre les tentatives alliées en Manche en 1944." *La Revue Maritime* 181 (October 1961): 1220–1233.

Rohwer, Jürgen, and Gerhard Hümmelchen. *Chronology of the War at Sea, 1939–1945.* Translated by Derek Masters. 1992.

JÜRGEN ROHWER

ULTRA. The code word Ultra was the word British authorities attached to signals and documents that disseminated Special Intelligence—that is, the contents of the decrypts of enemy high-grade and medium-grade ciphers as distinct from tactical or low-grade codes and ciphers. It covered all such ciphers, whether German, Italian, Japanese, or indeed, Vichy French, and not merely Enigma, the German code machine. It was introduced in June 1941, replacing earlier labels indicating utmost or top secrecy, including Hydro (which had been used by the Admiralty since January 1940) and Boniface (which so took Winston Churchill's fancy that he continued to use it in telegrams and memoranda until late in the war).

Its introduction coincided with the standardization of existing regulations for safeguarding the security of Special Intelligence. These had to be made more detailed and explicit in view of the need to distribute a growing volume of decrypts to a growing number of recipients. They controlled eligibility for indoctrination, restricted distribution to special ciphers, radio links, and staff, and specified the precautions recipients had to observe when making use of the intelligence for operational purposes.

The U.S. authorities introduced the code word Magic to perform these functions for Japanese decrypts. From early in 1942, as a result of the exchange of Special Intelligence, Ultra and Magic became to some extent interchangeable in both countries, but in general each used

Ultra for European and Atlantic theaters and Magic for the Far East.

[*See also* Intelligence.]

BIBLIOGRAPHY

Hinsley, F. H. *British Intelligence in the Second World War*. Vol. 1, 1979.

F. H. HINSLEY

UNITED STATES OF AMERICA. The numerous defeats inflicted by Japan on America, beginning with the Pearl Harbor attack on 7 December 1941, were disheartening, but they were misleading, too, since the United States would be a far more formidable enemy than the Axis powers supposed. Its unreadiness was a result of indecision, not of national weakness. Until the Japanese attacked Hawaii, Americans could not bring themselves to support entry into a war that was being fought so far from home. But Pearl Harbor, followed by Germany's declaration of war on 11 December, united the nation.

The Home Front. A national mythology had evolved holding that the United States had been tricked into entering World War I. This had prevented President Franklin D. Roosevelt from forming alliances with other democratic states before the European war broke out in 1939, and from rendering effective assistance afterward. Thus, while the program of aid to the Allies called Lend-Lease was enacted in March 1941, few arms made their way to Britain and Russia before Pearl Harbor, and fewer still afterward until America's own basic needs had been met. These needs were great because antiwar sentiment had also made Roosevelt reluctant to build up the armed forces.

Yet, though the nation was practically unarmed on 7 December, America's potential was immense. Its more than 130 million people gave it the third largest population on the Allied side (after China and the Soviet Union) and perhaps the best educated. High school attendance had become nearly universal since the previous war, so that whereas the doughboy of World War I typically had a fifth-grade education, the GI, with eleven years of schooling behind him, was almost a high school graduate. In a war involving the highest technology to date, this would make a crucial difference. Further, although

DWIGHT D. EISENHOWER WITH SOME OF HIS GENERALS, 1945.   Seated, left to right: William H. Simpson (Ninth Army), George S. Patton, Jr. (Third Army), Carl Spaatz (commander, USSTAF), Dwight D. Eisenhower, Omar Bradley (12th Army Group), Courtney H. Hodges (First Army), and L. T. Gerow (Fifteenth Army). Standing: Ralph F. Stearley (IX TAC), Hoyt Vandenberg (Ninth Air Force), Walter Bedell Smith (chief of staff, SHAEF), Otto Weyland (XIX TAC), and Richard E. Nugent (XXIX TAC).

NATIONAL ARCHIVES

PRESIDENT HARRY S. TRUMAN AND DWIGHT D. EISEN-
HOWER.   NATIONAL ARCHIVES

composed of many ethnic groups—Hitler called them a "mongrel people"—Americans had assimilated most of their immigrants since World War I and possessed a common culture. This, too, would be a source of strength.

In addition, America's industrial might, though not at the time geared for war, gave it an overwhelming long-term advantage. In 1938 the American share of world manufacturing output was 28.7 percent, compared to Germany's 13.2 and Japan's 3.8 percent. Yet 1938 was still a Depression year and many plants, and many workers also, were idle. When war came, bringing with it full employment, the industrial advantage of the United States would become even greater. At the war's end, and only in part because so many German and Japanese plants had been destroyed, America would possess about 50 percent of the entire world's manufacturing capacity.

The eightfold increase in military production achieved between 1941 and 1943 (the peak year) would enable the United States to arm not only itself but its allies as well. By 1944 28.7 percent of all weapons used by Great Britain had been made in America. Russia, too, would in time benefit greatly from American support. When the war ended it possessed 665,000 motor vehicles, 400,000 of which—mostly trucks—had been provided by Lend-Lease. In addition, America supplied the Soviets with 2,000 locomotives, 11,000 freight cars, and 540,000 tons of rail. The

mobility of the Red Army was, therefore, largely an American achievement.

Its enormous resources also allowed the United States to make the fewest demands on its people of any great warring nation. Though many items were rationed, and shortages of consumer goods frequent, Americans ended the war better off materially than when they entered it. Thanks to effective anti-inflation policies, incomes rose faster than prices, the excess being only partially absorbed by higher levels of taxation. An economic curse for most, World War II brought prosperity to America; this circumstance, together with distance from the fighting fronts, made the American war experience unique.

These conditions help explain why politics continued as usual. All scheduled elections were held on time, unlike in Britain, for example, where the Parliament elected in 1935 sat for ten years. Although Roosevelt was reelected in 1944, and there were no serious challenges to his direction of the war, a coalition of conservative Democrats and Republicans controlled Congress. As a result, and because, unlike in Britain, there was no popular demand for reform, certain New Deal social programs were canceled, and remarkably little was done by government to help people overcome the dislocations of wartime. In part for the same reason, mobilization in the United States was less extensive than elsewhere. Though labor unions were restricted, there was no labor draft. And while millions of women did enter the work force, many more would have done so if day care and other support services had been provided on the necessary scale.

Although American democracy remained strong during the war, it failed several crucial tests. The internment of nearly all Japanese Americans in 1942 solely because of their race (all those suspected of disloyalty had been arrested immediately after war broke out) was a shameful stain on the national honor. So also was the segregation of African Americans by the military, and their assignment for the most part to noncombat occupations. A number of violent clashes took place as a result of racial tension, the worst being the Detroit Race Riot of 1943, which left thirty-five Americans dead—most of them black. Yet many blacks obtained well-paying jobs in industry for the first time, as a result of which the National Association for the Advancement of Colored People grew tenfold during the war. This explosive growth, and the broadening effects of military service on blacks, would contribute importantly to the successful civil rights struggle that began a few years later.

The Armed Forces. Although the army, including its air arm, numbered almost 1.5 million men when Pearl Harbor was attacked, nearly all were still in training. The army possessed only one combat-ready division. The Army Air Forces, as they were officially called, had just a few hundred modern aircraft, most of which were

RACIAL SEGREGATION.   Cases of food being loaded by soldiers for delivery to the front, a typical noncombat assignment for African American soldiers in the segregated U.S. military.   IMPERIAL WAR MUSEUM

destroyed in the Pacific within a matter of days. The navy had only 284,000 men, the Marines another 54,000. Because the navy had to deploy many of its warships in Atlantic waters, the Pacific Fleet was far smaller than the Imperial Japanese Navy. Thus even if the United States had not been taken by surprise, Japan's great military edge would have assured it of early dominance.

Yet in a remarkably short time these defects would be remedied. The U.S. army and its air forces would ultimately comprise over eight million men and women. The U.S. Navy and Marine Corps would exceed four million. In 1940, when President Roosevelt called for the production of 50,000 military aircraft a year, they were being turned out at an annual rate of only 2,000. But in 1941 production would reach 20,000 for the year, and ultimately a total of 300,000 aircraft would be built. Similarly, when naval construction programs going back as far as 1933 matured ten years later, the navy quickly became the world's largest.

So rapid an expansion enabled the United States to conduct major operations against both Germany and Japan. However, until Hitler was defeated, the demands of one war could not be met except at some expense to the other. A further difficulty was that, while Roosevelt was committed to a policy of defeating Germany first, the polls showed Japan to be far and away the most hated enemy.

Roosevelt agreed to the invasion of North Africa in 1942 primarily to get American troops into action against Germany soon, before domestic pressures to concentrate on the Pacific war became impossible to resist. As it was, at the end of 1942 total American troop strength in the Pacific exceeded that in Britain and North Africa combined (460,000 compared with 380,000).

This would continue to be a problem, since every slackening of the war against Germany resulted in American men and ships being diverted to the Pacific. Consequently, on D-day there would be fewer American troops available to fight in France than if the invasion had gone forward the previous year, as originally intended. Only seventeen U.S. divisions were in Britain on 6 June 1944, whereas twenty-four had been scheduled for the invasion in 1943. On the other hand, 13,000 American airplanes supported Operation OVERLORD, considerably more than would have been available the previous year.

Additionally complicating OVERLORD was the military manpower shortage. It was decided in 1943 to freeze the U.S. Army at ninety divisions, a small number compared to those of the enemy. The theory was that fewer divisions maintained at full strength through replacements would be better than the larger number of shrinking divisions characteristic of many armies. But even before D-day it was becoming evident that the army would be stretched thin, and that replacements in the required numbers would be difficult to obtain. The military draft was not broad enough, and in 1944 Congress refused to expand it. Also, there were too few volunteers for the Women's Army Corps (WAC).

As D-day neared, Americans experienced powerfully mixed emotions. All wished to see the war end as quickly as possible. All knew that to defeat Hitler, Germany would have to be invaded by way of France. But all shrank from what *Life* magazine referred to a few months before D-day as "the coming leap into the blood bath." The Normandy invasion would be just that, but thanks to the foresight of U.S. Army Chief of Staff George Marshall, there would be enough fighting men to win it.

Early in 1944 General Marshall began to close down the aviation cadet schools, and also the Army Specialized Training Program (ASTP), under which soldiers were sent to college campuses for advanced training. Most of the men thus released ended up in the ground forces. The U.S. Army in Europe would never have enough fighting men, infantry-trained replacements especially. However, various expedients combined to keep the army growing after its breakout from Normandy. By the end of the year General Dwight D. Eisenhower would have seventy-three divisions under his command, forty-nine of them American, facing seventy German divisions—a dangerously narrow margin.

A peculiarity of the American army was that the longer the war lasted, the better it became. By 1944 Germany had long since lost the best of its fighting men and, on the Eastern front, its ability to conduct armored operations. After D-day General Bernard L. Montgomery was forced to cannibalize existing British divisions in order to provide replacements for those on the line. But the flow of fresh American divisions continued up to V-E Day. The quality of these divisions improved as well, thanks to more realistic training methods and the influx of better educated men from the canceled ASTP and air force cadet programs. This marked the end of "skimming," whereby the ablest men were placed in the air force or in advanced technical fields, leaving for the ground forces only those who scored lowest in army qualification tests.

Another factor that made it possible for the army to conduct offensive operations against an enemy who, at times, almost equaled it in size, was air superiority. Although the United States, like Great Britain, devoted too much of its resources to high-altitude "strategic" bombing attacks on industrial targets in Germany that were only marginally useful, American production was large enough to permit the deployment of powerful "tactical" air forces in Europe. The numerous medium bombers and fighter-bombers assigned to ground support

prevented the Wehrmacht from launching effective counteroffensives. The German attack in the Battle of the Bulge, a partial exception to this rule, was feasible only because bad weather had grounded Allied tactical aircraft.

As the United States was never bombed, few American civilians were killed during the war—except for merchant seamen, thousands of whom gave their lives to the cause of freedom. Over 400,000 service personnel died of all causes; 291,557 were killed in battle. Each of these was a tragic loss, yet in total, a small fraction of the over sixteen million men and women who served in the armed forces. The returning veterans, who had spent on average three years in uniform, were welcomed by a grateful nation and rewarded for their service. In 1944 Congress had passed the so-called GI Bill of Rights, which provided them with low-interest home mortgages and small business loans, as well as educational benefits that eased their transition into civilian life. At the war's end, therefore, Americans enjoyed not only the thrill of victory, but a wide variety of material benefits that became the foundation of postwar prosperity.

[See also Roosevelt, Franklin D.]

BIBLIOGRAPHY

Burns, James MacGregor. *Roosevelt: The Soldier of Freedom, 1940–1945*. 1970.

Perret, Geoffrey. *Days of Sadness, Years of Triumph: The American People, 1939–1945*. 1973.

Perret, Geoffrey. *There's a War to be Won: The United States Army in World War II*. 1991.

Sherry, Michael S. *The Rise of American Air Power: The Creation of Armageddon*. 1987.

Spector, Ronald H. *Eagle against the Sun: The American War with Japan*. 1985.

Weigley, Russell F. *Eisenhower's Lieutenants: The Campaigns of France and Germany, 1944–1945*. 1981.

WILLIAM L. O'NEILL

U.S. STRATEGIC AIR FORCES (USSTAF).

USSTAF, located in London adjacent to the Supreme Headquarters, Allied Expeditionary Force, and the senior U.S. Army Air Forces (AAF) headquarters in Europe, was an independent command that did not fall under General Dwight D. Eisenhower's direction. The Anglo-American Combined Chiefs of Staff (CCS) approved its establishment in early December 1943 as U.S. Strategic Air Forces in Europe (USSAFE). Its commander, Lt. Gen. Carl Spaatz, had operational control over the U.S. Eighth Air Force in Britain and the U.S. Fifteenth Air Force in Italy. He also had administrative control (including military justice, personnel, and promotion) over the U.S. Eighth and Ninth air forces in Britain. In February 1944, Spaatz redesignated the command U.S. Strategic Air Forces (USSTAF).

Because General Spaatz disliked bureaucratic trivia, USSTAF had an unusual internal organization designed to keep his desk clear of detail and free him for major decisions. Instead of the normal staff organization with several assistants reporting to the commander, USSTAF had a chief of staff and two deputies, one for operations (operations, plans, intelligence, and weather) and one for administration (maintenance, supply, personnel, and technical services), reporting to the commander. In practice USSTAF controlled all AAF forces in Britain.

USSTAF had two missions. The AAF created it to oversee a daylight precision strategic bombing campaign against Germany. Separate air forces operating from Britain and Italy required a coordinating headquarters. In addition, the bombing of Germany had not proceeded according to plan and the AAF needed to reinvigorate it. Second, USSTAF would have to support OVERLORD directly to ensure its success. Spaatz wished to bomb deep into Germany, but he recognized that USSTAF must aid the invasion on the coast. These conflicting objectives plagued USSTAF until D-day.

The arrival of long-range P-51 fighters and new jettisonable gas tanks for the P-38s and P-47s, plus the decision allowing American fighters to leave the bombers and attack German fighters, enabled USSTAF to engage Luftwaffe fighters in a battle of attrition and to successfully bomb the German aircraft industry. The American fighters crushed their opponents. By mid-April USSTAF had gained air superiority over Germany and imposed ruinous pilot and aircraft losses on the Luftwaffe. However, this effort required maximum assistance from Ninth Air Force aircraft, delaying their transitioning and training for tactical air support of OVERLORD. USSTAF retained effective control over the Ninth until 1 April 1944.

In the meantime a dispute arose between supporters of rival plans for a preinvasion bombing campaign. Air Chief Marshal Trafford Leigh-Mallory (Eisenhower's tactical air leader) and others supported the Transportation Plan, which emphasized attritional attacks on German lines of communications in Belgium and France, particularly rail marshaling yards. USSTAF espoused the Oil Plan, which provided for attacks against the German synthetic oil industry. Also, Eisenhower questioned USSTAF's independent status and requested that the CCS place it under his control, which it did in mid-April. Eisenhower delegated responsibility for overseeing the strategic bombers to his deputy supreme commander, Air Chief Marshal Arthur Tedder, who continued the task until mid-September. Leigh-Mallory would have operational control of USSTAF for the week before the invasion.

On 25 March 1944 Eisenhower selected the Transportation Plan over the Oil Plan, but USSTAF did not hit its first transportation plan target for four more weeks. In the interim Spaatz obtained Eisenhower's permission to conduct two synthetic oil attacks, which the Eighth flew on 12 and 28 May. The attacks halved total German production. Meanwhile Fifteenth Air Force attacks in April and May on Ploesti, Romania, halved exports from Germany's major source of natural petroleum. Taken together, these attacks severely affected Luftwaffe training and operations and German ground forces' mobility. During May and the first week of June the Eighth's bombers destroyed or heavily damaged their twenty-three transportation targets, while the Eighth's fighters attacked French engines and rolling stock, assorted motor vehicles, and military transport. In addition, the Eighth and Fifteenth joined to attack German airfields throughout France.

On 6 June the Eighth bombed German defenses and attacked transportation targets. In the weeks following the invasion the Eighth flew several missions in direct support of ground forces. In Operation COBRA on 25 July, it assisted the American breakout from the Normandy peninsula. USSTAF contributed to OVERLORD in three areas. The strategic air campaign smashed the Luftwaffe and guaranteed it could not oppose the invasion in strength. Its bombing of German oil lessened the mobility of the German Army. Finally, its help in wrecking the French rail system slowed reinforcements and supplies to the beachhead, enabling the Allies to consolidate their lodgment.

[See also Air Strategy, article on Allied Air Strategy; Eighth Air Force; Fifteenth Air Force; Ninth Air Force; Railroads; Spaatz, Carl.]

BIBLIOGRAPHY

Craven, Wesley Frank, and James Lea Cate, eds. Europe: ARGUMENT to V-E Day, January 1944 to May 1945. Vol. 3 of The Army Air Forces in World War II. 1951.

Pogue, Forrest C. The Supreme Command. U.S. Army in World War II: The European Theater of Operations. 1954.

RICHARD G. DAVIS

UTAH BEACH. See American Beaches, article on Utah Beach.

VANDENBERG, HOYT (1899–1954), American, major general and deputy commander of the Allied Expeditionary Air Force. After graduating from West Point in 1923, Hoyt S. Vandenberg served as a fighter pilot and attended the appropriate military schools for the next sixteen years. From 1939 to 1942 he served in the Air Staff Plans Division, where he was heavily involved with mobilization planning. In mid-1942 he became an air planner for TORCH, the North African invasion, and soon was named chief of staff of the Twelfth Air Force for that operation. After a brief tour in Moscow, where he arranged an agreement for American aircraft to use bases in the Ukraine for shuttle bombing missions, Vandenberg was made an air planner for OVERLORD.

In February 1944 he was promoted to major general and named deputy commander of the Allied Expeditionary Air Force. This proved a challenging assignment because it placed him between a difficult and widely disliked superior, Air Chief Marshal Sir Trafford Leigh-Mallory, and the senior American airman in Europe, Lt. Gen. Carl Spaatz, commander of the U.S. Strategic Air Forces. Although working directly for Leigh-Mallory, he was told by Spaatz (and Eisenhower confirmed it) that his first loyalty was to the "American contingent." Vandenberg found himself juggling the needs and desires of his two superiors while at the same time working primarily to defeat Germany. Most of his disagreements with Leigh-Mallory arose over targeting policy; Vandenberg thought that using heavy bombers against minor tactical targets such as bridges was a waste of air power. He argued that medium bombers should be used for such targets, while heavy bombers concentrated on strategic objectives like railroad marshaling yards and oil refineries. Nonetheless, Vandenberg was remarkably successful in this delicate role, winning the confidence and respect of both Leigh-Mallory and Spaatz.

On D-day Vandenberg broke away from headquarters at Stanmore, near London, and flew his P-38 over the Normandy beaches. Upon returning to Stanmore and entering the situation room, he noted that maps for the American beaches were not being updated by the mostly British staff. When he questioned why this was the case, he was told that reconnaissance flights had been made only over the British and Canadian beaches. Angered, he ordered this rectified immediately.

In August 1944 Vandenberg was given command of the Ninth Air Force, the largest tactical air unit in history, which he led until the end of the war. His airmen complemented the activities of Gen. Omar Bradley's Twelfth Army Group. After Germany surrendered, Vandenberg, now a lieutenant general, returned to the Air Staff in Washington. In 1946 President Truman made him director of Central Intelligence. After one year he returned to uniform, received his fourth star, and in June 1948 became chief of staff of the new independent air force, replacing Spaatz. He served in this capacity for over five years, leading his service through the Berlin Airlift, the formation of NATO, and the Korean War. He retired in June 1953 and died of cancer the following year.

[*See also* Air Force, *article on* Allied Expeditionary Air Force.]

BIBLIOGRAPHY

Meilinger, Phillip S. *Hoyt S. Vandenberg: The Life of a General.* 1989.

Reynolds, Jon A. "Education and Training for High Command: Hoyt S. Vandenberg's Early Career." Ph.D. diss., Duke University, 1980.

PHILLIP S. MEILINGER

VETERANS' ASSOCIATION. *See* Associations and Organizations.

VIAN, PHILIP (1894–1968), British, rear admiral, naval commander, Eastern Task Force. Philip Vian joined

PHILIP VIAN.   NATIONAL ARCHIVES

the Royal Navy as a cadet in 1907 and served at sea throughout World War I, principally in destroyers. Qualifying as a gunnery officer after the war, he served in cruisers and battleships until 1932, when he returned to destroyers, leading a division and then a destroyer flotilla of the Mediterranean Fleet. Shortly after the outbreak of World War II, Captain Vian was appointed to command the large Tribal-class ships of the Home Fleet's 4th Destroyer Flotilla. Commanding HMS *Cossack,* Vian led the flotilla with distinction for eighteen months, and participated in the sinking of the German battleship *Bismarck* in May 1941. Promoted to rear admiral in July 1941, he was sent to command the 15th Cruiser Squadron in the eastern Mediterranean. During a Malta convoy operation in March 1942, his light cruisers held off the Italian battle fleet in the Second Battle of Sirte, an exploit for which he was created a Knight of the British Empire. Established as one of the Royal Navy's outstanding tactical commanders, Vian was introduced to amphibious operations in early 1943, on appointment as naval commander of one of the four British sectors for the invasion of Sicily on 10 July 1943. Two months later, at the Salerno invasion, Vian was in command of an escort carrier group.

On return to Britain, in November 1943 Vian was appointed to command Force J, the assault force for Juno Beach, which had already been training for two months, based on the Isle of Wight. Under Vian's direction there were repeated assault and ferry exercises and a number of successful beach reconnaissance missions in the Courseulles sector. In February 1944 Vian became overall assault commander of the (British) Eastern Task Force, responsible for the training of all three assault forces and for planning the cross-Channel passage. A final full-scale landing rehearsal was carried out to the east of Portsmouth in early May 1944, followed later in the month by a major defense exercise off Brighton, where the ships were subjected to dummy air, E-boat, midget submarine, and minelaying attacks.

Vian was allocated the antiaircraft cruiser HMS *Scylla* as his flagship for the crossing and assault. Although he was separated from the military commander, who was in Adm. Bertram H. Ramsay's flagship, the cruiser's high speed and mobility permitted Vian to exercise personal control over his entire sector and, on occasion, to provide gunfire support at critical points. *Scylla* also acted as the control ship for the seaward defense of the anchorages, for which Vian was responsible. On 23 June *Scylla* was badly damaged by a pressure mine while proceeding to its night defense anchorage, and Vian had to hand over his command to Vice Adm. F. H. G. Dalrymple-Hamilton for several hours, until he could resume control from HMS *Hilary*. On 24 June Rear Adm. J. W. Rivett-Carnac established the headquarters ashore of flag officer, British Assault Area; on 30 June Vian handed over control and withdrew, hauling down his flag as Eastern Task Force commander. For his part in the success of Operation NEPTUNE, he was created a Knight Commander of the Order of the Bath and appointed to the Legion of Merit and the Légion d'Honneur by the U.S. and French governments respectively; the French government also awarded him the Croix de Guerre.

Between November 1944 and the end of the war in the Pacific, Vian commanded the 1st Aircraft Carrier Squadron, thereafter serving as second-in-command of the British Pacific Fleet. He served as 5th Sea Lord after his return to Britain, and his final appointment was as Commander-in-Chief, Home Fleet, 1950–1952. He was promoted to admiral of the fleet on his retirement on 1 June 1952.

[*See also* Eastern Task Force; Scylla, HMS.]

BIBLIOGRAPHY

Barnett, Correlli. *Engage the Enemy More Closely: The Royal Navy in the Second World War.* 1991.
Vian, Philip. *Action This Day.* 1960.

DAVID BROWN

W

WAR-GAMING. D-day began with a war game. German officers were war-gaming a possible Allied invasion when the actual invasion took place. The war game was ordered to continue to serve as a means of keeping track of what was going on and to enable the German commanders to better control their operations. Ten years later, the German style of war-gaming, developed in the nineteenth century as an elaborate form of chess, became a commercial product in the United States. The first American war-game publishers basically reinvented the German war game (*Kriegsspiel*). Ten years later there were only a dozen war games in print, but these had acquired a loyal following.

In 1961 a war game called "D-day" was published, and, as the name implies, it covered the Allied invasion and also the subsequent battle for France. After the initial "D-day" game, it was eight years until the next game, "Normandy," appeared in 1969. This one covered only the invasion and the battle to establish a large enough beachhead to support the breakout. From the late 1960s to the present there was an explosive growth in the number of war games published—over a thousand titles—and several dozen of these covered D-day. Until the mid-1980s, over a dozen of the games that dealt with D-day were manual, but from the mid-1980s on, nearly all the new D-day games were computer-based, reflecting the shift of war-gamer tastes.

Both manual and computer-based D-day games have covered the situation on one of three scales. The strategic level has been common, and this was the perspective of the 1961 "D-Day," where the player controlled division-size units. Several other strategic-level games have followed in both manual and computer formats. There are several tactical-level treatments of the battle, with the player controlling platoons, squads, or individual soldiers, but these games are rather generic, as is all warfare at the tac-

tical level. Operational-level games, with the player controlling companies, battalions, or regiments, allow for considerable detail while still dealing with a situation that is obviously unique to D-day.

One of the more recent D-day games (1992) was a computer-based one called "V for Victory: Utah Beach." This particular game is operational in scale and stunning in execution. It requires a powerful personal computer to play it on, but it presents the invasion and subsequent fighting in sharp and easily played detail.

For over thirty years there has been an unending stream of D-day war games, and the trend will probably continue. Some have sold over a hundred thousand copies, and sales increase as personal computers proliferate. War games are an excellent way to understand the nuances of the campaign and a fitting complement to the many books on the subject of the invasion.

BIBLIOGRAPHY

Dunnigan, James F. *The Complete Wargames Handbook.* 1992.
Perla, Peter. *The Art of Wargaming.* 1990.

JAMES F. DUNNIGAN

WEATHER. For Allied invasion planners studying the meteorological records of the English Channel, early June had emerged as something of an anticyclonic "singularity": that is, a time during which the weather was more likely to be fine and settled than it was over the summer as a whole. However, things did not work out thus in 1944. Instead, the North Atlantic witnessed a sequence of depressions more characteristic of midwinter. Yet the launching of Operation OVERLORD required several days of benign weather. The wind over the beaches was not to be more than a "moderate breeze" of 10 to 15 knots. There had to be no heavy swell, though this could be an all-too-natural legacy from any rough seas in previous days and perhaps quite distant places. The forward visibility sought was three to five miles. To permit close air support, any low cloud needed to be well broken with its base 1,000 feet above the surface. For the airborne landings, an absence of low cloud was desirable.

Prediction of these limits was difficult owing to the transitional state of meteorology as a science. Its last great conceptual breakthrough had been the frontal theory evolved by the Bergen School of meteorologists during World War I. During World War II the big thrust in observation and theory was toward the upper air. By 1943 the Allies had adequate facilities for recording pressure contours, winds, and temperatures up to 30,000 feet over much of the Atlantic and Europe. In 1944, however, the interpretation of this data was still at the experimental stage. The techniques that had been introduced—most notably at Britain's Central Forecasting Office at Dunstable on the Bedfordshire Downs, and at its U.S. Army Air Forces counterpart at Widewing near Teddington in the lower Thames Valley—assisted forecasting at these two centers. Even so, this upper-air analysis figured little in the pre–D-day briefings or the multilateral conferences that preceded them. Yet potentially it held the key to an understanding of vertical air motion, a big factor in the life cycle of any anticyclone (i.e., core of high atmospheric pressure) or of any depression.

Again, much progress had been made since 1941 on the empirical prediction of waves on the open sea, as judged from the wind to be expected overhead. But applying these correlations to how waves plunge on particular shores was harder in theory as well as practice. So was the forecasting of swell. Also, little systematic work had yet been done on the total interaction (important to any longer-range forecast) between sea and air. One thing the meteorologists serving OVERLORD were always in agreement about was how hazardous forecasting could be when projected more than a day or so ahead.

To cap everything there were, during those critical days in early June, serious deficiencies in reporting from an area west of Scotland crucial to an analysis of the westerly flow of air then dominant. Nonetheless, Group Capt. J. M. Stagg, the chief meteorological officer to General Eisenhower, enjoyed two overriding operational advantages. One was that the Allies had a much wider spread of observations than did the Germans, especially to westward, as witness the desperate attempts of Berlin surreptitiously to establish weather stations in Greenland or even Labrador. The other was that, from late April, there had been regular telephone conferences among the main weather centers in Britain to get all concerned into that routine for generating the five-day forecasts that the military leaders saw as minimal. The three places mainly involved were Dunstable, Widewing, and the Admiralty in London.

From 1 June onward, there was continual dispute between Widewing and Dunstable about the prospects for D-day, the 5th. Invariably, the former inclined to optimism and the latter to apprehension. Mostly the Admiralty sought compromise, but on 3 June threw its weight behind pessimism. So, too, did Stagg in his briefing that evening to Eisenhower and his staff. Stagg's concern was that a ridge of high atmospheric pressure extending toward the British Isles from the Azores anticyclone had started to slide southward, soon to leave the Channel more under the influence of the Atlantic depressions. Early on the 4th, Widewing was still hopeful and still unable to persuade Stagg. His next briefing to Eisenhower and staff, given at 0415, effectively clinched the decision to defer D-day to the 6th, a prime concern being that low cloud might compromise air support. A cold front that by noon would be into the west of Ireland was driving bad weather eastward. Its parent depression, L5, was slow-moving off northwest Scotland and the next in line, L6, was centered just east of Newfoundland and developing strongly. Postponement was a good move.

Soon Widewing was arguing that the diversion of energy into L6's development would slow its movement down while, at the same time, L6 would turn north. Likewise at Eisenhower's briefing at 2130 on the 4th, Stagg felt able to dispense some cheer. He foresaw a fair interlude for a day or two at least, as a slender ridge built up behind the cold front. Hard upon this advice, Eisenhower gave the order to make ready to land on the 6th. As he did so, wind and rain raged outside. When he had ordered the twenty-four-hour delay, the skies above had been clear and calm. When his order was confirmed early on the 5th, the weather locally was fair.

By the 6th, the center of L6 was moving northward along the east coast of Greenland, closely in line with what Widewing had anticipated, rather than along Dunstable's projected track of eastward toward Norway. Meanwhile a ridge was building behind the cold front of L5. The inability of the German weather service to discern this easement had led to the garrisons along the French coast being left on low alert.

Had a further postponement of D-day been authorized, the invasion would have been delayed until 19 June, with an irreversible commitment to go being made on the 17th or early 18th during what looked like an enduring calm spell. But on the 19th what proved to be the most protracted Channel storm in that season for decades suddenly arrived. Over the next three days, it wreaked havoc on the invasion buildup, disabling one of the two Mulberry artificial harbors. Had D-day been rearranged for then, the impact on OVERLORD would have been catastrophic.

BIBLIOGRAPHY

Giles, Brian D. *Meteorology and World War II.* 1987.
Kimble, George. *The Weather.* 1943.
Stagg, J. M. *Forecast for Overlord.* 1971.

NEVILLE G. BROWN

WESSEX DIVISION. *See* 43d (Wessex) Infantry Division.

WESTERN DEFENSE FORCE. Germany's *Western Defense Force* was divided into seagoing forces and shore-based forces; both were subordinated to the Commander in Chief Naval Group Command West at Paris (Adm. Theodor Krancke). Seagoing vessels were subordinated to the commander of the *Western Defense Force* at Paris (Rear Adm. Erich Alfred Breuning). He had three defense divisions under his command.

2d Defense Division at Souverin-Moulin near Boulogne (Comdr. Adalbert von Blanc) was responsible for the area from the Schelde Estuary to the Cotentin Peninsula. Under this command were:

2d Gun Carrier (Artillerieträger) Flotilla at Boulogne (Lt. Comdr. Elmershaus von Haxthausen)
6th Gun Carrier (Artillerieträger) Flotilla at the Channel Islands (Lt. Comdr. Friedrich Schad)
36th Fleet Minesweeper (Minensuch) Flotilla at Ostend (Reserve Comdr. Walter Grosse)
38th Fleet Minesweeper (Minensuch) Flotilla at Le Havre (Comdr. Otto Ulrich)
2d Motor Minesweeper (Räumboot) Flotilla at Dunkirk (Comdr. Georg Pinkepank)
4th Motor Minesweeper (Räumboot) Flotilla at Wimereux-Boulogne (Lt. Comdr. Wilhelm Anhalt)
8th Motor Minesweeper (Räumboot) Flotilla at Bruges (Lt. Comdr. Albert Muser)
10th Motor Minesweeper (Räumboot) Flotilla at Ouistreham (Lt. Comdr. Herbert Nau)
14th Motor Minesweeper (Räumboot) Flotilla at Dieppe (Lt. Comdr. Otto Nordt)
15th Patrol (Vorposten) Flotilla at Le Havre (Reserve Comdr. Viktor Rall)
18th Patrol (Vorposten) Flotilla at Bruges (Reserve Comdr. Albrecht Boit)

3d Defense Division at Nostang, near Lorient (Capt. Karl Bergelt), was responsible for the area from the Cotentin Peninsula to Lorient. Attached were:

2d Fleet Minesweeper (Minensuch) Flotilla at Bénodet (Comdr. Wilhelm Ambrosius)

6th Fleet Minesweeper (Minensuch) Flotilla at Concarneau (Comdr. Eberhard Homeyer)
24th Fleet Minesweeper (Minensuch) Flotilla at Brest (Reserve Comdr. Fritz Breithaupt)
40th Fleet Minesweeper (Minensuch) Flotilla at Brest (Reserve Comdr. Horst von Treufels)
46th Fleet Minesweeper (Minensuch) Flotilla at Saint-Malo (Lt. Comdr. Armin Zimmermann)
6th Mine Destruction (Sperrbrecher) Flotilla at Concarneau (Reserve Comdr. Bodo Notholt)
2d Patrol (Vorposten) Flotilla at Saint-Malo (Senior Reserve Comdr. Otto Lensch)
7th Patrol (Vorposten) Flotilla at Brest (Reserve Comdr. Kurt Hamacher)
14th Submarine Chaser (U-Jagd) Flotilla at Lorient (Lt. Comdr. Heinz Roscher)

4th Defense Division at La Rochelle (Capt. Hans John) was responsible for the French west coast from Lorient to the Spanish border. Attached were:

8th Fleet Minesweeper (Minensuch) Flotilla at Royan (Comdr. Arnulf Hölzerkopf)
10th Fleet Minesweeper (Minensuch) Flotilla at Paimboeuf (Reserve Comdr. Walter Josephi)
26th Fleet Minesweeper (Minensuch) Flotilla at Couëron (Lt. Comdr. Max von Lueder)
28th Fleet Minesweeper (Minensuch) Flotilla at Pauillac (Senior Comdr. Gerhard Bidlingmeier)
42d Fleet Minesweeper (Minensuch) Flotilla at Les Sables d'Olonne (Reserve Comdr. Louis Max de Laporte)
44th Fleet Minesweeper (Minensuch) Flotilla at La Pallice (Reserve Comdr. Günther Gelpke)
2d Mine Destruction (Sperrbrecher) Flotilla at Royan (Senior Comdr. Fritz Drevin)
4th Patrol (Vorposten) Flotilla at Bordeaux (Reserve Comdr. Wilhelm Cyrus)
6th Patrol (Vorposten) Flotilla at Saint-Nazaire (Reserve Comdr. Georg Behrmann)

Shore-based forces were subordinated to two admirals. Commanding admiral, Channel Coast, at Trouville (Vice Adm. Friedrich Rieve) was responsible for the area from the Dutch-Belgian border to Saint-Malo. Subordinated to him was commander, Coastal Defense Pas de Calais (Rear Adm. Friedrich Frisius), at Wimille near Boulogne, responsible for the area south of Antwerp to the Somme Estuary. He commanded:

Harbor captains at Zeebrugge, Ostend, Dunkirk, Gravelines, Calais, and Boulogne
Marine artillery commander, Pas de Calais
Marine D/F (direction-finder) and marine radar battalions

Commander, Coastal Defense Seine–Somme, at Le Havre (Rear Adm. Hans-Udo von Treskow) was responsible for the area from the Somme to the Orne rivers. Under his command were:

Harbor captains at Le Tréport, Dieppe, Fécamp, Le Havre, Rouen, Trouville, and Caen
Marine artillery commander, Seine–Somme

Commander, Coastal Defense Normandy, at Cherbourg (Rear Adm. Walter Hennecke) was responsible for the area from the Orne Estuary to the Cotentin Peninsula and Saint-Malo. He commanded:

Harbor captains at Cherbourg, Granville, and Saint-Malo
Marine Artillery Battalion 260 at Cherbourg

Commander, Coastal Defense Channel Islands, at Guernsey (Captain Julius Steinbach) was responsible for the Channel Islands. He commanded:

Harbor captains at Guernsey, Jersey, and Alderney
Marine Artillery Battalions 604 and 605
Harbor Defense Flotilla, Channel Islands

The second commanding admiral was the commanding admiral, Atlantic Coast, at Erigné near Angers (Vice Adm. Ernst Schirlitz), responsible for Brittany and the French coast to the Spanish border. Subordinated to him was commander, Coastal Defense Brittany, at Brest (Rear Adm. Otto Kähler), responsible for Brittany south to Carnac. He commanded:

Harbor captains at Brest and Lorient
Island commanders, Île de Groix and Belle Île
Marine Artillery Battalions 262, 264 and 681
Marine Antiaircraft Brigades III and IV
Marine D/F (Direction-Finder) Battalion, Brittany

Commander, Coastal Defense Loire, at Saint-Nazaire (Rear Adm. Hans Mirow) was responsible for the area between Carnac and the Seudre Estuary. He commanded:

Harbor captains at Saint-Nazaire, Nantes, La Pallice/La Rochelle
Island commanders, Île de Noirmoutier, Île d'Yeu, Île de Ré, and Île d'Oléron
Marine Artillery Battalions 280, 282, 684, 685, 686, 687, and Antiaircraft Battalion 812
Marine Antiaircraft Brigade V

Commander, Coastal Defense Gascogne, at Royan (Capt. Ernst Michahelles) was responsible for the area from the Seudre Estuary to the Spanish border. He commanded:

Harbor captains at Bordeaux and Bayonne
Marine Artillery Battalions 284 and 286
Antiaircraft Battalion 618

Losses of the Western Defense Force, 6 June–31 August 1944

TYPE	AIR ATTACK	SURFACE ENGAGEMENT	MINES	SCUTTLED	OTHER CAUSES	TOTAL SUNK
Minesweepers	12	5	1	10	–	28
Motor minesweepers	12	3	3	8	2	28
Auxiliary minesweepers	19	5	2	4	–	30
Submarine chasers	2	3	–	1	–	6
Patrol boats	21	13	–	15	–	49
Gun carriers	14	10	2	3	–	29
Mine destruction vessels	8	2	1	10	–	21
Total	88	41	9	51	2	191

The seagoing units of the *Western Defense Force* consisted mostly of auxiliary vessels. They could only be used for patrol, minesweeping, and escort duties, and were incapable of fighting the destroyers and heavier ships that covered the Allied landings. When Allied cruiser-destroyer task forces or motor torpedo boats attacked the convoys escorted by the auxiliaries, the latter's losses were great. But the heaviest losses came from the Allied air attacks on the ports, as the table above shows.

BIBLIOGRAPHY
Lohmann, Walter, and Hans H. Hildebrand. *Die deutsche Kriegsmarine 1939–1945.* 2 vols. 1956–1964.

JÜRGEN ROHWER

WESTERN TASK FORCE. The Western Task Force (Task Force 122, or TF 122) was the Allied naval force that supported the landing by the U.S. First Army (Gen. Omar Bradley) on Utah and Omaha beaches. It was commanded by Rear Adm. Alan G. Kirk, USN. Organized into Task Force 125 (TF 125, Force U for Utah) and Task Force 124 (TF 124, Force O for Omaha), it comprised 2,010 vessels (counting landing craft carried aboard ships), 931 of which crossed the Channel on their own. The missions of the task force included naval gunfire support, minesweeping, and transportation of men and equipment.

Rear Admiral Kirk was subordinate operationally to Adm. Bertram H. Ramsay, RN, naval commander in chief of the Allied Expeditionary Force. Administratively, Kirk came under Adm. Harold Stark, commander of the U.S. Naval Forces in Europe.

The great danger that the entire operation faced was mines. Thus Operation NEPTUNE included the largest minesweeping operation to date in the war. Admiral

Ramsay's plan called for the assault forces to move coastwise in convoy from their assembly points in the south of England to a designated rendezvous point twenty-four kilometers (fifteen miles) southeast of the Isle of Wight.

The rendezvous point for all units in the Western Task Force was centered on an imaginary Point Z at 50°, 25′ North, 0°, 58′ West. A circle with a radius of eight kilometers (about five miles) was swept, through which all the convoys passed before turning south to Normandy. From this circle, nicknamed "Picadilly Circus," minesweepers cleared five lanes to the French coast, one for each task force. To expedite the passage, each of the five lanes became two about halfway across the Channel, so that fast convoys, which were the last to sail, could overtake the slow convoys without losing formation. Beginning on the night of 31 May–1 June, fast harbor-defense motor launches dropped buoys to mark the northern approaches to the ten swept channels. These buoys were timed to transmit between the hours of 1400 and 2200 for six successive days, beginning on 4 June. Many of the ships in the convoys had receivers that enabled them to calculate their position with information from the Gee and Decca radio navigation systems. Navigators could reckon their location by observing the time taken to receive pulse signals from three separate ground stations.

Planners had worried that the minesweepers of the Western Task Force would arrive so early as to alert the Germans, but the Germans did not react, although the minesweepers were within sight of Cape Barfleur as early as 2000 on 5 June. Many of the minesweepers had been fitted with electronic countermeasures that they activated after 2130 on 5 June. Thus the minesweeping did not cost the Allies the element of surprise.

The approaches from the various Channel ports to Picadilly Circus were those that normal traffic followed, so they were regularly swept for mines. In addition, for the convoys to follow this approach initially minimized German suspicions. The great danger from the mines lay ahead. The Allies knew that a German mine barrier lay across the line of advance in the middle of the Channel, so minesweepers preceded the assault forces. The Germans had earlier laid defensive mine fields in the Bay of the Seine as well, and in May had intensified their mining in this area. Because the Germans had kept a narrow channel swept near the French coast for their coastal traffic, the safest place to lower landing craft was between eleven and sixteen kilometers (seven to ten miles) offshore. But this choice of position put the transports well

USS *AUGUSTA*, FLAGSHIP OF ADMIRAL KIRK.   As landing craft approach the Normandy shore.

within range of shore batteries when they were most vulnerable, so heavy bombardment units had to be available to silence these batteries. Fearing what shore batteries might do to his landing ships, Admiral Kirk elected to anchor the landing ships and lower landing craft from a position sixteen to twenty kilometers (ten to twelve miles) out. This decision exposed the landing craft to rough waters and required a longer passage in to the beach.

German coastal defense batteries ranged from modern 210-mm rifles protected by reinforced concrete two meters (seven feet) thick to older French 75-mm guns dating from World War I. Most coastal batteries were sited close to the beaches, although howitzers were positioned well inland on reverse slopes. The first targets for the heavy ships were twenty coast defense batteries selected because of the threat they posed to the assault shipping. Although American and British heavy bombers would bombard these batteries, experience indicated that only the heaviest naval guns could neutralize such artillery for the prolonged period required to land the U.S. First Army.

Admiral Ramsay's basic plan was to silence all enemy batteries capable of firing on the sea approaches to the landing beaches or on the beaches themselves, and then to destroy beach defenses during the final approach by landing forces. The Western Task Force would begin with a brief but heavy bombardment to knock out identified enemy strong points, and then force the German defenders in emplacements near the shore to take cover by laying down a high volume of fire from lighter weapons. The great danger was that the Germans would rush reinforcements to any landing site, so the bombardment had to be abbreviated, lest a prolonged shelling such as was common in the Pacific eliminate whatever element of surprise remained. After the landing began, ships were to engage mobile enemy batteries, counterattacking forces, and such strong points as Allied forces might encounter.

Because ordinary spotting aircraft were vulnerable in a heavily defended environment, the British provided 104 high-speed fighter aircraft, specifically five RAF squadrons of Spitfires and Mustangs and four Fleet Air Arm squadrons of Seafires, to act as spotters. In addition, eighteen shore fire-control parties landed with the troops, as did nine paratroop naval gunfire spotters.

Beginning on the night of 7–8 June, German E-boats sortied nightly from Cherbourg to attack the Western Task Force and raid convoy lanes in mid-Channel. On the night of 8–9 June they sank two LSTs (Landing Ships, Tank). On 11 June they sank fleet tug *Partridge* near Omaha Beach.

The reserve battleships HMS *Rodney* and *Nelson* arrived off the beaches on 11 June and contributed the fire of their 16-inch guns through 18 June in response to numerous requests from army units ashore. The entire Cotentin Peninsula lay within range of naval gunfire, and until the battle moved beyond that range, the bombardment ships of Admirals Deyo and Bryant continued to pound targets as requested. On 15 June Admiral Kirk put the naval gunfire ships from both the eastern and western bombardment groups under Admiral Deyo, and on that day *Texas, Glasgow,* and *Bellona* fired the last rounds, for the battle had now moved beyond the range of even their main armament. On 19 June Admiral Kirk suspended all naval gunfire support.

[*See also* American Beaches; Kirk, Alan G.; Task Force 124; Task Force 125; Ramsay, Bertram H.]

BIBLIOGRAPHY

Barnett, Correlli. *Engage the Enemy More Closely: The Royal Navy in the Second World War.* 1991.

Ellis, L. F., et al. *The Battle of Normandy.* Vol. 1 of *Victory in the West.* 1962.

Morison, Samuel E. *The Invasion of France and Germany, 1944–1945.* Vol. 11 of *History of United States Naval Operations in World War II.* 1957.

Ramsay, Bertram H. "The Assault Phase of the Normandy Landings." Dispatch dated 16 October 1944, printed in *The London Gazette*, 30 October 1947.

Roskill, Stephen W. *The Offensive.* Vol. 3, pt. 2, of *The War at Sea, 1939–1945.* 1961.

MARK JACOBSEN

Western Task Force
List of Ships and Commanders Involved
TF 122 Western Naval Task Force
Rear Adm. Alan G. Kirk, USN

Force Flagship Group

Heavy cruiser *Augusta* (Capt. E. H. Jones, USN)
Destroyer *Thompson* (Lt. Comdr. A. L. Gebelin, USN)

TF 125 Assault Force U for Utah Beach
Rear Adm. Don P. Moon, USN

Force Flagship Group

Attack transport *Bayfield* (Capt. Lyndon Spencer, USCG)
Attack transport *Forrest* (Comdr. K. P. Letts, USN)

Minesweeper Group (Comdr. M. H. Brown, RN)

Sweep Unit 1 (Comdr. Brown)
  HMS *Shippigan, Tadoussac, Ilfracombe, Beaumaris, Dornock, Parrsboro, Qualicum,* and *Wedgeport*
Sweep Unit 2 (Comdr. G. W. A. T. Irvine, RNVR)

HMS *Romney, Guysborough, Seaham, Rye, Whitehaven, Poole, Vegreville,* and *Kenova*

Sweep Unit 3 (Comdr. Henry Plander, USN)
USS *Pheasant, Auk, Broadbill, Chicadee, Nuthatch, Staff, Swift, Threat, Tide, Raven,* and *Osprey*

Sweep Unit 4 (Lt. H. J. White, USNR)
11 coastal minesweepers

Sweep Unit 5 (Lt. C. L. Rich, USNR)
7 coastal minesweepers

Sweep Unit 6 (Lt. Comdr. J. A. Ludlow, RNVR)
9 motor minesweepers

Sweep Unit 7 (Lt. [j.g.] Irving Kramer, USNR)
16 landing craft

Assault Groups

Beach Green Assault Group (Comdr. A. L. Warburton, USN)
Attack transport *Joseph T. Dickman* (Capt. R. J. Mauerman, USCG), 141 landing craft

Beach Red Assault Group (Comdr. E. W. Wilson, USNR)
Attack transport *Barnett* (Comdr. S. S. Reynolds, USN)
Attack transport *Bayfield* (Capt. Spencer, USN), 151 landing craft

Escort Group (Comdr. W. W. Outerbridge, USN)

Destroyers *O'Brien* (Comdr. Outerbridge), *Jeffers* (Lt. Comdr. H. Q. Murray, USN), *Glennon* (Comdr. C. A. Johnson, USN), *Walke* (Comdr. J. C. Zahm, USN), *Barton* (Comdr. J. W. Callahan, USN), *Laffey* (Comdr. F. J. Becton, USN), *Meredith* (Comdr. George Kneupfer, USN)
Three British antisubmarine trawlers
French corvettes *Aconit* (Lt. de V. Le Millier) and *Renoncule* (Lt. de V. Mithois)
21 small craft

Bombardment Group (Rear Adm. Morton L. Deyo, USN)

Heavy cruisers *Tuscaloosa* (Capt. J. B. W. Waller, USN), *Quincy* (Capt. E. N. Senn, USN), HMS *Hawkins* (Capt. J. W. Josselyn, RN)
Battleship *Nevada* (Capt. P. M. Rhea, USN)
Monitor HMS *Erebus* (Capt. J. S. P. Colquhoun, RN)
Light cruisers HMS *Enterprise* (Capt. H. T. W. Grant, RCN) and HMS *Black Prince* (Capt. D. M. Lees, RN)
Dutch gunboat *Soemba* (Lt. Cdr. H. H. L. Propper, RNN)·
Destroyers *Fitch* (Comdr. K. C. Walpole, USN), *Forrest* (Comdr. Letts, USN), *Corry* (Lt. Comdr. G. D. Hoffman, USN), *Hobson* (Lt. Kenneth Loveland, USN), *Herndon* (Comdr. G. A. Moore, USN), *Shubrick* (Lt.

Comdr. William Blenman, USN), *Butler* (Comdr. M. D. Matthews, USN), *Gherardi* (Comdr. N. R. Curtin, USN)
Destroyer escorts *Bates* (Lt. Comdr. H. A. Wilmerding, USNR) and *Rich* (Lt. Comdr. E. A. Michel, USN)

Far Shore Service Group (Capt. J. E. Arnold, USNR)

Two steamships, 75 landing ships, 5 fueling trawlers, 23 barges, and many small landing craft
Sea Rescue Group (Lt. Comdr. A. V. Stewart, USCGR)
10 U. S. Coast Guard cutters
Follow-up Convoy Group (Comdr. W. S. Blair, USNR)
25 landing ships
Motor torpedo boats (Lt. R. R. Read, USNR)
13 patrol torpedo boats

TF 124 Assault Force O for Omaha Beach
Rear Adm. John L. Hall, USN

Amphibious force flagship *Ancon* (Comdr. M. G. Pearson USN)

Minesweeper Group (Comdr. J. S. Cochrane, RN)

Sweep Unit 1 (Comdr. Cochrane)
HMS *Kellett, Pangbourne, Albury, Sutton, Lydd, Selkirk, Ross, Saltash, Thunder*
4 motor launches

Sweep Unit 2 (Comdr. A. H. G. Storrs, RCNR)
HMCS *Caraquet, Blairmore, Cowichan, Fort William, Malpeque, Vegrebille, Minas, Wasaga, Mulgrave*
4 motor launches

Sweep Unit 3 (Lt. Heath, RNR)
10 coastal minesweepers

Sweep Unit 4 (Lt. Bennett, RNVR)
10 motor minesweepers

Reserve units included cruisers USS *Augusta* and HMS *Bellona*, 17 U.S. destroyers, and battleship HMS *Nelson*, held back at Milford Haven (Pembroke Dockyard), Wales

Assault Groups

Assault Group O-1 for beaches Easy Red and Fox Green (Capt. E. H. Fritzsche, USCG)
Attack transports *Samuel Chase* (Capt. Fritzsche) and *Henrico* (Comdr. J. H. Willis, USN)
LSI *Empire Anvil* (British)
1 LCH, 6 LST, 5 LCI, 53 LCT, 18 LCM, 2 patrol craft, 2 submarine chasers, 2 motor launches, and 2 LCC

Assault Group O-2 for beaches Dog and Easy Green (Capt. W. O. Bailey, USN)
Attack transports *Charles Carroll* (Capt. Harold Biese-

meier, USN) and *Thomas Jefferson* (Comdr. J. R. Barbaro, USN)

LSI *Empire Javelin* (British)

1 LCH, 6 LST, 17 LCI, 54 LCT, 18 LCM, 4 patrol craft, 4 submarine chasers, 2 motor launches, and 3 LCC

Assault Group O-3 for beaches Fox Green and Easy Red (Capt. L. B. Schulten, USN)

Transports *Anne Arundel* (Capt. W. S. Campbell, USN), *Dorothea L. Dix* (Comdr. W. I. Leahy, USN), and *Thurston* (Comdr. R. B. Vanasse, USN)

1 LCH, 12 LST, 11 LCI, 39 LCT, 1 LSB, 1 LSD, 3 patrol craft, and 2 motor launches

Assault Group O-4 for Pointe du Hoc and Dog Green (Comdr. S. H. Dennis, RN)

British LSI *Prince Charles* (Comdr. Dennis), *Prince Baudouin* (Lt. Comdr. W. E. Gelling, RNR), *Prince Leopold* (Lt. Comdr. J. A. Lowe, RNR), *Ben-My-Chree* (Master R. Duggan), *Amsterdam* (Master Pickering), *Princess Maud*

1 LCT and 2 motor launches

Escort Group (Capt. Harry Sanders, USN)

Destroyers *Frankford* (Lt. Comdr. J. L. Semmes, USN), *Nelson* (Lt. Comdr. T. D. McGrath, USN), *Murphy* (Comdr. R. A. Wolverton, USN), *Plunkett* (Comdr. William Outerson, USN)

Destroyers in bombardment group listed below

HMS *Vesper* (Lt. Comdr. V. D. Ravenscroft, RNR) and *Vidette* (Lt. Comdr. G. S. Woolley, RNVR)

Destroyer escorts *Borum* (Lt. Comdr. J. K. Davis, USN), *Amesbury* (Lt. Comdr. A. B. Wilbor, USNR), and *Blessman* (Lt. Comdr. J. A. Gillis, USNR)

French frigates *L'Aventure* (Capt. de F. Querville) and *L'Escarmouche* (Capt. de C. Duplessis-Casso)

British antisubmarine trawlers *Coll, Bressay,* and *Skye*

9 patrol craft, 6 submarine chasers, 12 motor launches, 7 motor torpedo boats, 2 harbor defense motor launches, and 6 British steam gunboats

Close Gunfire Support Group (Capt. L. S. Sabin, USN)

1 LCH, 7 LCR, 5 LCG, 9 LCT(R), 28 LCP, 9 LCT(A), and 10 LCT(HE)

Bombardment Group (Rear Adm. C. F. Bryant, USN)

Battleships *Texas* (Capt. C. A. Baker, USN) and *Arkansas* (Capt. F. G. Richards, USN)

Light cruisers HMS *Glasgow* (Capt. C. P. Clarke, RN), HMS *Bellona* (Capt. C. W. F. Norris, RN), and Free French *Montcalm* (Capt. de V. Deprez) and *Georges Leygues* (Capt. de V. Laurin, with Rear Admiral

Jaujard in overall command of French units)

Destroyers *Frankford, McCook* (Lt. Comdr. R. L. Ramey, USN), *Carmick* (Comdr. R. O. Beer, USN), *Doyle* (Comdr. J. G. Marshall, USN), *Emmons* (Comdr. E. B. Billingsley, USN), *Baldwin* (Lt. Comdr. E. S. Powell, USN), *Harding* (Comdr. G. G. Palmer, USN), *Satterlee* (Lt. Comdr. R. W. Leach, USN, with commander of Destroyer Division 36, Comdr. W. J. Marshall, USN), *Thompson* (Lt. Comdr. A. L. Gebelin, USN), HMS *Tanatside* (Comdr. B. de St. Croix, RN), *Talybont* (Lt. Comdr. E. F. Baines, RNR), and *Melbreak* (Lt. G. J. Kirkby, RN)

Far Shore Service Group (Capt. Chauncey Camp, USNR)

Steamship *Eleazar Wheelock,* repair ship *Adonis*

12 LCM, 4 LCI, 4 LCH, 72 LCT, 20 RHF, 139 LCM, 72 LBV, 9 fueling trawlers, 16 LBE, 20 LBO, 5 LBW, and 2 LBK

Rescue Vessels (Lt. Comdr. A. Stewart, USCG)

15 USCG cutters

TF 126 Follow-up Force B
Como. C. D. Edgar, USN

Destroyer escort *Maloy* (Lt. Comdr. F. D. Kellogg, USNR)

Convoy B-1 (Capt. J. R. Johannesen, USN) in *LST 511*

18 LST and 46 British LCT (Lt. Comdr. A. D. S. Dunne, RN), escorted by destroyer *Rodman* (Comdr. J. F. Foley, USN), destroyer escorts HMS *Brissenden* (Lt. D. D. E. Vivian, RN) and *Wensleydale* (Lt. Comdr. W .P. Goodfellow, RNVR)

British antisubmarine trawlers *Gateshead, Olivina,* and *Lindisfarne,* 2 submarine chasers, and 2 USCG cutters

Convoy B-2 (Comdr. T. F. Cameron, USN) in *LCI 414*

Attack freighter *Achernar* (Comdr. H. R. Stevens, USN), 1 LCH, and 12 LCI, escorted by destroyer *Ellyson* (Comdr. E. W. Longton, USN, with Commander of Destroyer Squadron 10, Capt. A. F. Converse, USN)

HM corvettes *Azalea* and *Kitchener,* 2 patrol craft, and 1 USCG cutter

Convoy B-3 (Comdr. T. W. Greene, USN) in *LST 266*

34 LST towing 26 barges

Convoy B-4 (Comdr. B. J. Skahill, USN) in *LST 515*

9 LST towing 9 barges, escorted by destroyer *Hambleton* (Comdr. H. A. Renken, USN), HM corvettes *Boadicea* and *Bluebell,* HM destroyers *Volunteer* and *Vimy*

HM antisubmarine trawlers *Ellesmere, Cornelian,* and *Pearl,* and 2 USCG cutters

Mulberry A (Capt. A. Dayton Clark, USN, in SC 1329)

Numerous tugboats, net layers, bar vessels, trawlers, etc.

Salvage and Firefighting Group (Como. W. A. Sullivan, USN)

British wreck dispersal vessels *Marie, Admiral Sir John Lawford, Tehana, Help,* and *Abigail*
USN salvage vessels *Brant, Diver,* and *Swivel*
USN rescue tugs *Pinto, Arikara, Kiowa,* and *Bannock,* and various small craft

Area Screen (Capt. Harry Sanders, USN, in Frankford)

Destroyers and destroyer escorts in the escort and bombardment groups
Patrol craft and submarine chasers assigned; Lt. Comdr. John D. Bulkeley, USN, commanding 12 patrol torpedo boats of MTB Squadron 34 and several motor torpedo boats from British 53d and 63d flotillas
Far Shore Shuttle Control (Capt. Edward C. Kline, USN, in light cruiser HMS *Capetown,* Capt. H. F. Nash, RN).

SOURCE: Morison, Samuel Eliot. *The Invasion of France and Germany, 1944–1945.* Vol. 11 of *History of United States Naval Operations in World War II.* 1957.

WEST RIDING DIVISION. *See* 49th (West Riding) Infantry Division.

WEYLAND, OTTO P. ("OPIE") (1902–1979), American, brigadier general commanding XIX Tactical Air Command (XIX TAC). After graduating from Texas A&M in 1923, Weyland joined the Air Corps Reserve, then took a regular commission. In the 1920s and 1930s he held various Army Air Force commands, and graduated from the Air Corps Tactical School in 1938, and from the army's Command and General Staff School in 1939.

When war came, Weyland served in progressively more important staff assignments in Europe. In November 1943 he put his experience in air-ground cooperation to the test when he joined the U.S. Ninth Air Force as commanding general of the 84th Fighter Group. He became deputy commander of IX Fighter Command and, in February 1944, head of the XIX Air Support Command (redesignated XIX TAC in April). IX Fighter Command conducted the air-ground training for Ninth Air Force fighter-bomber groups and tactical air commands. XIX

TAC would supply direct fighter-bomber close air support to the U.S. Third Army, commanded by Lt. Gen. George S. Patton, Jr. Fighters had the range to cover an army's frontage. Patton described their relationship as "love at first sight" and the two officers worked well together throughout the war.

Allied plans provided for Third Army and XIX TAC to become operational after the Allied breakout from the Normandy beachhead, which they did on 1 August 1944. Patton's and Weyland's commands fought together across France, participated in the Battle of the Bulge, and drove deep into Germany. Patton called Weyland "the best damn general in the Air Force."

After the war Weyland served in the Pentagon, then assumed command of the U.S. Air Forces in Korea in June 1951. During his stay in the Far East he was credited with being the "father" of the new Japanese Air Force. He retired from the service in 1959. Weyland attributed his career-long success in working with the army to his ability to lay his cards on the table and negotiate in good faith.

[*See also* XIX Tactical Air Command.]

BIBLIOGRAPHY

Kohn, Richard H., and Joseph Hanrahan, eds. *Condensed Analysis of the Ninth Air Force in the European Theater of Operations.* Reprint, 1984.
Spires, David N. *Air Power for Patton's Army: The XIX Tactical Air Command in the Second World War.* Forthcoming late 1993.

RICHARD G. DAVIS

WHARTON, JAMES E. (1894–1944), American, brigadier general, commanding general, 1st Engineer Special Brigade. Born in Elk, New Mexico, on 2 December 1894, Wharton was commissioned in the infantry through the Officers' Reserve Corps. Wharton served with the 62d Infantry in World War I without leaving the United States. Between the wars, he went to the Philippines, then alternated attendance at several army schools with service with troops and with the Civilian Conservation Corps. Graduating from the Army Industrial College in June 1940, he remained in Washington with the Officers' Branch, Personnel Division, G-1, of the War Department General Staff.

Wharton was made director of the Military Personnel Division of the Services of Supply in March 1942, then in July of that year became assistant division commander of the 80th Infantry Division. At Slapton Sands in England on 9 May 1944, he took command of the 1st Engineer Special Brigade, rebuilding it after a surprise naval attack. German craft, presumably E-boats, had caught eight LSTs of the 1st Engineer Special Brigade by surprise during

Operation TIGER, a final rehearsal for the D-day landings off Portland on 28 April 1944. According to one report, over 700 were killed and more than 300 wounded from the brigade alone, necessitating the rebuilding which led to Wharton's appointment. Wharton perfected the internal organization of the brigade, simplified its operating procedures, and developed the supply plan for the operation of the U.S. VII Corps against Cherbourg.

On D-day Wharton landed at Utah Beach at 0730 and directed his brigade's work during the early hours of the assault, emphasizing beach clearance and road development to move the large numbers of men and equipment coming ashore rapidly through to the front.

On 2 July 1944 Wharton became assistant division commander of the U.S. 9th Infantry Division during a regrouping of the First Army. On 9 July, and later as part of Operation COBRA on 25 July, his division participated in the Allied offensive west of Saint-Lô.

Again rebuilding a unit, Wharton was given the 28th Infantry Division of the XIX Corps on 12 August during its attacks to tighten the Argentan-Falaise pocket and exploit the Saint-Lô breakthrough. German artillery wounded Wharton a few hours later and he died that evening.

General Wharton was an able administrator, and was twice given commands where rebuilding was needed. He also proved himself a capable combat commander under enemy fire.

[See also American Beaches, article on Utah Beach; Engineers, article on American Engineers; 9th Infantry Division; Shore Party.]

BIBLIOGRAPHY

Beck, Alfred M., Abe Bortz, Charles W. Lynch, et al. *The Technical Services, The Corps of Engineers: The War against Germany.* The United States Army in World War II. 1985.
Wharton, James E. Biography Files. Research Collections, Office of History, Headquarters, U.S. Army Corps of Engineers.

MARTIN K. GORDON

WILKE, GUSTAV (1898–?), German, major general, commander of the *5th Parachute Division.* Wilke was born 6 March 1898 in Deutsch-Eylau, eastern Prussia. He entered the Prussian *4th Grenadier Regiment* on 27 December 1916 as a cadet and was promoted to second lieutenant in January 1918. He had to leave active service, however, as a result of the Versailles treaty on 1 January 1920. He reentered the army on 1 February 1925, joining the *2d Infantry Regiment* of the German Reichswehr. He was promoted to first lieutenant in February 1927 and to captain in April 1934, when he became commander of the *9th Company* in the *2d Infantry Regiment.*

On 1 October 1935, Wilke switched services and was trained as a military pilot in the German air force. In April 1937, he was promoted to major and placed in command of a bomber squadron. He became a company commander in the *25th Air Force Basic Training Regiment* and then battalion commander in April 1939. That November, he attained the rank of lieutenant colonel.

Wilke entered World War II as a group (battalion) commander with the *1st Glider Wing (Luftlandegeschwader 1),* whose commander he became in August 1940. From September 1941 to April 1942 he was detached to the aircraft works Messerschmitt-Werke, where he was responsible for the development and construction of large cargo gliders. In May 1942, as a colonel, he commanded an air force field regiment in the Eastern theater and from September to the end of 1943, the *1st Luftwaffe Field Division.* In December 1943, having been promoted to brigadier general, he was placed in command of the *2d Parachute Division (2 Fallschirmjägerdivision)* when its commander, Maj. Gen. Bernhard Hermann Ramcke, fell ill.

In April 1944 Wilke was assigned to organize and train the new *5th Parachute Division* and was promoted to major general the next month. During operations against the Allied invasion in Normandy, his division was not committed as a whole, and most of it was seized in the Falaise pocket. Wilke commanded the remnants of his division under the tactical control of the German *LXXX Corps* through 1944. In January 1945 he was ordered to set up the *9th Parachute Division.* After three months in the commanders' reserve of the Luftwaffe High Command, he began to organize the *10th Parachute Infantry Division,* but on 5 May he was captured by American forces. He was not released until July 1947.

Wilke, who in the course of his career won the Iron Cross and the Knight's Cross, belonged to the generation of German officers who fought in World War I as volunteers. After the armistice of November 1918, they defended the new German republic against both Communist revolution and Polish territorial claims, but they were forced to leave the army as a result of the Versailles Treaty. The rearmament of Germany after 1928 and the buildup of a modern air force gave these men a chance to resume military service. But, politically uneducated, they did not realize that through their activities they were helping pave the way for World War II.

[See also 5th Parachute Division.]

BIBLIOGRAPHY

Thomas, Franz, and Günter Wegmann. "Fallschirmjäger." Part 2 of *Die Ritterkreuzträger der deutschen Wehrmacht, 1939–1945.* 1986.
Wilke, Gustav. Personnel records. Bundesarchiv-Militärarchiv, Freiburg, Germany.

FLORIAN BERBERICH

WILKES, JOHN (1895–1957), American, rear admiral, commander of Landing Craft and Bases. John Wilkes was born on 26 May 1895 at Charlotte, North Carolina. He was commissioned in June 1916 upon graduation from the U.S. Naval Academy. During his years as an officer he served primarily in the submarine force, including a tour of duty in the Southwest Pacific early in World War II. As a captain Wilkes commanded the light cruiser *Birmingham* from January through August 1943 and participated in the invasion of Sicily.

Promoted to the rank of rear admiral, Wilkes proceeded in late August 1943 to Falmouth in Cornwall, where he became commander of Landing Craft and Bases, Amphibious Force, Europe. In this capacity he was responsible for training thousands of army and navy personnel who would operate landing craft and ships during the invasion of France. He was charged as well with the physical preparation and logistic support of those landing craft. The amphibious training bases under his command dotted the south coast of England on the English Channel, and there were bases as well in Wales, Scotland, and Northern Ireland. In assessing the training commander's role, historian Samuel Eliot Morison observed, "Admiral Wilkes, a bundle of nervous energy, had plenty of objects on which to expend it." Rear Adm. Alan G. Kirk, commander of the invasion task force, credited Wilkes with delivering more than 99 percent of the assigned landing craft to the French coast.

From July 1944 to March 1945, in the aftermath of the invasion, Wilkes served as commander of U.S. Ports and Bases France, headquartered at Cherbourg. Because of the need for continuing logistic support of Allied troops pushing eastward across France toward Germany, Wilkes had an important role in ensuring that large amounts of cargo moved through the French ports, particularly Cherbourg. This included the salvage work necessary to clear Cherbourg harbor of mines and sunken ships. After the war the admiral commanded amphibious and then submarine forces before his final tour, 1948–1951, as commander of U.S. Naval Forces in Germany. At the time of retirement he was promoted to vice admiral on the basis of his combat service. Admiral Wilkes died 20 July 1957 in the naval hospital at Bethesda, Maryland.

[*See also* Amphibious Assault Training.]

BIBLIOGRAPHY

Morison, Samuel Eliot. *The Invasion of France and Germany, 1944–1945.* Vol. 11 of *History of United States Naval Operations in World War II.* 1957. Reprint, 1988.
Wilkes, John. Biographical file. Operational Archives, Naval Historical Center, Washington, D.C.

PAUL STILLWELL

WILLIAMS, PAUL (1894–1968), American, major general commanding IX Troop Carrier Command. Paul L. Williams graduated from Stanford University and joined the army in April 1917, transferring into the Aviation Section in October 1917. A pilot in the 1920s, he served as a flight training officer in the 1930s at Randolph Field, Texas. From 1937 to 1942 he commanded attack and light bomber groups, units specializing in support of ground forces. After assuming charge of XII Air Support Command in Tunisia in January 1943, he worked closely with Lt. Gens. George S. Patton, Jr., and Omar Bradley. In June 1943 he resumed command of 51st Troop Carrier Wing, leading it through the landings in Sicily and at Salerno.

Upon returning to England in February 1944 he perfected the organization of the previously activated IX Troop Carrier Command, the force slated to conduct all American airborne operations. By May 1944 he led 1,226 transport aircraft. On D-day 900 of Williams's transports and 100 of his gliders carried portions of the 82d and 101st airborne divisions, the first American troops into Normandy, to their drop zones behind German coastal defenses. Although many of the drops were scattered, enough of the paratroops landed at their objectives to render material assistance to forces attacking the invasion beaches.

Although Williams's command did not conduct any further airborne operations during the campaign, its aircraft flew in time-sensitive supplies and evacuated casualties to England. It also provided the airborne forces with air-dropped supplies, troop-carrying glider reinforcements, and other support until those units withdrew in late June for refitting for future operations.

In July 1944 Williams and two-thirds of his command went to the Mediterranean to assist in the invasion of southern France. They returned in September 1944 to participate in Operation MARKET GARDEN, the airborne landings in Holland, which attempted to breach the Rhine River barrier.

After the war Williams commanded, at various times, the Third, Ninth, Second, and Tenth air forces. Before retiring in 1950 he also served as a member of the Air Force Personnel Board.

[*See also* IX Troop Carrier Command.]

BIBLIOGRAPHY

Craven, Wesley Frank, and James Lea Cate, eds. *Europe: ARGUMENT to V-E Day, January 1944 to May 1945.* Vol. 3 of *The Army Air Forces in World War II.* 1951.
Kohn, Richard H., and Joseph Hanrahan, eds. *Condensed Analysis of the Ninth Air Force in the European Theater of Operations.* Reprint, 1984.

RICHARD G. DAVIS

WILLIAMS, ROBERT B. (1901–1977), American, major general commanding 1st Bombardment Division, Eighth Air Force. Robert B. Williams graduated from Texas A&M in 1923 and immediately joined the Air Service. Subsequently, he served in Texas and in Panama, and in 1933 he attended the Air Corps Tactical School, after which he became an instructor pilot. In 1937 he graduated from the Army Command and Staff College and became operations officer of the 2d Bombardment Group (which had the only operational B-17s in the Air Corps) at Langley Field, Virginia. In November 1939 he took part in the flight of the "Flying Forts" to Rio de Janeiro, Brazil. Now a major, he served as a military observer in England from late 1940 to early 1941, an assignment that was intended to provide the future leaders of the air service with a firsthand look at combat operations. After various command assignments over bombardment units within the United States during the first eighteen months of the war, Williams, a brigadier general, was sent to England in June 1943.

Shortly afterward Williams took command of the Eighth Air Force's largest and most experienced division, the 1st Bombardment Division. He led this division, composed entirely of B-17 groups, through the most difficult period of the Eighth Air Force's existence, including major attacks on Germany, the pre–D-day attacks on the enemy transportation network, the bombing of the beachheads, and the tactical bombing that preceded the Saint-Lô breakout. He became a major general in May 1944. In the weeks before the D-day invasion the division pounded German transportation targets and airfields within 210 kilometers (130 miles) of the invasion site. The German airfields were bombed so that German planes would be forced to use more distant airfields, thus equalizing the flying distances to the invasion site for both German and Allied planes.

On 6 June 1944 the 1st Bombardment Division, which contained twelve bomb groups (91BG, 92BG, 303BG, 305BG, 306BG, 351BG, 379BG, 381BG, 384BG, 398BG, 401BG, and 457BG), bombed Omaha and the British invasion beaches. The bombardiers, however, to ensure that no bombs fell among the invasion shipping, released their bombs a fraction too late, so that the bombs overshot the beaches and did little damage to the German defenses. In a second mission that day, the 1st Bombardment Division hit transportation choke points in Normandy.

In July 1944 the division participated in the strategic bombing offensive against German synthetic oil plants and in three attacks in close support of Anglo-American ground offensives. The ground support bombing mission of 25 July 1944 (Operation COBRA) pulverized the *Panzer Lehr Division* and eased the American breakthrough at Saint-Lô. General Williams's bombardiers appear not to have dropped their bombs short in this attack, an error that was committed by the Eighth Air Force's other two bombardment divisions. In October 1944 Williams returned to the United States to assume the post of commanding general of the Special Air Force, the principal bomber-training air force of the U.S. Army Air Forces. General Williams retired in June 1946 and died in San Antonio, Texas, on 10 February 1977.

[*See also* Eighth Air Force; 1st Bombardment Division.]

BIBLIOGRAPHY

Center for Air Force History. Official biography of Robert Boyd Williams [ca. 1951]. Retired Generals Collection, Bolling AFB, Washington, D.C.
Freeman, Roger. *Mighty Eighth War Diary*. 1981.

RICHARD G. DAVIS

WITT, FRITZ (1908–1944), German, Gruppenführer, commander of the *12th SS Panzer Division "Hitlerjugend"*. Witt chose a military career in 1931, when he joined the Nazi party and the SS. When the *Leibstandarte SS,* Hitler's bodyguard formation, was created in the spring of 1933, Witt was among the first 120 men to volunteer for that elite formation. In June, he completed an infantry junior commanders' course and took over a platoon in the *Leibstandarte*'s 2d Company. He was later seconded to the paramilitary auxiliary police formations known as *Verfügungstruppen*.

Shortly before the outbreak of World War II, Witt was selected to serve with the *Army/SS Panzer Division "Kempf"* and during the Polish campaign of September 1939 commanded a company. In the course of one patrol to the west of Modlin, Witt carried a wounded man on his back and brought him to safety. In Poland he won both classes of the Iron Cross; the citation records that Witt was the first member of the *"Kempf" Division* to be so honored and that the award was a recognition of his courage and of his company's achievements.

In October 1939, Witt was promoted and given command of the *1st Battalion* of the *"Deutschland" Regiment* in the newly created *SS Verfügungs Division*. He led this battalion in the 1940 campaign in the West, fighting first in Holland and then in France, where his battalion's part in the capture of 22,000 French soldiers on the Langres Plateau gained for him the Knight's Cross.

Witt returned from the *Verfügungs Division* to the *Leibstandarte Regiment* with the rank of Sturmbannführer, took over command of its *1st Battalion,* and led it in the 1941 campaigns in Yugoslavia and in Greece. He and his men spearheaded the assault to open the Klidi Pass, an operation that, according to the *Leibstandarte* history, contributed significantly to the swift conclusion of the Greek

FRITZ WITT.   BIBLIOTHEK FÜR ZEITGESCHICHTE, STUTTGART

campaign. He served with the regiment on the Eastern front and for his achievements in the battles along the Mius River was awarded the German Cross in Gold as well as the Infantry Assault Badge.

When the *Leibstandarte* expanded to become a division, Witt took over the *1st SS Panzer Grenadier Regiment,* served temporarily as divisional commander in January 1943, and during the winter battles of February of that year, led one of the battle groups that closed a gap in the German line at Merefa to the south of Kharkov. He later participated in the recapture of that city. The award of Oak Leaves to the Knight's Cross and promotion to Oberführer were recognition of his achievements in the Kharkov fighting.

In the spring of 1943, Witt was among a group of *Leibstandarte* officers and men charged with raising the *"Hitlerjugend" Division*. Because of his powers of leadership and organization, Witt was given command of that formation, becoming, at the age of thirty-five, the second youngest divisional commander in the German armed forces.

During a preinvasion reconnaissance in Normandy, Witt predicted that the *716th Division*'s sector would be a main Allied objective because it held the best tank coun-

try in the area and had an airfield at Carpiquet. His reading of the ground proved correct, for in that sector were Gold, Juno, and Sword beaches.

On D-day conflicting orders from German senior commanders dispersed the *"Hitlerjugend" Division* so widely that when a major counterattack was ordered to be launched on 7 June, aimed at driving the Allies into the sea, less than half of the *12th SS* was immediately available. Witt, whose motto had always been "attack," nevertheless committed his men to battle, and although his division lacked the strength to carry out the High Command's orders, it was able to create a perimeter strong enough to thwart the British Second Army's first attempts to capture Caen.

It was Witt's custom to visit a unit of his command each day, but on 14 June he remained in divisional headquarters at Venoix. During the late morning, shells fell around the house and Witt, who was in the garden, was struck in the head and died of his wounds. He was first buried in the garden of the château at Tillières-sur-Avre but was disinterred by the Allies and eventually laid to rest in a German military cemetery in Normandy. Witt's epitaph must surely be the *"Hitlerjugend" Division*, which gained for itself a fearsome reputation among the soldiers who fought against it in the Normandy battles.

[*See also* 12th SS Panzer Division.]

BIBLIOGRAPHY

Ellis, L. F., et al. *The Battle of Normandy.* Vol. 1 of *Victory in the West.* 1962.

Klietmann, K. G. *Die Waffen SS: Eine Dokumentation.* 1965.

Kratschmer, E. G. *Die Ritterkreuzträger der Waffen SS.* 1982.

Tessin, Georg. *Verbände und Truppen der deutschen Wehrmacht und Waffen-SS im Zweiten Weltkrieg, 1939–1945.* 1973–1980.

Weidinger, O. *Tulle und Oradour: A Franco-German Tragedy.* 1985.

JAMES LUCAS

WOOD, MYRON (1892–1946), American, brigadier general, commander of the IX Air Force Service Command. During the D-day Campaign Wood led the IX Air Force Service Command, which provided the logistics and maintenance support for the U.S. Ninth Air Force. The IX Service Command, which by June 1944 contained 62,000 men, was the largest unit of the Ninth Air Force.

Myron Wood graduated from the University of Colorado. He joined the Air Service in 1918 and became a pilot that same year. Early in his career Wood became involved in logistics and procurement for the air corps. His logistics specialization began when he was appointed purchasing officer at Kelly Field in 1920. In the interwar period Wood attended the Army Industrial College, America's premier school for logistics planning, and served with the planning section of the air corps's Matériel Division at Wright Field. In 1940 he was appointed aircraft procurement chief for the Army Air Corps. His experience as a command pilot and observer gave him a thorough understanding of air operations as well as logistics.

Wood was sent to England in 1942 as the chief of supply for the Eighth Air Force. He was promoted to brigadier general in June 1943, and the next year was given command of the IX Air Force Service Command. His extensive experience made him the logical choice for one of the most difficult logistics missions of the war—providing repair, maintenance, and supply support for the Ninth Air Force. After D-day the Ninth Air Force would have to operate from rough forward airfields on the Continent with support brought over the Normandy beaches; it would take huge quantities of bombs, fuel, and parts to keep it flying.

Upon taking charge of the IX Service Command, Wood introduced many innovations. As the Allies landed in Normandy, he created a series of forward depots, streamlined the supply system, and transferred logistics operations to France as quickly as possible. But as the Ninth Air Force units deployed to France, the insufficient port facilities resulted in a critical parts shortage. So, using Ninth Air Force transports, Wood improvised an airlift force to rush parts to maintenance units at forward airfields. This program and Wood's policy of sending most of his maintenance units to forward depots helped keep 70 percent of the Ninth Air Force units operational even during the heavy combat action and severe losses of 1944.

Wood commanded the IX Service Command until the end of the war. His organizational ability and logistics competence had enabled him to overcome difficult problems and resulted in the Ninth Air Force having fuel, bombs, and bullets as they were needed.

[See also IX Air Force Service Command.]

BIBLIOGRAPHY

Ninth Air Force. Operational Records. USAF Historical Research Agency, Maxwell Air Force Base, Alabama.

JAMES S. CORUM

WYCHE, IRA T.

WYCHE, IRA T. (1887–1981), American, major general, commander, 79th Infantry Division. General Wyche was born on Ocracoke Island, North Carolina, on 16 October 1887. Graduating from West Point in 1911, he was commissioned a second lieutenant of infantry, but transferred to the field artillery in 1917 and served in France from May to August 1918. For the next two decades he held various field artillery assignments and commands and was graduated from the Field Artillery School, the Command and General Staff School, and the Army War College. Promoted to major general in April 1942, he briefly commanded the 74th Field Artillery Brigade and in May took command of the about-to-be activated 79th Infantry Division. Wyche oversaw the activation and organization of the division and drove it through a long period of hard training, the importance of which he repeatedly emphasized. In April 1944 he took the division to England, where it prepared to take part in the upcoming invasion of Normandy.

Although the 79th Division was not scheduled to land until D plus 8 (14 June), Wyche led an advance party ashore at Utah Beach on D plus 6. The rest of his command followed over the next two days. As part of Maj. Gen. J. Lawton Collins's U.S. VII Corps, the 79th Division was chosen to play a major role in the drive to capture the key port of Cherbourg at the northern end of the Cotentin Peninsula.

Wyche moved his division into the Golleville-Urville sector, relieving the U.S. 90th Division in the center of the VII Corps front facing north toward Cherbourg. The attack opened on 19 June. After overcoming initial strong resistance that day, the 79th Division drove steadily ahead and by nightfall of 21 June was up against the final German defenses. Wyche's division finally captured the stronghold of Fort du Roule on 25 June and entered Cherbourg itself. Its patrols were the first to do so, but several more days of fighting were necessary before the city was secured.

General Wyche commanded the 79th Division throughout its subsequent battles against the Germans. His troops were the first to cross the Seine River, withstood a German counteroffensive in Alsace, took part in the assault crossing of the Rhine, and helped clear the Ruhr pocket. The division's excellent combat record can be attributed in many ways to Wyche's continued emphasis on training, even while his men were supposedly resting between combat missions.

In May 1945 General Wyche took command of the U.S. VIII Corps, before returning to the United States in December. In January 1947 he became Inspector General of the Army. He retired on 30 September 1948 to Pinehurst, North Carolina, where he died on 8 July 1981 at the age of ninety-three.

[See also 79th Infantry Division.]

BIBLIOGRAPHY

Harrison, Gordon A. *Cross-Channel Attack.* U.S. Army in World War II: The European Theater of Operations. 1951.
His son-in-law [sic]. "Ira Thomas Wyche." *Assembly,* December 1982, 122–123.

STANLEY L. FALK

Synoptic Outline of Contents

The following outline is divided into seven sections, reflecting the systematic organization of the encyclopedia and its focus on D-day and the twelve days that followed. The first heading, Normandy Campaign, refers to articles about Allied preparations for the invasion of Europe in 1944, German plans for defense, and general discussions about the campaign. The second heading includes articles about the nations that were involved in the battle and the landing beaches on D-day. Army, naval, and air force topics are each listed separately. The sixth section lists all biographical entries in the encyclopedia. The last section lists articles concerned with the memory and honor of those who fought in the Normandy campaign and refers to entries that give guidance concerning further research on D-day.

Guide to German Military Units

In most cases, this work refers to German military units by using English forms of their German designations. The following provides the German military name and its English equivalent.

GERMAN DESIGNATION	ENGLISH FORM
Afrika Korps	Africa Corps
Bodenständigedivision	Static Division
Fallschirmjägerdivision	Parachute Division
Fallschirmjägerregiment	Parachute Infantry Regiment
Fallschirmkorps	Parachute Corps
Feldersatzbataillon	Field Replacement Battalion
Flakabteilung	Antiaircraft Artillery Battalion
Fliegerdivision	Air Division
Fliegerkorps	Air Corps
Geschwader	Wing
Granatwerferbataillon	Mortar Battalion
Grosse Generalstab	High Command General Staff
Gruppe	Group
Jagddivision	Fighter Division
Jagdgeschwader	Fighter Wing
Jagdkorps	Fighter Corps
Jägerdivision	Jäger (Light) Division
Kampfgeschwader	Bomber Wing
Kriegsmarine	German Navy
Luftflotte 3	Third Air Force
Luftflotte Reich	Home Air Force
Luftlandedivision	Air Landing Division
Luftnachrichtenabteilung	Signal Battalion
Luftwaffe	German Air Force
Nachschubstruppen	Supply Corps
Panzerjägerabteilung	Antitank Battalion
Pionierbataillon	Engineer Battalion
Schlachtgeschwader	Ground Attack Wing
Staffel	Squadron
Wehrmacht	German Armed Forces

Table of Comparative Ranks

American	British	German	SS
ARMY			
–	–	Reichsmarshall	–
General of the Army	Field Marshal	Generalfeldmarschall	Reichsführer
General	General	Generaloberst	Oberstgruppenführer
Lieutenant General	Lieutenant General	General der Artillerie, Infanterie, etc.	Obergruppenführer
Major General	Major General	Generalleutnant	Gruppenführer
Brigadier General	Brigadier	Generalmajor	Brigadeführer
–	–	–	Oberführer
Colonel	Colonel	Oberst	Standartenführer
Lieutenant Colonel	Lieutenant Colonel	Oberstleutnant	Obersturmbann-führer
Major	Major	Major	Sturmbannführer
Captain	Captain	Hauptmann	Hauptsturmführer
Captain (Cavalry)	Captain (Cavalry)	Rittmeister	–
First Lieutenant	Lieutenant	Oberleutnant	Obersturmführer
Second Lieutenant	Second Lieutenant	Leutnant	Untersturmführer
NAVY			
Fleet Admiral	Admiral of the Fleet	Grossadmiral	–
Admiral	Admiral	General Admiral	–
Vice Admiral	Vice Admiral	Vizeadmiral	–
Rear Admiral	Rear Admiral	Konteradmiral	–
Commodore	Commodore	–	–
Captain	Captain	Kapitän zur See	–
Commander	Commander	Fregattenkapitän	–
Lieutenant Commander	Lieutenant Commander	Korvettenkapitän	–
Lieutenant	Lieutenant	Kapitänleutnant	–
Lieutenant Junior Grade	Sub-Lieutenant	Oberleutnant zur See	–
Ensign	Acting Sub-Lieutenant	Leutnant zur See	–
Air Force			
–	Marshal of the RAF	Reichsmarshall	–
General	Air Chief Marshal	Generaloberst	–
Lieutenant General	Air Marshal	General der . . . [unit]	–
Major General	Air Vice Marshal	Generalleutnant	–
Brigadier General	Air Commodore	Generalmajor	–
Colonel	Group Captain	Oberst	–
Lieutenant Colonel	Wing Commander	Oberstleutnant	–
Major	Squadron Leader	Major	–
Captain	Flight Lieutenant	Hauptmann	–
First Lieutenant	Flying Officer	Oberleutnant	–
Second Lieutenant	Pilot Officer	Leutnant	–

607

Glossary of Acronyms, Code Names, and Special Terms

Code names are indicated in small capital letters, as in ANVIL.

For a table of common abbreviations, see page li. *For a guide to German military units, see page 605.*
For a comparative guide to military ranks, see page 607.

AAF	Army Air Forces
ACM	Air Chief Marshal
ADGB	Air Defence of Great Britain
AEAF	Allied Expeditionary Air Force
AEF	Allied Expeditionary Force
AFHQ	Allied Force Headquarters
AFSC	Air Force Service Command
AGC	Command ship
ANCXF	Allied Naval Commander, Expeditionary Force
ANVIL	Planned 1944 Allied invasion of southern France in the Toulon-Marseilles area
AOC	Air officer commanding
AP	Transport craft (British)
APA	Attack transport craft (British)
APDS	Armor-piercing discarding sabot
ARCADIA	U.S.–British staff conference at Washington, December 1941–January 1942
ARGONAUT	Yalta Conference, February 1945
ATA	Rescue tugs
AVM	Air vice marshal
AVRE	Armoured Vehicle Royal Engineers
BAGRATION	Massive Soviet attack against the German *Army Group Center,* June 1944
BENEFICIARY	Plan for breaking out of the Normandy lodgment by means of a combined airborne-amphibious attack on Saint-Malo
BIGOT	Code used for access to top-secret Allied planning at various headquarters in England for the Normandy invasion
Blitzkrieg	German for "lightning war": a surprise offensive conducted with great speed and force
BLUES	British plan for carrier-based air attacks on southern Norway, June 1944
BODYGUARD	Allied deception plan to mask the Normady invasion, adopted in January 1944
BOLERO	Buildup of troops and supplies in the United Kingdom in preparation for a cross-Channel attack
BYMS	British Yard Minesweeper
CCOS	Combined Chiefs of Staff
Chaff	Aluminum strips dropped by Allied aircraft to confuse German radar

GLOSSARY

COBRA	Operation launched by U.S. First Army on 25 July 1944 to break out of the Normandy lodgment
COMET	British plan, not carried out, for an air drop on 7 September 1944 in the Arnhem-Nijmegen area of the Netherlands
CONEBO	Allied Coastal Command operations against German light surface forces
CORK	Allied patrol operation in May and June 1944 to prevent U-boats from entering the western end of the Channel
COSSAC	Chief of Staff to the Supreme Allied Commander
CROSSBOW	RAF operations against German V-weapons in 1944
DD	Duplex Drive (amphibious tank)
DIVER	British defense against and attacks on German V-weapons in 1944
DRAGOON	Allied invasion of southern France, 15 August 1944, planned under the code name ANVIL
DUKW	Amphibious truck
E-boat	Allied name for German S-boat (*Schnellboot*); a small, fast motor torpedo boat
EPSOM	British offensive near Caen, July 1944
ETF	Eastern Task Force
ETO	European Theater of Operations
EUREKA	Teheran Conference, November–December 1943
FABIUS	Amphibious landing exercises for the Normandy invasion in May 1944
FFI	French Forces of the Interior
FORTITUDE	Cover operations to conceal the Normandy invasion
FTD	Fighter direction tenders
GARDEN	See MARKET-GARDEN
GHQ	General headquarters
GOC	General officer commanding
Gold	Allied name for the Normandy beach where troops of the British XXX Corps landed on D-day
GOODWOOD	British attack to break out of the Normandy lodgment, late July 1944, coinciding with U.S. Operation COBRA
Gooseberries	Artificial harbors for OVERLORD created by sinking block ships
GYMNAST	1941 plan for the Allied invasion of North Africa
HANDS UP	Plan for breaking out of the Normandy lodgment by means of a combined airborne-amphibious attack on Quiberon Bay in Brittany
HE	High explosive
HORNPIPE	Code designation for a message to alert Allied forces of a twenty-four-hour delay in the Normandy assault
JAEL	An early Allied deception plan, abandoned in late 1943, to convince the Germans that the Allies would attack in Italy and the Balkans rather than in France
Juno	Allied name for the Normandy beach where the 3d Canadian Division landed on D-day
(L)	Large [following abbreviations for landing craft, as in LCS(L)]
LBE	Landing Barge, Emergency Repair
LCA	Landing Craft, Assault
LCA(HR)	Landing Craft, Assault (Hedgerow)
LCE	Landing Craft, Emergency Repair
LCF	Landing Craft, Flak

610

LCG	Landing Craft, Gun
LCH	Landing Craft, Headquarters
LCI	Landing Craft, Infantry
LCM	Landing Craft, Mechanized
LCP	Landing Craft, Personnel
LCS	Landing Craft, Support
LCT	Landing Craft, Tank
LCT(A)	Landing Craft, Tank (Armored)
LCT(HE)	Landing Craft, Tank (High Explosive)
LCT(R)	Landing Craft, Tank (Rocket)
LCVP	Landing Craft, Vehicle and Personnel
LOOK	Code name for General Dwight D. Eisenhower
LSD	Landing Ship, Dock
LSE	Landing Ship, Emergency Repair
LSH	Landing Ship, Headquarters
LSI	Landing Ship, Infantry
LSI(H)	Landing Ship, Infantry (Hand)
LST	Landing Ship, Tank
LUCKY STRIKE	21st Army Group plan, considered in May and June 1944, calling for an eastward drive to capture the Seine ports, as an alternative to plans for the earlier capture of Brittany
(M)	Medium [following abbreviations of landing craft, as in LCS(M)]
Maquis	Units of the French Resistance
MARKET-GARDEN	Allied airborne operation intended to establish a bridgehead across the Rhine in the Netherlands, September 1944
MASTER	Signal for U.S. First Army, 1944-1945
Matériel	Equipment, apparatus, supplies
MOWT	Ministry of War transport
MTB	Motor torpedo boat
MTO	Mediterranean Theater of Operations
Mulberries	Artificial harbors for OVERLORD created by sinking concrete caissons
MV	Motor vessel
NCETF	Naval Commander, Eastern Task Force
NEPTUNE	Naval operations in support of OVERLORD
NEST EGG	Plan for occupation of Channel Islands in case of German collapse or surrender
NOBALL	Air force term referring to target sites in attacks on long-range weapons
OB West	Oberbefehlshaber West (Commander in Chief West)
OKH	Oberkommando des Heeres (Army High Command)
OKL	Oberkommando der Luftwaffe (Luftwaffe High Command)
OKM	Oberkommando der Kriegsmarine (Navy High Command)
OKW	Oberkommando der Wehrmacht (Armed Forces High Command)
Omaha	Allied name for the Normandy beach where troops of the U.S. V Corps landed on D-day
Osttruppen	Eastern troops; anti-Communist citizens of the Soviet Union who were enlisted in the German Army
OVERLORD	The Normandy invasion, D-day, 6 June 1944
PC	Patrol craft
PIRATE	1943 exercise by British and Canadian Task Force J
PLUTO	Pipe Line Under The Ocean, Allied plan for supplying fuel to the invasion forces
POINTBLANK	Combined Bomber Offensive from the United Kingdom against Germany

GLOSSARY

QUADRANT	First Quebec Conference, August 1943
RA	Royal Artillery
RAAF	Royal Australian Air Force
RAF	Royal Air Force
RANVR	Royal Australian Naval Volunteer Reserve
RATTLE	Conference held by the Combined Operation Headquarters in 1943 to discuss amphibious tactics and techniques
R-boat	*Räumboot:* German motor minesweeper
RCN	Royal Canadian Navy
RE	Royal Engineers
RHA	Royal Horse Artillery
RN	Royal Navy
RNZNVR	Royal New Zealand Naval Volunteer Reserve
ROUNDHAMMER	Code name used at the Washington Conference in May 1943 to designate a modified ROUNDUP invasion
ROUNDUP	Various 1941–1943 plans for a cross-Channel attack in the final phases of the war
(S)	Small [following abbreviations of landing craft, as in LCS(S)]
S-boat	*Schnellboot:* a small, fast German motor torpedo boat, called E-boat by the Allies
SEELÖWE (SEALION)	The German planned invasion of England in 1940–1941
SEXTANT	Cairo Conference, 22–26 November 1943
SHAEF	Supreme Headquarters Allied Expeditionary Force
SHARPENER	Supreme Commander's advance command post at Portsmouth, May 1944
SHELLBURST	Advance headquarters of SHAEF in Normandy, June 1944
SHIPMATE	Enlarged SHAEF advance headquarters near Portsmouth, replacing SHARPENER
Sigint	Allied Signals Intelligence
SKYSCRAPER	A cross-Channel attack plan drawn by the Combined Commanders in the spring of 1943
SLEDGEHAMMER	Plan for a limited-objective attack across the Channel in 1942, designed either to take advantage of a crack in German morale or as a "sacrifice" operation to aid the Russians
Snorkel	Tube housing air intake and exhaust pipes, protruding above the surface when a U-boat was submerged
SOS	Services of Supply (U.S. Army)
SPRING	Canadian attack in Normandy, July 1944, coinciding with Operation COBRA
SS	Schutzstaffeln (Protection Squads): Nazi paramilitary units that originated as bodyguard units. Waffen-SS was the collective designation for combat units of the SS.
SWAMP	Intensive RAF Coastal Command attack on German U-boats in support of Operation OVERLORD
Sword	Allied name for the Normandy beach where the British 3d Division landed on D-day
SWORDHILT	Allied plan for a combined airborne-amphibious operation to seize the area east of Brest in August 1944
SYMBOL	Casablanca Conference, January 1943
TAC	Tactical Air Command
TD	Tank Destroyer
TIGER	Invasion exercise of Force U (U.S. VII Corps)
TOPFLIGHT	Signal for the release of press information on the D-day assault
TORCH	Allied invasion of Morocco and Algeria in November 1942
TRIDENT	Washington Conference, May 1943

GLOSSARY

U-boat	*Unterseeboot:* German submarine
Ultra	British designation for Special Intelligence signals and documents, indicating high-level secrecy
USAAF	U.S. Army Air Forces
USCG	U.S. Coast Guard
USN	U.S. Navy
USSAFE	U.S. Strategic Air Forces in Europe (later USSTAF)
USSTAF	U.S. Strategic Air Forces
Utah	Allied name for the Normandy beach where troops of the U.S. VII Corps landed on D-day
V-1	German Vergeltungswaffen 1 (Vengeance Weapon 1); the Flying Bomb
Volksdeutsche	Ethnic German residents of central and eastern European countries, repatriated for political reasons by the Nazi regime
WIDEWING	SHAEF headquarters at Bushy Park, near London
Window	Aluminum strips (chaff) released by Allied aircraft to simulate an invasion fleet on German radar
XAP	Assault transport craft
ZEBRA	USAAF mass drop of supplies to the French Maquis on 25 June 1944
ZEPPELIN	Simulated Allied threats to the Balkans and southern France in the spring of 1944, to mask the Normandy invasion

Appendix 1

The Supreme Commander's Orders of the Day

Soldiers, Sailors and Airmen of the Allied Expeditionary Force:

You are about to embark upon the Great Crusade, toward which we have striven these many months. The eyes of the world are upon you. The hopes and prayers of liberty-loving people everywhere march with you. In company with our brave Allies and brothers-in-arms on other Fronts you will bring about the destruction of the German war machine, the elimination of Nazi tyranny over oppressed peoples of Europe, and security for ourselves in a free world.

Your task will not be an easy one. Your enemy is well trained, well equipped and battle-hardened. He will fight savagely.

But this is the year 1944! Much has happened since the Nazi triumphs of 1940-41. The United Nations have inflicted upon the Germans great defeats, in open battle, man-to-man. Our air offensive has seriously reduced their strength in the air and their capacity to wage war on the ground. Our Home Fronts have given us an overwhelming superiority in weapons and munitions of war, and placed at our disposal great reserves of trained fighting men. The tide has turned! The free men of the world are marching together to Victory!

I have full confidence in your courage, devotion to duty and skill in battle. We will accept nothing less than full victory!

Good luck! And let us all beseech the blessing of Almighty God upon this great and noble undertaking.

DWIGHT D. EISENHOWER

6 June 1944

This message was distributed to the troops with the D-day statement.

You are soon to be engaged in a great undertaking—the invasion of Europe. Our purpose is to bring about, in company with our Allies, and our comrades on other fronts, the total defeat of Germany. Only by such a complete victory can we free ourselves and our homelands from the fear and threat of the Nazi tyranny.

A further element of our mission is the liberation of those people of Western Europe now suffering under German oppression.

Before embarking on this operation, I have a personal message for you as to your own individual responsibility, in relation to the inhabitants of our Allied countries.

As a representative of your country, you will be welcomed with deep gratitude by the liberated people, who for years have longed for this deliverance. It is of the utmost importance that this feeling of friendliness and goodwill be in no way impaired by careless or indifferent behavior on your part. By a courteous and considerate demeanor, you can on the other hand do much to strengthen that feeling.

The inhabitants of Nazi-occupied Europe have suffered great privation, and you will find that many of them lack even the barest necessities. You, on the other hand, have been, and will continue to be, provided adequate food, clothes and other necessities. You must not deplete the already meager local stocks of food and other supplies by indiscriminate buying, thereby fostering the "Black Market," which can only increase the hardship of the inhabitants.

The rights of individuals, as to their persons and property, must be scrupulously respected, as though in your own country. You must remember, always, that these people are our friends and Allies.

I urge each of you to bear constantly in mind that by your actions not only you as an individual, but your country as well, will be judged. By establishing a relationship with the liberated peoples, based on mutual understanding and respect, we shall enlist their wholehearted assistance in the defeat of our common enemy. Thus shall we lay the foundation for a lasting peace, without which our great effort will have been in vain.

DWIGHT D. EISENHOWER

615

Führer Headquarters
3 November 1943

Top Secret

The Führer
OKW/WFSt/Op.No. 662656/43 g.K. Chefs

27 Copies
Copy No. . . .

Directive No. 51

For the last two and one-half years the bitter and costly struggle against Bolshevism has made the utmost demands upon the bulk of our military resources and energies. This commitment was in keeping with the seriousness of the danger, and the over-all situation. The situation has since changed. The threat from the East remains, but an even greater danger looms in the West: the Anglo-American landing! In the East, the vastness of the space will, as a last resort, permit a loss of territory even on a major scale, without suffering a mortal blow to Germany's chance for survival. Not so in the West! If the enemy here succeeds in penetrating our defenses on a wide front, consequences of staggering proportions will follow within a short time. All signs point to an offensive against the Western Front of Europe no later than spring, and perhaps earlier.

For that reason, I can no longer justify the further weakening of the West in favor of other theaters of war. I have therefore decided to strengthen the defenses in the West, particularly at places from which we shall launch our long-range war against England. For those are the very points at which the enemy must and will attack; there—unless all indications are misleading—will be fought the decisive invasion battle.

Holding attacks and diversions on other fronts are to be expected. Not even the possibility of a large-scale offensive against Denmark may be excluded. It would pose greater nautical problems and could be less effectively supported from the air, but would nevertheless produce the greatest political and strategic impact if it were to succeed.

During the opening phase of the battle, the entire striking power of the enemy will of necessity be directed against our forces manning the coast. Only an all-out effort in the construction of fortifications, an unsurpassed effort that will enlist all available manpower and physical resources of Germany and the occupied areas, will be able to strengthen our defenses along the coasts within the short time that still appears to be left to us.

Stationary weapons (heavy AT [antitank] guns, immobile tanks to be dug in, coast artillery, shore-defense guns, mines, etc.) arriving in Denmark and the occupied West within the near future will be heavily concentrated in points of main defensive effort at the most vulnerable coastal sectors. At the same time, we must take the calculated risk that for the present we may be unable to improve our defenses in less threatened sectors.

Should the enemy nevertheless force a landing by concentrating his armed might, he must be hit by the full fury of our counterattack. For this mission ample and speedy reinforcements of men and materiel, as well as intensive training must transform available larger units into first-rate, fully mobile general reserves suitable for offensive operations. The counterattack of these units will prevent the enlargement of the beachhead, and throw the enemy back into the sea.

In addition, well-planned emergency measures, prepared down to the last detail, must enable us instantly to throw against the invader every fit man and machine from coastal sectors not under attack and from the home front.

The anticipated strong attacks by air and sea must be relentlessly countered by Air Force and Navy with all their available resources. I therefore order the following:
A) Army:

1.) The Chief of the Army General Staff and the Inspector General of Panzer Troops will submit to me as soon as possible a schedule covering arms, tanks, assault guns, motor vehicles, and ammunition to be allocated to the Western Front and Denmark within the next three months.

That schedule will conform to the new situation. The following considerations will be basic:

a) Sufficient mobility for all panzer and panzer grenadier divisions in the West, and equipment of each of those units by December 1943 with 93 Mark IV tanks or assault guns, as well as large numbers of antitank weapons.

Accelerated reorganization of the 20 Luftwaffe field divisions into an effective mobile reserve force by the end of 1943. This reorganization is to include the issue of assault guns.

Accelerated issue of all authorized weapons to the SS Panzer Grenadier Division Hitlerjugend, the 21st Panzer Division, and the infantry and reserve divisions stationed in Jutland.

b) Additional shipments of Mark IV tanks, assault guns, and heavy AT guns to the reserve panzer divisions stationed in the West and in Denmark, as well as to the Assault Gun Training Battalion in Denmark.

c) In November and December, monthly allotments of 100 heavy AT guns models 40 and 43 (half of these to be mobile) in addition to those required for newly activated units in the West and in Denmark.

d) Allotment of large numbers of weapons (including about 1,000 machine guns) for augmenting the armament of those static divisions that are committed for coastal defense in the West and in Denmark, and for standardizing the equipment of elements that are to be withdrawn from sectors not under attack.

e) Ample supply of close-combat AT weapons to units in vulnerable sectors.

f) Improvement of artillery and AT defenses in units stationed in Denmark, as well as those committed for coastal protection in the occupied West. Strengthening of GHQ artillery.

2.) The units and elements stationed in the West or in Denmark, as well as panzer, assault gun, and AT units to be activated in the West, must not be transferred to other fronts without my permission. The Chief of the Army General Staff or the Inspector General of Panzer Troops will submit to me a report through the Armed Forces Operations Staff as soon as the issue of equipment to the panzer and assault gun battalions, as well as to the AT battalions and companies, has been completed.

3.) Beyond similar measures taken in the past, the Commander in Chief West will establish timetables for, and conduct maneuvers and command post exercises on, the procedure for bringing up units from sectors not under attack. These units will be made capable of performing offensive missions, however limited. In that connection I demand that sectors not threatened by the enemy be ruthlessly stripped of all forces except small guard detachments. For sectors from which reserves are withdrawn, security and guard detachments must be set aside from security and alarm units. Labor forces drawn largely from the native population must likewise be organized in those sectors, in order to keep open whatever roads might be destroyed by the enemy air force.

4.) The Commander of German Troops in Denmark will take measures in the area under his control in compliance with paragraph 3 above.

5.) Pursuant to separate orders, the Chief of Army Equipment and Commander of the Replacement Army will form Kampfgruppen in regimental strength, security battalions, and engineer construction battalions from training cadres, trainees, schools, and instruction and convalescent units in the Zone of the Interior. These troops must be ready for shipment on 48 hours' notice.

Furthermore, other available personnel are to be organized into battalions of replacements and equipped with the available weapons, so that the anticipated heavy losses can quickly be replaced.

B)   Luftwaffe:

The offensive and defensive effectiveness of Luftwaffe units in the West and in Denmark will be increased to meet the changed situation. To that end, preparations will be made for the release of units suited for commitment in the anti-invasion effort, that is, all flying units and mobile flak artillery that can be spared from the air defenses of the home front, and from schools and training units in the Zone of the Interior. All those units are to be earmarked for the West and possibly Denmark.

The Luftwaffe ground organization in southern Norway, Denmark, northwestern Germany, and the West will be expanded and supplied in a way that will—by the most far-reaching decentralization of own forces—deny targets to the enemy bombers, and split the enemy's offensive effort in case of large-scale operations. Particularly important in that connection will be our fighter forces. Possibilities for their commitment must be increased by the establishment of numerous advance landing fields. Special emphasis is to be placed on good camouflage. I expect also that the Luftwaffe will unstintingly furnish all available forces, by stripping them from less threatened areas.

C)   <u>Navy</u>

The Navy will prepare the strongest possible forces suitable for attacking the enemy landing fleets. Coastal defense installations in the process of construction will be completed with the utmost speed. The emplacing of additional coastal batteries and the possibility of laying further flanking mine fields should be investigated.

All school, training, and other shore-based personnel fit for ground combat must be prepared for commitment so that, without undue delay, they can at least be employed as security forces within the zone of the enemy landing operations.

While preparing the reinforcement of the defenses in the West, the Navy must keep in mind that it might be called upon to repulse simultaneous enemy landings in Norway and Denmark. In that connection, I attach particular importance to the assembly of numerous U-boats in the northern area. A temporary weakening of U-boat forces in the Atlantic must be risked.

D)   <u>SS:</u>

The Reichsführer-SS will determine what Waffen SS and police forces he can release for combat, security, and guard duty. He is to prepare to organize effective combat and security forces from training, replacement, and convalescent units, as well as schools and other home-front establishments.

E)   The commanders in chief of the services, the Reichsführer-SS, the Chief of the Army General Staff, the Commander in Chief West, the Chief of Army Equipment and Commander of the Replacement Army, the Inspector General of Panzer Troops, as well as the Commander of German Troops in Denmark will report to me <u>by 15 November</u> all measures taken or planned.

I expect that all agencies will make a supreme effort toward utilizing every moment of the remaining time in preparing for the decisive battle in the West.

All authorities will guard against wasting time and energy in useless jurisdictional squabbles, and will direct all their efforts toward strengthening our defensive and offensive power.

signed: Adolf Hitler

The following is a digest of the plan for Operation OVERLORD
prepared by the Offices of the War Cabinet, 30 July 1943.

Digest of Operation "OVERLORD"

Object.

1. The object of Operation "Overlord" is to mount and carry out an operation, with forces and equipment established in the United Kingdom, and with target date the 1st May, 1944, to secure a lodgement on the Continent from which further offensive operations can be developed. The lodgement area must contain sufficient port facilities to maintain a force of some twenty-six to thirty divisions, and enable that force to be augmented by follow-up shipments from the United States or elsewhere of additional divisions and supporting units at the rate of three to five divisions per month.

Selection of a Lodgement Area.

2. In order to provide sufficient port facilities to maintain these large forces, it will be necessary to select a lodgement area which includes a group of major ports. We must plan on the assumption that ports, on capture, will be seriously damaged and probably blocked. It will take some time to restore normal facilities. We shall thus be forced to rely on maintenance over beaches for an extended period.

3. A study of the beaches on the Belgian and Channel coasts shows that the beaches with the highest capacity for passing vehicles and stores inland are those in the Pas de Calais,* and the Caen†— Cotentin‡ area. Of these, the Caen beaches are the most favourable, as they are, unlike the others, sheltered from the prevailing winds. Naval and air considerations point to the area between the Pas de Calais and the Cotentin as the most suitable for the initial landing, air factors of optimum air support and rapid provision of airfields indicating the Pas de Calais as the best choice, with Caen as an acceptable alternative.

4. Thus, taking beach capacity and air and naval considerations together, it appears that either the Pas de Calais area or the Caen-Cotentin area is the most suitable for the initial main landing.

5. As the area for the initial landing, the Pas de Calais has many obvious advantages such that good air support and quick turn round for our shipping can be achieved. On the other hand, it is a focal point of the enemy fighters disposed for defence, and maximum enemy air activity can be brought to bear over this area with the minimum movement of his air forces. Moreover, the Pas de Calais is the most strongly defended area on the whole French coast. The defences would require very heavy and sustained bombardment from sea and air: penetration would be slow, and the result of the bombardment of beach exits would severely limit the rate of build-up. Further, this area does not offer good opportunities for expansion. It would be necessary to develop the bridgehead to include either the Belgian ports as far as Antwerp or the Channel ports Westwards to include Havre and Rouen. But both an advance to Antwerp across the numerous water obstacles, and a long flank march of some 120 miles to the Seine ports must be considered unsound operations of war unless the German forces are in a state not far short of final collapse.

6. In the Caen-Cotentin area it would be possible to make our initial landing either partly on the Cotentin Peninsula and partly on the Caen beaches, wholly in the Cotentin or wholly on the Caen beaches. An attack with part of our forces in the Cotentin and part on the Caen beaches, is, however, considered to be unsound. It would entail dividing our limited forces by the low-lying marshy ground and intricate river system at the neck of the Cotentin Peninsula; thus exposing them to defeat in detail.

7. An attack against the Cotentin Peninsula, on the other hand, has a reasonable chance of success, and would ensure the early capture of the port of Cherbourg. Unfortunately, very few

---

* "Pas de Calais area" has been assumed as the area between Gravelines and the River Somme.
† "Caen area" is taken as that between the River Orne and the base of the Cotentin Peninsula.
‡ The "Cotentin" Peninsula is the peninsula in which Cherbourg is situated.

airfields exist in the Cotentin, and that area is not suitable for rapid airfield development. Furthermore, the narrow neck of the Peninsula would give the Germans an easy task in preventing us from breaking out and expanding our initial bridgehead. Moreover, during the period of our consolidation in the Cotentin the Germans would have time to reinforce their coastal troops in the Caen area, rendering a subsequent amphibious assault in that area much more difficult.

8. There remains the attack on the Caen beaches. The Caen sector is weakly held; the defences are relatively light and the beaches are of high capacity and sheltered from the prevailing winds. Inland the terrain is suitable for airfield development and for the consolidation of the initial bridgehead; and much of it is unfavourable for counter-attacks by panzer divisions. Maximum enemy air opposition can only be brought to bear at the expense of the enemy air defence screen covering the approaches to Germany; and the limited number of enemy airfields within range of the Caen area facilitates local neutralisation of the German fighter force. The sector suffers from the disadvantage that considerable effort will be required to provide adequate air support to our assault forces and some time must elapse before the capture of a major port.

After a landing in the Caen sector it would be necessary to seize either the Seine group of ports or the Brittany group of ports. To seize the Seine ports would entail forcing a crossing of the Seine, which is likely to require greater forces than we can build up through the Caen beaches and the port of Cherbourg. It should, however, be possible to seize the Brittany ports between Cherbourg and Nantes and on them build up sufficient forces for our final advance Eastwards.

Provided that the necessary air situation can first be achieved, the chances of a successful attack and of rapid subsequent development are so much greater in this sector than in any other that it is considered that the advantages far outweigh the disadvantages.

The Lodgement Area Selected.

9. In the light of these factors, it is considered that our initial landing on the Continent should be effected in the Caen area, with a view to the eventual seizure of a lodgement area comprising the Cherbourg-Brittany group of ports (from Cherbourg to Nantes).

Opening Phase up to the Capture of Cherbourg.

10. The opening phase in the seizing of this lodgement area would be the effecting of a landing in the Caen sector with a view to the early capture and development of airfield sites in the Caen area, and of the port of Cherbourg.

11. The main limiting factors affecting such an operation are the possibility of attaining the necessary air situation; the number of offensive divisions which the enemy can make available for counter attack in the Caen area; the availability of landing ships and craft and of transport aircraft; and the capacity of the beaches and ports in the sector.

12. Although the strength of the G.A.F. available in 1944 on the Western front cannot be forecast at this stage, we can confidently expect that we shall have a vast numerical superiority in bomber forces. The first-line strength of the German fighter force is, however, showing a steady increase and although it is unlikely to equal the size of the force at our disposal, there is no doubt that our fighters will have a very large commitment entailing dispersal and operations at maximum intensity. Our fighters will also be operating under serious tactical disadvantages in the early stages, which will largely offset their numerical superiority. Before the assault takes place, therefore, it will be necessary to reduce the effectiveness of the G.A.F., particularly that part which can be brought to bear against the Caen area.

13. The necessary air situation to ensure a reasonable chance of success will therefore require that the maximum number of German fighter forces are contained in the Low Countries and North-West Germany, that the effectiveness of the fighter defence in the Caen area is reduced and that air reinforcements are prevented from arriving in the early stages from the Mediterranean. Above all, it will be necessary to reduce the overall strength of the German fighter force between now and the date of the operation by destruction of the sources of supply, by the infliction of casualties by bringing on air battles, and, immediately prior to the assault, by the disorganization of G.A.F. installations and control system in the Caen area.

14. As it is impossible to forecast with any accuracy the number and location of German formations in reserve in 1944, while, on the other hand, the forces available to us have been laid down, an attempt has been made in this paper to determine the wisest employment of our own forces and then to determine the maximum number of German formations which they can reasonably overcome. Apart from the air situation, which is an over-riding factor, the practicabili-

ty of this plan will depend principally on the number, effectiveness, and availability of German divisions present in France and the Low Countries in relation to our own capabilities. This consideration is discussed below (paragraph 35).

15. A maximum of thirty and a minimum of twenty-six equivalent divisions are likely to be available in the United Kingdom for cross-Channel operations on the 1st May 1944. Further build-up can be at the rate of three to five divisions per month.

16. Landing ships and craft have been provided to lift the equivalent of three assault divisions and two follow-up divisions, without "overheads," and it has been assumed that the equivalent of an additional two divisions can be afloat in ships.

17. Airborne forces amounting to two airborne divisions and some five or six parachute regiments will be available, but, largely owing to shortage of transport aircraft, it is only possible to lift the equivalent of two-thirds of one airborne division simultaneously, on the basis of present forecasts.

18. Even if additional landing-ships and craft could be made available, the beaches in the Caen area would preclude the landing of forces greater than the equivalent of the three assault and two follow-up divisions, for which craft have already been provided. Nevertheless, an all-round increase of at least 10 per cent. in landing ships and craft is highly desirable in order to provide a greater margin for contingencies within the framework of the existing plan. Furthermore, sufficient lift for a further assault division could most usefully be employed in an additional landing on other beaches.

19. There is no port of any capacity within the sector although there are a number of small ports of limited value. Maintenance will, therefore, of necessity be largely over the beaches until it is possible to capture and open up the port of Cherbourg. In view of the possibilities of interruption by bad weather it will be essential to provide early some form of improvised sheltered waters.

20. Assuming optimum weather conditions, it should be possible to build up the force over the beaches to a total by D plus 6 of the equivalent of some eleven divisions and five tank brigades and thereafter to land one division a day until about D plus 24.

Proposed Plan.

Preliminary Phase.

21. During the preliminary phase, which must start forthwith, all possible means including air and sea action, propaganda, political and economic pressure, and sabotage, must be integrated into a combined offensive aimed at softening the German resistance. In particular, air action should be directed towards the reduction of the German air forces on the Western front, the progressive destruction of the German economic system and the undermining of German morale.

22. In order to contain the maximum German forces away from the Caen area diversionary operations should be staged against other areas such as the Pas de Calais and the Mediterranean Coast of France.

Preparatory Phase.

23. During this phase air action will be intensified against the G.A.F., particularly in North-West France, with a view to reducing the effectiveness of the G.A.F. in that area, and will be extended to include attacks against communications more directly associated with movement of German reserves which might affect the Caen area. Three naval assault forces will be assembled with the naval escorts and loaded at ports along the South Coast of England. Two naval assault forces carrying the follow-up forces will also be assembled and loaded, one in the Thames Estuary and one on the West Coast.

The Assault.

24. After a very short air bombardment of the beach defences three assault divisions will be landed simultaneously on the Caen beaches, followed up on D Day by the equivalent of two tank brigades (United States regiments) and a brigade group (United States regimental combat team). At the same time, airborne forces will be used to seize the town of Caen; and subsidiary operations by commandos and possibly by airborne forces will be undertaken to neutralize certain coast defences and seize certain important river crossings. The object of the assault forces will be to seize the general line Grandcamp—Bayeux—Caen.

Follow-up and Build-up Phase.

25. Subsequent action will take the form of a strong thrust Southwards and South-Westwards with a view to destroying enemy forces, acquiring sites for airfields, and gaining depth for a

turning movement into the Cotentin Peninsula directed on Cherbourg. When sufficient depth has been gained a force will advance into the Cotentin and seize Cherbourg. At the same time a thrust will be made to deepen the bridgehead South-Eastwards in order to cover the construction and operation of additional airfields in the area South-East of Caen.

26. It is considered that, within fourteen days of the initial assault, Cherbourg should be captured and the bridgehead extended to include the general line Trouville—Alencon—Mont St. Michel. By this date, moreover, it should have been possible to land some eighteen divisions and to have in operation about fourteen airfields from which twenty-eight to thirty-three fighter-type squadrons should be operating.

Further Developments after Capture of Cherbourg.

27. After the capture of Cherbourg the Supreme Allied Commander will have to decide whether to initiate operations to seize the Seine ports or whether he must content himself with first occupying the Brittany ports. In this decision he will have to be guided largely by the situation of the enemy forces. If the German resistance is sufficiently weak, an immediate advance could be made to seize Havre and Rouen. On the other hand, the more probable situation is that the Germans will have retired with the bulk of their forces to hold Paris and the line of the Seine, where they can best be covered by their air forces from North-East France and where they may possibly be reinforced by formations from Russia. Elsewhere they may move a few divisions from Southern France to hold the crossings of the Loire and will leave the existing defensive divisions in Brittany.

It will therefore most probably be necessary for us to seize the Brittany ports first, in order to build up sufficient forces with which we can eventually force the passage of the Seine.

28. Under these circumstances, the most suitable plan would appear to be to secure first the left flank and to gain sufficient airfields for subsequent operations. This would be done by extending the bridgehead to the line of the River Eure from Dreux to Rouen and thence along the line of the Seine to the sea, seizing at the same time Chartres, Orleans and Tours.

29. Under cover of these operations a force would be employed in capturing the Brittany ports; the first step being a thrust Southwards to seize Nantes and St. Nazaire, followed by subsidiary operations to capture Brest and the various small ports of the Brittany Peninsula.

30. This action would complete the occupation of our initial lodgement area and would secure sufficient major ports for the maintenance of at least thirty divisions. As soon as the organization of the L. of C. in this lodgement area allowed, and sufficient air forces had been established, operations would then be begun to force the line of the Seine, and to capture Paris and the Seine ports. As opportunity offered, subsidiary action would also be taken to clear the Germans from the Biscay ports to facilitate the entry of additional American troops and the feeding of the French population.

Command and Control.

31. In carrying out Operation "Overlord" administrative control would be greatly simplified if the principle were adopted that the United States forces were normally on the right of the line and the British and Canadian forces on the left.

Major Conditions Affecting Success of the Operation.

32. It will be seen that the plan for the initial landing is based on two main principles— concentration of force and tactical surprise. Concentration of the assault forces is considered essential if we are to ensure adequate air support and if our limited assault forces are to avoid defeat in detail. An attempt has been made to obtain tactical surprise by landing in a lightly defended area—presumably lightly defended as, due to its distance from a major port, the Germans consider a landing there unlikely to be successful. This action, of course, presupposes that we can offset the absence of a port in the initial stages by the provision of improvised sheltered waters. It is believed that this can be accomplished.

33. The operation calls for a much higher standard of performance on the part of the naval assault forces than any previous operation. This will depend upon their being formed in sufficient time to permit of adequate training.

34. Above all, it is essential that there should be an over-all reduction in the German fighter force between now and the time of the surface assault. From now onwards every practical method of achieving this end must be employed. This condition, above all others, will dictate the date by which the amphibious assault can be launched.

35. The next condition is that the number of German offensive divisions in reserve must not exceed a certain figure on the target date if the operation is to have a reasonable chance of success. The German reserves in France and the Low Countries as a whole, excluding divisions holding the coast, G.A.F. divisions and training divisions, should not exceed on the day of the assault twelve full-strength first-quality divisions. In addition, the Germans should not be able to transfer more than fifteen first-quality divisions from Russia during the first two months. Moreover, on the target date the divisions in reserve should be so located that the number of first-quality divisions which the Germans could deploy in the Caen area to support the divisions holding the coast should not exceed three divisions on D Day, five divisions on D plus 2, or nine divisions by D plus 8.

During the preliminary period, therefore, every effort must be made to dissipate and divert German formations, lower their fighting efficiency and disrupt communications.

36. Finally, there is the question of maintenance. Maintenance will have to be carried out over beaches for a period of some three months for a number of formations, varying from a maximum of eighteen divisions in the first month to twelve divisions in the second month, rapidly diminishing to nil in the third month. Unless adequate measures are taken to provide sheltered waters by artificial means, the operation will be at the mercy of the weather. Moreover, special facilities and equipment will be required to prevent undue damage to craft during this extended period. Immediate action for the provision of the necessary requirements is essential.

37. Given these conditions—a reduced G.A.F., a limitation in the number or effectiveness of German offensive formations in France, and adequate arrangements to provide improvised sheltered waters—it is considered that Operation "Overlord" has a reasonable prospect of success. To ensure these conditions being attained by the 1st May, 1944, action must start *now* and every possible effort made by all means in our power to soften German resistance and to speed up our own preparations.

Offices of the War Cabinet, S. W. 1,
30th July, 1943

Index

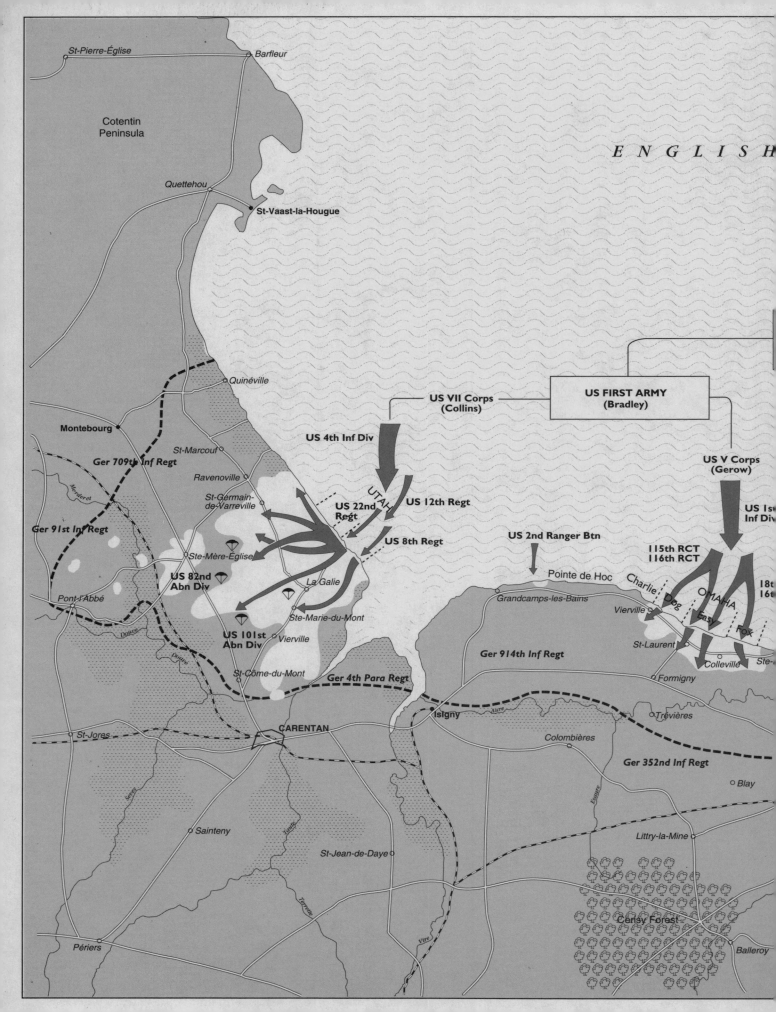

St-Pierre-Église · Barfleur

Cotentin
Peninsula

Quettehou

St-Vaast-la-Hougue

E N G L I S H

Quinéville

Montebourg

Ger 709th Inf Regt

St-Marcouf

Ravenoville

US VII Corps
(Collins)

**US FIRST ARMY
(Bradley)**

US 4th Inf Div

St-Germain-
de-Varreville

UTAH

**US 22nd
Regt**

US 12th Regt

US V Corps
(Gerow)

Ger 91st Inf Regt

Ste-Mère-Église

US 8th Regt

US 2nd Ranger Btn

US 1st
Inf Div

**US 82nd
Abn Div**

La Galie

Pointe de Hoc

Grandcamps-les-Bains

Charlie Dog

115th RCT
116th RCT

OMAHA

18t
16t

Pont-l'Abbé

Douve

Ste-Marie-du-Mont

Vierville

St-Laurent

**US 101st
Abn Div**

Vierville

Ger 914th Inf Regt

Colleville

Ste-

St-Côme-du-Mont

Ger 4th Para Regt

Formigny

St-Jores

Isigny

Aure

Trévières

CARENTAN

Sèves

Colombières

Sainteny

Taute

Ger 352nd Inf Regt

Blay

Littry-la-Mine

St-Jean-de-Daye

Terrette

Cerisy Forest

Périers

Vire

Balleroy